Redgauntlet. the Betrothed. the Talisman
by Sir Walter Scott

Address:
HardPress
8345 NW 66TH ST #2561
MIAMI FL 33166-2626
USA
Email: info@hardpress.net

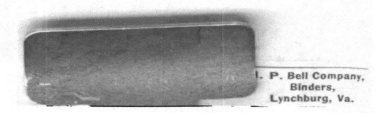

W. C. McClure

PETER PEEBLES DISCOVERING HIS COUNSEL ALAN FAIRFORD

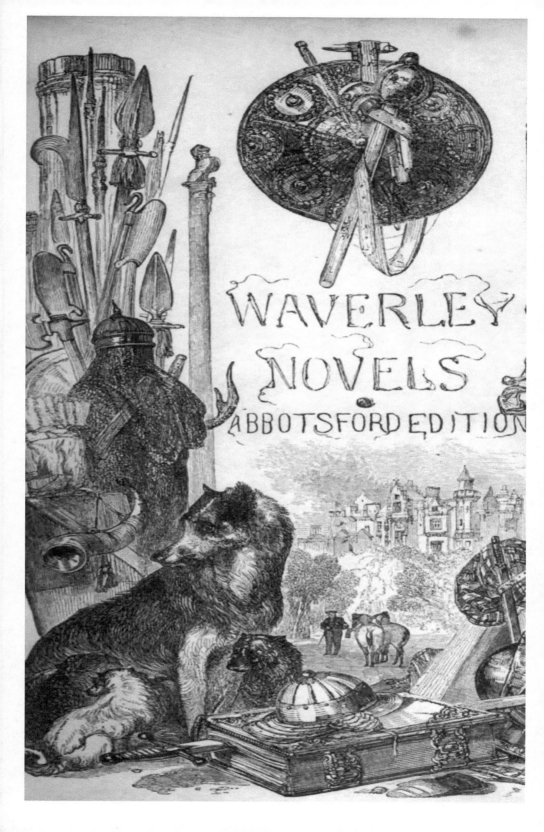

WAVERLEY
NOVELS
ABBOTSFORD EDITION

Abbotsford Edition.

THE

WAVERLEY NOVELS,

BY

SIR WALTER SCOTT.

COMPLETE

IN TWELVE VOLUMES.

PRINTED

From the latest English Editions.

EMBRACING

THE AUTHOR'S LAST CORRECTIONS, PREFACES, AND NOTES.

VOL. IX.

REDGAUNTLET — THE BETROTHED — THE TALISMAN.

PHILADELPHIA:

J. B. LIPPINCOTT & CO.

1856.

271122

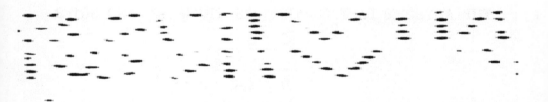

REDGAUNTLET.

A TALE OF THE EIGHTEENTH CENTURY.

Master, go on; and I will follow thee,
To the last gasp, with truth and loyalty.
As You Like It.

INTRODUCTION — (1832.)

THE Jacobite enthusiasm of the eighteenth century, particularly during the rebellion of 1745, afforded a theme, perhaps the finest that could be selected, for fictitious composition, founded upon real or probable incident. This civil war, and its remarkable events, were remembered by the existing generation without any degree of the bitterness of spirit which seldom fails to attend internal dissension. The Highlanders, who formed the principal strength of Charles Edward's army, were an ancient and high-spirited race, peculiar in their habits of war and of peace, brave to romance, and exhibiting a character turning upon points more adapted to poetry than to the prose of real life. Their Prince, young, valiant, patient of fatigue, and despising danger, heading his army on foot in the most toilsome marches, and defeating a regular force in three battles, all these were circumstances fascinating to the imagination, and might well be supposed to seduce young and enthusiastic minds to the cause in which they were found united, although wisdom and reason frowned upon the enterprise.

The adventurous Prince, as is well known, proved to be one of those personages who distinguish themselves during some single and extraordinarily brilliant period of their lives, like the course of a shooting star, at which men wonder, as well on account of the briefness, as the brilliancy of its splendour. A long trace of darkness overshadowed the subsequent life of a man, who, in his youth, showed himself so capable of great undertakings; and, without the painful task of tracing his course farther, we may say the latter pursuits and habits of this unhappy Prince, are those painfully evincing a broken heart, which seeks refuge from its own thoughts in sordid enjoyments.

Still, however, it was long ere Charles Edward appeared to be, perhaps it was long ere he altogether became, so much degraded from his original self; as he enjoyed for a time the lustre attending the progress and termination of his enterprise. Those who thought they discerned in his subsequent conduct an insensibility to the distresses of his followers, coupled with that egotistical attention to his own interests, which has been often attributed to the Stewart Family, and which is the natural effect of the principles of divine right in which they were brought up, were now generally

A 2
(5)

considered as dissatisfied and splenetic persons, who, displeased with the issue of their adventure, and finding themselves involved in the ruins of a falling cause, indulged themselves in undeserved reproaches against their leader. Indeed, such censures were by no means frequent among those of his followers, who, if what was alleged had been just, had the best right to complain. Far the greater number of those unfortunate gentlemen suffered with the most dignified patience, and were either too proud to take notice of ill treatment on the part of their Prince, or so prudent as to be aware their complaints would meet with little sympathy from the world. It may be added, that the greater part of the banished Jacobites, and those of high rank and consequence, were not much within reach of the influence of the Prince's character and conduct, whether well regulated or otherwise.

In the meantime, that great Jacobite conspiracy, of which the insurrection of 1745–6 was but a small part, precipitated into action on the failure of a far more general scheme, was resumed and again put into motion by the Jacobites of England, whose force had never been broken, as they had prudently avoided bringing it into the field. The surprising effect which had been produced by small means, in 1745–6, animated their hopes for more important successes, when the whole nonjuring interest of Britain, identified as it then was with great part of the landed gentlemen, should come forward to finish what had been gallantly attempted by a few Highland chiefs.

It is probable, indeed, that the Jacobites of the day were incapable of considering that the very small scale on which the effort was made, was in one great measure the cause of its unexpected success. The remarkable speed with which the insurgents marched, the singularly good discipline which they preserved, the union and unanimity which for some time animated their councils, were all in a considerable degree produced by the smallness of their numbers. Notwithstanding the discomfiture of Charles Edward, the nonjurors of the period long continued to nurse unlawful schemes, and to drink treasonable toasts, until age stole upon them. Another generation arose, who did not share the sentiments which they cherished ; and at length the sparkles of disaffection, which had long smouldered, but had never been heated enough to burst into actual flame, became entirely extinguished. But in proportion as the political enthusiasm died gradually away among men of ordinary temperament, it influenced those of warm imaginations and weak understandings, and hence wild schemes were formed, as desperate as they were adventurous.

Thus a young Scottishman of rank is said to have stooped so low as to plot the surprisal of St. James's palace, and the assassination of the royal family. While these ill-digested and desperate conspiracies were agitated among the few Jacobites who still adhered with more obstinacy to their purpose, there is no question but that other plots might have been brought to an open explosion, had it not suited the policy of Sir Robert Walpole, rather to prevent or disable the conspirators in their projects, than to promulgate the tale of danger, which might thus have been believed to be more widely diffused than was really the case.

In one instance alone this very prudential and humane line of conduct was departed from, and the event seemed to confirm the policy of the general course. Doctor Archibald Cameron, brother of the celebrated Donald Cameron of Lochiel, attainted for the rebellion of 1745, was found by a party of soldiers lurking with a comrade in the wilds of Loch Katrine, five or six years after the battle of Culloden, and was there seized. There were circumstances in his case, so far as was made known to the public, which attracted much compassion, and gave to the judicial proceedings against him an appearance of cold-blooded revenge on the part of government ; and the following argument of a zealous Jacobite in his favour, was received as conclusive by Dr. Johnson, and other persons who might pretend to impartiality. Dr. Cameron had never borne arms, although engaged in the Rebellion, but used his medical skill for the service, indifferently, of the wounded of both parties. His return to Scotland was ascribed exclusively to family affairs. His behaviour at the bar was decent, firm, and respectful. His wife threw herself, on three different occasions, before George II. and the members of his family, was rudely repulsed from their presence, and at length placed, it was said, in the same prison with her husband, and confined with unmanly severity.

Dr. Cameron was finally executed, with all the severities of the law of treason; and his death remains in popular estimation a dark blot upon the memory of George II., being almost publicly imputed to a mean and personal hatred of Donald Cameron of Lochiel, the sufferer's heroic brother.

Yet the fact was, that whether the execution of Archibald Cameron was political or otherwise, it might certainly have been justified, had the King's ministers so pleased, upon reasons of a public nature. The unfortunate sufferer had not come to the Highlands solely upon his private affairs, as was the general belief; but it was not judged prudent by the English ministry to let it be generally known that he came to inquire about a considerable sum of money which had been remitted from France to the friends of the exiled family. He had also a commission to hold intercourse with the well-known M'Pherson of Cluny, chief of the clan Vourich, whom the Chevalier had left behind at his departure from Scotland in 1746, and who remained during ten years of proscription and danger, skulking from place to place in the Highlands, and maintaining an uninterrupted correspondence between Charles and his friends. That Dr. Cameron should have held a commission to assist this chief in raking together the dispersed embers of disaffection, is in itself sufficiently natural, and, considering his political principles, in no respect dishonourable to his memory. But neither ought it to be imputed to George II., that he suffered the laws to be enforced against a person taken in the act of breaking them. When he lost his hazardous game, Dr. Cameron only paid the forfeit which he must have calculated upon. The ministers, however, thought it proper to leave Dr. Cameron's new schemes in concealment, lest, by divulging them, they had indicated the channel of communication which, it is now well known, they possessed to all the plots of Charles Edward. But it was equally ill advised and ungenerous to sacrifice the character of the king to the policy of the administration. Both points might have been gained by sparing the life of Dr. Cameron after conviction, and limiting his punishment to perpetual exile.

These repeated and successive Jacobite plots rose and burst like bubbles on a fountain; and one of them, at least, the Chevalier judged of importance enough to induce him to risk himself within the dangerous precincts of the British capital. This appears from Dr. King's Anecdotes of his Own Times.

"September, 1750.—I received a note from my Lady Primrose, who desired to see me immediately. As soon as I waited on her, she led me into her dressing-room, and presented me to ——," [the Chevalier, doubtless.] "If I was surprised to find him there, I was still more astonished when he acquainted me with the motives which had induced him to hazard a journey to England at this juncture. The impatience of his friends who were in exile, had formed a scheme which was impracticable; but although it had been as feasible as they had represented it to him, yet no preparation had been made, nor was any thing ready to carry it into execution. He was soon convinced that he had been deceived; and, therefore, after a stay in London of five days only, he returned to the place from whence he came." Dr. King was in 1750 a keen Jacobite, as may be inferred from the visit made by him to the Prince under such circumstances, and from his being one of that unfortunate person's chosen correspondents. He, as well as other men of sense and observation, began to despair of making their fortune in the party which they had chosen. It was indeed sufficiently dangerous; for, during the short visit just described, one of Dr. King's servants remarked the stranger's likeness to Prince Charles, whom he recognized from the common busts.

The occasion taken for breaking up the Stewart interest, we shall tell in Dr. King's own words:—"When he (Charles Edward) was in Scotland, he had a mistress whose name was Walkinshaw, and whose sister was at that time, and is still, housekeeper at Leicester House. Some years after he was released from his prison, and conducted out of France, he sent for this girl, who soon acquired such a dominion over him, that she was acquainted with all his schemes, and trusted with his most secret correspondence. As soon as this was known in England, all those persons of distinction who were attached to him were greatly alarmed: they imagined that this wench had been placed in his family by the English ministers; and, considering her sister's situation, they seemed to have some ground for their suspicion; wherefore, they despatched a gentleman to Paris, where the Prince then was, who had instructions to insist that Mrs. Walkinshaw should be removed to a convent for a certain term; but her gallant absolutely refused to comply with this demand; and although Mr. M'Namara, the gentleman who was sent to him, who has a natural eloquence, and an excellent understanding, urged the most cogent reason, and used all the arts of persuasion, to induce him to part with his mistress, and even proceeded so far as to assure him, according to his instructions, that an immediate interruption of all correspondence with his most powerful friends in England, and, in short, that the ruin of his interest, which was now daily increasing, would be the infallible consequence of his refusal; yet he continued inflexible, and all M'Namara's entreaties and remonstrances were ineffectual. M'Namara staid in Paris some days beyond the time prescribed him, endeavouring to reason the Prince into a better temper; but finding him obstinately persevere in his first answer, he took his leave with concern and indignation, saying, as he passed out, 'What has your family done, sir, thus to draw down the vengeance of Heaven on every branch of it, through so many ages?' It is worthy of remark, that in all the conferences which M'Namara had with the Prince on this occasion, the latter declared that it was not a violent passion, or indeed any particular regard, which attached him to Mrs. Walkinshaw, and that he could see her removed from him without any concern; but he would not receive directions, in respect to his private conduct, from any man alive. When M'Namara returned to London, and reported the Prince's answer to the gentlemen who had employed him, they were astonished and confounded. However, they soon resolved on the measures which they were to pursue for the future, and determined no longer to serve a man who could not be persuaded to serve himself, and chose rather to endanger the lives of his best and most faithful friends, than part with an harlot, whom, as he often declared, he neither loved nor esteemed."

From this anecdote, the general truth of which is indubitable, the principal fault of Charles Edward's temper is sufficiently obvious. It was a high sense of his own importance, and an obstinate adherence to what he had once determined on—qualities which, if he had succeeded in his bold attempt, gave the nation little room to hope that he would have been found free from the love of prerogative and desire of arbitrary power, which characterized his unhappy grandfather. He gave a notable instance how far this was the leading feature of his character, when, for no reasonable cause that can be assigned, he placed his own single will in opposition to the necessities of France, which, in order to purchase a peace become necessary to the kingdom, was reduced to gratify Britain by prohibiting the residence of Charles within any part of the French dominions. It was in vain that France endeavoured to lessen the disgrace of this step by making the most flattering offers, in hopes to induce the Prince of himself to anticipate this disagreeable alternative, which, if seriously enforced, as it was likely to be, he had no means whatever of resisting, by leaving the kingdom as of his own free-will. Inspired, however, by the spirit of hereditary obstinacy, Charles preferred a useless resistance to a dignified submission, and, by a series of idle bravadoes, laid the French Court under the necessity of arresting their late ally, and sending him to close confinement in the Bastile, from which he was afterwards sent out of the French dominions, much in the manner in which a convict is transported to the place of his destination.

In addition to these repeated instances of a rash and inflexible temper, Dr. King also adds faults alleged to belong to the Prince's character, of a kind less consonant with his noble birth and high pretensions. He is said by this author to have been avaricious, or parsimonious at least, to such a degree of meanness, as to fail, even when he had ample means, in relieving the sufferers who had lost their fortune, and sacrificed all in his ill-fated attempt.* We must receive, however, with some degree of jealousy what is said by Dr. King on this subject, recollecting that he had left at least, if he did not desert, the standard of the unfortunate Prince, and was not therefore a person who was likely to form the fairest estimate of his virtues and faults. We must also remember, that if the exiled Prince gave little, he had but little to give, especially considering how late he nourished the scheme of another expedition to Scotland, for which he was long endeavouring to hoard money.

The case, also, of Charles Edward must be allowed to have been a difficult one. He had to satisfy numerous persons, who, having lost their all in his cause, had, with that all, seen the extinction of hopes which they accounted nearly as good as certainties; some of these were perhaps clamorous in their applications, and certainly ill-pleased with their want of success. Other parts of the Chevalier's conduct may have afforded grounds for charging him with coldness to the sufferings of his devoted followers. One of these was a sentiment which has nothing in it that is generous, but it was certainly a principle in which the young Prince was trained, and which may be too probably denominated peculiar to his family, educated in all the high notions of passive obedience and non-resistance. If the unhappy Prince gave implicit faith to the professions of statesmen holding such notions, which is implied by his whole conduct, it must have led to the natural, though ungracious inference, that the services of a subject could not, to whatever degree of ruin they might bring the individual, create a debt against his sovereign. Such a person could only boast that he had done his duty; nor was he entitled to be a claimant for a greater reward than it was convenient for the Prince to bestow, or to hold his sovereign his debtor for losses which he had sustained through his loyalty. To a certain extent the Jacobite principles inevitably led to this cold and egotistical mode of reasoning on the part of the sovereign; nor, with all our natural pity for the situation of royalty in distress, do we feel entitled to affirm that Charles did not use this opiate to his feelings, on viewing the misery of his followers, while he certainly possessed, though in no great degree, the means of affording them more relief than he practised.

---

* The reproach is thus expressed by Dr. King, who brings the charge :— " But the most odious part of his character is his love of money, a vice which I do not remember to have been imputed by our historians to any of his ancestors, and is the certain index of a base and little mind. I know it may be urged in his vindication, that a Prince in exile ought to be an economist. And so he ought ; but, nevertheless, his purse should be always open as long as there is any thing in it, to relieve the necessities of his friends and adherents. King Charles II., during his banishment, would have shared the last pistole in his pocket with his little family. But I have known this gentleman with two thousand louis-d'ors in his strong box, pretend he was in great distress, and borrow money from a lady in Paris who was not in affluent circumstances. His most faithful servants, who had closely attended him in all his difficulties, were ill rewarded." — *King's Memoirs.*

His own history, after leaving France, is brief and melancholy. For a time he seems to have held the firm belief that Providence, which had borne him through so many hazards, still reserved him for some distant occasion, in which he should be empowered to vindicate the honours of his birth. But opportunity after opportunity slipt by unimproved, and the death of his father gave him the fatal proof that none of the principal powers of Europe were, after that event, likely to interest themselves in his quarrel. They refused to acknowledge him under the title of the King of England, and, on his part, he declined to be then recognized as the Prince of Wales.

Family discord came to add its sting to those of disappointed ambition; and, though a humiliating circumstance, it is generally acknowledged, that Charles Edward, the adventurous, the gallant, and the handsome, the leader of a race of pristine valour, whose romantic qualities may be said to have died along with him, had, in his latter days, yielded to those humiliating habits of intoxication, in which the meanest mortals seek to drown the recollection of their disappointments and miseries. Under such circumstances, the unhappy Prince lost the friendship even of those faithful followers who had most devoted themselves to his misfortunes, and was surrounded, with some honourable exceptions, by men of a lower description, regardless of the character which he was himself no longer able to protect.

It is a fact consistent with the author's knowledge, that persons totally unentitled to, and unfitted for, such a distinction, were presented to the unfortunate Prince in moments unfit for presentation of any kind. Amid these clouds was at length extinguished the torch which once shook itself over Britain with such terrific glare, and at last sunk in its own ashes, scarce remembered and scarce noticed.

Meantime, while the life of Charles Edward was gradually wasting in disappointed solitude, the number of those who had shared his misfortunes and dangers had shrunk into a small handful of veterans, the heroes of a tale which had been told. Most Scottish readers who can count the number of sixty years, must recollect many respected acquaintances of their youth, who, as the established phrase gently worded it, had been *out in the Forty-five*. It may be said, that their political principles and plans no longer either gained proselytes or attracted terror, — those who held them had ceased to be the subjects either of fear or opposition. Jacobites were looked upon in society as men who had proved their sincerity by sacrificing their interest to their principles; and in well-regulated companies, it was held a piece of ill-breeding to injure their feelings or ridicule the compromises by which they endeavoured to keep themselves abreast of the current of the day. Such, for example, was the evasion of a gentleman of fortune in Perthshire, who, in having the newspapers read to him, caused the King and Queen to be designated by the initial letters of K. and Q., as if, by naming the full word, he might imply an acquiescence in the usurpation of the family of Hanover. George III., having heard of this gentleman's custom in the above and other particulars, commissioned the member for Perthshire to carry his compliments to the steady Jacobite — "that is," said the excellent old King, "not the compliments of the King of England, but those of the Elector of Hanover, and tell him how much I respect him for the steadiness of his principles."

Those who remember such old men, will probably agree that the progress of time, which has withdrawn all of them from the field, has removed, at the same time, a peculiar and striking feature of ancient manners. Their love of past times, their tales of bloody battles fought against romantic odds, were all dear to their imagination, and their idolatry of locks of hair, pictures, rings, ribbons, and other memorials of the time in which they still seemed to live, was an interesting enthusiasm; and although their political principles, had they existed in the relation of fathers, might have rendered them dangerous to the existing dynasty, yet, as we now recollect them, there could not be on the earth supposed to exist persons better qualified to sustain the capacity of innocuous and respectable grandsires.

It was while reflecting on these things that the novel of Redgauntlet was undertaken. But various circumstances in the composition induced the author to alter its purport considerably, as it passed through his hands, and to carry the action to that point of time when the Chevalier Charles Edward, though fallen into the sere and yellow leaf, was yet meditating a second attempt, which could scarcely have been more hopeless than his first; although one, to which, as we have seen, the unfortunate Prince, at least as late as seventeen hundred and fifty-three, still looked with hope and expectation.

1st April, 1832.

REDGAUNTLET.

LETTER I.

DARSIE LATIMER TO ALAN FAIRFORD.

DUMFRIES.

Cur me exanimas querelis tuis? — In plain English, **Why do you deafen me with your croaking?** The disconsolate tone in which you bade me farewell at Noble-House,* and mounted your miserable hack to return to your law drudgery, still sounds in my ears. It seemed to say, "Happy dog! you can ramble at pleasure over hill and dale, pursue every object of curiosity that presents itself, and relinquish the chase when it loses interest; while I, your senior and your better, must, in this brilliant season, return to my narrow chamber and my musty books."

Such was the import of the reflections with which you saddened our parting bottle of claret, and thus I must needs interpret the terms of your melancholy adieu.

And why should this be so, Alan? Why the deuce should you not be sitting precisely opposite to me at this moment, in the same comfortable George Inn; thy heels on the fender, and thy juridical brow expanding its plications as a pun rose in your fancy? Above all, why, when I fill this very glass of wine, cannot I push the bottle to you, and say, "Fairford, you are chased!" Why, I say, should not all this be, except because Alan Fairford has not the same true sense of friendship as Darsie Latimer, and will not regard our purses as common, as well as our sentiments?

I am alone in the world; my only guardian writes to me of a large fortune, which will be mine when I reach the age of twenty-five complete; my present income is, thou knowest, more than sufficient for all my wants; and yet thou — traitor as thou art to the cause of friendship — dost deprive me of the pleasure of thy society, and submittest, besides, to self-denial on thine own part, rather than my wanderings should cost me a few guineas more! Is this regard for my purse, or for thine own pride? Is it not equally absurd and unreasonable, whichever source it springs from? For myself, I tell thee, I have, and shall have, more than enough for both. This same methodical Samuel Griffiths, of Ironmonger-Lane, Guildhall, London, whose letter arrives as duly as quarter-day, has sent me, as I told thee, double allowance for this my twenty-first birth-day, and an assurance, in his brief fashion, that it will be again doubled for the succeeding years, until I enter into possession of my own property. Still I am to refrain from visiting England until my twenty-fifth year expires; and it is recommended that I shall forbear all inquiries concerning my family, and so forth, for the present.

Were it not that I recollect my poor mother in her deep widow's weeds, with a countenance that never smiled but when she looked on me — and

---

* The first stage on the road from Edinburgh to Dumfries and Moffat.

then, in such wan and woful sort, as the sun when he glances through an April cloud,—were it not, I say, that her mild and matron-like form and countenance forbid such a suspicion, I might think myself the son of some Indian director, or rich citizen, who had more wealth than grace, and a handful of hypocrisy to boot, and who was breeding up privately, and obscurely enriching, one of whose existence he had some reason to be ashamed. But, as I said before, I think on my mother, and am convinced as much as of the ▓▓▓▓▓ my own soul, that no touch of shame could arise from ▓▓▓ ▓▓▓▓ was implicated. Meantime, I am wealthy, and I am ale▓ my friend scruple to share my wealth?

▓▓▓ly friend? and have you not acquired a right to share my ▓▓▓ ▓▓▓▓ me that, Alan Fairford. When I was brought from the ▓▓▓ mother's dwelling into the tumult of the Gaite Class at the ▓▓▓▓ ▓▓—when I was mocked for my English accent—▓▓▓▓▓ with snow ▓▓▓ ▓thern—rolled in the gutter for a Saxon pock-pudding,—who with ▓▓▓ ▓rguments, and stouter blows, stood forth my defender?—why, Alan Fairford. Who beat me soundly when I brought the arrogance of an only son, and of course a spoiled urchin, to the forms of the little republic? —why, Alan. And who taught me to smoke a cobbler, pin a lozen, head a bicker, and hold the bannets?*—Alan, once more. If I became the pride of the Yards, and the dread of the hucksters in the High-School Wynd, it was under thy patronage; and, but for thee, I had been contented with humbly passing through the Cowgate-Port, without climbing over the top of it, and had never seen the *Kittle nine-steps*† nearer than from Bareford's Parks. You taught me to keep my fingers off the weak, and to clench my fist against the strong—to carry no tales out of school—to stand forth like a true man—obey the stern order of a *Pande manum*, and endure my pawnmies without wincing, like one that is determined not to be the better for them. In a word, before I knew thee, I knew nothing.

At College it was the same. When I was incorrigibly idle, your example and encouragement roused me to mental exertion, and showed me the way to intellectual enjoyment. You made me an historian, a metaphysician, (*invita Minerva*) — nay, by Heaven! you had almost made an advocate of me, as well as of yourself. Yes, rather than part with you, Alan, I attended a weary season at the Scotch Law Class; a wearier at the Civil; and with what excellent advantage, my note-book, filled with caricatures of the professors and my fellow-students, is it not yet extant to testify?

> "Thus far have I held on with thee untired;"

and, to say truth, purely and solely that I might travel the same road with thee. But it will not do, Alan. By my faith, man, I could as soon think of being one of those ingenious traders who cheat little Master Jackies on the outside of the partition with tops, balls, bats, and battledores, as a member of the long-robed fraternity within, who impose on grown country gentlemen with bouncing brocards of law.‡ Now, don't you read this to your worthy father, Alan — he loves me well enough, I know, of a Saturday night; but he thinks me but idle company for any other day of the

---

* Break a window, head a skirmish with stones, and hold the bonnet, or handkerchief, which used to divide high-school boys when fighting.

† A pass on the very brink of the Castle-rock to the north, by which it is just possible for a goat, or a high-school boy, to turn the corner of the building where it rises from the edge of the precipice. This was so favourite a feat with the "hail and neck boys" of the higher classes, that at one time sentinels were posted to prevent its repetition. One of the nine-steps was rendered more secure because the climber could take hold of the root of a nettle, as precarious were the means of passing this celebrated spot. The manning the Cowgate-Port, especially in snow-ball time, was also a choice amusement, as it offered an inaccessible station for the boys who used these missiles to the annoyance of the passengers. The gateway is now demolished; and probably most of its garrison lie as low as the fortress. To recollect that the author himself, however naturally disqualified, was one of those juvenile dreadnoughts, is a sad reflection to one who cannot now step over a brook without assistance.

‡ The Hall of the Parliament House of Edinburgh was, in former days, divided into two unequal portions by a partition, the inner side of which was consecrated to the use of the Courts of Justice and the gentlemen of the law; while the outer station was occupied by the stalls of stationers, toymen, and the like, as in a modern bazaar. From the old play of the Plain Dealer, it seems such was formerly the case with Westminster Hall. Minos has now purified his courts in both cities from all traffic but his own.

week. And here, I suspect, lies your real objection to taking a ramble with me through the southern counties in this delicious weather. I know the good gentleman has hard thoughts of me for being so unsettled as to leave Edinburgh before the Session rises; perhaps, too, he quarrels a little — I will not say, with my want of ancestry, but with my want of connections. He reckons me a lone thing in this world, Alan, and so, in good truth, I am; and it seems a reason to him why you should not attach yourself to me, that I can claim no interest in the general herd.

Do not suppose I forget what I owe him, for permitting ██████ for four years under his roof: My obligations to him are ████████ the greater, if he never heartily loved me. He is angry, ███, ██████ not, or cannot, both lawyer, and, with reference to you, considers my ████ inclination ████ as *pessimi exempli*, as he might say.

But ████ not be afraid that a lad of your steadiness will be influenced by such a reed shaken by the winds as I am. You will go on doubting with Dirleton, and resolving those doubts with Stewart,* until the cramp speech† has been spoken *more solito* from the corner of the bench, and with covered head — until you have sworn to defend the liberties and privileges of the College of Justice — until the black gown is hung on your shoulders, and you are free as any of the Faculty to sue or defend. Then will I step forth, Alan, and in a character which even your father will allow may be more useful to you than had I shared this splendid termination of your legal studies. In a word, if I cannot be a counsel, I am determined to be a *client*, a sort of person without whom a lawsuit would be as dull as a supposed case. Yes, I am determined to give you your first fee. One can easily, I am assured, get into a lawsuit — it is only the getting out which is sometimes found troublesome; — and, with your kind father for an agent, and you for my counsel learned in the law, and the worshipful Master Samuel Griffiths to back me, a few sessions shall not tire my patience. In short, I will make my way into Court, even if it should cost me the committing a *delict*, or at least a *quasi delict*. — You see all is not lost of what Erskine wrote, and Wallace taught.

Thus far I have fooled it off well enough; and yet, Alan, all is not at ease within me. I am affected with a sense of loneliness, the more depressing, that it seems to me to be a solitude peculiarly my own. In a country where all the world have a circle of consanguinity, extending to sixth cousins at least, I am a solitary individual, having only one kind heart to throb in unison with my own. If I were condemned to labour for my bread, methinks I should less regard this peculiar species of deprivation. The necessary communication of master and servant would be at least a tie which would attach me to the rest of my kind — as it is, my very independence seems to enhance the peculiarity of my situation. I am in the world as a stranger in the crowded coffeehouse, where he enters, calls for what refreshment he wants, pays his bill, and is forgotten so soon as the waiter's mouth has pronounced his " Thank ye, sir."

I know your good father would term this *sinning my mercies*,‡ and ask how I should feel if, instead of being able to throw down my reckoning, I were obliged to deprecate the resentment of the landlord for consuming that which I could not pay for. I cannot tell how it is; but, though this very reasonable reflection comes across me, and though I do confess that

---

* " Sir John Nisbett of Dirleton's Doubts and Questions upon the Law, especially of Scotland ;" and " Sir James Stewart's Dirleton's Doubts and Questions on the Law of Scotland resolved and answered," are works of authority in Scottish jurisprudence. As is generally the case, the Doubts are held more in respect than the solution.

† Till of late years, every advocate who entered at the Scottish bar made a Latin address to the Court, faculty, and audience, in set terms, and said a few words upon a text of the civil law, to show his Latinity and jurisprudence. He also wore his hat for a minute, in order to vindicate his right of being covered before the Court, which is said to have originated from the celebrated lawyer, Sir Thomas Hope, having two sons on the bench while he himself remained at the bar. Of late this ceremony has been dispensed with, as occupying the time of the Court unnecessarily. The entrant lawyer merely takes the oaths to government, and swears to maintain the rules and privileges of his order.

‡ A peculiar Scottish phrase expressive of ingratitude for the favours of Providence.

four hundred a-year in possession, eight hundred in near prospect, and the L—d knows how many hundreds more in the distance, are very pretty and comfortable things, yet I would freely give one half of them to call your father *father*, though he should scold me for my idleness every hour of the day, and to call you *brother*, though a brother whose merits would throw my own so completely into the shade.

The faint, yet not improbable belief has often come across me, that your father knows something more about my birth and condition than he is willing to communicate; it is so unlikely that I should be left in Edinburgh at six years old, without any other recommendation than the regular payment of my board to old M——* of the High School. Before that time, as I have often told you, I have but a recollection of unbounded indulgence on my mother's part, and the most tyrannical exertion of caprice on my own. I remember still how bitterly she sighed, how vainly she strove to soothe me, while, in the full energy of despotism, I roared like ten bull-calves, for something which it was impossible to procure for me. She is dead, that kind, that ill-rewarded mother! I remember the long faces—the darkened rooms—the black hangings—the mysterious impression made upon my mind by the hearse and mourning coaches, and the difficulty which I had to reconcile all this to the disappearance of my mother. I do not think I had before this event formed any idea of death, or that I had even heard of that final consummation of all that lives. The first acquaintance which I formed with it deprived me of my only relation.

A clergyman of venerable appearance, our only visiter, was my guide and companion in a journey of considerable length; and in the charge of another elderly man, substituted in his place, I know not how or why, I completed my journey to Scotland—and this is all I recollect.

I repeat the little history now, as I have a hundred times before, merely because I would wring some sense out of it. Turn, then, thy sharp, wire-drawing, lawyer-like ingenuity to the same task—make up my history as though thou wert shaping the blundering allegations of some blue-bonneted, hard-headed client, into a condescendence of facts and circumstances, and thou shalt be, not my Apollo—*quid tibi cum lyra?*—but my Lord Stair.† Meanwhile, I have written myself out of my melancholy and blue devils, merely by prosing about them; so I will now converse half an hour with Roan Robin in his stall—the rascal knows me already, and snickers whenever I cross the threshold of the stable.

The black which you bestrode yesterday morning, promises to be an admirable roadster, and ambled as easily with Sam and the portmanteau, as with you and your load of law-learning. Sam promises to be steady, and has hitherto been so. No long trial, you will say. He lays the blame of former inaccuracies on evil company—the people who were at the livery-stable were too seductive, I suppose—he denies he ever did the horse injustice—would rather have wanted his own dinner, he says. In this I believe him, as Roan Robin's ribs and coat show no marks of contradiction. However, as he will meet with no saints in the inns we frequent, and as oats are sometimes as speedily converted into ale as John Barleycorn himself, I shall keep a look-out after Master Sam. Stupid fellow! had he not abused my good nature, I might have chatted to him to keep my tongue in exercise; whereas now, I must keep him at a distance.

Do you remember what Mr. Fairford said to me on this subject—it did not become my father's son to speak in that manner to Sam's father's son? I asked you what your father could possibly know of mine; and you answered, "As much, you supposed, as he knew of Sam's—it was a proverbial expression." This did not quite satisfy me, though I am sure I

* Probably Mathieson, the predecessor of Dr. Adams, to whose memory the author and his contemporaries owe a deep debt of gratitude.
† Celebrated as a Scottish lawyer.

cannot tell why it should not. But I am returning to a fruitless and exhausted subject. Do not be afraid that I shall come back on this welltrodden yet pathless field of conjecture. I know nothing so useless, so utterly feeble and contemptible, as the groaning forth one's helpless lamentations into the ears of our friends.

I would fain promise you, that my letters shall be as entertaining as I am determined they shall be regular and well filled. We have an advantage over the dear friends of old, every pair of them. Neither David and Jonathan, nor Orestes and Pylades, nor Damon and Pythias — although, in the latter case particularly, a letter by post would have been very acceptable — ever corresponded together; for they probably could not write, and certainly had neither post nor franks to speed their effusions to each other; whereas yours, which you had from the old peer, being handled gently, and opened with precaution, may be returned to me again, and serve to make us free of his Majesty's post-office, during the whole time of my proposed tour.[*] Mercy upon us, Alan! what letters I shall have to send to you, with an account of all that I can collect, of pleasant or rare, in this wild-goose jaunt of mine! All I stipulate is that you do not communicate them to the Scots Magazine; for though you used, in a left-handed way, to compliment me on my attainments in the lighter branches of literature, at the expense of my deficiency in the weightier matters of the law, I am not yet audacious enough to enter the portal which the learned Ruddiman so kindly opened for the acolytes of the Muses. — *Vale sis memor mei.* D. L.

P. S. — Direct to the Post-Office here. I shall leave orders to forward your letters wherever I may travel.

LETTER II.

ALAN FAIRFORD TO DARSIE LATIMER.

NEGATUR, my dear Darsie — you have logic and law enough to understand the word of denial. I deny your conclusion. The premises I admit, namely, that when I mounted on that infernal hack, I might utter what seemed a sigh, although I deemed it lost amid the puffs and groans of the broken-winded brute, matchless in the complication of her complaints by any save she, the poor man's mare, renowned in song, that died

"A mile aboon Dundee." [†]

But credit me, Darsie, the sigh which escaped me, concerned thee more than myself, and regarded neither the superior mettle of your cavalry, nor your greater command of the means of travelling. I could certainly have cheerfully ridden on with you for a few days; and assure yourself I would not have hesitated to tax your better filled purse for our joint expenses. But you know my father considers every moment taken from the law as a

* It is well known and remembered, that when Members of Parliament enjoyed the unlimited privilege of franking by the mere writing the name on the cover, it was extended to the most extraordinary occasions. One noble lord, to express his regard for a particular regiment, franked a letter for every rank and file. It was customary also to save the covers and return them, in order that the correspondence might be carried on as long as the envelopes could hold together.

† Alluding, as all Scotsmen knew, to the humorous old song : —
"The auld man's mare's dead,
The puir man's mare's dead,
The auld man's mare's dead,
A mile aboon Dundee."

step down hill; and I owe much to his anxiety on my account, although its effects are sometimes troublesome. For example:

I found, on my arrival at the shop in Brown's Square, that the old gentleman had returned that very evening, impatient, it seems, of remaining a night out of the guardianship of the domestic Lares. Having this information from James, whose brow wore rather an anxious look on the occasion, I despatched a Highland chairman to the livery stable with my Bucephalus, and slunk, with as little noise as might be, into my own den, where I began to mumble certain half-gnawed and not half-digested doctrines of our municipal code. I was not long seated, when my father's visage was thrust, in a peering sort of way, through the half-opened door; and withdrawn, on seeing my occupation, with a half-articulated *humph !* which seemed to convey a doubt of the seriousness of my application. If it were so, I cannot condemn him; for recollection of thee occupied me so entirely during an hour's reading, that although Stair lay before me, and notwithstanding that I turned over three or four pages, the sense of his lordship's clear and perspicuous style so far escaped me, that I had the mortification to find my labour was utterly in vain.

Ere I had brought up my lee-way, James appeared with his summons to our frugal supper — radishes, cheese, and a bottle of the old ale — only two plates though — and no chair set for Mr. Darsie, by the attentive James Wilkinson. Said James, with his long face, lank hair, and very long pigtail in its leathern strap, was placed, as usual, at the back of my father's chair, upright as a wooden sentinel at the door of a puppet-show. "You may go down, James," said my father; and exit Wilkinson. — What is to come next? thought I; for the weather is not clear on the paternal brow.

My boots encountered the first glance of displeasure, and he asked me, with a sneer, which way I had been riding. He expected me to answer, "No where," and would then have been at me with his usual sarcasm, touching the humour of walking in shoes at twenty shillings a pair. But I answered with composure, that I had ridden out to dinner as far as Noble-House. He started, (you know his way,) as if I had said that I had dined at Jericho; and as I did not choose to seem to observe his surprise, but continued munching my radishes in tranquillity, he broke forth in ire.

"To Noble-House, sir ! and what had you to do at Noble-House, sir ? — Do you remember you are studying law, sir ? — that your Scots law trials are coming on, sir ? — that every moment of your time just now is worth hours at another time ? — and have you leisure to go to Noble-House, sir ? — and to throw your books behind you for so many hours ? — Had it been a turn in the Meadows, or even a game at golf — but Noble-House, sir !"

"I went so far with Darsie Latimer, sir, to see him begin his journey."

"Darsie Latimer ?" he replied in a softened tone — "Humph ! — Well, I do not blame you for being kind to Darsie Latimer ; but it would have done as much good if you had walked with him as far as the toll-bar, and then made your farewells — it would have saved horse-hire—and your reckoning, too, at dinner."

"Latimer paid that, sir !" I replied, thinking to soften the matter ; but I had much better have left it unspoken.

"The reckoning, sir !" replied my father. "And did you sponge upon any man for a reckoning? Sir, no man should enter the door of a public-house without paying his lawing."

"I admit the general rule, sir," I replied ; "but this was a parting-cup between Darsie and me ; and I should conceive it fell under the exception of *Doch an dorroch.*"

"You think yourself a wit," said my father, with as near an approach to a smile as ever he permits to gild the solemnity of his features ; "but I reckon you did not eat your dinner standing, like the Jews at their Passover ? and it was decided in a case before the town-bailies of Cupar-Angus, when

Luckie Simpson's cow had drunk up Luckie Jamieson's browst of ale, while it stood in the door to cool, that there was no damage to pay, because the crummie drank without sitting down; such being the very circumstance constituting *Doch an dorroch*, which is a standing drink, for which no reckoning is paid. Ha, sir! what says your advocateship (*fieri*) to that? *Exceptio firmat regulam*— But come, fill your glass, Alan; I am not sorry ye have shown this attention to Darsie Latimer, who is a good lad, as times go; and having now lived under my roof since he left the school, why, there is really no great matter in coming under this small obligation to him."

As I saw my father's scruples were much softened by the consciousness of his superiority in the legal argument, I took care to accept my pardon as a matter of grace, rather than of justice; and only replied, we should feel ourselves duller of an evening, now that you were absent. I will give you my father's exact words in reply, Darsie. You know him so well, that they will not offend you; and you are also aware, that there mingles with the good man's preciseness and formality, a fund of shrewd observation and practical good sense.

"It is very true," he said; "Darsie was a pleasant companion — but over waggish, over waggish, Alan, and somewhat scatter-brained. — By the way, Wilkinson must get our ale bottled in English pints now, for a quart bottle is too much, night after night, for you and me, without his assistance. But Darsie, as I was saying, is an arch lad, and somewhat light in the upper-story— I wish him well through the world; but he has little solidity, Alan, little solidity."

I scorn to desert an absent friend, Darsie, so I said for you a little more than my conscience warranted; but your defection from your legal studies had driven you far to leeward in my father's good opinion.

"Unstable as water, he shall not excel," said my father; "or, as the Septuagint hath it, *Effusa est sicut aqua—non crescat.* He goeth to dancing-houses, and readeth novels — *sat est.*"

I endeavoured to parry these texts by observing, that the dancing-houses amounted only to one night at La Pique's ball—the novels (so far as matter of notoriety, Darsie) to an odd volume of Tom Jones.

"But he danced from night to morning," replied my father; "and he read the idle trash, which the author should have been scourged for, at least twenty times over. It was never out of his hand."

I then hinted, that in all probability your fortune was now so easy as to dispense with your prosecuting the law any farther than you had done; and therefore you might think you had some title to amuse yourself. This was the least palatable argument of all.

"If he cannot amuse himself with the law," said my father, snappishly, "it is the worse for him. If he needs not law to teach him to make a fortune, I am sure he needs it to teach him how to keep one; and it would better become him to be learning this, than to be scouring the country like a land-louper, going he knows not where, to see he knows not what, and giving treats at Noble-House to fools like himself," (an angry glance at poor me.) "Noble-House, indeed!" he repeated, with elevated voice and sneering tone, as if there was something offensive to him in the name, though I will venture to say that any place in which you had been extravagant enough to spend five shillings, would have stood as deep in his reprobation.

Mindful of your idea, that my father knows more of your real situation than he thinks proper to mention, I thought I would hazard a fishing observation. "I did not see," I said, "how the Scottish law would be useful to a young gentleman whose fortune would seem to be vested in England."— I really thought my father would have beat me.

"D'ye mean to come round me, sir, *per ambages*, as Counsellor Pest says? What is it to you where Darsie Latimer's fortune is vested, or whether he hath any fortune, ay or no? — And what ill would the Scottish law do to him, though he had as much of it as either Stair or Bankton, sir? Is not the foundation of our municipal law the ancient code of the Roman Empire, devised at a time when it was so much renowned for its civil polity, sir, and wisdom? Go to your bed, sir, after your expedition to Noble-House, and see that your lamp be burning and your book before you ere the sun peeps. *Ars longa, vita brevis*, — were it not a sin to call the divine science of the law by the inferior name of art."

So my lamp did burn, dear Darsie, the next morning, though the owner took the risk of a domiciliary visitation, and lay snug in bed, trusting its glimmer might, without farther inquiry, be received as sufficient evidence of his vigilance. And now, upon this the third morning after your departure, things are but little better; for though the lamp burns in my den, and Voet on the Pandects hath his wisdom spread open before me, yet as I only use him as a reading-desk on which to scribble this sheet of nonsense to Darsie Latimer, it is probable the vicinity will be of little furtherance to my studies.

And now, methinks, I hear thee call me an affected hypocritical varlet, who, living under such a system of distrust and restraint as my father chooses to govern by, nevertheless pretends not to envy you your freedom and independence.

Latimer, I will tell you no lies. I wish my father would allow me a little more exercise of my free will, were it but that I might feel the pleasure of doing what would please him of my own accord. A little more spare time, and a little more money to enjoy it, would, besides, neither misbecome my age nor my condition; and it is, I own, provoking to see so many in the same situation winging the air at freedom, while I sit here, caged up like a cobbler's linnet, to chant the same unvaried lesson from sunrise to sunset, not to mention the listening to so many lectures against idleness, as if I enjoyed or was making use of the means of amusement! But then I cannot at heart blame either the motive or the object of this severity. For the motive, it is and can only be my father's anxious, devoted, and unremitting affection and zeal for my improvement, with a laudable sense of the honour of the profession to which he has trained me.

As we have no near relations, the tie betwixt us is of even unusual closeness, though in itself one of the strongest which nature can form. I am, and have all along been, the exclusive object of my father's anxious hopes, and his still more anxious and engrossing fears; so what title have I to complain, although now and then these fears and hopes lead him to take a troublesome and incessant charge of all my notions? Besides, I ought to recollect, and, Darsie, I do recollect, that my father upon various occasions, has shown that he can be indulgent as well as strict. The leaving his old apartments in the Luckenbooths was to him like divorcing the soul from the body; yet, Dr. R—— did but hint that the better air of this new district was more favourable to my health, as I was then suffering under the penalties of too rapid a growth, when he exchanged his old and beloved quarters, adjacent to the very Heart of Mid-Lothian, for one of those new tenements [entire within themselves] which modern taste has so lately introduced. Instance also the inestimable favour which he conferred on me by receiving you into his house, when you had only the unpleasant alternative of remaining, though a grown-up lad, in the society of mere boys.* This was a thing so contrary to all my father's ideas of seclusion, of economy, and of the safety to my morals and industry, which he wished to attain, by preserving me from the society of other young people, that, upon

---

* The diminutive and obscure *place* called Brown's Square, was hailed about the time of its erection as an extremely elegant improvement upon the style of designing and erecting Edinburgh residences. Each house was, in the phrase used by appraisers, " finished within itself," or, in the still newer phraseology, "self-contained." It was built about the year 1763-4; and the old part of the city being near and accessible, this square soon received many inhabitants, who ventured to remove to so moderate a distance from the ——— street.

my word, I am always rather astonished how I should have had the impudence to make the request, than that he should have complied with it.

Then for the object of his solicitude — Do not laugh, or hold up your hands, my good Darsie; but upon my word I like the profession to which I am in the course of being educated, and am serious in prosecuting the preliminary studies. The law is my vocation—in an especial, and, I may say, in an hereditary way, my vocation; for although I have not the honour to belong to any of the great families who form in Scotland, as in France, the noblesse of the robe, and with us, at least, carry their heads as high, or rather higher, than the noblesse of the sword,—for the former consist more frequently of the "first-born of Egypt," yet my grandfather, who, I dare say, was a most excellent person, had the honour to sign a bitter protest against the Union, in the respectable character of town-clerk to the ancient Borough of Birlthegroat; and there is some reason—shall I say to hope, or to suspect?—that he may have been a natural son of a first cousin of the then Fairford of that Ilk, who had been long numbered among the minor barons. Now my father mounted a step higher on the ladder of legal promotion, being, as you know as well as I do, an eminent and respected Writer to his Majesty's Signet; and I myself am destined to mount a round higher still, and wear the honoured robe which is sometimes supposed, like Charity, to cover a multitude of sins. I have, therefore, no choice but to climb upwards, since we have mounted thus high, or else to fall down at the imminent risk of my neck. So that I reconcile myself to my destiny; and while you are looking from mountain peaks, at distant lakes and friths, I am, *de apicibus juris*, consoling myself with visions of crimson and scarlet gowns — with the appendages of handsome cowls, well lined with salary.

You smile, Darsie, *more tuo*, and seem to say it is little worth while to cozen one's self with such vulgar dreams; yours being, on the contrary, of a high and heroic character, bearing the same resemblance to mine, that a bench, covered with purple cloth, and plentifully loaded with session papers, does to some Gothic throne, rough with Barbaric pearl and gold. But what would you have? — *Sua quemque trahit voluptas.* And my visions of preferment, though they may be as unsubstantial at present, are nevertheless more capable of being realized, than your aspirations after the Lord knows what. What says my father's proverb? "Look to a gown of gold, and you will at least get a sleeve of it." Such is my pursuit; but what dost thou look to? The chance that the mystery, as you call it, which at present overclouds your birth and connections, will clear up into something inexpressibly and inconceivably brilliant; and this without any effort or exertion of your own, but purely by the goodwill of Fortune. · I know the pride and naughtiness of thy heart, and sincerely do I wish that thou hadst more beatings to thank me for, than those which thou dost acknowledge so gratefully. Then had I thumped these Quixotical expectations out of thee, and thou hadst not, as now, conceived thyself to be the hero of some romantic history, and converted, in thy vain imaginations, honest Griffiths, citizen and broker, who never bestows more than the needful upon his quarterly epistles, into some wise Alcander or sage Alquife, the mystical and magical protector of thy peerless destiny. But I know not how it was, thy skull got harder, I think, and my knuckles became softer; not to mention that at length thou didst begin to show about thee a spark of something dangerous, which I was bound to respect at least, if I did not fear it.

And while I speak of this, it is not much amiss to advise thee to correct a little this cock-a-hoop courage of thine. I fear much that, like a hot-mettled horse, it will carry the owner into some scrape, out of which he will find it difficult to extricate himself, especially if the daring spirit which bore thee thither should chance to fail thee at a pinch. Remember, Darsie, thou art not naturally courageous; on the contrary, we have long since agreed, that, quiet as I am, I have the advantage in this important particular. My courage consists, I think, in strength of nerves and constitutional indifference to danger; which, though it never pushes me on adventure, secures me in full use of my recollection, and tolerably complete self-possession, when danger actually arrives. Now, thine seems more what may be called intellectual courage; highness of spirit, and desire of distinction; impulses which render thee alive to the love of fame, and deaf to the apprehension of danger, until it forces itself suddenly upon thee. I own, that whether it is from my having caught my father's apprehensions, or that I have reason to entertain doubts of my own, I often think that this wildfire chase, of romantic situation and adventure, may lead thee into some mischief; and then what would become of Alan Fairford? They might make whom they pleased Lord-Advocate or Solicitor-General, I should never have the heart to strive for it. All my exertions are intended to vindicate myself one day in your eyes; and I think I should not care a farthing for the embroidered silk gown, more than for an old woman's apron, unless I had hopes that thou shouldst be walking the boards to admire, and perhaps to envy me.

That this may be the case, I prithee — beware! See not a Dulcinea in every slipshod girl, who, with blue eyes, fair hair, a tattered plaid, and a willow-wand in her gripe, drives out the village cows to the loaming. Do not think you will meet a gallant Valentine in every English rider, or an Orson in every Highland drover. View things as they are, and not as they may be magnified through thy teeming fancy. I have seen thee look at an old gravel pit, till thou madest out capes, and bays, and inlets, crags and precipices, and the whole stupendous scenery of the Isle of Feroe, in what was, to all ordinary eyes, a mere horse-pond. Besides, did I not once find thee gazing with respect at a lizard, in the attitude of one who looks upon a crocodile? Now this is, doubtless, so far a harmless exercise of your imagination, for the puddle cannot drown you, nor the Lilliputian alligator eat you up. But it is different in society, where you cannot mistake the character of those you converse with, or suffer your fancy to exaggerate their qualities, good or bad, without exposing yourself not only to ridicule, but to great and serious inconveniences. Keep guard, therefore, on your imagination, my dear Darsie; and let your old friend assure you, it is the point of your character most pregnant with peril to its good and generous owner. Adieu! let not the franks of the worthy peer remain unemployed; above all, *Sis memor mei.*

A. F.

LETTER III.

DARSIE LATIMER TO ALAN FAIRFORD.

SHEPHERD'S BUSH.

I HAVE received thine absurd and most conceited epistle. It is well for thee that, Lovelace and Belford-like, we came under a convention to pardon every species of liberty which we may take with each other; since, upon my word, there are some reflections in your last, which would otherwise have obliged me to return forthwith to Edinburgh, merely to show you I was not what you took me for.

Why, what a pair of prigs hast thou made of us!—I plunging into scrapes, without having courage to get out of them — thy sagacious self, afraid to put one foot before the other, lest it should run away from its companion:

and so standing still like a post, out of mere faintness and coldness of heart, while all the world are driving full speed past thee. Thou a portrait-painter!—I tell thee, Alan, I have seen a better seated on the fourth round of a ladder, and painting a bare-breeched Highlander, holding a pint-stoup as big as himself, and a booted Lowlander, in a bobwig, supporting a glass of like dimensions; the whole being designed to represent the sign of the Salutation.

How hadst thou the heart to represent thine own individual self, with all thy motions, like those of a great Dutch doll, depending on the pressure of certain springs, as duty, reflection, and the like; without the impulse of which, thou wouldst doubtless have me believe thou wouldst not budge an inch! But have I not seen Gravity out of his bed at midnight; and must I, in plain terms, remind thee of certain mad pranks? Thou hadst ever, with the gravest sentiments in thy mouth, and the most starched reserve in thy manner, a kind of lumbering proclivity towards mischief, although with more inclination to set it a-going, than address to carry it through; and I cannot but chuckle internally, when I think of having seen my most venerable monitor, the future President of some high Scottish Court, puffing, blowing, and floundering, like a clumsy cart-horse in a bog, where his efforts to extricate himself only plunged him deeper at every awkward struggle, till some one—I myself, for example—took compassion on the moaning monster, and dragged him out by mane and tail.

As for me, my portrait is, if possible, even more scandalously caricatured. *I* fail or quail in spirit at the upcome! Where canst thou show me the least symptom of the recreant temper with which thou hast invested me, (as I trust,) merely to set off the solid and impassible dignity of thine own stupid indifference? If you ever saw me tremble, be assured that my flesh, like that of the old Spanish general, only quaked at the dangers into which my spirit was about to lead it. Seriously, Alan, this imputed poverty of spirit is a shabby charge to bring against your friend. I have examined myself as closely as I can, being, in very truth, a little hurt at your having such hard thoughts of me, and on my life I can see no reason for them. I allow you have, perhaps, some advantage of me in the steadiness and indifference of your temper; but I should despise myself, if I were conscious of the deficiency in courage which you seem willing enough to impute to me. However, I suppose this ungracious hint proceeds from sincere anxiety for my safety; and so viewing it, I swallow it as I would do medicine from a friendly doctor, although I believed in my heart he had mistaken my complaint.

This offensive insinuation disposed of, I thank thee, Alan, for the rest of thy epistle. I thought I heard your good father pronouncing the word Noble-House, with a mixture of contempt and displeasure, as if the very name of the poor little hamlet were odious to him, or, as if you had selected, out of all Scotland, the very place at which you had no call to dine. But if he had had any particular aversion to that blameless village, and very sorry inn, is it not his own fault that I did not accept the invitation of the Laird of Glengallacher, to shoot a buck in what he emphatically calls "his country?" Truth is, I had a strong desire to have complied with his Laird-ship's invitation. To shoot a buck! Think how magnificent an idea to one who never shot any thing but hedge-sparrows, and that with a horse-pistol, purchased at a broker's stand in the Cowgate!—You, who stand upon your courage, may remember that I took the risk of firing the said pistol for the first time, while you stood at twenty yards' distance; and that, when you were persuaded it would go off without bursting, forgetting all law but that of the biggest and strongest, you possessed yourself of it exclusively for the rest of the holydays. Such a day's sport was no complete introduction to the noble art of deer-stalking, as it is practised in the Highlands; but I should not have scrupled to accept honest Glengallacher's invitation, at the risk of firing a rifle for the first time, had it not been for the outcry which your father made at my proposal, in the full ardour of his zeal for King George, the Hanover succession, and the Presbyterian faith. I wish I had stood out, since I have gained so little upon his good opinion by submission. All his impressions concerning the Highlanders are taken from the recollections of the Forty-five, when he retreated from the West-Port with his brother volunteers, each to the fortalice of his own separate dwelling, so soon as they heard the Adventurer was arrived with his clans as near them as Kirkliston. The flight of Falkirk — *parma non bene selecta* — in which I think your sire had his share with the undaunted western regiment, does not seem to have improved his taste for the company of Highlanders; (quære, Alan, dost thou derive the courage thou makest such boast of from an hereditary source?) — and stories of Rob Roy Macgregor, and Sergeant Alan Mhor Cameron,* have served to paint them in still more sable colours to his imagination.

Now, from all I can understand, these ideas, as applied to the present state of the country, are absolutely chimerical. The Pretender is no more remembered in the Highlands, than if the poor gentleman were gathered to his hundred and eight fathers, whose portraits adorn the ancient walls of Holyrood; the broadswords have passed into other hands; the targets are used to cover the butter churns; and the race has sunk, or is fast sinking, from ruffling bullies into tame cheaters. Indeed, it was partly my conviction that there is little to be seen in the north, which, arriving at your father's conclusions, though from different premises, inclined my course in this direction, where perhaps I shall see as little.

One thing, however, I *have* seen; and it was with pleasure the more indescribable, that I was debarred from treading the land which my eyes were permitted to gaze upon, like those of the dying prophet from the top of Mount Pisgah, — I have seen, in a word, the fruitful shores of merry England; merry England! of which I boast myself a native, and on which I gaze, even while raging floods and unstable quicksands divide us, with the filial affection of a dutiful son.

Thou canst not have forgotten, Alan — for when didst thou ever forget what was interesting to thy friend? — that the same letter from my friend Griffiths, which doubled my income, and placed my motions at my own free disposal, contained a prohibitory clause, by which, reason none assigned, I was prohibited, as I respected my present safety and future fortunes, from visiting England; every other part of the British dominions, and a tour, if I pleased, on the Continent, being left to my own choice. — Where is the tale, Alan, of a covered dish in the midst of a royal banquet, upon which the eyes of every guest were immediately fixed, neglecting all the dainties with which the table was loaded? This cause of banishment from England — from my native country — from the land of the brave, and the wise, and the free — affects me more than I am rejoiced by the freedom and independence assigned to me in all other respects. Thus, in seeking this extreme boundary of the country which I am forbidden to tread, I resemble the poor tethered horse, which, you may have observed, is always grazing on the very verge of the circle to which it is limited by its halter.

Do not accuse me of romance for obeying this impulse towards the South; nor suppose that, to satisfy the imaginary longing of an idle curiosity, I am in any danger of risking the solid comforts of my present condition. Whoever has hitherto taken charge of my motions, has shown me, by convincing proofs, more weighty than the assurances which they have withheld, that my real advantage is their principal object. I should be, therefore, worse than a fool did I object to their authority, even when it seems some-

---

* Of Rob Roy we have had more than enough. Alan Cameron, commonly called Sergeant Mhor, a freebooter of the same period, was equally remarkable for strength, courage, and generosity.

what capriciously exercised; for assuredly, at my age, I might—intrusted as I am with the care and management of myself in every other particular—expect that the cause of excluding me from England should be frankly and fairly stated for my own consideration and guidance.   However, I will not grumble about the matter.   I shall know the whole story one day, I suppose; and perhaps, as you sometimes surmise, I shall not find there is any mighty matter in it after all.

Yet one cannot help wondering—but plague on it, if I wonder any longer, my letter will be as full of wonders as one of Katterfelto's advertisements.   I have a month's mind, instead of this damnable iteration of guesses and forebodings, to give thee the history of a little adventure which befell me yesterday; though I am sure you will, as usual, turn the opposite side of the spy-glass on my poor narrative, and reduce *more tuo*, to the most petty trivialities, the circumstance to which thou accusest me of giving undue consequence.   Hang thee, Alan, thou art as unfit a confidant for a youthful gallant with some spice of imagination, as the old taciturn secretary of Facardin of Trebizond.   Nevertheless, we' must each perform our separate destinies.   I am doomed to see, act, and tell;—thou, like a Dutchman, enclosed in the same Diligence with a Gascon, to hear, and shrug thy shoulders.

Of Dumfries, the capital town of this county, I have but little to say, and will not abuse your patience by reminding you, that it is built on the gallant river Nith, and that its churchyard, the highest place of the old town, commands an extensive and fine prospect.   Neither will I take the traveller's privilege of inflicting upon you the whole history of Bruce poniarding the Red Comyn in the Church of the Dominicans at this place, and becoming a king and patriot, because he had been a church-breaker and a murderer.   The present Dumfriezers remember and justify the deed, observing it was only a papist church—in evidence whereof, its walls have been so completely demolished, that no vestiges of them remain.   They are a sturdy set of true-blue Presbyterians, these burghers of Dumfries; men after your father's own heart, zealous for the Protestant succession—the rather that many of the great families around are suspected to be of a different way of thinking, and shared, a great many of them, in the insurrection of the Fifteen, and some of the more recent business of the Forty-five.   The town itself suffered in the latter era; for Lord Elcho, with a large party of the rebels, levied a severe contribution upon Dumfries, on account of the citizens having annoyed the rear of the Chevalier during his march into England.

Many of these particulars I learned from Provost C——, who, happening to see me in the market-place, remembered that I was an intimate of your father's, and very kindly asked me to dinner.   Pray tell your father that the effects of his kindness to me follow me every where.   I became tired, however, of this pretty town in the course of twenty-four hours, and crept along the coast eastwards, amusing myself with looking out for objects of antiquity, and sometimes making, or attempting to make, use of my new angling-rod.   By the way, old Cotton's instructions, by which I hoped to qualify myself for one of the gentle society of anglers, are not worth a farthing for this meridian.   I learned this by mere accident, after I had waited four mortal hours.   I shall never forget an impudent urchin, a cowherd, about twelve years old, without either brogue or bonnet, barelegged, and with a very indifferent pair of breeches—how the villain grinned in scorn at my landing-net, my plummet, and the gorgeous jury of flies which I had assembled to destroy all the fish in the river.   I was induced at last to lend the rod to the sneering scoundrel, to see what he would make of it? and he had not only half filled my basket in an hour, but literally taught me to kill two trouts with my own hand.   This, and Sam having found the hay and oats, not forgetting the ale, very good at this small inn, first made me take the fancy of resting here for a day or two; and I have got my grinning blackguard of a Piscator leave to attend on me, by paying sixpence a-day for a herdboy in his stead.

A notably clean Englishwoman keeps this small house, and my bedroom is sweetened with lavender, has a clean sash-window, and the walls are, moreover, adorned with ballads of Fair Rosamond and Cruel Barbara Allan. The woman's accent, though uncouth enough, sounds yet kindly in my ear; for I have never yet forgotten the desolate effect produced on my infant organs, when I heard on all sides your slow and broad northern pronunciation, which was to me the tone of a foreign land. I am sensible I myself have since that time acquired Scotch in perfection, and many a Scotticism withal. Still the sound of the English accentuation comes to my ears as the tones of a friend; and even when heard from the mouth of some wandering beggar, it has seldom failed to charm forth my mite. You Scotch, who are so proud of your own nationality, must make due allowance for that of other folks.

On the next morning I was about to set forth to the stream where I had commenced angler the night before, but was prevented, by a heavy shower of rain, from stirring abroad the whole forenoon; during all which time, I heard my varlet of a guide as loud with his blackguard jokes in the kitchen, as a footman in the shilling gallery;—so little are modesty and innocence the inseparable companions of rusticity and seclusion.

When after dinner the day cleared, and we at length sallied out to the river side, I found myself subjected to a new trick on the part of my accomplished preceptor. Apparently, he liked fishing himself better than the trouble of instructing an awkward novice, such as I; and in hopes of exhausting my patience, and inducing me to resign the rod, as I had done the preceding day, my friend contrived to keep me thrashing the water more than an hour with a pointless hook. I detected this trick at last, by observing the rogue grinning with delight when he saw a large trout rise and dash harmless away from the angle. I gave him a sound cuff, Alan; but the next moment was sorry, and, to make amends, yielded possession of the fishing-rod for the rest of the evening, he undertaking to bring me home a dish of trouts for my supper, in atonement for his offences.

Having thus got honourably rid of the trouble of amusing myself in a way I cared not for, I turned my steps towards the sea, or rather the Solway Firth, which here separates the two sister kingdoms, and which lay at about a mile's distance, by a pleasant walk over sandy-knolls, covered with short herbage, which you call Links, and we English, Downs.

But the rest of my adventure would weary out my fingers, and must be deferred until to-morrow, when you shall hear from me, by way of continuation; and, in the meanwhile, to prevent over-hasty conclusions, I must just hint to you, we are but yet on the verge of the adventure which it is my purpose to communicate.

LETTER IV.

THE SAME TO THE SAME.

SHEPHERD'S BUSH.

I MENTIONED in my last, that having abandoned my fishing-rod as an unprofitable implement, I crossed over the open downs which divided me from the margin of the Solway. When I reached the banks of the great estuary, which are here very bare and exposed, the waters had receded

c

from the large and level space of sand, through which a stream, now feeble and fordable, found its way to the ocean. The whole was illuminated by the beams of the low and setting sun, who showed his ruddy front, like a warrior prepared for defence, over a huge battlemented and turreted wall of crimson and black clouds, which appeared like an immense Gothic fortress, into which the Lord of day was descending. His setting rays glimmered bright upon the wet surface of the sands, and the numberless pools of water by which it was covered, where the inequality of the ground had occasioned their being left by the tide.

The scene was animated by the exertions of a number of horsemen, who were actually employed in hunting salmon. Ay, Alan, lift up your hands and eyes as you will, I can give their mode of fishing no name so appropriate; for they chased the fish at full gallop, and struck them with their barbed spears, as you see hunters spearing boars in the old tapestry. The salmon, to be sure, take the thing more quietly than the boars; but they are so swift in their own element, that to pursue and strike them is the task of a good horseman, with a quick eye, a determined hand, and full command both of his horse and weapon. The shouts of the fellows as they galloped up and down in the animating exercise — their loud bursts of laughter when any of their number caught a fall — and still louder acclamations when any of the party made a capital stroke with his lance — gave so much animation to the whole scene, that I caught the enthusiasm of the sport, and ventured forward a considerable space on the sands. The feats of one horseman, in particular, called forth so repeatedly the clamorous applause of his companions, that the very banks rang again with their shouts. He was a tall man, well mounted on a strong black horse, which he caused to turn and wind like a bird in the air, carried a longer spear than the others, and wore a sort of fur cap or bonnet, with a short feather in it, which gave him on the whole rather a superior appearance to the other fishermen. He seemed to hold some sort of authority among them, and occasionally directed their motions both by voice and hand; at which times I thought his gestures were striking, and his voice uncommonly sonorous and commanding.

The riders began to make for the shore, and the interest of the scene was almost over, while I lingered on the sands, with my looks turned to the shores of England, still gilded by the sun's last rays, and, as it seemed, scarce distant a mile from me. The anxious thoughts which haunt me began to muster in my bosom, and my feet slowly and insensibly approached the river which divided me from the forbidden precincts, though without any formed intention, when my steps were arrested by the sound of a horse galloping; and as I turned, the rider (the same fisherman whom I had formerly distinguished) called out to me, in an abrupt manner, "Soho, brother! you are too late for Bowness to-night — the tide will make presently."

I turned my head and looked at him without answering; for, to my thinking, his sudden appearance (or rather, I should say, his unexpected approach) had, amidst the gathering shadows and lingering light, something in it which was wild and ominous.

"Are you deaf?" he added — "or are you mad? — or have you a mind for the next world?"

"I am a stranger," I answered, "and had no other purpose than looking on at the fishing — I am about to return to the side I came from."

"Best make haste then," said he. "He that dreams on the bed of the Solway, may wake in the next world. The sky threatens a blast that will bring in the waves three feet a-breast."

So saying he turned his horse and rode off, while I began to walk back towards the Scottish shore, a little alarmed at what I had heard; for the tide advances with such rapidity upon these fatal sands, that well-mounted horsemen lay aside hopes of safety, if they see its white surge advancing while they are yet at a distance from the bank.

These recollections grew more agitating, and, instead of walking deliberately, I began a race as fast as I could, feeling, or thinking I felt, each pool of salt water through which I splashed, grow deeper and deeper. At length the surface of the sand did seem considerably more intersected with pools and channels full of water — either that the tide was really beginning to influence the bed of the estuary, or, as I must own is equally probable, that I had, in the hurry and confusion of my retreat, involved myself in difficulties which I had avoided in my more deliberate advance. Either way, it was rather an unpromising state of affairs, for the sands at the same time turned softer, and my footsteps, as soon as I had passed, were instantly filled with water. I began to have odd recollections concerning the snugness of your father's parlour, and the secure footing afforded by the pavement of Brown's Square and Scot's Close, when my better genius, the tall fisherman, appeared once more close to my side, he and his sable horse looming gigantic in the now darkening twilight.

"Are you mad?" he said, in the same deep tone which had before thrilled on my ear, "or are you weary of your life?—You will be presently amongst the quicksands." — I professed my ignorance of the way, to which he only replied, "There is no time for prating — get up behind me."

He probably expected me to spring from the ground with the activity which these Borderers have, by constant practice, acquired in every thing relating to horsemanship; but as I stood irresolute, he extended his hand, and grasping mine, bid me place my foot on the toe of his boot, and thus raised me in a trice to the croupe of his horse. I was scarcely securely seated, ere he shook the reins of his horse, who instantly sprung forward; but annoyed, doubtless, by the unusual burden, treated us to two or three bounds, accompanied by as many flourishes of his hind heels. The rider sat like a tower, notwithstanding that the unexpected plunging of the animal threw me forward upon him. The horse was soon compelled to submit to the discipline of the spur and bridle, and went off at a steady hand gallop; thus shortening the devious, for it was by no means a direct path, by which the rider, avoiding the loose quicksands, made for the northern bank.

My friend, perhaps I may call him my preserver, — for to a stranger, my situation was fraught with real danger, — continued to press on at the same speedy pace, but in perfect silence, and I was under too much anxiety of mind to disturb him with any questions. At length we arrived at a part of the shore with which I was utterly unacquainted, when I alighted and began to return, in the best fashion I could, my thanks for the important service which he had just rendered me.

The stranger only replied by an impatient "pshaw!" and was about to ride off, and leave me to my own resources, when I implored him to complete his work of kindness, by directing me to Shepherd's Bush, which was, as I informed him, my home for the present.

"To Shepherd's Bush?" he said; "it is but three miles, but if you know not the land better than the sand, you may break your neck before you get there; for it is no road for a moping boy in a dark night; and, besides, there are the brook and the fens to cross."

I was a little dismayed at this communication of such difficulties as my habits had not called on me to contend with. Once more the idea of thy father's fireside came across me; and I could have been well contented to have swop'd the romance of my situation, together with the glorious independence of control, which I possessed at the moment, for the comforts of the chimney-corner, though I were obliged to keep my eyes chained to Erskine's Larger Institutes.

I asked my new friend whether he could not direct me to any house of public entertainment for the night; and supposing it probable he was himself a poor man, I added, with the conscious dignity of a well-filled pocket-book, that I could make it worth any man's while to oblige me. The fisherman making no answer, I turned away from him with as gallant an appearance of indifference as I could command, and began to take, as I thought, the path which he had pointed out to me.

His deep voice immediately sounded after me to recall me. "Stay, young man, stay — you have mistaken the road already. — I wonder your friends sent out such an inconsiderate youth, without some one wiser than himself to take care of him."

"Perhaps they might not have done so," said I, "if I had any friends who cared about the matter."

"Well, sir," he said, "it is not my custom to open my house to strangers, but your pinch is like to be a smart one; for, besides the risk from bad roads, fords, and broken ground, and the night, which looks both black and gloomy, there is bad company on the road sometimes — at least it has a bad name, and some have come to harm; so that I think I must for once make my rule give way to your necessity, and give you a night's lodging in my cottage."

Why was it, Alan, that I could not help giving an involuntary shudder at receiving an invitation so seasonable in itself, and so suitable to my naturally inquisitive disposition? I easily suppressed this untimely sensation; and as I returned thanks, and expressed my hope that I should not disarrange his family, I once more dropped a hint of my desire to make compensation for any trouble I might occasion. The man answered very coldly, "Your presence will no doubt give me trouble, sir, but it is of a kind which your purse cannot compensate; in a word, although I am content to receive you as my guest, I am no publican to call a reckoning."

I begged his pardon, and, at his instance, once more seated myself behind him upon the good horse, which went forth steady as before — the moon, whenever she could penetrate the clouds, throwing the huge shadow of the animal, with its double burden, on the wild- and bare ground over which we passed.

Thou mayest laugh till thou lettest the letter fall if thou wilt, but it reminded me of the Magician Atlantes on his hippogriff, with a knight trussed up behind him, in the manner Ariosto has depicted that matter. Thou art, I know, matter-of-fact enough to affect contempt of that fascinating and delicious poem; but think not that, to conform with thy bad taste, I shall forbear any suitable illustration which now or hereafter may occur to me.

On we went, the sky blackening around us, and the wind beginning to pipe such a wild and melancholy tune as best suited the hollow sounds of the advancing tide, which I could hear at a distance, like the roar of some immense monster defrauded of its prey.

At length, our course was crossed by a deep dell or dingle, such as they call in some parts of Scotland a den, and in others a cleuch, or narrow glen. It seemed, by the broken glances which the moon continued to throw upon it, to be steep, precipitous, and full of trees, which are, generally speaking, rather scarce upon these shores. The descent by which we plunged into this dell was both steep and rugged, with two or three abrupt turnings; but neither danger nor darkness impeded the motion of the black horse, who seemed rather to slide upon his haunches, than to gallop down the pass, throwing me again on the shoulders of the athletic rider, who, sustaining no inconvenience by the circumstance, continued to press the horse forward with his heel, steadily supporting him at the same time by raising his bridle hand, until we stood in safety at the bottom of the steep — not a little to my consolation, as, friend Alan, thou mayst easily conceive.

A very short advance up the glen, the bottom of which we had attained by this ugly descent, brought us in front of two or three cottages, one of which another blink of moonshine enabled me to rate as rather better than those of the Scottish peasantry in this part of the world; for the sashes seemed glazed, and there were what are called storm-windows in the roof, giving symptoms of the magnificence of a second story. The scene around was very interesting; for the cottages, and the yards or crofts annexed to them, occupied a *haugh*, or holm, of two acres, which a brook of some consequence (to judge from its roar) had left upon one side of tho little glen while finding its course close to the farther bank, and which appeared to be covered and darkened with trees, while the level space beneath enjoyed such stormy smiles as the moon had that night to bestow.

I had little time for observation, for my companion's loud whistle, seconded by an equally loud balloo, speedily brought to the door of the principal cottage a man and a woman, together with two large Newfoundland dogs, the deep baying of which I had for some time heard. A yelping terrier or two, which had joined the concert, were silent at the presence of my conductor, and began to whine, jump up, and fawn upon him. The female drew back when she beheld a stranger; the man who had a lighted lantern, advanced, and without any observation, received the horse from my host, and led him, doubtless, to stable, while I followed my conductor into the house. When we had passed the *hallan*,* we entered a well-sized apartment, with a clean brick floor, where a fire blazed (much to my contentment) in the ordinary projecting sort of a chimney, common in Scottish houses. There were stone seast within the chimney, and ordinary utensils, mixed with fishing-spears, nets, and similar implements of sport, were hung around the walls of the place. The female who had first appeared at the door, had now retreated into a side apartment. She was presently followed by my guide, after he had silently motioned me to a seat; and their place was supplied by an elderly woman, in a gray stuff gown, with a check apron and *toy*, obviously a menial, though neater in her dress than is usual in her apparent rank — an advantage which was counterbalanced by a very forbidding aspect. But the most singular part of her attire, in this very Protestant country, was a rosary, in which the smaller beads were black oak, and those indicating the *pater-noster* of silver, with a crucifix of the same metal.

This person made preparations for supper, by spreading a clean though coarse cloth over a large oaken table, placing trenchers and salt upon it, and arranging the fire to receive a gridiron. I observed her motions in silence; for she took no sort of notice of me, and as her looks were singularly forbidding, I felt no disposition to commence conversation.

When this duenna had made all preliminary arrangements, she took from the well-filled pouch of my conductor, which he had hung up by the door, one or two salmon, or *grilses*, as the smaller sort are termed, and selecting that which seemed best, and in highest season, began to cut it into slices, and to prepare a *grillade;* the savoury smell of which affected me so powerfully, that I began sincerely to hope that no delay would intervene between the platter and the lip.

As this thought came across me, the man who had conducted the horse to the stable entered the apartment, and discovered to me a countenance yet more uninviting than that of the old crone who was performing with such dexterity the office of cook to the party. He was perhaps sixty years old; yet his brow was not much furrowed, and his jet black hair was only grizzled, not whitened, by the advance of age. All his motions spoke strength unabated; and, though rather undersized, he had very broad shoulders, was square-made, thin-flanked, and apparently combined in his

---

* The partition which divides a Scottish cottage.

frame muscular strength and activity; the last somewhat impaired perhaps by years, but the first remaining in full vigour. A hard and harsh countenance — eyes far sunk under projecting eyebrows, which were grizzled like his hair — a wide mouth, furnished from ear to ear with a range of unimpaired teeth, of uncommon whiteness, and a size and breadth which might have become the jaws of an ogre, completed this delightful portrait. He was clad like a fisherman, in jacket and trowsers of the blue cloth commonly used by seamen, and had a Dutch case-knife, like that of a Hamburgh skipper, stuck into a broad buff belt, which seemed as if it might occasionally sustain weapons of a description still less equivocally calculated for violence.

This man gave me an inquisitive, and, as I thought, a sinister look upon entering the apartment; but without any farther notice of me, took up the office of arranging the table, which the old lady had abandoned for that of cooking the fish, and with more address than I expected from a person of his coarse appearance, placed two chairs at the head of the table, and two stools below; accommodating each seat to a cover, beside which he placed an allowance of barley-bread, and a small jug, which he replenished with ale from a large black jack. Three of these jugs were of ordinary earthenware, but the fourth, which he placed by the right-hand cover at the upper end of the table, was a flagon of silver, and displayed armorial bearings. Beside this flagon he placed a salt-cellar of silver, handsomely wrought, containing salt of exquisite whiteness, with pepper and other spices. A sliced lemon was also presented on a small silver salver. The two large water-dogs, who seemed perfectly to understand the nature of the preparations, seated themselves one on each side of the table, to be ready to receive their portion of the entertainment. I never saw finer animals, or which seemed to be more influenced by a sense of decorum, excepting that they slobbered a little as the rich scent from the chimney was wafted past their noses. The small dogs ensconced themselves beneath the table.

I am aware that I am dwelling upon trivial and ordinary circumstances, and that perhaps I may weary out your patience in doing so. But conceive me alone in this strange place, which seemed, from the universal silence, to be the very temple of Harpocrates—remember that this is my first excursion from home — forget not that the manner in which I had been brought hither had the dignity of danger and something the air of an adventure, and that there was a mysterious incongruity in all I had hitherto witnessed; and you will not, I think, be surprised that these circumstances, though trifling, should force themselves on my notice at the time, and dwell in my memory afterwards.

That a fisher, who pursued the sport perhaps for his amusement as well as profit, should be well mounted and better lodged than the lower class of peasantry, had in it nothing surprising; but there was something about all that I saw which seemed to intimate, that I was rather in the abode of a decayed gentleman, who clung to a few of the forms and observances of former rank, than in that of a common peasant, raised above his fellows by comparative opulence.

Besides the articles of plate which I have already noticed, the old man now lighted and placed on the table a silver lamp, or *cruisie*, as the Scottish term it, filled with very pure oil, which in burning diffused an aromatic fragrance, and gave me a more perfect view of the cottage walls, which I had hitherto only seen dimly by the light of the fire. The *bink*,* with its usual arrangement of pewter and earthenware, which was most strictly and critically clean, glanced back the flame of the lamp merrily from one side of the apartment. In a recess, formed by the small bow of a latticed window, was a large writing-desk of walnut-tree wood, curiously carved,

---

* The frame of wooden shelves placed in a Scottish kitchen for holding plates.

above which arose shelves of the same, which supported a few books and papers. The opposite side of the recess contained (as far as I could discern, for it lay in shadow, and I could at any rate have seen it but imperfectly from the place where I was seated) one or two guns, together with swords, pistols, and other arms — a collection which, in a poor cottage, and in a country so peaceful, appeared singular at least, if not even somewhat suspicious.

All these observations, you may suppose, were made much sooner than I have recorded, or you (if you have not skipped) have been able to read them. They were already finished, and I was considering how I should open some communication with the mute inhabitants of the mansion, when my conductor re-entered from the side-door by which he had made his exit.

He had now thrown off his rough riding-cap, and his coarse jockey-coat, and stood before me in a gray jerkin trimmed with black, which sat close to, and set off, his large and sinewy frame, and a pair of trowsers of a lighter colour, cut as close to the body as they are used by Highlandmen. His whole dress was of finer cloth than that of the old man; and his linen, so minute was my observation, clean and unsullied. His shirt was without ruffles, and tied at the collar with a black riband, which showed his strong and muscular neck rising from it, like that of an ancient Hercules. His head was small, with a large forehead, and well-formed ears. He wore neither peruke nor hair powder; and his chestnut locks, curling close to his head, like those of an antique statue, showed not the least touch of time, though the owner must have been at least fifty. His features were high and prominent in such a degree, that one knew not whether to term them harsh or handsome. In either case, the sparkling gray eye, aquiline nose, and well-formed mouth, combined to render his physiognomy noble and expressive. An air of sadness, or severity, or of both, seemed to indicate a melancholy, and, at the same time, a haughty temper. I could not help running mentally over the ancient heroes, to whom I might assimilate the noble form and countenance before me. He was too young, and evinced too little resignation to his fate, to resemble Belisarius. Coriolanus, standing by the hearth of Tullus Aufidius, came nearer the mark; yet the gloomy and haughty look of the stranger had, perhaps, still more of Marius, seated among the ruins of Carthage.

While I was lost in these imaginations, my host stood by the fire, gazing on me with the same attention which I paid to him, until, embarrassed by his look, I was about to break silence at all hazards. But the supper, now placed upon the table, reminded me, by its appearance, of those wants which I had almost forgotten while I was gazing on the fine form of my conductor. He spoke at length, and I almost started at the deep rich tone of his voice, though what he said was but to invite me to sit down to the table. He himself assumed the seat of honour, beside which the silver flagon was placed, and beckoned to me to sit down beside him.

Thou knowest thy father's strict and excellent domestic discipline has trained me to hear the invocation of a blessing before we break the daily bread, for which we are taught to pray — I paused a moment, and, without designing to do so, I suppose my manner made him sensible of what I expected. The two domestics, or inferiors, as I should have before observed, were already seated at the bottom of the table, when my host shot a glance of a very peculiar expression towards the old man, observing, with something approaching to a sneer, "Cristal Nixon, say grace — the gentleman expects one."

"The foul fiend shall be clerk, and say amen, when I turn chaplain," growled out the party addressed, in tones which might have become the condition of a dying bear; "if the gentleman is a whig, he may please himself with his own mummery. My faith is neither in word nor writ, but in barley bread and brown ale."

"Mabel Moffat," said my guide, looking at the old woman, and raising his sonorous voice, probably because she was hard of hearing, "canst thou ask a blessing upon our victuals?"

The old woman shook her head, kissed the cross which hung from her rosary, and was silent.

"Mabel will say grace for no heretic," said the master of the house, with the same latent sneer on his brow and in his accent.

At the same moment, the side-door already mentioned opened, and the young woman (so she proved) whom I had first seen at the door of the cottage, advanced a little way into the room, then stopped bashfully, as if she had observed that I was looking at her, and asked the master of the house, "if he had called?"

"Not louder than to make old Mabel hear me," he replied; "and yet," he added, as she turned to retire, "it is a shame a stranger should see a house where not one of the family can or will say a grace—do thou be our chaplain."

The girl, who was really pretty, came forward with timid modesty, and, apparently unconscious that she was doing any thing uncommon, pronounced the benediction in a silver-toned voice, and with affecting simplicity—her cheek colouring just so much as to show that on a less solemn occasion, she would have felt more embarrassed.

Now, if thou expectest a fine description of this young woman, Alan Fairford, in order to entitle thee to taunt me with having found a Dulcinea in the inhabitant of a fisherman's cottage on the Solway Frith, thou shalt be disappointed: for, having said she seemed very pretty, and that she was a sweet and gentle-speaking creature, I have said all concerning her that I can tell thee. She vanished when the benediction was spoken.

My host, with a muttered remark on the cold of our ride, and the keen air of the Solway Sands, to which he did not seem to wish an answer, loaded my plate from Mabel's grillade, which, with a large wooden bowl of potatoes, formed our whole meal. A sprinkling from the lemon gave a much higher zest than the usual condiment of vinegar; and I promise you that, whatever I might hitherto have felt, either of curiosity or suspicion, did not prevent me from making a most excellent supper, during which little passed betwixt me and my entertainer, unless that he did the usual honours of the table with courtesy, indeed, but without even the affectation of hearty hospitality, which those in his (apparent) condition generally affect on such occasions, even when they do not actually feel it. On the contrary, his manner seemed that of a polished landlord towards an unexpected and unwelcome guest, whom, for the sake of his own credit, he receives with civility, but without either good-will or cheerfulness.

If you ask how I learned all this, I cannot tell you; nor, were I to write down at length the insignificant intercourse which took place between us, would it perhaps serve to justify these observations. It is sufficient to say, that in helping his dogs, which he did from time to time with great liberality, he seemed to discharge a duty much more pleasing to himself, than when he paid the same attention to his guest. Upon the whole, the result on my mind was as I tell it you.

When supper was over, a small case-bottle of brandy, in a curious frame of silver filigree, circulated to the guests. I had already taken a small glass of the liquor, and, when it had passed to Mabel and to Cristal, and was again returned to the upper end of the table, I could not help taking the bottle in my hand, to look more at the armorial bearings, which were chased with considerable taste on the silver framework. Encountering the eye of my entertainer, I instantly saw that my curiosity was highly distasteful; he frowned, bit his lip, and showed such uncontrollable signs of impatience, that, setting the bottle immediately down, I attempted some apology. To this he did not deign to reply, or even to listen; and Cristal,

at a signal from his master, removed the object of my curiosity, as well as
the cup, upon which the same arms were engraved.

There ensued an awkward pause, which I endeavoured to break by
observing, that "I feared my intrusion upon his hospitality had put his
family to some inconvenience."

"I hope you see no appearance of it, sir," he replied, with cold civility.
"What inconvenience a family so retired as ours may suffer from receiving
an unexpected guest is like to be trifling, in comparison of what the visiter
himself sustains from want of his accustomed comforts. So far, therefore,
as our connection stands, our accounts stand clear."

Notwithstanding this discouraging reply, I blundered on, as is usual in
such cases, wishing to appear civil, and being, perhaps, in reality the very
reverse. "I was afraid," I said, "that my presence had banished one of
the family" (looking at the side-door) "from his table."

"If," he coldly replied, "I meant the young woman whom I had seen in
the apartment, he bid me observe that there was room enough at the table
for her to have seated herself, and meat enough, such as it was, for her
supper. I might, therefore, be assured, if she had chosen it, she would
have supped with us."

There was no dwelling on this or any other topic longer; for my entertainer, taking up the lamp, observed, that "my wet clothes might reconcile
me for the night to their custom of keeping early hours; that he was under
the necessity of going abroad by peep of day to-morrow morning, and
would call me up at the same time, to point out the way by which I was to
return to the Shepherd's Bush."

This left no opening for farther explanation; nor was there room for it
on the usual terms of civility; for, as he neither asked my name, nor
expressed the least interest concerning my condition, I—the obliged person
—had no pretence to trouble him with such inquiries on my part.

He took up the lamp, and led me through the side-door into a very small
room, where a bed had been hastily arranged for my accommodation, and,
putting down the lamp, directed me to leave my wet clothes on the outside
of the door, that they might be exposed to the fire during the night. He
then left me, having muttered something which was meant to pass for good-
night.

I obeyed his directions with respect to my clothes, the rather that in
despite of the spirits which I had drunk, I felt my teeth begin to chatter,
and received various hints from an aguish feeling, that a town-bred youth,
like myself, could not at once rush into all the hardihood of country sports
with impunity. But my bed, though coarse and hard, was dry and clean;
and I soon was so little occupied with my heats and tremors, as to listen
with interest to a heavy foot, which seemed to be that of my landlord,
traversing the boards (there was no ceiling, as you may believe) which
roofed my apartment. Light glancing through these rude planks, became
visible as soon as my lamp was extinguished; and as the noise of the slow,
solemn, and regular step continued, and I could distinguish that the person
turned and returned as he reached the end of the apartment, it seemed clear
to me that the walker was engaged in no domestic occupation, but merely
pacing to and fro for his own pleasure. "An odd amusement this," I
thought, "for one who had been engaged at least a part of the preceding
day in violent exercise, and who talked of rising by the peep of dawn on
the ensuing morning."

Meantime I heard the storm, which had been brewing during the evening,
begin to descend with a vengeance; sounds, as of distant thunder, (the
noise of the more distant waves, doubtless, on the shore,) mingled with the
roaring of the neighbouring torrent, and with the crashing, groaning, and
even screaming of the trees in the glen, whose boughs were tormented by
the gale. Within the house, windows clattered, and doors clapped, and the

walls, thought sufficiently substantial for a building of the kind, seemed to
me to totter in the tempest.

But still the heavy steps perambulating the apartment over my head,
were distinctly heard amid the roar and fury of the elements. I thought
more than once I even heard a groan; but I frankly own, that, placed in
this unusual situation, my fancy may have misled me. I was tempted
several times to call aloud, and ask whether the turmoil around us did not
threaten danger to the building which we inhabited; but when I thought
of the secluded and unsocial master of the dwelling, who seemed to avoid
human society, and to remain unperturbed amid the elemental war, it
seemed, that to speak to him at that moment, would have been to address
the spirit of the tempest himself, since no other being, I thought, could
have remained calm and tranquil while winds and waters were thus raging
around.

In process of time, fatigue prevailed over anxiety and curiosity. The
storm abated, or my senses became deadened to its terrors, and I fell asleep
ere yet the mysterious paces of my host had ceased to shake the flooring
over my head.

It might have been expected that the novelty of my situation, although
it did not prevent my slumbers, would have at least diminished their pro-
foundness, and shortened their duration. It proved otherwise, however;
for I never slept more soundly in my life, and only awoke when, at morning
dawn, my landlord shook me by the shoulder, and dispelled some dream,
of which, fortunately for you, I have no recollection, otherwise you would
have been favoured with it, in hopes you might have proved a second Daniel
upon the occasion.

"You sleep sound—" said his full deep voice; "ere five years have
rolled over your head, your slumbers will be lighter — unless ere then you
are wrapped in the sleep which is never broken."

"How!" said I, starting up in the bed; "do you know any thing of me
—of my prospects—of my-views in life?"

"Nothing," he answered, with a grim smile; "but it is evident you are
entering upon the world young, inexperienced, and full of hopes, and I do
but prophesy to you what I would to any one in your condition. — But
come; there lie your clothes — a brown crust and a draught of milk wait
you, if you choose to break your fast; but you must make haste."

"I must first," I said, "take the freedom to spend a few minutes alone,
before beginning the ordinary works of the day."

"Oh! — umph! — I cry your devotions pardon," he replied, and left the
apartment.

Alan, there is something terrible about this man.

I joined him, as I had promised, in the kitchen where we had supped
over night, where I found the articles which he had offered me for breakfast, without butter or any other addition.

He walked up and down while I partook of the bread and milk; and the
slow measured weighty step seemed identified with those which I had heard
last night. His pace, from its funereal slowness, seemed to keep time with
some current of internal passion, dark, slow, and unchanged. — "We run
and leap by the side of a lively and bubbling brook," thought I, internally,
"as if we would run a race with it; but beside waters deep, slow, and
lonely, our pace is sullen and silent as their course. What thoughts may
be now corresponding with that furrowed brow, and bearing time with that
heavy step?"

"If you have finished," said he, looking up to me with a glance of impatience, as he observed that I ate no longer, but remained with my eyes
fixed upon him, "I wait to show you the way."

We went out together, no individual of the family having been visible
excepting my landlord. I was disappointed of the opportunity which I

watched for of giving some gratuity to the domestics, as they seemed to be. As for offering any recompense to the master of the household, it seemed to me impossible to have attempted it.

What would I have given for a share of thy composure, who wouldst have thrust half-a-crown into a man's hand whose necessities seemed to crave it, conscious that you did right in making the proffer, and not caring sixpence whether you hurt the feelings of him whom you meant to serve! I saw thee once give a penny to a man with a long beard, who, from the dignity of his exterior, might have represented Solon. I had not thy courage, and therefore I made no tender to my mysterious host, although, notwithstanding his display of silver utensils, all around the house bespoke narrow circumstances, if not actual poverty.

We left the place together. But I hear thee murmur thy very new and appropriate ejaculation, *Ohe, jam satis !* — The rest for another time. Perhaps I may delay farther communication till I learn how my favours are valued.

LETTER V.

ALAN FAIRFORD TO DARSIE LATIMER.

I HAVE thy two last epistles, my dear Darsie, and expecting the third, have been in no hurry to answer them. Do not think my silence ought to be ascribed to my failing to take interest in them, for, truly, they excel (though the task was difficult) thy usual excellings. Since the moon-calf who earliest discovered the Pandemonium of Milton in an expiring wood-fire — since the first ingenious urchin who blew bubbles out of soap and water, thou, my best of friends, hast the highest knack at making histories out of nothing. Wert thou to plant the bean in the nursery-tale, thou wouldst make out, so soon as it began to germinate, that the castle of the giant was about to elevate its battlements on the top of it. All that happens to thee gets a touch of the wonderful and the sublime from thy own rich imagination. Didst ever see what artists call a Claude Lorraine glass, which spreads its own particular hue over the whole landscape which you see through it? — thou beholdest ordinary events just through such a medium.

I have looked carefully at the facts of thy last long letter, and they are just such as might have befallen any little truant of the High School, who had got down to Leith Sands, gone beyond the *prawn-dub*, wet his hose and shoon, and, finally, had been carried home, in compassion, by some high-kilted fishwife, cursing all the while the trouble which the brat occasioned her.

I admire the figure which thou must have made, clinging for dear life behind the old fellow's back — thy jaws chattering with fear, thy muscles cramped with anxiety. Thy execrable supper of broiled salmon, which was enough to ensure the nightmare's regular visits for a twelvemonth, may be termed a real affliction ; but as for the storm of Thursday last, (such, I observe, was the date,) it roared, whistled, howled, and bellowed, as fearfully amongst the old chimney heads in the Candlemaker-row, as it could on the Solway shore, for the very wind of it — *teste me per totam noctem vigilante.* And then in the morning again, when—Lord help you—in your sentimental delicacy you bid the poor man adieu, without even tendering him half-a-crown for supper and lodging !

You laugh at me for giving a penny (to be accurate, though, thou shouldst have said sixpence) to an old fellow, whom thou, in thy high flight, wouldst have sent home supperless, because he was like Solon or Belisarius. But you forget that the affront descended like a benediction into the pouch of the old gaberlunzie, who overflowed in blessings upon the generous donor—Long ere he would have thanked thee, Darsie, for thy barren veneration of his beard and his bearing. Then you laugh at my good father's retreat from Falkirk, just as if it were not time for a man to trudge when three or four mountain knaves, with naked claymores, and heels as light as their fingers, were scampering after him, crying *furinish.* You remember what he said himself when the Laird of Bucklivat told him that *furinish* signified "stay a while." "What the devil," he said, surprised out of his Presbyterian correctness by the unreasonableness of such a request under the circumstances, "would the scoundrels have had me stop to have my head cut off?"

Imagine such a train at your own heels, Darsie, and ask yourself whether you would not exert your legs as fast as you did in flying from the Solway tide. And yet you impeach my father's courage. I tell you he has courage enough to do what is right, and to spurn what is wrong—courage enough to defend a righteous cause with hand and purse, and to take the part of the poor man against his oppressor, without fear of the consequences to himself. This is civil courage, Darsie; and it is of little consequence to most men in this age and country, whether they ever possess military courage or no.

Do not think I am angry with you, though I thus attempt to rectify your opinions on my father's account. I am well aware that, upon the whole, he is scarce regarded with more respect by me than by thee. And, while I am in a serious humour, which it is difficult to preserve with one who is perpetually tempting me to laugh at him, pray, dearest Darsie, let not thy ardour for adventure carry thee into more such scrapes as that of the Solway Sands. The rest of the story is a mere imagination; but that stormy evening might have proved, as the Clown says to Lear, "a naughty night to swim in."

As for the rest, if you can work mysterious and romantic heroes out of old cross-grained fishermen, why, I for one will reap some amusement by the metamorphosis. Yet hold! even there, there is some need of caution. This same female chaplain—thou sayest so little of her, and so much of every one else, that it excites some doubt in my mind. *Very pretty* she is, it seems—and that is all thy discretion informs me of. There are cases in which silence implies other things than consent. Wert thou ashamed or afraid, Darsie, to trust thyself with the praises of the very pretty grace-sayer?—As I live, thou blushest! Why, do I not know thee an inveterate Squire of Dames? and have I not been in thy confidence? An elegant elbow, displayed when the rest of the figure was muffled in a cardinal, or a neat well-turned ankle and instep, seen by chance as its owner tripped up the Old Assembly Close,* turned thy brain for eight days. Thou wert once caught, if I remember rightly, with a single glance of a single matchless eye, which, when the fair owner withdrew her veil, proved to be single in the literal sense of the word. And, besides, were you not another time enamoured of a voice—a mere voice, that mingled in the psalmody at the Old Greyfriars' Church—until you discovered the proprietor of that dulcet organ to be Miss Dolly MacIzzard, who is both "back and breast," as our saying goes?

All these things considered, and contrasted with thy artful silence on the subject of this grace-saying Nereid of thine, I must beg thee to be more explicit upon that subject in thy next, unless thou wouldst have me form the conclusion that thou thinkest more of her than thou carest to talk of.

---

* Of old this almost deserted alley formed the most common access betwixt the High Street and the southern suburbs

You will not expect much news from this quarter, as you know the monotony of my life, and are aware it must at present be devoted to uninterrupted
study.   You have said a thousand times, that I am only qualified to make
my way by dint of plodding, and therefore plod I must.

My father seems to be more impatient of your absence than he was after
your first departure.   He is sensible, I believe, that our solitary meals want
the light which your gay humour was wont to throw over them, and feels
melancholy as men do when the light of the sun is no longer upon the landscape.   If it is thus with him, thou mayest imagine it is much more so
with me, and canst conceive how heartily I wish that thy frolic were ended,
and thou once more our inmate.

I resume my pen, after a few hours' interval, to say that an incident has
occurred, on which you will yourself be building a hundred castles in the
air, and which even I, jealous as I am of such baseless fabrics, cannot but
own affords ground for singular conjecture.

My father has of late taken me frequently along with him when he
attends the Courts, in his anxiety to see me properly initiated into the practical forms of business.   I own I feel something on his account and my
own from this over-anxiety, which, I dare say, renders us both ridiculous.
But what signifies my repugnance ? my father drags me up to his counsel
learned in the law, — " Are you quite ready to come on to-day, Mr. Crossbite ? — This is my son, designed for the bar — I take the liberty to bring
him with me to-day to the consultation, merely that he may see how these
things are managed."

Mr. Crossbite smiles and bows, as a lawyer smiles on the solicitor who
employs him, and I dare say, thrusts his tongue into his cheek, and whispers
into the first great wig that passes him, " What the d—l does old Fairford
mean by letting loose his whelp on me ?"

As I stood beside them, too much vexed at the childish part I was made
to play to derive much information from the valuable arguments of Mr.
Crossbite, I observed a rather elderly man, who stood with his eyes firmly
bent on my father, as if he only waited an end of the business in which
he was engaged, to address him.   There was something, I thought, in the
gentleman's appearance which commanded attention. — Yet his dress was
not in the present taste, and though it had once been magnificent, was now
antiquated and unfashionable.   His coat was of blanched velvet, with a
satin lining, a waistcoat of violet-coloured silk, much embroidered ; his
breeches the same stuff as the coat.   He wore square-toed shoes, with fore-
tops, as they are called ; and his silk stockings were rolled up over his
knee, as you may have seen in pictures ; and here and there on some of
those originals who seem to pique themselves on dressing after the mode
of Methuselah.   A *chapeau bras* and sword necessarily completed his
equipment, which, though out of date, showed that it belonged to a man of
distinction.

The instant Mr. Crossbite had ended what he had to say, this gentleman
walked up to my father, with, " Your servant, Mr. Fairford — it is long
since you and I met."

My father, whose politeness, you know, is exact and formal, bowed, and
hemmed, and was confused, and at length professed that the distance since
they had met was so great, that though he remembered the face perfectly,
the name, he was sorry to say, had — really — somehow — escaped his
memory.

" Have you forgot Herries of Birrenswork ?" said the gentleman, and my
father bowed even more profoundly than before ; though I think his reception of his old friend seemed to lose some of the respectful civility which
he bestowed on him while his name was yet unknown.   It now seemed to

D

be something like the lip-courtesy which the heart would have denied had ceremony permitted.

My father, however, again bowed low, and hoped he saw him well.

"So well, my good Mr. Fairford, that I come hither determined to renew my acquaintance with one or two old friends, and with you in the first place. I halt at my old resting-place — you must dine with me to-day, at Paterson's, at the head of the Horse Wynd — it is near your new fashionable dwelling, and I have business with you."

My father excused himself respectfully, and not without embarrassment — "he was particularly engaged at home."

"Then I will dine with you, man," said Mr. Herries of Birrenswork; "the few minutes you can spare me after dinner will suffice for my business; and I will not prevent you a moment from minding your own — I am no bottle-man."

You have often remarked that my father, though a scrupulous observer of the rites of hospitality, seems to exercise them rather as a duty than as a pleasure; indeed, but for a conscientious wish to feed the hungry and receive the stranger, his doors would open to guests much seldomer than is the case. I never saw so strong an example of this peculiarity, (which I should otherwise have said is caricatured in your description,) as in his mode of homologating the self-given invitation of Mr. Herries. The embarrassed brow, and the attempt at a smile which accompanied his "We will expect the honour of seeing you in Brown Square at three o'clock,"-could not deceive any one, and did not impose upon the old Laird. — It was with a look of scorn that he replied, "I will relieve you then till that hour, Mr. Fairford;" and his whole manner seemed to say, "It is my pleasure to dine with you, and I care not whether I am welcome or no."

When he turned away, I asked my father who he was.

"An unfortunate gentleman," was the reply.

"He looks pretty well on his misfortunes," replied I. "I should not have suspected that so gay an outside was lacking a dinner."

"Who told you that he does?" replied my father; "he is *omni suspicione major*, so far as worldly circumstances are concerned. — It is to be hoped he makes a good use of them; though, if he does, it will be for the first time in his life."

"He has then been an irregular liver?" insinuated I.

My father replied by that famous brocard with which he silences all unacceptable queries, turning in the slightest degree upon the failings of our neighbours, — "If we mend our own faults, Alan, we shall all of us have enough to do, without sitting in judgment upon other folks."

Here I was again at fault; but rallying once more, I observed, he had the air of a man of high rank and family.

"He is well entitled," said my father, "representing Herries of Birrenswork; a branch of that great and once powerful family of Herries, the elder branch whereof merged in the house of Nithesdale at the death of Lord Robin the Philosopher, Anno Domini sixteen hundred and sixty-seven."

"Has he still," said I, "his patrimonial estate of Birrenswork?"

"No," replied my father; "so far back as his father's time, it was a mere designation — the property being forfeited by Herbert Herries following his kinsman the Earl of Derwentwater, to the Preston affair in 1715. But they keep up the designation, thinking, doubtless, that their claims may be revived in more favourable times for Jacobites and for popery; and folks who in no way partake of their fantastic capriccios, do yet allow it to pass unchallenged, *ex comitate*, if not *ex misericordia*. — But were he the Pope and the Pretender both, we must get some dinner ready for him, since he has thought fit to offer himself. So hasten home, my lad, and tell Hannah, Cook Epps, and James Wilkinson, to do their best; and do thou look out a pint or two of Maxwell's best — it is in the fifth bin — there are the keys of the wine-cellar. — Do not leave them in the lock — you know poor James's failing, though he is an honest creature under all other temptations — and I have but two bottles of the old brandy left — we must keep it for medicine, Alan."

Away went I — made my preparations — the hour of dinner came, and so did Mr. Herries of Birrenswork.

If I had thy power of imagination and description, Darsie, I could make out a fine, dark, mysterious, Rembrandt-looking portrait of this same stranger, which should be as far superior to thy fisherman, as a shirt of chain-mail is to a herring-net. I can assure you there is some matter for description about him; but knowing my own imperfections, I can only say, I thought him eminently disagreeable and ill-bred.—No, *ill-bred* is not the proper word; on the contrary, he appeared to know the rules of good-breeding perfectly, and only to think that the rank of the company did not require that he should attend to them—a view of the matter infinitely more offensive than if his behaviour had been that of uneducated and proper rudeness. While my father said grace, the Laird did all but whistle aloud; and when I, at my father's desire, returned thanks, he used his toothpick, as if he had waited that moment for its exercise.

So much for Kirk — with King, matters went even worse. My father, thou knowest, is particularly full of deference to his guests; and in the present case, he seemed more than usually desirous to escape every cause of dispute. He so far compromised his loyalty, as to announce merely " The King," as his first toast after dinner, instead of the emphatic " King George," which is his usual formula. Our guest made a motion with his glass, so as to pass it over the water-decanter which stood beside him, and added, "Over the water."

My father coloured, but would not seem to hear this. Much more there was of careless and disrespectful, in the stranger's manner and tone of conversation; so that though I know my father's prejudices in favour of rank and birth, and though I am aware his otherwise masculine understanding has never entirely shaken off the slavish awe of the great, which in his earlier days they had so many modes of commanding, still I could hardly excuse him for enduring so much insolence—such it seemed to be—as this self-invited guest was disposed to offer to him at his own table.

One can endure a traveller in the same carriage, if he treads upon your toes by accident, or even through negligence; but it is very different when, knowing that they are rather of a tender description, he continues to pound away at them with his hoofs. In my poor opinion — and I am a man of peace—you can, in that case, hardly avoid a declaration of war.

I believe my father read my thoughts in my eye; for, pulling out his watch, he said, "Half-past four, Alan—you should be in your own room by this time—Birrenswork will excuse you."

Our visitor nodded carelessly, and I had no longer any pretence to remain. But as I left the room, I heard this Magnate of Nithesdale distinctly mention the name of Latimer. I lingered; but at length a direct hint from my father obliged me to withdraw; and when, an hour afterwards, I was summoned to partake of a cup of tea, our guest had departed. He had business that evening in the High Street, and could not spare time even to drink tea. I could not help saying, I considered his departure as a relief from incivility. "What business has he to upbraid us," I said, "with the change of our dwelling from a more inconvenient to a better quarter of the town? What was it to him if we chose to imitate some of the conveniences or luxuries of an English dwelling-house, instead of living piled up above each other in flats? Have his patrician birth and aristocratic fortunes given him any right to censure those who dispose of the fruits of their own industry, according to their own pleasure?"

My father took a long pinch of snuff, and replied, "Very well, Alan; very well indeed. I wish Mr. Crossbite or Counsellor Pest had heard you; they must have acknowledged that you have a talent for forensic elocution; and it may not be amiss to try a little declamation at home now and then, to gather audacity and keep yourself in breath. But touching the subject of this paraffle of words, it's not worth a pinch of tobacco. D'ye think that I care for Mr. Herries of Birrenswork more than any other gentleman who comes here about business, although I do not care to go tilting at his throat, because he speaks like a gray goose, as he is? But to say no more about him, I want to have Darsie Latimer's present direction; for it is possible I may have to write the lad a line with my own hand—and yet I do not well know—but give me the direction at all events."

I did so, and if you have heard from my father accordingly, you know more, probably, about the subject of this letter than I who write it. But if you have not, then shall I have discharged a friend's duty, in letting you know that there certainly is something afloat between this disagreeable Laird and my father, in which you are considerably interested.

Adieu! and although I have given thee a subject for waking dreams, beware of building a castle too heavy for the foundation; which in the present instance, is barely the word Latimer occurring in a conversation betwixt a gentleman of Dumfriesshire and a W. S. of Edinburgh — *Cætera prorsus ignoro.*

LETTER VI.

DARSIE LATIMER TO ALAN FAIRFORD.

[In continuation of Letters III. and IV.]

I TOLD thee I walked out into the open air with my grave and stern landlord. I could now see more perfectly than on the preceding night the secluded glen in which stood the two or three cottages which appeared to be the abode of him and his family.

It was so narrow, in proportion to its depth, that no ray of the morning sun was likely to reach it till it should rise high in the horizon. Looking up the dell, you saw a brawling brook issuing in foamy haste from a covert of underwood, like a race-horse impatient to arrive at the goal; and, if you gazed yet more earnestly, you might observe part of a high waterfall glimmering through the foliage, and giving occasion, doubtless, to the precipitate speed of the brook. Lower down, the stream became more placid, and opened into a quiet piece of water, which afforded a rude haven to two or three fishermen's boats, then lying high and dry on the sand, the tide being out. Two or three miserable huts could be seen beside this little haven, inhabited probably by the owners of the boats, but inferior in every respect to the establishment of mine host, though that was miserable enough.

I had but a minute or two to make these observations, yet during that space my companion showed symptoms of impatience, and more than once shouted, "Cristal — Cristal Nixon!" until the old man of the preceding evening appeared at the door of one of the neighbouring cottages or outhouses, leading the strong black horse which I before commemorated, ready bridled and saddled. My conductor made Cristal a sign with his finger, and, turning from the cottage door, led the way up the steep path or ravine which connected the sequestered dell with the open country.

Had I been perfectly aware of the character of the road down which I had been hurried with so much impetuosity on the preceding evening, I greatly question if I should have ventured the descent; for it deserved no better name than the channel of a torrent, now in a good measure filled with water, that dashed in foam and fury into the dell, being swelled with the rains of the preceding night. I ascended this ugly path with some difficulty, although on foot, and felt dizzy when I observed, from such traces as the rains had not obliterated, that the horse seemed almost to have slid down it upon his haunches the evening before.

My host threw himself on his horse's back, without placing a foot in the stirrup—passed me in the perilous ascent, against which he pressed his steed as if the animal had had the footing of a wild cat. The water and mud splashed from his heels in his reckless course, and a few bounds placed him on the top of the bank, where I presently joined him, and found the horse and rider standing still as a statue; the former panting and expanding his broad nostrils to the morning wind, the latter motionless, with his eye fixed on the first beams of the rising sun, which already began to peer above the eastern horizon, and gild the distant mountains of Cumberland and Liddesdale.

He seemed in a reverie, from which he started at my approach, and, putting his horse in motion, led the way, at a leisurely pace, through a broken and sandy road, which traversed a waste, level, and uncultivated tract of downs, intermixed with morass, much like that in the neighbourhood of my quarters at Shepherd's Bush. Indeed, the whole open ground of this district, where it approaches the sea, has, except in a few favoured spots, the same uniform and dreary character.

Advancing about a hundred yards from the brink of the glen, we gained a still more extensive command of this desolate prospect, which seemed even more dreary, as contrasted with the opposite shores of Cumberland, crossed and intersected by ten thousand lines of trees growing in hedge rows, shaded with groves and woods of considerable extent, animated by hamlets and villas, from which thin clouds of smoke already gave sign of human life and human industry.

My conductor had extended his arm, and was pointing the road to Shepherd's Bush, when the step of a horse was heard approaching us. He looked sharply round, and having observed who was approaching, proceeded in his instructions to me, planting himself at the same time in the very middle of the path, which, at the place where we halted, had a slough on the one side, and a sand-bank on the other.

I observed that the rider who approached us slackened his horse's pace from a slow trot to a walk, as if desirous to suffer us to proceed, or at least to avoid passing us at a spot where the difficulty of doing so must have brought us very close to each other. You know my old failing, Alan, and that I am always willing to attend to any thing in preference to the individual who has for the time possession of the conversation.

Agreeably to this amiable propensity, I was internally speculating concerning the cause of the rider keeping aloof from us, when my companion, elevating his deep voice so suddenly and so sternly, as at once to recall my wandering thoughts, exclaimed, " In the name of the devil, young man, do you think that others have no better use for their time than you have, that you oblige me to repeat the same thing to you three times over?—Do you see, I say, yonder thing at a mile's distance, that looks like a finger-post, or rather like a gallows?—I would it had a dreaming fool hanging upon it, as an example to all meditative moon-calves!—Yon gibbet-looking pole will guide you to the bridge, where you must pass the large brook; then proceed straight forward, till several roads divide at a cairn.—Plague on thee, thou art wandering again !"

It is indeed quite true, that at this moment the horseman approached us, and my attention was again called to him as I made way to let him pass.

His whole exterior at once showed that he belonged to the Society of Friends, or, as the world and the world's law calls them, Quakers. A strong and useful iron-gray galloway showed, by its sleek and good condition, that the merciful man was merciful to his beast. His accoutrements were in the usual unostentatious, but clean and serviceable order, which characterizes these sectaries. His long surtout of dark-gray superfine cloth descended down to the middle of his leg, and was buttoned up to his chin, to defend him against the morning air. As usual, his ample beaver hung down without button or loop, and shaded a comely and placid countenance, the gravity of which appeared to contain some seasoning of humour, and had nothing in common with the pinched puritanical air affected by devotees in general. The brow was open and free from wrinkles, whether of age or hypocrisy. The eye was clear, calm, and considerate, yet appeared to be disturbed by apprehension, not to say fear, as pronouncing the usual salutation of, " I wish thee a good morrow, friend," he indicated, by turning his palfrey close to one side of the path, a wish to glide past with as little trouble as possible —just as a traveller would choose to pass a mastiff of whose peaceable intentions he is by no means confident.

But my friend, not meaning, perhaps, that he should get off so easily, put his horse quite across the path, so that, without plunging into the slough, or scrambling up the bank, the Quaker could not have passed him. Neither of these was an experiment without hazard greater than the passenger seemed willing to incur. He halted, therefore, as if waiting till my companion should make way for him ; and, as they sat fronting each other, I could not help thinking that they might have formed no bad emblem of Peace and War ; for, although my conductor was unarmed, yet the whole of his manner, his stern look, and his upright seat on horseback, were entirely those of a soldier in undress. He accosted the Quaker in these words,—" So ho ! friend Joshua—thou art early to the road this morning. Has the spirit moved thee and thy righteous brethren to act with some honesty, and pull down yonder tide-nets that keep the fish from coming up the river ?"

" Surely, friend, not so," answered Joshua, firmly, but good-humouredly at the same time ; " thou canst not expect that our own hands should pull down what our purses established. Thou killest the fish with spear, line, and coble-net ; and we, with snares and with nets, which work by the ebb and the flow of the tide. Each doth what seems best in his eyes to secure a share of the blessing which Providence hath bestowed on the river, and that within his own bounds. I prithee seek no quarrel against us, for thou shalt have no wrong at our hand."

" Be assured I will take none at the hand of any man, whether his hat be cocked or broad-brimmed," answered the fisherman. " I tell you in fair terms, Joshua Geddes, that you and your partners are using unlawful craft to destroy the fish in the Solway by stake-nets and wears ; and that we, who fish fairly, and like men, as our fathers did, have daily and yearly less sport and less profit. Do not think gravity or hypocrisy can carry it off as you have done. The world knows you, and we know you. You will destroy the salmon which makes the livelihood of fifty poor families, and then wipe your mouth, and go to make a speech at Meeting. But do not hope it will last thus. I give you fair warning, we will be upon you one morning soon, when we will not leave a stake standing in the pools of the Solway ; and down the tide they shall every one go, and well if we do not send a lessee along with them."

" Friend," replied Joshua, with a constrained smile, " but that I know thou dost not mean as thou say'st, I would tell thee we are under the protection of this country's laws ; nor do we the less trust to obtain their protection, that our principles permit us not, by any act of violent resistance, to protect ourselves."

· "All villanous cant and cowardice," exclaimed the fisherman, "and assumed merely as a cloak to your hypocritical avarice."

"Nay, say not cowardice, my friend," answered the Quaker, "since thou knowest there may be as much courage in enduring as in acting; and I will be judged by this youth, or by any one else, whether there is not more cowardice — even in the opinion of that world whose thoughts are the breath in thy nostrils — in the armed oppressor who doth injury, than in the defenceless and patient sufferer, who endureth it with constancy."

"I will change no more words with you on the subject," said the fisherman, who, as if something moved at the last argument which Mr. Geddes had used, now made room for him to pass forward on his journey. — "Do not forget, however," he added, "that you have had fair warning, nor suppose that we will accept of fair words in apology for foul play. These nets of yours are unlawful — they spoil our fishings — we will have them down at all risks and hazards. I am a man of my word, friend Joshua."

"I trust thou art," said the Quaker; "but thou art the rather bound to be cautious in rashly affirming what thou wilt never execute. For I tell thee, friend, that though there is as great a difference between thee and one of our people, as there is between a lion and a sheep, yet I know and believe thou hast so much of the lion in thee, that thou wouldst scarce employ thy strength and thy rage upon that which professeth no means of resistance. Report says so much good of thee, at least, if it says little more."

"Time will try," answered the fisherman; "and hark thee, Joshua, before we part I will put thee in the way of doing one good deed, which, credit me, is better than twenty moral speeches. Here is a stranger youth, whom Heaven has so scantily gifted with brains, that he will bewilder himself in the Sands, as he did last night, unless thou wilt kindly show him the way to Shepherd's Bush; for I have been in vain endeavouring to make him comprehend the road thither — Hast thou so much charity under thy simplicity, Quaker, as to do this good turn?"

"Nay, it is thou, friend," answered Joshua, "that dost lack charity, to suppose any one unwilling to do so simple a kindness."

"Thou art right — I should have remembered it can cost thee nothing.— Young gentleman, this pious pattern of primitive simplicity will teach thee the right way to the Shepherd's Bush—ay, and will himself shear thee like a sheep, if you come to buying and selling with him."

He then abruptly asked me, how long I intended to remain at Shepherd's Bush.

I replied, I was at present uncertain — as long, probably, as I could amuse myself in the neighbourhood.

"You are fond of sport?" he added, in the same tone of brief inquiry.

I answered in the affirmative, but added, I was totally inexperienced.

"Perhaps if you reside here for some days," he said, "we may meet again, and I may have the chance of giving you a lesson."

Ere I could express either thanks or assent, he turned short round with a wave of his hand, by way of adieu, and rode back to the verge of the dell from which we had emerged together; and as he remained standing upon the banks, I could long hear his voice while he shouted down to those within its recesses.

Meanwhile the Quaker and I proceeded on our journey for some time in silence; he restraining his soberminded steed to a pace which might have suited a much less active walker than myself, and looking on me from time to time with an expression of curiosity, mingled with benignity. For my part, I cared not to speak first. It happened I had never before been in company with one of this particular sect, and afraid that in addressing him I might unwittingly infringe upon some of their prejudices or peculiarities,

I patiently remained silent. At length he asked me, whether I had been long in the service of the Laird, as men called him.

I repeated the words "in his service," with such an accent of surprise, as induced him to say, "Nay, but, friend, I mean no offence; perhaps I should have said in his society—an inmate, I mean, in his house?"

"I am totally unknown to the person from whom we have just parted," said I, "and our connection is only temporary—He had the charity to give me his guidance from the Sands, and a night's harbourage from the tempest. So our acquaintance began, and there it is likely to end; for you may observe that our friend is by no means apt to encourage familiarity."

"So little so," answered my companion, "that thy case is, I think, the first in which I ever heard of his receiving any one into his house; that is, if thou hast really spent the night there."

"Why should you doubt it?" replied I; "there is no motive I can have to deceive you, nor is the object worth it."

"Be not angry with me," said the Quaker; "but thou knowest that thine own people do not, as we humbly endeavour to do, confine themselves within the simplicity of truth, but employ the language of falsehood, not only for profit, but for compliment, and sometimes for mere diversion. I have heard various stories of my neighbour; of most of which I only believe a small part, and even then they are difficult to reconcile with each other. But this being the first time I ever heard of his receiving a stranger within his dwelling, made me express some doubts. I pray thee let them not offend thee."

"He does not," said I, "appear to possess in much abundance the means of exercising hospitality, and so may be excused from offering it in ordinary cases."

"That is to say, friend," replied Joshua, "thou hast supped ill, and perhaps breakfasted worse. Now my small tenement, called Mount Sharon, is nearer to us by two miles than thine inn; and although going thither may prolong thy walk, as taking thee off the straighter road to Shepherd's Bush, yet methinks exercise will suit thy youthful limbs, as well as a good plain meal thy youthful appetite. What say'st thou, my young acquaintance?"

"If it puts you not to inconvenience," I replied; "for the invitation was cordially given, and my bread and milk had been hastily swallowed, and in small quantity."

"Nay," said Joshua, "use not the language of compliment with those who renounce it. Had this poor courtesy been very inconvenient, perhaps I had not offered it."

"I accept the invitation then," said I, "in the same good spirit in which you give it."

The Quaker smiled, reached me his hand, I shook it, and we travelled on in great cordiality with each other. The fact is, I was much entertained by contrasting in my own mind, the open manner of the kind-hearted Joshua Geddes, with the abrupt, dark, and lofty demeanour of my entertainer on the preceding evening. Both were blunt and unceremonious; but the plainness of the Quaker had the character of devotional simplicity, and was mingled with the more real kindness, as if honest Joshua was desirous of atoning, by his sincerity, for the lack of external courtesy. On the contrary, the manners of the fisherman were those of one to whom the rules of good behaviour might be familiar, but who, either from pride or misanthropy, scorned to observe them. Still I thought of him with interest and curiosity, notwithstanding so much about him that was repulsive; and I promised myself, in the course of my conversation with the Quaker, to learn all that he knew on the subject. He turned the conversation, however, into a different channel, and inquired into my own condition of life, and views in visiting this remote frontier.

I only thought it necessary to mention my name, and add, that I had been educated to the law, but finding myself possessed of some independence, I had of late permitted myself some relaxation, and was residing at Shepherd's Bush to enjoy the pleasure of angling.

"I do thee no harm, young man," said my new friend, "in wishing thee a better employment for thy grave hours, and a more humane amusement (if amusement thou must have) for those of a lighter character."

"You are severe, sir," I replied. "I heard you but a moment since refer yourself to the protection of the laws of the country — if there be laws, there must be lawyers to explain, and judges to administer them."

Joshua smiled, and pointed to the sheep which were grazing on the downs over which we were travelling. — "Were a wolf," he said, "to come even now upon yonder flocks, they would crowd for protection, doubtless, around the shepherd and his dogs; yet they are bitten and harassed daily by the one, shorn, and finally killed and eaten by the other. But I say not this to shock you; for, though laws and lawyers are evils, yet they are necessary evils in this probationary state of society, till man shall learn to render unto his fellows that which is their due, according to the light of his own conscience, and through no other compulsion. Meanwhile, I have known many righteous men who have followed thy intended profession in honesty and uprightness of walk. The greater their merit, who walk erect in a path which so many find slippery."

"And angling," said I, — "you object to that also as an amusement, you who, if I understood rightly what passed between you and my late landlord, are yourself a proprietor of fisheries."

"Not a proprietor," he replied, "I am only, in copartnery with others, a tacksman or lessee of some valuable salmon fisheries a little down the coast. But mistake me not. The evil of angling, with which I class all sports, as they are called, which have the sufferings of animals for their end and object, does not consist in the mere catching and killing those animals with which the bounty of Providence hath stocked the earth for the good of man, but in making their protracted agony a principle of delight and enjoyment. I do indeed cause these fisheries to be conducted for the necessary taking, killing, and selling the fish; and, in the same way, were I a farmer, I should send my lambs to market. But I should as soon think of contriving myself a sport and amusement out of the trade of the butcher as out of that of the fisher."

We argued the point no farther; for though I thought his arguments a little too high-strained, yet as my mind acquitted me of having taken delight in aught but the theory of field-sports, I did not think myself called upon stubbornly to advocate a practice which had afforded me so little pleasure.

We had by this time arrived at the remains of an old finger-post, which my host had formerly pointed out as a landmark. Here, a ruinous wooden bridge, supported by long posts resembling crutches, served me to get across the water, while my new friend sought a ford a good way higher up, for the stream was considerably swelled.

As I paused for his rejoining me, I observed an angler at a little distance pouching trout after trout, as fast almost as he could cast his line; and I own, in spite of Joshua's lecture on humanity, I could not but envy his adroitness and success, — so natural is the love of sport to our minds, or so easily are we taught to assimilate success in field-sports with ideas of pleasure, and with the praise due to address and agility. I soon recognized in the successful angler little Benjie, who had been my guide and tutor in that gentle art, as you have learned from my former letters. I called — I whistled — the rascal recognized me, and, starting like a guilty thing, seemed hesitating whether to approach or to run away; and when he determined on the former, it was to assail me with a loud, clamorous, and exaggerated report of the anxiety of all at the Shepherd's Bush for my personal safety; how my landlady had wept, how Sam and the ostler had not the heart to go to bed, but sat up all night drinking — and how he himself had been up long before day-break to go in quest of me.

"And you were switching the water, I suppose," said I, "to discover my dead body?"

This observation produced a long "Na—a—a" of acknowledged detection; but, with his natural impudence, and confidence in my good-nature, he immediately added, "that he thought I would like a fresh trout or twa for breakfast, and the water being in such a rare trim for the saumon raun,* he couldna help taking a cast."

While we were engaged in this discussion, the honest Quaker returned to the farther end of the wooden bridge to tell me he could not venture to cross the brook in its present state, but would be under the necessity to ride round by the stone bridge, which was a mile and a half higher up than his own house. He was about to give me directions how to proceed without him, and inquire for his sister, when I suggested to him, that if he pleased to trust his horse to little Benjie, the boy might carry him round by the bridge, while we walked the shorter and more pleasant road.

Joshua shook his head, for he was well acquainted with Benjie, who, he said, was the naughtiest varlet in the whole neighbourhood. Nevertheless, rather than part company, he agreed to put the pony under his charge for a short season, with many injunctions that he should not attempt to mount, but lead the pony (even Solomon) by the bridle, under the assurances of sixpence in case of proper demeanour, and penalty that if he transgressed the orders given him, "verily he should be scourged."

Promises cost Benjie nothing, and he showered them out wholesale; till the Quaker at length yielded up the bridle to him, repeating his charges, and enforcing them by holding up his forefinger. On my part, I called to Benjie to leave the fish he had taken at Mount Sharon, making, at the same time, an apologetic countenance to my new friend, not being quite aware whether the compliment would be agreeable to such a condemner of field-sports.

He understood me at once, and reminded me of the practical distinction betwixt catching the animals as an object of cruel and wanton sport, and eating them as lawful and gratifying articles of food, after they were killed. On the latter point he had no scruples; but, on the contrary, assured me, that this brook contained the real red trout, so highly esteemed by all connoisseurs, and that, when eaten within an hour of their being caught, they had a peculiar firmness of substance and delicacy of flavour, which rendered them an agreeable addition to a morning meal, especially when earned, like ours, by early rising, and an hour or two's wholesome exercise.

But to thy alarm be it spoken, Alan, we did not come so far as the frying of our fish without farther adventure. So it is only to spare thy patience, and mine own eyes, that I pull up for the present, and send thee the rest of my story in a subsequent letter.

---

* The bait made of salmon-roe salted and preserved. In a swollen river, and about the month of October it is a most deadly bait.

LETTER VII.

THE SAME TO THE SAME.

[In continuation.]

LITTLE BENJIE, with the pony, having been sent off on the left side of the brook, the Quaker and I sauntered on, like the cavalry and infantry of the same army occupying the opposite banks of a river, and observing the same line of march. But, while my worthy companion was assuring me of a pleasant greensward walk to his mansion, little Benjie, who had been charged to keep in sight, chose to deviate from the path assigned him, and, turning to the right, led his charge, Solomon, out of our vision.

"The villain means to mount him!" cried Joshua, with more vivacity than was consistent with his profession of passive endurance.

I endeavoured to appease his apprehensions, as he pushed on, wiping his brow with vexation, assuring him, that if the boy did mount, he would, for his own sake, ride gently.

"You do not know him," said Joshua, rejecting all consolation; "he do any thing gently!—no, he will gallop Solomon—he will misuse the sober patience of the poor animal who has borne me so long! Yes, I was given over to my own devices when I ever let him touch the bridle, for such a little miscreant there never was before him in this country."

He then proceeded to expatiate on every sort of rustic enormity of which he accused Benjie. He had been suspected of snaring partridges—was detected by Joshua himself in liming singing-birds—stood fully charged with having worried several cats, by aid of a lurcher which attended him, and which was as lean, and ragged, and mischievous, as his master. Finally, Benjie stood accused of having stolen a duck, to hunt it with the said lurcher, which was as dexterous on water as on land. I chimed in with my friend, in order to avoid giving him further irritation, and declared, I should be disposed, from my own experience, to give up Benjie as one of Satan's imps. Joshua Geddes began to censure the phrase as too much exaggerated, and otherwise unbecoming the mouth of a reflecting person; and, just as I was apologizing for it, as being a term of common parlance, we heard certain sounds on the opposite side of the brook, which seemed to indicate that Solomon and Benjie were at issue together. The sand-hills behind which Benjie seemed to take his course, had concealed from us, as doubtless he meant they should, his ascent into the forbidden saddle, and, putting Solomon to his mettle, which he was seldom called upon to exert, they had cantered away together in great amity, till they came near to the ford from which the palfrey's legitimate owner had already turned back.

Here a contest of opinions took place between the horse and his rider. The latter, according to his instructions, attempted to direct Solomon towards the distant bridge of stone; but Solomon opined that the ford was the shortest way to his own stable. The point was sharply contested, and we heard Benjie gee-hupping, tchek-tcheking, and, above all, flogging in great style; while Solomon, who, docile in his general habits, was now stirred beyond his patience, made a great trampling and recalcitration; and it was their joint noise which we heard, without being able to see, though Joshua might too well guess, the cause of it.

Alarmed at these indications, the Quaker began to shout out, "Benjie—thou varlet!—Solomon—thou fool!" when the couple presented themselves in full drive, Solomon having now decidedly obtained the better of the conflict, and bringing his unwilling rider in high career down to the ford. Never was there anger changed so fast into humane fear, as that of my good companion. "The varlet will be drowned!" he exclaimed — "a widow's son! — her only son! — and drowned! — let me go ———" And he struggled with me stoutly as I hung upon him, to prevent him from plunging into the ford.

I had no fear whatever for Benjie; for the blackguard vermin, though he could not manage the refractory horse, stuck on his seat like a monkey. Solomon and Benjie scrambled through the ford with little inconvenience, and resumed their gallop on the other side.

It was impossible to guess whether on this last occasion Benjie was running off with Solomon, or Solomon with Benjie; but, judging from character and motives, I rather suspected the former. I could not help laughing as the rascal passed me, grinning betwixt terror and delight, perched on the very pommel of the saddle, and holding with extended arms by bridle and mane; while Solomon, the bit secured between his teeth, and his head bored down betwixt his fore-legs, passed his master in this unwonted guise as hard as he could pelt.

"The mischievous bastard!" exclaimed the Quaker, terrified out of his usual moderation of speech — "the doomed gallows-bird! — he will break Solomon's wind to a certainty."

I prayed him to be comforted — assured him a brushing gallop would do his favourite no harm — and reminded him of the censure he had bestowed on me a minute before for applying a harsh epithet to the boy.

But Joshua was not without his answer; — "Friend youth," he said, "thou didst speak of the lad's soul, which thou didst affirm belonged to the enemy, and of that thou couldst say nothing of thine own knowledge; on the contrary, I did but speak of his outward man, which will assuredly be suspended by a cord, if he mendeth not his manners. Men say that, young as he is, he is one of the Laird's gang."

"Of the Laird's gang!" said I, repeating the words in surprise — "Do you mean the person with whom I slept last night? — I heard you call him the Laird — Is he at the head of a gang?"

"Nay, I meant not precisely a gang," said the Quaker, who appeared in his haste to have spoken more than he intended — "a company, or party, I should have said; but thus it is, friend Latimer, with the wisest men, when they permit themselves to be perturbed with passion, and speak as in a fever, or as with the tongue of the foolish and the forward. And although thou hast been hasty to mark my infirmity, yet I grieve not that thou hast been a witness to it, seeing that the stumbles of the wise may be no less a caution to youth and inexperience. than is the fall of the foolish."

This was a sort of acknowledgment of what I had already begun to suspect — that my new friend's real goodness of disposition, joined to the acquired quietism of his religious sect, had been unable entirely to check the effervescence of a temper naturally warm and hasty.

Upon the present occasion, as if sensible he had displayed a greater degree of emotion than became his character, Joshua avoided farther allusion to Benjie and Solomon, and proceeded to solicit my attention to the natural objects around us, which increased in beauty and interest, as, still conducted by the meanders of the brook, we left the common behind us, and entered a more cultivated and enclosed country, where arable and pasture ground was agreeably varied with groves and hedges. Descending now almost close to the stream, our course lay through a little gate, into a pathway, kept with great neatness, the sides of which were decorated with trees and flowering shrubs of the hardier species; until, ascending by a gentle slope, we issued from the grove, and stood almost at once in front of a low but very neat building, of an irregular form; and my guide, shaking me cordially by the hand, made me welcome to Mount Sharon.

The wood through which we had approached this little mansion was thrown around it both on the north and north-west, but, breaking off into different directions, was intersected by a few fields well watered and sheltered. The house fronted to the south-east, and from thence the pleasure-ground, or, I should rather say, the gardens, sloped down to the water. I afterwards understood that the father of the present proprietor had a considerable taste for horticulture, which had been inherited by his son, and had formed these gardens, which, with their shaven turf pleached alleys, wildernesses, and exotic trees and shrubs, greatly excelled any thing of the kind which had been attempted in the neighbourhood.

If there was a little vanity in the complacent smile with which Joshua Geddes saw me gaze with delight on a scene so different from the naked waste we had that day traversed in company, it might surely be permitted to one, who, cultivating and improving the beauties of nature, had found therein, as he said, bodily health, and a pleasing relaxation for the mind. At the bottom of the extended gardens the brook wheeled round in a wide semi-circle, and was itself their boundary. The opposite side was no part of Joshua's domain, but the brook was there skirted by a precipitous rock of limestone, which seemed a barrier of Nature's own erecting around his little Eden of beauty, comfort, and peace.

"But I must not let thee forget," said the kind Quaker, "amidst thy admiration of these beauties of our little inheritance, that thy breakfast has been a light one."

So saying, Joshua conducted me to a small sashed door, opening under a porch amply mantled by honeysuckle and clematis, into a parlour of moderate size; the furniture of which, in plainness and excessive cleanliness, bore the characteristic marks of the sect to which the owner belonged.

Thy father's Hannah is generally allowed to be an exception to all Scottish housekeepers, and stands unparalleled for cleanliness among the women of Auld Reekie; but the cleanliness of Hannah is sluttishness, compared to the scrupulous purifications of these people, who seem to carry into the minor decencies of life that conscientious rigour which they affect in their morals.

The parlour would have been gloomy, for the windows were small and the ceiling low; but the present proprietor had rendered it more cheerful by opening one end into a small conservatory, roofed with glass, and divided from the parlour by a partition of the same. I have never before seen this very pleasing manner of uniting the comforts of an apartment with the beauties of a garden, and I wonder it is not more practised by the great. Something of the kind is hinted at in a paper of the Spectator.

As I walked towards the conservatory to view it more closely, the parlour chimney engaged my attention. It was a pile of massive stone, entirely out of proportion to the size of the apartment. On the front had once been an armorial scutcheon; for the hammer, or chisel, which had been employed to deface the shield or crest, had left uninjured the scroll beneath, which bore the pious motto, "*Trust in God.*" Black-letter, you know, was my early passion, and the tombstones in the Greyfriars' Church-yard early yielded up to my knowledge as a decipherer what little they could tell of the forgotten dead.

Joshua Geddes paused when he saw my eye fixed on this relic of antiquity. "Thou canst read it?" he said.

I repeated the motto, and added, there seemed vestiges of a date.

"It should be 1537," said he; "for so long ago, at the least computation, did my ancestors, in the blinded times of Papistry, possess these lands, and in that year did they build their house."

"It is an ancient descent," said I, looking with respect upon the monument. "I am sorry the arms have been defaced."

It was perhaps impossible for my friend, Quaker as he was, to seem altogether void of respect for the pedigree which he began to recount to me, disclaiming all the while the vanity usually connected with the subject; in short, with the air of mingled melancholy, regret, and conscious dignity, with which Jack Fawkes used to tell us, at College, of his ancestor's unfortunate connection with the Gunpowder Plot.

"Vanity of vanities, saith the preacher,"—thus harangued Joshua Geddes of Mount Sharon;—"if we ourselves are nothing in the sight of Heaven, how much less than nothing must be our derivation from rotten bones and mouldering dust, whose immortal spirits have long since gone to their private account? Yes, friend Latimer, my ancestors were renowned among the ravenous and bloodthirsty men who then dwelt in this vexed country; and so much were they famed for successful freebooting, robbery, and bloodshed, that they are said to have been called Geddes, as likening them to the fish called a Jack, Pike, or Luce, and in our country tongue, a *Ged* —a goodly distinction truly for Christian men! Yet did they paint this shark of the fresh waters upon their shields, and these profane priests of a wicked idolatry, the empty boasters called heralds, who make engraven images of fishes, fowls, and fourfooted beasts, that men may fall down and worship them, assigned the Ged for the device and escutcheon of my fathers, and hewed it over their chimneys, and placed it above their tombs; and the men were elated in mind, and became yet more Ged-like, slaying, leading into captivity, and dividing the spoil, until the place where they dwelt obtained the name of Sharing-Knowe, from the booty which was there divided amongst them and their accomplices. But a better judgment was given to my father's father, Philip Geddes, who, after trying to light his candle at some of the vain wild-fires then held aloft at different meetings and steeple-houses, at length obtained a spark from the lamp of the blessed George Fox, who came into Scotland spreading light among darkness, as he himself hath written, as plentifully as fly the sparkles from the hoof of the horse which gallops swiftly along the stony road."—Here the good Quaker interrupted himself with, "And that is very true, I must go speedily to see after the condition of Solomon."

A Quaker servant here entered the room with a tray, and inclining his head towards his master, but not after the manner of one who bows, said composedly, "Thou art welcome home, friend Joshua, we expected thee not so early; but what hath befallen Solomon thy horse?"

"What hath befallen him, indeed?" said my friend; "hath he not been returned hither by the child whom they call Benjie?"

"He hath," said his domestic, "but it was after a strange fashion; for he came hither at a swift and furious pace, and flung the child Benjie from his back, upon the heap of dung which is in the stable-yard."

"I am glad of it," said Joshua, hastily,—"glad of it, with all my heart and spirit!—But stay he is the child of the widow—hath the boy any hurt?"

"Not so," answered the servant, "for he rose and fled swiftly."

Joshua muttered something about a scourge, and then inquired after Solomon's present condition.

"He seetheth like a steaming caldron," answered the servant; "and Bauldie, the lad, walketh him about the yard with a halter, lest he take cold."

Mr. Geddes hastened to the stable-yard to view personally the condition of his favourite, and I followed, to offer my counsel as a jockey—Don't laugh, Alan, sure I have jockeyship enough to assist a Quaker—in this unpleasing predicament.

The lad who was leading the horse seemed to be no Quaker, though his intercourse with the family had given him a touch of their prim sobriety of look and manner. He assured Joshua that his horse had received no injury, and I even hinted that the exercise would be of service to him. Solomon himself neighed towards his master, and rubbed his head against the good Quaker's shoulder, as if to assure him of his being quite well; so that Joshua returned in comfort to his parlour, where breakfast was now about to be displayed.

I have since learned that the affection of Joshua for his pony is considered as inordinate by some of his own sect; and that he has been much blamed for permitting it to be called by the name of Solomon, or any other name whatever; but he has gained so much respect and influence among them that they overlook these foibles.

I learned from him (whilst the old servant, Jehoiachim, entering and re-entering, seemed to make no end of the materials which he brought in for breakfast) that his grandfather Philip, the convert of George Fox, had suffered much from the persecution to which these harmless devotees were subjected on all sides during that intolerant period, and much of their family estate had been dilapidated. But better days dawned on Joshua's father, who, connecting himself by marriage with a wealthy family of Quakers in Lancashire, engaged successfully in various branches of commerce, and redeemed the remnants of the property, changing its name in sense, without much alteration of sound, from the Border appellation of Sharing-Knowe, to the evangelical appellation of Mount Sharon.

This Philip Geddes, as I before hinted, had imbibed the taste for horticulture and the pursuits of the florist, which are not uncommon among the peaceful sect he belonged to. He had destroyed the remnants of the old peel-house, substituting the modern mansion in its place; and while he reserved the hearth of his ancestors, in memory of their hospitality, as also the pious motto which they had chanced to assume, he failed not to obliterate the worldly and military emblems displayed upon the shield and helmet, together with all their blazonry.

In a few minutes after Mr. Geddes had concluded the account of himself and his family, his sister Rachel, the only surviving member of it, entered the room. Her appearance is remarkably pleasing, and although her age is thirty at least, she still retains the shape and motion of an earlier period. The absence of every thing like fashion or ornament was, as usual, atoned for by the most perfect neatness and cleanliness of her dress; and her simple close cap was particularly suited to eyes which had the softness and simplicity of the dove's. Her features were also extremely agreeable, but had suffered a little through the ravages of that professed enemy to beauty, the small-pox; a disadvantage which was in part counterbalanced by a well-formed mouth, teeth like pearls, and a pleasing sobriety of smile, that seemed to wish good here and hereafter to every one she spoke to. You cannot make any of your vile inferences here, Alan, for I have given a full-length picture of Rachel Geddes; so that you cannot say, in this case, as in the letter I have just received, that she was passed over as a subject on which I feared to dilate. More of this anon.

Well, we settled to our breakfast after a blessing, or rather an extempore prayer, which Joshua made upon the occasion, and which the spirit moved him to prolong rather more than I felt altogether agreeable. Then, Alan, there was such a despatching of the good things of the morning, as you have not witnessed since you have seen Darsie Latimer at breakfast. Tea and chocolate, eggs, hams, and pastry, not forgetting the broiled fish, disappeared with a celerity which seemed to astonish the good-humoured Quakers, who kept loading my plate with supplies, as if desirous of seeing whether they could, by any possibility, tire me out. One hint, however, I received, which put me in mind where I was. Miss Geddes had offered me some sweet-cake, which, at the moment, I declined; but presently afterwards, seeing it within my reach, I naturally enough helped myself to a slice, and had just deposited it beside my plate, when Joshua, mine host, not with the authority air of Sancho's doctor, Tirtea Fuera, but in a very calm and quiet manner, lifted it away and replaced it on the dish, observing only, " Thou didst refuse it before, friend Latimer."

These good folks, Alan, make no allowance for what your good father calls the Aberdeen-man's privilege, of " taking his word again ;" or what the wise call second thoughts.

Bating this slight hint, that I was among a precise generation, there was nothing in my reception that was peculiar — unless, indeed, I were to notice the solicitous and uniform kindness with which all the attentions of my new friends were seasoned, as if they were anxious to assure me that the neglect of worldly compliments interdicted by their sect, only served to render their hospitality more sincere.   At length my hunger was satisfied, and the worthy Quaker, who, with looks of great good-nature, had watched my progress, thus addressed his sister :—

" This young man, Rachel, hath last night sojourned in the tents of our neighbour, whom men call the Laird. . I am sorry I had not met him the evening before, for our neighbour's hospitality is too unfrequently exercised to be well prepared with the means of welcome."

" Nay, but, Joshua," said Rachel, " if our neighbour hath done a kindness, thou shouldst not grudge him the opportunity ; and if our young friend hath fared ill for a night, he will the better relish what Providence may send him of better provisions."

" And that he may do so at leisure," said Joshua, " we will pray him, Rachel, to tarry a day or twain with us : he is young, and is but now entering upon the world, and our habitation may, if he will, be like a resting-place, from which he may look abroad upon the pilgrimage which he must take, and the path which he has to travel. — What sayest thou, friend Latimer ?   We constrain not our friends to our ways, and thou art, I think, too wise to quarrel with us for following our own fashions ; and if we should even give thee a word of advice, thou wilt not, I think, be angry, so that it is spoken in season."

You know, Alan, how easily I am determined by any thing resembling cordiality — and so, though a little afraid of the formality of my host and hostess, I accepted their invitation, provided I could get some messenger to send to Shepherd's Bush for my servant and portmanteau.

" Why, truly, friend," said Joshua, " thy outward frame would be improved by cleaner garments ; but I will do thine errand myself to the Widow Gregson's house of reception, and send thy lad hither with thy clothes. Meanwhile, Rachel will show thee these little gardens, and then will put thee in some way of spending thy time usefully, till our meal calls us together at the second hour after noon.   I bid thee farewell for the present, having some space to walk, seeing I must leave the animal Solomon to his refreshing rest."

With these words, Mr. Joshua Geddes withdrew.   Some ladies we have known would have felt, or at least affected, reserve or embarrassment, at being left to do the honours of the grounds to (it will be out, Alan) — a smart young fellow — an entire stranger.   She went out for a few minutes, and returned in her plain cloak and bonnet, with her beaver gloves, prepared to act as my guide, with as much simplicity as if she had been to wait upon thy father.   So forth I sallied with my fair Quakeress.

If the house at Mount Sharon be merely a plain and convenient dwelling, of moderate size, and small pretensions, the gardens and offices, though not extensive, might rival an earl's in point of care and expense.   Rachel carried me first to her own favourite resort, a poultry-yard, stocked with a variety of domestic fowls, of the more rare as well as the most ordinary kinds, furnished with every accommodation which may suit their various habits.   A rivulet which spread into a pond for the convenience of the aquatic birds, trickled over gravel as it passed through the yards dedicated to the land poultry, which were thus amply supplied with the means they use for digestion.

All these creatures seemed to recognize the presence of their mistress, and some especial favourites hastened to her feet, and continued to follow her as far as their limits permitted. She pointed out their peculiarities and qualities, with the discrimination of one who had made natural history her study; and I own I never looked on barn-door fowls with so much interest before — at least until they were boiled or roasted. I could not help asking the trying question, how she could order the execution of any of the creatures of which she seemed so careful.

"It was painful," she said, "but it was according to the law of their being. They must die; but they knew not when death was approaching; and in making them comfortable while they lived, we contributed to their happiness as much as the conditions of their existence permitted to us."

I am not quite of her mind, Alan. I do not believe either pigs or poultry would admit that the chief end of their being was to be killed and eaten. However, I did not press the argument, from which my Quaker seemed rather desirous to escape; for, conducting me to the greenhouse, which was extensive, and filled with the choicest plants, she pointed out an aviary which occupied the farther end, where, she said, she employed herself with attending the inhabitants, without being disturbed with any painful recollections concerning their future destination.

I will not trouble you with any account of the various hot-houses and gardens, and their contents. No small sum of money must have been expended in erecting and maintaining them in the exquisite degree of good order which they exhibited. The family, I understood, were connected with that of the celebrated Millar, and had imbibed his taste for flowers, and for horticulture. But instead of murdering botanical names, I will rather conduct you to the *policy, or pleasure-garden,* which the taste of Joshua or his father, had extended on the banks betwixt the house and river. This also, in contradistinction to the prevailing simplicity, was ornamented in an unusual degree. There were various compartments, the connection of which was well managed, and although the whole ground did not exceed five or six acres, it was so much varied as to seem four times larger. The space contained close alleys and open walks; a very pretty artificial water-fall; a fountain also, consisting of a considerable jet-d'eau, whose streams glittered in the sunbeams, and exhibited a continual rainbow. There was a cabinet of verdure, as the French call it, to cool the summer heat, and there was a terrace sheltered from the north-east by a noble holly hedge, with all its glittering spears, where you might have the full advantage of the sun in the clear frosty days of winter.

I know that you, Alan, will condemn all this as bad and antiquated; for, ever since Dodsley has described the Leasowes, and talked of Brown's imitations of nature, and Horace Walpole's late Essay on Gardening, you are all for simple nature — condemn walking up and down stairs in the open air, and declare for wood and wilderness. But *ne quid nimis.* I would not deface a scene of natural grandeur or beauty, by the introduction of crowded artificial decorations; yet such may, I think, be very interesting where the situation, in its natural state, otherwise has no particular charms.

So that when I have a country-house (who can say how soon?) you may look for grottoes, and cascades, and fountains; nay, if you vex me by contradiction, perhaps I may go the length of a temple—so provoke me not, for you see of what enormities I am capable.

At any rate, Alan, had you condemned as artificial the rest of Friend Geddes's grounds, there is a willow walk by the very verge of the stream, so sad, so solemn, and so silent, that it must have commanded your admiration. The brook, restrained at the ultimate boundary of the grounds by a natural dam-dike or ledge of rocks, seemed, even in its present swoln state, scarcely to glide along: and the pale willow-trees, drooping their long branches into the stream, gathered around them little coronals of the foam that floated down from the more rapid stream above. The high rock, which formed the opposite bank of the brook, was seen dimly through the branches, and its pale and splintered front, garlanded with long streamers of briers and other creeping plants, seemed a barrier between the quiet path which we trode, and the toiling and bustling world beyond. The path itself, following the sweep of the stream, made a very gentle curve; enough, however, served by its inflection completely to hide the end of the walk, until you arrived at it. A deep and sullen sound, which increased as you proceeded, prepared you for this termination, which was indeed only a plain root-seat, from which you looked on a fall of about six or seven feet, where the brook flung itself over the ledge of natural rock I have already mentioned, which there crossed its course.

The quiet and twilight seclusion of this walk rendered it a fit scene for a confidential communing; and having nothing more interesting to say to my fair Quaker, I took the liberty of questioning her about the Laird; for you are, or ought to be, aware, that next to discussing the affairs of the heart, the fair sex are most interested in those of their neighbours.

I did not conceal either my curiosity, or the check which it had received from Joshua, and I saw that my companion answered with embarrassment. "I must not speak otherwise than truly," she said; "and therefore I tell thee, that my brother dislikes, and that I fear, the man of whom thou hast asked me. Perhaps we are both wrong — but he is a man of violence, and hath great influence over many, who, following the trade of sailors and fishermen, become as rude as the elements with which they contend. He hath no certain name among them, which is not unusual, their rude fashion being to distinguish each other by nicknames; and they have called him the Laird of the Lakes, (not remembering there should be no one called Lord, save one only,) in idle derision; the pools of salt water left by the tide among the sands being called the Lakes of Solway."

"Has he no other revenue than he derives from these sands?" I asked.

"That I cannot answer," replied Rachel; "men say that he wants not money, though he lives like an ordinary fisherman, and that he imparts freely of his means to the poor around him. They intimate that he is a man of consequence, once deeply engaged in the unhappy affair of the rebellion, and even still too much in danger from the government to assume his own name. He is often absent from his cottage at Broken-burn-cliffs, for weeks and months."

"I should have thought," said I, "that the government would scarce, at this time of day, be likely to proceed against any one even of the most obnoxious rebels. Many years have passed away——"

"It is true," she replied; "yet such persons may understand that their being connived at depends on their living in obscurity. But indeed there can nothing certain be known among these rude people. The truth is not in them — most of them participate in the unlawful trade betwixt these parts and the neighbouring shore of England; and they are familiar with every species of falsehood and deceit."

"It is a pity," I remarked, "your brother should have neighbours of such a description, especially as I understand he is at some variance with them."

"Where, when, and about what matter?" answered Miss Geddes, with an eager and timorous anxiety, which made me regret having touched on the subject.

I told her, in a way as little alarming as I could devise, the purport of what passed betwixt this Laird of the Lakes and her brother, at their morning's interview.

"You affright me much," answered she; "it is this very circumstance which has scared me in the watches of the night. When my brother Joshua withdrew from an active share in the commercial concerns of my father, being satisfied with the portion of worldly substance which he already possessed, there were one or two undertakings in which he retained an interest, either because his withdrawing might have been prejudicial to friends, or because he wished to retain some mode of occupying his time. Amongst the more important of these, is a fishing station, on the coast, where, by certain improved modes of erecting snares, opening at the advance of the tide, and shutting at the reflux, many more fish are taken than can be destroyed by those who, like the men of Broken-burn, use only the boat-net and spear, or fishing-rod. They complain of these tide-nets, as men call them, as an innovation, and pretend to a right to remove and destroy them by the strong hand. I fear me, this man of violence, whom they call the Laird, will execute these his threats, which cannot be without both loss and danger to my brother."

"Mr. Geddes," said I, "ought to apply to the civil magistrate; there are soldiers at Dumfries who would be detached for his protection."

"Thou speakest, friend Latimer," answered the lady, "as one who is still in the gall of bitterness and bond of iniquity. God forbid that we should endeavour to preserve nets of flax and stakes of wood, or the Mammon of gain which they procure for us, by the hands of men of war, and at the risk of spilling human blood."

"I respect your scruples," I replied; "but since such is your way of thinking, your brother ought to avert the danger by compromise or submission."

"Perhaps it would be best," answered Rachel; "but what can I say? Even in the best-trained temper there may remain some leaven of the old Adam; and I know not whether it is this or a better spirit that maketh my brother Joshua determine, that though he will not resist force by force, neither will he yield up his right to mere threats, or encourage wrong to others by yielding to menaces. His partners, he says, confide in his steadiness; and that he must not disappoint them by yielding up their right for the fear of the threats of man, whose breath is in his nostrils."

This observation convinced me that the spirit of the old sharers of the spoil was not utterly departed even from the bosom of the peaceful Quaker; and I could not help confessing internally that Joshua had the right, when he averred that there was as much courage in sufferance as in exertion.

As we approached the farther end of the willow walk, the sullen and continuous sound of the dashing waters became still more and more audible, and at length rendered it difficult for us to communicate with each other. The conversation dropped, but apparently my companion continued to dwell upon the apprehensions which it had excited. At the bottom of the walk, we obtained a view of the cascade, where the swollen brook flung itself in foam and tumult over the natural barrier of rock, which seemed in vain to attempt to bar its course. I gazed with delight, and, turning to express my sentiment to my companion, I observed that she had folded her hands in an attitude of sorrowful resignation, which showed her thoughts were far from the scene which lay before her. When she saw that her abstraction was observed, she resumed her former placidity of manner; and having given me sufficient time to admire this termination of our sober and secluded walk, proposed that we should return to the house through her brother's farm. "Even we Quakers, as we are called, have our little pride," she said; "and my brother Joshua would not forgive me, were I not to show thee the fields which he taketh delight to cultivate, after the newest and best fashion; for which, I promise thee, he hath received much praise from good judges, as well as some ridicule from those who think it folly to improve on the customs of our ancestors."

As she spoke, she opened a low door, leading through a moss and ivy-covered wall, the boundary of the pleasure-ground, into the open fields;

through which we moved by a convenient path, leading, with good taste and simplicity, by stile and hedge-row, through pasturage, and arable, and woodland; so that in all ordinary weather, the good man might, without even soiling his shoes, perform his perambulation round the farm. There were seats also, on which to rest; and though not adorned with inscriptions, nor quite so frequent in occurrence as those mentioned in the account of the Leasowes, their situation was always chosen with respect to some distant prospect to be commanded, or some home-view to be enjoyed.

But what struck me most in Joshua's domain, was the quantity and the tameness of the game. The hen partridge scarce abandoned the roost at the foot of the hedge where she had assembled her covey, though the path went close beside her; and the hare, remaining on her form, gazed at us as we passed, with her full dark eve, or rising lazily and hopping to a little distance, stood erect to look at us with more curiosity than apprehension. I observed to Miss Geddes the extreme tameness of these timid and shy animals, and she informed me that their confidence arose from protection in the summer, and relief during the winter.

"They are pets," she said, "of my brother, who considers them as the better entitled to his kindness that they are a race persecuted by the world in general. He denieth himself," she said, "even the company of a dog, that these creatures may here at least enjoy undisturbed security. Yet this harmless or humane propensity, or humour, hath given offence," she added, "to our dangerous neighbours."

She explained this, by telling me that my host of the preceding night was remarkable for his attachment to field-sports, which he pursued without much regard to the wishes of the individuals over whose property he followed them. The undefined mixture of respect and fear with which he was generally regarded, induced most of the neighbouring landholders to connive at what they would perhaps in another have punished as a trespass; but Joshua Geddes would not permit the intrusion of any one upon his premises, and as he had before offended several country neighbours, who, because he would neither shoot himself nor permit others to do so, compared him to the dog in the manger, so he now aggravated the displeasure which the Laird of the Lakes had already conceived against him, by positively debarring him from pursuing his sport over his grounds—"So that," said Rachel Geddes, "I sometimes wish our lot had been cast elsewhere than in these pleasant borders, where, if we had less of beauty around us, we might have had a neighbourhood of peace and good-will."

We at length returned to the house, where Miss Geddes showed me a small study, containing a little collection of books, in two separate presses.

"These," said she, pointing to the smaller press, "will, if thou bestowest thy leisure upon them, do thee good; and these," pointing to the other and larger cabinet, "can, I believe, do thee little harm. Some of our people do indeed hold, that every writer who is not with us is against us; but brother Joshua is mitigated in his opinions, and correspondeth with our friend John Scot of Amwell, who hath himself constructed verses well approved of even in the world. I wish thee many good thoughts till our family meet at the hour of dinner."

Left alone, I tried both collections; the first consisted entirely of religious and controversial tracts, and the latter formed a small selection of history and of moral writers, both in prose and verse.

Neither collection promising much amusement, thou hast, in these close pages, the fruits of my tediousness; and truly, I think, writing history (one's self being the subject) is as amusing as reading that of foreign countries, at any time.

Sam, still more drunk than sober, arrived in due time with my portmanteau, and enabled me to put my dress into order, better befitting this temple of cleanliness and decorum, where (to conclude) I believe I shall be a sojourner for more days than one.*

P. S.—I have noted your adventure, as you home-bred youths may perhaps term it, concerning the visit of your doughty Laird. We travellers hold such an incident of no great consequence, though it may serve to embellish the uniform life of Brown's Square. But art thou not ashamed to attempt to interest one who is seeing the world at large, and studying human nature on a large scale, by so bald a narrative? Why, what does it amount to, after all, but that a Tory Laird dined with a Whig Lawyer? no very uncommon matter, especially as you state Mr. Herries to have lost the estate, though retaining the designation. The Laird behaves with haughtiness and impertinence — nothing out of character in that: is *not* kicked down stairs, as he ought to have been, were Alan Fairford half the man that he would wish his friends to think him. — Ay, but then, as the young lawyer, instead of showing his friend the door, chose to make use of it himself, he overheard the Laird aforesaid ask the old lawyer concerning Darsie Latimer — no doubt earnestly inquiring after the handsome, accomplished inmate of his family, who has so lately made Themis his bow, and declined the honour of following her farther. You laugh at me for my air-drawn castles; but confess, have they not surer footing, in general, than two words spoken by such a man as Herries? And yet—and yet—I would rally the matter off, Alan; but in dark nights, even the glow-worm becomes an object of lustre, and to one plunged in my uncertainty and ignorance, the slightest gleam that promises intelligence, is interesting. My life is like the subterranean river in the Peak of Derby, visible only where it crosses the celebrated cavern. I am here, and this much I know; but where I have sprung from, or whither my course of life is like to tend, who shall tell me? Your father, too, seemed interested and alarmed, and talked of writing; would to Heaven he may!—I send daily to the post-town for letters.

LETTER VIII.

ALAN FAIRFORD TO DARSIE LATIMER.

THOU mayst clap thy wings and crow as thou pleasest. You go in search of adventures, but adventures come to me unsought for; and oh! in what a pleasing shape came mine, since it arrived in the form of a client — and a fair client to boot! What think you of that, Darsie! you who are such a sworn squire of dames? Will this not match my adventures with thine, that hunt salmon on horseback, and will it not, besides, eclipse the history of a whole tribe of Broadbrims?—but I must proceed methodically.

When I returned to-day from the College, I was surprised to see a broad grin distending the adust countenance of the faithful James Wilkinson, which, as the circumstance seldom happens above once a-year, was matter

* In explanation of this circumstance, I cannot help adding a note not very necessary for the reader, which yet I record with pleasure, from recollection of the kindness which it evinces. In early youth I resided for a considerable time in the vicinity of the beautiful village of Kelso, where my life passed in a very solitary manner. I had few acquaintances, scarce any companions, and books, which were at the time almost essential to my happiness, were difficult to come by. It was then that I was particularly indebted to the liberality and friendship of an old lady of the Society of Friends, eminent for her benevolence and charity. Her deceased husband had been a medical man of eminence, and left her, with other valuable property, a small and well-selected library. This the kind old lady permitted me to rummage at pleasure, and carry home what volumes I chose, on condition that I should take, at the same time, some of the tracts printed for encouraging and extending the doctrines of her own sect. She did not even exact any promise that I would read these performances, being too justly afraid of involving me in a breach of promise, but was merely desirous that I should have the chance of instruction within my reach, in case whim, curiosity, or accident, might induce me to have recourse to it.

of some surprise. Moreover, he had a knowing glance with his eye, which I should have as soon expected from a dumb-waiter—an article of furniture to which James, in his usual state, may be happily assimilated. "What the devil is the matter, James?"

"The devil may be in the matter, for aught I ken," said James, with another provoking grin; "for here has been a woman calling for you, Maister Alan."

"A woman calling for me?" said I in surprise; for you know well, that excepting old Aunt Peggy, who comes to dinner of a Sunday, and the still older Lady Bedrooket, who calls ten times a-year for the quarterly payment of her jointure of four hundred merks, a female scarce approaches our threshold, as my father visits all his female clients at their own lodgings. James protested, however, that there had been a lady calling, and for me. "As bonny a lass as I have seen," added James, "since I was in the Fusileers, and kept company with Peg Baxter." Thou knowest all James's gay recollections go back to the period of his military service, the years he has spent in ours having probably been dull enough.

"Did the lady leave no name nor place of address?"

"No," replied James; "but she asked when you wad be at hame, and I appointed her for twelve o'clock, when the house wad be quiet, and your father at the Bank."

"For shame, James! how can you think my father's being at home or abroad could be of consequence?—The lady is of course a decent person?"

"I'se uphaud her that, sir—she is none of your—*whew*"—[Here James supplied a blank with a low whistle]—"but I didna ken—my maister makes an unco wark if a woman comes here."

I passed into my own room, not ill-pleased that my father was absent, notwithstanding I had thought it proper to rebuke James for having so contrived it. I disarranged my books, to give them the appearance of a graceful confusion on the table, and laying my foils (useless since your departure) across the mantelpiece, that the lady might see I was *tam Marte quam Mercurio*—I endeavoured to dispose my dress so as to resemble an elegant morning dishabille—gave my hair the general shade of powder which marks the gentleman—laid my watch and seals on the table, to hint that I understood the value of time;—and when I had made all these arrangements, of which I am a little ashamed when I think of them, I had nothing better to do than to watch the dial-plate till the index pointed to noon. Five minutes elapsed, which I allowed for variation of clocks—five minutes more rendered me anxious and doubtful—and five minutes more would have made me impatient.

Laugh as thou wilt; but remember, Darsie, I was a lawyer, excepting his first client—a young man, how strictly bred up I need not remind you, expecting a private interview with a young and beautiful woman. But ere the third term of five minutes had elapsed, the door-bell was heard to tinkle low and modestly, as if touched by some timid hand.

James Wilkinson, swift in nothing, is, as thou knowest, peculiarly slow in answering the door-bell; and I reckoned on five minutes good, ere his solemn step should have ascended the stair. Time enough, thought I, for a peep through the blinds, and was hastening to the window accordingly. But I reckoned without my host; for James, who had his own curiosity as well as I, was lying *perdu* in the lobby, ready to open at the first tinkle; and there was, "This way, ma'am—Yes, ma'am—The lady, Mr. Alan," before I could get to the chair in which I proposed to be discovered, seated in all legal dignity. The consciousness of being half caught in the act of peeping, joined to that native air of awkward bashfulness of which I am told the law will soon free me, kept me standing on the floor in some confusion; while the lady, disconcerted on her part, remained on the threshold of the room. James Wilkinson, who had his senses most about him, and was perhaps willing to prolong his stay in the apartment, busied himself in setting a chair for the lady, and recalled me to my good-breeding by the hint. I invited her to take possession of it, and bid James withdraw.

My visitor was undeniably a lady, and probably considerably above the ordinary rank — very modest, too, judging from the mixture of grace and timidity with which she moved, and at my entreaty sat down. Her dress was, I should suppose, both handsome and fashionable; but it was much concealed by a walking-cloak of green silk, fancifully embroidered; in which, though heavy for the season, her person was enveloped, and which, moreover, was furnished with a hood.

The devil take that hood, Darsie! for I was just able to distinguish that, pulled as it was over the face, it concealed from me, as I was convinced, one of the prettiest countenances I have seen, and which, from a sense of embarrassment, seemed to be crimsoned with a deep blush. I could see her complexion was beautiful — her chin finely turned — her lips coral — and her teeth rivals to ivory. But farther the deponent sayeth not; for a clasp of gold, ornamented with a sapphire, closed the envious mantle under the incognita's throat, and the cursed hood concealed entirely the upper part of the face.

I ought to have spoke first, that is certain; but ere I could get my phrases well arranged, the young lady, rendered desperate, I suppose, by my hesitation, opened the conversation herself.

"I fear I am an intruder, sir—I expected to meet an elderly gentleman."

This brought me to myself. "My father, madam, perhaps. But you inquired for Alan Fairford — my father's name is Alexander."

"It is Mr. Alan Fairford, undoubtedly, with whom I wished to speak," she said, with greater confusion; "but I was told that he was advanced in life."

"Some mistake, madam, I presume, betwixt my father and myself — our Christian names have the same initials, though the terminations are different. — I — I — I would esteem it a most fortunate mistake if I could have the honour of supplying my father's place in any thing that could be of service to you."

"You are very obliging, sir." A pause, during which she seemed undetermined whether to rise or sit still.

"I am just about to be called to the bar, madam," said I, in hopes to remove her scruples to open her case to me; "and if my advice or opinion could be of the slightest use, although I cannot presume to say that they are much to be depended upon, yet——"

The lady arose. "I am truly sensible of your kindness, sir; and I have no doubt of your talents. I will be very plain with you — it *is* you whom I came to visit; although, now that we have met, I find it will be much better that I should commit my communication to writing."

"I hope, madam, you will not be so cruel — so tantalizing, I would say. Consider, you are my first client — your business my first consultation — do not do me the displeasure of withdrawing your confidence because I am a few years younger than you seem to have expected — My attention shall make amends for my want of experience."

"I have no doubt of either," said the lady, in a grave tone, calculated to restrain the air of gallantry with which I had endeavoured to address her. "But when you have received my letter you will find good reasons assigned why a written communication will best suit my purpose. I wish you, sir, a good morning." And she left the apartment, her poor baffled counsel scraping, and bowing, and apologizing for any thing that might have been disagreeable to her, although the front of my offence seems to be my having been discovered to be younger than my father.

The door was opened — out she went — walked along the pavement, turned down the close, and put the sun, I believe, into her pocket when she disappeared, so suddenly did dulness and darkness sink down on the square, when she was no longer visible. I stood for a moment as if I had been senseless, not recollecting what a fund of entertainment I must have supplied to our watchful friends on the other side of the green. Then it darted on my mind that I might dog her, and ascertain at least who or what she was. Off I set — ran down the close, where she was no longer to be seen, and demanded of one of the dyer's lads whether he had seen a lady go down the close or had observed which way she turned.

"A leddy !"—said the dyer, staring at me with his rainbow countenance. "Mr. Alan, what takes you out, rinning like daft, without your hat ?"

"The devil take my hat !" answered I, running back, however, in quest of it ; snatched it up, and again sallied forth. But as I reached the head of the close once more, I had sense enough to recollect that all pursuit would be now in vain. Besides, I saw my friend, the journeyman dyer, in close confabulation with a pea-green personage of his own profession, and was conscious, like Scrub, that they talked of me, because they laughed consumedly. I had no mind, by a second sudden appearance, to confirm the report that Advocate Fairford was " gaen daft," which had probably spread from Campbell's close-foot to the Mealmarket Stairs ; and so slunk back within my own hole again.

My first employment was to remove all traces of that elegant and fanciful disposition of my effects, from which I had hoped for so much credit ; for I was now ashamed and angry at having thought an instant upon the mode of receiving a visit which had commenced so agreeably, but terminated in a manner so unsatisfactory. I put my folios in their places — threw the foils into the dressing-closet — tormenting myself all the while with the fruitless doubt, whether I had missed an opportunity or escaped a stratagem, or whether the young person had been really startled, as she seemed to intimate, by the extreme youth of her intended legal adviser. The mirror was not unnaturally called in to aid ; and that cabinet-counsellor pronounced me rather short, thick-set, with a cast of features fitter, I trust, for the bar than the ball — not handsome enough for blushing virgins to pine for my sake, or even to invent sham cases to bring them to my chambers — yet not ugly enough either to scare those away who came on real business — dark, to be sure, but—*nigri sunt hyacinthi*—there are pretty things to be said in favour of that complexion.

At length — as common sense will get the better in all cases, when a man will but give it fair play — I began to stand convicted in my own mind, as an ass before the interview, for having expected too much — an ass during the interview, for having failed to extract the lady's real purpose — and an especial ass, now that it was over, for thinking so much about it. But I can think of nothing else, and therefore I am determined to think of this to some good purpose.

You remember Murtough O'Hara's defence of the Catholic doctrine of confession ; because, " by his soul, his sins were always a great burden to his mind, till he had told them to the priest ; and once confessed, he never thought more about them." I have tried his receipt, therefore ; and having poured my secret mortification into thy trusty ear, I will think no more about this maid of the mist,

> " Who, with no face, as 'twere, outfaced me."

-------- Four o'Clock.

Plague on her green mantle, she can be nothing better than a fairy ; she keeps possession of my head yet ! All during dinner time I was terribly absent ; but, luckily, my father gave the whole credit of my reverie to the abstract nature of the doctrine, *Vinco vincentem, ergo vinco te ;* upon which brocard of law the Professor this morning lectured. So I got an early dismissal to my own crib, and here am I studying, in one sense, *vincere vincentem*, to get the better of the silly passion of curiosity — I think — I think it amounts to nothing else — which has taken such possession of my imagination, and is perpetually worrying me with the question — will she write or no? She will not — she will not! So says Reason, and adds, Why should she take the trouble to enter into correspondence with one, who, instead of a bold, alert, prompt gallant, proved a chicken-hearted boy, and left her the whole awkwardness of explanation, which he should have met half-way? But then, says Fancy, she *will* write, for she was not a bit that sort of person whom you, Mr. Reason, in your wisdom, take her to be. She was disconcerted enough, without my adding to her distress by any impudent conduct on my part. And she will write, for —— By Heaven, she HAS written, Darsie, and with a vengeance!—Here is her letter, thrown into the kitchen by a cadi, too faithful to be bribed, either by money or whisky, to say more than that he received it, with sixpence, from an ordinary-looking woman, as he was plying on his station near the Cross.

"FOR ALAN FAIRFORD, ESQUIRE, BARRISTER.
    "SIR,
    "Excuse my mistake of to-day. I had accidentally learnt that Mr. Darsie Latimer had an intimate friend and associate in Mr. A. Fairford. When I inquired for such a person, he was pointed out to me at the Cross, (as I think the Exchange of your city is called,) in the character of a respectable elderly man — your father, as I now understand. On inquiry at Brown's Square, where I understood he resided, I used the full name of Alan, which naturally occasioned you the trouble of this day's visit. Upon farther inquiry, I am led to believe that you are likely to be the person most active in the matter to which I am now about to direct your attention; and I regret much that circumstances, arising out of my own particular situation, prevent my communicating to you personally what I now apprise you of in this matter.

    "Your friend, Mr. Darsie Latimer, is in a situation of considerable danger. You are doubtless aware, that he has been cautioned not to trust himself in England — Now, if he has not absolutely transgressed this friendly injunction, he has at least approached as nearly to the menaced danger as he could do, consistently with the letter of the prohibition. He has chosen his abode in a neighbourhood very perilous to him; and it is only by a speedy return to Edinburgh, or at least by a removal to some more remote part of Scotland, that he can escape the machinations of those whose enmity he has to fear. I must speak in mystery, but my words are not the less certain; and, I believe, you know enough of your friend's fortunes to be aware, that I could not write this much without being even more intimate with them than you are.

    "If he cannot, or will not, take the advice here given, it is my opinion that you should join him, if possible, without delay, and urge, by your personal presence and entreaty, the arguments which may prove ineffectual in writing. One word more, and I implore of your candour to take it as it is meant. No one supposes that Mr. Fairford's zeal in his friend's service needs to be quickened by mercenary motives. But report says, that Mr. Alan Fairford not having entered on his professional career, may, in such a case as this, want the means, though he cannot want the inclination, to act with promptitude. The enclosed note, Mr. Alan Fairford must be pleased to consider as his first professional emolument; and she who sends it hopes it will be the omen of unbounded success, though the fee comes from a hand so unknown as that of   "GREEN MANTLE."

    A bank note of 20*l*. was the enclosure, and the whole incident left me speechless with astonishment. I am not able to read over the beginning

F

of my own letter, which forms the introduction to this extraordinary communication. I only know that, though mixed with a quantity of foolery, (God knows very much different from my present feelings,) it gives an account sufficiently accurate, of the mysterious person from whom this letter comes, and that I have neither time nor patience to separate the absurd commentary from the text, which it is so necessary you should know.

Combine this warning, so strangely conveyed, with the caution impressed on you by your London correspondent, Griffiths, against your visiting England—with the character of your Laird of the Solway Lakes—with the lawless habits of the people on that frontier country, where warrants are not easily executed, owing to the jealousy entertained by either country of the legal interference of the other; remember, that even Sir John Fielding said to my father, that he could never trace a rogue beyond the Briggend of Dumfries—think that the distinctions of Whig and Tory, Papist and Protestant, still keep that country in a loose and comparatively lawless state—think of all this, my dearest Darsie, and remember that, while at this Mount Sharon of yours, you are residing with a family actually menaced with forcible interference, and who, while their obstinacy provokes violence, are by principle bound to abstain from resistance.

Nay, let me tell you, professionally, that the legality of the mode of fishing practised by your friend Joshua, is greatly doubted by our best lawyers; and that, if the stake-nets be considered as actually an unlawful obstruction raised in the channel of the estuary, an assembly of persons who shall proceed, *via facti*, to pull down and destroy them, would not, in the eye of the law, be esteemed guilty of a riot. So, by remaining where you are, you are likely to be engaged in a quarrel with which you have nothing to do, and thus to enable your enemies, whoever these may be, to execute, amid the confusion of a general hubbub, whatever designs they may have against your personal safety. Black-fishers, poachers, and smugglers, are a sort of gentry that will not be much checked, either by your Quaker's texts, or by your chivalry. If you are Don Quixote enough to lay lance in rest, in defence of those of the stake-net, and of the sad-coloured garment, I pronounce you but a lost knight; for, as I said before, I doubt if these potent redressers of wrongs, the justices and constables, will hold themselves warranted to interfere. In a word, return, my dear Amadis; the adventure of the Solway-nets is not reserved for your worship. Come back, and I will be your faithful Sancho Panza upon a more hopeful quest. We will beat about together, in search of this Urganda, the Unknown She of the Green Mantle, who can read this, the riddle of thy fate, better than wise Eppie of Buckhaven,* or Cassandra herself.

I would fain trifle, Darsie; for, in debating with you, jests will sometimes go farther than arguments; but I am sick at heart and cannot keep the ball up. If you have a moment's regard for the friendship we have so often vowed to each other, let my wishes for once prevail over your own venturous and romantic temper. I am quite serious in thinking, that the information communicated to my father by this Mr. Herries, and the admonitory letter of the young lady, bear upon each other; and that, were you here, you might learn something from one or other, or from both, that might throw light on your birth and parentage. You will not, surely, prefer an idle whim to the prospect which is thus held out to you?

I would, agreeably to the hint I have received in the young lady's letter, (for I am confident that such is her condition,) have ere now been with you to urge these things, instead of pouring them out upon paper. But you know that the day for my trials is appointed; I have already gone through the form of being introduced to the examinators, and have gotten my titles

---

* Well known in the Chap-Book, called the History of Buckhaven.

assigned me. All this should not keep me at home, but my father would view any irregularity upon this occasion as a mortal blow to the hopes which he has cherished most fondly during his life; viz. my being called to the bar with some credit. For my own part, I know there is no great difficulty in passing these formal examinations, else how have some of our acquaintance got through them? But, to my father, these formalities compose an august and serious solemnity, to which he has long looked forward, and my absenting myself at this moment would well-nigh drive him distracted. Yet I shall go altogether distracted myself, if I have not an instant assurance from you that you are hastening hither——Meanwhile I have desired Hannah to get your little crib into the best order possible. I cannot learn that my father has yet written to you; nor has he spoken more of his communication with Birrenswork; but when I let him have some inkling of the dangers you are at present incurring, I know my request that you will return immediately, will have his cordial support.

Another reason yet——I must give a dinner, as usual, upon my admission, to our friends; and my father, laying aside all his usual considerations of economy, has desired it may be in the best style possible. Come hither then, dear Darsie! or, I protest to you, I shall send examination, admission-dinner, and guests, to the devil, and come, in person, to fetch you with a vengeance. Thine, in much anxiety, A. F.

LETTER IX.

ALEXANDER FAIRFORD, W.S., TO MR. DARSIE LATIMER.

Dear Mr. Darsie,

Having been your factor *loco tutoris*, or, rather, I ought to say, in correctness, (since I acted without warrant from the Court,) your *negotiorum gestor;* that connection occasions my present writing. And although having rendered an account of my intromissions, which have been regularly approved of, not only by yourself, (whom I could not prevail upon to look at more than the docket and sum total,) but also by the worthy Mr. Samuel Griffiths of London, being the hand through whom the remittances were made, I may, in some sense, be considered as to you *functus officio;* yet, to speak facetiously, I trust you will not hold me accountable as a vicious intromitter, should I still consider myself as occasionally interested in your welfare. My motives for writing, at this time, are twofold.

I have met with a Mr. Herries of Birrenswork, a gentleman of very ancient descent, but who hath in time past been in difficulties, nor do I know if his affairs are yet well redd. Birrenswork says, that he believes he was very familiar with your father, whom he states to have been called Ralph Latimer of Langcote-Hall, in Westmoreland; and he mentioned family affairs, which it may be of the highest importance to you to be acquainted with; but as he seemed to decline communicating them to me, I could not civilly urge him thereanent. Thus much I know, that Mr. Herries had his own share in the late desperate and unhappy matter of 1745, and was in trouble about it, although that is probably now over. Moreover, although he did not profess the Popish religion openly, he had an eye that way. And both of these are reasons why I have hesitated to recommend him to a youth who maybe hath not altogether so well founded his opinions concerning Kirk and State, that they might not be changed by some sudden wind of doctrine. For I have observed ye, Master Darsie, to be rather tinctured with the old leaven of prelacy — this under your leave; and although God forbid that you should be in any manner disaffected to the Protestant Hanoverian line, yet ye have ever loved to hear the blawing, blazing stories which the Hieland gentlemen tell of those troublous times, which, if it were their will, they had better pretermit, as tending rather to shame than to honour. It is come to me also by a side-wind, as I may say, that you have been neighbouring more than was needful among some of the pestilent sect of Quakers — a people who own neither priest, nor king, nor civil magistrate, nor the fabric of our law, and will not depone either *in civilibus* or *criminalibus*, be the loss to the lieges what it may. Anent which heresies, it were good ye read "the Snake in the Grass," or, "the Foot out of the Snare," being both well-approved tracts, touching these doctrines.

Now, Mr. Darsie, ye are to judge for yourself whether ye can safely to your soul's weal remain longer among these Papists and Quakers; these defections on the right hand, and fallings away on the left; and truly if you can confidently resist these evil examples of doctrine, I think ye may as well tarry in the bounds where ye are, until you see Mr. Herries of Birrenswork, who does assuredly know more of your matters than I thought had been communicated to any man in Scotland. I would fain have precognosced him myself on these affairs, but found him unwilling to speak out, as I have partly intimated before.

To call a new cause—I have the pleasure to tell you, that Alan has passed his private Scots Law examinations with good approbation — a great relief to my mind; especially as worthy Mr. Pest told me in my ear there was no fear of "the callant," as he familiarly called him, which gives me great heart. His public trials, which are nothing in comparison save a mere form, are to take place, by order of the Honourable Dean of Faculty, on Wednesday first; and on Friday he puts on the gown, and gives a bit chack of dinner to his friends and acquaintances, as is, you know, the custom. Your company will be wished for there, Master Darsie, by more than him, which I regret to think is impossible to have, as well by your engagements, as that our cousin, Peter Fairford, comes from the West on purpose, and we have no place to offer him but your chamber in the wall. And, to be plain with you, after my use and wont, Master Darsie, it may be as well that Alan and you do not meet till he is hefted as it were to his new calling. You are a pleasant gentleman, and full of daffing, which may well become you, as you have enough (as I understand) to uphold your merry humour. If you regard the matter wisely, you would perchance consider that a man of substance should have a douce and staid demeanour; yet you are so far from growing grave and considerate with the increase of your annual income, that the richer you become, the merrier I think you grow. But this must be at your own pleasure, so far as you are concerned. Alan, however, (overpassing my small savings,) has the world to win; and louping and laughing, as you and he were wont to do, would soon make the powder flee out of his wig, and the pence out of his pocket. Nevertheless, I trust you will meet when you return from your rambles; for there is a time, as the wise man sayeth, for gathering, and a time for casting away; it is always the part of a man of sense to take the gathering time first. I remain, dear sir, your well-wishing friend, and obedient to command,

                                        ALEXANDER FAIRFORD.

P. S.—Alan's Thesis is upon the title *De periculo et commodo rei venditæ*, and is a very pretty piece of Latinity.—Ross-House, in our neighbourhood, is nearly finished, and is thought to excel Duff-House in ornature.

LETTER X.

DARSIE LATIMER TO ALAN FAIRFORD.

THE plot thickens, Alan. I have your letter, and also one from your father. The last makes it impossible for me to comply with the kind request which the former urges. No — I cannot be with you, Alan; and that, for the best of all reasons—I cannot and ought not to counteract your father's anxious wishes. I do not take it unkind of him that he desires my absence. It is natural that he should wish for his son what his son so well deserves—the advantage of a wiser and steadier companion than I seem to him. And yet I am sure I have often laboured hard enough to acquire that decency of demeanour which can no more be suspected of breaking bounds, than an owl of catching a butterfly.

But it was in vain that I have knitted my brows till I had the headach, in order to acquire the reputation of a grave, solid, and well-judging youth. Your father always has discovered, or thought that he discovered, a hare-brained eccentricity lying folded among the wrinkles of my forehead, which rendered me a perilous associate for the future counsellor and ultimate judge. Well, Corporal Nym's philosophy must be my comfort — "Things must be as they may." — I cannot come to your father's house, where he wishes not to see me; and as to your coming hither,—by all that is dear to me, I vow that if you are guilty of such a piece of reckless folly — not to say undutiful cruelty, considering your father's thoughts and wishes — I will never speak to you again as long as I live! I am perfectly serious. And besides, your father, while he in a manner prohibits me from returning to Edinburgh, gives me the strongest reasons for continuing a little while longer in this country, by holding out the hope that I may receive from your old friend, Mr. Herries of Birrenswork, some particulars concerning my origin, with which that ancient recusant seems to be acquainted.

That gentleman mentioned the name of a family in Westmoreland, with which he supposes me connected. My inquiries here after such a family have been ineffectual, for the borderers, on either side, know little of each other. But I shall doubtless find some English person of whom to make inquiries, since the confounded fetterlock clapped on my movements by old Griffiths, prevents me repairing to England in person. At least, the prospect of obtaining some information is greater here than elsewhere; it will be an apology for my making a longer stay in this neighbourhood, a line of conduct which seems to have your father's sanction, whose opinion must be sounder than that of your wandering damoselle.

If the road were paved with dangers which leads to such a discovery, I cannot for a moment hesitate to tread it. But in fact there is no peril in the case. If the Tritons of the Solway shall proceed to pull down honest Joshua's tide-nets, I am neither Quixote enough in disposition, nor Goliath enough in person, to attempt their protection. I have no idea of attempting to prop a falling house, by putting my shoulders against it. And indeed, Joshua gave me a hint, that the company which he belongs to, injured in the way threatened, (some of them being men who thought after the fashion of the world,) would pursue the rioters at law, and recover damages, in which probably his own ideas of non-resistance will not prevent his participating. Therefore the whole affair will take its course as law will, as I only mean to interfere when it may be necessary to direct the course of the plaintiffs to thy chambers; and I request they may find thee intimate with all the Scottish statutes concerning salmon fisheries, from the *Lex Aquarum*, downward.

As for the Lady of the Mantle, I will lay a wager that the sun so bedazzled thine eyes on that memorable morning, that every thing thou didst look upon seemed green; and notwithstanding James Wilkinson's experience in the fusileers, as well as his negative whistle, I will venture to hold a crown that she is but a what-shall-call-'um after all. Let not even the gold persuade you to the contrary. She may make a shift to cause you to disgorge that, and (immense spoil!) a session's fees to boot, if you look not all the sharper about you. Or if it should be otherwise, and if indeed there lurk some mystery under this visitation, credit me, it is one which thou canst not penetrate, nor can I as yet even attempt to explain it; since, if I prove mistaken, and mistaken I may easily be, I would be fain to creep into Phalaris's bull, were it standing before me ready heated, rather than be roasted with thy raillery. Do not tax me with want of confidence; for the instant I can throw any light on the matter thou shalt have it; but while I am only blundering about in the dark, I do not choose to call wise folks to see me, perchance, break my nose against a post. So if you marvel at this,

> "E'en marvel on till time makes all things plain."

In the meantime, kind Alan, let me proceed in my diurnal.

On the third or fourth day after my arrival at Mount Sharon, Time, that bald sexton to whom I have just referred you, did certainly limp more heavily along with me than he had done at first. The quaint morality of Joshua, and Huguenot simplicity of his sister, began to lose much of their raciness with their novelty, and my mode of life, by dint of being very quiet, began to feel abominably dull. It was, as thou say'st, as if the Quakers had put the sun in their pockets — all around was soft and mild, and even pleasant; but there was, in the whole routine, a uniformity, a want of interest, a helpless and hopeless languor, which rendered life insipid. No doubt, my worthy host and hostess felt none of this void, this want of excitation, which was becoming oppressive to their guest. They had their little round of occupations, charities, and pleasures; Rachel had her poultry-yard and conservatory, and Joshua his garden. Besides this, they enjoyed, doubtless, their devotional meditations; and, on the whole, time glided softly and imperceptibly on with them, though to me, who long for stream and cataract, it seemed absolutely to stand still. I meditated returning to Shepherd's Bush, and began to think, with some hankering, after little Benjie and the rod. The imp has ventured hither, and hovers about to catch a peep of me now and then; I suppose the little sharper is angling for a few more sixpences. But this would have been, in Joshua's eyes, a return of the washed sow to wallowing in the mire, and I resolved, while I remained his guest, to spare him so violent a shock to his prejudices. The next point was, to shorten the time of my proposed stay; but, alas! that I felt to be equally impossible. I had named a week; and however rashly my promise had been pledged, it must be held sacred, even according to the letter, from which the Friends permit no deviation.

All these considerations wrought me up to a kind of impatience yesterday evening; so that I snatched up my hat, and prepared for a sally beyond the cultivated farm and ornamented grounds of Mount Sharon, just as if I were desirous to escape from the realms of art, into those of free and unconstrained nature.

I was scarcely more delighted when I first entered this peaceful demesne, than I now was—such is the instability and inconsistency of human nature! —when I escaped from it to the open downs, which had formerly seemed so waste and dreary. The air I breathed felt purer and more bracing. The clouds, riding high upon a summer breeze, drove, in gay succession, over my head, now obscuring the sun, now letting its rays stream in transient flashes upon various parts of the landscape, and especially upon the broad mirror of the distant Firth of Solway.

I advanced on the scene with the light step of a liberated captive; and, like John Bunyan's Pilgrim, could have found in my heart to sing as I went on my way. It seemed as if my gaiety had accumulated while suppressed, and that I was, in my present joyous mood, entitled to expend the savings of the previous week. But just as I was about to uplift a merry stave, I heard, to my joyful surprise, the voices of three or more choristers, singing with considerable success, the lively old catch,

> " For all our men were very very merry,
>   And all our men were drinking:
>   There were two men of mine.
>   Three men of thine,
>   And three that belonged to old Sir Thom o' Lyne;
>   As they went to the ferry, they were very very merry,
>   And all our men were drinking." *

As the chorus ended, there followed a loud and hearty laugh by way of cheers. Attracted by sounds which were so congenial to my present feelings, I made towards the spot from which they came,—cautiously however, for the downs, as had been repeatedly hinted to me, had no good name; and the attraction of the music, without rivalling that of the Syrens in melody, might have been followed by similarly inconvenient consequences to an incautious amateur.

I crept on, therefore, trusting that the sinuosities of the ground, broken as it was into knolls and sand-pits, would permit me to obtain a sight of the musicians before I should be observed by them. As I advanced, the old ditty was again raised. The voices seemed those of a man and two boys; they were rough, but kept good time, and were managed with too much skill to belong to the ordinary country people.

> " Jack looked at the sun, and cried, Fire, fire, fire;
>   Tom stabled his keffel in Birkendale mire;
>   Jem started a calf, and halloo'd for a stag;
>   Will mounted a gate-post instead of his nag:
>   For all our men were very very merry,
>   And all our men were drinking.
>   There were two men of mine,
>   Three men of thine,
>   And three that belonged to old Sir Thom o' Lyne:
>   As they went to the ferry, they were very very merry,
>   For all our men were drinking."

The voices, as they mixed in their several parts, and ran through them, untwisting and again entwining all the links of the merry old catch, seemed to have a little touch of the bacchanalian spirit which they celebrated, and showed plainly that the musicians were engaged in the same joyous revel as the *menyie* of old Sir Thom o' Lyne. At length I came within sight of them, three in number, where they sat cosily niched into what you might call a *bunker*, a little sand-pit, dry and snug, and surrounded by its banks, and a screen of whins in full bloom.

The only one of the trio whom I recognized as a personal acquaintance was the notorious little Benjie, who, having just finished his stave, was cramming a huge luncheon of pie-crust into his mouth with one hand, while in the other he held a foaming tankard, his eyes dancing with all the glee of a forbidden revel; and his features, which have at all times a mischie-

---

* The original of this catch is to be found in Cowley's witty comedy of the Guardian, the first edition. It does not exist in the second and revised edition, called the Cutter of Coleman Street.
"Captain Blade. Ha, ha, boys, another catch.
>   And all our men were very very merry,
>   And all our men were drinking.

> Cutter.   One man of mine.
> Dogrel.   Two men of mine.
> Blade.   Three men of mine.
> Cutter.   And one man of mine.
> Omnes.   As we went by the way we were drunk, drunk, damnably drunk,
>   And all our men were very very merry," &c.

Such are the words, which are somewhat altered and amplified in the text. The play was acted in presence of Charles II., then Prince of Wales, in 1641. The catch in the text has been happily set to music

vous archness of expression, confessing the full sweetness of stolen waters, and bread eaten in secret.

There was no mistaking the profession of the male and female, who were partners with Benjie in these merry doings. The man's long loose-bodied great-coat, (wrap-rascal as the vulgar term it,) the fiddle-case, with its straps, which lay beside him, and a small knapsack which might contain his few necessaries; a clear gray eye; features which, in contending with many a storm, had not lost a wild and careless expression of glee, animated at present, when he was exercising for his own pleasure the arts which he usually practised for bread,—all announced one of those peripatetic followers of Orpheus, whom the vulgar call a strolling fiddler. Gazing more attentively, I easily discovered that though the poor musician's eyes were open, their sense was shut, and that the ecstacy with which he turned them up to Heaven, only derived its apparent expression from his own internal emotions, but received no assistance from the visible objects around. Beside him sat his female companion, in a man's hat, a blue coat, which seemed also to have been an article of male apparel, and a red petticoat. She was cleaner, in person and in clothes, than such itinerants generally are; and, having been in her day a strapping *bona roba*, she did not even yet neglect some attention to her appearance; wore a large amber necklace, and silver ear-rings, and had her plaid fastened across her breast with a brooch of the same metal.

The man also looked clean, notwithstanding the meanness of his attire, and had a decent silk handkerchief well knotted about his throat, under which peeped a clean owerlay. His beard, also, instead of displaying a grizzly stubble, unmowed for several days, flowed in thick and comely abundance over the breast, to the length of six inches, and mingled with his hair, which was but beginning to exhibit a touch of age. To sum up his appearance, the loose garment which I have described, was secured around him by a large old-fashioned belt, with brass studs, in which hung a dirk, with a knife and fork, its usual accompaniments. Altogether, there was something more wild and adventurous-looking about the man, than I could have expected to see in an ordinary modern crowder; and the bow which he now and then drew across the violin, to direct his little choir, was decidedly that of no ordinary performer.

You must understand, that many of these observations were the fruits of after remark; for I had scarce approached so near as to get a distinct view of the party, when my friend Benjie's lurching attendant, which he calls by the appropriate name of Hemp, began to cock his tail and ears, and, sensible of my presence, flew, barking like a fury, to the place where I had meant to lie concealed till I heard another song. I was obliged, however, to jump on my feet, and intimidate Hemp, who would otherwise have bit me, by two sound kicks on the ribs, which sent him howling back to his master.

Little Benjie seemed somewhat dismayed at my appearance; but, calculating on my placability, and remembering, perhaps, that the ill-used Solomon was no palfrey of mine, he speedily affected great glee, and almost in one breath assured the itinerants that I was "a grand gentleman, and had plenty of money, and was very kind to poor folk;" and informed me that this was "Willie Steenson — Wandering Willie — the best fiddler that ever kittled thairm with horse-hair."

The woman rose and curtsied; and Wandering Willie sanctioned his own praises with a nod, and the ejaculation, "All is true that the little boy says."

I asked him if he was of this country.

"*This* country!" replied the blind man — "I am of every country in broad Scotland, and a wee bit of England to the boot. But yet I am, in some sense, of this country; for I was born within hearing of the roar of Solway. Will I give your honour a touch of the auld bread-winner?"

He preluded as he spoke, in a manner which really excited my curiosity; and then taking the old tune of Galashiels for his theme, he graced it with a number of wild, complicated, and beautiful variations; during which, it was wonderful to observe how his sightless face was lighted up under the conscious pride and heartfelt delight in the exercise of his own very considerable powers.

"What think you of that, now, for threescore and twa?"

I expressed my surprise and pleasure.

"A rant, man — an auld rant," said Willie; "naething like the music ye hae in your ballhouses and your playhouses in Edinbro'; but it's weel aneugh anes in a way at a dyke-side — Here's another — it's no a Scotch tune, but it passes for ane — Oswald made it himsell, I reckon — he has cheated mony ane, but he canna cheat Wandering Willie."

He then played your favourite air of Roslin Castle, with a number of beautiful variations, some of which I am certain were almost extempore.

"You have another fiddle there, my friend," said I — "Have you a comrade?" But Willie's ears were deaf, or his attention was still busied with the tune.

The female replied in his stead, "O ay, sir — troth we have a partner — a gangrel body like oursells. No but my binny might have been better if he had liked; for mony a bein nook in mony a braw house has been offered to my binny Willie, if he wad but just bide still and play to the gentles."

"Whisht, woman! whisht!" said the blind man, angrily, shaking his locks; "dinna deave the gentleman wi' your havers. Stay in a house and play to the gentles! — strike up when my leddy pleases, and lay down the bow when my lord bids! Na, na, that's nae life for Willie. — Look out, Maggie — peer out, woman, and see if ye can see Robin coming. — De'il be in him! he has got to the lee-side of some smuggler's punch-bowl, and he wunna budge the night, I doubt."

"That is your consort's instrument," said I — "Will you give me leave to try my skill?" I slipped at the same time a shilling into the woman's hand.

"I dinna ken whether I dare trust Robin's fiddle to ye," said Willie, bluntly. His wife gave him a twitch. "Hout awa, Maggie," he said in contempt of the hint; "though the gentleman may hae gien ye siller, he may have nae bow-hand for a' that, and I'll no trust Robin's fiddle wi' an ignoramus. — But that's no sae muckle amiss," he added, as I began to touch the instrument; "I am thinking ye have some skill o' the craft."

To confirm him in this favourable opinion, I began to execute such a complicated flourish as I thought must have turned Crowdero into a pillar of stone with envy and wonder. I scaled the top of the finger-board, to dive at once to the bottom — skipped with flying fingers, like Timotheus, from shift to shift — struck arpeggios and harmonic tones, but without exciting any of the astonishment which I had expected.

Willie indeed listened to me with considerable attention; but I was no sooner finished, than he immediately mimicked on his own instrument the fantastic complication of tones which I had produced, and made so whimsical a parody of my performance, that, although somewhat angry, I could not help laughing heartily, in which I was joined by Benjie, whose reverence for me held him under no restraint; while the poor dame, fearful, doubtless, of my taking offence at this familiarity, seemed divided betwixt her conjugal reverence for her Willie, and her desire to give him a hint for his guidance.

At length the old man stopped of his own accord, and, as if he had sufficiently rebuked me by his mimicry, he said, "But for a' that, ye will play very weel wi' a little practice and some gude teaching. **But ye maun** learn to put the heart into it, man — to put the heart into it."

I played an air in simpler taste, and received more decided approbation.

"That's something like it, man. Od, ye are a clever birkie!"

The woman touched his coat again. "The gentleman is a gentleman, Willie — ye maunna speak that gate to him, hinnie."

"The deevil I maunna!" said Willie; "and what for maunna I? — If he was ten gentles, he canna draw a bow like me, can he?"

"Indeed I cannot, my honest friend," said I; "and if you will go with me to a house hard by, I would be glad to have a night with you."

Here I looked round, and observed Benjie smothering in a laugh, which I was sure had mischief in it. I seized him suddenly by the ear, and made him confess that he was laughing at the thoughts of the reception which a fiddler was likely to get from the Quakers at Mount Sharon. I chucked him from me, not sorry that his mirth had reminded me in time of what I had for the moment forgotten; and invited the itinerant to go with me to Shepherd's Bush, from which I proposed to send word to Mr. Geddes that I should not return home that evening. But the minstrel declined this invitation also. He was engaged for the night, he said, to a dance in the neighbourhood, and vented a round execration on the laziness or drunkenness of his comrade, who had not appeared at the place of rendezvous.

"I will go with you instead of him," said I, in a sudden whim; "and I will give you a crown to introduce me as your comrade."

"*You* gang instead of Rob the Rambler! My certie, freend, ye are no blate!" answered Wandering Willie, in a tone which announced death to my frolic.

But Maggie, whom the offer of the crown had not escaped, began to open on that scent with a maundering sort of lecture. "Oh Willie! hinny Willie, whan will ye learn to be wise? There's a crown to be win for naething but saying ae man's name instead of anither. And, wae's me! I hae just a shilling of this gentleman's gieing, and a boodle of my ain; and ye wunna bend your will sae muckle as to take up the siller that's flung at your feet! Ye will die the death of a cadger's powney, in a wreath of drift! and what can I do better than lie doun and die wi' you? for ye winna let me win siller to keep either you or mysell leevin."

"Haud your nonsense tongue, woman," said Willie, but less absolutely than before. "Is he a real gentleman, or ane of the player-men?"

"I'se uphaud him a real gentleman," said the woman.

"I'se uphaud ye ken little of the matter," said Willie; "let us see haud of your hand, neebor, gin ye like."

I gave him my hand. He said to himself, "Ay, ay, here are fingers that have seen canny service." Then running his hand over my hair, my face, and my dress, he went on with his soliloquy; "Ay, ay, muisted hair, braidclaith o' the best, and seenteen hundred linen on his back, at the least o' it. — And how do you think, my braw birkie, that you are to pass for a tramping fiddler?"

"My dress is plain," said I, — indeed I had chosen my most ordinary suit, out of compliment to my Quaker friends, —"and I can easily pass for a young farmer out upon a frolic. Come, I will double the crown I promised you."

"Damn your crowns!" said the disinterested man of music. "I would like to have a round wi' you, that's certain; — but a farmer, and with a hand that never held pleughstilt, or pettle, that will never do. Ye may pass for a trades-lad from Dumfries, or a student upon the ramble, or the like o' that. — But hark ye, lad; if ye expect to be ranting among the queans o' lasses where ye are gaun, ye will come by the waur, I can tell ye; for the fishers are wild chaps, and will bide nae taunts."

I promised to be civil and cautious; and, to smooth the good woman, I slipped the promised piece into her hand. The acute organs of the blind man detected this little manœuvre.

"Are ye at it again wi' the siller, ye jaud? I'll be sworn ye wad rather hear ae twalpenny clink against another, than have a sprig from Rory Dall,[*] if he was coming alive again anes errand. Gang doun the gate to Lucky Gregson's and get the things ye want, and bide there till ele'en hours in the morn ; and if you see Robin, send him on to me."

"Am I no gaun to the ploy, then?" said Maggie, in a disappointed tone.

"And what for should ye?" said her lord and master; "to dance a' night, I'se warrant, and no to be fit to walk your tae's-length the morn, and we have ten Scots miles afore us? Na, na. Stable the steed, and pit your wife to bed, when there's night wark to do."

"Aweel, aweel, Willie, hinnie, ye ken best; but oh, take an unco care o' yoursell, and mind ye haena the blessing o' sight."

"Your tongue gars me whiles tire of the blessing of hearing, woman," replied Willie, in answer to this tender exhortation.

But I now put in for my interest. "Hollo, good folks, remember that I am to send the boy to Mount Sharon, and if you go to the Shepherd's Bush, honest woman, how the deuce am I to guide the blind man where he is going? I know little or nothing of the country."

"And ye ken mickle less of my hinnie, sir," replied Maggie, "that think he needs ony guiding; he's the best guide himsell, that ye'll find between Criffell and Carlisle. Horse-road and foot-path, parish-road and kirk-road, high-road and cross-road, he kens ilka foot of ground in Nithsdale."

"Ay, ye might have said in braid Scotland, gude-wife," added the fiddler. "But gang your ways, Maggie, that's the first wise word ye hae spoke the day. I wish it was dark night, and rain, and wind, for the gentleman's sake, that I might show him there is whiles when ane had better want een than have them; for I am as true a guide by darkness as by daylight."

Internally as well pleased that my companion was not put to give me this last proof of his skill, I wrote a note with a pencil, desiring Samuel to bring my horse at midnight, when I thought my frolic would be well-nigh over, to the place to which the bearer should direct him, and I sent little Benjie with an apology to the worthy Quakers.

As we parted in different directions, the good woman said, "Oh, sir, if ye wad but ask Willie to tell ye ane of his tales to shorten the gate! He can speak like ony minister frae the pu'pit, and he might have been a minister himsell, but——"

"Haud your tongue, ye fule!" said Willie, —— "But stay, Meg —— gie me a kiss, we maunna part in anger, neither."——And thus our society separated.[†]

LETTER XI.

THE SAME TO THE SAME.

You are now to conceive us proceeding in our different directions across the bare downs. Yonder flies little Benjie to the northward, with Hemp scampering at his heels, both running as if for dear life, so long as the rogue is within sight of his employer, and certain to take the walk very easy,

---

[*] Blind Rorie, a famous musician according to tradition.

[†] It is certain that in many cases the blind have, by constant exercise of their other organs, learned to overcome a defect which one would think incapable of being supplied. Every reader must remember the celebrated Blind Jack of Knaresborough, who lived by laying out roads.

so soon as he is out of ken. Stepping westward, you see Maggie's tall form and high-crowned hat, relieved by the fluttering of her plaid upon the left shoulder, darkening as the distance diminishes her size, and as the level sunbeams begin to sink upon the sea. She is taking her quiet journey to the Shepherd's Bush.

Then, stoutly striding over the lea, you have a full view of Darsie Latimer, with his new acquaintance, Wandering Willie, who, bating that he touched the ground now and then with his staff, not in a doubtful groping manner, but with the confident air of an experienced pilot, heaving the lead when he has the soundings by heart, walks as firmly and boldly as if he possessed the eyes of Argus. There they go, each with his violin slung at his back, but one of them at least totally ignorant whither their course is directed.

And wherefore did you enter so keenly into such a mad frolic? says my wise counsellor — Why, I think, upon the whole, that as a sense of loneliness, and a longing for that kindness which is interchanged in society, led me to take up my temporary residence at Mount Sharon, the monotony of my life there, the quiet simplicity of the conversation of the Geddeses, and the uniformity of their amusements and employments, wearied out my impatient temper, and prepared me for the first escapade which chance might throw in my way.

What would I have given that I could have procured that solemn grave visage of thine, to dignify this joke, as it hath done full many a one of thine own! Thou hast so happy a knack of doing the most foolish things in the wisest manner, that thou mightst pass thy extravagancies for rational actions, even in the eyes of Prudence herself.

From the direction which my guide observed, I began to suspect that the dell at Brokenburn was our probable destination; and it became important to me to consider whether I could, with propriety, or even perfect safety, intrude myself again upon the hospitality of my former host. I therefore asked Willie, whether we were bound for the Laird's, as folk called him.

"Do ye ken the Laird?" said Willie, interrupting a sonata of Corelli, of which he had whistled several bars with great precision.

"I know the Laird a little," said I; "and therefore I was doubting whether I ought to go to his town in disguise."

"I should doubt, not a little only, but a great deal, before I took ye there, my chap," said Wandering Willie; "for I am thinking it wad be worth little less than broken banes baith to you and me. Na, na, chap, we are no ganging to the Laird's, but to a blithe birling at the Brokenburn-foot, where there will be mony a braw lad and lass; and maybe there may be some of the Laird's folks, for he never comes to sic splores himsell. He is all for fowling-piece and salmon-spear, now that pike and musket are out of the question."

"He has been a soldier, then?" said I.

"I'se warrant him a soger," answered Willie; "but take my advice, and speer as little about him as he does about you. Best to let sleeping dogs lie. Better say naething about the Laird, my man, and tell me instead, what sort of a chap ye are, that are sae ready to cleik in with an auld gaberlunzie fiddler? Maggie says ye're gentle, but a shilling maks a' the difference that Maggie kens, between a gentle and a simple, and your crowns wad mak ye a prince of the blood in her een. But I am ane that ken full weel that ye may wear good claithes, and have a saft hand, and yet that may come of idleness as weel as gentrice."

I told him my name, with the same addition I had formerly given to Mr. Joshua Geddes; that I was a law-student, tired of my studies, and rambling about for exercise and amusement.

"And are ye in the wont of drawing up wi' a' the gangrel bodies that ye meet on the high road, or find cowering in a sand-bunker upon the links?" demanded Willie.

"Oh no; only with honest folks like yourself, Willie," was my reply.

"Honest folks like me!—How do ye ken whether I am honest, or what I am?—I may be the deevil himsell for what ye ken; for he has power to come disguised like an angel of light; and besides he is a prime fiddler. He played a sonata to Corelli, ye ken."

There was something odd in this speech, and the tone in which it was said. It seemed as if my companion was not always in his constant mind, or that he was willing to try if he could frighten me. I laughed at the extravagance of his language, however, and asked him in reply, if he was fool enough to believe that the foul fiend would play so silly a masquerade.

"Ye ken little about it—little about it," said the old man, shaking his head and beard, and knitting his brows—"I could tell ye something about that."

What his wife mentioned of his being a tale-teller, as well as a musician, now occurred to me; and as you know I like tales of superstition, I begged to have a specimen of his talent as we went along.

"It is very true," said the blind man, "that when I am tired of scraping thairm or singing ballants, I while mak a tale serve the turn among the country bodies; and I have some fearsome anes, that make the auld carlines shake on the settle, and the bits o' bairns skirl on their minnies out frae their beds. But this that I am gaun to tell you was a thing that befell in our ain house in my father's time—that is, my father was then a hafflins callant; and I tell it to you, that it may be a lesson to you, that are but a young, thoughtless chap, wha ye draw up wi' on a lonely road; for muckle was the dool and care that came o't to my gudesire."

He commenced his tale accordingly, in a distinct narrative tone of voice, which he raised and depressed with considerable skill; at times sinking almost into a whisper, and turning his clear but sightless eyeballs upon my face, as if it had been possible for him to witness the impression which his narrative made upon my features. I will not spare you a syllable of it, although it be of the longest; so I make a dash——and begin

Wandering Willie's Tale.

Ye maun have heard of Sir Robert Redgauntlet of that Ilk, who lived in these parts before the dear years. The country will lang mind him; and our fathers used to draw breath thick if ever they heard him named. He was out wi' the Hielandmen in Montrose's time; and again he was in the hills wi' Glencairn in the saxteen hundred and fifty-twa; and sae when King Charles the Second came in, wha was in sic favour as the Laird of Redgauntlet? He was knighted at Lonnon court, wi' the King's ain sword; and being a redhot prelatist, he came down here, rampauging like a lion, with commissions of lieutenancy, (and of lunacy, for what I ken,) to put down a' the Whigs and Covenanters in the country. Wild wark they made of it; for the Whigs were as dour as the Cavaliers were fierce, and it was which should first tire the other. Redgauntlet was aye-for the strong hand; and his name is kend as wide in the country as Claverhouse's or Tam Dalyell's. Glen, nor dargle, nor mountain, nor cave, could hide the puir hill-folk when Redgauntlet was out with bugle and bloodhound after them, as if they had been sae mony deer. And troth when they fand them, they didna mak muckle mair ceremony than a Hielandman wi' a roebuck—It was just, "Will ye tak the test?"—If not, "Make ready—present—fire!"—and there lay the recusant.

Far and wide was Sir Robert hated and feared. Men thought he had a direct compact with Satan—that he was proof against steel—and that bullets happed aff his buff-coat like hailstanes from a hearth—that he had a mear that would turn a hare on the side of Carrifra-gawns*—and muckle

* A precipitous side of a mountain in Moffatdale.

G

to the same purpose, of whilk mair anon.　The best blessing they wared on him wus, "Deil scoowp wi' Redgauntlet!"　He wasna a bad master to his ain folk, though, and was weel aneugh liked by his tenants; and as for the lackies and troopers that raid out wi' him to the persecutions, as the Whigs caa'd those killing times, they wad hae drunken themsells blind to his health at ony time.

Now you are to ken that my gudesire lived on Redgauntlet's grund—they ca' the place Primrose-Knowe.　We had lived on the grund, and under the Redgauntlets, since the riding days, and lang before.　It was a pleasant bit; and I think the air is callerer and fresher there than ony where else in the country.　It's a' deserted now; and I sat on the broken door-cheek three days since, and was glad I couldna see the plight the place was in; but that's a' wide o' the mark.　There dwelt my gudesire, Steenie Steenson, a rambling, rattling chiel' he had been in his young days, and could play weel on the pipes; he was famous at "Hoopers and Girders"—a' Cumberland couldna touch him at "Jockie Lattin"—and he had the finest finger for the back-lilt botween Berwick and Carlisle.　The like o' Steenie wasna the sort that they made Whigs o'.　And so he became a Tory, as they ca' it, which we now ca' Jacobites, just out of a kind of needcessity, that he might belang to some side or other.　He had nae ill-will to the Whig bodies, and liked little to see the blude rin, though, being obliged to follow Sir Robert in hunting and hoisting, watching and warding, he saw muckle mischief, and maybe did some, that he couldna avoid.

Now Steenie was a kind of favourite with his master, and kend a' the folks about the castle, and was often sent for to play the pipes when they were at their merriment.　Auld Dougal MacCallum, the butler, that had followed Sir Robert through gude and ill, thick and thin, pool and stream, was specially fond of the pipes, and aye gae my gudesire his gude word wi' the Laird; for Dougal could turn his master round his finger.

Weel, round came the Revolution, and it had like to have broken the hearts baith of Dougal and his master.　But the change was not a'thegither sae great as they feared, and other folk thought for.　The Whigs made an unco crawing what they wad do with their auld enemies, and in special wi' Sir Robert Redgauntlet.　But there were ower mony great folks dipped in the same doings, to mak a spick and span new warld.　So Parliament passed it a' ower easy; and Sir Robert, bating that he was held to hunting foxes instead of Covenanters, remained just the man he was.*　His revel was as loud, and his hall as weel lighted, as ever it had been, though maybe he lacked the fines of the nonconformists, that used to come to stock his larder and cellar; for it is certain he began to be keener about the rents than his tenants used to find him before, and they behoved to be prompt to the rent-day, or else the Laird wasna pleased.　And he was sic an awsome body, that naebody cared to anger him; for the oaths he swore, and the rage that he used to get into, and the looks that he put on, made men sometimes think him a devil incarnate.

Weel, my gudesire was nae manager—no that he was a very great misguider—but he hadna the saving gift, and he got twa terms' rent in arrear. He got the first brash at Whitsunday put ower wi' fair word and piping; but when Martinmas came, there was a summons from the grund-officer to come wi' the rent on a day preceese, or else Steenie behoved to flitt.　Sair wark he had to get the siller; but he was weel-freended, and at last he got the haill scraped thegether—a thousand merks—the maist of it was from a neighbour they ca'd Laurie Lapraik—a sly tod.　Laurie had walth o' gear—could hunt wi' the hound and rin wi' the hare—and be Whig or Tory.

---

* The caution and moderation of King William III., and his principles of unlimited toleration, deprived the Cameronians of the opportunity they ardently desired, to retaliate the injuries which they had received during the reign of prelacy, and purify the land, as they called it, from the pollution of blood. They esteemed the Revolution, therefore, only a half measure, which neither comprehended the rebuilding the Kirk in its full splendour, nor the revenge of the death of the Saints on their persecutors.

saunt or sinner, as the wind stood. He was a professor in this Revolution warld, but he liked an orra sough of this warld, and a tune on the pipes weel aneugh at a by time; and abune a', he thought he had gude security for the siller he lent my gudesire ower the stocking at Primrose-Knowe.

Away trots my gudesire to Redgauntlet Castle wi' a heavy purse and a light heart, glad to be out of the Laird's danger. Weel, the first thing he learned at the Castle was, that Sir Robert had fretted himsell into a fit of the gout, because he did not appear before twelve o'clock. It wasna a'thegether for sake of the money, Dougal thought; but because he didna like to part wi' my gudesire aff the grund. Dougal was glad to see Steenie, and brought him into the great oak parlour, and there sat the Laird his leesome lane, excepting that he had beside him a great, ill-favoured jackanape, that was a special pet of his; a cankered beast it was, and mony an ill-natured trick it played—ill to please it was, and easily angered—ran about the haill castle, chattering and yowling, and pinching, and biting folk, specially before ill-weather, or disturbances in the state. Sir Robert caa'd it Major Weir, after the warlock that was burnt;* and few folk liked either the name or the conditions of the creature—they thought there was something in it by ordinar — and my gudesire was not just easy in mind when the door shut on him, and he saw himself in the room wi' naebody but the Laird, Dougal MacCallum, and the Major, a thing that hadna chanced to him before.

Sir Robert sat, or, I should say, lay, in a great armed chair, wi' his grand velvet gown, and his feet on a cradle; for he had baith gout and gravel, and his face looked as gash and ghastly as Satan's. Major Weir sat opposite to him, in a red laced coat, and the Laird's wig on his head; and aye as Sir Robert girned wi' pain, the jackanape girned too, like a sheep's-head between a pair of tangs — an ill-faur'd, fearsome couple they were. The Laird's buff-coat was hung on a pin behind him, and his roadsword and his pistols within reach; for he keepit up the auld fashion of having the weapons ready, and a horse saddled day and night, just as he used to do when he was able to loup on horseback, and away after ony of the hill-folk he could get speerings of. Some said it was for fear of the Whigs taking vengeance, but I judge it was just his auld custom — he wasna gien to fear ony thing. The rental-book, wi' its black cover and brass clasps, was lying beside him; and a book of sculduddry sangs was put betwixt the leaves, to keep it open at the place where it bore evidence against the Goodman of Primrose-Knowe, as behind the hand with his mails and duties. Sir Robert gave my gudesire a look, as if he would hae withered his heart in his bosom. Ye maun ken he had a way of bending his brows, that men saw the visible mark of a horse-shoe in his forehead, deep dinted, as if it had been stamped there.

"Are ye come light-handed, ye son of a toom whistle?" said Sir Robert. "Zounds! if you are——"

My gudesire, with as gude a countenance as he could put on, made a leg, and placed the bag of money on the table wi' a dash, like a man that does something clever. The Laird drew it to him hastily — "Is it all here, Steenie, man?"

"Your honour will find it right," said my gudesire.

"Here, Dougal," said the Laird, "gie Steenie a tass of brandy down stairs, till I count the siller and write the receipt."

But they werena weel out of the room, when Sir Robert gied a yelloch that garr'd the Castle rock. Back ran Dougal — in flew the livery-men — yell on yell gied the Laird, ilk ane mair awfu' than the ither. My gudesire knew not whether to stand or flee, but he ventured back into the parlour, where a' was gaun birdy-girdie — naebody to say 'come in,' or 'gae out.'

---

* A celebrated wizard, executed at Edinburgh for sorcery and other crimes.

Terribly the Laird roared for cauld water to his feet, and wine to cool his throat; and Hell, hell, hell, and its flames, was aye the word in his mouth. They brought him water, and when they plunged his swoln feet into the tub, he cried out it was burning; and folk say that it *did* bubble and sparkle like a seething caldron. He flung the cup at Dougal's head, and said he had given him blood instead of burgundy; and, sure aneugh, the lass washed clotted blood aff the carpet the neist day. The jackanape they ca'd Major Weir, it jibbered and cried as if it was mocking its master; my gudesire's head was like to turn — he forgot baith siller and receipt, and down stairs he banged; but as he ran, the shrieks came faint and fainter; there was a deep-drawn shivering groan, and word gaed through the Castle, that the Laird was dead.

Weel, away came my gudesire, wi' his finger in his mouth, and his best hope was, that Dougal had seen the money-bag, and heard the Laird speak of writing the receipt. The young Laird, now Sir John, came from Edinburgh, to see things put to rights. Sir John and his father never gree'd weel. Sir John had been bred an advocate, and afterwards sat in the last Scots Parliament and voted for the Union, having gotten, it was thought, a rug of the compensations — if his father could have come out of his grave, he would have brained him for it on his awn hearthstane. Some thought it was easier counting with the auld rough Knight than the fair-spoken young ane—but mair of that anon.

Dougal MacCallum, poor body, neither grat nor grained, but gaed about the house looking like a corpse, but directing, as was his duty, a' the order of the grand funeral. Now, Dougal looked aye waur and waur when night was coming, and was aye the last to gang to his bed, whilk was in a little round just opposite the chamber of dais, whilk his master occupied while he was living, an were he now lay in state, as they ca'd it, weel-a-day! The night before the funeral, Dougal could keep his awn counsel nae langer; he came doun with his proud spirit, and fairly asked auld Hutcheon to sit in his room with him for an hour. When they were in the round, Dougal took ae tass of brandy to himsell, and gave another to Hutcheon, and wished him all health and lang life, and said that, for himsell, he wasna lang for this world; for that, every night since Sir Robert's death, his silver call had sounded from the state chamber, just as it used to do at nights in his life-time, to call Dougal to help to turn him in his bed. Dougal said, that being alone with the dead on that floor of the tower, (for naebody cared to wake Sir Robert Redgauntlet like another corpse,) he had never daured to answer the call, but that now his conscience checked him for neglecting his duty; for, "though death breaks service," said MacCallum, "it shall never break my service to Sir Robert; and I will answer his next whistle, so be you will stand by me, Hutcheon."

Hutcheon had nae will to the wark, but he had stood by Dougal in battle and broil, and he wad not fail him at this pinch; so down the carles sat ower a stoup of brandy, and Hutcheon, who was something of a clerk, would have read a chapter of the Bible; but Dougal would hear naething but a blaud of Davie Lindsay, whilk was the waur preparation.

When midnight came, and the house was quiet as a grave, sure enough the silver whistle sounded as sharp and shrill as if Sir Robert were blowing it, and up got the twa auld serving-men, and tottered into the room where the dead man lay. Hutcheon saw aneugh at the first glance; for there were torches in the room, which showed him the foul fiend, in his ain shape, sitting on the Laird's coffin! Ower he cowped as if he had been dead. He could not tell how lang he lay in a trance at the door, but when he gathered himself, he cried on his neighbour, and getting nae answer, raised the house, when Dougal was found lying dead within twa steps of the bed where his master's coffin was placed. As for the whistle, it was gaen anes and aye; but mony a time was it heard at the top of the house on the bartizan, and amang the auld chimneys and turrets where the howlets have their nests. Sir John hushed the matter up, and the funeral passed over without mair bogle-wark.

But when a' was ower, and the Laird was beginning to settle his affairs, every tenant was called up for his arrears, and my gudesire for the full sum that stood against him in the rental-book. Weel, away he trots to the Castle, to tell his story, and there he is introduced to Sir John, sitting in his father's chair, in deep mourning, with weepers and hanging cravat, and a small walking rapier by his side, instead of the auld broadsword that had a hundred-weight of steel about it, what with blade, chape, and basket-hilt. I have heard their communing so often tauld ower, that I almost think I was there mysell, though I couldna be born at the time. (In fact, Alan, my companion mimicked, with a good deal of humour, the flattering, conciliating tone of the tenant's address, and the hypocritical melancholy of the Laird's reply. His grandfather, he said, had, while he spoke, his eye fixed on the rental-book, as if it were a mastiff-dog that he was afraid would spring up and bite him.)

"I wuss ye joy, sir, of the head seat, and the white loaf, and the braid lairdship. Your father was a kind man to friends and followers; muckle grace to you, Sir John, to fill his shoon—his boots, I suld say, for he seldom wore shoon, unless it were muils when he had the gout."

"Ay, Steenie," quoth the Laird, sighing deeply, and putting his napkin to his een, "his was a sudden call, and he will be missed in the country; no time to set his house in order—weel prepared Godward, no doubt, which is the root of the matter—but left us behind a tangled heap to wind, Steenie. —Hem! hem! We maun go to business, Steenie; much to do, and little time to do it in."

Here he opened the fatal volume. I have heard of a thing they call Doomsday-book — I am clear it has been a rental of back-ganging tenants.

"Stephen," said Sir John, still in the same soft, sleekit tone of voice — "Stephen Stevenson, or Steenson, ye are down here for a year's rent behind the hand — due at last term."

Stephen. "Please your honour, Sir John, I paid it to your father."

Sir John. "Ye took a receipt, then, doubtless, Stephen; and can produce it."

Stephen. "Indeed I hadna time, an it like your honour; for nae sooner had I set doun the siller, and just as his honour, Sir Robert, that's gaen, drew it till him to count it, and write out the receipt, he was ta'en wi' the pains that removed him."

"That was unlucky," said Sir John, after a pause. "But ye maybe paid it in the presence of somebody. I want but a *talis qualis* evidence, Stephen. I would go ower strictly to work with no poor man."

Stephen. "Troth, Sir John, there was naebody in the room but Dougal MacCallum the butler. But, as yer honour kens, he has e'en followed his auld master."

"Very unlucky again, Stephen," said Sir John, without altering his voice a single note. "The man to whom ye paid the money is dead — and the man who witnessed the payment is dead too — and the siller, which should have been to the fore, is neither seen nor heard tell of in the repositories. How am I to believe a' this?"

Stephen. "I dinna ken, your honour; but there is a bit memorandum note of the very coins; for, God help me! I had to borrow out of twenty purses; and I am sure that ilka man there set down will take his grit oath for what purpose I borrowed the money."

Sir John. "I have little doubt ye *borrowed* the money, Steenie. It is the *payment* to my father that I want to have some proof of."

Stephen. "The siller maun be about the house, Sir John. And since your honour never got it, and his honour that was canna have taen it wi' him, maybe some of the family may have seen it."

Sir John. "We will examine the servants, Stephen; that is but reasonable."

But lackey and lass, and page and groom, all denied stoutly that they had ever seen such a bag of money as my gudesire described. What was waur, he had unluckily not mentioned to any living soul of them his purpose of paying his rent. Ae quaen had noticed something under his arm, but she took it for the pipes.

Sir John Redgauntlet ordered the servants out of the room, and then said to my gudesire, " Now, Steenie, ye see ye have fair play ; and, as I have little doubt ye ken better where to find the siller than ony other body, I beg, in fair terms, and for your own sake, that you will end this fasherie ; for, Stephen, ye maun pay or flitt.'

" The Lord forgie your opinion," said Stephen, driven almost to his wit's end — " I am an honest man."

" So am I, Stephen," said his honour; "and so are all the folks in the house, I hope. But if there be a knave amongst us, it must be he that tells the story he cannot prove." He paused, and then added, mair sternly, " If I understand your trick, sir, you want to take advantage of some malicious reports concerning things in this family, and particularly respecting my father's sudden death, thereby to cheat me out of the money, and perhaps take away my character, by insinuating that I have received the rent I am demanding. — Where do you suppose this money to be ? — I insist upon knowing."

My gudesire saw every thing look so muckle against him, that he grew nearly desperate — however, he shifted from one foot to another, looked to every corner of the room, and made no answer.

" Speak out, sirrah," said the Laird, assuming a look of his father's, a very particular ane, which he had when he was angry — it seemed as if the wrinkles of his frown made that self-same fearful shape of a horse's shoe in the middle of his brow ;—" Speak out, sir ! I *will* know your thoughts ; — do you suppose that I have this money ?"

" Far be it frae me to say so," said Stephen.

" Do you charge any of my people with having taken it ?"

" I wad be laith to charge them that may be innocent," said my gudesire ; " and if there be any one that is guilty, I have nae proof."

" Somewhere the money must be, if there is a word of truth in your story," said Sir John ; " I ask where you think it is — and demand a correct answer."

" In hell, if you *will* have my thoughts of it," said my gudesire, driven to extremity —" in hell ! with your father, his jackanape, and his silver whistle."

Down the stairs he ran, (for the parlour was nae place for him after such a word,) and he heard the Laird swearing blood and wounds, behind him, as fast as ever did Sir Robert, and roaring for the bailie and the baron-officer.

Away rode my gudesire to his chief creditor, (him they caa'd Laurie Lapraik,) to try if he could make ony thing out of him ; but when he tauld his story, he got but the worst word in his wame — thief, beggar, and dyvour, were the saftest terms ; and to the boot of these hard terms, Laurie brought up the auld story of his dipping his hand in the blood of God's saunts, just as if a tenant could have helped riding with the Laird, and that a laird like Sir Robert Redgauntlet. My gudesire was, by this time, far beyond the bounds of patience, and, while he and Laurie were at deil speed the liars, he was wanchancie aneugh to abuse Lapraik's doctrine as weel as the man, and said things that garr'd folks' flesh grue that heard them ; — he wasna just himsell, and he had lived wi' a wild set in his day.

At last they parted, and my gudesire was to ride hame through the wood of Pitmurkie, that is a' fou of black firs, as they say. — I ken the wood, but the firs may be black or white for what I can tell.—At the entry of the wood there is a wild common, and on the edge of the common, a little lonely change-house, that was keepit then by an ostler-wife, they suld hae caa'd her Tibbie Faw, and there puir Steenie cried for a mutchkin of brandy, for he had had no refreshment the haill day. Tibbie was earnest wi' him to take a bite of meat, but he couldna think o't, nor would he take his foot out of the stirrup, and took off the brandy wholely at two draughts, and named a toast at each ;— the first was, the memory of Sir Robert Redgauntlet, and might he never lie quiet in his grave till he had righted his poor bond-tenant; and the second was, a health to Man's Enemy, if he would but get him back the pock of siller, or tell him what came o't, for he saw the haill world was like to regard him as a thief and a cheat, and he took that waur than even the ruin of his house and hauld.

On he rode, little caring where. It was a dark night turned, and the trees made it yet darker, and he let the beast take its ain road through the wood ; when all of a sudden, from tired and wearied that it was before, the nag began to spring, and flee, and stend, that my gudesire could hardly keep the saddle — Upon the whilk, a horseman, suddenly riding up beside him, said, "That's a mettle beast of yours, freend ; will you sell him ?"— So saying, he touched the horse's neck with his riding-wand, and it fell into its auld heigh-ho of a stumbling trot. "But his spunk's soon out of him, I think," continued the stranger, "and that is like mony a man's courage, that thinks he wad do great things till he come to the proof."

My gudesire scarce listened to this, but spurred his horse, with "Gude e'en to you, freend."

But it's like the stranger was ane that doesna lightly yield his point ; for, ride as Steenie liked, he was aye beside him at the self-same pace. At last my gudesire, Steenie Steenson, grew half angry, and, to say the truth, half feared.

"What was it that ye want with me, freend?" he said. "If ye be a robber, I have nae money ; if ye be a leal man, wanting company, I have nae heart to mirth or speaking ; and if ye want to ken the road, I scarce ken it mysell."

"If you will tell me your grief," said the stranger, "I am one that, though I have been sair miscaa'd in the world, am the only hand for helping my freends."

So my gudesire, to ease his ain heart, mair than from any hope of help, told him the story from beginning to end.

"It's a hard pinch," said the stranger ; "but I think I can help you."

"If you could lend the money, sir, and take a lang day — I ken nae other help on earth," said my gudesire.

"But there may be some under the earth," said the stranger. "Come, I'll be frank wi' you ; I could lend you the money on bond, but you would maybe scruple my terms. Now, I can tell you, that your auld Laird is disturbed in his grave by your curses, and the wailing of your family, and if ye daur venture to go to see him, he will give you the receipt."

My gudesire's hair stood on end at this proposal, but he thought his companion might be some humorsome chield that was trying to frighten him, and might end with lending him the money. Besides, he was bauld wi' brandy, and desperate wi' distress ; and he said he had courage to go to the gate of hell, and a step farther, for that receipt.—The stranger laughed.

Weel, they rode on through the thickest of the wood, when, all of a sudden, the horse stopped at the door of a great house ; and, but that he knew the place was ten miles off, my father would have thought he was at Redgauntlet Castle. They rode into the outer court-yard, through the muckle faulding yetts, and aneath the auld portcullis ; and the whole front of the house was lighted, and there were pipes and fiddles, and as much dancing and deray within as used to be at Sir Robert's house at Pace and Yule, and such high seasons. They lap off, and my gudesire, as seemed to him, fastened his horse to the very ring he had tied him to that morning, when he gaed to wait on the young Sir John.

"God!" said my gudesire, "if Sir Robert's death be but a dream!"

He knocked at the ha' door just as he was wont, and his auld acquaintance, Dougal MacCallum,—just after his wont, too,—came to open the door, and said, "Piper Steenie, are ye there, lad? Sir Robert has been crying for you."

My gudesire was like a man in a dream—he looked for the stranger, but he was gane for the time. At last he just tried to say, "Ha! Dougal Driveower, are ye living? I thought ye had been dead."

"Never fash yoursell wi' me," said Dougal, "but look to yoursell; and see ye tak naething frae ony body here, neither meat, drink, or siller, except just the receipt that is your ain."

So saying, he led the way out through halls and trances that were weel kend to my gudesire, and into the auld oak parlour; and there was as much singing of profane sangs, and birling of red wine, and speaking blasphemy and sculduddry, as had ever been in Redgauntlet Castle when it was at the blithest.

But, Lord take us in keeping, what a set of ghastly revellers they were that sat around that table!—My gudesire kend mony that had long before gane to their place, for often had he piped to the most part in the hall of Redgauntlet. There was the fierce Middleton, and the dissolute Rothes, and the crafty Lauderdale; and Dalyell, with his bald head, and a beard to his girdle; and Earlshall, with Cameron's blude on his hand; and wild Bonshaw, that tied blessed Mr. Cargill's limbs till the blude sprung; and Dunbarton Douglas, the twice-turned traitor baith to country and king. There was the Bluidy Advocate MacKenyie, who, for his worldly wit and wisdom had been to the rest as a god. And there was Claverhouse, as beautiful as when he lived, with his long, dark, curled locks, streaming down over his laced buff-coat, and his left hand always on his right spule-blade, to hide the wound that the silver bullet had made.* He sat apart from them all, and looked at them with a melancholy, haughty countenance; while the rest halloed, and sung, and laughed, that the room rang. But their smiles were fearfully contorted from time to time; and their laugh passed into such wild sounds, as made my gudesire's very nails grow blue, and chilled the marrow in his banes.

They that waited at the table were just the wicked serving-men and troopers, that had done their work and cruel bidding on earth. There was the Lang Lad of the Nethertown, that helped to take Argyle; and the Bishop's summoner, that they called the Deil's Rattle-bag; and the wicked guardsmen in their laced coats; and the savage Highland Amorites, that shed blood like water; and many a proud serving-man, haughty of heart and bloody of hand, cringing to the rich, and making them wickeder than they would be; grinding the poor to powder, when the rich had broken them to fragments. And mony, mony mair were coming and ganging, a' as busy in their vocation as if they had been alive.

---

* The personages here mentioned are most of them characters of historical fame; but those less known and remembered may be found in the tract entitled, "The Judgment and Justice of God Exemplified, or, a Brief Historical Account of some of the Wicked Lives and Miserable Deaths of some of the most remarkable Apostates and Bloody Persecutors, from the Reformation till after the Revolution." This constitutes a sort of postscript or appendix to John Howie of Lochgoin's "Account of the Lives of the most eminent Scots Worthies." The author has, with considerable ingenuity, reversed his reasoning upon the inference to be drawn from the prosperity or misfortunes which befall individuals in this world, either in the course of their lives or in the hour of death. In the account of the martyrs' sufferings, such inflictions are mentioned only as trials permitted by Providence, for the better and brighter display of their faith, and constancy of principle. But when similar afflictions befell the opposite party, they are imputed to the direct vengeance of Heaven upon their impiety. If, indeed, the life of any person obnoxious to the historian's censures happened to have passed in unusual prosperity, the mere fact of its being finally concluded by death, is assumed as an undeniable token of the judgment of Heaven, and, to render the conclusion inevitable, his last scene is generally garnished with some singular circumstances. Thus the Duke of Lauderdale is said, through old age but immense corpulence, to have become so sunk in spirits, "that his heart was not the bigness of a walnut."

REDGAUNTLET.

Sir Robert Redgauntlet, in the midst of a' this fearful riot, cried, wi' a voice like thunder, on Steenie Piper to come to the board-head where he was sitting; his legs stretched out before him, and swathed up with flannel, with his holster pistols aside him, while the great broadsword rested against his chair, just as my gudesire had seen him the last time upon earth — the very cushion for the jackanape was close to him, but the creature itself was not there — it wasna its hour, it's likely; for he heard them say as he came forward, "Is not the Major come yet?" And another answered, "The jackanape will be here betimes the morn." And when my gudesire came forward, Sir Robert, or his ghaist, or the deevil in his likeness, said, "Weel, piper, hae ye settled wi' my son for the year's rent?"

With much ado my father gat breath to say, that Sir John would not settle without his honour's receipt.

"Ye shall hae that for a tune of the pipes, Steenie," said the appearance of Sir Robert—"Play us up 'Weel hoddled, Luckie.' "

Now this was a tune my gudesire learned frae a warlock, that heard it when they were worshipping Satan at their meetings; and my gudesire had sometimes played it at the ranting suppers in Redgauntlet Castle, but never very willingly; and now he grew cauld at the very name of it, and said, for excuse, he hadna his pipes wi' him.

"MacCallum, ye limb of Beelzebub," said the fearfu' Sir Robert, "bring Steenie the pipes that I am keeping for him!"

MacCallum brought a pair of pipes might have served the piper of Donald of the Isles. But he gave my gudesire a nudge as he offered them; and looking secretly and closely, Steenie saw that the chanter was of steel, and heated to a white heat; so he had fair warning not to trust his fingers with it. So he excused himself again, and said, he was faint and frightened, and had not wind aneugh to fill the bag.

"Then ye maun eat and drink, Steenie," said the figure; "for we do little else here; and it's ill speaking between a fou man and a fasting."

Now these were the very words that the bloody Earl of Douglas said to keep the King's messenger in hand, while he cut the head off MacLellan of Bombie, at the Threave Castle,* and that put Steenie mair and mair on his guard. So he spoke up like a man, and said he came neither to eat, or drink, or make minstrelsy; but simply for his ain — to ken what was come o' the money he had paid, and to get a discharge for it; and he was so stout-hearted by this time, that he charged Sir Robert for conscience-sake —(he had no power to say the holy name)—and as he hoped for peace and rest, to spread no snares for him, but just to give him his ain.

The appearance gnashed its teeth and laughed, but it took from a large pocket-book the receipt, and handed it to Steenie. "There is your receipt, ye pitiful cur; and for the money, my dog-whelp of a son may go look for it in the Cat's Cradle."

My gudesire uttered mony thanks, and was about to retire, when Sir Robert roared aloud, "Stop, though, thou sack-doudling son of a whore! I am not done with thee. HERE we do nothing for nothing; and you must return on this very day twelvemonth, to pay your master the homage that you owe me for my protection."

My father's tongue was loosed of a suddenty, and he said aloud, "I refer mysell to God's pleasure, and not to yours."

He had no sooner uttered the word than all was dark around him; and he sunk on the earth with such a sudden shock, that he lost both breath and sense.

How lang Steenie lay there, he could not tell; but when he came to himsell, he was lying in the auld kirkyard of Redgauntlet parochine just at the door of the family aisle, and the skutcheon of the auld knight, Sir Robert,

prayer
to plead
called to
the bed
of the
sick,
He
was
thought
to pray
better
when he
held a
stick of
curious
caper —
& was
exe-
1676 —
by burning
& his
eester
who was
an ill
beetle —
also
was
exe-
See
was
made —
both
confused
in one
crime

* The reader is referred for particulars to Pitscottie's History of Scotland.

hanging over his head. There was a deep morning fog on grass and grave-stane around him, and his horse was feeding quietly beside the minister's twa cows. Steenie would have thought the whole was a dream, but he had the receipt in his hand, fairly written and signed by the auld Laird; only the last letters of his name were a little disorderly, written like one seized with sudden pain.

Sorely troubled in his mind, he left that dreary place, rode through the mist to Redgauntlet Castle, and with much ado he got speech of the Laird.

"Well, you dyvour bankrupt," was the first word, "have you brought me my rent?"

"No," answered my gudesire, "I have not; but I have brought your honour Sir Robert's receipt for it."

"How, sirrah?—Sir Robert's receipt!—You told me he had not given you one."

"Will your honour please to see if that bit line is right?"

Sir John looked at every line, and at every letter, with much attention; and at last, at the date, which my gudesire had not observed,—"*From my appointed place*," he read, "*this twenty-fifth of November.*"—"What!—That is yesterday!—Villain, thou must have gone to hell for this!"

"I got it from your honour's father—whether he be in heaven or hell, I know not," said Steenie.

"I will delate you for a warlock to the Privy Council!" said Sir John. "I will send you to your master, the devil, with the help of a tar-barrel and a torch!"

"I intend to delate mysell to the Presbytery," said Steenie, "and tell them all I have seen last night, whilk are things fitter for them to judge of than a borrel man like me."

Sir John paused, composed himsell, and desired to hear the full history; and my gudesire told it him from point to point, as I have told it you—word for word, neither more nor less.

Sir John was silent again for a long time, and at last he said, very com-posedly, "Steenie, this story of yours concerns the honour of many a noble family besides mine; and if it be a leasing-making, to keep yourself out of my danger, the least you can expect is to have a redhot iron driven through your tongue, and that will be as bad as scauding your fingers wi' a redhot chanter. But yet it may be true, Steenie; and if the money cast up, I shall not know what to think of it. — But where shall we find the Cat's Cradle? There are cats enough about the old house, but I think they kitten without the ceremony of bed or cradle."

"We were best ask Hutcheon," said my gudesire; "he kens a' the odd corners about as weel as — another serving man that is now gane, and that I wad not like to name."

Aweel, Hutcheon, when he was asked, told them, that a ruinous turret, lang disused, next to the clock-house, only accessible by a ladder, for the opening was on the outside, and far above the battlements, was called of old the Cat's Cradle.

"There will I go immediately," said Sir John; and he took (with what purpose, Heaven kens) one of his father's pistols from the hall-table, where they had lain since the night he died, and hastened to the battlements.

It was a dangerous place to climb, for the ladder was auld and frail, and wanted ane or twa rounds. However, up got Sir John, and entered at the turret door, where his body stopped the only little light that was in the bit turret. Something flees at him wi' a vengeance, maist dang him back ower — bang gaed the knight's pistol, and Hutcheon, that held the ladder, and my gudesire that stood beside him, hears a loud skelloch. A minute after, Sir John flings the body of the jackanape down to them, and cries that the siller is fund, and that they should come up and help him. And there was the bag of siller sure eneugh, and mony orra thing besides, that had been missing for mony a day. And Sir John, when he had riped turret weel, led my gudesire into the dining-parlour, and took him hand, and spoke kindly to him, and said he was sorry he shoul doubted his word, and that he would hereafter be a good master to make amends.

"And now, Steenie," said Sir John, "although this vision of yours on the whole, to my father's credit, as an honest man, that he should, even after his death, desire to see justice done to a poor man like you, yet you are sensible that ill-dispositioned men might make bad constructions upon it, concerning his soul's health. So, I think, we had better lay the haill dirdum on that ill-deedie creature, Major Weir, and say naething about your dream in the wood of Pitmurkie. You had taken ower muckle brandy to be very certain about ony thing; and, Steenie, this receipt," (his hand shook while he held it out,) — "it's but a queer kind of document, and we will do best, I think, to put it quietly in the fire."

"Od, but for as queer as it is, it's a' the voucher I have for my rent," said my gudesire, who was afraid, it may be, of losing the benefit of Sir Robert's discharge.

"I will bear the contents to your credit in the rental-book, and give you a discharge under my own hand," said Sir John, "and that on the spot. And, Steenie, if you can hold your tongue about this matter, you shall sit, from this term downward, at an easier rent."

"Mony thanks to your honour," said Steenie, who saw easily in what corner the wind was; "doubtless I will be conformable to all your honour's commands; only I would willingly speak wi' some powerful minister on the subject, for I do not like the sort of soumons of appointment whilk your honour's father ——"

"Do not call the phantom my father!" said Sir John, interrupting him.

"Weel, then, the thing that was so like him," said my gudesire; "he spoke of my coming back to see him this time twelvemonth, and it's a weight on my conscience."

"Aweel, then," said Sir John, "if you be so much distressed in mind, you may speak to our minister of the parish; he is a douce man, regards the honour of our family, and the mair that he may look for some patronage from me."

Wi' that, my father readily agreed that the receipt should be burnt, and the Laird threw it into the chimney with his ain hand. Burn it would not for them, though; but away it flew up the lumb, wi' a lang train of sparks at its tail, and a hissing noise like a squib.

My grandsire gaed down to the Manse, and the minister, when he had heard the story, said, it was his real opinion, that though my gudesire had gaen very far in tampering with dangerous matters, yet, as he had refused the devil's arles, (for such was the offer of meat and drink,) and had refused to do homage by piping at his bidding, he hoped, that if he held a circumspect walk hereafter, Satan could take little advantage by what was come and gane. And, indeed, my gudesire, of his ain accord, lang foreswore baith the pipes and the brandy — it was not even till the year was out, and the fatal day past, that he would so much as take the fiddle, or drink usquebaugh or tippeny.

Sir John made up his story about the jackanape as he liked himsell; and some believe till this day there was no more in the matter than the filching nature of the brute. Indeed, ye'll no hinder some to threap, that it was nane o' the auld Enemy that Dougal and my gudesire saw in the Laird's room, but only that wanchancy creature, the Major, capering on the coffin; and that, as to the blawing on the Laird's whistle that was heard after he was dead, the filthy brute could do that as weel as the Laird himsell, if no better. But Heaven kens the truth, whilk first came out by the minister's wife, after Sir John and her ain gude man were baith in the moulds. And then my gudesire, wha was failed in his limbs, but not in his judgment or memory — at least nothing to speak of — was obliged to tell the real narrative to his friends, for the credit of his good name. He might else have been charged for a warlock.*

THE shades of evening were growing thicker around us as my conductor finished his long narrative with this moral—"Ye see, birkie, it is nae chancy thing to tak a stranger traveller for a guide, when you are in an uncouth land."

"I should not have made that inference," said I. "Your grandfather's adventure was fortunate for himself, whom it saved from ruin and distress; and fortunate for his landlord also, whom it prevented from committing a gross act of injustice."

"Ay, but they had baith to sup the sauce o't sooner or later," said Wandering Willie—"what was fristed wasna forgiven. Sir John died before he was much over three-score; and it was just like of a moment's illness. And for my gudesire, though he departed in fullness of life, yet there was my father, a yauld man of forty-five, fell down betwixt the stilts of his pleugh, and raise never again, and left nae bairn but me, a puir sightless, fatherless motherless creature, could neither work nor want. Things gaed weel enough at first; for Sir Redwald Redgauntlet, the only son of Sir John, and the oye of auld Sir Robert, and, waes me! the last of the honourable house, took the farm aff our hands, and brought me into his household to have care of me. He liked music, and I had the best teachers baith England and Scotland could gie me. Mony a merry year was I wi' him; but waes me! he gaed out with other pretty men in the forty-five—I'll say nae mair about

* I have heard in my youth some such wild tale as that placed in the mouth of the blind fiddler, of which, I think, the hero was Sir Robert Grierson of Lagg, the famous persecutor. But the belief was general throughout Scotland, that the excessive lamentation over the loss of friends disturbed the repose of the dead, and broke even the rest of the grave. There are several instances of this in tradition, but one struck me particularly, as I heard it from the lips of one who professed receiving it from those of a ghost-seer. This was a Highland lady, named Mrs. C—— of B——, who probably believed firmly in the truth of an apparition, which seems to have originated in the weakness of her nerves and strength of her imagination. She had been lately left a widow by her husband, with the office of guardian to their only child. The young man added to the difficulties of his charge by an extreme propensity for a military life, which his mother was unwilling to give way to, while she found it impossible to repress it. About this time the Independent Companies, formed for the preservation of the peace of the Highlands, were in the course of being levied; and as a gentleman named Cameron, nearly connected with Mrs. C——, commanded one of those companies, she was at length persuaded to compromise the matter with her son, by permitting him to enter this company in the capacity of a cadet, thus gratifying his love of a military life without the dangers of foreign service, to which no one then thought these troops were at all liable to be exposed, while even their active service at home was not likely to be attended with much danger. She readily obtained a promise from her relative that he would be particular in his attention to her son, and therefore concluded she had accommodated matters between her son's wishes and his safety in a way sufficiently attentive to both. She set off to Edinburgh to get what was a wanting for his outfit, and shortly afterwards received melancholy news from the Highlands. The Independent Company into which her son was to enter had a skirmish with a party of caterans engaged in some act of spoil, and her friend the captain being wounded, and out of the reach of medical assistance, died in consequence. This news was a thunder-bolt to the poor mother, who was at once deprived of her kinsman's advice and assistance, and instructed by his fate of the unexpected danger to which her son's new calling exposed him. She remained also in great sorrow for her relative, whom she loved with sisterly affection. These conflicting causes of anxiety, together with her uncertainty, whether to continue or change her son's destination, were terminated in the following manner :—

The house in which Mrs. C—— resided in the old town of Edinburgh, was a flat or story of a land accessible, as was then universal, by a common stair. The family who occupied the story beneath were her acquaintances, and she was in the habit of drinking tea with them every evening. It was accordingly about six o'clock, when, recovering herself from a deep fit of anxious reflection, she was about to leave the parlour in which she sat in order to attend this engagement. The door through which she was to pass opened, as was very common in Edinburgh, into a dark passage. In this passage, and within a yard of her when she opened the door, stood the apparition of her kinsman, the deceased officer, in his full tartans, and wearing his bonnet. Terrified at what she saw, or thought she saw, she closed the door hastily, and, sinking on her knees by a chair, prayed to be delivered from the horrors of the vision. She remained in that posture till her friends below tapped on the floor to intimate that tea was ready. Recalled to herself by the signal, she arose, and, on opening the apartment door, again was confronted by the visionary Highlander, whose bloody brow bore token, on this second appearance, to the death he had died. Unable to endure this repetition of her terrors, Mrs. C—— sunk on the floor in a swoon. Her friends below, startled with the noise, came up stairs, and, alarmed at the situation in which they found her, insisted on her going to bed and taking some medicine, in order to compose what they took for a nervous attack. They had no sooner left her in quiet, than the apparition of the soldier was once more visible in the apartment. This time she took courage and said, "In the name of God, Donald, why do you haunt one who respected and loved you when living?" To which he answered readily, in Gaelic, "Cousin, why did you not speak sooner? My rest is disturbed by your unnecessary lamentation—your tears scald me in my shroud. I come to tell you that my untimely death ought to make no difference in your views for your son; God will raise patrons to supply my place, and he will live to the fulness of years, and die honoured and at peace." The lady of course followed her kinsman's advice; and as she was accounted a person of strict veracity, we may conclude the first apparition an illusion on the fancy, the final one a lively dream, suggested by the other two.

it—My head never settled weel since I lost him; and if I say another word about it, deil a bar will I have the heart to play the night.—Look out, my gentle chap," he resumed in a different tone, "ye should see the lights at Brokenburn Glen by this time."

LETTER XII.

THE SAME TO THE SAME.

Tam Luter was their minstrel meet,
Gude Lord as he could lance,
He play'd me shrill, and sang me sweet,
Till Towsie took a trance.
Auld Lightfoot there he did forlest,
And counterfeited France;
He used himself as man discreet,
And up took Morrice danse
See loud,
At Christ's Kirk on the Green that day.
KING JAMES I.

I CONTINUE to scribble at length, though the subject may seem somewhat deficient in interest. Let the grace of the narrative, therefore, and the concern we take in each other's matters, make amends for its tenuity. We fools of fancy, who suffer ourselves, like Malvolio, to be cheated with our own visions, have, nevertheless, this advantage over the wise ones of the earth, that we have our whole stock of enjoyments under our own command, and can dish for ourselves an intellectual banquet with most moderate assistance from external objects. It is, to be sure, something like the feast which the Barmecide served up to Alnaschar; and we cannot expect to get fat upon such diet. But then, neither is there repletion nor nausea, which often succeed the grosser and more material revel. On the whole, I still pray, with the Ode to Castle Building—

"Give me thy hope which sickens not the heart;
Give me thy wealth which has no wings to fly;
Give me the bliss thy visions can impart:
Thy friendship give me, warm in poverty!"

And so, despite thy solemn smile and sapient shake of the head, I will go on picking such interest as I can out of my trivial adventures, even though that interest should be the creation of my own fancy; nor will I cease to inflict on thy devoted eyes the labour of perusing the scrolls in which I shall record my narrative.

My last broke off as we were on the point of descending into the glen at Brokenburn, by the dangerous track which I had first travelled *en croupe*, behind a furious horseman, and was now again to brave under the precarious guidance of a blind man.

It was now getting dark; but this was no inconvenience to my guide, who moved on, as formerly, with instinctive security of step, so that we soon reached the bottom, and I could see lights twinkling in the cottage which had been my place of refuge on a former occasion. It was not thither, however, that our course was directed. We left the habitation of the Laird to the left, and turning down the brook, soon approached the small hamlet which had been erected at the mouth of the stream, probably on account of the convenience which it afforded as a harbour to the fishing-boats. A large, low cottage, full in our front, seemed highly illuminated; for the light not only glanced from every window and aperture in its frail

H

walls, but was even visible from rents and fractures in the roof, composed of tarred shingles, repaired in part by thatch and *divot*.

While these appearances engaged my attention, that of my companion was attracted by a regular succession of sounds, like a bouncing on the floor, mixed with a very faint noise of music, which Willie's acute organs at once recognized and accounted for, while to me it was almost inaudible. The old man struck the earth with his staff in a violent passion. "The whoreson fisher rabble! They have brought another violer upon my walk! They are such smuggling blackguards, that they must run in their very music; but I'll sort them waur than ony gauger in the country. — Stay — hark — it's no a fiddle neither — it's the pipe and tabor bastard, Simon of Sowport, frae the Nicol Forest; but I'll pipe and tabor him! — Let me hae ance my left hand on his cravat, and ye shall see what my right will do. Come away, chap — come away, gentle chap — nae time to be picking and waling your steps." And on he passed with long and determined strides, dragging me along with him.

I was not quite easy in his company; for, now that his minstrel pride was hurt, the man had changed from the quiet, decorous, I might almost say respectable person, which he seemed while he told his tale, into the appearance of a fierce, brawling, dissolute stroller. So that when he entered the large hut, where a great number of fishers, with their wives and daughters, were engaged in eating, drinking, and dancing, I was somewhat afraid that the impatient violence of my companion might procure us an indifferent reception.

But the universal shout of welcome with which Wandering Willie was received—the hearty congratulations—the repeated "Here's t' ye, Willie!" — "Whare hae ye been, ye blind deevil?" and the call upon him to pledge them — above all, the speed with which the obnoxious pipe and tabor were put to silence, gave the old man such effectual assurance of undiminished popularity and importance, as at once put his jealousy to rest, and changed his tone of offended dignity, into one better fitted to receive such cordial greetings. Young men and women crowded round, to tell how much they were afraid some mischance had detained him, and how two or three young fellows had set out in quest of him.

"It was nae mischance, praised be Heaven," said Willie, "but the absence of the lazy loon Rob the Rambler, my comrade, that didna come to meet me on the Links; but I hae gotten a braw consort in his stead, worth a dozen of him, the unhanged blackguard."

"And wha is't tou's gotten, Wullie, lad?" said half a score of voices, while all eyes were turned on your humble servant, who kept the best countenance he could, though not quite easy at becoming the centre to which all eyes were pointed.

"I ken him by his bemmed cravat," said one fellow; "it's Gil Hobson, the souple tailor frae Burgh.—Ye are welcome to Scotland, ye prick-the-clout loon," he said, thrusting forth a paw much the colour of a badger's back, and of most portentous dimensions.

"Gil Hobson? Gil whoreson!" exclaimed Wandering Willie; "it's a gentle chap that I judge to be an apprentice wi' auld Joshua Geddes, to the quaker-trade."

"What trade be's that, man?" said he of the badger-coloured fist.

"Canting and lying,"—said Willie, which produced a thundering laugh; "but I am teaching the callant a better trade, and that is, feasting and fiddling."

Willie's conduct in thus announcing something like my real character, was contrary to compact; and yet I was rather glad he did so, for the consequence of putting a trick upon these rude and ferocious men, might, in case of discovery, have been dangerous to us both, and I was at the same time delivered from the painful effort to support a fictitious character.

The good company, except perhaps one or two of the young women, whose looks expressed some desire for better acquaintance, gave themselves no farther trouble about me; but, while the seniors resumed their places near an immense bowl, or rather reeking caldron of brandy-punch, the younger arranged themselves on the floor, and called loudly on Willie to strike up.

With a brief caution to me, to "mind my credit, for fishers have ears, though fish have none," Willie led off in capital style, and I followed, certainly not so as to disgrace my companion, who, every now and then, gave me a nod of approbation. The dances were, of course, the Scottish jigs, and reels, and "twasome dances," with a strathspey or hornpipe for interlude; and the want of grace, on the part of the performers, was amply supplied by truth of ear, vigour and decision of step, and the agility proper to the northern performers. My own spirits rose with the mirth around me, and with old Willie's admirable execution, and frequent "weel dune, gentle chap, yet;"—and, to confess the truth, I felt a great deal more pleasure in this rustic revel, than I have done at the more formal balls and concerts in your famed city, to which I have sometimes made my way. Perhaps this was because I was a person of more importance to the presiding matron of Brokenburn-foot, than I had the means of rendering myself to the far-famed Miss Nickie Murray, the patroness of your Edinburgh assemblies. The person I mean was a buxom dame of about thirty, her fingers loaded with many a silver ring, and three or four of gold; her ankles liberally displayed from · under her numerous, blue, white, and scarlet short petticoats, and attired in hose of the finest and whitest lamb's-wool, which arose from shoes of Spanish cordwain, fastened with silver buckles. She took the lead in my favour, and declared, "that the brave young gentleman should not weary himself to death wi' playing, but take the floor for a dance or twa."

"And what's to come of me, Dame Martin?" said Willie.

"Come o' thee?" said the dame; "mishanter on the auld beard o' ye! ye could play for twenty hours on end, and tire out the haill country-side wi' dancing before ye laid down your bow, saving for a by-drink or the like o' that."

"In troth, dame," answered Willie, "ye are no sae far wrang; sae if my comrade is to take his dance, ye maun gie me my drink, and then bob it away like Madge of Middlebie."

The drink was soon brought; but while Willie was partaking of it, a party entered the hut, which arrested my attention at once, and intercepted the intended gallantry with which I had proposed to present my hand to the fresh-coloured, well-made, white-ankled Thetis, who had obtained me manumission from my musical task.

This was nothing less than the sudden appearance of the old woman whom the Laird had termed Mabel; Cristal Nixon, his male attendant; and the young person who said grace to us when I supped with him.

This young person—Alan, thou art in thy way a bit of a conjurer—this young person whom I *did not* describe, and whom you, for that very reason, suspected was not an indifferent object to me — is, I am sorry to say it, in very fact not so much so as in prudence she ought. I will not use the name of *love* on this occasion; for I have applied it too often to transient whims and fancies to escape your satire, should I venture to apply it now. For it is a phrase, I must confess, which I have used—a romancer would say, profaned — a little too often, considering how few years have passed over my head. But seriously, the fair chaplain of Brokenburn has been often in my head when she had no business there; and if this can give thee any clew for explaining my motives in lingering about the country, and assuming the character of Willie's companion, why, hang thee, thou art welcome to make use of it—a permission for which thou need'st not thank me much, as thou wouldst not have failed to assume it whether it were given or no.

Such being my feelings, conceive how they must have been excited, when, like a beam upon a cloud, I saw this uncommonly beautiful girl enter the apartment in which they were dancing; not, however, with the air of an equal, but that of a superior, come to grace with her presence the festival of her dependents. The old man and woman attended, with looks as sinister as hers were lovely, like two of the worst winter months waiting upon the bright-eyed May.

When she entered—wonder if thou wilt—she wore *a green mantle*, such as thou hast described as the garb of thy fair client, and confirmed what I had partly guessed from thy personal description, that my chaplain and thy visiter were the same person. There was an alteration on her brow the instant she recognized me. She gave her cloak to her female attendant, and, after a momentary hesitation, as if uncertain whether to advance or retire, she walked into the room with dignity and composure, all making way, the men unbonneting, and the women curtsying respectfully, as she assumed a chair which was reverently placed for her accommodation, apart from others.

There was then a pause, until the bustling mistress of the ceremonies, with awkward, but kindly courtesy, offered the young lady a glass of wine, which was at first declined, and at length only thus far accepted, that, bowing round to the festive company, the fair visiter wished them all health and mirth, and just touching the brim with her lip, replaced it on the salver. There was another pause; and I did not immediately recollect, confused as I was by this unexpected apparition, that it belonged to me to break it. At length a murmur was heard around me, being expected to exhibit, nay, to lead down the dance,—in consequence of the previous conversation.

"Deil's in the fiddler lad," was muttered from more quarters than one— "saw folk ever sic a thing as a shamefaced fiddler before?"

At length a venerable Triton, seconding his remonstrances with a hearty thump on my shoulder, cried out, "To the floor—to the floor, and let us see how ye can fling—the lasses are a' waiting."

Up I jumped, sprung from the elevated station which constituted our orchestra, and, arranging my ideas as rapidly as I could, advanced to the head of the room, and, instead of offering my hand to the white-footed Thetis aforesaid, I venturously made the same proposal to her of the Green Mantle.

The nymph's lovely eyes seemed to open with astonishment at the audacity of this offer; and, from the murmurs I heard around me, I also understood that it surprised, and perhaps offended, the bystanders. But after the first moment's emotion, she wreathed her neck, and drawing herself haughtily up, like one who was willing to show that she was sensible of the full extent of her own condescension, extended her hand towards me, like a princess gracing a squire of low degree.

There is affectation in all this, thought I to myself, if the Green Mantle has borne true evidence—for young ladies do not make visits, or write letters to counsel learned in the law, to interfere in the motions of those whom they hold as cheap as this nymph seems to do me; and if I am cheated by a resemblance of cloaks, still I am interested to show myself, in some degree, worthy of the favour she has granted with so much state and reserve. The dance to be performed was the old Scots Jigg, in which you are aware I used to play no sorry figure at La Pique's, when thy clumsy movements used to be rebuked by raps over the knuckles with that great professor's fiddlestick. The choice of the tune was left to my comrade Willie, who, having finished his drink, feloniously struck up the well-known and popular measure,

"Merrily danced the Quaker's wife
And merrily danced the Quaker."

An astounding laugh arose at my expense, and I should have been annihilated, but that the smile which mantled on the lip of my partner, had a different expression from that of ridicule, and seemed to say, "Do not take this to heart." And I did not, Alan—my partner danced admirably, and I like one who was determined, if outshone, which I could not help, not to be altogether thrown into the shade.

I assure you our performance, as well as Willie's music, deserved more polished spectators and auditors; but we could not then have been greeted with such enthusiastic shouts of applause as attended while I handed my partner to her seat, and took my place by her side, as one who had a right to offer the attentions usual on such an occasion. She was visibly embarrassed, but I was determined not to observe her confusion, and to avail myself of the opportunity of learning whether this beautiful creature's mind was worthy of the casket in which nature had lodged it.

Nevertheless, however courageously I formed this resolution, you cannot but too well guess the difficulties I must needs have felt in carrying it into execution; since want of habitual intercourse with the charmers of the other sex has rendered me a sheepish cur, only one grain less awkward than thyself. Then she was so very beautiful, and assumed an air of so much dignity, that I was like to fall under the fatal error of supposing she should only be addressed with something very clever; and in the hasty raking which my brains underwent in this persuasion, not a single idea occurred that common sense did not reject as fustian on the one hand, or weary, flat, and stale triticism on the other. I felt as if my understanding were no longer my own, but was alternately under the dominion of Aldeborontiphoscophornio, and that of his facetious friend Rigdum-Funnidos. How did I envy at that moment our friend Jack Oliver, who produces with such happy complacence his fardel of small talk, and who, as he never doubts his own powers of affording amusement, passes them current with every pretty woman he approaches, and fills up the intervals of chat by his complete acquaintance with the exercise of the fan, the *flagon*, and the other duties of the *Cavaliere serviente*. Some of these I attempted, but I suppose it was awkwardly; at least the Lady Greenmantle received them as a princess accepts the homage of a clown.

Meantime the floor remained empty, and as the mirth of the good meeting was somewhat checked, I ventured, as a dernier resort, to propose a minuet. She thanked me, and told me haughtily enough, "she was here to encourage the harmless pleasures of these good folks, but was not disposed to make an exhibition of her own indifferent dancing for their amusement."

She paused a moment, as if she expected me to suggest something; and as I remained silent and rebuked, she bowed her head more graciously, and said, "Not to affront you, however, a country-dance, if you please."

What an ass was I, Alan, not to have anticipated her wishes! Should I not have observed that the ill-favoured couple, Mabel and Cristal, had placed themselves on each side of her seat, like the supporters of the royal arms? the man, thick, short, shaggy, and hirsute, as the lion; the female, skin-dried, tight-laced, long, lean, and hungry-faced, like the unicorn. I ought to have recollected, that under the close inspection of two such watchful salvages, our communication, while in repose, could not have been easy; that the period of dancing a minuet was not the very choicest time for conversation; but that the noise, the exercise, and the mazy confusion of a country-dance, where the inexperienced performers were every now and then running against each other, and compelling the other couples to stand still for a minute at a time, besides the more regular repose afforded by the intervals of the dance itself, gave the best possible openings for a word or two spoken in season, and without being liable to observation.

We had but just led down, when an opportunity of the kind occurred, and my partner said, with great gentleness and modesty, "It is not perhaps very proper in me to acknowledge an acquaintance that is not claimed; but I believe I speak to Mr. Darsie Latimer?"

"Darsie Latimer was indeed the person that had now the honour and happiness——"

I would have gone on in the false gallop of compliment, but she cut me short. "And why," she said, "is Mr. Latimer here, and in disguise, or at least assuming an office unworthy of a man of education?—I beg pardon," she continued, — "I would not give you pain, but surely making an associate of a person of that description——"

She looked towards my friend Willie, and was silent. I felt heartily ashamed of myself, and hastened to say it was an idle frolic, which want of occupation had suggested, and which I could not regret, since it had procured me the pleasure I at present enjoyed.

Without seeming to notice my compliment, she took the next opportunity to say, "Will Mr. Latimer permit a stranger who wishes him well to ask, whether it is right that, at his active age, he should be in so far void of occupation, as to be ready to adopt low society for the sake of idle amusement?"

"You are severe, madam," I answered; "but I cannot think myself degraded by mixing with any society where I meet——"

Here I stopped short, conscious that I was giving my answer an unhandsome turn. The *argumentum ad hominem*, the last to which a polite man has recourse, may, however, be justified by circumstances, but seldom or never the *argumentum ad fœminam*.

She filled up the blank herself which I had left. "Where you meet *me*, I suppose you would say? But the case is different. I am, from my unhappy fate, obliged to move by the will of others, and to be in places which I would by my own will gladly avoid. Besides, I am, except for these few minutes, no participator of the revels — a spectator only, and attended by my servants. Your situation is different—you are here by choice, the partaker and minister of the pleasures of a class below you in education, birth, and fortunes. If I speak harshly, Mr. Latimer," she added, with much sweetness of manner, "I mean kindly."

I was confounded by her speech, "severe in youthful wisdom;" all of *naive* or lively, suitable to such a dialogue, vanished from my recollection, and I answered with gravity like her own, "I am, indeed, better educated than these poor people; but you, madam, whose kind admonition I am grateful for, must know more of my condition than I do myself—I dare not say I am their superior in birth, since I know nothing of my own, or in fortunes, over which hangs an impenetrable cloud."

"And why should your ignorance on these points drive you into low society and idle habits?" answered my female monitor. "Is it manly to wait till fortune cast her beams upon you, when by exertion of your own energy you might distinguish yourself? — Do not the pursuits of learning lie open to you — of manly ambition — of war?—But no — not of war, that has already cost you too dear."

"I will be what you wish me to be," I replied with eagerness — "You have but to choose my path, and you shall see if I do not pursue it with energy, were it only because you command me."

"Not because I command you," said the maiden, "but because reason, common sense, manhood, and, in one word, regard for your own safety, give the same counsel."

"At least permit me to reply, that reason and sense never assumed a fairer form—of persuasion," I hastily added; for she turned from me—nor did she give me another opportunity of continuing what I had to say till the next pause of the dance, when, determined to bring our dialogue to a point, I said, "You mentioned manhood also, and in the same breath, personal danger. My ideas of manhood suggest that it is cowardice to retreat before dangers of a doubtful character. You, who appear to know so much of my fortunes that I might call you my guardian angel, tell me what these dangers are, that I may judge whether manhood calls on me to face or to fly them."

She was evidently perplexed by this appeal.

"You make me pay dearly for acting as your humane adviser," she replied at last: "I acknowledge an interest in your fate, and yet I dare not tell you whence it arises; neither am I at liberty to say why, or from whom; you are in danger; but it is not less true that danger is near and imminent. Ask me no more, but, for your own sake, begone from this country. Elsewhere you are safe — here you do but invite your fate."

"But am I doomed to bid thus farewell to almost the only human being who-has showed an interest in my welfare? — Do not say so — say that we shall meet again, and the hope shall be the leading star to regulate my course!"

"It is more than probable," she said — "much more than probable, that we may never meet again. The help which I now render you is all that may be in my power; it is such as I should render to a blind man whom I might observe approaching the verge of a precipice; it ought to excite no surprise, and requires no gratitude."

So saying, she again turned from me, nor did she address me until the dance was on the point of ending, when she said, "Do not attempt to speak to, or approach me again in the course of the night; leave the company as soon as you can, but not abruptly, and God be with you."

I handed her to her seat, and did not quit the fair palm I held, without expressing my feelings by a gentle pressure. She coloured slightly, and withdrew her hand, but not angrily. Seeing the eyes of Cristal and Mabel sternly fixed on me, I bowed deeply, and withdrew from her; my heart saddening, and my eyes becoming dim in spite of me, as the shifting crowd hid us from each other.

It was my intention to have crept back to my comrade Willie, and resumed my bow with such spirit as I might, although, at the moment, I would have given half my income for an instant's solitude. But my retreat was cut off by Dame Martin, with the frankness—if it is not an inconsistent phrase — of rustic coquetry, that goes straight up to the point.

"Ay, lad, ye seem unca sune weary, to dance sae lightly? Better the nag that ambles a' the day, than him that makes a brattle for a mile, and then's dune wi' the road."

This was a fair challenge, and I could not decline accepting it. Besides, I could see Dame Martin was queen of the revels; and so many were the rude and singular figures about me, that I was by no means certain whether I might not need some protection. I seized on her willing hand, and we took our places in the dance, where, if I did not acquit myself with all the accuracy of step and movement which I had before attempted, I at least came up to the expectations of my partner, who said, and almost swore, "I was prime at it;" while, stimulated to her utmost exertions, she herself frisked like a kid, snapped her fingers like castanets, whooped like a Bacchanal, and bounded from the floor like a tennis-ball, — ay, till the colour of her garters was no particular mystery. She made the less secret of this, perhaps, that they were sky-blue, and fringed with silver.

The time has been that this would have been special fun; or, rather, last night was the only time I can recollect these four years when it would not have been so; yet at this moment, I cannot tell you how I longed to be rid of Dame Martin. I almost wished she would sprain one of those "many-twinkling" ankles, which served her so alertly; and when, in the midst of her exuberant caprioling, I saw my former partner leaving the apartment, and with eyes, as I thought, towards me, this unwillingness to carry on the dance increased to such a point, that I was almost about to feign a sprain or a dislocation myself, in order to put an end to the performance.   But there were around me scores of old women, all of whom looked as if they might have some sovereign recipe for such an accident; and, remembering Gil Blas, and his pretended disorder in the robbers' cavern, I thought it as wise to play Dame Martin fair, and dance till she thought proper to dismiss me. What I did I resolved to do strenuously, and in the latter part of the exhibition, I cut and sprang from the floor as high and as perpendicularly as Dame Martin herself; and received, I promise you, thunders of applause, for the common people always prefer exertion and agility to grace.   At length Dame Martin could dance no more, and, rejoicing at my release, I led her to a seat, and took the privilege of a partner to attend her.

"Hegh, sirs," exclaimed Dame Martin; "I am sair fourfoughen! Troth, callant, I think ye hae been amaist the death o' me."

I could only atone for the alleged offence by fetching her some refreshment, of which she readily partook.

"I have been lucky in my partners," I said, "first that pretty young lady, and then you, Mrs. Martin."

"Hout wi' your fleeching," said Dame Martin.   "Gae wa — gae wa, lad; dinna blaw in folk's lugs that gate; me and Miss Lilias even'd thegither! Na, na, lad — od, she is maybe four or five years younger than the like o' me, — bye and attour her gentle havings."

"She is the Laird's daughter?" said I, in as careless a tone of inquiry as I could assume.

"His daughter, man?   Na, na, only his niece — and sib aneugh to him, I think."

"Ay, indeed," I replied; "I thought she had borne his name?"

"She bears her ain name, and that's Lilias."

"And has she no other name?" asked I.

"What needs she another till she gets a gudeman?" answered my Thetis, a little miffed perhaps — to use the women's phrase — that I turned the conversation upon my former partner, rather than addressed it to herself.

There was a little pause, which was interrupted by Dame Martin observing, "They are standing up again."

"True," said I, having no mind to renew my late violent *capriole*, "and I must go help old Willie."

Ere I could extricate myself, I heard poor Thetis address herself to a sort of Merman in a jacket of seaman's blue, and a pair of trowsers, (whose hand, by the way, she had rejected at an earlier part of the evening,) and intimate that she was now disposed to take a trip.

"Trip away, then, dearie," said the vindictive man of the waters, without offering his hand; "there," pointing to the floor, "is a roomy berth for you."

Certain I had made one enemy, and perhaps two, I hastened to my original seat beside Willie, and began to handle my bow.   But I could see that my conduct had made an unfavourable impression; the words, "flory conceited chap," — "haffins gentle," and at length, the still more alarming epithet of "spy," began to be buzzed about, and I was heartily glad when the apparition of Sam's visage at the door, who was already possessed of and draining a can of punch, gave me assurance that my means of retreat were at hand.   I intimated as much to Willie, who probably had heard more of the murmurs of the company than I had, for he whispered, "Ay, ay — awa wi' ye — ower lang here — slide out canny — dinna let them see ye are on the tramp."

I slipped half-a-guinea into the old man's hand, who answered, "Truts! pruts! nonsense! but I'se no refuse, trusting ye can afford it — Awa wi' ye — and if ony body stops ye, cry on me."

I glided, by his advice, along the room as if looking for a partner, joined

Sam, whom I disengaged with some difficulty from his can, and we left the cottage together in a manner to attract the least possible observation. The horses were tied in a neighbouring shed, and as the moon was up, and I was now familiar with the road, broken and complicated as it is, we soon reached the Shepherd's Bush, where the old landlady was sitting up waiting for us, under some anxiety of mind, to account for which she did not hesitate to tell me that some folks had gone to Brokenburn from her house, or neighbouring towns, that did not come so safe back again. "Wandering Willie," she said, "was doubtless a kind of protection."

Here Willie's wife, who was smoking in the chimney corner, took up the praises of her "hinnie," as she called him, and endeavoured to awaken my generosity afresh, by describing the dangers from which, as she was pleased to allege, her husband's countenance had assuredly been the means of preserving me. I was not, however, to be fooled out of more money at this time, and went to bed in haste, full of various cogitations.

I have since spent a couple of days betwixt Mount Sharon and this place, and betwixt reading, writing to thee this momentous history, forming plans for seeing the lovely Lilias, and — partly, I think, for the sake of contradiction — angling a little in spite of Joshua's scruples — though I am rather liking the amusement better as I begin to have some success in it.

And now, my dearest Alan, you are in full possession of my secret—let me as frankly into the recesses of your bosom. How do you feel towards this fair ignis fatuus, this lily of the desert? Tell me honestly; for however the recollection of her may haunt my own mind, my love for Alan Fairford surpasses the love of woman. I know, too, that when you *do* love, it will be to

"Love once and love no more."

A deep-consuming passion, once kindled in a breast so steady as yours, would never be extinguished but with life. I am of another and more volatile temper, and though I shall open your next with a trembling hand, and uncertain heart, yet let it bring a frank confession that this fair unknown has made a deeper impression on your gravity than you reckoned for, and you will see I can tear the arrow from my own wound, barb and all. In the meantime, though I have formed schemes once more to see her, I will, you may rely on it, take no step for putting them into practice. I have refrained from this hitherto, and I give you my word of honour, I shall continue to do so; yet why should you need any farther assurance from one who is so entirely yours as   D. L.

P. S. — I shall be on thorns till I receive your answer. I read, and re-read your letter, and cannot for my soul discover what your real sentiments are. Sometimes I think you write of her as one in jest — and sometimes I think that cannot be. Put me at ease as soon as possible.

LETTER XIII.

ALAN FAIRFORD TO DARSIE LATIMER.

I WRITE on the instant, as you direct; and in a tragi-comic humour, for I have a tear in my eye, and a smile on my cheek. Dearest Darsie, sure never a being but yourself could be so generous — sure never a being but yourself could be so absurd! I remember when you were a boy you wished to make your fine new whip a present to old aunt Peggy, merely because she admired it; and now, with like unreflecting and inappropriate liberality, you would resign your beloved to a smoke-dried young sophister, who cares not one of the hairs which it is his occupation to split, for all the daughters of Eve. *I* in love with your Lilias—your Green-mantle—your unknown enchantress!—why I scarce saw her for five minutes, and even then only the tip of her chin was distinctly visible. She was well made, and the tip of her chin was of a most promising cast for the rest of the face; but, Heaven save you! she came upon business! and for a lawyer to fall in love with a pretty client on a single consultation, would be as wise as if he became enamoured of a particularly bright sunbeam which chanced for a moment to gild his bob-wig. I give you my word I am heart-whole; and moreover, I assure you, that before I suffer a woman to sit near my heart's core, I must see her full face, without mask or mantle, ay, know a good deal of her mind into the bargain. So never fret yourself on my account, my kind and generous Darsie; but, for your own sake, have a care, and let not an idle attachment, so lightly taken up, lead you into serious danger.

On this subject I feel so apprehensive, that now when I am decorated with the honours of the gown, I should have abandoned my career at the very starting to come to you, but for my father having contrived to clog my heels with fetters of a professional nature. I will tell you the matter at length, for it is comical enough; and why should not you list to my juridical adventures, as well as I to those of your fiddling knight-errantry?

It was after dinner, and I was considering how I might best introduce to my father the private resolution I had formed to set off for Dumfriesshire, or whether I had not better run away at once, and plead my excuse by letter, when assuming the peculiar look with which he communicates any of his intentions respecting me, that he suspects may not be altogether acceptable, "Alan," he said, "ye now wear a gown — ye have opened shop, as we would say of a more mechanical profession; and, doubtless, ye think the floor of the courts is strewed with guineas, and that ye have only to stoop down to gather them?"

"I hope I am sensible, sir," I replied, "that I have some knowledge and practice to acquire, and must stoop for that in the first place."

"It is well said," answered my father; and, always afraid to give too much encouragement, added, "Very well said, if it be well acted up to — Stoop to get knowledge and practice is the very word. Ye know very well, Alan, that in the other faculty who study the *Ars medendi*, before the young doctor gets to the bedsides of palaces, he must, as they call it, walk the hospitals; and cure Lazarus of his sores, before he be admitted to prescribe for Dives, when he has gout or indigestion ——"

"I am aware, sir, that ——"

"Whisht — do not interrupt the court—Well—also the chirurgeons have an useful practice, by which they put their apprentices and *tyrones* to work upon senseless dead bodies, to which, as they can do no good, so they certainly can do as little harm; while at the same time the *tyro*, or apprentice, gains experience, and becomes fit to whip off a leg or arm from a living subject, as cleanly as ye would slice an onion."

"I believe I guess your meaning, sir," answered I; "and were it not for a very particular engagement ——"

"Do not speak to me of engagements; but whisht — there is a good lad — and do not interrupt the court."

My father, you know, is apt — be it said with all filial duty — to be a little prolix in his harangues. I had nothing for it but to lean back and listen.

"Maybe you think, Alan, because I have, doubtless, the management of some actions in dependence, whilk my worthy clients have intrusted me with, that I may think of airting them your way *instanter;* and so setting you up in practice, so far as my small business or influence may go; and, doubtless, Alan, that is a day whilk I hope may come round. But then, before I give, as the proverb hath it, 'My own fish-guts to my own sea-maws,' I must, for the sake of my own character, be very sure that my sea-maw can pick them to some purpose. What say ye?"

"I am so far," answered I, "from wishing to get early into practice, sir, that I would willingly bestow a few days ——"

"In farther study, ye would say, Alan. But that is not the way either — ye must walk the hospitals — ye must cure Lazarus — ye must cut and carve on a departed subject, to show your skill."

"I am sure," I replied, "I will undertake the cause of any poor man with pleasure, and bestow as much pains upon it as if it were a Duke's; but for the next two or three days ——"

"They must be devoted to close study, Alan — very close study indeed; for ye must stand primed for a hearing, *in presentia Dominorum* upon Tuesday next."

"I, sir?" I replied in astonishment — "I have not opened my mouth in the Outer-House yet!"

"Never mind the Court of the Gentiles, man," said my father; "we will have you into the Sanctuary at once — over shoes, over boots."

"But, sir, I should really spoil any cause thrust on me so hastily."

"Ye cannot spoil it, Alan," said my father, rubbing his hands with much complacency; "that is the very cream of the business, man — it is just, as I said before, a subject upon whilk all the *tyrones* have been trying their whittles for fifteen years; and as there have been about ten or a dozen agents concerned, and each took his own way, the case is come to that pass, that Stair or Arniston could not mend it; and I do not think even you, Alan, can do it much harm — ye may get credit by it, but ye can lose none."

"And pray what is the name of my happy client, sir?" said I, ungraciously enough, I believe.

"It is a well-known name in the Parliament-House," replied my father. "To say the truth, I expect him every moment; it is Peter Peebles."[*]

"Peter Peebles!" exclaimed I, in astonishment; "he is an insane beggar — as poor as Job, and as mad as a March hare!"

"He has been pleaing in the court for fifteen years," said my father, in a tone of commiseration, which seemed to acknowledge that this fact was enough to account for the poor man's condition both in mind and circumstances.

"Besides, sir," I added, "he is on the Poor's Roll; and you know there are advocates regularly appointed to manage those cases; and for me to presume to interfere ——"

"Whisht, Alan! — never interrupt the court — all *that* is managed for ye like a tee'd ball;" (my father sometimes draws his similes from his once favourite game of golf;) — "you must know, Alan, that Peter's cause was to have been opened by young Dumtoustie — ye may ken the lad, a son of Dumtoustie of that ilk, member of Parliament for the county of ——, and a nephew of the Laird's younger brother, worthy Lord Bladderskate, whilk ye are aware sounds as like being akin to a peatship† and a sheriffdom, as a sieve is sib to a riddle. Now, Peter Drudgeit, my lord's clerk, came to me this morning in the House, like ane bereft of his wits; for it seems that young Dumtoustie is ane of the Poor's Lawyers, and Peter Peebles's process had been remitted to him of course. But so soon as the harebrained goose

---

* This unfortunate litigant (for a person named Peter Peebles actually flourished) frequented the courts of justice in Scotland about the year 1792, and the sketch of his appearance is given from recollection. The author is of opinion, that he himself had at one time the honour to be counsel for Peter Peebles, whose voluminous morse of litigation served as a sort of assay-pieces to mint young men who were called to the bar. The scene of the consultation is entirely imaginary.

† Formerly, a lawyer, supposed to be under the peculiar patronage of any particular judge, was invidiously termed his post or pet.

saw the pokes* (as indeed, Alan, they are none of the least,) he took fright,
called for his nag, lap on, and away to the country is he gone; and so, said
Peter, my lord is at his wit's end wi' vexation and shame, to see his nevoy
break off the course at the very starting. 'I'll tell you, Peter,' said I,
'were I my lord, and a friend or kinsman of mine should leave the town
while the court was sitting, that kinsman, or be he what he liked, should
never darken my door again.' And then, Alan, I thought to turn the ball
our own way; and I said that you were a gey sharp birkie, just off the
irons, and if it would oblige my lord, and so forth, you would open Peter's
cause on Tuesday, and make some handsome apology for the necessary
absence of your learned friend, and the loss which your client and the court
had sustained, and so forth. Peter lap at the proposition like a cock at a
grossart; for, he said, the only chance was to get a new hand, that he did
not ken the charge he was taking upon him; for there was not a lad of two
Session's standing that was not dead-sick of Peter Peebles and his cause;
and he advised me to break the matter gently to you at the first; but I told
him you were a good bairn, Alan, and had no will and pleasure in these
matters but mine."

What could I say, Darsie, in answer to this arrangement, so very well
meant—so very vexatious at the same time?—To imitate the defection and
flight of young Dumtoustie, was at once to destroy my father's hopes of me
for ever; nay, such is the keenness with which he regards all connected
with his profession, it might have been a step to breaking his heart. I was
obliged, therefore, to bow in sad acquiescence, when my father called to
James Wilkinson to bring the two bits of pokes he would find on his
table.

Exit James, and presently re-enters, bending under the load of two huge
leathern bags, full of papers to the brim, and labelled on the greasy backs
with the magic impress of the clerks of court, and the title, *Peebles against
Plainstanes.* This huge mass was deposited on the table, and my father,
with no ordinary glee in his countenance, began to draw out the various
bundles of papers, secured by none of your red tape or whip-cord, but stout,
substantial casts of tarred rope, such as might have held small craft at their
moorings.

I made at last a desperate effort to get rid of the impending job. "I am
really afraid, sir, that this case seems so much complicated, and there is so
little time to prepare, that we had better move the Court to supersede it till
next Session."

"How, sir — how, Alan?" said my father — "Would you approbate and
reprobate, sir?—You have accepted the poor man's cause, and if you have
not his fee in your pocket, it is because he has none to give you; and now
would you approbate and reprobate in the same breath of your mouth?—
Think of your oath of office, Alan, and your duty to your father, my dear
boy."

Once more, what could I say?—I saw from my father's hurried and
alarmed manner, that nothing could vex him so much as failing in the point
he had determined to carry, and once more intimated my readiness to do
my best, under every disadvantage.

"Well, well, my boy," said my father, "the Lord will make your days
long in the land, for the honour you have given to your father's gray hairs.
You may find wiser advisers, Alan, but none that can wish you better."

My father, you know, does not usually give way to expressions of affection,
and they are interesting in proportion to their rarity. My eyes began to
fill at seeing his glisten; and my delight at having given him such sensible
gratification would have been unmixed but for the thoughts of you. These
out of the question, I could have grappled with the bags, had they been as

---

* Process-bags.

large as corn-sacks. But, to turn what was grave into farce, the door opened, and Wilkinson ushered in Peter Peebles.

You must have seen this original, Darsie, who, like others in the same predicament, continues to haunt the courts of justice, where he has made shipwreck of time, means, and understanding. Such insane paupers have sometimes seemed to me to resemble wrecks lying upon the shoals on the Goodwin Sands, or in Yarmouth Roads, warning other vessels to keep aloof from the banks on which they have been lost; or rather, such ruined clients are like scarecrows and potatoe-bogles, distributed through the courts to scare away fools from the scene of litigation.

The identical Peter wears a huge great-coat, threadbare and patched itself, yet carefully so disposed and secured by what buttons remain, and many supplementary pins, as to conceal the still more infirm state of his under garments. The shoes and stockings of a ploughman were, however, seen to meet at his knees with a pair of brownish, blackish breeches; a rusty-coloured handkerchief, that has been black in its day, surrounded his throat, and was an apology for linen. His hair, half gray, half black, escaped in elf-locks around a huge wig, made of tow, as it seemed to me, and so much shrunk, that it stood up on the very top of his head; above which he plants, when covered, an immense cocked hat, which, like the chieftain's banner in an ancient battle, may be seen any sederunt day betwixt nine and ten, high towering above all the fluctuating and changeful scene in the Outer-House, where his eccentricities often make him the centre of a group of petulant and teasing boys, who exercise upon him every art of ingenious torture. His countenance, originally that of a portly, comely burgess, is now emaciated with poverty and anxiety, and rendered wild by an insane lightness about the eyes; a withered and blighted skin and complexion; features begrimed with snuff, charged with the self-importance peculiar to insanity; and a habit of perpetually speaking to himself. Such was my fortunate client; and I must allow, Darsie, that my profession had need to do a great deal of good, if, as is much to be feared, it brings many individuals to such a pass.

After we had been, with a good deal of form, presented to each other, at which time I easily saw by my father's manner that he was desirous of supporting Peter's character in my eyes, as much as circumstances would permit, "Alan," he said, "this is the gentleman who has agreed to accept of you as his counsel, in place of young Dumtoustie."

"Entirely out of favour to my old acquaintance your father," said Peter, with a benign and patronising countenance, "out of respect to your father, and my old intimacy with Lord Bladderskate. Otherwise, by the *Regiam Majestatem!* I would have presented a petition and complaint against Daniel Dumtoustie, Advocate, by name and surname—I would, by all the practiques!—I know the forms of process; and I am not to be trifled with."

My father here interrupted my client, and reminded him that there was a good deal of business to do, as he proposed to give the young counsel an outline of the state of the conjoined process, with a view to letting him into the merits of the cause, disencumbered from the points of form. "I have made a short abbreviate, Mr. Peebles," said he; "having sat up late last night, and employed much of this morning in wading through these papers, to save Alan some trouble, and I am now about to state the result."

"I will state it myself," said Peter, breaking in without reverence upon his solicitor.

"No, by no means," said my father; "I am your agent for the time."

"Mine eleventh in number," said Peter; "I have a new one every year; I wish I could get a new coat as regularly."

"Your agent for the time," resumed my father; "and you, who are acquainted with the forms, know that the client states the cause to the agent—the agent to the counsel——"

"The counsel to the Lord Ordinary," continued Peter, once set-a-going, like the peal of an alarm-clock, "the Ordinary to the Inner-House, the President to the Bench. It is just like the rope to the man, the man to the ox, the ox to the water, the water to the fire——"

"Hush, for Heaven's sake, Mr. Peebles," said my father, cutting his recitation short; "time wears on — we must get to business — you must not interrupt the court, you know. — Hem, hem! From this abbreviate it appears——"

"Before you begin," said Peter Peebles, "I'll thank you to order me a morsel of bread and cheese, or some cauld meat, or broth, or the like alimentary provision; I was so anxious to see your son, that I could not eat a mouthful of dinner."

Heartily glad, I believe, to have so good a chance of stopping his client's mouth effectually, my father ordered some cold meat; to which James Wilkinson, for the honour of the house, was about to add the brandy bottle, which remained on the sideboard, but, at a wink from my father, supplied its place with small beer. Peter charged the provisions with the rapacity of a famished lion; and so well did the diversion engage him, that though, while my father stated the case, he looked at him repeatedly, as if he meant to interrupt his statement, yet he always found more agreeable employment for his mouth, and returned to the cold beef with an avidity which convinced me he had not had such an opportunity for many a day of satiating his appetite. Omitting much formal phraseology, and many legal details, I will endeavour to give you, in exchange for your fiddler's tale, the history of a litigant, or rather, the history of his lawsuit.

"Peter Peebles and Paul Plainstanes," said my father, "entered into partnership, in the year——, as mercers and linendrapers, in the Luckenbooths, and carried on a great line of business to mutual advantage. But the learned counsel needeth not to be told, *societas est mater discordiarum*, partnership oft makes pleaship. The company being dissolved by mutual consent, in the year ——, the affairs had to be wound up, and after certain attempts to settle the matter extra-judicially, it was at last brought into the Court, and has branched out into several distinct processes, most of whilk have been conjoined by the Ordinary. It is to the state of these processes that counsel's attention is particularly directed. There is the original action of Peebles *v.* Plainstanes, convening him for payment of 3000*l.*, less or more, as alleged balance due by Plainstanes. 2dly, There is a counter action, in which Plainstanes is pursuer and Peebles defender, for 2500*l.*, less or more, being balance alleged *per contra*, to be due by Peebles. 3dly, Mr. Peebles's seventh agent advised an action of Compt and Reckoning at his instance, wherein what balance should prove due on either side might be fairly struck and ascertained. 4thly, To meet the hypothetical case, that Peebles might be found liable in a balance to Plainstanes, Mr. Wildgoose, Mr. Peebles's eighth agent, recommended a Multiplepoinding, to bring all parties concerned into the field."

My brain was like to turn at this account of lawsuit within lawsuit, like a nest of chip-boxes, with all of which I was expected to make myself acquainted.

"I understand," I said, "that Mr. Peebles claims a sum of money from Plainstanes — how then can he be his debtor? and if not his debtor, how can he bring a Multiplepoinding, the very summons of which sets forth, that the pursuer does owe certain monies, which he is desirous to pay by warrant of a judge?"*

"Ye know little of the matter, I doubt, friend," said Mr. Peebles; "a Multiplepoinding is the safest *remedium juris* in the whole form of process. I have known it conjoined with a declarator of marriage. — Your beef is

---

* Multiplepoinding is, I believe, equivalent to what is called in England a case of Double Distress.

excellent," he said to my father, who in vain endeavoured to resume his legal disquisition; "but something highly powdered — and the twopenny is undeniable; but it is small swipes — small swipes — more of hop than malt—with your leave, I'll try your black bottle."

My father started to help him with his own hand, and in due measure; but, infinitely to my amusement, Peter got possession of the bottle by the neck, and my father's ideas of hospitality were far too scrupulous to permit his attempting, by any direct means, to redeem it; so that Peter returned to the table triumphant, with his prey in his clutch.

"Better have a wine-glass, Mr. Peebles," said my father, in an admonitory tone, "you will find it pretty strong."

"If the kirk is ower muckle, we can sing mass in the quire," said Peter, helping himself in the goblet out of which he had been drinking the small beer. "What is it, usquebaugh?—BRANDY, as I am an honest man! I had almost forgotten the name and taste of brandy. — Mr. Fairford, elder, your good health," (a mouthful of brandy) — "Mr. Alan Fairford, wishing you well through your arduous undertaking," (another go-down of the comfortable liquor.) "And now, though you have given a tolerable breviate of this great lawsuit, of whilk every body has heard something that has walked the boards in the Outer-House, (here's to ye again, by way of interim decreet,) yet ye have omitted to speak a word of the arrestments."

"I was just coming to that point, Mr. Peebles."

"Or of the action of suspension of the charge on the bill."

"I was just coming to that."

"Or the advocation of the Sheriff-Court process."

"I was just coming to it."

"As Tweed comes to Melrose, I think," said the litigant; and then filling his goblet about a quarter full of brandy, as if in absence of mind, "Oh, Mr. Alan Fairford, ye are a lucky man to buckle to such a cause as mine at the very outset! it is like a specimen of all causes, man. By the Regiam, there is not a *remedium juris* in the practiques but ye'll find a spice o't. Here's to your getting weel through with it — Pshut—I am drinking naked spirits, I think. But if the heathen be ower strong, we'll christen him with the brewer," (here he added a little small beer to his beverage, paused, rolled his eyes, winked, and proceeded,—"Mr. Fairford—the action of assault and battery, Mr. Fairford, when I compelled the villain Plainstanes to pull my nose within two steps of King Charles's statue, in the Parliament Close — there I had him in a hose-net. Never man could tell me how to shape that process—no counsel that ever selled wind could condescend and say whether it were best to proceed by way of petition and complaint, *ad vindictam publicam*, with consent of his Majesty's advocate, or by action on the statute for battery *pendente lite*, whilk would be the winning my plea at once, and so getting a back-door out of Court.—By the Regiam, that beef and brandy is unco het at my heart—I maun try the ale again" (sipped a little beer;) "and the ale's but cauld, I maun e'en put in the rest of the brandy."

He was as good as his word, and proceeded in so loud and animated a style of elocution, thumping the table, drinking and snuffing alternately, that my father, abandoning all attempts to interrupt him, sat silent and ashamed, suffering, and anxious for the conclusion of the scene.

"And then to come back to my pet process of all — my battery and assault process, when I had the good luck to provoke him to pull my nose at the very threshold of the Court, whilk was the very thing I wanted—Mr. Pest, ye ken him, Daddie Fairford? Old Pest was for making it out *hamesucken*, for he said the Court might be said—said—ugh!—to be my dwelling-place. I dwell mair there than ony gate else, and the essence of hamesucken is to strike a man in his dwelling-place—mind that, young advocate —and so there's hope Plainstanes may be hanged, as many has for a less matter; for, my Lords,—will Pest say to the Justiciary bodies,—my Lords, the Parliament House is Peebles's place of dwelling, says he—being *commune forum*, and *commune forum est commune domicilium*—Lass, fetch another glass of whisky, and score it—time to gae hame—by the practiques, I cannot find the jug—yet there's twa of them, I think. By the Regiain, Fairford—Daddie Fairford—lend us twal pennies to buy sneeshing, mine is done—Macer, call another cause."

The box fell from his hands, and his body would at the same time have fallen from the chair, had not I supported him.

"This is intolerable," said my father—"Call a chairman, James Wilkinson, to carry this degraded, worthless, drunken beast home."

When Peter Peebles was removed from this memorable consultation, under the care of an able-bodied Celt, my father hastily bundled up the papers, as a showman, whose exhibition has miscarried, hastes to remove his booth. "Here are my memoranda, Alan," he said, in a hurried way; "look them carefully over—compare them with the processes, and turn it in your head before Tuesday. Many a good speech has been made for a beast of a client; and hark ye, lad, hark ye—I never intended to cheat you of your fee when all was done, though I would have liked to have heard the speech first; but there is nothing like corning the horse before the journey. Here are five goud guineas in a silk purse—of your poor mother's netting, Alan—she would have been a blithe woman to have seen her young son with a gown on his back—but no more of that—be a good boy, and to the work like a tiger."

I did set to work, Darsie; for who could resist such motives? With my father's assistance, I have mastered the details, confused as they are; and on Tuesday, I shall plead as well for Peter Peebles, as I could for a duke. Indeed, I feel my head so clear on the subject, as to be able to write this long letter to you; into which, however, Peter and his lawsuit have insinuated themselves so far, as to show you how much they at present occupy my thoughts. Once more, be careful of yourself, and mindful of me, who am ever thine, while   ALAN FAIRFORD.

From circumstances, to be hereafter mentioned, it was long ere this letter reached the person to whom it was addressed.

Chapter the First.

NARRATIVE.

THE advantage of laying before the reader, in the words of the actors themselves, the adventures which we must otherwise have narrated in our own, has given great popularity to the publication of epistolary correspondence, as practised by various great authors, and by ourselves in the preceding chapters. Nevertheless, a genuine correspondence of this kind (and Heaven forbid it should be in any respect sophisticated by interpolations of our own!) can seldom be found to contain all in which it is necessary to instruct the reader for his full comprehension of the story. Also it must often happen that various prolixities and redundancies occur in the course of an interchange of letters, which must hang as a dead weight on the progress of the narrative. To avoid this dilemma, some biographers

+ Scott's own father — as described ?
Drop were like Scott's father + others like
his mother

REDGAUNTLET.   101

have used the letters of the personages concerned, or liberal extracts from them, to describe particular incidents, or express the sentiments which they entertained; while they connect them occasionally with such portions of narrative, as may serve to carry on the thread of the story.

It is thus that the adventurous travellers who explore the summit of Mont Blanc, now move on through the crumbling snow-drift so slowly, that their progress is almost imperceptible, and anon abridge their journey by springing over the intervening chasms which cross their path, with the assistance of their pilgrim-staves. Or, to make a briefer simile, the course of story-telling which we have for the present adopted, resembles the original discipline of the dragoons, who were trained to serve either on foot or horseback, as the emergencies of the service required. With this explanation, we shall proceed to narrate some circumstances which Alan Fairford did not, and could not, write to his correspondent.

Our reader, we trust, has formed somewhat approaching to a distinct idea of the principal characters who have appeared before him during our narrative; but in case our good opinion of his sagacity has been exaggerated, and in order to satisfy such as are addicted to the laudable practice of *skipping*, (with whom we have at times a strong fellow-feeling,) the following particulars may not be superfluous.

Mr. Saunders Fairford, as he was usually called, was a man of business of the old school, moderate in his charges, economical and even niggardly in his expenditure, strictly honest in conducting his own affairs, and those of his clients, but taught by long experience to be wary and suspicious in observing the motions of others. Punctual as the clock of Saint Giles tolled nine, the neat dapper form of the little hale old gentleman was seen at the threshold of the Court hall, or at farthest, at the head of the Back Stairs, trimly dressed in a complete suit of snuff-coloured brown, with stockings of silk or woollen, as suited the weather; a bob-wig, and a small cocked hat; shoes blacked as Warren would have blacked them; silver shoe-buckles, and a gold stock-buckle. A nosegay in summer, and a sprig of holly in winter, completed his well-known dress and appearance. His manners corresponded with his attire, for they were scrupulously civil, and not a little formal. He was an elder of the kirk, and, of course, zealous for King George and the government even to slaying, as he had showed by taking up arms in their cause. But then, as he had clients and connections of business among families of opposite political tenets, he was particularly cautious to use all the conventional phrases which the civility of the time had devised, as an admissible mode of language betwixt the two parties. Thus he spoke sometimes of the Chevalier, but never either of the Prince, which would have been sacrificing his own principles, or of the Pretender, which would have been offensive to those of others. Again, he usually designated the Rebellion as the *affair* of 1745, and spoke of any one engaged in it as a person who had been *out* at a certain period.* So that, on the whole, Mr. Fairford was a man much liked and respected on all sides, though his friends would not have been sorry if he had given a dinner more frequently, as his little cellar contained some choice old wine, of which, on such rare occasions, he was no niggard.

The whole pleasure of this good old-fashioned man of method, besides that which he really felt in the discharge of his daily business, was the hope to see his son Alan, the only fruit of a union which death early dissolved, attain what in the father's eyes was the proudest of all distinctions — the rank and fame of a well-employed lawyer.

Every profession has its peculiar honours, and Mr. Fairford's mind was

* *Old-fashioned Scottish Civility.* — Such were literally the points of politeness observed in general society during the author's youth, where it was by no means unusual in a company assembled by chance, to find individuals who had borne arms on one side or other in the civil broils of 1745. Nothing, according to my recollection, could be more gentle and decorous than the respect these old enemies paid to each other's prejudices. But in this I speak generally. I have witnessed one or two explosions.

I 2

constructed upon so limited and exclusive a plan, that he valued nothing, save the objects of ambition which his own presented. He would have shuddered at Alan's acquiring the renown of a hero, and laughed with scorn at the equally barren laurels of literature; it was by the path of the law alone that he was desirous to see him rise to eminence, and the probabilities of success or disappointment were the thoughts of his father by day, and his dream by night.

The disposition of Alan Fairford, as well as his talents, were such as to encourage his father's expectations. He had acuteness of intellect, joined to habits of long and patient study, improved no doubt by the discipline of his father's house; to which, generally speaking, he conformed with the utmost docility, expressing no wish for greater or more frequent relaxation than consisted with his father's anxious and severe restrictions. When he did indulge in any juvenile frolics, his father had the candour to lay the whole blame upon his more mercurial companion, Darsie Lartimer.

This youth, as the reader must be aware, had been received as an inmate into the family of Mr. Fairford, senior, at a time when some of the delicacy of constitution which had abridged the life of his consort, began to show itself in the son, and when the father was, of course, peculiarly disposed to indulge his slightest wish. That the young Englishman was able to pay a considerable board, was a matter of no importance to Mr. Fairford; it was enough that his presence seemed to make his son cheerful and happy. He was compelled to allow that "Darsie was a fine lad, though unsettled," and he would have had some difficulty in getting rid of him, and the apprehensions which his levities excited, had it not been for the voluntary excursion which gave rise to the preceding correspondence, and in which Mr. Fairford secretly rejoiced, as affording the means of separating Alan from his gay companion, at least until he should have assumed, and become accustomed to, the duties of his dry and laborious profession.

But the absence of Darsie was far from promoting the end which the elder Mr. Fairford had expected and desired. The young men were united by the closest bonds of intimacy; and the more so, that neither of them sought nor desired to admit any others into their society. Alan Fairford was averse to general company, from a disposition naturally reserved, and Darsie Latimer from a painful sense of his own unknown origin, peculiarly afflicting in a country where high and low are professed genealogists. The young men were all in all to each other; it is no wonder, therefore, that their separation was painful, and that its effects upon Alan Fairford, joined to the anxiety occasioned by the tenor of his friend's letters, greatly exceeded what the senior had anticipated. The young man went through his usual duties, his studies, and the examinations to which he was subjected, but with nothing like the zeal and assiduity which he had formerly displayed; and his anxious and observant father saw but too plainly that his heart was with his absent comrade.

A philosopher would have given way to this tide of feeling, in hopes to have diminished its excess, and permitted the youths to have been some time together, that their intimacy might have been broken off by degrees; but Mr. Fairford only saw the more direct mode of continued restraint, which, however, he was desirous of veiling under some plausible pretext. In the anxiety which he felt on this occasion, he had held communication with an old acquaintance, Peter Drudgeit, with whom the reader is partly acquainted. "Alan," he said, "was ance wud, and aye waur; and he was expecting every moment when he would start off in a wildgoose-chase after the callant Latimer; Will Sampson, the horse-hirer in Candlemaker-Row, had given him a hint that Alan had been looking for a good hack, to go to the country for a few days. And then to oppose him downright—he could not but think on the way his poor mother was removed—Would to Heaven he was yoked to some tight piece of business, no matter whether well or ill paid, but some job that would hamshackle him at least until the Courts rose, if it were but for decency's sake.

Peter Drudgeit sympathized, for Peter had a son, who, reason or none, would needs exchange the torn and inky fustian sleeves for the blue jacket and white lapelle; and he suggested, as the reader knows, the engaging our friend Alan in the matter of Poor Peter Peebles, just opened by the desertion of young Dumtoustie, whose defection would be at the same time concealed; and this, Drudgeit said, " would be felling two dogs with one stone."

With these explanations, the reader will hold a man of the elder Fairford's sense and experience free from the hazardous and impatient curiosity with which boys fling a puppy into a deep pond, merely to see if the creature can swim. However confident in his son's talents, which were really considerable, he would have been very sorry to have involved him in the duty of pleading a complicated and difficult case, upon his very first appearance at the bar, had he not resorted to it as an effectual way to prevent the young man from taking a step, which his habits of thinking represented as a most fatal one at his outset of life.

Betwixt two evils, Mr. Fairford chose that which was in his own apprehension the least; and, like a brave officer sending forth his son to battle, rather chose he should die upon the breach, than desert the conflict with dishonour. Neither did he leave him to his own unassisted energies. Like Alpheus preceding Hercules, he himself encountered the Augean mass of Peter Peebles's law-matters. It was to the old man a labour of love to place in a clear and undistorted view the real merits of this case, which the carelessness and blunders of Peter's former solicitors had converted into a huge chaotic mass of unintelligible technicality; and such was his skill and industry, that he was able, after the severe toil of two or three days, to present to the consideration of the young counsel the principal facts of the case, in a light equally simple and comprehensible. With the assistance of a solicitor so affectionate and indefatigable, Alan Fairford was enabled, when the day of trial arrived, to walk towards the Court, attended by his anxious yet encouraging parent, with some degree of confidence that he would lose no reputation upon this arduous occasion.

They were met at the door of the Court by Peter Peebles in his usual plenitude of wig and celsitude of hat. He seized on the young pleader like a lion on his prey. " How is a' wi' you, Mr. Alan — how is a' wi' you, man ? — The awfu' day is come at last — a day that will be lang minded in this house. Poor Peter Peebles against Plainstanes—conjoined processes—Hearing in presence — stands for the Short Roll for this day — I have not been able to sleep for a week for thinking of it, and, I dare to say, neither has the Lord President himsell — for such a cause!! But your father garr'd me tak a wee drap ower muckle of his pint bottle the other night; it's no right to mix brandy wi' business, Mr. Fairford. I would have been the waur o' liquor if I would have drank as muckle as you twa would have had me. But there's a time for a' things, and if ye will dine with me after the case is heard, or whilk is the same, or maybe better, *I'll* gang my ways hame wi' *you*, and I winna object to a cheerfu' glass, within the bounds of moderation."

Old Fairford shrugged his shoulders and hurried past the client, saw his son wrapt in the sable bombazine, which, in his eyes, was more venerable than an archbishop's lawn, and could not help fondly patting his shoulder, and whispering to him to take courage, and show he was worthy to wear it. The party entered the Outer Hall of the Court, (once the place of meeting of the ancient Scottish Parliament,) and which corresponds to the use of Westminster Hall in England, serving as a vestibule to the Inner-House, as it is termed, and a place of dominion to certain sedentary personages called Lords Ordinary.

The earlier part of the morning was spent by old Fairford in reiterating his instructions to Alan, and in running from one person to another, from whom he thought he could still glean some grains of information, either concerning the point at issue, or collateral cases. Meantime, Poor Peter Peebles, whose shallow brain was altogether unable to bear the importance of the moment, kept as close to his young counsel as shadow to substance, affected now to speak loud, now to whisper in his ear, now to deck his ghastly countenance with wreathed smiles, now to cloud it with a shade of deep and solemn importance, and anon to contort it with the sneer of scorn and derision. These moods of the client's mind were accompanied with singular "mockings and mowings," fantastic gestures, which the man of rags and litigation deemed appropriate to his changes of countenance. Now he brandished his arm aloft, now thrust his fist straight out, as if to knock his opponent down. Now he laid his open palm on his bosom, and now flinging it abroad, he gallantly snapped his fingers in the air.

These demonstrations, and the obvious shame and embarrassment of Alan Fairford, did not escape the observation of the juvenile idlers in the hall. They did not, indeed, approach Peter with their usual familiarity, from some feeling of deference towards Fairford, though many accused him of conceit in presuming to undertake, at this early stage of his practice, a case of considerable difficulty. But Alan, notwithstanding this forbearance, was not the less sensible that he and his companion were the subjects of many a passing jest, and many a shout of laughter, with which that region at all times abounds.

At length the young counsel's patience gave way, and as it threatened to carry his presence of mind and recollection along with it, Alan frankly told his father, that unless he was relieved from the infliction of his client's personal presence and instructions, he must necessarily throw up his brief, and decline pleading the case.

"Hush, hush, my dear Alan," said the old gentleman, almost at his own wit's end upon hearing this dilemma; "dinna mind the silly ne'er-do-weel; we cannot keep the man from hearing his own cause, though he be not quite right in the head."

"On my life, sir," answered Alan, "I shall be unable to go on, he drives every thing out of my remembrance; and if I attempt to speak seriously of the injuries he has sustained, and the condition he is reduced to, how can I expect but that the very appearance of such an absurd scarecrow will turn it all into ridicule."

"There is something in that," said Saunders Fairford, glancing a look at Poor Peter, and then cautiously inserting his forefinger under his bob-wig, in order to rub his temple and aid his invention; "he is no figure for the fore-bar to see without laughing; but how to get rid of him? To speak sense, or any thing like it, is the last thing he will listen to. Stay, ay — Alan, my darling, hae patience; I'll get him off on the instant, like a gowff ba'."

So saying, he hastened to his ally, Peter Drudgeit, who on seeing him with marks of haste in his gait, and care upon his countenance, clapped his pen behind his ear, with "What's the stir now, Mr. Saunders? — Is there aught wrang?"

"Here's a dollar, man," said Saunders; "now, or never, Peter, do me a good turn. Yonder's your namesake, Peter Peebles, will drive the swine through our bonny hanks of yarn;* get him over to John's Coffee-house, man — gie him his meridian — keep him there, drunk or sober, till the hearing is over."

"Eneugh said," quoth Peter Drudgeit, no way displeased with his own share in the service required, — "We'se do your bidding."

---

* The simile is obvious, from the old manufacture of Scotland, when the gude-wife's thrift, as the yarn wrought in the winter was called, when laid down to bleach by the barn-side, was peculiarly exposed to the inroads of pigs, seldom well regulated about a Scottish farm-house.

Accordingly, the scribe was presently seen whispering in the ear of Peter Peebles, whose responses came forth in the following broken form: —

"Leave the Court for ae minute on this great day of judgment? — not I, by the Reg——Eh! what? Brandy, did ye say — French brandy?——couldna ye fetch a stoup to the bar under your coat, man? — Impossible?—Nay, if it's clean impossible, and if we have an hour good till they get through the single bill and the summar-roll, I carena if I cross the close wi' you; I am sure I need something to keep my heart up this awful day; but I'll no stay above an instant — not above a minute of time — nor drink aboon a single gill."

In a few minutes afterwards, the two Peters were seen moving through the Parliament Close, (which new-fangled affectation has termed a Square,) the triumphant Drudgeit leading captive the passive Peebles, whose legs conducted him towards the dramshop, while his reverted eyes were fixed upon the court. They dived into the Cimmerian abysses of John's coffee-house,* formerly the favourite rendezvous of the classic and genial Doctor Pitcairn, and were for the present seen no more.

Relieved from his tormentor, Alan Fairford had time to rally his recollections, which in the irritation of his spirits, had nearly escaped him, and to prepare himself for a task, the successful discharge or failure in which must, he was aware, have the deepest influence upon his fortunes. He had pride, was not without a consciousness of talent, and the sense of his father's feelings upon the subject impelled him to the utmost exertion. Above all, he had that sort of self-command which is essential to success in every arduous undertaking, and he was constitutionally free from that feverish irritability, by which those, whose over-active imaginations exaggerate difficulties, render themselves incapable of encountering such when they arrive.

Having collected all the scattered and broken associations which were necessary, Alan's thoughts reverted to Dumfries-shire, and the precarious situation in which he feared his beloved friend had placed himself; and once and again he consulted his watch, eager to have his present task commenced and ended, that he might hasten to Darsie's assistance. The hour and moment at length arrived. The Macer shouted, with all his well-remembered brazen strength of lungs, "Poor Peter Peebles *versus* Plainstanes, *per* Dumtoustie *et* Tough! — Maister Da-a-niel Dumtoustie!" Dumtoustie answered not the summons, which, deep and swelling as it was, could not reach across the Queensferry; but our Maister Alan Fairford appeared in his place.

The Court was very much crowded; for much amusement had been received on former occasions when Peter had volunteered his own oratory, and had been completely successful in routing the gravity of the whole procedure, and putting to silence, not indeed the counsel of the opposite party, but his own.

Both bench and audience seemed considerably surprised at the juvenile appearance of the young man who appeared in the room of Dumtoustie, for the purpose of opening this complicated and long depending process, and the common herd were disappointed at the absence of Peter the client, the Punchinello of the expected entertainment. The Judges looked with a very favourable countenance on our friend Alan, most of them being acquainted, more or less, with so old a practitioner as his father, and all, or almost all, affording, from civility, the same fair play to the first pleading of a counsel

---

* This small dark coffee-house, now burnt down, was the resort of such writers and clerks belonging to the Parliament House above thirty years ago, as retained the ancient Scottish custom of a meridian, as it was called, or noontide dram of spirits. If their proceedings were watched, they might be seen to turn fidgety about the hour of noon, and exchange looks with each other from their separate desks, till at length some one of formal and dignified presence assumed the honour of leading the band, when away they went, threading the crowd like a string of wild-fowl, crossed the square or close, and following each other into the coffee-house received in turn from the hand of the waiter, the meridian, which was placed ready at the bar. This they did, day by day; and though they did not speak to each other, they seemed to attach a certain degree of sociability to performing the ceremony in company.

which the House of Commons yields to the maiden speech of one of its members.

Lord Bladderskate was an exception to this general expression of benevolence. He scowled upon Alan, from beneath his large, shaggy, gray eyebrows, just as if the young lawyer had been usurping his nephew's honours, instead of covering his disgrace; and, from feelings which did his lordship little honour, he privately hoped the young man would not succeed in the cause which his kinsman had abandoned.

Even Lord Bladderskate, however, was, in spite of himself, pleased with the judicious and modest tone in which Alan began his address to the Court, apologizing for his own presumption, and excusing it by the sudden illness of his learned brother, for whom the labour of opening a cause of some difficulty and importance had been much more worthily designed. He spoke of himself as he really was, and of young Dumtoustie as what he ought to have been, taking care not to dwell on either topic a moment longer than was necessary. The old Judge's looks became benign; his family pride was propitiated, and, pleased equally with the modesty and civility of the young man whom he had thought forward and officious, he relaxed the scorn of his features into an expression of profound attention; the highest compliment, and the greatest encouragement, which a judge can render to the counsel addressing him.

Having succeeded in securing the favourable attention of the Court, the young lawyer, using the lights which his father's experience and knowledge of business had afforded him, proceeded with an address and clearness, unexpected from one of his years, to remove from the case itself those complicated formalities with which it had been loaded, as a surgeon strips from a wound the dressings which had been hastily wrapped round it, in order to proceed to his cure *secundum artem*. Developed of the cumbrous and complicated technicalities of litigation, with which the perverse obstinacy of the client, the inconsiderate haste or ignorance of his agents, and the evasions of a subtle adversary, had invested the process, the cause of Poor Peter Peebles, standing upon its simple merits, was no bad subject for the declamation of a young counsel, nor did our friend Alan fail to avail himself of its strong points.

He exhibited his client as a simple-hearted, honest, well-meaning man, who, during a copartnership of twelve years, had gradually become impoverished, while his partner, (his former clerk,) having no funds but his share of the same business, into which he had been admitted without any advance of stock, had become gradually more and more wealthy.

"Their association," said Alan, and the little flight was received with some applause, "resembled the ancient story of the fruit which was carved with a knife poisoned on one side of the blade only, so that the individual to whom the envenomed portion was served, drew decay and death from what afforded savour and sustenance to the consumer of the other moiety." He then plunged boldly into the *mare magnum* of accompts between the parties; he pursued each false statement from the waste-book to the day-book, from the day-book to the bill-book, from the bill-book to the ledger; placed the artful interpolations and insertions of the fallacious Plainstanes in array against each other, and against the fact; and availing himself to the utmost of his father's previous labours, and his own knowledge of accompts, in which he had been sedulously trained, he laid before the Court a clear and intelligible statement of the affairs of the copartnery, showing, with precision, that a large balance must, at the dissolution, have been due to his client, sufficient to have enabled him to have carried on business on his own account, and thus to have retained his situation in society, as an independent and industrious tradesman. "But instead of this justice being voluntarily rendered by the former clerk to his former master,—by the party obliged to his benefactor,— by one honest man to another,— his wretched client had been compelled to follow his quondam clerk, his present debtor, from Court to Court; had found his just claims met with well-invented but unfounded counter-claims, had seen his party shift his character of pursuer or defender, as often as Harlequin effects his transformations, till, in a chase so varied and so long, the unhappy litigant had lost substance, reputation, and almost the use of reason itself, and came before their Lordships an object of thoughtless derision to the unreflecting, of compassion to the better-hearted, and of awful meditation to every one, who considered that, in a country where excellent laws were administered by upright and incorruptible judges, a man might pursue an almost indisputable claim through all the mazes of litigation; lose fortune, reputation, and reason itself in the chase, and now come before the Supreme Court of his country in the wretched condition of his unhappy client, a victim to protracted justice, and to that hope delayed which sickens the heart."

The force of this appeal to feeling made as much impression on the Bench, as had been previously effected by the clearness of Alan's argument. The absurd form of Peter himself, with his tow-wig, was fortunately not present to excite any ludicrous emotion, and the pause that took place when the young lawyer had concluded his speech, was followed by a murmur of approbation, which the ears of his father drank in as the sweetest sounds that had ever entered them. Many a hand of gratulation was thrust out to his grasp, trembling as it was with anxiety, and finally with delight; his voice faltering as he replied, " Ay, ay, I kend Alan was the lad to make a spoon or spoil a horn."[*]

The counsel on the other side arose, an old practitioner, who had noted too closely the impression made by Alan's pleading, not to fear the consequences of an immediate decision. He paid the highest compliments to his very young brother—" the Benjamin, as he would presume to call him, of the learned Faculty—said the alleged hardships of Mr. Peebles were compensated, by his being placed in a situation where the benevolence of their Lordships had assigned him gratuitously such assistance as he might not otherwise have obtained at a high price — and allowed his young brother had put many things in such a new point of view, that, although he was quite certain of his ability to refute them, he was honestly desirous of having a few hours to arrange his answer, in order to be able to follow Mr. Fairford from point to point. He had farther to observe, there was one point of the case to which his brother, whose attention had been otherwise so wonderfully comprehensive, had not given the consideration which he expected; it was founded on the interpretation of certain correspondence which had passed betwixt the parties soon after the dissolution of the copartnery."

The Court having heard Mr. Tough, readily allowed him two days for preparing himself, hinting at the same time, that he might find his task difficult, and affording the young counsel, with high encomiums upon the mode in which he had acquitted himself, the choice of speaking, either now or at the next calling of the cause, upon the point which Plainstanes's lawyer had adverted to.

Alan modestly apologized for what in fact had been an omission very pardonable in so complicated a case, and professed himself instantly ready to go through that correspondence, and prove that it was in form and substance exactly applicable to the view of the case he had submitted to their lordships. He applied to his father, who sat behind him, to hand him, from time to time, the letters, in the order in which he meant to read and comment upon them.

Old Counsellor Tough had probably formed an ingenious enough scheme to blunt the effect of the young lawyer's reasoning, by thus obliging him to

---

[*] Said of an adventurous gipsy, who resolves at all risks to convert a sheep's horn into a spoon.

follow up a process of reasoning, clear and complete in itself, by a hasty and extemporary appendix. If so, he seemed likely to be disappointed; for Alan was well prepared on this, as on other parts of the cause, and recommenced his pleading with a degree of animation, which added force even to what he had formerly stated, and might perhaps have occasioned the old gentleman to regret his having again called him up; when his father, as he handed him the letters, put one into his hand which produced a singular effect on the pleader.

At the first glance, he saw that the paper had no reference to the affairs of Peter Peebles; but the first glance also showed him, what, even at that time, and in that presence, he could not help reading; and which, being read, seemed totally to disconcert his ideas. He stopped short in his harangue—gazed on the paper with a look of surprise and horror—uttered an exclamation, and flinging down the brief which he had in hand, hurried out of court without returning a single word of answer to the various questions, "What was the matter?"—"Was he taken unwell?"—"Should not a chair be called?" &c. &c. &c.

The elder Mr. Fairford, who remained seated, and looking as senseless as if he had been made of stone, was at length recalled to himself by the anxious inquiries of the judges and the counsel after his son's health. He then rose with an air, in which was mingled the deep habitual reverence in which he held the Court, with some internal cause of agitation, and with difficulty mentioned something of a mistake — a piece of bad news — Alan, he hoped, would be well enough to-morrow. But unable to proceed farther, he clasped his hands together, exclaiming, "My son! my son!" and left the court hastily, as if in pursuit of him.

"What's the matter with the auld bitch next?"* said an acute metaphysical judge, though somewhat coarse in his manners, aside to his brethren. "This is a daft cause, Bladderskate — first, it drives the poor man mad that aught it—then your nevoy goes daft with fright, and flies the pit — then this smart young hopeful is aff the hooks with too hard study, I fancy — and now auld Saunders Fairford is as lunatic as the best of them. What say ye till't, ye bitch?"

"Nothing, my lord," answered Bladderskate, much too formal to admire the levities in which his philosophical brother sometimes indulged—"I say nothing, but pray to Heaven to keep our own wits."

"Amen, amen," answered his learned brother; "for some of us have but few to spare."

The Court then arose, and the audience departed, greatly wondering at the talent displayed by Alan Fairford at his first appearance in a case so difficult and so complicated, and assigning an hundred conjectural causes, each different from the others, for the singular interruption which had clouded his day of success. The worst of the whole was, that six agents, who had each come to the separate resolution of thrusting a retaining fee into Alan's hand as he left the court, shook their heads as they returned the money into their leathern pouches, and said, "that the lad was clever, but they would like to see more of him before they engaged him in the way of business—they did not like his lowping away like a flea in a blanket."

---

* Tradition ascribes this whimsical style of language to the ingenious and philosophical Lord Kaimes.

Chapter the Second.

HAD our friend Alexander Fairford known the consequences of his son's abrupt retreat from the Court, which are mentioned in the end of the last chapter, it might have accomplished the prediction of the lively old judge, and driven him utterly distracted. As it was, he was miserable enough. His son had risen ten degrees higher in his estimation than ever, by his display of juridical talents, which seemed to assure him that the applause of the judges and professors of the law, which, in his estimation, was worth that of all mankind besides, authorized to the fullest extent the advantageous estimate which even his parental partiality had been induced to form of Alan's powers. On the other hand, he felt that he was himself a little humbled, from a disguise which he had practised towards this son of his hopes and wishes.

The truth was, that on the morning of this eventful day, Mr. Alexander Fairford had received from his correspondent and friend, Provost Crosbie of Dumfries, a letter of the following tenor :—

" DEAR SIR,

" YOUR respected favour of 25th ultimo, per favour of Mr. Darsie Latimer, reached me in safety, and I showed to the young gentleman such attention as he was pleased to accept of. The object of my present writing is twofold. First, the council are of opinion that you should now begin to stir in the thirlage cause ; and they think they will be able, from evidence *noviter repertum*, to enable you to amend your condescendence upon the use and wont of the burgh, touching the *grana invecta et illata*. So you will please consider yourself as authorized to speak to Mr. Pest, and lay before him the papers which you will receive by the coach. The council think that a fee of two guineas may be sufficient on this occasion, as Mr. Pest had three for drawing the original condescendence.

" I take the opportunity of adding, that there has been a great riot among the Solway fishermen, who have destroyed, in a masterful manner, the stake-nets set up near the mouth of this river ; and have beside attacked the house of Quaker Geddes, one of the principal partners of the Tide-net Fishing Company, and done a great deal of damage. Am sorry to add, young Mr. Latimer was in the fray, and has not since been heard of. Murder is spoke of, but that may be a word of course. As the young gentleman has behaved rather oddly while in these parts, as in declining to dine with me more than once, and going about the country with strolling fiddlers and such like, I rather hope that his present absence is only occasioned by a frolic ; but as his servant has been making inquiries of me respecting his master, I thought it best to acquaint you in course of post. I have only to add, that our sheriff has taken a precognition, and committed one or two of the rioters. If I can be useful in this matter, either by advertising for Mr. Latimer as missing, publishing a reward, or otherwise, I will obey your respected instructions, being your most obedient to command,

" WILLIAM CROSBIE."

When Mr. Fairford received this letter, and had read it to an end, his first idea was to communicate it to his son, that an express might be instantly despatched, or a King's messenger sent with proper authority to search after his late guest.

The habits of the fishers were rude, as he well knew, though not absolutely sanguinary or ferocious ; and there had been instances of their transporting persons who had interfered in their smuggling trade to the Isle of Man, and elsewhere, and keeping them under restraint for many weeks. On this account, Mr. Fairford was naturally led to feel anxiety concerning the fate of his late inmate; and, at a less interesting moment, would certainly have set out himself, or licensed his son to go in pursuit of his friend.

But, alas! he was both a father and an agent. In the one capacity, he looked on his son as dearer to him than all the world besides; in the other, the lawsuit which he conducted was to him like an infant to its nurse, and the case of Poor Peter Peebles against Plainstanes was, he saw, adjourned, perhaps *sine die*, should this document reach the hands of his son. The mutual and enthusiastical affection betwixt the young men was well known to him; and he concluded, that if the precarious state of Latimer were made known to Alan Fairford, it would render him not only unwilling, but totally unfit, to discharge the duty of the day, to which the old gentleman attached such ideas of importance.

On mature reflection, therefore, he resolved, though not without some feelings of compunction, to delay communicating to his son the disagreeable intelligence which he had received, until the business of the day should be ended. The delay, he persuaded himself, could be of little consequence to Darsie Latimer, whose folly, he dared to say, had led him into some scrape which would meet an appropriate punishment, in some accidental restraint, which would be thus prolonged for only a few hours longer. Besides, he would have time to speak to the Sheriff of the county — perhaps to the King's Advocate — and set about the matter in a regular manner, or as he termed it, as summing up the duties of a solicitor, to *age as accords.**

The scheme, as we have seen, was partially successful, and was only ultimately defeated, as he confessed to himself with shame, by his own very unbusiness-like mistake of shuffling the Provost's letter, in the hurry and anxiety of the morning, among some papers belonging to Peter Peebles's affairs, and then handing it to his son, without observing the blunder. He used to protest, even till the day of his death, that he never had been guilty of such an inaccuracy as giving a paper out of his hand without looking at the docketing, except on that unhappy occasion, when, of all others, he had such particular reason to regret his negligence.

Disturbed by these reflections, the old gentleman had, for the first time in his life, some disinclination, arising from shame and vexation, to face his own son; so that to protract for a little the meeting, which he feared would be a painful one, he went to wait upon the Sheriff-depute, who he found had set off for Dumfries, in great haste, to superintend in person the investigation which had been set on foot by his Substitute. This gentleman's clerk could say little on the subject of the riot, excepting that it had been serious, much damage done to property, and some personal violence offered to individuals; but, as far as he had yet heard, no lives lost on the spot.

Mr. Fairford was compelled to return home with this intelligence; and on inquiring at James Wilkinson where his son was, received for answer, that "Maister Alan was in his own room, and very busy."

"We must have our explanation over," said Saunders Fairford to himself. "Better a finger off, as aye wagging;" and going to the door of his son's apartment, he knocked at first gently—then more loudly—but received no answer. Somewhat alarmed at this silence, he opened the door of the chamber—it was empty—clothes lay mixed in confusion with the law-books and papers, as if the inmate had been engaged in hastily packing for a journey. As Mr. Fairford looked around in alarm, his eye was arrested by a sealed letter lying upon his son's writing-table, and addressed to himself. It contained the following words: —

---

* A Scots law phrase, of no very determinate import, meaning, generally, to do what is fitting.

"MY DEAREST FATHER,

"You will not, I trust, be surprised, nor perhaps very much displeased, to learn that I am on my way to Dumfries-shire, to learn, by my own personal investigation, the present state of my dear friend, and afford him such relief as may be in my power, and which, I trust, will be effectual. I do not presume to reflect upon you, dearest sir, for concealing from me information of so much consequence to my peace of mind and happiness; but I hope your having done so will be, if not an excuse, at least some mitigation of my present offence, in taking a step of consequence without consulting your pleasure; and, I must farther own, under circumstances which perhaps might lead to your disapprobation of my purpose. I can only say, in farther apology, that if any thing unhappy, which Heaven forbid! shall have occurred to the person who, next to yourself, is dearest to me in this world, I shall have on my heart, as a subject of eternal regret, that being in a certain degree warned of his danger, and furnished with the means of obviating it, I did not instantly hasten to his assistance, but preferred giving my attention to the business of this unlucky morning. No view of personal distinction, nothing, indeed, short of your earnest and often expressed wishes, could have detained me in town till this day; and having made this sacrifice to filial duty, I trust you will hold me excused, if I now obey the calls of friendship and humanity. Do not be in the least anxious on my account; I shall know, I trust, how to conduct myself with due caution in any emergence which may occur, otherwise my legal studies for so many years have been to little purpose. I am fully provided with money, and also with arms, in case of need; but you may rely on my prudence in avoiding all occasions of using the latter, short of the last necessity. God Almighty bless you, my dearest father! and grant that you may forgive the first, and, I trust, the last act approaching towards premeditated disobedience, of which I either have now, or shall hereafter have, to accuse myself. I remain, till death, your dutiful and affectionate son,

"ALAN FAIRFORD."

"P. S. — I shall write with the utmost regularity, acquainting you with my motions, and requesting your advice. I trust my stay will be very short, and I think it possible that I may bring back Darsie along with me."

The paper dropped from the old man's hand when he was thus assured of the misfortune which he apprehended. His first idea was to get a post-chaise and pursue the fugitive; but he recollected, that, upon the very rare occasions when Alan had shown himself indocile to the *patria potestas*, his natural ease and gentleness of disposition seemed hardened into obstinacy, and that now, entitled, as arrived at the years of majority, and a member of the learned Faculty, to direct his own motions, there was great doubt, whether, in the event of his overtaking his son, he might be able to prevail upon him to return back. In such a risk of failure, he thought it wiser to desist from his purpose, especially as even his success in such a pursuit would give a ridiculous *éclat* to the whole affair, which could not be otherwise than prejudicial to his son's rising character.

Bitter, however, were Saunders Fairford's reflections, as, again picking up the fatal scroll, he threw himself into his son's leathern easy-chair, and bestowed upon it a disjointed commentary. "Bring back Darsie? little doubt of that—the bad shilling is sure enough to come back again. I wish Darsie no worse ill than that he were carried where the silly fool, Alan, should never see him again. It was an ill hour that he darkened my doors in, for, ever since that, Alan has given up his ain old-fashioned mother-wit, for the tother's capernoited maggots and nonsense.—Provided with money? you must have more than I know of, then, my friend, for I trow I kept you pretty short, for your own good. — Can he have gotten more fees? or, does he think five guineas has neither beginning nor end?—Arms! What would he do with arms, or what would any man do with them that is not a regular soldier under government, or else a thief-taker? I have had enough of arms, I trow, although I carried them for King George and the government. But this is a worse strait than Falkirk-field yet.—God guide us, we are poor inconsistent creatures! To think the lad should have made so able an appearance, and then bolted off this gate, after a glaiket ne'er-do-weel, like a hound upon a false scent!—Las-a-day! it's a sore thing to see a stunkard cow kick down the pail when it's reaming fou.—But, after all, it's an ill bird that defiles its ain nest. I must cover up the scandal as well as I can. —What's the matter now, James?"

"A message, sir," said James Wilkinson, "from my Lord President; and he hopes Mr. Alan is not seriously indisposed."

"From the Lord President? the Lord preserve us!—I'll send an answer this instant; bid the lad sit down, and ask him to drink, James.—Let me see," continued he, taking a sheet of gilt paper, "how we are to draw our answers."

Ere his pen had touched the paper, James was in the room again.

"What now, James?"

"Lord Bladderskate's lad is come to ask how Mr. Alan is, as he left the Court——"

"Ay, ay, ay," answered Saunders, bitterly; "he has e'en made a moonlight flitting, like my lord's ain nevoy."

"Shall I say sae, sir?" said James, who, as an old soldier, was literal in all things touching the service.

"The devil! no, no!—Bid the lad sit down and taste our ale. I will write his lordship an answer."

Once more the gilt paper was resumed, and once more the door was opened by James.

"Lord —— sends his servitor to ask after Mr. Alan."

"Oh, the deevil take their civility!" said poor Saunders. "Sit him down to drink too—I will write to his lordship."

"The lads will bide your pleasure, sir, as lang as I keep the bicker fou; but this ringing is like to wear out the bell, I think; there are they at it again."

He answered the fresh summons accordingly, and came back to inform Mr. Fairford, that the Dean of Faculty was below, inquiring for Mr. Alan. —"Will I set him down to drink, too?" said James.

"Will you be an idiot, sir?" said Mr. Fairford. "Show Mr. Dean into the parlour."

In going slowly down stairs, step by step, the perplexed man of business had time enough to reflect, that if it be possible to put a fair gloss upon a true story, the verity always serves the purpose better than any substitute which ingenuity can devise. He therefore told his learned visiter, that although his son had been incommoded by the heat of the court, and the long train of hard study, by day and night, preceding his exertions, yet he had fortunately so far recovered, as to be in condition to obey upon the instant a sudden summons which had called him to the country, on a matter of life and death.

"It should be a serious matter indeed that takes my young friend away at this moment," said the good-natured Dean. "I wish he had stayed to finish his pleading, and put down old Tough. Without compliment, Mr. Fairford, it was as fine a first appearance as I ever heard. I should be sorry your son did not follow it up in a reply. Nothing like striking while the iron is hot."

Mr. Saunders Fairford made a bitter grimace as he acquiesced in an opinion which was indeed decidedly his own; but he thought it most prudent to reply, "that the affair which rendered his son Alan's presence in the country absolutely necessary, regarded the affairs of a young gentleman of great fortune, who was a particular friend of Alan's, and who never took any material step in his affairs, without consulting his counsel learned in the law."

"Well, well, Mr. Fairford, you know best," answered the learned Dean; "if there be death or marriage in the case, a will or a wedding is to be preferred to all other business. I am happy Mr. Alan is so much recovered as to be able for travel, and wish you a very good morning."

Having thus taken his ground to the Dean of Faculty, Mr. Fairford hastily wrote cards in answer to the inquiry of the three judges, accounting for Alan's absence in the same manner. These, being properly sealed and addressed, he delivered to James, with directions to dismiss the parti-coloured gentry, who, in the meanwhile, had consumed a gallon of twopenny ale, while discussing points of law, and addressing each other by their masters' titles.*

The exertions which these matters demanded, and the interest which so many persons of legal distinction appeared to have taken in his son, greatly relieved the oppressed spirit of Saunders Fairford, who continued to talk mysteriously of the very important business which had interfered with his son's attendance during the brief remainder of the session. He endeavoured to lay the same unction to his own heart; but here the application was less fortunate, for his conscience told him, that no end, however important, which could be achieved in Darsie Latimer's affairs, could be balanced against the reputation which Alan was like to forfeit, by deserting the cause of Poor Peter Peebles.

In the meanwhile, although the haze which surrounded the cause, or causes, of that unfortunate litigant had been for a time dispelled by Alan's eloquence, like a fog by the thunder of artillery, yet it seemed once more to settle down upon the mass of litigation, thick as the palpable darkness of Egypt, at the very sound of Mr. Tough's voice, who, on the second day after Alan's departure, was heard in answer to the opening counsel. Deep-mouthed, long-breathed, and pertinacious, taking a pinch of snuff betwixt every sentence, which otherwise seemed interminable—the veteran pleader prosed over all the themes which had been treated so luminously by Fairford: he quietly and imperceptibly replaced all the rubbish which the other had cleared away; and succeeded in restoring the veil of obscurity and unintelligibility which had for many years darkened the case of Peebles against Plainstanes; and the matter was once more hung up by a remit to an accountant, with instruction to report before answer. So different a result from that which the public had been led to expect from Alan's speech, gave rise to various speculations.

The client himself opined, that it was entirely owing, first, to his own absence during the first day's pleading, being, as he said, deboshed with brandy, usquebaugh, and other strong waters, at John's Coffee-house, *per ambages* of Peter Drudgeit, employed to that effect by and through the device, counsel, and covyne of Saunders Fairford, his agent, or pretended agent. Secondly, by the flight and voluntary desertion of the younger Fairford, the advocate; on account of which he served both father and son with a petition and complaint against them, for malversation in office. So that the apparent and most probable issue of this cause seemed to menace the melancholy Mr. Saunders Fairford with additional subject for plague and mortification; which was the more galling, as his conscience told him that the case was really given away, and that a very brief resumption of the former argument, with reference to the necessary authorities and points of evidence,

---

* The Scottish Judges are distinguished by the title of lord prefixed to their own temporal designation. As the ladies of these official dignitaries do not bear any share in their husbands' honours, they are distinguished only by their lords' family name. They were not always contented with this species of Salique law, which certainly is somewhat inconsistent. But their pretensions to title are said to have been long since repelled by James V., the Sovereign who founded the College of Justice. "I," said he, "made the carles lords, but who the devil made the carlines ladies?"

K 2

would have enabled Alan, by the mere breath, as it were, of his mouth, to blow away the various cobwebs with which Mr. Tough had again invested the proceedings. But it went, he said, just like a decreet in absence, and was lost for want of a contradictor.

In the meanwhile, nearly a week passed over without Mr. Fairford hearing a word directly from his son. He learned, indeed, by a letter from Mr. Crosbie, that the young counsellor had safely reached Dumfries, but had left that town upon some ulterior researches, the purpose of which he had not communicated. The old man, thus left to suspense, and to mortifying recollections, deprived also of the domestic society to which he had been habituated, began to suffer in body as well as in mind. He had formed the determination of setting out in person for Dumfries-shire, when, after having been dogged, peevish, and snappish to his clerks and domestics, to an unusual and almost intolerable degree, the acrimonious humours settled in a hissing-hot fit of the gout, which is a well-known tamer of the most froward spirits, and under whose discipline we shall, for the present, leave him, as the continuation of this history assumes, with the next division, a form somewhat different from direct narrative and epistolary correspondence, though partaking of the character of both.

Chapter the Third.

JOURNAL OF DARSIE LATIMER.

[The following Address is written on the inside of the envelope which contained the Journal.]

INTO what hands soever these leaves may fall, they will instruct him, during a certain time at least, in the history of the life of an unfortunate young man, who, in the heart of a free country, and without any crime being laid to his charge, has been, and is, subjected to a course of unlawful and violent restraint. He who opens this letter, is therefore conjured to apply to the nearest magistrate, and, following such indications as the papers may afford, to exert himself for the relief of one, who, while he possesses every claim to assistance which oppressed innocence can give, has, at the same time, both the inclination and the means of being grateful to his deliverers. Or, if the person obtaining these letters shall want courage or means to effect the writer's release, he is, in that case, conjured, by every duty of a man to his fellow mortals, and of a Christian towards one who professes the same holy faith, to take the speediest measures for conveying them with speed and safety to the hands of Alan Fairford, Esq., Advocate, residing in the family of his father, Alexander Fairford, Esq., Writer to the Signet, Brown's Square, Edinburgh. He may be assured of a liberal reward, besides the consciousness of having discharged a real duty to humanity.

MY DEAREST ALAN,

Feeling as warmly towards you in doubt and in distress, as I ever did in the brightest days of our intimacy, it is to you whom I address a history which may perhaps fall into very different hands. A portion of my former spirit descends to my pen, when I write your name, and indulging the happy thought that you may be my deliverer from my present uncomfortable and alarming situation, as you have been my guide and counsellor on every former occasion, I will subdue the dejection which would otherwise overwhelm me. Therefore, as, Heaven knows, I have time enough to write, I will endeavour to pour my thoughts out, as fully and freely as of old, though probably without the same gay and happy levity.

If the papers should reach other hands than yours, still I will not regret this exposure of my feelings; for, allowing for an ample share of the folly incidental to youth and inexperience, I fear not that I have much to be ashamed of in my narrative; nay, I even hope, that the open simplicity and frankness with which I am about to relate every singular and distressing circumstance, may prepossess even a stranger in my favour; and that, amid the multitude of seemingly trivial circumstances which I detail at length, a clew may be found to effect my liberation.

Another chance certainly remains—the Journal, as I may call it, may never reach the hands, either of the dear friend to whom it is addressed, or those of an indifferent stranger, but may become the prey of the persons by whom I am at present treated as a prisoner. Let it be so—they will learn from it little but what they already know; that, as a man, and an Englishman, my soul revolts at the usage which I have received; that I am determined to essay every possible means to obtain my freedom; that captivity has not broken my spirit, and that, although they may doubtless complete their oppression by murder, I am still willing to bequeath my cause to the justice of my country. Undeterred, therefore, by the probability that my papers may be torn from me, and subjected to the inspection of one in particular, who, causelessly my enemy already, may be yet farther incensed at me for recording the history of my wrongs, I proceed to resume the history of events which have befallen me since the conclusion of my last letter to my dear Alan Fairford, dated, if I mistake not, on the 5th day of this still current month of August.

Upon the night preceding the date of that letter, I had been present, for the purpose of an idle frolic, at a dancing-party at the village of Brokenburn, about six miles from Dumfries; many persons must have seen me there, should the fact appear of importance sufficient to require investigation. I danced, played on the violin, and took part in the festivity till about midnight, when my servant, Samuel Owen, brought me my horses, and I rode back to a small inn called Shepherd's Bush, kept by Mrs. Gregson, which had been occasionally my residence for about a fortnight past. I spent the earlier part of the forenoon in writing a letter, which I have already mentioned, to you, my dear Alan, and which, I think, you must have received in safety. Why did I not follow your advice, so often given me? Why did I linger in the neighbourhood of a danger, of which a kind voice had warned me? These are now unavailing questions; I was blinded by a fatality, and remained, fluttering like a moth around the candle, until I have been scorched to some purpose.

The greater part of the day had passed, and time hung heavy on my hands. I ought, perhaps, to blush at recollecting what has been often objected to me by the dear friend to whom this letter is addressed, viz. the facility with which I have, in moments of indolence, suffered my motions to be directed by any person who chanced to be near me, instead of taking the labour of thinking or deciding for myself. I had employed for some time, as a sort of guide and errand-boy, a lad named Benjamin, the son of one widow Coltherd, who lives near the Shepherd's Bush, and I cannot but remember that, upon several occasions, I had of late suffered him to possess more influence over my motions, than at all became the difference of our age and condition. At present, he exerted himself to persuade me that it was the finest possible sport to see the fish taken out from the nets placed in the Solway at the reflux of the tide, and urged my going thither this evening so much, that, looking back on the whole circumstances, I cannot but think he had some especial motive for his conduct. These particulars

I have mentioned, that if these papers fall into friendly hands, the boy may be sought after and submitted to examination.

His eloquence being unable to persuade me that I should take any pleasure in seeing the fruitless struggles of the fish when left in the nets, and deserted by the tide, he artfully suggested, that Mr. and Miss Geddes, a respectable Quaker family well known in the neighbourhood, and with whom I had contracted habits of intimacy, would possibly be offended if I did not make them an early visit. Both, he said, had been particularly inquiring the reasons of my leaving their house rather suddenly on the previous day. I resolved, therefore, to walk up to Mount Sharon and make my apologies; and I agreed to permit the boy to attend upon me, and wait my return from the house, that I might fish on my way homeward to Shepherd's Bush, for which amusement, he assured me, I would find the evening most favourable. I mention this minute circumstance, because I strongly suspect that this boy had a presentiment how the evening was to terminate with me, and entertained the selfish though childish wish of securing to himself an angling rod which he had often admired, as a part of my spoils. I may do the boy wrong, but I had before remarked in him the peculiar art of pursuing the trifling objects of cupidity proper to his age, with the systematic address of much riper years.

When we had commenced our walk, I upbraided him with the coolness of the evening, considering the season, the easterly wind, and other circumstances, unfavourable for angling. He persisted in his own story, and made a few casts, as if to convince me of my error, but caught no fish; and, indeed, as I am now convinced, was much more intent on watching my motions, than on taking any. When I ridiculed him once more on his fruitless endeavours, he answered with a sneering smile, that " the trouts would not rise, because there was thunder in the air;" an intimation which, in one sense, I have found too true.

I arrived at Mount Sharon; was received by my friends there with their wonted kindness; and after being a little rallied on my having suddenly left them on the preceding evening, I agreed to make atonement by staying all night, and dismissed the lad who attended with my fishing-rod, to carry that information to Shepherd's Bush. It may be doubted whether he went thither, or in a different direction.

Betwixt eight and nine o'clock, when it began to become dark, we walked on the terrace to enjoy the appearance of the firmament, glittering with ten million of stars; to which a slight touch of early frost gave tenfold lustre. As we gazed on this splendid scene, Miss Geddes, I think, was the first to point out to our admiration a shooting or falling star, which, she said, drew a long train after it. Looking to the part of the heavens which she pointed out, I distinctly observed two successive sky-rockets arise and burst in the sky.

"These meteors," said Mr. Geddes, in answer to his sister's observation, " are not formed in heaven, nor do they bode any good to the dwellers upon earth."

As he spoke, I looked to another quarter of the sky, and a rocket, as if a signal in answer to those which had already appeared, rose high from the earth, and burst apparently among the stars.

Mr. Geddes seemed very thoughtful for some minutes, and then said to his sister, " Rachel, though it waxes late, I must go down to the fishing station, and pass the night in the overseer's room there."

"Nay, then," replied the lady, "I am but too well assured that the sons of Belial are menacing these nets and devices. Joshua, art thou a man of peace, and wilt thou willingly and wittingly thrust thyself, where thou mayst be tempted by the old man Adam within thee, to enter into debate and strife?"

"I am a man of peace, Rachel," answered Mr. Geddes, " even to the utmost extent which our friends can demand of humanity; and neither have I ever used, nor, with the help of God, will I at any future time employ, the arm of flesh to repel or to revenge injuries. But if I can, by mild reasons and firm conduct, save those rude men from committing a crime, and the property belonging to myself and others from sustaining damage, surely I do but the duty of a man and a Christian."

With these words, he ordered his horse instantly; and his sister ceasing to argue with him, folded her arms upon her bosom, and looked up to heaven with a resigned and yet sorrowful countenance.

These particulars may appear trivial; but it is better, in my present condition, to exert my faculties in recollecting the past, and in recording it, than waste them in vain and anxious anticipations of the future.

It would have been scarcely proper in me to remain in the house, from which the master was thus suddenly summoned away; and I therefore begged permission to attend him to the fishing station, assuring his sister that I would be a guarantee for his safety.

The proposal seemed to give much pleasure to Miss Geddes. "Let it be so, brother," she said; "and let the young man have the desire of his heart, that there may be a faithful witness to stand by thee in the hour of need, and to report how it shall fare with thee."

"Nay, Rachel," said the worthy man, "thou art to blame in this, that to quiet thy apprehensions on my account, thou shouldst thrust into danger— if danger it shall prove to be—this youth, our guest; for whom, doubtless, in case of mishap, as many hearts will ache as may be afflicted on our account."

"No, my good friend," said I, taking Mr. Geddes's hand, "I am not so happy as you suppose me. Were my span to be concluded this evening, few would so much as know that such a being had existed for twenty years on the face of the earth; and of these few, only one would sincerely regret me. Do not, therefore, refuse me the privilege of attending you; and of showing, by so trifling an act of kindness, that if I have few friends, I am at least desirous to serve them."

"Thou hast a kind heart, I warrant thee," said Joshua Geddes, returning the pressure of my hand. "Rachel, the young man shall go with me. Why should he not face danger, in order to do justice and preserve peace? There is that within me," he added, looking upwards, and with a passing enthusiasm which I had not before observed, and which perhaps rather belonged to the sect than to his own personal character—"I say, I have that within which assures me, that though the ungodly may rage even like the storm of the ocean, they shall not have freedom to prevail against us."

Having spoken thus, Mr. Geddes appointed a pony to be saddled for my use; and having taken a basket with some provisions, and a servant to carry back the horses, for which there was no accommodation at the fishing station, we set off about nine o'clock at night, and after three quarters of an hour's riding, arrived at our place of destination.

The station consists, or then consisted, of huts for four or five fishermen, a cooperage and shed, and a better sort of cottage, at which the superintendent resided. We gave our horses to the servant, to be carried back to Mount Sharon; my companion expressing himself humanely anxious for their safety—and knocked at the door of the house. At first we only heard a barking of dogs; but these animals became quiet on snuffing beneath the door, and acknowledging the presence of friends. A hoarse voice then demanded, in rather unfriendly accents, who we were and what we wanted; and it was not until Joshua named himself, and called upon his superintendent to open, that the latter appeared at the door of the hut, attended by three large dogs of the Newfoundland breed. He had a flambeau in his hand, and two large heavy ship-pistols stuck into his belt. He was a stout, elderly man, who had been a sailor, as I learned, during the earlier part of his life, and was now much confided in by the Fishing Company, whose concerns he directed under the orders of Mr. Geddes.

"Thou didst not expect me to-night, friend Davies?" said my friend to the old man, who was arranging seats for us by the fire.

"No, Master Geddes," answered he, "I did not expect you, nor, to speak the truth, did I wish for you either."

"These are plain terms, John Davies," answered Mr. Geddes.

"Ay, ay, sir, I know your worship loves no holiday speeches."

"Thou dost guess, I suppose, what brings us here so late, John Davies?" said Mr. Geddes.

"I do suppose, sir," answered the superintendent, "that it was because those d——d smuggling wreckers on the coast are showing their lights to gather their forces, as they did the night before they broke down the dam-dike and wears up the country, but if that same be the case, I wish once more you had staid away, for your worship carries no fighting tackle aboard, I think; and there will be work for such ere morning, your worship."

"Worship is due to Heaven only, John Davies," said Geddes. "I have often desired thee to desist from using that phrase to me."

"I won't, then," said John; "no offence meant: but how the devil can a man stand picking his words, when he is just going to come to blows?"

"I hope not, John Davies," said Joshua Geddes. "Call in the rest of the men, that I may give them their instructions."

"I may cry till doomsday, Master Geddes, ere a soul answers—the cowardly lubbers have all made sail — the cooper, and all the rest of them, so soon as they heard the enemy were at sea. They have all taken to the long-boat, and left the ship among the breakers, except little Phil and myself—they have, by ——!"

"Swear not at all, John Davies—thou art an honest man; and I believe, without an oath, that thy comrades love their own bones better than my goods and chattels. And so thou hast no assistance but little Phil against a hundred men or two?"

"Why, there are the dogs, your honour knows, Neptune and Thetis—and the puppy may do something; and then though your worship—I beg pardon —though your honour be no great fighter, this young gentleman may bear a hand."

"Ay, and I see you are provided with arms," said Mr. Geddes; "let me see them."

"Ay, ay, sir; here be a pair of buffers will bite as well as bark — these will make sure of two rogues at least. It would be a shame to strike without firing a shot.—Take care, your honour, they are double-shotted."

"Ay, John Davies, I will take care of them," throwing the pistols into a tub of water beside him; "and I wish I could render the whole generation of them useless at the same moment."

A deep shade of displeasure passed over John Davies's weatherbeaten countenance. "Belike your honour is going to take the command yourself, then?" he said, after a pause. "Why, I can be of little use now; and since your worship, or your honour, or whatever you are, means to strike quietly, I believe you will do it better without me than with me, for I am like enough to make mischief, I admit; but I'll never leave my post without orders."

"Then you have mine, John Davies, to go to Mount Sharon directly, and take the boy Phil with you. Where is he?"

"He is on the outlook for these scums of the earth," answered Davies; "but it is to no purpose to know when they come, if we are not to stand to our weapons."

"We will use none but those of sense and reason, John."

"And you may just as well cast chaff against the wind, as speak sense and reason to the like of them."

"Well, well, be it so," said Joshua; "and now, John Davies, I know thou art what the world calls a brave fellow, and I have ever found thee an honest one. And now I command you to go to Mount Sharon, and let Phil lie on the bank-side—see the poor boy hath a sea-cloak, though—and watch what happens there, and let him bring you the news; and if any violence shall be offered to the property there, I trust to your fidelity to carry my sister to Dumfries, to the house of our friends the Corsacks, and inform the civil authorities of what mischief hath befallen."

The old seaman paused a moment. "It is hard lines for me," he said, "to leave your honour in tribulation; and yet, staying here, I am only like to make bad worse; and your honour's sister, Miss Rachel, must be looked to, that's certain; for if the rogues once get their hand to mischief, they will come to Mount Sharon after they have wasted and destroyed this here snug little road-stead, where I thought to ride at anchor for life."

"Right, right, John Davies," said Joshua Geddes; "and best call the dogs with you."

"Ay, ay, sir," said the veteran, "for they are something of my mind, and would not keep quiet if they saw mischief doing; so maybe they might come to mischief, poor dumb creatures. So God bless your honour—I mean your worship—I cannot bring my mouth to say fare you well.—Here, Neptune, Thetis! come, dogs, come."

So saying, and with a very crest-fallen countenance, John Davies left the hut.

"Now there goes one of the best and most faithful creatures that ever was born," said Mr. Geddes, as the superintendent shut the door of the cottage. "Nature made him with a heart that would not have suffered him to harm a fly; but thou seest, friend Latimer, that as men arm their bull-dogs with spiked collars, and their game-cocks with steel spurs, to aid them in fight, so they corrupt, by education, the best and mildest natures, until fortitude and spirit become stubbornness and ferocity. Believe me, friend Latimer, I would as soon expose my faithful household dog to a vain combat with a herd of wolves, as yon trusty creature to the violence of the enraged multitude. But I need say little on this subject to thee, friend Latimer, who, I doubt not, art trained to believe that courage is displayed and honour attained, not by doing and suffering, as becomes a man, that which fate calls us to suffer, and justice commands us to do, but because thou art ready to retort violence for violence, and considerest the lightest insult as a sufficient cause for the spilling of blood, nay, the taking of life. — But, leaving these points of controversy to a more fit season, let us see what our basket of provision contains; for in truth, friend Latimer, I am one of those whom neither fear nor anxiety deprive of their ordinary appetite."

We found the means of good cheer accordingly, which Mr. Geddes seemed to enjoy as much as if it had been eaten in a situation of perfect safety; nay, his conversation appeared to be rather more gay than on ordinary occasions. After eating our supper, we left the hut together, and walked for a few minutes on the banks of the sea. It was high water, and the ebb had not yet commenced. The moon shone broad and bright upon the placid face of the Solway Firth, and showed a slight ripple upon the stakes, the tops of which were just visible above the waves, and on the dark-coloured buoys which marked the upper edge of the enclosure of nets. At a much greater distance, — for the estuary is here very wide, — the line of the English coast was seen on the verge of the water, resembling one of those fog-banks on which mariners are said to gaze, uncertain whether it be land or atmospherical delusion.

"We shall be undisturbed for some hours," said Mr. Geddes; "they will not come down upon us till the state of the tide permits them to destroy the tide nets. Is it not strange to think that human passions will so soon transform such a tranquil scene as this, into one of devastation and confusion ?"

It was indeed a scene of exquisite stillness; so much so, that the restless waves of the Solway seemed, if not absolutely to sleep, at least to slumber; — on the shore no night-bird was heard — the cock had not sung his first matins, and we ourselves walked more lightly than by day, as if to suit the sounds of our own paces to the serene tranquillity around us. At length, the plaintive cry of a dog broke the silence, and on our return to the cottage, we found that the younger of the three animals which had gone along with John Davies, unaccustomed, perhaps, to distant journeys, and the duty of following to heel, had strayed from the party, and unable to rejoin them, had wandered back to the place of its birth.

"Another feeble addition to our feeble garrison," said Mr. Geddes, as he caressed the dog, and admitted it into the cottage. "Poor thing! as thou art incapable of doing any mischief, I hope thou wilt sustain none. At least thou mayst do us the good service of a sentinel, and permit us to enjoy a quiet repose, under the certainty that thou wilt alarm us when the enemy is at hand."

There were two beds in the superintendent's room, upon which we threw ourselves. Mr. Geddes, with his happy equanimity of temper, was asleep in the first five minutes. I lay for some time in doubtful and anxious thought, watching the fire and the motions of the restless dog, which, disturbed probably at the absence of John Davies, wandered from the hearth to the door and back again, then came to the bedside and licked my hands and face, and at length, experiencing no repulse to its advances, established itself at my feet, and went to sleep, an example which I soon afterwards followed.

The rage of narration, my dear Alan—for I will never relinquish the hope that what I am writing may one day reach your hands — has not forsaken me, even in my confinement, and the extensive though unimportant details into which I have been hurried, renders it necessary that I commence another sheet. Fortunately, my pigmy characters comprehend a great many words within a small space of paper.

Chapter the Fourth.

DARSIE LATIMER'S JOURNAL, IN CONTINUATION.

THE morning was dawning, and Mr. Geddes and I myself were still sleeping soundly, when the alarm was given by my canine bedfellow, who first growled deeply at intervals, and at length bore more decided testimony to the approach of some enemy. I opened the door of the cottage, and perceived, at the distance of about two hundred yards, a small but close column of men, which I would have taken for a dark hedge, but that I could perceive it was advancing rapidly and in silence.

The dog flew towards them, but instantly ran howling back to me, having probably been chastised by a stick or a stone. Uncertain as to the plan of tactics or of treaty which Mr. Geddes might think proper to adopt, I was about to retire into the cottage, when he suddenly joined me at the door, and slipping his arm through mine, said, "Let us go to meet them manfully; we have done nothing to be ashamed of. Friends," he said, raising his voice as we approached them, "who and what are you, and with what purpose are you here on my property ?"

A loud cheer was the answer returned, and a brace of fiddlers who occupied the front of the march immediately struck up the insulting air, the words of which begin,

> "Merrily danced the Quaker's wife,
> And merrily danced the Quaker."

Even at that moment of alarm, I think I recognized the tones of the blind fiddler, Will, known by the name of Wandering Willie, from his itinerant habits. They continued to advance swiftly and in great order in their front

> "The fiery fiddlers playing martial airs;"

when, coming close up, they surrounded us by a single movement, and there was a universal cry, "Whoop, Quaker! whoop, Quaker!—Here have we them both, the wet Quaker and the dry one."

"Hang up the wet Quaker to dry, and wet the dry one with a ducking," answered another voice.

"Where is the sea-otter, John Davies, that destroyed more fish than any sealch upon Ailsay Craig?" exclaimed a third voice. "I have an old crow to pluck with him, and a pock to put the feathers in."

We stood perfectly passive; for, to have attempted resistance against more than a hundred men, armed with guns, fish-spears, iron-crows, spades, and bludgeons, would have been an act of utter insanity. Mr. Geddes, with his strong sonorous voice, answered the question about the superintendent in a manner, the manly indifference of which compelled them to attend to him.

"John Davies," he said, "will, I trust, soon be at Dumfries——"

"To fetch down redcoats and dragoons against us, you canting old villain!"

A blow was, at the same time, levelled at my friend, which I parried by interposing the stick I had in my hand. I was instantly struck down, and have a faint recollection of hearing some crying, "Kill the young spy!" and others, as I thought, interposing on my behalf. But a second blow on the head, received in the scuffle, soon deprived me of sense and consciousness, and threw me into a state of insensibility, from which I did not recover immediately. When I did come to myself, I was lying on the bed from which I had just risen before the fray, and my poor companion, the Newfoundland puppy, its courage entirely cowed by the tumult of the riot, had crept as close to me as it could, and lay trembling and whining, as if under the most dreadful terror. I doubted at first whether I had not dreamed of the tumult, until, as I attempted to rise, a feeling of pain and dizziness assured me that the injury I had sustained was but too real. I gathered together my senses — listened — and heard at a distance the shouts of the rioters, busy, doubtless, in their work of devastation. I made a second effort to rise, or at least to turn myself, for I lay with my face to the wall of the cottage, but I found that my limbs were secured, and my motions effectually prevented — not indeed by cords, but by linen or cloth bandages swathed around my ankles, and securing my arms to my sides. Aware of my utterly captive condition, I groaned betwixt bodily pain and mental distress.

A voice by my bedside whispered, in a whining tone, "Whist a-ye, hinnie — whisht a-ye; haud your tongue, like a gude bairn—ye have cost us dear aneugh already. My hinnie's clean gane now."

Knowing, as I thought, the phraseology of the wife of the itinerant musician, I asked her where her husband was, and whether he had been hurt.

"Broken," answered the dame, "all broken to pieces; fit for nought but to be made spunks of — the best blood that was in Scotland."

"Broken? — blood? — is your husband wounded; has there been bloodshed — broken limbs?"

L

"Broken limbs — I wish," answered the beldam, "that my hinnie had broken the best bane in his body, before he had broken his fiddle, that was the best blood in Scotland — it was a cremony, for aught that I ken."

"Pshaw — only his fiddle?" said I.

"I dinna ken what waur your honour could have wished him to do, unless he had broken his neck; and that is muckle the same to my hinnie Willie, and me. Chaw, indeed! It is easy to say *chaw*, but wha is to gie us ony thing to chaw? — the bread-winner's gane, and we may e'en sit down and starve."

"No, no," I said, "I will pay you for twenty such fiddles."

"Twenty such! is that a' ye ken about it? the country hadna the like o't. But if your honour were to pay us, as nae doubt wad be to your credit here and hereafter, where are ye to get the siller?"

"I have enough of money," said I, attempting to reach my hand towards my side-pocket; "unloose these bandages, and I will pay you on the spot."

This hint appeared to move her, and she was approaching the bedside, as I hoped, to liberate me from my bonds, when a nearer and more desperate shout was heard, as if the rioters were close by the hut.

"I daurna — I daurna," said the poor woman, "they would murder me and my hinnie Willie baith, and they have misguided us eneugh already;— but if there is any thing worldly I could do for your honour, leave out loosing ye?"

What she said recalled me to my bodily suffering. Agitation, and the effects of the usage I had received, had produced a burning thirst. I asked for a drink of water.

"Heaven Almighty forbid that Epps Ainslie should gie ony sick gentleman cauld well-water, and him in a fever. Na, na, hinnie, let me alane, I'll do better for ye than the like of that."

"Give me what you will," I replied; "let it but be liquid and cool."

The woman gave me a large horn accordingly, filled with spirits and water, which, without minute inquiry concerning the nature of its contents, I drained at a draught. Either the spirits taken in such a manner, acted more suddenly than usual on my brain, or else there was some drug mixed with the beverage. I remember little after drinking it off, only that the appearance of things around me became indistinct; that the woman's form seemed to multiply itself, and to flit in various figures around me, bearing the same lineaments as she herself did. I remember also that the discordant noises and cries of those without the cottage, seemed to die away in a hum like that with which a nurse hushes her babe. At length I fell into a deep sound sleep, or rather, a state of absolute insensibility.

I have reason to think this species of trance lasted for many hours; indeed, for the whole subsequent day and part of the night. It was not uniformly so profound, for my recollection of it is chequered with many dreams, all of a painful nature, but too faint and too indistinct to be remembered. At length the moment of waking came, and my sensations were horrible.

A deep sound, which, in the confusion of my senses, I identified with the cries of the rioters, was the first thing of which I was sensible; next, I became conscious that I was carried violently forward in some conveyance, with an unequal motion, which gave me much pain. My position was horizontal, and when I attempted to stretch my hands in order to find some mode of securing myself against this species of suffering, I found I was bound as before, and the horrible reality rushed on my mind, that I was in the hands of those who had lately committed a great outrage on property, and were now about to kidnap, if not to murder me. I opened my eyes, it was to no purpose — all around me was dark, for a day had passed over during my captivity. A dispiriting sickness oppressed my head—my heart seemed on fire, while my feet and hands were chilled and benumbed with want of circulation. It was with the utmost difficulty that I at length, and gradually, recovered in a sufficient degree the power of observing external sounds and circumstances; and when I did so, they presented nothing consolatory.

Groping with my hands, as far as the bandages would permit, and receiving the assistance of some occasional glances of the moonlight, I became aware that the carriage in which I was transported was one of the light carts of the country, called *tumblers*, and that a little attention had been paid to my accommodation, as I was laid upon some sacks covered with matting, and filled with straw. Without these, my condition would have been still more intolerable, for the vehicle, sinking now on one side, and now on the other, sometimes sticking absolutely fast, and requiring the utmost exertions of the animal which drew it to put it once more in motion, was subjected to jolts in all directions, which were very severe. At other times it rolled silently and smoothly over what seemed to be wet sand; and, as I heard the distant roar of the tide, I had little doubt that we were engaged in passing the formidable estuary which divides the two kingdoms.

There seemed to be at least five or six people about the cart, some on foot, others on horseback; the former lent assistance whenever it was in danger of upsetting, or sticking fast in the quicksand; the others rode before and acted as guides, often changing the direction of the vehicle as the precarious state of the passage required.

I addressed myself to the men around the cart, and endeavoured to move their compassion. I had harmed, I said, no one, and for no action in my life had deserved such cruel treatment. I had no concern whatever in the fishing station which had incurred their displeasure, and my acquaintance with Mr. Geddes was of a very late date. Lastly, and as my strongest argument, I endeavoured to excite their fears, by informing them that my rank in life would not permit me to be either murdered or secreted with impunity; and to interest their avarice, by the promises I made them of reward, if they would effect my deliverance. I only received a scornful laugh in reply to my threats; my promises might have done more, for the fellows were whispering together as if in hesitation, and I began to reiterate and increase my offers, when the voice of one of the horsemen, who had suddenly come up, enjoined silence to the men on foot, and, approaching the side of the cart, said to me, with a strong and determined voice, "Young man, there is no personal harm designed to you. If you remain silent and quiet, you may reckon on good treatment; but if you endeavour to tamper with these men in the execution of their duty, I will take such measures for silencing you, as you shall remember the longest day you have to live."

I thought I knew the voice which uttered these threats; but, in such a situation, my perceptions could not be supposed to be perfectly accurate. I was contented to reply, "Whoever you are that speak to me, I entreat the benefit of the meanest prisoner, who is not to be subjected legally to greater hardship than is necessary for the restraint of his person. I entreat that these bonds, which hurt me so cruelly, may be slackened at least, if not removed altogether."

"I will slacken the belts," said the former speaker; "nay, I will altogether remove them, and allow you to pursue your journey in a more convenient manner, provided you will give me your word of honour that you will not attempt an escape?"

"*Never!*" I answered, with an energy of which despair alone could have rendered me capable — "I will *never* submit to loss of freedom a moment longer than I am subjected to it by force."

"Enough," he replied; "the sentiment is natural; but do not on your side complain that I, who am carrying on an important undertaking, use the only means in my power for ensuring its success."

I entreated to know what it was designed to do with me; but my conductor, in a voice of menacing authority, desired me to be silent on my peril; and my strength and spirits were too much exhausted to permit my continuing a dialogue so singular, even if I could have promised myself any good result by doing so.

It is proper here to add, that, from my recollections at the time, and from what has since taken place, I have the strongest possible belief that the man with whom I held this expostulation, was the singular person residing at Brokenburn, in Dumfries-shire, and called by the fishers of that hamlet, the Laird of the Solway Lochs. The cause for his inveterate persecution I can not pretend even to guess at.

In the meantime, the cart was dragged heavily and wearily on, until the nearer roar of the advancing tide excited the apprehension of another danger. I could not mistake the sound, which I had heard upon another occasion, when it was only the speed of a fleet horse which saved me from perishing in the quicksands. Thou, my dear Alan, canst not but remember the former circumstances; and now, wonderful contrast! the very man, to the best of my belief, who then saved me from peril, was the leader of the lawless band who had deprived me of my liberty. I conjectured that the danger grew imminent; for I heard some words and circumstances which made me aware that a rider hastily fastened his own horse to the shafts of the cart, in order to assist the exhausted animal which drew it, and the vehicle was now pulled forward at a faster pace, which the horses were urged to maintain by blows and curses. The men, however, were inhabitants of the neighbourhood; and I had strong personal reason to believe, that one of them, at least, was intimately acquainted with all the depths and shallows of the perilous paths in which we were engaged. But they were in imminent danger themselves; and if so, as from the whispering and exertions to push on with the cart, was much to be apprehended, there was little doubt that I should be left behind as a useless encumbrance, and that while I was in a condition which rendered every chance of escape impracticable. These were awful apprehensions; but it pleased Providence to increase them to a point which my brain was scarcely able to endure.

As we approached very near to a black line, which, dimly visible as it was, I could make out to be the shore, we heard two or three sounds, which appeared to be the report of fire-arms. Immediately all was bustle among our party to get forward. Presently a fellow galloped up to us, crying out, " Ware hawk! ware hawk! the land-sharks are out from Burgh, and Allonby Tom will lose his cargo if you do not bear a hand."

Most of my company seemed to make hastily for the shore on receiving this intelligence. A driver was left with the cart; but at length, when, after repeated and hair-breadth escapes, it actually stuck fast in a slough or quicksand, the fellow, with an oath, cut the harness, and, as I presume, departed with the horses, whose feet I heard splashing over the wet sand, and through the shallows, as he galloped off.

The dropping sound of fire-arms was still continued, but lost almost entirely in the thunder of the advancing surge. By a desperate effort I raised myself in the cart, and attained a sitting posture, which served only to show me the extent of my danger. There lay my native land—my own England —the land where I was born, and to which my wishes, since my earliest age, had turned with all the prejudices of national feeling — there it lay, within a furlong of the place where I yet was; that furlong, which an infant would have raced over in a minute, was yet a barrier effectual to divide me for ever from England and from life. I soon not only heard the roar of this dreadful torrent, but saw, by the fitful moonlight, the foamy crests of the devouring waves, as they advanced with the speed and fury of a pack of hungry wolves.

The consciousness that the slightest ray of hope, or power of struggling, was not left me, quite overcame the constancy which I had hitherto main tained. My eyes began to swim—my head grew giddy and mad with fear—I chattered and howled to the howling and roaring sea. One or two great waves had already reached the cart, when the conductor of the party whom I have mentioned so often, was, as if by magic, at my side. He sprang from his horse into the vehicle, cut the ligatures which restrained me, and bade me get up and mount in the fiend's name.

Seeing I was incapable of obeying, he seized me, as if I had been a child of six months old, threw me across the horse, sprung on behind, supporting me with one hand, while he directed the animal with the other. In my helpless and painful posture, I was unconscious of the degree of danger which we incurred; but I believe at one time the horse was swimming, or nearly so; and that it was with difficulty that my stern and powerful assistant kept my head above water. I remember particularly the shock which I felt when the animal, endeavouring to gain the bank, reared, and very nearly fell back on his burden. The time during which I continued in this dreadful condition did not probably exceed two or three minutes, yet so strongly were they marked with horror and agony, that they seem to my recollection a much more considerable space of time.

When I had been thus snatched from destruction, I had only power to say to my protector,—or oppressor,—for he merited either name at my hand, "You do not, then, design to murder me?"

He laughed as he replied, but it was a sort of laughter which I scarce desire to hear again,—"Else you think I had let the waves do the work? But remember, the shepherd saves his sheep from the torrent — is it to preserve its life? — Be silent, however, with questions or entreaties. What I mean to do, thou canst no more discover or prevent, than a man, with his bare palm, can scoop dry the Solway."

I was too much exhausted to continue the argument; and, still numbed and torpid in all my limbs, permitted myself without reluctance to be placed on a horse brought for the purpose. My formidable conductor rode on the one side, and another person on the other, keeping me upright in the saddle. In this manner we travelled forward at a considerable rate, and by by-roads, with which my attendant seemed as familiar as with the perilous passages of the Solway.

At length, after stumbling through a labyrinth of dark and deep lanes, and crossing more than one rough and barren heath, we found ourselves on the edge of a high-road, where a chaise and four awaited, as it appeared, our arrival. To my great relief, we now changed our mode of conveyance; for my dizziness and headach had returned in so strong a degree, that I should otherwise have been totally unable to keep my seat on horseback, even with the support which I received.

My doubted and dangerous companion signed to me to enter the carriage —the man who had ridden on the left side of my horse stepped in after me, and drawing up the blinds of the vehicle, gave the signal for instant departure.

I had obtained a glimpse of the countenance of my new companion, as by the aid of a dark lantern the driver opened the carriage door, and I was well-nigh persuaded that I recognized in him the domestic of the leader of this party, whom I had seen at his house in Brokenburn on a former occasion. To ascertain the truth of my suspicion, I asked him whether his name was not Cristal Nixon.

"What is other folk's names to you," he replied, gruffly, "who cannot tell your own father and mother?"

"You know them, perhaps!" I exclaimed eagerly. "You know them! and with that secret is connected the treatment which I am now receiving? It must be so, for in all my life have I never injured any one. Tell me the cause of my misfortunes, or rather, help me to my liberty, and I will reward you richly."

"Ay, ay," replied my keeper; "but what use to give you liberty, who know nothing how to use it like a gentleman, but spend your time with Quakers and fiddlers, and such like raff! If I was your—hem, hem, hem!"

Here Cristal stopped short, just on the point, as it appeared, when some information was likely to escape him. I urged him once more to be my friend, and promised him all the stock of money which I had about me, and it was not inconsiderable, if he would assist in my escape.

He listened, as if to a proposition which had some interest, and replied, but in a voice rather softer than before, "Ay, but men do not catch old birds with chaff, my master. Where have you got the rhino you are so flush of?"

"I will give you earnest directly, and that in bank-notes," said I; but thrusting my hand into my side-pocket, I found my pocket-book was gone. I would have persuaded myself that it was only the numbness of my hands which prevented my finding it; but Cristal Nixon, who bears in his countenance that cynicism which is especially entertained with human misery, no longer suppressed his laughter.

"Oh, ho! my young master," he said; "we have taken good enough care you have not kept the means of bribing poor folk's fidelity. What, man, they have souls as well as other people, and to make them break trust is a deadly sin. And as for me, young gentleman, if you would fill Saint Mary's Kirk with gold, Cristal Nixon would mind it no more than so many chucky-stones."

I would have persisted, were it but in hopes of his letting drop that which it concerned me to know, but he cut off farther communication, by desiring me to lean back in the corner and go to sleep.

"Thou art cock-brained enough already," he added, "and we shall have thy young pate addled entirely, if you do not take some natural rest."

I did indeed require repose, if not slumber; the draught which I had taken continued to operate, and satisfied in my own mind that no attempt on my life was designed, the fear of instant death no longer combated the torpor which crept over me—I slept, and slept soundly, but still without refreshment.

When I awoke, I found myself extremely indisposed; images of the past, and anticipations of the future, floated confusedly through my brain. I perceived, however, that my situation was changed, greatly for the better. I was in a good bed, with the curtains drawn round it; I heard the lowered voice, and cautious step of attendants, who seemed to respect my repose; it appeared as if I was in the hands either of friends, or of such as meant me no personal harm.

I can give but an indistinct account of two or three broken and feverish days which succeeded, but if they were chequered with dreams and visions of terror, other and more agreeable objects were also sometimes presented. Alan Fairford will understand me when I say, I am convinced I saw G. M. during this interval of oblivion. I had medical attendance, and was bled more than once. I also remember a painful operation performed on my head, where I had received a severe blow on the night of the riot. My hair was cut short, and the bone of the skull examined, to discover if the cranium had received any injury.

On seeing the physician, it would have been natural to have appealed to him on the subject of my confinement, and I remember more than once attempting to do so. But the fever lay like a spell upon my tongue, and when I would have implored the doctor's assistance, I rambled from the subject, and spoke I know not what nonsense. Some power, which I was unable to resist, seemed to impel me into a different course of conversation from what I intended, and though conscious, in some degree, of the failure,

I could not mend it; and resolved, therefore, to be patient, until my capacity of steady thought and expression was restored to me with my ordinary health, which had sustained a severe shock from the vicissitudes to which I had been exposed.*

Chapter the Fifth.

DARSIE LATIMER'S JOURNAL, IN CONTINUATION.

Two or three days, perhaps more, perhaps less, had been spent in bed, where I was carefully attended, and treated, I believe, with as much judgment as the case required, and I was at length allowed to quit my bed, though not the chamber. I was now more able to make some observation on the place of my confinement.

The room, in appearance and furniture, resembled the best apartment in a farmer's house; and the window, two stories high, looked into a backyard, or court, filled with domestic poultry. There were the usual domestic offices about this yard. I could distinguish the brewhouse and the barn, and I heard, from a more remote building, the lowing of the cattle, and other rural sounds, announcing a large and well-stocked farm. These were sights and sounds qualified to dispel any apprehension of immediate violence. Yet the building seemed ancient and strong, a part of the roof was battlemented, and the walls were of great thickness; lastly, I observed, with some unpleasant sensations, that the windows of my chamber had been lately secured with iron stanchions, and that the servants who brought me victuals, or visited my apartment to render other menial offices, always looked the door when they retired.

The comfort and cleanliness of my chamber were of true English growth, and such as I had rarely seen on the other side of the Tweed; the very old wainscot, which composed the floor and the panelling of the room, was scrubbed with a degree of labour which the Scottish housewife rarely bestows on her most costly furniture.

The whole apartments appropriated to my use consisted of the bedroom, a small parlour adjacent, within which was a still smaller closet, having a narrow window, which seemed anciently to have been used as a shot-hole, admitting, indeed, a very moderate portion of light and air, but without its being possible to see any thing from it except the blue sky, and that only by mounting on a chair. There were appearances of a separate entrance into this cabinet, besides that which communicated with the parlour, but it had been recently built up, as I discovered, by removing a piece of tapestry which covered the fresh mason-work. I found some of my clothes here, with linen and other articles, as well as my writing-case, containing pen, ink, and paper, which enables me, at my leisure, (which, God knows, is

* It may be here mentioned, that a violent and popular attack upon what the country people of this district considered as an invasion of their fishing right, is by no means an improbable fiction. Shortly after the close of the American war, Sir James Graham of Netherby constructed a dam-dike, or cauld, across the Esk, at a place where it flowed through his estate, though it has its origin, and the principal part of its course, in Scotland. The new barrier at Netherby was considered as an encroachment calculated to prevent the salmon from ascending into Scotland; and the right of erecting it being an international question of law betwixt the sister kingdoms, there was no court in either competent to its decision. In this dilemma, the Scots people assembled in numbers by signal of rocket lights, and, rudely armed with fowling-pieces, fish-spears, and such rustic weapons, marched to the banks of the river for the purpose of pulling down the dam-dike objected to. Sir James Graham armed many of his own people to protect his property, and had some military from Carlisle for the same purpose. A renewal of the Border wars had nearly taken place in the eighteenth century, when prudence and moderation on both sides saved much tumult, and perhaps some bloodshed. The English proprietor consented that a breach should be made in his dam-dike sufficient for the passage of the fish, and thus removed the Scottish grievance. I believe the river has since that time taken the matter into its own disposal, and entirely swept away the dam-dike in question.

undisturbed enough,) to make this record of my confinement. It may be well believed, however, that I do not trust to the security of the bureau, but carry the written sheets about my person, so that I can only be deprived of them by actual violence. I also am cautious to write in the little cabinet only, so that I can hear any person approach me through the other apartments, and have time enough to put aside my journal before they come upon me.

The servants, a stout country-fellow, and a very pretty milkmaid-looking lass, by whom I am attended, seem of the true Joan and Hodge school, thinking of little, and desiring nothing, beyond the very limited sphere of their own duties or enjoyments, and having no curiosity whatever about the affairs of others. Their behaviour to me in particular, is, at the same time, very kind and very provoking. My table is abundantly supplied, and they seem anxious to comply with my taste in that department. But whenever I make inquiries beyond "what's for dinner," the brute of a lad baffles me by his *anan*, and his *dunna knaw*, and, if hard pressed, turns his back on me composedly, and leaves the room. The girl, too, pretends to be as simple as he; but an arch grin, which she cannot always suppress, seems to acknowledge that she understands perfectly well the game which she is playing, and is determined to keep me in ignorance. Both of them, and the wench in particular, treat me as they would do a spoiled child, and never directly refuse me any thing which I ask, taking care, at the same time, not to make their words good by effectually granting my request. Thus, if I desire to go out, I am promised by Dorcas that I shall walk in the park at night, and see the cows milked, just as she would propose such an amusement to a child. But she takes care never to keep her word, if it is in her power to do so.

In the meantime there has stolen on me insensibly an indifference to my freedom — a carelessness about my situation, for which I am unable to account, unless it be the consequence of weakness and loss of blood. I have read of men who, immured as I am, have surprised the world by the address with which they have successfully overcome the most formidable obstacles to their escape; and when I have heard such anecdotes, I have said to myself, that no one who is possessed only of a fragment of freestone, or a rusty nail, to grind down rivets and to pick locks, having his full leisure to employ in the task, need continue the inhabitant of a prison. Here, however, I sit, day after day, without a single effort to effect my liberation.

Yet my inactivity is not the result of despondency, but arises, in part at least, from feelings of a very different cast. My story, long a mysterious one, seems now upon the verge of some strange development; and I feel a solemn impression that I ought to wait the course of events, to struggle against which is opposing my feeble efforts to the high will of fate. Thou, my Alan, will treat as timidity this passive acquiescence, which has sunk down on me like a benumbing torpor; but if thou hast remembered by what visions my couch was haunted, and dost but think of the probability that I am in the vicinity, perhaps under the same roof with G. M., thou wilt acknowledge that other feelings than pusillanimity have tended in some degree to reconcile me to my fate.

Still I own it is unmanly to submit with patience to this oppressive confinement. My heart rises against it, especially when I sit down to record my sufferings in this Journal; and I am determined, as the first step to my deliverance, to have my letters sent to the post-house.

I am disappointed. When the girl Dorcas, upon whom I had fixed for a messenger, heard me talk of sending a letter, she willingly offered her services, and received the crown which I gave her, (for my purse had not taken flight with the more valuable contents of my pocket-book,) with a smile which showed her whole set of white teeth.

But when, with the purpose of gaining some intelligence respecting my present place of abode, I asked to which post-town she was to send or carry the letter, a stolid "*Anan*" showed me she was either ignorant of the nature of a post-office, or that, for the present, she chose to seem so.— "Simpleton!" I said, with some sharpness.

"O Lord, sir!" answered the girl, turning pale, which they always do when I show any sparks of anger,—"Don't put yourself in a passion—I'll put the letter in the post."

"What! and not know the name of the post-town?" said I, out of patience. "How on earth do you propose to manage that?"

"La you there, good master. What need you frighten a poor girl that is no schollard, bating what she learned at the Charity-School of Saint Bees?"

"Is Saint Bees far from this place, Dorcas?—Do you send your letters there?" said I, in a manner as insinuating, and yet careless, as I could assume.

"Saint Bees!—La, who but a madman—begging your honour's pardon—it's a matter of twenty years since fader lived at Saint Bees, which is twenty, or forty, or I dunna know not how many miles from this part, to the West, on the coast side; and I would not have left Saint Bees, but that fader——"

"Oh, the devil take your father!" replied I.

To which she answered, "Nay, but thof your honour be a little how-come-so, you should't damn folk's faders; and I won't stand to it, for one."

. "Oh, I beg you a thousand pardons—I wish your father no ill in the world — he was a very honest man in his way."

"*Was* an honest man!" she exclaimed; for the Cumbrians are, it would seem, like their neighbours the Scotch, ticklish on the point of ancestry, — "He *is* a very honest man as ever led nag with halter on head to Staneshaw-Bank Fair — Honest! — He is a horse-couper."

"Right, right," I replied; "I know it—I have heard of your father—as honest as any horse-couper of them all. Why, Dorcas, I mean to buy a horse of him."

"Ah, your honour," sighed Dorcas, "he is the man to serve your honour well — if ever you should get round again — or thof you were a bit off the hooks, he would no more cheat you than ——"

"Well, well, we will deal, my girl, you may depend on't. But tell me now, were I to give you a letter, what would you do to get it forward?"

"Why, put it into Squire's own bag that hangs in hall," answered poor Dorcas. "What else could I do? He sends it to Brampton, or to Carloisle, or where it pleases him, once a week, and that gate."

"Ah!" said I; "and I suppose your sweetheart John carries it?"

"Noa,—disn't now — and Jan is no sweetheart of mine, ever since he danced at his mother's feast with Kitty Rutlege, and let me sit still; that a did."

"It was most abominable in Jan, and what I could never have thought of him," I replied.

"Oh, but a did though — a let me sit still on my seat, a did."

"Well, well, my pretty May, you will get a handsomer fellow than Jan — Jan's not the fellow for you, I see that."

"Noa, noa," answered the damsel; "but he's weel aneugh for a' that, mon. But I carena a button for him; for there is the miller's son, that suitored me last Appleby Fair, when I went wi' oncle, is a gway canny lad as you will see in the sunshine."

"Ay, a fine stout fellow — Do you think he would carry my letter to Carlisle?"

. "To Carloisle! 'Twould be all his life is worth; he maun wait on clap and hopper, as they say. Odd, his father would brain him if he went to

Carloisle, hating to wrestling for the belt, or sic loike. But I ha' more bachelors than him; there is the schoolmaster, can write almaist as weel as tou canst, mon."

"Then he is the very man to take charge of a letter; he knows the trouble of writing one."

"Ay, marry does he, an tou comest to that, mon; only it takes him four hours to write as mony lines. Tan, it is a great round hand loike, that one can read easily, and not loike your honour's, that are like madge's taes. But for ganging to Carloisle, he's dead foundered, man, as cripple as Eckie's mear."

"In the name of God," said I, "how is it that you propose to get my letter to the post?"

"Why, just to put it into Squire's bag loike." reiterated Dorcas; "he sends it by Cristal Nixon to poat, as you call it, when such is his pleasure."

Here I was, then, not much edified by having obtained a list of Dorcas's bachelors; and by finding myself, with respect to any information which I desired, just exactly at the point where I set out. It was of consequence to me, however, to accustom the girl to converse with me familiarly. If she did so, she could not always be on her guard, and something, I thought, might drop from her which I could turn to advantage.

"Does not the Squire usually look into his letter-bag, Dorcas?" said I, with as much indifference as I could assume.

"That a does," said Dorcas; "and a threw out a letter of mine to Raff Miller, because a said——"

"Well, well, I won't trouble him with mine," said I, "Dorcas; but, instead, I will write to himself, Dorcas. But how shall I address him?"

"Anan?" was again Dorcas's resource.

"I mean how is he called?—What is his name?"

"Sure your honour should know best," said Dorcas.

"I know?—The devil!—You drive me beyond patience."

"Noa, noa! donna your honour go beyond patience—donna ye now," implored the wench. "And for his neame, they say he has mair nor ane in Westmoreland and on the Scottish side. But he is but seldom wi' us, excepting in the cocking season; and then we just call him Squire loike; and so do my measter and dame."

"And is he here at present?" said I.

"Not he, not he; he is a buck-hoonting, as they tell me, somewhere up the Patterdale way; but he comes and gangs like a flap of a whirlwind, or sic loike."

I broke off the conversation, after forcing on Dorcas a little silver to buy ribbons, with which she was so much delighted, that she exclaimed, "God! Cristal Nixon may say his worst on thee; but thou art a civil gentleman for all him; and a quoit man wi' woman folk loike."

There is no sense in being too quiet with women folk, so I added a kiss with my crown piece; and I cannot help thinking that I have secured a partisan in Dorcas. At least, she blushed, and pocketed her little compliment with one hand, while, with the other, she adjusted her cherry-coloured ribbons, a little disordered by the struggle it cost me to attain the honour of a salute.

As she unlocked the door to leave the apartment, she turned back, and looking on me with a strong expression of compassion, added the remarkable words, "La—be'st mad or no, thou'se a mettled lad, after all."

There was something very ominous in the sound of these farewell words, which seemed to afford me a clew to the pretext under which I was detained in confinement. My demeanour was probably insane enough, while I was agitated at once by the frenzy incident to the fever, and the anxiety arising from my extraordinary situation. But is it possible they can now establish any cause for confining me arising out of the state of my mind?

If this be really the pretext under which I am restrained from my liberty, nothing but the sedate correctness of my conduct can remove the prejudices which these circumstances may have excited in the minds of all who have approached me during my illness. I have heard—dreadful thought!—of men who, for various reasons, have been trepanned into the custody of the keepers of private madhouses, and whose brain, after years of misery, became at length unsettled, through irresistible sympathy with the wretched beings among whom they were classed. This shall not be my case, if, by strong internal resolution, it is in human nature to avoid the action of exterior and contagious sympathies.

Meantime I sat down to compose and arrange my thoughts, for my purposed appeal to my jailer—so I must call him—whom I addressed in the following manner; having at length, and after making several copies, found language to qualify the sense of resentment which burned in the first draughts of my letter, and endeavoured to assume a tone more conciliating. I mentioned the two occasions on which he had certainly saved my life, when at the utmost peril; and I added, that whatever was the purpose of the restraint now practised on me, as I was given to understand, by his authority, it could not certainly be with any view to ultimately injuring me. He might, I said, have mistaken me for some other person; and I gave him what account I could of my situation and education, to correct such an error. I supposed it next possible, that he might think me too weak for travelling, and not capable of taking care of myself; and I begged to assure him, that I was restored to perfect health, and quite able to endure the fatigue of a journey. Lastly, I reminded him, in firm though measured terms, that the restraint which I sustained was an illegal one, and highly punishable by the laws which protect the liberties of the subject. I ended by demanding, that he would take me before a magistrate; or, at least, that he would favour me with a personal interview, and explain his meaning with regard to me.

Perhaps this letter was expressed in a tone too humble for the situation of an injured man, and I am inclined to think so when I again recapitulate its tenor. But what could I do? I was in the power of one whose passions seem as violent as his means of gratifying them appeared unbounded. I had reason, too, to believe [this to thee, Alan] that all his family did not approve of the violence of his conduct towards me; my object, in fine, was freedom, and who would not sacrifice much to attain it?

I had no means of addressing my letter excepting, "For the Squire's own hand." He could be at no great distance, for in the course of twenty-four hours I received an answer. It was addressed to Darsie Latimer, and contained these words:—"You have demanded an interview with me. You have required to be carried before a magistrate. Your first wish shall be granted—perhaps the second also. Meanwhile, be assured that you are a prisoner for the time, by competent authority, and that such authority is supported by adequate power. Beware, therefore, of struggling with a force sufficient to crush you, but abandon yourself to that train of events by which we are both swept along, and which it is impossible that either of us can resist."

These mysterious words were without signature of any kind, and left me nothing more important to do than to prepare myself for the meeting which they promised. For that purpose I must now break off, and make sure of the manuscript,—so far as I can, in my present condition, be sure of any thing,—by concealing it within the lining of my coat, so as not to be found without strict search.

Chapter the Sixth.

LATIMER'S JOURNAL, IN CONTINUATION.

THE important interview expected at the conclusion of my last took place sooner than I had calculated; for the very day I received the letter, and just when my dinner was finished, the Squire, or whatever he is called, entered the room so suddenly, that I almost thought I beheld an apparition. The figure of this man is peculiarly noble and stately, and his voice has that deep fulness of accent which implies unresisted authority. I had risen involuntarily as he entered; we gazed on each other for a moment in silence, which was at length broken by my visiter.

"You have desired to see me," he said. "I am here; if you have aught to say, let me hear it; my time is too brief to be consumed in childish dumbshows."

"I would ask of you," said I, "by what authority I am detained in this place of confinement, and for what purpose?"

"I have told you already," said he, "that my authority is sufficient, and my power equal to it; this is all which it is necessary for you at present to know."

"Every British subject has a right to know why he suffers restraint," I replied; "nor can he be deprived of liberty without a legal warrant.— Show me that by which you confine me thus."

"You shall see more," he said; "you shall see the magistrate by whom it is granted, and that without a moment's delay."

This sudden proposal fluttered and alarmed me; I felt, nevertheless, that I had the right cause, and resolved to plead it boldly, although I could well have desired a little farther time for preparation. He turned, however, threw open the door of the apartment, and commanded me to follow him. I felt some inclination, when I crossed the threshold of my prison-chamber, to have turned and run for it; but I knew not where to find the stairs—had reason to think the outer-doors would be secured—and, to conclude, so soon as I had quitted the room to follow the proud step of my conductor, I observed that I was dogged by Cristal Nixon, who suddenly appeared within two paces of me, and with whose great personal strength, independent of the assistance he might have received from his master, I saw no chance of contending. I therefore followed, unresistingly, and in silence, along one or two passages of much greater length than consisted with the ideas I had previously entertained of the size of the house. At length a door was flung open, and we entered a large, old-fashioned parlour, having coloured glass in the windows, oaken panelling on the wall, a huge grate, in which a large fagot or two smoked under an arched chimney-piece of stone, which bore some armorial device, whilst the walls were adorned with the usual number of heroes in armour, with large wigs instead of helmets, and ladies in sacques, smelling to nosegays.

Behind a long table, on which were several books, sat a smart underbred-looking man, wearing his own hair tied in a club, and who, from the quire of paper laid before him, and the pen which he handled at my entrance, seemed prepared to officiate as clerk. As I wish to describe these persons as accurately as possible, I may add, he wore a dark-coloured coat, corduroy breeches, and spatterdashes. At the upper end of the same table, in an ample easy-chair, covered with black leather, reposed a fat personage, about fifty years old, who either was actually a country justice, or was well selected to represent such a character. His leathern breeches were faultless in make, his jockey boots spotless in the varnish, and a handsome and flourishing pair of boot-garters, as they are called, united the one part of his garments to the other; in fine, a richly-laced scarlet waistcoat, and a purple coat, set off the neat though corpulent figure of the little man, and threw an additional bloom upon his plethoric aspect. I suppose he had dined, for it was two hours past noon, and he was amusing himself, and aiding digestion, with a pipe of tobacco. There was an air of importance in his manner which corresponded to the rural dignity of his exterior, and a habit which he had of throwing out a number of interjectional sounds, uttered with a strange variety of intonation running from bass up to treble in a very extraordinary manner, or breaking off his sentences with a whiff of his pipe, seemed adopted to give an air of thought and mature deliberation to his opinions and decisions. Notwithstanding all this, Alan, it might be *dooted*, as our old Professor used to say, whether the Justice was any thing more than an ass. Certainly, besides a great deference for the legal opinion of his clerk, which might be quite according to the order of things, he seemed to be wonderfully under the command of his brother Squire, if squire either of them were, and indeed much more than was consistent with so much assumed consequence of his own.

"Ho—ha—ay—so—so—Hum—Humph—this is the young man, I suppose—Hum—ay—seems sickly—Young gentleman, you may sit down."

I used the permission given, for I had been much more reduced by my illness than I was aware of, and felt myself really fatigued, even by the few paces I had walked, joined to the agitation I suffered.

"And your name, young man, is—humph—ay—ha—what is it?"

"Darsie Latimer."

"Right—ay—humph—very right. Darsie Latimer is the very thing—ha—ay—where do you come from?"

"From Scotland, sir," I replied.

"A native of Scotland—a—humph—eh—how is it?"

"I am an Englishman by birth, sir."

'Right—ay—yes, you are so. But pray, Mr. Darsie Latimer, have you always been called by that name, or have you any other?—Nick, write down his answers, Nick."

"As far as I remember, I never bore any other," was my answer.

"How, no?—well, I should not have thought so—Hey, neighbour, would you?"

Here he looked towards the other Squire, who had thrown himself into a chair; and, with his legs stretched out before him, and his arms folded on his bosom, seemed carelessly attending to what was going forward. He answered the appeal of the Justice by saying, that perhaps the young man's memory did not go back to a very early period.

"Ah — he — ha — you hear the gentleman — Pray, how far may your memory be pleased to run back to?—umph?"

"Perhaps, sir, to the age of three years, or a little farther."

"And will you presume to say, sir," said the Squire, drawing himself suddenly erect in his seat, and exerting the strength of his powerful voice, "that you *then* bore your present name."

I was startled at the confidence with which this question was put, and in vain rummaged my memory for the means of replying. "At least," I said, "I always remember being called Darsie; children, at that early age, seldom get more than their Christian name?"

"Oh, I thought so," he replied, and again stretched himself on his seat, in the same lounging posture as before.

"So you were called Darsie in your infancy," said the Justice; "and—hum—ay—when did you first take the name of Latimer?"

"I did not take it, sir; it was given to me."

"I ask you," said the lord of the mansion, but with less severity in his voice than formerly, "whether you can remember that you were ever called Latimer, until you had the name given you in Scotland?"

"I will be candid: I cannot recollect an instance that I was so called when in England, but neither can I recollect when the name was first given me; and if any thing is to be founded on these queries and my answers, I desire my early childhood may be taken into consideration."

"Hum—ay—yes," said the justice; "all that requires consideration shall be duly considered. Young man — eh — I beg to know the name of your father and mother?"

This was galling a wound that has festered for years, and I did not endure the question so patiently as those which preceded it; but replied, "I demand, in my turn, to know if I am before an English Justice of the Peace?"

"His worship, Squire Foxley, of Foxley Hall, has been of the quorum these twenty years," said Master Nicholas.

"Then he ought to know, or you, sir, as his clerk, should inform him," said I, "that I am the complainer in this case, and that my complaint ought to be heard before I am subjected to cross-examination."

"Humph—hoy—what, ay—there is something in that, neighbour," said the poor Justice, who, blown about by every wind of doctrine, seemed desirous to attain the sanction of his brother Squire.

"I wonder at you, Foxley," said his firm-minded acquaintance; "how can you render the young man justice unless you know who he is?"

"Ha—yes—egad that's true," said Mr. Justice Foxley; "and now—looking into the matter more closely—there is, eh, upon the whole—nothing at all in what he says — so, sir, you must tell your father's name, and surname."

"It is out of my power, sir; they are not known to me, since you must needs know so much of my private affairs."

The Justice collected a great *afflatus* in his cheeks, which puffed them up like those of a Dutch cherub, while his eyes seemed flying out of his head, from the effort with which he retained his breath. He then blew it forthwith,—"Whew!—Hoom—poof—ha!—not know your parents, youngster?—Then I must commit you for a vagrant, I warrant you. *Omne ignotum pro terribili*, as we used to say at Appleby school; that is, every one that is not known to the Justice, is a rogue and a vagabond. Ha! — ay, you may sneer, sir; but I question if you would have known the meaning of that Latin, unless I had told you."

I acknowledged myself obliged for a new edition of the adage, and an interpretation which I could never have reached alone and unassisted. I then proceeded to state my case with greater confidence. The Justice was an ass, that was clear; but it was scarcely possible he could be so utterly ignorant as not to know what was necessary in so plain a case as mine. I therefore informed him of the riot which had been committed on the Scottish side of the Solway Frith, explained how I came to be placed in my present situation, and requested of his worship to set me at liberty. I pleaded my cause with as much earnestness as I could, casting an eye from time to time upon the opposite party, who seemed entirely indifferent to all the animation with which I accused him.

As for the Justice, when at length I had ceased, as really not knowing what more to say in a case so very plain, he replied, "Ho—ay—ay—yes—wonderful! and so this is all the gratitude you show to this good gentleman for the great charge and trouble he hath with respect to and concerning of you?"

"He saved my life, sir, I acknowledge, on one occasion certainly, and most probably on two; but his having done so gives him no right over my person. I am not, however, asking for any punishment or revenge; on the contrary, I am content to part friends with the gentleman, whose motives

I am unwilling to suppose are bad, though his actions have been, towards me, unauthorized and violent."

This moderation, Alan, thou wilt comprehend, was not entirely dictated by my feelings towards the individual of whom I complained; there were other reasons, in which regard for him had little share. It seemed, however, as if the mildness with which I pleaded my cause had more effect upon him than any thing I had yet said. He was moved to the point of being almost out of countenance; and took snuff repeatedly, as if to gain time to stifle some degree of emotion.

But on Justice Foxley, on whom my eloquence was particularly designed to make impression, the result was much less favourable. He consulted in a whisper with Mr. Nicholas his clerk — pshawed, hemmed, and elevated his eyebrows, as if in scorn of my supplication. At length, having apparently made up his mind, he leaned back in his chair, and smoked his pipe with great energy, with a look of defiance, designed to make me aware that all my reasoning was lost on him.

At length, when I stopped, more from lack of breath than want of argument, he opened his oracular jaws, and made the following reply, interrupted by his usual interjectional ejaculations, and by long volumes of smoke :—" Hem—ay—eh—poof—And, youngster, do you think Matthew Foxley, who has been one of the quorum for these twenty years, is to be come over with such trash as would hardly cheat an apple-woman ?—Poof —poof—eh ! Why, man—eh—dost thou not know the charge is not a bailable matter—and that—hum—ay—the greatest man—poof—the Baron of Graystock himself, must stand committed ? and yet you pretend to have been kidnapped by this gentleman, and robbed of property, and what not; and—eh—poof—you would persuade me all you want is to get away from him ?—I do believe—eh—that it *is* all you want. Therefore, as you are a sort of a slip-string gentleman, and—ay—hum—a kind of idle apprentice, and something cock-brained with all, as the honest folks of the house tell me—why, you must e'en remain under custody of your guardian, till your coming of age, or my Lord Chancellor's warrant, shall give you the management of your own affairs, which, if you can gather your brains again, you will even then not be—ay—hem—poof—in particular haste to assume."

The time occupied by his worship's hums, and haws, and puffs of tobacco smoke, together with the slow and pompous manner in which he spoke, gave me a minute's space to collect my ideas, dispersed as they were by the extraordinary purport of this annunciation.

" I cannot conceive, sir," I replied, " by what singular tenure this person claims my obedience as a guardian; it is a barefaced imposture — I never in my life saw him, until I came unhappily to this country, about four weeks since."

" Ay, sir—we—he—know, and are aware—that—poof—you do not like to hear some folk's names; and that—eh—you understand me—there are things, and sounds, and matters, conversations about names, and such like, which put you off the hooks—which I have no humour to witness. Nevertheless, Mr. Darsie—or—poof—Mr. Darsie Latimer—or—poof, poof—eh— ay, Mr. Darsie without the Latimer — you have acknowledged as much to-day as assures me you will best be disposed of under the honourable care of my friend here—all your confessions—besides that—poof—eh—I know him to be a most responsible person—a—hay—ay—most responsible and honourable person—Can you deny this ?"

" I know nothing of him," I repeated; " not even his name; and I have not, as I told you, seen him in the course of my whole life, till a few weeks since."

" Will you swear to that ?" said the singular man, who seemed to await the result of this debate, secure as a rattlesnake is of the prey which has once felt its fascination. And while he said these words in deep under-tone, he withdrew his chair a little behind that of the Justice, so as to be unseen by him or his clerk, who sat upon the same side; while he bent on me a frown so portentous, that no one who has witnessed the look can forget it during the whole of his life. The furrows of the brow above the eyes became livid and almost black, and were bent into a semicircular, or rather an elliptical form, above the junction of the eyebrows. I had heard such a look described in an old tale of *diablerie*, which it was my chance to be entertained with not long since; when this deep and gloomy contortion of the frontal muscles was not unaptly described, as forming the representation of a small horseshoe.

The tale, when told, awakened a dreadful vision of infancy, which the withering and blighting look now fixed on me again forced on my recollection, but with much more vivacity. Indeed I was so much surprised, and I must add, terrified, at the vague ideas which were awakened in my mind by this fearful sign, that I kept my eyes fixed on the face in which it was exhibited, as on a frightful vision; until, passing his handkerchief a moment across his countenance, this mysterious man relaxed at once the look which had for me something so appalling. "The young man will no longer deny that he has seen me before," said he to the Justice, in a tone of complacency; "and I trust he will now be reconciled to my temporary guardianship, which may end better for him than he expects."

"Whatever I expect," I replied, summoning my scattered recollections together, "I see I am neither to expect justice nor protection from this gentleman, whose office it is to render both to the lieges. For you, sir, how strangely you have wrought yourself into the fate of an unhappy young man, or what interest you can pretend in me, you yourself only can explain. That I have seen you before, is certain; for none can forget the look with which you seem to have the power of blighting those upon whom you cast it."

The Justice seemed not very easy under this hint. "Ha!—ay," he said, "it is time to be going, neighbour. I have a many miles to ride, and care not to ride darkling in these parts.—You and I, Mr. Nicholas, must be jogging."

The Justice fumbled with his gloves, in endeavouring to draw them on hastily, and Mr. Nicholas bustled to get his great-coat and whip. Their landlord endeavoured to detain them, and spoke of supper and beds. Both pouring forth many thanks for his invitation, seemed as if they would much rather not; and Mr. Justice Foxley was making a score of apologies, with at least a hundred cautionary hems and eh-ehs, when the girl Dorcas burst into the room, and announced a gentleman on justice business.

"What gentleman?—and whom does he want?"

"He is cuome post on his ten toes," said the wench; "and on justice business to his worship loike. I'se uphald him a gentleman, for he speaks as good Latin as the schulemeaster; but, lack-a-day! he has gotten a queer mop of a wig."

The gentleman, thus announced and described, bounced into the room. But I have already written as much as fills a sheet of my paper, and my singular embarrassments press so hard on me, that I have matter to fill another from what followed the intrusion of—my dear Alan—your crazy client—Poor Peter Peebles!

Chapter the Seventh.

LATIMER'S JOURNAL, IN CONTINUATION.

Sheet 2.

I HAVE rarely in my life, till the last alarming days, known what it was to sustain a moment's real sorrow. What I called such, was, I am now well convinced, only the weariness of mind, which, having nothing actually present to complain of, turns upon itself, and becomes anxious about the past and the future; those periods with which human life has so little connection, that Scripture itself hath said, "Sufficient for the day is the evil thereof."

If, therefore, I have sometimes abused prosperity, by murmuring at my unknown birth and uncertain rank in society, I will make amends by bearing my present real adversity with patience and courage, and, if I can, even with gaiety. What can they—dare they, do to me?—Foxley, I am persuaded, is a real Justice of Peace, and country gentleman of estate, though (wonderful to tell!) he is an ass notwithstanding; and his functionary in the drab coat must have a shrewd guess at the consequences of being accessary to an act of murder or kidnapping. Men invite not such witnesses to deeds of darkness. I have also—Alan, I *have* hopes, arising out of the family of the oppressor himself. I am encouraged to believe that G. M. is likely again to enter on the field. More I dare not here say; nor must I drop a hint which another eye than thine might be able to construe. Enough, my feelings are lighter than they have been; and, though fear and wonder are still around me, they are unable entirely to overcloud the horizon.

Even when I saw the spectral form of the old scarecrow of the Parliament-House rush into the apartment where I had undergone so singular an examination, I thought of thy connection with him, and could almost have parodied Lear—

"Death!—nothing could have thus subdued nature
To such a lowness, but his 'learned lawyers.' "

He was e'en as we have seen him of yore, Alan, when, rather to keep thee company than to follow my own bent, I formerly frequented the halls of justice. The only addition to his dress, in the capacity of a traveller, was a pair of boots, that seemed as if they might have seen the field of Sheriff-moor; so large and heavy, that tied as they were to the creature's wearied hams with large bunches of worsted tape of various colours, they looked as if he had been dragging them along, either for a wager, or by way of penance.

Regardless of the surprised looks of the party on whom he thus intruded himself, Peter blundered into the middle of the apartment, with his head charged like a ram's in the act of butting, and saluted them thus:—

"Gude day to ye, gude day to your honours—Is't here they sell the fugie warrants?"

I observed that on his entrance, my friend—or enemy—drew himself back, and placed himself as if he would rather avoid attracting the observation of the new-comer. I did the same myself, as far as I was able; for I thought it likely that Mr. Peebles might recognize me, as indeed I was too frequently among the group of young juridical aspirants who used to amuse themselves by putting cases for Peter's solution, and playing him worse tricks; yet I was uncertain whether I had better avail myself of our acquaintance to have the advantage, such as it might be, of his evidence before the magistrate, or whether to make him, if possible, bearer of a letter which might procure me more effectual assistance. I resolved, therefore, to be guided by circumstances, and to watch carefully that nothing might escape me. I drew back as far as I could, and even reconnoitred the door and passage, to consider whether absolute escape might not be practicable. But there paraded Cristal Nixon, whose little black eyes, sharp as those of a basilisk, seemed, the instant when they encountered mine, to penetrate my purpose.

I sat down, as much out of sight of all parties as I could, and listened to the dialogue which followed — a dialogue how much more interesting to me than any I could have conceived, in which Peter Peebles was to be one of the *Dramatis Personæ!*

"Is it here where ye sell the warrants — the fugies, ye ken?" said Peter.

"Hey — eh — what!" said Justice Foxley; "what the devil does the fellow mean? — What would you have a warrant for?"

"It is to apprehend a young lawyer that is *in meditatione fugæ;* for he has ta'en my memorial and pleaded my cause, and a good fee I gave him, and as muckle brandy as he could drink that day at his father's house—he loes the brandy ower weel for sae youthful a creature."

"And what has this drunken young dog of a lawyer done to you, that you are come to me — eh — ha? Has he robbed you? Not unlikely if he be a lawyer — eh — Nick — ha?" said Justice Foxley.

"He has robbed me of himself, sir," answered Peter; "of his help, comfort, aid, maintenance, and assistance, whilk, as a counsel to a client, he is bound to yield me *ratione officii* — that is it, ye see. He has pouched my fee, and drunken a mutchkin of brandy, and now he's ower the march, and left my cause, half won half lost — as dead a heat as e'er was run ower the back-sands. Now I was advised by some cunning laddies that are used to crack a bit law wi' me in the House, that the best thing I could do was to take heart o' grace and set out after him; so I have taken post on my ain shanks, forby a cast in a cart, or the like. I got wind of him in Dumfries, and now I have run him ower to the English side, and I want a fugie warrant against him."

How did my heart throb at this information, dearest Alan! Thou art near me then, and I well know with what kind purpose; thou hast abandoned all to fly to my assistance; and no wonder that, knowing thy friendship and faith, thy sound sagacity and persevering disposition, "my bosom's lord should now sit lightly on his throne;" that gaiety should almost involuntarily hover on my pen; and that my heart should beat like that of a general, responsive to the drums of his advancing ally, without whose help the battle must have been lost.

I did not suffer myself to be startled by this joyous surprise, but continued to bend my strictest attention to what followed, among this singular party. That Poor Peter Peebles had been put on this wildgoose chase, by some of his juvenile advisers in the Parliament House, he himself had intimated; but he spoke with much confidence, and the Justice, who seemed to have some secret apprehension of being put to trouble in the matter, and, as sometimes occurs on the English frontier, a jealousy lest the superior acuteness of their northern neighbours might overreach their own simplicity, turned to his clerk with a perplexed countenance.

"Eh — oh — Nick — d—n thee — Hast thou got nothing to say? This is more Scots law, I take it, and more Scotsmen." (Here he cast a sideglance at the owner of the mansion, and winked to his clerk.) "I would Solway were as deep as it is wide, and we had then some chance of keeping of them out."

Nicholas conversed an instant aside with the supplicant, and then reported:—

"The man wants a border-warrant, I think; but they are only granted for debt — now he wants one to catch a lawyer."

"And what for no?" answered Peter Peebles, doggedly; "what for no, I would be glad to ken? If a day's labourer refuse to work, ye'll grant a warrant to gar him do out his daurg — if a wench quean rin away from her hairst, ye'll send her back to her heuck again — if sae mickle as a collier or a salter make a moonlight flitting, ye will cleek him by the back-spaul in a minute of time,—and yet the damage canna amount to mair than a creelfu' of coals, and a forpit or twa of saut; and here is a chield taks leg from his engagement, and damages me to the tune of sax thousand punds sterling; that is, three thousand that I should win, and three thousand mair that I am like to lose; and you that ca' yourself a justice canna help a poor man to catch the rinaway? A bonny like justice I am like to get amang ye!"

"The fellow must be drunk," said the clerk.

"Black fasting from all but sin," replied the supplicant; "I havna had mair than a mouthful of cauld water since I passed the Border, and deil a ane of ye is like to say to me, 'Dog, will ye drink?'"

The Justice seemed moved by this appeal. "Hem—tush, man," replied he; "thou speak'st to us as if thou wert in presence of one of thine own beggarly justices — get down stairs — get something to eat, man, (with permission of my friend to make so free in his house,) and a mouthful to drink, and I warrant we get ye such justice as will please ye."

"I winna refuse your neighbourly offer," said Poor Peter Peebles, making his bow; "muckle grace be wi' your honour, and wisdom to guide you in this extraordinary cause."

When I saw Peter Peebles about to retire from the room, I could not forbear an effort to obtain from him such evidence as might give me some credit with the justice. I stepped forward, therefore, and, saluting him, asked him if he remembered me?

After a stare or two, and a long pinch of snuff, recollection seemed suddenly to dawn on Peter Peebles. "Recollect ye!" he said; "by my troth do I.—Haud him a grip, gentlemen!—constables, keep him fast! where that ill-deedy hempy is, ye are sure that Alan Fairford is not far off.—Haud him fast, Master Constable; I charge ye wi' him, for I am mista'en if he is not at the bottom of this rinaway business. He was aye getting the silly callant Alan awa wi' gigs, and horse, and the like of that, to Roslin, and Prestonpans, and a' the idle gates he could think of. He's a rinaway apprentice, that ane."

"Mr. Peebles," I said, "do not do me wrong. I am sure you can say no harm of me justly, but can satisfy these gentlemen, if you will, that I am a student of law in Edinburgh — Darsie Latimer by name."

"Me satisfy! how can I satisfy the gentlemen," answered Peter, "that am sae far from being satisfied mysell? I ken naething about your name, and can only testify, *nihil novit in causa.*"

"A pretty witness you have brought forward in your favour," said Mr. Foxley. "But—ha—ay—I'll ask him a question or two.—Pray, friend, will you take your oath to this youth being a runaway apprentice?"

"Sir," said Peter, "I will make oath to ony thing in reason; when a case comes to my oath it's a won cause: But I am in some haste to prie your worship's good cheer;" for Peter had become much more respectful in his demeanour towards the Justice, since he had heard some intimation of dinner.

"You shall have—eh—hum—ay—a bellyful, if it be possible to fill it. First let me know if this young man be really what he pretends. — Nick, make his affidavit."

"Ow, he is just a wud harum-scarum creature, that wad never take to his studies; daft, sir, clean daft."

"Deft!" said the justice; "what d'ye mean by deft — eh?"

"Just Fifish," replied Peter; "wowf—a wee bit by the East-Nook or

sae; it's a common case—the ae half of the warld thinks the tither daft. I
have met with folk in my day, that thought I was daft mysell; and, for my
part, I think our Court of Session clean daft, that have had the great cause
of Peebles against Plainstanes before them for this score of years, and have
never been able to ding the bottom out of it yet."

"I cannot make out a word of his cursed brogue," said the Cumbrian
justice; "can you, neighbour—eh? What can he mean by *deft?*"

"He means *mad*," said the party appealed to, thrown off his guard by
impatience of this protracted discussion.

"Ye have it—ye have it," said Peter; "that is, not clean skivie,
but ——"

"Here he stopped, and fixed his eye on the person he addressed with an
air of joyful recognition. — "Ay, ay, Mr. Herries of Birrenswork, is this
your ainsell in blood and bane? I thought ye had been hanged at Ken-
nington Common, or Hairiebie, or some of these places, after the bonny
ploy ye made in the forty-five."

"I believe you are mistaken, friend," said Herries, sternly, with whose
name and designation I was thus made unexpectedly acquainted.

"The deil a bit," answered the undaunted Peter Peebles; "I mind ye
weel, for ye lodged in my house the great year of forty-five, for a great year
it was; the Grand Rebellion broke out, and my cause—the great cause—
Peebles against Plainstanes, *et per contra*—was called in the beginning of
the winter Session, and would have been heard, but that there was a sur-
cease of justice, with your plaids, and your piping, and your nonsense."

"I tell you, fellow," said Herries, yet more fiercely, "you have confused
me with some of the other furniture of your crazy pate."

"Speak like a gentleman, sir," answered Peebles; "these are not legal
phrases, Mr. Herries of Birrenswork. Speak in form of law, or I sall bid
ye gude day, sir. I have nae pleasure in speaking to proud folk, though I
am willing to answer ony thing in a legal way; so if ye are for a crack
about auld langsyne, and the splores that you and Captain Redgimlet used
to breed in my house, and the girded cask of brandy that ye drank and
ne'er thought of paying for it, (not that I minded it muckle in thae days,
though I have felt a lack of it sin syne,) why I will waste an hour on ye at
ony time.—And where is Captain Redgimlet now? he was a wild chap, like
yoursell, though they arena sae keen after you poor bodies for these some
years bygane; the heading and hanging is weel ower now — awful job—
awful job—will ye try my sneeshing?"

He concluded his desultory speech by thrusting out his large bony paw,
filled with a Scottish mull of huge dimensions, which Herries, who had
been standing like one petrified by the assurance of this unexpected address, rejected with a contemptuous motion of his hand, which spilled some
of the contents of the box.

"Aweel, aweel," said Peter Peebles, totally unabashed by the repulse,
"e'en as ye like, a wilful man maun hae his way; but," he added, stooping
down and endeavouring to gather the spilled snuff from the polished floor,
"I canna afford to lose my sneeshing for a' that ye are gumple-foisted wi'
me."

My attention had been keenly awakened, during this extraordinary and
unexpected scene. I watched, with as much attention as my own agitation
permitted me to command, the effect produced on the parties concerned. It
was evident that our friend, Peter Peebles, had unwarily let out something
which altered the sentiments of Justice Foxley and his clerk towards Mr.
Herries, with whom, until he was known and acknowledged under that
name, they had appeared to be so intimate. They talked with each other
aside, looked at a paper or two which the clerk selected from the contents
of a huge black pocketbook, and seemed, under the influence of fear and
uncertainty, totally at a loss what line of conduct to adopt.

Herries made a different, and far more interesting figure. However little Peter Peebles might resemble the angel Ithuriel, the appearance of Herries, his high and scornful demeanour, vexed at what seemed detection, yet fear less of the consequences, and regarding the whispering magistrate and his clerk with looks in which contempt predominated over anger or anxiety, bore, in my opinion, no slight resemblance to

———"the regal port
And faded splendour wan"—

with which the poet has invested the detected King of the powers of the air.

As he glanced round, with a look which he had endeavoured to compose to haughty indifference, his eye encountered mine, and, I thought, at the first glance sunk beneath it. But he instantly rallied his natural spirit, and returned me one of those extraordinary looks, by which he could contort so strangely the wrinkles on his forehead. I started; but, angry at myself for my pusillanimity, I answered him by a look of the same kind, and catching the reflection of my countenance in a large antique mirror which stood before me, I started again at the real or imaginary resemblance which my countenance, at that moment, bore to that of Herries. Surely my fate is somehow strangely interwoven with that of this mysterious individual. I had no time at present to speculate upon the subject, for the subsequent conversation demanded all my attention.

The Justice addressed Herries, after a pause of about five minutes, in which all parties seemed at some loss how to proceed. He spoke with embarrassment, and his faltering voice, and the long intervals which divided his sentences, seemed to indicate fear of him whom he addressed.

"Neighbour," he said, "I could not have thought this; or, if I—eh—did think—in a corner of my own mind as it were—that you, I say—that you might have unluckily engaged in—eh—the matter of the forty-five—there was still time to have forgot all that."

"And is it so singular that a man should have been out in the forty-five?" said Herries, with contemptuous composure;—"your father, I think, Mr. Foxley, was out with Derwentwater in the fifteen."

"And lost half of his estate," answered Foxley, with more rapidity than usual; "and was very near—hem—being hanged into the boot. But this is—another guess job—for—eh—fifteen is not forty-five; and my father had a remission, and you, I take it, have none."

"Perhaps I have," said Herries, indifferently; "or if I have not, I am but in the case of half a dozen others whom government do not think worth looking after at this time of day, so they give no offence or disturbance."

"But you have given both, sir," said Nicholas Faggot, the clerk, who, having some petty provincial situation, as I have since understood, deemed himself bound to be zealous for government. "Mr. Justice Foxley cannot be answerable for letting you pass free, now your name and surname have been spoken plainly out. There are warrants out against you from the Secretary of State's office."

"A proper allegation, Mr. Attorney! that, at the distance of so many years, the Secretary of State should trouble himself about the unfortunate relics of a ruined cause," answered Mr. Herries.

"But if it be so," said the clerk, who seemed to assume more confidence upon the composure of Herries's demeanour; "and if cause has been given by the conduct of a gentleman himself, who hath been, it is alleged, raking up old matters, and mixing them with new subjects of disaffection—I say, if it be so, I should advise the party, in his wisdom, to surrender himself quietly into the lawful custody of the next Justice of Peace—Mr. Foxley, suppose—where, and by whom, the matter should be regularly inquired into. I am only putting a case," he added, watching with apprehension

the effect which his words were likely to produce upon the party to whom
they were addressed.

"And were I to receive such advice," said Herries, with the same composure as before — "putting the case, as you say, Mr. Faggot — I should
request to see the warrant which countenanced such a scandalous proceeding."

Mr. Nicholas, by way of answer, placed in his hand a paper, and seemed
anxiously to expect the consequences which were to ensue. Mr. Herries
looked it over with the same equanimity as before, and then continued,
"And were such a scrawl as this presented to me in my own house, I would
throw it into the chimney, and Mr. Faggot upon the top of it."

Accordingly, seconding the word with the action, he flung the warrant
into the fire with one hand, and fixed the other, with a stern and irresistible
gripe, on the breast of the attorney, who, totally unable to contend with
him, in either personal strength or mental energy, trembled like a chicken
in the raven's clutch. He got off, however, for the fright; for Herries,
having probably made him fully sensible of the strength of his grasp, released him, with a scornful laugh.

"Deforcement—spulzie—stouthrief—masterful rescue!" exclaimed Peter
Peebles, scandalized at the resistance offered to the law in the person of
Nicholas Faggot. But his shrill exclamations were drowned in the thundering voice of Herries, who, calling upon Cristal Nixon, ordered him to
take the brawling fool down stairs, fill his belly, and then give him a
guinea, and thrust him out of doors. Under such injunctions, Peter easily
suffered himself to be withdrawn from the scene.

Herries then turned to the Justice, whose visage, wholly abandoned by
the rubicund hue which so lately beamed upon it, hung out the same pale
livery as that of his dismayed clerk. "Old friend and acquaintance," he
said, "you came here at my request, on a friendly errand, to convince this
silly young man of the right which I have over his person for the present.
I trust you do not intend to make your visit the pretext of disquieting me
about other matters? All the world knows that I have been living at large,
in these northern counties, for some months, not to say years, and might
have been apprehended at any time, had the necessities of the state required, or my own behaviour deserved it. But no English magistrate has
been ungenerous enough to trouble a gentleman under misfortune, on account of political opinions and disputes, which have been long ended by the
success of the reigning powers. I trust, my good friend, you will not endanger yourself, by taking any other view of the subject than you have done
ever since we were acquainted?"

The Justice answered with more readiness, as well as more spirit than
usual, "Neighbour Ingoldsby—what you say—is—eh—in some sort true;
and when you were coming and going at markets, horse-races, and cock-
fights, fairs, hunts, and such like—it was—eh—neither my business nor my
wish to dispel—I say—to inquire into and dispel the mysteries which hung
about you; for while you were a good companion in the field, and over a
bottle now and then—I did not—eh—think it necessary to ask—into your
private affairs. And if I thought you were—ahem—somewhat unfortunate
in former undertakings, and enterprises, and connections, which might
cause you to live unsettledly and more private, I could have — eh — very
little pleasure—to aggravate your case by interfering, or requiring explanations, which are often more easily asked than given. But when there are
warrants and witnesses to names—and those names, Christian and surname,
belong to — eh — an attainted person — charged — I trust falsely — with —
ahem—taking advantage of modern broils and heart-burnings to renew our
civil disturbances, the case is altered; and I must—ahem—do my duty."

The Justice got on his feet as he concluded this speech, and looked as
bold as he could. I drew close beside him and his clerk, Mr. Faggot,

thinking the moment favourable for my own liberation, and intimated to Mr. Foxley my determination to stand by him. But Mr. Herries only laughed at the menacing posture which we assumed. "My good neighbour," said he, "you talk of a witness — Is you crazy beggar a fit witness in an affair of this nature?"

"But you do not deny that you are Mr. Herries of Birrenswork, mentioned in the Secretary of State's warrant?" said Mr. Foxley.

"How can I deny or own any thing about it?" said Herries, with a sneer. "There is no such warrant in existence now; its ashes, like the poor traitor whose doom it threatened, have been dispersed to the four winds of heaven. There is now no warrant in the world."

"But you will not deny," said the Justice, "that you were the person named in it; and that — eh — your own act destroyed it?"

"I will neither deny my name nor my actions, Justice," replied Mr. Herries, "when called upon by competent authority to avow or defend them. But I will resist all impertinent attempts either to intrude into my private motives, or to control my person. I am quite well prepared to do so; and I trust that you, my good neighbour and brother sportsman, in your expostulation, and my friend Mr. Nicholas Faggot here, in his humble advice and petition that I should surrender myself, will consider yourselves as having amply discharged your duty to King George and Government."

The cold and ironical tone in which he made this declaration; the look and attitude, so nobly expressive of absolute confidence in his own superior strength and energy, seemed to complete the indecision which had already shown itself on the side of those whom he addressed.

The Justice looked to the Clerk — the Clerk to the Justice; the former *ha'd, eh'd*, without bringing forth an articulate syllable; the latter only said, "As the warrant is destroyed, Mr. Justice, I presume you do not mean to proceed with the arrest?"

"Hum—ay—why, no—Nicholas—it would not be quite advisable—and as the Forty-five was an old affair—and — hem — as my friend here will, I hope, see his error — that is, if he has not seen it already — and renounce the Pope, the Devil, and the Pretender — I mean no harm, neighbour — I think we—as we have no *posse*, or constables, or the like—should order our horses — and, in one word, look the matter over."

"Judiciously resolved," said the person whom this decision affected; "but before you go, I trust you will drink and be friends?"

"Why," said the Justice, rubbing his brow, "our business has been — hem—rather a thirsty one."

"Cristal Nixon," said Mr. Herries, "let us have a cool tankard instantly, large enough to quench the thirst of the whole commission."

While Cristal was absent on this genial errand, there was a pause, of which I endeavoured to avail myself, by bringing back the discourse to my own concerns. "Sir," I said to Justice Foxley, "I have no direct business with your late discussion with Mr. Herries, only just thus far — You leave me, a loyal subject of King George, an unwilling prisoner in the hands of a person whom you have reason to believe unfriendly to the King's cause. I humbly submit that this is contrary to your duty as a magistrate, and that you ought to make Mr. Herries aware of the illegality of his proceedings, and take steps for my rescue, either upon the spot, or, at least, as soon as possible after you have left this case——"

"Young man," said Mr. Justice Foxley, "I would have you remember you are under the power, the lawful power—ahem—of your guardian."

"He calls himself so, indeed," I replied; "but he has shown no evidence to establish so absurd a claim; and if he had, his circumstances, as an attainted traitor excepted from pardon, would void such a right if it existed. I do therefore desire you, Mr. Justice, and you, his clerk, to consider my situation, and afford me relief at your peril."

"Here is a young fellow now," said the Justice, with much embarrassed looks, "thinks that I carry the whole statute law of England in my head, and a *posse comitatus* to execute them in my pocket! Why, what good would my interference do?—but—hum—eh—I will speak to your guardian in your favour."

He took Mr. Herries aside, and seemed indeed to urge something upon him with much earnestness; and perhaps such a species of intercession was all which, in the circumstances, I was entitled to expect from him.

They often looked at me as they spoke together; and as Cristal Nixon entered with a huge four-pottle tankard, filled with the beverage his master had demanded, Herries turned away from Mr. Foxley somewhat impatiently, saying with emphasis, "I give you my word of honour, that you have not the slightest reason to apprehend any thing on his account." He then took up the tankard, and saying aloud in Gaelic, "*Slaint an Rey*,"* just tasted the liquor, and handed the tankard to Justice Foxley, who, to avoid the dilemma of pledging him to what might be the Pretender's health, drank to Mr. Herries's own, with much pointed solemnity, but in a draught far less moderate.

The clerk imitated the example of his principal, and I was fain to follow their example, for anxiety and fear are at least as thirsty as sorrow is said to be. In a word, we exhausted the composition of ale, sherry, lemon-juice, nutmeg, and other good things, stranded upon the silver bottom of the tankard the huge toast, as well as the roasted orange, which had whileome floated jollily upon the brim, and rendered legible Dr. Byrom's celebrated lines engraved thereon—

> "God bless the King!—God bless the Faith's defender!
> God bless—No harm in blessing the Pretender.
> Who that Pretender is, and who that King,—
> God bless us all!—is quite another thing."

I had time enough to study this effusion of the Jacobite muse, while the Justice was engaged in the somewhat tedious ceremony of taking leave. That of Mr. Faggot was less ceremonious; but I suspect something besides empty compliment passed betwixt him and Mr. Herries; for I remarked that the latter slipped a piece of paper into the hand of the former, which might perhaps be a little atonement for the rashness with which he had burnt the warrant, and imposed no gentle hand on the respectable minion of the law by whom it was exhibited; and I observed that he made this propitiation in such a manner as to be secret from the worthy clerk's principal.

When this was arranged, the party took leave of each other, with much formality on the part of Squire Foxley, amongst whose adieus the following phrase was chiefly remarkable: — "I presume you do not intend to stay long in these parts?"

"Not for the present, Justice, you may be sure; there are good reasons to the contrary. But I have no doubt of arranging my affairs so that we shall speedily have sport together again."

He went to wait upon the Justice to the court-yard; and, as he did so, commanded Cristal Nixon to see that I returned into my apartment. Knowing it would be to no purpose to resist or tamper with that stubborn functionary, I obeyed in silence, and was once more a prisoner in my former quarters.

---

* The King's health.

Chapter the Eighth.

LATIMER'S JOURNAL, IN CONTINUATION.

I SPENT more than an hour, after returning to the apartment which I may call my prison, in reducing to writing the singular circumstances which I had just witnessed. Methought I could now form some guess at the character of Mr. Herries, upon whose name and situation the late scene had thrown considerable light;—one of those fanatical Jacobites, doubtless, whose arms, not twenty years since, had shaken the British throne, and some of whom, though their party daily diminished in numbers, energy, and power, retained still an inclination to renew the attempt they had found so desperate. He was indeed perfectly different from the sort of zealous Jacobites whom it had been my luck hitherto to meet with. Old ladies of family over their hyson, and gray-haired lairds over their punch, I had often heard utter a little harmless treason; while the former remembered having led down a dance with the Chevalier, and the latter recounted the feats they had performed at Preston, Clifton, and Falkirk.

The disaffection of such persons was too unimportant to excite the attention of government. I had heard, however, that there still existed partisans of the Stewart family, of a more daring and dangerous description; men who, furnished with gold from Rome, moved, secretly and in disguise, through the various classes of society, and endeavoured to keep alive the expiring zeal of their party.

I had no difficulty in assigning an important post among this class of persons, whose agency and exertion are only doubted by those who look on the surface of things, to this Mr. Herries, whose mental energies, as well as his personal strength and activity, seemed to qualify him well to act so dangerous a part; and I knew that, all along the Western Border, both in England and Scotland, there are so many Nonjurors, that such a person may reside there with absolute safety, unless it becomes, in a very especial degree, the object of the government to secure his person; and which purpose, even then, might be disappointed by early intelligence, or, as in the case of Mr. Foxley, by the unwillingness of provincial magistrates to interfere in what is now considered an invidious pursuit of the unfortunate.

There have, however, been rumours lately, as if the present state of the nation, or at least of some discontented provinces, agitated by a variety of causes, but particularly by the unpopularity of the present administration, may seem to this species of agitators, a favourable period for recommencing their intrigues; while, on the other hand, government may not, at such a crisis, be inclined to look upon them with the contempt which a few years ago would have been their most appropriate punishment.

That men should be found rash enough to throw away their services and lives in a desperate cause, is nothing new in history, which abounds with instances of similar devotion—that Mr. Herries is such an enthusiast, is no less evident; but all this explains not his conduct towards *me*. Had he sought to make me a proselyte to his ruined cause, violence and compulsion were arguments very unlikely to prevail with any generous spirit. But even if such were his object, of what use could be to him the acquisition of a single reluctant partisan, who could bring only his own person to support any quarrel which he might adopt? He had claimed over me the rights of a guardian; he had more than hinted that I was in a state of mind which could not dispense with the authority of such a person. Was this man, so sternly desperate in his purpose,—he who seemed willing to take on his own shoulders the entire support of a cause which had been ruinous to thousands, — was he the person that had the power of deciding on my fate? Was it from him those dangers flowed, to secure me against which I had been educated under such circumstances of secrecy and precaution?

And if this was so, of what nature was the claim which he asserted? — Was it that of propinquity? And did I share the blood, perhaps the features, of this singular being? — Strange as it may seem, a thrill of awe, which shot across my mind at that instant, was not unmingled with a wild and mysterious feeling of wonder, almost amounting to pleasure. I remembered the reflection of my own face in the mirror, at one striking moment during the single interview of the day, and I hastened to the outward apartment to consult a glass which hung there, whether it were possible for my countenance to be again contorted into the peculiar frown which so much resembled the terrific look of Herries. But I folded my brows in vain into a thousand complicated wrinkles, and I was obliged to conclude, either that the supposed mark on my brow was altogether imaginary, or that it could not be called forth by voluntary effort; or, in fine, what seemed most likely, that it was such a resemblance as the imagination traces in the embers of a wood fire, or among the varied veins of marble, distinct at one time, and obscure or invisible at another, according as the combination of lines strikes the eye, or impresses the fancy.

While I was moulding my visage like a mad player, the door suddenly opened, and the girl of the house entered. Angry and ashamed at being detected in my singular occupation, I turned round sharply, and, I suppose, chance produced the change on my features which I had been in vain labouring to call forth.

The girl started back, with her "Don't ye look so now — don't ye, for love's sake — you be as like the ould Squoire as — But here a comes," she said, huddling away out of the room; "and if you want a third, there is none but ould Harry, as I know of, that can match ye for a brent broo!"

As the girl muttered this exclamation, and hastened out of the room, Herries entered. He stopped on observing that I had looked again to the mirror, anxious to trace the look by which the wench had undoubtedly been terrified. He seemed to guess what was passing in my mind, for, as I turned towards him, he observed, "Doubt not that it is stamped on your forehead—the fatal mark of our race; though it is not now so apparent as it will become when age and sorrow, and the traces of stormy passions, and of bitter penitence, shall have drawn their furrows on your brow."

"Mysterious man," I replied, "I know not of what you speak; your language is as dark as your purposes."

"Sit down, then," he said, "and listen; thus far, at least, must the veil of which you complain be raised. When withdrawn, it will only display guilt and sorrow — guilt followed by strange penalty, and sorrow, which Providence has entailed upon the posterity of the mourners."

He paused a moment, and commenced his narrative, which he told with the air of one, who, remote as the events were which he recited, took still the deepest interest in them. The tone of his voice, which I have already described as rich and powerful, aided by its inflections the effects of his story, which I will endeavour to write down, as nearly as possible, in the very words which he used.

"It was not of late years that the English learned, that their best chance of conquering their independent neighbours must be by introducing amongst them division and civil war. You need not be reminded of the state of thraldom to which Scotland was reduced by the unhappy wars betwixt the domestic factions of Bruce and Baliol; nor how, after Scotland had been emancipated from a foreign yoke, by the conduct and valour of the immortal Bruce, the whole fruits of the triumphs of Bannockburn were lost in the dreadful defeats of Dupplin and Halidon; and Edward Baliol, the minion and feudatory of his namesake of England, seemed, for a brief season, in safe and uncontested possession of the throne so lately occupied by the greatest general and wisest prince in Europe. But the experience of Bruce had not died with him. There were many who had shared his martial labours, and all remembered the successful efforts by which, under circumstances as disadvantageous as those of his son, he had achieved the liberation of Scotland.

"The usurper, Edward Baliol, was feasting with a few of his favourite retainers in the Castle of Annan, when he was suddenly surprised by a chosen band of insurgent patriots. Their chiefs were, Douglas, Randolph, the young Earl of Moray, and Sir Simon Fraser; and their success was so complete, that Baliol was obliged to fly for his life scarcely clothed, and on a horse which there was no leisure to saddle. It was of importance to seize his person, if possible, and his flight was closely pursued by a valiant knight of Norman descent, whose family had been long settled in the marches of Dumfries-shire. Their Norman appellation was Fitz-Aldin, but this knight, from the great slaughter which he had made of the Southron, and the reluctance which he had shown to admit them to quarter during the former war of that bloody period, had acquired the name of Redgauntlet, which he transmitted to his posterity——"

"Redgauntlet!" I involuntarily repeated.

"Yes, Redgauntlet," said my alleged guardian, looking at me keenly; "does that name recall any associations to your mind?"

"No," I replied, "except that I had lately heard it given to the hero of a supernatural legend."

"There are many such current concerning the family," he answered; and then proceeded in his narrative.

"Alberick Redgauntlet, the first of his house so termed, was, as may be supposed from his name, of a stern and implacable disposition, which had been rendered more so by family discord. An only son, now a youth of eighteen, shared so much the haughty spirit of his father, that he became impatient of domestic control, resisted paternal authority, and finally fled from his father's house, renounced his political opinions, and awakened his mortal displeasure by joining the adherents of Baliol. It was said that his father cursed, in his wrath, his degenerate offspring, and swore that if they met, he should perish by his hand. Meantime, circumstances seemed to promise atonement for this great deprivation. The lady of Alberick Redgauntlet was again, after many years, in a situation which afforded her husband the hope of a more dutiful heir.

"But the delicacy and deep interest of his wife's condition did not prevent Alberick from engaging in the undertaking of Douglas and Moray. He had been the most forward in the attack of the castle, and was now foremost in the pursuit of Baliol, eagerly engaged in dispersing or cutting down the few daring followers who endeavoured to protect the usurper in his flight.

"As these were successively routed or slain, the formidable Redgauntlet, the mortal enemy of the House of Baliol, was within two lances' length of the fugitive Edward Baliol, in a narrow pass, when a youth, one of the last who attended the usurper in his flight, threw himself between them, received the shock of the pursuer, and was unhorsed and overthrown. The helmet rolled from his head, and the beams of the sun, then rising over the Solway, showed Redgauntlet the features of his disobedient son, in the livery, and wearing the cognizance, of the usurper.

"Redgauntlet beheld his son lying before his horse's feet; but he also saw Baliol, the usurper of the Scottish crown, still, as it seemed, within his grasp, and separated from him only by the prostrate body of his overthrown adherent. Without pausing to inquire whether young Edward was wounded, he dashed his spurs into his horse, meaning to leap over him, but was unhappily frustrated in his purpose. The steed made indeed a bound forward, but was unable to clear the body of the youth, and with its hind foot struck him in the forehead, as he was in the act of rising. The blow was mortal. It is needless to add, that the pursuit was checked, and Baliol escaped.

"Redgauntlet, ferocious as he is described, was yet overwhelmed with the thoughts of the crime he had committed. When he returned to his castle, it was to encounter new domestic sorrows. His wife had been prematurely seized with the pangs of labour, upon hearing the dreadful catastrophe which had taken place. The birth of an infant boy cost her her life. Redgauntlet sat by her corpse for more than twenty-four hours without changing either feature or posture, so far as his terrified domestics could observe. The Abbot of Dundrennan preached consolation to him in vain. Douglas, who came to visit in his affliction a patriot of such distinguished zeal, was more successful in rousing his attention. He caused the trumpets to sound an English point of war in the court-yard, and Redgauntlet at once sprung to his arms, and seemed restored to the recollection, which had been lost in the extent of his misery.

"From that moment, whatever he might feel inwardly, he gave way to no outward emotion. Douglas caused his infant to be brought; but even the iron-hearted soldiers were struck with horror to observe, that, by the mysterious law of nature, the cause of his mother's death, and the evidence of his father's guilt, was stamped on the innocent face of the babe, whose brow was distinctly marked by the miniature resemblance of a horseshoe. Redgauntlet himself pointed it out to Douglas, saying, with a ghastly smile, 'It should have been bloody.'

"Moved, as he was, to compassion for his brother-in-arms, and steeled against all softer feelings by the habits of civil war, Douglas shuddered at this sight, and displayed a desire to leave the house which was doomed to be the scene of such horrors. As his parting advice, he exhorted Alberick Redgauntlet to make a pilgrimage to Saint Ninian's of Whitehorne, then esteemed a shrine of great sanctity; and departed with a precipitation, which might have aggravated, had that been possible, the forlorn state of his unhappy friend. But that seems to have been incapable of admitting any addition. Sir Alberick caused the bodies of his slaughtered son and the mother to be laid side by side in the ancient chapel of his house, after he had used the skill of a celebrated surgeon of that time to embalm them; and it was said, that for many weeks he spent some hours nightly in the vault where they reposed.

"At length he undertook the proposed pilgrimage to Whitehorne, where he confessed himself for the first time since his misfortune, and was shrived by an aged monk, who afterwards died in the odour of sanctity. It is said, that it was then foretold to the Redgauntlet, that on account of his unshaken patriotism, his family should continue to be powerful amid the changes of future times; but that, in detestation of his unrelenting cruelty to his own issue, Heaven had decreed that the valour of his race should always be fruitless, and that the cause which they espoused should never prosper.

"Submitting to such penance as was there imposed, Sir Alberick went, it is thought, on a pilgrimage either to Rome, or to the Holy Sepulchre itself. He was universally considered as dead; and it was not till thirteen years afterwards, that, in the great battle of Durham, fought between David Bruce and Queen Philippa of England, a knight, bearing a horseshoe for his crest, appeared in the van of the Scottish army, distinguishing himself by his reckless and desperate valour; who being at length overpowered and slain, was finally discovered to be the brave and unhappy Sir Alberick Redgauntlet."

"And has the fatal sign," said I, when Herries had ended his narrative, "descended on all the posterity of this unhappy house?"

"It has been so handed down from antiquity, and is still believed," said

Herries. "But perhaps there is, in the popular evidence, something of that fancy which creates what it sees. Certainly, as other families have peculiarities by which they are distinguished, this of Redgauntlet is marked in most individuals by a singular indenture of the forehead, supposed to be derived from the son of Alberick, their ancestor, and brother to the unfortunate Edward, who had perished in so piteous a manner. It is certain there seems to have been a fate upon the House of Redgauntlet, which has been on the losing side in almost all the civil broils which have divided the kingdom of Scotland from David Bruce's days, till the late valiant and unsuccessful attempt of the Chevalier Charles Edward."

He concluded with a deep sigh, as one whom the subject had involved in a train of painful reflections.

"And am I then," I exclaimed, "descended from this unhappy race? — Do you belong to it? — And if so, why do I sustain restraint and hard usage at the hands of a relation?"

"Inquire no farther for the present," he said. "The line of conduct which I am pursuing towards you, is dictated not by choice, but by necessity. You were withdrawn from the bosom of your family, and the care of your legal guardian, by the timidity and ignorance of a doting mother, who was incapable of estimating the arguments or feelings of those who prefer honour and principle to fortune, and even to life. The young hawk, accustomed only to the fostering care of its dam, must be tamed by darkness and sleeplessness, ere it is trusted on the wing for the purposes of the falconer."

I was appalled at this declaration, which seemed to threaten a long continuance, and a dangerous termination, of my captivity. I deemed it best, however, to show some spirit, and at the same time to mingle a tone of conciliation. "Mr. Herries," I said, "(if I call you rightly by that name,) let us speak upon this matter without the tone of mystery and fear in which you seem inclined to envelope it. I have been long, alas! deprived of the care of that affectionate mother to whom you allude—long under the charge of strangers—and compelled to form my own resolutions upon the reasoning of my own mind. Misfortune—early deprivation—has given me the privilege of acting for myself; and constraint shall not deprive me of an Englishman's best privilege."

"The true cant of the day," said Herries, in a tone of scorn. "The privilege of free action belongs to no mortal—we are tied down by the fetters of duty—our mortal path is limited by the regulations of honour—our most indifferent actions are but meshes of the web of destiny by which we are all surrounded."

He paced the room rapidly, and proceeded in a tone of enthusiasm which, joined to some other parts of his conduct, seems to intimate an over-excited imagination, were it not contradicted by the general tenor of his speech and conduct.

"Nothing," he said, in an earnest yet melancholy voice—"nothing is the work of chance—nothing is the consequence of free-will—the liberty of which the Englishman boasts gives as little real freedom to its owner, as the despotism of an Eastern Sultan permits to his slave. The usurper, William of Nassau, went forth to hunt, and thought, doubtless, that it was by an act of his own royal pleasure that the horse of his murdered victim was prepared for his kingly sport. But Heaven had other views; and before the sun was high, a stumble of that very animal over an obstacle so inconsiderable as a mole-hillock, cost the haughty rider his life and his usurped crown. Do you think an inclination of the rein could have avoided that trifling impediment? I tell you, it crossed his way as inevitably as all the long chain of Caucasus could have done. Yes, young man, in doing and suffering, we play but the part allotted by Destiny, the manager of this strange drama, stand bound to act no more than is prescribed, to say no more than is set down for us; and yet, we mouth about free-will, and freedom of thought and action, as if Richard must not die, or Richmond conquer, exactly where the Author has decreed it shall be so!"

He continued to pace the room after this speech, with folded arms and downcast looks; and the sound of his steps and the tone of his voice brought to my remembrance, that I had heard this singular person, when I met him on a former occasion, uttering such soliloquies in his solitary chamber. I observed that, like other Jacobites, in his inveteracy against the memory of King William, he had adopted the party opinion, that the monarch, on the day he had his fatal accident, rode upon a horse once the property of the unfortunate Sir John Friend, executed for High Treason in 1696.

It was not my business to aggravate, but, if possible, rather to soothe him in whose power I was so singularly placed. When I conceived that the keenness of his feelings had in some degree subsided, I answered him as follows:—"I will not—indeed I feel myself incompetent to argue a question of such metaphysical subtlety, as that which involves the limits betwixt free-will and predestination. Let us hope we may live honestly and die hopefully, without being obliged to form a decided opinion upon a point so far beyond our comprehension."

"Wisely resolved," he interrupted, with a sneer—"there came a note from some Geneva Sermon."

"But," I proceeded, "I call your attention to the fact, that I, as well as you, am acted upon by impulses, the result either of my own free will, or the consequences of the part which is assigned to me by destiny. These may be—nay, at present they are—in direct contradiction to those by which you are actuated; and how shall we decide which shall have precedence?— *You* perhaps feel yourself destined to act as my jailer. I feel myself, on the contrary, destined to attempt and effect my escape. One of us must be wrong, but who can say which errs till the event has decided betwixt us?"

"I shall feel myself destined to have recourse to severe modes of restraint," said he, in the same tone of half jest, half earnest, which I had used.

"In that case," I answered, "it will be my destiny to attempt every thing for my freedom."

"And it may be mine, young man," he replied, in a deep and stern tone, "to take care that you should rather die than attain your purpose."

"This was speaking out indeed, and I did not allow him to go unanswered. "You threaten me in vain," said I; "the laws of my country will protect me; or whom they cannot protect, they will avenge."

I spoke this firmly, and he seemed for a moment silenced; and the scorn with which he at last answered me, had something of affectation in it.

"The laws!" he said; "and what, stripling, do you know of the laws of your country?—Could you learn jurisprudence under a base-born blotter of parchment, such as Saunders Fairford; or from the empty pedantic coxcomb, his son, who now, forsooth, writes himself advocate?—When Scotland was herself, and had her own King and Legislature, such plebeian cubs, instead of being called to the bar of her Supreme Courts, would scarce have been admitted to the honour of bearing a sheepskin process-bag."

Alan, I could not bear this, but answered indignantly, that he knew not the worth and honour from which he was detracting.

"I know as much of these Fairfords as I do of you," he replied.

"As much," said I, "and as little; for you can neither estimate their real worth nor mine. I know you saw them when last in Edinburgh."

"Ha!" he exclaimed, and turned on me an inquisitive look.

"It is true," said I; "you cannot deny it; and having thus shown you that I know something of your motions, let me warn you I have modes of communication with which you are not acquainted. Oblige me not to use them to your prejudice."

"Prejudice *me!*" he replied. "Young man, I smile at, and forgive your folly. Nay, I will tell you that of which you are not aware, namely, that it was from letters received from these Fairfords that I first suspected, what the result of my visit to them confirmed, that you were the person whom I had sought for years."

"If you learned this," said I, "from the papers which were about my person on the night when I was under the necessity of becoming your guest at Brokenburn, I do not envy your indifference to the means of acquiring information. It was dishonourable to——"

"Peace, young man," said Herries, more calmly than I might have expected; "the word dishonour must not be mentioned as in conjunction with my name. Your pocket-book was in the pocket of your coat, and did not escape the curiosity of another, though it would have been sacred from mine. My servant, Cristal Nixon, brought me the intelligence after you were gone. I was displeased with the manner in which he had acquired his information; but it was not the less my duty to ascertain its truth, and for that purpose I went to Edinburgh. I was in hopes to persuade Mr. Fairford to have entered into my views; but I found him too much prejudiced to permit me to trust him. He is a wretched, yet a timid slave of the present government, under which our unhappy country is dishonourably enthralled; and it would have been altogether unfit and unsafe to have intrusted him with the secret either of the right which I possess to direct your actions, or of the manner in which I purpose to exercise it."

I was determined to take advantage of his communicative humour, and obtain, if possible, more light upon his purpose. He seemed most accessible to being piqued on the point of honour, and I resolved to avail myself, but with caution, of his sensibility upon that topic. "You say," I replied, "that you are not friendly to indirect practices, and disapprove of the means by which your domestic obtained information of my name and quality—Is it honourable to avail yourself of that knowledge which is dishonourably obtained?"

"It is boldly asked," he replied; "but, within certain necessary limits, I dislike not boldness of expostulation. You have, in this short conference, displayed more character and energy than I was prepared to expect. You will, I trust, resemble a forest plant, which has indeed, by some accident, been brought up in the greenhouse, and thus rendered delicate and effeminate, but which regains its native firmness and tenacity, when exposed for a season to the winter air. I will answer your question plainly. In business, as in war, spies and informers are necessary evils, which all good men detest; but which yet all prudent men must use, unless they mean to fight and act blindfold. But nothing can justify the use of falsehood and treachery in our own person."

"You said to the elder Mr. Fairford," continued I, with the same boldness, which I began to find was my best game, "that I was the son of Ralph Latimer of Langcote-Hall?—How do you reconcile this with your late assertion that my name is not Latimer?"

He coloured as he replied, "The doting old fool lied; or perhaps mistook my meaning. I said, that gentleman *might* be your father. To say truth, I wished you to visit England, your native country; because, when you might do so, my rights over you would revive."

This speech fully led me to understand a caution which had been often impressed upon me, that, if I regarded my safety, I should not cross the southern Border; and I cursed my own folly, which kept me fluttering like a moth around the candle, until I was betrayed into the calamity, with which I had dallied. "What are those rights," I said, "which you claim over me?—To what end do you propose to turn them?"

"To a weighty one, you may be certain," answered Mr. Herries; "but I do not, at present, mean to communicate to you either its nature or extent. You may judge of its importance, when, in order entirely to possess myself of your person, I condescended to mix myself with the fellows who destroyed the fishing station of yon wretched Quaker. That I held him in contempt, and was displeased at the greedy devices with which he ruined a manly sport, is true enough; but, unless as it favoured my designs on you, he might have, for me, maintained his stake-nets till Solway should cease to ebb and flow."

"Alas!" I said, "it doubles my regret to have been the unwilling cause of misfortune to an honest and friendly man."

"Do not grieve for that," said Herries; "honest Joshua is one of those who, by dint of long prayers, can possess themselves of widows' houses—he will quickly repair his losses. - When he sustains any mishap, he and the other canters set it down as a debt against Heaven, and by way of set-off, practise rogueries without compunction, till they make the balance even, or incline it to the winning side. Enough of this for the present.—I must immediately shift my quarters; for, although I do not fear the over-zeal of Mr. Justice Foxley or his clerk will lead them to any extreme measure, yet that mad scoundrel's unhappy recognition of me may make it more serious for them to connive at me, and I must not put their patience to an over severe trial. You must prepare to attend me, either as a captive or a companion; if as the latter, you must give your parole of honour to attempt no escape. Should you be so ill advised as to break your word once pledged, be assured that I will blow your brains out, without a moment's scruple."

"I am ignorant of your plans and purposes," I replied, "and cannot but hold them dangerous. I do not mean to aggravate my present situation by any unavailing resistance to the superior force which detains me; but I will not renounce the right of asserting my natural freedom should a favourable opportunity occur. I will, therefore, rather be your prisoner than your confederate."

"That is spoken fairly," he said; "and yet not without the canny caution of one brought up in the Gude Town of Edinburgh. On my part, I will impose no unnecessary hardship upon you; but, on the contrary, your journey shall be made as easy as is consistent with your being kept safely. Do you feel strong enough to ride on horseback as yet, or would you prefer a carriage? The former mode of travelling is best adapted to the country through which we are to travel, but you are at liberty to choose between them."

I said, "I felt my strength gradually returning, and that I should much prefer travelling on horseback. A carriage," I added, "is so close——"

"And so easily guarded," replied Herries, with a look as if he would have penetrated my very thoughts,—"that, doubtless, you think horseback better calculated for an escape."

"My thoughts are my own," I answered; "and though you keep my person prisoner, these are beyond your control."

"Oh, I can read the book," he said, "without opening the leaves. But I would recommend to you to make no rash attempt, and it will be my care to see that you have no power to make any that is likely to be effectual. Linen, and all other necessaries for one in your circumstances, are amply provided. Cristal Nixon will act as your valet, — I should rather, perhaps, say, your *femme de chambre*. Your travelling dress you may perhaps consider as singular; but it is such as the circumstances require; and, if you object to use the articles prepared for your use, your mode of journeying will be as personally unpleasant as that which conducted you hither. — Adieu — We now know each other better than we did — it will not be my fault if the consequences of farther intimacy be not a more favourable mutual opinion."

He then left me, with a civil good night, to my own reflections, and only turned back to say, that we should proceed on our journey at daybreak next morning, at farthest; perhaps earlier, he said; but complimented me by supposing that, as I was a sportsman, I must always be ready for a sudden start.

We are then at issue, this singular man and myself. His personal views are to a certain point explained. He has chosen an antiquated and desperate line of politics, and he claims, from some pretended tie of guardianship, or relationship, which he does not deign to explain, but which he seems to have been able to pass current on a silly country Justice and his knavish clerk, a right to direct and to control my motions. The danger which awaited me in England, and which I might have escaped had I remained in Scotland, was doubtless occasioned by the authority of this man. But what my poor mother might fear for me as a child — what my English friend, Samuel Griffiths, endeavoured to guard against during my youth and nonage, is now, it seems, come upon me; and, under a legal pretext, I am detained in what must be a most illegal manner, by a person, too, whose own political immunities have been forfeited by his conduct. It matters not — my mind is made up — neither persuasion nor threats shall force me into the desperate designs which this man meditates. Whether I am of the trifling consequence which my life hitherto seems to intimate, or whether I have (as would appear from my adversary's conduct) such importance, by birth or fortune, as may make me a desirable acquisition to a political faction, my resolution is taken in either case. Those who read this Journal, if it shall be perused by impartial eyes, shall judge of me truly; and if they consider me as a fool in encountering danger unnecessarily, they shall have no reason to believe me a coward or a turncoat, when I find myself engaged in it. I have been bred in sentiments of attachment to the family on the throne, and in these sentiments I will live and die. I have, indeed, some idea that Mr. Herries has already discovered that I am made of different and more unmalleable metal than he had at first believed. There were letters from my dear Alan Fairford, giving a ludicrous account of my instability of temper, in the same pocket-book, which, according to the admission of my pretended guardian, fell under the investigation of his domestic, during the night I passed at Brokenburn, where, as I now recollect, my wet clothes, with the contents of my pockets, were, with the thoughtlessness of a young traveller, committed too rashly to the care of a strange servant. And my kind friend and hospitable landlord, Mr. Alexander Fairford, may also, and with justice, have spoken of my levities to this man. But he shall find he has made a false estimate upon these plausible grounds, since ——

I must break off for the present.

Chapter the Ninth.

LATIMER'S JOURNAL, IN CONTINUATION.

THERE is at length a halt—at length I have gained so much privacy as to enable me to continue my Journal. It has become a sort of task of duty to me, without the discharge of which I do not feel that the business of the day is performed. True, no friendly eye may ever look upon these labours, which have amused the solitary hours of an unhappy prisoner. Yet, in the meanwhile, the exercise of the pen seems to act as a sedative upon my own agitated thoughts and tumultuous passions. I never lay it down but I rise stronger in resolution, more ardent in hope. A thousand vague fears, wild expectations, and indigested schemes, hurry through one's thoughts in seasons of doubt and of danger. But by arresting them as they flit across the mind, by throwing them on paper, and even by that mechanical act compelling ourselves to consider them with scrupulous and minute attention, we may perhaps escape becoming the dupes of our own excited imagination; just as a young horse is cured of the vice of starting, by being made to stand still and look for some time without any interruption at the cause of its terror.

There remains but one risk, which is that of discovery. But besides the small characters, in which my residence in Mr. Fairford's house enabled me to excel, for the purpose of transferring as many scroll sheets as possible to a huge sheet of stamped paper, I have, as I have elsewhere intimated, had hitherto the comfortable reflection, that if the record of my misfortunes should fall into the hands of him by whom they are caused, they would, without harming any one, show him the real character and disposition of the person who has become his prisoner — perhaps his victim. Now, however, that other names, and other characters, are to be mingled with the register of my own sentiments, I must take additional care of these papers, and keep them in such a manner that, in case of the least hazard of detection, I may be able to destroy them at a moment's notice. I shall not soon or easily forget the lesson I have been taught, by the prying disposition which Cristal Nixon, this man's agent and confederate, manifested at Brokenburn, and which proved the original cause of my sufferings.

My laying aside the last sheet of my Journal hastily, was occasioned by the unwonted sound of a violin, in the farm-yard beneath my windows. It will not appear surprising to those who have made music their study, that, after listening to a few notes, I became at once assured that the musician was no other than the itinerant, formerly mentioned as present at the destruction of Joshua Geddes's stake-nets, the superior delicacy and force of whose execution would enable me to swear to his bow amongst a whole orchestra. I had the less reason to doubt his identity, because he played twice over the beautiful Scottish air called Wandering Willie; and I could not help concluding that he did so for the purpose of intimating his own presence, since what the French called the *nom de guerre* of the performer was described by the tune.

Hope will catch at the most feeble twig for support in extremity. I knew this man, though deprived of sight, to be bold, ingenious, and perfectly capable of acting as a guide. I believed I had won his good-will, by having, in a frolic, assumed the character of his partner; and I remembered that, in a wild, wandering, and disorderly course of life, men as they become loosened from the ordinary bonds of civil society, hold those of comradeship more closely sacred; so that honour is sometimes found among thieves, and faith and attachment in such as the law has termed vagrants. The history of Richard Cœur de Lion and his minstrel, Blondel, rushed, at the same time, on my mind, though I could not even then suppress a smile at the dignity of the example, when applied to a blind fiddler and myself. Still there was something in all this to awaken a hope, that if I could open a correspondence with this poor violer, he might be useful in extricating me from my present situation.

His profession furnished me with some hope that this desired communication might be attained; since it is well known that, in Scotland, where there is so much national music, the words and airs of which are generally known, there is a kind of free-masonry amongst performers, by which they can, by the mere choice of a tune, express a great deal to the hearers. Personal allusions are often made in this manner, with much point and pleasantry; and nothing is more usual at public festivals, than that the air played to accompany a particular health or toast, is made the vehicle of compliment, of wit, and sometimes of satire.*

While these things passed through my mind rapidly, I heard my friend beneath recommence, for the third time, the air from which his own name had been probably adopted, when he was interrupted by his rustic auditors.

"If thou canst play no other spring but that, mon, ho hadst best put up bo's pipes and be jogging. Squoire will be back anon, or Master Nixon, and we'll see who will pay poiper then."

Oho, thought I, if I have no sharper ears than those of my friends Jan and Dorcas to encounter, I may venture an experiment upon them; and, as most expressive of my state of captivity, I sung two or three lines of the 137th Psalm—

"By Babel's streams we sat and wept."

The country people listened with attention, and when I ceased, I heard them whisper together in tones of commiseration, "Lack-a-day, poor soul! so pretty a man to be beside his wits!"

"An he be that gate," said Wandering Willie, in a tone calculated to reach my ears, "I ken naething will raise his spirits like a spring." And he struck up, with great vigour and spirit, the lively Scottish air, the words of which instantly occurred to me,—

"Oh whistle and I'll come t' ye, my lad,
Oh whistle and I'll come t' ye, my lad:
Though father and mother and a' should gae mad,
Oh whistle and I'll come t' ye, my lad."

I soon heard a clattering noise of feet in the court-yard, which I concluded to be Jan and Dorcas dancing a jig in their Cumberland wooden clogs. Under cover of this din, I endeavoured to answer Willie's signal by whistling, as loud as I could,

"Come back again and loe me
When a' the lave are gane."

He instantly threw the dancers out, by changing his air to

"There's my thumb, I'll ne'er beguile thee."

I no longer doubted that a communication betwixt us was happily established, and that, if I had an opportunity of speaking to the poor musician, I should find him willing to take my letter to the post, to invoke the assistance of some active magistrate, or of the commanding-officer of Carlisle Castle, or, in short, to do whatever else I could point out, in the compass of his power, to contribute to my liberation. But to obtain speech of him, I must have run the risk of alarming the suspicions of Dorcas, if not of her yet more stupid Corydon. My ally's blindness prevented his receiving any communication by signs from the window — even if I could have ventured to make them, consistently with prudence — so that, notwithstanding the mode of intercourse we had adopted was both circuitous and peculiarly liable to misapprehension, I saw nothing I could do better than to continue it, trusting my own and my correspondent's acuteness, in applying to the airs the meaning they were intended to convey. I thought of singing the words themselves of some significant song, but feared I might, by doing so, attract suspicion. I endeavoured, therefore, to intimate my speedy departure from my present place of residence, by whistling the well-known air with which festive parties in Scotland usually conclude the dance.—

"Good-night, and joy be wi' ye a',
For here nae langer maun I stay;
There's neither friend nor foe of mine
But wishes that I were away."

* Every one must remember instances of this festive custom, in which the adaptation of the tune to the toast was remarkably felicitous. Old Niel Gow and his son Nathaniel, were peculiarly happy on such occasions.

It appeared that Willie's powers of intelligence were much more active than mine, and that, like a deaf person, accustomed to be spoken to by signs, he comprehended, from the very first notes, the whole meaning I intended to convey; and he accompanied me in the air with his violin, in such a manner as at once to show he understood my meaning, and to prevent my whistling from being attended to.

His reply was almost immediate, and was conveyed in the old martial air of "Hey, Johnnie lad, cock up your beaver." I ran over the words, and fixed on the following stanzas, as most applicable to my circumstances:—

> "Cock up your beaver, and cock it fu' sprush,
> We'll over the border and give them a brush;
> There's somebody there we'll teach better behaviour,
> Hey, Johnnie lad, cock up your beaver."

If these sounds alluded, as I hope they do, to the chance of assistance from my Scottish friends, I may indeed consider that a door is open to hope and freedom. I immediately replied with,

> "My heart's in the Highlands, my heart is not here;
> My heart's in the Highlands, a-chasing the deer;
> A-chasing the wild deer, and following the roe,
> My heart's in the Highlands wherever I go.
>
> "Farewell to the Highlands! farewell to the North!
> The birth-place of valour, the cradle of worth;
> Wherever I wander, wherever I rove,
> The hills of the Highlands for ever I love."

Willie instantly played, with a degree of spirit which might have awakened hope in Despair herself, if Despair could be supposed to understand Scotch music, the fine old Jacobite air,

> "For a' that, and a' that,
> And twice as much as a' that."

I next endeavoured to intimate my wish to send notice of my condition to my friends; and, despairing to find an air sufficiently expressive of my purpose, I ventured to sing a verse, which, in various forms, occurs so frequently in old ballads—

> "Whare will I get a bonny boy
> That will win hose and shoon;
> That will gae down to Durisdeer,
> And bid my merry men come!"

He drowned the latter part of the verse by playing, with much emphasis,

> "Kind Robin loes me."

Of this, though I ran over the verses of the song in my mind, I could make nothing; and before I could contrive any mode of intimating my uncertainty, a cry arose in the court-yard that Cristal Nixon was coming. My faithful Willie was obliged to retreat; but not before he had half played, half hummed, by way of farewell,

> "Leave thee—leave thee, lad—
> I'll never leave thee;
> The stars shall gae withershins
> Ere I will leave thee."

I am thus, I think, secure of one trusty adherent in my misfortunes; and, however whimsical it may be to rely much on a man of his idle profession, and deprived of sight withal, it is deeply impressed on my mind, that his services may be both useful and necessary. There is another quarter from which I look for succour, and which I have indicated to thee, Alan, in more than one passage of my Journal. Twice, at the early hour of daybreak, I have seen the individual alluded to in the court of the farm, and twice she made signs of recognition in answer to the gestures by which I endeavoured to make her comprehend my situation; but on both occasions she pressed her finger on her lips, as expressive of silence and secrecy.

The manner in which G. M. entered upon the scene for the first time, seems to assure me of her good-will, so far as her power may reach; and I have many reasons to believe it is considerable. Yet she seemed hurried and frightened during the very transitory moments of our interview, and I think was, upon the last occasion, startled by the entrance of some one into the farm-yard, just as she was on the point of addressing me. You must not ask whether I am an early riser, since such objects are only to be seen at daybreak; and although I have never again seen her, yet I have reason to think she is not distant. It was but three nights ago, that, worn out by the uniformity of my confinement, I had manifested more symptoms of despondence than I had before exhibited, which I conceive may have attracted the attention of the domestics, through whom the circumstance might transpire. On the next morning, the following lines lay on my table; but how conveyed there, I cannot tell. The hand in which they were written is a beautiful Italian manuscript:—

> " As lords their labourers' hire delay,
>   Fate quits our toil with hopes to come,
> Which, if far short of present pay,
>   Still owns a debt and names a sum.
>
> " Quit not the pledge, frail sufferer, then,
>   Although a distant date be given;
> Despair is treason towards man,
>   And blasphemy to Heaven."

That those lines were written with the friendly purpose of inducing me to keep up my spirits, I cannot doubt; and I trust the manner in which I shall conduct myself may show that the pledge is accepted.

The dress is arrived in which it seems to be my self-elected guardian's pleasure that I shall travel; and what does it prove to be?—A skirt, or upper-petticoat of camlet, like those worn by country ladies of moderate rank when on horseback, with such a riding-mask as they frequently use on journeys to preserve their eyes and complexion from the sun and dust, and sometimes, it is suspected, to enable them to play off a little coquetry. From the gayer mode of employing the mask, however, I suspect I shall be precluded; for instead of being only pasteboard, covered with black velvet, I observe with anxiety that mine is thickened with a plate of steel, which, like Quixote's visor, serves to render it more strong and durable.

This apparatus, together with a steel clasp for securing the mask behind me with a padlock, gave me fearful recollections of the unfortunate being, who, never being permitted to lay aside such a visor, acquired the well-known historical epithet of the Man in the Iron Mask. I hesitated a moment whether I should so far submit to the acts of oppression designed against me as to assume this disguise, which was, of course, contrived to aid their purposes. But then I remembered Mr. Herries's threat, that I should be kept close prisoner in a carriage, unless I assumed the dress which should be appointed for me; and I considered the comparative degree of freedom which I might purchase by wearing the mask and female dress, as easily and advantageously purchased. Here, therefore, I must pause for the present, and await what the morning may bring forth.

[To carry on the story from the documents before us, we think it proper here to drop the Journal of the captive Darsie Latimer, and adopt, instead, a narrative of the proceedings of Alan Fairford in pursuit of his friend, which forms another series in this history.]

Chapter the Tenth.

NARRATIVE OF ALAN FAIRFORD.

THE reader ought, by this time, to have formed some idea of the character of Alan Fairford. He had a warmth of heart which the study of the law and of the world could not chill, and talents which they had rendered unusually acute. Deprived of the personal patronage enjoyed by most of his contemporaries, who assumed the gown under the protection of their aristocratic alliances and descents, he early saw that he should have that to achieve for himself which fell to them as a right of birth. He laboured hard in silence and solitude, and his labours were crowned with success. But Alan doted on his friend Darsie, even more than he loved his profession, and, as we have seen, threw every thing aside when he thought Latimer in danger; forgetting fame and fortune, and hazarding even the serious displeasure of his father, to rescue him whom he loved with an elder brother's affection. Darsie, though his parts were more quick and brilliant than those of his friend, seemed always to the latter a being under his peculiar charge, whom he was called upon to cherish and protect, in cases where the youth's own experience was unequal to the exigency; and now, when, the fate of Latimer seeming worse than doubtful, Alan's whole prudence and energy were to be exerted in his behalf, an adventure which might have seemed perilous to most youths of his age, had no terrors for him. He was well acquainted with the laws of his country, and knew how to appeal to them; and, besides his professional confidence, his natural disposition was steady, sedate, persevering, and undaunted. With these requisites he undertook a quest which, at that time, was not unattended with actual danger, and had much in it to appal a more timid disposition.

Fairford's first inquiry concerning his friend was of the chief magistrate of Dumfries, Provost Crosbie, who had sent the information of Darsie's disappearance. On his first application, he thought he discerned in the honest dignitary a desire to get rid of the subject. The Provost spoke of the riot at the fishing station as an "outbreak among those lawless loons the fishermen, which concerned the Sheriff," he said, "more than us poor Town-Council bodies, that have enough to do to keep peace within burgh, amongst such a set of commoners as the town are plagued with."

"But this is not all, Provost Crosbie," said Mr. Alan Fairford; "A young gentleman of rank and fortune has disappeared amongst their hands — you know him. My father gave him a letter to you—Mr. Darsie Latimer."

"Lack-a-day, yes! lack-a-day, yes!" said the Provost; "Mr. Darsie Latimer—he dined at my house—I hope he is well."

"I hope so too," said Alan, rather indignantly; "but I desire more certainty on that point. You yourself wrote my father that he had disappeared."

"Troth, yes, and that is true," said the Provost. "But did he not go back to his friends in Scotland? it was not natural to think he would stay here."

"Not unless he is under restraint," said Fairford, surprised at the coolness with which the Provost seemed to take up the matter.

"Rely on it, sir," said Mr. Crosbie, "that if he has not returned to his friends in Scotland, he must have gone to his friends in England."

"I will rely on no such thing," said Alan; "if there is law or justice in Scotland, I will have the thing cleared to the very bottom."

"Reasonable, reasonable," said the Provost, "so far as is possible; but you know I have no power beyond the ports of the burgh."

"But you are in the commission besides, Mr. Crosbie; a Justice of Peace for the county."

"True, very true—that is," said the cautious magistrate, "I will not say but my name may stand on the list, but I cannot remember that I have ever qualified."*

"Why, in that case," said young Fairford, "there are ill-natured people might doubt your attachment to the Protestant line, Mr. Crosbie."

"God forbid, Mr. Fairford! I who have done and suffered in the forty-five. I reckon the Highlandmen did me damage to the amount of 100l. Scots, forby all they ate and drank—no, no, sir, I stand beyond challenge; but as for plaguing myself with county business, let them that aught the mare shoe the mare. The Commissioners of Supply would see my back broken before they would help me in the burgh's work, and all the world kens the difference of the weight between public business in burgh and landward. What are their riots to me? have we not riots enough of our own?—But I must be getting ready, for the council meets this forenoon. I am blithe to see your father's son on the causeway of our ancient burgh, Mr. Alan Fairford. Were you a twelvemonth aulder, we would make a burgess of you, man. I hope you will come and dine with me before you go away. What think you of to-day at two o'clock—just a roasted chucky and a drappit egg?"

Alan Fairford resolved that his friend's hospitality should not, as it seemed the inviter intended, put a stop to his queries. "I must delay you for a moment," he said, "Mr. Crosbie; this is a serious affair; a young gentleman of high hopes, my own dearest friend, is missing—you cannot think it will be passed over slightly, if a man of your high character and known zeal for the government, do not make some active inquiry. Mr. Crosbie, you are my father's friend, and I respect you as such—but to others it will have a bad appearance."

The withers of the Provost were not unwrung; he paced the room in much tribulation, repeating, "But what can I do, Mr. Fairford? I warrant your friend casts up again—he will come back again, like the ill shilling—he is not the sort of gear that tynes—a hellicat boy, running through the country with a blind fiddler, and playing the fiddle to a parcel of blackguards, who can tell where the like of him may have scampered to?"

"There are persons apprehended, and in the jail of the town, as I understand from the Sheriff-Substitute," said Mr. Fairford; "you must call them before you, and inquire what they know of this young gentleman."

"Ay, ay—the Sheriff-Depute did commit some poor creatures, I believe—wretched ignorant fishermen bodies, that had been quarrelling with Quaker Geddes and his stakenets, whilk, under favour of your gown be it spoken, Mr. Fairford, are not over and above lawful, and the Town-Clerk thinks that they may be lawfully removed *via facti* — but that is by the by. But, sir, the creatures were a' dismissed for want of evidence; the Quaker would not swear to them, and what could the Sheriff and me do but just let them loose? Come awa, cheer up, Master Alan, and take a walk till dinner time—I must really go to the council."

"Stop a moment, Provost," said Alan; "I lodge a complaint before you as a magistrate, and you will find it serious to slight it over. You must have these men apprehended again."

"Ay, ay — easy said; but catch them that can," answered the Provost; "they are ower the March by this time, or by the point of Cairn. — Lord help ye! they are a kind of amphibious deevils, neither land nor water beasts—neither English nor Scots—neither county nor stewartry, as we say — they are dispersed like so much quicksilver. You may as well try to whistle a sealgh out of the Solway, as to get hold of one of them till all the fray is over."

---

* By taking the oaths to Government.

"Mr. Crosbie, this will not do," answered the young counsellor; "there is a person of more importance than such wretches as you describe concerned in this unhappy business — I must name to you a certain Mr. Herries."

He kept his eye on the Provost as he uttered the name, which he did rather at a venture, and from the connection which that gentleman, and his real or supposed niece, seemed to have with the fate of Darsie Latimer, than from any distinct cause of suspicions which he entertained. He thought the Provost seemed embarrassed, though he showed much desire to assume an appearance of indifference, in which he partly succeeded.

"Herries!" he said—"What Herries?—There are many of that name—not so many as formerly, for the old stocks are wearing out; but there is Herries of Heathgill, and Herries of Auchintullock, and Herries ——"

"To save you farther trouble, this person's designation is Herries of Birrenswork."

"Of Birrenswork?" said Mr. Crosbie; "I have you now, Mr. Alan. Could you not as well have said, the Laird of Redgauntlet?"

Fairford was too wary to testify any surprise at this identification of names, however unexpected. "I thought," said he, "he was more generally known by the name of Herries. I have seen and been in company with him under that name, I am sure."

"Oh ay; in Edinburgh, belike. You know Redgauntlet was unfortunate a great while ago, and though he was maybe not deeper in the mire than other folk, yet, for some reason or other, he did not get so easily out."

"He was attainted, I understand; and has no remission," said Fairford.

The cautious Provost only nodded, and said, "You may guess, therefore, why it is so convenient he should hold his mother's name, which is also partly his own, when he is about Edinburgh. To bear his proper name might be accounted a kind of flying in the face of government, ye understand. But he has been long connived at—the story is an old story—and the gentleman has many excellent qualities, and is of a very ancient and honourable house—has cousins among the great folk—counts kin with the Advocate and with the Sheriff—hawks, you know, Mr. Alan, will not pike out hawks' een—he is widely connected—my wife is a fourth cousin of Red gauntlet's."

Hinc illæ lachrymæ! thought Alan Fairford to himself; but the hint presently determined him to proceed by soft means and with caution. "I beg you to understand," said Fairford, "that in the investigation I am about to make, I design no harm to Mr. Herries, or Redgauntlet — call him what you will. All I wish is, to ascertain the safety of my friend. I know that he was rather foolish in once going upon a mere frolic, in disguise, to the neighbourhood of this same gentleman's house. In his circumstances, Mr. Redgauntlet may have misinterpreted the motives, and considered Darsie Latimer as a spy. His influence, I believe, is great, among the disorderly people you spoke of but now?"

The Provost answered with another sagacious shake of his head, that would have done honour to Lord Burleigh in the Critic.

"Well, then," continued Fairford, "is it not possible that, in the mistaken belief that Mr. Latimer was a spy, he may, upon such suspicion, have caused him to be carried off and confined somewhere?—Such things are done at elections, and on occasions less pressing than when men think their lives are in danger from an informer."

"Mr. Fairford," said the Provost, very earnestly, "I scarce think such a mistake possible: or if, by any extraordinary chance, it should have taken place, Redgauntlet, whom I cannot but know well, being, as I have said, my wife's first cousin, (fourth cousin, I should say,) is altogether incapable of doing any thing harsh to the young gentleman—he might send him over to Ailsay for a night or two, or maybe land him on the north coast of Ireland, or in Islay, or some of the Hebrides; but depend upon it, he is incapable of harming a hair of his head."

"I am determined not to trust to that, Provost," answered Fairford, firmly; "and I am a good deal surprised at your way of talking so lightly of such an aggression on the liberty of the subject. You are to consider, and Mr. Herries or Mr. Redgauntlet's friends would do very well also to consider, how it would sound in the ears of an English Secretary of State, that an attainted traitor (for such is this gentleman) has not only ventured to take up his abode in this realm—against the King of which he has been in arms—but is suspected of having proceeded, by open force and violence, against the person of one of the lieges, a young man, who is neither without friends nor property to secure his being righted."

The Provost looked at the young counsellor with a face in which distrust, alarm, and vexation seemed mingled. "A fashious job," he said at last, "a fashious job; and it will be dangerous meddling with it. I should like ill to see your father's son turn informer against an unfortunate gentleman."

"Neither do I mean it," answered Alan, "provided that unfortunate gentleman and his friends give me a quiet opportunity of securing my friend's safety. If I could speak with Mr. Redgauntlet, and hear his own explanation, I should probably be satisfied. If I am forced to denounce him to government, it will be in his new capacity of a kidnapper. I may not be able, nor is it my business, to prevent his being recognized in his former character of an attainted person, excepted from the general pardon."

"Master Fairford," said the Provost, "would ye ruin the poor innocent gentleman on an idle suspicion?"

"Say no more of it, Mr. Crosbie; my line of conduct is determined—unless that suspicion is removed."

"Weel, sir," said the Provost, "since so it be, and since you say that you do not seek to harm Redgauntlet personally, I'll ask a man to dine with us to-day that kens as much about his matters as most folk. You must think, Mr. Alan Fairford, though Redgauntlet be my wife's near relative, and though, doubtless, I wish him weel, yet I am not the person who is like to be intrusted with his incomings and outgoings. I am not a man for that—I keep the kirk, and I abhor Popery—I have stood up for the House of Hanover, and for liberty and property—I carried arms, sir, against the Pretender, when three of the Highlandmen's baggage-carts were stopped at Ecclefechan; and I had an especial loss of a hundred pounds——"

"Scots," interrupted Fairford. "You forget you told me all this before."

"Scots or English, it was too much for me to lose," said the Provost; "so you see I am not a person to pack or peel with Jacobites, and such unfreemen as poor Redgauntlet."

"Granted, granted, Mr. Crosbie; and what then?" said Alan Fairford.

"Why, then, it follows, that if I am to help you at this pinch, it cannot be by and through my ain personal knowledge, but through some fitting agent or third person."

"Granted again," said Fairford. "And pray who may this third person be?"

"Wha but Pate Maxwell of Summertrees—him they call Pate-in-Peril."

"An old forty-five man, of course?" said Fairford.

"Ye may swear that," replied the Provost—"as black a Jacobite as the auld leaven can make him; but a sonsy, merry companion, that none of us think it worth while to break wi' for all his brags and his clavers. You would have thought, if he had had but his own way at Derby, he would have marched Charlie Stewart through between Wade and the Duke, as a thred goes through the needle's ee, and seated him in Saint-James's before you could have said haud your hand. But though he is a windy body when he gets on his auld-warld stories, he has mair gumption in him than most people—knows business, Mr. Alan, being bred to the law; but never took the gown, because of the oaths, which kept more folk out then than they do now — the more's the pity."

"What! are you sorry, Provost, that Jacobitism is upon the decline?" said Fairford.

"No, no," answered the Provost — "I am only sorry for the folks losing the tenderness of conscience which they used to have. I have a son breeding to the bar, Mr. Fairford; and, no doubt, considering my services and sufferings, I might have looked for some bit postie to him; but if the muckle tikes come in—I mean a' these Maxwells, and Johnstones, and great lairds, that the oaths used to keep out lang syne — the bits o' meesan dogies, like my son, and maybe like your father's son, Mr. Alan, will be sair put to the wall."

"But to return to the subject, Mr. Crosbie," said Fairford, "do you really think it likely that this Mr. Maxwell will be of service in this matter?"

"It's very like he may be, for he is the tongue of the trump to the whole squad of them," said the Provost; "and Redgauntlet, though he will not stick at times to call him a fool, takes more of his counsel than any man's else that I am aware of. If Pate can bring him to a communing, the business is done. "He's a sharp chield, Pate-in-Peril."

"Pate-in-Peril!" repeated Alan; "a very singular name."

"Ay, and it was in as queer a way he got it; but I'll say naething about that," said the Provost, "for fear of forestalling his market; for ye are sure to hear it once at least, however oftener, before the punch-bowl gives place to the tea-pot.—And now, fare ye weel; for there is the council-bell clinking in earnest; and if I am not there before it jows in, Bailie Laurie will be trying some of his manœuvres."

The Provost, repeating his expectation of seeing Mr. Fairford at two o'clock, at length effected his escape from the young counsellor, and left him at a considerable loss how to proceed. The Sheriff, it seems, had returned to Edinburgh, and he feared to find the visible repugnance of the Provost to interfere with this Laird of Birrenswork, or Redgauntlet, much stronger amongst the country gentlemen, many of whom were Catholics as well as Jacobites, and most others unwilling to quarrel with kinsmen and friends, by prosecuting with severity political offences which had almost run a prescription.

To collect all the information in his power, and not to have recourse to the higher authorities until he could give all the light of which the case was capable, seemed the wiser proceeding in a choice of difficulties. He had some conversation with the Procurator-Fiscal, who, as well as the Provost, was an old correspondent of his father. Alan expressed to that officer a purpose of visiting Brokenburn, but was assured by him, that it would be a step attended with much danger to his own person, and altogether fruitless; that the individuals who had been ringleaders in the riot were long since safely sheltered in their various lurking-holes in the Isle of Man, Cumberland, and elsewhere; and that those who might remain would undoubtedly commit violence on any who visited their settlement with the purpose of inquiring into the late disturbances.

There were not the same objections to his hastening to Mount Sharon, where he expected to find the latest news of his friend; and there was time enough to do so, before the hour appointed for the Provost's dinner. Upon the road, he congratulated himself on having obtained one point of almost certain information. The person who had in a manner forced himself upon his father's hospitality, and had appeared desirous to induce Darsie Latimer to visit England, against whom, too, a sort of warning had been received from an individual connected with and residing in his own family, proved to be a promoter of the disturbance in which Darsie had disappeared.

What could be the cause of such an attempt on the liberty of an inoffensive and amiable man? It was impossible it could be merely owing to Redgauntlet's mistaking Darsie for a spy; for though that was the solution which Fairford had offered to the Provost, he well knew that, in point of fact, he himself had been warned by his singular visiter of some danger to which his friend was exposed, before such suspicion could have been entertained; and the injunctions received by Latimer from his guardian, or him who acted as such, Mr. Griffiths of London, pointed to the same thing. He was rather glad, however, that he had not let Provost Crosbie into his secret, farther than was absolutely necessary; since it was plain that the connection of his wife with the suspected party was likely to affect his impartiality as a magistrate.

When Alan Fairford arrived at Mount Sharon, Rachel Geddes hastened to meet him, almost before the servant could open the door. She drew back in disappointment when she beheld a stranger, and said, to excuse her precipitation, that "she had thought it was her brother Joshua returned from Cumberland."

"Mr. Geddes is then absent from home?" said Fairford, much disappointed in his turn.

"He hath been gone since yesterday, friend," answered Rachel, once more composed to the quietude which characterizes her sect, but her pale cheek and red eye giving contradiction to her assumed equanimity.

"I am," said Fairford, hastily, "the particular friend of a young man not unknown to you, Miss Geddes—the friend of Darsie Latimer—and am come hither in the utmost anxiety, having understood from Provost Crosbie, that he had disappeared in the night when a destructive attack was made upon the fishing-station of Mr. Geddes."

"Thou dost afflict me, friend, by thy inquiries," said Rachel, more affected than before; "for although the youth was like those of the worldly generation, wise in his own conceit, and lightly to be moved by the breath of vanity, yet Joshua loved him, and his heart clave to him as if he had been his own son. And when he himself escaped from the sons of Belial, which was not until they had tired themselves with reviling, and with idle reproach, and the jests of the scoffer, Joshua, my brother, returned to them once and again, to give ransom for the youth called Darsie Latimer, with offers of money and with promise of remission, but they would not hearken to him. Also, he went before the Head Judge, whom men call the Sheriff, and would have told him of the youth's peril; but he would in no way hearken to him unless he would swear unto the truth of his words, which thing he might not do without sin, seeing it is written, Swear not at all — also, that our conversation shall be yea or nay. Therefore, Joshua returned to me disconsolate, and said, 'Sister Rachel, this youth hath run into peril for my sake; assuredly I shall not be guiltless if a hair of his head be harmed, seeing I have sinned in permitting him to go with me to the fishing-station when such evil was to be feared. Therefore, I will take my horse, even Solomon, and ride swiftly into Cumberland, and I will make myself friends with Mammon of Unrighteousness, among the magistrates of the Gentiles, and among their mighty men; and it shall come to pass that Darsie Latimer shall be delivered, even if it were at the expense of half my substance.' And I said, 'Nay, my brother, go not, for they will but scoff at and revile thee; but hire with thy silver one of the scribes, who are eager as hunters in pursuing their prey, and he shall free Darsie Latimer from the men of violence by his cunning, and thy soul shall be guiltless of evil towards the lad.' But he answered and said, 'I will not be controlled in this matter.' And he is gone forth, and hath not returned, and I fear me that he may never return; for though he be peaceful, as becometh one who holds all violence as offence against his own soul, yet neither the floods of water, nor the fear of the snare, nor the drawn sword of the adversary brandished in the path, will overcome his purpose. Wherefore the Solway may swallow him up, or the sword of the enemy may devour him — nevertheless, my hope is better in Him who directeth all things, and ruleth over the waves of the sea, and overruleth the devices of the wicked, and who can redeem us even as a bird from the fowler's net."

This was all that Fairford could learn from Miss Geddes; but he heard with pleasure, that the good Quaker, her brother, had many friends among those of his own profession in Cumberland, and without exposing himself to so much danger as his sister seemed to apprehend, he trusted he might be able to discover some traces of Darsie Latimer. He himself rode back to Dumfries, having left with Miss Geddes his direction in that place, and an earnest request that she would forward thither whatever information she might obtain from her brother.

On Fairford's return to Dumfries he employed the brief interval which remained before dinner-time, in writing an account of what had befallen Latimer, and of the present uncertainty of his condition, to Mr. Samuel Griffiths, through whose hands the remittances for his friend's service had been regularly made, desiring he would instantly acquaint him with such parts of his history as might direct him in the search which he was about to institute through the border counties, and which he pledged himself not to give up until he had obtained news of his friend, alive or dead. The young lawyer's mind felt easier when he had despatched this letter. He could not conceive any reason why his friend's life should be aimed at; he knew Darsie had done nothing by which his liberty could be legally affected ; and although, even of late years, there had been singular histories of men, and women also, who had been trepanned, and concealed in solitudes and distant islands, in order to serve some temporary purpose, such violences had been chiefly practised by the rich on the poor, and by the strong on the feeble ; whereas, in the present case, this Mr. Herries, or Redgauntlet, being amenable, for more reasons than one, to the censure of the law, must be the weakest in any struggle in which it could be appealed to. It is true, that his friendly anxiety whispered, that the very cause which rendered this oppressor less formidable, might make him more desperate. Still, recalling his language, so strikingly that of the gentleman, and even of the man of honour, Alan Fairford concluded, that though, in his feudal pride, Redgauntlet might venture on the deeds of violence exercised by the aristocracy in other times, he could not be capable of any action of deliberate atrocity. And in these convictions he went to dine with Provost Crosbie, with a heart more at ease than might have been expected.*

Chapter the Eleventh.

NARRATIVE OF ALAN FAIRFORD, CONTINUED.

FIVE minutes had elapsed after the town-clock struck two, before Alan Fairford, who had made a small detour to put his letter into the post-house, reached the mansion of Mr. Provost Crosbie, and was at once greeted by the voice of that civic dignitary, and the rural dignitary his visiter, as by the voices of men impatient for their dinner.

---

* Scotland, in its half-civilized state, exhibited too many examples of the exertion of arbitrary force and violence, rendered easy by the dominion which lairds exerted over their tenants, and chiefs over their clans. The captivity of Lady Grange, in the desolate cliffs of Saint Kilda, is in the recollection of every one. At the supposed date of the novel also, a man of the name of Merrilees, a tanner in Leith, absconded from his country to escape his creditors ; and after having slain his own mastiff dog, and put a bit of red cloth in its mouth, as if it had died in a contest with soldiers, and involved his own existence in as much mystery as possible, made his escape into Yorkshire. Here he was detected by persons sent in search of him, to whom he gave a portentous account of his having been carried off and concealed in various places. Mr. Merrilees was, in short, a kind of male Elizabeth Canning, but did not trespass on the public credulity quite so long.

· "Come away, Mr. Fairford—the Edinburgh time is later than ours," said the Provost.

And, "Come away, young gentleman," said the Laird; "I remember your father weel, at the Cross, thirty years ago—I reckon you are as late in Edinburgh as at London, four o'clock hours—eh?"

"Not quite so degenerate," replied Fairford; "but certainly many Edinburgh people are so ill-advised as to postpone their dinner till three, that they may have full time to answer their London correspondents."

"London correspondents!" said Mr. Maxwell; "and pray, what the devil have the people of Auld Reekie to do with London correspondents?"*

"The tradesmen must have their goods," said Fairford.

"Can they not buy our own Scottish manufactures, and pick their customers' pockets in a more patriotic manner?"

"Then the ladies must have fashions," said Fairford.

"Can they not busk the plaid over their heads, as their mothers did? A tartan screen, and once a-year a new cockernony from Paris, should serve a countess. But ye have not many of them left, I think—Mareschal, Airley, Winton, Wemyss, Balmerino, all passed and gone—ay, ay, the countesses and ladies of quality will scarce take up too much of your ball-room floor with their quality hoops now-a-days."

"There is no want of crowding, however, sir," said Fairford; "they begin to talk of a new Assembly-Room."

"A new Assembly-Room!" said the old Jacobite Laird—"Umph—I mind quartering three hundred men in the old Assembly-Room †—But come, come —I'll ask no more questions—the answers all smell of new lords new lands, and do but spoil my appetite, which were a pity, since here comes Mrs. Crosbie to say our mutton's ready."

It was even so. Mrs. Crosbie had been absent, like Eve, "on hospitable cares intent," a duty which she did not conceive herself exempted from, either by the dignity of her husband's rank in the municipality, or the splendour of her Brussels silk gown, or even by the more highly prized lustre of her birth; for she was born a Maxwell, and allied, as her husband often informed his friends, to several of the first families in the county. She had been handsome, and was still a portly, good-looking woman of her years; and though her peep into the kitchen had somewhat heightened her complexion, it was no more than a modest touch of rouge might have done.

The Provost was certainly proud of his lady, nay, some said he was afraid of her; for, of the females of the Redgauntlet family there went a rumour, that, ally where they would, there was a gray mare as surely in the stables of their husbands, as there is a white horse in Wouverman's pictures. The good dame, too, was supposed to have brought a spice of politics into Mr. Crosbie's household along with her; and the Provost's enemies at the Council-table of the burgh used to observe, that he uttered there many a bold harangue against the Pretender, and in favour of King George and government, of which he dared not have pronounced a syllable in his own bed-chamber; and that, in fact, his wife's predominating influence had now and then occasioned his acting, or forbearing to act, in a manner very different from his general professions of zeal for Revolution principles. If this was in any respect true, it was certain, on the other hand, that Mrs. Crosbie, in all external points, seemed to acknowledge "the lawful sway and right supremacy" of the head of the house, and if she did not in truth reverence her husband, she at least seemed to do so.

This stately dame received Mr. Maxwell (a cousin of course) with cordiality, and Fairford with civility; answering at the same time with respect,

---

* Not much in those days, for within my recollection the London post was brought north in a small mail-cart; and men are yet alive who recollect when it came down with only one single letter for Edinburgh, addressed to the manager of the British Linen Company.

† I remember hearing this identical answer given by an old Highland gentleman of the Forty-Five, when he heard of the opening of the New Assembly-Rooms in George Street.

to the magisterial complaints of the Provost, that dinner was just coming up. "But since you changed poor Peter MacAlpin, that used to take care of the town-clock, my dear, it has never gone well a single day."

"Peter MacAlpin, my dear," said the Provost, "made himself too busy for a person in office, and drunk healths and so forth, which it became no man to drink or to pledge, far less one that is in point of office a servant of the public. I understand that he lost the music bells in Edinburgh for playing 'Ower the Water to Charlie,' upon the tenth of June. He is a black sheep, and deserves no encouragement."

"Not a bad tune though, after all," said Summertrees; and, turning to the window, he half hummed, half whistled, the air in question, then sang the last verse aloud:

"Oh I loe weel my Charlie's name,
    Though some there be that abhor him;
But oh to see the deil gang hame
    Wi' a' the Whigs before him!
Over the water, and over the sea,
    And over the water to Charlie;
Come weal, come wo, we'll gather and go
    And live or die with Charlie."

Mrs. Crosbie smiled furtively on the Laird, wearing an aspect at the same time of deep submission; while the Provost, not choosing to hear his visiter's ditty, took a turn through the room, in unquestioned dignity and independence of authority.

"Aweel, aweel, my dear," said the lady, with a quiet smile of submission, "ye ken these matters best, and you will do your pleasure — they are far above my hand — only, I doubt if ever the town-clock will go right, or your meals be got up so regular as I should wish, till Peter MacAlpin gets his office back again. The body's auld, and can neither work nor want, but he is the only hand to set a clock."

It may be noticed in passing, that, notwithstanding this prediction, which, probably, the fair Cassandra had the full means of accomplishing, it was not till the second council-day thereafter that the misdemeanours of the Jacobite clock-keeper were passed over, and he was once more restored to his occupation of fixing the town's time, and the Provost's dinner-hour.

Upon the present occasion the dinner passed pleasantly away. Summertrees talked and jested with the easy indifference of a man who holds himself superior to his company. He was indeed an important person, as was testified by his portly appearance; his hat laced with *point d'Espagne;* his coat and waistcoat once richly embroidered, though now almost threadbare; the splendour of his solitaire, and laced ruffles, though the first was sorely creased, and the other sullied; not to forget the length of his silver-hilted rapier. His wit, or rather humour, bordered on the sarcastic, and intimated a discontented man; and although he showed no displeasure when the Provost attempted a repartee, yet it seemed that he permitted it upon mere sufferance, as a fencing-master, engaged with a pupil, will sometimes permit the tyro to hit him, solely by way of encouragement. The Laird's own jests, in the meanwhile, were eminently successful, not only with the Provost and his lady, but with the red-cheeked and red-ribboned servant-maid who waited at table, and who could scarce perform her duty with propriety, so effectual were the explosions of Summertrees. Alan Fairford alone was unmoved among all this mirth; which was the less wonderful, that, besides the important subject which occupied his thoughts, most of the Laird's good things consisted in sly allusions to little parochial or family incidents, with which the Edinburgh visiter was totally unacquainted: so that the laughter of the party sounded in his ear like the idle crackling of thorns under the pot, with this indifference, that they did not accompany or second any such useful operation as the boiling thereof.

Fairford was glad when the cloth was withdrawn; and when Provost Crosbie (not without some points of advice from his lady, touching the precise mixture of the ingredients) had accomplished the compounding of a noble bowl of punch, at which the old Jacobite's eyes seemed to glisten, the glasses were pushed round it, filled, and withdrawn each by its owner, when the Provost emphatically named the toast, "The King," with an important look to Fairford, which seemed to say, You can have no doubt whom I mean, and therefore there is no occasion to particularize the individual.

Summertrees repeated the toast, with a sly wink to the lady, while Fairford drank his glass in silence.

"Well, young advocate," said the landed proprietor, "I am glad to see there is some shame, if there is little honesty, left in the Faculty. Some of your black-gowns, now-a-days, have as little of the one as of the other."

"At least, sir," replied Mr. Fairford, "I am so much of a lawyer as not willingly to enter into disputes which I am not retained to support—it would be but throwing away both time and argument."

"Come, come," said the lady, "we will have no argument in this house about Whig or Tory—the Provost kens what he maun say, and I ken what he should think; and for a' that has come and gane yet, there may be a time coming when honest men may say what they think, whether they be Provosts or not."

"D'ye hear that, Provost?" said Summertrees; "your wife's a witch, man; you should nail a horse-shoe on your chamber door—Ha, ha, ha!"

This sally did not take quite so well as former efforts of the Laird's wit. The lady drew up, and the Provost said, half aside, "The sooth bourd is nae bourd.* You will find the horse-shoe hissing hot, Summertrees."

"You can speak from experience, doubtless, Provost," answered the Laird; "but I crave pardon—I need not tell Mrs. Crosbie that I have all respect for the auld and honourable house of Redgauntlet."

"And good reason ye have, that are sae sib to them," quoth the lady, "and kend weel baith them that are here, and them that are gane."

"In troth, and ye may say sae, madam," answered the Laird; "for poor Harry Redgauntlet, that suffered at Carlisle, was hand and glove with me; and yet we parted on short leave-taking."

"Ay, Summertrees," said the Provost; "that was when you played Cheat-the-woodie, and gat the by-name of Pate-in-Peril. I wish you would tell the story to my young friend here. He likes weel to hear of a sharp trick, as most lawyers do."

"I wonder at your want of circumspection, Provost," said the Laird,—much after the manner of a singer when declining to sing the song that is quivering upon his tongue's very end. "Ye should mind there are some auld stories that cannot be ripped up again with entire safety to all concerned. Tace is Latin for a candle."

"I hope," said the lady, "you are not afraid of any thing being said out of this house to your prejudice, Summertrees? I have heard the story before; but the oftener I hear it, the more wonderful I think it."

"Yes, madam; but it has been now a wonder of more than nine days, and it is time it should be ended," answered Maxwell.

Fairford now thought it civil to say, "that he had often heard of Mr. Maxwell's wonderful escape, and that nothing could be more agreeable to him than to hear the right version of it."

But Summertrees was obdurate, and refused to take up the time of the company with such "auld warld nonsense."

"Weel, weel," said the Provost, "a wilful man maun hae his way. What do your folk in the country think about the disturbances that are beginning to spunk out in the colonies?"

"Excellent, sir, excellent. When things come to the worst they will mend; and to the worst they are coming. But as to that nonsense ploy

---

* The true joke is no joke.

of mine, if ye insist on hearing particulars,"—said the Laird, who began to be sensible that the period of telling his story gracefully was gliding fast away.

"Nay," said the Provost, "it was not for myself, but this young gentleman."

"Aweel, what for should I not pleasure the young gentleman?—I'll just drink to honest folk at hame and abroad, and deil ane else. And then— but you have heard it before, Mrs. Crosbie?"

"Not so often as to think it tiresome, I assure ye," said the lady; and without farther preliminaries, the Laird addressed Alan Fairford.

"Ye have heard of a year they call the *forty-five*, young gentleman: when the Southron's heads made their last acquaintance with Scottish claymores? There was a set of rampauging chields in the country then that they called rebels — I never could find out what for — Some men should have been wi' them that never came, Provost — Skye and the Bush aboon Traquair for that, ye ken. — Weel, the job was settled at last. Cloured crowns were plenty, and raxed necks came into fashion. I dinna mind very weel what I was doing, swaggering about the country with dirk and pistol at my belt for five or six months, or thereaway; but I had a weary waking out of a wild dream. Then did I find myself on foot in a misty morning, with my hand, just for' fear of going astray, linked into a handcuff, as they call it, with poor Harry Redgauntlet's fastened into the other; and there we were, trudging along, with about a score more that had thrust their horns ower deep in the bog, just like ourselves, and a sergeant's guard of redcoats, with twa file of dragoons, to keep all quiet, and give us heart to the road. Now, if this mode of travelling was not very pleasant, the object did not particularly recommend it; for, you understand, young man, that they did not trust these poor rebel bodies to be tried by juries of their ain kindly countrymen, though ane would have thought they would have found Whigs enough in Scotland to hang us all; but they behoved to trounce us away to be tried at Carlisle, where the folk had been so frightened, that had you brought a whole Highland clan at once into the court, they would have put their hands upon their een, and cried, 'hang them a',' just to be quit of them."

"Ay, ay," said the Provost, "that was a snell law, I grant ye."

"Snell!" said the wife, "snell! I wish they that passed it had the jury I would recommend them to!"

"I suppose the young lawyer thinks it all very right," said Summertrees, looking at Fairford—"an *old* lawyer might have thought otherwise. However, the cudgel was to be found to beat the dog, and they chose a heavy one. Well, I kept my spirits better than my companion, poor fellow; for I had the luck to have neither wife nor child to think about, and Harry Redgauntlet had both one and t'other. — You have seen Harry, Mrs. Crosbie?"

"In troth have I," said she, with the sigh which we give to early recollections, of which the object is no more. "He was not so tall as his brother, and a gentler lad every way. After he married the great English fortune, folk called him less of a Scottishman than Edward."

"Folk lee'd, then," said Summertrees; "poor Harry was none of your bold-speaking, ranting reivers, that talk about what they did yesterday, or what they will do to-morrow; it was when something was to do at the moment that you should have looked at Harry Redgauntlet. I saw him at Culloden, when all was lost, doing more than twenty of these bleezing braggarts, till the very soldiers that took him, cried not to hurt him — for all somebody's orders, Provost — for he was the bravest fellow of them all. Weel, as I went by the side of Harry, and felt him raise my hand up in the mist of the morning, as if he wished to wipe his eye — for he had not that freedom without my leave — my very heart was like to break for him, poor fellow. In the meanwhile, I had been trying and trying to make my hand as fine as a lady's, to see if I could slip it out of my iron wristband. You may think," he said, laying his broad bony hand on the table, "I had work enough with such a shoulder-of-mutton fist; but if you observe, the shackle-bones are of the largest, and so they were obliged to keep the handcuff wide; at length I got my hand slipped out, and slipped in again; and poor Harry was sae deep in his ain thoughts, I could not make him sensible what I was doing."

"Why not?" said Alan Fairford, for whom the tale began to have some interest.

"Because there was an unchancy beast of a dragoon riding close beside us on the other side; and if I had let him into my confidence as well as Harry, it would not have been long before a pistol-ball slapped through my bonnet. Well, I had little for it but to do the best I could for myself; and, by my conscience, it was time, when the gallows was staring me in the face. We were to halt for breakfast at Moffat. Well did I know the moors we were marching over, having hunted and hawked on every acre of ground in very different times. So I waited, you see, till I was on the edge of Errickstane brae—Ye ken the place they call the Marquis's Beef-stand, because the Annandale loons used to put their stolen cattle in there?"

Fairford intimated his ignorance.

"Ye must have seen it as ye came this way; it looks as if four hills were laying their heads together, to shut out daylight from the dark hollow space between them. A d—d deep, black, blackguard-looking abyss of a hole it is, and goes straight down from the road-side, as perpendicular as it can do, to be a heathery brae. At the bottom, there is a small bit of a brook, that you would think could hardly find its way out from the hills that are so closely jammed round it."

"A bad pass, indeed," said Alan.

"You may say that," continued the Laird. "Bad as it was, sir, it was my only chance; and though my very flesh creeped when I thought what a rumble I was going to get, yet I kept my heart up all the same. And so, just when we came on the edge of this Beef-stand of the Johnstones, I slipped out my hand from the handcuff, cried to Harry Gauntlet, 'Follow me!'—whisked under the belly of the dragoon horse—flung my plaid round me with the speed of lightning—threw myself on my side, for there was no keeping my feet, and down the brae hurled I, over heather and fern, and blackberries, like a barrel down Chalmers's Close, in Auld Reekie. G—, sir, I never could help laughing when I think how the scoundrel redcoats must have been bumbazed; for the mist being, as I said, thick, they had little notion, I take it, that they were on the verge of such a dilemma. I was half way down—for rowing is faster wark than rinning—ere they could get at their arms; and then it was flash, flash, flash—rap, rap, rap—from the edge of the road; but my head was too jumbled to think any thing either of that or the hard knocks I got among the stones. I kept my senses thegither, whilk has been thought wonderful by all that ever saw the place; and I helped myself with my hands as gallantly as I could, and to the bottom I came. There I lay for half a moment; but the thoughts of a gallows is worth all the salts and scent-bottles in the world, for bringing a man to himself. Up I sprung, like a four-year-auld colt. All the hills were spinning round with me, like so many great big humming-tops. But there was nae time to think of that neither; more especially as the mist had risen a little with the firing. I could see the villains, like sae mony craws on the edge of the brae; and I reckon that they saw me; for some of the loons were beginning to crawl down the hill, but liker auld wives in their red cloaks, coming frae a field preaching, than such a souple lad as I was. Accordingly, they soon began to stop and load their pieces. Good-e'en to you, gentlemen, thought I, if that is to be the gate of it. If you have any

P

farther word with me, you maun come as far as Carriefraw-gauns. And so off I set, and never buck went faster ower the braes than I did; and I never stopped till I had put three waters, reasonably deep, as the season was rainy, half-a-dozen mountains, and a few thousand acres of the worst moss and ling in Scotland, betwixt me and my friends the redcoats."

"It was that job which got you the name of Pate-in-Peril," said the Provost, filling the glasses, and exclaiming with great emphasis, while his guest, much animated with the recollections which the exploit excited, looked round with an air of triumph for sympathy and applause,—"Here is to your good health; and may you never put your neck in such a venture again."*

"Humph!—I do not know," answered Summertrees. "I am not like to be tempted with another opportunity† — Yet who knows?" And then he made a deep pause.

"May I ask what became of your friend, sir?" said Alan Fairford.

"Ah, poor Harry!" said Summertrees. "I'll tell you what, sir, it takes time to make up one's mind to such a venture, as my friend the Provost calls it; and I was told by Neil Maclean,—who was next file to us, but had the luck to escape the gallows by some slight-of-hand trick or other,—that, upon my breaking off, poor Harry stood like one motionless, although all our brethren in captivity made as much tumult as they could, to distract the attention of the soldiers. And run he did at last; but he did not know the ground, and either from confusion, or because he judged the descent altogether perpendicular, he fled up the hill to the left, instead of going down at once, and so was easily pursued and taken. If he had followed my example, he would have found enough among the shepherds to hide him, and feed him, as they did me, on bear-meal scones and braxy mutton,‡ till better days came round again."

"He suffered then for his share in the insurrection?" said Alan.

"You may swear that," said Summertrees. "His blood was too red to be spared when that sort of paint was in request. He suffered, sir, as you call it — that is, he was murdered in cold blood, with many a pretty fellow besides.—Well, we may have our day next—what is fristed is not forgiven — they think us all dead and buried — but——" Here he filled his glass, and muttering some indistinct denunciations, drank it off, and assumed his usual manner, which had been a little disturbed towards the end of the narrative.

"What became of Mr. Redgauntlet's child?" said Fairford.

"*Mister* Redgauntlet!—He was Sir Henry Redgauntlet, as his son, if the child now lives, will be Sir Arthur—I called him Harry from intimacy, and Redgauntlet, as the chief of his name — His proper style was Sir Henry Redgauntlet."

"His son, therefore, is dead?" said Alan Fairford. "It is a pity so brave a line should draw to a close."

"He has left a brother," said Summertrees, "Edward Hugh Redgauntlet, who has now the representation of the family. And well it is; for though he be unfortunate in many respects, he will keep up the honour of the house better than a boy bred up amongst these bitter Whigs, the relations of his elder brother Sir Henry's lady. Then they are on no good terms with the Redgauntlet line—bitter Whigs they are in every sense. It was a runaway match betwixt Sir Henry and his lady. Poor thing, they would not allow her to see him when in confinement—they had even the meanness to leave him without pecuniary assistance; and as all his own property was seized upon and plundered, he would have wanted common necessaries, but for the attachment of a fellow who was a famous fiddler—a blind man—I have seen him with Sir Henry myself, both before the affair broke out and while it was going on. I have heard that he fiddled in the streets of Carlisle, and carried what money he got to his master, while he was confined in the castle."

"I do not believe a word of it," said Mrs. Crosbie, kindling with indignation. "A Redgauntlet would have died twenty times before he had touched a fiddler's wages."

"Hout fye—hout fye—all nonsense and pride," said the Laird of Summertrees. "Scornful dogs will eat dirty puddings, cousin Crosbie — ye little ken what some of your friends were obliged to do yon time for a sowp of brose, or a bit of bannock.—G—d, I carried a cutler's wheel for several weeks, partly for need, and partly for disguise — there I went bizz — bizz —whizz—zizz, at every auld wife's door; and if ever you want your shears sharpened, Mrs. Crosbie, I am the lad to do it for you, if my wheel was but in order."

"You must ask my leave, first," said the Provost; "for I have been told you had some queer fashions of taking a kiss instead of a penny, if you liked your customer."

"Come, come, Provost," said the lady, rising, "if the maut gets abune the meal with you, it is time for me to take myself away — And you will come to my room, gentlemen, when you want a cup of tea."

Alan Fairford was not sorry for the lady's departure. She seemed too much alive to the honour of the house of Redgauntlet, though only a fourth cousin, not to be alarmed by the inquiries which he proposed to make after the whereabout of its present head. Strange confused suspicions arose in his mind, from his imperfect recollection of the tale of Wandering Willie, and the idea forced itself upon him, that his friend Darsie Latimer might be the son of the unfortunate Sir Henry. But before indulging in such speculations, the point was, to discover what had actually become of him. If he were in the hands of his uncle, might there not exist some rivalry in fortune, or rank, which might induce so stern a man as Redgauntlet to use unfair measures towards a youth whom he would find himself unable to mould to his purpose? He considered these points in silence, during several revolutions of the glasses as they wheeled in galaxy round the bowl, waiting until the Provost, agreeably to his own proposal, should mention the subject, for which he had expressly introduced him to Mr. Maxwell of Summertrees.

Apparently the Provost had forgot his promise, or at least was in no great haste to fulfil it. He debated with great earnestness upon the stamp act, which was then impending over the American colonies, and upon other political subjects of the day, but said not a word of Redgauntlet. Alan soon saw that the investigation he meditated must advance, if at all, on his own special motion, and determined to proceed accordingly.

Acting upon this resolution, he took the first opportunity afforded by a pause in the discussion of colonial politics, to say, "I must remind you, Provost Crosbie, of your kind promise to procure some intelligence upon the subject I am so anxious about."

"Gadso!" said the Provost, after a moment's hesitation, "it is very true. —Mr. Maxwell, we wish to consult you on a piece of important business. You must know — indeed I think you must have heard, that the fishermen at Brokenburn, and higher up the Solway, have made a raid upon Quaker Geddes's stake-nets, and levelled all with the sands."

"In troth I heard it, Provost, and I was glad to hear the scoundrels had so much pluck left, as to right themselves against a fashion which would make the upper heritors a sort of clocking-hens, to hatch the fish that folk below them were to catch and eat."

"Well, sir," said Alan, "that is not the present point. But a young friend of mine was with Mr. Geddes at the time this violent procedure took place, and he has not since been heard of. Now, our friend, the Provost, thinks that you may be able to advise——"

Here he was interrupted by the Provost and Summertrees speaking out both at once, the first endeavouring to disclaim all interest in the question, and the last to evade giving an answer.

"Me think!" said the Provost; "I never thought twice about it, Mr. Fairford; it was neither fish, nor flesh, nor salt herring of mine."

"And I 'able to advise!'" said Mr. Maxwell of Summertrees; "what the devil can I advise you to do, excepting to send the bellman through the town to cry your lost sheep, as they do spaniel dogs or stray ponies?"

"With your pardon," said Alan, calmly, but resolutely, "I must ask a more serious answer."

"Why, Mr. Advocate," answered Summertrees, "I thought it was your business to give advice to the lieges, and not to take it from poor stupid country gentlemen."

"If not exactly advice, it is sometimes our duty to ask questions, Mr. Maxwell."

"Ay, sir, when you have your bag-wig and your gown on, we must allow you the usual privilege of both gown and petticoat, to ask what questions you please. But when you are out of your canonicals, the case is altered. How come you, sir, to suppose that I have any business with this riotous proceeding, or should know more than you do what happened there? the question proceeds on an uncivil supposition."

"I will explain," said Alan, determined to give Mr. Maxwell no opportunity of breaking off the conversation. "You are an intimate of Mr. Redgauntlet—he is accused of having been engaged in this affray, and of having placed under forcible restraint the person of my friend, Darsie Latimer, a young man of property and consequence, whose fate I am here for the express purpose of investigating. This is the plain state of the case; and all parties concerned,—your friend, in particular,—will have reason to be thankful for the temperate manner in which it is my purpose to conduct the matter, if I am treated with proportionate frankness."

"You have misunderstood me," said Maxwell, with a tone changed to more composure; "I told you I was the friend of the late Sir Henry Redgauntlet, who was executed, in 1745, at Hairibie, near Carlisle, but I know no one who at present bears the name of Redgauntlet."

"You know Mr. Herries of Birrenswork," said Alan, smiling, "to whom the name of Redgauntlet belongs?"

Maxwell darted a keen reproachful look towards the Provost, but instantly smoothed his brow, and changed his tone to that of confidence and candour.

"You must not be angry, Mr. Fairford, that the poor persecuted nonjurors are a little upon the *qui vive* when such clever young men as you are making inquiries after us. I myself now, though I am quite out of the scrape, and may cock my hat at the Cross as I best like, sunshine or moonshine, have been yet so much accustomed to walk with the lap of my cloak cast over my face, that, faith, if a redcoat walk suddenly up to me, I wish for my wheel and whetstone again for a moment. Now Redgauntlet, poor fellow, is far worse off — he is, you may have heard, still under the lash of the law,—the mark of the beast is still on his forehead, poor gentleman,— and that makes us cautious — very cautious, which I am sure there is no occasion to be towards you, as no one of your appearance and manners would wish to trepan a gentleman under misfortune."

"On the contrary, sir," said Fairford, "I wish to afford Mr. Redgauntlet's friends an opportunity to get him out of the scrape, by procuring the instant liberation of my friend Darsie Latimer. I will engage, that if he has sustained no greater bodily harm than a short confinement, the matter may be passed over quietly, without inquiry ; but to attain this end, so desirable for the man who has committed a great and recent infraction of the laws, which he had before grievously offended, very speedy reparation of the wrong must be rendered."

Maxwell seemed lost in reflection, and exchanged a glance or two, not of the most comfortable or congratulatory kind, with his host the Provost. Fairford rose and walked about the room, to allow them an opportunity of conversing together ; for he was in hopes that the impression he had visibly made upon Summertrees was likely to ripen into something favourable to his purpose. They took the opportunity, and engaged in whispers to each other, eagerly and reproachfully on the part of the Laird, while the Provost answered in an embarrassed and apologetical tone. Some broken words of the conversation reached Fairford, whose presence they seemed to forget, as he stood at the bottom of the room, apparently intent upon examining the figures upon a fine Indian screen, a present to the Provost from his brother, captain of a vessel in the Company's service. What he overheard made it evident that his errand, and the obstinacy with which he pursued it, occasioned altercation between the whisperers.

Maxwell at length let out the words, "A good fright ; and so send him home with his tail scalded, like a dog, that has come a privateering on strange premises."

The Provost's negative was strongly interposed—"Not to be thought of" — "making bad worse" — "my situation" — "my utility" — "you cannot conceive how obstinate—just like his father."

They then whispered more closely, and at length the Provost raised his drooping crest, and spoke in a cheerful tone. "Come, sit down to your glass, Mr. Fairford ; we have laid our heads thegither, and you shall see it will not be our fault if you are not quite pleased, and Mr. Darsie Latimer let loose to take his fiddle under his neck again. But Summertrees thinks it will require you to put yourself into some bodily risk, which maybe you may not be so keen of."

"Gentlemen," said Fairford, "I will not certainly shun any risk by which my object may be accomplished ; but I bind it on your consciences — on yours, Mr. Maxwell, as a man of honour and a gentleman ; and on yours, Provost, as a magistrate and a loyal subject, that you do not mislead me in this matter."

"Nay, as for me," said Summertrees, "I will tell you the truth at once, and fairly own that I can certainly find you the means of seeing Redgauntlet, poor man ; and that I will do, if you require it, and conjure him also to treat you as your errand requires ; but poor Redgauntlet is much changed —indeed, to say truth, his temper never was the best in the world ; however, I will warrant you from any very great danger."

"I will warrant myself from such," said Fairford, "by carrying a proper force with me."

"Indeed," said Summertrees, "you will do no such thing ; for, in the first place, do you think that we will deliver up the poor fellow into the hands of the Philistines, when, on the contrary, my only reason for furnishing you with the clew I am to put into your hands, is to settle the matter amicably on all sides? And secondly, his intelligence is so good, that were you coming near him with soldiers, or constables, or the like, I shall answer for it, you will never lay salt on his tail."

Fairford mused for a moment. He considered that to gain sight of this man, and knowledge of his friend's condition, were advantages to be purchased at every personal risk ; and he saw plainly, that were he to take the course most safe for himself, and call in the assistance of the law, it was clear he would either be deprived of the intelligence necessary to guide him, or that Redgauntlet would be apprized of his danger, and might probably leave the country, carrying his captive along with him. He therefore repeated, " I put myself on your honour, Mr. Maxwell; and I will go alone to visit your friend. I have little doubt I shall find him amenable to reason; and that I shall receive from him a satisfactory account of Mr. Latimer."

" I have little doubt that you will," said Mr. Maxwell of Summertrees; " but still I think it will be only in the long run, and after having sustained some delay and inconvenience. My warrandice goes no farther."

" I will take it as it is given," said Alan Fairford. " But let me ask, would it not be better, since you value your friend's safety so highly, and surely would not willingly compromise mine, that the Provost or you should go with me to this man, if he is within any reasonable distance, and try to make him hear reason?"

" Me!—I will not go my foot's length," said the Provost; " and that, Mr. Alan, you may be well assured of. Mr. Redgauntlet is my wife's fourth cousin, that is undeniable; but were he the last of her kin and mine both, it would ill befit my office to be communing with rebels."

" Ay, or drinking with nonjurors," said Maxwell, filling his glass. " I would as soon expect to have met Claverhouse at a field-preaching. And as for myself, Mr. Fairford, I cannot go, for just the opposite reason. It would be *infra dig.* in the Provost of this most flourishing and loyal town to associate with Redgauntlet; and for me it would be *noscitur a socio.* There would be post to London, with the tidings that two such Jacobites as Redgauntlet and I had met on a braeside — the Habeas Corpus would be suspended—Fame would sound a charge from Carlisle to the Land's-end— and who knows but the very wind of the rumour might blow my estate from between my fingers, and my body over Errickstane-brae again? No, no; bide a gliff— I will go into the Provost's closet, and write a letter to Redgauntlet, and direct you how to deliver it."

" There is pen and ink in the office," said the Provost, pointing to the door of an inner apartment, in which he had his walnut-tree desk, and east-country cabinet.

"A pen that can write, I hope?" said the old Laird.

" It can write and spell baith in right hands," answered the Provost, as the Laird retired and shut the door behind him.

<hr />

Chapter the Twelfth.

NARRATIVE OF ALAN FAIRFORD, CONTINUED.

THE room was no sooner deprived of Mr. Maxwell of Summertrees's presence, than the Provost looked very warily above, beneath, and around the apartment, hitched his chair towards that of his remaining guest, and began to speak in a whisper which could not have startled "the smallest mouse that creeps on floor."

" Mr. Fairford," said he, " you are a good lad; and, what is more, you are my auld friend your father's son. Your father has been agent for this burgh for years, and has a good deal to say with the council; so there have been a sort of obligations between him and me; it may have been now on this side and now on that; but obligations there have been. I am but a plain man, Mr. Fairford; but I hope you understand me?"

"I believe you mean me well, Provost; and I am sure," replied Fairford, "you can never better show your kindness than on this occasion."

"That's it — that's the very point I would be at, Mr. Alan," replied the Provost; "besides, I am, as becomes well my situation, a stanch friend to Kirk and King, meaning this present establishment in church and state; and so, as I was saying, you may command my best — advice."

"I hope for your assistance and co-operation also," said the youth.

"Certainly, certainly," said the wary magistrate. "Well, now, you see one may love the Kirk, and yet not ride on the rigging of it; and one may love the King, and yet not be cramming him eternally down the throat of the unhappy folk that may chance to like another King better. I have friends and connections among them, Mr. Fairford, as your father may have clients—they are flesh and blood like ourselves, these poor Jacobite bodies —sons of Adam and Eve, after all; and therefore—I hope you understand me!—I am a plain-spoken man."

"I am afraid I do *not* quite understand you," said Fairford; "and if you have any thing to say to me in private, my dear Provost, you had better come quickly out with it, for the Laird of Summertrees must finish his letter in a minute or two."

"Not a bit, man—Pate is a lang-headed fellow, but his pen does not clear the paper as his grayhound does the Tinwald-furs. I gave him a wipe about that, if you noticed; I can say any thing to Pate-in-Peril — Indeed, he is my wife's near kinsman."

"But your advice, Provost," said Alan, who perceived that, like a shy horse, the worthy magistrate always started off from his own purpose just when he seemed approaching to it.

"Weel, you shall have it in plain terms, for I am a plain man. — Ye see, we will suppose that any friend like yourself were in the deepest hole in the Nith, and making a sprattle for your life. Now, you see, such being the case, I have little chance of helping you, being a fat, short-armed man, and no swimmer, and what would be the use of my jumping in after you?—"

"I understand you, I think," said Alan Fairford. "You think that Darsie Latimer is in danger of his life."

"Me!—I think nothing about it, Mr. Alan; but if he were, as I trust he is not, he is nae drap's blood akin to you, Mr. Alan."

"But here your friend, Summertrees," said the young lawyer, "offers me a letter to this Redgauntlet of yours — What say you to that?"

"Me!" ejaculated the Provost, "me, Mr. Alan? I say neither buff nor stye to it—But ye dinna ken what it is to look a Redgauntlet in the face;— better try my wife, who is but a fourth cousin, before ye venture on the Laird himself—just say something about the Revolution, and see what a look she can gie you."

"I shall leave you to stand all the shots from that battery, Provost," replied Fairford. "But speak out like a man — Do you think Summertrees means fairly by me?"

"Fairly—he is just coming—fairly? I am a plain man, Mr. Fairford— but ye said *fairly?*"

"I do so," replied Alan, "and it is of importance to me to know, and to you to tell me if such is the case; for if you do not, you may be an accomplice to murder before the fact, and that under circumstances which may bring it near to murder under trust."

"Murder!—who spoke of murder?" said the Provost. "No danger of that, Mr. Alan — only, if I were you—to speak my plain mind"—Here he approached his mouth to the ear of the young lawyer, and, after another acute pang of travail, was safely delivered of his advice in the following abrupt words: — "Take a keek into Pate's letter before ye deliver it."

Fairford started, looked the Provost hard in the face, and was silent; while Mr. Crosbie, with the self-approbation of one who has at length brought himself to the discharge of a great duty, at the expense of a considerable sacrifice, nodded and winked to Alan, as if enforcing his advice; and then, swallowing a large glass of punch, concluded, with the sigh of a man released from a heavy burden, " I am a plain man, Mr. Fairford."

" A plain man?" said Maxwell, who entered the room at that moment, with the letter in his hand,—" Provost, I never heard you make use of the word, but when you had some sly turn of your own to work out."

The Provost looked silly enough, and the Laird of Summertrees directed a keen and suspicious glance upon Alan Fairford, who sustained it with professional intrepidity.—There was a moment's pause.

" I was trying," said the Provost, " to dissuade our young friend from his wildgoose expedition."

" And I," said Fairford, " am determined to go through with it. Trusting myself to you, Mr. Maxwell, I conceive that I rely, as I before said, on the word of a gentleman."

" I will warrant you," said Maxwell, " from all serious consequences — some inconveniences you must look to suffer."

" To these I shall be resigned," said Fairford, " and stand prepared to run my risk."

" Well, then," said Summertrees, " you must go ——"

" I will leave you to yourselves, gentlemen," said the Provost, rising; when you have done with your crack, you will find me at my wife's tea-table."

" And a more accomplished old woman never drank cat-lap," said Maxwell, as he shut the door ; " the last word has him, speak it who will—and yet because he is a whilly-whaw body, and has a plausible tongue of his own, and is well enough connected, and especially because nobody could ever find out whether he is Whig or Tory, this is the third time they have made him Provost!—But to the matter in hand. This letter, Mr. Fairford," putting a sealed one into his hand, " is addressed, you observe, to Mr. H—— of B——, and contains your credentials for that gentleman, who is also known by his family name of Redgauntlet, but less frequently addressed by it, because it is mentioned something invidiously in a certain act of Parliament. I have little doubt he will assure you of your friend's safety, and in a short time place him at freedom — that is, supposing him under present restraint. But the point is, to discover where he is — and, before you are made acquainted with this necessary part of the business, you must give me your assurance of honour that you will acquaint no one, either by word or letter, with the expedition which you now propose to yourself."

" How, sir?" answered Alan, " can you expect that I will not take the precaution of informing some person of the route I am about to take, that in case of accident it may be known where I am, and with what purpose I have gone thither?"

" And can you expect," answered Maxwell, in the same tone, " that I am to place my friend's safety, not merely in your hands, but in those of any person you may choose to confide in, and who may use the knowledge to his destruction?—Na—na—I have pledged my word for your safety, and you must give me yours to be private in the matter—giff gaff—you know."

Alan Fairford could not help thinking that this obligation to secrecy gave a new and suspicious colouring to the whole transaction ; but, considering that his friend's release might depend upon his accepting the condition, he gave it in the terms proposed, and with the purpose of abiding by it.

" And now, sir," he said, " whither am I to proceed with this letter? Is Mr. Herries at Brokenburn?"

" He is not; I do not think he will come thither again, until the business of the stake-nets be hushed up, nor would I advise him to do so — the Quakers, with all their demureness, can bear malice as long as other folk; and though I have not the prudence of Mr. Provost, who refuses to ken where his friends are concealed during adversity, lest, perchance, he should be asked to contribute to their relief, yet I do not think it necessary or prudent to inquire into Redgauntlet's wanderings, poor man, but wish to remain at perfect freedom to answer, if asked at, that I ken nothing of the matter. You must, then, go to old Tom Trumbull's at Annan,—Tam Turnpenny, as they call him,—and he is sure either to know where Redgauntlet is himself, or to find some one who can give a shrewd guess. But you must attend that old Turnpenny will answer no question on such a subject without you give him the passport, which at present you must do, by asking him the age of the moon: if he answers, 'Not light enough to land a cargo,' you are to answer, 'Then plague on Aberdeen Almanacks, and upon that he will hold free intercourse with you. — And now, I would advise you to lose no time, for the parole is often changed — and take care of yourself among these moonlight lads, for laws and lawyers do not stand very high in their favour."

"I will set out this instant," said the young barrister; "I will but bid the Provost and Mrs. Crosbie farewell, and then get on horseback so soon as the hostler of the George Inn can saddle him; — as for the smugglers, I am neither gauger nor supervisor, and, like the man who met the devil, if they have nothing to say to me, I have nothing to say to them."

"You are a mettled young man," said Summertrees, evidently with increasing good will, on observing an alertness and contempt of danger, which perhaps he did not expect from Alan's appearance and profession, — "a very mettled young fellow indeed! and it is almost a pity" —— Here he stopped short.

"What is a pity?" said Fairford.

"It is almost a pity that I cannot go with you myself, or at least send a trusty guide."

They walked together to the bedchamber of Mrs. Crosbie, for it was in that asylum that the ladies of the period dispensed their tea, when the parlour was occupied by the punch-bowl.

"You have been good bairns to-night, gentlemen," said Mrs. Crosbie; "I am afraid, Summertrees, that the Provost has given you a bad browst; you are not used to quit the lee-side of the punch-bowl in such a hurry. I say nothing to you, Mr. Fairford, for you are too young a man yet for stoup and bicker; but I hope you will not tell the Edinburgh fine folk that the Provost has scrimped you of your cogie, as the sang says?"

"I am much obliged for the Provost's kindness, and yours, madam," replied Alan; "but the truth is, I have still a long ride before me this evening, and the sooner I am on horseback the better."

"This evening?" said the Provost, anxiously; "had you not better take daylight with you to-morrow morning?"

"Mr. Fairford will ride as well in the cool of the evening," said Summertrees, taking the word out of Alan's mouth.

The Provost said no more, nor did his wife ask any questions, nor testify any surprise at the suddenness of their guest's departure.

Having drunk tea, Alan Fairford took leave with the usual ceremony. The Laird of Summertrees seemed studious to prevent any farther communication between him and the Provost, and remained lounging on the landing-place of the stair while they made their adieus—heard the Provost ask if Alan proposed a speedy return, and the latter reply, that his stay was uncertain, and witnessed the parting shake of the hand, which, with a pressure more warm than usual, and a tremulous, "God bless and prosper you!" Mr. Crosbie bestowed on his young friend. Maxwell even strolled with Fairford as far as the George, although resisting all his attempts at farther inquiry into the affairs of Redgauntlet, and referring him to Tom Trumbull, alias Turnpenny, for the particulars which he might find it necessary to inquire into.

At length Alan's hack was produced — an animal long in neck, and high in bone, accoutred with a pair of saddle-bags containing the rider's travelling wardrobe. Proudly surmounting his small stock of necessaries, and no way ashamed of a mode of travelling which a modern Mr. Silvertongue would consider as the last of degradations, Alan Fairford took leave of the old Jacobite, Pate-in-Peril, and set forward on the road to the loyal burgh of Annan. His reflections during his ride were none of the most pleasant. He could not disguise from himself that he was venturing rather too rashly into the power of outlawed and desperate persons; for with such only, a man in the situation of Redgauntlet could be supposed to associate. There were other grounds for apprehension. Several marks of intelligence betwixt Mrs. Crosbie and the Laird of Summertrees had not escaped Alan's acute observation; and it was plain that the Provost's inclinations towards him, which he believed to be sincere and good, were not firm enough to withstand the influence of this league between his wife and friend. The Provost's adieus, like Macbeth's amen, had stuck in his throat, and seemed to intimate that he apprehended more than he dared give utterance to.

Laying all these matters together, Alan thought, with no little anxiety, on the celebrated lines of Shakspeare,

> ——— "A drop,
> That in the ocean seeks another drop," &c.

But pertinacity was a strong feature in the young lawyer's character. He was, and always had been, totally unlike the "horse hot at hand," who tires before noon through his own over eager exertions in the beginning of the day. On the contrary, his first efforts seemed frequently inadequate to accomplishing his purpose, whatever that for the time might be; and it was only as the difficulties of the task increased, that his mind seemed to acquire the energy necessary to combat and subdue them. If, therefore, he went anxiously forward upon his uncertain and perilous expedition, the reader must acquit him of all idea, even in a passing thought, of the possibility of abandoning his search, and resigning Darsie Latimer to his destiny.

A couple of hours' riding brought him to the little town of Annan, situated on the shores of the Solway, between eight and nine o'clock. The sun had set, but the day was not yet ended; and when he had alighted and seen his horse properly cared for at the principal inn of the place, he was readily directed to Mr. Maxwell's friend, old Tom Trumbull, with whom every body seemed well acquainted. He endeavoured to fish out from the lad that acted as a guide, something of this man's situation and profession; but the general expressions of "a very decent man" — "a very honest body" — "weel to pass in the world," and such like, were all that could be extracted from him; and while Fairford was following up the investigation with closer interrogatories, the lad put an end to them by knocking at the door of Mr. Trumbull, whose decent dwelling was a little distance from the town, and considerably nearer to the sea. It was one of a little row of houses running down to the waterside, and having gardens and other accommodations behind. There was heard within the uplifting of a Scottish psalm; and the boy saying, "They are at exercise, sir," gave intimation they might not be admitted till prayers were over.

When, however, Fairford repeated the summons with the end of his whip, the singing ceased, and Mr. Trumbull himself, with his psalm-book in his hand, kept open by the insertion of his forefinger between the leaves, came to demand the meaning of this unseasonable interruption.

Nothing could be more different than his whole appearance seemed to be from the confidant of a desperate man, and the associate of outlaws in their unlawful enterprises. He was a tall, thin, bony figure, with white hair combed straight down on each side of his face, and an iron-gray hue of complexion; where the lines, or rather, as Quin said of Macklin, the cordage, of his countenance were so sternly adapted to a devotional and even ascetic expression, that they left no room for any indication of reckless daring, or sly dissimulation. In short, Trumbull appeared a perfect specimen of the rigid old Covenanter, who said only what he thought right, acted on no other principle but that of duty, and, if he committed errors, did so under the full impression that he was serving God rather than man.

"Do you want me, sir?" he said to Fairford, whose guide had slunk to the rear, as if to escape the rebuke of the severe old man, — "We were engaged, and it is the Saturday night."

Alan Fairford's preconceptions were so much deranged by this man's appearance and manner, that he stood for a moment bewildered, and would as soon have thought of giving a cant pass-word to a clergyman descending from the pulpit, as to the respectable father of a family just interrupted in his prayers for and with the objects of his care. Hastily concluding Mr. Maxwell had passed some idle jest on him, or rather that he had mistaken the person to whom he was directed, he asked if he spoke to Mr. Trumbull.

"To Thomas Trumbull," answered the old man — "What may be your business, sir?" And he glanced his eye to the book he held in his hand, with a sigh like that of a saint desirous of dissolution.

"Do you know Mr. Maxwell of Summertrees?" said Fairford.

"I have heard of such a gentleman in the country-side, but have no acquaintance with him," answered Mr. Trumbull; "he is, as I have heard, a Papist; for the whore that sitteth on the seven hills ceaseth not yet to pour forth the cup of her abomination on these parts."

"Yet he directed me hither, my good friend," said Alan. "Is there another of your name in this town of Annan?"

"None," replied Mr. Trumbull, "since my worthy father was removed; he was indeed a shining light. — I wish you goodeven, sir."

"Stay one single instant," said Fairford; "this is a matter of life and death."

"Not more than the casting of the burden of our sins where they should be laid," said Thomas Trumbull, about to shut the door in the inquirer's face.

"Do you know," said Alan Fairford, "the Laird of Redgauntlet?"

"Now Heaven defend me from treason and rebellion!" exclaimed Trumbull. "Young gentleman, you are importunate. I live here among my own people, and do not consort with Jacobites and mass-mongers."

He seemed about to shut the door, but did *not* shut it, a circumstance which did not escape Alan's notice.

"Mr. Redgauntlet is sometimes," he said, "called Herries of Birrenswork; perhaps you may know him under that name?"

"Friend, you are uncivil," answered Mr. Trumbull; "honest men have enough to do to keep one name undefiled. I ken nothing about those who have two. Good-even to you, friend."

He was now about to slam the door in his visitor's face without farther ceremony, when Alan, who had observed symptoms that the name of Redgauntlet did not seem altogether so indifferent to him as he pretended, arrested his purpose by saying, in a low voice, "At least you can tell me what age the moon is?"

The old man started, as if from a trance, and before answering, surveyed the querist with a keen penetrating glance, which seemed to say, "Are you really in possession of this key to my confidence, or do you speak from mere accident?"

To this keen look of scrutiny, Fairford replied by a smile of intelligence. The iron muscles of the old man's face did not, however, relax, as he dropped, in a careless manner, the countersign, "Not light enough to land a cargo."

"Then plague of all Aberdeen Almanacks!"

"And plague of all fools that waste time," said Thomas Trumbull. "Could you not have said as much at first? — And standing wasting time, and encouraging lookers-on, in the open street too? Come in by — in by."

He drew his visiter into the dark entrance of the house, and shut the door carefully; then putting his head into an apartment which the murmurs within announced to be filled with the family, he said aloud, "A work of necessity and mercy — Malachi, take the book — You will sing six double verses of the hundred and nineteen — and then you may lecture out of the Lamentations. And, Malachi,"—this he said in an under-tone,—"see you give them a screed of doctrine that will last them till I come back; or else these inconsiderate lads will be out of the house, and away to the publics, wasting their precious time, and, it may be, putting themselves in the way of missing the morning tide."

An inarticulate answer from within intimated Malachi's acquiescence in the commands imposed; and Mr. Trumbull, shutting the door, muttered something about fast bind, fast find, turned the key and put it into his pocket; and then bidding his visiter have a care of his steps, and make no noise, he led him through the house, and out at a back-door, into a little garden. Here a plaited alley conducted them, without the possibility of their being seen by any neighbour, to a door in the garden-wall, which being opened, proved to be a private entrance into a three-stalled stable; in one of which was a horse, that whinnied on their entrance. "Hush, hush!" cried the old man, and presently seconded his exhortations to silence by throwing a handful of corn into the manger, and the horse soon converted his acknowledgment of their presence into the usual sound of munching and grinding his provender.

As the light was now failing fast, the old man, with much more alertness than might have been expected from the rigidity of his figure, closed the window-shutters in an instant, produced phosphorus and matches, and lighted a stable-lantern, which he placed on the corn-bin, and then addressed Fairford. "We are private here, young man; and as some time has been wasted already, you will be so kind as to tell me what is your errand. Is it about the way of business, or the other job?"

"My business with you, Mr. Trumbull, is to request you will find me the means of delivering this letter, from Mr. Maxwell of Summertrees to the Laird of Redgauntlet."

"Humph — fashious job! — Pate Maxwell will still be the auld man — always Pate-in-Peril — Craig-in-Peril, for what I know. Let me see the letter from him."

He examined it with much care, turning it up and down, and looking at the seal very attentively. "All's right, I see; it has the private mark for haste and speed. I bless my Maker that I am no great man, or great man's fellow; and so I think no more of these passages than just to help them forward in the way of business. You are an utter stranger in these parts, I warrant?"

Fairford answered in the affirmative.

"Ay — I never saw them make a wiser choice — I must call some one to direct you what to do — Stay, we must go to him, I believe. You are well recommended to me, friend, and doubtless trusty; otherwise you may see more than I would like to show, or am in the use of showing in the common line of business."

Saying this, he placed his lantern on the ground, beside the post of one of the empty stalls, drew up a small spring-bolt which secured it to the floor, and then forcing the post to one side, discovered a small trap-door.

"Follow me," he said, and dived into the subterranean descent to which this secret aperture gave access.

Fairford plunged after him, not without apprehensions of more kinds than one, but still resolved to prosecute the adventure.

The descent, which was not above six feet, led to a very narrow passage, which seemed to have been constructed for the precise purpose of excluding every one who chanced to be an inch more in girth than was his conductor. A small vaulted room, of about eight feet square, received them at the end of this lane. Here Mr. Trumbull left Fairford alone, and returned for an instant, as he said, to shut his concealed trap-door.

Fairford liked not his departure, as it left him in utter darkness; besides that his breathing was much affected by a strong and stifling smell of spirits, and other articles of a savour more powerful than agreeable to the lungs. He was very glad, therefore, when he heard the returning steps of Mr. Trumbull, who, when once more by his side, opened a strong though narrow door in the wall, and conveyed Fairford into an immense magazine of spirit-casks, and other articles of contraband trade.

There was a small light at the end of this range of well-stocked subterranean vaults, which, upon a low whistle, began to flicker and move towards them. An undefined figure, holding a dark lantern, with the light averted, approached them, whom Mr. Trumbull thus addressed:—"Why were you not at worship, Job; and this Saturday at e'en?"

"Swanston was loading the Jenny, sir; and I stayed to serve out the article."

"True — a work of necessity, and in the way of business. Does the Jumping Jenny sail this tide?"

"Ay, ay, sir; she sails for ——"

"I did not ask you *where* she sailed for, Job," said the old gentleman, interrupting him. "I thank my Maker, I know nothing of their incomings or outgoings. I sell my article fairly and in the ordinary way of business; and I wash my hands of every thing else. But what I wished to know is, whether the gentleman called the Laird of the Solway Lakes is on the other side of the Border even now?"

"Ay, ay," said Job, "the Laird is something in my own line, you know — a little contraband or so. There is a statute for him — But no matter; he took the sands after the splore at the Quaker's fish-traps yonder; for he has a leal heart, the Laird, and is always true to the country-side. But avast — is all snug here?"

So saying, he suddenly turned on Alan Fairford the light side of the lantern he carried, who, by the transient gleam which it threw in passing on the man who bore it, saw a huge figure, upwards of six feet high, with a rough hairy cap on his head, and a set of features corresponding to his bulky frame. He thought also he observed pistols at his belt.

"I will answer for this gentleman," said Mr. Trumbull; "he must be brought to speech of the Laird."

"That will be kittle steering," said the subordinate personage; "for I understood that the Laird and his folk were no sooner on the other side than the land-sharks were on them, and some mounted lobsters from Carlisle; and so they were obliged to split and squander. There are new brooms out to sweep the country for them, they say; of the brush was a hard one; and they say there was a lad drowned;—he was not one of the Laird's gang, so there was the less matter."

"Peace! prithee, peace, Job Rutledge," said honest, pacific Mr. Trumbull. "I wish thou couldst remember, man, that I desire to know nothing of your roars and splores, your brooms and brushes. I dwell here among my own people; and I sell my commodity to him who comes in the way of business; and so wash my hands of all consequences, as becomes a quiet subject and an honest man. I never take payment, save in ready money."

Q

"Ay, ay," muttered he with the lantern, "your worship, Mr. Trumbull, understands that in the way of business."

"Well, I hope you will one day know, Job," answered Mr. Trumbull, — "the comfort of a conscience void of offence, and that fears neither gauger nor collector, neither excise nor customs. The business is to pass this gentleman to Cumberland upon earnest business, and to procure him speech with the Laird of the Solway Lakes — I suppose that can be done? Now I think Nanty Ewart, if he sails with the brig this morning tide, is the man to set him forward."

"Ay, ay, truly is he," said Job; "never man knew the Border, dale and fell, pasture and ploughland, better than Nanty; and he can always bring him to the Laird, too, if you are sure the gentleman's right. But indeed that's his own look-out; for were he the best man in Scotland, and the chairman of the d—d Board to boot, and had fifty men at his back, he were as well not visit the Laird for any thing but good. As for Nanty, he is word and blow, a d—d deal fiercer than Cristie Nixon that they keep such a din about. I have seen them both tried, by ——"

Fairford now found himself called upon to say something; yet his feelings, upon finding himself thus completely in the power of a canting hypocrite, and of his retainer, who had so much the air of a determined ruffian, joined to the strong and abominable fume which they snuffed up with indifference, while it almost deprived him of respiration, combined to render utterance difficult. He stated, however, that he had no evil intentions towards the Laird, as they called him, but was only the bearer of a letter to him on particular business, from Mr. Maxwell of Summertrees.

"Ay, ay," said Job, "that may be well enough; and if Mr. Trumbull is satisfied that the service is right, why, we will give you a cast in the Jumping Jenny this tide, and Nanty Ewart will put you on a way of finding the Laird, I warrant you."

"I may for the present return, I presume, to the inn where I left my horse?" said Fairford.

"With pardon," replied Mr. Trumbull, "you have been ower far ben with us for that; but Job will take you to a place where you may sleep rough till he calls you. I will bring you what little baggage you can need — for those who go on such errands must not be dainty. I will myself see after your horse, for a merciful man is merciful to his beast — a matter too often forgotten in our way of business."

"Why, Master Trumbull," replied Job, "you know that when we are chased, it's no time to shorten sail, and so the boys do ride whip and spur" — He stopped in his speech, observing the old man had vanished through the door by which he had entered — "That's always the way with old Turnpenny," he said to Fairford; "he cares for nothing of the trade but the profit — now, d—me, if I don't think the fun of it is better worth while. But come along, my fine chap; I must stow you away in safety until it is time to go aboard."

Chapter the Thirteenth.

NARRATIVE OF ALAN FAIRFORD, CONTINUED.

FAIRFORD followed his gruff guide among a labyrinth of barrels and puncheons, on which he had more than once like to have broken his nose, and from thence into what, by the glimpse of the passing lantern upon a desk and writing materials, seemed to be a small office for the despatch of business. Here there appeared no exit; but the smuggler, or smuggler's ally, availing himself of a ladder, removed an old picture, which showed a door about seven feet from the ground, and Fairford, still following him, involved in another tortuous and dark passage, which involuntarily reminded him of Peter Peebles's lawsuit. At the end of this labyrinth, when he had little guess where he had been conducted, and was, according to the French phrase, totally *desorienté*, Job suddenly set down the lantern, and availing himself of the flame to light two candles which stood on the table, asked if Alan would choose any thing to eat, recommending, at all events, a slug of brandy to keep out the night air. Fairford declined both, but inquired after his baggage.

" The old master will take care of that himself," said Job Rutledge; and drawing back in the direction in which he had entered, he vanished from the farther end of the apartment, by a mode which the candles, still shedding an imperfect light, gave Alan no means of ascertaining. Thus the adventurous young lawyer was left alone in the apartment to which he had been conducted by so singular a passage.

In this condition, it was Alan's first employment to survey, with some accuracy, the place where he was; and accordingly, having trimmed the lights, he walked slowly round the apartment, examining its appearance and dimensions. It seemed to be such a small dining-parlour as is usually found in the house of the better class of artisans, shopkeepers, and such persons, having a recess at the upper end, and the usual furniture of an ordinary description. He found a door, which he endeavoured to open, but it was locked on the outside. A corresponding door on the same side of the apartment admitted him into a closet, upon the front shelves of which were punch-bowls, glasses, tea-cups, and the like, while on one side was hung a horseman's great-coat of the coarsest materials, with two great horse-pistols peeping out of the pocket, and on the floor stood a pair of well-spattered jack-boots, the usual equipment of the time, at least for long journeys.

Not greatly liking the contents of the closet, Alan Fairford shut the door, and resumed his scrutiny round the walls of the apartment, in order to discover the mode of Job Rutledge's retreat. The secret passage was, however, too artificially concealed, and the young lawyer had nothing better to do than to meditate on the singularity of his present situation. He had long known that the excise laws had occasioned an active contraband trade betwixt Scotland and England, which then, as now, existed, and will continue to exist, until the utter abolition of the wretched system which establishes an inequality of duties betwixt the different parts of the same kingdom; a system, be it said in passing, mightily resembling the conduct of a pugilist, who should tie up one arm that he might fight the better with the other. But Fairford was unprepared for the expensive and regular establishments by which the illicit traffic was carried on, and could not have conceived that the capital employed in it should have been adequate to the erection of these extensive buildings, with all their contrivances for secrecy of communication. He was musing on these circumstances, not without some anxiety for the progress of his own journey, when suddenly, as he lifted his eyes, he discovered old **Mr. Trumbull** at the upper end of the apartment, bearing in one hand a small bundle, in the other his dark lantern, the light of which, as he advanced, he directed full upon Fairford's countenance.

Though such an apparition was exactly what he expected, yet he did not see the grim, stern old man present himself thus suddenly without emotion; especially when he recollected, what to a youth of his pious education was peculiarly shocking, that the grizzled hypocrite was probably that instant arisen from his knees to Heaven, for the purpose of engaging in the mysterious transactions of a desperate and illegal trade.

The old man, accustomed to judge with ready sharpness of the physiognomy of those with whom he had business, did not fail to remark something like agitation in Fairford's demeanour. "Have ye taken the rue?" said he. "   ye take the sheaf from the mare, and give up the venture?"

"   er!" said Fairford, firmly, stimulated at once by his natural spirit, and   recollection of his friend; "never, while I have life and strength to follow it out!"

"I have brought you," said Trumbull, "a clean shirt, and some stockings, which is all the baggage you can conveniently carry, and I will cause one of the lads lend you a horseman's coat, for it is ill sailing or riding without one; and, touching your valise, it will be as safe in my poor house, were it full of the gold of Ophir, as if it were in the depth of the mine."

"I have no doubt of it," said Fairford.

"And now," said Trumbull, again, "I pray you to tell me by what name I am to name you to Nanty [which is Antony] Ewart?"

"By the name of Alan Fairford," answered the young lawyer.

"But that," said Mr. Trumbull, in reply, "is your own proper name and surname."

"And what other should I give?" said the young man; "do you think I have any occasion for an alias? And, besides, Mr. Trumbull," added Alan, thinking a little raillery might intimate confidence of spirit, "you blessed yourself, but a little while since, that you had no acquaintance with those who defiled their names so far as to be obliged to change them."

"True, very true," said Mr. Trumbull; "nevertheless, young man, my gray hairs stand unreproved in this matter; for, in my line of business, when I sit under my vine and my fig-tree, exchanging the strong waters of the north for the gold which is the price thereof, I have, I thank Heaven, no disguises to keep with any man, and wear my own name of Thomas Trumbull, without any chance that the same may be polluted. Whereas, thou, who art to journey in miry ways, and amongst a strange people, mayst do well to have two names, as thou hast two shirts, the one to keep the other clean."

Here he emitted a chuckling grunt, which lasted for two vibrations of the pendulum exactly, and was the only approach towards laughter in which old Turnpenny, as he was nicknamed, was ever known to indulge.

"You are witty, Mr. Trumbull," said Fairford; "but jests are no arguments — I shall keep my own name."

"At your own pleasure," said the merchant; "there is but one name which," &c. &c. &c.

We will not follow the hypocrite through the impious cant which he added, in order to close the subject.

Alan followed him, in silent abhorrence, to the recess in which the beaufet was placed, and which was so artificially made as to conceal another of those traps with which the whole building abounded. This concealment admitted them to the same winding passage by which the young lawyer had been brought thither. The path which they now took amid these mazes, differed from the direction in which he had been guided by Rutledge. It led upwards, and terminated beneath a garret window. Trumbull opened it, and with more agility than his age promised, clambered out upon the leads. If Fairford's journey had been hitherto in a stifled and subterranean atmosphere, it was now open, lofty, and airy enough; for he had to follow his guide over leads and slates, which the old smuggler traversed with the dexterity of a cat. It is true, his course was facilitated by knowing exactly where certain stepping-places and holdfasts were placed, of which Fairford could not so readily avail himself; but, after a difficult and somewhat perilous progress along the roofs of two or three houses, they at length descended by a skylight into a garret room, and from thence by the stairs into a public-house; for such it appeared, by the ringing of bells, whistling for waiters and attendance, bawling of "House, house, here!" chorus of sea songs, and the like noises.

Having descended to the second story, and entered a room there, in which there was a light, old Mr. Trumbull rung the bell of the apartment thrice, with an interval betwixt each, during which, he told deliberately the number twenty. Immediately after the third ringing the landlord appeared, with stealthy step, and appearance of mystery on his buxom visage. He greeted Mr. Trumbull, who was his landlord as it proved, with great respect, and expressed some surprise at seeing him so late, as he termed it, "on Saturday e'en."

"And I, Robin Hastie," said the landlord to the tenant, "am more surprised than pleased, to hear sae muckle din in your house, Robie, so near the honourable Sabbath; and I must mind you, that it is contravening the terms of your tack, whilk stipulates, that you should shut your public on Saturday at nine o'clock, at latest."

"Yes, sir," said Robin Hastie, no way alarmed at the gravity of the rebuke, "but you must take tent that I have admitted naebody but you, Mr. Trumbull, (who by the way admitted yoursell,) since nine o'clock; for the most of the folk have been here for several hours about the lading, and so on, of the brig. It is not full tide yet, and I cannot put the men out into the street. If I did, they would go to some other public, and their souls would be nane the better, and my purse muckle the waur; for how am I to pay the rent, if I do not sell the liquor?"

"Nay, then," said Thomas Trumbull, "if it is a work of necessity, and in the honest independent way of business, no doubt there is balm in Gilead. But prithee, Robin, wilt thou see if Nanty Ewart be, as is most likely, amongst these unhappy topers; and if so, let him step this way cannily, and speak to me and this young gentleman. And it's dry talking, Robin— you must minister to us a bowl of punch — ye ken my gage."

"From a mutchkin to a gallon, I ken your honour's taste, Mr. Thomas Trumbull," said mine host; "and ye shall hang me over the sign-post if there be a drap mair lemon or a curn less sugar than just suits you. There are three of you—you will be for the auld Scots peremptory pint-stoup* for the success of the voyage?"

"Better pray for it than drink for it, Robin," said Mr. Trumbull. "Yours is a dangerous trade, Robin; it hurts mony a ane — baith host and guest. But ye will get the blue bowl, Robin — the blue bowl — that will sloken all their drouth, and prevent the sinful repetition of whipping for an eke of a Saturday at e'en. Ay, Robin, it is a pity of Nanty Ewart — Nanty likes the turning up of his little finger unco weel, and we maunna stint him, Robin, so as we leave him sense to steer by."

"Nanty Ewart could steer through the Pentland Firth though he were as drunk as the Baltic Ocean," said Robin Hastie; and instantly tripping down stairs, he speedily returned with the materials for what he called his

* The Scottish pint of liquid measure comprehends four English measures of the same denomination. The jest is well known of my poor countryman, who, driven to extremity by the raillery of the Southern, on the small denomination of the Scottish coin, at length answered, "Ay, ay! But the deil tak them that his the least pint-stoup."

browst, which consisted of two English quarts of spirits, in a huge blue bowl, with all the ingredients for punch, in the same formidable proportion. At the same time he introduced Mr. Antony or Nanty Ewart, whose person, although he was a good deal flustered with liquor, was different from what Fairford expected. His dress was what is emphatically termed the shabby genteel—a frock with tarnished lace—a small cocked-hat, ornamented in a similar way — a scarlet waistcoat, with faded embroidery, breeches of the same, with silver knee-bands, and he wore a smart hanger and a pair of pistols in a sullied sword-belt.

"Here I come, patron," he said, shaking hands with Mr. Trumbull. "Well, I see you have got some grog aboard."

"It is not my custom, Mr. Ewart," said the old gentleman, "as you well know, to become a chamberer or carouser thus late on Saturday at e'en; but I wanted to recommend to your attention a young friend of ours, that is going upon a something particular journey, with a letter to our friend the Laird from Pate-in-Peril, as they call him."

"Ay—indeed?—he must be in high trust for so young a gentleman. I wish you joy, sir," bowing to Fairford. "By'r lady, as Shakspeare says, you are bringing up a neck for a fair end.—Come, patron, we will drink to Mr. What-shall-call-um—What is his name?—Did you tell me?—And have I forgot it already?"

"Mr. Alan Fairford," said Trumbull.

"Ay, Mr. Alan Fairford—a good name for a fair trader—Mr. Alan Fairford; and may he be long withheld from the topmost round of ambition, which I take to be the highest round of a certain ladder."

While he spoke, he seized the punch ladle, and began to fill the glasses. But Mr. Trumbull arrested his hand, until he had, as he expressed himself, sanctified the liquor by a long grace; during the pronunciation of which, he shut indeed his eyes, but his nostrils became dilated, as if he were snuffing up the fragrant beverage with peculiar complacency.

When the grace was at length over, the three friends sat down to their beverage, and invited Alan Fairford to partake. Anxious about his situation, and disgusted as he was with his company, he craved, and with difficulty obtained permission, under the allegation of being fatigued, heated, and the like, to stretch himself on a couch which was in the apartment, and attempted at least to procure some rest before high-water, when the vessel was to sail.

He was at length permitted to use his freedom, and stretched himself on the couch, having his eyes for some time fixed on the jovial party he had left, and straining his ears to catch if possible a little of their conversation. This he soon found was to no purpose; for what did reach his ears was disguised so completely by the use of cant words, and the thieves Latin called slang, that even when he caught the words, he found himself as far as ever from the sense of their conversation. At length he fell asleep.

It was after Alan had slumbered for three or four hours, that he was wakened by voices bidding him rise up and prepare to be jogging. He started up accordingly, and found himself in presence of the same party of boon companions, who had just despatched their huge bowl of punch. To Alan's surprise, the liquor had made but little innovation on the brains of men, who were accustomed to drink at all hours, and in the most inordinate quantities. The landlord indeed spoke a little thick, and the texts of Mr. Thomas Trumbull stumbled on his tongue; but Nanty was one of those topers, who, becoming early what *bon vivants* term flustered, remain whole nights and days at the same point of intoxication; and, in fact, as they are seldom entirely sober, can be as rarely seen absolutely drunk. Indeed, Fairford, had he not known how Ewart had been engaged whilst he himself was asleep, would almost have sworn when he awoke, that the man was more sober than when he first entered the room.

He was confirmed in this opinion when they descended below, where two or three sailors and ruffian-looking fellows awaited their commands. Ewart took the whole direction upon himself, gave his orders with briefness and precision, and looked to their being executed with the silence and celerity which that peculiar crisis required. All were now dismissed for the brig, which lay, as Fairford was given to understand, a little farther down the river, which is navigable for vessels of light burden, till almost within a mile of the town.

When they issued from the inn, the landlord bid them good-by. Old Trumbull walked a little way with them, but the air had probably considerable effect on the state of his brain; for after reminding Alan Fairford that the next day was the honourable Sabbath, he became extremely excursive in an attempt to exhort him to keep it holy. At length, being perhaps sensible that he was becoming unintelligible, he thrust a volume into Fairford's hand—hiccuping at the same time—"Good book—good book—fine hymn-book—fit for the honourable Sabbath, whilk awaits us to-morrow morning." — Here the iron tongue of time told five from the town steeple of Annan, to the farther confusion of Mr. Trumbull's already disordered ideas. "Ay? Is Sunday come and gone already?—Heaven be praised! Only it is a marvel the afternoon is sae dark for the time of the year—Sabbath has slipped ower quietly, but we have reason to bless oursells it has not been altogether misemployed. I heard little of the preaching—a cauld moralist, I doubt, served that out—but, eh—the prayer—I mind it as if I had said the words mysell."—Here he repeated one or two petitions, which were probably a part of his family devotions, before he was summoned forth to what he called the way of business. "I never remember a Sabbath pass so cannily off in my life."—Then he recollected himself a little, and said to Alan, "You may read that book, Mr. Fairford, to-morrow, all the same, though it be Monday; for, you see, it was Saturday when we were thegither, and now it's Sunday and it's dark night — so the Sabbath has slipped clean away through our fingers like water through a sieve, which abideth not; and we have to begin again to-morrow morning, in the weariful, base, mean, earthly employments, whilk are unworthy of an immortal spirit—always excepting the way of business."

Three of the fellows were now returning to the town, and, at Ewart's command, they cut short the patriarch's exhortation, by leading him back to his own residence. The rest of the party then proceeded to the brig, which only waited their arrival to get under weigh and drop down the river. Nanty Ewart betook himself to steering the brig, and the very touch of the helm seemed to dispel the remaining influence of the liquor which he had drunk, since, through a troublesome and intricate channel, he was able to direct the course of his little vessel with the most perfect accuracy and safety.

Alan Fairford, for some time, availed himself of the clearness of the summer morning to gaze on the dimly seen shores betwixt which they glided, becoming less and less distinct as they receded from each other, until at length, having adjusted his little bundle by way of pillow, and wrapt around him the great-coat with which old Trumbull had equipped him, he stretched himself on the deck, to try to recover the slumber out of which he had been awakened. Sleep had scarce begun to settle on his eyes, ere he found something stirring about his person. With ready presence of mind he recollected his situation, and resolved to show no alarm until the purpose of this became obvious; but he was soon relieved from his anxiety, by finding it was only the result of Nanty's attention to his comfort, who was wrapping around him, as softly as he could, a great boat-cloak, in order to defend him from the morning air.

"Thou art but a cockerel," he muttered, "but 'twere pity thou wert knocked off the porch before seeing a little more of the sweet and sour of this world — though, faith, if thou hast the usual luck of it, the best way were to leave thee to the chance of a seasoning fever."

These words, and the awkward courtesy with which the skipper of the little brig tucked the sea-coat round Fairford, gave him a confidence of safety which he had not yet thoroughly possessed. He stretched himself in more security on the hard planks, and was speedily asleep, though his slumbers were feverish and unfreshing.

It has been elsewhere intimated that Alan Fairford inherited from his mother a delicate constitution, with a tendency to consumption; and, being an only child, with such a cause for apprehension, care, to the verge of effeminacy, was taken to preserve him from damp beds, wet feet, and those various emergencies, to which the Caledonian boys of much higher birth, but more active habits, are generally accustomed. In man, the spirit sustains the constitutional weakness, as in the winged tribes the feathers bear aloft the body. But there is a bound to these supporting qualities; and as the pinions of the bird must at length grow weary, so the *vis animi* of the human struggler becomes broken down by continued fatigue.

When the voyager was awakened by the light of the sun now riding high in Heaven, he found himself under the influence of an almost intolerable headach, with heat, thirst, shooting across the back and loins, and other symptoms intimating violent cold, accompanied with fever. The manner in which he had passed the preceding day and night, though perhaps it might have been of little consequence to most young men, was to him, delicate in constitution and nurture, attended with bad and even perilous consequences. He felt this was the case, yet would fain have combated the symptoms of indisposition, which, indeed, he imputed chiefly to sea-sickness. He sat up on deck, and looked on the scene around, as the little vessel, having borne down the Solway Firth, was beginning, with a favourable northerly breeze, to bear away to the southward, crossing the entrance of the Wampole river, and preparing to double the most northerly point of Cumberland.

But Fairford felt annoyed with deadly sickness, as well as by pain of a distressing and oppressive character; and neither Criffel, rising in majesty on the one hand, nor the distant yet more picturesque outline of Skiddaw and Glaramara upon the other, could attract his attention in the manner in which it was usually fixed by beautiful scenery, and especially that which had in it something new as well as striking. Yet it was not in Alan Fairford's nature to give way to despondence, even when seconded by pain. He had recourse, in the first place, to his pocket; but instead of the little Sallust he had brought with him, that the perusal of a classical author might help to pass away a heavy hour, he pulled out the supposed hymn-book with which he had been presented a few hours before, by that temperate and scrupulous person, Mr. Thomas Trumbull, *alias* Turnpenny. The volume was bound in sable, and its exterior might have become a psalter. But what was Alan's astonishment to read on the titlepage the following words: "Merry Thoughts for Merry Men; or Mother Midnight's Miscellany for the Small Hours;" and turning over the leaves, he was disgusted with profligate tales, and more profligate songs, ornamented with figures corresponding in infamy with the letter-press.

"Good God!" he thought, "and did this hoary reprobate summon his family together, and, with such a disgraceful pledge of infamy in his bosom, venture to approach the throne of his Creator? It must be so; the book is bound after the manner of those dedicated to devotional subjects, and doubtless, the wretch, in his intoxication, confounded the books he carried with him, as he did the days of the week."—Seized with the disgust with which the young and generous usually regard the vices of advanced life, Alan, having turned the leaves of the book over in hasty disdain, flung it from him, as far as he could, into the sea. He then had recourse to the Sallust, which he had at first sought for in vain. As he opened the book, Nanty Ewart, who had been looking over his shoulder, made his own opinion heard.

"I think now, brother, if you are so much scandalized at a little piece of sculduddery, which, after all, does nobody any harm, you had better have given it to me than have flung it into the Solway."

"I hope, sir," answered Fairford, civilly, "you are in the habit of read- ing better books."

"Faith," answered Nanty, "with help of a little Geneva text, I could read my Sallust as well as you can;" and snatching the book from Alan's hand, he began to read, in the Scottish accent.—"*Igitur ex divitiis juven- tutem luxuria atque avaritia cum superbiâ invasêre: rapere, consumere; sua parvi pendere, aliena cupere; pudorem, amicitiam, pudicitiam, divina atque humana promiscua, nihil pensi neque moderati habere.*'* —There is a slap in the face now, for an honest fellow that has been buccaniering! Never could keep a groat of what he got, or hold his fingers from what belonged to another, said you? Fie, fie, friend Crispus, thy morals are as crabbed and austere as thy style—the one has as little mercy as the other has grace. By my soul, it is unhandsome to make personal reflections on an old ac- quaintance, who seeks a little civil intercourse with you after nigh twenty years' separation. On my soul, Master Sallust deserves to float on the Sol- way better than Mother Midnight herself."

"Perhaps, in some respects, he may merit better usage at our hands," said Alan; "for if he has described vice plainly, it seems to have been for the purpose of rendering it generally abhorred."

"Well," said the seaman, "I have heard of the Sortes Virgilianæ, and I daresay the Sortes Sallustianæ are as true every tittle. I have consulted honest Crispus on my own account, and have had a cuff for my pains. But now see, I open the book on your behalf, and behold what occurs first to my eye!—Lo you there—'*Catilina . . . omnium flagitiosorum atque facino- rosorum circum se habebat.*' And then again—'*Etiam si quis à culpâ vacuus in amicitiam ejus inciderat, quotidiano usu par cimilisque cæteris efficiebatur.*'† That is what I call plain speaking on the part of the old Roman, Mr. Fair- ford. By the way, that is a capital name for a lawyer."

"Lawyer as I am," said Fairford, "I do not understand your innuendo."

"Nay, then," said Ewart, "I can try it another way, as well as the hypocritical old rascal Turnpenny himself could do. I would have you to know that I am well acquainted with my Bible-book, as well as with my friend Sallust." He then, in a snuffling and canting tone, began to repeat the Scriptural text—"'*David therefore departed thence, and went to the cave of Adullam. And every one that was in distress, and every one that was in debt, and every one that was discontented, gathered themselves together unto him, and he became a captain over them.*' What think you of that?" he said, suddenly changing his manner. "Have I touched you now, sir?"

"You are as far off as ever," replied Fairford.

"What the devil! and you a repeating frigate between Summertrees and the Laird! Tell that to the marines—the sailors won't believe it. But you are right to be cautious, since you can't say who are right, who not. — But you look ill; it's but the cold morning air—Will you have a can of flip, or a jorum of hot rumbo? — or will you splice the main-brace" — (showing a spirit-flask)—"Will you have a quid—or a pipe—or a cigar?—a pinch of snuff, at least, to clear your brains and sharpen your apprehension?"

---

* The translation of the passage is thus given by Sir Henry Steuart of Allanton :—"The youth, taught to look up to riches as the sovereign good, became apt pupils in the school of Luxury. Rapacity and profusion went hand in hand. Careless of their own fortunes, and eager to possess those of others, shame and re- morse, modesty and moderation, every principle gave way."—*Works of Sallust, with Original Essays,* vol. ii., p. 17.

† After enumerating the evil qualities of Catiline's associates, the author adds, "If it happened that any as yet uncontaminated by vice were fatally drawn into his friendship, the effects of intercourse and snares artfully spread, subdued every scruple, and early assimilated them to their conductors."—*Ibidem,* p. 19.

Fairford rejected all these friendly propositions.

"Why, then," continued Ewart, "if you will do nothing for the free trade, I must patronise it myself."

So saying, he took a large glass of brandy.

"A hair of the dog that bit me," he continued, — "of the dog that will worry me one day soon ; and yet, and be d—d to me for an idiot, I must always have him at my throat. But, says the old catch"—— Here he sung, and sung well—

> "'Let's drink—let's drink — while life we have ;
> We'll find but cold drinking, cold drinking in the grave.'

All this," he continued, "is no charm against the headach. I wish I had any thing that could do you good. — Faith, and we have tea and coffee aboard ! I'll open a chest or a bag, and let you have some in an instant. You are at the age to like such catlap better than better stuff."

Fairford thanked him, and accepted his offer of tea.

Nanty Ewart was soon heard calling about, "Break open yon chest — take out your capful, you bastard of a powder-monkey ; we may want it again.—No sugar ?—all used up for grog, say you ?—knock another loaf to pieces, can't ye ? — and get the kettle boiling, ye hell's baby, in no time at all !"

By dint of these energetic proceedings he was in a short time able to return to the place where his passenger lay sick and exhausted, with a cup, or rather a canful, of tea ; for every thing was on a large scale on board of the Jumping Jenny. Alan drank it eagerly, and with so much appearance of being refreshed, that Nanty Ewart swore he would have some too, and only laced it, as his phrase went, with a single glass of brandy.*

Chapter the Fourteenth.

NARRATIVE OF ALAN FAIRFORD, CONTINUED.

WE left Alan Fairford on the deck of the little smuggling brig, in that disconsolate situation, when sickness and nausea attack a heated and fevered frame, and an anxious mind. His share of sea-sickness, however, was not so great as to engross his sensations entirely, or altogether to divert his attention from what was passing around. If he could not delight in the swiftness and agility with which the "little frigate" walked the waves, or amuse himself by noticing the beauty of the sea-views around him, where the distant Skiddaw raised his brow, as if in defiance of the clouded eminence of Criffel, which lorded it over the Scottish side of the estuary,

---

* I am sorry to say, that the modes of concealment described in the imaginary premises of Mr. Trumbull, are of a kind which have been common on the frontiers of late years. The neighbourhood of two nations having different laws, though united in government, still leads to a multitude of transgressions on the Border, and extreme difficulty in apprehending delinquents. About twenty years since, as far as my recollection serves, there was along the frontier an organized gang of coiners, forgers, smugglers, and other malefactors, whose operations were conducted on a scale not inferior to what is here described. The chief of the party was one Richard Mendham, a carpenter, who rose to opulence, although ignorant even of the arts of reading and writing. But he had found a short road to wealth, and had taken singular measures for conducting his operations. Amongst these, he found means to build, in a suburb of Berwick called Spittal, a street of small houses, as if for the investment of property. He himself inhabited one of these ; another, a species of public-house, was open to his confederates, who held secret and unsuspected communication with him by crossing the roofs of the intervening houses, and descending by a trap-stair, which admitted them into the alcove of the dining-room of Dick Mendham's private mansion. A vault, too, beneath Mendham's stable, was accessible in the manner mentioned in the novel. The post of one of the stalls turned round on a bolt being withdrawn, and gave admittance to a subterranean place of concealment for contraband and stolen goods, to a great extent. Richard Mendham, the head of this very formidable conspiracy, which involved malefactors of every kind, was tried and executed at Jedburgh, where the author was present as Sheriff of Selkirkshire. Mendham had previously been tried, but escaped by want of proof and the ingenuity of his counsel.

he had spirits and composure enough to pay particular attention to the master of the vessel, on whose character his own safety in all probability was dependent.

Nanty Ewart had now given the helm to one of his people, a bald-pated, grizzled old fellow, whose whole life had been spent in evading the revenue laws, with now and then the relaxation of a few months' imprisonment, for deforcing officers, resisting seizures, and the like offences.

Nanty himself sat down by Fairford, helped him to his tea, with such other refreshments as he could think of, and seemed in his way sincerely desirous to make his situation as comfortable as things admitted. Fairford had thus an opportunity to study his countenance and manners more closely.

It was plain, Ewart, though a good seaman, had not been bred upon that element. He was a reasonably good scholar, and seemed fond of showing it, by recurring to the subject of Sallust and Juvenal; while, on the other hand, sea-phrases seldom chequered his conversation. He had been in person what is called a smart little man; but the tropical sun had burnt his originally fair complexion to a dusty red; and the bile which was diffused through his system, had stained it with a yellowish black — what ought to have been the white part of his eyes, in particular, had a hue as deep as the topaz. He was very thin, or rather emaciated, and his countenance, though still indicating alertness and activity, showed a constitution exhausted with excessive use of his favourite stimulus.

"I see you look at me hard," said he to Fairford. "Had you been an officer of the d——d customs, my terriers' backs would have been up." He opened his breast, and showed Alan a pair of pistols disposed between his waistcoat and jacket, placing his finger at the same time upon the cock of one of them. "But come, you are an honest fellow, though you're a close one. I dare say you think me a queer customer; but I can tell you, they that see the ship leave harbour, know little of the seas she is to sail through. My father, honest old gentleman, never would have thought to see me master of the Jumping Jenny."

Fairford said, it seemed very clear indeed that Mr. Ewart's education was far superior to the line he at present occupied.

"Oh, Criffel to Solway Moss!" said the other. "Why, man, I should have been an expounder of the word, with a wig like a snow-wreath, and a stipend like—like—like a hundred pounds a-year, I suppose. I can spend thrice as much as that, though, being such as I am." Here he sung a scrap of an old Northumbrian ditty, mimicking the burr of the natives of that county:—

> "Willy Foster's gone to sea,
> Siller buckles at his knee,
> He'll come back and marry me—
> Canny Willie Foster."

"I have no doubt," said Fairford, "your present occupation is more lucrative; but I should have thought the church might have been more——"

He stopped, recollecting that it was not his business to say any thing disagreeable.

"More respectable, you mean, I suppose?" said Ewart, with a sneer, and squirting the tobacco-juice through his front-teeth; then was silent for a moment, and proceeded in a tone of candour which some internal touch of conscience dictated. "And so it would, Mr. Fairford — and happier, too, by a thousand degrees — though I have had my pleasures too. But there was my father, (God bless the old man!) a true chip of the old Presbyterian block, walked his parish like a captain on the quarter-deck, and was always ready to do good to rich and poor — Off went the laird's hat to the minister, as fast as the poor man's bonnet. When the eye saw him—Pshaw! what have I to do with that now?—Yes, he was, as Virgil hath it, '*Vir sapientia et pietate gravis.*' But he might have been the wiser man, had he kept me at home, when he sent me at nineteen to study Divinity at the head of the highest stair in the Covenant-Close. It was a cursed mistake in the old gentleman. What though Mrs. Cantrips of Kittlebasket (for she wrote herself no less) was our cousin five times removed, and took me on that account to board and lodging, at six shillings, instead of seven shillings a-week? it was a d——d bad saving, as the case proved. Yet her very dignity might have kept me in order; for she never read a chapter excepting out of a Cambridge Bible, printed by Daniel, and bound in embroidered velvet. I think I see it at this moment! And on Sundays, when we had a quart of twopenny ale, instead of butter-milk, to our porridge, it was always served up in a silver posset-dish. Also she used silver-mounted spectacles, whereas even my father's were cased in mere horn. These things had their impression at first, but we get used to grandeur by degrees. Well, sir!—Gad, I can scarce get on with my story—it sticks in my throat —must take a trifle to wash it down. Well, this dame had a daughter— Jess Cantrips, a black-eyed, bouncing wench—and, as the devil would have it, there was the d——d five-story stair—her foot was never from it, whether I went out or came home from the Divinity Hall. I would have eschewed her, sir—I would, on my soul; for I was as innocent a lad as ever came from Lammermuir; but there was no possibility of escape, retreat, or flight, unless I could have got a pair of wings, or made use of a ladder seven stories high, to scale the window of my attic. It signifies little talking—you may suppose how all this was to end—I would have married the girl, and taken my chance—I would, by Heaven! for she was a pretty girl, and a good girl, till she and I met; but you know the old song, 'Kirk would not let us be.' A gentleman, in my case, would have settled the matter with the Kirk-treasurer for a small sum of money; but the poor stibbler, the penniless dominie, having married his cousin of Kettlebasket, must next have proclaimed her frailty to the whole parish, by mounting the throne of Presbyterian penance, and proving, as Othello says, 'his love a whore,' in face of the whole congregation.

"In this extremity I dared not stay where I was, and so thought to go home to my father. But first I got Jack Hadaway, a lad from the same parish, and who lived in the same infernal stair, to make some inquiries how the old gentleman had taken the matter. I soon, by way of answer, learned, to the great increase of my comfortable reflections, that the good old man made as much clamour, as if such a thing as a man's eating his wedding dinner without saying grace, had never happened since Adam's time. He did nothing for six days but cry out, 'Ichabod, Ichabod, the glory is departed from my house!' and on the seventh he preached a sermon, in which he enlarged on this incident as illustrative of one of the great occasions for humiliation, and causes of national defection. I hope the course he took comforted himself—I am sure it made me ashamed to show my nose at home. So I went down to Leith, and, exchanging my hoddin gray coat of my mother's spinning for such a jacket as this, I entered my name at the rendezvous as an able-bodied landsman, and sailed with the tender round to Plymouth, where they were fitting out a squadron for the West Indies. There I was put aboard the Fearnought, Captain Daredevil —among whose crew I soon learned to fear Satan, (the terror of my early youth,) as little as the toughest Jack on board. I had some qualms at first, but I took the remedy" (tapping the case-bottle) "which I recommend to you, being as good for sickness of the soul as for sickness of the stomach— What, you won't?—very well, I must, then—here is to ye."

"You would, I am afraid, find your education of little use in your new condition?" said Fairford.

"Pardon me, sir," resumed the Captain of the Jumping Jenny; "my handful of Latin, and small pinch of Greek, were as useless as old junk, to be sure; but my reading, writing, and accompting, stood me in good stead, and brought me forward; I might have been schoolmaster — ay, and master, in time; but that valiant liquor, rum, made a conquest of me rather too often, and so, make what sail I could, I always went to leeward. We were four years broiling in that blasted climate, and I came back at last with a little prize-money.—I always had thoughts of putting things to rights in the Covenant-Close, and reconciling myself to my father. I found out Jack Hadaway, who was *Tuptowing* away with a dozen of wretched boys, and a fine string of stories he had ready to regale my ears withal. My father had lectured on what he called 'my falling away,' for seven Sabbaths, when, just as his parishioners began to hope that the course was at an end, he was found dead in his bed on the eighth Sunday morning. Jack Hadaway assured me, that if I wished to atone for my errors, by undergoing the fate of the first martyr, I had only to go to my native village, where the very stones of the street would rise up against me as my father's murderer. Here was a pretty item — well, my tongue clove to my mouth for an hour, and was only able at last to utter the name of Mrs. Cantrips. Oh, this was a new theme for my Job's comforter. My sudden departure — my father's no less sudden death — had prevented the payment of the arrears of my board and lodging—the landlord was a haberdasher, with a heart as rotten as the muslin wares he dealt in. Without respect to her age, or gentle kin, my Lady Kittlebasket was ejected from her airy habitation — her porridge-pot, silver posset-dish, silver-mounted spectacles, and Daniel's Cambridge Bible, sold, at the Cross of Edinburgh, to the cadie who would bid highest for them, and she herself driven to the work-house, where she got in with difficulty, but was easily enough lifted out, at the end of the month, as dead as her friends could desire. Merry tidings this to me, who had been the d—d" (he paused a moment) "*origo mali*—Gad, I think my confession would sound better in Latin than in English!

"But the best jest was behind — I had just power to stammer out something about Jess — by my faith he *had* an answer! I had taught Jess one trade, and, like a prudent girl, she had found out another for herself; unluckily, they were both contraband, and Jess Cantrips, daughter of the Lady Kittlebasket, had the honour to be transported to the plantations, for street-walking and pocket-picking, about six months before I touched shore."

He changed the bitter tone of affected pleasantry into an attempt to laugh, then drew his swarthy hand across his swarthy eyes, and said in a more natural accent, "Poor Jess!"

There was a pause—until Fairford, pitying the poor man's state of mind, and believing he saw something in him that, but for early error and subsequent profligacy, might have been excellent and noble, helped on the conversation by asking, in a tone of commisération, how he had been able to endure such a load of calamity.

"Why, very well," answered the seaman; "exceedingly well — like a tight ship in a brisk gale.—Let me recollect.—I remember thanking Jack, very composedly, for the interesting and agreeable communication; I then pulled out my canvass pouch, with my hoard of moidores, and taking out two pieces, I bid Jack keep the rest till I came back, as I was for a cruise about Auld Reekie. The poor devil looked anxiously, but I shook him by the hand, and ran down stairs, in such confusion of mind, that notwithstanding what I had heard, I expected to meet Jess at every turning.

"It was market-day, and the usual number of rogues and fools were assembled at the Cross. I observed every body looked strange on me, and I thought some laughed. I fancy I had been making queer faces enough, and perhaps talking to myself. When I saw myself used in this manner, I held out my clenched fists straight before me, stooped my head, and, like a ram when he makes his race, darted off right down the street, scattering groups of weatherbeaten lairds and periwigged burgesses, and bearing down all before me. I heard the cry of 'Seize the madman!' echoed, in Celtic sounds, from the City Guard, with 'Ceaze ta matman!'—but pursuit and opposition were in vain. I pursued my career; the smell of the sea, I suppose, led me to Leith, where, soon after, I found myself walking very quietly, on the shore, admiring the tough round and sound cordage of the vessels, and thinking how a loop, with a man at the end of one of them, would look, by way of tassel.

"I was opposite to the rendezvous, formerly my place of refuge—in I bolted—found one or two old acquaintances, made half-a-dozen new ones—drank for two days—was put aboard the tender—off to Portsmouth—then landed at the Haslaar hospital in a fine hissing-hot fever. Never mind—I got better—nothing can kill me—the West Indies were my lot again, for since I did not go where I deserved in the next world, I had something as like such quarters as can be had in this—black devils for inhabitants—flames and earthquakes, and so forth, for your element. Well, brother, something or other I did or said—I can't tell what—How the devil should I, when I was as drunk as David's sow, you know?—But I was punished, my lad—made to kiss the wench that never speaks but when she scolds, and that's the gunner's daughter, comrade. Yes, the minister's son of—no matter where—has the cat's scratch on his back! This roused me, and when we were ashore with the boat, I gave three inches of the dirk, after a tussle, to the fellow I blamed most, and so took the bush for it. There were plenty of wild lads then along shore—and, I don't care who knows—I went on the account, look you—sailed under the black flag and marrow-bones—was a good friend to the sea, and an enemy to all that sailed on it."

Fairford, though uneasy in his mind at finding himself, a lawyer, so close to a character so lawless, thought it best, nevertheless, to put a good face on the matter, and asked Mr. Ewart, with as much unconcern as he could assume, "whether he was fortunate as a rover?"

"No, no—d—n it, no," replied Nanty; "the devil a crumb of butter was ever churned that would stick upon my bread. There was no order among us—he that was captain to-day, was swabber to-morrow; and as for plunder—they say old Avery, and one or two close hunks, made money; but in my time, all went as it came; and reason good, for if a fellow had saved five dollars, his throat would have been cut in his hammock—And then it was a cruel, bloody work.—Pah,—we'll say no more about it. I broke with them at last, for what they did on board of a bit of a snow—no matter what it was—bad enough, since it frightened me—I took French leave, and came in upon the proclamation, so I am free of all that business. And here I sit, the skipper of the Jumping Jenny—a nutshell of a thing, but goes through the water like a dolphin. If it were not for yon hypocritical scoundrel at Annan, who has the best end of the profit, and takes none of the risk, I should be well enough—as well as I want to be. Here is no lack of my best friend,"—touching his case-bottle;—"but, to tell you a secret, he and I have got so used to each other, I begin to think he is like a professed joker, that makes your sides sore with laughing, if you see him but now and then; but if you take up house with him, he can only make your head stupid. But I warrant the old fellow is doing the best he can for me, after all."

"And what may that be?" said Fairford.

"He is KILLING me," replied Nanty Ewart; "and I am only sorry he is so long about it."

So saying, he jumped on his feet, and, tripping up and down the deck, gave his orders with his usual clearness and decision, notwithstanding the considerable quantity of spirits which he had contrived to swallow while recounting his history.

Although far from feeling well, Fairford endeavoured to rouse himself and walk to the head of the brig, to enjoy the beautiful prospect, as well as to take some note of the course which the vessel held. To his great surprise, instead of standing across to the opposite shore from which she had departed, the brig was going down the Firth, and apparently steering into the Irish Sea. He called to Nanty Ewart, and expressed his surprise at the course they were pursuing, and asked why they did not stand straight across the Firth for some port in Cumberland.

"Why, this is what I call a reasonable question, now," answered Nanty; "as if a ship could go as straight to its port, as a horse to the stable, or a free-trader could sail the Solway as securely as a King's cutter! Why, I'll tell ye, brother—if I do not see a smoke on Bowness, that is the village upon the headland yonder, I must stand out to sea for twenty-four hours a least, for we must keep the weathergage if there are hawks abroad."

"And if you do see the signal of safety, Master Ewart, what is to be done then?"

"Why then, and in that case, I must keep off till night, and then run you, with the kegs and the rest of the lumber, ashore at Skinburness."

"And then I am to meet with this same Laird whom I have the letter for?" continued Fairford.

"That," said Ewart, "is thereafter as it may be; the ship has its course—the fair trader has his port—but it is not easy to say where the Laird may be found. But he will be within twenty miles of us, off or on—and it will be my business to guide you to him."

Fairford could not withstand the passing impulse of terror which crossed him, when thus reminded that he was so absolutely in the power of a man, who, by his own account, had been a pirate, and who was at present, in all probability, an outlaw as well as a contraband trader. Nanty Ewart guessed the cause of his involuntary shuddering.

"What the devil should I gain," he said, "by passing so poor a card as you are?—Have I not had ace of trumps in my hand, and did I not play it fairly?—Ay, I say the Jumping Jenny can run in other ware as well as kegs. Put *sigma* and *tau* to *Ewart*, and see how that will spell—D'ye take me now?"

"No indeed," said Fairford; "I am utterly ignorant of what you allude to."

"Now, by Jove!" said Nanty Ewart, "thou art either the deepest or the shallowest fellow I ever met with—or you are not right after all. I wonder where Summertrees could pick up such a tender along-shore. Will you let me see his letter?"

Fairford did not hesitate to gratify his wish, which, he was aware, he could not easily resist. The master of the Jumping Jenny looked at the direction very attentively, then turned the letter to and fro, and examined each flourish of the pen, as if he were judging of a piece of ornamented manuscript; then handed it back to Fairford, without a single word of remark.

"Am I right now?" said the young lawyer.

"Why, for that matter," answered Nanty, "the letter is right, sur enough; but whether *you* are right or not, is your own business rather than mine."—And, striking upon a flint with the back of a knife, he kindled a cigar as thick as his finger, and began to smoke away with great perseverance.

Alan Fairford continued to regard him with a melancholy feeling, divided betwixt the interest he took in the unhappy man, and a not unnatural apprehension for the issue of his own adventure.

Ewart, notwithstanding the stupifying nature of his pastime, seemed to guess what was working in his passenger's mind; for, after they had remained some time engaged in silently observing each other, he suddenly dashed his cigar on the deck, and said to him, "Well then, if you are sorry for me, I am sorry for you. D—n me, if I have cared a button for man or mother's son, since two years since, when I had another peep of Jack Hadaway. The fellow was got as fat as a Norway whale — married to a great Dutch built quean that had brought him six children. I believe he did not know me, and thought I was come to rob his house; however, I made up a poor face, and told him who I was. Poor Jack would have given me shelter and clothes, and began to tell me of the moidores that were in bank, when I wanted them. Egad, he changed his note when I told him what my life had been, and only wanted to pay me my cash and get rid of me. I never saw so terrified a visage. I burst out a-laughing in his face, told him it was all a humbug, and that the moidores were all his own, henceforth and for ever, and so ran off. I caused one of our people send him a bag of tea and a keg of brandy, before I left—poor Jack! I think you are the second person these ten years, that has cared a tobacco-stopper for Nanty Ewart."

"Perhaps, Mr. Ewart," said Fairford, "you live chiefly with men too deeply interested for their own immediate safety, to think much upon the distress of others?"

"And with whom do you yourself consort, I pray?" replied Nanty, smartly. "Why, with plotters, that can make no plot to better purpose than their own hanging; and incendiaries, that are snapping the flint upon wet tinder. You'll as soon raise the dead as raise the Highlands—you'll as soon get a grunt from a dead sow as any comfort from Wales or Cheshire. You think because the pot is boiling, that no scum but yours can come uppermost — I know better, by ——. All these rackets and riots that you think are trending your way, have no relation at all to your interest; and the best way to make the whole kingdom friends again at once, would be the alarm of such an undertaking as these mad old fellows are trying to launch into."

"I really am not in such secrets as you seem to allude to," said Fairford; and, determined at the same time to avail himself as far as possible of Nanty's communicative disposition, he added, with a smile, "And if I were, I should not hold it prudent to make them much the subject of conversation. But I am sure, so sensible a man as Summertrees and the Laird may correspond together without offence to the state."

"I take you, friend — I take you," said Nanty Ewart, upon whom, at length, the liquor and tobacco-smoke began to make considerable innovation. "As to what gentlemen may or may not correspond about, why we may pretermit the question, as the old Professor used to say at the Hall; and as to Summertrees, I will say nothing, knowing him to be an old fox. But I say that this fellow the Laird is a firebrand in the country; that he is stirring up all the honest fellows who should be drinking their brandy quietly, by telling them stories about their ancestors and the forty-five; and that he is trying to turn all waters into his own mill-dam, and to set his sails to all winds. And because the London people are roaring about for some pinches of their own, he thinks to win them to his turn with a wet finger. And he gets encouragement from some, because they want a spell of money from him; and from others, because they fought for the cause once, and are ashamed to go back; and others, because they have nothing to lose; and others, because they are discontented fools. But if he has brought you, or any one, I say not whom, into this scrape, with the hope of doing any good, he's a d——d decoy-duck, and that's all I can say for him; and you are geese, which is worse than being decoy-ducks, or lame-ducks either. And so here is to the prosperity of King George the Third, and the true Presbyterian religion, and confusion to the Pope, the Devil, and the Pretender!—I'll tell you what, Mr. Fairbairn, I am but tenth owner of this bit of a craft, the Jumping Jenny — but tenth owner — and must sail her by my owners' directions. But if I were whole owner, I would not have the brig be made a ferry-boat for your jacobitical, old-fashioned Popish riff-raff, Mr. Fairport — I would not, by my soul; they should walk the plank, by the gods, as I have seen better men do when I sailed under the What-d'ye-callum colours. But being contraband goods, and on board my vessel, and I with my sailing orders in my hand, why, I am to forward them as directed — I say, John Roberts, keep her up a bit with the helm.—And so, Mr. Fairweather, what I do is—as the d—d villain Turnpenny says—all in the way of business."

He had been speaking with difficulty for the last five minutes, and now at length dropped on the deck, fairly silenced by the quantity of spirits which he had swallowed, but without having showed any glimpse of the gaiety, or even of the extravagance of intoxication.

The old sailor stepped forward and flung a sea-cloak over the slumberer's shoulders, and added, looking at Fairford, "Pity of him he should have this fault; for without it, he would have been as clever a fellow as ever trode a plank with ox leather."

"And what are we to do now?" said Fairford.

"Stand off and on, to be sure, till we see the signal, and then obey orders."

So saying, the old man turned to his duty, and left the passenger to amuse himself with his own meditations. Presently afterward a light column of smoke was seen rising from the little headland.

"I can tell you what we are to do now, master," said the sailor. "We'll stand out to sea, and then run in again with the evening tide, and make Skinburness; or, if there's not light, we can run into the Wampool river, and put you ashore about Kirkbride or Leaths, with the long-boat."

Fairford, unwell before, felt this destination condemned him to an agony of many hours, which his disordered stomach and aching head were ill able to endure. There was no remedy, however, but patience, and the recollection that he was suffering in the cause of friendship. As the sun rose high, he became worse; his sense of smell appeared to acquire a morbid degree of acuteness, for the mere purpose of inhaling and distinguishing all the various odours with which he was surrounded, from that of pitch, to all the complicated smells of the hold. His heart, too, throbbed under the heat, and he felt as if in full progress towards a high fever.

The seamen, who were civil and attentive, considering their calling, observed his distress, and one contrived to make an awning out of an old sail, while another compounded some lemonade, the only liquor which their passenger could be prevailed upon to touch. After drinking it off, he obtained, but could not be said to enjoy, a few hours of troubled slumber.

Chapter the Fifteenth.

NARRATIVE OF ALAN FAIRFORD, CONTINUED.

ALAN FAIRFORD's spirit was more ready to encounter labour than his frame was adequate to support it. In spite of his exertions, when he awoke, after five or six hours' slumber, he found that he was so much disabled by dizziness in his head, and pains in his limbs, that he could not raise himself without assistance. He heard with some pleasure that they were now running right for the Wampool river, and that he would be put on shore in a very short time. The vessel accordingly lay to, and presently showed a weft in her ensign, which was hastily answered by signals from on shore. Men and horses were seen to come down the broken path which leads to the shore; the latter all properly tackled for carrying their loading. Twenty fishing barks were pushed afloat at once, and crowded round the brig with much clamour, laughter, cursing, and jesting. Amidst all this apparent confusion there was the essential regularity. Nanty Ewart again walked his quarterdeck as if he had never tasted spirits in his life, issued the necessary orders with precision, and saw them executed with punctuality. In half an hour the loading of the brig was in a great measure disposed in the boats; in a quarter of an hour more, it was landed on the beach, and another interval of about the same duration was sufficient to distribute it on the various strings of packhorses which waited for that purpose, and which instantly dispersed, each on its own proper adventure. More mystery was observed in loading the ship's boat with a quantity of small barrels, which seemed to contain ammunition. This was not done until the commercial customers had been dismissed; and it was not until this was performed that Ewart proposed to Alan, as he lay stunned with pain and noise, to accompany him ashore.

It was with difficulty that Fairford could get over the side of the vessel, and he could not seat himself in the stern of the boat without assistance from the captain and his people. Nanty Ewart, who saw nothing in this worse than an ordinary fit of sea-sickness, applied the usual topics of consolation. He assured his passenger that he would be quite well by and by, when he had been half an hour on terra firma, and that he hoped to drink a can and smoke a pipe with him at Father Crackenthorp's, for all that he felt a little out of the way for riding the wooden horse.

"Who is Father Crackenthorp?" said Fairford, though scarcely able to articulate the question.

"As honest a fellow as is of a thousand," answered Nanty. "Ah, how much good brandy he and I have made little of in our day! By my soul, Mr. Fairbird, he is the prince of skinkers, and the father of the free trade—not a stingy hypocritical devil like old Turnpenny Skinflint, that drinks drunk on other folk's cost, and thinks it sin when he has to pay for it—but a real hearty old cock;—the sharks have been at and about him this many a day, but Father Crackenthorp knows how to trim his sails—never a warrant but he hears of it before the ink's dry. He is *bonus socius* with headborough and constable. The King's Exchequer could not bribe a man to inform against him. If any such rascal were to cast up, why, he would miss his ears next morning, or be sent to seek them in the Solway. He is a statesman,* though he keeps a public; but, indeed, that is only for convenience, and to excuse his having cellarage and folk about him; his wife's a canny woman—and his daughter Doll too. Gad, you'll be in port there till you get round again; and I'll keep my word with you, and bring you to speech of the Laird. Gad, the only trouble I shall have is to get you out of the house; for Doll is a rare wench, and my dame a funny old one, and Father Crackenthorp the rarest companion! He'll drink you a bottle of rum or brandy without stopping, but never wet his lips with the nasty Scottish stuff that the canting old scoundrel Turnpenny has brought into fashion. He is a gentleman, every inch of him, old Crackenthorp; in his own way, that is; and besides, he has a share in the Jumping Jenny, and many a moonlight outfit besides. He can give Doll a pretty penny, if he likes the tight fellow that would turn in with her for life."

In the midst of this prolonged panegyric on Father Crackenthorp, the boat touched the beach, the rowers backed their oars to keep her afloat, whilst the other fellows jumped into the surf, and, with the most rapid dexterity, began to hand the barrels ashore.

"Up with them higher on the beach, my hearties," exclaimed Nanty Ewart—"High and dry—high and dry—this gear will not stand wetting. Now, out with our spare hand here - - high and dry with him too. What's

---

* A small landed proprietor.

that?—the galloping of horse! Oh, I hear the jingle of the packsaddles—they are our own folk."

By this time all the boat's load was ashore, consisting of the little barrels; and the boat's crew, standing to their arms, ranged themselves in front, waiting the advance of the horses which came clattering along the beach. A man, overgrown with corpulence, who might be distinguished in the moonlight, panting with his own exertions, appeared at the head of the cavalcade, which consisted of horses linked together, and accommodated with packsaddles, and chains for securing the kegs, which made a dreadful clattering.

"How now, Father Crackenthorp?" said Ewart—"Why this hurry with your horses?—We mean to stay a night with you, and taste your old brandy, and my dame's home-brewed. The signal is up, man, and all is right."

"All is wrong, Captain Nanty," cried the man to whom he spoke; "and you are the lad that is like to find it so, unless you bundle off—there are new brooms bought at Carlisle yesterday to sweep the country of you and the like of you — so you were better be jogging inland."

"How many rogues are the officers?—If not more than ten, I will make fight."

"The devil you will!" answered Crackenthorp. "You were better not, for they have the bloody-backed dragoons from Carlisle with them."

"Nay, then," said Nanty, "we must make sail.—Come, Master Fairlord, you must mount and ride.—He does not hear me—he has fainted, I believe —What the devil shall I do?— Father Crackenthorp, I must leave this young fellow with you till the gale blows out — hark ye—goes between the Laird and the t'other old one; he can neither ride nor walk — I must send him up to you."

"Send him up to the gallows!" said Crackenthorp; "there is Quartermaster Thwacker, with twenty men, up yonder; an he had not some kindness for Doll, I had never got hither for a start — but you must get off, or they will be here to seek us, for his orders are woundy particular; and these kegs contain worse than whisky—a hanging matter, I take it."

"I wish they were at the bottom of Wampool river, with them they belong to," said Nanty Ewart. "But they are part of cargo; and what to do with the poor young fellow ——"

"Why, many a better fellow has roughed it on the grass with a cloak o'er him," said Crackenthorp. "If he hath a fever, nothing is so cooling as the night air."

"Yes, he would be cold enough in the morning, no doubt; but it's a kind heart and shall not cool so soon, if I can help it," answered the Captain of the Jumping Jenny.

"Well, Captain, an ye will risk your own neck for another man's, why not take him to the old girls at Fairladies?"

"What, the Miss Arthurets! — The Papist jades!—But never mind; it will do—I have known them take in a whole sloop's crew that were stranded on the sands."

"You may run some risk, though, by turning up to Fairladies; for I tell you they are all up through the country."

"Never mind—I may chance to put some of them down again," said Nanty, cheerfully.—"Come, lads, bustle to your tackle. Are you all loaded?"

"Ay, ay, Captain; we will be ready in a jiffy," answered the gang.

"D—n your Captains!—Have you a mind to have me hanged if I am taken?—All's hail-fellow, here."

"A sup at parting," said Father Crackenthorp, extending a flask to Nanty Ewart.

"Not the twentieth part of a drop," said Nanty. "No Dutch courage

for me—my heart is always high enough when there's a chance of fighting;
besides, if I live drunk, I should like to die sober. — Here, old Jephson —
you are the best natured brute amongst them—get the lad between us on a
quiet horse, and we will keep him upright, I warrant."

As they raised Fairford from the ground, he groaned heavily, and asked
faintly where they were taking him to.

"To a place where you will be as snug and quiet as a mouse in his hole,"
said Nanty, "if so be that we can get you there safely. — Good-by, Father
Crackenthorp—poison the quartermaster, if you can."

The loaded horses then sprang forward at a hard trot, following each other
in a line, and every second horse being mounted by a stout fellow in a
smock-frock, which served to conceal the arms with which most of these
desperate men were provided. Ewart followed in the rear of the line, and,
with the occasional assistance of old Jephson, kept his young charge erect
in the saddle. He groaned heavily from time to time; and Ewart, more
moved with compassion for his situation than might have been expected from
his own habits, endeavoured to amuse him and comfort him, by some account of the place to which they were conveying him — his words of consolation being, however, frequently interrupted by the necessity of calling to
his people, and many of them being lost amongst the rattling of the barrels,
and clinking of the tackle and small chains by which they are secured on
such occasions.

"And you see, brother, you will be in safe quarters at Fairladies — good
old scrambling house—good old maids enough, if they were not Papists. —
Hollo, you Jack Lowther; keep the line can't ye, and shut your rattle-trap,
you broth of a ——? And so, being of a good family, and having enough,
the old lasses have turned a kind of saints, and nuns, and so forth. The
place they live in was some sort of nun-shop long ago, as they have them
still in Flanders; so folk call them the Vestals of Fairladies — that may
be, or may not be; and I care not whether it be or no. — Blinkinsop, hold
your tongue, and be d—d! — And so, betwixt great alms and good dinners,
they are well thought of by rich and poor, and their trucking with Papists
is looked over. There are plenty of priests, and stout young scholars, and
such like, about the house—it's a hive of them—More shame that government
send dragoons out after a few honest fellows that bring the old women of
England a drop of brandy, and let these ragamuffins smuggle in as much
papistry and — Hark! — was that a whistle? — No, it's only a plover. You,
Jem Collier, keep a look-out a-head — we'll meet them at the High Whins,
or Brotthole bottom, or no where. Go a furlong a-head, I say, and look
sharp.—These Misses Arthurets feed the hungry, and clothe the naked, and
such like acts — which my poor father used to say were filthy rags, but he
dressed himself out with as many of them as most folk. — D—n that stumbling horse! Father Crackenthorp should be d—d himself for putting an
honest fellow's neck in such jeopardy."

Thus, and with much more to the same purpose, Nanty ran on, increasing, by his well-intended annoyance, the agony of Alan Fairford, who, tormented by a racking pain along the back and loins, which made the rough
trot of the horse torture to him, had his aching head still farther rended
and split by the hoarse voice of the sailor, close to his ear. Perfectly passive, however, he did not even essay to give any answer; and indeed his
own bodily distress was now so great and engrossing, that to think of his
situation was impossible, even if he could have mended it by doing so.

Their course was inland; but in what direction, Alan had no means of
ascertaining. They passed at first over heaths and sandy downs; they
crossed more than one brook, or *beck*, as they are called in that country —
some of them of considerable depth — and at length reached a cultivated
country, divided, according to the English fashion of agriculture, into very
small fields or closes, by high banks, overgrown with underwood, and sur-

mounted by hedge-row trees, amongst which winded a number of impracticable and complicated lanes, where the boughs projecting from the embankments on each side, intercepted the light of the moon, and endangered the safety of the horsemen. But through this labyrinth the experience of the guides conducted them without a blunder, and without even the slackening of their pace. In many places, however, it was impossible for three men to ride abreast; and therefore the burden of supporting Alan Fairford fell alternately to old Jephson, and to Nanty; and it was with much difficulty that they could keep him upright in his saddle.

At length, when his powers of sufferance were quite worn out, and he was about to implore them to leave him to his fate in the first cottage or shed—or under a haystack or a hedge—or any where, so he was left at ease, Collier, who rode a-head, passed back the word that they were at the avenue to Fairladies—"Was he to turn up?"

Committing the charge of Fairford to Jephson, Nanty dashed up to the head of the troop, and gave his orders.—"Who knows the house best?"

"Sam Skelton's a Catholic," said Lowther.

"A d—d bad religion," said Nanty, of whose Presbyterian education, a hatred of Popery seemed to be the only remnant. "But I am glad there is one amongst us, any how.—You, Sam, being a Papist, know Fairladies, and the old maidens, I dare say; so do you fall out of the line, and wait here with me; and do you, Collier, carry on to Walinford bottom, then turn down the beck till you come to the old mill, and Goodman Grist the Miller, or old Peel-the-Causeway, will tell you where to stow; but I will be up with you before that."

The string of loaded horses then struck forward at their former pace, while Nanty, with Sam Skelton, waited by the road-side till the rear came up, when Jephson and Fairford joined them, and, to the great relief of the latter, they began to proceed at an easier pace than formerly, suffering the gang to precede them, till the clatter and clang attending their progress began to die away in the distance. They had not proceeded a pistol-shot from the place where they parted, when a short turning brought them in front of an old mouldering gateway, whose heavy pinnacles were decorated in the style of the seventeenth century, with clumsy architectural ornaments; several of which had fallen down from decay, and lay scattered about, no farther care having been taken than just to remove them out of the direct approach to the avenue. The great stone pillars, glimmering white in the moonlight, had some fanciful resemblance to supernatural apparitions, and the air of neglect all around, gave an uncomfortable idea of the habitation to those who passed its avenue.

"There used to be no gate here," said Skelton, finding their way unexpectedly stopped.

"But there is a gate now, and a porter too," said a rough voice from within. "Who be you, and what do you want at this time of night?"

"We want to come to speech of the ladies—of the Misses Arthuret," said Nanty; "and to ask lodging for a sick man."

"There is no speech to be had of the Miss Arthurets at this time of night, and you may carry your sick man to the doctor," answered the fellow from within, gruffly; "for as sure as there is savour in salt, and scent in rosemary, you will get no entrance—put your pipes up and be jogging on."

"Why, Dick Gardener," said Skelton, "be thou then turned porter?"

"What, do you know who I am?" said the domestic sharply.

"I know you by your by-word," answered the other; "What, have you forgot little Sam Skelton, and the brock in the barrel?"

"No, I have not forgotten you," answered the acquaintance of Sam Skelton; "but my orders are peremptory to let no one up the avenue this night, and therefore——"

"But we are armed, and will not be kept back," said Nanty. "Hark ye, fellow, were it not better for you to take a guinea and let us in, than to have us break the door first, and thy pate afterwards? for I won't see my comrade die at your door—be assured of that."

"Why, I dunna know," said the fellow; "but what cattle were those that rode by in such hurry?"

"Some of our folk from Bowness, Stoniecultrum, and thereby," answered Skelton; "Jack Lowther, and old Jephson, and broad Will Lamplugh, and such like."

"Well," said Dick Gardener, "as sure as there is savour in salt, and scent in rosemary, I thought it had been the troopers from Carlisle and Wigton, and the sound brought my heart to my mouth."

"Had thought thou wouldst have known the clatter of a cask from the clash of a broadsword, as well as e'er a quaffer in Cumberland," said Skelton.

"Come, brother, less of your jaw and more of your legs, if you please," said Nanty; "every moment we stay is a moment lost. Go to the ladies, and tell them that Nanty Ewart, of the Jumping Jenny, has brought a young gentleman, charged with letters from Scotland, to a certain gentleman of consequence in Cumberland — that the soldiers are out, and the gentleman is very ill, and if he is not received at Fairladies, he must be left either to die at the gate, or to be taken, with all his papers about him, by the redcoats."

Away ran Dick Gardener with this message; and, in a few minutes, lights were seen to flit about, which convinced Fairford, who was now, in consequence of the halt, a little restored to self-possession, that they were traversing the front of a tolerably large mansion-house.

"What if thy friend, Dick Gardener, comes not back again?" said Jephson to Skelton.

"Why, then," said the person addressed, "I shall owe him just such a licking as thou, old Jephson, had from Dan Cooke, and will pay as duly and truly as he did."

The old man was about to make an angry reply, when his doubts were silenced by the return of Dick Gardener, who announced that Miss Arthuret was coming herself as far as the gateway to speak with them.

Nanty Ewart cursed in a low tone, the suspicions of old maids and the churlish scruples of Catholics, that made so many obstacles to helping a fellow-creature, and wished Miss Arthuret a hearty rheumatism or toothach as the reward of her excursion; but the lady presently appeared, to cut short farther grumbling. She was attended by a waiting-maid with a lantern, by means of which she examined the party on the outside, as closely as the imperfect light, and the spars of the newly-erected gate, would permit."

"I am sorry we have disturbed you so late, Madam Arthuret," said Nanty; "but the case is this ——"

"Holy Virgin," said she, "why do you speak so loud? Pray, are you not the Captain of the Sainte Genevieve?"

"Why, ay, ma'am," answered Ewart, "they call the brig so at Dunkirk, sure enough; but along shore here, they call her the Jumping Jenny."

"You brought over the holy Father Buonaventure, did you not?"

"Ay, ay, madam, I have brought over enough of them black cattle," answered Nanty.

"Fie! fie! friend," said Miss Arthuret; "it is a pity that the saints should commit these good men to a heretic's care."

"Why, no more they would, ma'am," answered Nanty, "could they find a Papist lubber that knew the coast as I do; then I am trusty as steel to owners, and always look after cargo—live lumber, or dead flesh, or spirits, all is one to me; and your Catholics have such d—d large hoods, with pardon, ma'am, that they can sometimes hide two faces under them. But here is a gentleman dying, with letters about him from the Laird of Summertrees to the Laird of the Lochs, as they call him, along Solway, and every minute he lies here is a nail in his coffin."

"Saint Mary! what shall we do?" said Miss Arthuret; "we must admit him, I think, at all risks. — You, Richard Gardener, help one of these men to carry the gentleman up to the Place; and you, Selby, see him lodged at the end of the long gallery. — You are a heretic, Captain, but I think you are trusty, and I know you have been trusted—but if you are imposing on me ——"

"Not I, madam—never attempt to impose on ladies of your experience— my practice that way has been all among the young ones.—Come, cheerly, Mr. Fairford—you will be taken good care of—try to walk."

Alan did so; and, refreshed by his halt, declared himself able to walk to the house with the sole assistance of the gardener.

"Why, that's hearty. Thank thee, Dick, for lending him thine arm,"— and Nanty slipped into his hand the guinea he had promised.—"Farewell, then, Mr. Fairford, and farewell, Madam Arthuret, for I have been too long here."

So saying, he and his two companions threw themselves on horseback, and went off at a gallop. Yet, even above the clatter of their hoofs did the incorrigible Nanty hollow out the old ballad—

> "A lovely lass to a friar came,
> To confession a-morning early ;—
> ' In what, my dear, are you to blame?
> Come tell me most sincerely?'
> ' Alas! my fault I dare not name—
> But my lad he loved me dearly.'"

"Holy Virgin!" exclaimed Miss Seraphina, as the unhallowed sounds reached her ears; "what profane heathens be these men, and what frights and pinches we be put to among them! The saints be good to us, what a night has this been!—the like never seen at Fairladies.—Help me to make fast the gate, Richard, and thou shalt come down again to wait on it, lest there come more unwelcome visiters—Not that you are unwelcome, young gentleman, for it is sufficient that you need such assistance as we can give you, to make you welcome to Fairladies—only, another time would have done as well—but, hem! I dare say it is all for the best. The avenue is none of the smoothest, sir, look to your feet. Richard Gardener should have had it mown and levelled, but he was obliged to go on a pilgrimage to Saint Winifred's Well, in Wales."—(Here Dick gave a short dry cough, which, as if he had found it betrayed some internal feeling a little at variance with what the lady said, he converted into a muttered *Sancta Winifreda, ora pro nobis.* Miss Arthuret, meantime, proceeded)—"We never interfere with our servants' vows or penances, Master Fairford—I know a very worthy father of your name, perhaps a relation—I say, we never interfere with our servants' vows. Our Lady forbid they should not know some difference between our service and a heretic's.—Take care, sir, you will fall if you have not a care. Alas! by night and day there are many stumbling-blocks in our paths!"

With more talk to the same purpose, all of which tended to show a charitable, and somewhat silly woman, with a strong inclination to her superstitious devotion, Miss Arthuret entertained her new guest, as, stumbling at every obstacle which the devotion of his guide, Richard, had left in the path, he at last, by ascending some stone steps decorated on the side with griffins, or some such heraldic anomalies, attained a terrace extending in front of the Place of Fairladies; an old-fashioned gentleman's house of some consequence, with its range of notched gable-ends and narrow windows, relieved by here and there an old turret about the size of a pepper-box. The door was locked, during the brief absence of the mistress; a dim light glimmered through the sashed door of the hall, which opened beneath a huge stone porch, loaded with jessamine and other creepers. All the windows were dark as pitch.

Miss Arthuret tapped at the door. "Sister, sister Angelica."

"Who is there?" was answered from within; "is it you, sister Seraphina?"

"Yes, yes, undo the door; do you not know my voice?"

"No doubt, sister," said Angelica, undoing bolt and bar: "but you know our charge, and the enemy is watchful to surprise us—*incedit sicut leo vorans*, saith the breviary.—Whom have you brought here? Oh, sister, what have you done!"

"It is a young man," said Seraphina, hastening to interrupt her sister's remonstrance, "a relation, I believe, of our worthy Father Fairford; left at the gate by the captain of that blessed vessel the Sainte Genevieve—almost dead—and charged with despatches to——"

She lowered her voice as she mumbled over the last words.

"Nay, then, there is no help," said Angelica; "but it is unlucky."

During this dialogue between the vestals of Fairladies, Dick Gardener deposited his burden in a chair, where the young lady, after a moment of hesitation, expressing a becoming reluctance to touch the hand of a stranger, put her finger and thumb upon Fairford's wrist, and counted his pulse.

"There is fever here, sister," she said; "Richard must call Ambrose, and we must send some of the febrifuge."

Ambrose arrived presently, a plausible and respectable-looking old servant, bred in the family, and who had risen from rank to rank in the Arthuret service, till he was become half-physician, half-almoner, half-butler, and entire governor; that is, when the Father Confessor, who frequently eased him of the toils of government, chanced to be abroad. Under the direction, and with the assistance, of this venerable personage, the unlucky Alan Fairford was conveyed to a decent apartment at the end of a long gallery, and, to his inexpressible relief, consigned to a comfortable bed. He did not attempt to resist the prescription of Mr. Ambrose, who not only presented him with the proposed draught, but proceeded so far as to take a consider, able quantity of blood from him, by which last operation he probably did his patient much service.

Chapter the Sixteenth.

NARRATIVE OF ALAN FAIRFORD, CONTINUED.

On the next morning, when Fairford awoke, after no very refreshing slumbers, in which were mingled many wild dreams of his father, and of Darsie Latimer,—of the damsel in the green mantle, and the vestals of Fairladies,—of drinking small beer with Nanty Ewart, and being immersed in the Solway with the Jumping Jenny,—he found himself in no condition to dispute the order of Mr. Ambrose, that he should keep his bed, from which, indeed, he could not have raised himself without assistance. He became sensible that his anxiety, and his constant efforts for some days past, had been too much for his health, and that, whatever might be his impatience, he could not proceed in his undertaking until his strength was re-established.

In the meanwhile, no better quarters could have been found for an invalid. The attendants spoke under their breath, and moved only on tiptoe—nothing was done unless *par ordonnance du medecin* — Esculapius reigned paramount in the premises at Fairladies. Once a-day, the ladies came in great state to wait upon him, and enquire after his health, and it was then that Alan's natural civility, and the thankfulness which he expressed for their timely and charitable assistance, raised him considerably in their esteem. He was on the third day removed to a better apartment than that in which he had been at first accommodated. When he was permitted to drink a glass of wine, it was of the first quality; one of those curious old-fashioned cobwebbed bottles being produced on the occasion, which are only to be found in the crypts of old country-seats, where they may have lurked undisturbed for more than half a century.

But however delightful a residence for an invalid, Fairladies, as its present inmate became soon aware, was not so agreeable to a convalescent. When he dragged himself to the window so soon as he could crawl from bed, behold it was closely grated, and commanded no view except of a little paved court. This was nothing remarkable, most old Border-houses having their windows so secured. But then Fairford observed, that whosoever entered or left the room, always locked the door with great care and circumspection; and some proposals which he made to take a walk in the gallery, or even in the garden, were so coldly received, both by the ladies and their prime minister, Mr. Ambrose, that he saw plainly such an extension of his privileges as a guest would not be permitted.

Anxious to ascertain whether this excessive hospitality would permit him his proper privilege of free-agency, he announced to this important functionary, with grateful thanks for the care with which he had been attended, his purpose to leave Fairladies next morning, requesting only as a continuance of the favours with which he had been loaded, the loan of a horse to the next town; and, assuring Mr. Ambrose that his gratitude would not be limited by such a trifle, he slipped three guineas into his hand, by way of seconding his proposal. The fingers of that worthy domestic closed as naturally upon the *honorarium*, as if a degree in the learned faculty had given him a right to clutch it; but his answer concerning Alan's proposed departure was at first evasive, and when he was pushed, it amounted to a peremptory assurance that he could not be permitted to depart to-morrow; it was as much as his life was worth, and his ladies would not authorize it.

"I know best what my own life is worth," said Alan; "and I do not value it in comparison to the business which requires my instant attention."

Receiving still no satisfactory answer from Mr. Ambrose, Fairford thought it best to state his resolution to the ladies themselves, in the most measured, respectful, and grateful terms; but still such as expressed a firm determination to depart on the morrow, or next day at farthest. After some attempts to induce him to stay, on the alleged score of health, which were so expressed that he was convinced they were only used to delay his departure, Fairford plainly told them that he was intrusted with despatches of consequence to the gentleman known by the name of Herries, Redgauntlet, and the Laird of the Lochs; and that it was matter of life and death to deliver them early.

"I dare say, Sister Angelica," said the elder Miss Arthuret, "that the gentleman is honest; and if he is really a relation of Father Fairford, we can run no risk."

"Jesu Maria!" exclaimed the younger. "Oh, fie, Sister Seraphina! Fie, fie! — *Vade retro* — get thee behind me!"

"Well, well; but, sister — Sister Angelica — let me speak with you in the gallery."

So out the ladies rustled in their silks and tissues, and it was a good half hour ere they rustled in again, with importance and awe on their countenances.

"To tell you the truth, Mr. Fairford, the cause of our desire to delay you is — there is a religious gentleman in the house at present——"

"A most excellent person indeed"—said the Sister Angelica.

"An anointed of his Master!" echoed Seraphina, — "and we should be glad that, for conscience' sake, you would hold some discourse with him before your departure."

"Oho!" thought Fairford, "the murder is out — here is a design of conversion! — I must not affront the good ladies, but I shall soon send off the priest, I think." — He then answered aloud, "that he should be happy to converse with any friend of theirs — that in religious matters he had the greatest respect for every modification of Christianity, though, he must say, his belief was made up to that in which he had been educated; nevertheless, if his seeing the religious person they recommended could in the least show his respect——"

"It is not quite that," said Sister Seraphina, "although I am sure the day is too short to hear him — Father Buonaventure, I mean — speak upon the concerns of our souls; but——"

"Come, come, Sister Seraphina," said the younger, "it is needless to talk so much about it. His — his Eminence — I mean Father Buonaventure — will himself explain what he wants this gentleman to know."

"His Eminence!" said Fairford, surprised — "Is this gentleman so high in the Catholic Church?—The title is given only to Cardinals, I think"

"He is not a Cardinal as yet," answered Seraphina; "but I assure you, Mr. Fairford, he is as high in rank as he is eminently endowed with good gifts, and——"

"Come away," said Sister Angelica. "Holy Virgin, how you do talk! —What has Mr. Fairford to do with Father Buonaventure's rank? — Only, sir, you will remember that the Father has been always accustomed to be treated with the most profound deference; indeed——"

"Come away, sister," said Sister Seraphina, in her turn; "who talks now, I pray you? Mr. Fairford will know how to comport himself."

"And we had best both leave the room," said the younger lady, "for here his Eminence comes."

She lowered her voice to a whisper as she pronounced the last words; and as Fairford was about to reply, by assuring her that any friend of hers should be treated by him with all the ceremony he could expect, she imposed silence on him, by holding up her finger.

A solemn and stately step was now heard in the gallery; it might have proclaimed the approach not merely of a bishop or cardinal, but of the Sovereign Pontiff himself. Nor could the sound have been more respectfully listened to by the two ladies, had it announced that the Head of the Church was approaching in person. They drew themselves, like sentinels on duty, one on each side of the door by which the long gallery communicated with Fairford's apartment, and stood there immovable, and with countenances expressive of the deepest reverence.

The approach of Father Buonaventure was so slow, that Fairford had time to notice all this, and to marvel in his mind what wily and ambitious priest could have contrived to subject his worthy but simple-minded hostesses to such superstitious trammels. Father Buonaventure's entrance and appearance in some degree accounted for the whole.

He was a man of middle life, about forty, or upwards; but either care, or fatigue, or indulgence, had brought on the appearance of premature old age, and given to his fine features a cast of seriousness or even sadness. A noble countenance, however, still remained; and though his complexion was altered, and wrinkles stamped upon his brow in many a melancholy fold, still the lofty forehead, the full and well-opened eye, and the well-formed nose, showed how handsome in better days he must have been. He was tall, but lost the advantage of his height by stooping; and the cane which he wore always in his hand, and occasionally used, as well as his slow though majestic gait, seemed to intimate that his form and limbs felt already some touch of infirmity. The colour of his hair could not be discovered, as, according to the fashion he wore a periwig. He was handsomely, though gravely dressed in a secular habit, and had a cockade in his hat; circumstances which did not surprise Fairford, who knew that a military disguise was very often assumed by the seminary priests, whose visits to England, or residence there, subjected them to legal penalties.

As this stately person entered the apartment, the two ladies facing inward, like soldiers on their post when about to salute a superior officer, dropped on either hand of the Father a curtsy so profound, that the hoop petticoats which performed the feat seemed to sink down to the very floor, nay, through it, as if a trap-door had opened for the descent of the dames who performed this act of reverence.

The Father seemed accustomed to such homage, profound as it was; he turned his person a little way first towards one sister, and then towards the other, while, with a gracious inclination of his person, which certainly did not amount to a bow, he acknowledged their courtesy. But he passed forward without addressing them, and seemed, by doing so, to intimate that their presence in the apartment was unnecessary.

They accordingly glided out of the room, retreating backwards, with hands clasped and eyes cast upwards, as if imploring blessings on the religious man whom they venerated so highly. The door of the apartment was shut after them, but not before Fairford had perceived that there were one or two men in the gallery, and that, contrary to what he had before observed, the door, though shut, was not locked on the outside.

"Can the good souls apprehend danger from me to this god of their idolatry?" thought Fairford. But he had no time to make farther observations, for the stranger had already reached the middle of his apartment.

Fairford rose to receive him respectfully, but as he fixed his eyes on the visiter, he thought that the Father avoided his looks. His reasons for remaining incognito were cogent enough to account for this, and Fairford hastened to relieve him, by looking downwards in his turn; but when again he raised his face, he found the broad light eye of the stranger so fixed on him, that he was almost put out of countenance by the steadiness of his gaze. During this time they remained standing.

"Take your seat, sir," said the Father; "you have been an invalid."

He spoke with the tone of one who desires an inferior to be seated in his presence, and his voice was full and melodious.

Fairford, somewhat surprised to find himself overawed by the airs of superiority, which could be only properly exercised towards one over whom religion gave the speaker influence, sat down at his bidding, as if moved by springs, and was at a loss how to assert the footing of equality on which he felt that they ought to stand. The stranger kept the advantage which he had obtained.

"Your name, sir, I am informed, is Fairford?" said the Father.

Alan answered by a bow.

"Called to the Scottish bar," continued his visiter. "There is, I believe, in the West, a family of birth and rank called Fairford of Fairford."

Alan thought this a strange observation from a foreign ecclesiastic, as his name intimated Father Buonaventure to be; but only answered he believed there was such a family.

"Do you count kindred with them, Mr. Fairford?" continued the inquirer.

"I have not the honour to lay such a claim," said Fairford. "My father's industry has raised his family from a low and obscure situation—I have no hereditary claim to distinction of any kind.—May I ask the cause of these inquiries?"

"You will learn it presently," said Father Buonaventure, who had given a dry and dissatisfied *hem* at the young man's acknowledging a plebeian descent. He then motioned to him to be silent, and proceeded with his queries.

"Although not of condition, you are, doubtless, by sentiments and education, a man of honour and a gentleman?"

"I hope so, sir," said Alan, colouring with displeasure. "I have not been accustomed to have it questioned."

"Patience, young man," said the unperturbed querist — "we are on serious business, and no idle etiquette must prevent its being discussed seriously. — You are probably aware, that you speak to a person proscribed by the severe and unjust laws of the present government?"

"I am aware of the statute 1700, chapter 3," said Alan, "banishing from the realm Priests and trafficking Papists, and punishing by death, on summary conviction, any such person who being so banished may return. But I have no means of knowing you, sir, to be one of those persons; and I think your prudence may recommend to you to keep your own counsel."

"It is sufficient, sir; and I have no apprehensions of disagreeable consequences from your having seen me in this house," said the Priest.

"Assuredly no," said Alan. "I consider myself as indebted for my life to the Mistresses of Fairladies; and it would be a vile requital on my part to pry into or make known what I may have seen or heard under this hospitable roof. If I were to meet the Pretender himself in such a situation, he should, even at the risk of a little stretch to my loyalty, be free from any danger from my indiscretion."

"The Pretender!" said the Priest, with some angry emphasis, but immediately softened his tone, and added, "No doubt, however, that person is a pretender; and some people think his pretensions are not ill founded. But before running into politics, give me leave to say, that I am surprised to find a gentleman of your opinions in habits of intimacy with Mr. Maxwell of Summertrees and Mr. Redgauntlet, and the medium of conducting the intercourse betwixt them."

"Pardon me, sir," replied Alan Fairford; "I do not aspire to the honour of being reputed their confidant or go-between. My concern with those gentlemen is limited to one matter of business, dearly interesting to me, because it concerns the safety — perhaps the life — of my dearest friend."

"Would you have any objection to intrust me with the cause of your journey?" said Father Buonaventure. "My advice may be of service to you, and my influence with one or both these gentlemen is considerable."

Fairford hesitated a moment, and hastily revolving all circumstances, concluded that he might perhaps receive some advantage from propitiating this personage; while, on the other hand, he endangered nothing by communicating to him the occasion of his journey. He, therefore, after stating shortly, that he hoped Mr. Buonaventure would render him the same confidence which he required on his part, gave a short account of Darsie Latimer—of the mystery which hung over his family—and of the disaster which had befallen him. Finally, of his own resolution to seek for his friend, and to deliver him at the peril of his own life.

The Catholic Priest, whose manner it seemed to be to avoid all conversation which did not arise from his own express motion, made no remarks upon what he had heard, but only asked one or two abrupt questions, where Alan's narrative appeared less clear to him; then rising from his seat, he took two turns through the apartment, muttering between his teeth, with emphasis, the word "Madman!" But apparently he was in the habit of keeping all violent emotions under restraint; for he presently addressed Fairford with the most perfect indifference.

"If," said he, "you thought you could do so without breach of confidence, I wish you would have the goodness to show me the letter of Mr. Maxwell of Summertrees. I desire to look particularly at the address."

Seeing no cause to decline this extension of his confidence, Alan, without hesitation, put the letter into his hand. Having turned it round as old Trumbull and Nanty Ewart had formerly done, and, like them, having examined the address with much minuteness, he asked whether he had observed these words, pointing to a pencil-writing upon the under side of the letter. Fairford answered in the negative, and looking at the letter, read with surprise, "*Cave ne literas Bellerophontis adferres;*" a caution which coincided so exactly with the Provost's admonition, that he would do well to inspect the letter of which he was bearer, that he was about to spring up and attempt an escape, he knew not wherefore, or from whom.

"Sit still, young man," said the Father, with the same tone of authority which reigned in his whole manner, although mingled with stately courtesy. "You are in no danger—my character shall be a pledge for your safety.—By whom do you suppose these words have been written?"

Fairford could have answered, "By Nanty Ewart," for he remembered seeing that person scribble something with a pencil, although he was not well enough to observe with accuracy, where or upon what. But not knowing what suspicions, or what worse consequences, the seaman's interest in his affairs might draw upon him, he judged it best to answer that he knew not the hand.

Father Buonaventure was again silent for a moment or two, which he employed in surveying the letter with the strictest attention; then stepped to the window, as if to examine the address and writing of the envelop with the assistance of a stronger light, and Alan Fairford beheld him, with no less amazement than high displeasure, coolly and deliberately break the seal, open the letter, and peruse the contents.

"Stop, sir, hold!" he exclaimed, so soon as his astonishment permitted him to express his resentment in words; "by what right do you dare——"

"Peace, young gentleman," said the Father, repelling him with a wave of his hand; "be assured I do not act without warrant—nothing can pass betwixt Mr. Maxwell and Mr. Redgauntlet, that I am not fully entitled to know."

"It may be so," said Alan, extremely angry; "but though you may be these gentlemen's father confessor, you are not mine; and in breaking the seal of a letter intrusted to my care, you have done me——"

"No injury, I assure you," answered the unperturbed priest; "on the contrary, it may be a service."

"I desire no advantage at such a rate, or to be obtained in such a manner," answered Fairford; "restore me the letter instantly, or——"

"As you regard your own safety," said the priest, "forbear all injurious expressions, and all menacing gestures. I am not one who can be threatened or insulted with impunity; and there are enough within hearing to chastise any injury or affront offered to me, in case I may think it unbecoming to protect or avenge myself with my own hand."

In saying this, the Father assumed an air of such fearlessness and calm authority, that the young lawyer, surprised and overawed, forbore, as he had intended, to snatch the letter from his hand, and confined himself to bitter complaints of the impropriety of his conduct, and of the light in which he himself must be placed to Redgauntlet, should he present him a letter with a broken seal.

"That," said Father Buonaventure, "shall be fully cared for. I will myself write to Redgauntlet, and enclose Maxwell's letter, provided always you continue to desire to deliver it, after perusing the contents."

He then restored the letter to Fairford, and, observing that he hesitated to peruse it, said emphatically, "Read it, for it concerns you."

This recommendation, joined to what Provost Crosbie had formerly recommended, and to the warning, which he doubted not that Nanty intended to convey by his classical allusion, decided Fairford's resolution. "If these correspondents," he thought, "are conspiring against my person, I have a right to counterplot them; self-preservation, as well as my friend's safety, require that I should not be too scrupulous."

So thinking, he read the letter, which was in the following words:—

"DEAR RUGGED AND DANGEROUS,

"WILL you never cease meriting your old nick-name? You have springed your dottrel, I find, and what is the consequence?—why, that there will be hue and cry after you presently. The bearer is a pert young lawyer, who has brought a formal complaint against you, which, luckily, he has preferred in a friendly court. Yet, favourable as the judge was disposed to be, it was with the utmost difficulty that cousin Jenny and I could keep him to his tackle. He begins to be timid, suspicious, and untractable, and I fear Jenny will soon bend her brows on him in vain. I know not what to advise—the lad who carries this is a good lad—active for his friend—and I have pledged my honour he shall have no personal ill-usage—Pledged my honour, remark these words, and remember I can be rugged and dangerous as well as my neighbours. But I have not ensured him against a short captivity, and as he is a stirring active fellow, I see no remedy but keeping him out of the way till this business of the good Father B—— is safely blown over, which God send it were!—Always thine, even should I be once more

"CRAIG-IN-PERIL."

"What think you, young man, of the danger you have been about to encounter so willingly?"

"As strangely," replied Alan Fairford, "as of the extraordinary means which you have been at present pleased to use for the discovery of Mr. Maxwell's purpose."

"Trouble not yourself to account for my conduct," said the Father; "I have a warrant for what I do, and fear no responsibility. But tell me what is your present purpose."

"I should not perhaps name it to you, whose own safety may be implicated."

"I understand you," answered the Father; "you would appeal to the existing government?— That can at no rate be permitted—we will rather detain you at Fairladies by compulsion."

"You will probably," said Fairford, "first weigh the risk of such a proceeding in a free country."

"I have incurred more formidable hazard," said the priest, smiling; "yet I am willing to find a milder expedient. Come; let us bring the matter to a compromise."—And he assumed a conciliating graciousness of manner, which struck Fairford as being rather too condescending for the occasion; "I presume you will be satisfied to remain here in seclusion for a day or two longer, provided I pass my solemn word to you, that you shall meet with the person whom you seek after—meet with him in perfect safety, and, I trust, in good health, and be afterwards both at liberty to return to Scotland, or dispose of yourselves as each of you may be minded?"

"I respect the *verbum sacerdotis* as much as can reasonably be expected from a Protestant," answered Fairford; "but methinks, you can scarce expect me to repose so much confidence in the word of an unknown person, as is implied in the guarantee which you offer me."

"I am not accustomed, sir," said the Father, in a very haughty tone, "to have my word disputed. But," he added, while the angry hue passed from his cheek, after a moment's reflection, "you know me not, and ought to be excused. I will repose more confidence in your honour than you seem willing to rest upon mine; and, since we are so situated that one must rely upon the other's faith, I will cause you to be set presently at liberty, and furnished with the means of delivering your letter as addressed, provided that now, knowing the contents, you think it safe for yourself to execute the commission."

Alan Fairford paused. "I cannot see," he at length replied, "how I can proceed with respect to the accomplishment of my sole purpose, which is the liberation of my friend, without appealing to the law, and obtaining the assistance of a magistrate. If I present this singular letter of Mr. Maxwell, with the contents of which I have become so unexpectedly acquainted, I shall only share his captivity."

"And if you apply to a magistrate, young man, you will bring ruin on these hospitable ladies, to whom, in all human probability, you owe your life. You cannot obtain a warrant for your purpose, without giving a clear detail of all the late scenes through which you have passed. A magistrate would oblige you to give a complete account of yourself, before arming you with his authority against a third party; and in giving such an account, the safety of these ladies will necessarily be compromised. A hundred spies have had, and still have, their eyes upon this mansion; but God will protect his own." — He crossed himself devoutly, and then proceeded. — "You can take an hour to think of your best plan, and I will pledge myself to forward it thus far, provided it be not asking you to rely more on my word than your prudence can warrant. You shall go to Redgauntlet, — I name him plainly, to show my confidence in you, — and you shall deliver him this letter of Mr. Maxwell's, with one from me, in which I will enjoin him to set your friend at liberty, or at least to make no attempts upon your own person, either by detention or otherwise. If you can trust me thus far," he said, with a proud emphasis on the words, "I will on my side see you depart from this place with the most perfect confidence that you will not return armed with powers to drag its inmates to destruction. You are young and inexperienced — bred to a profession also which sharpens suspicion, and gives false views of human nature. I have seen much of the world, and have known better than most men, how far mutual confidence is requisite in managing affairs of consequence."

He spoke with an air of superiority, even of authority, by which Fairford, notwithstanding his own internal struggles, was silenced and overawed so much, that it was not till the Father had turned to leave the apartment that he found words to ask him what the consequences would be, should he decline to depart on the terms proposed.

"You must then, for the safety of all parties, remain for some days an inhabitant of Fairladies, where we have the means of detaining you, which self-preservation will in that case compel us to make use of. Your captivity will be short; for matters cannot long remain as they are—The cloud must soon rise, or it must sink upon us for ever.—*Benedicite!*"

With these words he left the apartment.

Fairford, upon his departure, felt himself much at a loss what course to pursue. His line of education, as well as his father's tenets in matters of church and state, had taught him a holy horror for Papists, and a devout belief in whatever had been said of the punic faith of Jesuits, and of the expedients of mental reservation, by which the Catholic priests in general were supposed to evade keeping faith with heretics. Yet there was something of majesty, depressed indeed, and overclouded, but still grand and imposing, in the manner and words of Father Buonaventure, which it was difficult to reconcile with those preconceived opinions which imputed subtlety and fraud to his sect and order. Above all, Alan was aware, that if he accepted not his freedom upon the terms offered him, he was likely to be detained by force; so that, in every point of view, he was a gainer by accepting them.

A qualm, indeed, came across him, when he considered, as a lawyer, that this Father was probably, in the eye of law, a traitor; and that there was an ugly crime on the Statute Book, called Misprision of Treason On the other hand, whatever he might think or suspect, he could not take upon him to say that the man was a priest, whom he had never seen in the dress of his order, or in the act of celebrating mass; so that he felt himself at liberty to doubt of that, respecting which he possessed no legal proof. He therefore arrived at the conclusion, that he would do well to accept his liberty, and proceed to Redgauntlet under the guarantee of Father Buonaventure, which he scarce doubted would be sufficient to save him from personal inconvenience. Should he once obtain speech of that gentleman, he felt the same confidence as formerly, that he might be able to convince him of the rashness of his conduct, should he not consent to liberate Darsie Latimer. At all events, he should learn where his friend was, and how circumstanced.

Having thus made up his mind, Alan waited anxiously for the expiration of the hour which had been allowed him for deliberation. He was not kept on the tenter-hooks of impatience an instant longer than the appointed moment arrived, for, even as the clock struck, Ambrose appeared at the door of the gallery, and made a sign that Alan should follow him. He did so, and after passing through some of the intricate avenues common in old houses, was ushered into a small apartment, commodiously fitted up, in which he found Father Buonaventure reclining on a couch, in the attitude of a man exhausted by fatigue or indisposition. On a small table beside him, a silver embossed salver sustained a Catholic book of prayer, a small flask of medicine, a cordial, and a little tea-cup of old china. Ambrose did not enter the room — he only bowed profoundly, and closed the door with the least possible noise, so soon as Fairford had entered.

"Sit down, young man," said the Father, with the same air of condescension which had before surprised, and rather offended Fairford. "You have been ill, and I know too well by my own case, that indisposition requires indulgence.—Have you," he continued, so soon as he saw him seated, "resolved to remain, or to depart?"

"To depart," said Alan, "under the agreement that you will guarantee my safety with the extraordinary person who has conducted himself in such a lawless manner toward my friend, Darsie Latimer."

"Do not judge hastily, young man," replied the Father. "Redgauntlet has the claims of a guardian over his ward, in respect to the young gentleman, and a right to dictate his place of residence, although he may have been injudicious in selecting the means by which he thinks to enforce his authority."

"His situation as an attainted person abrogates such rights," said Fairford, hastily.

"Surely," replied the priest, smiling at the young lawyer's readiness; "in the eye of those who acknowledge the justice of the attainder—but that do not I. However, sir, here is the guarantee—look at its contents, and do not again carry the letters of Uriah."

Fairford read these words:—

"GOOD FRIEND,

"We send you hither a young man desirous to know the situation of your ward, since he came under your paternal authority, and hopeful of dealing with you for having your relative put at large. This we recommend to your prudence, highly disapproving, at the same time, of any force or coercion, when such can be avoided, and wishing, therefore, that the bearer's negotiation may be successful. At all rates, however, the bearer hath our pledged word for his safety and freedom, which, therefore, you are to see strictly observed, as you value our honour and your own. We farther wish to converse with you, with as small loss of time as may be, having matters of the utmost confidence to impart. For this purpose we desire you to repair hither with all haste, and thereupon we bid you heartily farewell

P. B."

"You will understand, sir," said the Father, when he saw that Alan had perused his letter, "that, by accepting charge of this missive, you bind yourself to try the effect of it before having recourse to any legal means, as you term them, for your friend's release."

"There are a few ciphers added to this letter," said Fairford, when he had perused the paper attentively,—"may I inquire what their import is?"

"They respect my own affairs," answered the Father, briefly; "and have no concern whatever with yours."

"It seems to me, however," replied Alan, "natural to suppose——"

"Nothing must be supposed incompatible with my honour," replied the priest, interrupting him; "when such as I am confer favours, we expect that they shall be accepted with gratitude, or declined with thankful respect —not questioned or discussed."

"I will accept your letter, then," said Fairford, after a minute's consideration, "and the thanks you expect shall be most liberally paid, if the result answer what you teach me to expect."

"God only commands the issue," said Father Buonaventure. "Man uses means.—You understand, that, by accepting this commission, you engage yourself in honour to try the effect of my letter upon Mr. Redgauntlet, before you have recourse to informations or legal warrants?"

"I hold myself bound, as a man of good faith and honour, to do so," said Fairford.

"Well, I trust you," said the Father. "I will now tell you, that an express, despatched by me last night, has, I hear, brought Redgauntlet to a spot many miles nearer this place, where he will not find it safe to attempt any violence on your friend, should he be rash enough to follow the advice of Mr. Maxwell of Summertrees rather than my commands. We now understand each other."

He extended his hand towards Alan, who was about to pledge his faith in the usual form by grasping it with his own, when the Father drew back hastily. Ere Alan had time to comment upon this repulse, a small side-door, covered with tapestry, was opened; the hangings were drawn aside, and a lady, as if by sudden apparition, glided into the apartment. It was neither of the Misses Arthuret, but a woman in the prime of life, and in the full-blown expansion of female beauty, tall, fair, and commanding in her aspect. Her locks, of paly gold, were taught to fall over a brow, which, with the stately glance of the large, open, blue eyes, might have become Juno herself; her neck and bosom were admirably formed, and of a dazzling whiteness. She was rather inclined to *embonpoint*, but not more than became her age, of apparently thirty years. Her step was that of a queen, but it was of Queen Vashti, not Queen Esther—the bold and commanding, not the retiring beauty.

Father Buonaventure raised himself on the couch, angrily, as if displeased by this intrusion. "How now, madam," he said, with sternness; "why have we the honour of your company?"

"Because it is my pleasure," answered the lady, composedly.

"Your pleasure, madam!" he repeated in the same angry tone.

"My pleasure, sir," she continued, "which always keeps exact pace with my duty. I had heard you were unwell—let me hope it is only business which produces this seclusion."

"I am well," he replied; "perfectly well, and I thank you for your care —but we are not alone, and this young man——"

"That young man?" she said, bending her large and serious eye on Alan Fairford, as if she had been for the first time aware of his presence—"may I ask who he is?"

"Another time, madam; you shall learn his history after he is gone. His presence renders it impossible for me to explain farther."

"After he is gone may be too late," said the lady; "and what is his presence to me, when your safety is at stake? He is the heretic lawyer whom those silly fools, the Arthurets, admitted into this house at a time when they should have let their own father knock at the door in vain, though the night had been a wild one. You will not surely dismiss him?"

"Your own impatience can alone make that step perilous," said the Father; "I have resolved to take it—do not let your indiscreet zeal, however excellent its motive, add any unnecessary risk to the transaction."

"Even so?" said the lady, in a tone of reproach, yet mingled with respect and apprehension. "And thus you will still go forward, like a stag upon the hunter's snares, with undoubting confidence, after all that has happened?"

"Peace, madam," said Father Buonaventure, rising up; "be silent, or quit the apartment; my designs do not admit of female criticism."

To this peremptory command the lady seemed about to make a sharp reply; but she checked herself, and pressing her lips strongly together, as if to secure the words from bursting from them which were already formed upon her tongue, she made a deep reverence, partly as it seemed in reproach, partly in respect, and left the room as suddenly as she had entered it.

The Father looked disturbed at this incident, which he seemed sensible could not but fill Fairford's imagination with an additional throng of bewildering suspicions; he bit his lip and muttered something to himself as he walked through the apartment; then suddenly turned to his visiter with a smile of much sweetness, and a countenance in which every rougher expression was exchanged for those of courtesy and kindness.

"The visit we have been just honoured with, my young friend, has given you," he said, "more secrets to keep than I would have wished you burdened with. The lady is a person of condition — of rank and fortune—but nevertheless is so circumstanced, that the mere fact of her being known to be in this country would occasion many evils. I should wish you to observe secrecy on this subject, even to Redgauntlet or Maxwell, however much I trust them in all that concerns my own affairs."

"I can have no occasion," replied Fairford, "for holding any discussion with these gentlemen, or with any others, on the circumstance which I have just witnessed — it could only have become the subject of my conversation by mere accident, and I will now take care to avoid the subject entirely."

"You will do well, sir, and I thank you," said the Father, throwing much dignity into the expression of obligation which he meant to convey. "The time may perhaps come when you will learn what it is to have obliged one of my condition. As to the lady, she has the highest merit, and nothing can be said of her justly which would not redound to her praise. Nevertheless—in short, sir, we wander at present as in a morning mist—the sun will, I trust, soon rise and dispel it, when all that now seems mysterious will be fully revealed — or it will sink into rain," he added, in a solemn tone, "and then explanation will be of little consequence. — Adieu, sir; I wish you well."

He made a graceful obeisance, and vanished through the same side-door by which the lady had entered; and Alan thought he heard their voices high in dispute in the adjoining apartment.

Presently afterwards, Ambrose entered, and told him that a horse and guide awaited him beneath the terrace.

"The good Father Buonaventure," added the butler, "has been graciously pleased to consider your situation, and desired me to inquire whether you have any occasion for a supply of money?"

"Make my respects to his reverence," answered Fairford, "and assure him I am provided in that particular. I beg you also to make my acknowledgments to the Misses Arthuret, and assure them that their kind hospitality, to which I probably owe my life, shall be remembered with gratitude as long as that life lasts. You yourself, Mr. Ambrose, must accept of my kindest thanks for your skill and attention."

Mid these acknowledgments they left the house, descended the terrace, and reached the spot where the gardener, Fairford's old acquaintance, waited for him, mounted upon one horse and leading another.

Bidding adieu to Ambrose, our young lawyer mounted, and rode down the avenue, often looking back to the melancholy and neglected dwelling in which he had witnessed such strange scenes, and musing upon the character of its mysterious inmates, especially the noble and almost regal seeming priest, and the beautiful but capricious dame, who, if she was really Father Buonaventure's penitent, seemed less docile to the authority of the church, than, as Alan conceived, the Catholic discipline permitted. He could not indeed help being sensible that the whole deportment of these persons differed much from his preconceived notions of a priest and devotee. Father Buonaventure, in particular, had more natural dignity and less art and affectation in his manner, than accorded with the idea which Calvinists were taught to entertain of that wily and formidable person, a Jesuitical missionary.

While reflecting on these things, he looked back so frequently at the house, that Dick Gardener, a forward, talkative fellow, who began to tire of silence, at length said to him, "I think you will know Fairladies when you see it again, sir?"

"I dare say I shall, Richard," answered Fairford good-humouredly. "I wish I knew as well where I am to go next. But you can tell me, perhaps."

"Your worship should know better than I," said Dick Gardener; "nevertheless, I have a notion you are going where all you Scotsmen should be sent, whether you will or no."

"Not to the devil, I hope, good Dick?" said Fairford.

"Why, no. That is a road which you may travel as heretics; but as Scotsmen, I would only send you three-fourths of the way — and that is back to Scotland again—always craving your honour's pardon."

"Does our journey lie that way?" said Fairford. "As far as the water-side," said Richard. "I am to carry you to old Father Crackenthorp's, and then you are within a spit and a stride of Scotland, as the saying is. But mayhap you may think twice of going thither, for all that; for Old England is fat feeding-ground for north-country cattle.

Chapter the Seventeenth.

NARRATIVE OF DARSIE LATIMER.

Our history must now, as the old romancers wont to say, "leave to tell" of the quest of Alan Fairford, and instruct our readers of the adventures which befell Darsie Latimer, left as he was in the precarious custody of his self-named tutor, the Laird of the Lochs of Solway, to whose arbitrary pleasure he found it necessary for the present to conform himself.

In consequence of this prudent resolution, and although he did not assume such a disguise without some sensations of shame and degradation, Darsie permitted Cristal Nixon to place over his face, and secure by a string, one of those silk masks which ladies frequently wore to preserve their complexions, when exposed to the air during long journeys on horseback. He remonstrated somewhat more vehemently against the long riding-skirt, which converted his person from the waist into the female guise, but was obliged to concede this point also.

The metamorphosis was then complete; for the fair reader must be informed, that in those rude times, the ladies, when they honoured the masculine dress by assuming any part of it, wore just such hats, coats, and waistcoats, as the male animals themselves made use of, and had no notion of the elegant compromise betwixt male and female attire, which has now acquired, *par excellence*, the name of a *habit*. Trolloping things our mothers must have looked, with long square-cut coats, lacking collars, and with waistcoats plentifully supplied with a length of pocket, which hung far downwards from the middle. But then they had some advantage from the splendid colours, lace, and gay embroidery, which masculine attire then exhibited; and, as happens in many similar instances, the finery of the materials made amends for the want of symmetry and grace of form in the garments themselves. But this is a digression.

In the court of the old mansion, half manor-place, half farm-house, or rather a decayed manor-house, converted into an abode for a Cumberland tenant, stood several saddled horses. Four or five of them were mounted by servants or inferior retainers, all of whom were well armed with sword, pistol, and carabine. But two had riding furniture for the use of females —the one being accoutred with a side-saddle, the other with a pillion attached to the saddle.

Darsie's heart beat quicker within him; he easily comprehended that one of these was intended for his own use; and his hopes suggested that the other was designed for that of the fair Green-Mantle, whom, according to his established practice, he had adopted for the queen of his affections, although his opportunities of holding communication with her had not exceeded the length of a silent supper on one occasion, and the going down a country-dance on another. This, however, was no unwonted mood of passion with Darsie Latimer, upon whom Cupid was used to triumph only in the degree of a Mahratta conqueror, who overruns a province with the rapidity of lightning, but finds it impossible to retain it beyond a very brief space. Yet this new love was rather more serious than the scarce skinned-up wounds which his friend Fairford used to ridicule. The damsel had shown a sincere interest in his behalf; and the air of mystery with which that interest was veiled, gave her, to his lively imagination, the character of a benevolent and protecting spirit, as much as that of a beautiful female.

At former times, the romance attending his short-lived attachments had been of his own creating, and had disappeared as soon as ever he approached more closely to the object with which he had invested it. On the present occasion it really flowed from external circumstances, which might have interested less susceptible feelings, and an imagination less lively than that of Darsie Latimer, young, inexperienced, and enthusiastic as he was.

He watched, therefore, anxiously to whose service the palfrey bearing the lady's saddle was destined. But ere any female appeared to occupy it, he was himself summoned to take his seat on the pillion behind Cristal Nixon, amid the grins of his old acquaintance Jan, who helped him to horse, and the unrestrained laughter of Cicely, who displayed on the occasion a case of teeth which might have rivalled ivory.

Latimer was at an age when being an object of general ridicule even to clowns and milkmaids, was not a matter of indifference, and he longed heartily to have laid his horsewhip across Jan's shoulders. That, however, was a solacement of his feelings which was not at the moment to be thought of; and Cristal Nixon presently put an end to his unpleasant situation, by ordering the riders to go on. He himself kept the centre of the troop, two men riding before and two behind him, always, as it seemed to Darsie, having their eye upon him, to prevent any attempt to escape. He could see from time to time, when the straight line of the road, or the advantage of an ascent permitted him, that another troop of three or four riders followed them at about a quarter of a mile's distance, amongst whom he could discover the tall form of Redgauntlet, and the powerful action of his gallant black horse. He had little doubt that Green-Mantle made one of the party, though he was unable to distinguish her from the others.

In this manner they travelled from six in the morning until nearly ten of the clock, without Darsie exchanging a word with any one; for he loathed the very idea of entering into conversation with Cristal Nixon, against whom he seemed to feel an instinctive aversion; nor was that domestic's saturnine and sullen disposition such as to have encouraged advances, had he thought of making them.

At length the party halted for the purpose of refreshment; but as they had hitherto avoided all villages and inhabited places upon their route, so they now stopped at one of those large ruinous Dutch barns, which are sometimes found in the fields, at a distance from the farm-house to which they belong. Yet in this desolate place some preparations had been made for their reception. There were in the end of the barn, racks filled with provender for the horses, and plenty of provisions for the party were drawn from the trusses of straw, under which the baskets that contained them had been deposited. The choicest of these were selected and arranged apart by Cristal Nixon, while the men of the party threw themselves upon the rest, which he abandoned to their discretion. In a few minutes afterwards the rearward party arrived and dismounted, and Redgauntlet himself entered the barn with the green-mantled maiden by his side. He presented her to Darsie with these words:—

"It is time you two should know each other better. I promised you my confidence, Darsie, and the time is come for reposing it. But first we will have our breakfast; and then, when once more in the saddle, I will tell you that which it is necessary that you should know. Salute Lilias, Darsie."

The command was sudden, and surprised Latimer, whose confusion was increased by the perfect ease and frankness with which Lilias offered at once her cheek and her hand, and pressing his as she rather took it than gave her own, said very frankly, "Dearest Darsie, how rejoiced I am that our uncle has at last permitted us to become acquainted!"

Darsie's head turned round; and it was perhaps well that Redgauntlet called on him to sit down, as even that movement served to hide his confusion. There is an old song which says—

—"when ladies are willing,
A man can but look like a fool;"

And on the same principle Darsie Latimer's looks at this unexpected frankness of reception, would have formed an admirable vignette for illustrating the passage. "Dearest Darsie," and such a ready, nay, eager salute of lip and hand!—It was all very gracious, no doubt—and ought to have been received with much gratitude; but constituted as our friend's temper was, nothing could be more inconsistent with his tone of feeling. If a hermit had proposed to him to club for a pot of beer, the illusion of his reverend sanctity could not have been dispelled more effectually than the divine qualities of Green-Mantle faded upon the ill-imagined frank-heartedness of poor Lilias. Vexed with her forwardness, and affronted at having once more cheated himself, Darsie could hardly help muttering two lines of the song we have already quoted:

The fruit that must fall without shaking
Is rather too mellow for me."

And yet it was pity for her too — she was a very pretty young woman — his fancy had scarcely overrated her in that respect — and the slight derangement of the beautiful brown locks which escaped in natural ringlets from under her riding-hat, with the bloom which exercise had brought into her cheek, made her even more than usually fascinating. Redgauntlet

T

modified the sternness of his look when it was turned towards her, and in addressing her, used a softer tone than his usual deep bass. Even the grim features of Cristal Nixon relaxed when he attended on her, and it was then, if ever, that his misanthropical visage expressed some sympathy with the rest of humanity.

"How can she," thought Latimer, "look so like an angel, yet be so mere a mortal after all?—How could so much seeming modesty have so much forwardness of manner, when she ought to have been most reserved? How can her conduct be reconciled to the grace and ease of her general deportment?"

The confusion of thoughts which occupied Darsie's imagination, gave to his looks a disordered appearance, and his inattention to the food which was placed before him, together with his silence and absence of mind, induced Lilias solicitously to inquire, whether he did not feel some return of the disorder under which he had suffered so lately. This led Mr. Redgauntlet, who seemed also lost in his own contemplations, to raise his eyes, and join in the same inquiry with some appearance of interest. Latimer explained to both that he was perfectly well.

"It is well it is so," answered Redgauntlet; "for we have that before us which will brook no delay from indisposition—we have not, as Hotspur says, leisure to be sick."

Lilias, on her part, endeavoured to prevail upon Darsie to partake of the food which she offered him, with a kindly and affectionate courtesy, corresponding to the warmth of the interest she had displayed at their meeting; but so very natural, innocent, and pure in its character, that it would have been impossible for the vainest coxcomb to have mistaken it for coquetry, or a desire of captivating a prize so valuable as his affection. Darsie, with no more than the reasonable share of self-opinion common to most youths when they approach twenty-one, knew not how to explain her conduct.

Sometimes he was tempted to think that his own merits had, even during the short intervals when they had seen each other, secured such a hold of the affections of a young person, who had probably been bred up in ignorance of the world and its forms, that she was unable to conceal her partiality. Sometimes he suspected that she acted by her guardian's order, who, aware that he, Darsie, was entitled to a considerable fortune, might have taken this bold stroke to bring about a marriage betwixt him and so near a relative.

But neither of these suppositions was applicable to the character of the parties. Miss Lilias's manners, however soft and natural, displayed in their ease and versatility considerable acquaintance with the habits of the world, and in the few words she said during the morning repast, there were mingled a shrewdness and good sense, which could scarce belong to a miss capable of playing the silly part of a love-smitten maiden so broadly. As for Redgauntlet, with his stately bearing, his fatal frown, his eye of threat and of command, it was impossible, Darsie thought, to suspect him of a scheme having private advantage for its object;—he could as soon have imagined Cassius picking Cæsar's pocket, instead of drawing his poniard on the Dictator.

While he thus mused, unable either to eat, drink, or answer to the courtesy of Lilias, she soon ceased to speak to him, and sat silent as himself.

They had remained nearly an hour in their halting place, when Redgauntlet said aloud, "Look out, Cristal Nixon. If we hear nothing from Fairladies, we must continue our journey."

Cristal went to the door, and presently returned and said to his master, in a voice as harsh as his features, "Gilbert Gregson is coming, his horse as white with foam as if a fiend had ridden him."

Redgauntlet threw from him the plate on which he had been eating, and hastened towards the door of the barn, which the courier at that moment entered; a smart jockey with a black velvet hunting-cap, and a broad belt drawn tight round his waist, to which was secured his express-bag. The variety of mud with which he was splashed from cap to spur, showed he had had a rough and rapid ride. He delivered a letter to Mr. Redgauntlet, with an obeisance, and then retired to the end of the barn, where the other attendants were sitting or lying upon the straw, in order to get some refreshment.

Redgauntlet broke the letter open with haste, and read it with anxious and discomposed looks. On a second perusal, his displeasure seemed to increase, his brow darkened, and was distinctly marked with the fatal sign peculiar to his family and house. Darsie had never before observed his frown bear such a close resemblance to the shape which tradition as signed it.

Redgauntlet held out the open letter with one hand, and struck it with the forefinger of the other, as, in a suppressed and displeased tone, he said to Cristal Nixon, "Countermanded — ordered northward once more! — Northward, when all our hopes lie to the south — a second Derby direction, when we turned our back on glory, and marched in quest of ruin!"

Cristal Nixon took the letter and ran it over, then returned it to his master with the cold observation, "A female influence predominates."

"But it shall predominate no longer," said Redgauntlet; "it shall wane as ours rises in the horizon. Meanwhile, I will on before—and you, Cristal, will bring the party to the place assigned in the letter. You may now permit the young persons to have unreserved communication together; only mark that you watch the young man closely enough to prevent his escape, if he should be idiot enough to attempt it, but not approaching so close as to watch their free conversation."

"I care nought about their conversation," said Nixon, surlily.

"You bear my commands, Lilias," said the Laird, turning to the young lady. "You may use my permission and authority, to explain so much of our family matters as you yourself know. At our next meeting I will complete the task of disclosure, and I trust I shall restore one Redgauntlet more to the bosom of our ancient family. Let Latimer, as he calls himself, have a horse to himself; he must for some time retain his disguise.—My horse— my horse!"

In two minutes they heard him ride off from the door of the barn, followed at speed by two of the armed men of his party.

The commands of Cristal Nixon, in the meanwhile, put all the remainder of the party in motion, but the Laird himself was long out of sight ere they were in readiness to resume their journey. When at length they set out, Darsie was accommodated with a horse and side-saddle, instead of being obliged to resume his place on the pillion behind the detestable Nixon. He was obliged, however, to retain his riding-skirt, and to reassume his mask. Yet, notwithstanding this disagreeable circumstance, and although he observed that they gave him the heaviest and slowest horse of the party, and that, as a farther precaution against escape, he was closely watched on every side, yet riding in company with the pretty Lilias was an advantage which overbalanced these inconveniences.

It is true, that this society, to which that very morning he would have looked forward as a glimpse of heaven, had, now that it was thus unexpectedly indulged, something much less rapturous than he had expected.

It was in vain that, in order to avail himself of a situation so favourable for indulging his romantic disposition, he endeavoured to coax back, if I may so express myself, that delightful dream of ardent and tender passion; he felt only such a confusion of ideas at the difference between the being whom he had imagined, and her with whom he was now in contact, that it seemed to him like the effect of witchcraft. What most surprised him was, that this sudden flame should have died away so rapidly, notwithstanding that the maiden's personal beauty was even greater than he had expected — her demeanour, unless it should be deemed over kind towards himself, as graceful and becoming as he could have fancied it, even in his gayest dreams. It were judging hardly of him to suppose that the mere belief of his having attracted her affections more easily than he expected, was the cause of his ungratefully undervaluing a prize too lightly won, or that his transient passion played around his heart with the flitting radiance of a wintry sunbeam flashing against an icicle, which may brighten it for a moment, but cannot melt it. Neither of these was precisely the case, though such fickleness of disposition might also have some influence in the change.

The truth is, perhaps, the lover's pleasure, like that of the hunter, is in the chase; and that the brightest beauty loses half its merit, as the fairest flower its perfume, when the willing hand can reach it too easily. There must be doubt—there must be danger—there must be difficulty; and if, as the poet says, the course of ardent affection never does run smooth, it is perhaps because, without some intervening obstacle, that which is called the romantic passion of love, in its high poetical character and colouring, can hardly have an existence;—any more than there can be a current in a river, without the stream being narrowed by steep banks, or checked by opposing rocks.

Let not those, however, who enter into a union for life without those embarrassments which delight a Darsie Latimer, or a Lydia Languish, and which are perhaps necessary to excite an enthusiastic passion in breasts more firm than theirs, augur worse of their future happiness, because their own alliance is formed under calmer auspices. Mutual esteem, an intimate knowledge of each other's character, seen, as in their case, undisguised by the mists of too partial passion — a suitable proportion of parties in rank and fortune, in taste and pursuits — are more frequently found in a marriage of reason, than in a union of romantic attachment; where the imagination, which probably created the virtues and accomplishments with which it invested the beloved object, is frequently afterwards employed in magnifying the mortifying consequences of its own delusion, and exasperating all the stings of disappointment. Those who follow the banners of Reason are like the well-disciplined battalion, which, wearing a more sober uniform, and making a less dazzling show, than the light troops commanded by Imagination, enjoy more safety, and even more honour, in the conflicts of human life. All this, however, is foreign to our present purpose.

Uncertain in what manner to address her whom he had been lately so anxious to meet with, and embarrassed by a *tête-à-tête* to which his own timid inexperience gave some awkwardness, the party had proceeded more than a hundred yards before Darsie assumed courage to accost, or even to look at, his companion. Sensible, however, of the impropriety of his silence, he turned to speak to her; and observing that, although she wore her mask, there was something like disappointment and dejection in her manner, he was moved by self-reproach for his own coldness, and hastened to address her in the kindest tone he could assume.

"You must think me cruelly deficient in gratitude, Miss Lilias, that I have been thus long in your company, without thanking you for the interest which you have deigned to take in my unfortunate affairs?"

"I am glad you have at length spoken," she said, "though I own it is more coldly than I expected. — *Miss* Lilias! *Deign* to take interest!—In whom, dear Darsie, *can* I take interest but in you; and why do you put this barrier of ceremony betwixt us, whom adverse circumstances have already separated for such a length of time?"

Darsie was again confounded at the extra candour, if we may use the term, of this frank avowal—"One must love partridge very well," thought he, "to accept it when thrown in one's face — if this is not plain speaking, there is no such place as downright Dunstable in being!"

Embarrassed with these reflections, and himself of a nature fancifully, almost fastidiously, delicate, he could only in reply stammer forth an acknowledgment of his companion's goodness, and his own gratitude. She answered in a tone partly sorrowful and partly impatient, repeating, with displeased emphasis, the only distinct words he had been able to bring forth—"Goodness—gratitude!—O Darsie! should these be the phrases between you and me?—Alas! I am too sure you are displeased with me, though I cannot even guess on what account. Perhaps you think I have been too free venturing upon my visit to your friend. But then remember, it was in your behalf, and that I knew no better way to put you on your guard against the misfortunes and restraint which you have been subjected to, and are still enduring.".

"Dear lady"—said Darsie, rallying his recollection, and suspicious of some error in apprehension,—a suspicion which his mode of address seemed at once to communicate to Lilias, for she interrupted him,—

"*Lady!* dear *lady!*—For whom, or for what, in Heaven's name, do you take me, that you address me so formally?'"

Had the question been asked in that enchanted hall in Fairyland, where all interrogations must be answered with absolute sincerity, Darsie had certainly replied, that he took her for the most frank-hearted and ultra-liberal lass that had ever lived since Mother Eve eat the pippin without paring. But as he was still on middle-earth, and free to avail himself of a little polite deceit, he barely answered, that he believed he had the honour of speaking to the niece of Mr. Redgauntlet.

"Surely," she replied; "but were it not as easy for you to have said, to your own only sister ?".

Darsie started in his saddle, as if he had received a pistol-shot.

"My sister !" he exclaimed.

"And you did *not* know it, then?" said she. "I thought your reception of me was cold and indifferent!"

A kind and cordial embrace took place betwixt the relatives; and so light was Darsie's spirit, that he really felt himself more relieved, by getting quit of the embarrassments of the last half hour, during which he conceived himself in danger of being persecuted by the attachment of a forward girl, than disappointed by the vanishing of so many day-dreams as he had been in the habit of encouraging during the time when the greenmantled maiden was goddess of his idolatry. He had been already flung from his romantic Pegasus, and was too happy at length to find himself with bones unbroken, though with his back on the ground. He was, besides, with all his whims and follies, a generous, kind-hearted youth, and was delighted to acknowledge so beautiful and amiable a relative, and to assure her in the warmest terms of his immediate affection and future protection, so soon as they should be extricated from their present situation. Smiles and tears mingled on Lilias's cheeks, like showers and sunshine in April weather.

"Out on me," she said, "that I should be so childish as to cry at what makes me so sincerely happy! since, God knows, family-love is what my heart has most longed after, and to which it has been most a stranger. My uncle says that you and I, Darsie, are but half Redgauntlets, and that the metal of which our father's family was made, has been softened to effeminacy in our mother's offspring."

"Alas!" said Darsie, "I know so little of our family story, that I almost doubted that I belonged to the House of Redgauntlet, although the chief of the family himself intimated so much to me."

"The Chief of the family!" said Lilias. "You must know little of your own descent indeed, if you mean my uncle by that expression. You yourself, my dear Darsie, are the heir and representative of our ancient House, for our father was the elder brother—that brave and unhappy Sir Henry

Darsie Redgauntlet, who suffered at Carlisle in the year 1746. He took the name of Darsie, in conjunction with his own, from our mother, heiress to a Cumberland family of great wealth and antiquity, of whose large estates you are the undeniable heir, although those of your father have been involved in the general doom of forfeiture. But all this must be necessarily unknown to you."

"Indeed I hear it for the first time in my life," answered Darsie.

"And you knew not that I was your sister?" said Lilias. "No wonder you received me so coldly. What a strange, wild, forward young person you must have thought me — mixing myself in the fortunes of a stranger whom I had only once spoken to—corresponding with him by signs—Good Heaven! what can you have supposed me?"

"And how should I have come to the knowledge of our connection?" said Darsie. "You are aware I was not acquainted with it when we danced together at Brokenburn."

"I saw that with concern, and fain I would have warned you," answered Lilias; "but I was closely watched, and before I could find or make an opportunity of coming to a full explanation with you on a subject so agitating, I was forced to leave the room. What I did say was, you may remember, a caution to leave the southern border, for I foresaw what has since happened. But since my uncle has had you in his power, I never doubted he had communicated to you our whole family history."

"He has left me to learn it from you, Lilias; and assure yourself that I will hear it with more pleasure from your lips than from his. I have no reason to be pleased with his conduct towards me."

"Of that," said Lilias, "you will judge better when you have heard what I have to tell you;" and she began her communication in the following manner.

Chapter the Eighteenth.

NARRATIVE OF DARSIE LATIMER, CONTINUED.

"THE House of Redgauntlet," said the young lady, "has for centuries been supposed to lie under a doom, which has rendered vain their courage, their talents, their ambition, and their wisdom. Often making a figure in history, they have been ever in the situation of men striving against both wind and tide, who distinguish themselves by their desperate exertions of strength, and their persevering endurance of toil, but without being able to advance themselves upon their course, by either vigour or resolution. They pretended to trace this fatality to a legendary history, which I may tell you at a less busy moment."

Darsie intimated, that he had already heard the tragic story of Sir Alberick Redgauntlet.

"I need only say, then," proceeded Lilias, "that our father and uncle felt the family doom in its full extent. They were both possessed of considerable property, which was largely increased by our father's marriage, and were both devoted to the service of the unhappy House of Stewart; but (as our mother at least supposed) family considerations might have withheld her husband from joining openly in the affair of 1745, had not the high influence which the younger brother possessed over the elder, from his more decided energy of character, hurried him along with himself into that undertaking.

"When, therefore, the enterprise came to the fatal conclusion which bereaved our father of his life, and consigned his brother to exile, Lady Redgauntlet fled from the north of England, determined to break off all communication with her late husband's family, particularly his brother, whom she regarded as having, by their insane political enthusiasm, been the means of his untimely death; and determined that you, my brother, an infant, and that I, to whom she had just given birth, should be brought up as adherents of the present dynasty. Perhaps she was too hasty in this determination — too timidly anxious to exclude, if possible, from the knowledge of the very spot where we existed, a relation so nearly connected with us as our father's only brother. But you must make allowance for what she had suffered. See, brother," she said, pulling her glove off, "these five blood-specks on my arm are a mark by which mysterious Nature has impressed, on an unborn infant, a record of its father's violent death and its mother's miseries."*

"You were not, then, born when my father suffered?" said Darsie.

"Alas, no!" she replied; "nor were you a twelvemonth old. It was no wonder that my mother, after going through such scenes of agony, became irresistibly anxious for the sake of her children—of her son in particular; the more especially as the late Sir Henry, her husband, had, by a settlement of his affairs, confided the custody of the persons of her children, as well as the estates which descended to them, independently of those which fell under his forfeiture, to his brother Hugh, in whom he placed unlimited confidence."

"But my mother had no reason to fear the operation of such a deed, conceived in favour of an attainted man," said Darsie.

"True," replied Lilias; "but our uncle's attainder might have been reversed, like that of so many other persons, and our mother, who both feared and hated him, lived in continual terror that this would be the case, and that she should see the author, as she thought him, of her husband's death, come armed with legal powers, and in a capacity to use them, for the purpose of tearing her children from her protection. Besides, she feared, even in his incapacitated condition, the adventurous and pertinacious spirit of her brother-in-law, Hugh Redgauntlet, and felt assured that he would make some attempt to possess himself of the persons of the children. On the other hand, our uncle, whose proud disposition might, perhaps, have been soothed by the offer of her confidence, revolted against the distrustful and suspicious manner in which Lady Darsie Redgauntlet acted towards him. She basely abused, he said, the unhappy circumstances in which he was placed, in order to deprive him of his natural privilege of protecting and educating the infants, whom nature and law, and the will of their father, had committed to his charge, and he swore solemnly he would not submit to such an injury. Report of his threats was made to Lady Redgauntlet, and tended to increase those fears which proved but two well founded. While you and I, children at that time of two or three years old, were playing together in a walled orchard, adjacent to our mother's residence, which she had fixed somewhere in Devonshire, my uncle suddenly scaled the wall with several men, and I was snatched up and carried off to a boat which waited for them. My mother, however, flew to your rescue, and as she seized on and held you fast, my uncle could not, as he has since told me, possess himself of your person, without using unmanly violence to his brother's widow. Of this he was incapable; and, as people began to assemble upon my mother's screaming, he withdrew, after darting upon you

---

* Several persons have brought down to these days the impressions which Nature had thus recorded, when they were yet babes unborn. One lady of quality, whose father was long under sentence of death, previous to the Rebellion, was marked on the back of the neck by the sign of a broad axe. Another, whose kinsmen had been slain in battle, and died on the scaffold, to the number of seven, bore a child spattered on the right shoulder, and down the arm, with scarlet drops, as if of blood. Many other instances might be quoted.

and her one of those fearful looks, which, it is said, remain with our family, as a fatal bequest of Sir Alberick, our ancestor."

"I have some recollection of the scuffle which you mention," said Darsie; "and I think it was my uncle himself (since my uncle he is) who recalled the circumstance to my mind on a late occasion. I can now account for the guarded seclusion under which my poor mother lived—for her frequent tears, her starts of hysterical alarm, and her constant and deep melancholy. Poor lady! what a lot was hers, and what must have been her feelings when it approached to a close!"

"It was then that she adopted," said Lilias, "every precaution her ingenuity could suggest, to keep your very existence concealed from the person whom she feared—nay, from yourself; for she dreaded, as she is said often to have expressed herself, that the wildfire blood of Redgauntlet would urge you to unite your fortunes to those of your uncle, who was well known still to carry on political intrigues, which most other persons had considered as desperate. It was also possible that he, as well as others, might get his pardon, as government showed every year more lenity towards the remnant of the Jacobites, and then he might claim the custody of your person, as your legal guardian. Either of these events she considered as the direct road to your destruction."

"I wonder she had not claimed the protection of Chancery for me," said Darsie; "or confided me to the care of some powerful friend."

"She was on indifferent terms with her relations, on account of her marriage with our father," said Lilias, "and trusted more in secreting you from your uncle's attempts, than to any protection which law might afford against them. Perhaps she judged unwisely, but surely not unnaturally, for one rendered irritable by so many misfortunes and so many alarms. Samuel Griffiths, an eminent banker, and a worthy clergyman now dead, were, I believe, the only persons whom she intrusted with the execution of her last will; and my uncle believes that she made them both swear to observe profound secrecy concerning your birth and pretensions, until you should come to the age of majority, and, in the meantime, to breed you up in the most private way possible, and that which was most likely to withdraw you from my uncle's observation."

"And I have no doubt," said Darsie, "that betwixt change of name and habitation, they might have succeeded perfectly, but for the accident—lucky or unlucky, I know not which to term it—which brought me to Brokenburn, and into contact with Mr. Redgauntlet. I see also why I was warned against England, for in England——"

"In England alone, if I understand rightly," said Miss Redgauntlet, "the claims of your uncle to the custody of your person could have been enforced, in case of his being replaced in the ordinary rights of citizenship, either by the lenity of the government or by some change in it. In Scotland, where you possess no property, I understand his authority might have been resisted, and measures taken to put you under the protection of the law. But, pray, think it not unlucky that you have taken the step to visit Brokenburn—I feel confident that the consequences must be ultimately fortunate, for, have they not already brought us into contact with each other?"

So saying, she held out her hand to her brother, who grasped it with a fondness of pressure very different from the manner in which they first clasped hands that morning. There was a moment's pause, while the hearts of both were overflowing with a feeling of natural affection, to which circumstances had hitherto rendered them strangers.

At length Darsie broke silence; "I am ashamed," he said, "my dearest Lilias, that I have suffered you to talk so long about matters concerning myself only, while I remain ignorant of your story, and your present situation."

"The former is none of the most interesting, nor the latter the most safe or agreeable," answered Lilias; "but now, my dearest brother, I shall have the inestimable support of your countenance and affection; and were I but sure that we could weather the formidable crisis which I find so close at hand, I should have little apprehensions for the future."

"Let me know," said Darsie, "what our present situation is; and rely upon my utmost exertions· both in your defence and my own. For what reason can my uncle desire to detain me a prisoner?—If in mere opposition to the will of my mother, she has long been no more; and I see not why he should wish, at so much trouble and risk, to interfere with the free will of one, to whom a few months will give a privilege of acting for himself, with which he will have no longer any pretence to interfere."

"My dearest Arthur," answered Lilias—"for that name, as well as Darsie, properly belongs to you—it is the leading feature in my uncle's character, that he has applied every energy of his powerful mind to the service of the exiled family of Stewart. The death of his brother, the dilapidation of his own fortunes, have only added to his hereditary zeal for the House of Stewart, a deep and almost personal hatred against the present reigning family. He is, in short, a political enthusiast of the most dangerous character, and proceeds in his agency with as much confidence, as if he felt himself the very Atlas, who is alone capable of supporting a sinking cause."

"And where or how did you, my Lilias, educated, doubtless, under his auspices, learn to have a different view of such subjects?"

"By a singular chance," replied Lilias, "in the nunnery where my uncle placed me. Although the Abbess was a person exactly after his own heart, my education as a pensioner devolved much on an excellent old mother who had adopted the tenets of the Jansenists, with perhaps a still farther tendency towards the reformed doctrines, than those of Porte-Royale. The mysterious secrecy with which she inculcated these tenets, gave them charms to my young mind, and I embraced them the rather that they were in direct opposition to the doctrines of the Abbess, whom I hated so much for her severity, that I felt a childish delight in setting her control at defiance, and contradicting in my secret soul all that I was openly obliged to listen to with reverence. Freedom of religious opinion brings on, I suppose, freedom of political creed; for I had no sooner renounced the Pope's infallibility, than I began to question the doctrine of hereditary and indefeasible right. In short, strange as it may seem, I came out of a Parisian convent, not indeed an instructed Whig and Protestant, but with as much inclination to be so as if I had been bred up, like you, within the presbyterian sound of Saint Giles's chimes."

"More so, perhaps," replied Darsie; "for the nearer the church —— the proverb is somewhat musty. But how did these liberal opinions of yours agree with the very opposite prejudices of my uncle?"

"They would have agreed like fire and water," answered Lilias, "had I suffered mine to become visible; but as that would have subjected me to constant reproach and upbraiding, or worse, I took great care to keep my own secret; so that occasional censures for coldness, and lack of zeal for the good cause, were the worst I had to undergo; and these were bad enough."

"I applaud your caution," said Darsie.

"You have reason," replied his sister; "but I got so terrible a specimen of my uncle's determination of character, before I had been acquainted with him for much more than a week, that it taught me at what risk I should contradict his humour. I will tell you the circumstances; for it will better teach you to appreciate the romantic and resolved nature of his character, than any thing which I could state of his rashness and enthusiasm.

"After I had been many a long year at the convent, I was removed from thence, and placed with a meagre old Scottish lady of high rank, the daughter of an unfortunate person, whose head had in the year 1715 been placed on

Temple-bar. She subsisted on a small pension from the French Court, aided by an occasional gratuity from the Stewarts; to which the annuity paid for my board formed a desirable addition. She was not ill-tempered, nor very covetous—neither beat me nor starved me—but she was so completely trammelled by rank and prejudices, so awfully profound in genealogy, and so bitterly keen, poor lady, in British politics, that I sometimes thought it pity that the Hanoverians, who murdered, as she used to tell me, her poor dear father, had left his dear daughter in the land of the living. Delighted, therefore, was I, when my uncle made his appearance, and abruptly announced his purpose of conveying me to England. My extravagant joy at the idea of leaving Lady Rachel Rougedragon, was somewhat qualified by observing the melancholy look, lofty demeanour, and commanding tone of my near relative. He held more communication with me on the journey, however, than consisted with his taciturn demeanour in general, and seemed anxious to ascertain my tone of character, and particularly in point of courage. Now, though I am a tamed Redgauntlet, yet I have still so much of our family spirit as enables me to be as composed in danger as most of my sex; and upon two occasions in the course of our journey—a threatened attack by banditti, and the overturn of our carriage—I had the fortune so to conduct myself, as to convey to my uncle a very favourable idea of my intrepidity. Probably this encouraged him to put in execution the singular scheme which he had in agitation.

"Ere we reached London we changed our means of conveyance, and altered the route by which we approached the city, more than once; then, like a hare which doubles repeatedly at some distance from the seat she means to occupy, and at last leaps into her form from a distance so great as she can clear by a spring, we made a forced march, and landed in private and obscure lodgings in a little old street in Westminster, not far from the Cloisters.

"On the morning of the day on which we arrived my uncle went abroad, and did not return for some hours. Meantime I had no other amusement than to listen to the tumult of noises which succeeded each other, or reigned in confusion together during the whole morning. Paris I had thought the most noisy capital in the world, but Paris seemed midnight silence compared to London. Cannon thundered near and at a distance—drums, trumpets, and military music of every kind, rolled, flourished, and pierced the clouds, almost without intermission. To fill up the concert, bells pealed incessantly from a hundred steeples. The acclamations of an immense multitude were heard from time to time, like the roaring of a mighty ocean, and all this without my being able to glean the least idea of what was going on, for the windows of our apartment looked upon a waste back-yard, which seemed totally deserted. My curiosity became extreme, for I was satisfied, at length, that it must be some festival of the highest order which called forth these incessant sounds.

"My uncle at length returned, and with him a man of an exterior singularly unprepossessing. I need not describe him to you, for—do not look round—he rides behind us at this moment."

"That respectable person, Mr. Cristal Nixon, I suppose?" said Darsie.

"The same," answered Lilias; "make no gesture, that may intimate we are speaking of him."

Darsie signified that he understood her, and she pursued her relation.

"They were both in full dress, and my uncle, taking a bundle from Nixon, said to me, 'Lilias, I am come to carry you to see a grand ceremony—put on as hastily as you can the dress you will find in that parcel, and prepare to attend me.' I found a female dress, splendid and elegant, but somewhat bordering upon the antique fashion. It might be that of England, I thought, and I went to my apartment full of curiosity, and dressed myself with all speed.

"My uncle surveyed me with attention — 'She may pass for one of the flower-girls,' he said to Nixon, who only answered with a nod.

"We left the house together, and such was their knowledge of the lanes, courts, and bypaths, that though there was the roar of a multitude in the broad streets, those which we traversed were silent and deserted ; and the strollers whom we met, tired of gazing upon gayer figures, scarcely honoured us with a passing look, although, at any other time, we should, among these vulgar suburbs, have attracted a troublesome share of observation. We crossed at length a broad street, where many soldiers were on guard, while others, exhausted with previous duty, were eating, drinking, smoking, and sleeping beside their piled arms.

"'One day, Nixon,' whispered my uncle, 'we will make these redcoated gentry stand to their muskets more watchfully.'

"'Or it will be the worse for them,' answered his attendant, in a voice as unpleasant as his physiognomy.

"Unquestioned and unchallenged by any one, we crossed among the guards, and Nixon tapped thrice at a small postern door in a huge ancient building, which was straight before us. It opened, and we entered without my perceiving by whom we were admitted. A few dark and narrow passages at length conveyed us into an immense Gothic hall, the magnificence of which baffles my powers of description.

"It was illuminated by ten thousand wax lights, whose splendour at first dazzled my eyes, coming as we did from these dark and secret avenues. But when my sight began to become steady, how shall I describe what I beheld? Beneath were huge ranges of tables, occupied by princes and nobles in their robes of state—high officers of the crown, wearing their dresses and badges of authority — reverend prelates and judges, the sages of the church and law, in their more sombre, yet not less awful robes — with others whose antique and striking costume announced their importance, though I could not even guess who they might be. But at length the truth burst on me at once — it was, and the murmurs around confirmed it, the Coronation Feast. At a table above the rest, and extending across the upper end of the hall, sat enthroned the youthful Sovereign himself, surrounded by the princes of the blood, and other dignitaries, and receiving the suit and homage of his subjects. Heralds and pursuivants, blazing in their fantastic yet splendid armorial habits, and pages of honour, gorgeously arrayed in the garb of other days, waited upon the princely banqueters. In the galleries with which this spacious hall was surrounded, shone all, and more than all, that my poor imagination could conceive, of what was brilliant in riches, or captivating in beauty. Countless rows of ladies, whose diamonds, jewels, and splendid attire, were their least powerful charms, looked down from their lofty seats on the rich scene beneath, themselves forming a show as dazzling and as beautiful as that of which they were spectators. Under these galleries, and behind the banqueting tables, were a multitude of gentlemen, dressed as if to attend a court, but whose garb, although rich enough to have adorned a royal drawingroom, could not distinguish them in such a high scene as this. Amongst these we wandered for a few minutes, undistinguished and unregarded. I saw several young persons dressed as I was, so was under no embarrassment from the singularity of my habit, and only rejoiced, as I hung on my uncle's arm, at the magical splendour of such a scene, and at his goodness for procuring me the pleasure of beholding it.

"By and by, I perceived that my uncle had acquaintances among those who were under the galleries, and seemed, like ourselves, to be mere spectators of the solemnity. They recognized each other with a single word, sometimes only with a gripe of the hand — exchanged some private signs, doubtless — and gradually formed a little group, in the centre of which we were placed.

" 'Is it not a grand sight, Lilias?' said my uncle. 'All the noble, and all the wise, and all the wealthy of Britain, are there assembled.'

" 'It is indeed,' said I, 'all that my mind could have fancied of regal power and splendour.'

" 'Girl,' he whispered,—and my uncle can make his whispers as terribly emphatic as his thundering voice or his blighting look — 'all that is noble and worthy in this fair land are there assembled — but it is to bend like slaves and sycophants before the throne of a new usurper.'

" I looked at him, and the dark hereditary frown of our unhappy ancestor was black upon his brow.

" 'For God's sake,' I whispered, 'consider where we are.'

" 'Fear nothing,' he said ; 'we are surrounded by friends.' — As he proceeded, his strong and muscular frame shook with suppressed agitation. 'See,' he said, 'yonder bends Norfolk, renegade to his Catholic faith ; there stoops the Bishop of ——, traitor to the Church of England ; and,—shame of shames! yonder the gigantic form of Errol bows his head before the grandson of his father's murderer ! But a sign shall be seen this night amongst them — *Mene, Mene, Tekel, Upharsin*, shall be read on these walls, as distinctly as the spectral hand-writing made them visible on those of Belshazzar!'

" 'For God's sake,' said I, dreadfully alarmed, 'it is impossible you can meditate violence in such a presence !'

" 'None is intended, fool,' he answered, 'nor can the slightest mischance happen, provided you will rally your boasted courage, and obey my directions. But do it coolly and quickly, for there are an hundred lives at stake.'

" 'Alas! what can I do?' I asked in the utmost terror.

" 'Only be prompt to execute my bidding,' said he ; 'it is but to lift a glove—Here, hold this in your hand—throw the train of your dress over it, be firm, composed, and ready—or, at all events, I step forward myself.'

" 'If there is no violence designed,' I said, taking, mechanically, the iron glove he put into my hand.

" I could not conceive his meaning ; but, in the excited state of mind in which I beheld him, I was convinced that disobedience on my part would lead to some wild explosion. I felt, from the emergency of the occasion, a sudden presence of mind, and resolved to do any thing that might avert violence and bloodshed. I was not long held in suspense. A loud flourish of trumpets, and the voice of heralds, were mixed with the clatter of horses' hoofs, while a champion, armed at all points, like those I had read of in romances, attended by squires, pages, and the whole retinue of chivalry, pranced forward, mounted upon a barbed steed. His challenge, in defiance of all who dared impeach the title of the new sovereign, was recited aloud— once, and again.

" 'Rush in at the third sounding,' said my uncle to me ; 'bring me the parader's gage, and leave mine in lieu of it.'

" I could not see how this was to be done, as we were surrounded by people on all sides. But, at the third sounding of the trumpets, a lane opened as if by word of command, betwixt me and the champion, and my uncle's voice said, 'Now, Lilias, NOW !'

" With a swift and yet steady step, and with a presence of mind for which I have never since been able to account, I discharged the perilous commission. I was hardly seen, I believe, as I exchanged the pledges of battle, and in an instant retired. 'Nobly done, my girl !' said my uncle, at whose side I found myself, shrouded as I was before, by the interposition of the bystanders. 'Cover our retreat, gentlemen,' he whispered to those around him.

" Room was made for us to approach the wall, which seemed to open, and we were again involved in the dark passages through which we had formerly passed. In a small anteroom, my uncle stopped, and hastily muffling me in a mantle which was lying there, we passed the guards—threaded the labyrinth of empty streets and courts, and reached our retired lodgings without attracting the least attention."

"I have often heard," said Darsie, "that a female, supposed to be a man in disguise,—and yet, Lilias, you do not look very masculine,—had taken up the champion's gauntlet at the present King's Coronation, and left in its place a gage of battle, with a paper, offering to accept the combat, provided a fair field should be allowed for it. I have hitherto considered it as an idle tale. I little thought how nearly I was interested in the actors of a scene so daring—How could you have courage to go through with it?"*

"Had I the leisure for reflection," answered his sister, "I should have refused, from a mixture of principle and of fear. But, like many people who do daring actions, I went on because I had no time to think of retreating. The matter was little known, and it is said the King had commanded that it should not be farther inquired into;—from prudence, as I suppose, and lenity, though my uncle chooses to ascribe the forbearance of the Elector of Hanover, as he calls him, sometimes to pusillanimity, and sometimes to a presumptuous scorn of the faction who opposes his title."

"And have your subsequent agencies under this frantic enthusiast," said Darsie, "equalled this in danger?"

"No—nor in importance," replied Lilias; "though I have witnessed much of the strange and desperate machinations, by which, in spite of every obstacle, and in contempt of every danger, he endeavours to awaken the courage of a broken party. I have traversed, in his company, all England and Scotland, and have visited the most extraordinary and contrasted scenes; now lodging at the castles of the proud gentry of Cheshire and Wales, where the retired aristocrats, with opinions as antiquated as their dwellings and their manners, still continue to nourish jacobitical principles; and the next week, perhaps, spent among outlawed smugglers, or Highland banditti. I have known my uncle often act the part of a hero, and sometimes that of a mere vulgar conspirator, and turn himself, with the most surprising flexibility, into all sorts of shapes to attract proselytes to his cause."

"Which, in the present day," said Darsie, "he finds, I presume, no easy task."

"So difficult," said Lilias, "that, I believe, he has, at different times, disgusted with the total falling away of some friends, and the coldness of others, been almost on the point of resigning his undertaking. How often have I known him affect an open brow and a jovial manner, joining in the games of the gentry, and even in the sports of the common people, in order to invest himself with a temporary degree of popularity; while, in fact, his heart was bursting to witness what he called the degeneracy of the times, the decay of activity among the aged, and the want of zeal in the rising generation. After the day has been spent in the hardest exercise, he has

---

* In excuse of what may be considered as a violent infraction of probability in the foregoing chapter, the author is under the necessity of quoting a tradition which many persons may recollect having heard. It was always said, though with very little appearance of truth, that upon the Coronation of the late George III. when the Champion of England, Dymock, or his representative, appeared in Westminster Hall, and in the language of chivalry, solemnly wagered his body to defend in single combat the right of the young King to the crown of these realms, at the moment when he flung down his gauntlet as the gage of battle, an unknown female stepped from the crowd and lifted the pledge, leaving another gage in room of it, with a paper expressing, that if a fair field of combat should be allowed, a champion of rank and birth would appear with equal arms to dispute the claim of King George to the British kingdoms. The story is probably one of the numerous fictions which were circulated to keep up the spirits of a sinking faction. The incident was, however, possible, if it could be supposed to be attended by any motive adequate to the risk, and might be imagined to occur to a person of Redgauntlet's enthusiastic character. George III. it is said, had a police of his own, whose agency was so efficient, that the Sovereign was able to tell his prime minister upon one occasion, to his great surprise, that the Pretender was in London. The prime minister began immediately to talk of measures to be taken, warrants to be procured, messengers and guards to be put in readiness. "Pooh, pooh," said the good-natured Sovereign, "since I have found him out, leave me alone to deal with him."—"And what," said the minister, "is your Majesty's purpose, in so important a case?"—"To leave the young man to himself," said George III.; "and when he tires he will go back again." The truth of this story does not depend on that of the lifting of the gauntlet; and while the latter could be but an idle bravade the former expresses George III.'s goodness of heart and soundness of policy.

spent the night in pacing his solitary chamber, bewailing the downfall of the cause, and wishing for the bullet of Dundee, or the axe of Balmerino."

"A strange delusion," said Darsie; "and it is wonderful that it does not yield to the force of reality."

"Ah, but," replied Lilias, "realities of late have seemed to flutter his hopes. The general dissatisfaction with the peace — the unpopularity of the minister, which has extended itself even to the person of his master — the various uproars which have disturbed the peace of the metropolis, and a general state of disgust and disaffection, which seems to affect the body of the nation, have given unwonted encouragement to the expiring hopes of the Jacobites, and induced many, both at the Court of Rome, and, if it can be called so, of the Pretender, to lend a more favourable ear than they had hitherto done to the insinuations of those, who, like my uncle, hope, when hope is lost to all but themselves. Nay, I really believe that at this moment they meditate some desperate effort. My uncle has been doing all in his power, of late, to conciliate the affections of those wild communities that dwell on the Solway, over whom our family possessed a seignorial interest before the forfeiture, and amongst whom, on the occasion of 1745, our unhappy father's interest, with his own, raised a considerable body of men. But they are no longer willing to obey his summons; and, as one apology among others, they allege your absence as their natural head and leader. This has increased his desire to obtain possession of your person, and, if he possibly can, to influence your mind, so as to obtain your authority to his proceedings."

"That he shall never obtain," answered Darsie; "my principles and my prudence alike forbid such a step. Besides, it would be totally unavailing to his purpose. Whatever these people may pretend, to evade your uncle's importunities, they cannot, at this time of day, think of subjecting their necks again to the feudal yoke, which was effectually broken by the act of 1748, abolishing vassalage and hereditary jurisdictions."

"Ay, but that my uncle considers as the act of an usurping government," said Lilias.

"Like enough he may think so," answered her brother, "for he is a superior, and loses his authority by the enactment. But the question is, what the vassals will think of it, who have gained their freedom from feudal slavery, and have now enjoyed that freedom for many years? However, to cut the matter short, if five hundred men would rise at the wagging of my finger, that finger shall not be raised in a cause which I disapprove of, and upon that my uncle may reckon."

"But you may temporize," said Lilias, upon whom the idea of her uncle's displeasure made evidently a strong impression, — "you may temporize, as most of the gentry in this country do, and let the bubble burst of itself; for it is singular how few of them venture to oppose my uncle directly. I entreat you to avoid direct collision with him. To hear you, the head of the House of Redgauntlet, declare against the family of Stewart, would either break his heart, or drive him to some act of desperation."

"Yes, but, Lilias, you forget that the consequences of such an act of complaisance might be, that the House of Redgauntlet and I might lose both our heads at one blow."

"Alas!" said she, "I had forgotten that danger. I have grown familiar with perilous intrigues, as the nurses in a pest-house are said to become accustomed to the air around them, till they forget even that it is noisome."

"And yet," said Darsie, "if I could free myself from him without coming to an open rupture — Tell me, Lilias, do you think it possible that he can have any immediate attempt in view?"

"To confess the truth," answered Lilias, "I cannot doubt that he has. There has been an unusual bustle among the Jacobites of late. They have hopes, as I told you, from circumstances unconnected with their own strength. Just before you came to the country, my uncle's desire to find you out, became, if possible, more eager than ever—he talked of men to be presently brought together, and of your name and influence for raising them. At this very time, your first visit to Brokenburn took place. A suspicion arose in my uncle's mind, that you might be the youth he sought, and it was strengthened by papers and letters which the rascal Nixon did not hesitate to take from your pocket. Yet a mistake might have occasioned a fatal explosion; and my uncle therefore posted to Edinburgh to follow out the clew he had obtained, and fished enough of information from old Mr. Fairford to make him certain that you were the person he sought. Meanwhile, and at the expense of some personal and perhaps too bold exertion, I endeavoured, through your friend young Fairford, to put you on your guard."

" Without success," said Darsie, blushing under his mask, when he recollected how he had mistaken his sister's meaning.

" I do not wonder that my warning was fruitless," said she; " the thing was doomed to be. Besides, your escape would have been difficult. You were dogged the whole time you were at the Shepherd's Bush and at Mount Sharon, by a spy who scarcely ever left you."

" The wretch, little Benjie!" exclaimed Darsie. " I will wring the monkey's neck round, the first time we meet."

" It was he indeed who gave constant information of your motions to Cristal Nixon," said Lilias.

" And Cristal Nixon—I owe him, too, a day's work in harvest," said Darsie; " for I am mistaken if he was not the person that struck me down when I was made prisoner among the rioters."

" Like enough; for he has a head and hand for any villany. My uncle was very angry about it; for though the riot was made to have an opportunity of carrying you off in the confusion, as well as to put the fishermen at variance with the public law, it would have been his last thought to have injured a hair of your head. But Nixon has insinuated himself into all my uncle's secrets, and some of these are so dark and dangerous, that though there are few things he would *not* dare, I doubt if he dare quarrel with him. — And yet I know that of Cristal, would move my uncle to pass his sword through his body."

" What is it, for Heaven's sake?" said Darsie. " I have a particular desire for wishing to know."

" The old, brutal desperado, whose face and mind are a libel upon human nature, has had the insolence to speak to his master's niece as one whom he was at liberty to admire; and when I turned on him with the anger and contempt he merited, the wretch grumbled out something, as if he held the destiny of our family in his hand."

" I thank you, Lilias," said Darsie, eagerly, — " I thank you with all my heart for this communication. I have blamed myself as a Christian man for the indescribable longing I felt from the first moment I saw that rascal, to send a bullet through his head; and now you have perfectly accounted for and justified this very laudable wish. I wonder my uncle, with the powerful sense you describe him to be possessed of, does not see through such a villain."

" I believe he knows him to be capable of much evil," answered Lilias— " selfish, obdurate, brutal, and a man-hater. But then he conceives him to possess the qualities most requisite for a conspirator — undaunted courage, imperturbable coolness and address, and inviolable fidelity. In the last particular he may be mistaken. I have heard Nixon blamed for the manner in which our poor father was taken after Culloden."

" Another reason for my innate aversion," said Darsie; " but I will be on my guard with him."

" See, he observes us closely," said Lilias. " What a thing is conscience!

— He knows we are now speaking of him, though he cannot have heard a word that we have said."

It seemed as if she had guessed truly; for Cristal Nixon at that moment rode up to them, and said, with an affectation of jocularity, which sat very ill on his sullen features, "Come, young ladies, you have had time enough for your chat this morning, and your tongues, I think, must be tired. We are going to pass a village, and I must beg you to separate — you, Miss Lilias, to ride a little behind—and you, Mrs., or Miss, or Master, whichever you choose to be called, to be jogging a little before."

Lilias checked her horse without speaking, but not until she had given her brother an expressive look, recommending caution; to which he replied by a signal, indicating that he understood and would comply with her request.

Chapter the Nineteenth.

NARRATIVE OF DARSIE LATIMER, CONTINUED.

LEFT to his solitary meditations, Darsie (for we will still term Sir Arthur Darsie Redgauntlet of that Ilk, by the name to which the reader is habituated) was surprised not only at the alteration of his own state and condition, but at the equanimity with which he felt himself disposed to view all these vicissitudes.

His fever-fit of love had departed like a morning's dream, and left nothing behind but a painful sense of shame, and a resolution to be more cautious ere he again indulged in such romantic visions. His station in society was changed from that of a wandering, unowned youth, in whom none appeared to take an interest, excepting the strangers by whom he had been educated, to the heir of a noble house, possessed of such influence and such property, that it seemed as if the progress or arrest of important political events were likely to depend upon his resolution. Even this sudden elevation, the more than fulfilment of those wishes which had haunted him ever since he was able to form a wish on the subject, was contemplated by Darsie, volatile as his disposition was, without more than a few thrills of gratified vanity.

It is true, there were circumstances in his present situation to counterbalance such high advantages. To be a prisoner in the hands of a man so determined as his uncle, was no agreeable consideration, when he was calculating how he might best dispute his pleasure, and refuse to join him in the perilous enterprise which he seemed to meditate. Outlawed and desperate himself, Darsie could not doubt that his uncle was surrounded by men capable of any thing — that he was restrained by no personal considerations — and therefore what degree of compulsion he might apply to his brother's son, or in what manner he might feel at liberty to punish his contumacy, should he disavow the Jacobite cause, must depend entirely upon the limits of his own conscience; and who was to answer for the conscience of a heated enthusiast, who considers opposition to the party he has espoused, as treason to the welfare of his country? After a short interval, Cristal Nixon was pleased to throw some light upon the subject which agitated him.

When that grim satellite rode up without ceremony close to Darsie's side, the latter felt his very flesh creep with abhorrence, so little was he able to endure his presence, since the story of Lilias had added to his instinctive hatred of the man.

His voice, too, sounded like that of a screech-owl, as he said, "So, my young cook of the north, you now know it all, and no doubt are blessing your uncle for stirring you up to such an honourable action."

"I will acquaint my uncle with my sentiments on the subject, before I make them known to any one else," said Darsie, scarcely prevailing on his tongue to utter even these few words in a civil manner.

"Umph," murmured Cristal betwixt his teeth. "Close as wax, I see; and perhaps not quite so pliable.—But take care, my pretty youth," he added, scornfully; "Hugh Redgauntlet will prove a rough colt-breaker—he will neither spare whipcord nor spur-rowel, I promise you."

"I have already said, Mr. Nixon," answered Darsie, "that I will canvass those matters of which my sister has informed me, with my uncle himself, and with no other person."

"Nay, but a word of friendly advice would do you no harm, young master," replied Nixon. "Old Redgauntlet is apter at a blow than a word—likely to bite before he barks—the true man for giving Scarborough warning, first knock you down, then bid you stand.—So, methinks, a little kind warning as to consequences were not amiss, lest they come upon you unawares."

"If the warning is really kind, Mr. Nixon," said the young man, "I will hear it thankfully; and indeed, if otherwise, I must listen to it whether I will or no, since I have at present no choice of company or conversation."

"Nay, I have but little to say," said Nixon, affecting to give to his sullen and dogged manner the appearance of an honest bluntness; "I am as little apt to throw away words as any one. But here is the question—Will you join heart and hand with your uncle, or no?"

"What if I should say Ay?" said Darsie, determined, if possible, to conceal his resolution from this man.

"Why, then," said Nixon, somewhat surprised at the readiness of his answer, "all will go smooth, of course—you will take share in this noble undertaking, and, when it succeeds, you will exchange your open helmet for an Earl's coronet perhaps."

"And how if it fails?" said Darsie.

"Thereafter as it may be," said Nixon; "they who play at bowls must meet with rubbers."

"Well, but suppose, then, I have some foolish tenderness for my windpipe, and that, when my uncle proposes the adventure to me, I should say No—how then, Mr. Nixon?"

"Why, then, I would have you look to yourself, young master—There are sharp laws in France against refractory pupils—*lettres de cachet* are easily come by, when such men as we are concerned with interest themselves in the matter."

"But we are not in France," said poor Darsie, through whose blood ran a cold shivering at the idea of a French prison.

"A fast-sailing lugger will soon bring you there though, snug stowed under hatches, like a cask of moonlight."

"But the French are at peace with us," said Darsie, "and would not dare ——"

"Why, who would ever hear of you?" interrupted Nixon; "do you imagine that a foreign Court would call you up for judgment, and put the sentence of imprisonment in the *Courrier de l'Europe*, as they do at the Old Bailey? —No, no, young gentleman—the gates of the Bastile, and of Mont Saint Michel, and the Castle of Vincennes, move on d—d easy hinges when they let folk in—not the least jar is heard. There are cool cells there for hot heads—as calm, and quiet, and dark, as you could wish in Bedlam—and the dismissal comes when the carpenter brings the prisoner's coffin, and not sooner."

"Well, Mr. Nixon," said Darsie, affecting a cheerfulness which he was far from feeling, "mine is a hard case—a sort of hanging choice, you will allow — since I must either offend our own government here, and run the risk of my life for doing so, or be doomed to the dungeons of another country, whose laws I have never offended, since I have never trod its soil — Tell me what you would do if you were in my place."

" I'll tell you that when I *am* there," said Nixon, and, checking his horse, fell back to the rear of the little party.

" It is evident," thought the young man, " that the villain believes me completely noosed, and perhaps has the ineffable impudence to suppose that my sister must eventually succeed to the possessions which have occasioned my loss of freedom, and that his own influence over the destinies of our unhappy family may secure him possession of the heiress; but he shall perish by my hand first! — I must now be on the alert to make my escape, if possible, before I am forced on shipboard — Blind Willie will not, I think, desert me without an effort on my behalf, especially if he has learned that I am the son of his late unhappy patron. — What a change is mine! Whilst I possessed neither rank nor fortune, I lived safely and unknown, under the protection of the kind and respectable friends whose hearts Heaven had moved towards me — Now that I am the head of an honourable house, and that enterprises of the most daring character await my decision, and retainers and vassals seem ready to rise at my beck, my safety consists chiefly in the attachment of a blind stroller!"

While he was revolving these things in his mind, and preparing himself for the interview with his uncle, which could not but be a stormy one, he saw Hugh Redgauntlet come riding slowly back to meet them without any attendants. Cristal Nixon rode up as he approached, and, as they met, fixed on him a look of inquiry.

" The fool, Crackenthorp," said Redgauntlet, " has let strangers into his house. Some of his smuggling comrades, I believe; we must ride slowly to give him time to send them packing."

" Did you see any of your friends?" said Cristal.

" Three, and have letters from many more. They are unanimous on the subject you wot of — and the point must be conceded to them, or, far as the matter has gone, it will go no farther."

" You will hardly bring the Father to stoop to his flock," said Cristal, with a sneer.

" He must and shall!" answered Redgauntlet, briefly. " Go to the front, Cristal — I would speak with my nephew. — I trust, Sir Arthur Redgauntlet, you are satisfied with the manner in which I have discharged my duty to your sister?"

" There can be no fault found to her manners or sentiments," answered Darsie; " I am happy in knowing a relative so amiable."

" I am glad of it," answered Mr. Redgauntlet. " I am no nice judge of women's qualifications, and my life has been dedicated to one great object; so that since she left France she has had but little opportunity of improvement. I have subjected her, however, as little as possible to the inconveniences and privations of my wandering and dangerous life. From time to time she has resided for weeks and months with families of honour and respectability, and I am glad that she has, in your opinion, the manners and behaviour which become her birth."

Darsie expressed himself perfectly satisfied, and there was a little pause, which Redgauntlet broke by solemnly addressing his nephew.

" For you, my nephew, I also hoped to have done much. The weakness and timidity of your mother sequestered you from my care, or it would have been my pride and happiness to have trained up the son of my unhappy brother in those paths of honour in which our ancestors have always trod."

" Now comes the storm," thought Darsie to himself, and began to collect his thoughts, as the cautious master of a vessel furls his sails, and makes his ship snug, when he discerns the approaching squall.

"My mother's conduct in respect to me, might be misjudged," he said, "but it was founded on the most anxious affection."

"Assuredly," said his uncle, "and I have no wish to reflect on her memory, though her mistrust has done so much injury, I will not say to me, but to the cause of my unhappy country. Her scheme was, I think, to have made you that wretched pettifogging being, which they still continue to call in derision by the once respectable name of a Scottish Advocate; one of those mongrel things, that must creep to learn the ultimate decision of his causes to the bar of a foreign Court, instead of pleading before the independent and august Parliament of his own native kingdom."

"I did prosecute the study of law for a year or two," said Darsie, "but I found I had neither taste nor talents for the science."

"And left it with scorn, doubtless?" said Mr. Redgauntlet. "Well, I now bold up to you, my dearest nephew, a more worthy object of ambition. Look eastward — do you see a monument standing on yonder plain, near a hamlet?"

Darsie replied that he did.

"The hamlet is called Burgh-upon-sands, and yonder monument is erected to the memory of the tyrant Edward I. The just hand of Providence overtook him on that spot, as he was leading his bands to complete the subjugation of Scotland, whose civil dissensions began under his accursed policy. The glorious career of Bruce might have been stopped in its outset; the field of Bannockburn might have remained a bloodless turf, if God had not removed, in the very crisis, the crafty and bold tyrant who had so long been Scotland's scourge. Edward's grave is the cradle of our national freedom. It is within sight of that great landmark of our liberty that I have to propose to you an undertaking, second in honour and importance to none since the immortal Bruce stabbed the Red Comyn, and grasped with his yet bloody hand, the independent crown of Scotland."

He paused for an answer; but Darsie, overawed by the energy of his manner, and unwilling to commit himself by a hasty explanation, remained silent.

"I will not suppose," said Hugh Redgauntlet, after a pause, "that you are either so dull as not to comprehend the import of my words—or so dastardly as to be dismayed by my proposal—or so utterly degenerate from the blood and sentiments of your ancestors, as not to feel my summons as the horse hears the war-trumpet."

"I will not pretend to misunderstand you, sir," said Darsie; "but an enterprise directed against a dynasty now established for three reigns requires strong arguments, both in point of justice and of expediency, to recommend it to men of conscience and prudence."

"I will not," said Redgauntlet, while his eyes sparkled with anger, — "I will not hear you speak a word against the justice of that enterprise, for which your oppressed country calls with the voice of a parent, entreating her children for aid—or against that noble revenge which your father's blood demands from his dishonoured grave. His skull is yet standing over the Rikargate,* and even its bleak and mouldered jaws command you to be a man. I ask you, in the name of God, and of your country, will you draw your sword and go with me to Carlisle, were it but to lay your father's head, now the perch of the obscene owl and carrion crow, and the scoff of every ribald clown, in consecrated earth, as befits his long ancestry?"

Darsie, unprepared to answer an appeal urged with so much passion, and not doubting a direct refusal would cost him his liberty or life, was again silent.

"I see," said his uncle, in a more composed tone, "that it is not deficiency of spirit, but the grovelling habits of a confined education, among the poor-

* The northern gate of Carlisle was long garnished with the heads of the Scottish rebels executed in 1746.

spirited class you were condemned to herd with, that keeps you silent. You scarce yet believe yourself a Redgauntlet; your pulse has not yet learned the genuine throb that answers to the summons of honour and of patriotism.

"I trust," replied Darsie, at last, "that I shall never be found indifferent to the call of either; but to answer them with effect—even were I convinced that they now sounded in my ear—I must see some reasonable hope of success in the desperate enterprise in which you would involve me. I look around me, and I see a settled government— an established authority — a born Briton on the throne —the very Highland mountaineers, upon whom alone the trust of the exiled family reposed, assembled into regiments, which act under the orders of the existing dynasty.* France has been utterly dismayed by the tremendous lessons of the last war, and will hardly provoke another. All without and within the kingdom is adverse to encountering a hopeless struggle, and you alone, sir, seem willing to undertake a desperate enterprise.

"And would undertake it were it ten times more desperate; and have agitated it when ten times the obstacles were interposed. Have I forgot my brother's blood?— Can I — dare I even now repeat the Pater Noster, since my enemies and the murderers remain unforgiven?—Is there an art I have not practised — a privation to which I have not submitted, to bring on the crisis, which I now behold arrived?— Have I not been a vowed and a devoted man, foregoing every comfort of social life, renouncing even the exercise of devotion, unless when I might name in prayer my prince and country, submitting to every thing to make converts to this noble cause?— Have I done all this, and shall I now stop short?"— Darsie was about to interrupt him, but he pressed his hand affectionately upon his shoulder, and enjoining, or rather imploring silence,—"Peace," he said, "heir of my ancestors' fame—heir of all my hopes and wishes—Peace, son of my slaughtered brother! I have sought for thee, and mourned for thee, as a mother for an only child. Do not let me again lose you in the moment when you are restored to my hopes. Believe me, I distrust so much my own impatient temper, that I entreat you, as the dearest boon, do nought to awaken it at this crisis."

Darsie was not sorry to reply, that his respect for the person of his relation would induce him to listen to all which he had to apprise him of, before he formed any definite resolution upon the weighty subjects of deliberation which he proposed to him.

"Deliberation!" repeated Redgauntlet, impatiently; "and yet it is not ill said. I wish there had been more warmth in thy reply, Arthur; but I must recollect, were an eagle bred in a falcon's mew, and hooded like a reclaimed hawk, he could not at first gaze steadily on the sun. Listen to me, my dearest Arthur. The state of this nation no more implies prosperity, than the florid colour of a feverish patient is a symptom of health. All is false and hollow. The apparent success of Chatham's administration has plunged the country deeper in debt than all the barren acres of Canada are worth, were they as fertile as Yorkshire—the dazzling lustre of the victories of Minden and Quebec have been dimmed by the disgrace of the hasty peace — by the war, England, at immense expense, gained nothing but honour, and that she has gratuitously resigned. Many eyes, formerly cold and indifferent, are now looking towards the line of our ancient and rightful monarchs, as the only refuge in the approaching storm—the rich are alarmed — the nobles are disgusted — the populace are inflamed — and a band of patriots, whose measures are more safe than their numbers are few, have resolved to set up King Charles's standard."

"But the military," said Darsie—"how can you, with a body of unarmed

---

* The Highland regiments were first employed by the celebrated Earl of Chatham, who assumed to himself no small degree of praise for having called forth to the support of the country and the government, the valour which had been too often directed against both.

and disorderly insurgents, propose to encounter a regular army? The Highlanders are now totally disarmed."

"In a great measure, perhaps," answered Redgauntlet; "but the policy which raised the Highland regiments has provided for that. We have already friends in these corps; nor can we doubt for a moment what their conduct will be, when the white cockade is once more mounted. The rest of the standing army has been greatly reduced since the peace; and we reckon confidently on our standard being joined by thousands of the disbanded troops."

"Alas!" said Darsie, "and is it upon such vague hopes as these, the inconstant humour of a crowd, or of a disbanded soldiery, that men of honour are invited to risk their families, their property, their life?"

"Men of honour, boy," said Redgauntlet, his eyes glancing with impatience, "set life, property, family, and all at stake, when that honour commands it! We are not now weaker than when seven men, landing in the wilds of Moidart, shook the throne of the usurper till it tottered — won two pitched fields, besides overrunning one kingdom and the half of another, and, but for treachery, would have achieved what their venturous successors are now to attempt in their turn."

"And will such an attempt be made in serious earnest?" said Darsie. "Excuse me, my uncle, if I can scarce believe a fact so extraordinary. Will there really be found men of rank and consequence sufficient to renew the adventure of 1745?"

"I will not give you my confidence by halves, Sir Arthur," replied his uncle—"Look at that scroll—what say you to these names?—Are they not the flower of the western shires — of Wales — of Scotland?"

"The paper contains indeed the names of many that are great and noble," replied Darsie, after perusing it; "but——"

"But what?" asked his uncle, impatiently; "do you doubt the ability of those nobles and gentlemen to furnish the aid in men and money, at which they are rated?"

"Not their ability, certainly," said Darsie, "for of that I am no competent judge; but I see in this scroll the name of Sir Arthur Darsie Redgauntlet of that Ilk, rated at an hundred men and upwards—I certainly am ignorant how he is to redeem that pledge."

"I will be responsible for the men," replied Hugh Redgauntlet.

"But, my dear uncle," added Darsie, "I hope for your sake, that the other individuals, whose names are here written, have had more acquaintance with your plan than I have been indulged with."

"For thee and thine I can be myself responsible," said Redgauntlet; "for if thou hast not the courage to head the force of thy house, the leading shall pass to other hands, and thy inheritance shall depart from thee, like vigour and verdure from a rotten branch. For these honourable persons, a slight condition there is which they annex to their friendship — something so trifling that it is scarce worthy of mention. This boon granted to them by him who is most interested, there is no question they will take the field in the manner there stated."

Again Darsie perused the paper, and felt himself still less inclined to believe that so many men of family and fortune were likely to embark in an enterprise so fatal. It seemed as if some rash plotter had put down at a venture the names of all whom common report tainted with Jacobitism; or if it was really the act of the individuals named, he suspected that they must be aware of some mode of excusing themselves from compliance with its purport. It was impossible, he thought, that Englishmen, of large fortune, who had failed to join Charles when he broke into England at the head of a victorious army, should have the least thoughts of encouraging a descent when circumstances were so much less propitious. He therefore concluded the enterprise would fall to pieces of itself, and that his best way was, in the meantime, to remain silent, unless the actual approach of a crisis (which might, however, never arrive) should compel him to give a downright refusal to his uncle's proposition; and if, in the interim, some door for escape should be opened, he resolved within himself not to omit availing himself of it.

Hugh Redgauntlet watched his nephew's looks for some time, and then, as if arriving from some other process of reasoning at the same conclusion, he said, "I have told you, Sir Arthur, that I do not urge your immediate accession to my proposal: indeed the consequences of a refusal would be so dreadful to yourself, so destructive to all the hopes which I have nursed, that I would not risk, by a moment's impatience, the object of my whole life. Yes, Arthur, I have been a self-denying hermit at one time — at another, the apparent associate of outlaws and desperadoes — at another, the subordinate agent of men whom I felt in every way my inferiors — not for any selfish purpose of my own, no, not even to win for myself the renown of being the principal instrument in restoring my King and freeing my country. My first wish on earth is for that restoration and that freedom — my next, that my nephew, the representative of my house, and of the brother of my love, may have the advantage and the credit of all my efforts in the good cause. But," he added, darting on Darsie one of his withering frowns, "if Scotland and my father's house cannot stand and flourish together, then perish the very name of Redgauntlet! perish the son of my brother, with every recollection of the glories of my family, of the affections of my youth, rather than my country's cause should be injured in the tithing of a barleycorn! The spirit of Sir Alberick is alive within me at this moment," he continued, drawing up his stately form and sitting erect in his saddle, while he pressed his finger against his forehead; "and if you yourself crossed my path in opposition, I swear, by the mark that darkens my brow, that a new deed should be done — a new doom should be deserved!"

He was silent, and his threats were uttered in a tone of voice so deeply resolute, that Darsie's heart sunk within him, when he reflected on the storm of passion which he must encounter, if he declined to join his uncle in a project to which prudence and principle made him equally adverse. He had scarce any hope left but in temporizing until he could make his escape, and resolved to avail himself for that purpose of the delay which his uncle seemed not unwilling to grant. The stern, gloomy look of his companion became relaxed by degrees, and presently afterwards he made a sign to Miss Redgauntlet to join the party, and began a forced conversation on ordinary topics; in the course of which Darsie observed that his sister seemed to speak under the most cautious restraint, weighing every word before she uttered it, and always permitting her uncle to give the tone to the conversation, though of the most trifling kind. This seemed to him (such an opinion had he already entertained of his sister's good sense and firmness) the strongest proof he had yet received of his uncle's peremptory character, since he saw it observed with so much deference by a young person, whose sex might have given her privileges, and who seemed by no means deficient either in spirit or firmness.

The little cavalcade was now approaching the house of Father Crackenthorp, situated, as the reader knows, by the side of the Solway, and not far distant from a rude pier, near which lay several fishing-boats, which frequently acted in a different capacity. The house of the worthy publican was also adapted to the various occupations which he carried on, being a large scrambling assemblage of cottages attached to a house of two stories, roofed with flags of sandstone — the original mansion, to which the extensions of Mr. Crackenthorp's trade had occasioned his making many additions. Instead of the single long watering-trough which usually distinguishes the front of the English public-house of the second class, there were three conveniences of that kind, for the use, as the landlord used to say, of the troop-horses, when the soldiers came to search his house; while a knowing leer and a nod let you understand what species of troops he was thinking of. A huge ash-tree before the door, which had reared itself to a great size and height, in spite of the blasts from the neighbouring Solway, overshadowed, as usual, the ale-bench, as our ancestors called it, where, though it was still early in the day, several fellows, who seemed to be gentlemen's servants, were drinking beer and smoking. One or two of them wore liveries, which seemed known to Mr. Redgauntlet, for he muttered between his teeth, "Fools, fools! were they on a march to hell, they must have their rascals in livery with them, that the whole world might know who were going to be damned."

As he thus muttered, he drew bridle before the door of the place, from which several other lounging guests began to issue, to look with indolent curiosity, as usual, upon an *arrival*.

Redgauntlet sprung from his horse, and assisted his niece to dismount; but, forgetting, perhaps, his nephew's disguise, he did not pay him the attention which his female dress demanded.

The situation of Darsie was indeed something awkward; for Cristal Nixon, out of caution perhaps to prevent escape, had muffled the extreme folds of the riding-skirt with which he was accoutred, around his ankles and under his feet, and there secured it with large corking-pins. We presume that gentlemen-cavaliers may sometimes cast their eyes to that part of the person of the fair equestrians whom they chance occasionally to escort; and if they will conceive their own feet, like Darsie's, muffled in such a labyrinth of folds and amplitude of robe, as modesty doubtless induces the fair creatures to assume upon such occasions, they will allow that, on a first attempt, they might find some awkwardness in dismounting. Darsie, at least, was in such a predicament, for, not receiving adroit assistance from the attendant of Mr. Redgauntlet, he stumbled as he dismounted from the horse, and might have had a bad fall, had it not been broken by the gallant interposition of a gentleman, who probably was, on his part, a little surprised at the solid weight of the distressed fair one whom he had the honour to receive in his embrace. But what was his surprise to that of Darsie's, when the hurry of the moment, and of the accident, permitted him to see that it was his friend Alan Fairford in whose arms he found himself! A thousand apprehensions rushed on him, mingled with the full career of hope and joy, inspired by the unexpected appearance of his beloved friend at the very crisis, it seemed, of his fate.

He was about to whisper in his ear, cautioning him at the same time to be silent; yet he hesitated for a second or two to effect his purpose, since, should Redgauntlet take the alarm from any sudden exclamation on the part of Alan, there was no saying what consequences might ensue.

Ere he could decide what was to be done, Redgauntlet, who had entered the house, returned hastily, followed by Cristal Nixon. "I'll release you of the charge of this young lady, sir;" he said, haughtily, to Alan Fairford, whom he probably did not recognize.

"I had no desire to intrude, sir," replied Alan; "the lady's situation seemed to require assistance—and—but have I not the honour to speak to Mr. Herries of Birrenswork?"

"You are mistaken, sir," said Redgauntlet, turning short off, and making a sign with his hand to Cristal, who hurried Darsie, however unwillingly, into the house, whispering in his ear, "Come, miss, let us have no making of acquaintance from the windows. Ladies of fashion must be private. Show us a room, Father Crackenthorp."

So saying, he conducted Darsie into the house, interposing at the same time his person betwixt the supposed young lady and the stranger of whom he was suspicious, so as to make communication by signs impossible. As they entered, they heard the sound of a fiddle in the stone-floored and well-sanded kitchen, through which they were about to follow their corpulent host, and where several people seemed engaged in dancing to its strains.

"D—n thee," said Nixon to Crackenthorp, "would you have the lady go through all the mob of the parish?—Hast thou no more private way to our sitting-room?"

"None that is fit for my travelling," answered the landlord, laying his hand on his portly stomach. "I am not Tom Turnpenny, to creep like a lizard through keyholes."

So saying, he kept moving on through the revellers in the kitchen; and Nixon, holding Darsie by his arm, as if to offer the lady support, but in all probability to frustrate any effort at escape, moved through the crowd, which presented a very motley appearance, consisting of domestic servants, country fellows, seamen, and other idlers, whom Wandering Willie was regaling with his music.

To pass another friend without intimation of his presence would have been actual pusillanimity; and just when they were passing the blind man's elevated seat, Darsie asked him with some emphasis, whether he could not play a Scottish air?—The man's face had been the instant before devoid of all sort of expression, going through his performance like a clown through a beautiful country, too much accustomed to consider it as a task, to take any interest in the performance, and, in fact, scarce seeming to hear the noise that he was creating. In a word, he might at the time have made a companion to my friend Wilkie's inimitable blind crowder. But with Wandering Willie this was only an occasional, and a rare fit of dullness, such as will at times creep over all the professors of the fine arts, arising either from fatigue, or contempt of the present audience, or that caprice which so often tempts painters and musicians, and great actors, in the phrase of the latter, to *walk through* their part, instead of exerting themselves with the energy which acquired their fame. But when the performer heard the voice of Darsie, his countenance became at once illuminated, and showed the complete mistake of those who suppose that the principal point of expression depends upon the eyes. With his face turned to the point from which the sound came, his upper lip a little curved, and quivering with agitation, and with a colour which surprise and pleasure had brought at once into his faded cheek, he exchanged the humdrum hornpipe which he had been sawing out with reluctant and lazy bow, for the fine Scottish air,

"You're welcome, Charlie Stewart,"

which flew from his strings as if by inspiration, and after a breathless pause of admiration among the audience, was received with a clamour of applause, which seemed to show that the name and tendency, as well as the execution of the tune, was in the highest degree acceptable to all the party assembled.

In the meantime, Cristal Nixon, still keeping hold of Darsie, and following the landlord, forced his way with some difficulty through the crowded kitchen, and entered a small apartment on the other side of it, where they found Lilias Redgauntlet already seated. Here Nixon gave way to his suppressed resentment, and turning sternly on Crackenthorp, threatened him with his master's severest displeasure, because things were in such bad order to receive his family, when he had given such special advice that he desired to be private. But Father Crackenthorp was not a man to be browbeaten.

"Why, brother Nixon, thou art angry this morning," he replied; "hast risen from thy wrong side, I think. You know, as well as I, that most of this mob is of the Squire's own making — gentlemen that come with their servants, and so forth, to meet him in the way of business, as old Tom Turnpenny says — the very last that came was sent down with Dick Gardener from Fairladies."

"But the blind scraping scoundrel yonder," said Nixon, "how dared you take such a rascal as that across your threshold at such a time as this?—If the Squire should dream you have a thought of peaching—I am only speaking for your good, Father Crackenthorp."

"Why, look ye, brother Nixon," said Crackenthorp, turning his quid with great composure, "the Squire is a very worthy gentleman, and I'll never deny it; but I am neither his servant nor his tenant, and so he need send me none of his orders till he hears I have put on his livery. As for turning away folk from my door, I might as well plug up the ale-tap, and pull down the sign—and as for peaching, and such like, the Squire will find the folk here are as honest to the full as those he brings with him."

"How, you impudent lump of tallow," said Nixon, "what do you mean by that?"

"Nothing," said Crackenthorp, "but that I can tour out as well as another—you understand me—keep good lights in my upper story—know a thing or two more than most folk in this country. If folk will come to my house on dangerous errands, egad they shall not find Joe Crackenthorp a cat's-paw. I'll keep myself clear, you may depend on it, and let every man answer for his own actions—that's my way—Any thing wanted, Master Nixon?"

"No—yes—begone!" said Nixon, who seemed embarrassed with the landlord's contumacy, yet desirous to conceal the effect it produced on him.

The door was no sooner closed on Crackenthorp, than Miss Redgauntlet, addressing Nixon, commanded him to leave the room, and go to his proper place.

"How, madam?" said the fellow sullenly, yet with an air of respect, "Would you have your uncle pistol me for disobeying his orders?"

"He may perhaps pistol you for some other reason, if you do not obey mine," said Lilias, composedly.

"You abuse your advantage over me, madam—I really dare not go—I am on guard over this other Miss here; and if I should desert my post, my life were not worth five minutes' purchase."

"Then know your post, sir," said Lilias, "and watch on the outside of the door. You have no commission to listen to our private conversation, I suppose? Begone, sir, without farther speech or remonstrance, or I will tell my uncle that which you would have reason to repent he should know."

The fellow looked at her with a singular expression of spite, mixed with deference. "You abuse your advantages, madam," he said, "and act as foolishly in doing so, as I did in affording you such a hank over me. But you are a tyrant; and tyrants have commonly short reigns."

So saying, he left the apartment.

"The wretch's unparalleled insolence," said Lilias to her brother, "has given me one great advantage over him. For knowing that my uncle would shoot him with as little remorse as a wood-cock, if he but guessed at his brazen-faced assurance towards me, he dares not since that time assume, so far as I am concerned, the air of insolent domination which the possession of my uncle's secrets, and the knowledge of his most secret plans, have led him to exert over others of his family."

"In the meantime," said Darsie, "I am happy to see that the landlord of the house does not seem so devoted to him as I apprehended; and this aids the hope of escape which I am nourishing for you and for myself. O Lilias! the truest of friends, Alan Fairford, is in pursuit of me, and is here at this moment. Another humble, but, I think, faithful friend, is also within these dangerous walls."

Lilias laid her finger on her lips, and pointed to the door. Darsie took the hint, lowered his voice, and informed her in whispers of the arrival of Fairford, and that he believed he had opened a communication with Wandering Willie. She listened with the utmost interest, and had just begun to reply, when a loud noise was heard in the kitchen, caused by several contending voices, amongst which Darsie thought he could distinguish that of Alan Fairford.

Forgetting how little his own condition permitted him to become the assistant of another, Darsie flew to the door of the room, and finding it locked and bolted on the outside, rushed against it with all his force, and made the most desperate efforts to burst it open, notwithstanding the entreaties of his sister that he would compose himself, and recollect the condition in which he was placed. But the door, framed to withstand attacks from excisemen, constables, and other personages, considered as worthy to use what are called the King's keys,* "and therewith to make lockfast places open and patent," set his efforts at defiance. Meantime the noise continued without, and we are to give an account of its origin in our next chapter.

Chapter the Twentieth.

NARRATIVE OF DARSIE LATIMER, CONTINUED.

Joe Crackenthorp's public-house had never, since it first reared its chimneys on the banks of the Solway, been frequented by such a miscellaneous group of visiters as had that morning become its guests. Several of them were persons whose quality seemed much superior to their dresses and modes of travelling. The servants who attended them contradicted the inferences to be drawn from the garb of their masters, and, according to the custom of the knights of the rainbow, gave many hints that they were not people to serve any but men of first-rate consequence. These gentlemen, who had come thither chiefly for the purpose of meeting with Mr. Redgauntlet, seemed moody and anxious, conversed and walked together, apparently in deep conversation, and avoided any communication with the chance travellers whom accident brought that morning to the same place of resort.

As if Fate had set herself to confound the plans of the Jacobite conspirators, the number of travellers was unusually great, their appearance respectable, and they filled the public tap-room of the inn, where the political guests had already occupied most of the private apartments.

Amongst others, honest Joshua Geddes had arrived, travelling, as he said, in the sorrow of the soul, and mourning for the fate of Darsie Latimer as he would for his first-born child. He had skirted the whole coast of the Solway, besides making various trips into the interior, not shunning, on such occasions, to expose himself to the laugh of the scorner, nay, even to serious personal risk, by frequenting the haunts of smugglers, horse-jockeys, and other irregular persons, who looked on his intrusion with jealous eyes, and were apt to consider him as an exciseman in the disguise of a Quaker. All this labour and peril, however, had been undergone in vain. No search he could make obtained the least intelligence of Latimer, so that he began to fear the poor lad had been spirited abroad ; for the practice of kidnapping was then not infrequent, especially on the western coasts of Britain, if indeed he had escaped a briefer and more bloody fate.

---

* In common parlance, a crowbar and hatchet.

With a heavy heart, he delivered his horse, even Solomon, into the hands of the hostler, and walking into the inn, demanded from the landlord breakfast and a private room. Quakers, and such hosts as old Father Crackenthorp, are no congenial spirits; the latter looked askew over his shoulder, and replied, "If you would have breakfast here, friend, you are like to eat it where other folk eat theirs."

"And wherefore can I not," said the Quaker, "have an apartment to myself, for my money?"

"Because, Master Jonathan, you must wait till your betters be served, or else eat with your equals."

Joshua Geddes argued the point no farther, but sitting quietly down on the seat which Quackenthorp indicated to him, and calling for a pint of ale, with some bread, butter, and Dutch cheese, began to satisfy the appetite which the morning air had rendered unusually alert.

While the honest Quaker was thus employed, another stranger entered the apartment, and sat down near to the table on which his victuals were placed. He looked repeatedly at Joshua, licked his parched and chopped lips as he saw the good Quaker masticate his bread and cheese, and sucked up his thin chops when Mr. Geddes applied the tankard to his mouth, as if the discharge of these bodily functions by another had awakened his sympathies in an uncontrollable degree. At last, being apparently unable to withstand his longings, he asked, in a faltering tone, the huge landlord, who was tramping through the room in all corpulent impatience, "whether he could have a plack-pie?"

"Never heard of such a thing, master," said the landlord, and was about to trudge onward; when the guest, detaining him, said, in a strong Scottish tone, "Ye will maybe have nae whey then, nor buttermilk, nor ye couldna exhibit a souter's clod?"

"Can't tell what ye are talking about, master," said Crackenthorp.

"Then ye will have nae breakfast that will come within the compass of a shilling Scots?"

"Which is a penny sterling," answered Crackenthorp, with a sneer. "Why, no, Sawney, I can't say as we have—we can't afford it; but you shall have a bellyful for love, as we say in the bull-ring."

"I shall never refuse a fair offer," said the poverty-stricken guest; "and I will say that for the English, if they were deils, that they are a ceeveleesed people to gentlemen that are under a cloud."

"Gentlemen!—humph!" said Crackenthorp—"not a blue-cap among them but halts upon that foot." Then seizing on a dish which still contained a huge cantle of what had been once a princely mutton pasty, he placed it on the table before the stranger, saying, "There, master gentleman; there is what is worth all the black pies, as you call them, that were ever made of sheep's head."

"Sheep's head is a gude thing, for a' that," replied the guest; but not being spoken so loud as to offend his hospitable entertainer, the interjection might pass for a private protest against the scandal thrown out against the standing dish of Caledonia.

This premised, he immediately began to transfer the mutton and pie-crust from his plate to his lips, in such huge gobbets, as if he was refreshing after a three days' fast, and laying in provisions against a whole Lent to come.

Joshua Geddes in his turn gazed on him with surprise, having never, he thought, beheld such a gaunt expression of hunger in the act of eating. "Friend," he said, after watching him for some minutes, "if thou gorgest thyself in this fashion, thou wilt assuredly choke. Wilt thou not take a draught out of my cup to help down all that dry meat?"

"Troth," said the stranger, stopping and looking at the friendly pro-

pounder, "that's nae bad overture, as they say in the General Assembly.
I have heard waur motions than that frae wiser counsel."

Mr. Geddes ordered a quart of home-brewed to be placed before our
friend Peter Peebles; for the reader must have already conceived that this
unfortunate litigant was the wanderer in question.

The victim of Themis had no sooner seen the flagon, than he seized it
with the same energy which he had displayed in operating upon the pie—
puffed off the froth with such emphasis, that some of it lighted on Mr.
Geddes's head—and then said, as if with a sudden recollection of what was
due to civility, "Here's to ye, friend.—What! are ye ower grand to give
me an answer, or are ye dull o' hearing?"

"I prithee drink thy liquor, friend," said the good Quaker; "thou meanest
it in civility, but we care not for these idle fashions."

"What! ye are a Quaker, are ye?" said Peter; and without further
ceremony reared the flagon to his head, from which he withdrew it not
while a single drop of "barley-broo" remained.—"That's done you and me
muckle gude," he said, sighing as he set down his pot; "but twa mutchkins
o' yill between twa folk is a drappie ower little measure. What say ye to
anither pot? or shall we cry in a blithe Scots pint at ance?—The yill is no
amiss?"

"Thou mayst call for what thou wilt on thine own charges, friend," said
Geddes; "for myself, I willingly contribute to the quenching of thy natural
thirst; but I fear it were no such easy matter to relieve thy acquired and
artificial drought."

"That is to say, in plain terms, ye are for withdrawing your caution
with the folk of the house? You Quaker folk are but fause comforters;
but since ye have garred me drink sae muckle cauld yill—me that am no
used to the like of it in the forenoon—I think ye might as weel have offered
me a glass of brandy or usquebae—I'm nae nice body—I can drink ony
thing that's wet and toothsome."

"Not a drop at my cost, friend," quoth Geddes. "Thou art an old man,
and hast perchance a heavy and long journey before thee. Thou art, moreover, my countryman, as I judge from thy tongue; and I will not give thee
the means of dishonouring thy gray hairs in a strange land."

"Gray hairs, neighbour!" said Peter, with a wink to the by-standers,
whom this dialogue began to interest, and who were in hopes of seeing
the Quaker played off by the crazed beggar, for such Peter Peebles appeared
to be.—"Gray hairs! The Lord mend your eyesight, neighbour, that disna
ken gray hairs frae a tow wig!"

This jest procured a shout of laughter, and, what was still more acceptable than dry applause, a man who stood beside called out, "Father Crackenthorp, bring a uipperkin of brandy. I'll bestow a dram on this fellow,
were it but for that very word."

The brandy was immediately brought by a wench who acted as bar-maid;
and Peter, with a grin of delight, filled a glass, quaffed it off, and then
saying, "God bless me! I was so unmannerly as not to drink to ye—I think
the Quaker has smitten me wi' his ill-bred havings,"—he was about to fill
another, when his hand was arrested by his new friend; who said at the
same time, "No, no, friend—fair play's a jewel—time about, if you please."
And filling a glass for himself, emptied it as gallantly as Peter could have
done. "What say you to that, friend?" he continued, addressing the
Quaker.

"Nay, friend," answered Joshua, "it went down thy throat, not mine;
and I have nothing to say about what concerns me not; but if thou art a
man of humanity, thou wilt not give this poor creature the means of debauchery. Bethink thee that they will spurn him from the door, as they
would do a houseless and masterless dog, and that he may die on the sands

or on the common. And if he has through thy means been rendered incapable of helping himself, thou shalt not be innocent of his blood."

"Faith, Broadbrim, I believe thou art right, and the old gentleman in the flaxen jazy shall have no more of the comforter—Besides, we have business in hand to-day, and this fellow, for as mad as he looks, may have a nose on his face after all.—Hark ye, father,—what is your name, and what brings you into such an out-of-the-way corner?"

"I am not just free to condescend on my name," said Peter; "and as for my business—there is a wee dribble of brandy in the stoup—it would be wrang to leave it to the lass—it is learning her bad usages."

"Well, thou shalt have the brandy, and be d——d to thee, if thou wilt tell me what you are making here."

"Seeking a young advocate chap that they ca' Alan Fairford, that has played me a slippery trick, and ye maun ken a' about the cause," said Peter.

"An advocate, man!" answered the Captain of the Jumping Jenny—for it was he, and no other, who had taken compassion on Peter's drought; "why, Lord help thee, thou art on the wrong side of the Firth to seek advocates, whom I take to be Scottish lawyers, not English."

"English lawyers, man!" exclaimed Peter, "the deil a lawyer's in a' England."

"I wish from my soul it were true," said Ewart; "but what the devil put that in your head?"

"Lord, man, I got a grip of ane of their attorneys in Carlisle, and he tauld me that there wasna a lawyer in England ony mair than himsell, that kend the nature of a multiplepoinding! And when I told him how this loopy lad, Alan Fairford, had served me, he said I might bring an action on the case—just as if the case hadna as mony actions already as one case can weel carry. By my word, it is a gude case, and muckle has it borne, in its day, of various procedure—but it's the barley-pickle breaks the naig's back, and wi' my consent it shall not hae ony mair burden laid upon it."

"But this Alan Fairford?" said Nanty—"come—sip up the drop of brandy, man, and tell me some more about him, and whether you are seeking him for good or for harm."

"For my ain gude, and for his harm, to be sure," said Peter. "Think of his having left my cause in the dead-thraw between the tyneing and the winning, and capering off into Cumberland here, after a wild loup-the-tether lad they ca' Darsie Latimer."

"Darsie Latimer!" said Mr. Geddes, hastily; "Do you know any thing of Darsie Latimer?"

"Maybe I do, and maybe I do not," answered Peter; "I am no free to answer every body's interrogatory, unless it is put judicially, and by form of law—specially where folk think so much of a caup of sour yill, or a thimblefu' of brandy. But as for this gentleman, that has shown himself a gentleman at breakfast, and will show himself a gentleman at the meridian, I am free to condescend upon any points in the cause that may appear to bear upon the question at issue."

"Why, all I want to know from you, my friend, is, whether you are seeking to do this Mr. Alan Fairford good or harm; because if you come to do him good, I think you could maybe get speech of him—and if to do him harm, I will take the liberty to give you a cast across the Firth, with fair warning not to come back on such an errand, lest worse come of it."

The manner and language of Ewart were such, that Joshua Geddes resolved to keep cautious silence, till he could more plainly discover whether he was likely to aid or impede him in his researches after Darsie Latimer. He therefore determined to listen attentively to what should pass between Peter and the seaman, and to watch for an opportunity of questioning the former, so soon as he should be separated from his new acquaintance.

"I wad by no means," said Peter Peebles, "do any substantial harm to the poor lad Fairford, who has had mony a gowd guinea of mine, as weel as his father before him; but I wad hae him brought back to the minding of my business and his ain; and maybe I wadna insist farther in my action of damages against him, than for refunding the fees, and for some annual rent on the principal sum, due frae the day on which he should have recovered it for me, plack and bawbee, at the great advising; for ye are aware, that is the least that I can ask *nomine damni;* and I have nae thought to break down the lad bodily a'thegither—we maun live and let live—forgie and forget."

"The deuce take me, friend Broadbrim," said Nanty Ewart, looking to the Quaker, "if I can make out what this old scarecrow means. If I thought it was fitting that Master Fairford should see him, why perhaps it is a matter that could be managed. Do you know any thing about the old fellow?—you seemed to take some charge of him just now."

"No more than I should have done by any one in distress," said Geddes, not sorry to be appealed to; "but I will try what I can do to find out who he is, and what he is about in this country—But are we not a little too public in this open room?"

"It's well thought of," said Nanty; and at his command the bar-maid ushered the party into a side booth, Peter attending them in the instinctive hope that there would be more liquor drunk among them before parting. They had scarce sat down in their new apartment, when the sound of a violin was heard in the room which they had just left.

"I'll awa back yonder," said Peter, rising up again; "yon's the sound of a fiddle, and when there is music, there's aye something ganging to eat or drink."

"I am just going to order something here," said the Quaker; "but in the meantime, have you any objection, my good friend, to tell us your name?"

"None in the world, if you are wanting to drink to me by name and surname," answered Peebles; "but, otherwise, I would rather evite your interrogatories."

"Friend," said the Quaker, "it is not for thine own health, seeing thou hast drunk enough already—however—Here, hand-maiden—bring me a gill of sherry."

"Sherry's but shilpit drink, and a gill's a sma' measure for twa gentlemen to crack ower at their first acquaintance.—But let us see your sneaking gill of sherry," said Poor Peter, thrusting forth his huge hand to seize on the diminutive pewter measure, which, according to the fashion of the time, contained the generous liquor freshly drawn from the butt.

"Nay, hold, friend," said Joshua, "thou hast not yet told me what name and surname I am to call thee by."

"D—n sly in the Quaker," said Nanty, apart, "to make him pay for his liquor before he gives it him. Now, I am such a fool, that I should have let him get too drunk to open his mouth, before I thought of asking him a question."

"My name is Peter Peebles, then," said the litigant, rather sulkily, as one who thought his liquor too sparingly meted out to him; "and what have you to say to that?"

"Peter Peebles?" repeated Nanty Ewart, and seemed to muse upon something which the words brought to his remembrance, while the Quaker pursued his examination.

"But I prithee, Peter Peebles, what is thy farther designation?—Thou knowest, in our country, that some men are distinguished by their craft and calling, as cordwainers, fishers, weavers, or the like, and some by their titles as proprietors of land, (which savours of vanity)—Now, how may you be distinguished from others of the same name?"

"As Peter Peebles of the great plea of Poor Peter Peebles against Plainstanes, *et per contra* — if I am laird of naething else, I am aye a *dominus litis.*"

"It's but a poor lairdship, I doubt," said Joshua.

"Pray, Mr. Peebles," said Nanty, interrupting the conversation abruptly, "were not you once a burgess of Edinburgh?"

"*Was* I a burgess!" said Peter, indignantly, "and *am* I not a burgess even now? I have done nothing to forfeit my right, I trow — once provost and aye my lord."

"Well, Mr. Burgess, tell me farther, have you not some property in the Gude Town?" continued Ewart.

"Troth have I—that is, before my misfortunes, I had twa or three bonny bits of mailings amang the closes and wynds, forby the shop and the story abune it. But Plainstanes has put me to the causeway now. Never mind though, I will be upsides with him yet."

"Had not you once a tenement in the Covenant Close?" again demanded Nanty.

"You have hit it, lad, though ye look not like a Covenanter," said Peter; "we'll drink to its memory—[Hout! the heart's at the mouth o' that ill-faur'd bit stoup already!]—it brought a rent, reckoning from the crawstep to the groundsill, that ye might ca' fourteen punds a-year, forby the laigh cellar that was let to Lucky Littleworth."

"And do you not remember that you had a poor old lady for your tenant, Mrs. Cantripe of Kittlebasket?" said Nanty, suppressing his emotion with difficulty.

"Remember! G—d, I have gude cause to remember her," said Peter, "for she turned a dyvour on my hands, the auld besom! and, after a' that the law could do to make me satisfied and paid, in the way of poinding and distrenzieing, and sae forth, as the law will, she ran awa to the Charity Workhouse, a matter of twenty punds Scots in my debt—it's a great shame and oppression that Charity Workhouse, taking in bankrupt dyvours that canna pay their honest creditors."

"Methinks, friend," said the Quaker, "thine own rags might teach thee compassion for other people's nakedness."

"Rags!" said Peter, taking Joshua's words literally; "does ony wise body put on their best coat when they are travelling, and keeping company with Quakers, and such other cattle as the road affords?"

"The old lady *died*, I have heard," said Nanty, affecting a moderation which was belied by accents that faltered with passion.

"She might live or die, for what I care," answered Peter the Cruel; "what business have folk to do to live, that canna live as law will, and satisfy their just and lawful creditors?"

"And you—you that are now yourself trodden down in the very kennel, are you not sorry for what you have done? Do you not repent having occasioned the poor widow woman's death?"

"What for should I repent?" said Peter; "the law was on my side — a decreet of the Bailies, followed by poinding, and an act of warding—a suspension intented, and the letters found orderly proceeded. I followed the auld rudas through twa Courts — she cost me mair money than her lugs were worth."

"Now, by Heaven!" said Nanty, "I would give a thousand guineas, if I had them, to have you worth my beating! Had you said you repented, it had been between God and your conscience; but to hear you boast of your villany—Do you think it little to have reduced the aged to famine, and the young to infamy — to have caused the death of one woman, the ruin of another, and to have driven a man to exile and despair? By him that made me, I can scarce keep hands off you!"

"Off me?—I defy ye!" said Peter. "I take this honest man to witness, that if ye stir the neck of my collar, I will have my action for stouthreif, spulzie, oppression, assault and battery. Here's a bra' din, indeed, about an auld wife gaun to the grave, a young limmer to the close-heads and causeway, and a sticket stibbler* to the sea instead of the gallows!"

"Now, by my soul," said Nanty, "this is too much! and since you can feel no otherwise, I will try if I cannot beat some humanity into your head and shoulders."

He drew his hanger as he spoke, and although Joshua, who had in vain endeavoured to interrupt the dialogue, to which he foresaw a violent termination, now threw himself between Nanty and the old litigant, he could not prevent the latter from receiving two or three sound slaps over the shoulder with the flat side of the weapon.

Poor Peter Peebles, as inglorious in his extremity as he had been presumptuous in bringing it on, now ran and roared, and bolted out of the apartment and house itself, pursued by Nanty, whose passion became high in proportion to his giving way to its dictates, and by Joshua, who still interfered at every risk, calling upon Nanty to reflect on the age and miserable circumstances of the offender, and upon Poor Peter to stand and place himself under his protection. In front of the house, however, Peter Peebles found a more efficient protector than the worthy Quaker.

Chapter the Twenty-First.

NARRATIVE OF ALAN FAIRFORD.

OUR readers may recollect, that Fairford had been conducted by Dick Gardener from the House of Fairladies, to the inn of old Father Crackenthorp, in order, as he had been informed by the mysterious Father Buonaventure, that he might have the meeting which he desired with Mr. Redgauntlet, to treat with him for the liberty of his friend Darsie. His guide, by the special direction of Mr. Ambrose, had introduced him into the public-house by a back-door, and recommended to the landlord to accommodate him with a private apartment, and to treat him with all civility; but in other respects to keep his eye on him, and even to secure his person, if he saw any reason to suspect him to be a spy. He was not, however, subjected to any direct restraint, but was ushered into an apartment, where he was requested to await the arrival of the gentleman with whom he wished to have an interview, and who, as Crackenthorp assured him with a significant nod, would be certainly there in the course of an hour. In the meanwhile, he recommended to him, with another significant sign, to keep his apartment, "as there were people in the house who were apt to busy themselves about other folk's matters."

Alan Fairford complied with the recommendation, so long as he thought it reasonable; but when, among a large party riding up to the house, he discerned Redgauntlet, whom he had seen under the name of Mr. Herries of Birrenswork, and whom, by his height and strength, he easily distinguished from the rest, he thought it proper to go down to the front of the house, in hopes that, by more closely reconnoitering the party, he might discover if his friend Darsie was among them.

The reader is aware that, by doing so, he had an opportunity of breaking Darsie's fall from his side-saddle, although his disguise and mask prevented his recognizing his friend. It may be also recollected, that while Nixon

---

* A student of divinity who has not been able to complete his studies on theology.

hurried Miss Redgauntlet and her brother into the house, their uncle, somewhat chafed at an unexpected and inconvenient interruption, remained himself in parley with Fairford, who had already successively addressed him by the names of Herries and Redgauntlet; neither of which, any more than the acquaintance of the young lawyer, he seemed at the moment willing to acknowledge, though an air of haughty indifference, which he assumed, could not conceal his vexation and embarrassment.

"If we must needs be acquainted, sir," he said at last—"for which I am unable to see any necessity, especially as I am now particularly disposed to be private—I must entreat you will tell me at once what you have to say, and permit me to attend to matters of more importance."

"My introduction," said Fairford, "is contained in this letter.—Delivering that of Maxwell.)—I am convinced that, under whatever name it may be your pleasure for the present to be known, it is into your hands, and yours only, that it should be delivered."

Redgauntlet turned the letter in his hand—then read the contents—then again looked upon the letter, and sternly observed, "The seal of the letter has been broken. Was this the case, sir, when it was delivered into your hand?"

Fairford despised a falsehood as much as any man,—unless, perhaps, as Tom Turnpenny might have said, "in the way of business." He answered readily and firmly, "The seal was whole when the letter was delivered to me by Mr. Maxwell of Summertrees."

"And did you dare, sir, to break the seal of a letter addressed to me?" said Redgauntlet, not sorry, perhaps, to pick a quarrel upon a point foreign to the tenor of the epistle.

"I have never broken the seal of any letter committed to my charge," said Alan; "not from fear of those to whom such letter might be addressed, but from respect to myself."

"That is well worded," said Redgauntlet; "and yet, young Mr. Counsellor, I doubt whether your delicacy prevented your reading my letter, or listening to the contents as read by some other person after it was opened."

"I certainly did hear the contents read over," said Fairford; "and they were such as to surprise me a good deal."

"Now that," said Redgauntlet, "I hold to be pretty much the same, in foro conscientiæ, as if you had broken the seal yourself. I shall hold myself excused from entering upon farther discourse with a messenger so faithless; and you may thank yourself if your journey has been fruitless."

"Stay, sir," said Fairford; "and know that I became acquainted with the contents of the paper without my consent—I may even say, against my will; for Mr. Buonaventure——"

"Who?" demanded Redgauntlet, in a wild and alarmed manner—"Whom was it you named?"

"Father Buonaventure," said Alan,—"a Catholic priest, as I apprehend, whom I saw at the Misses Arthuret's house, called Fairladies."

"Misses Arthuret!—Fairladies!—A Catholic priest!—Father Buonaventure!" said Redgauntlet, repeating the words of Alan with astonishment.— "Is it possible that human rashness can reach such a point of infatuation? —Tell me the truth, I conjure you, sir—I have the deepest interest to know whether this is more than an idle legend, picked up from hearsay about the country. You are a lawyer, and know the risk incurred by the Catholic clergy, whom the discharge of their duty sends to these bloody shores."

"I am a lawyer, certainly," said Fairford; "but my holding such a respectable condition in life warrants that I am neither an informer nor a spy. Here is sufficient evidence that I have seen Father Buonaventure."

He put Buonaventure's letter into Redgauntlet's hand, and watched his looks closely while he read it. "Double-dyed infatuation!" he muttered, with looks in which sorrow, displeasure, and anxiety were mingled. "'Save me from the indiscretion of my friends,' says the Spaniard; 'I can save myself from the hostility of my enemies.'"

He then read the letter attentively, and for two or three minutes was lost in thought, while some purpose of importance seemed to have gathered and sit brooding upon his countenance. He held up his finger towards his satellite, Cristal Nixon, who replied to his signal with a prompt nod; and with one or two of the attendants approached Fairford in such a manner as to make him apprehensive they were about to lay hold of him.

At this moment a noise was heard from withinside of the house, and presently rushed forth Peter Peebles, pursued by Nanty Ewart with his drawn hanger, and the worthy Quaker, who was endeavouring to prevent mischief to others, at some risk of bringing it on himself.

A wilder and yet a more absurd figure can hardly be imagined, than that of Poor Peter clattering along as fast as his huge boots would permit him, and resembling nothing so much as a flying scarecrow; while the thin emaciated form of Nanty Ewart, with the hue of death on his cheek, and the fire of vengeance glancing from his eye, formed a ghastly contrast with the ridiculous object of his pursuit.

Redgauntlet threw himself between them. "What extravagant folly is this?" he said. "Put up your weapon, Captain. Is this a time to indulge in drunken brawls, or is such a miserable object as that a fitting antagonist for a man of courage?"

"I beg pardon," said the Captain, sheathing his weapon—"I was a little bit out of the way, to be sure; but to know the provocation, a man must read my heart, and that I hardly dare to do myself. But the wretch is safe from me. Heaven has done its own vengeance on us both."

While he spoke in this manner, Peter Peebles, who had at first crept behind Redgauntlet in bodily fear, began now to reassume his spirits. Pulling his protector by the sleeve, "Mr. Herries — Mr. Herries," he whispered, eagerly, "ye have done me mair than ae gude turn, and if ye will but do me anither at this dead pinch, I'll forgie the girded keg of brandy that you and Captain Sir Harry Redgimlet drank out yon time. Ye sall hae an ample discharge and renunciation, and, though I should see you walking at the Cross of Edinburgh, or standing at the bar of the Court of Justiciary, no the very thumbikins themselves should bring to my memory that ever I saw you in arms yon day."

He accompanied this promise by pulling so hard at Redgauntlet's cloak, that he at last turned round. "Idiot! speak in a word what you want."

"Aweel, aweel. In a word, then," said Peter Peebles, "I have a warrant on me to apprehend that man that stands there, Alan Fairford by name, and advocate by calling. I bought it from Maister Justice Foxley's clerk, Maister Nicholas Faggot, wi' the guinea that you gied me."

"Ha!" said Redgauntlet, "hast thou really such a warrant? let me see it. Look sharp that no one escape, Cristal Nixon."

Peter produced a huge, greasy, leathern pocket-book, too dirty to permit its original colour to be visible, filled with scrolls of notes, memorials to counsel, and Heaven knows what besides. From amongst this precious mass he culled forth a paper, and placed it in the hands of Redgauntlet, or Herries, as he continued to call him, saying, at the same time, "It's a formal and binding warrant, proceeding on my affidavy made, that the said Alan Fairford, being lawfully engaged in my service, had slipped the tether and fled over the Border, and was now lurking there and thereabouts, to elude and evite the discharge of his bounden duty to me; and therefore granting warrant to constables and others, to seek for, take, and apprehend him, that he may be brought before the honourable Justice Foxley for examination, and, if necessary, for commitment. Now, though a' this be fairly set down, as I tell ye, yet where am I to get an officer to execute this warrant in sic a country as this, where swords and pistols flee out at a word's speaking, and folk care as little for the peace of King George, as the peace of Auld King Coul?—There's that drunken skipper, and that wet Quaker, enticed me into the public this morning, and because I wadna gie them as much brandy as wad have made them blind-drunk, they baith fell on me, and were in the way of guiding me very ill."

While Peter went on in this manner, Redgauntlet glanced his eye over the warrant, and immediately saw it must be a trick passed by Nicholas Faggot, to cheat the poor insane wretch out of his solitary guinea. But the Justice had actually subscribed it, as he did whatever his clerk presented to him, and Redgauntlet resolved to use it for his own purposes.

Without making any direct answer, therefore, to Peter Peebles, he walked up gravely to Fairford, who had waited quietly for the termination of a scene in which he was not a little surprised to find his client, Mr. Peebles, a conspicuous actor.

"Mr. Fairford," said Redgauntlet, "there are many reasons which might induce me to comply with the request, or rather the injunctions, of the excellent Father Buonaventure, that I should communicate with you upon the present condition of my ward, whom you know under the name of Darsie Latimer; but no man is better aware than you that the law must be obeyed, even in contradiction to our own feelings; now this poor man has obtained a warrant for carrying you before a magistrate, and, I am afraid, there is a necessity of your yielding to it, although to the postponement of the business which you may have with me."

"A warrant against me!" said Alan, indignantly; "and at that poor miserable wretch's instance?—why, this is a trick, a mere and most palpable trick."

"It may be so," replied Redgauntlet, with great equanimity; "doubtless you know best; only the writ appears regular, and with that respect for the law which has been," he said, with hypocritical formality, "a leading feature of my character through life, I cannot dispense with giving my poor aid to the support of a legal warrant. Look at it yourself, and be satisfied it is no trick of mine."

Fairford ran over the affidavit and the warrant, and then exclaimed once more, that it was an impudent imposition, and that he would hold those who acted upon such a warrant liable in the highest damages. "I guess at your motive, Mr. Redgauntlet," he said, "for acquiescing in so ridiculous a proceeding. But be assured you will find that, in this country, one act of illegal violence will not be covered or atoned for by practising another. You cannot, as a man of sense and honour, pretend to say you regard this as a legal warrant."

"I am no lawyer, sir," said Redgauntlet; "and pretend not to know what is or is not law—the warrant is quite formal, and that is enough for me."

"Did ever any one hear," said Fairford, "of an advocate being compelled to return to his task, like a collier or a salter* who has deserted his master?"

"I see no reason why he should not," said Redgauntlet, dryly, "unless on the ground that the services of the lawyer are the most expensive and least useful of the two."

"You cannot mean this in earnest," said Fairford; "you cannot really mean to avail yourself of so poor a contrivance, to evade the word pledged by your friend, your ghostly father, in my behalf. I may have been a fool for trusting it too easily, but think what you must be if you can abuse my

* The persons engaged in these occupations were at this time bondsmen; and in case they left the ground of the farm to which they belonged, and as pertaining to which their services were bought or sold, they were liable to be brought back by a summary process. The existence of this species of slavery being thought irreconcilable with the spirit of liberty, colliers and salters were declared free, and put upon the same footing with other servants, by the Act 15 Geo. III. chapter 28th. They were so far from desiring or prizing the blessing conferred on them, that they esteemed the interest taken in their freedom to be a mere desire on the part of the proprietors to get rid of what they called head and harigald money, payable to them when a female of their number, by bearing a child, made an addition to the live stock of their master's property.

confidence in this manner. I entreat you to reflect that this usage releases me from all promises of secrecy or connivance at what I am apt to think are very dangerous practices, and that ——"

"Hark ye, Mr. Fairford," said Redgauntlet; "I must here interrupt you for your own sake. One word of betraying what you may have seen, or what you may have suspected, and your seclusion is like to have either a very distant or a very brief termination; in either case a most undesirable one. At present, you are sure of being at liberty in a very few days — perhaps much sooner."

"And my friend," said Alan Fairford, "for whose sake I have run myself into this danger, what is to become of him? — Dark and dangerous man!" he exclaimed, raising his voice, "I will not be again cajoled by deceitful promises ——"

"I give you my honour that your friend is well," interrupted Redgauntlet; "perhaps I may permit you to see him, if you will but submit with patience to a fate which is inevitable."

But Alan Fairford, considering his confidence as having been abused, first by Maxwell, and next by the Priest, raised his voice, and appealed to all the King's lieges within hearing, against the violence with which he was threatened. He was instantly seized on by Nixon and two assistants, who, holding down his arms, and endeavouring to stop his mouth, were about to hurry him away.

The honest Quaker, who had kept out of Redgauntlet's presence, now came boldly forward.

"Friend," said he, "thou dost more than thou canst answer. Thou knowest me well, and thou art aware, that in me thou hast a deeply injured neighbour, who was dwelling beside thee in the honesty and simplicity of his heart."

"Tush, Jonathan," said Redgauntlet; "talk not to me, man; it is neither the craft of a young lawyer, nor the *simplicity* of an old hypocrite, can drive me from my purpose."

"By my faith," said the Captain, coming forward in his turn, "this is hardly fair, General; and I doubt," he added, "whether the will of my owners can make me a party to such proceedings.—Nay, never fumble with your sword-bilt, but out with it like a man, if you are for a tilting."— He unsheathed his hanger, and continued — "I will neither see my comrade Fairford, nor the old Quaker, abused. D—n all warrants, false or true — curse the justice — confound the constable!—and here stands little Nanty Ewart to make good what he says against gentle and simple, in spite of horse-shoe or horse-radish either."

The cry of "Down with all warrants!" was popular in the ears of the militia of the inn, and Nanty Ewart was no less so. Fishers, ostlers, seamen, smugglers, began to crowd to the spot. Crackenthorp endeavoured in vain to mediate. The attendants of Redgauntlet began to handle their firearms; but their master shouted to them to forbear, and, unsheathing his sword as quick as lightning, he rushed on Ewart in the midst of his bravade, and struck his weapon from his hand with such address and force, that it flew three yards from him. Closing with him at the same moment, he gave him a severe fall, and waved his sword over his head, to show he was absolutely at his mercy.

"There, you drunken vagabond," he said, "I give you your life—you are no bad fellow, if you could keep from brawling among your friends. — But we all know Nanty Ewart," he said to the crowd around, with a forgiving laugh, which, joined to the awe his prowess had inspired, entirely confirmed their wavering allegiance.

They shouted, "The Laird for ever!" while poor Nanty, rising from the earth, on whose lap he had been stretched so rudely, went in quest of his hanger, lifted it, wiped it, and, as he returned the weapon to the scabbard, muttered between his teeth, "It is true they say of him, and the devil will stand his friend till his hour come; I will cross him no more."

So saying, he slunk from the crowd, cowed and disheartened by his defeat.

"For you, Joshua Geddes," said Redgauntlet, approaching the Quaker, who, with lifted hands and eyes, had beheld the scene of violence, "I shall take the liberty to arrest thee for a breach of the peace, altogether unbecoming thy pretended principles; and I believe it will go hard with thee both in a Court of Justice and among thine own Society of Friends, as they call themselves, who will be but indifferently pleased to see the quiet tenor of their hypocrisy insulted by such violent proceedings."

"*I* violent!" said Joshua; "*I* do aught unbecoming the principles of the Friends! I defy thee, man, and I charge thee, as a Christian, to forbear vexing my soul with such charges: it is grievous enough to me to have seen violences which I was unable to prevent."

"O Joshua, Joshua!" said Redgauntlet, with a sardonic smile; "thou light of the faithful in the town of Dumfries and the places adjacent, wilt thou thus fall away from the truth? Hast thou not, before us all, attempted to rescue a man from the warrant of law? Didst thou not encourage that drunken fellow to draw his weapon—and didst thou not thyself flourish thy cudgel in the cause? Think'st thou that the oaths of the injured Peter Peebles, and the conscientious Cristal Nixon, besides those of such gentlemen as look on this strange scene, who not only put on swearing as a garment, but to whom, in Custom-House matters, oaths are literally meat and drink, — dost thou not think, I say, that these men's oaths will go farther than thy Yea and Nay in this matter?"

"I will swear to any thing," said Peter. "All is fair when it comes to an oath *ad litem.*"

"You do me foul wrong," said the Quaker, undismayed by the general laugh. "I encouraged no drawing of weapons, though I attempted to move an unjust man by some use of argument—I brandished no cudgel, although it may be that the ancient Adam struggled within me, and caused my hand to grasp mine oaken staff firmer than usual, when I saw innocence borne down with violence. — But why talk I what is true and just to thee, who hast been a man of violence from thy youth upwards? Let me rather speak to thee such language as thou canst comprehend. Deliver these young men up to me," he said, when he had led Redgauntlet a little apart from the crowd, "and I will not only free thee from the heavy charge of damages which thou hast incurred by thine outrage upon my property, but I will add ransom for them and for myself. What would it profit thee to do the youths wrong, by detaining them in captivity?"

"Mr. Geddes," said Redgauntlet, in a tone more respectful than he had hitherto used to the Quaker, "your language is disinterested, and I respect the fidelity of your friendship. Perhaps we have mistaken each other's principles and motives; but if so, we have not at present time for explanation. Make yourself easy. I hope to raise your friend Darsie Latimer to a pitch of eminence which you will witness with pleasure; — nay, do not attempt to answer me. The other young man shall suffer restraint a few days, probably only a few hours, — it is not more than due for his pragmatical interference in what concerned him not. Do you, Mr. Geddes, be so prudent as to take your horse and leave this place, which is growing every moment more unfit for the abode of a man of peace. You may wait the event in safety at Mount Sharon."

"Friend," replied Joshua, "I cannot comply with thy advice; I will remain here, even as thy prisoner, as thou didst but now threaten, rather than leave the youth who hath suffered by and through me and my misfortunes, in his present state of doubtful safety. Wherefore I will not mount my steed Solomon; neither will I turn his head towards Mount Sharon, until I see an end of this matter."

"A prisoner, then, you must be," said Redgauntlet. "I have no time to dispute the matter farther with you. — But tell me for what you fix your eyes so attentively on yonder people of mine."

"To speak the truth," said the Quaker, "I admire to behold among them a little wretch of a boy called Benjie, to whom I think Satan has given the power of transporting himself wheresoever mischief is going forward; so that it may be truly said, there is no evil in this land wherein he hath not a finger, if not a whole hand."

The boy, who saw their eyes fixed on him as they spoke, seemed embarrassed, and rather desirous of making his escape; but at a signal from Redgauntlet he advanced, assuming the sheepish look and rustic manner with which the jackanapes covered much acuteness and roguery.

"How long have you been with the party, sirrah?" said Redgauntlet.

"Since the raid on the stake-nets," said Benjie, with his finger in his mouth.

"And what made you follow us?"

"I dauredna stay at hame for the constables," replied the boy.

"And what have you been doing all this time?"

"Doing, sir? — I dinna ken what ye ca' doing — I have been doing naething," said Benjie; then seeing something in Redgauntlet's eye which was not to be trifled with, he added, "Naething but waiting on Maister Cristal Nixon."

"Hum! — ay — indeed?" muttered Redgauntlet. "Must Master Nixon bring his own retinue into the field? — This must be seen to."

He was about to pursue his inquiry, when Nixon himself came to him with looks of anxious haste. "The Father is come," he whispered, "and the gentlemen are getting together in the largest room of the house, and they desire to see you. Yonder is your nephew, too, making a noise like a man in Bedlam."

"I will look to it all instantly," said Redgauntlet. "Is the Father lodged as I directed?"

Cristal nodded.

"Now, then, for the final trial," said Redgauntlet. He folded his hands —looked upwards—crossed himself—and after this act of devotion, (almost the first which any one had observed him make use of,) he commanded Nixon to keep good watch — have his horses and men ready for every emergence—look after the safe custody of the prisoners—but treat them at the same time well and civilly. And these orders given, he darted hastily into the house.

Chapter the Twenty-Second.

NARRATIVE CONTINUED.

REDGAUNTLET's first course was to the chamber of his nephew. He unlocked the door, entered the apartment, and asked what he wanted, that he made so much noise.

"I want my liberty," said Darsie, who had wrought himself up to a pitch of passion in which his uncle's wrath had lost its terrors. "I desire my liberty, and to be assured of the safety of my beloved friend Alan Fairford, whose voice I heard but now."

"Your liberty shall be your own within half an hour from this period —

your friend shall be also set at freedom in due time — and you yourself be permitted to have access to his place of confinement."

"This does not satisfy me," said Darsie; "I must see my friend instantly; he is here, and he is here endangered on my account only — I have heard violent exclamations — the clash of swords. You will gain no point with me unless I have ocular demonstration of his safety."

"Arthur — dearest nephew," answered Redgauntlet, "drive me not mad! Thine own fate — that of thy house — that of thousands — that of Britain herself, are at this moment in the scales; and you are only occupied about the safety of a poor insignificant pettifogger!"

"He has sustained injury at your hands, then?" said Darsie, fiercely. "I know he has; but if so, not even our relationship shall protect you."

"Peace, ungrateful and obstinate fool!" said Redgauntlet. "Yet stay — Will you be satisfied if you see this Alan Fairford, the bundle of bombazine — this precious friend of yours — well and sound? — Will you, I say, be satisfied with seeing him in perfect safety without attempting to speak to or converse with him?" — Darsie signified his assent. "Take hold of my arm, then," said Redgauntlet; "and do you, niece Lilias, take the other; and beware, Sir Arthur, how you bear yourself."

Darsie was compelled to acquiesce, sufficiently aware that his uncle would permit him no interview with a friend whose influence would certainly be used against his present earnest wishes, and in some measure contented with the assurance of Fairford's personal safety.

Redgauntlet led them through one or two passages, (for the house, as we have before said, was very irregular, and built at different times), until they entered an apartment, where a man with shouldered carabine kept watch at the door, but readily turned the key for their reception. In this room they found Alan Fairford and the Quaker, apparently in deep conversation with each other. They looked up as Redgauntlet and his party entered; and Alan pulled off his hat and made a profound reverence, which the young lady, who recognized him, — though, masked as she was, he could not know her, — returned with some embarrassment, arising probably from the recollection of the bold step she had taken in visiting him.

Darsie longed to speak, but dared not. His uncle only said, "Gentlemen, I know you are as anxious on Mr. Darsie Latimer's account as he is upon yours. I am commissioned by him to inform you, that he is as well as you are — I trust you will all meet soon. Meantime, although I cannot suffer you to be at large, you shall be as well treated as is possible under your temporary confinement."

He passed on, without pausing to hear the answers which the lawyer and the Quaker were hastening to prefer; and only waving his hand by way of adieu, made his exit, with the real and the seeming lady whom he had under his charge, through a door at the upper end of the apartment, which was fastened and guarded like that by which they entered.

Redgauntlet next led the way into a very small room; adjoining which, but divided by a partition, was one of apparently larger dimensions; for they heard the trampling of the heavy boots of the period, as if several persons were walking to and fro, and conversing in low and anxious whispers.

"Here," said Redgauntlet to his nephew, as he disencumbered him from the riding-skirt and the mask, "I restore you to yourself, and trust you will lay aside all effeminate thoughts with this feminine dress. Do not blush at having worn a disguise to which kings and heroes have been reduced. It is when female craft or female cowardice find their way into a manly bosom, that he who entertains these sentiments should take eternal shame to himself for thus having resembled womankind. Follow me, while Lilias remains here. I will introduce you to those whom I hope to see associated with you in the most glorious cause that hand ever drew sword in."

Darsie paused. "Uncle," he said, "my person is in your hands; but remember, my will is my own. I will not be hurried into any resolution of importance. Remember what I have already said — what I now repeat — that I will take no step of importance but upon conviction."

"But canst thou be convinced, thou foolish boy, without hearing and understanding the grounds on which we act?"

So saying he took Darsie by the arm, and walked with him to the next room —a large apartment, partly filled with miscellaneous articles of commerce, chiefly connected with contraband trade; where, among bales and barrels, sat, or walked to and fro, several gentlemen, whose manners and looks seemed superior to the plain riding dresses which they wore.

There was a grave and stern anxiety upon their countenances, when, on Redgauntlet's entrance, they drew from their separate coteries into one group around him, and saluted him with a formality, which had something in it of ominous melancholy. As Darsie looked around the circle, he thought he could discern in it few traces of that adventurous hope which urges men upon desperate enterprises; and began to believe that the conspiracy would dissolve of itself, without the necessity of his placing himself in direct opposition to so violent a character as his uncle, and incurring the hazard with which such opposition must be attended.

Mr. Redgauntlet, however, did not, or would not, see any such marks of depression of spirit amongst his coadjutors, but met them with cheerful countenance, and a warm greeting of welcome. "Happy to meet you here, my lord," he said, bowing low to a slender young man. "I trust you come with the pledges of your noble father of B——, and all that loyal house.— Sir Richard, what news in the west? I am told you had two hundred men on foot to have joined when the fatal retreat from Derby was commenced. When the White Standard is again displayed, it shall not be turned back so easily, either by the force of its enemies, or the falsehood of its friends. —Doctor Grumball, I bow to the representative of Oxford, the mother of learning and loyalty.— Pengwinion, you Cornish chough, has this good wind blown you north? — Ah, my brave Cambro-Britons, when was Wales last in the race of honour?"

Such and such-like compliments he dealt around, which were in general answered by silent bows; but when he saluted one of his own countrymen by the name of MacKellar, and greeted Maxwell of Summertrees by that of Pate-in-Peril, the latter replied, "that if Pate were not a fool, he would be Pate-in-Safety;" and the former, a thin old gentleman, in tarnished embroidery, said bluntly, "Ay, troth, Redgauntlet, I am here just like yourself; I have little to lose — they that took my land the last time, may take my life this; and that is all I care about it."

The English gentlemen, who were still in possession of their paternal estates, looked doubtfully on each other, and there was something whispered among them of the fox which had lost his tail.

Redgauntlet hastened to address them. "I think, my lords and gentlemen," he said, "that I can account for something like sadness which has crept upon an assembly gathered together for so noble a purpose. Our numbers seem, when thus assembled, too small and inconsiderable to shake the firm-seated usurpation of half a century. But do not count us by what we are in thewe and muscle, but by what our summons can do among our countrymen. In this small party are those who have power to raise battalions, and those who have wealth to pay them. And do not believe our friends who are absent are cold or indifferent to the cause. Let us once light the signal, and it will be hailed by all who retain love for the Stewart, and by all—a more numerous body—who hate the Elector. Here I have letters from ——"

Sir Richard Glendale interrupted the speaker. "We all confide, Redgauntlet, in your valour and skill — we admire your perseverance; and probably nothing short of your strenuous exertions, and the emulation awakened by your noble and disinterested conduct, could have brought so many of us, the scattered remnant of a disheartened party, to meet together once again in solemn consultation;—for I take it, gentlemen," he said, looking round, "this is only a consultation."

"Nothing more," said the young lord.

"Nothing more," said Doctor Grumball, shaking his large academical peruke.

And, "Only a consultation," was echoed by the others.

Redgauntlet bit his lip. "I had hopes," he said, "that the discourses I have held with most of you, from time to time, had ripened into more maturity than your words imply, and that we were here to execute as well as to deliberate; and for this we stand prepared. I can raise five hundred men with my whistle."

"Five hundred men!" said one of the Welsh squires; "Cot bless us! and pray you, what cood could five hundred men do?"

"All that the priming does for the cannon, Mr. Meredith," answered Redgauntlet; "it will enable us to seize Carlisle, and you know what our friends have engaged for in that case."

"Yes — but," said the young nobleman, "you must not hurry us on too fast, Mr. Redgauntlet; we are all, I believe, as sincere and truehearted in this business as you are, but we will not be driven forward blindfold. We owe caution to ourselves and our families, as well as to those whom we are empowered to represent on this occasion."

"Who hurries you, my lord? Who is it that would drive this meeting forward blindfold? I do not understand your lordship," said Redgauntlet.

"Nay," said Sir Richard Glendale, "at least do not let us fall under our old reproach of disagreeing among ourselves. What my lord means, Redgauntlet, is, that we have this morning heard it is uncertain whether you could even bring that body of men whom you count upon; your countryman, Mr. MacKellar, seemed, just before you came in, to doubt whether your people would rise in any force, unless you could produce the authority of your nephew."

"I might ask," said Redgauntlet, "what right MacKellar, or any one, has to doubt my being able to accomplish what I stand pledged for?—But our hopes consist in our unity. — Here stands my nephew. — Gentlemen, I present to you my kinsman, Sir Arthur Darsie Redgauntlet of that Ilk."

"Gentlemen," said Darsie, with a throbbing bosom, for he felt the crisis a very painful one, "Allow me to say, that I suspend expressing my sentiments on the important subject under discussion until I have heard those of the present meeting."

"Proceed in your deliberations, gentlemen," said Redgauntlet; "I will show my nephew such reasons for acquiescing in the result, as will entirely remove any scruples which may hang around his mind."

Dr. Grumball now coughed, "shook his ambrosial curls," and addressed the assembly.

"The principles of Oxford," he said, "are well understood, since she was the last to resign herself to the Arch-Usurper,—since she has condemned, by her sovereign authority, the blasphemous, atheistical, and anarchical tenets of Locke, and other deluders of the public mind. Oxford will give men, money, and countenance, to the cause of the rightful monarch. But we have been often deluded by foreign powers, who have availed themselves of our zeal to stir up civil dissensions in Britain, not for the advantage of our blessed though banished monarch, but to stir up disturbances by which they might profit, while we, their tools, are sure to be ruined. Oxford, therefore, will not rise, unless our Sovereign comes in person to claim our allegiance, in which case, God forbid we should refuse him our best obedience."

"It is a very good advice," said Mr. Meredith.

"In troth," said Sir Richard Glendale, "it is the very keystone of our enterprise, and the only condition upon which I myself and others could ever have dreamt of taking up arms. No insurrection which has not Charles Edward himself at its head, will ever last longer than till a single foot company of redcoats march to disperse it."

"This is my own opinion, and that of all my family," said the young nobleman already mentioned; "and I own I am somewhat surprised at being summoned to attend a dangerous rendezvous such as this, before something certain could have been stated to us on this most important preliminary point."

"Pardon me, my lord," said Redgauntlet; "I have not been so unjust either to myself or my friends. I had no means of communicating to our distant confederates (without the greatest risk of discovery) what is known to some of my honourable friends. As courageous, and as resolved, as when, twenty years since, he threw himself into the wilds of Moidart, Charles Edward has instantly complied with the wishes of his faithful subjects. Charles Edward is in this country — Charles Edward is in this house! — Charles Edward waits but your present decision, to receive the homage of those who have ever called themselves his loyal liegemen. He that would now turn his coat, and change his note, must do so under the eye of his sovereign."

There was a deep pause. Those among the conspirators whom mere habit, or a desire of preserving consistency, had engaged in the affair, now saw with terror their retreat cut off; and others, who at a distance had regarded the proposed enterprise as hopeful, trembled when the moment of actually embarking in it was thus unexpectedly and almost inevitably precipitated.

"How now, my lords and gentlemen!" said Redgauntlet; "is it delight and rapture that keeps you thus silent? where are the eager welcomes that should be paid to your rightful King, who a second time confides his person to the care of his subjects, undeterred by the hairbreadth escapes and severe privations of his former expedition? I hope there is no gentleman here that is not ready to redeem, in his Prince's presence, the pledge of fidelity which he offered in his absence."

"I, at least," said the young nobleman resolutely, and laying his hand on his sword, "will not be that coward. If Charles is come to these shores, I will be the first to give him welcome, and to devote my life and fortune to his service."

"Before Cot," said Mr. Meredith, "I do not see that Mr. Redcantlet has left us any thing else to do."

"Stay," said Summertrees, "there is yet one other question. Has he brought any of those Irish rapparees with him, who broke the neck of our last glorious affair?"

"Not a man of them," said Redgauntlet.

"I trust," said Dr. Grumball, "that there are no Catholic priests in his company. I would not intrude on the private conscience of my Sovereign, but, as an unworthy son of the Church of England, it is my duty to consider her security."

"Not a Popish dog or cat is there, to bark or mew about his Majesty," said Redgauntlet. "Old Shaftesbury himself could not wish a prince's person more secure from Popery — which may not be the worst religion in the world, notwithstanding. Any more doubts, gentlemen? can no more plausible reasons be discovered for postponing the payment of our duty, and discharge of our oaths and engagements? Meantime your King waits your declaration — by my faith he hath but a frozen reception!"

"Redgauntlet," said Sir Richard Glendale, calmly, "your reproaches shall not goad me into any thing of which my reason disapproves. That I respect my engagement as much as you do, is evident, since I am here, ready to support it with the best blood in my veins. But has the King really come hither entirely unattended?"

"He has no man with him but young ——, as aid-de-camp, and a single valet-de-chambre."

"No man;—but, Redgauntlet, as you are a gentleman, has he no woman with him?"

Redgauntlet cast his eyes on the ground and replied, "I am sorry to say —he has."

The company looked at each other, and remained silent for a moment. At length Sir Richard proceeded. "I need not repeat to you, Mr. Redgauntlet, what is the well-grounded opinion of his Majesty's friends concerning that most unhappy connection; there is but one sense and feeling amongst us upon the subject. I must conclude that our humble remonstrances were communicated by you, sir, to the King?"

"In the same strong terms in which they were couched," replied Redgauntlet. "I love his Majesty's cause more than I fear his displeasure."

"But, apparently, our humble expostulation has produced no effect. This lady, who has crept into his bosom, has a sister in the Elector of Hanover's Court, and yet we are well assured that our most private communication is placed in her keeping."

"*Varium et mutabile super femina,*" said Dr. Grumball.

"She puts his secrets into her work-bag," said Maxwell; "and out they fly whenever she opens it. If I must hang, I would wish it to be in somewhat a better rope than the string of a lady's hussey."

"Are you, too, turning dastard, Maxwell?" said Redgauntlet, in a whisper.

"Not I," said Maxwell; "let us fight for it, and let them win and wear us; but to be betrayed by a brimstone like that——"

"Be temperate, gentlemen," said Redgauntlet; "the foible of which you complain so heavily has always been that of kings and heroes; which I feel strongly confident the king will surmount, upon the humble entreaty of his best servants, and when he sees them ready to peril their all in his cause, upon the slight condition of his resigning the society of a female favourite, of whom I have seen reason to think he hath been himself for some time wearied. But let us not press upon him rashly with our well-meant zeal. He has a princely will, as becomes his princely birth, and we, gentlemen, who are royalists, should be the last to take advantage of circumstances to limit its exercise. I am as much surprised and hurt as you can be, to find that he has made her the companion of this journey, increasing every chance of treachery and detection. But do not let us insist upon a sacrifice so humiliating, while he has scarce placed a foot upon the beach of his kingdom. Let us act generously by our Sovereign; and when we have shown what we will do for him, we shall be able, with better face, to state what it is we expect him to concede."

"Indeed, I think it is but a pity," said MacKellar, "when so many pretty gentlemen are got together, that they should part without the flash of a sword among them."

"I should be of that gentleman's opinion," said Lord ——, "had I nothing to lose but my life; but I frankly own, that the conditions on which our family agreed to join having been, in this instance, left unfulfilled, I will not peril the whole fortunes of our house on the doubtful fidelity of an artful woman."

"I am sorry to see your lordship," said Redgauntlet, "take a course, which is more likely to secure your house's wealth than to augment its honours."

"How am I to understand your language, sir?" said the young nobleman, haughtily.

"Nay, gentlemen," said Dr. Grumball, interposing, "do not let friends quarrel; we are all zealous for the cause — but truly, although I know the license claimed by the great in such matters, and can, I hope, make due allowance, there is, I may say, an indecorum in a prince who comes to claim the allegiance of the Church of England, arriving on such an errand with such a companion—*si non casté, cauté tamen.*"

"I wonder how the Church of England came to be so heartily attached to his merry old namesake," said Redgauntlet.

Sir Richard Glendale then took up the question, as one whose authority and experience gave him right to speak with much weight.

"We have no leisure for hesitation," he said; "it is full time that we decide what course we are to hold. I feel as much as you, Mr. Redgauntlet, the delicacy of capitulating with our Sovereign in his present condition. But I must also think of the total ruin of the cause, the confiscation and bloodshed which will take place among his adherents, and all through the infatuation with which he adheres to a woman who is the pensionary of the present minister, as she was for years Sir Robert Walpole's. Let his Majesty send her back to the continent, and the sword on which I now lay my hand shall instantly be unsheathed, and, I trust, many hundred others at the same moment."

The other persons present testified their unanimous acquiescence in what Sir Richard Glendale had said.

"I see you have taken your resolutions, gentlemen," said Redgauntlet; "unwisely I think, because I believe that, by softer and more generous proceedings, you would have been more likely to carry a point which I think as desirable as you do. But what is to be done if Charles should refuse, with the inflexibility of his grandfather, to comply with this request of yours? Do you mean to abandon him to his fate?"

"God forbid!" said Sir Richard, hastily; "and God forgive you, Mr. Redgauntlet, for breathing such a thought. No! I for one will, with all duty and humility, see him safe back to his vessel, and defend him with my life against whosoever shall assail him. But when I have seen his sails spread, my next act will be to secure, if I can, my own safety, by retiring to my house; or, if I find our engagement, as is too probable, has taken wind, by surrendering myself to the next Justice of Peace, and giving security that hereafter I shall live quiet, and submit to the ruling powers."

Again the rest of the persons present intimated their agreement in opinion with the speaker.

"Well, gentlemen," said Redgauntlet, "it is not for me to oppose the opinion of every one; and I must do you the justice to say, that the King has, in the present instance, neglected a condition of your agreement which was laid before him in very distinct terms. The question now is, who is to acquaint him with the result of this conference; for I presume you would not wait on him in a body to make the proposal, that he should dismiss a person from his family as the price of your allegiance."

"I think Mr. Redgauntlet should make the explanation," said Lord ——. "As he has, doubtless, done justice to our remonstrances by communicating them to the King, no one can, with such propriety and force, state the natural and inevitable consequence of their being neglected."

"Now, I think," said Redgauntlet, "that those who make the objection should state it, for I am confident the King will hardly believe, on less authority than that of the heir of the loyal House of B——, that he is the first to seek an evasion of his pledge to join him."

"An evasion, sir!" repeated Lord ——, fiercely. "I have borne too much from you already, and this I will not endure. Favour me with your company to the downs."

Redgauntlet laughed scornfully, and was about to follow the fiery young man, when Sir Richard again interposed. "Are we to exhibit," he said

" the last symptoms of the dissolution of our party, by turning our swords against each other ?—Be patient, Lord ——; in such conferences as this, much must pass unquestioned which might brook challenge elsewhere. There is a privilege of party as of parliament—men cannot, in emergency, stand upon picking phrases.—Gentlemen, if you will extend your confidence in me so far, I will wait upon his Majesty, and I hope my Lord —— and Mr. Redgauntlet will accompany me. I trust the explanation of this unpleasant matter will prove entirely satisfactory, and that we shall find ourselves at liberty to render our homage to our Sovereign without reserve, when I for one will be the first to peril all in his just quarrel."

Redgauntlet at once stepped forward. " My lord," he said, " if my zeal made me say anything in the slightest degree offensive, I wish it unsaid, and ask your pardon. A gentleman can do no more."

" I could not have asked Mr. Redgauntlet to do so much," said the young nobleman, willingly accepting the hand which Redgauntlet offered. " I know no man living from whom I could take so much reproof without a sense of degradation, as from himself."

" Let me then hope, my lord, that you will go with Sir Richard and me to the presence. Your warm blood will heat our zeal—our colder resolves will temper yours."

The young lord smiled, and shook his head. " Alas! Mr. Redgauntlet," he said, " I am ashamed to say, that in zeal you surpass us all. But I will not refuse this mission, provided you will permit Sir Arthur, your nephew, also to accompany us."

" My nephew?" said Redgauntlet, and seemed to hesitate, then added, " Most certainly.—I trust," he said, looking at Darsie, " he will bring to his Prince's presence such sentiments as fit the occasion."

It seemed however to Darsie, that his uncle would rather have left him behind, had he not feared that he might in that case have been influenced by, or might perhaps himself influence, the unresolved confederates with whom he must have associated during his absence.

" I will go," said Redgauntlet, " and request admission."

In a moment after he returned, and without speaking, motioned for the young nobleman to advance. He did so, followed by Sir Richard Glendale and Darsie, Redgauntlet himself bringing up the rear. A short passage, and a few steps, brought them to the door of the temporary presence-chamber, in which the Royal Wanderer was to receive their homage. It was the upper loft of one of those cottages which made additions to the old inn, poorly furnished, dusty, and in disorder; for rash as the enterprise might be considered, they had been still careful not to draw the attention of strangers by any particular attentions to the personal accommodation of the Prince. He was seated, when the deputies, as they might be termed, of his remaining adherents entered; and as he rose, and came forward and bowed, in acceptance of their salutation, it was with a dignified courtesy which at once supplied whatever was deficient in external pomp, and converted the wretched garret into a saloon worthy of the occasion.

It is needless to add, that he was the same personage already introduced in the character of Father Buonaventure, by which name he was distinguished at Fairladies. His dress was not different from what he then wore, excepting that he had a loose riding-coat of camlet, under which he carried an efficient cut-and-thrust sword, instead of his walking rapier, and also a pair of pistols.

Redgauntlet presented to him successively the young Lord ——, and his kinsman, Sir Arthur Darsie Redgauntlet, who trembled as, bowing and kissing his hand, he found himself surprised into what might be construed an act of high treason, which yet he saw no safe means to avoid.

Sir Richard Glendale seemed personally known to Charles Edward, who received him with a mixture of dignity and affection, and seemed to sympathize with the tears which rushed into that gentleman's eyes as he bade his Majesty welcome to his native kingdom.

"Yes, my good Sir Richard," said the unfortunate Prince in a tone melancholy, yet resolved, "Charles Edward is with his faithful friends once more —not, perhaps, with his former gay hopes which undervalued danger, but with the same determined contempt of the worst which can befall him, in claiming his own rights and those of his country."

"I rejoice, sire—and yet, alas! I must also grieve, to see you once more on the British shores," said Sir Richard Glendale, and stopped short— a tumult of contradictory feelings preventing his farther utterance.

"It is the call of my faithful and suffering people which alone could have induced me to take once more the sword in my hand. For my own part, Sir Richard, when I have reflected how many of my loyal and devoted friends perished by the sword and by proscription, or died indigent and neglected in a foreign land, I have often sworn that no view to my personal aggrandizement should again induce me to agitate a title which has cost my followers so dear. But since so many men of worth and honour conceive the cause of England and Scotland to be linked with that of Charles Stewart, I must follow their brave example, and, laying aside all other considerations, once more stand forward as their deliverer. I am, however, come hither upon your invitation; and as you are so completely acquainted with circumstances to which my absence must necessarily have rendered me a stranger, I must be a mere tool in the hands of my friends. I know well I never can refer myself implicitly to more loyal hearts or wiser heads, than Herries Redgauntlet, and Sir Richard Glendale. Give me your advice, then, how we are to proceed, and decide upon the fate of Charles Edward."

Redgauntlet looked at Sir Richard, as if to say, "Can you press any additional or unpleasant condition at a moment like this?" And the other shook his head and looked down, as if his resolution was unaltered, and yet as feeling all the delicacy of the situation.

There was a silence, which was broken by the unfortunate representative of an unhappy dynasty, with some appearance of irritation. "This is strange, gentlemen," he said; "you have sent for me from the bosom of my family, to head an adventure of doubt and danger; and when I come, your own minds seem to be still irresolute. I had not expected this on the part of two such men."

"For me, sire," said Redgauntlet, "the steel of my sword is not truer than the temper of my mind."

"My Lord ——'s and mine are equally so," said Sir Richard; "but you had in charge, Mr. Redgauntlet, to convey our request to his Majesty, coupled with certain conditions."

"And I discharged my duty to his Majesty and to you," said Redgauntlet.

"I looked at no condition, gentlemen," said their King, with dignity, "save that which called me here to assert my rights in person. *That* I have fulfilled at no common risk. Here I stand to keep my word, and I expect of you to be true to yours."

"There was, or should have been, something more than that in our proposal, please your Majesty," said Sir Richard. "There was a condition annexed to it."

"I saw it not," said Charles, interrupting him. "Out of tenderness towards the noble hearts of whom I think so highly, I would neither see nor read any thing which could lessen them in my love and my esteem. Conditions can have no part betwixt Prince and subject."

"Sire," said Redgauntlet, kneeling on one knee, "I see from Sir Richard's countenance he deems it my fault that your Majesty seems ignorant of what your subjects desired that I should communicate to your Majesty. For Heaven's sake! for the sake of all my past services and sufferings, leave not such a stain upon my honour! The note, Number D., of which this is a copy, referred to the painful subject to which Sir Richard again directs your attention."

"You press upon me, gentlemen," said the Prince, colouring highly, " recollections, which, as I hold them most alien to your character, I would willingly have banished from my memory. I did not suppose that my loyal subjects would think so poorly of me, as to use my depressed circumstances as a reason for forcing themselves into my domestic privacies, and stipulating arrangements with their King regarding matters, in which the meanest hinds claim the privilege of thinking for themselves. In affairs of state and public policy, I will ever be guided, as becomes a prince, by the advice of my wisest counsellors; in those which regard my private affections, and my domestic arrangements, I claim the same freedom of will which I allow to all my subjects, and without which a crown were less worth wearing than a beggar's bonnet."

"May it please your Majesty," said Sir Richard Glendale, " I see it must be my lot to speak unwilling truths; but believe me, I do so with as much profound respect as deep regret. It is true, we have called you to head a mighty undertaking, and that your Majesty, preferring honour to safety, and the love of your country to your own ease, has condescended to become our leader. But we also pointed out as a necessary and indispensable preparatory step to the achievement of our purpose — and, I must say, as a positive condition of our engaging in it — that an individual, supposed, — I presume not to guess how truly, — to have your Majesty's more intimate confidence, and believed, I will not say on absolute proof, but upon the most pregnant suspicion, to be capable of betraying that confidence to the Elector of Hanover, should be removed from your royal household and society."

"This is too insolent, Sir Richard !" said Charles Edward. "Have you inveigled me into your power to bait me in this unseemly manner ? — And you, Redgauntlet, why did you suffer matters to come to such a point as this, without making me more distinctly aware what insults were to be practised on me ?"

"My gracious Prince," said Redgauntlet, " I am so far to blame in this, that I did not think so slight an impediment as that of a woman's society could have really interrupted an undertaking of this magnitude. I am a plain man, Sire, and speak but bluntly; I could not have dreamt but what, within the first five minutes of this interview, either Sir Richard and his friends would have ceased to insist upon a condition so ungrateful to your Majesty, or that your Majesty would have sacrificed this unhappy attachment to the sound advice, or even to the over-anxious suspicions, of so many faithful subjects. I saw no entanglement in such a difficulty, which on either side might not have been broken through like a cobweb."

"You were mistaken, sir," said Charles Edward, " entirely mistaken—as much so as you are at this moment, when you think in your heart my refusal to comply with this insolent proposition is dictated by a childish and romantic passion for an individual. I tell you, sir, I could part with that person to-morrow, without an instant's regret—that I have had thoughts of dismissing her from my court, for reasons known to myself; but that I will never betray my rights as a sovereign and a man, by taking this step to secure the favour of any one, or to purchase that allegiance which, if you owe it to me at all, is due to me as my birthright."

"I am sorry for this," said Redgauntlet; " I hope both your Majesty and Sir Richard will reconsider your resolutions, or forbear this discussion, in a conjuncture so pressing. I trust your Majesty will recollect that you are on hostile ground; that our preparations cannot have so far escaped notice as to permit us now with safety to retreat from our purpose; insomuch, that it is with the deepest anxiety of heart I foresee even danger to your own royal person, unless you can generously give your subjects the satisfaction, which Sir Richard seems to think they are obstinate in demanding."

"And deep indeed your anxiety ought to be," said the Prince. "Is it in these circumstances of personal danger in which you expect to overcome a resolution, which is founded on a sense of what is due to me as a man or a prince? If the axe and scaffold were ready before the windows of Whitehall, I would rather tread the same path with my great-grandfather, than concede the slightest point in which my honour is concerned."

He spoke these words with a determined accent, and looked around him on the company, all of whom (excepting Darsie, who saw, he thought, a fair period to a most perilous enterprise) seemed in deep anxiety and confusion. At length, Sir Richard spoke in a solemn and melancholy tone.

"If the safety," he said, "of poor Richard Glendale were alone concerned in this matter, I have never valued my life enough to weigh it against the slightest point of your Majesty's service. But I am only a messenger—a commissioner, who must execute my trust, and upon whom a thousand voices will cry, Curse and wo, if I do it not with fidelity. All of your adherents, even Redgauntlet himself, see certain ruin to this enterprise—the greatest danger to your Majesty's person—the utter destruction of all your party and friends, if they insist not on the point, which, unfortunately, your Majesty is so unwilling to concede. I speak it with a heart full of anguish—with a tongue unable to utter my emotions—but it must be spoken—the fatal truth—that if your royal goodness cannot yield to us a boon which we hold necessary to our security and your own, your Majesty with one word disarms ten thousand men, ready to draw their swords in your behalf; or, to speak yet more plainly, you annihilate even the semblance of a royal party in Great Britain."

"And why do you not add," said the Prince, scornfully, "that the men who have been ready to assume arms in my behalf, will atone for their treason to the Elector, by delivering me up to the fate for which so many proclamations have destined me? Carry my head to St. James's, gentlemen; you will do a more acceptable and a more honourable action, than, having inveigled me into a situation which places me so completely in your power, to dishonour yourselves by propositions which dishonour me."

"My God, sire!" exclaimed Sir Richard, clasping his hands together, in impatience, "of what great and inexpiable crime can your Majesty's ancestors have been guilty, that they have been punished by the infliction of judicial blindness on their whole generation!—Come, my Lord——, we must to our friends."

"By your leave, Sir Richard," said the young nobleman, "not till we have learned what measures can be taken for his Majesty's personal safety."

"Care not for me, young man," said Charles Edward; "when I was in the society of Highland robbers and cattle-drovers, I was safer than I now hold myself among the representatives of the best blood in England.—Farewell, gentlemen—I will shift for myself."

"This must never be," said Redgauntlet. "Let me that brought you to the point of danger, at least provide for your safe retreat."

So saying, he hastily left the apartment, followed by his nephew. The Wanderer, averting his eyes from Lord —— and Sir Richard Glendale, threw himself into a seat at the upper end of the apartment, while they, in much anxiety, stood together, at a distance from him, and conversed in whispers.

Chapter the Twenty-Third.

NARRATIVE CONTINUED.

WHEN Redgauntlet left the room, in haste and discomposure, the first person he met on the stair, and indeed so close by the door of the apartment that Darsie thought he must have been listening there, was his attendant Nixon.

"What the devil do you here?" he said, abruptly and sternly.

"I wait your orders," said Nixon. "I hope all's right!—excuse my zeal."

"All is wrong, sir—Where is the seafaring fellow—Ewart—what do you call him?"

"Nanty Ewart, sir—I will carry your commands," said Nixon.

"I will deliver them myself to him," said Redgauntlet; "call him hither."

"But should your honour leave the presence?" said Nixon, still lingering.

"'Sdeath, sir, do you prate to me?" said Redgauntlet, bending his brows. "I, sir, transact my own business; you, I am told, act by a ragged deputy."

Without farther answer, Nixon departed, rather disconcerted, as it seemed to Darsie.

"That dog turns insolent and lazy," said Redgauntlet; "but I must bear with him for a while."

A moment after, Nixon returned with Ewart.

"Is this the smuggling fellow?" demanded Redgauntlet.

Nixon nodded.

"Is he sober now?—he was brawling anon."

"Sober enough for business," said Nixon.

"Well then, hark ye, Ewart—man your boat with your best hands, and have her by the pier—get your other fellows on board the brig—if you have any cargo left, throw it overboard; it shall be all paid, five times over—and be ready for a start to Wales or the Hebrides, or perhaps for Sweden or Norway."

Ewart answered sullenly enough, "Ay, ay, sir."

"Go with him, Nixon," said Redgauntlet, forcing himself to speak with some appearance of cordiality to the servant with whom he was offended; "see he does his duty."

Ewart left the house sullenly, followed by Nixon. The sailor was just in that species of drunken humour which made him jealous, passionate, and troublesome, without showing any other disorder than that of irritability. As he walked towards the beach he kept muttering to himself, but in such a tone that his companion lost not a word, "Smuggling fellow—Ay, smuggler—and, start your cargo into the sea—and be ready to start for the Hebrides, or Sweden—or the devil, I suppose. Well, and what if I said in answer—Rebel, Jacobite—traitor—I'll make you and your d—d confederates walk the plank—I have seen better men do it—half-a-score of a morning—when I was across the Line."

"D—d unhandsome terms those Redgauntlet used to you, brother," said Nixon.

"Which do you mean?" said Ewart, starting, and recollecting himself. "I have been at my old trade of thinking aloud, have I?"

"No matter," answered Nixon, "none but a friend heard you. You cannot have forgotten how Redgauntlet disarmed you this morning."

"Why, I would bear no malice about that—only he is so cursedly high and saucy," said Ewart.

x

"And then," said Nixon, "I know you for a true-hearted Protestant."

"That I am, by G——," said Ewart. "No, the Spaniards could never get my religion from me."

"And a friend to King George, and the Hanover line of succession," said Nixon, still walking and speaking very slow.

"You may swear I am, excepting in the way of business, as Turnpenny says. I like King George, but I can't afford to pay duties."

"You are outlawed, I believe," said Nixon.

"Am I?—faith, I believe I am," said Ewart. "I wish I were *inlawed* again with all my heart—But come along, we must get all ready for our peremptory gentleman, I suppose."

"I will teach you a better trick," said Nixon. "There is a bloody pack of rebels yonder."

"Ay, we all know that," said the smuggler; "but the snowball's melting, I think."

"There is some one yonder, whose head is worth—thirty—thousand—pounds—of sterling money," said Nixon, pausing between each word, as if to enforce the magnificence of the sum.

"And what of that?" said Ewart, quickly.

"Only that instead of lying by the pier with your men on their oars, if you will just carry your boat on board just now, and take no notice of any signal from the shore, by G—d, Nanty Ewart, I will make a man of you for life!"

"Oh ho! then the Jacobite gentry are not so safe as they think themselves?" said Nanty.

"In an hour or two," replied Nixon, "they will be made safer in Carlisle Castle."

"The devil they will!" said Ewart; "and you have been the informer, I suppose?"

"Yes; I have been ill paid for my service among the Redgauntlets—have scarce got dog's wages—and been treated worse than ever dog was used. I have the old fox and his cubs in the same trap now, Nanty; and we'll see how a certain young lady will look then. You see I am frank with you, Nanty."

"And I will be as frank with you," said the smuggler. "You are a d—d old scoundrel—traitor to the man whose bread you eat! Me help to betray poor devils, that have been so often betrayed myself!—Not if they were a hundred Popes, Devils, and Pretenders. I will back and tell them their danger—they are part of cargo—regularly invoiced—put under my charge by the owners—I'll back——"

"You are not stark mad?" said Nixon, who now saw he had miscalculated in supposing Nanty's wild ideas of honour and fidelity could be shaken even by resentment, or by his Protestant partialities. "You shall not go back—it is all a joke."

"I'll back to Redgauntlet, and see whether it is a joke he will laugh at."

"My life is lost if you do," said Nixon—"hear reason."

They were in a clump or cluster of tall furze at the moment they were speaking, about half way between the pier and the house, but not in a direct line, from which Nixon, whose object it was to gain time, had induced Ewart to diverge insensibly.

He now saw the necessity of taking a desperate resolution. "Hear reason," he said; and added, as Nanty still endeavoured to pass him, "Or else hear this!" discharging a pocket-pistol into the unfortunate man's body.

Nanty staggered, but kept his feet. "It has cut my back-bone asunder," he said; "you have done me the last good office, and I will not die ungrateful."

As he uttered the last words, he collected his remaining strength, stood firm for an instant, drew his hanger, and, fetching a stroke with both hands, cut Cristal Nixon down. The blow, struck with all the energy of a desperate and dying man, exhibited a force to which Ewart's exhausted frame might have seemed inadequate; — it cleft the hat which the wretch wore, though secured by a plate of iron within the lining, bit deep into his skull, and there left a fragment of the weapon, which was broke by the fury of the blow.

One of the seamen of the lugger, who strolled up, attracted by the firing of the pistol, though, being a small one, the report was very trifling, found both the unfortunate men stark dead. Alarmed at what he saw, which he conceived to have been the consequence of some unsuccessful engagement betwixt his late commander and a revenue officer, (for Nixon chanced not to be personally known to him,) the sailor hastened back to the boat, in order to apprize his comrades of Nanty's fate, and to advise them to take off themselves and the vessel.

Meantime Redgauntlet, having, as we have seen, despatched Nixon for the purpose of securing a retreat for the unfortunate Charles, in case of extremity, returned to the apartment where he had left the Wanderer. He now found him alone.

"Sir Richard Glendale," said the unfortunate Prince, "with his young friend, has gone to consult their adherents now in the house. Redgauntlet, my friend, I will not blame you for the circumstances in which I find myself, though I am at once placed in danger, and rendered contemptible. But you ought to have stated to me more strongly the weight which these gentlemen attached to their insolent proposition. You should have told me that no compromise would have any effect — that they desire not a Prince to govern them, but one, on the contrary, over whom they were to exercise restraint on all occasions, from the highest affairs of the state, down to the most intimate and private concerns of his own privacy, which the most ordinary men desire to keep secret and sacred from interference."

"God knows," said Redgauntlet, in much agitation, "I acted for the best when I pressed your Majesty to come hither — I never thought that your Majesty, at such a crisis, would have scrupled, when a kingdom was in view, to sacrifice an attachment, which ——"

"Peace, sir!" said Charles; "it is not for you to estimate my feelings upon such a subject."

Redgauntlet coloured high, and bowed profoundly. "At least," he resumed, "I hoped that some middle way might be found, and it shall — and must — Come with me, nephew. We will to these gentlemen, and I am confident I will bring back heart-stirring tidings."

"I will do much to comply with them, Redgauntlet. I am loath, having again set my foot on British land, to quit it without a blow for my right. But this which they demand of me is a degradation, and compliance is impossible."

Redgauntlet, followed by his nephew, the unwilling spectator of this extraordinary scene, left once more the apartment of the adventurous Wanderer, and was met on the top of the stairs by Joe Crackenthorp. "Where are the other gentlemen?" he said.

"Yonder, in the west barrack," answered Joe; "but, Master Ingoldsby," — that was the name by which Redgauntlet was most generally known in Cumberland, — "I wish to say to you that I must put yonder folk together in one room."

"What folk?" said Redgauntlet, impatiently.

"Why, them prisoner stranger folk, as you bid Cristal Nixon look after. Lord love you! this is a large house enow, but we cannot have separate lock-ups for folk, as they have in Newgate or in Bedlam. Yonder's a mad beggar, that is to be a great man when he wins a lawsuit, Lord help him! — Yonder's a Quaker and a lawyer charged with a riot; and, ecod, I must make one key and one lock keep them, for we are chokeful, and you have sent off old Nixon, that could have given one some help in this confusion. Besides, they take up every one a room, and call for noughts on earth, — excepting the old man, who calls lustily enough, — but he has not a penny to pay shot."

"Do as thou wilt with them," said Redgauntlet, who had listened impatiently to his statement; "so thou dost but keep them from getting out and making some alarm in the country, I care not."

"A Quaker and a lawyer!" said Darsie. "This must be Fairford and Geddes. — Uncle, I must request of you——"

"Nay, nephew," interrupted Redgauntlet, "this is no time for asking questions. You shall yourself decide upon their fate in the course of an hour — no harm whatever is designed them."

So saying, he hurried towards the place where the Jacobite gentlemen were holding their council, and Darsie followed him, in the hope that the obstacle which had arisen to the prosecution of their desperate adventure would prove unsurmountable, and spare him the necessity of a dangerous and violent rupture with his uncle. The discussions among them were very eager; the more daring part of the conspirators, who had little but life to lose, being desirous to proceed at all hazards; while the others, whom a sense of honour and a hesitation to disavow long-cherished principles had brought forward, were perhaps not ill satisfied to have a fair apology for declining an adventure, into which they had entered with more of reluctance than zeal.

Meanwhile Joe Crackenthorp, availing himself of the hasty permission attained from Redgauntlet, proceeded to assemble in one apartment those whose safe custody had been thought necessary; and, without much considering the propriety of the matter, he selected for the common place of confinement, the room which Lilias had, since her brother's departure, occupied alone. It had a strong lock, and was double-hinged, which probably led to the preference assigned to it as a place of security.

Into this, Joe, with little ceremony, and a good deal of noise, introduced the Quaker and Fairford; the first descanting on the immorality, the other on the illegality, of his proceedings; and he turned a deaf ear both to the one and the other. Next he pushed in, almost in headlong fashion, the unfortunate litigant, who having made some resistance at the threshold, had received a violent thrust in consequence, came rushing forward, like a ram in the act of charging, with such impetus, as must have carried him to the top of the room, and struck the cocked hat which sat perched on the top of his tow wig against Miss Redgauntlet's person, had not the honest Quaker interrupted his career by seizing him by the collar, and bringing him to a stand. "Friend," said he, with the real good-breeding which so often subsists independently of ceremony, "thou art no company for that young person; she is, thou seest, frightened at our being so suddenly thrust in hither; and although that be no fault of ours, yet it will become us to behave civilly towards her. Wherefore come thou with me to this window, and I will tell thee what it concerns thee to know."

"And what for should I no speak to the leddy, friend?" said Peter, who was now about half seas over. "I have spoke to leddies before now, man — What for should she be frightened at me? — I am nae bogle, I ween. — What are ye pooin' me that gate for? — Ye will rive my coat, and I will have a good action for having myself made *sartum atque tectum* at your expenses."

Notwithstanding this threat, Mr. Geddes, whose muscles were as strong as his judgment was sound and his temper sedate, led Poor Peter, under the sense of a control against which he could not struggle, to the farther corner of the apartment, where, placing him, whether he would or no, in a chair, he sat down beside him, and effectually prevented his annoying the young lady, upon whom he had seemed bent upon conferring the delights of his society.

If Peter had immediately recognised his counsel learned in the law, it is probable that not even the benevolent efforts of a Quaker could have kept him in a state of restraint; but Fairford's back was turned towards his client, whose optics, besides being somewhat dazzled with ale and brandy, were speedily engaged in contemplating a half-crown which Joshua held between his finger and his thumb, saying, at the same time, "Friend, thou art indignant and improvident. This will, well employed, procure thee sustentation of nature for more than a single day; and I will bestow it on thee if thou wilt sit here and keep me company: for neither thou nor I, friend, are fit company for ladies."

"Speak for yourself, friend," said Peter, scornfully; "I was aye kend to be agreeable to the fair sex; and when I was in business I served the ladies wi' anither sort of decorum than Plainstanes, the d—d awkward scoundrel! It was one of the articles of dittay between us."

"Well, but, friend," said the Quaker, who observed that the young lady still seemed to fear Peter's intrusion, "I wish to hear thee speak about this great lawsuit of thine, which has been matter of such celebrity."

"Celebrity!—Ye may swear that," said Peter, for the string was touched to which his crazy imagination always vibrated. "And I dinna wonder that folk that judge things by their outward grandeur, should think me something worth their envying. It's very true that it is grandeur upon earth to hear ane's name thundered out along the long-arched roof of the Outer-House,—' Poor Peter Peebles against Plainstanes *et per contra*;' a' the best lawyers in the house fleeing like eagles to the prey; some because they are in the cause, and some because they want to be thought engaged (for there are tricks in other trades by selling muslins)—to see the reporters mending their pens to take down the debate — the Lords themselves pooin' in their chairs, like folk sitting down to a gude dinner, and crying on the clerks for parts and pendicils of the process, who, puir bodies, can do little mair than cry on their closet-keepers to help them. To see a' this," continued Peter, in a tone of sustained rapture, "and to ken that naething will be said or dune amang a' the grand folk, for maybe the feck of three hours, saving what concerns you and your business — Oh, man, nae wonder that ye judge this to be earthly glory! — And yet, neighbour, as I was saying, there be unco drawbacks — I whiles think of my bit house, where dinner, and supper, and breakfast, used to come without the crying for, just as if fairies had brought it — and the gude bed at e'en — and the needfu' penny in the pouch. — And then to see a' ane's warldly substance capering in the air in a pair of weigh-bauks, now up, now down, as the breath of judge or counsel inclines it for pursuer or defender, — troth, man, there are times I rue having ever begun the plea wark, though, maybe, when ye consider the renown and credit I have by it, ye will hardly believe what I am saying."

"Indeed, friend," said Joshua, with a sigh, "I am glad thou hast found anything in the legal contention which compensates thee for poverty and hunger; but I believe, were other human objects of ambition looked upon as closely, their advantages would be found as chimerical as those attending thy protracted litigation."

"But never mind, friend," said Peter, "I'll tell you the exact state of the conjunct processes, and make you sensible that I can bring mysell round with a wet finger, now I have my finger and my thumb on this loup-the-dike loon, the lad Fairford."

Alan Fairford was in the act of speaking to the masked lady, (for Miss Redgauntlet had retained her riding vizard,) endeavouring to assure her, as he perceived her anxiety, of such protection as he could afford, when his own name, pronounced in a loud tone, attracted his attention. He looked round, and seeing Peter Peebles, as hastily turned to avoid his notice, in which he succeeded, so earnest was Peter upon his colloquy with one of the most respectable auditors whose attention he had ever been able to engage. And by this little motion, momentary as it was, Alan gained an unexpected advantage; for while he looked round, Miss Lilias, I could never ascertain why, took the moment to adjust her mask, and did it so awkwardly, that when her companion again turned his head, he recognized as much of her features as authorized him to address her as his fair client, and to press his offers of protection and assistance with the boldness of a former acquaintance.

Lilias Redgauntlet withdrew the mask from her crimsoned cheek. "Mr. Fairford," she said, in a voice almost inaudible, "you have the character of a young gentleman of sense and generosity; but we have already met in one situation which you must think singular; and I must be exposed to misconstruction, at least, for my forwardness, were it not in a cause in which my dearest affections were concerned."

"Any interest in my beloved friend Darsie Latimer," said Fairford, stepping a little back, and putting a marked restraint upon his former advances, "gives me a double right to be useful to ——" He stopped short.

"To his sister, your goodness would say," answered Lilias.

"His sister, madam!" replied Alan, in the extremity of astonishment— "Sister, I presume, in affection only?"

"No, sir; my dear brother Darsie and I are connected by the bonds of actual relationship; and I am not sorry to be the first to tell this to the friend he most values."

Fairford's first thought was on the violent passion which Darsie had expressed towards the fair unknown. "Good God!" he exclaimed, "how did he bear the discovery?"

"With resignation, I hope," said Lilias, smiling. "A more accomplished sister he might easily have come by, but scarcely could have found one who could love him more than I do."

"I meant—I only meant to say," said the young counsellor, his presence of mind failing him for an instant—"that is, I meant to ask where Darsie Latimer is at this moment."

"In this very house, and under the guardianship of his uncle, whom I believe you knew as a visitor of your father, under the name of Mr. Herries of Birrenswork."

"Let me hasten to him," said Fairford; "I have sought him through difficulties and dangers—I must see him instantly."

"You forget you are a prisoner," said the young lady.

"True—true; but I cannot be long detained—the cause alleged is too ridiculous."

"Alas!" said Lilias, "our fate—my brother's and mine, at least—must turn on the deliberations perhaps of less than an hour. — For you, sir, I believe and apprehend nothing but some restraint; my uncle is neither cruel nor unjust, though few will go farther in the cause which he has adopted."

"Which is that of the Pretend—"

"For God's sake speak lower!" said Lilias, approaching her hand, as if to stop him. "The word may cost you your life. You do not know—indeed you do not—the terrors of the situation in which we at present stand, and in which I fear you also are involved by your friendship for my brother."

"I do not indeed know the particulars of our situation," said Fairford; "but, be the danger what it may, I shall not grudge my share of it for the sake of my friend; or," he added, with more timidity, "of my friend's sister. Let me hope," he said, "my dear Miss Latimer, that my presence may be of some use to you; and that it may be so, let me entreat a share of your confidence, which I am conscious I have otherwise no right to ask."

He led her, as he spoke, towards the recess of the farther window of the room, and observing to her that, unhappily, he was particularly exposed to interruption from the mad old man whose entrance had alarmed her, he disposed of Darsie Latimer's riding skirt, which had been left in the apartment, over the back of two chairs, forming thus a sort of screen, behind which he ensconced himself with the maiden of the green mantle; feeling at the moment, that the danger in which he was placed was almost compensated by the intelligence which permitted those feelings towards her to revive, which justice to his friend had induced him to stifle in the birth.

The relative situation of adviser and advised, of protector and protected, is so peculiarly suited to the respective condition of man and woman, that great progress towards intimacy is often made in very short space; for the circumstances call for confidence on the part of the gentleman, and forbid coyness on that of the lady, so that the usual barriers against easy intercourse are at once thrown down.

Under these circumstances, securing themselves as far as possible from observation, conversing in whispers, and seated in a corner, where they were brought into so close contact that their faces nearly touched each other, Fairford heard from Lilias Redgauntlet the history of her family, particularly of her uncle; his views upon her brother, and the agony which she felt, lest at that very moment he might succeed in engaging Darsie in some desperate scheme, fatal to his fortune, and perhaps to his life.

Alan Fairford's acute understanding instantly connected what he had heard with the circumstances he had witnessed at Fairladies. His first thought was, to attempt, at all risks, his instant escape, and procure assistance powerful enough to crush, in the very cradle, a conspiracy of such a determined character. This he did not consider as difficult; for, though the door was guarded on the outside, the window, which was not above ten feet from the ground, was open for escape, the common on which it looked was unenclosed, and profusely covered with furze. There would, he thought, be little difficulty in effecting his liberty, and in concealing his course after he had gained it.

But Lilias exclaimed against this scheme. Her uncle, she said, was a man, who, in his moments of enthusiasm, knew neither remorse nor fear. He was capable of visiting upon Darsie any injury which he might conceive Fairford had rendered him—he was her near kinsman also, and not an unkind one, and she deprecated any effort, even in her brother's favour, by which his life must be exposed to danger. Fairford himself remembered Father Buonaventure, and made little question but that he was one of the sons of the old Chevalier de Saint George; and with feelings which, although contradictory of his public duty, can hardly be much censured, his heart recoiled from being the agent by whom the last scion of such a long line of Scottish Princes should be rooted up. He then thought of obtaining an audience, if possible, of this devoted person, and explaining to him the utter hopelessness of his undertaking, which he judged it likely that the ardour of his partisans might have concealed from him. But he relinquished this design as soon as formed. He had no doubt, that any light which he could throw on the state of the country, would come too late to be serviceable to one who was always reported to have his own full share of the hereditary obstinacy which had cost his ancestors so dear, and who, in drawing the sword, must have thrown from him the scabbard.

Lilias suggested the advice which, of all others, seemed most suited to the occasion, that, yielding, namely, to the circumstances of their situation, they should watch carefully when Darsie should obtain any degree of freedom, and endeavour to open a communication with him, in which case their joint flight might be effected, and without endangering the safety of any one.

Their youthful deliberation had nearly fixed in this point, when Fairford, who was listening to the low sweet whispering tones of Lilias Redgauntlet, rendered yet more interesting by some slight touch of foreign accent, was startled by a heavy hand which descended with full weight on his shoulder, while the discordant voice of Peter Peebles, who had at length broke loose from the well-meaning Quaker, exclaimed in the ear of his truant counsel—"Aha, lad! I think ye are catched—An' so ye are turned chamber-counsel, are ye?—And ye have drawn up wi' clients in scarfs and hoods? But bide a wee, billie, and see if I dinna sort ye when my petition and complaint comes to be discussed, with or without answers, under certification."

Alan Fairford had never more difficulty in his life to subdue a first emotion, than he had to refrain from knocking down the crazy blockhead who had broken in upon him at such a moment. But the length of Peter's address gave him time, fortunately perhaps for both parties, to reflect on the extreme irregularity of such a proceeding. He stood silent, however, with vexation, while Peter went on.

"Weel, my bonnie man, I see ye are thinking shame o' yoursell, and nae great wonder. Ye maun leave this quean—the like of her is ower light company for you. I have heard honest Mr. Pest say, that the gown grees ill wi' the petticoat. But come awa hame to your puir father, and I'll take care of you the haill gate, and keep you company, and deil a word we will speak about, but just the state of the conjoined processes of the great cause of Poor Peter Peebles against Plainstanes."

"If thou canst endure to hear as much of that suit, friend," said the Quaker, "as I have heard out of mere compassion for thee, I think verily thou wilt soon be at the bottom of the matter, unless it be altogether bottomless."

Fairford shook off, rather indignantly, the large bony hand which Peter had imposed upon his shoulder, and was about to say something peevish, upon so unpleasant and insolent a mode of interruption, when the door opened, a treble voice saying to the sentinel, "I tell you I maun be in, to see if Mr. Nixon's here;" and Little Benjie thrust in his mop-head and keen black eyes. Ere he could withdraw it, Peter Peebles sprang to the door, seized on the boy by the collar, and dragged him forward into the room.

"Let me see it," he said, "ye ne'er-do-weel limb of Satan—I'll gar you satisfy the production, I trow—I'll hae first and second diligence against you, ye deevil's buckie!"

"What dost thou want?" said the Quaker, interfering; "why dost thou frighten the boy, friend Peebles?"

"I gave the bastard a penny to buy me snuff," said the pauper, "and he has rendered no account of his intromissions; but I'll gar him as gude."

So saying, he proceeded forcibly to rifle the pockets of Benjie's ragged jacket, of one or two snares for game, marbles, a half-bitten apple, two stolen eggs, (one of which Peter broke in the eagerness of his research,) and various other unconsidered trifles, which had not the air of being very honestly come by. The little rascal, under this discipline, bit and struggled like a fox-cub, but, like that vermin, uttered neither cry nor complaint, till a note, which Peter tore from his bosom, flew as far as Lilias Redgauntlet, and fell at her feet. It was addressed to C. N.

"It is for the villain Nixon," she said to Alan Fairford; "open it without scruple; that boy is his emissary; we shall now see what the miscreant is driving at."

Little Benjie now gave up all further struggle, and suffered Peebles to take from him, without resistance, a shilling, out of which Peter declared he would pay himself principal and interest, and account for the balance. The boy, whose attention seemed fixed on something very different, only said, "Maister Nixon will murder me!"

Alan Fairford did not hesitate to read the little scrap of paper, on which was written, "All is prepared — keep them in play until I come up — You may depend on your reward.—C. C."

"Alas, my uncle—my poor uncle!" said Lilias; "this is the result of his confidence. Methinks, to give him instant notice of his confidant's treachery, is now the best service we can render all concerned — if they break up their undertaking, as they must now do, Darsie will be at liberty."

In the same breath, they were both at the half-opened door of the room, Fairford entreating to speak with the Father Buonaventure, and Lilias, equally vehemently, requesting a moment's interview with her uncle. While the sentinel hesitated what to do, his attention was called to a loud noise at the door, where a crowd had been assembled in consequence of the appalling cry, that the enemy were upon them, occasioned, as it afterwards proved, by some stragglers having at length discovered the dead bodies of Nanty Ewart and of Nixon.

Amid the confusion occasioned by this alarming incident, the sentinel ceased to attend to his duty; and, accepting Alan Fairford's arm, Lilias found no opposition in penetrating even to the inner apartment, where the principal persons in the enterprise, whose conclave had been disturbed by this alarming incident, were now assembled in great confusion, and had been joined by the Chevalier himself.

"Only a mutiny among these smuggling scoundrels," said Redgauntlet.

"*Only* a mutiny, do you say?" said Sir Richard Glendale; "and the lugger, the last hope of escape for"—he looked towards Charles,—"stands out to sea under a press of sail!"

"Do not concern yourself about me," said the unfortunate Prince; "this is not the worst emergency in which it has been my lot to stand; and if it were, I fear it not. Shift for yourselves, my lords and gentlemen."

"No, never!" said the young Lord ——. "Our only hope now is in an honourable resistance."

"Most true," said Redgauntlet; "let despair renew the union amongst us which accident disturbed. I give my voice for displaying the royal banner instantly, and —— How now!" he concluded, sternly, as Lilias, first soliciting his attention by pulling his cloak, put into his hand the scroll, and added, it was designed for that of Nixon.

Redgauntlet read — and, dropping it on the ground, continued to stare upon the spot where it fell, with raised hands and fixed eyes. Sir Richard Glendale lifted the fatal paper, read it, and saying, "Now all is indeed over," handed it to Maxwell, who said aloud, "Black Colin Campbell, by G—d! I heard he had come post from London last night."

As if in echo to his thoughts, the violin of the blind man was heard, playing with spirit, "The Campbells are coming," a celebrated clan-march.

"The Campbells are coming in earnest," said MacKellar; "they are upon us with the whole battalion from Carlisle."

There was a silence of dismay, and two or three of the company began to drop out of the room.

Lord —— spoke with the generous spirit of a young English nobleman. "If we have been fools, do not let us be cowards. We have one here more precious than us all, and come hither on our warranty — let us save him at least."

"True, most true," answered Sir Richard Glendale. "Let the King be first cared for."

"That shall be my business," said Redgauntlet; "if we have but time to bring back the brig, all will be well—I will instantly despatch a party in a fishing skiff to bring her to."—He gave his commands to two or three of the most active among his followers.—"Let him be once on board," he said, "and there are enough of us to stand to arms and cover his retreat."

"Right, right," said Sir Richard, "and I will look to points which can be made defensible; and the old powder-plot boys could not have made a more desperate resistance than we shall. — Redgauntlet," continued he, "I see some of our friends are looking pale; but methinks your nephew has more mettle in his eye now than when we were in cold deliberation, with danger at a distance."

"It is the way of our house," said Redgauntlet; "our courage ever kindles highest on the losing side. I, too, feel that the catastrophe I have brought on must not be survived by its author. Let me first," he said, addressing Charles, "see your Majesty's sacred person in such safety as can now be provided for it, and then——"

"You may spare all considerations concerning me, gentlemen," again repeated Charles; "yon mountain of Criffel shall fly as soon as I will."

Most threw themselves at his feet with weeping and entreaty; some one or two slunk in confusion from the apartment, and were heard riding off. Unnoticed in such a scene, Darsie, his sister, and Fairford, drew together, and held each other by the hands, as those who, when a vessel is about to founder in the storm, determine to take their chance of life and death together.

Amid this scene of confusion, a gentleman, plainly dressed in a riding-habit, with a black cockade in his hat, but without any arms except a *couteau-de-chasse*, walked into the apartment without ceremony. He was a tall, thin, gentlemanly man, with a look and bearing decidedly military. He had passed through their guards, if in the confusion they now maintained any, without stop or question, and now stood, almost unarmed, among armed men, who nevertheless, gazed on him as on the angel of destruction.

"You look coldly on me, gentlemen," he said. "Sir Richard Glendale —my Lord ——, we were not always such strangers. Ha, Pate-in-Peril, how is it with you? and you, too, Ingoldsby—I must not call you by any other name—why do you receive an old friend so coldly? But you guess my errand."

"And are prepared for it, General," said Redgauntlet; "we are not men to be penned up like sheep for the slaughter."

"Pshaw! you take it too seriously—let me speak but one word with you."

"No words can shake our purpose," said Redgauntlet, "were your whole command, as I suppose is the case, drawn round the house."

"I am certainly not unsupported," said the General; "but if you would hear me——"

"Hear *me*, sir," said the Wanderer, stepping forward; "I suppose I am the mark you aim at—I surrender myself willingly, to save these gentlemen's danger—let this at least avail in their favour."

An exclamation of "Never, never!" broke from the little body of partisans, who threw themselves round the unfortunate Prince, and would have seized or struck down Campbell, had it not been that he remained with his arms folded, and a look, rather indicating impatience because they would not hear him, than the least apprehension of violence at their hand.

At length he obtained a moment's silence. "I do not," he said, "know this gentleman"—(making a profound bow to the unfortunate Prince)—"I do not wish to know him; it is a knowledge which would suit neither of us."

"Our ancestors, nevertheless, have been well acquainted," said Charles, unable to suppress, even at that hour of dread and danger, the painful recollections of fallen royalty.

"In one word, General Campbell," said Redgauntlet, "is it to be peace or war?—You are a man of honour, and we can trust you."

"I thank you, sir," said the General; "and I reply, that the answer to your question rests with yourself. Come, do not be fools, gentlemen; there was perhaps no great harm meant or intended by your gathering together in this obscure corner, for a bear-bait or a cock-fight, or whatever other amusement you have intended, but it was a little imprudent, considering how you stand with government, and it has occasioned some anxiety. Exaggerated accounts of your purpose have been laid before government by the information of a traitor in your own councils; and I was sent down post to take the command of a sufficient number of troops, in case these calumnies should be found to have any real foundation. I have come here, of course, sufficiently supported both with cavalry and infantry, to do whatever might be necessary; but my commands are—and I am sure they agree with my inclination—to make no arrests, nay, to make no farther inquiries of any kind, if this good assembly will consider their own interest so far as to give up their immediate purpose, and return quietly home to their own houses."

"What!—all?" exclaimed Sir Richard Glendale—"all, without exception?"

"ALL, without one single exception," said the General; "such are my orders. If you accept my terms, say so, and make haste; for things may happen to interfere with his Majesty's kind purposes towards you all."

"His Majesty's kind purposes!" said the Wanderer. "Do I hear you aright, sir?"

"I speak the King's very words, from his very lips," replied the General. "'I will,' said his Majesty, 'deserve the confidence of my subjects by reposing my security in the fidelity of the millions who acknowledge my title—in the good sense and prudence of the few who continue, from the errors of education, to disown it.'—His Majesty will not even believe that the most zealous Jacobites who yet remain can nourish a thought of exciting a civil war, which must be fatal to their families and themselves, besides spreading bloodshed and ruin through a peaceful land. He cannot even believe of his kinsman, that he would engage brave and generous, though mistaken men, in an attempt which must ruin all who have escaped former calamities; and he is convinced, that, did curiosity or any other motive lead that person to visit this country, he would soon see it was his wisest course to return to the continent; and his Majesty compassionates his situation too much to offer any obstacle to his doing so."

"Is this real?" said Redgauntlet. "Can you mean this?—Am I—are all, are any of these gentlemen at liberty, without interruption, to embark in yonder brig, which, I see, is now again approaching the shore?"

"You, sir—all—any of the gentlemen present," said the General,—"all whom the vessel can contain, are at liberty to embark uninterrupted by me; but I advise none to go off who have not powerful reasons unconnected with the present meeting, for this will be remembered against no one."

"Then, gentlemen," said Redgauntlet, clasping his hands together as the words burst from him, "the cause is lost for ever!"

General Campbell turned away to the window, as if to avoid hearing what they said. Their consultation was but momentary; for the door of escape which thus opened was as unexpected as the exigence was threatening.

"We have your word of honour for our protection," said Sir Richard Glendale, "if we dissolve our meeting in obedience to your summons?"

"You have, Sir Richard," answered the General.

"And I also have your promise," said Redgauntlet, "that I may go on board yonder vessel, with any friend whom I may choose to accompany me?"

"Not only that, Mr. Ingoldsby—or I will call you Mr. Redgauntlet once more—you may stay in the offing for a tide, until you are joined by any person who may remain at Fairladies. After that, there will be a sloop of war on the station, and I need not say your condition will then become perilous."

"Perilous it should not be, General Campbell," said Redgauntlet, "or more perilous to others than to us, if others thought as I do even in this extremity."

"You forget yourself, my friend," said the unhappy Adventurer; "you forget that the arrival of this gentleman only puts the cope-stone on already adopted resolution to abandon our bull-fight, or by whatever wild name this headlong enterprise may be termed. I bid *you* farewell (bowing to the General,) "my friendly foe—I leave this strand as I landed upon it, alone and to return no more!"

"Not alone," said Redgauntlet, "while there is blood in the veins of my father's son."

"Not alone," said the other gentlemen present, stung with feelings which almost overpowered the better reasons under which they had acted. "We will not disown our principles, or see your person endangered."

"If it be only your purpose to see the gentleman to the beach," said General Campbell, "I will myself go with you. My presence among you, unarmed, and in your power, will be a pledge of my friendly intentions, and will overawe, should such be offered, any interruption on the part of officious persons."

"Be it so," said the Adventurer, with the air of a Prince to a subject, not of one who complied with the request of an enemy too powerful to be resisted.

They left the apartment—they left the house—an unauthenticated and dubious, but appalling, sensation of terror had already spread itself among the inferior retainers, who had so short time before strutted, and bustled, and thronged the doorway and the passages. A report had arisen, of which the origin could not be traced, of troops advancing towards the spot in considerable numbers; and men who, for one reason or other, were most of them amenable to the arm of power, had either shrunk into stables or corners, or fled the place entirely. There was solitude on the landscape excepting the small party which now moved towards the rude pier, where a boat lay manned, agreeably to Redgauntlet's orders previously given.

The last heir of the Stewarts leant on Redgauntlet's arm as they walked towards the beach; for the ground was rough, and he no longer possessed the elasticity of limb and of spirit which had, twenty years before, carried him over many a Highland hill, as light as one of their native deer. His adherents followed, looking on the ground, their feelings struggling against the dictates of their reason.

General Campbell accompanied them with an air of apparent ease and indifference, but watching, at the same time, and no doubt with some anxiety, the changing features of those who acted in this extraordinary scene.

Darsie and his sister naturally followed their uncle, whose violence they no longer feared, while his character attracted their respect, and Alan Fairford attended them from interest in their fate, unnoticed in a party where all were too much occupied with their own thoughts and feelings, as well as with the impending crisis, to attend to his presence.

Half way betwixt the house and the beach, they saw the bodies of Nanty Ewart and Cristal Nixon blackening in the sun.

"That was your informer?" said Redgauntlet, looking back to General Campbell, who only nodded his assent.

"Caitiff wretch!" exclaimed Redgauntlet;—"and yet the name were better bestowed on the fool who could be misled by thee."

"That sound broadsword cut," said the General, "has saved us the shame of rewarding a traitor."

They arrived at the place of embarkation. The Prince stood a moment with folded arms, and looked around him in deep silence. A paper was then slipped into his hands—he looked at it, and said, "I find the two friends I have left at Fairladies are apprized of my destination, and propose to embark from Bowness. I presume this will not be an infringement of the conditions under which you have acted?"

"Certainly not," answered General Campbell; "they shall have all facility to join you."

"I wish, then," said Charles, "only another companion. Redgauntlet, the air of this country is as hostile to you as it is to me. These gentlemen have made their peace, or rather they have done nothing to break it. But you—come you and share my home where chance shall cast it. We shall never see these shores again; but we will talk of them, and of our disconcerted bull-fight."

"I follow you, Sire, through life," said Redgauntlet, "as I would have followed you to death. Permit me one moment."

The Prince then looked round, and seeing the abashed countenances of his other adherents, bent upon the ground, he hastened to say, "Do not think that you, gentlemen, have obliged me less because your zeal was mingled with prudence, entertained, I am sure, more on my own account, and on that of your country, than from selfish apprehensions."

He stepped from one to another, and, amid sobs and bursting tears, received the adieus of the last remnant which had hitherto supported his lofty pretensions, and addressed them individually with accents of tenderness and affection.

The General drew a little aloof, and signed to Redgauntlet to speak with him while this scene proceeded. "It is now all over," he said, "and Jacobite will be henceforward no longer a party name. When you tire of foreign parts, and wish to make your peace, let me know. Your restless zeal alone has impeded your pardon hitherto."

"And now I shall not need it," said Redgauntlet. "I leave England for ever; but I am not displeased that you should hear my family adieus. Nephew, come hither. In presence of General Campbell, I tell you, that though to breed you up in my own political opinions has been for many years my anxious wish, I am now glad that it could not be accomplished. You pass under the service of the reigning Monarch without the necessity of changing your allegiance—a change, however," he added, looking around him, "which sits more easy on honourable men than I could have anticipated; but some wear the badge of their loyalty on their sleeve, and others in the heart. You will, from henceforth, be uncontrolled master of all the property of which forfeiture could not deprive your father—of all that belonged to him—excepting this, his good sword," (laying his hand on the weapon he wore,) "which shall never fight for the House of Hanover; and as my hand will never draw weapon more, I shall sink it forty fathoms deep in the wide ocean. Bless you, young man! If I have dealt harshly with you, forgive me. I had set my whole desires on one point,—God knows, with no selfish purpose; and I am justly punished by this final termination of my views, for having been too little scrupulous in the means by which I pursued them. Niece, farewell, and may God bless you also!"

"No, sir," said Lilias, seizing his hand eagerly. "You have been hitherto my protector,—you are now in sorrow, let me be your attendant and your comforter in exile."

"I thank you, my girl, for your unmerited affection; but it cannot and must not be. The curtain here falls between us. I go to the house of another—If I leave it before I quit the earth, it shall be only for the House of God. Once more, farewell both! The fatal doom," he said, with a melancholy smile, "will, I trust, now depart-from the House of Redgauntlet, since its present representative has adhered to the winning side. I am convinced he will not change it, should it in turn become the losing one."

The unfortunate Charles Edward had now given his last adieus to his downcast adherents. He made a sign with his hand to Redgauntlet, who came to assist him into the skiff. General Campbell also offered his assistance, the rest appearing too much affected by the scene which had taken place to prevent him.

T

"You are not sorry, General, to do me this last act of courtesy," said the Chevalier; "and, on my part, I thank you for it. You have taught me the principle on which men on the scaffold feel forgiveness and kindness even for their executioner.—Farewell!"

They were seated in the boat, which presently pulled off from the land. The Oxford divine broke out into a loud benediction, in terms which General Campbell was too generous to criticise at the time, or to remember afterwards;—nay, it is said, that, Whig and Campbell as he was, he could not help joining in the universal Amen! which resounded from the shore.

CONCLUSION, BY DR. DRYASDUST,

IN A LETTER TO THE AUTHOR OF WAVERLEY.

I am truly sorry, my worthy and much-respected sir, that my anxious researches have neither, in the form of letters, nor of diaries, or other memoranda, been able to discover more than I have hitherto transmitted, of the history of the Redgauntlet family. But I observe in an old newspaper called the Whitehall Gazette, of which I fortunately possess a file for several years, that Sir Arthur Darsie Redgauntlet was presented to his late Majesty at the drawing-room, by Lieut.-General Campbell — upon which the Editor observes, in the way of comment, that we were going, *remis atque velis*, into the interests of the Pretender, since a Scot had presented a Jacobite at Court. I am sorry I have not room (the frank being only uncial) for his farther observations, tending to show the apprehensions entertained by many well-instructed persons of the period, that the young King might himself be induced to become one of the Stewarts' faction, — a catastrophe from which it has pleased Heaven to preserve these kingdoms.

I perceive also, by a marriage contract in the family repositories, that Miss Lilias Redgauntlet of Redgauntlet, about eighteen months after the transactions you have commemorated, intermarried with Alan Fairford, Esq. Advocate of Clinkdollar, who, I think, we may not unreasonably conclude to be the same person whose name occurs so frequently in the pages of your narration. In my last excursion to Edinburgh, I was fortunate enough to discover an old cadie, from whom, at the expense of a bottle of whisky, and half a pound of tobacco, I extracted the important information, that he knew Peter Peebles very well, and had drunk many a mutchkin with him in Cadie Fraser's time. He said that he lived ten years after King George's accession, in the momentary expectation of winning his cause every day in the Session time, and every hour in the day, and at last fell down dead, in what my informer called a "Perplexity fit," upon a proposal for a composition being made to him in the Outer-House. I have chosen to retain my informer's phrase, not being able justly to determine whether it is a corruption of the word apoplexy, as my friend Mr. Oldbuck supposes, or the name of some peculiar disorder incidental to those who have concern in the Courts of Law, as many callings and conditions of men have diseases appropriate to themselves. The same cadie also remembered Blind Willie Stevenson, who was called Wandering Willie, and who ended his days "unco beinly, in Sir Arthur Redgauntlet's ha' neuk." "He had done the family some good turn," he said, "specially when ane of the Argyle gentlemen was coming down on a wheen of them that had the 'auld leaven' about them, and wad hae taen every man of them, and nae less nor headed and hanged them. But Willie, and a friend they had, called Robin the Rambler, gae them warning, by playing tunes such as, 'the Campbells are

have altogether defaced the effigies of the knight and lady on the tomb. The particulars are preserved in Mr. Roby's Traditions of Lancashire,* to which the reader is referred for further particulars. It does not appear that Sir William Braidshaigh was irreparably offended against the too hasty Lady Mabel, although he certainly showed himself of a more fiery mould than the Scottish and German barons who were heroes of the former tales. The tradition, which the author knew very early in life, was told to him by the late Lady Balcarras. He was so much struck with it, that being at that time profuse of legendary lore, he inserted it in the shape of a note to Waverley, the first of his romantic offences. Had he then known, as he now does, the value of such a story, it is likely that, as directed in the inimitable receipt for making an epic poem, preserved in the Guardian, he would have kept it for some future opportunity.

As, however, the tale had not been completely told, and was a very interesting one, and as it was sufficiently interwoven with the Crusades, the wars between the Welsh and the Norman lords of the Marches was selected as a period when all freedoms might be taken with the strict truth of history without encountering any well known fact which might render the narrative improbable. Perhaps, however, the period which vindicates the probability of the tale, will, with its wars and murders, be best found described in the following passage of Gryffyth Ap Edwin's wars.

"This prince in conjunction with Algar, Earl of Chester, who had been banished from England as a traitor, in the reign of Edward the Confessor, marched into Herefordshire and wasted all that fertile country with fire and sword, to revenge the death of his brother Rhees, whose head had been brought to Edward in pursuance of an order sent by the King on account of the depredations which he had committed against the English on the borders. To stop these ravages the Earl of Hereford, who was nephew to Edward, advanced with an army, not of English alone, but of mercenary Normans and French, whom he had entertained in his service, against Gryffyth and Algar. He met them near Hereford, and offered them battle, which the Welsh monarch, who had won five pitched battles before, and never had fought without conquering, joyfully accepted. The earl had commanded his English forces to fight on horseback, in imitation of the Normans, against their usual custom; but the Welsh making a furious and desperate charge, that nobleman himself, and the foreign cavalry led by him, were so daunted at the view of them, that they shamefully fled without fighting; which being seen by the English, they also turned their backs on the enemy, who, having killed or wounded as many of them as they could come up with in their flight, entered triumphantly into Hereford, spoiled and fired the city, razed the walls to the ground, slaughtered some of the citizens, led many of them captive, and (to use the words of the Welsh Chronicle) left nothing in the town but blood and ashes. After this exploit they immediately returned into Wales, undoubtedly from a desire of securing their prisoners, and the rich plunder they had gained. The King of England hereupon commanded Earl Harold to collect a great army from all parts of the kingdom, and assembling them at Gloucester, advanced from thence to invade the dominions of Gryffyth in North Wales. He performed his orders, and penetrated into that country without resistance from the Welsh; Gryffyth and Algar returning into some parts of South Wales. What were their reasons for this conduct we are not well informed; nor why Harold did not pursue his advantage against them; but it appears that he thought it more advisable at this time to treat with, than subdue, them; for he left North Wales, and employed himself in rebuilding the walls of Hereford, while negotiations were carrying on with Gryffyth which soon after produced the restoration of Algar, and a peace with that king,

---

* A very elegant work, 2 vols. 1829. By J. Roby, M.R.S.L.

not very honourable to England, as he made no satisfaction for the mischief he had done in the war, nor any submissions to Edward. Harold must doubtless have had some private and forcible motives to conclude such a treaty. The very next year the Welsh monarch, upon what quarrel we know not, made a new incursion into England, and killed the Bishop of Hereford, the Sheriff of the county, and many more of the English, both ecclesiastics and laymen. Edward was counselled by Harold, and Leofrick, Earl of Mercia, to make peace with him again; which he again broke; nor could he be restrained by any means, from these barbarous inroads, before the year one thousand and sixty-three; when Edward, whose patience and pacific disposition had been too much abused, commissioned Harold to assemble the whole strength of the kingdom, and make war upon him in his own country till he had subdued or destroyed him. That general acted so vigorously, and with so much celerity, that he had like to have surprised him in his palace: but just before the English forces arrived at his gate, having notice of the danger that threatened him, and seeing no other means of safety, he threw himself with a few of his household into one of his ships which happened at the instant to be ready to sail and put to sea."—LYTTLE-TON's *Hist. of England*, vol. ii. p. 338.

This passage will be found to bear a general resemblance to the fictitious tale told, in the Romance.

ABBOTSFORD, *1st June,* 1832.

~~~~~~~~~~~~~~~~~~~~~~~~~~~~

INTRODUCTION.

**MINUTES OF SEDERUNT OF A GENERAL MEETING OF THE SHAREHOLDERS DESIGN-
ING TO FORM A JOINT-STOCK COMPANY, UNITED FOR THE PURPOSE OF WRITING
AND PUBLISHING THE CLASS OF WORKS CALLED THE WAVERLEY NOVELS,**

HELD IN THE WATERLOO TAVERN, REGENT'S BRIDGE, EDINBURGH,
1st June, 1825.

[The reader must have remarked, that the various editions of the proceedings at this meeting were given in the public papers with rather more than usual inaccuracy. The cause of this was no ill-timed delicacy on the part of the gentlemen of the press to assert their privilege of universal presence wherever a few are met together, and to commit to the public prints whatever may then and there pass of the most private nature. But very unusual and arbitrary methods were resorted to on the present occasion to prevent the reporters using a right which is generally conceded to them by almost all meetings, whether of a political or commercial description. Our own reporter, indeed, was bold enough to secrete himself under the Secretary's table, and was not discovered till the meeting was well-nigh over. We are sorry to say, he suffered much in person from fists and toes, and two or three principal pages were torn out of his note-book, which occasions his report to break off abruptly. We cannot but consider this behaviour as more particularly illiberal on the part of men who are themselves a kind of gentlemen of the press; and they ought to consider themselves as fortunate that the misused reporter has sought no other vengeance than from the tone of acidity with which he has seasoned his account of their proceedings.—*Edinburgh Newspaper.*]

A MEETING of the gentlemen and others interested in the celebrated publications called the Waverley Novels, having been called by public advertisement, the same was respectably attended by various literary characters of eminence. And it being in the first place understood that individuals were to be denominated by the names assigned to them in the publications in question, the Eidolon, or image of the author, was unanimously called to the chair, and Jonathan Oldbuck, Esq. of Monkbarns, was requested to act as Secretary.

The Preses then addressed the meeting to the following purpose:—

"Gentlemen,

"I need scarcely remind you, that we have a joint interest in the valuable property which has accumulated under our common labours. While the public have been idly engaged in ascribing to one individual or another the immense mass of various matter, which the labours of many had accumulated, you, gentlemen, well know, that every person in this numerous assembly has had his share in the honours and profits of our common success. It is, indeed, to me a mystery, how the sharp-sighted could suppose so huge a mass of sense and nonsense, jest and earnest, humorous and pathetic, good, bad, and indifferent, amounting to scores of volumes, could be the work of one hand, when we know the doctrine so well laid down by the immortal Adam Smith, concerning the division of labour. Were those who entertained an opinion so strange, not wise enough to know, that it requires twenty pairs of hands to make a thing so trifling as a pin—twenty couple of dogs to kill an animal so insignificant as a fox?——"

"Hout, man!" said a stout countryman, "I have a grew-bitch at hame will worry the best tod in Pomoragrains, before ye could say, Dumpling."

"Who is that person?" said the Preses, with some warmth, as it appeared to us.

"A son of Dandy Dinmont's," answered the unabashed rustic. "God, ye may mind him, I think!—ane o' the best in your aught, I reckon. And, ye see, I am come into the farm, and maybe something mair, and a wheen shares in this buik-trade of yours."

": Well, well," replied the Preses, "peace, I pray thee, peace. Gentlemen, when thus interrupted, I was on the point of introducing the business of this meeting, being, as is known to most of you, the discussion of a proposition now on your table, which I myself had the honour to suggest at last meeting, namely, that we do apply to the Legislature for an Act of Parliament in ordinary, to associate us into a corporate body, and give us a *personi standi in judicio*, with full power to prosecute and bring to conviction all encroachers upon our exclusive privilege, in the manner therein to be made and provided. In a letter from the ingenious Mr. Dousterswivel which I have received——"

Oldbuck, warmly—"I object to that fellow's name being mentioned; he is a common swindler."

"For shame, Mr. Oldbuck," said the Preses, "to use such terms respecting the ingenious inventor of the great patent machine erected at Groningen, where they put in raw hemp at one end, and take out ruffled shirts at the other, without the aid of hackle or rippling-comb—loom, shuttle, or weaver—scissors, needle, or seamstress. He had just completed it, by the addition of a piece of machinery to perform the work of the laundress; but when it was exhibited before his honour the burgomaster, it had the inconvenience of heating the smoothing-irons red-hot; excepting which, the experiment was entirely satisfactory. He will become as rich as a Jew."

"Well," added Mr. Oldbuck, "if the scoundrel——"

"Scoundrel, Mr. Oldbuck," said the Preses, "is a most unseemly expression, and I must call you to order. Mr. Dousterswivel is only an eccentric genius."

"Pretty much the same in the Greek," muttered Mr. Oldbuck; and then said aloud, "and if this eccentric genius has work enough in singeing the Dutchman's linen, what the devil has he to do here?"

"Why, he is of opinion, that at the expense of a little mechanism, some part of the labour of composing these novels might be saved by the use of steam."

There was a murmur of disapprobation at this proposal, and the words, "Blown up," and "Bread taken out of our mouths," and "They might as well construct a steam parson," were whispered. And it was not without repeated calls to order, that the Preses obtained an opportunity of resuming his address.

"Order!—Order! Pray, support the chair. Hear, hear, hear the chair!"

"Gentlemen, it is to be premised, that this mechanical operation can only apply to those parts of the narrative which are at present composed out of commonplaces, such as the love-speeches of the hero, the description of the heroine's person, the moral observations of all sorts, and the distribution of happiness at the conclusion of the piece. Mr. Dousterswivel has sent me some drawings, which go far to show, that by placing the words and phrases technically employed on these subjects, in a sort of framework, like that of the Sage of Laputa, and changing them by such a mechanical process as that by which weavers of damask alter their patterns, many new and happy combinations cannot fail to occur, while the author, tired of pumping his own brains, may have an agreeable relaxation in the use of his fingers."

"I speak for information, Mr. Preses," said the Rev. Mr. Lawrence Templeton; "but I am inclined to suppose the late publication of Walladmor to have been the work of Dousterswivel, by the help of the steam-engine."[*]

"For shame, Mr. Templeton," said the Preses; "there are good things in Walladmor, I assure you, had the writer known any thing about the country in which he laid the scene."

"Or had he had the wit, like some of ourselves, to lay the scene in such a remote or distant country that nobody should be able to back-speer[†] him," said Mr. Oldbuck.

"Why, as to that," said the Preses, "you must consider the thing was got up for the German market, where folks are no better judges of Walsh manners than of Welsh crw."[‡]

"I make it my prayer that this be not found the fault of our own next venture," said Dr. Dryasdust, pointing to some books which lay on the table. "I fear the manners expressed in that 'Betrothed' of ours, will scarce meet the approbation of the Cymmerodion; I could have wished that Llhuyd had been looked into—that Powel had been consulted—that Lewis's History had been quoted, the preliminary dissertations particularly, in order to give due weight to the work."

"Weight!" said Captain Clutterbuck; "by my soul, it is heavy enough already, Doctor."

"Speak to the chair," said the Preses, rather peevishly.

"To the chair, then, I say it," said Captain Clutterbuck, "that 'The Betrothed' is heavy enough to break down the chair of John of Gaunt, or Cador-Edris itself. I must add, however, that, in my poor mind, 'The Talisman' goes more trippingly off."[‖]

"It is not for me to speak," said the worthy minister of Saint Ronan's Well; "but yet I must say, that being so long engaged upon the Siege of Ptolemais, my work ought to have been brought out, humble though it be, before any other upon a similar subject at least."

"Your Siege, Parson!" said Mr. Oldbuck, with great contempt; "will you speak of your paltry prose-doings in my presence, whose great Historical Poem, in twenty books, with notes in proportion, has been postponed ad Græcas Kalendas?"

---

* A Romance, by the Author of Waverley, having been expected about this time at the great commercial mart of literature, the Fair of Leipsic, an ingenious gentleman of Germany, finding that none such appeared, was so kind as to supply its place with a work, in three volumes, called Walladmor, to which he prefixed the Christian and surname at full length. The character of this work is given with tolerable fairness in the text.
† Scottish for cross-examine him.
‡ The ale of the ancient British is called crw in their native language.
‖ This was an opinion universally entertained among the friends of the author.

The Preses, who appeared to suffer a great deal during this discussion, now spoke with dignity and determination. "Gentlemen," he said, "this sort of discussion is highly irregular. There is a question before you, and to that, gentlemen, I must confine your attention. Priority of publication, let me remind you, gentlemen, is always referred to the Committee of Criticism, whose determination on such subjects is without appeal. I declare I will leave the chair, if any more extraneous matter be introduced.—And now, gentlemen, that we are once more in order, I would wish to have some gentleman speak upon the question, whether, as associated to carry on a joint-stock trade in fictitious narrative, in prose and verse, we ought not to be incorporated by Act of Parliament? What say you, gentlemen, to the proposal? *Vis unita fortior*, is an old and true adage."

"*Societas mater discordiarum*, is a brocard as ancient and as veritable," said Oldbuck, who seemed determined, on this occasion, to be pleased with no proposal that was announced by the chair.

"Come, Monkbarns," said the Preses, in his most coaxing manner, "you have studied the monastic institutions deeply, and know there must be a union of persons and talents to do any thing respectable, and attain a due ascendance over the spirit of the age. *Tres faciunt collegium* — it takes three monks to make a convent."

"And nine tailors to make a man," replied Oldbuck, not in the least softened in his opposition; "a quotation as much to the purpose as the other."

"Come, come," said the Preses, "you know the Prince of Orange said to Mr. Seymour, 'Without an association, we are a rope of sand.'"

"I know," replied Oldbuck, "it would have been as seemly that none of the old leaven had been displayed on this occasion, though you be the author of a Jacobite novel. I know nothing of the Prince of Orange after 1688; but I have heard a good deal of the immortal William the Third."

"And to the best of my recollection," said Mr. Templeton, whispering to Oldbuck, "it was Seymour made the remark to the Prince, not the Prince to Seymour. But this is a specimen of our friend's accuracy, poor gentleman: He trusts too much to his memory! of late years—failing fast, sir—breaking up."

"And breaking down, too," said Mr. Oldbuck. "But what can you expect of a man too fond of his own hasty and flashy compositions, to take the assistance of men of reading and of solid parts?"

"No whispering—no caballing—no private business, gentlemen," said the unfortunate Preses, who reminded us somewhat of a Highland drover engaged in gathering and keeping in the straight road his excursive black cattle.

"I have not yet heard," he continued, "a single reasonable objection to applying for the Act of Parliament, of which the draught lies on the table. You must be aware that the extremes of rude and of civilized society are, in these our days, on the point of approaching to each other. In the patriarchal period, a man is his own weaver, tailor, butcher, shoemaker, and so forth; and, in the age of Stock-companies, as the present may be called, an individual may be said, in one sense, to exercise the same plurality of trades. In fact, a man who has dipt largely into these speculations, may combine his own expenditure with the improvement of his own income, just like the ingenious hydraulic machine, which, by its very waste, raises its own supplies of water. Such a person buys his bread from his own Baking Company, his milk and cheese from his own Dairy Company, takes off a new coat for the benefit of his own Clothing Company, illuminates his house to advance his own Gas Establishment, and drinks an additional bottle of wine for the benefit of the General Wine Importation Company, of which he is himself a member. Every act, which would otherwise be one of mere extravagance, is, to such a person, seasoned with the *odor lucri*, and reconciled to prudence. Even if the price of the article consumed be extravagant, and the quality indifferent, the person, who is in a manner his own customer, is only imposed upon for his own benefit. Nay, if the Joint-stock

Company of Undertakers shall unite with the Medical Faculty, as proposed by the late facetious Doctor G——, under the firm of Death and the Doctor, the shareholder might contrive to secure to his heirs a handsome slice of his own death-bed and funeral expenses. In short, Stock-Companies are the fashion of the age, and an Incorporating Act will, I think, be particularly useful in bringing back the body, over whom I have the honour to preside, to a spirit of subordination, highly necessary to success in every enterprise where joint wisdom, talent, and labour, are to be employed. It is with regret that I state, that, besides several differences amongst yourselves, I have not myself for some time been treated with that deference among you which circumstances entitled me to expect."

"*Hinc illæ lachrymæ,*" muttered Mr. Oldbuck.

"But," continued the Chairman, "I see other gentlemen impatient to deliver their opinions, and I desire to stand in no man's way. I therefore — my place in this chair forbidding me to originate the motion — beg some gentleman may move a committee for revising the draught of the bill now upon the table, and which has been duly circulated among those having interest, and take the necessary measures to bring it before the House early next session."

There was a short murmur in the meeting, and at length Mr. Oldbuck again rose. "It seems, sir," he said, addressing the chair, "that no one present is willing to make the motion you point at. I am sorry no more qualified person has taken upon him to show any reasons in the contrair, and that it has fallen on me, as we Scotsmen say, to bell-the-cat with you; anent whilk phrase, Pitscottie hath a pleasant jest of the great Earl of Angus—"

Here a gentleman whispered to the speaker, "Have a care of Pitscottie!" and Mr. Oldbuck, as if taking the hint, went on.

"But that's neither here nor there—Well, gentlemen, to be short, I think it unnecessary to enter into the general reasonings whilk have this day been delivered, as I may say, *ex cathedra;* nor will I charge our worthy Preses with an attempt to obtain over us, *per ambages,* and under colour of an Act of Parliament, a despotic authority, inconsistent with our freedom. But this I will say, that times are so much changed above stairs, that whereas last year you might have obtained an act incorporating a Stock Company for riddling ashes, you will not be able to procure one this year for gathering pearls. What signifies, then, wasting the time of the meeting, by inquiring whether or not we ought to go in at a door which we know to be bolted and barred in our face, and in the face of all the companies for fire or air, land or water, which we have of late seen blighted!"

Here there was a general clamour, seemingly of approbation, in which the words might be distinguished, "Needless to think of it" — "Money thrown away" — "Lost before the committee," &c. &c. &c. But above the tumult, the voices of two gentlemen, in different corners of the room, answered each other clear and loud, like the blows of the two figures on Saint Dunstan's clock; and although the Chairman, in much agitation, endeavoured to silence them, his interruption had only the effect of cutting their words up into syllables, thus,—

First Voice. "The Lord Chan ——"
Second Voice. "The Lord Lau ——"
Chairman, (loudly.) "Scandalum magnatum!"
First Voice. "The Lord Chancel ——"
Second Voice. "The Lord Lauder ——"
Chairman, (louder yet.) "Breach of Privilege!"
First Voice. "The Lord Chancellor ——"
Second Voice. "My Lord Lauderdale ——"
Chairman, (at the highest pitch of his voice.) "Called before the House!"
Both Voices together. "Will never consent to such a bill."

A general assent seemed to follow this last proposition, which was propounded with as much emphasis as could be contributed by the united clappers of the whole meeting, joined to those of the voices already mentioned.

Several persons present seemed to consider the business of the meeting as ended, and were beginning to handle their hats and canes, with a view to departure, when the Chairman, who had thrown himself back in his chair, with an air of manifest mortification and displeasure, again drew himself up, and commanded attention. All stopped, though some shrugged their shoulders, as if under the predominating influence of what is called a *bore*. But the tenor of his discourse soon excited anxious attention.

"I perceive, gentlemen," he said, "that you are like the young birds, who are impatient to leave their mother's nest — take care your own pen-feathers are strong enough to support you; since, as for my part, I am tired of supporting on my wing such a set of ungrateful gulls. But it signifies nothing speaking—I will no longer avail myself of such weak ministers as you—I will discard you—I will unbeget you, as Sir Anthony Absolute says —I will leave you and your whole hacked stock in trade—your caverns and your castles — your modern antiques, and your antiquated moderns — your confusion of times, manners, and circumstances—your properties, as player-folk say of scenery and dresses — the whole of your exhausted expedients, to the fools who choose to deal with them. I will vindicate my own fame with my own right hand, without appealing to such halting assistants,

'Whom I have used for sport, rather than need.'

—I will lay my foundations better than on quicksands — I will rear my structure of better materials than painted cards; in a word, I will write HISTORY!"

There was a tumult of surprise, amid which our reporter detected the following expressions:—"The devil you will!"—"You, my dear sir, *you?*" — "The old gentleman forgets that he is the greatest liar since Sir John Mandeville."

"Not the worse historian for that," said Oldbuck, "since history, you know, is half fiction."

"I'll answer for that half being forthcoming," said the former speaker; "but for the scantling of truth which is necessary after all, Lord help us!— Geoffrey of Monmouth will be Lord Clarendon to him."

As the confusion began to abate, more than one member of the meeting was seen to touch his forehead significantly, while Captain Clutterbuck humm'd

Be by your friends advised,
Too rash, too hasty, dad,
Maugre your bolts and wise head,
The world will think you mad.

"The world, and you, gentlemen, may think what you please," said the Chairman, elevating his voice; "but I intend to write the most wonderful book which the world ever read — a book in which every incident shall be incredible, yet strictly true — a work recalling recollections with which the ears of this generation once tingled, and which shall be read by our children with an admiration approaching to incredulity. Such shall be the LIFE OF NAPOLEON BONAPARTE by the AUTHOR OF WAVERLEY."

In the general start and exclamation which followed this annunciation, Mr. Oldbuck dropped his snuff-box; and the Scottish rappee, which dispersed itself in consequence, had effects upon the nasal organs of our reporter, ensconced as he was under the secretary's table, which occasioned his being discovered and extruded in the illiberal and unhandsome manner we have mentioned, with threats of farther damage to his nose, ears, and other portions of his body, on the part especially of Captain Clutterbuck. Undismayed by these threats, which indeed those of his profession are accustomed to hold at defiance, our young man hovered about the door of the tavern, but could only bring us the farther intelligence, that the meeting had broken up in about a quarter of an hour after his expulsion, "in much-admired disorder."

z 2

THE BETROTHED.

Chapter the First.

Now in these days were hotte wars upon the Marches of Wales.
Lewis's *History*.

THE Chronicles, from which this narrative is extracted, assure us, that during the long period when the Welsh princes maintained their independence, the year 1187 was peculiarly marked as favourable to peace betwixt them and their warlike neighbours, the Lords Marchers, who inhabited those formidable castles on the frontiers of the ancient British, on the ruins of which the traveller gazes with wonder. This was the time when Baldwin, Archbishop of Canterbury, accompanied by the learned Giraldus de Barri, afterwards Bishop of Saint David's, preached the Crusade from castle to castle, from town to town; awakened the inmost valleys of his native Cambria with the call to arms for recovery of the Holy Sepulchre; and, while he deprecated the feuds and wars of Christian men against each other, held out to the martial spirit of the age a general object of ambition, and a scene of adventure, where the favour of Heaven, as well as earthy renown, was to reward the successful champions.

Yet the British chieftains, among the thousands whom this spirit-stirring summons called from their native land to a distant and perilous expedition, had perhaps the best excuse for declining the summons. The superior skill of the Anglo-Norman knights, who were engaged in constant inroads on the Welsh frontier, and who were frequently detaching from it large portions, which they fortified with castles, thus making good what they had won, was avenged, indeed, but not compensated, by the furious inroads of the British, who, like the billows of a retiring tide, rolled on successively, with noise, fury, and devastation; but, on each retreat, yielded ground insensibly to their invaders.

A union among the native princes might have opposed a strong and permanent barrier to the encroachments of the strangers; but they were, unhappily, as much at discord among themselves as they were with the Normans, and were constantly engaged in private war with each other, of which the common enemy had the sole advantage.

The invitation to the Crusade promised something at least of novelty to a nation peculiarly ardent in their temper; and it was accepted by many, regardless of the consequences which must ensue, to the country which they left defenceless. Even the most celebrated enemies of the Saxon and Norman race laid aside their enmity against the invaders of their country, to enrol themselves under the banners of the Crusade.

Amongst these was reckoned Gwenwyn, (or more properly Gwenwynwen, though we retain the briefer appellative,) a British prince who continued exercising a precarious sovereignty over such parts of Powys-Land as had not been subjugated by the Mortimers, Guarines, Latimers, FitzAlans, and

(294)

other Norman nobles, who, under various pretexts, and sometimes contemning all other save the open avowal of superior force, had severed and appropriated large portions of that once extensive and independent principality, which, when Wales was unhappily divided into three parts on the death of Roderick Mawr, fell to the lot of his youngest son, Mervyn. The undaunted resolution and stubborn ferocity of Gwenwyn, descendant of that prince, had long made him beloved among the "Tall men," or Champions of Wales; and he was enabled, more by the number of those who served under him, attracted by his reputation, than by the natural strength of his dilapidated principality, to retaliate the encroachments of the English by the most wasteful inroads.

Yet even Gwenwyn on the present occasion seemed to forget his deeply sworn hatred against his dangerous neighbours. The Torch of Pengwern (for so Gwenwyn was called, from his frequently laying the province of Shrewsbury in conflagration) seemed at present to burn as calmly as a taper in the bower of a lady; and the Wolf of Plinlimmon, another name with which the bards had graced Gwenwyn, now slumbered as peacefully as the shepherd's dog on the domestic hearth.

But it was not alone the eloquence of Baldwin or of Girald which had lulled into peace a spirit so restless and fierce. It is true, their exhortations had done more towards it than Gwenwyn's followers had thought possible. The Archbishop had induced the British Chief to break bread, and to mingle in silvan sports, with his nearest, and hitherto one of his most determined enemies, the old Norman warrior Sir Raymond Berenger, who, sometimes beaten, sometimes victorious, but never subdued, had, in spite of Gwenwyn's hottest incursions, maintained his Castle of Garde Doloureuse, upon the marches of Wales; a place strong by nature, and well fortified by art, which the Welsh prince had found it impossible to conquer, either by open force or by stratagem, and which, remaining with a strong garrison in his rear, often checked his incursions, by rendering his retreat precarious.

On this account, Gwenwyn of Powys-Land had an hundred times vowed the death of Raymond Berenger, and the demolition of his castle; but the policy of the sagacious old warrior, and his long experience in all warlike practice, were such as, with the aid of his more powerful countrymen, enabled him to defy the attempts of his fiery neighbour. If there was a man, therefore, throughout England, whom Gwenwyn hated more than another, it was Raymond Berenger; and yet the good Archbishop Baldwin could prevail on the Welsh prince to meet him as a friend and ally in the cause of the Cross. He even invited Raymond to the autumn festivities of his Welsh palace, where the old knight, in all honourable courtesy, feasted and hunted for more than a week in the dominions of his hereditary foe.

To requite this hospitality, Raymond invited the Prince of Powys, with a chosen but limited train, during the ensuing Christmas, to the Garde Doloureuse, which some antiquaries have endeavoured to identify with the Castle of Colune, on the river of the same name. But the length of time, and some geographical difficulties, throw doubts upon this ingenious conjecture.

As the Welshman crossed the drawbridge, he was observed by his faithful bard to shudder with involuntary emotion; nor did Cadwallon, experienced as he was in life, and well acquainted with the character of his master, make any doubt that he was at that moment strongly urged by the apparent opportunity, to seize upon the strong fortress which had been so long the object of his cupidity, even at the expense of violating his good faith.

Dreading lest the struggle of his master's conscience and his ambition should terminate unfavourably for his fame, the bard arrested his attention by whispering in their native language, that "the teeth which bite hardest are those which are out of sight;" and Gwenwyn looking around him, became aware that, though only unarmed squires and pages appeared in the court-yard, yet the towers and battlements connecting them were garnished with archers and men-at-arms.

They proceeded to the banquet, at which Gwenwyn, for the first time, beheld Eveline Berenger, the sole child of the Norman castellane, the inheritor of his domains and of his supposed wealth, aged only sixteen, and the most beautiful damsel upon the Welsh marches. Many a spear had already been shivered in maintenance of her charms; and the gallant Hugo de Lacy, Constable of Chester, one of the most redoubted warriors of the time, had laid at Eveline's feet the prize which his chivalry had gained in a great tournament held near that ancient town. Gwenwyn considered these triumphs as so many additional recommendations to Eveline; her beauty was incontestable, and she was heiress of the fortress which he so much longed to possess, and which he began now to think might be acquired by means more smooth than those with which he was in the use of working out his will.

Again, the hatred which subsisted between the British and their Saxon and Norman invaders; his long and ill-extinguished feud with this very Raymond Berenger; a general recollection that alliances between the Welsh and English had rarely been happy; and a consciousness that the measure which he meditated would be unpopular among his followers, and appear a dereliction of the systematic principles on which he had hitherto acted, restrained him from speaking his wishes to Raymond or his daughter. The idea of the rejection of his suit did not for a moment occur to him; he was convinced he had but to speak his wishes, and that the daughter of a Norman castellane, whose rank or power were not of the highest order among the nobles of the frontiers, must be delighted and honoured by a proposal for allying his family with that of the sovereign of a hundred mountains.

There was indeed another objection, which in later times would have been of considerable weight—Gwenwyn was already married. But Brengwain was a childless bride; sovereigns (and among sovereigns the Welsh prince ranked himself) marry for lineage, and the Pope was not likely to be scrupulous, where the question was to oblige a prince who had assumed the Cross with such ready zeal, even although, in fact, his thoughts had been much more on the Garde Doloureuse than on Jerusalem. In the meanwhile, if Raymond Berenger (as was suspected) was not liberal enough in his opinions to permit Eveline to hold the temporary rank of concubine, which the manners of Wales warranted Gwenwyn to offer as an interim arrangement, he had only to wait for a few months, and sue for a divorce through the Bishop of Saint David's, or some other intercessor at the Court of Rome.

Agitating these thoughts in his mind, Gwenwyn prolonged his residence at the Castle of Berenger, from Christmas till Twelfthday; and endured the presence of the Norman cavaliers who resorted to Raymond's festal halls, although, regarding themselves, in virtue of their rank of knighthood, equal to the most potent sovereigns, they made small account of the long descent of the Welsh prince, who, in their eyes, was but the chief of a semibarbarous province; while he, on his part, considered them little better than a sort of privileged robbers, and with the utmost difficulty restrained himself from manifesting his open hatred, when he beheld them careering in the exercises of chivalry, the habitual use of which rendered them such formidable enemies to his country. At length, the term of feasting was ended, and knight and squire departed from the castle, which once more assumed the aspect of a solitary and guarded frontier fort.

But the Prince of Powys-Land, while pursuing his sports on his own mountains and valleys, found that even the abundance of the game, as well as his release from the society of the Norman chivalry, who affected to treat him as an equal, profited him nothing, so long as the light and beautiful form of Eveline, on her white palfrey, was banished from the train of sportsmen. In short, he hesitated no longer, but took into his confidence his chaplain, an able and sagacious man, whose pride was flattered by his patron's communication, and who, besides, saw in the proposed scheme some contingent advantages for himself and his order. By his counsel, the proceedings for Gwenwyn's divorce were prosecuted under favourable auspices, and the unfortunate Brengwain was removed to a nunnery, which perhaps she found a more cheerful habitation than the lonely retreat in which she had led a neglected life, ever since Gwenwyn had despaired of her bed being blessed with issue. Father Einion also dealt with the chiefs and elders of the land, and represented to them the advantage which in future wars they were certain to obtain by the possession of the Garde Doloureuse, which had for more than a century covered and protected a considerable tract of country, rendered their advance difficult, and their retreat perilous, and, in a word, prevented their carrying their incursions as far as the gates of Shrewsbury. As for the union with the Saxon damsel, the fetters which it was to form might not (the good father hinted) be found more permanent than those which had bound Gwenwyn to her predecessor, Brengwain.

These arguments, mingled with others adapted to the views and wishes of different individuals, were so prevailing, that the chaplain in the course of a few weeks was able to report to his princely patron, that this proposed match would meet with no opposition from the elders and nobles of his dominions. A golden bracelet, six ounces in weight, was the instant reward of the priest's dexterity in negotiation, and he was appointed by Gwenwyn to commit to paper those proposals, which he doubted not were to throw the Castle of Garde Doloureuse, notwithstanding its melancholy name, into an ecstasy of joy. With some difficulty the chaplain prevailed on his patron to say nothing in this letter upon his temporary plan of concubinage, which he wisely judged might be considered as an affront both by Eveline and her father. The matter of the divorce he represented as almost entirely settled, and wound up his letter with a moral application, in which were many allusions to Vashti, Esther, and Ahasuerus.

Having despatched this letter by a swift and trusty messenger, the British prince opened in all solemnity the feast of Easter, which had come round during the course of these external and internal negotiations.

Upon the approaching Holy-tide, to propitiate the minds of his subjects and vassals, they were invited in large numbers to partake of a princely festivity at Castell-Coch, or the Red-Castle, as it was then called, since better known by the name of Powys-Castle, and in latter times the princely seat of the Duke of Beaufort. The architectural magnificence of this noble residence is of a much later period than that of Gwenwyn, whose palace, at the time we speak of, was a low, long-roofed edifice of red stone, whence the castle derived its name ; while a ditch and palisade were, in addition to the commanding situation, its most important defences.

Chapter the Second.

In Madoc's tent the clarion sounds,
With rapid clangor hurried far;
Each hill and dale the note rebounds,
But when return the sons of war?
Then, born of stern Necessity,
Dull Peace! the valley yields to thee,
And owns thy melancholy sway.
          WELSH POEM.

THE feasts of the ancient British princes usually exhibited all the rude splendour and liberal indulgence of mountain hospitality, and Gwenwyn was, on the present occasion, anxious to purchase popularity by even an unusual display of profusion; for he was sensible that the alliance which he meditated might indeed be tolerated, but could not be approved, by his subjects and followers.

The following incident, trifling in itself, confirmed his apprehensions. Passing one evening, when it was become nearly dark, by the open window of a guard-room, usually occupied by some few of his most celebrated soldiers, who relieved each other in watching his palace, he heard Morgan, a man distinguished for strength, courage, and ferocity, say to the companion with whom he was sitting by the watch-fire, "Gwenwyn is turned to a priest, or a woman! When was it before these last months, that a follower of his was obliged to gnaw the meat from the bone so closely, as I am now peeling the morsel which I hold in my hand?"*

"Wait but a while," replied his comrade, "till the Norman match be accomplished; and so small will be the prey we shall then drive from the Saxon churls, that we may be glad to swallow, like hungry dogs, the very bones themselves."

Gwenwyn heard no more of their conversation; but this was enough to alarm his pride as a soldier, and his jealousy as a prince. He was sensible, that the people over whom he ruled were at once fickle in their disposition, impatient of long repose, and full of hatred against their neighbours; and he almost dreaded the consequences of the inactivity to which a long truce might reduce them. The risk was now incurred, however; and to display even more than his wonted splendour and liberality, seemed the best way of reconciling the wavering affections of his subjects.

A Norman would have despised the barbarous magnificence of an entertainment, consisting of kine and sheep roasted whole, of goat's flesh and deer's flesh seethed in the skins of the animals themselves; for the Normans piqued themselves on the quality rather than the quantity of their food, and, eating rather delicately than largely, ridiculed the coarser taste of the Britons, although the last were in their banquets much more moderate than were the Saxons; nor would the oceans of *Crw* and hydromel, which overwhelmed the guests like a deluge, have made up, in their opinion, for the absence of the more elegant and costly beverage which they had learnt to love in the south of Europe. Milk, prepared in various ways, was another material of the British entertainment, which would not have received their approbation, although a nutriment which, on ordinary occasions, often supplied the want of all others among the ancient inhabitants, whose country was rich in flocks and herds, but poor in agricultural produce.

The banquet was spread in a long low hall, built of rough wood lined

---

* It is said in Highland tradition, that one of the Macdonalds of the Isles, who had suffered his broadsword to remain sheathed for some months after his marriage with a beautiful woman, was stirred to a sudden and furious expedition against the mainland by hearing conversation to the above purpose among his bodyguard.

with shingles, having a fire at each end, the smoke of which, unable to find its way through the imperfect chimneys in the roof, rolled in cloudy billows above the heads of the revellers, who sat on low seats, purposely to avoid its stifling fumes.* The mien and appearance of the company assembled was wild, and, even in their social hours, almost terrific. Their prince himself had the gigantic port and fiery eye fitted to sway an unruly people, whose delight was in the field of battle; and the long mustaches which he and most of his champions wore, added to the formidable dignity of his presence. Like most of those present, Gwenwyn was clad in a simple tunic of white linen cloth, a remnant of the dress which the Romans had introduced into provincial Britain; and he was distinguished by the Eudorchawg, or chain of twisted gold links, with which the Celtic tribes always decorated their chiefs. The collar, indeed, representing in form the species of links made by children out of rushes, was common to chieftains of inferior rank, many of whom bore it in virtue of their birth, or had won it by military exploits; but a ring of gold, bent around the head, intermingled with Gwenwyn's hair—for he claimed the rank of one of three diademed princes of Wales, and his armlets and anklets, of the same metal, were peculiar to the Prince of Powys, as an independent sovereign. Two squires of his body, who dedicated their whole attention to his service, stood at the Prince's back; and at his feet sat a page, whose duty it was to keep them warm by chafing and by wrapping them in his mantle. The same right of sovereignty, which assigned to Gwenwyn his golden crownlet, gave him a title to the attendance of the foot-bearer, or youth, who lay on the rushes, and whose duty it was to cherish the Prince's feet in his lap or bosom.†

Notwithstanding the military disposition of the guests, and the danger arising from the feuds into which they were divided, few of the feasters wore any defensive armour, except the light goat-skin buckler, which hung behind each man's seat. On the other hand, they were well provided with offensive weapons; for the broad, sharp, short, two-edged sword was another legacy of the Romans. Most added a wood-knife or poniard; and there were store of javelins, darts, bows, and arrows, pikes, halberds, Danish axes, and Welsh hooks and bills; so, in case of ill-blood arising during the banquet, there was no lack of weapons to work mischief.

But although the form of the feast was somewhat disorderly, and that the revellers were unrestrained by the stricter rules of good-breeding which the laws of chivalry imposed, the Easter banquet of Gwenwyn possessed, in the attendance of twelve eminent bards, one source of the most exalted pleasure, in a much higher degree than the proud Normans could themselves boast. The latter, it is true, had their minstrels, a race of men trained to the profession of poetry, song, and music; but although those arts were highly honoured, and the individual professors, when they attained to eminence, were often richly rewarded, and treated with distinction, the order of minstrels, as such, was held in low esteem, being composed chiefly of worthless and dissolute strollers, by whom the art was assumed, in order to escape from the necessity of labour, and to have the means of pursuing a wandering and dissipated course of life. Such, in all times, has been the censure upon the calling of those who dedicate themselves to the public

* The Welsh houses, like those of the cognate tribes in Ireland and in the Highlands of Scotland, were very imperfectly supplied with chimneys. Hence, in the History of the Gwydir Family, the striking expression of a Welsh chieftain who, the house being assaulted and set on fire by his enemies, exhorted his friends to stand to their defence, saying he had seen as much smoke in the hall upon a Christmas even.

† See Madoc for this literal foot page's office and duties. Mr. Southey's notes inform us: "The font-bearer shall hold the feet of the King in his lap, from the time he reclines at the board till he goes to rest, and he shall chafe them with a towel; and during all that time shall watch that no harm befalls the King. He shall eat of the same dish from which the King takes his food; he shall light the first candle before the King." Such are the instructions given for this part of royal ceremonial in the laws of Howell Dha. It may be added, that probably upon this Celtic custom was founded one of those absurd and incredible representations which were propagated at the time of the French revolution, to stir up the peasants against their feudal superiors. It was pretended that some feudal seigneurs asserted their right to kill and disembowel a peasant, in order to put their own feet within the expiring body, and so recover them from the chill.

amusement; among whom those distinguished by individual excellence are sometimes raised high in the social circle, while far the more numerous professors, who only reach mediocrity, are sunk into the lower scale.   But such was not the case with the order of bards in Wales, who, succeeding to the dignity of the Druids, under whom they had originally formed a subordinate fraternity, had many immunities, were held in the highest reverence and esteem, and exercised much influence with their countrymen.   Their power over the public mind even rivalled that of the priests themselves, to whom indeed they bore some resemblance; for they never wore arms, were initiated into their order by secret and mystic solemnities, and homage was rendered to their *Awen*, or flow of poetic inspiration, as if it had been indeed marked with a divine character.   Thus possessed of power and consequence, the bards were not unwilling to exercise their privileges, and sometimes, in doing so, their manners frequently savoured of caprice.

This was perhaps the case with Cadwallon, the chief bard of Gwenwyn, and who, as such, was expected to have poured forth the tide of song in the banqueting-hall of his prince.   But neither the anxious and breathless expectation of the assembled chiefs and champions — neither the dead silence which stilled the roaring hall, when his harp was reverently placed before him by his attendant — nor even the commands or entreaties of the Prince himself—could extract from Cadwallon more than a short and interrupted prelude upon the instrument, the notes of which arranged themselves into an air inexpressibly mournful, and died away in silence.   The Prince frowned darkly on the bard, who was himself far too deeply lost in gloomy thought, to offer any apology, or even to observe his displeasure. Again he touched a few wild notes, and, raising his looks upward, seemed to be on the very point of bursting forth into a tide of song similar to those with which this master of his art was wont to enchant his hearers.   But the effort was in vain — he declared that his right hand was withered, and pushed the instrument from him.

A murmur went round the company, and Gwenwyn read in their aspects that they received the unusual silence of Cadwallon on this high occasion as a bad omen.   He called hastily on a young and ambitious bard, named Caradoc of Menwygent, whose rising fame was likely soon to vie with the established reputation of Cadwallon, and summoned him to sing something which might command the applause of his sovereign and the gratitude of the company.   The young man was ambitious, and understood the arts of a courtier.   He commenced a poem, in which, although under a feigned name, he drew such a poetic picture of Eveline Berenger, that Gwenwyn was enraptured; and while all who had seen the beautiful original at once recognized the resemblance, the eyes of the Prince confessed at once his passion for the subject, and his admiration of the poet.   The figures of Celtic poetry, in themselves highly imaginative, were scarce sufficient for the enthusiasm of the ambitious bard, rising in his tone as he perceived the feelings which he was exciting.   The praises of the Prince mingled with those of the Norman beauty; and " as a lion," said the poet, " can only be led by the hand of a chaste and beautiful maiden, so a chief can only acknowledge the empire of the most virtuous, the most lovely of her sex.   Who asks of the noonday sun, in what quarter of the world he was born? and who shall ask of such charms as hers, to what country they owe their birth?"

Enthusiasts in pleasure as in war, and possessed of imaginations which answered readily to the summons of their poets, the Welsh chiefs and leaders united in acclamations of applause; and the song of the bard went farther to render popular the intended alliance of the Prince, than had all the graver arguments of his priestly precursor in the same topic.

Gwenwyn himself, in a transport of delight, tore off the golden bracelets which he wore, to bestow them upon a bard whose song had produced an effect so desirable; and said, as he looked at the silent and sullen Cadwallon, "The silent harp was never strung with golden wires."

"Prince," answered the bard, whose pride was at least equal to that of Gwenwyn himself, "you pervert the proverb of Taliessin — it is the flattering harp which never lacked golden strings."

Gwenwyn, turning sternly towards him, was about to make an angry answer, when the sudden appearance of Jorworth, the messenger whom he had despatched to Raymond Berenger, arrested his purpose. This rude envoy entered the hall bare-legged, excepting the sandals of goat-skin which he wore, and having on his shoulder a cloak of the same, and a short javelin in his hand. The dust on his garments, and the flush on his brow, showed with what hasty zeal his errand had been executed. Gwenwyn demanded of him eagerly, "What news from Garde Doloureuse, Jorworth ap Jevan?"

"I bear them in my bosom," said the son of Jevan; and, with much reverence, he delivered to the Prince a packet, bound with silk, and sealed with the impression of a swan, the ancient cognizance of the House of Berenger. Himself ignorant of writing or reading, Gwenwyn, in anxious haste, delivered the letter to Cadwallon, who usually acted as secretary when the chaplain was not in presence, as chanced then to be the case. Cadwallon, looking at the letter, said briefly, "I read no Latin. Ill betide the Norman, who writes to a Prince of Powys in other language than that of Britain! and well was the hour, when that noble tongue alone was spoken from Tintadgel to Cairleoil!"

Gwenwyn only replied to him with an angry glance.

"Where is Father Einion?" said the impatient Prince.

"He assists in the church," replied one of his attendants, "for it is the feast of Saint——"

"Were it the feast of Saint David," said Gwenwyn, "and were the pyx between his hands, he must come hither to me instantly!"

One of the chief henchmen sprung off, to command his attendance, and, in the meantime, Gwenwyn eyed the letter containing the secret of his fate, but which it required an interpreter to read, with such eagerness and anxiety, that Caradoc, elated by his former success, threw in a few notes to divert, if possible, the tenor of his patron's thoughts during the interval. A light and lively air, touched by a hand which seemed to hesitate, like the submissive voice of an inferior, fearing to interrupt his master's meditations, introduced a stanza or two applicable to the subject.

"And what though thou, O scroll," he said, apostrophizing the letter, which lay on the table before his master, "dost speak with the tongue of the stranger? Hath not the cuckoo a harsh note, and yet she tells us of green buds and springing flowers? What if thy language be that of the stoled priest, is it not the same which binds hearts and hands together at the altar? And what though thou delayest to render up thy treasures, are not all pleasures most sweet, when enhanced by expectation? What were the chase, if the deer dropped at our feet the instant he started from the cover—or what value were there in the love of the maiden, were it yielded without coy delay?"

The song of the bard was here broken short by the entrance of the priest, who, hasty in obeying the summons of his impatient master, had not tarried to lay aside even the stole, which he had worn in the holy service; and many of the elders thought it was no good omen, that, so habited, a priest should appear in a festive assembly, and amid profane minstrelsy.

The priest opened the letter of the Norman Baron, and, struck with surprise at the contents, lifted his eyes in silence.

"Read it!" exclaimed the fierce Gwenwyn.

"So please you," replied the more prudent chaplain, "a smaller company were a fitter audience."

"Read it aloud!" repeated the Prince, in a still higher tone; "there are none here who respect not the honour of their prince, or who deserve not his confidence. Read it, I say, aloud! and by Saint David, if Raymond the Norman hath dared——"

He stopped short, and, reclining on his seat, composed himself to an attitude of attention; but it was easy for his followers to fill up the breach in his exclamation which prudence had recommended.

The voice of the chaplain was low and ill-assured as he read the following epistle:—

"Raymond Berenger, the noble Norman Knight, Seneschal of the Garde Doloureuse, to Gwenwyn, Prince of Powys, (may peace be between them!) sendeth health.

"Your letter, craving the hand of our daughter Eveline Berenger, was safely delivered to us by your servant, Jorworth ap Jevan, and we thank you heartily for the good meaning therein expressed to us and to ours. But, considering within ourselves the difference of blood and lineage, with the impediments and causes of offence which have often arisen in like cases, we hold it fitter to match our daughter among our own people; and this by no case in disparagement of you, but solely for the weal of you, of ourselves, and of our mutual dependants, who will be the more safe from the risk of quarrel betwixt us, that we essay not to draw the bonds of our intimure close than beseemeth. The sheep and the goats feed together in peace on the same pastures, but they mingle not in blood, or race, the one with the other. Moreover, our daughter Eveline hath been sought in marriage by a noble and potent Lord of the Marches, Hugo de Lacy, the Constable of Chester, to which most honourable suit we have returned a favourable answer. It is therefore impossible that we should in this matter grant to you the boon you seek; nevertheless, you shall at all times find us, in other matters, willing to pleasure you; and hereunto we call God, and Our Lady, and Saint Mary Magdalene of Quatford, to witness; to whose keeping we heartily recommend you.

"Written by our command, at our Castle of Garde Doloureuse, within the Marches of Wales, by a reverend priest, Father Aldrovand, a black monk of the house of Wenlock; and to which we have appended our seal, upon the eve of the blessed martyr Saint Alphegius, to whom be honour and glory!"

The voice of Father Einion faltered, and the scroll which he held in his hand trembled in his grasp, as he arrived at the conclusion of this epistle; for well he knew that insults more slight than Gwenwyn would hold the least word it contained, were sure to put every drop of his British blood into the most vehement commotion. Nor did it fail to do so. The Prince had gradually drawn himself up from the posture of repose in which he had prepared to listen to the epistle; and when it concluded, he sprung on his feet like a startled lion, spurning from him as he rose the foot-bearer, who rolled at some distance on the floor. "Priest," he said, "hast thou read that accursed scroll fairly? for if thou hast added, or diminished, one word, or one letter, I will have thine eyes so handled, that thou shalt never read letter more!"

The monk replied, trembling, (for he was well aware that the sacerdotal character was not uniformly respected among the irascible Welshmen,) "By the oath of my order, mighty prince, I have read word for word, and letter for letter."

There was a momentary pause, while the fury of Gwenwyn, at this unexpected affront, offered to him in the presence of all his Uckelwyr, (i. e. noble chiefs, literally men of high stature,) seemed too big for utterance, when the silence was broken by a few notes from the hitherto mute harp of Cadwallon. The Prince looked round at first with displeasure at the interruption, for he was himself about to speak; but when he beheld the bard bending over his harp with an air of inspiration, and blending together, with unexampled skill, the wildest and most exalted tones of his art, he himself became an auditor instead of a speaker, and Cadwallon, not the Prince, seemed to become the central point of the assembly, on whom all eyes were bent, and to whom each ear was turned with breathless eagerness, as if his strains were the responses of an oracle.

"We wed not with the stranger,"—thus burst the song from the lips of the poet. "Vortigern wedded with the stranger; thence came the first wo upon Britain, and a sword upon her nobles, and a thunderbolt upon her palace. We wed not with the enslaved Saxon — the free and princely stag seeks not for his bride the heifer whose neck the yoke bath worn. We wed not with the rapacious Norman — the noble hound scorns to seek a mate from the herd of ravening wolves. When was it heard that the Cymry, the descendants of Brute, the true children of the soil of fair Britain, were plundered, oppressed, bereft of their birthright, and insulted even in their last retreats? — when, but since they stretched their hand in friendship to the stranger, and clasped to their bosoms the daughter of the Saxon? Which of the two is feared? — the empty water-course of summer, or the channel of the headlong winter torrent? — A maiden smiles at the summer-shrunk brook while she crosses it, but a barbed horse and his rider will fear to stem the wintry flood. Men of Mathravel and Powys, be the dreaded flood, winter — Gwenwyn, son of Cyverliock! — may thy plume be the topmost of its waves!"

All thoughts of peace, thoughts which, in themselves, were foreign to the hearts of the warlike British, passed before the song of Cadwallon like dust before the whirlwind, and the unanimous shout of the assembly declared for instant war. The Prince himself spoke not, but, looking proudly around him, flung abroad his arm, as one who cheers his followers to the attack.

The priest, had he dared, might have reminded Gwenwyn, that the Cross which he had assumed on his shoulder, had consecrated his arm to the Holy War, and precluded his engaging in any civil strife. But the task was too dangerous for Father Einion's courage, and he shrunk from the hall to the seclusion of his own convent. Caradoc, whose brief hour of popularity was past, also retired, with humbled and dejected looks, and not without a glance of indignation at his triumphant rival, who had so judiciously reserved his display of art for the theme of war, that was ever most popular with the audience.

The chiefs resumed their seats no longer for the purpose of festivity, but to fix, in the hasty manner customary among these prompt warriors, where they were to assemble their forces, which, upon such occasions, comprehended almost all the able-bodied males of the country, — for all, excepting the priests and the bards, were soldiers, — and to settle the order of their descent upon the devoted marches, where they proposed to signalize, by general ravage, their sense of the insult which their Prince had received, by the rejection of his suit.

Chapter the Third.

The sands are number'd, that make up my life;
Here must I stay, and here my life must end.
                              HENRY VI. ACT. I. SCENE IV.

WHEN Raymond Berenger had despatched his mission to the Prince of Powys, he was not unsuspicious, though altogether fearless, of the result. He sent messengers to the several dependants who held their fiefs by the tenure of *cornage*, and warned them to be on the alert, that he might receive instant notice of the approach of the enemy. These vassals, as is well known, occupied the numerous towers, which, like so many falcon-nests, had been built on the points most convenient to defend the frontiers, and were bound to give signal of any incursion of the Welsh, by blowing their horns; which sounds, answered from tower to tower, and from station to station, gave the alarm for general defence. But although Raymond considered these precautions as necessary, from the fickle and precarious temper of his neighbours, and for maintaining his own credit as a soldier, he was far from believing the danger to be imminent; for the preparations of the Welsh, though on a much more extensive scale than had lately been usual, were as secret, as their resolution of war had been suddenly adopted.

It was upon the second morning after the memorable festival of Castell-Coch, that the tempest broke on the Norman frontier. At first a single, long, and keen bugle-blast, announced the approach of the enemy; presently the signals of alarm were echoed from every castle and tower on the borders of Shropshire, where every place of habitation was then a fortress. Beacons were lighted upon crags and eminences, the bells were rung backward in the churches and towns, while the general and earnest summons to arms announced an extremity of danger which even the inhabitants of that unsettled country had not hitherto experienced.

Amid this general alarm, Raymond Berenger, having busied himself in arranging his few but gallant followers and adherents, and taken such modes of procuring intelligence of the enemy's strength and motions as were in his power, at length ascended the watch-tower of the castle, to observe in person the country around, already obscured in several places by the clouds of smoke, which announced the progress and the ravages of the invaders. He was speedily joined by his favourite squire, to whom the unusual heaviness of his master's looks was cause of much surprise, for till now they had ever been blithest at the hour of battle. The squire held in his hand his master's helmet, for Sir Raymond was all armed, saving the head.

"Dennis Morolt," said the veteran soldier, "are our vassals and liegemen all mustered?"

"All, noble sir, but the Flemings, who are not yet come in."

"The lazy hounds, why tarry they?" said Raymond. "Ill policy it is to plant such sluggish natures in our borders. They are like their own steers, fitter to tug a plough than for aught that requires mettle."

"With your favour," said Dennis, "the knaves can do good service notwithstanding. That Wilkin Flammock of the Green can strike like the hammers of his own fulling-mill."

"He will fight, I believe, when he cannot help it," said Raymond; "but he has no stomach for such exercise, and is as slow and as stubborn, as a mule."

"And therefore are his countrymen rightly matched against the Welsh," replied Dennis Morolt, "that their solid and unyielding temper may be a fit foil to the fiery and headlong dispositions of our dangerous neighbours, just as restless waves are best opposed by steadfast rocks. — Hark, sir, I hear Wilkin Flammock's step ascending the turret-stair, as deliberately as ever monk mounted to matins."

Step by step the heavy sound approached, until the form of the huge and substantial Fleming at length issued from the turret-door to the platform where they were conversing. Wilkin Flammock was cased in bright armour, of unusual weight and thickness, and cleaned with exceeding care, which marked the neatness of his nation; but, contrary to the custom of the Normans, entirely plain, and void of carving, gilding, or any sort of ornament. The basenet, or steel-cap, had no visor, and left exposed a broad countenance, with heavy and unpliable features, which announced the character of his temper and understanding. He carried in his hand a heavy mace.

" So, Sir Fleming," said the Castellane, " you are in no hurry, methinks, to repair to the rendezvous."

" So please you," answered the Fleming, " we were compelled to tarry, that we might load our wains with our bales of cloth and other property."

" Ha! wains?—how many wains have you brought with you?"

" Six, noble sir," replied Wilkin.

" And how many men?" demanded Raymond Berenger.

" Twelve, valiant sir," answered Flammock.

" Only two men to each baggage-wain? I wonder you would thus encumber yourself," said Berenger.

" Under your favour, sir, once more," replied Wilkin, " it is only the value which I and my comrades set upon our goods, that inclines us to defend them with our bodies; and, had we been obliged to leave our cloth to the plundering clutches of yonder vagabonds, I should have seen small policy in stopping here to give them the opportunity of adding murder to robbery. Gloucester should have been my first halting-place."

The Norman knight gazed on the Flemish artisan, for such was Wilkin Flammock, with such a mixture of surprise and contempt, as excluded indignation. " I have heard much," he said, " but this is the first time that I have heard one with a beard on his lip avouch himself a coward."

" Nor do you hear it now," answered Flammock, with the utmost composure—" I am always ready to fight for life and property; and my coming to this country, where they are both in constant danger, shows that I care not much how often I do so. But a sound skin is better than a slashed one, for all that."

" Well," said Raymond Berenger, " fight after thine own fashion, so thou wilt but fight stoutly with that long body of thine. We are like to have need for all that we can do. — Saw you aught of these rascaille Welsh? — have they Gwenwyn's banner amongst them?"

" I saw it with the white dragon displayed," replied Wilkin; " I could not but know it, since it was broidered in my own loom."

Raymond looked so grave upon this intelligence, that Dennis Morolt, unwilling the Fleming should mark it, thought it necessary to withdraw his attention. " I can tell thee," he said to Flammock, " that when the Constable of Chester joins us with his lances, you shall see your handiwork, the dragon, fly faster homeward than ever flew the shuttle which wove it."

" It must fly before the Constable comes up, Dennis Morolt," said Berenger, " else it will fly triumphant over all our bodies."

" In the name of God and the Holy Virgin!" said Dennis, " what may you mean, Sir Knight?—not that we should fight with the Welsh before the Constable joins us?"— He paused, and then, well understanding the firm, yet melancholy glance, with which his master answered the question, he proceeded, with yet more vehement earnestness—" You cannot mean it — you cannot intend that we shall quit this castle, which we have so often made good against them, and contend in the field with two hundred men against thousands?—Think better of it, my beloved master, and let not the rashness of your old age blemish that character for wisdom and warlike skill, which your former life has so nobly won."

"I am not angry with you for blaming my purpose, Dennis," answered the Norman, "for I know you do it in love to me and mine. But, Dennis Morolt, this thing must be—we must fight the Welshmen within these three hours, or the name of Raymond Berenger must be blotted from the genealogy of his house."

"And so we will—we will fight them, my noble master," said the esquire; "fear not cold counsel from Dennis Morolt, where battle is the theme. But we will fight them under the walls of the castle, with honest Wilkin Flammock and his crossbows on the wall to protect our flanks, and afford us some balance against the numerous odds."

"Not so, Dennis," answered his master — "In the open field we must fight them, or thy master must rank but as a mansworn knight. Know, that when I feasted yonder wily savage in my halls at Christmas, and when the wine was flowing fastest around, Gwenwyn threw out some praises of the fastness and strength of my castle, in a manner which intimated it was these advantages alone that had secured me in former wars from defeat and captivity. I spoke in answer, when I had far better been silent; for what availed my idle boast, but as a fetter to bind me to a deed next to madness? If, I said, a prince of the Cymry shall come in hostile fashion before the Garde Doloureuse, let him pitch his standard down in yonder plain by the bridge, and, by the word of a good knight, and the faith of a Christian man, Raymond Berenger will meet him as willingly, be he many or be he few, as ever Welshman was met withal."

Dennis was struck speechless when he heard of a promise so rash, so fatal; but his was not the casuistry which could release his master from the fetters with which his unwary confidence had bound him. It was otherwise with Wilkin Flammock. He stared—he almost laughed, notwithstanding the reverence due to the Castellane, and his own insensibility to risible emotions. "And is this all?" he said. "If your honour had pledged yourself to pay one hundred florins to a Jew or to a Lombard, no doubt you must have kept the day, or forfeited your pledge; but surely one day is as good as another to keep a promise for fighting, and that day is best in which the promiser is strongest. But indeed, after all, what signifies any promise over a wine flagon?"

"It signifies as much as a promise can do that is given elsewhere. The promiser," said Berenger, "escapes not the sin of a word-breaker, because he hath been a drunken braggart."

"For the sin," said Dennis, "sure I am, that rather than you should do such a deed of dole, the Abbot of Glastonbury would absolve you for a florin."

"But what shall wipe out the shame?" demanded Berenger—"how shall I dare to show myself again among press of knights, who have broken my word of battle pledged, for fear of a Welshman and his naked savages? No! Dennis Morolt, speak on it no more. Be it for weal or wo, we fight them to-day, and upon yonder fair field."

"It may be," said Flammock, "that Gwenwyn may have forgotten the promise, and so fail to appear to claim it in the appointed space; for, as we heard, your wines of France flooded his Welsh brains deeply."

"He again alluded to it on the morning after it was made," said the Castellane—"trust me, he will not forget what will give him such a chance of removing me from his path for ever."

As he spoke, they observed that large clouds of dust, which had been seen at different points of the landscape, were drawing down towards the opposite side of the river, over which an ancient bridge extended itself to the appointed place of combat. They were at no loss to conjecture the cause. It was evident that Gwenwyn, recalling the parties who had been engaged in partial devastation, was bending with his whole forces towards the bridge and the plain beyond it.

"Let us rush down and secure the pass," said Dennis Morolt; "we may debate with them with some equality by the advantage of defending the bridge. Your word bound you to the plain as to a field of battle, but it did not oblige you to forego such advantages as the passage of the bridge would afford. Our men, our horses, are ready—let our bowmen secure the banks, and my life on the issue."

"When I promised to meet him in yonder field, I meant," replied Raymond Berenger, "to give the Welshman the full advantage of equality of ground. I so meant it—he so understood it; and what avails keeping my word in the letter, if I break it in the sense? We move not till the last Welshman has crossed the bridge; and then ——"

"And then," said Dennis, "we move to our death!—May God forgive our sins!—But ——"

"But what?" said Berenger; "something sticks in thy mind that should have vent."

"My young lady, your daughter the Lady Eveline ——"

"I have told her what is to be. She shall remain in the castle, where I will leave a few chosen veterans, with you, Dennis, to command them. In twenty-four hours the siege will be relieved, and we have defended it longer with a slighter garrison. Then to her aunt, the Abbess of the Benedictine sisters—thou, Dennis, wilt see her placed there in honour and safety, and my sister will care for her future provision as her wisdom shall determine."

"*I* leave you at this pinch!" said Dennis Morolt, bursting into tears—"*I* shut myself up within walls, when my master rides to his last of battles! —*I* become esquire to a lady, even though it be to the Lady Eveline, when he lies dead under his shield!—Raymond Berenger, is it for this that I have buckled thy armour so often?"

The tears gushed from the old warrior's eyes as fast as from those of a girl who weeps for her lover; and Raymond, taking him kindly by the hand, said, in a soothing tone, "Do not think, my good old servant, that, were honour to be won, I would drive thee from my side. But this is a wild and an inconsiderate deed, to which my fate or my folly has bound me. I die to save my name from dishonour; but, alas! I must leave on my memory the charge of imprudence."

"Let me share your imprudence, my dearest master," said Dennis Morolt, earnestly—"the poor esquire has no business to be thought wiser than his master. In many a battle my valour derived some little fame from partaking in thee deeds which won your renown—deny me not the right to share in that blame which your temerity may incur; let them not say, that so rash was his action, even his old esquire was not permitted to partake in it! I am part of yourself—it is murder to every man whom you take with you, if you leave me behind."

"Dennis," said Berenger, "you make me feel yet more bitterly the folly I have yielded to. I would grant you the boon you ask, sad as it is—But my daughter ——"

"Sir Knight," said the Fleming, who had listened to this dialogue with somewhat less than his usual apathy, "it is not my purpose this day to leave this castle; now, if you could trust my troth to do what a plain man may for the protection of my Lady Eveline ——"

"How, sirrah!" said Raymond; "you do not propose to leave the castle? Who gives you right to propose or dispose in the case, until my pleasure is known?"

"I shall be sorry to have words with you, Sir Castellane," said the imperturbable Fleming;—"but I hold here, in this township, certain mills, tenements, cloth-yards, and so forth, for which I am to pay man-service in defending this Castle of the Garde Doloureuse, and in this I am ready. But if you call on me to march from hence, leaving the same castle defenceless, and to offer up my life in a battle which you acknowledge to be desperate, I must needs say my tenure binds me not to obey thee."

"Base mechanic!" said Morolt, laying his hand on his dagger, and menacing the Fleming.

But Raymond Berenger interfered with voice and hand—"Harm him not, Morolt, and blame him not. He hath a sense of duty, though not after our manner; and he and his knaves will fight best behind stone walls. They are taught also, these Flemings, by the practice of their own country, the attack and defence of walled cities and fortresses, and are especially skilful in working of mangonels and military engines. There are several of his countrymen in the castle, besides his own followers. These I propose to leave behind; and I think they will obey him more readily than any but thyself—how think'st thou? Thou wouldst not, I know, from a misconstrued point of honour, or a blind love to me, leave this important place, and the safety of Eveline, in doubtful hands?"

"Wilkin Flammock is but a Flemish clown, noble sir," answered Dennis, as much overjoyed as if he had obtained some important advantage; "but I must needs say he is as stout and true as any whom you might trust; and, besides, his own shrewdness will teach him there is more to be gained by defending such a castle as this, than by yielding it to strangers, who may not be likely to keep the terms of surrender, however fairly they may offer them."

"It is fixed then," said Raymond Berenger. "Then, Dennis, thou shalt go with me, and he shall remain behind.—Wilkin Flammock," he said, addressing the Fleming solemnly, "I speak not to thee the language of chivalry, of which thou knowest nothing; but, as thou art an honest man, and a true Christian, I conjure thee to stand to the defence of this castle. Let no promise of the enemy draw thee to any base composition—no threat to any surrender. Relief must speedily arrive, if you fulfil your trust to me and to my daughter, Hugo de Lacy will reward you richly—if you fail, he will punish you severely."

"Sir Knight," said Flammock, "I am pleased you have put your trust so far in a plain handicraftsman. For the Welsh, I am come from a land for which we were compelled—yearly compelled—to struggle with the sea; and they who can deal with the waves in a tempest, need not fear an undisciplined people in their fury. Your daughter shall be as dear to me as mine own; and in that faith you may prick forth—if, indeed, you will not still, like a wiser man, shut gate, down portcullis, up drawbridge, and let your archers and my crossbows man the wall, and tell the knaves you are not the fool that they take you for."

"Good fellow, that must not be," said the Knight. "I hear my daughter's voice," he added hastily; "I would not again meet her, again to part from her. To Heaven's keeping I commit thee, honest Fleming.—Follow me, Dennis Morolt."

The old Castellane descended the stair of the southern tower hastily, just as his daughter Eveline ascended that of the eastern turret, to throw herself at his feet once more. She was followed by the Father Aldrovand, chaplain of her father; by an old and almost invalid huntsman, whose more active services in the field and the chase had been for some time chiefly limited to the superintendence of the Knight's kennels, and the charge especially of his more favourite hounds; and by Rose Flammock, the daughter of Wilkin, a blue-eyed Flemish maiden, round, plump, and shy as a partridge, who had been for some time permitted to keep company with the high-born Norman damsel, in a doubtful station, betwixt that of an humble friend and a superior domestic.

Eveline rushed upon the battlements, her hair disl.vslled, and her eyes drowned in tears, and eagerly demanded of the Fleming where her father was.

Flammock made a clumsy reverence, and attempted some answer; but his voice seemed to fail him. He turned his back upon Eveline without ceremony, and totally disregarding the anxious inquiries of the huntsman and the chaplain, he said hastily to his daughter, in his own language, "Mad work! mad work! look to the poor maiden, Roschen—*Der alter Herr ist verruckt.*" *

Without farther speech he descended the stairs, and never paused till he reached the buttery. Here he called like a lion for the controller of these regions, by the various names of Kammerer, Keller-master, and so forth, to which the old Reinold, an ancient Norman esquire, answered not, until the Netherlander fortunately recollected his Anglo-Norman title of butler. This, his regular name of office, was the key to the buttery-hatch, and the old man instantly appeared, with his gray cassock and high rolled hose, a ponderous bunch of keys suspended by a silver chain to his broad leathern girdle, which, in consideration of the emergency of the time, he had thought it right to balance on the left side with a huge falchion, which seemed much too weighty for his old arm to wield.

"What is your will," he said, "Master Flammock? or what are your commands, since it is my lord's pleasure that they shall be laws to me for a time?"

"Only a cup of wine, good Meister Keller-master — butler, I mean."

"I am glad you remember the name of mine office," said Reinold, with some of the petty resentment of a spoiled domestic, who thinks that a stranger has been irregularly put in command over him.

"A flagon of Rhenish, if you love me," answered the Fleming, "for my heart is low and poor within me, and I must needs drink of the best."

"And drink you shall," said Reinold, "if drink will give you the courage which perhaps you want." — He descended to the secret crypts, of which he was the guardian, and returned with a silver flagon, which might contain about a quart. — "Here is such wine," said Reinold, "as thou hast seldom tasted," and was about to pour it out into a cup.

"Nay, the flagon—the flagon, friend Reinold; I love a deep and solemn draught when the business is weighty," said Wilkin. He seized on the flagon accordingly, and drinking a preparatory mouthful, paused as if to estimate the strength and flavour of the generous liquor. Apparently he was pleased with both, for he nodded in approbation to the butler; and, raising the flagon to his mouth once more, he slowly and gradually brought the bottom of the vessel parallel with the roof of the apartment, without suffering one drop of the contents to escape him.

"That hath savour, Herr Keller-master," said he, while he was recovering his breath by intervals, after so long a suspense of respiration; "but, may Heaven forgive you for thinking it the best I have ever tasted! You little know the cellars of Ghent and of Ypres."

"And I care not for them," said Reinold; "those of gentle Norman blood hold the wines of Gascony and France, generous, light, and cordial, worth all the acid potations of the Rhine and the Neckar."

"All is matter of taste," said the Fleming; "but hark ye — Is there much of this wine in the cellar?"

"Methought but now it pleased not your dainty palate?" said Reinold.

"Nay, nay, my friend," said Wilkin, "I said it had savour—I may have drunk better—but this is right good, where better may not be had.—Again, now much of it hast thou?"

"The whole butt, man," answered the butler; "I have broached a fresh piece for you."

---

* The old lord is frantic.

"Good," replied Flammock; "get the quart-pot of Christian measure; heave the cask up into this same buttery, and let each soldier of this castle be served with such a cup as I have here swallowed. I feel it hath done me much good—my heart was sinking when I saw the black smoke arising from mine own fulling-mills yonder. Let each man, I say, have a full quart-pot—men defend not castles on thin liquors."

"I must do as you will, good Wilkin Flammock," said the butler; "but I pray you, remember all men are not alike. That which will but warm you, Flemish hearts, will put wildfire into Norman brains; and what may only encourage your countrymen to man the walls, will make ours fly over the battlements."

"Well, you know the conditions of your own countrymen best; serve out to them what wines and measure you list—only let each Fleming have a solemn quart of Rhenish.—But what will you do for the English churls, of whom there are a right many left with us?"

The old butler paused, and rubbed his brow. —"There will be a strange waste of liquor," he said; "and yet I may not deny that the emergency may defend the expenditure. But for the English, they are, as you wot, a mixed breed, having much of your German sullenness, together with a plentiful touch of the hot blood of yonder Welsh furies. Light wines stir them not; strong heavy draughts would madden them. What think you of ale, an invigorating, strengthening liquor, that warms the heart without inflaming the brain?"

"Ale!" said the Fleming.—"Hum—ha—is your ale mighty, Sir Butler? —is it double ale?"

'Do you doubt my skill?" said the butler. —"March and October have witnessed me ever as they came round, for thirty years, deal with the best barley in Shropshire.—You shall judge."

He filled, from a large hogshead in the corner of the buttery, the flagon which the Fleming had just emptied, and which was no sooner replenished than Wilkin again drained it to the bottom.

"Good ware," he said, "Master Butler, strong stinging ware. The English churls will fight like devils upon it—let them be furnished with mighty ale along with their beef and brown bread. And now, having given you your charge, Master Reinold, it is time I should look after mine own."

Wilkin Flammock left the buttery, and with a mien and judgment alike undisturbed by the deep potations in which he had so recently indulged, undisturbed also by the various rumours concerning what was passing without doors, he made the round of the castle and its outworks, mustered the little garrison, and assigned to each their posts, reserving to his own countrymen the management of the arblasts, or crossbows, and of the military engines which were contrived by the proud Normans, and were incomprehensible to the ignorant English, or, more properly, Anglo-Saxons, of the period, but which his more adroit countrymen managed with great address. The jealousies entertained by both the Normans and English, at being placed under the temporary command of a Fleming, gradually yielded to the military and mechanical skill which he displayed, as well as to a sense of the emergency, which became greater with every moment.

Chapter the Fourth.

Beside you brigg out ower yon burn,
   Where the water bickereth bright and sheen,
Shall many a falling courser spurn,
   And knights shall die in battle keen.
       PROPHECY OF THOMAS THE RHYMER.

THE daughter of Raymond Berenger, with the attendants whom we have mentioned, continued to remain upon the battlements of the Garde Douloureuse, in spite of the exhortations of the priest that she would rather await the issue of this terrible interval in the chapel, and amid the rites of religion. He perceived, at length, that she was incapable, from grief and fear, of attending to, or understanding his advice; and, sitting down beside her, while the huntsman and Rose Flammock stood by, endeavoured to suggest such comfort as perhaps he scarcely felt himself.

"This is but a sally of your noble father's," he said; "and though it may seem it is made on great hazard, yet who ever questioned Sir Raymond Berenger's policy of wars?—He is close and secret in his purposes. I guess right well he had not marched out as he proposes, unless he knew that the noble Earl of Arundel, or the mighty Constable of Chester, were close at hand."

"Think you this assuredly, good father?—Go, Raoul—go, my dearest Rose—look to the east—see if you cannot descry banners or clouds of dust.—Listen—listen—hear you no trumpets from that quarter?"

"Alas! my lady," said Raoul, "the thunder of heaven could scarce be heard amid the howling of yonder Welsh wolves." Eveline turned as he spoke, and looking towards the bridge, she beheld an appalling spectacle.

The river, whose stream washes on three sides the base of the proud eminence on which the castle is situated, curves away from the fortress and its corresponding village on the west, and the hill sinks downward to an extensive plain, so extremely level as to indicate its alluvial origin. Lower down, at the extremity of this plain, where the banks again close on the river, were situated the manufacturing houses of the stout Flemings, which were now burning in a bright flame. The bridge, a high, narrow combination of arches of unequal size, was about half a mile distant from the castle, in the very centre of the plain. The river itself ran in a deep rocky channel, was often unfordable, and at all times difficult of passage, giving considerable advantage to the defenders of the castle, who had spent on other occasions many a dear drop of blood to defend the pass, which Raymond Berenger's fantastic scruples now induced him to abandon. The Welshmen, seizing the opportunity with the avidity with which men grasp an unexpected benefit, were fast crowding over the high and steep arches, while new bands, collecting from different points upon the farther bank, increased the continued stream of warriors, who, passing leisurely and uninterrupted, formed their line of battle on the plain opposite to the castle.

At first Father Aldrovand viewed their motions without anxiety, nay, with the scornful smile of one who observes an enemy in the act of falling into the snare spread for them by superior skill. Raymond Berenger, with his little body of infantry and cavalry, were drawn up on the easy hill which is betwixt the castle and the plain, ascending from the former towards the fortress; and it seemed clear to the Dominican, who had not entirely forgotten in the cloister his ancient military experience, that it was the Knight's purpose to attack the disordered enemy when a certain number had crossed the river, and the others were partly on the farther side, and partly engaged in the slow and perilous manoeuvre of effecting their passage. But when large bodies of the white-mantled Welshmen were permitted

without interruption to take such order on the plain as their habits of
fighting recommended, the monk's countenance, though he still endeavoured
to speak encouragement to the terrified Eveline, assumed a different and an
anxious expression; and his acquired habits of resignation contended
strenuously with his ancient military ardour. "Be patient," he said, "my
daughter, and be of good comfort; thine eyes shall behold the dismay of
yonder barbarous enemy. Let but a minute elapse, and thou shalt see
them scattered like dust.—Saint George! they will surely cry thy name
now, or never!"

The monk's beads passed meanwhile rapidly through his hands, but many
an expression of military impatience mingled itself with his orisons. He
could not conceive the cause why each successive throng of mountaineers,
led under their different banners, and headed by their respective chieftains,
was permitted, without interruption, to pass the difficult defile, and extend
themselves in battle array on the near side of the bridge, while the English,
or rather Anglo-Norman cavalry, remained stationary, without so much as
laying their lances in rest. There remained, as he thought, but one hope
—one only rational explanation of this unaccountable inactivity—this
voluntary surrender of every advantage of ground, when that of numbers
was so tremendously on the side of the enemy. Father Aldrovand concluded,
that the succours of the Constable of Chester, and other Lord Marchers,
must be in the immediate vicinity, and that the Welsh were only permitted
to pass the river without opposition, that their retreat might be the more
effectually cut off, and their defeat, with a deep river in their rear, rendered
the more signally calamitous. But even while he clung to this hope, the
monk's heart sunk within him, as, looking in every direction from which
the expected succours might arrive, he could neither see nor hear the
slightest token which announced their approach. In a frame of mind approaching more nearly to despair than to hope, the old man continued
alternately to tell his beads, to gaze anxiously around, and to address some
words of consolation in broken phrases to the young lady, until the general
shout of the Welsh, ringing from the bank of the river to the battlements
of the castle, warned him, in a note of exultation, that the very last of the
British had defiled through the pass, and that their whole formidable array
stood prompt for action upon the hither side of the river.

This thrilling and astounding clamour, to which each Welshman lent
his voice with all the energy of defiance, thirst of battle, and hope of conquest, was at length answered by the blast of the Norman trumpets,—the
first sign of activity which had been exhibited on the part of Raymond
Berenger. But cheerily as they rang, the trumpets, in comparison of the
shout which they answered, sounded like the silver whistle of the stout
boatswain amid the howling of the tempest.

At the same moment when the trumpets were blown, Berenger gave
signal to the archers to discharge their arrows, and the men-at-arms to
advance under a hail-storm of shafts, javelins, and stones, shot, darted, and
slung by the Welsh against their steel-clad assailants.

The veterans of Raymond, on the other hand, stimulated by so many
victorious recollections, confident in the talents of their accomplished leader,
and undismayed even by the desperation of their circumstances, charged
the mass of the Welshmen with their usual determined valour. It was a
gallant sight to see this little body of cavalry advance to the onset, their
plumes floating above their helmets, their lances in rest, and projecting six
feet in length before the breasts of their coursers; their shields hanging
from their necks, that their left hands might have freedom to guide their
horses; and the whole body rushing on with an equal front, and a momentum of speed which increased with every second. Such an onset might
have startled naked men, (for such were the Welsh, in respect of the mail-
sheathed Normans,) but it brought no terrors to the ancient British, wh

had long made it their boast that they exposed their bare bosoms and white tunics to the lances and swords of the men-at-arms, with as much confidence as if they had been born invulnerable. It was not indeed in their power to withstand the weight of the first shock, which, breaking their ranks, densely as they were arranged, carried the barbed horses into the very centre of their host, and well-nigh up to the fatal standard, to which Raymond Berenger, bound by his fatal vow, had that day conceded so much vantage-ground. But they yielded like the billows, which give way, indeed, to the gallant ship, but only to assail her sides, and to unite in her wake. With wild and horrible clamours, they closed their tumultuous ranks around Berenger and his devoted followers, and a deadly scene of strife ensued.

The best warriors of Wales had on this occasion joined the standard of Gwenwyn; the arrows of the men of Gwentland, whose skill in archery almost equalled that of the Normans themselves, rattled on the helmets of the men-at-arms; and the spears of the people of Deheubarth, renowned for the sharpness and temper of their steel heads, were employed against the cuirasses not without fatal effect, notwithstanding the protection which these afforded to the rider.

It was in vain that the archery belonging to Raymond's little band, stout yeomen, who, for the most part, held possession by military tenure, exhausted their quivers on the broad mark afforded them by the Welsh army. It is probable, that every shaft carried a Welshman's life on its point; yet, to have afforded important relief to the cavalry, now closely and inextricably engaged, the slaughter ought to have been twenty-fold at least. Meantime, the Welsh, galled by this incessant discharge, answered it by volleys from their own archers, whose numbers made some amends for their inferiority, and who were supported by numerous bodies of darters and slingers. So that the Norman archers, who had more than once attempted to descend from their position to operate a diversion in favour of Raymond and his devoted band, were now so closely engaged in front, as obliged them to abandon all thoughts of such a movement.

Meanwhile, that chivalrous leader, who from the first had hoped for no more than an honourable death, laboured with all his power to render his fate signal, by involving in it that of the Welsh Prince, the author of the war. He cautiously avoided the expenditure of his strength by hewing among the British; but, with the shock of his managed horse, repelled the numbers who pressed on him, and leaving the plebeians to the swords of his companions, shouted his war-cry, and made his way towards the fatal standard of Gwenwyn, beside which, discharging at once the duties of a skilful leader and a brave soldier, the Prince had stationed himself. Raymond's experience of the Welsh disposition, subject equally to the highest flood, and most sudden ebb of passion, gave him some hope that a successful attack upon this point, followed by the death or capture of the Prince, and the downfall of his standard, might even yet strike such a panic, as should change the fortunes of the day, otherwise so nearly desperate. The veteran, therefore, animated his comrades to the charge by voice and example; and, in spite of all opposition, forced his way gradually onward. But Gwenwyn in person, surrounded by his best and noblest champions, offered a defence as obstinate as the assault was intrepid. In vain they were borne to the earth by the barbed horses, or hewed down by the invulnerable riders. Wounded and overthrown, the Britons continued their resistance, clung round the legs of the Norman steeds, and cumbered their advance; while their brethren, thrusting with pikes, proved every joint and crevice of the plate and mail, or grappling with the men-at-arms, strove to pull them from their horses by main force, or beat them down with their bills and Welsh hooks. And wo betide those who were by these various means dismounted, for the long sharp knives worn by the Welsh soon pierced them

2 B

with a hundred wounds, and were then only merciful when the first inflicted was deadly.

The combat was at this point, and had raged for more than half an hour, when Berenger, having forced his horse within two spears' length of the British standard, he and Gwenwyn were so near to each other as to exchange tokens of mutual defiance.

"Turn thee, Wolf of Wales," said Berenger, "and abide, if thou darest, one blow of a good knight's sword! Raymond Berenger spits at thee and thy banner."

"False Norman churl!" said Gwenwyn, swinging around his head a mace of prodigious weight, and already clottered with blood, "thy iron head-piece shall ill protect thy lying tongue, with which I will this day feed the ravens."

Raymond made no farther answer, but pushed his horse towards the Prince, who advanced to meet him with equal readiness. But ere they came within reach of each other's weapons, a Welsh champion, devoted like the Romans who opposed the elephants of Pyrrhus, finding that the armour of Raymond's horse resisted the repeated thrusts of his spear, threw himself under the animal, and stabbed him in the belly with his long knife. The noble horse reared and fell, crushing with his weight the Briton who had wounded him; the helmet of the rider burst its clasps in the fall, and rolled away from his head, giving to view his noble features and gray hairs. He made more than one effort to extricate himself from the fallen horse, but ere he could succeed, received his death-wound from the hand of Gwenwyn, who hesitated not to strike him down with his mace while in the act of extricating himself.

During the whole of this bloody day, Dennis Morolt's horse had kept pace for pace, and his arm blow for blow, with his master's. It seemed as if two different bodies had been moving under one act of volition. He husbanded his strength, or put it forth, exactly as he observed his knight did, and was close by his side, when he made the last deadly effort. At that fatal moment, when Raymond Berenger rushed on the chief, the brave squire forced his way up to the standard, and, grasping it firmly, struggled for possession of it with a gigantic Briton, to whose care it had been confided, and who now exerted his utmost strength to defend it. But even while engaged in this mortal struggle, the eye of Morolt scarcely left his master; and when he saw him fall, his own force seemed by sympathy to abandon him, and the British champion had no longer any trouble in laying him prostrate among the slain.

The victory of the British was now complete. Upon the fall of their leader, the followers of Raymond Berenger would willingly have fled or surrendered. But the first was impossible, so closely had they been enveloped; and in the cruel wars maintained by the Welsh upon their frontiers, quarter to the vanquished was out of question. A few of the men-at-arms were lucky enough to disentangle themselves from the tumult, and, not even attempting to enter the castle, fled in various directions, to carry their own fears among the inhabitants of the marches, by announcing the loss of the battle, and the fate of the far-renowned Raymond Berenger.

The archers of the fallen leader, as they had never been so deeply involved in the combat, which had been chiefly maintained by the cavalry, became now, in their turn, the sole object of the enemy's attack. But when they saw the multitude come roaring towards them like a sea, with all its waves, they abandoned the bank which they had hitherto bravely defended, and began a regular retreat to the castle in the best order which they could, as the only remaining means of securing their lives. A few of their light-footed enemies attempted to intercept them, during the execution of this prudent manœuvre, by outstripping them in their march, and throwing themselves into the hollow way which led to the castle, to oppose their retreat. But the coolness of the English archers, accustomed to extremities of every kind, supported them on the present occasion. While a part of them, armed with glaives and bills, dislodged the Welsh from the hollow way, the others, facing in the opposite direction, and parted into divisions, which alternately halted and retreated, maintained such a countenance as to check pursuit, and exchange a severe discharge of missiles with the Welsh, by which both parties were considerable sufferers.

At length, having left more than two-thirds of their brave companions behind them, the yeomanry attained the point, which, being commanded by arrows and engines from the battlements, might be considered as that of comparative safety. A volley of large stones, and square-headed bolts of great size and thickness, effectually stopped the farther progress of the pursuit, and those who had led it drew back their desultory forces to the plain, where, with shouts of jubilee and exultation, their countrymen were employed in securing the plunder of the field ; while some, impelled by hatred and revenge, mangled and mutilated the limbs of the dead Normans, in a manner unworthy of their national cause and their own courage. The fearful yells with which this dreadful work was consummated, while it struck horror into the minds of the slender garrison of the Garde Douloureuse, inspired them at the same time with the resolution rather to defend the fortress to the last extremity, than to submit to the mercy of so vengeful an enemy.*

Chapter the Fifth.

That baron he to his castle fled,
    To Barnard Castle then fled he ;
The uttermost walls were eathe to win,
    The Earls have won them speedilie ;—
The uttermost walls were stone and brick ;
    But though they won them soon anoa,
Long are they won the inmost walls,
    For they were hewn in rock of stone.

PERCY'S RELICS OF ANCIENT POETRY.

THE unhappy fate of the battle was soon evident to the anxious spectators upon the watch-towers of the Garde Douloureuse, which name the castle that day too well deserved. With difficulty the confessor mastered his own emotions to control those of the females on whom he attended, and who were now joined in their lamentation by many others — women, children, and infirm old men, the relatives of those whom they saw engaged in this unavailing contest. These helpless beings had been admitted to the castle for security's sake, and they had now thronged to the battlements, from which Father Aldrovand found difficulty in making them descend, aware that the sight of them on the towers, that should have appeared lined with armed men, would be an additional encouragement to the exertions of the assailants. He urged the Lady Eveline to set an example to this group of helpless, yet intractable mourners.

Preserving, at least endeavouring to preserve, even in the extremity of grief, that composure which the manners of the times enjoined—for chivalry

* This is by no means exaggerated in the text. A very honourable testimony was given to their valour by King Henry II., in a letter to the Greek Emperor, Emanuel Commenos. This prince having desired that an account might be sent him of all that was remarkable in the island of Great Britain, Henry, in answer to that request, was pleased to take notice, among other particulars, of the extraordinary courage and fierceness of the Welsh, who were not afraid to fight unarmed with enemies armed at all points, valiantly shedding their blood in the cause of their country, and purchasing glory at the expense of their lives.

had its stoicism as well as philosophy—Eveline replied in a voice which she would fain have rendered firm, and which was tremulous in her despite — "Yes, father, you say well—here is no longer aught left for maidens to look upon. Warlike meed and honoured deed sunk when yonder white plume touched the bloody ground. — Come, maidens, there is no longer aught left us to see—To mass, to mass—the tourney is over!"

There was wildness in her tone, and when she rose, with the air of one who would fain lead out a procession, she staggered, and would have fallen, but for the support of the confessor. Hastily wrapping her head in her mantle, as if ashamed of the agony of grief which she could not restrain, and of which her sobs and the low moaning sounds that issued from under the folds enveloping her face, declared the excess, she suffered Father Aldrovand to conduct her whither he would.

"Our gold," he said, "has changed to brass, our silver to dross, our wisdom to folly—it is His will, who confounds the counsels of the wise, and shortens the arm of the mighty. To the chapel—to the chapel, Lady Eveline; and instead of vain repining, let us pray to God and the saints to turn away their displeasure, and to save the feeble remnant from the jaws of the devouring wolf."

Thus speaking, he half led, half supported Eveline, who was at the moment almost incapable of thought and action, to the castle-chapel, where, sinking before the altar, she assumed the attitude at least of devotion, though her thoughts, despite the pious words which her tongue faltered out mechanically, were upon the field of battle, beside the body of her slaughtered parent. The rest of the mourners imitated their young lady in her devotional posture, and in the absence of her thoughts. The consciousness that so many of the garrison had been cut off in Raymond's incautious sally, added to their sorrows the sense of personal insecurity, which was exaggerated by the cruelties which were too often exercised by the enemy, who, in the heat of victory, were accustomed to spare neither sex nor age.

The monk, however, assumed among them the tone of authority which his character warranted, rebuked their wailing and ineffectual complaints, and having, as he thought, brought them to such a state of mind as better became their condition, he left them to their private devotions to indulge his own anxious curiosity by inquiring into the defences of the castle. Upon the outward walls he found Wilkin Flammock, who, having done the office of a good and skilful captain in the mode of managing his artillery, and beating back, as we have already seen, the advanced guard of the enemy, was now with his own hand measuring out to his little garrison no stinted allowance of wine.

"Have a care, good Wilkin," said the father, "that thou dost not exceed in this matter. Wine is, thou knowest, like fire and water, an excellent servant, but a very bad master."

"It will be long ere it overflow the deep and solid skulls of my countrymen," said Wilkin Flammock. "Our Flemish courage is like our Flanders horses—the one needs the spur, and the other must have a taste of the winepot; but, credit me, father, they are of an enduring generation, and will not shrink in the washing.—But indeed, if I were to give the knaves a cup more than enough, it were not altogether amiss, since they are like to have a platter the less."

"How do you mean?" cried the monk, starting; "I trust in the saints the provisions have been cared for?"

"Not so well as in your convent, good father," replied Wilkin, with the same immoveable stolidity of countenance. "We had kept, as you know, too jolly a Christmas to have a very fat Easter. Yon Welsh hounds, who helped to eat up our victuals, are now like to get into our hold for the lack of them."

"Thou talkest mere folly," answered the monk; "orders were last evening given by our lord (whose soul God assoilzie!) to fetch in the necessary supplies from the country around!"

"Ay, but the Welsh were too sharp set to permit us to do that at our ease this morning, which should have been done weeks and months since. Our lord deceased, if deceased he be, was one of those who trusted to the edge of the sword, and even so hath come of it. Commend me to a crossbow and a well-victualled castle, if I must needs fight at all. — You look pale, my good father, a cup of wine will revive you."

The monk motioned away from him the untasted cup, which Wilkin pressed him to with clownish civility. "We have now, indeed," he said, "no refuge, save in prayer!"

"Most true, good father;" again replied the impassible Fleming; "pray therefore as much as you will. I will content myself with fasting, which will come whether I will or no."—At this moment a horn was heard before the gate.—"Look to the portcullis and the gate, ye knaves!—What news, Neil Hansen?"

"A messenger from the Welsh tarries at the Mill-hill, just within shot of the cross-bows; he has a white flag, and demands admittance."

"Admit him not, upon thy life, till we be prepared for him," said Wilkin. "Bend the bonny mangonel upon the place, and shoot him if he dare to stir from the spot where he stands till we get all prepared to receive him," said Flammock in his native language. "And, Neil, thou houndsfoot, bestir thyself — let every pike, lance, and pole in the castle be ranged along the battlements, and pointed through the shot-holes—cut up some tapestry into the shape of banners, and show them from the highest towers. — Be ready when I give a signal, to strike *naker*,* and blow trumpets, if we have any; if not, some cow-horns—anything for a noise. And hark ye, Neil Hansen, do you, and four or five of your fellows, go to the armoury and slip on coats-of-mail; our Netherlandish corslets do not appal them so much. Then let the Welsh thief be blindfolded and brought in amongst us — Do you hold up your heads and keep silence — leave me to deal with him — only have a care there be no English among us."

The monk, who in his travels had acquired some slight knowledge of the Flemish language, had well-nigh started when he heard the last article in Wilkin's instructions to his countryman, but commanded himself, although a little surprised, both at this suspicious circumstance, and at the readiness and dexterity with which the rough-hewn Fleming seemed to adapt his preparations to the rules of war and of sound policy.

Wilkin, on his part, was not very certain whether the monk had not heard and understood more of what he said to his countryman, than what he had intended. As if to lull asleep any suspicion which Father Aldrovand might entertain, he repeated to him in English most of the directions which he had given, adding, "Well, good father, what think you of it?"

"Excellent well," answered the father, "and done as if you had practised war from the cradle, instead of weaving broad-cloth."

"Nay, spare not your jibes, father," answered Wilkin. — "I know full well that you English think that Flemings have nought in their brainpan but sodden beef and cabbage; yet you see there goes wisdom to weaving of webs."

"Right, Master Wilkin Flammock," answered the father; "but, good Fleming, wilt thou tell me what answer thou wilt make to the Welsh Prince's summons?"

"Reverend father, first tell me what the summons will be," replied the Fleming.

"To surrender this castle upon the instant," answered the monk. "What will be your reply?"

"My answer will be, Nay—unless upon good composition."

"How, Sir Fleming! dare you mention composition and the castle of the Garde Doloureuse in one sentence?" said the monk.

"Not if I may do better," answered the Fleming. "But would your reverence have me dally until the question amongst the garrison be, whether a plump priest or a fat Fleming will be the better flesh to furnish their shambles?"

"Pshaw!" replied Father Aldrovand, "thou canst not mean such folly. Relief must arrive within twenty-four hours at farthest. Raymond Berenger expected it for certain within such a space."

"Raymond Berenger has been deceived this morning in more matters than one," answered the Fleming.

"Hark thee, Flanderkin," answered the monk, whose retreat from the world had not altogether quenched his military habits and propensities, "I counsel thee to deal uprightly in this matter, as thou dost regard thine own life; for here are as many English left alive, notwithstanding the slaughter of to-day, as may well suffice to fling the Flemish bull-frogs into the castle-ditch, should they have cause to think thou meanest falsely, in the keeping of this castle, and the defence of the Lady Eveline."

"Let not your reverence be moved with unnecessary and idle fears," replied Wilkin Flammock—"I am castellane in this house, by command of its lord, and what I hold for the advantage of mine service, that will I do."

"But I," said the angry monk, "I am the servant of the Pope—the chaplain of this castle, with power to bind and unloose. I fear me thou art no true Christian, Wilkin Flammock, but dost lean to the heresy of the mountaineers. Thou hast refused to take the blessed cross—thou hast breakfasted, and drunk both ale and wine, ere thou hast heard mass. Thou art not to be trusted, man, and I will not trust thee—I demand to be present at the conference betwixt thee and the Welshman."

"It may not be, good father," said Wilkin, with the same smiling, heavy countenance, which he maintained on all occasions of life, however urgent. "It is true, as thou sayest, good father, that I have mine own reasons for not marching quite so far as the gates of Jericho at present; and lucky I have such reasons, since I had not else been here to defend the gate of the Garde Doloureuse. It is also true that I may have been sometimes obliged to visit my mills earlier than the chaplain was called by his zeal to the altar, and that my stomach brooks not working ere I break my fast. But for this, father, I have paid a mulct even to your worshipful reverence, and methinks since you are pleased to remember the confession so exactly, you should not forget the penance and the absolution."

The monk, in alluding to the secrets of the confessional, had gone a step beyond what the rules of his order and of the church permitted. He was baffled by the Fleming's reply, and finding him unmoved by the charge of heresy, he could only answer, in some confusion, "You refuse, then, to admit me to the conference with the Welshman?"

"Reverend father," said Wilkin, "it altogether respecteth secular matters. If aught of religious tenor should intervene, you shall be summoned without delay."

"I will be there in spite of thee, thou Flemish ox," muttered the monk to himself, but in a tone not to be heard by the by-standers; and so speaking, he left the battlements.

Wilkin Flammock, a few minutes afterwards, having first seen that all was arranged on the battlements, so as to give an imposing idea of a strength which did not exist, descended to a small guard-room, betwixt the outer and inner gate, where he was attended by half-a-dozen of his own people, disguised in the Norman armour which they had found in the armoury of the castle,—their strong, tall, and bulky forms, and motionless postures, causing them to look rather like trophies of some past age, than living and existing soldiers. Surrounded by these huge and inanimate figures, in a little vaulted room which almost excluded daylight, Flammock received the Welsh envoy, who was led in blindfolded betwixt two Flemings, yet not so carefully watched but that they permitted him to have a glimpse of the preparations on the battlements, which had, in fact, been made chiefly for the purpose of imposing on him. For the same purpose an occasional clatter of arms was made without; voices were heard as if officers were going their rounds; and other sounds of active preparation seemed to announce that a numerous and regular garrison was preparing to receive an attack.

When the bandage was removed from Jorworth's eyes,—for the same individual who had formerly brought Gwenwyn's offer of alliance, now bare his summons of surrender,—he looked haughtily around him and demanded to whom he was to deliver the commands of his master, the Gwenwyn, son of Cyvelioc, Prince of Powys.

"His highness," answered Flammock, with his usual smiling indifference of manner, "must be contented to treat with Wilkin Flammock of the Fulling-mills, deputed governor of the Garde Doloureuse."

"Thou deputed governor!" exclaimed Jorworth; "thou?—a Low-country weaver!—it is impossible. Low as they are, the English Crogan * cannot have sunk to a point so low, as to be commanded by *thee!*—these men seem English, to them I will deliver my message."

"You may if you will," replied Wilkin, "but if they return you any answer save by signs, you shall call me *schelm.*"

"Is this true?" said the Welsh envoy, looking towards the men-at-arms, as they seemed, by whom Flammock was attended; "are you really come to this pass? I thought that the mere having been born on British earth, though the children of spoilers and invaders, had inspired you with too much pride to brook the yoke of a base mechanic. Or, if you are not courageous, should you not be cautious?—Well speaks the proverb, Wo to him that will trust a stranger! Still mute — still silent? — answer me by word or sign — Do you really call and acknowledge him as your leader?"

The men in armour with one accord nodded their casques in reply to Jorworth's question, and then remained motionless as before.

The Welshman, with the acute genius of his country, suspected there was something in this which he could not entirely comprehend, but, preparing himself to be upon his guard, he proceeded as follows: "Be it as it may, I care not who hears the message of my sovereign, since it brings pardon and mercy to the inhabitants of this Castell an Carrig,† which you have called the Garde Doloureuse, to cover the usurpation of the territory by the change of the name. Upon surrender of the same to the Prince of Powys, with its dependencies, and with the arms which it contains, and with the maiden Eveline Berenger, all within the castle shall depart unmolested, and have safe-conduct wheresoever they will, to go beyond the marches of the Cymry."

"And how, if we obey not this summons?" said the imperturbable Wilkin Flammock.

"Then shall your portion be with Raymond Berenger, your late leader," replied Jorworth, his eyes, while he was speaking, glancing with the vindictive ferocity which dictated his answer. "So many strangers as be here amongst ye, so many bodies to the ravens, so many heads to the gibbet! —It is long since the kites have had such a banquet of lurdane Flemings and false Saxons."

"Friend Jorworth," said Wilkin, "if such be thy only message, bear mine answer back to thy master. That wise men trust not to the words of others that safety, which they can secure by their own deeds. We have walls high and strong enough, deep moats, and plenty of munition, both

---

* This is a somewhat contumelious epithet applied by the Welsh to the English.
† Castle of the Craig.

longbow and arblast. We will keep the castle, trusting the castle will keep us, till God shall send us succour."

"Do not peril your lives on such an issue," said the Welsh emissary, changing his language to the Flemish, which, from occasional communication with those of that nation in Pembrokeshire, he spoke fluently, and which he now adopted, as if to conceal the purport of his discourse from the supposed English in the apartment. "Hark thee hither," he proceeded, "good Fleming. Knowest thou not that he in whom is your trust, the Constable De Lacy, hath bound himself by his vow to engage in no quarrel till he crosses the sea, and cannot come to your aid without perjury? He and the other Lords Marchers have drawn their forces far northward to join the host of Crusaders. What will it avail you to put us to the toil and trouble of a long siege, when you can hope no rescue?"

"And what will it avail me more," said Wilkin, answering in his native language and looking at the Welshman fixedly, yet with a countenance from which all expression seemed studiously banished, and which exhibited, upon features otherwise tolerable, a remarkable compound of dulness and simplicity, "what will it avail me whether your trouble be great or small?"

"Come, friend Flammock," said the Welshman, "frame not thyself more unapprehensive than nature hath formed thee. The glen is dark, but a sunbeam can light the side of it. Thy utmost efforts cannot prevent the fall of this castle; but thou mayst hasten it, and the doing so shall avail thee much." Thus speaking, he drew close up to Wilkin, and sunk his voice to an insinuating whisper, as he said, "Never did the withdrawing of a bar, or the raising of a portcullis, bring such vantage to Fleming as they may to thee, if thou wilt."

"I only know," said Wilkin, "that the drawing the one, and the dropping the other, have cost me my whole worldly subsistence."

"Fleming, it shall be compensated to thee with an overflowing measure. The liberality of Gwenwyn is as the summer rain."

"My whole mills and buildings have been this morning burnt to the earth——"

"Thou shalt have a thousand marks of silver, man, in the place of thy goods," said the Welshman; but the Fleming continued, without seeming to hear him, to number up his losses.

"My lands are forayed, twenty kine driven off, and——"

"Threescore shall replace them," interrupted Jorworth, "chosen from the most bright-skinned of the spoil."

"But my daughter — but the Lady Eveline"—said the Fleming, with some slight change in his monotonous voice, which seemed to express doubt and perplexity—"You are cruel conquerors, and——"

"To those who resist us we are fearful," said Jorworth, "but not to such as shall deserve clemency by surrender. Gwenwyn will forget the contumelies of Raymond, and raise his daughter to high honour among the daughters of the Cymry. For thine own child, form but a wish for her advantage, and it shall be fulfilled to the uttermost. Now, Fleming, we understand each other."

"I understand thee, at least," said Flammock.

"And I thee, I trust?" said Jorworth, bending his keen, wild blue eye on the stolid and unexpressive face of the Netherlander, like an eager student who seeks to discover some hidden and mysterious meaning in a passage of a classic author, the direct import of which seems trite and trivial.

"You believe that you understand me," said Wilkin; "but here lies the difficulty,—which of us shall trust the other?"

"Darest thou ask?" answered Jorworth. "Is it for thee, or such as thee, to express doubt of the purposes of the Prince of Powys?"

"I know them not, good Jorworth, but through thee; and well I wot thou art not one who will let thy traffic miscarry for want of aid from the breath of thy mouth."

"As I am a Christian man," said Jorworth, hurrying asseveration on asseveration —"by the soul of my father— by the faith of my mother — by the black rood of ——"

"Stop, good Jorworth — thou heapest thine oaths too thickly on each other, for me to value them to the right estimate," said Flammock;. "that which is so lightly pledged, is sometimes not thought worth redeeming. Some part of the promised guerdon in hand the whilst, were worth an hundred oaths."

"Thou suspicious churl, darest thou doubt my word?"

"No — by no means," answered Wilkin; — "ne'ertheless, I will believe thy deed more readily."

"To the point, Fleming," said Jorworth — "What wouldst thou have of me?"

"Let me have some present sight of the money thou didst promise, and I will think of the rest of thy proposal."

"Base silver-broker!" answered Jorworth, "thinkest thou the Prince of Powys has as many money-bags, as the merchants of thy land of sale and barter? He gathers treasures by his conquests, as the waterspout sucks up water by its strength, but it is to disperse them among his followers, as the cloudy column restores its contents to earth and ocean. The silver that I promise thee has yet to be gathered out of the Saxon chests—nay, the casket of Berenger himself must be ransacked to make up the tale."

"Methinks I could do that myself, (having full power in the castle,) and so save you a labour," said the Fleming.

"True," answered Jorworth, "but it would be at the expense of a cord and a noose, whether the Welsh took the place or the Normans relieved it —the one would expect their booty entire—the other their countryman's treasures to be delivered undiminished."

"I may not gainsay that," said the Fleming. "Well, say I were content to trust you thus far, why not return my cattle, which are in your own hands, and at your disposal? If you do not pleasure me in something beforehand, what can I expect of you afterwards?"

"I would pleasure you in a greater matter," answered the equally suspicious Welshman. "But what would it avail thee to have thy cattle within the fortress? They can be better cared for on the plain beneath."

"In faith," replied the Fleming, "thou sayst truth—they will be but a trouble to us here, where we have so many already provided for the use of the garrison.—And yet, when I consider it more closely, we have enough of forage to maintain all we have, and more. Now, my cattle are of a peculiar stock, brought from the rich pastures of Flanders, and I desire to have them restored ere your axes and Welsh hooks be busy with their hides."

"You shall have them this night, hide and horn," said Jorworth; "it is but a small earnest of a great loan."

"Thanks to your munificence," said the Fleming; "I am a simple-minded man, and bound my wishes to the recovery of my own property."

"Thou wilt be ready, then, to deliver the castle?" said Jorworth.

"Of that we will talk farther to-morrow," said Wilkin Flammock; "if these English and Normans should suspect such a purpose, we should have wild work—they must be fully dispersed ere I can hold farther communication on the subject. Meanwhile, I pray thee, depart suddenly, and as if offended with the tenor of our discourse."

"Yet would I fain know something more fixed and absolute," said Jorworth.

"Impossible—impossible," said the Fleming; "see you not yonder tall fellow begins already to handle his dagger—Go hence in haste, and angrily—and forget not the cattle."

"I will not forget them," said Jorworth; "but if thou keep not faith with us——"

So speaking, he left the apartment with a gesture of menace, partly really directed to Wilkin himself, partly assumed in consequence of his advice. Flammock replied in English, as if that all around might understand what he said,

"Do thy worst, Sir Welshman! I am a true man; I defy the proposals of rendition, and will hold out this castle to thy shame and thy master's!—Here—let him be blindfolded once more, and returned in safety to his attendants without; the next Welshman who appears before the gate of the Garde Doloureuse, shall be more sharply received."

The Welshman was blindfolded and withdrawn, when, as Wilkin Flammock himself left the guardroom, one of the seeming men-at-arms, who had been present at this interview, said in his ear, in English, "Thou art a false traitor, Flammock, and shalt die a traitor's death!"

Startled at this, the Fleming would have questioned the man farther, but he had disappeared so soon as the words were uttered. Flammock was disconcerted by this circumstance, which showed him that his interview with Jorworth had been observed, and its purpose known or conjectured, by some one who was a stranger to his confidence, and might thwart his intentions; and he quickly after learned that this was the case.

Chapter the Sixth.

Blessed Mary, mother dear,
To a maiden bend thine ear,
Virgin undefiled, to thee
A wretched virgin bends the knee.
                    HYMN TO THE VIRGIN.

THE daughter of the slaughtered Raymond had descended from the elevated station whence she had beheld the field of battle, in the agony of grief natural to a child whose eyes have beheld the death of an honoured and beloved father. But her station, and the principles of chivalry in which she had been trained up, did not permit any prolonged or needless indulgence of inactive sorrow. In raising the young and beautiful of the female sex to the rank of princesses, or rather goddesses, the spirit of that singular system exacted from them, in requital, a tone of character, and a line of conduct, superior and something contradictory to that of natural or merely human feeling. Its heroines frequently resembled portraits shown by an artificial light—strong and luminous, and which placed in high relief the objects on which it was turned; but having still something of adventitious splendour, which, compared with that of the natural day, seemed glaring and exaggerated.

It was not permitted to the orphan of the Garde Doloureuse, the daughter of a line of heroes, whose stem was to be found in the race of Thor, Balder, Odin, and other deified warriors of the North, whose beauty was the theme of a hundred minstrels, and her eyes the leading star of half the chivalry of the warlike marches of Wales, to mourn her sire with the ineffectual tears of a village maiden. Young as she was, and horrible as was the incident which she had but that instant witnessed, it was not altogether so appalling to her as to a maiden whose eye had not been accustomed to the rough, and often fatal sports of chivalry, and whose residence had not been among scenes and men where war and death had been the unceasing theme of every tongue, whose imagination had not been familiarized with wild and bloody events, or, finally, who had not been trained up to consider an honourable " death under shield," as that of a field of battle was termed, as a more desirable termination to the life of a warrior, than that lingering and unhonoured fate which comes slowly on, to conclude the listless and helpless inactivity of prolonged old age. Eveline, while she wept for her father, felt her bosom glow when she recollected that he died in the blaze of his fame, and amidst heaps of his slaughtered enemies; and when she thought of the exigencies of her own situation, it was with the determination to defend her own liberty, and to avenge her father's death, by every means which Heaven had left within her power.

The aids of religion were not forgotten; and according to the custom of the times, and the doctrines of the Roman church, she endeavoured to propitiate the favour of Heaven by vows as well as prayers. In a small crypt, or oratory, adjoining to the chapel, was hung over an altar-piece, on which a lamp constantly burned, a small picture of the Virgin Mary, revered as a household and peculiar deity by the family of Berenger, one of whose ancestors had brought it from the Holy Land, whither he had gone upon pilgrimage. It was of the period of the Lower Empire, a Grecian painting, not unlike those which in Catholic countries are often imputed to the Evangelist Luke. The crypt in which it was placed was accounted a shrine of uncommon sanctity — nay, supposed to have displayed miraculous powers; and Eveline, by the daily garland of flowers which she offered before the painting, and by the constant prayers with which they were accompanied, had constituted herself the peculiar votaress of Our Lady of the Garde Doloureuse, for so the picture was named.

Now, apart from others, alone, and in secrecy, sinking in the extremity of her sorrow before the shrine of her patroness, she besought the protection of kindred purity for the defence of her freedom and honour, and invoked vengeance on the wild and treacherous chieftain who had slain her father, and was now beleaguering her place of strength. Not only did she vow a large donative in lands to the shrine of the protectress whose aid she implored; but the oath passed her lips, (even though they faltered, and though something within her remonstrated against the vow,) that whatsoever favoured knight Our Lady of the Garde Doloureuse might employ for her rescue, should obtain from her in guerdon whatever boon she might honourably grant, were it that of her virgin hand at the holy altar. Taught as she was to believe, by the assurances of many a knight, that such a surrender was the highest boon which Heaven could bestow, she felt as discharging a debt of gratitude when she placed herself entirely at the disposal of the pure and blessed patroness in whose aid she confided. Perhaps there lurked in this devotion some earthly hope of which she was herself scarce conscious, and which reconciled her to the indefinite sacrifice thus freely offered. The Virgin, (this flattering hope might insinuate,) kindest and most benevolent of patronesses, will use compassionately the power resigned to her, and he will be the favoured champion of Maria, upon whom her votaress would most willingly confer favour.

But if there was such a hope, as something selfish will often mingle with our noblest and purest emotions, it arose unconscious of Eveline herself, who, in the full assurance of implicit faith, and fixing on the representative of her adoration, eyes in which the most earnest supplication, the most humble confidence, struggled with unbidden tears, was perhaps more beautiful than when, young as she was, she was selected to bestow the prize of chivalry in the lists of Chester. It was no wonder that, in such a moment of high excitation, when prostrated in devotion before a being of whose power to protect her, and to make her protection assured by a visible sign, she doubted nothing, the Lady Eveline conceived she saw with her own eyes the acceptance of her vow. As she gazed on the picture with an over-strained eye, and an imagination heated with enthusiasm, the expression seemed to alter from the hard outline, fashioned by the Greek painter; the eyes appeared to become animated, and to return with looks of compassion the suppliant entreaties of the votaress, and the mouth visibly arranged itself into a smile of inexpressible sweetness. It even seemed to her that the head made a gentle inclination.

Overpowered by supernatural awe at appearances, of which her faith permitted her not to question the reality, the Lady Eveline folded her arms on her bosom, and prostrated her forehead on the pavement, as the posture most fitting to listen to divine communication.

But her vision went not so far; there was neither sound nor voice, and when, after stealing her eyes all around the crypt in which she knelt, she again raised them to the figure of Our Lady, the features seemed to be in the form in which the limner had sketched them, saving that, to Eveline's imagination, they still retained an august and yet gracious expression, which she had not before remarked upon the countenance. With awful reverence, almost amounting to fear, yet comforted, and even elated, with the visitation she had witnessed, the maiden repeated again and again the orisons which she thought most grateful to the ear of her benefactress; and rising at length, retired backwards, as from the presence of a sovereign, until she attained the outer chapel.

Here one or two females still knelt before the saints which the walls and niches presented for adoration; but the rest of the terrified suppliants, too anxious to prolong their devotions, had dispersed through the castle to learn tidings of their friends, and to obtain some refreshment, or at least some place of repose for themselves and their families.

Bowing her head, and muttering an ave to each saint as she passed his image, (for impending danger makes men observant of the rites of devotion,) the Lady Eveline had almost reached the door of the chapel, when a man-at-arms, as he seemed, entered hastily; and, with a louder voice than suited the holy place, unless when need was most urgent, demanded the Lady Eveline. Impressed with the feelings of veneration which the late scene had produced, she was about to rebuke his military rudeness, when he spoke again, and in anxious haste, "Daughter, we are betrayed!" and though the form, and the coat-of-mail which covered it, were those of a soldier, the voice was that of Father Aldrovand, who, eager and anxious at the same time, disengaged himself from the mail hood, and showed his countenance.

"Father," she said, "what means this? Have you forgotten the confidence in Heaven which you are wont to recommend, that you bear other arms than your order assigns to you?"

"It may come to that ere long," said Father Aldrovand; "for I was a soldier ere I was a monk. But now I have donn'd this harness to discover treachery, not to resist force. Ah! my beloved daughter — we are dreadfully beset—foemen without—traitors within!—The false Fleming, Wilkin Flammock, is treating for the surrender of the castle!"

"Who dares say so?" said a veiled female, who had been kneeling unnoticed in a sequestered corner of the chapel, but who now started up and came boldly betwixt Lady Eveline and the monk.

"Go hence, thou saucy minion," said the monk, surprised at this bold interruption; "this concerns not thee."

"But it *doth* concern me," said the damsel, throwing back her veil, and discovering the juvenile countenance of Rose, the daughter of Wilkin Flammock, her eyes sparkling, and her cheeks blushing with anger, the vehemence of which made a singular contrast with the very fair complexion, and almost infantine features of the speaker, whose whole form and figure was that of a girl who has scarce emerged from childhood, and indeed whose general manners were as gentle and bashful as they now seemed bold, impassioned, and undaunted.—"Doth it not concern me," she said, "that my father's honest name should be tainted with treason? Doth it not concern the stream when the fountain is troubled? It *doth* concern me, and I will know the author of the calumny."

"Damsel," said Eveline, "restrain thy useless passion; the good father, though he cannot intentionally calumniate thy father, speaks, it may be, from false report."

"As I am an unworthy priest," said the father, "I speak from the report of my own ears. Upon the oath of my order, myself heard this Wilkin Flammock chaffering with the Welshman for the surrender of the Garde Douloureuse. By help of this hauberk and mail hood, I gained admittance to a conference where he-thought there were no English ears. They spoke Flemish too, but I knew the jargon of old."

"The Flemish," said the angry maiden, whose headstrong passion led her to speak first in answer to the last insult offered, "is no jargon like your piebald English, half Norman, half Saxon, but a noble Gothic tongue, spoken by the brave warriors who fought against the Roman Kaisars, when Britain bent the neck to them—and as for this he has said of Wilkin Flammock," she continued, collecting her ideas into more order as she went on, "believe it not, my dearest lady; but, as you value the honour of your own noble father, confide, as in the Evangelists, in the honesty of mine!" This she spoke with an imploring tone of voice, mingled with sobs, as if her heart had been breaking.

Eveline endeavoured to soothe her attendant. "Rose," she said, "in this evil time suspicions will light on the best men, and misunderstandings will arise among the best friends. Let us hear the good father state what he hath to charge upon your parent. Fear not but that Wilkin shall be heard in his defence. Thou wert wont to be quiet and reasonable."

"I am neither quiet nor reasonable on this matter," said Rose, with redoubled indignation; "and it is ill of you, lady, to listen to the falsehoods of that reverend mummer, who is neither true priest nor true soldier. But I will fetch one who shall confront him either in casque or cowl."

So saying, she went hastily out of the chapel, while the monk, after some pedantic circumlocution, acquainted the Lady Eveline with what he had overheard betwixt Jorworth and Wilkin; and proposed to her to draw together the few English who were in the castle, and take possession of the innermost square tower; a keep which, as usual in Gothic fortresses of the Norman period, was situated so as to make considerable defence, even after the exterior works of the castle, which it commanded, were in the hand of the enemy.

"Father," said Eveline, still confident in the vision she had lately witnessed, "this were good counsel in extremity; but otherwise, it were to create the very evil we fear, by setting our garrison at odds amongst themselves. I have a strong, and not unwarranted confidence, good father, in our blessed Lady of the Garde Douloureuse, that we shall attain at once vengeance on our barbarous enemies, and escape from our present jeopardy; and I call you to witness the vow I have made, that to him whom Our Lady should employ to work us succour, I will refuse nothing, were it my father's inheritance, or the hand of his daughter."

"*Ave Maria! Ave Regina Cœli!*" said the priest; "on a rock more sure you could not have founded your trust.—But, daughter," he continued after the proper ejaculation had been made, "have you never heard, even by a hint, that there was a treaty for your hand betwixt our much honoured lord, of whom we are cruelly bereft, (may God assoilzie his soul!) and the great house of Lacy?"

2 c

"Something I may have heard," said Eveline, dropping her eyes, while a slight tinge suffused her cheek; "but I refer me to the disposal of our Lady of Succour and Consolation."

As she spoke, Rose entered the chapel with the same vivacity she had shown in leaving it, leading by the hand her father, whose sluggish though firm step, vacant countenance, and heavy demeanour, formed the strongest contrast to the rapidity of her motions, and the anxious animation of her address. Her task of dragging him forward might have reminded the spectator of some of those ancient monuments, on which a small cherub, singularly inadequate to the task, is often represented as hoisting upward towards the empyrean the fleshy bulk of some ponderous tenant of the tomb, whose disproportioned weight bids fair to render ineffectual the benevolent and spirited exertions of its fluttering guide and assistant.

"Roschen—my child—what grieves thee?" said the Netherlander, as he yielded to his daughter's violence with a smile, which, being on the countenance of a father, had more of expression and feeling than those which seemed to have made their constant dwelling upon his lips.

"Here stands my father," said the impatient maiden; "impeach him with treason, who can or dare! There stands Wilkin Flammock, son of Dieterick, the Cramer of Antwerp, — let those accuse him to his face who slandered him behind his back!"

"Speak, Father Aldrovand," said the Lady Eveline; "we are young in our lordship, and, alas! the duty hath descended upon us in an evil hour; yet we will, so may God and Our Lady help us, hear and judge of your accusation to the utmost of our power."

"This Wilkin Flammock," said the monk, "however bold he hath made himself in villany, dares not deny that I heard him with my own ears treat for the surrender of the castle."

"Strike him, father!" said the indignant Rose, — "strike the disguised mummer! The steel hauberk may be struck, though not the monk's frock —strike him, or tell him that he lies foully!"

"Peace, Roschen, thou art mad," said her father, angrily; "the monk hath more truth than sense about him, and I would his ears had been farther off when he thrust them into what concerned him not."

Rose's countenance fell when she heard her father bluntly avow the treasonable communication of which she had thought him incapable—she dropt the hand by which she had dragged him into the chapel, and stared on the Lady Eveline, with eyes which seemed starting from their sockets, and a countenance from which the blood, with which it was so lately highly coloured, had retreated to garrison the heart.

Eveline looked upon the culprit with a countenance in which sweetness and dignity were mingled with sorrow. "Wilkin," she said, "I could not have believed this. What! on the very day of thy confiding benefactor's death, canst thou have been tampering with his murderers, to deliver up the castle, and betray thy trust! — But I will not upbraid thee — I deprive thee of the trust reposed in so unworthy a person, and appoint thee to be kept in ward in the western tower, till God send us relief; when, it may be, thy daughter's merits shall atone for thy offences, and save farther punishment.—See that our commands be presently obeyed."

"Yes — yes — yes!" exclaimed Rose, hurrying one word on the other as fast and vehemently as she could articulate—"Let us go — let us go to the darkest dungeon—darkness befits us better than light."

The monk, on the other hand, perceiving that the Fleming made no motion to obey the mandate of arrest, came forward, in a manner more suiting his ancient profession, and present disguise, than his spiritual character; and with the words, "I attach thee, Wilkin Flammock, of acknowledged treason to your liege lady," would have laid hand upon him, had not the Fleming stepped back and warned him off, with a menacing and determined gesture, while he said,—"Ye are mad!—all of you English are mad when the moon is full, and my silly girl hath caught the malady.—Lady, your honoured father gave me a charge, which I propose to execute to the best for all parties, and you cannot, being a minor, deprive me of it at your idle pleasure.—Father Aldrovand, a monk makes no lawful arrests.—Daughter Roschen, hold your peace and dry your eyes—you are a fool."

"I am, I am," said Rose, drying her eyes and regaining her elasticity of manner—"I am indeed a fool, and worse than a fool, for a moment to doubt my father's probity.—Confide in him, dearest lady; he is wise though he is grave, and kind though he is plain and homely in his speech. Should he prove false he will fare the worse! for I will plunge myself from the pinnacle of the Warder's Tower to the bottom of the moat, and he shall lose his own daughter for betraying his master's."

"This is all frenzy," said the monk—"Who trusts avowed traitors?—Here, Normans, English, to the rescue of your liege lady—Bows and bills—bows and bills!"

"You may spare your throat for your next homily, good father," said the Netherlander, "or call in good Flemish, since you understand it, for to no other language will those within hearing reply."

He then approached the Lady Eveline with a real or affected air of clumsy kindness, and something as nearly approaching to courtesy as his manners and features could assume. He bade her good-night, and assuring her that he would act for the best, left the chapel. The monk was about to break forth into revilings, but Eveline, with more prudence, checked his zeal.

"I cannot," she said, "but hope that this man's intentions are honest——"

"Now, God's blessing on you, lady, for that very word!" said Rose, eagerly interrupting her, and kissing her hand.

"But if unhappily they are doubtful," continued Eveline, "it is not by reproach that we can bring him to a better purpose. Good father, give an eye to the preparations for resistance, and see nought omitted that our means furnish for the defence of the castle."

"Fear nothing, my dearest daughter," said Aldrovand; "there are still some English hearts amongst us, and we will rather kill and eat the Flemings themselves, than surrender the castle."

"That were food as dangerous to come by as bear's venison, father," answered Rose, bitterly, still on fire with the idea that the monk treated her nation with suspicion and contumely.

On these terms they separated—the women to indulge their fears and sorrows in private grief, or alleviate them by private devotion; the monk to try to discover what were the real purposes of Wilkin Flammock, and to counteract them if possible, should they seem to indicate treachery. His eye, however, though sharpened by strong suspicion, saw nothing to strengthen his fears, excepting that the Fleming had, with considerable military skill, placed the principal posts of the castle in the charge of his own countrymen, which must make any attempt to dispossess him of his present authority both difficult and dangerous. The monk at length retired, summoned by the duties of the evening service, and with the determination to be stirring with the light the next morning.

Chapter the Seventh.

Oh, sadly shines the morning sun
On leaguer'd castle wall,
When bastion, tower, and battlement,
Seemed nodding to their fall.
                                    OLD BALLAD.

TRUE to his resolution, and telling his beads as he went, that he might lose no time, Father Aldrovand began his rounds in the castle so soon as daylight had touched the top of the eastern horizon. A natural instinct led him first to those stalls which, had the fortress been properly victualled for a siege, ought to have been tenanted by cattle; and great was his delight to see more than a score of fat kine and bullocks in the place which had last night been empty! One of them had already been carried to the shambles, and a Fleming or two, who played butchers on the occasion, were dividing the carcass for the cook's use. The good father had well-nigh cried out, a miracle; but, not to be too precipitate, he limited his transport to a private exclamation in honour of Our Lady of the Garde Doloureuse.

"Who talks of lack of provender?—who speaks of surrender now?" he said. "Here is enough to maintain us till Hugo de Lacy arrives, were he to sail back from Cyprus to our relief. I did purpose to have fasted this morning, as well to save victuals as on a religious score; but the blessings of the saints must not be slighted.—Sir Cook, let me have half a yard or so of broiled beef presently; bid the pantler send me a manchet, and the butler a cup of wine. I will take a running breakfast on the western battlements."[*]

At this place, which was rather the weakest point of the Garde Doloureuse, the good father found Wilkin Flammock anxiously superintending the necessary measures of defence. He greeted him courteously, congratulated him on the stock of provisions with which the castle had been supplied during the night, and was inquiring how they had been so happily introduced through the Welsh besiegers, when Wilkin took the first occasion to interrupt him.

"Of all this another time, good father; but I wish at present, and before other discourse, to consult thee on a matter which presses my conscience, and moreover deeply concerns my worldly estate."

"Speak on, my excellent son," said the father, conceiving that he should thus gain the key to Wilkin's real intentions. "Oh, a tender conscience is a jewel! and he that will not listen when it saith, 'Pour out thy doubts into the ear of the priest,' shall one day have his own dolorous outcries choked with fire and brimstone. Thou wert ever of a tender conscience, son Wilkin, though thou hast but a rough and borrel bearing."

"Well, then," said Wilkin, "you are to know, good father, that I have had some dealings with my neighbour, Jan Vanwelt, concerning my daughter Rose, and that he has paid me certain gilders on condition I will match her to him."

"Pshaw, pshaw! my good son," said the disappointed confessor, "this gear can lie over—this is no time for marrying or giving in marriage, when we are all like to be murdered."

"Nay, but hear me, good father," said the Fleming, "for this point of conscience concerns the present case more nearly than you wot of.—You must know I have no will to bestow Rose on this same Jan Vanwelt, who is

---

* Old Henry Jenkins, in his Recollections of the Abbacies before their dissolution, has preserved the fact that roast-beef was delivered out to the guests not by weight, but by measure.

old, and of ill conditions; and I would know of you whether I may, in conscience, refuse him my consent?"

"Truly," said Father Aldrovand, "Rose is a pretty lass, though somewhat hasty; and I think you may honestly withdraw your consent, always on paying back the gilders you have received."

"But there lies the pinch, good father," said the Fleming—"the refunding this money will reduce me to utter poverty. The Welsh have destroyed my substance; and this handful of money is all, God help me! on which I must begin the world again."

"Nevertheless, son Wilkin," said Aldrovand, "thou must keep thy word, or pay the forfeit; for what saith the text? *Quis habitabit in tabernaculo, quis requiescet in monte sancta?*—Who shall ascend to the tabernacle, and dwell in the holy mountain? Is it not answered again, *Qui jurat proximo et non decipit?*—Go to, my son—break not thy plighted word for a little filthy lucre—better is an empty stomach and an hungry heart with a clear conscience, than a fatted ox with iniquity and wordbreaking.—Sawest thou not our late noble lord, who (may his soul be happy!) chose rather to die in unequal battle, like a true knight, than live a perjured man, though he had but spoken a rash word to a Welshman over a wine flask?"

"Alas! then," said the Fleming, "this is even what I feared! We must e'en render up the castle, or restore to the Welshman, Jorworth, the cattle, by means of which I had schemed to victual and defend it."

"How—wherefore—what dost thou mean?" said the monk, in astonishment. "I speak to thee of Rose Flammock, and Jan Van-devil, or whatever you call him, and you reply with talk about cattle and castles, and I wot not what!"

"So please you, holy father, I did but speak in parables. This castle was the daughter I had promised to deliver over—the Welshman is Jan Vanwelt, and the gilders were the cattle he has sent in, as a part-payment beforehand of my guerdon."

"Parables!" said the monk, colouring with anger at the trick put on him; "what has a boor like thee to do with parables?—But I forgive thee—I forgive thee."

"I am therefore to yield the castle to the Welshman, or restore him his cattle?" said the impenetrable Dutchman.

"Sooner yield thy soul to Satan!" replied the monk.

"I fear it must be the alternative," said the Fleming; "for the example of thy honourable lord——"

"The example of an honourable fool"—answered the monk; then presently subjoined, "Our Lady be with her servant!—This Belgic-brained boor makes me forget what I would say."

"Nay, but the holy text which your reverence cited to me even now," continued the Fleming.

"Go to," said the monk; "what hast thou to do to presume to think of texts?—knowest thou not the letter of the Scripture slayeth, and that it is the exposition which maketh to live?—Art thou not like one who, coming to a physician, conceals from him half the symptoms of the disease?—I tell thee, thou foolish Fleming, the text speaketh but of promises made unto Christians, and there is in the Rubric a special exception of such as are made to Welshmen." At this commentary the Fleming grinned so broadly as to show his whole case of broad strong white teeth. Father Aldrovand himself grinned in sympathy, and then proceeded to say,—"Come, come, I see how it is. Thou hast studied some small revenge on me for doubting of thy truth; and, in verity, I think thou hast taken it wittily enough. But wherefore didst thou not let me into the secret from the beginning? I promise thee I had foul suspicions of thee."

"What!" said the Fleming, "is it possible I could ever think of involving your reverence in a little matter of deceit? Surely Heaven hath sent me more grace and manners.—Hark, I hear Jorworth's horn at the gate."

" He blows like a town swineherd," said Aldrovand, in disdain.

" It is not your reverence's pleasure that I should restore the cattle unto them, then ?" said Flammock.

" Yes, thus far. Prithee, deliver him straightway over the walls such a tub of boiling water as shall scald the hair from his goatskin cloak. And, hark thee, do thou, in the first place, try the temperature of the kettle with thy forefinger, and that shall be thy penance for the trick thou hast played me."

The Fleming answered this with another broad grin of intelligence, and they proceeded to the outer gate, to which Jorworth had come alone. Placing himself at the wicket, which, however, he kept carefully barred, and speaking through a small opening, contrived for such purpose, Wilkin Flammock demanded of the Welshman his business.

" To receive rendition of the castle, agreeable to promise," said Jorworth.

" Ay ? and art thou come on such errand alone ?" said Wilkin.

" No, truly," answered Jorworth ; " I have some two score of men concealed among yonder bushes."

" Then thou hadst best lead them away quickly," answered Wilkin, " before our archers let fly a sheaf of arrows among them."

" How, villain ! Dost thou not mean to keep thy promise ?" said the Welshman.

" I gave thee none," said the Fleming ; " I promised but to think on what thou didst say. I have done so, and have communicated with my ghostly father, who will in no respect hear of my listening to thy proposal."

" And wilt thou," said Jorworth, " keep the cattle, which I simply sent into the castle on the faith of our agreement ?"

" I will excommunicate and deliver him over to Satan," said the monk, unable to wait the phlegmatic and lingering answer of the Fleming, " if he give horn, hoof, or hair of them, to such an uncircumcised Philistine as thou or thy master."

" It is well, shorn priest," answered Jorworth in great anger. " But mark me—reckon not on your frock for ransom. When Gwenwyn hath taken this castle, as it shall not longer shelter such a pair of faithless traitors, I will have you sewed up each into the carcass of one of these kine, for which your penitent has forsworn himself, and lay you where wolf and eagle shall be your only companions."

" Thou wilt work thy will when it is matched with thy power," said the sedate Netherlander.

" False Welshman, we defy thee to thy teeth !" answered, in the same breath, the more irascible monk. " I trust to see hounds gnaw thy joints ere that day come that ye talk of so proudly."

By way of answer to both, Jorworth drew back his arm with his levelled javelin, and shaking the shaft till it acquired a vibratory motion, he hurled it with equal strength and dexterity right against the aperture in the wicket. It whizzed through the opening at which it was aimed, and flew (harmlessly, however) between the heads of the monk and the Fleming ; the former of whom started back, while the latter only said, as he looked at the javelin, which stood quivering in the door of the guard-room, " That was well aimed, and happily baulked."

Jorworth, the instant he had flung his dart, hastened to the ambush which he had prepared, and gave them at once the signal and the example of a rapid retreat down the hill. Father Aldrovand would willingly have followed them with a volley of arrows, but the Fleming observed that ammunition was too precious with them to be wasted on a few runaways. Perhaps the honest man remembered that they had come within the danger of such a salutation, in some measure, on his own assurance.

: When the noise of the hasty retreat of Jorworth and his followers had died away, there ensued a dead silence, well corresponding with the coolness and calmness of that early hour in the morning.

"This will not last long," said Wilkin to the monk, in a tone of foreboding seriousness, which found an echo in the good father's bosom.

"It will not, and it cannot," answered Aldrovand; "and we must expect a shrewd attack, which I should mind little, but that their numbers are great, ours few; the extent of the walls considerable, and the obstinacy of these Welsh fiends almost equal to their fury. But we will do the best. I will to the Lady Eveline — She must show herself upon the battlements — She is fairer in feature than becometh a man of my order to speak of; and she has withal a breathing of her father's lofty spirit. The look and the word of such a lady will give a man double strength in the hour of need."

"It may be," said the Fleming; "and I will go see that the good break-fast which I have appointed be presently served forth; it will give my Flemings more strength than the sight of the ten thousand virgins — may their help be with us! — were they all arranged on a fair field."

Chapter the Eighth.

'Twas when ye raised, 'mid sap and siege,
The banner of your rightful liege
At your she captain's call,
Who, miracle of womankind,
Lent mettle to the meanest hind
That mann'd her castle wall.
WILLIAM STEWART ROSE.

THE morning light was scarce fully spread abroad, when Eveline Berenger, in compliance with her confessor's advice, commenced her progress around the walls and battlements of the beleaguered castle, to confirm, by her personal entreaties, the minds of the valiant, and to rouse the more timid to hope and to exertion. She wore a rich collar and bracelets, as ornaments which indicated her rank and high descent; and her under tunic, in the manner of the times, was gathered around her slender waist by a girdle, embroidered with precious stones, and secured by a large buckle of gold. From one side of the girdle was suspended a pouch or purse, splendidly adorned with needle-work, and on the left side it sustained a small dagger of exquisite workmanship. A dark-coloured mantle, chosen as emblematic of her clouded fortunes, was flung loosely around her; and its hood was brought forward, so as to shadow, but not hide, her beautiful countenance. Her looks had lost the high and ecstatic expression which had been inspired by supposed revelation, but they retained a sorrowful and mild, yet determined character — and, in addressing the soldiers, she used a mixture of entreaty and command — now throwing herself upon their protection — now demanding in her aid the just tribute of their allegiance.

The garrison was divided, as military skill dictated, in groups, on the points most liable to attack, or from which an assailing enemy might be best annoyed; and it was this unavoidable separation of their force into small detachments, which showed to disadvantage the extent of walls, compared with the number of the defenders; and though Wilkin Flammock had contrived several means of concealing this deficiency of force from the enemy, he could not disguise it from the defenders of the castle, who cast mournful glances on the length of battlements which were unoccupied save by sentinels, and then looked out to the fatal field of battle, loaded with the bodies of those who ought to have been their comrades in this hour of peril.

The presence of Eveline did much to rouse the garrison from this state of discouragement. She glided from post to post, from tower to tower of the old gray fortress, as a gleam of light passes over a clouded landscape, and touching its various points in succession, calls them out to beauty and effect. Sorrow and fear sometimes make sufferers eloquent. She addressed the various nations who composed her little garrison, each in appropriate language. To the English, she spoke as children of the soil — to the Flemings, as men who had become denizens by the right of hospitality — to the Normans, as descendants of that victorious race, whose sword had made them the nobles and sovereigns of every land where its edge had been tried. To them she used the language of chivalry, by whose rules the meanest of that nation regulated, or affected to regulate, his actions. The English she reminded of their good faith and honesty of heart; and to the Flemings she spoke of the destruction of their property, the fruits of their honest industry. To all she proposed vengeance for the death of their leader and his followers — to all she recommended confidence in God and Our Lady of the Garde Doloureuse; and she ventured to assure all, of the strong and victorious bands that were already in march to their relief.

"Will the gallant champions of the cross," she said, "think of leaving their native land, while the wail of women and of orphans is in their ears? — it were to convert their pious purpose into mortal sin, and to derogate from the high fame they have so well won. Yes — fight but valiantly, and perhaps, before the very sun that is now slowly rising shall sink in the sea, you will see it shining on the ranks of Shrewsbury and Chester. When did the Welshmen wait to hear the clangour of their trumpets, or the rustling of their silken banners? Fight bravely — fight freely but a while! — our castle is strong — our munition ample — your hearts are good — your arms are powerful — God is nigh to us, and our friends are not far distant. Fight, then, in the name of all that is good and holy — fight for yourselves, for your wives, for your children, and for your property — and oh! fight for an orphan maiden, who hath no other defenders but what a sense of her sorrows, and the remembrance of her father, may raise up among you!"

Such speeches as these made a powerful impression on the men to whom they were addressed, already hardened, by habits and sentiments, against a sense of danger. The chivalrous Normans swore, on the cross of their swords, they would die to a man ere they would surrender their posts — the blunter Anglo-Saxons cried, "Shame on him who would render up such a lamb as Eveline to a Welsh wolf, while he could make her a bulwark with his body!" — Even the cold Flemings caught a spark of the enthusiasm with which the others were animated, and muttered to each other praises of the young lady's beauty, and short but honest resolves to do the best they might in her defence.

Rose Flammock, who accompanied her lady with one or two attendants upon her circuit around the castle, seemed to have relapsed into her natural character of a shy and timid girl, out of the excited state into which she had been brought by the suspicions which in the evening before had attached to her father's character. She tripped closely but respectfully after Eveline, and listened to what she said from time to time, with the awe and admiration of a child listening to its tutor, while only her moistened eye expressed how far she felt or comprehended the extent of the danger, or the force of the exhortations. There was, however, a moment when the youthful maiden's eye became more bright, her step more confident, her looks more elevated. This was when they approached the spot where her father, having discharged the duties of commander of the garrison, was now exercising those of engineer, and displaying great skill, as well as wonderful personal strength, in directing and assisting the establishment of a large mangonel, (a military engine used for casting stones,) upon a station commanding an exposed postern gate, which led from the western side of the castle down to the plain ; and where a severe assault was naturally to be expected. The greater part of his armour lay beside him, but covered with his cassock to screen it from morning dew ; while in his leathern doublet, with arms bare to the shoulder, and a huge sledge-hammer in his hand, he set an example to the mechanics who worked under his direction.

In slow and solid natures there is usually a touch of shamefacedness, and a sensitiveness to the breach of petty observances. Wilkin Flammock had been unmoved even to insensibility at the imputation of treason so lately cast upon him ; but he coloured high, and was confused, while, hastily throwing on his cassock, he endeavoured to conceal the dishabille in which he had been surprised by the Lady Eveline. Not so his daughter. Proud of her father's zeal, her eye gleamed from him to her mistress with a look of triumph, which seemed to say, "And this faithful follower is he who was suspected of treachery !"

Eveline's own bosom made her the same reproach ; and anxious to atone for her momentary doubt of his fidelity, she offered for his acceptance a ring of value ; "in small amends," she said, "of a momentary misconstruction."

"It needs not, lady," said Flammock, with his usual bluntness, "unless I have the freedom to bestow the gaud on Rose ; for I think she was grieved enough at that which moved me little,—as why should it ?"

"Dispose of it as thou wilt," said Eveline ; "the stone it bears is as true as thine own faith."

Here Eveline paused, and looking on the broad expanded plain which extended between the site of the castle and the river, observed how silent and still the morning was rising over what had so lately been a scene of such extensive slaughter.

"It will not be so long," answered Flammock ; "we shall have noise enough, and that nearer to our ears than yesterday."

"Which way lie the enemy?" said Eveline ; "methinks I can spy neither tents nor pavilions."

"They use none, lady," answered Wilkin Flammock. "Heaven has denied them the grace and knowledge to weave linen enough for such a purpose — Yonder they lie on both sides of the river, covered with nought but their white mantles. Would one think that a host of thieves and cutthroats could look so like the finest object in nature—a well-spread bleaching-field ! — Hark ! — hark — the wasps are beginning to buzz ; they will soon be plying their stings."

In fact, there was heard among the Welsh army a low and indistinct murmur, like that of

"Bees alarmed and arming in their hives."

Terrified at the hollow menacing sound, which grew louder every moment, Rose, who had all the irritability of a sensitive temperament, clung to her father's arm, saying, in a terrified whisper, "It is like the sound of the sea the night before the great inundation."

"And it betokens too rough weather for woman to be abroad in," said Flammock. "Go to your chamber, Lady Eveline, if it be your will — and go you too, Roschen — God bless you both — ye do but keep us idle here."

And, indeed, conscious that she had done all that was incumbent upon her, and fearful lest the chill which she felt creeping over her own heart should infect others, Eveline took her vassal's advice, and withdrew slowly to her own apartment, often casting back her eye to the place where the Welsh, now drawn out and under arms, were advancing their ridgy battalions, like the waves of an approaching tide.

The Prince of Powys had, with considerable military skill, adopted a plan of attack suitable to the fiery genius of his followers, and calculated to alarm on every point the feeble garrison.

The three sides of the castle which were defended by the river, were watched each by a numerous body of the British, with instructions to confine themselves to the discharge of arrows, unless they should observe that some favourable opportunity of close attack should occur. But far the greater part of Gwenwyn's forces, consisting of three columns of great strength, advanced along the plain on the western side of the castle, and menaced, with a desperate assault, the walls, which, in that direction, were deprived of the defence of the river. The first of these formidable bodies consisted entirely of archers, who dispersed themselves in front of the beleaguered place, and took advantage of every bush and rising ground which could afford them shelter; and then began to bend their bows and shower their arrows on the battlements and loop-holes, suffering, however, a great deal more damage than they were able to inflict, as the garrison returned their shot in comparative safety, and with more secure and deliberate aim.* Under cover, however, of their discharge of arrows, two very strong bodies of Welsh attempted to carry the outer defences of the castle by storm. They had axes to destroy the palisades, then called barriers; faggots to fill up the external ditches; torches to set fire to aught combustible which they might find; and, above all, ladders to scale the walls.

These detachments rushed with incredible fury towards the point of attack, despite a most obstinate defence, and the great loss which they sustained by missiles of every kind, and continued the assault for nearly an hour, supplied by reinforcements which more than recruited their diminished numbers. When they were at last compelled to retreat, they seemed to adopt a new and yet more harassing species of attack. A large body assaulted one exposed point of the fortress with such fury as to draw thither as many of the besieged as could possibly be spared from other defended posts, and when there appeared a point less strongly manned than was adequate to defence, that, in its turn, was furiously assailed by a separate body of the enemy.

Thus the defenders of the Garde Douloureuse resembled the embarrassed traveller, engaged in repelling a swarm of hornets, which, while he brushes them from one part, fix in swarms upon another, and drive him to despair by their numbers, and the boldness and multiplicity of their attacks. The postern being of course a principal point of attack, Father Aldrovand, whose anxiety would not permit him to be absent from the walls, and who, indeed, where decency would permit, took an occasional share in the active defence of the place, hasted thither, as the point chiefly in danger.

Here he found the Fleming, like a second Ajax, grim with dust and blood, working with his own hands the great engine which he had lately helped to erect, and at the same time giving heedful eye to all the exigencies around.

"How thinkest thou of this day's work?" said the monk in a whisper.

"What skills it talking of it, father?" replied Flammock; "thou art no soldier, and I have no time for words."

"Nay, take thy breath," said the monk, tucking up the sleeves of his frock; "I will try to help thee the whilst — although, our Lady pity me, I know nothing of these strange devices,—not even the names. But our rule commands us to labour; there can be no harm, therefore, in turning this

<hr/>

* The Welsh were excellent bowmen: but, under favour of Lord Lyttleton, they probably did not use the long bow, the formidable weapon of the Normans, and afterwards of the English yeomen. That of the Welsh most likely rather resembled the bow of the cognate Celtic tribes of Ireland, and of the Highlanders of Scotland. It was shorter than the Norman long bow, as being drawn to the breast, not to the ear, more loosely strung, and the arrow having a heavy iron head; altogether, in short, a less effective weapon. It appears, from the following anecdote, that there was a difference between the Welsh arrow and those of the English.

In 1122, Henry the II., marching into Powys-land to chastise Meredith ap Blethyn and certain rebels, in passing a defile, was struck by an arrow on the breast. Repelled by the excellence of his breast-plate, the shaft fell to the ground. When the King felt the blow, and saw the shaft, he swore his usual oath, by the death of our Lord, that the arrow came not from a Welsh but an English bow; and, inflamed by this belief, hastily put an end to the war.

winch—or in placing this steel-headed piece of wood opposite to the chord, (suiting his actions to his words,) nor see I aught uncanonical in adjusting the lever thus, or in touching the spring."

The large bolt whizzed through the air as he spoke, and was so successfully aimed, that it struck down a Welsh chief of eminence, to which Gwenwyn himself was in the act of giving some important charge.

"Well driven, *trebuchet*—well flown, *quarrel!*" cried the monk, unable to contain his delight, and giving, in his triumph, the true technical names to the engine, and the javelin which it discharged.

"And well aimed, monk," added Wilkin Flammock; "I think thou knowest more than is in thy breviary."

"Care not thou for that," said the father; "and now that thou seest I can work an engine, and that the Welsh knaves seem something low in stomach, what think'st thou of our estate?"

"Well enough — for a bad one — if we may hope for speedy succour; but men's bodies are of flesh, not of iron, and we may be at last wearied out by numbers. Only one soldier to four yards of wall, is a fearful odds; and the villains are aware of it, and keep us to sharp work."

The renewal of the assault here broke off their conversation, nor did the active enemy permit them to enjoy much repose until sunset; for, alarming them with repeated menaces of attack upon different points, besides making two or three formidable and furious assaults, they left them scarce time to breathe, or to take a moment's refreshment. Yet the Welsh paid a severe price for their temerity; for, while nothing could exceed the bravery with which their men repeatedly advanced to the attack, those which were made latest in the day had less of animated desperation than their first onset; and it is probable, that the sense of having sustained great loss, and apprehension of its effects on the spirits of his people, made nightfall, and the interruption of the contest, as acceptable to Gwenwyn as to the exhausted garrison of the Garde Doloureuse.

But in the camp or leaguer of the Welsh there was glee and triumph, for the loss of the past day was forgotten in recollection of the signal victory which had preceded this siege; and the dispirited garrison could hear from their walls the laugh and the song, the sound of harping and gaiety, which triumphed by anticipation over their surrender.

The sun was for some time sunk, the twilight deepened, and night closed with a blue and cloudless sky, in which the thousand spangles that deck the firmament received double brilliancy from some slight touch of frost, although the paler planet, their mistress, was but in her first quarter. The necessities of the garrison were considerably aggravated by that of keeping a very strong and watchful guard, ill according with the weakness of their numbers, at a time which appeared favourable to any sudden nocturnal alarm; and, so urgent was this duty, that those who had been more slightly wounded on the preceding day, were obliged to take their share in it, notwithstanding their hurts. The monk and Fleming, who now perfectly understood each other, went in company around the walls at midnight, exhorting the warders to be watchful, and examining with their own eyes the state of the fortress. It was in the course of these rounds, and as they were ascending an elevated platform by a range of narrow and uneven steps, something galling to the monk's tread, that they perceived on the summit to which they were ascending, instead of the black corslet of the Flemish sentinel who had been placed there, two white forms, the appearance of which struck Wilkin Flammock with more dismay than he had shown during any of the doubtful events of the preceding day's fight.

"Father," he said, "betake yourself to your tools—*es spuckt*—there are hobgoblins here."

The good father had not learned as a priest to defy the spiritual host, whom, as a soldier, he had dreaded more than any mortal enemy; but he began to recite, with chattering teeth, the exorcism of the church, "*Conjuro vos omnes, spiritus maligni, magni, atque parvi,*"—when he was interrupted by the voice of Eveline, who called out, "Is it you, Father Aldrovand?"

Much lightened at heart by finding they had no ghost to deal with, Wilkin Flammock and the priest advanced hastily to the platform, where they found the lady with her faithful Rose, the former with a half-pike in her hand, like a sentinel on duty.

"How is this, daughter?" said the monk; "how came you here, and thus armed? and where is the sentinel,—the lazy Flemish hound, that should have kept the post?"

"May he not be a lazy hound, yet not a Flemish one, father?" said Rose, who was ever awakened by anything which seemed a reflection upon her country; "methinks I have heard of such curs of English breed."

"Go to, Rose, you are too malapert for a young maiden," said her father. "Once more, where is Peterkin Vorst, who should have kept this post?"

"Let him not be blamed for my fault," said Eveline, pointing to a place where the Flemish sentinel lay in the shade of the battlement fast asleep—"He was overcome with toil—had fought hard through the day, and when I saw him asleep as I came hither, like a wandering spirit that cannot take slumber or repose, I would not disturb the rest which I envied. As he had fought for me, I might, I thought, watch an hour for him; so I took his weapon with the purpose of remaining here till some one should come to relieve him."

"I will relieve the schelm, with a vengeance!" said Wilkin Flammock, and saluted the slumbering and prostrate warder with two kicks, which made his corslet clatter. The man started to his feet in no small alarm, which he would have communicated to the next sentinels and to the whole garrison, by crying out that the Welsh were upon the walls, had not the monk covered his broad mouth with his hand just as the roar was issuing forth.—"Peace, and get thee down to the under bayley," said he;—"thou deservest death, by all the policies of war—but, look ye, varlet, and see who has saved your worthless neck, by watching while you were dreaming of swine's flesh and beer-pots."

The Fleming, although as yet but half awake, was sufficiently conscious of his situation, to sneak off without reply, after two or three awkward congees, as well to Eveline as to those by whom his repose had been so unceremoniously interrupted.

"He deserves to be tied neck and heel, the houndsfoot," said Wilkin. "But what would you have, lady? My countrymen cannot live without rest or sleep." So saying, he gave a yawn so wide, as if he had proposed to swallow one of the turrets at an angle of the platform on which he stood, as if it had only garnished a Christmas pasty.

"True, good Wilkin," said Eveline; "and do you therefore take some rest, and trust to my watchfulness, at least till the guards are relieved. I cannot sleep if I would, and I would not if I could."

"Thanks, lady," said Flammock; "and in truth, as this is a centrical place, and the rounds must pass in an hour at farthest, I will e'en close my eyes for such a space, for the lids feel as heavy as flood-gates."

"Oh, father, father!" exclaimed Rose, alive to her sire's unceremonious neglect of decorum—"think where you are, and in whose presence!"

"Ay, ay, good Flammock," said the monk, "remember the presence of a noble Norman maiden is no place for folding of cloaks and donning of night-caps."

"Let him alone, father," said Eveline, who in another moment might have smiled at the readiness with which Wilkin Flammock folded himself in his huge cloak, extended his substantial form on the stone bench, and gave the most decided tokens of profound repose, long ere the monk had done speaking.—"Forms and fashions of respect," she continued, "are for times of ease and nicety;—when in danger, the soldier's bedchamber is wherever he can find leisure for an hour's sleep—his eating-hall, wherever he can obtain food. Sit thou down by Rose and me, good father, and tell us of some holy lesson which may pass away these hours of weariness and calamity."

The father obeyed; but however willing to afford consolation, his ingenuity and theological skill suggested nothing better than a recitation of the penitentiary psalms, in which task he continued until fatigue became too powerful for him also, when he committed the same breach of decorum for which he had upbraided Wilkin Flammock, and fell fast asleep in the midst of his devotions.

Chapter the Ninth.

"Oh, night of wo," she said, and wept,
  "Oh, night foreboding sorrow!
"Oh, night of wo," she said and wept,
  "But more I dread the morrow!"
        Sir Gilbert Elliot.

THE fatigue which had exhausted Flammock and the monk, was unfelt by the two anxious maidens, who remained with their eyes bent, now upon the dim landscape, now on the stars by which it was lighted, as if they could have read there the events which the morrow was to bring forth. It was a placid and melancholy scene. Tree and field, and hill and plain, lay before them in doubtful light, while at greater distance, their eye could with difficulty trace one or two places where the river, hidden in general by banks and trees, spread its more expanded bosom to the stars, and the pale crescent. All was still, excepting the solemn rush of the waters, and now and then the shrill tinkle of a harp, which, heard from more than a mile's distance through the midnight silence, announced that some of the Welshmen still protracted their most beloved amusement. The wild notes, partially heard, seemed like the voice of some passing spirit; and, connected as they were with ideas of fierce and unrelenting hostility, thrilled on Eveline's ear, as if prophetic of war and wo, captivity and death. The only other sounds which disturbed the extreme stillness of the night, were the occasional step of a sentinel upon his post, or the hooting of the owls, which seemed to wail the approaching downfal of the moonlight turrets, in which they had established their ancient habitations.

The calmness of all around seemed to press like a weight on the bosom of the unhappy Eveline, and brought to her mind a deeper sense of present grief, and keener apprehension of future horrors, than had reigned there during the bustle, blood, and confusion of the preceding day. She rose up—she sat down—she moved to and fro on the platform—she remained fixed like a statue to a single spot, as if she were trying by variety of posture to divert her internal sense of fear and sorrow.

At length, looking at the monk and the Fleming as they slept soundly under the shade of the battlement, she could no longer forbear breaking silence. "Men are happy," she said, "my beloved Rose; their anxious thoughts are either diverted by toilsome exertion, or drowned in the insensibility which follows it. They may encounter wounds and death, but it is we who feel in the spirit a more keen anguish than the body knows, and in the gnawing sense of present ill and fear of future misery, suffer a living death, more cruel than that which ends our woes at once."

"Do not be thus downcast, my noble lady," said Rose; "be rather what you were yesterday, caring for the wounded, for the aged, for every one but yourself—exposing even your dear life among the showers of the Welsh arrows, when doing so could give courage to others; while I—shame on me—could but tremble, sob, and weep, and needed all the little wit I have to prevent my shouting with the wild cries of the Welsh, or screaming and groaning with those of our friends who fell around me."

"Alas! Rose," answered her mistress, "you may at pleasure indulge your fears to the verge of distraction itself—you have a father to fight and watch for you. Mine—my kind, noble, and honoured parent, lies dead on yonder field, and all which remains for me is to act as may best become his memory. But this moment is at least mine, to think upon and to mourn for him."

So saying, and overpowered by the long-repressed burst of filial sorrow, she sunk down on the banquette which ran along the inside of the embattled parapet of the platform, and murmuring to herself, "He is gone for ever!" abandoned herself to the extremity of grief. One hand grasped unconsciously the weapon which she held, and served, at the same time, to prop her forehead, while the tears, by which she was now for the first time relieved, flowed in torrents from her eyes, and her sobs seemed so convulsive, that Rose almost feared her heart was bursting. Her affection and sympathy dictated at once the kindest course which Eveline's condition permitted. Without attempting to control the torrent of grief in its full current, she gently sat her down beside the mourner, and possessing herself of the hand which had sunk motionless by her side, she alternately pressed it to her lips, her bosom, and her brow—now covered it with kisses, now bedewed it with tears, and amid these tokens of the most devoted and humble sympathy, waited a more composed moment to offer her little stock of consolation in such deep silence and stillness, that, as the pale light fell upon the two beautiful young women, it seemed rather to show a group of statuary, the work of some eminent sculptor, than beings whose eyes still wept, and whose hearts still throbbed. At a little distance, the gleaming corslet of the Fleming, and the dark garments of Father Aldrovand, as they lay prostrate on the stone steps, might represent the bodies of those for whom the principal figures were mourning.

After a deep agony of many minutes, it seemed that the sorrows of Eveline were assuming a more composed character; her convulsive sobs were changed for long, low, profound sighs, and the course of her tears, though they still flowed, was milder and less violent. Her kind attendant, availing herself of these gentler symptoms, tried softly to win the spear from her lady's grasp. "Let me be sentinel for a while," she said, "my sweet lady —I will at least scream louder than you, if any danger should approach." She ventured to kiss her cheek, and throw her arms around Eveline's neck while she spoke; but a mute caress, which expressed her sense of the faithful girl's kind intentions to minister if possible to her repose, was the only answer returned. They remained for many minutes silent in the same posture, — Eveline, like an upright and tender poplar, — Rose, who encircled her lady in her arms, like the woodbine which twines around it.

At length Rose suddenly felt her young mistress shiver in her embrace, and then Eveline's hand grasped her arm rigidly as she whispered, "Do you hear nothing?"

"No—nothing but the hooting of the owl," answered Rose, timorously.

"I heard a distant sound," said Eveline,—"I thought I heard it—hark, it comes again!—Look from the battlements, Rose, while I awaken the priest and thy father."

"Dearest lady," said Rose, "I dare not—what can this sound be that is heard by one only?—You are deceived by the rush of the river."

"I would not alarm the castle unnecessarily," said Eveline, pausing, "or even break your father's needful slumbers, by a fancy of mine—But hark—hark!—I hear it again—distinct amidst the intermitting sounds of the rushing water—a low tremulous sound, mingled with a tinkling like smiths or armourers at work upon their anvils."

Rose had by this time sprung up on the banquette, and flinging back her rich tresses of fair hair, had applied her hand behind her ear to collect the distant sound. "I hear it," she cried, "and it increases—Awake them, for Heaven's sake, and without a moment's delay!"

Eveline accordingly stirred the sleepers with the reversed end of the lance, and as they started to their feet in haste, she whispered in a hasty but cautious voice, "To arms—the Welsh are upon us!"

"What—where?" said Wilkin Flammock,—"where be they?"

"Listen, and you will hear them arming," she replied.

"The noise is but in thine own fancy, lady," said the Fleming, whose organs were of the same heavy character with his form and his disposition. "I would I had not gone to sleep at all, since I was to be awakened so soon."

"Nay, but listen, good Flammock—the sound of armour comes from the north-east."

"The Welsh lie not in that quarter, lady," said Wilkin; "and besides, they wear no armour."

"I hear it—I hear it!" said Father Aldrovand, who had been listening for some time. "All praise to St. Benedict!—Our Lady of the Garde Doloureuse has been gracious to her servants as ever!—It is the tramp of horses—it is the clash of armour—the chivalry of the Marches are coming to our relief—Kyrie Eleison!"

"I hear something too," said Flammock,—"something like the hollow sound of the great sea, when it burst into my neighbour Klinkerman's warehouse, and rolled his pots and pans against each other. But it were an evil mistake, father, to take foes for friends—we were best rouse the people."

"Tush!" said the priest, "talk to me of pots and kettles?—Was I squire of the body to Count Stephen Mauleverer for twenty years, and do I not know the tramp of a war-horse, or the clash of a mail-coat?—But call the men to the walls at any rate, and have me the best drawn up at the base-court—we may help them by a sally."

"That will not be rashly undertaken with my consent," murmured the Fleming; "but to the wall if you will, and in good time. But keep your Normans and English silent, Sir Priest, else their unruly and noisy joy will awaken the Welsh camp, and prepare them for their unwelcome visiters."

The monk laid his finger on his lip in sign of obedience, and they parted in opposite directions, each to rouse the defenders of the castle, who were soon heard drawing from all quarters to their posts upon the walls, with hearts in a very different mood from that in which they had descended from them. The utmost caution being used to prevent noise, the manning of the walls was accomplished in silence, and the garrison awaited in breathless expectation the success of the forces who were rapidly advancing to their relief.

The character of the sounds which now loudly awakened the silence of this eventful night, could no longer be mistaken. They were distinguishable from the rushing of a mighty river, or from the muttering sound of distant thunder, by the sharp and angry notes which the clashing of the rider's arms mingled with the deep bass of the horses' rapid tread. From the long continuance of the sounds, their loudness, and the extent of horizon from which they seemed to come, all in the castle were satisfied that the approaching relief consisted of several very strong bodies of horse.*　At once this mighty sound ceased, as if the earth on which they trod had either devoured the armed squadrons or had become incapable of resounding to their tramp.　The defenders of the Garde Doloureuse concluded that their friends had made a sudden halt, to give their horses breath, examine the leaguer of the enemy, and settle the order of attack upon them.　The pause, however, was but momentary.

The British, so alert at surprising their enemies, were themselves, on many occasions, liable to surprise.　Their men were undisciplined, and sometimes negligent of the patient duties of the sentinel; and, besides, their foragers and flying parties, who scoured the country during the preceding day, had brought back tidings which had lulled them into fatal security.　Their camp had been therefore carelessly guarded, and confident in the smallness of the garrison, they had altogether neglected the important military duty of establishing patrols and outposts at a proper distance from their main body.　Thus the cavalry of the Lords Marchers, notwithstanding the noise which accompanied their advance, had approached very near the British camp without exciting the least alarm.　But while they were arranging their forces into separate columns, in order to commence the assault, a loud and increasing clamour among the Welsh announced that they were at length aware of their danger.　The shrill and discordant cries by which they endeavoured to assemble their men, each under the banner of his chief, resounded from their leaguer.　But these rallying shouts were soon converted into screams, and clamours of horror and dismay, when the thundering charge of the barbed horses and heavily armed cavalry of the Anglo-Normans surprised their undefended camp.

Yet not even under circumstances so adverse did the descendants of the ancient Britons renounce their defence, or forfeit their old hereditary privilege, to be called the bravest of mankind.　Their cries of defiance and resistance were heard resounding above the groans of the wounded, the shouts of the triumphant assailants, and the universal tumult of the night-battle.　It was not until the morning light began to peep forth, that the slaughter or dispersion of Gwenwyn's forces was complete, and that the "earthquake voice of victory" arose in uncontrolled and unmingled energy of exultation.

Then the besieged, if they could be still so termed, looking from their towers over the expanded country beneath, witnessed nothing but one wide-spread scene of desultory flight and unrelaxed pursuit.　That the Welsh had been permitted to encamp in fancied security upon the hither side of the river, now rendered their discomfiture more dreadfully fatal.　The single pass by which they could cross to the other side was soon completely choked by fugitives, on whose rear raged the swords of the victorious Normans. Many threw themselves into the river, upon the precarious chance of gaining the farther side, and, except a few, who were uncommonly strong, skilful, and active, perished among the rocks and in the currents; others, more fortunate, escaped by fords, with which they had accidentally been made acquainted; many dispersed, or, in small bands, fled in reckless despair towards the castle, as if the fortress, which had beat them off when victorious, could be a place of refuge to them in their present forlorn condition; while others roamed wildly over the plain, seeking only escape from immediate and instant danger, without knowing whither they ran.

The Normans, meanwhile, divided into small parties, followed and slaughtered them at pleasure; while, as a rallying point for the victors, the banner of Hugo de Lacy streamed from a small mount, on which Gwenwyn

---

* Even the sharp and angry clang made by the iron scabbards of modern cavalry ringing against the steel tipp'd saddles and stirrup, betrays their approach from a distance.　The clash of the armour of knights, armed cap-a-pie, must have been much more easily discernible.

had lately pitched his own, and surrounded by a competent force, both of infantry and horsemen, which the experienced Baron permitted on no account to wander far from it.

The rest, as we have already said, followed the chase with shouts of exultation and of vengeance, ringing around the battlements, which resounded with the cries, "Ha, Saint Edward!—Ha, Saint Dennis!—Strike—slay—no quarter to the Welsh wolves—think on Raymond Berenger!"

The soldiers on the walls joined in these vengeful and victorious clamours, and discharged several sheaves of arrows upon such fugitives, as, in their extremity, approached too near the castle. They would fain have sallied to give more active assistance in the work of destruction; but the communication being now open with the Constable of Chester's forces, Wilkin Flammock considered himself and the garrison to be under the orders of that renowned chief, and refused to listen to the eager admonitions of Father Aldrovand, who would, notwithstanding his sacerdotal character, have willingly himself taken charge of the sally which he proposed.

At length, the scene of slaughter seemed at an end. The retreat was blown on many a bugle, and knights halted on the plain to collect their personal followers, muster them under their proper pennon, and then march them slowly back to the great standard of their leader, around which the main body were again to be assembled, like the clouds which gather around the evening sun — a fanciful simile, which might yet be drawn farther, in respect of the level rays of strong lurid light which shot from those dark battalions, as the beams were flung back from their polished armour.

The plain was in this manner soon cleared of the horsemen, and remained occupied only by the dead bodies of the slaughtered Welshmen. The bands who had followed the pursuit to a greater distance were also now seen returning, driving before them, or dragging after them, dejected and unhappy captives, to whom they had given quarter when their thirst of blood was satiated.

It was then that, desirous to attract the attention of his liberators, Wilkin Flammock commanded all the banners of the castle to be displayed, under a general shout of acclamation from those who had fought under them. It was answered by a universal cry of joy from De Lacy's army, which rung so wide, as might even yet have startled such of the Welsh fugitives, as, far distant from this disastrous field of flight, might have ventured to halt for a moment's repose.

Presently after this greeting had been exchanged, a single rider advanced from the Constable's army towards the castle, showing, even at a distance, an unusual dexterity of horsemanship and grace of deportment. He arrived at the drawbridge, which was instantly lowered to receive him, whilst Flammock and the monk (for the latter, as far as he could, associated himself with the former in all acts of authority) hastened to receive the envoy of their liberator. They found him just alighted from the raven-coloured horse, which was slightly flecked with blood as well as foam, and still panted with the exertions of the evening; though, answering to the caressing hand of its youthful rider, he arched his neck, shook his steel caparison, and snorted to announce his unabated mettle and unwearied love of combat. The young man's eagle look bore the same token of unabated vigour, mingled with the signs of recent exertion. His helmet hanging at his saddle-bow, showed a gallant countenance, coloured highly, but not inflamed, which looked out from a rich profusion of short chesnut-curls; and although his armour was of a massive and simple form, he moved under it with such elasticity and ease, that it seemed a graceful attire, not a burden or encumbrance. A furred mantle had not sat on him with more easy grace than the heavy hauberk, which complied with every gesture of his noble form. Yet his countenance was so juvenile, that only the down on the upper lip announced decisively the approach to manhood. The females, who thronged into the court to see the first envoy of their deliverers, could not forbear mixing praises of his beauty with blessings on his valour; and one comely middle-aged dame, in particular, distinguished by the tightness with which her scarlet hose sat on a well-shaped leg and ankle, and by the cleanness of her coif, pressed close up to the young squire, and, more forward than the rest, doubled the crimson hue of his cheek, by crying aloud, that Our Lady of the Garde Doloureuse had sent them news of their redemption by an angel from the sanctuary;—a speech which, although Father Aldrovand shook his head, was received by her companions with such general acclamation, as greatly embarrassed the young man's modesty.

"Peace, all of ye!" said Wilkin Flammock — "Know you no respects, you women, or have you never seen a young gentleman before, that you hang on him like flies on a honeycomb? Stand back, I say, and let us hear in peace what are the commands of the noble Lord of Lacy."

"These," said the young man, "I can only deliver in the presence of the right noble demoiselle, Eveline Berenger, if I may be thought worthy of such honour."

"That thou art, noble sir," said the same forward dame, who had before expressed her admiration so energetically; "I will uphold thee worthy of her presence, and whatever other grace a lady can do thee."

"Now, hold thy tongue, with a wanion!" said the monk; while in the same breath the Fleming exclaimed, "Beware the cucking-stool, Dame Scant-o'-Grace!" while he conducted the noble youth across the court.

"Let my good horse be cared for," said the cavalier, as he put the bridle into the hand of a menial; and in doing so got rid of some part of his female retinue, who began to pat and praise the steed as much as they had done the rider; and some, in the enthusiasm of their joy, hardly abstained from kissing the stirrups and horse furniture.

But Dame Gillian was not so easily diverted from her own point as were some of her companions. She continued to repeat the word *cucking-stool*, till the Fleming was out of hearing, and then became more specific in her objurgation.—"And why cucking-stool, I pray, Sir Wilkin Butterfirkin? You are the man would stop an English mouth with a Flemish damask napkin, I trow! Marry quep, my cousin the weaver! And why the cucking-stool, I pray?—because my young lady is comely, and the young squire is a man of mettle, reverence to his beard that is to come yet! Have we not eyes to see, and have we not a mouth and a tongue?"

"In troth, Dame Gillian, they do you wrong who doubt it," said Eveline's nurse, who stood by; "but I prithee, keep it shut now, were it but for womanhood."

"How now, mannerly Mrs. Margery?" replied the incorrigible Gillian; "is your heart so high, because you dandled our young lady on your knee fifteen years since?—Let me tell you, the cat will find its way to the cream, though it was brought up on an abbess's lap."

"Home, housewife — home!" exclaimed her husband, the old huntsman, who was weary of this public exhibition of his domestic termagant—"home, or I will give you a taste of my dog lash — Here are both the confessor and Wilkin Flammock wondering at your impudence."

"Indeed!" replied Gillian; "and are not two fools enough for wonderment, that you must come with your grave pate to make up the number three?"

There was a general laugh at the huntsman's expense, under cover of which he prudently withdrew his spouse, without attempting to continue the war of tongues, in which she had shown such a decided superiority.

This controversy, so light is the change in human spirits, especially among the lower class, awakened bursts of idle mirth among beings, who had so lately been in the jaws of danger, if not of absolute despair.

Chapter the Tenth.

They bore him barefaced on his bier,
Six proper youths and tall,
And many a tear bedew'd his grave
Within yon kirkyard wall.
THE FRIAR OF ORDERS GRAY.

WHILE these matters took place in the castle-yard, the young squire, Damian Lacy, obtained the audience which he had requested of Eveline Berenger, who received him in the great hall of the castle, seated beneath the dais, or canopy, and waited upon by Rose and other female attendants; of whom the first alone was permitted to use a tabouret or small stool in her presence, so strict were the Norman maidens of quality in maintaining their claims to high rank and observance.

The youth was introduced by the confessor and Flammock, as the spiritual character of the one, and the trust reposed by her late father in the other, authorized them to be present upon the occasion. Eveline naturally blushed, as she advanced two steps to receive the handsome youthful envoy; and her bashfulness seemed infectious, for it was with some confusion that Damian went through the ceremony of saluting the hand which she extended towards him in token of welcome. Eveline was under the necessity of speaking first.

"We advance as far as our limits will permit us," she said, "to greet with our thanks the messenger who brings us tidings of safety. We speak —unless we err—to the noble Damian of Lacy?"

"To the humblest of your servants," answered Damian, falling with some difficulty into the tone of courtesy which his errand and character required, "who approaches you on behalf of his noble uncle, Hugo de Lacy, Constable of Chester."

"Will not our noble deliverer in person honour with his presence the poor dwelling which he has saved?"

"My noble kinsman," answered Damian, "is now God's soldier, and bound by a vow not to come beneath a roof until he embark for the Holy Land. But by my voice he congratulates you on the defeat of your savage enemies, and sends you these tokens that the comrade and friend of your noble father hath not left his lamentable death many hours unavenged." So saying, he drew forth and laid before Eveline the gold bracelets, the coronet, and the eudorchawg, or chain of linked gold, which had distinguished the rank of the Welsh Prince.*

"Gwenwyn hath then fallen?" said Eveline, a natural shudder combating with the feelings of gratified vengeance, as she beheld that the trophies were speckled with blood,—"The slayer of my father is no more!"

"My kinsman's lance transfixed the Briton as he endeavoured to rally his flying people — he died grimly on the weapon which had passed more than a fathom through his body, and exerted his last strength in a furious but ineffectual blow with his mace."

"Heaven is just," said Eveline; "may his sins be forgiven to the man of blood, since he hath fallen by a death so bloody!—One question I would ask you, noble sir. My father's remains ——" She paused unable to proceed.

---

* Eudorchawg, or Gold Chains of the Welsh. These were the distinguished marks of rank and valour among the numerous tribes of Celtic extraction. Manlius, the Roman Champion, gained the name of Tor-quatus, or he of the chain, on account of an ornament of this kind, won, in single combat, from a gigantic Gaul. Aneurin, the Welsh bard, mentions, in his poem on the battle of Cattorath, that no less than three hundred of the British, who fell there, had their necks wreathed with the Eudorchawg. This seems to infer that the chain was a badge of distinction, and valour perhaps, but not of royalty; otherwise there would scarce have been so many kings present in one battle. This chain has been found accordingly in Ireland and Wales, and sometimes, though more rarely, in Scotland. Doubtless it was of too precious materials not to be usually converted into money by the enemy into whose hands it fell.

"An hour will place them at your disposal, most honoured lady," replied the squire, in the tone of sympathy which the sorrows of so young and so fair an orphan called irresistibly forth. "Such preparations as time admitted were making even when I left the host, to transport what was mortal of the noble Berenger from the field on which we found him amid a monument of slain which his own sword had raised. My kinsman's vow will not allow him to pass your portcullis; but, with your permission, I will represent him, if such be your pleasure, at these honoured obsequies, having charge to that effect."

"My brave and noble father," said Eveline, making an effort to restrain her tears, "will be best mourned by the noble and the brave." She would have continued, but her voice failed her, and she was obliged to withdraw abruptly, in order to give vent to her sorrow, and prepare for the funeral rites with such ceremony as circumstances should permit. Damian bowed to the departing mourner as reverently as he would have done to a divinity, and taking his horse, returned to his uncle's host, which had encamped hastily on the recent field of battle.

The sun was now high, and the whole plain presented the appearance of a bustle, equally different from the solitude of the early morning, and from the roar and fury of the subsequent engagement. The news of Hugo de Lacy's victory every where spread abroad with all alacrity of triumph, and had induced many of the inhabitants of the country, who had fled before the fury of the Wolf of Plinlimmon, to return to their desolate habitations. Numbers also of the loose and profligate characters which abound in a country subject to the frequent changes of war, had flocked thither in quest of spoil, or to gratify a spirit of restless curiosity. The Jew and the Lombard, despising danger where there was a chance of gain, might be already seen bartering liquors and wares with the victorious men-at-arms, for the blood-stained ornaments of gold lately worn by the defeated British. Others acted as brokers betwixt the Welsh captives and their captors; and where they could trust the means and good faith of the former, sometimes became bound for, or even advanced in ready money, the sums necessary for their ransom; whilst a more numerous class became themselves the purchasers of those prisoners who had no immediate means of settling with their conquerors.

That the spoil thus acquired might not long encumber the soldier, or blunt his ardour for farther enterprise, the usual means of dissipating military spoils were already at hand. Courtezans, mimes, jugglers, minstrels, and tale-tellers of every description, had accompanied the night-march; and, secure in the military reputation of the celebrated De Lacy, had rested fearlessly at some little distance until the battle was fought and won. These now approached, in many a joyous group, to congratulate the victors. Close to the parties which they formed for the dance, the song, or the tale, upon the yet bloody field, the countrymen, summoned in for the purpose, were opening large trenches for depositing the dead — leeches were seen tending the wounded — priests and monks confessing those in extremity — soldiers transporting from the field the bodies of the more honoured among the slain — peasants mourning over their trampled crops and plundered habitations—and widows and orphans searching for the bodies of husbands and parents, amid the promiscuous carnage of two combats. Thus wo mingled her wildest notes with those of jubilee and bacchanal triumph, and the plain of the Garde Doloureuse formed a singular parallel to the varied maze of human life, where joy and grief are so strangely mixed, and where the confines of mirth and pleasure often border on those of sorrow and of death.

About noon these various noises were at once silenced, and the attention alike of those who rejoiced or grieved was arrested by the loud and mournful sound of six trumpets, which, uplifting and uniting their thrilling tones in a wild and melancholy death-note, apprised all, that the obsequies of the valiant Raymond Berenger were about to commence. From a tent, which had been hastily pitched for the immediate reception of the body, twelve black monks, the inhabitants of a neighbouring convent, began to file out in pairs, headed by their abbot, who bore a large cross, and thundered forth the sublime notes of the Catholic *Miserere me, Domine.* Then came a chosen body of men-at-arms, trailing their lances, with their points reversed and pointed to the earth ; and after them the body of the valiant Berenger, wrapped in his own knightly banner, which, regained from the hands of the Welsh, now served its noble owner instead of a funeral pall. The most gallant Knights of the Constable's household (for, like other great nobles of that period, he had formed it upon a scale which approached to that of royalty) walked as mourners and supporters of the corpse, which was borne upon lances ; and the Constable of Chester himself, alone and fully armed, excepting the head, followed as chief mourner. A chosen body of squires, men-at-arms, and pages of noble descent, brought up the rear of the procession ; while their nakers and trumpets echoed back, from time to time, the melancholy song of the monks, by replying in a note as lugubrious as their own.

The course of pleasure was arrested, and even that of sorrow was for a moment turned from her own griefs, to witness the last honours bestowed on him, who had been in life the father and guardian of his people.

The mournful procession traversed slowly the plain which had been within a few hours the scene of such varied events ; and, pausing before the outer gate of the barricades of the castle, invited, by a prolonged and solemn flourish, the fortress to receive the remains of its late gallant defender. The melancholy summons was answered by the warder's horn—the drawbridge sunk — the portcullis rose — and Father Aldrovand appeared in the middle of the gateway, arrayed in his sacerdotal habit, whilst a little way behind him stood the orphaned damsel, in such weeds of mourning as time admitted, supported by her attendant Rose, and followed by the females of the household.

The Constable of Chester paused upon the threshold of the outer gate, and, pointing to the cross signed in white cloth upon his left shoulder, with a lowly reverence resigned to his nephew, Damian, the task of attending the remains of Raymond Berenger to the chapel within the castle. The soldiers of Hugo de Lacy, most of whom were bound by the same vow with himself, also halted without the castle gate, and remained under arms, while the death-peal of the chapel bell announced from within the progress of the procession.

It winded on through those narrow entrances, which were skilfully contrived to interrupt the progress of an enemy, even should he succeed in forcing the outer gate, and arrived at length in the great court-yard, where most of the inhabitants of the fortress, and those who, under recent circumstances, had taken refuge there, were drawn up, in order to look, for the last time, on their departed lord. Among these were mingled a few of the motley crowd from without, whom curiosity, or the expectation of a dole, had brought to the castle gate, and who, by one argument or another, had obtained from the warder permission to enter the interior.

The body was here set down before the door of the chapel, the ancient Gothic front of which formed one side of the court-yard, until certain prayers were recited by the priests, in which the crowd around were supposed to join with becoming reverence.

It was during this interval, that a man, whose peaked beard, embroidered girdle, and high-crowned hat of gray felt, gave him the air of a Lombard merchant, addressed Margery, the nurse of Eveline, in a whispering tone, and with a foreign accent. — "I am a travelling merchant, good sister, and am come hither in quest of gain—can you tell me whether I can have any custom in this castle?"

"You are come at an evil time, Sir Stranger—you may yourself see that this is a place for mourning and not for merchandise."

"Yet mourning times have their own commerce," said the stranger, approaching still closer to the side of Margery, and lowering his voice to a tone yet more confidential. "I have sable scarfs of Persian silk — black bugles, in which a princess might mourn for a deceased monarch—cyprus, such as the East hath seldom sent forth — black cloth for mourning hangings—all that may express sorrow and reverence in fashion and attire; and I know how to be grateful to those who help me to custom. Come, bethink you, good dame—such things must be had—I will sell as good ware and as cheap as another; and a kirtle to yourself, or, at your pleasure, a purse with five florins, shall be the meed of your kindness."

"I prithee peace, friend," said Margery, "and choose a better time for vaunting your wares — you neglect both place and season; and if you be farther importunate, I must speak to those who will show you the outward side of the castle gate. I marvel the warders would admit pedlars upon a day such as this—they would drive a gainful bargain by the bedside of their mother, were she dying, I trow." So saying, she turned scornfully from him.

While thus angrily rejected on the one side, the merchant felt his cloak receive an intelligent twitch upon the other, and, looking round upon the signal, he saw a dame, whose black kerchief was affectedly disposed, so as to give an appearance of solemnity to a set of light laughing features, which must have been captivating when young, since they retained so many good points when at least forty years had passed over them. She winked to the merchant, touching at the same time her under lip with her forefinger, to announce the propriety of silence and secrecy; then gliding from the crowd, retreated to a small recess formed by a projecting buttress of the chapel, as if to avoid the pressure likely to take place at the moment when the bier should be lifted. The merchant failed not to follow her example, and was soon by her side, when she did not give him the trouble of opening his affairs, but commenced the conversation herself.

"I have heard what you said to our Dame Margery—Mannerly Margery, as I call her — heard as much, at least, as led me to guess the rest, for I have got an eye in my head, I promise you."

"A pair of them, my pretty dame, and as bright as drops of dew in a May morning."

"Oh, you say so, because I have been weeping," said the scarlet-hosed Gillian, for it was even herself who spoke; "and to be sure, I have good cause, for our lord was always my very good lord, and would sometimes chuck me under the chin, and call me buxom Gillian of Croydon—not that the good gentleman was ever uncivil, for he would thrust a silver twopennies into my hand at the same time.—Oh! the friend that I have lost!— And I have had anger on his account too—I have seen old Raoul as sour as vinegar, and fit for no place but the kennel for a whole day about it; but, as I said to him, it was not for the like of me, to be affronting our master, and a great baron, about a chuck under the chin, or a kiss, or such like."

"No wonder you are so sorry for so kind a master, dame," said the merchant.

"No wonder, indeed," replied the dame, with a sigh; "and then what is to become of us?—It is like my young mistress will go to her aunt—or she will marry one of these Lacys that they talk so much of — or, at any rate, she will leave the castle; and it's like old Raoul and I will be turned to grass with the lord's old chargers. The Lord knows, they may as well hang him up with the old hounds, for he is both footless and fangless, and fit for nothing on earth that I know of."

"Your young mistress is that lady in the mourning mantle," said the merchant, "who so nearly sunk down upon the body just now?"

"In good troth is she, sir — and much cause she has to sink down. I am sure she will be to seek for such another father."

"I see you are a most discerning woman, gossip Gillian," answered the merchant; "and yonder youth that supported her is her bridegroom?"

"Much need she has for some one to support her," said Gillian; "and so have I for that matter, for what can poor old rusty Raoul do?"

"But as to your young lady's marriage?" said the merchant.

"No one knows more, than that such a thing was in treaty between our late lord and the great Constable of Chester, that came to-day but just in time to prevent the Welsh from cutting all our throats, and doing the Lord knoweth what mischief beside. But there is a marriage talked of, that is certain — and most folk think it must be for this smooth-cheeked boy, Damian, as they call him; for though the Constable has gotten a beard, which his nephew hath not, it is something too grizzled for a bridegroom's chin—Besides, he goes to the Holy Wars—fittest place for all elderly warriors—I wish he would take Raoul with him.—But what is all this to what you were saying about your mourning wares even now?—It is a sad truth, that my poor lord is gone — But what then? — Well-a-day, you know the good old saw,—

> 'Cloth must be wear,
> Eat beef and drink beer,
> Though the dead go to bier.'

And for your merchandising, I am as like to help you with my good word as Mannerly Margery, provided you bid fair for it; since, if the lady loves me not so much, I can turn the steward round my finger."

"Take this in part of your bargain, pretty Mistress Gillian," said the merchant; "and when my wains come up, I will consider you amply, if I get good sale by your favourable report.— But how shall I get into the castle again? for I would wish to consult you, being a sensible woman, before I come in with my luggage."

"Why," answered the complaisant dame, "if our English be on guard, you have only to ask for Gillian, and they will open the wicket to any single man at once; for we English stick all together, were it but to spite the Normans;— but if a Norman be on duty, you must ask for old Raoul, and say you come to speak of dogs and hawks for sale, and I warrant you come to speech of me that way. If the sentinel be a Fleming, you have but to say you are a merchant, and he will let you in for the love of trade."

The merchant repeated his thankful acknowledgment, glided from her side, and mixed among the spectators, leaving her to congratulate herself on having gained a brace of florins by the indulgence of her natural talkative humour; for which, on other occasions, she had sometimes dearly paid.

The ceasing of the heavy toll of the castle bell now gave intimation that the noble Raymond Berenger had been laid in the vault with his fathers. That part of the funeral attendants who had come from the host of De Lacy, now proceeded to the castle hall, where they partook, but with temperance, of some refreshments which were offered as a death-meal: and presently after left the castle, headed by young Damian, in the same slow and melancholy form in which they had entered. The monks remained within the castle to sing repeated services for the soul of the deceased, and for those of his faithful men-at-arms who had fallen around him, and who had been so much mangled during, and after, the contest with the Welsh, that it was scarce possible to know one individual from another; otherwise the body of Dennis Morolt would have obtained, as his faith well deserved, the honour of a separate funeral.*

Chapter the Eleventh.

—— The funeral baked meats
Did coldly furnish forth the marriage table.
HAMLET.

THE religious rites which followed the funeral of Raymond Berenger, endured without interruption for the period of six days; during which, alms were distributed to the poor, and relief administered, at the expense of the Lady Eveline, to all those who had suffered by the late inroad. Death-meals, as they were termed, were also spread in honour of the deceased; but the lady herself, and most of her attendants, observed a stern course of vigil, discipline, and fasts, which appeared to the Normans a more decorous manner of testifying their respect for the dead, than the Saxon and Flemish custom of banqueting and drinking inordinately upon such occasions.

Meanwhile, the Constable De Lacy retained a large body of his men encamped under the walls of the Garde Doloureuse, for protection against some new irruption of the Welsh, while with the rest he took advantage of his victory, and struck terror into the British by many well-conducted forays, marked with ravages scarcely less hurtful than their own. Among the enemy, the evils of discord were added to those of defeat and invasion: for two distant relations of Gwenwyn contended for the throne he had lately occupied, and on this, as on many other occasions, the Britons suffered as much from internal dissension as from the sword of the Normans. A worse politician, and a less celebrated soldier, than the sagacious and successful De Lacy, could not have failed, under such circumstances, to negotiate as he did an advantageous peace, which, while it deprived Powys of a part of its frontier, and the command of some important passes, in which it was the Constable's purpose to build castles, rendered the Garde Doloureuse more secure than formerly, from any sudden attack on the part of their fiery and restless neighbours. De Lacy's care also went to re-establishing those settlers who had fled from their possessions, and putting the whole lordship, which now descended upon an unprotected female, into a state of defence as perfect as its situation on a hostile frontier could possibly permit.

Whilst thus anxiously provident in the affairs of the orphan of the Garde Doloureuse, De Lacy during the space we have mentioned, sought not to disturb her filial grief by any personal intercourse. His nephew, indeed, was despatched by times every morning to lay before her his uncle's *devoirs*, in the high-flown language of the day, and acquaint her with the steps which he had taken in her affairs. As a meed due to his relative's high services, Damian was always admitted to see Eveline on such occasions, and returned charged with her grateful thanks, and her implicit acquiescence in whatever the Constable proposed for her consideration.

But when the days of rigid mourning were elapsed, the young de Lacy stated, on the part of his kinsman, that his treaty with the Welsh being

---

* The Welsh, a fierce and barbarous people, were often accused of mangling the bodies of their slain antagonists. Every one must remember Shakspeare's account, how

—— " the noble Mortimer,
Leading the men of Herefordshire to fight,
Against the irregular and wild Glendower—
Was, by the rude hands of that Welshman taken,
And a thousand of his people butchered;

Upon whose dead corpse there was such misuse,
Such beastly, shameless transformation,
By these Welshwomen done, as may not be,
Without much shame, retold or spoken of."

concluded, and all things in the district arranged as well as circumstances would permit, the Constable of Chester now proposed to return into his own territory, in order to resume his instant preparations for the Holy Land, which the duty of chastising her enemies had for some days interrupted.

"And will not the noble Constable, before he departs from this place," said Eveline, with a burst of gratitude which the occasion well merited, "receive the personal thanks of her that was ready to perish, when he so valiantly came to her aid?"

"It was even on that point that I was commissioned to speak," replied Damian; "but my noble kinsman feels diffident to propose to you that which he most earnestly desires—the privilege of speaking to your own ear certain matters of high import, and with which he judges it fit to intrust no third party."

"Surely," said the maiden, blushing, "there can be nought beyond the bounds of maidenhood, in my seeing the noble Constable whenever such is his pleasure."

"But his vow," replied Damian, "binds my kinsman not to come beneath a roof until he sets sail for Palestine; and in order to meet him, you must grace him so far as to visit his pavilion;—a condescension which, as a knight and Norman noble, he can scarcely ask of a damsel of high degree."

"And is that all?" said Eveline, who, educated in a remote situation, was a stranger to some of the nice points of etiquette which the damsels of the time observed in keeping their state towards the other sex. "Shall I not," she said, "go to render my thanks to my deliverer, since he cannot come hither to receive them? Tell the noble Hugo de Lacy, that, next to my gratitude to Heaven, it is due to him, and to his brave companions in arms. I will come to his tent as to a holy shrine; and, could such homage please him, I would come barefooted, were the road strewed with flints and with thorns."

"My uncle will be equally honoured and delighted with your resolve," said Damian; "but it will be his study to save you all unnecessary trouble, and with that view a pavilion shall be instantly planted before your castle gate, which, if it please you to grace it with your presence, may be the place for the desired interview."

Eveline readily acquiesced in what was proposed, as the expedient agreeable to the Constable, and recommended by Damian; but, in the simplicity of her heart, she saw no good reason why, under the guardianship of the latter, she should not instantly, and without farther form, have traversed the little familiar plain on which, when a child, she used to chase butterflies and gather king's-cups, and where of later years she was wont to exercise her palfrey on this well-known plain, being the only space, and that of small extent, which separated her from the camp of the Constable.

The youthful emissary, with whose presence she had now become familiar, retired to acquaint his kinsman and lord with the success of his commission; and Eveline experienced the first sensation of anxiety upon her own account which had agitated her bosom, since the defeat and death of Gwenwyn gave her permission to dedicate her thoughts exclusively to grief, for the loss which she had sustained in the person of her noble father. But now, when that grief, though not satiated, was blunted by solitary indulgence—now that she was to appear before the person of whose fame she had heard so much, of whose powerful protection she had received such recent proofs, her mind insensibly turned upon the nature and consequences of that important interview. She had seen Hugo de Lacy, indeed, at the great tournament at Chester, where his valour and skill were the theme of every tongue, and she had received the homage which he rendered her beauty when he assigned to her the prize, with all the gay flutterings of youthful vanity; but of his person and figure she had no distinct idea, excepting that he was a middle-sized man, dressed in peculiarly rich armour, and that

2 E

the countenance, which looked out from under the shade of his raised visor, seemed to her juvenile estimate very nearly as old as that of her father. This person, of whom she had such slight recollection, had been the chosen instrument employed by her tutelar protectress in rescuing her from captivity, and in avenging the loss of a father, and she was bound by her vow to consider him as the arbiter of her fate, if indeed he should deem it worth his while to become so. She wearied her memory with vain efforts to recollect so much of his features as might give her some means of guessing at his disposition, and her judgment toiled in conjecturing what line of conduct he was likely to pursue towards her.

The great Baron himself seemed to attach to their meeting a degree of consequence, which was intimated by the formal preparations which he made for it. Eveline had imagined that he might have ridden to the gate of the castle in five minutes, and that, if a pavilion were actually necessary to the decorum of their interview, a tent could have been transferred from his leaguer to the castle gate, and pitched there in ten minutes more. But it was plain that the Constable considered much more form and ceremony as essential to their meeting; for in about half an hour after Damian de Lacy had left the castle, not fewer than twenty soldiers and artificers, under the direction of a pursuivant, whose tabard was decorated with the armorial bearings of the house of Lacy, were employed in erecting before the gate of the Garde Doloureuse one of those splendid pavilions, which were employed at tournaments and other occasions of public state. It was of purple silk, valanced with gold embroidery, having the chords of the same rich materials. The door-way was formed by six lances, the staves of which were plaited with silver, and the blades composed of the same precious metal. These were pitched into the ground by couples, and crossed at the top, so as to form a sort of succession of arches, which were covered by drapery of sea-green silk, forming a pleasing contrast with the purple and gold.

The interior of the tent was declared by Dame Gillian and others, whose curiosity induced them to visit it, to be of a splendour agreeing with the outside. There were Oriental carpets, and there were tapestries of Ghent and Bruges mingled in gay profusion, while the top of the pavilion, covered with sky-blue silk, was arranged so as to resemble the firmament, and richly studded with a sun, moon, and stars, composed of solid silver. This gorgeous pavilion had been made for the use of the celebrated William of Ypres, who acquired such great wealth as general of the mercenaries of King Stephen, and was by him created Earl of Albemarle; but the chance of war had assigned it to De Lacy, after one of the dreadful engagements, so many of which occurred during the civil wars betwixt Stephen and the Empress Maude, or Matilda. The Constable had never before been known to use it; for although wealthy and powerful, Hugo de Lacy was, on most occasions, plain and unostentatious; which, to those who knew him, made his present conduct seem the more remarkable. At the hour of noon he arrived, nobly mounted, at the gate of the castle, and drawing up a small body of servants, pages, and equerries, who attended him in their richest liveries, placed himself at their head, and directed his nephew to intimate to the Lady of the Garde Doloureuse, that the humblest of her servants awaited the honour of her presence at the castle gate.

Among the spectators who witnessed his arrival, there were many who thought that some part of the state and splendour attached to his pavilion and his retinue, had been better applied to set forth the person of the Constable himself, as his attire was simple even to meanness, and his person by no means of such distinguished bearing as might altogether dispense with the advantages of dress and ornament. The opinion became yet more prevalent, when he descended from horseback, until which time his masterly management of the noble animal he bestrode, gave a dignity to his person and figure, which he lost upon dismounting from his steel saddle. In height, the celebrated Constable scarce attained the middle size, and his limbs, though strongly built and well knit, were deficient in grace and ease of movement. His legs were slightly curved outwards, which gave him advantage as a horseman, but showed unfavourably when he was upon foot. He halted, though very slightly, in consequence of one of his legs having been broken by the fall of a charger, and inartificially set by an inexperienced surgeon. This, also, was a blemish in his deportment; and though his broad shoulders, sinewy arms, and expanded chest, betokened the strength which he often displayed, it was strength of a clumsy and ungraceful character. His language and gestures were those of one seldom used to converse with equals, more seldom still with superiors; short, abrupt, and decisive, almost to the verge of sternness. In the judgment of those who were habitually acquainted with the Constable, there was both dignity and kindness in his keen eye and expanded brow; but such as saw him for the first time judged less favourably, and pretended to discover a harsh and passionate expression, although they allowed his countenance to have, on the whole, a bold and martial character. His age was in reality not more than five-and-forty, but the fatigues of war and of climate had added in appearance ten years to that period of time. By far the plainest dressed man of his train, he wore only a short Norman mantle, over the close dress of shamois-leather, which, almost always covered by his armour, was in some places slightly soiled by its pressure. A brown hat, in which he wore a sprig of rosemary in memory of his vow, served for his head-gear —his good sword and dagger hung at a belt made of seal-skin.

Thus accoutred, and at the head of a glittering and gilded band of retainers, who watched his lightest glance, the Constable of Chester awaited the arrival of the Lady Eveline Berenger, at the gate of her castle of Garde Douloureuse.

The trumpets from within announced her presence—the bridge fell, and, led by Damian de Lacy in his gayest habit, and followed by her train of females, and menial or vassal attendants, she came forth in her loveliness from under the massive and antique portal of her paternal fortress. She was dressed without ornaments of any kind, and in deep mourning weeds, as best befitted her recent loss; forming, in this respect, a strong contrast with the rich attire of her conductor, whose costly dress gleamed with jewels and embroidery, while their age and personal beauty made them in every other respect the fair counterpart of each other; a circumstance which probably gave rise to the delighted murmur and buzz which passed through the bystanders on their appearance, and which only respect for the deep mourning of Eveline prevented from breaking out into shouts of applause.

The instant that the fair foot of Eveline had made a step beyond the palisades which formed the outward barrier of the castle, the Constable de Lacy stepped forward to meet her, and, bending his right knee to the earth, craved pardon for the discourtesy which his vow had imposed on him, while he expressed his sense of the honour with which she now graced him, as one for which his life, devoted to her service, would be an inadequate acknowledgment.

The action and speech, though both in consistence with the romantic gallantry of the times, embarrassed Eveline; and the rather that this homage was so publicly rendered. She entreated the Constable to stand up, and not to add to the confusion of one who was already sufficiently at a loss how to acquit herself of the heavy debt of gratitude which she owed him. The Constable arose accordingly, after saluting her hand, which she extended to him, and prayed her, since she was so far condescending, to deign to enter the poor hut he had prepared for her shelter, and to grant him the honour of the audience he had solicited. Eveline, without farther answer than a bow, yielded him her hand, and desiring the rest of her train to remain where they were, commanded the attendance of Rose Flammock.

"Lady," said the Constable, "the matters of which I am compelled thus hastily to speak, are of a nature the most private."

"This maiden," replied Eveline, "is my bower-woman, and acquainted with my most inward thoughts; I beseech you to permit her presence at our conference."

"It were better otherwise," said Hugo de Lacy, with some embarrassment; "but your pleasure shall be obeyed."

He led the Lady Eveline into the tent, and entreated her to be seated on a large pile of cushions, covered with rich Venetian silk. Rose placed herself behind her mistress, half kneeling upon the same cushions, and watched the motions of the all-accomplished soldier and statesman, whom the voice of fame lauded so loudly; enjoying his embarrassment as a triumph of her sex, and scarcely of opinion that his shamois doublet and square form accorded with the splendour of the scene, or the almost angelic beauty of Eveline, the other actor therein.

"Lady," said the Constable, after some hesitation, "I would willingly say what it is my lot to tell you, in such terms as ladies love to listen to, and which surely your excellent beauty more especially deserves; but I have been too long trained in camps and councils to express my meaning otherwise than simply and plainly."

"I shall the more easily understand you, my lord," said Eveline, trembling, though she scarce knew why.

"My story, then, must be a blunt one. Something there passed between your honourable father and myself, touching a union of our houses." — He paused, as if he wished or expected Eveline to say something, but, as she was silent, he proceeded. "I would to God, that, as he was at the beginning of this treaty, it had pleased Heaven he should have conducted and concluded it with his usual wisdom; but what remedy? — he has gone the path which we must all tread."

"Your lordship," said Eveline, "has nobly avenged the death of your noble friend."

"I have but done my devoir, lady, as a good knight, in defence of an endangered maiden — a Lord Marcher in protection of the frontier — and a friend in avenging his friend. But to the point. — Our long and noble line draws near to a close. Of my remote kinsman, Randal Lacy, I will not speak; for in him I see nothing that is good or hopeful, nor have we been at one for many years. My nephew, Damian, gives hopeful promise to be a worthy branch of our ancient tree — but he is scarce twenty years old, and hath a long career of adventure and peril to encounter, ere he can honourably propose to himself the duties of domestic privacy or matrimonial engagements. His mother also is English, some abatement perhaps in the escutcheon of his arms; yet, had ten years more passed over him with the honours of chivalry, I should have proposed Damian de Lacy for the happiness to which I at present myself aspire."

"You—you, my lord!—it is impossible!" said Eveline, endeavouring at the same time to suppress all that could be offensive in the surprise which she could not help exhibiting.

"I do not wonder," replied the Constable, calmly,—for the ice being now broken, he resumed the natural steadiness of his manner and character,— "that you express surprise at this daring proposal. I have not perhaps the form that pleases a lady's eye, and I have forgotten,—that is, if I ever knew them, — the terms and phrases which please a lady's ear; but, noble Eveline, the Lady of Hugh de Lacy will be one of the foremost among the matronage of England."

"It will the better become the individual to whom so high a dignity is offered," said Eveline, "to consider how far she is capable of discharging its duties."

"Of that I fear nothing," said De Lacy. "She who hath been so excellent a daughter, cannot be less estimable in every other relation in life."

"I do not find that confidence in myself, my lord," replied the embarrassed maiden, "with which you are so willing to load me—And I—forgive me—must crave time for other inquiries, as well as those which respect myself."

"Your father, noble lady, had this union warmly at heart. This scroll, signed with his own hand, will show it." He bent his knee as he gave the paper. "The wife of De Lacy will have, as the daughter of Raymond Berenger merits, the rank of a princess; his widow, the dowry of a queen."

"Mock me not with your knee, my lord, while you plead to me the paternal commands, which, joined to other circumstances"—she paused, and sighed deeply—"leave me, perhaps, but little room for free will!"

Imboldened by this answer, De Lacy, who had hitherto remained on his knee, rose gently, and assuming a seat beside the Lady Eveline, continued to press his suit,—not, indeed, in the language of passion, but of a plain-spoken man, eagerly urging a proposal on which his happiness depended. The vision of the miraculous image was, it may be supposed, uppermost in the mind of Eveline, who, tied down by the solemn vow she had made on that occasion, felt herself constrained to return evasive answers, where she might perhaps have given a direct negative, had her own wishes alone been to decide her reply.

"You cannot," she said, "expect from me, my lord, in this my so recent orphan state, that I should come to a speedy determination upon an affair of such deep importance. Give me leisure of your nobleness for consideration with myself—for consultation with my friends."

"Alas! fair Eveline," said the Baron, "do not be offended at my urgency. I cannot long delay setting forward on a distant and perilous expedition; and the short time left me for soliciting your favour, must be an apology for my importunity."

"And is it in these circumstances, noble De Lacy, that you would encumber yourself with family ties?" asked the maiden, timidly.

"I am God's soldier," said the Constable, "and He, in whose cause I fight in Palestine, will defend my wife in England."

"Hear then my present answer, my lord," said Eveline Berenger, rising from her seat. "To-morrow I proceed to the Benedictine nunnery at Gloucester, where resides my honoured father's sister, who is Abbess of that reverend house. To her guidance I will commit myself in this matter."

"A fair and maidenly resolution," answered De Lacy, who seemed, on his part, rather glad that the conference was abridged, "and, as I trust, not altogether unfavourable to the suit of your humble suppliant, since the good Lady Abbess hath been long my honoured friend." He then turned to Rose, who was about to attend her lady:—"Pretty maiden," he said, offering a chain of gold, "let this carcanet encircle thy neck, and buy thy good will."

"My good will cannot be purchased, my lord," said Rose, putting back the gift which he proffered.

"Your fair word, then," said the Constable, again pressing it upon her.

"Fair words are easily bought," said Rose, still rejecting the chain, "but they are seldom worth the purchase-money."

"Do you scorn my proffer, damsel?" said De Lacy: "it has graced the neck of a Norman count."

"Give it to a Norman countess then, my lord," said the damsel; "I am plain Rose Flammock, the weaver's daughter. I keep my good word to go with my good will, and a latten chain will become me as well as beaten gold."

"Peace, Rose," said her lady; "you are over malapert to talk thus to the Lord Constable. — And you, my lord," she continued, "permit me now to depart, since you are possessed of my answer to your present proposal. I regret it had not been of some less delicate nature, that by granting it at once, and without delay, I might have shown my sense of your services."

The lady was handed forth by the Constable of Chester, with the same ceremony which had been observed at their entrance, and she returned to her own castle, sad and anxious in mind for the event of this important conference. She gathered closely round her the great mourning veil, that the alteration of her countenance might not be observed; and, without pausing to speak even to Father Aldrovand, she instantly withdrew to the privacy of her own bower.

Chapter the Twelfth.

Now all ye ladies of fair Scotland,
And ladies of England that happy would prove,
Marry never for houses, nor marry for land,
Nor marry for nothing but only love.
FAMILY QUARRELS.

WHEN the Lady Eveline had retired into her own private chamber, Rose Flammock followed her unbidden, and proffered her assistance in removing the large veil which she had worn while she was abroad; but the lady refused her permission, saying, "You are forward with service, maiden, when it is not required of you."

"You are displeased with me, lady!" said Rose.

"And if I am, I have cause," replied Eveline. "You know my difficulties —you know what my duty demands; yet, instead of aiding me to make the sacrifice, you render it more difficult."

"Would I had influence to guide your path!" said Rose; "you should find it a smooth one—ay, an honest and straight one, to boot."

"How mean you, maiden?" said Eveline.

"I would have you," answered Rose, "recall the encouragement — the consent, I may almost call it, you have yielded to this proud baron. He is too great to be loved himself—too haughty to love you as you deserve. If you wed him, you wed gilded misery, and, it may be, dishonour as well as discontent."

"Remember, damsel," answered Eveline Berenger, "his services towards us."

"His services?" answered Rose. "He ventured his life for us, indeed, but so did every soldier in his host. And am I bound to wed any ruffling blade among them, because he fought when the trumpet sounded? I wonder what is the meaning of their *devoir*, as they call it, when it shames them not to claim the highest reward woman can bestow, merely for discharging the duty of a gentleman, by a distressed creature. A gentleman, said I?— The coarsest boor in Flanders would hardly expect thanks for doing the duty of a man by women in such a case."

"But my father's wishes?" said the young lady.

"They had reference, without doubt, to the inclination of your father's daughter," answered the attendant. "I will not do my late noble lord — (may God assoilzie him!) — the injustice to suppose he would have urged aught in this matter which squared not with your free choice."

"Then my vow—my fatal vow, as I had well-nigh called it?" said Eveline. "May Heaven forgive me my ingratitude to my patroness!"

"Even this shakes me not," said Rose; "I will never believe our Lady of Mercy would exact such a penalty for her protection, as to desire me to wed the man I could not love. She smiled, you say, upon your prayer. Go—lay at her feet these difficulties which oppress you, and see if she will not smile again. Or seek a dispensation from your vow—seek it at the expense of the half of your estate,—seek it at the expense of your whole property. Go a pilgrimage barefooted to Rome—do any thing but give your hand where you cannot give your heart."

"You speak warmly, Rose," said Eveline, still sighing as she spoke.

"Alas! my sweet lady, I have cause. Have I not seen a household where love was not—where, although there was worth and good will, and enough of the means of life, all was imbittered by regrets, which were not only vain, but criminal?"

"Yet, methinks, Rose, a sense of what is due to ourselves and to others may, if listened to, guide and comfort us under such feelings even as thou hast described."

"It will save us from sin, lady, but not from sorrow," answered Rose; "and wherefore should we, with our eyes open, rush into circumstances where duty must war with inclination? Why row against wind and tide, when you may as easily take advantage of the breeze?"

"Because the voyage of my life lies where winds and currents oppose me," answered Eveline. "It is my fate, Rose."

"Not unless you make it such by choice," answered Rose. "Oh, could you but have seen the pale cheek, sunken eye, and dejected bearing of my poor mother!—I have said too much."

"It was then your mother," said her young lady, "of whose unhappy wedlock you have spoken?"

"It was—it was," said Rose, bursting into tears. "I have exposed my own shame to save you from sorrow. Unhappy she was, though most guiltless—so unhappy, that the breach of the dike, and the inundation in which she perished, were, but for my sake, to her welcome as night to the weary labourer. She had a heart like yours, formed to love and be loved; and it would be doing honour to yonder proud Baron, to say he had such worth as my father's.—Yet was she most unhappy. Oh! my sweet lady, be warned, and break off this ill-omened match!"

Eveline returned the pressure with which the affectionate girl, as she clung to her hand, enforced her well-meant advice, and then muttered with a profound sigh,—"Rose, it is too late."

"Never—never," said Rose, looking eagerly round the room. "Where are those writing materials?—Let me bring Father Aldrovand, and instruct him of your pleasure—or, stay, the good father hath himself an eye on the splendours of the world which he thinks he has abandoned—he will be no safe secretary.—I will go myself to the Lord Constable—me his rank cannot dazzle, or his wealth bribe, or his power overawe. I will tell him he doth no knightly part towards you, to press his contract with your father in such an hour of helpless sorrow—no pious part, in delaying the execution of his vows for the purpose of marrying or giving in marriage—no honest part, to press himself on a maiden whose heart has not decided in his favour—no wise part, to marry one whom he must presently abandon, either to solitude, or to the dangers of a profligate court."

"You have not courage for such an embassy, Rose," said her mistress, sadly smiling through her tears at her youthful attendant's zeal.

"Not courage for it!—and wherefore not?—Try me," answered the Flemish maiden, in return. "I am neither Saracen nor Welshman—his lance and sword scare me not. I follow not his banner—his voice of command concerns me not. I could, with your leave, boldly tell him he is a selfish man, veiling with fair and honourable pretexts his pursuit of objects which concern his own pride and gratification, and founding high claims on having rendered the services which common humanity demanded. And all for what?—Forsooth the great De Lacy must have an heir to his noble house, and his fair nephew is not good enough to be his representative, because his mother was of Anglo-Saxon strain, and the real heir must be pure unmixed Norman; and for this, Lady Eveline Berenger, in the first bloom of youth, must be wedded to a man who might be her father, and who, after leaving her unprotected for years, will return in such guise as might beseem her grandfather!"

"Since he is thus scrupulous concerning purity of lineage," said Eveline, "perhaps he may call to mind, what so good a herald as he is cannot fail to know—that I am of Saxon strain by my father's mother."

"Oh," replied Rose, "he will forgive that blot in the heiress of the Garde Doloureuse."

"Fie, Rose," answered her mistress, "thou dost him wrong in taxing him with avarice."

"Perhaps so," answered Rose; "but he is undeniably ambitious; and Avarice, I have heard, is Ambition's bastard brother, though Ambition be sometimes ashamed of the relationship."

"You speak too boldly, damsel," said Eveline; "and, while I acknowledge your affection, it becomes me to check your mode of expression."

"Nay, take that tone, and I have done," said Rose.—"To Eveline, whom I love, and who loves me, I can speak freely—but to the Lady of the Garde Doloureuse, the proud Norman damsel, (which when you choose to be you can be,) I can curtsy as low as my station demands, and speak as little truth as she cares to hear."

"Thou art a wild but a kind girl," said Eveline; "no one who did not know thee would think that soft and childish exterior covered such a soul of fire. Thy mother must indeed have been the being of feeling and passion you paint her; for thy father—nay, nay, never arm in his defence until he be attacked—I only meant to say, that his solid sense and sound judgment are his most distinguished qualities."

"And I would you would avail yourself of them, lady," said Rose.

"In fitting things I will; but he were rather an unmeet counsellor in that which we now treat of," said Eveline.

"You mistake him," answered Rose Flammock, "and underrate his value. Sound judgment is like to the graduated measuring-wand, which, though usually applied only to coarser cloths, will give with equal truth the dimensions of Indian silk, or of cloth of gold."

"Well—well—this affair presses not instantly at least," said the young lady. "Leave me now, Rose, and send Gillian the tirewoman hither—I have directions to give about the packing and removal of my wardrobe."

"That Gillian the tirewoman hath been a mighty favourite of late," said Rose; "time was when it was otherwise."

"I like her manners as little as thou dost," said Eveline; "but she is old Raoul's wife—she was a sort of half favourite with my dear father—who, like other men, was perhaps taken by that very freedom which we think unseemly in persons of our sex; and then there is no other woman in the Castle that hath such skill in empacketing clothes without the risk of their being injured."

"That last reason alone," said Rose, smiling, "is, I admit, an irresistible pretension to favour, and Dame Gillian shall presently attend you.—But take my advice, lady—keep her to her bales and her mails, and let her not prate to you on what concerns her not."

So saying, Rose left the apartment, and her young lady looked after her in silence—then murmured to herself—"Rose loves me truly; but she would willingly be more of the mistress than the maiden; and then she is somewhat jealous of every other person that approaches me.—It is strange, that I have not seen Damian de Lacy since my interview with the Constable. He anticipates, I suppose, the chance of his finding in me a severe aunt!"

But the domestics, who crowded for orders with reference to her removal early on the morrow, began now to divert the current of their lady's thoughts from the consideration of her own particular situation, which, as the prospect presented nothing pleasant, with the elastic spirit of youth, she willingly postponed till farther leisure.

Chapter the Thirteenth.

Too much rest is rust,
  There's ever cheer in changing;
We tyne by too much trust,
So we'll be up and ranging.
OLD SONG.

EARLY on the subsequent morning, a gallant company, saddened indeed by the deep mourning which their principals wore, left the well-defended Castle of the Garde Doloureuse, which had been so lately the scene of such remarkable events.

The sun was just beginning to exhale the heavy dews which had fallen during the night, and to disperse the thin gray mist which eddied around towers and battlements, when Wilkin Flammock, with six crossbowmen on horseback, and as many spearmen on foot, sallied forth from under the Gothic gate-way, and crossed the sounding drawbridge. After this advanced guard, came four household servants well mounted, and after them, as many inferior female attendants, all in mourning. Then rode forth the young Lady Eveline herself, occupying the centre of the little procession, and her long black robes formed a striking contrast to the colour of her milk-white palfrey. Beside her, on a Spanish jennet, the gift of her affectionate father,—who had procured it at a high rate, and who would have given half his substance to gratify his daughter,—sat the girlish form of Rose Flammock, who had so much of juvenile shyness in her manner, so much of feeling and of judgment in her thoughts and actions. Dame Margery followed, mixed in the party escorted by Father Aldrovand, whose company she chiefly frequented; for Margery affected a little the character of the devotee, and her influence in the family, as having been Eveline's nurse, was so great as to render her no improper companion for the chaplain, when her lady did not require her attendance on her own person. Then came old Raoul the huntsman, his wife, and two or three other officers of Raymond Berenger's household; the steward, with his golden chain, velvet cassock, and white wand, bringing up the rear, which was closed by a small band of archers, and four men-at-arms. The guards, and indeed the greater part of the attendants, were only designed to give the necessary degree of honour to the young lady's movements, by accompanying her a short space from the castle, where they were met by the Constable of Chester, who, with a retinue of thirty lances, proposed himself to escort Eveline as far as Gloucester, the place of her destination. Under his protection no danger was to be apprehended, even if the severe defeat so lately sustained by the Welsh had not of itself been likely to prevent any attempt, on the part of those hostile mountaineers, to disturb the safety of the marches for some time to come.

In pursuance of this arrangement, which permitted the armed part of Eveline's retinue to return for the protection of the castle, and the restoration of order in the district around, the Constable awaited her at the fatal bridge, at the head of the gallant band of selected horsemen whom he had ordered to attend upon him. The parties halted, as if to salute each other; but the Constable, observing that Eveline drew her veil more closely around her, and recollecting the loss she had so lately sustained on that luckless spot, had the judgment to confine his greeting to a mute reverence, so low that the lofty plume which he wore, (for he was now in complete armour,) mingled with the flowing mane of his gallant horse. Wilkin Flammock next halted, to ask the lady if she had any farther commands.

"None, good Wilkin," said Eveline; "but to be, as ever, true and watchful."

"The properties of a good mastiff," said Flammock. "Some rude sagacity, and a stout hand instead of a sharp case of teeth, are all that I can claim to be added to them—I will do my best.—Fare thee well, Roschen! Thou art going among strangers—forget not the qualities which made thee loved at home. The saints bless thee—farewell!"

The steward next approached to take his leave, but in doing so, had nearly met with a fatal accident. It had been the pleasure of Raoul, who was in his own disposition cross-grained, and in person rheumatic, to accommodate himself with an old Arab horse, which had been kept for the sake of the breed, as lean, and almost as lame as himself, and with a temper as vicious as that of a fiend. Betwixt the rider and the horse was a constant misunderstanding, testified on Raoul's part by oaths, rough checks with the curb, and severe digging with the spurs, which Mahound (so paganishly was the horse named) answered by plunging, bounding, and endeavouring by all expedients to unseat his rider, as well as striking and lashing out furiously at whatever else approached him. It was thought by many of the household, that Raoul preferred this vicious cross-tempered animal upon all occasions when he travelled in company with his wife, in order to take advantage by the chance, that amongst the various kicks, plunges, gambades, lashings out, and other eccentricities of Mahound, his heels might come in contact with Dame Gillian's ribs. And now, when as the important steward spurred up his palfrey to kiss his young lady's hand, and to take his leave, it seemed to the bystanders as if Raoul so managed his bridle and spur, that Mahound yerked out his hoofs at the same moment, one of which coming in contact with the steward's thigh, would have splintered it like a rotten reed, had the parties been a couple of inches nearer to each other. As it was, the steward sustained considerable damage; and they who observed the grin upon Raoul's vinegar countenance entertained little doubt, that Mahound's heels then and there avenged certain nods, and winks, and wreathed smiles, which had passed betwixt the gold-chained functionary and the coquettish tirewoman, since the party left the castle.

This incident abridged the painful solemnity of parting betwixt the Lady Eveline and her dependents, and lessened, at the same time, the formality of her meeting with the Constable, and, as it were, resigning herself to his protection.

Hugo de Lacy, having commanded six of his men-at-arms to proceed as an advanced-guard, remained himself to see the steward properly deposited on a litter, and then, with the rest of his followers, marched in military fashion about one hundred yards in the rear of Lady Eveline and her retinue, judiciously forbearing to present himself to her society while she was engaged in the orisons which the place where they met naturally suggested, and waiting patiently until the elasticity of youthful temper should require some diversion of the gloomy thoughts which the scene inspired.

Guided by this policy, the Constable did not approach the ladies until the advance of the morning rendered it politeness to remind them, that a pleasant spot for breaking their fast occurred in the neighbourhood, where he had ventured to make some preparations for rest and refreshment. Immediately after the Lady Eveline had intimated her acceptance of this courtesy, they came in sight of the spot he alluded to, marked by an ancient oak, which, spreading its broad branches far and wide, reminded the traveller of that of Mamre, under which celestial beings accepted the hospitality of the patriarch. Across two of these huge projecting arms was flung a piece of rose-coloured sarsanet, as a canopy to keep off the morning beams, which were already rising high. Cushions of silk, interchanged with others covered with the furs of animals of the chase, were arranged round a repast, which a Norman cook had done his utmost to distinguish, by the superior delicacy of his art, from the gross meals of the Saxons, and the penurious simplicity of the Welsh tables. A fountain, which bubbled from under a large mossy stone at some distance, refreshed the air with its sound, and the taste with its liquid crystal; while, at the same time, it formed a cistern for cooling two or three flasks of Gascon wine and hippocras, which were at that time the necessary accompaniments of the morning meal.

When Eveline, with Rose, the Confessor, and at some farther distance her faithful nurse, was seated at this silvan banquet, the leaves rustling to a gentle breeze, the water bubbling in the background, the birds twittering around, while the half-heard sounds of conversation and laughter at a distance announced that their guard was in the vicinity, she could not avoid making the Constable some natural compliment on his happy selection of a place of repose.

"You do me more than justice," replied the Baron; "the spot was selected by my nephew, who hath a fancy like a minstrel. Myself am but slow in imagining such devices."

Rose looked full at her mistress, as if she endeavoured to look into her very inmost soul; but Eveline answered with the utmost simplicity,—"And wherefore hath not the noble Damian waited to join us at the entertainment which he hath directed?"

"He prefers riding onward," said the Baron, "with some light-horsemen; for, notwithstanding there are now no Welsh knaves stirring, yet the marches are never free from robbers and outlaws; and though there is nothing to fear for a band like ours, yet you should not be alarmed even by the approach of danger."

"I have indeed seen but too much of it lately," said Eveline; and relapsed into the melancholy mood from which the novelty of the scene had for a moment awakened her.

Meanwhile, the Constable, removing, with the assistance of his squire, his mailed hood and its steel crest, as well as his gauntlets, remained in his flexible coat of mail, composed entirely of rings of steel curiously interwoven, his hands bare, and his brows covered with a velvet bonnet of a peculiar fashion, appropriated to the use of knights, and called a *mortier*, which permitted him both to converse and to eat more easily than when he wore the full defensive armour. His discourse was plain, sensible, and manly; and, turning upon the state of the country, and the precautions to be observed for governing and defending so disorderly a frontier, it became gradually interesting to Eveline, one of whose warmest wishes was to be the protectress of her father's vassals. De Lacy, on his part, seemed much pleased; for, young as Eveline was, her questions showed intelligence, and her mode of answering, both apprehension and docility. In short, familiarity was so far established betwixt them, that in the next stage of their journey, the Constable seemed to think his appropriate place was at the Lady Eveline's bridle-rein; and although she certainly did not countenance his attendance, yet neither did she seem willing to discourage it. Himself no ardent lover, although captivated both by the beauty and the amiable qualities of the fair orphan, De Lacy was satisfied with being endured as a companion, and made no efforts to improve the opportunity which this familiarity afforded him, by recurring to any of the topics of the preceding day.

A halt was made at noon in a small village, where the same purveyor had made preparations for their accommodation, and particularly for that of the Lady Eveline ; but, something to her surprise, he himself remained invisible. The conversation of the Constable of Chester was, doubtless, in the highest degree instructive ; but at Eveline's years, a maiden might be excused for wishing some addition to the society in the person of a younger and less serious attendant; and when she recollected the regularity with which Damian Lacy had hitherto made his respects to her, she rather wondered at his continued absence. But her reflection went no deeper than the passing thought of one who was not quite so much delighted with her present company, as not to believe it capable of an agreeable addition. She was lending a patient ear to the account which the Constable gave her of the descent and pedigree of a gallant knight of the distinguished family of Herbert, at whose castle he proposed to repose during the night, when one of the retinue announced a messenger from the Lady of Baldringham.

" My honoured father's aunt," said Eveline, arising to testify that respect for age and relationship which the manners of the time required.

" I knew not," said the Constable, " that my gallant friend had such a relative."

" She was my grandmother's sister," answered Eveline, " a noble Saxon lady ; but she disliked the match formed with a Norman house, and never saw her sister after the period of her marriage."

She broke off, as the messenger, who had the appearance of the steward of a person of consequence, entered the presence, and, bending his knee reverently, delivered a letter, which, being examined by Father Aldrovand, was found to contain the following invitation, expressed, not in French, then the general language of communication amongst the gentry, but in the old Saxon language, modified as it now was by some intermixture of French.

" If the grand-daughter of Aelfried of Baldringham hath so much of the old Saxon strain as to desire to see an ancient relation, who still dwells in the house of her forefathers, and lives after their manner, she is thus invited to repose for the night in the dwelling of Ermengarde of Baldringham."

" Your pleasure will be, doubtless, to decline the present hospitality ?" said the Constable De Lacy ; " the noble Herbert expects us, and has made great preparation."

" Your presence, my lord," said Eveline, " will more than console him for my absence. It is fitting and proper that I should meet my aunt's advances to reconciliation, since she has condescended to make them."

De Lacy's brow was slightly clouded, for seldom had he met with anything approaching to contradiction of his pleasure. " I pray you to reflect, Lady Eveline," he said, " that your aunt's house is probably defenceless, or at least very imperfectly guarded.—Would it not be your pleasure that I should continue my dutiful attendance ?"

" Of that, my lord, mine aunt can, in her own house, be the sole judge ; and methinks, as she has not deemed it necessary to request the honour of your lordship's company, it were unbecoming in me to permit you to take the trouble of attendance ; — you have already had but too much on my account."

" But for the sake of your own safety, madam," said De Lacy, unwilling to leave his charge.

" My safety, my lord, cannot be endangered in the house of so near a relative ; whatever precautions she may take on her own behalf, will doubtless be amply sufficient for mine."

"I hope it will be found so," said De Lacy; "and I will at least add to them the security of a patrol around the castle during your abode in it." He stopped, and then proceeded with some hesitation to express his hope, that Eveline, now about to visit a kinswoman whose prejudices against the Norman race were generally known, would be on her guard against what she might hear upon that subject.

Eveline answered with dignity, that the daughter of Raymond Berenger was unlikely to listen to any opinions which would affect the dignity of that good knight's nation and descent; and with this assurance, the Constable, finding it impossible to obtain any which had more special reference to himself and his suit, was compelled to remain satisfied. He recollected also that the castle of Herbert was within two miles of the habitation of the Lady of Baldringham, and that his separation from Eveline was but for one night; yet a sense of the difference betwixt their years, and perhaps of his own deficiency in those lighter qualifications by which the female heart is supposed to be most frequently won, rendered even this temporary absence matter of anxious thought and apprehension; so that, during their afternoon journey, he rode in silence by Eveline's side, rather meditating what might chance to-morrow, than endeavouring to avail himself of present opportunity. In this unsocial manner they travelled on until the point was reached where they were to separate for the evening.

This was an elevated spot, from which they could see, on the right hand, the castle of Amelot Herbert, rising high upon an eminence, with all its Gothic pinnacles and turrets; and on the left, low-embowered amongst oaken woods, the rude and lonely dwelling in which the Lady of Baldringham still maintained the customs of the Anglo-Saxons, and looked with contempt and hatred on all innovations that had been introduced since the battle of Hastings.

Here the Constable De Lacy, having charged a part of his men to attend the Lady Eveline to the house of her relation, and to keep watch around it with the utmost vigilance, but at such a distance as might not give offence or inconvenience to the family, kissed her hand, and took a reluctant leave. Eveline proceeded onwards by a path so little trodden, as to show the solitary condition of the mansion to which it led. Large kine, of an uncommon and valuable breed, were feeding in the rich pastures around; and now and then fallow deer, which appeared to have lost the shyness of their nature, tripped across the glades of the woodland, or stood and lay in small groups under some great oak. The transient pleasure which such a scene of rural quiet was calculated to afford, changed to more serious feelings, when a sudden turn brought her at once in front of the mansion-house of which she had seen nothing since she first beheld it from the point she parted with the Constable, and which she had more than one reason for regarding with some apprehension.

The house, for it could not be termed a castle, was only two stories high, low and massively built, with doors and windows forming the heavy round arch which is usually called Saxon;—the walls were mantled with various creeping plants, which had crept along them undisturbed—grass grew up to the very threshold, at which hung a buffalo's horn, suspended by a brass chain. A massive door of black oak closed a gate, which much resembled the ancient entrance to a ruined sepulchre, and not a soul appeared to acknowledge or greet their arrival.

"Were I you, my Lady Eveline," said the officious dame Gillian, "I would turn bridle yet; for this old dungeon seems little likely to afford food or shelter to Christian folk."

Eveline imposed silence on her indiscreet attendant, though herself exchanging a look with Rose which confessed something like timidity, as she commanded Raoul to blow the horn at the gate. "I have heard," she said, "that my aunt loves the ancient customs so well, that she is loath to

2 F

admit into her halls any thing younger than the time of Edward the Con
fessor."

Raoul, in the meantime, cursing the rude instrument which baffled his
skill in sounding a regular call, and gave voice only to a tremulous and discordant roar, which seemed to shake the old walls, thick as they were, repeated his summons three times before they obtained admittance.   On the
third sounding, the gate opened, and a numerous retinue of servants of both
sexes appeared in the dark and narrow hall, at the upper end of which a
great fire of wood was sending its furnace-blast up an antique chimney,
whose front, as extensive as that of a modern kitchen, was carved over with
ornaments of massive stone, and garnished on the top with a long range of
niches, from each of which frowned the image of some Saxon Saint, whose
barbarous name was scarce to be found in the Romish calendar.

The same officer who had brought the invitation from his lady to Eveline,
now stepped forward, as she supposed, to assist her from her palfrey; but
it was in reality to lead it by the bridle-rein into the paved hall itself, and
up to a raised platform, or dais, at the upper end of which she was at length
permitted to dismount.   Two matrons of advanced years, and four young
women of gentle birth, educated by the bounty of Ermengarde, attended
with reverence the arrival of her kinswoman.   Eveline would have inquired
of them for her grand-aunt, but the matrons with much respect laid their
fingers on their mouths, as if to enjoin her silence; a gesture which, united
to the singularity of her reception in other respects, still farther excited her
curiosity to see her venerable relative.

It was soon gratified; for, through a pair of folding doors, which opened
not far from the platform on which she stood, she was ushered into a large
low apartment hung with arras; at the upper end of which, under a species
of canopy, was seated the ancient Lady of Baldringham.   Fourscore years
had not quenched the brightness of her eyes, or bent an inch of her stately
height; her gray hair was still so profuse as to form a tier, combined as it
was with a chaplet of ivy leaves; her long dark-coloured gown fell in ample
folds, and the broidered girdle, which gathered it around her, was fastened
by a buckle of gold, studded with precious stones, which were worth an
Earl's ransom; her features, which had once been beautiful, or rather
majestic, bore still, though faded and wrinkled, an air of melancholy and
stern grandeur, that assorted well with her garb and deportment.   She had
a staff of ebony in her hand; at her feet rested a large aged wolf-dog, who
pricked his ears and bristled up his neck, as the step of a stranger, a sound
so seldom heard in those halls, approached the chair in which his aged mistress sat motionless.

"Thryme," said the venerable dame; "and thou, daughter of the
house of Baldringham, approach, and fear not their ancient servant."

The hound sunk down to his couchant posture when she spoke, and, excepting the red glare of his eyes, might have seemed a hieroglyphical
emblem, lying at the feet of some ancient priestess of Woden or Freya; so
strongly did the appearance of Ermengarde, with her rod and her chaplet,
correspond with the ideas of the days of Paganism.   Yet he who had thus
deemed of her would have done therein much injustice to a venerable
Christian matron, who had given many a hide of land to holy church, in
honour of God and Saint Dunstan.

Ermengarde's reception of Eveline was of the same antiquated and formal
cast with her mansion and her exterior.   She did not at first arise from her
seat when the noble maiden approached her, nor did she even admit her to
the salute which she advanced to offer; but, laying her hand on Eveline's
arm, stopped her as she advanced, and perused her countenance with an
earnest and unsparing eye of minute observation.

"Berwine," she said to the most favoured of the two attendants, "our
niece hath the skin and eyes of the Saxon hue; but the hue of her eye-brows

and hair is from the foreigner and alien.—Thou art, nevertheless, welcome to my house, maiden," she added, addressing Eveline, "especially if thou canst bear to hear that thou art not absolutely a perfect creature, as doubtless these flatterers around thee have taught thee to believe."

So saying, she at length arose, and saluted her niece with a kiss on the forehead. She released her not, however, from her grasp, but proceeded to give the attention to her garments which she had hitherto bestowed upon her features.

"Saint Dunstan keep us from vanity!" she said; "and so this is the new guise — and modest maidens wear such tunics as these, showing the shape of their persons as plain as if (Saint Mary defend us!) they were altogether without garments? And see, Berwine, these gauds on the neck, and that neck itself uncovered as low as the shoulder — these be the guises which strangers have brought into merry England! and this pouch, like a player's placket, hath but little to do with housewifery, I wot; and that dagger, too, like a glee-man's wife, that rides a mumming in masculine apparel—dost thou ever go to the wars, maiden, that thou wearest steel at thy girdle?"

Eveline, equally surprised and disobliged by the depreciating catalogue of her apparel, replied to the last question with some spirit,—"The mode may have altered, madam; but I only wear such garments as are now worn by those of my age and condition. For the poniard, may it please you, it is not many days since I regarded it as the last resource betwixt me and dishonour."

"The maiden speaks well and boldly, Berwine," said Dame Ermengarde; "and, in truth, pass we but over some of these vain fripperies, is attired in a comely fashion. Thy father, I hear, fell knight-like in the field of battle."

"He did so," answered Eveline, her eyes filling with tears at the recollection of her recent loss.

"I never saw him," continued Dame Ermengarde; "he carried the old Norman scorn towards the Saxon stock, whom they wed but for what they can make by them, as the bramble clings to the elm;—nay, never seek to vindicate him," she continued, "observing that Eveline was about to speak, "I have known the Norman spirit for many a year ere thou wert born."

At this moment the steward appeared in the chamber, and, after a long genuflection, asked his lady's pleasure concerning the guard of Norman soldiers who remained without the mansion.

"Norman soldiers so near the house of Baldringham!" said the old lady, fiercely; "who brings them hither, and for what purpose?"

"They came, as I think," said the sewer, "to wait on and this gracious young lady."

"What, my daughter," said Ermengarde, in a tone of melancholy reproach, "darest thou not trust thyself unguarded for one night in the castle of thy forefathers?"

"God forbid else!" said Eveline. "But these men are not mine, nor under my authority. They are part of the train of the Constable de Lacy, who left them to watch around the castle, thinking there might be danger from robbers."

"Robbers," said Ermengarde, "have never harmed the house of Baldringham, since a Norman robber stole from it its best treasure, the person of thy grandmother — And so, poor bird, thou art already captive — unhappy flutterer! But it is thy lot, and wherefore should I wonder or repine? When was there fair maiden, with a wealthy dower, but she was ere maturity destined to be the slave of some of those petty kings, who allow us to call nothing ours that their passions can covet? Well—I cannot aid thee—I am but a poor and neglected woman, feeble both from sex and age.—And to which of those De Lacys art thou the destined household drudge?"

A question so asked, and by one whose prejudices were of such a determined character, was not likely to draw from Eveline any confession of the real circumstances in which she was placed, since it was but too plain her Saxon relation could have afforded her neither sound counsel nor useful assistance. She replied therefore briefly, that as the Lacys, and the Normans in general, were unwelcome to her kinswoman, she would entreat of the commander of the patrol to withdraw it from the neighbourhood of Baldringham.

"Not so, my niece," said the old lady; "as we cannot escape the Norman neighbourhood, or get beyond the sound of their curfew, it signifies not whether they be near our walls or more far off, so that they enter them not. And, Berwine, bid Hundwolf drench the Normans with liquor, and gorge them with food—the food of the best, and liquor of the strongest. Let them not say the old Saxon hag is churlish of her hospitality. Broach a piece of wine, for I warrant their gentle stomachs brook no ale."

Berwine, her huge bunch of keys jangling at her girdle, withdrew to give the necessary directions, and presently returned. Meanwhile Ermengarde proceeded to question her niece more closely. "Is it that thou wilt not, or canst not, tell me to which of the De Lacys thou art to be bondawoman?—to the overweening Constable, who, sheathed in impenetrable armour, and mounted on a swift and strong horse as invulnerable as himself, takes pride that he rides down and stabs at his ease, and with perfect safety, the naked Welshmen?—or is it to his nephew, the beardless Damian?—or must thy possessions go to mend a breach in the fortunes of that other cousin, Randal Lacy, the decayed reveller, who, they say, can no longer ruffle it among the debauched crusaders for want of means?"

"My honoured aunt," replied Eveline, naturally displeased with this discourse, "to none of the Lacy's, and I trust to none other, Saxon or Norman, will your kinswoman become a household drudge. There was, before the death of my honoured father, some treaty betwixt him and the Constable, on which account I cannot at present decline his attendance; but what may be the issue of it, fate must determine."

"But I can show thee, niece, how the balance of fate inclines," said Ermengarde, in a low and mysterious voice. "Those united with us by blood have, in some sort, the privilege of looking forward beyond the points of present time, and seeing in their very bud the thorns or flowers which are one day to encircle their head."

"For my own sake, noble kinswoman," answered Eveline, "I would decline such foreknowledge, even were it possible to acquire it without transgressing the rules of the Church. Could I have foreseen what has befallen me within these last unhappy days, I had lost the enjoyment of every happy moment before that time."

"Nevertheless, daughter," said the Lady of Baldringham, "thou, like others of thy race, must within this house conform to the rule, of passing one night within the chamber of the Red-Finger.—Berwine, see that it be prepared for my niece's reception."

"I—I—have heard speak of that chamber, gracious aunt," said Eveline, timidly, "and it it may consist with your good pleasure, I would not now choose to pass the night there. My health has suffered by my late perils and fatigue, and with your good-will I will delay to another time the usage, which I have heard is peculiar to the daughters of the house of Baldringham."

"And which, notwithstanding, you would willingly avoid," said the old Saxon lady, bending her brows angrily. "Has not such disobedience cost your house enough already?"

"Indeed, honoured and gracious lady," said Berwine, unable to forbear interference, though well knowing the obstinacy of her patroness, "that chamber is in disrepair, and cannot easily on a sudden be made fit for the Lady Eveline; and the noble damsel looks so pale, and hath lately suffered so much, that, might I have the permission to advise, this were better delayed."

"Thou art a fool, Berwine," said the old lady, sternly; "thinkest thou I will bring anger and misfortune on my house, by suffering this girl to leave it without rendering the usual homage to the Red-Finger? Go to— let the room be made ready —small preparation may serve, if she cherish not the Norman nicety about bed and lodging. Do not reply; but do as I command thee.—And you, Eveline—are you so far degenerated from the brave spirit of your ancestry, that you dare not pass a few hours in an ancient apartment?"

"You are my hostess, gracious madam," said Eveline, "and must assign my apartment where you judge proper—my courage is such as innocence and some pride of blood and birth have given me. It has been, of late, severely tried: but, since such is your pleasure, and the custom of your house, my heart is yet strong enough to encounter what you propose to subject me to."

She paused here in displeasure; for she resented, in some measure, her aunt's conduct, as unkind and inhospitable. And yet when she reflected upon the foundation of the legend of the chamber to which she was consigned, she could not but regard the Lady of Baldringham as having considerable reason for her conduct, according to the traditions of the family, and the belief of the times, in which Eveline herself was devout.

~~~~~~~~~~~~~~~~~~

Chapter the Fourteenth.

Sometimes, methinks, I hear the groans of ghosts,
Then hollow sounds and lamentable screams;
Then, like a dying echo from afar,
My mother's voice, that cries, "Wed not, Almeyda—
Forewarn'd, Almeyda, marriage is thy crime."

DON SEBASTIAN.

THE evening at Baldringham would have seemed of portentous and unendurable length, had it not been that apprehended danger ... times pass quickly betwixt us and the dreaded hour, and that if Eveline felt little interested or amused by the conversation of her aunt and Berwine, which turned upon the long deduction of their ancestors from the warlike Horsa, and the feats of Saxon champions, and the miracles of Saxon monks, she was still better pleased to listen to these legends, than to anticipate her retreat to the destined and dreaded apartment where she was to pass the night. There lacked not, however, such amusement as the house of Baldringham could afford, to pass away the evening. Blessed by a grave old Saxon monk, the chaplain of the house, a sumptuous entertainment, which might have sufficed twenty hungry men, was served up before Ermengarde and her niece, whose sole assistants, beside the reverend man, were Berwine and Rose Flammock. Eveline was the less inclined to do justice to this excess of hospitality, that the dishes were all of the gross and substantial nature which the Saxons admired, but which contrasted disadvantageously with the refined and delicate cookery of the Normans, as did the moderate cup of light and high-flavoured Gascon wine, tempered with more than half its quantity of the purest water, with the mighty ale, the high-spiced pigment and hippocras, and the other potent liquors, which, one after another, were in vain proffered for her acceptance by the steward Hundwolf, in honour of the hospitality of Baldringham.

Neither were the stated amusements of evening more congenial to Eveline's taste, than the profusion of her aunt's solid refection. When the boards and tresses, on which the viands had been served, were withdrawn from the apartment, the menials, under direction of the steward, proceeded to light several long waxen torches, one of which was graduated for the purpose of marking the passing time, and dividing it into portions. These were announced by means of brazen balls, suspended by threads from the torch, the spaces betwixt them being calculated to occupy a certain time in burning; so that, when the flame reached the thread, and the balls fell, each in succession, into a brazen basin placed for its reception, the office of a modern clock was in some degree discharged. By this light the party was arranged for the evening.

The ancient Ermengarde's lofty and ample chair was removed, according to ancient custom, from the middle of the apartment to the warmest side of a large grate, filled with charcoal, and her guest was placed on her right, as the seat of honour. Berwine then arranged in due order the females of the household, and, having seen that each was engaged with her own proper task, sat herself down to ply the spindle and distaff. The men, in a more remote circle, betook themselves to the repairing of their implements of husbandry, or new furbishing weapons of the chase, under the direction of the steward Hundwolf. For the amusement of the family thus assembled, an old glee-man sung to a harp, which had but four strings, a long and apparently interminable legend, upon some religious subject, which was rendered almost unintelligible to Eveline, by the extreme and complicated affectation of the poet, who, in order to indulge in the alliteration which was accounted one great ornament of Saxon poetry, had sacrificed sense to sound, and used words in the most forced and remote sense, provided they could be compelled into his service. There was also all the obscurity arising from elision, and from the most extravagant and hyperbolical epithets.

Eveline, though well acquainted with the Saxon language, soon left off listening to the singer, to reflect for a moment on the gay *fabliaux* and imaginative *lais* of the Norman minstrels, and then to anticipate, with anxious apprehension, what nature of visitation she might be exposed to in the mysterious chamber in which she was doomed to pass the night.

The hour of parting at length approached. At half an hour before midnight, a period ascertained by the consumption of the huge waxen torch, the ball which was secured to it fell clanging into the brazen basin placed beneath, and announced to all the hour of rest. The old glee-man paused in his song, instantaneously, and in the middle of a stanza, and the household were all on foot at the signal, some retiring to their own apartments, others lighting torches or bearing lamps to conduct the visiters to their places of repose. Among these last was a bevy of bower-women, to whom the duty was assigned of conveying the Lady Eveline to her chamber for the night. Her aunt took a solemn leave of her, crossed her forehead, kissed it, and whispered in her ear, "Be courageous, and be fortunate."

"May not my bower-maiden, Rose Flammock, or my tire-woman, Dame Gillian, Raoul's wife, remain in the apartment with me for this night?" said Eveline.

"Flammock—Raoul!" repeated Ermengarde, angrily; "is thy household thus made up? The Flemings are the cold palsy to Britain, the Normans the burning fever."

"And the poor Welsh will add," said Rose, whose resentment began to surpass her awe for the ancient Saxon dame, "that the Anglo-Saxons were the original disease, and resemble a wasting pestilence."

"Thou art too bold, sweetheart," said the Lady Ermengarde, looking at the Flemish maiden from under her dark brows; "and yet there is wit in thy words. Saxon, Dane, and Norman, have rolled like successive billows over the land, each having strength to subdue what they lacked wisdom to keep. When shall it be otherwise?"

"When Saxon, and Briton, and Norman, and Fleming," answered Rose, boldly, "shall learn to call themselves by one name, and think themselves alike children of the land they were born in."

"Ha!" exclaimed the Lady of Baldringham, in the tone of one half surprised, half-pleased. Then turning to her relation, she said, "There are words and wit in this maiden; see that she use but do not abuse them."

"She is as kind and faithful, as she is prompt and ready-witted," said Eveline. "I pray you, dearest aunt, let me use her company for this night."

"It may not be—it were dangerous to both. Alone you must learn your destiny, as have all the females of our race, excepting your grandmother, and what have been the consequences of her neglecting the rules of our house? Lo! her descendant stands before me an orphan in the very bloom of youth."

"I will go, then," said Eveline with a sigh of resignation; "and it shall never be said I incurred future wo, to shun present terror."

"Your attendants," said the Lady Ermengarde, "may occupy the anteroom, and be almost within your call. Berwine will show you the apartment—I cannot; for we, thou knowest, who have once entered it, return not thither again. Farewell, my child, and may heaven bless thee!"

With more of human emotion and sympathy than she had yet shown, the Lady again saluted Eveline, and signed to her to follow Berwine, who, attended by two damsels bearing torches, waited to conduct her to the dreaded apartment.

Their torches glared along the rudely built walls and dark arched roofs of one or two long winding passages; these by their light enabled them to descend the steps of a winding stair, whose inequality and ruggedness showed its antiquity; and finally led into a tolerably large chamber on the lower story of the edifice, to which some old hangings, a lively fire on the hearth, the moonbeams stealing through a latticed window, and the boughs of a myrtle plant which grew around the casement, gave no uncomfortable appearance.

"This," said Berwine, "is the resting-place of your attendants," and she pointed to the couches which had been prepared for Rose and Dame Gillian; "we," she added, "proceed farther."

She then took a torch from the attendant maidens, both of whom seemed to shrink back with fear, which was readily caught by Dame Gillian, although she was not probably aware of the cause. But Rose Flammock, unbidden, followed her mistress without hesitation, as Berwine conducted her through a small wicket at the upper end of the apartment, clenched with many an iron nail, into a second but smaller anteroom or wardrobe, at the end of which was a similar door. This wardrobe had also its casement mantled with evergreens, and, like the former, it was faintly enlightened by the moonbeams.

Berwine paused here, and, pointing to Rose, demanded of Eveline, "Why does she follow?"

"To share my mistress's danger, be it what it may," answered Rose, with her characteristic readiness of speech and resolution. "Speak," she said, "my dearest lady," grasping Eveline's hand, while she addressed her; "you will not drive your Rose from you? If I am less high-minded than one of your boasted race, I am bold and quick-witted in all honest service. —You tremble like the aspen! Do not go into this apartment—do not be gulled by all this pomp and mystery of terrible preparation; bid defiance to this antiquated, and, I think, half-pagan superstition."

"The Lady Eveline must go, minion," replied Berwine, sternly; "and she must go without any malapert adviser or companion."

"Must go—*must* go?" repeated Rose. "Is this language to a free and noble maiden?—Sweet lady, give me once but the least hint that you wish it, and their '*must* go' shall be put to the trial. I will call from the casement on the Norman cavaliers, and tell them we have fallen into a den of witches, instead of a house of hospitality."

"Silence, madwoman," said Berwine, her voice quivering with anger and fear; "you know not who dwells in the next chamber."

"I will call those who will soon see to that," said Rose, flying to the casement, when Eveline, seizing her arm in her turn, compelled her to stop.

"I thank thy kindness, Rose," she said, "but it cannot help me in this matter. She who enters yonder door, must do so alone."

"Then I will enter it in your stead, my dearest lady," said Rose. "You are pale—you are cold—you will die with terror if you go on. There may be as much of trick as of supernatural agency in this matter—me they shall not deceive—or if some stern spirit craves a victim,—better Rose than her lady."

"Forbear, forbear," said Eveline, rousing up her own spirits; "you make me ashamed of myself. This is an ancient ordeal, which regards the females descended from the house of Baldringham as far as in the third degree, and them only. I did not indeed expect, in my present circumstances, to have been called upon to undergo it; but, since the hour summons me, I will meet it as freely as any of my ancestors."

So saying, she took the torch from the hand of Berwine, and wishing good-night to her and Rose, gently disengaged herself from the hold of the latter, and advanced into the mysterious chamber. Rose pressed after her so far as to see that it was an apartment of moderate dimensions, resembling that through which they had last passed, and lighted by the moon-beams, which came through a window lying on the same range with those of the anterooms. More she could not see, for Eveline turned on the threshold, and kissing her at the same time, thrust her gently back into the smaller apartment which she had just left, shut the door of communication, and barred and bolted it, as if in security against her well-meant intrusion.

Berwine now exhorted Rose, as she valued her life, to retire into the first anteroom, where the beds were prepared, and betake herself, if not to rest, at least to silence and devotion; but the faithful Flemish girl stoutly refused her entreaties, and resisted her commands.

"Talk not to me of danger," she said; "here I remain, that I may be at least within hearing of my mistress's danger, and wo betide those who shall offer her injury!—Take notice, that twenty Norman spears surround this inhospitable dwelling, prompt to avenge whatsoever injury shall be offered to the daughter of Raymond Berenger."

"Reserve your threats for those who are mortal," said Berwine, in a low, but piercing whisper; "the owner of yonder chamber fears them not. Farewell—thy danger be on thine own head!"

She departed, leaving Rose strangely agitated by what had passed, and somewhat appalled at her last words. "These Saxons," said the maiden, within herself, "are but half converted after all, and hold many of their old hellish rites in the worship of elementary spirits. Their very saints are unlike to the saints of any Christian country, and have, as it were, a look of something savage and fiendish—their very names sound pagan and diabolical. It is fearful being alone here—and all is silent as death in the apartment into which my lady has been thus strangely compelled. Shall I call up Gillian?—but no—she has neither sense, nor courage, nor principle, to aid me on such an occasion — better alone than have a false friend for company. I will see if the Normans are on their post, since it is to them I must trust, if a moment of need should arrive."

Thus reflecting, Rose Flammock went to the window of the little apartment, in order to satisfy herself of the vigilance of the sentinels, and to ascertain the exact situation of the corps de garde. The moon was at the full, and enabled her to see with accuracy the nature of the ground without. In the first place, she was rather disappointed to find, that instead of being so near the earth as she supposed, the range of windows which gave light as well to the two anterooms as to the mysterious chamber itself, looked down upon an ancient moat, by which they were divided from the level ground on the farther side. The defence which this fosse afforded seemed to have been long neglected, and the bottom, entirely dry, was choked in many places with bushes and low trees, which rose up against the wall of the castle, and by means of which it seemed to Rose the windows might be easily scaled, and the mansion entered. From the level plain beyond, the space adjoining to the castle was in a considerable degree clear, and the moonbeams slumbered on its close and beautiful turf, mixed with long shadows of the towers and trees. Beyond this esplanade lay the forest ground, with a few gigantic oaks scattered individually along the skirt of its dark and ample domain, like champions, who take their ground of defiance in front of a line of arrayed battle.

The calm beauty and repose of a scene so lovely, the stillness of all around, and the more matured reflections which the whole suggested, quieted, in some measure, the apprehensions which the events of the evening had inspired. "After all," she reflected, "why should I be so anxious on account of the Lady Eveline? There is among the proud Normans and the dogged Saxons scarce a single family of note, but must needs be held distinguished from others by some superstitious observance peculiar to their race, as if they thought it scorn to go to Heaven like a poor simple Fleming, such as I am. — Could I but see the Norman sentinel, I would hold myself satisfied with my mistress's security. — And yonder one stalks along the gloom, wrapt in his long white mantle, and the moon tipping the point of his lance with silver.—What ho, Sir Cavalier!"

The Norman turned his steps, and approached the ditch as she spoke. "What is your pleasure, damsel?" he demanded.

"The window next to mine is that of the Lady Eveline Berenger, whom you are appointed to guard. Please to give heedful watch upon this side of the castle."

"Doubt it not, lady," answered the cavalier; and enveloping himself in his long *chappe*, or military watch-cloak, he withdrew to a large tree at some distance, and stood there with folded arms, and leaning on his lance, more like a trophy of armour than a living warrior.

Imboldened by the consciousness, that in case of need succour was close at hand, Rose drew back into her little chamber, and having ascertained, by listening, that there was no noise or stirring in that of Eveline, she began to make some preparations for her own repose. For this purpose she went into the outward ante-room, where Dame Gillian, whose fears had given way to the soporiferous effects of a copious draught of *lithe-alos*, (mild ale, of the first strength and quality,) slept as sound a sleep as that generous Saxon beverage could procure.

Muttering an indignant censure on her sloth and indifference, Rose caught, from the empty couch which had been destined for her own use, the upper covering, and dragging it with her into the inner ante-room, disposed it so as, with the assistance of the rushes which strewed that apartment, to form a sort of couch, upon which, half seated, half reclined, she resolved to pass the night in as close attendance upon her mistress as circumstances permitted.

Thus seated, her eye on the pale planet which sailed in full glory through the blue sky of midnight, she proposed to herself that sleep should not visit her eyelids till the dawn of morning should assure her of Eveline's safety.

Her thoughts, meanwhile, rested on the boundless and shadowy world beyond the grave, and on the great and perhaps yet undecided question, whether the separation of its inhabitants from those of this temporal sphere is absolute and decided, or whether, influenced by motives which we cannot appreciate, they continue to hold shadowy communication with those yet existing in earthly reality of flesh and blood? To have denied this, would, in the age of crusades and of miracles, have incurred the guilt of heresy; but Rose's firm good sense led her to doubt at least the frequency of supernatural interference, and she comforted herself with an opinion, contradicted, however, by her own involuntary starts and shudderings at every leaf which moved, that, in submitting to the performance of the rite imposed on her, Eveline incurred no real danger, and only sacrificed to an obsolete family superstition.

As this conviction strengthened on Rose's mind, her purpose of vigilance began to decline — her thoughts wandered to objects towards which they were not directed, like sheep which stray beyond the charge of their shepherd—her eyes no longer brought back to her a distinct apprehension of the broad, round, silvery orb on which they continued to gaze. At length they closed, and seated on the folded mantle, her back resting against the wall of the apartment, and her white arms folded on her bosom, Rose Flammock fell fast asleep.

Her repose was fearfully broken by a shrill and piercing shriek from the apartment where her lady reposed. To start up and fly to the door was the work of a moment with the generous girl, who never permitted fear to struggle with love or duty. The door was secured with both bar and bolt; and another fainter scream, or rather groan, seemed to say, aid must be instant, or in vain. Rose next rushed to the window, and screamed rather than called to the Norman soldier, who, distinguished by the white folds of his watch-cloak, still retained his position under the old oak-tree.

At the cry of "Help, help! — the Lady Eveline is murdered!" the seeming statue, starting at once into active exertion, sped with the swiftness of a race-horse to the brink of the moat, and was about to cross it, opposite to the spot where Rose stood at the open casement, urging him to speed by voice and gesture.

"Not here —not here!" she exclaimed, with breathless precipitation, as she saw him make towards her — "the window to the right — scale it, for God's sake, and undo the door of communication."

The soldier seemed to comprehend her—he dashed into the moat without hesitation, securing himself by catching at the boughs of trees as he descended. In one moment he vanished among the underwood; and in another, availing himself of the branches of a dwarf oak, Rose saw him upon her right, and close to the window of the fatal apartment. One fear remained—the casement might be secured against entrance from without— but no! at the thrust of the Norman it yielded, and its clasps or fastenings being worn with time, fell inward with a crash which even Dame Gillian's slumbers were unable to resist.

Echoing scream upon scream, in the usual fashion of fools and cowards, she entered the cabinet from the ante-room, just as the door of Eveline's chamber opened, and the soldier appeared, bearing in his arms the half-undressed and lifeless form of the Norman maiden herself. Without speaking a word, he placed her in Rose's arms, and with the same precipitation with which he had entered, threw himself out of the opened window from which Rose had summoned him.

Gillian, half distracted with fear and wonder, heaped exclamations on questions, and mingled questions with cries for help, till Rose sternly rebuked her in a tone which seemed to recall her scattered senses. She became then composed enough to fetch a lamp which remained lighted in the room she had left, and to render herself at least partly useful in suggesting and applying the usual modes for recalling the suspended sense. In this they at length succeeded, for Eveline fetched a fuller sigh, and opened her eyes; but presently shut them again, and letting her head drop on Rose's bosom, fell into a strong shuddering fit; while her faithful damsel, chafing her hands and her temples alternately with affectionate assiduity, and mingling caresses with these efforts, exclaimed aloud, "She lives! — She is recovering! — Praised be God!"

"Praised be God!" was echoed in a solemn tone from the window of the apartment; and turning towards it in terror, Rose beheld the armed and plumed head of the soldier who had come so opportunely to their assistance, and who, supported by his arms, had raised himself so high as to be able to look into the interior of the cabinet.

Rose immediately ran towards him. "Go—go—good friend," she said; "the lady recovers — your reward shall await you another time. Go — begone! — yet stay—keep on your post, and I will call you if there is farther need. Begone—be faithful, and be secret."

The soldier obeyed without answering a word, and she presently saw him descend into the moat. Rose then returned back to her mistress, whom she found supported by Gillian, moaning feebly, and muttering hurried and unintelligible ejaculations, all intimating that she had laboured under a violent shock sustained from some alarming cause.

Dame Gillian had no sooner recovered some degree of self-possession, than her curiosity became active in proportion. "What means all this?" she said to Rose; "what has been doing among you?"

"I do not know," replied Rose.

"If you do not," said Gillian, "who should? — Shall I call the other women, and raise the house?"

"Not for your life," said Rose, "till my lady is able to give her own orders; and for this apartment, so help me Heaven, as I will do my best to discover the secrets it contains! — Support my mistress the whilst."

So saying, she took the lamp in her hand, and, crossing her brow, stepped boldly across the mysterious threshold, and, holding up the light, surveyed the apartment.

It was merely an old vaulted chamber, of very moderate dimensions. In one corner was an image of the Virgin, rudely cut, and placed above a Saxon font of curious workmanship. There were two seats and a couch, covered with coarse tapestry, on which it seemed that Eveline had been reposing. The fragments of the shattered casement lay on the floor; but that opening had been only made when the soldier forced it in, and she saw no other access by which a stranger could have entered an apartment, the ordinary access to which was barred and bolted.

Rose felt the influence of those terrors which she had hitherto surmounted; she cast her mantle hastily around her head, as if to shroud her sight from some blighting vision, and tripping back to the cabinet, with more speed and a less firm step than when she left it, she directed Gillian to lend her assistance in conveying Eveline to the next room; and having done so, carefully secured the door of communication, as if to p▓▓▓▓arrier betwixt them and the suspected danger.

The Lady Eveline was now so far recovered that she could sit up, and was trying to speak, though but faintly. "Rose," she said at length, "I have seen her — my doom is sealed."

Rose immediately recollected the imprudence of suffering Gillian to hear what her mistress might say at such an awful moment, and hastily adopting the proposal she had before declined, desired her to go and call other two maidens of their mistress's household.

"And where am I to find them in this house," said Dame Gillian, "where strange men run about one chamber at midnight, and devils, for aught I know, frequent the rest of the habitation?"

"Find them where you can," said Rose, sharply; "but begone presently."

Gillian withdrew lingeringly, and muttering at the same time something which could not distinctly be understood. No sooner was she gone, than Rose, giving way to the enthusiastic affection which she felt for her mistress, implored her, in the most tender terms, to open her eyes, (for she had again closed them,) and speak to Rose, her own Rose, who was ready, if necessary, to die by her mistress's side.

"To-morrow — to-morrow, Rose," murmured Eveline — "I cannot speak at present."

"Only disburden your mind with one word — tell what has thus alarmed you — what danger you apprehend."

"I have seen her," answered Eveline—"I have seen the tenant of yonder chamber—the vision fatal to my race! — Urge me no more — to-morrow you shall know all."*

As Gillian entered with two of the maidens of her mistress's household, they removed the Lady Eveline, by Rose's directions, into a chamber at some distance which the latter had occupied, and placed her in one of their beds, where Rose, dismissing the others (Gillian excepted) to seek repose where they could find it, continued to watch her mistress. For some time she continued very much disturbed, but, gradually, fatigue, and the influence of some narcotic which Gillian had sense enough to recommend and prepare, seemed to compose her spirits. She fell into a deep slumber, from which she did not awaken until the sun was high over the distant hills.

~~~~~~~~~~~~~~~

Chapter the Fifteenth.

> I see a hand you cannot see,
>   Which beckons me away;
> I hear a voice you cannot hear,
>   Which says I must not stay.
>
>   MALLET.

When Eveline first opened her eyes, it seemed to be without any recollection of what had passed on the night preceding. She looked round the

---

* The idea of the Buhr-Geist was taken from a passage in the Memoirs of Lady Fanshaw, which have since been given to the public, and received with deserved approbation.

The original runs as follows. Lady Fanshaw, shifting among her friends in Ireland, like other sound loyalists of the period, tells her story thus:—

"From thence we went to the Lady Honor O'Brien's, a lady that went for a maid, but few believed it. She was the youngest daughter of the Earl of Thomond. There we staid three nights — the first of which I was surprised at being laid in a chamber, where, when about one o'clock, I heard a voice that awakened me. I drew the curtain, and in the casement of the window I saw, by the light of the moon, a woman leaning through the casement into the room, in white, with red hair and pale and ghastly complexion. She spoke loud, and in a tone I had never heard, thrice, "A horse:" and then, with a sigh more like the wind than breath, she vanished, and to me her body looked more like a thick cloud than substance. I was so much frightened that my hair stood on end, and my night-clothes fell off. I pulled and pinched your father, who never ceased crying the disorder I was in, but at last was much surprised to see me in this fright, and more so when ... the story and showed him the window opened. Neither of us slept any more that night; but he entertained me by telling me how much more these apparitions were common in this country than in England; and we concluded the cause to be the great superstition of the Irish, and the want of that knowing faith which should defend them from the power of the devil, which he exercises among them very much. About five o'clock the lady of the house came to see us, saying, she had not been in bed all night, because a cousin O'Brien of hers, whose ancestors had owned that house, had desired her to stay with him in his chamber, and that he died at two o'clock; and she said, I wish you to have had no disturbance, for 'tis the custom of the place, that when any of the family are dying, the shape of a woman appears every night in the window until they be dead. This woman was many ages ago got with child by the owner of this place, who murdered her in his garden, and flung her into the river under the window; but truly I thought not of it when I lodged you here it being the best room in the house! We made little reply to her speech, but disposed ourselves to be gone suddenly."

apartment; which was coarsely and scantily furnished, as one destined for the use of domestics and menials, and said to Rose, with a smile, "Our good kinswoman maintains the ancient Saxon hospitality at a homely rate, so far as lodging is concerned. I could have willingly parted with last night's profuse supper, to have obtained a bed of a softer texture. Methinks my limbs feel as if I had been under all the flails of a Franklin's barn-yard."

"I am glad to see you so pleasant, madam," answered Rose, discreetly avoiding any reference to the events of the night before.

Dame Gillian was not so scrupulous. "Your ladyship last night lay down on a better bed than this," she said, "unless I am much mistaken; and Rose Flammock and yourself know best why you left it."

If a look could have killed, Dame Gillian would have been in deadly peril from that which Rose shot at her, by way of rebuke for this ill-advised communication. It had instantly the effect which was to be apprehended, for Lady Eveline seemed at first surprised and confused; then, as recollections of the past arranged themselves in her memory, she folded her hands, looked on the ground, and wept bitterly, with much agitation.

Rose entreated her to be comforted, and offered to fetch the old Saxon chaplain of the house to administer spiritual consolation, if her grief rejected temporal comfort.

"No — call him not," said Eveline, raising her head and drying her eyes —"I have had enough of Saxon kindness. What a fool was I to expect, in that hard and unfeeling woman, any commiseration for my youth — my late sufferings — my orphan condition! I will not permit her a poor triumph over the Norman blood of Berenger, by letting her see how much I have suffered under her inhuman infliction. But first, Rose, answer me truly, was any inmate of Baldringham witness to my distress last night?"

Rose assured her that she had been tended exclusively by her own retinue, herself and Gillian, Blanche and Ternotte. She seemed to receive satisfaction from this assurance. "Hear me, both of you," she said, "and observe my words, as you love and as you fear me. Let no syllable be breathed from your lips of what has happened this night. Carry the same charge to my maidens. Lend me thine instant aid, Gillian, and thine, my dearest Rose, to change these disordered garments, and arrange this dishevelled hair. It was a poor vengeance she sought, and all because of my country. I am resolved she shall not see the slightest trace of the sufferings she has inflicted."

As she spoke thus, her eyes flashed with indignation, which seemed to dry up the tears that had before filled them. Rose saw the change of her manner with a mixture of pleasure and concern, being aware that her mistress's predominant failing was incident to her, as a spoiled child, who, accustomed to be treated with kindness, deference, and indulgence, by all around her, was apt to resent warmly whatever resembled neglect or contradiction.

"God knows," said the faithful bower-maiden, "I would hold my hand out to catch drops of molten lead, rather than endure your tears; and yet, my sweet mistress, I would rather at present see you grieved than angry. This ancient lady hath, it would seem, but acted according to some old superstitious rite of her family, which is in part yours. Her name is respectable, both from her conduct and possessions; and hard pressed as you are by the Normans, with whom your kinswoman, the Prioress, is sure to take part, I was in hope you might have had some shelter and countenance from the Lady of Baldringham."

"Never, Rose, never," answered Eveline; "you know not — you cannot guess what she has made me suffer—exposing me to witchcraft and fiends. Thyself said it, and said it truly — the Saxons are still half Pagans, void of Christianity, as of nurture and kindliness."

"Ay, but," replied Rose, "I spoke then to dissuade you from a danger · now that the danger is passed and over, I may judge of it otherwise."

"Speak not for them, Rose," replied Eveline, angrily; "no innocent victim was ever offered up at the altar of a fiend with more indifference than my father's kinswoman delivered up me—me, an orphan, bereaved of my natural and powerful support. I hate her cruelty—I hate her house—I hate the thought of all that has happened here—of all, Rose, except thy matchless faith and fearless attachment. Go, bid our train saddle directly—I will be gone instantly—I will not attire myself," she added, rejecting the assistance she had at first required—"I will have no ceremony—tarry for no leave-taking."

In the hurried and agitated manner of her mistress, Rose recognized with anxiety another mood of the same irritable and excited temperament, which had before discharged itself in tears and fits. But perceiving, at the same time, that remonstrance was in vain, she gave the necessary orders for collecting their company, saddling, and preparing for departure; hoping, that as her mistress removed to a farther distance from the scene where her mind had received so severe a shock, her equanimity might, by degrees, be restored.

Dame Gillian, accordingly, was busied with arranging the packages of her lady, and all the rest of Lady Eveline's retinue in preparing for instant departure, when, preceded by her steward, who acted also as a sort of gentleman-usher, leaning upon her confidential Berwine, and followed by two or three more of the most distinguished of her household, with looks of displeasure on her ancient yet lofty brow, the Lady Ermengarde entered the apartment.

Eveline, with a trembling and hurried hand, a burning cheek, and other signs of agitation, was herself busied about the arrangement of some baggage, when her relation made her appearance. At once, to Rose's great surprise, she exerted a strong command over herself, and, repressing every external appearance of disorder, she advanced to meet her relation, with a calm and haughty stateliness equal to her own.

"I come to give you good morning, our niece," said Ermengarde, haughtily indeed, yet with more deference than she seemed at first to have intended, so much did the bearing of Eveline impose respect upon her;—"I find that you have been pleased to shift that chamber which was assigned you, in conformity with the ancient custom of this household, and betake yourself to the apartment of a menial."

"Are you surprised at that, lady?" demanded Eveline in her turn; "or are you disappointed that you find me not a corpse, within the limits of the chamber which your hospitality and affection allotted to me?"

"Your sleep, then, has been broken?" said Ermengarde, looking fixedly at the Lady Eveline, as she spoke.

"If I complain not, madam, the evil must be deemed of little consequence. What has happened is over and passed, and it is not my intention to trouble you with the recital."

"She of the ruddy finger," replied Ermengarde, triumphantly, "loves not the blood of the stranger."

"She had less reason, while she walked the earth, to love that of the Saxon," said Eveline, "unless her legend speaks false in that matter; and unless   I well suspect, your house is haunted, not by the soul of the dead   suffered within its walls, but by evil spirits, such as the descendants of Hengist and Horsa are said still in secret to worship."

"You are pleasant, maiden," replied the old lady, scornfully, "or, if your words are meant in earnest, the shaft of your censure has glanced aside. A house, blessed by the holy Saint Dunstan, and by the royal and holy Confessor, is no abode for evil spirits."

"The house of Baldringham," replied Eveline, "is no abode for those who fear such spirits; and as I will, with all humility, avow myself of the number, I shall presently leave it to the custody of Saint Dunstan."

"Not till you have broken your fast, I trust?" said the Lady of Baldringham; "you will not, I hope, do my years and our relationship such foul disgrace?"

"Pardon me, madam," replied the Lady Eveline; "those who have experienced your hospitality at night, have little occasion for breakfast in the morning.—Rose, are not those loitering knaves assembled in the court-yard, or are they yet on their couches, making up for the slumber they have lost by midnight disturbances?"

Rose announced that her train was in the court, and mounted; when, with a low reverence, Eveline endeavoured to pass her relation, and leave the apartment without farther ceremony. Ermengarde at first confronted her with a grim and furious glance, which seemed to show a soul fraught with more rage than the thin blood and rigid features of extreme old age had the power of expressing, and raised her ebony staff as if about even to proceed to some act of personal violence. But she changed her purpose, and suddenly made way for Eveline, who passed without farther parley; and as she descended the staircase, which conducted from the apartment to the gateway, she heard the voice of her aunt behind her, like that of an aged and offended sibyl, denouncing wrath and wo upon her insolence and presumption.

"Pride," she exclaimed, "goeth before destruction, and a haughty spirit before a fall. She who scorneth the house of her forefathers, a stone from its battlements shall crush her! She who mocks the gray hairs of a parent, never shall one of her own locks be silvered with age! She who weds with a man of war and of blood, her end shall neither be peaceful nor bloodless!"

Hurrying to escape from these and other ominous denunciations, Eveline rushed from the house, mounted her palfrey with the precipitation of a fugitive, and, surrounded by her attendants, who had caught a part of her alarm, though without conjecturing the cause, rode hastily into the forest; old Raoul, who was well acquainted with the country, acting as their guide.

Agitated more than she was willing to confess to herself, by thus leaving the habitation of so near a relation, loaded with maledictions, instead of the blessings which are usually bestowed on a departing kinswoman, Eveline hastened forward, until the huge oak-trees with intervening arms had hidden from her view the fatal mansion.

The trampling and galloping of horse was soon after heard, announcing the approach of the patrol left by the Constable for the protection of the mansion, and who now, collecting from their different stations, came prepared to attend the Lady Eveline on her farther road to Gloucester, great part of which lay through the extensive forest of Deane, then a silvan region of large extent, though now much denuded of trees for the service of the iron mines. The Cavaliers came up to join the retinue of Lady Eveline, with armour glittering in the morning rays, trumpets sounding, horses prancing, neighing, and thrown, each by his chivalrous rider, into the attitude best qualified to exhibit the beauty of the steed and dexterity of the horseman; while their lances, streaming with long penoncelles, were brandished in every manner which could display elation of heart and readiness of hand. The sense of the military character of her countrymen of Normandy gave to Eveline a feeling at once of security and of triumph, which operated towards the dispelling of her gloomy thoughts, and of the feverish disorder which affected her nerves. The rising sun also—the song of the birds among the bowers — the lowing of the cattle as they were driven to pasture — the sight of the hind, who, with her fawn trotting by her side, often crossed some forest glade within view of the travellers, — all contributed to dispel the terror of Eveline's nocturnal visions, and soothe to rest the more angry passions which had agitated her bosom at her departure from Baldringham. She suffered her palfrey to slacken his pace, and, with female attention to propriety, began to adjust her riding robes, and compose her head-dress, disordered in her hasty departure. Rose saw her cheek assume a paler but more settled hue, instead of the angry hectic which had coloured it — saw her eye become more steady as she looked with a sort of triumph upon her military attendants, and pardoned (what on other occasions she would probably have made some reply to) her enthusiastic exclamations in praise of her countrymen.

"We journey safe," said Eveline, "under the care of the princely and victorious Normans. Theirs is the noble wrath of the lion, which destroys or is appeased at once — there is no guile in their romantic affection, no sullenness mixed with their generous indignation — they know the duties of the hall as well as those of battle; and were they to be surpassed in the arts of war, (which will only be when Plinlimmon is removed from its base,) they would still remain superior to every other people in generosity and courtesy."

"If I do not feel all their merits so strongly as if I shared their blood," said Rose, "I am at least glad to see them around us, in woods which are said to abound with dangers of various kinds. And I confess, my heart is the lighter, that I can now no longer observe the least vestige of that ancient mansion, in which we passed so unpleasant a night, and the recollection of which will always be odious to me."

Eveline looked sharply at her. "Confess the truth, Rose; thou wouldst give thy best kirtle to know all of my horrible adventure."

"It is but confessing that I am a woman," answered Rose; "and did I say a man, I dare say the difference of sex would imply but a small abatement of curiosity."

"Thou makest no parade of other feelings, which prompt thee to inquire into my fortunes," said Eveline; "but, sweet Rose, I give thee not the less credit for them. Believe me, thou shalt know all — but, I think, not now."

"At your pleasure," said Rose; "and yet, methinks, the bearing in your solitary bosom such a fearful secret will only render the weight more intolerable. On my silence you may rely as on that of the Holy Image, which hears us confess what it never reveals. Besides, such things become familiar to the imagination when they have been spoken of, and that which is familiar gradually becomes stripped of its terrors."

"Thou speakest with reason, my prudent Rose; and surely in this gallant troop, borne like a flower on a bush by my good palfrey Yseulte — fresh gales blowing round us, flowers opening and birds singing, and having thee by my bridle-rein, I ought to feel this a fitting time to communicate what thou hast so good a title to know. And — yes! — thou shalt know all! — Thou art not, I presume, ignorant of the qualities of what the Saxons of this land call a *Bahr-geist?*"

"Pardon me, lady," answered Rose, "my father discouraged my listening to such discourses. I might see evil spirits enough, he said, without my imagination being taught to form such as were fantastical. The word Bahrgeist, I have heard used by Gillian and other Saxons; but to me it only conveys some idea of indefinite terror, of which I never asked nor received an explanation."

"Know then," said Eveline, "it is a spectre, usually the image of a departed person, who, either for wrong sustained in some particular place during life, or through treasure hidden there, or from some such other cause, haunts the spot from time to time, becomes familiar to those who dwell there, takes an interest in their fate, occasionally for good, in other instances or times for evil. The Bahr-geist is, therefore, sometimes regarded as the good genius, sometimes as the avenging fiend, attached to particular families and classes of men. It is the lot of the family of Baldringham (of no mean note in other respects) to be subject to the visits of such a being."

"May I ask the cause (if it be known) of such visitation?" said Rose, desirous to avail herself to the uttermost of the communicative mood of her young lady, which might not perhaps last very long.

"I know the legend but imperfectly," replied Eveline, proceeding with a degree of calmness, the result of strong exertion over her mental anxiety, "but in general it runs thus :—Baldrick, the Saxon hero who first possessed yonder dwelling, became enamoured of a fair Briton, said to have been descended from those Druids of whom the Welsh speak so much, and deemed not unacquainted with the arts of sorcery which they practised, when they offered up human sacrifices amid those circles of unhewn and living rock, of which thou hast seen so many. After more than two years' wedlock, Baldrick became weary of his wife to such a point, that he formed the cruel resolution of putting her to death. Some say he doubted her fidelity—some that the matter was pressed on him by the church, as she was suspected of heresy — some that he removed her to make way for a more wealthy marriage — but all agree in the result. He sent two of his Cnichts to the house of Baldringham, to put to death the unfortunate Vanda, and commanded them to bring him the ring which had circled her finger on the day of wedlock, in token that his orders were accomplished. The men were ruthless in their office ; they strangled Vanda in yonder apartment, and as the hand was so swollen that no effort could draw off the ring, they obtained possession of it by severing the finger. But long before the return of those cruel perpetrators of her death, the shadow of Vanda had appeared before her appalled husband, and holding up to him her bloody hand, made him fearfully sensible how well his savage commands had been obeyed. After haunting him in peace and war, in desert, court, and camp, until he died despairingly on a pilgrimage to the Holy Land, the Bahr-geist, or ghost of the murdered Vanda, became so terrible in the House of Baldringham, that the succour of Saint Dunstan was itself scarcely sufficient to put bounds to her visitation. Yea, the blessed saint, when he had succeeded in his exorcism, did, in requital of Baldrick's crime, impose a strong and enduring penalty upon every female descendant of the house in the third degree ; namely, that once in their lives, and before their twenty-first year, they should each spend a solitary night in the chamber of the murdered Vanda, saying therein certain prayers, as well for her repose, as for the suffering soul of her murderer. During that awful space, it is generally believed that the spirit of the murdered person appears to the female who observes the vigil, and shows some sign of her future good or bad fortune. If favourable, she appears with a smiling aspect, and crosses them with her unbloodied hand ; but she announces evil fortune by showing the hand from which the finger was severed, with a stern countenance, as if resenting upon the descendant of her husband his inhuman cruelty. Sometimes she is said to speak. These particulars I learned long since from an old Saxon dame, the mother of our Margery, who had been an attendant on my grandmother, and left the House of Baldringham when she made her escape from it with my father's father."

"Did your grandmother ever render this homage," said Rose, "which seems to me — under favour of St. Dunstan — to bring humanity into too close intercourse with a being of a doubtful nature?"

"My grandfather thought so, and never permitted my grandmother to revisit the house of Baldringham after her marriage ; hence disunion betwixt him and his son on the one part, and the members of that family on the other. They laid sundry misfortunes, and particularly the loss of male heirs which at that time befell them, to my parent's not having done the hereditary homage to the bloody-fingered Bahr-geist."

"And how could you, my dearest lady," said Rose, "knowing that they

held among them a usage so hideous, think of accepting the invitation of
Lady Ermengarde?"

"I can hardly answer you the question," answered Eveline. "Partly I
feared my father's recent calamity, to be slain (as I have heard him say his
aunt once prophesied of him) by the enemy he most despised, might be the
result of this rite having been neglected; and partly I hoped, that if my
mind should be appalled at the danger, when it presented itself closer to
my eye, it could not be urged on me in courtesy and humanity. You saw
how soon my cruel-hearted relative pounced upon the opportunity, and how
impossible it became for me, bearing the name, and, I trust, the spirit of
Berenger, to escape from the net in which I had involved myself."

"No regard for name or rank should have engaged me," replied Rose,
"to place myself where apprehension alone, even without the terrors of a
real visitation, might have punished my presumption with insanity. But
what, in the name of Heaven, did you see at this horrible rendezvous?"

"Ay, there is the question," said Eveline, raising her hand to her brow—
"how I could witness that which I distinctly saw, yet be able to retain
command of thought and intellect!—I had recited the prescribed devotions
for the murderer and his victim, and sitting down on the couch which was
assigned me, had laid aside such of my clothes as might impede my rest—
I had surmounted, in short, the first shock which I experienced in committing myself to this mysterious chamber, and I hoped to pass the night in
slumber as sound as my thoughts were innocent. But I was fearfully disappointed. I cannot judge how long I had slept, when my bosom was
oppressed by an unusual weight, which seemed at once to stifle my voice,
stop the beating of my heart, and prevent me from drawing my breath;
and when I looked up to discover the cause of this horrible suffocation, the
form of the murdered British matron stood over my couch taller than life,
shadowy, and with a countenance where traits of dignity and beauty were
mingled with a fierce expression of vengeful exultation. She held over me
the hand which bore the bloody marks of her husband's cruelty, and seemed
as if she signed the cross, devoting me to destruction; while, with an unearthly tone, she uttered these words:—

> 'Widow'd wife, and married maid,
> Betrothed, betrayer, and betray'd!'

The phantom stooped over me as she spoke, and lowered her gory fingers,
as if to touch my face, when, terror giving me the power of which it at first
deprived me, I screamed aloud—the casement of the apartment was thrown
open with a loud noise,—and—But what signifies my telling all this to thee,
Rose, who show so plainly, by the movement of eye and lip, that you consider me as a silly and childish dreamer?"

"Be not angry, my dear lady," said Rose; "I do indeed believe that the
witch we call Mara* has been dealing with you; but she, you know, is by
leeches considered as no real phantom, but solely the creation of our own
imagination, disordered by causes which arise from bodily indisposition."

"Thou art learned, maiden," said Eveline, rather peevishly; "but when
I assure thee that my better angel came to my assistance in a human form
—that at his appearance the fiend vanished—and that he transported me in
his arms out of the chamber of terror, I think thou wilt, as a good Christian, put more faith in that which I tell you."

"Indeed, indeed, my sweetest mistress, I cannot," replied Rose. "It is
even that circumstance of the guardian angel which makes me consider the
whole as a dream. A Norman sentinel, whom I myself called from his
post on purpose, did indeed come to your assistance, and, breaking into
your apartment, transported you to that where I myself received you from
his arms in a lifeless condition."

---

* Ephialtes, or Nightmare.

"A Norman soldier, ha!" said Eveline, colouring extremely; "and to whom, maiden, did you dare give commission to break into my sleeping chamber?"

"Your eyes flash anger, madam, but is it reasonable they should?—Did I not hear your screams of agony, and was I to stand fettered by ceremony at such a moment?—no more than if the castle had been on fire."

"I ask you again, Rose," said her mistress, still with discomposure, though less angrily than at first, "whom you directed to break into my apartment?"

"Indeed, I know not, lady," said Rose; "for beside that he was muffled in his mantle, little chance was there of my knowing his features, even had I seen them fully. But I can soon discover the cavalier; and I will set about it, that I may give him the reward I promised, and warn him to be silent and discreet in this matter."

"Do so," said Eveline; "and if you find him among those soldiers who attend us, I will indeed lean to thine opinion, and think that fantasy had the chief share in the evils I have endured the last night."

Rose struck her palfrey with the rod, and, accompanied by her mistress, rode up to Philip Guarine, the Constable's squire, who for the present commanded their little escort. "Good Guarine," she said, "I had talk with one of these sentinels last night from my window, and he did me some service, for which I promised him recompense—Will you inquire for the man, that I may pay him his guerdon?"

"Truly, I will owe him a guerdon, also, pretty maiden," answered the squire; "for if a lance of them approached near enough the house to hold speech from the windows, he transgressed the precise orders of his watch."

"Tush! you must forgive that for my sake," said Rose. "I warrant, had I called on yourself, stout Guarine, I should have had influence to bring you under my chamber window."

Guarine laughed, and shrugged his shoulders. "True it is," he said, "when women are in place, discipline is in danger."

He then went to make the necessary inquiries among his band, and returned with the assurance, that his soldiers, generally and severally, denied having approached the mansion of the Lady Ermengarde on the preceding night.

"Thou seest, Rose," said Eveline, with a significant look to her attendant.

"The poor rogues are afraid of Guarine's severity," said Rose, "and dare not tell the truth—I shall have some one in private claiming the reward of me."

"I would I had the privilege myself, damsel," said Guarine; "but for these fellows, they are not so timorous as you suppose them, being even too ready to avouch their roguery when it hath less excuse—Besides, I promised them impunity.—Have you any thing farther to order?"

"Nothing, good Guarine," said Eveline; "only this small donative to procure wine for thy soldiers, that they may spend the next night more merrily than the last.—And now he is gone,—Maiden, thou must, I think, be now well aware, that what thou sawest was no earthly being?"

"I must believe mine own ears and eyes, madam," replied Rose.

"Do—but allow me the same privilege," answered Eveline. "Believe me that my deliverer (for so I must call him) bore the features of one who neither was, nor could be, in the neighbourhood of Baldringham. Tell me but one thing—What dost thou think of this extraordinary prediction—

'Widow'd wife, and wedded maid,
Betrothed, betrayer, and betray'd!'

Thou wilt say it is an idle invention of my brain—but think it for a moment the speech of a true diviner, and what wouldst thou say of it?"

"That you may be betrayed, my dearest lady, but never can be a betrayer," answered Rose, with animation.

Eveline reached her hand out to her friend, and as she pressed affectionately that which Rose gave in return, she whispered to her with energy, "I thank thee for the judgment, which my own heart confirms."

A cloud of dust now announced the approach of the Constable of Chester and his retinue, augmented by the attendance of his host Sir William Herbert, and some of his neighbours and kinsmen, who came to pay their respects to the orphan of the Garde Doloureuse, by which appellation Eveline was known upon her passage through their territory.

Eveline remarked, that, at their greeting, De Lacy looked with displeased surprise at the disarrangement of her dress and equipage, which her hasty departure from Baldringham had necessarily occasioned.; and she was, on her part, struck with an expression of countenance which seemed to say, "I am not to be treated as an ordinary person, who may be received with negligence, and treated slightly with impunity." For the first time, she thought that, though always deficient in grace and beauty, the Constable's countenance was formed to express the more angry passions with force and vivacity, and that she who shared his rank and name must lay her account with the implicit surrender of her will and wishes to those of an arbitrary lord and master.

But the cloud soon passed from the Constable's brow; and in the conversation which he afterwards maintained with Herbert and the other knights and gentlemen, who from time to time came to greet and accompany them for a little way on their journey, Eveline had occasion to admire his superiority, both of sense and expression, and to remark the attention and deference with which his words were listened to by men too high in rank, and too proud, readily to admit any pre-eminence that was not founded on acknowledged merit. The regard of women is generally much influenced by the estimation which an individual maintains in the opinion of men; and Eveline, when she concluded her journey in the Benedictine nunnery in Gloucester, could not think without respect upon the renowned warrior, and celebrated politician, whose acknowledged abilities appeared to place him above every one whom she had seen approach him. His wife, Eveline thought, (and she was not without ambition,) if relinquishing some of those qualities in a husband which are in youth most captivating to the female imagination, must be still generally honoured and respected, and have contentment, if not romantic felicity, within her reach.

Chapter the Sixteenth.

THE Lady Eveline remained nearly four months with her aunt, the Abbess of the Benedictine nunnery, under whose auspices the Constable of Chester saw his suit advance and prosper as it would probably have done under that of the deceased Raymond Berenger, her brother. It is probable, however, that, but for the supposed vision of the Virgin, and the vow of gratitude which that supposed vision had called forth, the natural dislike of so young a person to a match so unequal in years, might have effectually opposed his success. Indeed Eveline, while honouring the Constable's virtues, doing justice to his high character, and admiring his talents, could never altogether divest herself of a secret fear of him, which, while it prevented her from expressing any direct disapprobation of his addresses, caused her sometimes to shudder, she scarce knew why, at the idea of their becoming successful.

The ominous words, "betraying and betrayed," would then occur to her memory; and when her aunt (the period of the deepest mourning being elapsed) had fixed a period for her betrothal, she looked forward to it with a feeling of terror, for which she was unable to account to herself, and which, as well as the particulars of her dream, she concealed even from Father Aldrovand in the hours of confession. It was not aversion to the Constable —it was far less preference to any other suitor—it was one of those instinctive movements and emotions by which Nature seems to warn us of approaching danger, though furnishing no information respecting its nature, and suggesting no means of escaping from it.

So strong were these intervals of apprehension, that if they had been seconded by the remonstrances of Rose Flammock, as formerly, they might perhaps have led to Eveline's yet forming some resolution unfavourable to the suit of the Constable. But, still more zealous for her lady's honour than even for her happiness, Rose had strictly forborne every effort which could affect Eveline's purpose, when she had once expressed her approbation of De Lacy's addresses; and whatever she thought or anticipated concerning 'the proposed marriage, she seemed from that moment to consider it as an event which must necessarily take place.

De Lacy himself, as he learned more intimately to know the merit of the prize which he was desirous of possessing, looked forward with different feelings towards the union, than those with which he had first proposed the measure to Raymond Berenger. It was then a mere match of interest and convenience, which had occurred to the mind of a proud and politic feudal lord, as the best mode of consolidating the power and perpetuating the line of his family. Nor did even the splendour of Eveline's beauty make that impression upon De Lacy, which it was calculated to do on the fiery and impassioned chivalry of the age. He was past that period of life when the wise are captivated by outward form, and might have said with truth, as well as with discretion, that he could have wished his beautiful bride several years older, and possessed of a more moderate portion of personal charms, in order to have rendered the match more fitted for his own age and disposition. This stoicism, however, vanished, when, on repeated interviews with his destined bride, he found that she was indeed inexperienced in life, but desirous to be guided by superior wisdom; and that, although gifted with high spirit, and a disposition which began to recover its natural elastic gaiety, she was gentle, docile, and, above all, endowed with a firmness of principle, which seemed to give assurance that she would tread uprightly, and without spot, the slippery paths in which youth, rank, and beauty, are doomed to move.

As feelings of a warmer and more impassioned kind towards Eveline began to glow in De Lacy's bosom, his engagements as a crusader became more and more burdensome to him. The Benedictine Abbess, the natural guardian of Eveline's happiness, added to these feelings by her reasoning and remonstrances. Although a nun and a devotee, she held in reverence the holy state of matrimony, and comprehended so much of it as to be aware, that its important purposes could not be accomplished while the whole continent of Europe was interposed betwixt the married pair; for as to a hint from the Constable, that his young spouse might accompany him into the dangerous and dissolute precincts of the Crusader's camp, the good lady crossed herself with horror at the proposal, and never permitted it to be a second time mentioned in her presence.

It was not, however, uncommon for kings, princes, and other persons of high consequence, who had taken upon them the vow to rescue Jerusalem, to obtain delays, and even a total remission of their engagement, by proper application to the Church of Rome. The Constable was sure to possess the full advantage of his sovereign's interest and countenance, in seeking permission to remain in England, for he was the noble to whose valour and policy Henry had chiefly intrusted the defence of the disorderly Welsh marches; and it was by no means with his good-will that so useful a subject had ever assumed the cross.

It was settled, therefore, in private betwixt the Abbess and the Constable, that the latter should solicit at Rome, and with the Pope's Legate in England, a remission of his vow for at least two years; a favour which it was thought could scarce be refused to one of his wealth and influence, backed as it was with the most liberal offers of assistance towards the redemption of the Holy Land. His offers were indeed munificent; for he proposed, if his own personal attendance were dispensed with, to send an hundred lances at his own cost, each lance accompanied by two squires, three archers, and a varlet or horse-boy; being double the retinue by which his own person was to have been accompanied. He offered besides to deposit the sum of two thousand bezants to the general expenses of the expedition, to surrender to the use of the Christian armament those equipped vessels which he had provided, and which even now awaited the embarkation of himself and his followers.

Yet, while making these magnificent proffers, the Constable could not help feeling they would be inadequate to the expectations of the rigid prelate Baldwin, who, as he had himself preached the crusade, and brought the Constable and many others into that holy engagement, must needs see with displeasure the work of his eloquence endangered, by the retreat of so important an associate from his favourite enterprise. To soften, therefore, his disappointment as much as possible, the Constable offered to the Archbishop, that, in the event of his obtaining license to remain in Britain, his forces should be led by his nephew, Damian Lacy, already renowned for his early feats of chivalry, the present hope of his house, and, failing heirs of his own body, its future head and support.

The Constable took the most prudent method of communicating this proposal to the Archbishop Baldwin, through a mutual friend, on whose good offices he could depend, and whose interest with the Prelate was regarded as great. But notwithstanding the splendour of the proposal, the Prelate heard it with sullen and obstinate silence, and referred for answer to a personal conference with the Constable at an appointed day, when concerns of the church would call the Archbishop to the city of Gloucester. The report of the mediator was such as induced the Constable to expect a severe struggle with the proud and powerful churchman; but, himself proud and powerful, and backed by the favour of his sovereign, he did not expect to be foiled in the contest.

The necessity that this point should be previously adjusted, as well as the recent loss of Eveline's father, gave an air of privacy to De Lacy's courtship, and prevented its being signalized by tournaments and feats of military skill, in which he would have been otherwise desirous to display his address in the eyes of his mistress. The rules of the convent prevented his giving entertainments of dancing, music, or other more pacific revels; and although the Constable displayed his affection by the most splendid gifts to his future bride and her attendants, the whole affair, in the opinion of the experienced Dame Gillian, proceeded more with the solemnity of a funeral, than the light pace of an approaching bridal.

The bride herself felt something of this, and thought occasionally it might have been lightened by the visits of young Damian, in whose age, so nearly corresponding to her own, she might have expected some relief from the formal courtship of his graver uncle. But he came not; and from what the Constable said concerning him, she was led to imagine that the relations had, for a time at least, exchanged occupations and character. The elder De Lacy continued, indeed, in nominal observance of his vow, to dwell in a pavilion by the gates of Gloucester; but he seldom donned his armour, substituted costly damask and silk for his war-worn shamois doublet, and affected at his advanced time of life more gaiety of attire than his contemporaries remembered as distinguishing his early youth. His nephew, on the contrary, resided almost constantly on the marches of Wales, occupied in settling by prudence, or subduing by main force, the various disturbances by which these provinces were continually agitated; and Eveline learned with surprise, that it was with difficulty his uncle had prevailed on him to be present at the ceremony of their being betrothed to each other, or, as the Normans entitled the ceremony, their *fiançailles.* This engagement, which preceded the actual marriage for a space more or less, according to circumstances, was usually celebrated with a solemnity corresponding to the rank of the contracting parties.

The Constable added, with expressions of regret, that Damian gave himself too little rest, considering his early youth, slept too little, and indulged in too restless a disposition—that his health was suffering—and that a learned Jewish leech, whose opinion had been taken, had given his advice that the warmth of a more genial climate was necessary to restore his constitution to its general and natural vigour.

Eveline heard this with much regret, for she remembered Damian as the angel of good tidings, who first brought her news of deliverance from the forces of the Welsh; and the occasions on which they had met, though mournful, brought a sort of pleasure in recollection, so gentle had been the youth's deportment, and so consoling his expressions of sympathy. She wished she could see him, that she might herself judge of the nature of his illness; for, like other damsels of that age, she was not entirely ignorant of the art of healing, and had been taught by Father Aldrovand, himself no mean physician, how to extract healing essences from plants and herbs gathered under planetary hours. She thought it possible that her talents in this art, slight as they were, might perhaps be of service to one already her friend and liberator, and soon about to become her very near relation.

It was therefore with a sensation of pleasure mingled with some confusion, (at the idea, doubtless, of assuming the part of medical adviser to so young a patient,) that one evening, while the convent was assembled about some business of their chapter, she heard Gillian announce that the kinsman of the Lord Constable desired to speak with her. She snatched up the veil, which she wore in compliance with the customs of the house, and hastily descended to the parlour, commanding the attendance of Gillian, who, nevertheless, did not think proper to obey the signal.

When she entered the apartment, a man whom she had never seen before advanced, kneeling on one knee, and taking up the hem of her veil, saluted it with an air of the most profound respect. She stepped back, surprised and alarmed, although there was nothing in the appearance of the stranger to justify her apprehension. He seemed to be about thirty years of age, tall of stature, and bearing a noble though wasted form, and a countenance on which disease, or perhaps youthful indulgence, had anticipated the traces of age. His demeanour seemed courteous and respectful, even in a degree which approached to excess. He observed Eveline's surprise, and said, in a tone of pride, mingled with emotion, "I fear that I have been mistaken, and that my visit is regarded as an unwelcome intrusion."

"Arise, sir," answered Eveline, "and let me know your name and business. I was summoned to a kinsman of the Constable of Chester."

"And you expected the stripling Damian," answered the stranger. "But the match with which England rings will connect you with others of the house besides that young person; and amongst these, with the luckless Randal de Lacy. Perhaps," continued he, "the fair Eveline Berenger may not even have heard his name breathed by his more fortunate kinsman—more fortunate in every respect, but *most* fortunate in his present prospects."

This compliment was accompanied by a deep reverence, and Eveline stood much embarrassed how to reply to his civilities; for although she now remembered to have heard this Randal slightly mentioned by the Constable when speaking of his family, it was in terms which implied there was no good understanding betwixt them. She therefore only returned his courtesy by general thanks for the honour of his visit, trusting he would then retire; but such was not his purpose.

"I comprehend," he said, "from the coldness with which the Lady Eveline Berenger receives me, that what she has heard of me from my kinsman (if indeed he thought me worthy of being mentioned to her at all) has been, to say the least, unfavourable. And yet my name once stood as high in fields and courts, as that of the Constable; nor is it aught more disgraceful than what is indeed often esteemed the worst of disgraces—poverty, which prevents my still aspiring to places of honour and fame. If my youthful follies have been numerous, I have paid for them by the loss of my fortune, and the degradation of my condition; and therein, my happy kinsman might, if he pleased, do me some aid—I mean not with his purse or estate; for, poor as I am, I would not live on alms extorted from the reluctant hand of an estranged friend; but his countenance would put him to no cost, and, in so far, I might expect some favour."

"In that my Lord Constable," said Eveline, "must judge for himself. I have—as yet, at least—no right to interfere in his family affairs; and if I should ever have such right, it will well become me to be cautious how I use it."

"It is prudently answered," replied Randal; "but what I ask of you is merely, that you, in your gentleness, would please to convey to my cousin a suit, which I find it hard to bring my ruder tongue to utter with sufficient submission. The usurers, whose claims have eaten like a canker into my means, now menace me with a dungeon—a threat which they dared not mutter, far less attempt to execute, were it not that they see me an outcast, unprotected by the natural head of my family, and regard me rather as they would some unfriended vagrant, than as a descendant of the powerful house of Lacy."

"It is a sad necessity," replied Eveline; "but I see not how I can help you in such extremity."

"Easily," replied Randal de Lacy. "The day of your betrothal is fixed, as I hear reported; and it is your right to select what witnesses you please to the solemnity, which may the saints bless! To every one but myself, presence or absence upon that occasion is a matter of mere ceremony—to me it is almost life or death. So am I situated, that the marked instance of slight or contempt, implied by my exclusion from this meeting of our family, will be held for the signal of my final expulsion from the House of the De Lacy's, and for a thousand bloodhounds to assail me without mercy or forbearance, whom, cowards as they are, even the slightest show of countenance from my powerful kinsman would compel to stand at bay. But why should I occupy your time in talking thus?—Farewell, madam—be happy—and do not think of me the more harshly, that for a few minutes I have broken the tenor of your happy thoughts, by forcing my misfortunes on your notice."

"Stay, sir," said Eveline, affected by the tone and manner of the noble suppliant; "you shall not have it to say that you have told your distress to Eveline Berenger, without receiving such aid as is in her power to give. I will mention your request to the Constable of Chester."

"You must do more, if you really mean to assist me," said Randal de Lacy, "you must make that request your own. You do not know," said he, continuing to bend on her a fixed and expressive look, "how hard it is to change the fixed purpose of a De Lacy—a twelvemonth hence you will probably be better acquainted with the firm texture of our resolutions. But, at present, what can withstand your wish should you deign to express it?"

"Your suit, sir, shall not be lost for want of my advancing it with my good word, and good wishes," replied Eveline; "but you must be well aware that its success or failure must rest with the Constable himself."

Randal de Lacy took his leave with the same air of deep reverence which had marked his entrance; only that, as he then saluted the skirt of Eveline's robe, he now rendered the same homage by touching her hand with his lip. She saw him depart with a mixture of emotions, in which compassion was predominant; although in his complaints of the Constable's unkindness to him there was something offensive, and his avowal of follies and excess seemed uttered rather in the spirit of wounded pride, than in that of contrition.

When Eveline next saw the Constable, she told him of the visit of Randal and of his request; and strictly observing his countenance while she spoke, she saw, that at the first mention of his kinsman's name, a gleam of anger shot along his features. He soon subdued it, however, and, fixing his eyes on the ground, listened to Eveline's detailed account of the visit, and her request "that Randal might be one of the invited witnesses to their *fiançailles.*"

The Constable paused for a moment, as if he were considering how to elude the solicitation. At length he replied, "You do not know for whom you ask this, or you would perhaps have forborne your request; neither are you apprized of its full import, though my crafty cousin well knows, that when I do him this grace which he asks, I bind myself, as it were, in the eye of the world once more — and it will be for the third time — to interfere in his affairs, and place them on such a footing as may afford him the means of re-establishing his fallen consequence, and repairing his numerous errors."

"And wherefore not, my lord?" said the generous Eveline. "If he has been ruined only through follies, he is now of an age when these are no longer tempting snares; and if his heart and hand be good, he may yet be an honour to the House of De Lacy."

The Constable shook his head. "He hath indeed," he said, "a heart and hand fit for service, God knoweth, whether in good or evil. But never shall it be said that you, my fair Eveline, made request of Hugh de Lacy, which he was not to his uttermost willing to comply with. Randal shall attend at our *fiançailles;* there is indeed the more cause for his attendance, as I somewhat fear we may lack that of our valued nephew Damian, whose malady rather increases than declines, and, as I hear, with strange symptoms of unwonted disturbance of mind and starts of temper, to which the youth had not hitherto been subject."

Chapter the Seventeenth.

Ring out the merry bell, the bride approaches,
The blush upon her cheek has shamed the morning,
For that is dawning palely. Grant, good saints,
These clouds betoken nought of evil omen!

OLD PLAY.

THE day of the *fiançailles,* or espousals, was now approaching; and it seems that neither the profession of the Abbess, nor her practice at least, were so rigid as to prevent her selecting the great parlour of the convent for that holy rite, although necessarily introducing many male guests within those vestal precincts, and notwithstanding that the rite itself was the preliminary to a state which the inmates of the cloister had renounced for ever.

The Abbess's Norman pride of birth, and the real interest which she took in her niece's advancement, overcame all scruples; and the venerable mother might be seen in unwonted bustle, now giving orders to the gardener for decking the apartment with flowers—now to her cellaress, her precentrix, and the lay-sisters of the kitchen, for preparing a splendid banquet, mingling her commands on these worldly subjects with an occasional ejaculation on their vanity and worthlessness, and every now and then converting the busy and anxious looks which she threw upon her preparations into a solemn turning upward of eyes and folding of hands, as one who sighed over the mere earthly pomp which she took such trouble in superintending. At another time the good lady might have been seen in close consultation with Father Aldrovand, upon the ceremonial, civil and religious, which was to accompany a solemnity of such consequence to her family.

Meanwhile the reins of discipline, although relaxed for a season, were not entirely thrown loose. The outer court of the convent was indeed for the time opened for the reception of the male sex; but the younger sisters and novices of the house being carefully secluded in the more inner apartments of the extensive building, under the immediate eye of a grim old nun, or, as the conventual rule designed her, an ancient, sad, and virtuous person, termed Mistress of the Novices, were not permitted to pollute their eyes by looking on waving plumes and rustling mantles. A few sisters, indeed, of the Abbess's own standing, were left at liberty, being such goods as it was thought could not, in shopman's phrase, take harm from the air, and which are therefore left lying on the counter. These antiquated dames went mumping about with much affected indifference, and a great deal of real curiosity, endeavouring indirectly to get information concerning names, and dresses, and decorations, without daring to show such interest in these vanities as actual questions on the subject might have implied.

A stout band of the Constable's spearmen guarded the gate of the nunnery, admitting within the hallowed precinct the few only who were to be present at the solemnity, with their principal attendants, and while the former were ushered with all due ceremony into the apartments dressed out for the occasion, the attendants, although detained in the outer court, were liberally supplied with refreshments of the most substantial kind; and had the amusement, so dear to the menial classes, of examining and criticising their masters and mistresses, as they passed into the interior apartments prepared for their reception.

Amongst the domestics who were thus employed were old Raoul the huntsman and his jolly dame — he gay and glorious, in a new cassock of green velvet, she gracious and comely, in a kirtle of yellow silk, fringed with minivair, and that at no mean cost, were equally busied in beholding the gay spectacle. The most inveterate wars have their occasional terms of truce; the most bitter and boisterous weather its hours of warmth and of calmness; and so was it with the matrimonial horizon of this amiable pair, which, usually cloudy, had now for brief space cleared up. The splendour of their new apparel, the mirth of the spectacle around them, with the aid, perhaps, of a bowl of muscadine quaffed by Raoul, and a cup of hippocras sipped by his wife, had rendered them rather more agreeable in each other's eyes than was their wont; good cheer being in such cases, as oil is to a rusty lock, the means of making those valves move smoothly and glibly, which otherwise work not together at all, or by shrieks and groans express their reluctance to move in union. The pair had stuck themselves into a kind of niche, three or four steps from the ground, which contained a small stone bench, whence their curious eyes could scrutinize with advantage every guest who entered the court.

Thus placed, and in their present state of temporary concord, Raoul with his frosty visage formed no unapt representative of January, the bitter father of the year; and though Gillian was past the delicate bloom of youthful

May, yet the melting fire of a full black eye, and the genial glow of a ripe and crimson cheek, made her a lively type of the fruitful and jovial August. Dame Gillian used to make it her boast, that she could please every body with her gossip, when she chose it, from Raymond Berenger down to Robin the horse-boy; and like a good housewife. who, to keep her hand in use, will sometimes even condescend to dress a dish for her husband's sole eating, she now thought proper to practise her powers of pleasing on old Raoul, fairly conquering, in her successful sallies of mirth and satire, not only his cynical temperament towards all human kind, but his peculiar and special disposition to be testy with his spouse. Her jokes, such as they were, and the coquetry with which they were enforced, had such an effect on this Timon of the woods, that he curled up his cynical nose, displayed his few straggling teeth like a cur about to bite, broke out into a barking laugh, which was more like the cry of one of his own hounds — stopped short in the explosion, as if he had suddenly recollected that it was out of character; yet, ere he resumed his acrimonious gravity, shot such a glance at Gillian as made his nut-cracker jaws, pinched eyes, and convolved nose, bear no small resemblance to one of those fantastic faces which decorate the upper end of old bass viols.

"Is not this better than laying your dog-leash on your loving wife, as if she were a brach of the kennel?" said August to January

"In troth is it," answered January, in a frost-bitten tone; — "and so it is also better than doing the brach-tricks which bring the leash into exercise."

"Humph!" said Gillian, in the tone of one who thought her husband's proposition might bear being disputed; but instantly changing the note to that of tender complaint, "Ah! Raoul," she said, "do you not remember how you once beat me because our late lord — Our Lady assoilzie him! — took my crimson breast-knot for a peony rose?"

"Ay, ay," said the huntsman; "I remember our old master would make such mistakes — Our Lady assoilzie him! as you say — The best hound will hunt counter."

"And how could you think, dearest Raoul, to let the wife of thy bosom go so long without a new kirtle?" said his helpmate.

"Why, thou hast got one from our young lady that might serve a countess," said Raoul, his concord jarred by her touching this chord — "how many kirtles wouldst thou have?"

"Only two, kind Raoul; just that folk may not count their children's age by the date of Dame Gillian's last new gown."

"Well, well — it is hard that a man cannot be in good-humour once and away without being made to pay for it. But thou shalt have a new kirtle at Michaelmas, when I sell the buck's hides for the season. The very antlers should bring a good penny this year."

"Ay, ay," said Gillian; "I ever tell thee, husband, the horns would be worth the hide in a fair market."

Raoul turned briskly round as if a wasp had stung him, and there is no guessing what his reply might have been to this seemingly innocent observation, had not a gallant horseman at that instant entered the court, and, dismounting like the others, gave his horse to the charge of a squire, or equerry, whose attire blazed with embroidery.

"By Saint Hubert, a proper horseman, and a *destrier* for an earl," said Raoul; "and my Lord Constable's liveries withal — yet I know not the gallant."

"But I do," said Gillian; "it is Randal de Lacy, the Constable's kinsman, and as good a man as ever came of the name!"

"Oh! by Saint Hubert, I have heard of him — men say he is a reveller, and a jangler, and a waster of his goods."

"Men lie now and then," said Gillian dryly.

"And women also," replied Raoul;—"why, methinks he winked on thee just now."

"That right eye of thine saw never true since our good lord—Saint Mary rest him!—flung a cup of wine in thy face, for pressing over boldly into his withdrawing-room."

"I marvel," said Raoul, as if he heard her not, "that yonder ruffler comes hither. I have heard that he is suspected to have attempted the Constable's life, and that they have not spoken together for five years."

"He comes on my young lady's invitation, and that I know full well," said Dame Gillian; "and he is less like to do the Constable wrong than to have wrong at his hand, poor gentleman, as indeed he has had enough of that already."

"And who told thee so?" said Raoul, bitterly.

"No matter, it was one who knew all about it very well," said the dame, who began to fear that, in displaying her triumph of superior information, she had been rather over-communicative.

"It must have been the devil, or Randal himself," said Raoul, "for no other mouth is large enough for such a lie. — But hark ye, Dame Gillian, who is he that presses forward next, like a man that scarce sees how he goes?"

"Even your angel of grace, my young Squire Damian," said Dame Gillian.

"It is impossible!" answered Raoul—"call me blind if thou wilt;—but I have never seen man so changed in a few weeks — and his attire is flung on him so wildly as if he wore a horse-cloth round him instead of a mantle —What can ail the youth? — he has made a dead pause at the door, as if he saw something on the threshold that debarred his entrance — Saint Hubert, but he looks as if he were elf-stricken!"

"You ever thought him such a treasure!" said Gillian; "and now look at him as he stands by the side of a real gentleman, how he stares and trembles as if he were distraught."

"I will speak to him," said Raoul, forgetting his lameness, and springing from his elevated station — "I will speak to him; and if he be unwell, I have my lancets and fleams to bleed man as well as brute."

"And a fit physician for such a patient," muttered Gillian,—"a dog-leech for a dreamy madman, that neither knows his own disease nor the way to cure it."

Meanwhile the old huntsman made his way towards the entrance, before which Damian remained standing, in apparent uncertainty whether he should enter or not, regardless of the crowd around, and at the same time attracting their attention by the singularity of his deportment.

Raoul had a private regard for Damian; for which, perhaps, it was a chief reason, that of late his wife had been in the habit of speaking of him in a tone more disrespectful than she usually applied to handsome young men. Besides, he understood the youth was a second Sir Tristrem in silvan sports by wood and river, and there needed no more to fetter Raoul's soul to him with bands of steel. He saw with great concern his conduct attract general notice, mixed with some ridicule.

"He stands," said the town-jester, who had crowded into the gay throng, "before the gate, like Balaam's ass in the Mystery, when the animal sees so much more than can be seen by any one else."

A cut from Raoul's ready leash rewarded the felicity of this application, and sent the fool howling off to seek a more favourable audience for his pleasantry. At the same time Raoul pressed up to Damian, and with an earnestness very different from his usual dry causticity of manner, begged him for God's sake not to make himself the general spectacle, by standing there as if the devil sat on the doorway, but either to enter, or, what might be as becoming, to retire, and make himself more fit in apparel for attending on a solemnity so nearly concerning his house.

"And what ails my apparel, old man?" said Damian, turning sternly on the huntsman, as one who has been hastily and uncivilly roused from a reverie.

"Only, with respect to your valour," answered the huntsman, "men do not usually put old mantles over new doublets; and methinks, with submission, that of yours neither accords with your dress, nor is fitted for this noble presence."

"Thou art a fool!" answered Damian, "and as green in wit as gray in years. Know you not that in these days the young and old consort together—contract together—wed together? and should we take more care to make our apparel consistent than our actions?"

"For God's sake, my lord," said Raoul, "forbear these wild and dangerous words! they may be heard by other ears than mine, and construed by worse interpreters. There may be here those who will pretend to track mischief from light words, as I would find a buck from his frayings. Your cheek is pale, my lord, your eye is blood-shot; for Heaven's sake, retire!"

"I will not retire," said Damian, with yet more distemperature of manner, "till I have seen the Lady Eveline."

"For the sake of all the saints," ejaculated Raoul, "not now!—You will do my lady incredible injury by forcing yourself into her presence in this condition."

"Do you think so!" said Damian, the remark seeming to operate as a sedative which enabled him to collect his scattered thoughts. — "Do you really think so?—I thought that to have looked upon her once more—but no—you are in the right, old man."

He turned from the door as if to withdraw, but ere he could accomplish his purpose, he turned yet more pale than before, staggered, and fell on the pavement ere Raoul could afford him his support, useless as that might have proved. Those who raised him were surprised to observe that his garments were soiled with blood, and that the stains upon his cloak, which had been criticised by Raoul, were of the same complexion. A grave-looking personage, wrapped in a sad-coloured mantle, came forth from the crowd.

"I knew how it would be," he said; "I made venesection this morning, and commanded repose and sleep according to the aphorisms of Hippocrates; but if young gentlemen will neglect the ordinance of their physician, medicine will avenge herself. It is impossible that my bandage or ligature, knit by these fingers, should have started, but to avenge the neglect of the precepts of art."

"What means this prate?" said the voice of the Constable, before which all others were silent. He had been summoned forth just as the rite of espousal or betrothing was concluded, on the confusion occasioned by Damian's situation, and now sternly commanded the physician to replace the bandages which had slipped from his nephew's arm, himself assisting in the task of supporting the patient, with the anxious and deeply agitated feelings of one who saw a near and justly valued relative—as yet, the heir of his fame and family—stretched before him in a condition so dangerous.

But the griefs of the powerful and the fortunate are often mingled with impatience of interrupted prosperity. "What means this?" he demanded sternly of the leech. "I sent you this morning to attend my nephew on the first tidings of his illness, and commanded that he should make no attempt to be present on this day's solemnity, yet I find him in this state, and in this place."

"So please your lordship," replied the leech, with a conscious self-importance, which even the presence of the Constable could not subdue — "*Curatio est canonica, non coacta;* which signifieth, my lord, that the physician acteth his cure by rules of art and science—by advice and prescription, but not by force or violence upon the patient, who cannot be at all benefited unless he be voluntarily amenable to the orders of his medicum."

"Tell me not of your jargon," said De Lacy; "if my nephew was light-headed enough to attempt to come hither in the heat of a delirious dis-temper, you should have had sense to prevent him, had it been by actual force."

"It may be," said Randal de Lacy, joining the crowd, who, forgetting the cause which had brought them together, were now assembled about Damian, "that more powerful was the magnet which drew our kinsman hither, than aught the leech could do to withhold him."

The Constable, still busied about his nephew, looked up as Randal spoke, and, when he was done, asked, with formal coldness of manner, "Ha, fair kinsman, of what magnet do you speak?"

"Surely of your nephew's love and regard to your lordship," answered Randal, "which, not to mention his respect for the lady Eveline, must have compelled him hither, if his limbs were able to bear him. — And here the bride comes, I think, in charity, to thank him for his zeal."

"What unhappy case is this?" said the Lady Eveline, pressing forward, much disordered with the intelligence of Damian's danger, which had been suddenly conveyed to her. "Is there nothing in which my poor service may avail?"

"Nothing, lady," said the Constable, rising from beside his nephew, and taking her hand; "your kindness is here mistimed. This motley assembly, this unseeming confusion, become not your presence."

"Unless it could be helpful, my lord," said Eveline, eagerly. "It is your nephew who is in danger — my deliverer — one of my deliverers, I would say."

"He is fitly attended by his chirurgeon," said the Constable, leading back his reluctant bride to the convent, while the medical attendant trium-phantly exclaimed,

"Well judgeth my Lord Constable, to withdraw his noble Lady from the host of petticoated empirics, who, like so many Amazons, break in upon and derange the regular course of physical practice, with their petulant prognostics, their rash recipes, their mithridate, their febrifuges, their amulets, and their charms. Well speaketh the Ethnic poet,

'Non audet, nisi quæ didicit, dare quod medicorum est;
Promittunt medici—tractant fabrilia fabri.'"

As he repeated these lines with much emphasis, the doctor permitted his patient's arm to drop from his hand, that he might aid the cadence with a flourish of his own. "There," said he to the spectators, "is what none of you understand—no, by Saint Luke, nor the Constable himself."

"But he knows how to whip in a hound that babbles when he should be busy," said Raoul; and, silenced by this hint, the chirurgeon betook him-self to his proper duty, of superintending the removal of young Damian to an apartment in the neighbouring street, where the symptoms of his disor-der seemed rather to increase than diminish, and speedily required all the skill and attention which the leech could bestow.

The subscription of the contract of marriage had, as already noticed, been just concluded, when the company assembled on the occasion were interrupted by the news of Damian's illness. When the Constable led his bride from the court-yard into the apartment where the company was as-sembled, there was discomposure and uneasiness on the countenance of both; and it was not a little increased by the bride pulling her hand hastily from the hold of the bridegroom, on observing that the latter was stained with recent blood, and had in truth left the same stamp upon her own. With a faint exclamation she showed the marks to Rose, saying at the same time, "What bodes this?—Is this the revenge of the Bloody-finger already commencing?"

"It bodes nothing, my dearest lady," said Rose — "it is our fears that are prophets, not those trifles which we take for augury. For God's sake, speak to my lord! He is surprised at your agitation."

"Let him ask me the cause himself," said Eveline; "fitter it should be told at his bidding, than be offered by me unasked."

The Constable, while his bride stood thus conversing with her maiden, had also observed, that in his anxiety to assist his nephew, he had transferred part of his blood from his own hands to Eveline's dress. He came forward to apologize for what at such a moment seemed almost ominous. "Fair lady," said he, "the blood of a true De Lacy can never bode aught but peace and happiness to you."

Eveline seemed as if she would have answered, but could not immediately find words. The faithful Rose, at the risk of incurring the censure of being over forward, hastened to reply to the compliment. "Every damsel is bound to believe what you say, my noble lord," was her answer, "knowing how readily that blood hath ever flowed for protecting the distressed, and so lately for our own relief."

"It is well spoken, little one," answered the Constable; "and the Lady Eveline is happy in a maiden who so well knows how to speak when it is her own pleasure to be silent. — Come, lady," he added, "let us hope this mishap of my kinsman is but like a sacrifice to fortune, which permits not the brightest hour to pass without some intervening shadow. Damian, I trust, will speedily recover; and be we mindful that the blood-drops which alarm you have been drawn by a friendly steel, and are symptoms rather of recovery than of illness. — Come, dearest lady, your silence discourages our friends, and wakes in them doubts whether we be sincere in the welcome due to them. Let me be your sewer," he said; and, taking a silver ewer and napkin from the standing cupboard, which was loaded with plate, he presented them on his knee to his bride.

Exerting herself to shake off the alarm into which she had been thrown by some supposed coincidence of the present accident with the apparition at Baldringham, Eveline, entering into her betrothed husband's humour, was about to raise him from the ground, when she was interrupted by the arrival of a hasty messenger, who, coming into the room without ceremony, informed the Constable that his nephew was so extremely ill, that if he hoped to see him alive, it would be necessary he should come to his lodgings instantly.

The Constable started up, made a brief adieu to Eveline and to the guests, who, dismayed at this new and disastrous intelligence, were preparing to disperse themselves, when, as he advanced towards the door, he was met by a Paritor, or Summoner of the Ecclesiastical Court, whose official dress had procured him unobstructed entrance into the precincts of the abbey.

"*Deus vobiscum*," said the paritor; "I would know which of this fair company is the Constable of Chester?"

"I am he," answered the elder De Lacy; "but if thy business be not the more hasty, I cannot now speak with thee — I am bound on matters of life and death."

"I take all Christian people to witness that I have discharged my duty," said the paritor, putting into the hand of the Constable a slip of parchment.

"How is this, fellow?" said the Constable, in great indignation — "for whom or what does your master the Archbishop take me, that he deals with me in this uncourteous fashion, citing me to compear before him more like a delinquent than a friend or a nobleman?"

"My gracious lord," answered the paritor, haughtily, "is accountable to no one but our Holy Father the Pope, for the exercise of the power which is intrusted to him by the canons of the Church. Your lordship's answer to my citation?"

"Is the Archbishop present in this city?" said the Constable, after a moment's reflection—"I knew not of his purpose to travel hither, still less of his purpose to exercise authority within these bounds."

"My gracious lord the Archbishop," said the paritor, "is but now arrived in this city, of which he is metropolitan; and, besides, by his apostolical commission, a legate *a latere* hath plenary jurisdiction throughout all England, as those may find (whatsoever be their degree) who may dare to disobey his summons."

"Hark thee, fellow," said the Constable, regarding the paritor with a grim and angry countenance, "were it not for certain respects, which I promise thee thy tawny hood hath little to do with, thou wert better have swallowed thy citation, seal and all, than delivered it to me with the addition of such saucy terms. Go hence, and tell your master I will see him within the space of an hour, during which time I am delayed by the necessity of attending a sick relation."

The paritor left the apartment with more humility in his manner than when he had entered, and left the assembled guests to look upon each other in silence and dismay.

The reader cannot fail to remember how severely the yoke of the Roman supremacy pressed both on the clergy and laity of England during the reign of Henry II. Even the attempt of that wise and courageous monarch to make a stand for the independence of his throne in the memorable case of Thomas à Becket, had such an unhappy issue, that, like a suppressed rebellion, it was found to add new strength to the domination of the Church. Since the submission of the king in that ill-fated struggle, the voice of Rome had double potency whenever it was heard, and the boldest peers of England held it more wise to submit to her imperious dictates, than to provoke a spiritual censure which had so many secular consequences. Hence the slight and scornful manner in which the Constable was treated by the prelate Baldwin struck a chill of astonishment into the assembly of friends whom he had collected to witness his espousals; and as he glanced his haughty eye around, he saw that many who would have stood by him through life and death in any other quarrel, had it even been with his sovereign, were turning pale at the very thought of a collision with the Church. Embarrassed, and at the same time incensed at their timidity, the Constable hasted to dismiss them, with the general assurance that all would be well—that his nephew's indisposition was a trifling complaint, exaggerated by a conceited physician, and by his own want of care—and that the message of the Archbishop, so unceremoniously delivered, was but the consequence of their mutual and friendly familiarity, which induced them sometimes, for the jest's sake, to reverse or neglect the ordinary forms of intercourse. —"If I wanted to speak with the prelate Baldwin on express business and in haste, such is the humility and indifference to form of that worthy pillar of the Church, that I should not fear offence," said the Constable, "did I send the meanest horseboy in my troop to ask an audience of him."

So he spoke—but there was something in his countenance which contradicted his words; and his friends and relations retired from the splendid and joyful ceremony of his espousals as from a funeral feast, with anxious thoughts and with downcast eyes.

Randal was the only person, who, having attentively watched the whole progress of the affair during the evening, ventured to approach his cousin as he left the house, and asked him, "in the name of their reunited friendship, whether he had nothing to command him?" assuring him, with a look more expressive than his words, that he would not find him cold in his service.

"I have nought which can exercise your zeal, fair cousin," replied the Constable, with the air of one who partly questioned the speaker's sincerity; and the parting reverence with which he accompanied his words, left Randal no pretext for continuing his attendance, as he seemed to have designed.

~~~~~~~~~~~~~~~~~~~~~~~~~~~~~~~~~~~~~~

Chapter the Eighteenth.

Oh, were I seated high as my ambition,
I'd place this naked foot on necks of monarchs!
MYSTERIOUS MOTHER.

THE most anxious and unhappy moment of Hugo de Lacy's life, was unquestionably that in which, by espousing Eveline with all civil and religious solemnity, he seemed to approach to what for some time he had considered as the prime object of his wishes. He was assured of the early possession of a beautiful and amiable wife, endowed with such advantage of worldly goods, as gratified his ambition as well as his affections — Yet, even in this fortunate moment, the horizon darkened around him, in a manner which presaged nought but storm and calamity. At his nephew's lodging he learned that the pulse of the patient had risen, and his delirium had augmented, and all around him spoke very doubtfully of his chance of recovery, or surviving a crisis which seemed speedily approaching. The Constable stole towards the door of the apartment which his feelings permitted him not to enter, and listened to the raving which the fever gave rise to. Nothing can be more melancholy than to hear the mind at work concerning its ordinary occupations, when the body is stretched in pain and danger upon the couch of severe sickness; the contrast betwixt the ordinary state of health, its joys or its labours, renders doubly affecting the actual helplessness of the patient before whom these visions are rising, and we feel a corresponding degree of compassion for the sufferer whose thoughts are wandering so far from his real condition.

The Constable felt this acutely, as he heard his nephew shout the war-cry of the family repeatedly, appearing, by the words of command and direction, which he uttered from time to time, to be actively engaged in leading his men-at-arms against the Welsh. At another time he uttered various terms of the *manege*, of falconry, and of the chase — he mentioned his uncle's name repeatedly on these occasions, as if the idea of his kinsman had been connected alike with his martial encounters, and with his sports by wood and river. Other sounds there were, which he muttered so low as to be altogether undistinguishable.

With a heart even still more softened towards his kinsman's sufferings from hearing the points on which his mind wandered, the Constable twice applied his hand to the latch of the door, in order to enter the bedroom, and twice forebore, his eyes running faster with tears than he chose should be witnessed by the attendants. At length, relinquishing his purpose, he hastily left the house, mounted his horse, and followed only by four of his personal attendants, rode towards the palace of the Bishop, where, as he learned from public rumour, the Archprelate Baldwin had taken up his temporary residence.

The train of riders and of led-horses, of sumpter mules, and of menials and attendants, both lay and ecclesiastical, which thronged around the gate of the Episcopal mansion, together with the gaping crowd of inhabitants who had gathered around, some to gaze upon the splendid show, some to have the chance of receiving the benediction of the Holy Prelate, was so great as to impede the Constable's approach to the palace-door; and when this obstacle was surmounted, he found another in the obstinacy of the Archbishop's attendants, who permitted him not, though announced by name and title, to cross the threshold of the mansion, until they should receive the express command of their master to that effect.

The Constable felt the full effect of this slighting reception. He had dismounted from his horse in full confidence of being instantly admitted into the palace at least, if not into the Prelate's presence; and as he now stood on foot among the squires, grooms, and horseboys of the spiritual lord, he was so much disgusted, that his first impulse was to remount his horse, and return to his pavilion, pitched for the time before the city walls, leaving it to the Bishop to seek him there, if he really desired an interview. But the necessity of conciliation almost immediately rushed on his mind, and subdued the first haughty impulse of his offended pride. "If our wise King," he said to himself, "hath held the stirrup of one Prelate of Canterbury when living, and submitted to the most degrading observances before his shrine when dead, surely I need not be more scrupulous towards his priestly successor in the same overgrown authority." Another thought, which he dared hardly to acknowledge, recommended the same humble and submissive course. He could not but feel that, in endeavouring to evade his vows as a crusader, he was incurring some just censure from the Church; and he was not unwilling to hope, that his present cold and scornful reception on Baldwin's part, might be meant as a part of the penance which his conscience informed him his conduct was about to receive.

After a short interval, De Lacy was at length invited to enter the palace of the Bishop of Gloucester, in which he was to meet the Primate of England; but there was more than one brief pause, in hall and anteroom, ere he at length was admitted to Baldwin's presence.

The successor of the celebrated Becket had neither the extensive views, nor the aspiring spirit, of that redoubted personage; but, on the other hand, saint as the latter had become, it may be questioned, whether, in his professions for the weal of Christendom, he was half so sincere as was the present Archbishop. Baldwin was, in truth, a man well qualified to defend the powers which the Church had gained, though perhaps of a character too sincere and candid to be active in extending them. The advancement of the Crusade was the chief business of his life, his success the principal cause of his pride; and, if the sense of possessing the powers of eloquent persuasion, and skill to bend the minds of men to his purpose, was blended with his religious zeal, still the tenor of his life, and afterwards his death before Ptolemais, showed that the liberation of the Holy Sepulchre from the infidels was the unfeigned object of all his exertions. Hugo de Lacy well knew this; and the difficulty of managing such a temper appeared much greater to him on the eve of the interview in which the attempt was to be made, than he had suffered himself to suppose when the crisis was yet distant.

The Prelate, a man of a handsome and stately form, with features rather too severe to be pleasing, received the Constable in all the pomp of ecclesiastical dignity. He was seated on a chair of oak, richly carved with Gothic ornaments, and placed above the rest of the floor under a niche of the same workmanship. His dress was the rich episcopal robe, ornamented with costly embroidery, and fringed around the neck and cuffs; it opened from the throat and in the middle, and showed an under vestment of embroidery, betwixt the folds of which, as if imperfectly concealed, peeped the close shirt of hair-cloth which the Prelate constantly wore under all his pompous attire. His mitre was placed beside him on an oaken table of the same workmanship with his throne, against which also rested his pastoral staff, representing a shepherd's crook of the simplest form, yet which had proved more powerful and fearful than lance or scimetar, when wielded by the hand of Thomas à Becket.

A chaplain in a white surplice kneeled at a little distance before a desk, and read forth from an illuminated volume some portion of a theological treatise, in which Baldwin appeared so deeply interested, that he did not appear to notice the entrance of the Constable, who, highly displeased at this additional slight, stood on the floor of the hall, undetermined whether to interrupt the reader, and address the Prelate at once, or to withdraw without saluting him at all. Ere he had formed a resolution, the chaplain had arrived at some convenient pause in the lecture, where the Archbishop stopped him with, " *Satis est, mi fili.*"

It was in vain that the proud secular Baron strove to conceal the embarrassment with which he approached the Prelate, whose attitude was plainly assumed for the purpose of impressing him with awe and solicitude. He tried, indeed, to exhibit a demeanour of such ease as might characterize their old friendship, or at least of such indifference as might infer the possession of perfect tranquillity; but he failed in both, and his address expressed mortified pride, mixed with no ordinary degree of embarrassment. The genius of the Catholic Church was on such occasions sure to predominate over the haughtiest of the laity.

" I perceive," said De Lacy, collecting his thoughts, and ashamed to find he had difficulty in doing so, — " I perceive that an old friendship is here dissolved. Methinks Hugo de Lacy might have expected another messenger to summon him to this reverend presence, and that another welcome should wait him on his arrival."

The Archbishop raised himself slowly in his seat, and made a half-inclination towards the Constable, who, by an instinctive desire of conciliation, returned it lower than he had intended, or than the scanty courtesy merited. The Prelate at the same time signing to his chaplain, the latter rose to withdraw, and receiving permission in the phrase " *Do veniam,*" retreated reverentially, without either turning his back or looking upwards, his eyes fixed on the ground, his hands still folded in his habit, and crossed over his bosom.

When this mute attendant had disappeared, the Prelate's brow became more open, yet retained a dark shade of grave displeasure, and he replied to the address of De Lacy, but still without rising from his seat. "It skills not now, my lord, to say what the brave Constable of Chester has been to the poor priest Baldwin, or with what love and pride we beheld him assume the holy sign of salvation, and, to honour Him by whom he has himself been raised to honour, vow himself to the deliverance of the Holy Land. If I still see that noble lord before me, in the same holy resolution, let me know the joyful truth, and I will lay aside rochet and mitre, and tend his horse like a groom, if it be necessary by such menial service to show the cordial respect I bear to him."

" Reverend father," answered De Lacy, with hesitation, " I had hoped that the propositions which were made to you on my part by the Dean of Hereford, might have seemed more satisfactory in your eyes." Then, regaining his native confidence, he proceeded with more assurance in speech and manner; for the cold inflexible looks of the Archbishop irritated him. "If these proposals can be amended, my lord, let me know in what points, and, if possible, your pleasure shall be done, even if it should prove somewhat unreasonable. I would have peace, my lord, with Holy Church, and am the last who would despise her mandates. This has been known by my deeds in field, and counsels in the state; nor can I think my services have merited cold looks and cold language from the Primate of England."

" Do you upbraid the Church with your services, vain man?" said Baldwin. " I tell thee, Hugo de Lacy, that what Heaven hath wrought for the Church by thy hand, could, had it been the divine pleasure, have been achieved with as much ease by the meanest horseboy in thy host. It is *thou* that art honoured, in being the chosen instrument by which great things have been wrought in Israel. — Nay, interrupt me not — I tell thee, proud baron, that, in the sight of Heaven, thy wisdom is but as folly—thy courage, which thou dost boast, but the cowardice of a village maiden—thy strength weakness — thy spear an osier, and thy sword a bulrush."

"All this I know, good father," said the Constable, "and have ever heard it repeated when such poor services as I may have rendered are gone and past. Marry, when there was need for my helping hand, I was the very good lord of priest and prelate, and one who should be honoured and prayed for with patrons and founders who sleep in the choir and under the high altar. There was no thought, I trow, of osier or of bulrush, when I have been prayed to couch my lance or draw my weapon; it is only when they are needless that they and their owner are undervalued. Well, my reverend father, be it so, — if the Church can cast the Saracens from the Holy Land by grooms and horseboys, wherefore do you preach knights and nobles from the homes and the countries which they are born to protect and defend?".

The Archbishop looked steadily on him as he replied, "Not for the sake of their fleshly arm do we disturb your knights and barons in their prosecution of barbarous festivities, and murderous feuds, which you call enjoying their homes and protecting their domains, — not that Omnipotence requires their arm of flesh to execute the great predestined work of liberation — but for the weal of their immortal souls." These last words he pronounced with great emphasis.

The Constable paced the floor impatiently, and muttered to himself, "Such is the airy guerdon for which hosts on hosts have been drawn from Europe to drench the sands of Palestine with their gore—such the vain promises for which we are called upon to barter our country, our lands, and our lives!"

"Is it Hugo de Lacy speaks thus?" said the Archbishop, arising from his seat, and qualifying his tone of censure with the appearance of shame and of regret — "Is it he who underprizes the renown of a knight — the virtue of a Christian — the advancement of his earthly honour — the more incalculable profit of his immortal soul? — Is it he who desires a solid and substantial recompense in lands or treasures, to be won by warring on his less powerful neighbours at home, while knightly honour and religious faith, his vow as a knight and his baptism as a Christian, call him to a more glorious and more dangerous strife? — Can it be indeed Hugo de Lacy, the mirror of the Anglo-Norman chivalry, whose thoughts can conceive such sentiments, whose words can utter them?"

"Flattery and fair speech, suitably mixed with taunts and reproaches, my lord," answered the Constable, colouring and biting his lip, "may carry your point with others; but I am of a temper too solid to be either wheedled or goaded into measures of importance. Forbear, therefore, this strain of affected amazement; and believe me, that whether he goes to the Crusade or abides at home, the character of Hugo de Lacy will remain as unimpeached in point of courage as that of the Archbishop Baldwin in point of sanctitude."

"May it stand much higher," said the Archbishop, "than the reputation with which you vouchsafe to compare it! but a blaze may be extinguished as well as a spark; and I tell the Constable of Chester, that the fame which has set on his basnet for so many years, may flit from it in one moment, never to be recalled."

"Who dares to say so?" said the Constable, trembling alive to the honour for which he had encountered so many dangers.

"A friend," said the Prelate, "whose stripes should be received as benefits. You think of pay, Sir Constable, and of guerdon, as if you still stood in the market, free to chaffer on the terms of your service. I tell you, you are no longer your own master — you are, by the blessed badge you have voluntarily assumed, the soldier of God himself; nor can you fly from your standard without such infamy as even coistrels or grooms are unwilling to incur."

"You deal all too hardly with us, my lord," said Hugo de Lacy, stopping short in his troubled walk. "You of the spirituality make us laymen the pack-horses of your own concerns, and climb to ambitious heights by the help of our over-burdened shoulders; but all hath its limits—Becket transgressed it, and——"

A gloomy and expressive look corresponded with the tone in which he spoke this broken sentence; and the Prelate, at no loss to comprehend his meaning, replied, in a firm and determined voice, "And he was *murdered!* —that is what you dare to hint to me — even to me, the successor of that glorified saint—as a motive for complying with your fickle and selfish wish to withdraw your hand from the plough. You know not to whom you address such a threat. True, Becket, from a saint militant on earth, arrived, by the bloody path of martyrdom, to the dignity of a saint in Heaven; and no less true is it, that, to attain a seat a thousand degrees beneath that of his blessed predecessor, the unworthy Baldwin were willing to submit, under Our Lady's protection, to whatever the worst of wicked men can inflict on his earthly frame."

"There needs not this show of courage, reverend father," said Lacy, recollecting himself, "where there neither is, nor can be, danger. I pray you, let us debate this matter more deliberately. I have never meant to break off my purpose for the Holy Land, but only to postpone it. Methinks the offers that I have made are fair, and ought to obtain for me what has been granted to others in the like case — a slight delay in the time of my departure."

"A slight delay on the part of such a leader as you, noble De Lacy," answered the Prelate, "were a death-blow to our holy and most gallant enterprise. To meaner men we might have granted the privilege of marrying and giving in marriage, even although they care not for the sorrows of Jacob; but you, my lord, are a main prop of our enterprise, and, being withdrawn, the whole fabric may fall to the ground. Who in England will deem himself obliged to press forward, when Hugo de Lacy falls back? Think, my lord, less upon your plighted bride, and more on your plighted word; and believe not that a union can ever come to good, which shakes your purpose towards our blessed undertaking for the honour of Christendom."

The Constable was embarrassed by the pertinacity of the Prelate, and began to give way to his arguments, though most reluctantly, and only because the habits and opinions of the time left him no means of combating his arguments, otherwise than by solicitation. "I admit," he said, "my engagements for the Crusade, nor have I — I repeat it — farther desire than that brief interval which may be necessary to place my important affairs in order. Meanwhile, my vassals, led by my nephew——"

"Promise that which is within thy power," said the Prelate. "Who knows whether, in resentment of thy seeking after other things than his most holy cause, thy nephew may not be called hence, even while we speak together?"

"God forbid!" said the Baron, starting up, as if about to fly to his nephew's assistance; then suddenly pausing, he turned on the Prelate a keen and investigating glance. "It is not well," he said, "that your reverence should thus trifle with the dangers which threaten my house. Damian is dear to me for his own good qualities—dear for the sake of my only brother.—May God forgive us both! he died when we were in unkindness with each other.—My lord, your words import that my beloved nephew suffers pain and incurs danger on account of my offences?"

2 I

The Archbishop perceived he had at length touched the chord to which his refractory penitent's heart-strings must needs vibrate. He replied with circumspection, as well knowing with whom he had to deal,—"Far be it from me to presume to interpret the counsels of Heaven! but we read in Scripture, that when the fathers eat sour grapes, the teeth of the children are set on edge. What so reasonable as that we should be punished for our pride and contumacy, by a judgment specially calculated to abate and bend that spirit of surquedry?* You yourself best know if this disease clung to thy nephew before you had meditated defection from the banner of the Cross."

Hugo de Lacy hastily recollected himself, and found that it was indeed true, that, until he thought of his union with Eveline, there had appeared no change in his nephew's health. His silence and confusion did not escape the artful Prelate. He took the hand of the warrior as he stood before him overwhelmed in doubt, lest his preference of the continuance of his own house to the rescue of the Holy Sepulchre should have been punished by the disease which threatened his nephew's life. "Come," he said, "noble De Lacy—the judgment provoked by a moment's presumption may be even yet averted by prayer and penitence. The dial went back at the prayer of the good King Hezekiah—down, down upon thy knees, and doubt not that, with confession, and penance, and absolution, thou mayst yet atone for thy falling away from the cause of Heaven."

Borne down by the dictates of the religion in which he had been educated, and by the fears lest his delay was punished by his nephew's indisposition and danger, the Constable sunk on his knees before the Prelate, whom he had shortly before well-nigh braved, confessed, as a sin to be deeply repented of, his purpose of delaying his departure for Palestine, and received, with patience at least, if not with willing acquiescence, the penance inflicted by the Archbishop; which consisted in a prohibition to proceed farther in his proposed wedlock with the Lady Eveline, until he was returned from Palestine, where he was bound by his vow to abide for the term of three years.

"And now, noble De Lacy," said the Prelate, "once more my best beloved and most honoured friend—is not thy bosom lighter since thou hast thus nobly acquitted thee of thy debt to Heaven, and cleansed thy gallant spirit from those selfish and earthly stains which dimmed its brightness?"

The Constable sighed. "My happiest thoughts at this moment," he said, "would arise from knowledge that my nephew's health is amended."

"Be not discomforted on the score of the noble Damian, your hopeful and valorous kinsman," said the Archbishop, "for well I trust shortly ye shall hear of his recovery; or that, if it shall please God to remove him to a better world, the passage shall be so easy, and his arrival in yonder haven of bliss so speedy, that it were better for him to have died than to have lived."

The Constable looked at him, as if to gather from his countenance more certainty of his nephew's fate than his words seemed to imply; and the Prelate, to escape being farther pressed on the subject on which he was perhaps conscious he had ventured too far, rung a silver bell which stood before him on the table, and commanded the chaplain who entered at the summons, that he should despatch a careful messenger to the lodging of Damian Lacy to bring particular accounts of his health.

"A stranger," answered the chaplain, "just come from the sick chamber of the noble Damian Lacy, waits here even now to have speech of my Lord Constable."

"Admit him instantly," said the Archbishop—"my mind tells me he brings us joyful tidings.—Never knew I such humble penitence,—such

---

* Self-importance, or assumption.

willing resignation of natural affections and desires to the doing of Heaven's service, but it was rewarded with a guerdon either temporal or spiritual."

As he spoke, a man singularly dressed entered the apartment. His garments, of various colours, and showily disposed, were none of the newest or cleanest, neither were they altogether fitting for the presence in which he now stood.

"How now, sirrah!" said the Prelate; "when was it that jugglers and minstrels pressed into the company of such as we without permission?"

"So please you," said the man, "my instant business was not with your reverend lordship, but with my lord the Constable, to whom I will hope that my good news may atone for my evil apparel."

"Speak, sirrah, does my kinsman live?" said the Constable eagerly.

"And is like to live, my lord," answered the man—"a favourable crisis (so the leeches call it) hath taken place in his disorder, and they are no longer under any apprehensions for his life."

"Now, God be praised, that hath granted me so much mercy!" said the Constable.

"Amen, amen!" replied the Archbishop solemnly.—"About what period did this blessed change take place?"

"Scarcely a quarter of an hour since," said the messenger, "a soft sleep fell on the sick youth, like dew upon a parched field in summer—he breathed freely—the burning heat abated—and, as I said, the leeches no longer fear for his life."

"Marked you the hour, my Lord Constable?" said the Bishop, with exultation—"Even then you stooped to those counsels which Heaven suggested through the meanest of its servants! But two words avouching penitence —but one brief prayer—and some kind saint has interceded for an instant hearing, and a liberal granting of thy petition. Noble Hugo," he continued, grasping his hand in a species of enthusiasm, "surely Heaven designs to work high things by the hand of him whose faults are thus readily forgiven —whose prayer is thus instantly heard. For this shall *Te Deum Laudamus* be said in each church, and each convent in Gloucester, ere the world be a day older."

The Constable, no less joyful, though perhaps less able to perceive an especial providence in his nephew's recovery, expressed his gratitude to the messenger of the good tidings, by throwing him his purse.

"I thank you, noble lord," said the man; "but if I stoop to pick up this taste of your bounty, it is only to restore it again to the donor."

"How now, sir?" said the Constable, "methinks thy coat seems not so well lined as needs make thee spurn at such a guerdon."

"He that designs to catch larks, my lord," replied the messenger, "must not close his net upon sparrows—I have a greater boon to ask of your lordship, and therefore I decline your present gratuity."

"A greater boon, ha!" said the Constable,—"I am no knight-errant, to bind myself by promise to grant it ere I know its import; but do thou come to my pavilion to-morrow, and thou wilt not find me unwilling to do what is reason."

So saying, he took leave of the Prelate, and returned homeward, failing not to visit his nephew's lodging as he passed, where he received the same pleasant assurances which had been communicated by the messenger of the particoloured mantle.

Chapter the Nineteenth.

He was a minstrel—in his mood
Was wisdom mix'd with folly;
A tame companion to the good,
But wild and fierce among the rude,
And jovial with the jolly.
ARCHIBALD ARMSTRONG.

THE events of the preceding day had been of a nature so interesting, and latterly so harrassing, that the Constable felt weary as after a severely contested battle-field, and slept soundly until the earliest beams of dawn saluted him through the opening of the tent. It was then that, with a mingled feeling of pain and satisfaction, he began to review the change which had taken place in his condition since the preceding morning. He had then risen an ardent bridegroom, anxious to find favour in the eyes of his fair bride, and scrupulous about his dress and appointments, as if he had been as young in years as in hopes and wishes. This was over, and he had now before him the painful task of leaving his betrothed for a term of years, even before wedlock had united them indissolubly, and of reflecting that she was exposed to all the dangers which assail female constancy in a situation thus critical. When the immediate anxiety for his nephew was removed, he was tempted to think that he had been something hasty in listening to the arguments of the Archbishop, and in believing that Damian's death or recovery depended upon his own accomplishing, to the letter, and without delay, his vow for the Holy Land. "How many princes and kings," he thought to himself, "have assumed the Cross, and delayed or renounced it, yet lived and died in wealth and honour, without sustaining such a visitation as that with which Baldwin threatened me; and in what case or particular did such men deserve more indulgence than I? But the die is now cast, and it signifies little to inquire whether my obedience to the mandates of the Church has saved the life of my nephew, or whether I have not fallen, as laymen are wont to fall, whenever there is an encounter of wits betwixt them and those of the spirituality. I would to God it may prove otherwise, since, girding on my sword as Heaven's champion, I might the better expect Heaven's protection for her whom I must unhappily leave behind me."

As these reflections passed through his mind, he heard the warders at the entrance of his tent challenge some one whose footsteps were heard approaching it. The person stopped on their challenge, and presently after was heard the sound of a rote, (a small species of lute,) the strings of which were managed by means of a small wheel. After a short prelude, a manly voice, of good compass, sung verses, which, translated into modern language, might run nearly thus:

I.

"Soldier, wake—the day is peeping,
Honour ne'er was won in sleeping,
Never when the sunbeams still
Lay unreflected on the hill :
'Tis when they are glinted back
From axe and armour, spear and jack,
That they promise future story
Many a page of deathless glory.
Shields that are the foeman's terror,
Ever are the morning's mirror.

II.

"Arm and up—the morning beam
Hath call'd the rustic to his team,
Hath call'd the falc'ner to the lake,
Hath call'd the huntsman to the brake;
The early student ponders o'er
His dusty tomes of ancient lore.
Soldier, wake—thy harvest, fame;
Thy study, conquest; war, thy game.
Shield, that would be foeman's terror,
Still should gleam the morning's mirror.

III.

"Poor hire repays the rustic's pain;
More paltry still the sportsman's gain;
Vainest of all, the student's theme
Ends in some metaphysic dream.

> Yet each is up, and each has toil'd
> Since first the peep of dawn has smiled;
> And each is eagerer in his aim
> Than he who barters life for fame.
> Up, up, and arm thee, son of terror!
> Be thy bright shield the morning's mirror."

When the song was finished, the Constable heard some talking without, and presently Philip Guarine entered the pavilion to tell that a person, come hither as he said by the Constable's appointment, waited permission to speak with him.

"By my appointment?" said De Lacy; "admit him immediately."

The messenger of the preceding evening entered the tent, holding in one hand his small cap and feather, in the other the rote on which he had been just playing. His attire was fantastic, consisting of more than one inner dress of various colours, all of the brightest and richest dyes, and disposed so as to contrast with each other—the upper garment was a very short Norman cloak, in bright green. An embroidered girdle sustained, in lieu of offensive weapons, an inkhorn with its appurtenances on the one side, on the other a knife for the purposes of the table. His hair was cut in imitation of the clerical tonsure, which was designed to intimate that he had arrived to a certain rank in his profession; for the Joyous Science, as the profession of minstrelsy was termed, had its various ranks, like the degrees in the church and in chivalry. The features and the manners of the man seemed to be at variance with his profession and habit; for, as the latter was gay and fantastic, the former had a cast of gravity, and almost of sternness, which, unless when kindled by the enthusiasm of his poetical and musical exertions, seemed rather to indicate deep reflection, than the thoughtless vivacity of observation which characterized most of his brethren. His countenance, though not handsome, had therefore something in it striking and impressive, even from its very contrast with the particoloured hues and fluttering shape of his vestments; and the Constable felt something inclined to patronize him, as he said, "Good-morrow, friend, and I thank thee for thy morning greeting; it was well sung and well meant, for when we call forth any one to bethink him how time passes, we do him the credit of supposing that he can employ to advantage that flitting treasure."

The man, who had listened in silence, seemed to pause and make an effort ere he replied, "My intentions, at least, were good, when I ventured to disturb my lord thus early; and I am glad to learn that my boldness hath not been evil received at his hand."

"True," said the Constable, "you had a boon to ask of me. Be speedy, and say thy request — my leisure is short."

"It is for permission to follow you to the Holy Land, my lord," said the man.

"Thou hast asked what I can hardly grant, my friend," answered De Lacy — "Thou art a minstrel, art thou not?"

"An unworthy graduate of the Gay Science, my lord," said the musician; "yet let me say for myself, that I will not yield to the king of minstrels, Geoffrey Rudel, though the King of England hath given him four manors for one song. I would be willing to contend with him in romance, lay, or fable, were the judge to be King Henry himself."

"You have your own good word, doubtless," said De Lacy; "nevertheless, Sir Minstrel, thou goest not with me. The Crusade has been already too much encumbered by men of thy idle profession; and if thou dost add to the number, it shall not be under my protection. I am too old to be charmed by thy art, charm thou never so wisely."

"He that is young enough to seek for, and to win, the love of beauty," said the minstrel, but in a submissive tone, as if fearing his freedom might give offence, "should not term himself too old to feel the charms of minstrelsy."

The Constable smiled, not insensible to the flattery which assigned to him the character of a younger gallant. "Thou art a jester," he said, "I warrant me, in addition to thy other qualities."

"No," replied the minstrel, "it is a branch of our profession which I have for some time renounced—my fortunes have put me out of tune for jesting."

"Nay, comrade," said the Constable, "if thou hast been hardly dealt with in the world, and canst comply with the rules of a family so strictly ordered as mine, it is possible we may agree together better than I thought. What is thy name and country? thy speech, methinks, sounds somewhat foreign."

"I am an Armorican, my lord, from the merry shores of Morbihan; and hence my tongue hath some touch of my country speech. My name is Renault Vidal."

"Such being the case, Renault," said the Constable, "thou shalt follow me, and I will give orders to the master of my household to have thee attired something according to thy function, but in more orderly guise than thou now appearest in. Dost thou understand the use of a weapon?"

"Indifferently, my lord," said the Armorican; at the same time taking a sword from the wall, he drew, and made a pass with it so close to the Constable's body as he sat on the couch, that he started up, crying, "Villain, forbear!"

"La you! noble sir," replied Vidal, lowering with all submission the point of his weapon—"I have already given you a proof of sleight which has alarmed even your experience—I have an hundred other besides."

"It may be so," said De Lacy, somewhat ashamed at having shown himself moved by the sudden and lively action of the juggler; "but I love not jesting with edge-tools, and have too much to do with sword and sword-blows in earnest, to toy with them; so I pray you let us have no more of this, but call me my squire and my chamberlain, for I am about to array me and go to mass."

The religious duties of the morning performed, it was the Constable's intention to visit the Lady Abbess, and communicate, with the necessary precautions and qualifications, the altered relations in which he was placed towards her niece, by the resolution he had been compelled to adopt, of departing for the Crusade before accomplishing his marriage, in the terms of the precontract already entered into. He was conscious that it would be difficult to reconcile the good lady to this change of measures, and he delayed some time ere he could think of the best mode of communicating and softening the unpleasant intelligence. An interval was also spent in a visit to his nephew, whose state of convalescence continued to be as favourable, as if in truth it had been a miraculous consequence of the Constable's having complied with the advice of the Archbishop.

From the lodging of Damian, the Constable proceeded to the convent of the Benedictine Abbess. But she had been already made acquainted with the circumstances which he came to communicate, by a still earlier visit from the Archbishop Baldwin himself. The Primate had undertaken the office of mediator on this occasion, conscious that his success of the evening before must have placed the Constable in a delicate situation with the relations of his betrothed bride, and willing, by his countenance and authority, to reconcile the disputes which might ensue. Perhaps he had better have left Hugo de Lacy to plead his own cause; for the Abbess, though she listened to the communication with all the respect due to the highest dignitary of the English Church, drew consequences from the Constable's change of resolution which the Primate had not expected. She ventured to oppose no obstacle to De Lacy's accomplishment of his vows, but strongly argued that the contract with her niece should be entirely set aside, and each party left at liberty to form a new choice.

It was in vain that the Archbishop endeavoured to dazzle the Abbess with the future honours to be won by the Constable in the Holy Land; the splendour of which would attach not to his lady alone, but to all in the remotest degree allied to or connected with her. All his eloquence was to no purpose, though upon so favourite a topic he exerted it to the utmost. The Abbess, it is true, remained silent for a moment after his arguments had been exhausted, but it was only to consider how she should intimate in a suitable and reverent manner, that children, the usual attendants of a happy union, and the existence of which she looked to for the continuation of the house of her father and brother, could not be hoped for with any probability, unless the precontract was followed by marriage, and the residence of the married parties in the same country. She therefore insisted, that the Constable having altered his intentions in this most important particular, the *fiançailles* should be entirely abrogated and set aside; and she demanded of the Primate, as an act of justice, that, as he had interfered to prevent the bridegroom's execution of his original purpose, he should now assist with his influence wholly to dissolve an engagement which had been thus materially innovated upon.

The Primate, who was sensible he had himself occasioned De Lacy's breach of contract, felt himself bound in honour and reputation to prevent consequences so disagreeable to his friend, as the dissolution of an engagement in which his interest and inclinations were alike concerned. He reproved the Lady Abbess for the carnal and secular views which she, a dignitary of the church, entertained upon the subject of matrimony, and concerning the interest of her house. He even upbraided her with selfishly preferring the continuation of the line of Berenger to the recovery of the Holy Sepulchre, and denounced to her that Heaven would be avenged of the shortsighted and merely human policy, which postponed the interests of Christendom to those of an individual family.

After this severe homily, the Prelate took his departure, leaving the Abbess highly incensed, though she prudently forbore returning any irreverent answer to his paternal admonition.

In this humour the venerable lady was found by the Constable himself, when with some embarrassment, he proceeded to explain to her the necessity of his present departure for Palestine.

She received the communication with sullen dignity; her ample black robe and scapular seeming, as it were, to swell out in yet prouder folds as she listened to the reasons and the emergencies which compelled the Constable of Chester to defer the marriage which he avowed was the dearest wish of his heart, until after his return from the Crusade, for which he was about to set forth.

"Methinks," replied the Abbess, with much coldness, "if this communication is meant for earnest, — and it were no fit business — I myself no fit person, — for jesting with—methinks the Constable's resolution should have been proclaimed to us yesterday before the *fiançailles* had united his troth with that of Eveline Berenger, under expectations very different from those which he now announces."

"On the word of a knight and a gentleman, reverend lady," said the Constable, "I had not then the slightest thought that I should be called upon to take a step no less distressing to me, than, as I see with pain, it is unpleasing to you."

"I can scarcely conceive," replied the Abbess, "the cogent reasons, which, existing as they must have done yesterday, have nevertheless delayed their operation until to-day."

"I own," said De Lacy, reluctantly, "that I entertained too ready hopes of obtaining a remission from my vow, which my Lord of Canterbury hath, in his zeal for Heaven's service, deemed it necessary to refuse me."

"At least, then," said the Abbess, veiling her resentment under the appearance of extreme coldness, "your lordship will do us the justice to place us in the same situation in which we stood yesterday morning; and, by joining with my niece and her friends in desiring the abrogation of a marriage contract, entered into with very different views from those which you now entertain, put a young person in that state of liberty of which she is at present deprived by her contract with you."

"Ah, madam!" said the Constable, "what do you ask of me? and in a tone how cold and indifferent do you demand me to resign hopes, the dearest which my bosom ever entertained since the life-blood warmed it!"

"I am unacquainted with language belonging to such feelings, my lord," replied the Abbess; "but methinks the prospects which could be so easily adjourned for years, might, by a little, and a very little, farther self-control, be altogether abandoned."

Hugo de Lacy paced the room in agitation, nor did he answer until after a considerable pause. "If your niece, madam, shares the sentiments which you have expressed, I could not, indeed, with justice to her, or perhaps to myself, desire to retain that interest in her, which our solemn espousals have given me. But I must know my doom from her own lips; and if it is as severe as that which your expressions lead me to fear, I will go to Palestine the better soldier of Heaven, that I shall have little left on earth that can interest me."

The Abbess, without farther answer, called on her Præcentrix, and desired her to command her niece's attendance immediately. The Præcentrix bowed reverently, and withdrew.

"May I presume to inquire," said De Lacy, "whether the Lady Eveline hath been possessed of the circumstances which have occasioned this unhappy alteration in my purpose?"

"I have communicated the whole to her from point to point," said the Abbess, "even as it was explained to me this morning by my Lord of Canterbury, (for with him I have already spoken upon the subject,) and confirmed but now by your lordship's own mouth."

"I am little obliged to the Archbishop," said the Constable, "for having forestalled my excuses in the quarter where it was most important for me that they should be accurately stated, and favourably received."

"That," said the Abbess, "is but an item of the account betwixt you and the Prelate,—it concerns not us."

"Dare I venture to hope," continued De Lacy, without taking offence at the dryness of the Abbess's manner, "that Lady Eveline has heard this most unhappy change of circumstances without emotion,—I would say, without displeasure?"

"She is the daughter of a Berenger, my lord," answered the Abbess, "and it is our custom to punish a breach of faith or to contemn it—never to grieve over it. What my niece may do in this case, I know not. I am a woman of religion, sequestered from the world, and would advise peace and Christian forgiveness, with a proper sense of contempt for the unworthy treatment which she has received. She has followers and vassals, and friends, doubtless, and advisers, who may not, in blinded zeal for worldly honour, recommend to her to sit down slightly with this injury, but desire she should rather appeal to the King, or to the arms of her father's followers, unless her liberty is restored to her by the surrender of the contract into which she has been enticed.—But she comes, to answer for herself."

Eveline entered at the moment, leaning on Rose's arm. She had laid aside mourning since the ceremony of the *fiançailles*, and was dressed in a kirtle of white, with an upper robe of pale blue. Her head was covered with a veil of white gauze, so thin, as to float about her like the misty cloud usually painted around the countenance of a seraph. But the face of Eveline, though in beauty not unworthy one of that angelic order, was at present far from resembling that of a seraph in tranquillity of expression. Her limbs trembled, her cheeks were pale, the tinge of red around the eyelids expressed recent tears; yet amidst these natural signs of distress and uncertainty, there was an air of profound resignation—a resolution to discharge her duty in every emergence reigning in the solemn expression of her eye and eyebrow, and showing her prepared to govern the agitation which she could not entirely subdue. And so well were these opposing qualities of timidity and resolution mingled on her cheek, that Eveline, in the utmost pride of her beauty, never looked more fascinating than at that instant; and Hugo de Lacy, hitherto rather an unimpassioned lover, stood in her presence with feelings as if all the exaggerations of romance were realized, and his mistress were a being of a higher sphere, from whose doom he was to receive happiness or misery, life or death.

It was under the influence of such a feeling, that the warrior dropped on one knee before Eveline, took the hand which she rather resigned than gave to him, pressed it to his lips fervently, and, ere he parted with it, moistened it with one of the few tears which he was ever known to shed. But, although surprised, and carried out of his character by a sudden impulse, he regained his composure on observing that the Abbess regarded his humiliation, if it can be so termed, with an air of triumph; and he entered on his defence before Eveline with a manly earnestness, not devoid of fervour, nor free from agitation, yet made in a tone of firmness and pride, which seemed assumed to meet and control that of the offended Abbess.

"Lady," he said, addressing Eveline, "you have heard from the venerable Abbess in what unhappy position I have been placed since yesterday by the rigour of the Archbishop—perhaps I should rather say by his just though severe interpretation of my engagement in the Crusade. I cannot doubt that all this has been stated with accurate truth by the venerable lady; but as I must no longer call her my friend, let me fear whether she has done me justice in her commentary upon the unhappy necessity which must presently compel me to leave my country, and with my country to forego—at best to postpone—the fairest hopes which man ever entertained. The venerable lady hath upbraided me, that being myself the cause that the execution of yesterday's contract is postponed, I would fain keep it suspended over your head for an indefinite term of years. No one resigns willingly such rights as yesterday gave me; and, let me speak a boastful word, sooner than yield them up to man of woman born, I would hold a fair field against all comers, with grinded sword and sharp spear, from sunrise to sunset, for three days' space. But what I would retain at the price of a thousand lives, I am willing to renounce if it would cost you a single sigh. If, therefore, you think you cannot remain happy as the betrothed of De Lacy, you may command my assistance to have the contract annulled, and make some more fortunate man happy."

He would have gone on, but felt the danger of being overpowered again by those feelings of tenderness so new to his steady nature, that he blushed to give way to them.

Eveline remained silent. The Abbess took the word. "Kinswoman," she said, "you hear that the generosity—or the justice—of the Constable of Chester, proposes, in consequence of his departure upon a distant and perilous expedition, to cancel a contract entered into upon the specific and precise understanding that he was to remain in England for its fulfilment. You cannot, methinks, hesitate to accept of the freedom which he offers you, with thanks for his bounty. For my part, I will reserve mine own until I shall see that your joint application is sufficient to win to your purpose his Grace of Canterbury, who may again interfere with the actions of his friend the Lord Constable, over whom he has already exerted so much influence—for the weal, doubtless, of his spiritual concerns."

"If it is meant by your words, venerable lady," said the Constable, "that I have any purpose of sheltering myself behind the Prelate's authority, to avoid doing that which I proclaim my readiness, though not my willingness, to do, I can only say, that you are the first who has doubted the faith of Hugo de Lacy."—And while the proud Baron thus addressed a female and a recluse, he could not prevent his eye from sparkling, and his cheek from flushing.

"My gracious and venerable kinswoman," said Eveline, summoning together her resolution, "and you, my kind lord, be not offended if I pray you not to increase by groundless suspicions and hasty resentments your difficulties and mine. My lord, the obligations which I lie under to you are such as I can never discharge, since they comprehend fortune, life, and honour. Know that, in my anguish of mind, when besieged by the Welsh in my castle of the Garde Doloureuse, I vowed to the Virgin, that (my honour safe) I would place myself at the disposal of him whom our Lady should employ as her instrument to relieve me from yonder hour of agony. In giving me a deliverer, she gave me a master; nor could I desire a more noble one than Hugo de Lacy."

"God forbid, lady," said the Constable, speaking eagerly, as if he was afraid his resolution should fail ere he could get the renunciation uttered, "that I should, by such a tie, to which you subjected yourself in the extremity of your distress, bind you to any resolution in my favour which can put force on your own inclinations!"

The Abbess herself could not help expressing her applause of this sentiment, declaring it was spoken like a Norman gentleman; but at the same time, her eyes, turned towards her niece, seemed to exhort her to beware how she declined to profit by the candour of De Lacy.

But Eveline proceeded, with her eyes fixed on the ground, and a slight colour overspreading her face, to state her own sentiments, without listening to the suggestions of any one. "I will own, noble sir," she said, "that when your valour had rescued me from approaching destruction, I could have wished—honouring and respecting you, as I had done your late friend, my excellent father—that you could have accepted a daughter's service from me. I do not pretend entirely to have surmounted these sentiments, although I have combated them, as being unworthy of me, and ungrateful to you. But, from the moment you were pleased to honour me by a claim on this poor hand, I have studiously examined my sentiments towards you, and taught myself so far to make them coincide with my duty, that I may call myself assured that De Lacy would not find in Eveline Berenger an indifferent, far less an unworthy bride. In this, sir, you may boldly confide, whether the union you have sought for takes place instantly, or is delayed till a longer season. Still farther, I must acknowledge that the postponement of these nuptials will be more agreeable to me than their immediate accomplishment. I am at present very young, and totally inexperienced. Two or three years will, I trust, render me yet more worthy the regard of a man of honour."

At this declaration in his favour, however cold and qualified, De Lacy had as much difficulty to restrain his transports as formerly to moderate his agitation.

"Angel of bounty and of kindness!" he said, kneeling once more, and again possessing himself of her hand, "perhaps I ought in honour to resign voluntarily those hopes which you decline to ravish from me forcibly. But who could be capable of such unrelenting magnanimity?—Let me hope that my devoted attachment—that which you shall hear of me when at a distance—that which you shall know of me when near you—may give to your sentiments a more tender warmth than they now express; and, in the meanwhile, blame me not that I accept your plighted faith anew, under the conditions which you attach to it. I am conscious my wooing has been too late in life to expect the animated returns proper to youthful passion—Blame me not if I remain satisfied with those calmer sentiments which make life happy, though they cannot make possession rapturous. Your hand remains in my grasp, but it acknowledges not my pressure — Can it be that it refuses to ratify what your lips have said?"

"Never, noble De Lacy!" said Eveline, with more animation than she had yet expressed; and it appeared that the tone was at length sufficiently encouraging, since her lover was emboldened to take the lips themselves for guarantee.

It was with an air of pride, mingled with respect, that, after having received this pledge of fidelity, he turned to conciliate and to appease the offended Abbess. "I trust, venerable mother," he said, "that you will resume your former kind thoughts of me, which I am aware were only interrupted by your tender anxiety for the interest of her who should be dearest to us both. Let me hope that I may leave this fair flower under protection of the honoured lady who is her next in blood, happy and secure as she must ever be, while listening to your counsels, and residing within these sacred walls."

But the Abbess was too deeply displeased to be propitiated by a compliment, which perhaps it had been better policy to have delayed till a calmer season. "My lord," she said, "and you, fair kinswoman, you ought needs to be aware how little my counsels — not frequently given where they are unwillingly listened to — can be of avail to those embarked in worldly affairs. I am a woman dedicated to religion, to solitude, and seclusion — to the service, in brief, of Our Lady and Saint Benedict. I have been already censured by my superior because I have, for love of you, fair niece, mixed more deeply in secular affairs than became the head of a convent of recluses — I will merit no farther blame on such an account; nor can you expect it of me. My brother's daughter, unfettered by worldly ties, had been the welcome sharer of my poor solicitude. But this house is too mean for the residence of the vowed bride of a mighty baron; nor do I, in my lowliness and inexperience, feel fitness to exercise over such an one that authority, which must belong to me over every one whom this roof protects. The grave tenor of our devotions, and the serener contemplation to which the females of this house are devoted," continued the Abbess, with increasing heat and vehemence, "shall not, for the sake of my worldly connections, be disturbed by the intrusion of one whose thoughts must needs be on the worldly toys of love and marriage."

"I do indeed believe, reverend mother," said the Constable, in his turn giving way to displeasure, "that a richly-dowered maiden, unwedded, and unlikely to wed, were a fitter and more welcome inmate to the convent, than one who cannot be separated from the world, and whose wealth is not likely to increase the House's revenues."

The Constable did the Abbess great injury in this hasty insinuation, and it only went to confirm her purpose of rejecting all charge of her niece during his absence. She was in truth as disinterested as haughty; and her only reason for anger against her niece was, that her advice had not been adopted without hesitation, although the matter regarded Eveline's happiness exclusively.

The ill-timed reflection of the Constable confirmed her in the resolution which she had already, and hastily adopted. "May Heaven forgive you, Sir Knight," she replied, "your injurious thoughts of His servants! It is indeed time, for your soul's sake, that you do penance in the Holy Land, having such rash judgments to repent of. — For you, my niece, you cannot want that hospitality, which, without verifying, or seeming to verify, unjust suspicions, I cannot now grant to you, while you have, in your kinswoman of Baldringham, a secular relation, whose nearness of blood approaches mine, and who may open her gates to you without incurring the unworthy censure, that she means to enrich herself at your cost."

The Constable saw the deadly paleness which came over Eveline's cheek at this proposal, and, without knowing the cause of her repugnance, he hastened to relieve her from the apprehensions which she seemed evidently to entertain. "No, reverend mother," he said, "since *you* so harshly reject the care of your kinswoman, she shall not be a burden to any of her other relatives. While Hugo de Lacy hath six gallant castles, and many a manor besides, to maintain fire upon their hearths, his betrothed bride shall burden no one with her society, who may regard it as otherwise than a great honour; and methinks I were much poorer than Heaven hath made me, could I not furnish friends and followers sufficient to serve, obey, and protect her."

"No, my lord," said Eveline, recovering from the dejection into which she had been thrown by the unkindness of her relative; "since some unhappy destiny separates me from the protection of my father's sister, to whom I could so securely have resigned myself, I will neither apply for shelter to any more distant relation, nor accept of that which you, my lord, so generously offer; since my doing so might excite harsh, and, I am sure, undeserved reproaches, against her by whom I was driven to choose a less advisable dwelling-place. I have made my resolution. I have, it is true, only one friend left, but she is a powerful one, and is able to protect me against the particular evil fate which seems to follow me, as well as against the ordinary evils of human life."

"The Queen, I suppose?" said the Abbess, interrupting her impatiently.

"The Queen of Heaven! venerable kinswoman," answered Eveline; "our Lady of the Garde Doloureuse, ever gracious to our house, and so lately my especial guardian and protectress. Methinks, since the vowed votaress of the Virgin rejects me, it is to her holy patroness whom I ought to apply for succour."

The venerable dame, taken somewhat at unawares by this answer, pronounced the interjection "Umph!" in a tone better befitting a Lollard or an Iconoclast, than a Catholic Abbess, and a daughter of the House of Berenger. Truth is, the Lady Abbess's hereditary devotion to the Lady of the Garde Doloureuse was much decayed since she had known the full merits of another gifted image, the property of her own convent.

Recollecting herself, however, she remained silent, while the Constable alleged the vicinity of the Welsh, as what might possibly again render the abode of his betrothed bride at the Garde Doloureuse as perilous as she had on a former occasion found it. To this Eveline replied, by reminding him of the great strength of her native fortress—the various sieges which it had withstood—and the important circumstance, that, upon the late occasion, it was only endangered, because, in compliance with a point of honour, her father Raymond had sallied out with the garrison, and fought at disadvantage a battle under the walls. She farther suggested, that it was easy for the Constable to name, from among his own vassals or hers, a seneschal of such approved prudence and valour, as might ensure the safety of the place, and of its lady.

Ere De Lacy could reply to her arguments the Abbess rose, and, pleading her total inability to give counsel in secular affairs, and the rules of her order, which called her, as she said, with a heightened colour and raised voice, "to the simple and peaceful discharge of her conventual duties," she left the betrothed parties in the locutory, or parlour, without any company, save Rose, who prudently remained at some distance.

The issue of their private conference seemed agreeable to both; and when Eveline told Rose that they were to return presently to the Garde Doloureuse, under a sufficient escort, and were to remain there during the period of the Crusade, it was in a tone of heartfelt satisfaction, which her follower had not heard her make use of for many days. She spoke also highly in praise of the kind acquiescence of the Constable in her wishes, and of his whole conduct, with a warmth of gratitude approaching to a more tender feeling.

"And yet, my dearest lady," said Rose, "if you will speak unfeignedly, you must, I am convinced, allow that you look upon this interval of years, interposed betwixt your contract and your marriage, rather as a respite than in any other light."

"I confess it," said Eveline, "nor have I concealed from my future lord that such are my feelings, ungracious as they may seem. But it is my youth, Rose, my extreme youth, which makes me fear the duties of De Lacy's wife. Then those evil auguries hang strangely about me. Devoted to evil by one kinswoman, expelled almost from the roof of another, I seem to myself, at present, a creature who must carry distress with her, pass where she will. This evil hour, and, what is more, the apprehensions of it, will give way to time. When I shall have attained the age of twenty, Rose, I shall be a full-grown woman, with all the soul of a Berenger strong within me, to overcome those doubts and tremors which agitate the girl of seventeen."

"Ah! my sweet mistress," answered Rose, "may God and our Lady of the Garde Doloureuse guide all for the best!—But I would that this contract had not taken place, or, having taken place, that it could have been fulfilled by your immediate union."

Chapter the Twentieth.

The King call'd down his merry men all,
By one, and by two, and by three;
Earl Marshal was wont to be the foremost man,
But the hindmost man was he.
OLD BALLAD.

IF the Lady Eveline retired satisfied and pleased from her private interview with De Lacy, the joy on the part of the Constable rose to a higher pitch of rapture than he was in the habit of feeling or expressing; and it was augmented by a visit of the leeches who attended his nephew, from whom he received a minute and particular account of his present disorder, with every assurance of a speedy recovery.

The Constable caused alms to be distributed to the convents and to the poor, masses to be said, and tapers to be lighted. He visited the Archbishop, and received from him his full approbation of the course which he proposed to pursue, with the promise, that out of the plenary power which he held from the Pope, the Prelate was willing, in consideration of his instant obedience, to limit his stay in the Holy Land to the term of three years, to become current from his leaving Britain, and to include the space necessary for his return to his native country. Indeed, having succeeded in the main point, the Archbishop judged it wise to concede every inferior consideration to a person of the Constable's rank and character, whose good-will to the proposed expedition was perhaps as essential to its success as his bodily presence.

In short, the Constable returned to his pavilion highly satisfied with the manner in which he had extricated himself from those difficulties which in the morning seemed almost insuperable; and when his officers assembled to disrobe him, (for great feudal lords had their levees and couchees, in imitation of sovereign princes,) he distributed gratuities amongst them, and jested and laughed in a much gayer humour than they had ever before witnessed.

"For thee," he said, turning to Vidal the minstrel, who, sumptuously dressed, stood to pay his respects among the other attendants, "I will give thee nought at present; but do thou remain by my bedside until I am asleep, and I will next morning reward thy minstrelsy as I like it."

"My lord," said Vidal, "I am already rewarded, both by the honour, and by the liveries, which better befit a royal minstrel than one of my mean fame; but assign me a subject, and I will do my best, not out of greed of future largess, but gratitude for past favours."

"Gramercy, good fellow," said the Constable. "Guarine," he added, addressing his squire, "let the watch be posted, and do thou remain within the tent—stretch thyself on the bear-hide, and sleep, or listen to the minstrelsy, as thou likest best. Thou thinkest thyself a judge, I have heard, of such gear."

It was usual, in those insecure times, for some faithful domestic to sleep at night within the tent of every great baron, that, if danger arose, he might not be unsupported or unprotected. Guarine accordingly drew his sword, and, taking it in his hand, stretched himself on the ground in such a manner, that, on the slightest alarm, he could spring up, sword in hand. His broad black eyes, in which sleep contended with a desire to listen to the music, were fixed on Vidal, who saw them glittering in the reflection of the silver lamp, like those of a dragon or a basilisk.

After a few preliminary touches on the chords of his rote, the minstrel requested of the Constable to name the subject on which he desired the exercise of his powers.

"The truth of woman," answered Hugo de Lacy, as he laid his head upon his pillow.

After a short prelude, the minstrel obeyed, by singing nearly as follows:—

I.	II.
"Woman's faith, and woman's trust—	"I have strain'd the spider's thread
Write the characters in dust;	'Gainst the promise of a maid;
Stamp them on the running stream,	I have weigh'd a grain of sand
Print them on the moon's pale beam,	'Gainst her plight of heart and hand;
And each evanescent letter.	I told my true love of the token,
Shall be clearer, firmer, better,	How her faith proved light, and her word was broken
And more permanent. I ween,	Again her word and truth she plight,
Than the thing these letters mean.	And I believed them again ere night."

"How now, sir knave," said the Constable, raising himself on his elbow, "from what drunken rhymer did you learn that half-witted satire?"

"From an old, ragged, crossgrained friend of mine, called Experience," answered Vidal. "I pray Heaven, he may never take your lordship, or any other worthy man, under his tuition."

"Go to, fellow," said the Constable, in reply; "thou art one of those wiseacres, I warrant me, that would fain be thought witty, because thou canst make a jest of those things which wiser men hold worthy of most worship—the honour of men, and the truth of women. Dost thou call thyself a minstrel, and hast no tale of female fidelity?"

"I had right many a one, noble sir, but I laid them aside when I disused my practice of the jesting part of the Joyous Science. Nevertheless, if it pleases your nobleness to listen, I can sing you an established lay upon such a subject."

De Lacy made a sign of acquiescence, and laid himself as if to slumber; while Vidal began one of those interminable and almost innumerable adventures concerning that paragon of true lovers, fair Ysolte; and of the constant and uninterrupted faith and affection which she displayed in numerous situations of difficulty and peril, to her paramour, the gallant Sir Tristrem, at the expense of her less favoured husband, the luckless King Mark of Cornwall; to whom, as all the world knows, Sir Tristrem was nephew.

This was not the lay of love and fidelity which De Lacy would have chosen; but a feeling like shame prevented his interrupting it, perhaps because he was unwilling to yield to or acknowledge the unpleasing sensations excited by the tenor of the tale. He soon fell asleep, or feigned to do so; and the harper, continuing for a time his monotonous chant, began at length himself to feel the influence of slumber; his words, and the notes which he continued to touch upon the harp, were broken and interrupted, and seemed to escape drowsily from his fingers and voice. At length the sounds ceased entirely, and the minstrel seemed to have sunk into profound repose, with his head reclining on his breast, and one arm dropped down by his side, while the other rested on his harp. His slumber, however, was not very long, and when he awoke from it, and cast his eyes around him, reconnoitering, by the light of the night-lamp, whatever was in the tent, he felt a heavy hand, which pressed his shoulder as if gently to solicit his attention. At the same time the voice of the vigilant Philip Guarine whispered in his ear, "Thine office for the night is ended — depart to thine own quarters with all the silence thou mayst."

The minstrel wrapt himself in his cloak without reply, though perhaps not without feeling some resentment at a dismissal so unceremonious.

Chapter the Twenty-First.

Oh! then I see Queen Mab has been with you.
ROMEO AND JULIET.

THE subject on which the mind has last been engaged at night is apt to occupy our thoughts even during slumber, when Imagination, uncorrected by the organs of sense, weaves her own fantastic web out of whatever ideas rise at random in the sleeper. It is not surprising, therefore, that De Lacy in his dreams had some confused idea of being identified with the unlucky Mark of Cornwall; and that he awakened from such unpleasant visions with a brow more clouded than when he was preparing for his couch on the evening before. He was silent, and seemed lost in thought, while his squire assisted at his levee with the respect now only paid to sovereigns. "Guarine," at length he said, "know you the stout Fleming, who was said to have borne him so well at the siege of the Garde Doloureuse? — a tall, big, brawny man."

"Surely, my lord," answered his squire; "I know Wilkin Flammock—I saw him but yesterday."

"Indeed!" replied the Constable — "Here, meanest thou? — In this city of Gloucester?"

"Assuredly, my good lord. He came hither partly about his merchandise, partly, I think, to see his daughter Rose, who is in attendance on the gracious young Lady Eveline."

"He is a stout soldier, is he not?"

"Like most of his kind—a rampart to a castle, but rubbish in the field," said the Norman squire.

"Faithful, also, is he not?" continued the Constable.

"Faithful as most Flemings, while you can pay for their faith," replied Guarine, wondering a little at the unusual interest taken in one whom he esteemed a being of an inferior order; when, after some farther inquiries, the Constable ordered the Fleming's attendance to be presently commanded.

Other business of the morning now occurred, (for his speedy departure required many arrangements to be hastily adopted,) when, as the Constable was giving audience to several officers of his troops, the bulky figure of Wilkin Flammock was seen at the entrance of the pavilion, in jerkin of white cloth, and having only a knife by his side.

"Leave the tent, my masters," said De Lacy, "but continue in attendance in the neighbourhood; for here comes one I must speak to in private."

The officers withdrew, and the Constable and Fleming were left alone "You are Wilkin Flammock, who fought well against the Welsh at the Garde Doloureuse?"

"I did my best, my lord," answered Wilkin — "I was bound to it by my bargain; and I hope ever to act like a man of credit."

"Methinks," said the Constable, "that you, so stout of limb, and, as I hear, so bold in spirit, might look a little higher than this weaving trade of thine."

"No one is reluctant to mend his station, my lord," said Wilkin; "yet I am so far from complaining of mine, that I would willingly consent it should never be better, on condition I could be assured it were never worse."

"Nay, but, Flammock," said the Constable, "I mean higher things for you than your modesty apprehends — I mean to leave thee in a charge of great trust."

"Let it concern bales of drapery, my lord, and no one will perform it better," said the Fleming.

"Away! thou art too lowly minded," said the Constable. "What think'st thou of being dubbed knight, as thy valour well deserves, and left as Chattelain of the Garde Doloureuse?"

"For the knighthood, my lord, I should crave your forgiveness; for it would sit on me like a gilded helmet on a hog. For any charge, whether of castle or cottage, I trust I might discharge it as well as another."

"I fear me thy rank must be in some way mended," said the Constable, surveying the unmilitary dress of the figure before him; "it is at present too mean to befit the protector and guardian of a young lady of high birth and rank."

"I the guardian of a young lady of birth and rank!" said Flammock, his light large eyes turning larger, lighter, and rounder as he spoke.

"Even thou," said the Constable. "The Lady Eveline proposes to take up her residence in her castle of the Garde Doloureuse. I have been casting about to whom I may intrust the keeping of her person as well as of the stronghold. Were I to choose some knight of name, as I have many in my household, he would be setting about to do deeds of vassalage upon the Welsh, and engaging himself in turmoils, which would render the safety of the castle precarious; or he would be absent on feats of chivalry, tournaments, and hunting parties; or he would, perchance, have shows of that light nature under the walls, or even within the courts of the castle, turning the secluded and quiet abode, which becomes the situation of the Lady Eveline, into the misrule of a dissolute revel.—Thee I can confide in—thou wilt fight when it is requisite, yet wilt not provoke danger for the sake of danger itself — thy birth, thy habits, will lead thee to avoid those gaieties, which, however fascinating to others, cannot but be distasteful to thee—thy management will be as regular, as I will take care that it shall be honourable; and thy relation to her favourite, Rose, will render thy guardianship more agreeable to the Lady Eveline, than, perchance, one of her own rank —And, to speak to thee a language which thy nation readily comprehends, the reward, Fleming, for the regular discharge of this most weighty trust, shall be beyond thy most flattering hope."

The Fleming had listened to the first part of this discourse with an expression of surprise, which gradually gave way to one of deep and anxious reflection. He gazed fixedly on the earth for a minute after the Constable had ceased speaking, and then raising up his eyes suddenly, said, "It is needless to seek for round-about excuses. This cannot be your earnest, my lord — but if it is, the scheme is naught."

"How and wherefore?" asked the Constable, with displeased surprise.

"Another man may grasp at your bounty," continued Wilkin, "and leave you to take chance of the value you were to receive for it; but I am a downright dealer, I will not take payment for service I cannot render."

"But I demand, once more, wherefore thou canst not, or rather wilt not, accept this trust?" said the Constable. "Surely, if I am willing to confer such confidence, it is well thy part to answer it."

"True, my lord," said the Fleming; "but methinks the noble Lord de Lacy should feel, and the wise Lord de Lacy should foresee, that a Flemish weaver is no fitting guardian for his plighted bride. Think her shut up in yonder solitary castle, under such respectable protection, and reflect how long the place will be solitary in this land of love and of adventure! We shall have minstrels singing ballads by the threave under our windows, and such twangling of harps as would be enough to frighten our walls from their foundations, as clerks say happened to those of Jericho — We shall have as many knights-errant around us as ever had Charlemagne, or King Arthur. Mercy on me! A less matter than a fine and noble recluse immured — so will they term it — in a tower, under the guardianship of an old Flemish weaver, would bring half the chivalry in England round us, to break lances, vow vows, display love-liveries, and I know not what follies besides.—Think you such gallants, with the blood flying through their veins like quicksilver, would much mind my bidding them begone?"

"Draw bolts, up with the drawbridge, drop portcullis," said the Constable, with a constrained smile.

"And thinks your lordship such gallants would mind these impediments? such are the very essence of the adventures which they come to seek. — The Knight of the Swan would swim through the moat — he of the Eagle would fly over the walls — he of the Thunderbolt would burst open the gates."

"Ply crossbow and mangonel," said de Lacy.

"And be besieged in form," said the Fleming, "like the Castle of Tintadgel in the old hangings, all for the love of fair lady? — And then those gay dames and demoiselles, who go upon adventure from castle to castle, from tournament to tournament, with bare bosoms, flaunting plumes, poniards at their sides, and javelins in their hands, chattering like magpies, and fluttering like jays, and, ever and anon, cooing like doves — how am I to exclude such from the Lady Eveline's privacy?"

"By keeping doors shut, I tell thee," answered the Constable, still in the same tone of forced jocularity; "a wooden bar will be thy warrant."

"Ay, but," answered Flammock, "if the Flemish weaver say shut, when the Norman young lady says open, think which has best chance of being obeyed. At a word, my lord, for the matter of guardianship, and such like, I wash my hands of it — I would not undertake to be guardian to the chaste Susannah, though she lived in an enchanted castle, which no living thing could approach."

"Thou holdest the language and thoughts," said De Lacy, "of a vulgar debauchee, who laughs at female constancy, because he has lived only with the most worthless of the sex. Yet thou shouldst know the contrary, having, as I know, a most virtuous daughter——"

"Whose mother was not less so," said Wilkin, breaking in upon the Constable's speech with somewhat more emotion than he usually displayed. "But law, my lord, gave me authority to govern and direct my wife, as both law and nature give me power and charge over my daughter. That which I can govern, I can be answerable for; but how to discharge me so well of a delegated trust, is another question.—Stay at home, my good lord," continued the honest Fleming, observing that his speech made some impression upon De Lacy; "let a fool's advice for once be of avail to change a wise man's purpose, taken, let me say, in no wise hour. Remain in your own land, rule your own vassals, and protect your own bride. You only can claim her cheerful love and ready obedience; and sure I am, that, without pretending to guess what she may do if separated from you, she will, under your own eye, do the duty of a faithful and a loving spouse."

"And the Holy Sepulchre?" said the Constable, with a sigh, his heart confessing the wisdom of the advice, which circumstances prevented him from following.

"Let those who lost the Holy Sepulchre regain it, my lord," replied Flammock. "If those Latins and Greeks, as they call them, are no better men than I have heard, it signifies very little whether they or the heathen have the country that has cost Europe so much blood and treasure."

"In good faith," said the Constable, "there is sense in what thou say'st; but I caution thee to repeat it not, lest thou be taken for a heretic or a Jew. For me, my word and oath are pledged beyond retreat, and I have only to consider whom I may best name for that important station, which thy caution has — not without some shadow of reason — induced thee to decline."

"There is no man to whom your lordship can so naturally or honourably transfer such a charge," said Wilkin Flammock, "as to the kinsman near to you, and possessed of your trust; yet much better would it be were there no such trust to be reposed in any one."

"If," said the Constable, "by my near kinsman, you mean Randal de Lacy, I care not if I tell you, that I consider him as totally worthless, and undeserving of honourable confidence."

"Nay, I mean another," said Flammock, "nearer to you by blood, and, unless I greatly mistake, much nigher also in affection—I had in mind your lordship's nephew, Damian de Lacy."

The Constable started as if a wasp had stung him; but instantly replied, with forced composure, "Damian was to have gone in my stead to Palestine — it now seems I must go in his; for, since this last illness, the leeches have totally changed their minds, and consider that warmth of the climate as dangerous, which they formerly decided to be salutary. But our learned doctors, like our learned priests, must ever be in the right, change their counsels as they may; and we poor laymen still in the wrong. I can, it is true, rely on Damian with the utmost confidence; but he is young, Flammock—very young — and in that particular, resembles but too nearly the party who might be otherwise committed to his charge."

"Then once more, my lord," said the plain-spoken Fleming, "remain at home, and be yourself the protector of what is naturally so dear to you."

"Once more, I repeat, that I cannot," answered the Constable. "The step which I have adopted as a great duty, may perhaps be a great error — I only know that it is irretrievable."

"Trust your nephew, then, my lord," replied Wilkin—"he is honest and true; and it is better trusting young lions than old wolves. He may err, perhaps, but it will not be from premeditated treachery."

"Thou art right, Flammock," said the Constable; "and perhaps I ought to wish I had sooner asked thy counsel, blunt as it is. But let what has passed be a secret betwixt us; and bethink thee of something that may advantage thee more than the privilege of speaking about my affairs."

"That account will be easily settled, my lord," replied Flammock; "for my object was to ask your lordship's favour to obtain certain extensions of our privileges, in yonder wild corner where we Flemings have made our retreat."

"Thou shalt have them, so they be not exorbitant," said the Constable. And the honest Fleming, among whose good qualities scrupulous delicacy was not the foremost, hastened to detail, with great minuteness, the particulars of his request or petition, long pursued in vain, but to which this interview was the means of insuring success.

The Constable, eager to execute the resolution which he had formed, hastened to the lodging of Damian de Lacy, and to the no small astonishment of his nephew, intimated to him his change of destination; alleging his own hurried departure, Damian's late and present illness, together with the necessary protection to be afforded to the Lady Eveline, as reasons why his nephew must needs remain behind him — to represent him during his absence — to protect the family rights, and assert the family honour of the house of De Lacy—above all, to act as the guardian of the young and beautiful bride, whom his uncle and patron had been in some measure compelled to abandon for a time.

Damian yet occupied his bed while the Constable communicated this change of purpose. Perhaps he might think the circumstance fortunate, that in this position he could conceal from his uncle's observation the various emotions which he could not help feeling; while the Constable, with the eagerness of one who is desirous of hastily finishing what he has to say on an unpleasant subject, hurried over an account of the arrangements which he had made, in order that his nephew might have the means of discharging, with sufficient effect, the important trust committed to him.

The youth listened as to a voice in a dream, which he had not the power of interrupting, though there was something within him which whispered there would be both prudence and integrity in remonstrating against his uncle's alteration of plan. Something he accordingly attempted to say, when the Constable at length paused; but it was too feebly spoken to shake a resolution fully though hastily adopted and explicitly announced, by one not in the use to speak before his purpose was fixed, or to alter it when it was declared.

The remonstrance of Damian, besides, if it could be termed such, was spoken in terms too contradictory to be intelligible. In one moment he professed his regret for the laurels which he had hoped to gather in Palestine, and implored his uncle not to alter his purpose, but permit him to attend his banner thither; and in the next sentence, he professed his readiness to defend the safety of Lady Eveline with the last drop of his blood. De Lacy saw nothing inconsistent in these feelings, though they were for the moment contradictory to each other. It was natural, he thought, that a young knight should be desirous to win honour — natural also that he should willingly assume a charge so honourable and important as that with which he proposed to invest him; and therefore he thought that it was no wonder that, assuming his new office willingly, the young man should yet feel regret at losing the prospect of honourable adventure, which he must abandon. He therefore only smiled in reply to the broken expostulations of his nephew; and, having confirmed his former arrangement, left the young man to reflect at leisure on his change of destination, while he himself, in a second visit to the Benedictine Abbey, communicated the purpose which he had adopted, to the Abbess, and to his bride-elect.

The displeasure of the former lady was in no measure abated by this communication; in which, indeed, she affected to take very little interest. She pleaded her religious duties, and her want of knowledge of secular affairs, if she should chance to mistake the usages of the world; yet she had always, she said, understood, that the guardians of the young and beautiful of her own sex were chosen from the more mature of the other.

"Your own unkindness, lady," answered the Constable, "leaves me no better choice than I have made. Since the Lady Eveline's nearest friends deny her the privilege of their roof, on account of the claim with which she has honoured me, I, on my side, were worse than ungrateful did I not secure for her the protection of my nearest male heir. Damian is young, but he is true and honourable; nor does the chivalry of England afford me a better choice."

Eveline seemed surprised, and even struck with consternation, at the resolution which her bridegroom thus suddenly announced; and perhaps it was fortunate that the remark of the Lady Abbess made the answer of the Constable necessary, and prevented him from observing that her colour shifted more than once from pale to deep red.

Rose, who was not excluded from the conference, drew close up to her mistress; and, by affecting to adjust her veil, while in secret she strongly pressed her hand, gave her time and encouragement to compose her mind for a reply. It was brief and decisive, and announced with a firmness which showed that the uncertainty of the moment had passed away or been suppressed. "In case of danger," she said, "she would not fail to apply to Damian de Lacy to come to her aid, as he had once done before; but she did not apprehend any danger at present, within her own secure castle of the Garde Doloureuse, where it was her purpose to dwell, attended only by her own household. She was resolved," she continued, "in consideration of her peculiar condition, to observe the strictest retirement, which she expected would not be violated even by the noble young knight who was to act as her guardian, unless some apprehension for her safety made his visit unavoidable."

The Abbess acquiesced, though coldly, in a proposal, which her ideas of decorum recommended; and preparations were hastily made for the Lady Eveline's return to the castle of her father. Two interviews which intervened before her leaving the convent, were in their nature painful. The first was when Damian was formally presented to her by his uncle, as the delegate to whom he had committed the charge of his own property, and, which was much dearer to him, as he affirmed, the protection of her person and interest.

Eveline scarce trusted herself with one glance; but that single look comprehended and reported to her the ravage which disease, aided by secret grief, had made on the manly form and handsome countenance of the youth before her. She received his salutation in a manner as embarrassed as that in which it was made; and, to his hesitating proffer of service, answered, that she trusted only to be obliged to him for his good-will during the interval of his uncle's absence.

Her parting with the Constable was the next trial which she was to undergo. It was not without emotion, although she preserved her modest composure, and De Lacy his calm gravity of deportment. His voice faltered, however, when he came to announce, "that it were unjust she should be bound by the engagement which she had been graciously contented to abide under. Three years he had assigned for its term; to which space the Archbishop Baldwin had consented to shorten the period of his absence. If I appear not when these are elapsed," he said, "let the Lady Eveline conclude that the grave holds De Lacy, and seek out for her mate some happier man. She cannot find one more grateful, though there are many who better deserve her."

On these terms they parted; and the Constable, speedily afterwards embarking, ploughed the narrow seas for the shores of Flanders, where he proposed to unite his forces with the Count of that rich and warlike country, who had lately taken the Cross, and to proceed by the route which should be found most practicable on their destination for the Holy Land. The broad pennon, with the arms of the Lacys, streamed forward with a favourable wind from the prow of the vessel, as if pointing to the quarter of the horizon where its renown was to be augmented; and, considering the fame of the leader, and the excellence of the soldiers who followed him, a more gallant band, in proportion to their numbers, never went to avenge on the Saracens the evils endured by the Latins of Palestine.

Meanwhile Eveline, after a cold parting with the Abbess, whose offended dignity had not yet forgiven the slight regard which she had paid to her opinion, resumed her journey homeward to her paternal castle, where her household was to be arranged in a manner suggested by the Constable, and approved of by herself.

The same preparations were made for her accommodation at every halting place which she had experienced upon her journey to Gloucester, and, as before, the purveyor was invisible, although she could be at little loss to guess his name. Yet it appeared as if the character of these preparations was in some degree altered. All the realities of convenience and accommodation, with the most perfect assurances of safety, accompanied her every where on the route; but they were no longer mingled with that display of tender gallantry and taste, which marked that the attentions were paid to a young and beautiful female. The clearest fountain-head, and the most shady grove, were no longer selected for the noontide repast; but the house of some franklin, or a small abbey, afforded the necessary hospitality. All seemed to be ordered with the most severe attention to rank and decorum— it seemed as if a nun of some strict order, rather than a young maiden of high quality and a rich inheritance, had been journeying through the land, and Eveline, though pleased with the delicacy which seemed thus to respect her unprotected and peculiar condition, would sometimes think it unnecessary, that, by so many indirect hints, it should be forced on her recollection.

She thought it strange also, that Damian, to whose care she had been so solemnly committed, did not even pay his respects to her on the road. Something there was which whispered to her, that close and frequent intercourse might be unbecoming—even dangerous; but surely the ordinary duties of a knight and gentleman enjoined him some personal communication with the maiden under his escort, were it only to ask if her accommodations had been made to her satisfaction, or if she had any special wish which was ungratified. The only intercourse, however, which took place betwixt them, was through means of Amelot, Damian de Lacy's youthful page, who came at morning and evening to receive Eveline's commands concerning their route, and the hours of journey and repose.

These formalities rendered the solitude of Eveline's return less endurable; and had it not been for the society of Rose, she would have found herself under an intolerably irksome degree of constraint. She even hazarded to her attendant some remarks upon the singularity of De Lacy's conduct, who, authorized as he was by his situation, seemed yet as much afraid to approach her as if she had been a basilisk.

Rose let the first observation of this nature pass as if it had been unheard; but when her mistress made a second remark to the same purpose, she answered, with the truth and freedom of her character, though perhaps with less of her usual prudence, "Damian de Lacy judges well, noble lady. He to whom the safe keeping of a royal treasure is intrusted, should not indulge himself too often by gazing upon it."

Eveline blushed, wrapt herself closer in her veil, nor did she again during their journey mention the name of Damian de Lacy.

When the gray turrets of the Garde Doloureuse greeted her sight on the evening of the second day, and she once more beheld her father's banner floating from its highest watch-tower in honour of her approach, her sensations were mingled with pain; but, upon the whole, she looked towards that ancient home as a place of refuge, where she might indulge the new train of thoughts which circumstances had opened to her, amid the same scenes which had sheltered her infancy and childhood.

She pressed forward her palfrey, to reach the ancient portal as soon as possible, bowed hastily to the well-known faces which showed themselves on all sides, but spoke to no one, until, dismounting at the chapel door, she had penetrated to the crypt, in which was preserved the miraculous painting. There, prostrate on the ground, she implored the guidance and protection of the Holy Virgin through those intricacies in which she had involved herself, by the fulfilment of the vow which she had made in her anguish before the same shrine. If the prayer was misdirected, its purport was virtuous and sincere; nor are we disposed to doubt that it attained that Heaven towards which it was devoutly addressed.

Chapter the Twenty-Second.

The Virgin's image falls—yet some, I ween,
Not unforgiven the suppliant knee might bend,
As to a visible power, in which might blend
All that was mix'd, and reconciled in her,
Of mother's love, with maiden's purity,
Of high with low, celestial with terrene.

WORDSWORTH.

THE household of the Lady Eveline, though of an establishment becoming her present and future rank, was of a solemn and sequestered character, corresponding to her place of residence, and the privacy connected with her situation, retired as she was from the class of maidens who are yet unengaged, and yet not united with that of matrons, who enjoy the protection of a married name. Her immediate female attendants, with whom the reader is already acquainted, constituted almost her whole society. The garrison of the castle, besides household servants, consisted of veterans of tried faith, the followers of Berenger and of De Lacy in many a bloody field, to whom the duties of watching and warding were as familiar as any of their more ordinary occupations, and whose courage, nevertheless, tempered by age and experience, was not likely to engage in any rash adventure or accidental quarrel. Those men maintained a constant and watchful guard, commanded by the steward, but under the eye of Father Aldrovand, who, besides discharging his ecclesiastical functions, was at times pleased to show some sparkles of his ancient military education.

Whilst this garrison afforded security against any sudden attempt on the part of the Welsh to surprise the castle, a strong body of forces were disposed within a few miles of the Garde Doloureuse, ready, on the least alarm, to advance to defend the place against any more numerous body of invaders, who, undeterred by the fate of Gwenwyn, might have the hardihood to form a regular siege. To this band, which, under the eye of Damian de Lacy himself, was kept in constant readiness for action, could be added on occasion all the military force of the Marches, comprising numerous bodies of Flemings, and other foreigners, who held their establishments by military tenure.

While the fortress was thus secure from hostile violence, the life of its inmates was so unvaried and simple, as might have excused youth and beauty for wishing for variety, even at the expense of some danger. The labours of the needle were only relieved by a walk round the battlements, where Eveline, as she passed arm in arm with Rose, received a military salute from each sentinel in turn, or in the court-yard, where the caps and bonnets of the domestics paid her the same respect which she received above from the pikes and javelins of the warders. Did they wish to extend their airing beyond the castle gate, it was not sufficient that doors and bridges were to be opened and lowered; there was, besides, an escort to get under arms, who, on foot or horseback as the case might require, attended for the security of the Lady Eveline's person. Without this military attendance they could not in safety move even so far as the mills, where honest Wilkin Flammock, his warlike deeds forgotten, was occupied with his mechanical labours. But if a farther disport was intended, and the Lady of the Garde Doloureuse proposed to hunt or hawk for a few hours, her safety was not confided to a guard so feeble as the garrison of the castle might afford. It was necessary that Raoul should announce her purpose to Damian by a special messenger despatched the evening before, that there might be time before daybreak to scour, with a body of light cavalry, the region in which she intended to take her pleasure; and sentinels were placed in all suspicious places while she continued in the field. In truth, she tried, upon one or two occasions, to make an excursion, without any formal annunciation of her intention; but all her purposes seemed to be known to Damian as soon as they were formed, and she was no sooner abroad than parties of archers and spearmen from his camp were seen scouring the valleys, and guarding the mountain-pass, and Damian's own plume was usually beheld conspicuous among the distant soldiers.

The formality of these preparations so much allayed the pleasure derived from the sport, that Eveline seldom resorted to amusement which was attended with such bustle, and put in motion so many persons.

The day being worn out as it best might, in the evening Father Aldrovand was wont to read out of some holy legend, or from the homilies of some departed saint, such passages as he deemed fit for the hearing of his little congregation. Sometimes also he read and expounded a chapter of the Holy Scripture; but in such cases, the good man's attention was so strangely turned to the military part of the Jewish history, that he was never able to quit the books of Judges and of Kings, together with the triumphs of Judas Maccabeus; although the manner in which he illustrated the victories of the children of Israel was much more amusing to himself than edifying to his female audience.

Sometimes, but rarely, Rose obtained permission for a strolling minstrel to entertain an hour with his ditty of love and chivalry; sometimes a pilgrim from a distant shrine, repaid by long tales of the wonders which he had seen in other lands, the hospitality which the Garde Doloureuse afforded; and sometimes also it happened, that the interest and intercession of the tiring-woman obtained admission for travelling merchants, or pedlars, who, at the risk of their lives, found profit by carrying from castle to castle the materials of rich dresses and female ornaments.

The usual visits of mendicants, of jugglers, of travelling jesters, are not to be forgotten in this list of amusements; and though his nation subjected him to close watch and observation, even the Welsh bard, with his huge harp strung with horse-hair, was sometimes admitted to vary the uniformity of their secluded life. But, saving such amusements, and saving also the regular attendance upon the religious duties at the chapel, it was impossible for life to glide away in more wearisome monotony than at the castle of the Garde Doloureuse. Since the death of its brave owner, to whom feasting and hospitality seemed as natural as thoughts of honour and deeds of chivalry, the gloom of a convent might be said to have enveloped the ancient mansion of Raymond Berenger, were it not that the presence of so many armed warders, stalking in solemn state on the battlements, gave it rather the aspect of a state-prison; and the temper of the inhabitants gradually became infected by the character of their dwelling.

The spirits of Eveline in particular felt a depression, which her naturally lively temper was quite inadequate to resist; and as her ruminations became graver, had caught that calm and contemplative manner, which is so often united with an ardent and enthusiastical temperament. She meditated deeply upon the former accidents of her life; nor can it be wondered that her thoughts repeatedly wandered back to the two several periods on which she had witnessed, or supposed that she had witnessed, a supernatural appearance. Then it was that it often seemed to her, as if a good and evil power strove for mastery over her destiny.

Solitude is favourable to feelings of self-importance; and it is when alone, and occupied only with their own thoughts, that fanatics have reveries, and imagined saints lose themselves in imaginary ecstasies. With Eveline the influence of enthusiasm went not such a length, yet it seemed to her as if in the vision of the night she saw sometimes the aspect of the Lady of the Garde Doloureuse, bending upon her glances of pity, comfort, and protection; sometimes the ominous form of the Saxon castle of Baldringham, holding up the bloody hand as witness of the injuries with which she had been treated while in life, and menacing with revenge the descendant of her murderer.

On awaking from such dreams, Eveline would reflect that she was the last branch of her house — a house to which the tutelage and protection of the miraculous Image, and the enmity and evil influence of the revengeful Vanda, had been peculiarly attached for ages. It seemed to her as if she were the prize, for the disposal of which the benign saint and vindictive fiend were now to play their last and keenest game.

Thus thinking, and experiencing little interruption of her meditations from any external circumstance of interest and amusement, she became pensive, absent, wrapt herself up in contemplations which withdrew her attention from the conversation around her, and walked in the world of reality like one who is still in a dream. When she thought of her engagement with the Constable of Chester, it was with resignation, but without a wish, and almost without an expectation, that she would be called upon to fulfil it. She had accomplished her vow by accepting the faith of her deliverer in exchange for her own; and although she held herself willing to redeem the pledge — nay, would scarce confess to herself the reluctance with which she thought of doing so — yet it is certain that she entertained unavowed hopes that Our Lady of the Garde Doloureuse would not be a severe creditor; but, satisfied with the readiness she had shown to accomplish her vow, would not insist upon her claim in its full rigour. It would have been the blackest ingratitude, to have wished that her gallant deliverer, whom she had so much cause to pray for, should experience any of those fatalities which in the Holy Land so often changed the laurel-wreath into cypress; but other accidents chanced, when men had been long abroad, to alter those purposes with which they had left home.

A strolling minstrel, who sought the Garde Doloureuse, had recited, for the amusement of the lady and household, the celebrated lay of the Count of Gleichen, who, already married in his own country, laid himself under so many obligations in the East to a Saracen princess, through whose means he achieved his freedom, that he married her also. The Pope and his conclave were pleased to approve of the double wedlock, in a case so extraordinary; and the good Count of Gleichen shared his nuptial bed between two wives of equal rank, and now sleeps between them under the same monument.

The commentaries of the inmates of the castle had been various and discrepant upon this legend. Father Aldrovand considered it as altogether false, and an unworthy calumny on the head of the church, in affirming his Holiness would countenance such irregularity. Old Margery, with the tender-heartedness of an ancient nurse, wept bitterly for pity during the tale, and, never questioning either the power of the Pope or the propriety of his decision, was pleased that a mode of extrication was found for a complication of love distresses which seemed almost inextricable. Dame Gillian declared it unreasonable, that, since a woman was only allowed one husband, a man should, under any circumstances, be permitted to have two wives; while Raoul, glancing towards her a look of verjuice, pitied the deplorable idiocy of the man who could be fool enough to avail himself of such a privilege.

"Peace, all the rest of you," said the Lady Eveline; "and do you, my dear Rose, tell me your judgment upon the Count of Gleichen and his two wives."

Rose blushed, and replied, "She was not much accustomed to think of such matters; but that, in her apprehension, the wife who could be contented with but one half of her husband's affections, had never deserved to engage the slightest share of them."

THE EARL OF LEICESTER CONFESSING HIS MARRIAGE.

"Thou art partly right, Rose," said Eveline; "and methinks the European lady, when she found herself outshone by the young and beautiful foreign princess, would have best consulted her own dignity in resigning the place, and giving the Holy Father no more trouble than in annulling the marriage, as has been done in cases of more frequent occurrence."

This she said with an air of indifference and even gaiety, which intimated to her faithful attendant with how little effort she herself could have made such a sacrifice, and served to indicate the state of her affections towards the Constable. But there was another than the Constable on whom her thoughts turned more frequently, though involuntarily, than perhaps in prudence they should have done.

The recollections of Damian de Lacy had not been erased from Eveline's mind. They were, indeed, renewed by hearing his name so often mentioned, and by knowing that he was almost constantly in the neighbourhood, with his whole attention fixed upon her convenience, interest, and safety; whilst, on the other hand, so far from waiting on her in person, he never even attempted, by a direct communication with herself, to consult her pleasure, even upon what most concerned her.

The messages conveyed by Father Aldrovand, or by Rose, to Amelot, Damian's page, while they gave an air of formality to their intercourse, which Eveline thought unnecessary, and even unkind, yet served to fix her attention upon the connection between them, and to keep it ever present to her memory. The remark by which Rose had vindicated the distance observed by her youthful guardian, sometimes arose to her recollection; and while her soul repelled with scorn the suspicion, that, in any case, his presence, whether at intervals or constantly, could be prejudicial to his uncle's interest, she conjured up various arguments for giving him a frequent place in her memory.—Was it not her duty to think of Damian often and kindly, as the Constable's nearest, best beloved, and most trusted relative?—Was he not her former deliverer and her present guardian?—And might he not be considered as an instrument specially employed by her divine patroness, in rendering effectual the protection with which she had graced her in more than one emergency?

Eveline's mind mutinied against the restrictions which were laid on their intercourse, as against something which inferred suspicion and degradation, like the compelled seclusion to which she had heard the Paynim infidels of the East subjected their females. Why should she see her guardian only in the benefits which he conferred upon her, and the cares he took for her safety, and bear his sentiments only by the mouth of others, as if one of them had been infected with the plague, or some other fatal or infectious disorder, which might render their meeting dangerous to the other?—And if they did meet occasionally, what else could be the consequence, save that the care of a brother towards a sister — of a trusty and kind guardian to the betrothed bride of his near relative and honoured patron, might render the melancholy seclusion of the Garde Doloureuse more easy to be endured by one so young in years, and, though dejected by present circumstances, naturally so gay in temper?

Yet, though this train of reasoning appeared to Eveline, when tracing it in her own mind, so conclusive, that she several times resolved to communicate her view of the case to Rose Flammock, it so chanced that, whenever she looked on the calm steady blue eye of the Flemish maiden, and remembered that her unblemished faith was mixed with a sincerity and plain dealing proof against every consideration, she feared lest she might be subjected in the opinion of her attendant to suspicions from which her own mind freed her; and her proud Norman spirit revolted at the idea of being obliged to justify herself to another, when she stood self-acquitted to her own mind. "Let things be as they are," she said; "and let us endure all the weariness of a life which might be so easily rendered more cheerful, rather than that

2 L

this zealous but punctilious friend should, in the strictness and nicety of her feelings on my account, conceive me capable of encouraging an intercourse which could lead to a less worthy thought of me in the mind of the most scrupulous of man — or of womankind." But even this vacillation of opinion and resolution tended to bring the image of the handsome young Damian more frequently before the Lady Eveline's fancy, than perhaps his uncle, had he known it, would altogether have approved of. In such reflections, however, she never indulged long, ere a sense of the singular destiny which had hitherto attended her, led her back into the more melancholy contemplations from which the buoyancy of her youthful fancy had for a short time emancipated her.

Chapter the Twenty-Third.

—— Ours is the skie,
Where at what fowl we please our hawk shall flie.
RANDOLPH.

ONE bright September morning, old Raoul was busy in the mews where he kept his hawks, grumbling all the while to himself as he surveyed the condition of each bird, and blaming alternately the carelessness of the under-falconer, and the situation of the building, and the weather, and the wind, and all things around him, for the dilapidation which time and disease had made in the neglected hawking establishment of the Garde Doloureuse. While in these unpleasing meditations, he was surprised by the voice of his beloved Dame Gillian, who seldom was an early riser, and yet more rarely visited him when he was in his sphere of peculiar authority. "Raoul, Raoul! where art thou, man? — Ever to seek for, when thou canst make aught of advantage for thyself or me!"

"And what want'st thou, dame?" said Raoul, "what means thy screaming worse than the seagull before wet weather? A murrain on thy voice! it is enough to fray every hawk from the perch."

"Hawk!" answered Dame Gillian; "it is time to be looking for hawks, when here is a cast of the bravest falcons come hither for sale, that ever flew by lake, brook, or meadow!"

"Kites! like her that brings the news," said Raoul.

"No, nor kestrils like him that hears it," replied Gillian; "but brave jerfalcons, with large nares, strongly armed, and beaks short and something bluish ——"

"Pshaw, with thy jargon! — Where came they from?" said Raoul, interested in the tidings, but unwilling to give his wife the satisfaction of seeing that he was so.

"From the Isle of Man," replied Gillian.

"They must be good, then, though it was a woman brought tidings of them," said Raoul, smiling grimly at his own wit; then, leaving the mews, he demanded to know where this famous falcon-merchant was to be met withal.

"Why, between the barriers and the inner gate," replied Gillian, "where other men are admitted that have wares to utter — Where should he be?"

"And who let him in?" demanded the suspicious Raoul.

"Why, Master Steward, thou owl!" said Gillian; "he came but now to my chamber, and sent me hither to call you."

"Oh, the steward — the steward — I might have guessed as much. And he came to thy chamber, doubtless, because he could not have as easily come hither to me himself.—Was it not so, sweetheart?"

"I do not know why he chose to come to me rather than to you, Raoul," said Gillian; "and if I did know, perhaps I would not tell you. Go to — miss your bargain, or make your bargain, I care not which — the man will not wait for you — he has good proffers from the Seneschal of Malpas, and the Welsh Lord of Dinevawr."

"I come — I come," said Raoul, who felt the necessity of embracing this opportunity of improving his hawking establishment, and hastened to the gate, where he met the merchant, attended by a servant, who kept in separate cages the three falcons which he offered for sale.

The first glance satisfied Raoul that they were of the best breed in Europe, and that, if their education were in correspondence to their race, there could scarce be a more valuable addition even to a royal mews. The merchant did not fail to enlarge upon all their points of excellence; the breadth of their shoulders, the strength of their train, their full and fierce dark eyes, the boldness with which they endured the approach of strangers, and the lively spirit and vigour with which they pruned their plumes, and shook, or, as it was technically termed, roused themselves. He expatiated on the difficulty and danger with which they were obtained from the rock of Ramsey, on which they were bred, and which was an eyry unrivalled even on the coast of Norway.

Raoul turned apparently a deaf ear to all these commendations. "Friend merchant," said he, "I know a falcon as well as thou dost, and I will not deny that thine are fine ones; but if they be not carefully trained and reclaimed, I would rather have a goss-hawk on my perch than the fairest falcon that ever stretched wing to weather."

"I grant ye," said the merchant; "but if we agree on the price, for that is the main matter, thou shalt see the birds fly if thou wilt, and then buy them or not as thou likest. I am no true merchant if thou ever saw'st birds beat them, whether at the mount or the stoop."

"That I call fair," said Raoul, "if the price be equally so."

"It shall be corresponding," said the hawk-merchant; "for I have brought six casts from the island, by the good favour of good King Reginald of Man, and I have sold every feather of them, save these; and so, having emptied my cages and filled my purse, I desire not to be troubled longer with the residue: and if a good fellow and a judge, as thou seemest to be, should like the hawks when he has seen them fly, he shall have the price of his own making."

"Go to," said Raoul, "we will have no blind bargains; my lady, if the hawks be suitable, is more able to pay for them than thou to give them away. Will a bezant be a conformable price for the cast?"

"A bezant, Master Falconer!—By my faith, you are no bold bodesman! nevertheless, double your offer, and I will consider it."

"If the hawks are well reclaimed," said Raoul, "I will give you a bezant and a half; but I will see them strike a heron ere I will be so rash as to deal with you."

"It is well," said the merchant, "and I had better take your offer than be longer cumbered with them; for were I to carry them into Wales, I might get paid in a worse fashion by some of their long knives. — Will you to horse presently?"

"Assuredly," said Raoul; "and, though March be the fitter month for hawking at the heron, yet I will show you one of these frogpeckers for the trouble of riding the matter of a mile by the water-side."

"Content, Sir Falconer," said the merchant. "But are we to go alone, or is there no lord or lady in the castle who would take pleasure to see a piece of game gallantly struck? I am not afraid to show these hawks to a countess."

"My lady used to love the sport well enough," said Raoul; "but, I wot not why, she is moped and mazed ever since her father's death, and lives in her fair castle like a nun in a cloister, without disport or revelry of any kind. Nevertheless, Gillian, thou canst do something with her—good now, do a kind deed for once, and move her to come out and look on this morning's sport—the poor heart hath seen no pastime this summer."

"That I will do," quoth Gillian; "and, moreover, I will show her such a new riding-tire for the head, that no woman born could ever look at without the wish to toss it a little in the wind."

As Gillian spoke, it appeared to her jealous-pated husband that he surprised a glance of more intelligence exchanged betwixt her and the trader than brief acquaintance seemed to warrant, even when allowance was made for the extreme frankness of Dame Gillian's disposition. He thought also, that, on looking more closely at the merchant, his lineaments were not totally unknown to him; and proceeded to say to him dryly, "We have met before, friend, but I cannot call to remembrance where."

"Like enough," said the merchant; "I have used this country often, and may have taken money of you in the way of trade. If I were in fitting place, I would gladly bestow a pottle of wine to our better acquaintance."

"Not so fast, friend," said the old huntsman; "ere I drink to better acquaintance with any one, I must be well pleased with what I already know of him. We will see thy hawks fly, and if their breeding match thy bragging, we may perhaps crush a cup together. — And here come grooms and equerries, in faith — my lady has consented to come forth."

The opportunity of seeing this rural pastime had offered itself to Eveline, at a time when the delightful brilliancy of the day, the temperance of the air, and the joyous work of harvest, proceeding in every direction around, made the temptation to exercise almost irresistible.

As they proposed to go no farther than the side of the neighbouring river, near the fatal bridge, over which a small guard of infantry was constantly maintained, Eveline dispensed with any farther escort, and, contrary to the custom of the castle, took no one in her train save Rose and Gillian, and one or two servants, who led spaniels, or carried appurtenances of the chase. Raoul, the merchant, and an equerry, attended her of course, each holding a hawk on his wrist, and anxiously adjusting the mode in which they should throw them off, so as best to ascertain the extent of their powers and training.

When these important points had been adjusted, the party rode down the river, carefully looking on every side for the object of their game; but no heron was seen stalking on the usual haunts of the bird, although there was a heronry at no great distance.

Few disappointments of a small nature are more teasing than that of a sportsman, who, having set out with all means and appliances for destruction of game, finds that there is none to be met with; because he conceives himself, with his full shooting trim, and his empty game-pouch, to be subjected to the sneer of every passing rustic. The party of the Lady Eveline felt all the degradation of such disappointment.

"A fair country this," said the merchant, "where, on two miles of river, you cannot find one poor heron!"

"It is the clatter those d—d Flemings make with their water-mills and fulling-mills," said Raoul; "they destroy good sport and good company wherever they come. But were my lady willing to ride a mile or so farther to the Red Pool, I could show you a long-shanked fellow who would make your hawks cancelier till their brains were giddy."

"The Red Pool!" said Rose; "thou knowest it is more than three miles beyond the bridge, and lies up towards the hills."

"Ay, ay," said Raoul, "another Flemish freak to spoil pastime! They are not so scarce on the Marches these Flemish wenches, that they should fear being hawked at by Welsh haggards."

"Raoul is right, Rose," answered Eveline: "it is absurd to be cooped up like birds in a cage, when all around us has been so uniformly quiet. I am determined to break out of bounds for once, and see sport in our old fashion, without being surrounded with armed men like prisoners of state. We will merrily to the Red Pool, wench, and kill a heron like free maids of the Marches."

"Let me but tell my father, at least, to mount and follow us," said Rose — for they were now near the re-established manufacturing houses of the stout Fleming.

"I care not if thou dost, Rose," said Eveline; "yet credit me, girl, we will be at the Red Pool, and thus far on our way home again, ere thy father has donned his best doublet, girded on his two-handed sword, and accoutred his strong Flanderkin elephant of a horse, which he judiciously names Sloth—nay, frown not, and lose not, in justifying thy father, the time that may be better spent in calling him out."

Rose rode to the mills accordingly, when Wilkin Flammock, at the command of his liege mistress, readily hastened to get his steel cap and habergeon, and ordered half-a-dozen of his kinsmen and servants to get on horseback. Rose remained with him, to urge him to more despatch than his methodical disposition rendered natural to him; but in spite of all her efforts to stimulate him, the Lady Eveline had passed the bridge more than half an hour ere her escort was prepared to follow her.

Meanwhile, apprehensive of no evil, and riding gaily on, with the sensation of one escaped from confinement, Eveline moved forward on her lively jennet, as light as a lark; the plumes with which Dame Gillian had decked her riding-bonnet dancing in the wind, and her attendants galloping behind her, with dogs, pouches, lines, and all other appurtenances of the royal sport of hawking. After passing the river, the wild green-sward path which they pursued began to wind upward among small eminences, sometimes bare and craggy, sometimes overgrown with hazel, sloethorn, and other dwarf shrubs, and at length suddenly descending, brought them to the verge of a mountain rivulet, that, like a lamb at play, leapt merrily from rock to rock, seemingly uncertain which way to run.

"This little stream was always my favourite, Dame Gillian," said Eveline, "and now methinks it leaps the lighter that it sees me again."

"Ah! lady," said Dame Gillian, whose turn for conversation never extended in such cases beyond a few phrases of gross flattery, "many a fair knight would leap shoulder-height for leave to look on you as free as the brook may! more especially now that you have donned that riding-cap, which, in exquisite delicacy of invention, methinks, is a bow-shot before aught that I ever invented—What thinkest thou, Raoul?"

"I think," answered her well-natured helpmate, "that women's tongues were contrived to drive all the game out of the country. — Here we come near to the spot where we hope to speed, or no where; wherefore, pray, my sweet lady, be silent yourself, and keep your followers as much so as their natures will permit, while we steal along the bank of the pool, under the wind, with our hawks' hoods cast loose, all ready for a flight."

As he spoke, they advanced about a hundred yards up the brawling stream, until the little vale through which it flowed, making a very sudden turn to one side, showed them the Red Pool, the superfluous water of which formed the rivulet itself.

This mountain-lake, or tarn, as it is called in some countries, was a deep basin of about a mile in circumference, but rather oblong than circular. On the side next to our falconers arose a ridge of rock, of a dark red hue, giving name to the pool, which, reflecting this massive and dusky barrier, appeared to partake of its colour. On the opposite side was a heathy hill, whose autumnal bloom had not yet faded from purple to russet; its surface was varied by the dark green furze and the fern, and in many

places gray cliffs, or loose stones of the same colour, formed a contrast to
the ruddy precipice to which they lay opposed. A natural road of beautiful sand was formed by a beach, which, extending all the way around the
lake, separated its waters from the precipitous rock on the one hand, and on
the other from the steep and broken hill; and being no where less than five
or six yards in breadth, and in most places greatly more, offered around its
whole circuit a tempting opportunity to the rider, who desired to exercise
and breathe the horse on which he was mounted. The verge of the pool
on the rocky side was here and there strewed with fragments of large size,
detached from the precipice above, but'not in such quantity as to encumber
this pleasant horse-course. Many of these rocky masses, having passed
the margin of the water in their fall, lay immersed there like small islets;
and, placed amongst a little archipelago, the quick eye of Raoul detected
the heron which they were in search of.

A moment's consultation was held to consider in what manner they
should approach the sad and solitary bird, which, unconscious that itself
was the object of a formidable ambuscade, stood motionless on a stone, by
the brink of the lake, watching for such small fish or water-reptiles as
might chance to pass by its lonely station. A brief debate took place betwixt Raoul and the hawk-merchant on the best mode of starting the quarry,
so as to allow Lady Eveline and her attendants the most perfect view of the
flight. The facility of killing the heron at the *far jettee* or at the *jettee
ferré*—that is, upon the hither or farther side of the pool—was anxiously
debated in language of breathless importance, as if some great and perilous
enterprise was about to be executed.

At length the arrangements were fixed, and the party began to advance
towards the aquatic hermit, who, by this time aware of their approach,
drew himself up to his full height, erected his long lean neck, spread his
broad fan-like wings, uttered his usual clanging cry, and, projecting his
length of thin legs far behind him, rose upon the gentle breeze. It was
then, with a loud whoop of encouragement, that the merchant threw off
the noble hawk he bore, having first unhooded her to give her a view of her
quarry.

Eager as a frigate in chase of some rich galleon, darted the falcon towards the enemy, which she had been taught to pursue; while, preparing
for defence, if he should be unable to escape by flight, the heron exerted
all his powers of speed to escape from an enemy so formidable. Plying
his almost unequalled strength of wing, he ascended high and higher in
the air, by short gyrations, that the hawk might gain no vantage ground
for pouncing at him; while his spiked beak, at the extremity of so long a
neck as enabled him to strike an object at a yard's distance in every direction, possessed for any less spirited assailant all the terrors of a Moorish
javelin.

Another hawk was now thrown off, and encouraged by the halloos of the
falconer to join her companion. Both kept mounting, or scaling the air,
as it were, by a succession of small circles, endeavouring to gain that superior height which the heron on his part was bent to preserve; and to the
exquisite delight of the spectators, the contest was continued until all three
were well-nigh mingled with the fleecy clouds, from which was occasionally
heard the harsh and plaintive cry of the quarry, appealing as it were to
the heaven which he was approaching, against the wanton cruelty of those
by whom he was persecuted.

At length one of the falcons had reached a pitch from which she ventured
to stoop at the heron; but so judiciously did the quarry maintain his defence, as to receive on his beak the stroke which the falcon, shooting down
at full descent, had made against his right wing; so that one of his enemies, spiked through the body by his own weight, fell fluttering into the

lake, very near the land, on the side farthest from the falconers, and perished there.

"There goes a gallant falcon to the fishes," said Raoul. "Merchant, thy cake is dough."

Even as he spoke, however, the remaining bird had avenged the fate of her sister; for the success which the heron met with on one side, did not prevent his being assailed on the other wing; and the falcon stooping boldly, and grappling with, or, as it is called in falconry, *binding* his prey, both came tumbling down together, from a great height in the air. It was then no small object on the part of the falconers to come in as soon as possible, lest the falcon should receive hurt from the beak or talons of the heron; and the whole party, the men setting spurs, and the females switching their palfreys, went off like the wind, sweeping along the fair and smooth beach betwixt the rock and the water.

Lady Eveline, far better mounted than any of her train, her spirits elated by the sport, and by the speed at which she moved, was much sooner than any of her attendants at the spot where the falcon and heron, still engaged in their mortal struggle, lay fighting upon the moss; the wing of the latter having been broken by the stoop of the former. The duty of a falconer in such a crisis was to run in and assist the hawk, by thrusting the heron's bill into the earth, and breaking his legs, and thus permitting the falcon to dispatch him on easy terms.

Neither would the sex nor quality of the Lady Eveline have excused her becoming second to the falcon in this cruel manner; but, just as she had dismounted for that purpose, she was surprised to find herself seized on by a wild form, who exclaimed in Welsh, that he seized her as a *waif*, for hawking on the demesnes of Dawfyd with the one eye. At the same time many other Welshmen, to the number of more than a score, showed themselves from behind crags and bushes, all armed at point with the axes called Welsh hooks, long knives, darts, and bows and arrows.

Eveline screamed to her attendants for assistance, and at the same time made use of what Welsh phrases she possessed, to move the fears or excite the compassion of the outlawed mountaineers, for she doubted not that she had fallen under the power of such a party. When she found her requests were unheeded, and she perceived it was their purpose to detain her prisoner, she disdained to use farther entreaties, but demanded at their peril that they should treat her with respect, promising in that case that she would pay them a large ransom, and threatening them with the vengeance of the Lords Marchers, and particularly of Sir Damian de Lacy, if they ventured to use her otherwise.

The men seemed to understand her, and although they proceeded to tie a bandage over her eyes, and to bind her arms with her own veil, yet they observed in these acts of violence a certain delicacy and attention both to her feelings and her safety, which led her to hope that her request had had some effect on them. They secured her to the saddle of her palfrey, and led her away with them through the recesses of the hills; while she had the additional distress to hear behind her the noise of a conflict, occasioned by the fruitless efforts of her retinue to procure her rescue.

Astonishment had at first seized the hawking party, when they saw from some distance their sport interrupted by a violent assault on their mistress. Old Raoul valiantly put spurs to his horse, and calling on the rest to follow him to the rescue, rode furiously towards the banditti; but, having no other arms save a hawking-pole and short sword, he and those who followed him in his meritorious but ineffectual attempt were easily foiled, and Raoul and one or two of the foremost severely beaten; the banditti exercising upon them their own poles till they were broken to splinters, but generously abstaining from the use of more dangerous weapons. The rest of the retinue, completely discouraged, dispersed to give the alarm, and the merchant and Dame Gillian remained by the lake, filling the air with shrieks of useless fear and sorrow. The outlaws, meanwhile, drawing together in a body, shot a few arrows at the fugitives, but more to alarm than to injure them, and then marched off in a body, as if to cover their companions who had gone before, with the Lady Eveline in their custody.

Chapter the Twenty-Fourth.

Four ruffians seized me yester morn—
Alas! a maiden most forlorn!
They choked my cries with wicked might,
And bound me on a palfrey white.

COLERIDGE.

SUCH adventures as are now only recorded in works of mere fiction, were not uncommon in the feudal ages, when might was so universally superior to right; and it followed that those whose conditions exposed them to frequent violence, were more prompt in repelling, and more patient in enduring it, than could otherwise have been expected from their sex and age.

The Lady Eveline felt that she was a prisoner, nor was she devoid of fears concerning the purposes of this assault; but she suffered neither her alarm, nor the violence with which she was hurried along, to deprive her of the power of observing and reflecting. From the noise of hoofs which now increased around, she concluded that the greater part of the ruffians by whom she had been seized had betaken themselves to their horses. This she knew was consonant to the practice of the Welsh marauders, who, although the small size and slightness of their nags made them totally unfit for service in battle, availed themselves of their activity and sureness of foot to transport them with the necessary celerity to and from the scenes of their rapine; ensuring thus a rapid and unperceived approach, and a secure and speedy retreat. These animals traversed without difficulty, and beneath the load of a heavy soldier, the wild mountain paths by which the country was intersected, and in one of which Lady Eveline Berenger concluded she was now engaged, from the manner in which her own palfrey, supported by a man on foot at either rein, seemed now to labour up some precipice, and anon to descend with still greater risk on the other side.

At one of those moments, a voice which she had not yet distinguished addressed her in the Anglo-Norman language, and asked, with apparent interest, if she sat safely on her saddle, offering at the same time to have her accoutrements altered at her pleasure and convenience.

"Insult not my condition with the mention of safety," said Eveline; "you may well believe that I hold my safety altogether irreconcilable with these deeds of violence. If I or my vassals have done injury to any of the _Cymry_,* let me know, and it shall be amended—If it is ransom which you desire, name the sum, and I will send an order to treat for it; but detain me not prisoner, for that can but injure me, and will avail you nothing."

"The Lady Eveline," answered the voice, still in a tone of courtesy inconsistent with the violence which she sustained, "will speedily find that our actions are more rough than our purposes."

"If you know who I am," said Eveline, "you cannot doubt that this atrocity will be avenged — you must know by whose banner my lands are at present protected."

* Cymbri, or Welsh.

"Under De Lacy's," answered the voice, with a tone of indifference. "Be it so—falcons fear not falcons."

At this moment there was a halt, and a confused murmur arose amongst those around her, who had hitherto been silent, unless when muttering to each other in Welsh, and as briefly as possible, directions which way to hold, or encouragement to use haste.

These murmurs ceased, and there was a pause of several minutes; at length Eveline again heard the voice which formerly addressed her, giving directions which she could not understand. He then spoke to herself, "You will presently see," he said, "whether I have spoken truly, when I said I scorned the ties by which you are fettered. But you are at once the cause of strife and the reward of victory—your safety must be cared for as time will admit; and, strange as the mode of protection is to which we are to intrust you, I trust the victor in the approaching struggle will find you uninjured."

"Do not, for the sake of the blessed Virgin, let there be strife and bloodshed!" said Eveline; "rather unbind my eyes, and let me speak to those whose approach you dread. If friends, as it would seem to me, I will be the means of peace between you."

"Despise peace," replied the speaker. "I have not undertaken a resolute and daring adventure, to resign it as a child doth his plaything, at the first frown of fortune. Please to alight, noble lady; or rather be not offended that I thus lift you from thy seat, and place you on the greensward."

As he spoke, Eveline felt herself lifted from her palfrey, and placed carefully and safely on the ground, in a sitting posture. A moment after, the same peremptory valet who had aided her to dismount, disrobed her of her cap, the masterpiece of Dame Gillian, and of her upper mantle. "I must yet farther require you," said the bandit leader, "to creep on hands and knees into this narrow aperture. Believe me, I regret the nature of the singular fortification to which I commit your person for safety."

Eveline crept forwards as directed, conceiving resistance to be of no avail, and thinking that compliance with the request of one who spoke like a person of consequence, might find her protection against the unbridled fury of the Welsh, to whom she was obnoxious, as being the cause of Gwenwyn's death, and the defeat of the Britons under the walls of the Garde Doloureuse.

She crept then forwards through a narrow and damp passage, built on either side with rough stones, and so low that she could not have entered it in any other posture. When she had proceeded about two or three yards, the passage opened into a concavity or apartment, high enough to permit her to sit at her ease, and of irregular, but narrow, dimensions. At the same time she became sensible, from the noise which she heard behind her, that the ruffians were stopping up the passage by which she had been thus introduced into the bowels of the earth. She could distinctly hear the clattering of stone with which they closed the entrance, and she became sensible that the current of fresh air, which had rushed through the opening, was gradually failing, and that the atmosphere of the subterranean apartment became yet more damp, earthy, and oppressive than at first.

At this moment came a distant sound from without, in which Eveline thought she could distinguish cries, blows, the trampling of horse, the oaths, shouts, and screams of the combatants, but all deadened by the rude walls of her prison, into a confused hollow murmur, conveying such intelligence to her ears as we may suppose the dead to hear from the world they have quitted.

Influenced by desperation, under circumstances so dreadful, Eveline struggled for liberty with such frantic energy, that she partly effected her purpose by forcing her arms from the bonds which confined them. But this only convinced her of the impossibility to escape; for, rending off the veil which wrapped her head, she found herself in total darkness, and flinging her arms hastily around her, she discovered she was cooped up in a subterranean cavern, of very narrow dimensions. Her hands, which groped around, encountered only pieces of decayed metal, and a substance which, at another moment, would have made her shudder, being, in truth, the mouldering bones of the dead. At present, not even this circumstance could add to her fears, immured as she seemed to be, to perish by a strange and subterranean death, while her friends and deliverers were probably within a few yards of her. She flung her arms wildly around in search of some avenue of escape, but every effort she made for liberating herself from the ponderous circumvallation, was as ineffectual as if directed against the dome of a cathedral.

The noise by which her ears were at first assailed increased rapidly, and at one moment it seemed as if the covering of the vault under which she lay sounded repeatedly to blows, or the shock of substances which had fallen, or been thrown, against it. It was impossible that a human brain could have withstood these terrors, operating upon it so immediately; but happily this extremity lasted not long. Sounds, more hollow, and dying away in distance, argued that one or other of the parties had retreated; and at length all was silent.

Eveline was now left to the undisturbed contemplation of her own disastrous situation. The fight was over, and, as circumstances led her to infer, her own friends were conquerors; for otherwise the victor would have relieved her from her place of confinement, and carried her away captive with him, as his words had menaced. But what could the success of her faithful friends and followers avail Eveline, who, pent up under a place of concealment which, whatever was its character, must have escaped their observation, was left on the field of battle, to become again the prize of the enemy, should their band venture to return, or die in darkness and privation, a death as horrid as ever tyrant invented, or martyr underwent, and which the unfortunate young lady could not even bear to think of without a prayer that her agony might at least be shortened.

In this hour of dread she recollected the poniard which she wore, and the dark thought crossed her mind, that, when life became hopeless, a speedy death was at least within her reach. As her soul shuddered at so dreadful an alternative, the question suddenly occurred, might not this weapon be put to a more hallowed use, and aid her emancipation, instead of abridging her sufferings?

This hope once adopted, the daughter of Raymond Berenger hastened to prove the experiment, and by repeated efforts succeeded, though with difficulty, in changing her posture, so as to admit of her inspecting her place of confinement all around, but particularly the passage by which she had entered, and by which she now attempted again to return to the light of day. She crept to the extremity, and found it, as she expected, strongly blocked up with large stones and earth, rammed together in such a manner as nearly to extinguish all hope of escape. The work, however, had been hastily performed, and life and liberty were prizes to stimulate exertion. With her poniard she cleared away the earth and sods — with her hands, little accustomed to such labour, she removed several stones, and advanced in her task so far as to obtain a glimmering of light, and, what was scarce less precious, a supply of purer air. But, at the same time, she had the misfortune to ascertain, that, from the size and massiveness of a huge stone which closed the extremity of the passage, there was no hope that her unassisted strength could effect her extrication. Yet her condition was improved by the admission of air and light, as well as by the opportunity afforded of calling out for assistance.

Such cries, indeed, were for some time uttered in vain—the field had probably been left to the dead and the dying; for low and indistinct groans were the only answer which she received for several minutes. At length, as she repeated her exclamation, a voice, faint as that of one just awakened from a swoon, pronounced these words in answer:—"Edris of the Earthen House, dost thou call from thy tomb to the wretch who just hastens to his own?—Are the boundaries broken down which connect me with the living? —And do I already hear, with fleshly ears, the faint and screaming accents of the dead?"

"It is no spirit who speaks," replied Eveline, overjoyed at finding she could at least communicate her existence to a living person—"no spirit, but a most unhappy maiden, Eveline Berenger by name, immured beneath this dark vault, and in danger to perish horribly, unless God send me rescue!"

"Eveline Berenger!" exclaimed he whom she addressed, in the accents of wonder. "It is impossible!—I watched her green mantle—I watched her plumy bonnet as I saw her hurried from the field, and felt my own inability to follow to the rescue; nor did force or exertion altogether leave me till the waving of the robe and the dancing of the feathers were lost to my eyes, and all hope of rescuing her abandoned my heart."

"Faithful vassal, or right true friend, or courteous stranger, whichsoever I may name thee," answered Eveline, "know thou hast been abused by the artifices of these Welsh banditti—the mantle and head-gear of Eveline Berenger they have indeed with them, and may have used them to mislead those true friends, who, like thee, are anxious for my fate. Wherefore, brave sir, devise some succour, if thou canst, for thyself and me; since I dread that these ruffians, when they shall have escaped immediate pursuit, will return hither, like the robber to the hoard where he has deposited his stolen booty."

"Now, the Holy Virgin be praised," said the wounded man, "that I can spend the last breath of my life in thy just and honourable service! I would not before blow my bugle, lest I recalled from the pursuit to the aid of my worthless self some of those who might be effectually engaged in thy rescue; may Heaven grant that the recall may now be heard, that my eyes may yet see the Lady Eveline in safety and liberty!"

The words, though spoken in a feeble tone, breathed a spirit of enthusiasm, and were followed by the blast of a horn, faintly winded, to which no answer was made save the echoing of the dell. A sharper and louder blast was then sent forth, but sunk so suddenly, that it seemed the breath of him who sounded the instrument had failed in the effort.—A strange thought crossed Eveline's mind even in that moment of uncertainty and terror. "That," she said, "was the note of a De Lacy—surely you cannot be my gentle kinsman, Sir Damian?"

"I am that unhappy wretch, deserving of death for the evil care which I have taken of the treasure intrusted to me.—What was my business to trust to reports and messengers? I should have worshipped the saint who was committed to my keeping, with such vigilance as avarice bestows on the dross which he calls treasure—I should have rested no where, save at your gate; outwatched the brightest stars in the horizon; unseen and unknown myself, I should never have parted from your neighbourhood; then had you not been in the present danger, and—much less important consequence —thou, Damian de Lacy, had not filled the grave of a forsworn and negligent caitiff!"

"Alas! noble Damian," said Eveline, "break not my heart by blaming yourself for an imprudence which is altogether my own. Thy succour was ever near when I intimated the least want of it; and it imbitters my own misfortune to know that my rashness has been the cause of your disaster. Answer me, gentle kinsman, and give me to hope that the wounds you have suffered are such as may be cured.—Alas! how much of your blood have I seen spilled, and what a fate is mine, that I should ever bring distress on all for whom I would most willingly sacrifice my own happiness!—But do not let us imbitter the moments given us in mercy, by fruitless repinings—Try what you can to stop thine ebbing blood, which is so dear to England—to Eveline—and to thine uncle."

Damian groaned as she spoke, and was silent; while, maddened with the idea that he might be perishing for want of aid, Eveline repeated her efforts to extricate herself for her kinsman's assistance as well as her own. It was all in vain, and she had ceased the attempt in despair; and, passing from one hideous subject of terror to another, she sat listening, with sharpened ear, for the dying groan of Damian, when—feeling of ecstasy!—the ground was shaken with horses' feet advancing rapidly. Yet this joyful sound, if decisive of life, did not assure her of liberty—It might be the banditti of the mountains returning to seek their captive. Even then they would surely allow her leave to look upon and bind up the wounds of Damian de Lacy; for to keep him as a captive might vantage them more in many degrees, than could his death. A horseman came up—Eveline invoked his assistance, and the first word she heard was an exclamation in Flemish from the faithful Wilkin Flammock, which nothing save some spectacle of the most unusual kind was ever known to compel from that phlegmatic person.

His presence, indeed, was particularly useful on this occasion; for, being informed by the Lady Eveline in what condition she was placed, and implored at the same time to look to the situation of Sir Damian de Lacy, he began, with admirable composure and some skill, to stop the wounds of the one, while his attendants collected levers, left by the Welsh as they retreated, and were soon ready to attempt the liberation of Eveline. With much caution, and under the experienced direction of Flammock, the stone was at length so much raised, that the Lady Eveline was visible, to the delight of all, and especially of the faithful Rose, who, regardless of the risk of personal harm, fluttered around her mistress's place of confinement, like a bird robbed of her nestlings around the cage in which the truant urchin has imprisoned them. Precaution was necessary to remove the stone, lest falling inwards it might do the lady injury.

At length the rocky fragment was so much displaced that she could issue forth; while her people, as in hatred of the coercion which she had sustained, ceased not to heave, with bar and lever, till, totally destroying the balance of the heavy mass, it turned over from the little flat on which it had been placed at the mouth of the subterranean entrance, and, acquiring force as it revolved down a steep declivity, was at length put to rapid motion, and rolled, crashed, and thundered, down the hill, amid flashes of fire which it forced from the rocks, and clouds of smoke and dust, until it alighted in the channel of a brook, where it broke into several massive fragments, with a noise that might have been heard some miles off.

With garments rent and soiled through the violence which she had sustained; with dishevelled hair, and disordered dress; faint from the stifling effect of her confinement, and exhausted by the efforts she had made to relieve herself, Eveline did not, nevertheless, waste a single minute in considering her own condition; but with the eagerness of a sister hastening to the assistance of her only brother, betook herself to examine the several severe wounds of Damian de Lacy, and to use proper means to stanch the blood and recall him from his swoon. We have said elsewhere, that, like other ladies of the time, Eveline was not altogether unacquainted with the surgical art, and she now displayed a greater share of knowledge than she had been thought capable of exerting. There was prudence, foresight, and tenderness, in every direction which she gave, and the softness of the female sex, with their officious humanity, ever ready to assist in alleviating human misery. seemed in her enhanced, and rendered dignified, by the sagacity of a strong and powerful understanding. After hearing with wonder for a minute or two the prudent and ready-witted directions of her mistress, Rose seemed at once to recollect that the patient should not be left to the exclusive care of the Lady Eveline, and joining, therefore, in the task, she rendered what assistance she could, while the attendants were employed in forming a litter, on which the wounded knight was to be conveyed to the castle of the Garde Doloureuse.

Chapter the Twenty-Fifth.

A merry place, 'tis said, in times of yore,
But something ails it now — the place is cursed.
                                        WORDSWORTH.

THE place on which the skirmish had occurred, and the deliverance of the Lady Eveline had been effected, was a wild and singular spot, being a small level plain, forming a sort of stage, or resting-place, between two very rough paths, one of which winded up the rivulet from below, and another continued the ascent above. Being surrounded by hills and woods, it was a celebrated spot for finding game, and, in former days, a Welsh prince, renowned for his universal hospitality, his love of *crw* and of the chase, had erected a forest-lodge, where he used to feast his friends and followers with a profusion unexampled in Cambria.

The fancy of the bards, always captivated with magnificence, and having no objections to the peculiar species of profusion practised by this potentate, gave him the surname of Edris of the Goblets; and celebrated him in their odes in terms as high as those which exalt the heroes of the famous Hirlas Horn. The subject of their praises, however, fell finally a victim to his propensities, having been stabbed to the heart in one of those scenes of confusion and drunkenness which were frequently the conclusion of his renowned banquets. Shocked at this catastrophe, the assembled Britons interred the relics of the Prince on the place where he had died, within the narrow vault where Eveline had been confined, and having barricaded the entrance of the sepulchre with fragments of rock, heaped over it an immense *cairn*, or pile of stones, on the summit of which they put the assassin to death. Superstition guarded the spot; and for many a year this memorial of Edris remained unviolated, although the lodge had gone to ruin, and its vestiges had totally decayed.

In latter years, some prowling band of Welsh robbers had discovered the secret entrance, and opened it with the view of ransacking the tomb for arms and treasures, which were in ancient times often buried with the dead. These marauders were disappointed, and obtained nothing by the violation of the grave of Edris, excepting the knowledge of a secret place, which might be used for depositing their booty, or even as a place of retreat for one of their number in a case of emergency.

When the followers of Damian, five or six in number, explained their part of the history of the day to Wilkin Flammock, it appeared that Damian had ordered them to horse at break of day, with a more considerable body, to act, as they understood, against a party of insurgent peasants, when of a sudden he had altered his mind, and, dividing his force into small bands, employed himself and them in reconnoitring more than one mountain-pass betwixt Wales and the Marches of the English country, in the neighbourhood of the Garde Doloureuse.

This was an occupation so ordinary for him, that it excited no particular notice. These manœuvres were frequently undertaken by the warlike marchers, for the purpose of intimidating the Welsh in general, more especially the bands of outlaws, who, independent of any regular government, infested these wild frontiers. Yet it escaped not comment, that, in undertaking such service at this moment, Damian seemed to abandon that of dispersing the insurgents, which had been considered as the chief object of the day.

It was about noon, when, falling in, as good fortune would have it, with one of the fugitive grooms, Damian and his immediate attendants received information of the violence committed on the Lady Eveline, and, by their perfect knowledge of the country, were able to intercept the ruffians at the Pass of Edris, as it was called, by which the Welsh rovers ordinarily returned to their strongholds in the interior. It is probable that the banditti were not aware of the small force which Damian headed in person, and at the same time knew that there would be an immediate and hot pursuit in their rear; and these circumstances led their leader to adopt the singular expedient of hiding Eveline in the tomb, while one of their own number, dressed in her clothes, might serve as a decoy to deceive their assailants, and lead them from the spot where she was really concealed, to which it was no doubt the purpose of the banditti to return, when they had eluded their pursuers.

Accordingly, the robbers had already drawn up before the tomb for the purpose of regularly retreating, until they should find some suitable place either for making a stand, or where, if overmatched, they might, by abandoning their horses, and dispersing among the rocks, evade the attack of the Norman cavalry. Their plan had been defeated by the precipitation of Damian, who, beholding as he thought the plumes and mantle of the Lady Eveline in the rear of the party, charged them without considering either the odds of numbers, or the lightness of his own armour, which, consisting only of a headpiece and a buff surcoat, offered but imperfect resistance to the Welsh knives and glaives. He was accordingly wounded severely at the onset, and would have been slain, but for the exertions of his few followers, and the fears of the Welsh, that, while thus continuing the battle in front, they might be assaulted in the rear by the followers of Eveline, whom they must now suppose were all in arms and motion. They retreated, therefore, or rather fled, and the attendants of Damian were despatched after them by their fallen master, with directions to let no consideration induce them to leave off the chase, until the captive Lady of the Garde Doloureuse was delivered from her ravishers.

The outlaws, secure in their knowledge of the paths, and the activity of their small Welsh horses, made an orderly retreat, with the exception of two or three of their rear-guard, cut down by Damian in his furious onset. They shot arrows, from time to time, at the men-at-arms, and laughed at the ineffectual efforts which these heavy-armed warriors, with their barbed horses, made to overtake them. But the scene was changed by the appearance of Wilkin Flammock, on his puissant war-horse, who was beginning to ascend the pass, leading a party consisting both of foot and horse. The fear of being intercepted caused the outlaws to have recourse to their last stratagem, and, abandoning their Welsh nags, they betook themselves to the cliffs, and, by superior activity and dexterity, baffled, generally speaking, the attempts of their pursuers on either hand. All of them, however, were not equally fortunate, for two or three fell into the hands of Flammock's party; amongst others, the person upon whom Eveline's clothes had been placed, and who now, to the great disappointment of those who had attached themselves to his pursuit, proved to be, not the lady whom they were emulous to deliver, but a fair-haired young Welshman, whose wild looks, and incoherent speech, seemed to argue a disturbed imagination. This would not have saved him from immediate death, the usual doom of captives taken in such skirmishes, had not the faint blast of Damian's horn, sounding from above, recalled his own party, and summoned that of Wilkin

flammock to the spot; while, in the confusion and hurry of their obeying
the signal, the pity or the contempt of his guards suffered the prisoner to
escape. They had, indeed, little to learn from him, even had he been disposed to give intelligence, or capable of communicating it. All were well
assured that their lady had fallen into an ambuscade, formed by Dawfyd
the one-eyed, a redoubted freebooter of the period, who had ventured upon
this hardy enterprise in the hope of obtaining a large ransom for the captive
Eveline, and all, incensed at his extreme insolence and audacity, devoted
his head and limbs to the eagles and the ravens.

These were the particulars which the followers of Flammock and of
Damian learned by comparing notes with each other, on the incidents of
the day. As they returned by the Red Pool they were joined by Dame
Gillian, who, after many exclamations of joy at the unexpected liberation
of her lady, and as many of sorrow at the unexpected disaster of Damian,
proceeded to inform the men-at-arms, that the merchant, whose hawks had
been the original cause of these adventures, had been taken prisoner by two
or three of the Welsh in their retreat, and that she herself and the wounded
Raoul would have shared the same fate, but that they had no horse left to
mount her upon, and did not consider old Raoul as worth either ransom or
the trouble of killing. One had, indeed, flung a stone at him as he lay on
the hill-side, but happily, as his dame said, it fell something short of him—
"It was but a little fellow who threw it," she said — "there was a big man
amongst them — if he had tried, it's like, by our Lady's grace, he had cast
it a thought farther." So saying, the dame gathered herself up, and adjusted
her dress for again mounting on horseback.

The wounded Damian was placed on a litter, hastily constructed of boughs,
and, with the females, was placed in the centre of the little troop, augmented by the rest of the young knight's followers, who began to rejoin his
standard. The united body now marched with military order and precaution, and winded through the passes with the attention of men prepared to
meet and to repel injury.

Chapter the Twenty-Sixth.

What! fair and young, and faithful too?
A miracle if this be true.
                            WALLER.

Rose, by nature one of the most disinterested and affectionate maidens
that ever breathed, was the first who, hastily considering the peculiar condition in which her lady was placed, and the marked degree of restraint
which had hitherto characterized her intercourse with her youthful guardian,
became anxious to know how the wounded knight was to be disposed of;
and when she came to Eveline's side for the purpose of asking this important
question, her resolution well-nigh failed her.

The appearance of Eveline was indeed such as might have made it almost
cruelty to intrude upon her any other subject of anxious consideration than
those with which her mind had been so lately assailed, and was still occupied. Her countenance was as pale as death could have made it, unless
where it was specked with drops of blood; her veil, torn and disordered,
was soiled with dust and with gore; her hair, wildly dishevelled, fell in
elf-locks on her brow and shoulders, and a single broken and ragged feather,
which was all that remained of her headgear, had been twisted among her

tresses and still flowed there, as if in mockery, rather than ornament. Her eyes were fixed on the litter where Damian was deposited, and she rode close beside it, without apparently wasting a thought on any thing, save the danger of him who was extended there.

Rose plainly saw that her lady was under feelings of excitation, which might render it difficult for her to take a wise and prudent view of her own situation. She endeavoured gradually to awaken her to a sense of it. "Dearest lady," said Rose, "will it please you to take my mantle?"

"Torment me not," answered Eveline, with some sharpness in her accent.

"Indeed, my lady," said Dame Gillian, bustling up as one who feared her functions as mistress of the robes might be interfered with—"indeed, my lady, Rose Flammock speaks truth; and neither your kirtle nor your gown are sitting as they should do; and, to speak truth, they are but barely decent. And so, if Rose will turn herself, and put her horse out of my way," continued the tire-woman, "I will put your dress in better order in the sticking in of a bodkin, than any Fleming of them all could do in twelve hours."

"I care not for my dress," replied Eveline, in the same manner as before.

"Care then for your honour—for your fame," said Rose, riding close to her mistress, and whispering in her ear; "think, and that hastily, how you are to dispose of this wounded young man."

"To the castle," answered Eveline aloud, as if scorning the affectation of secrecy; "lead to the castle, and that straight as you can."

"Why not rather to his own camp, or to Malpas?" said Rose—"dearest lady, believe, it will be for the best."

"Wherefore not—wherefore not?—wherefore not leave him on the way-side at once, to the knife of the Welshman, and the teeth of the wolf?—Once—twice—three times has he been my preserver. Where I go, he shall go; nor will I be in safety myself a moment sooner than I know that he is so."

Rose saw that she could make no impression on her mistress, and her own reflection told her that the wounded man's life might be endangered by a longer transportation than was absolutely necessary. An expedient occurred to her, by which she imagined this objection might be obviated; but it was necessary she should consult her father. She struck her palfrey with her riding-rod, and in a moment her diminutive, though beautiful figure, and her spirited little jennet, were by the side of the gigantic Fleming and his tall black horse, and riding, as it were, in their vast shadow. "My dearest father," said Rose, "the lady intends that Sir Damian be transported to the castle, where it is like he may be a long sojourner;—what think you?—is that wholesome counsel?"

"Wholesome for the youth, surely, Roschen," answered the Fleming, "because he will escape the better risk of a fever."

"True; but is it wise for my lady?" continued Rose.

"Wise enough, if she deal wisely. But wherefore shouldst thou doubt her, Roschen?"

"I know not," said Rose, unwilling to breathe even to her father the fears and doubts which she herself entertained; "but where there are evil tongues, there may be evil rehearsing. Sir Damian and my lady are both very young—Methinks it were better, dearest father, would you offer the shelter of your roof to the wounded knight, in the stead of his being carried to the castle."

"That I shall not, wench," answered the Fleming, hastily—"that I shall not, if I may help. Norman shall not cross my quiet threshold, nor Englishman neither, to mock my quiet thrift, and consume my substance. Thou dost not know them, because thou art ever with thy lady, and hast her good favour; but I know them well; and the best I can get from them is Lazy Flanderkin, and Greedy Flanderkin, and Flemish sot—I thank the saints they cannot say Coward Flanderkin, since Gwenwyn's Welsh uproar."

"I had ever thought, my father," answered Rose, "that your spirit was too calm to regard these base calumnies. Bethink you we are under this lady's banner, and that she has been my loving mistress, and her father was your good lord; to the Constable, too, are you beholden, for enlarged privileges. Money may pay debt, but kindness only can requite kindness; and I forebode that you will never have such an opportunity to do kindness to the houses of Berenger and De Lacy, as by opening the doors of your house to this wounded knight."

"The doors of my house!" answered the Fleming—"do I know how long I may call that, or any house upon earth, my own? Alas, my daughter, we came hither to fly from the rage of the elements, but who knows how soon we may perish by the wrath of men!"

"You speak strangely, my father," said Rose; "it holds not with your solid wisdom to augur such general evil from the rash enterprise of a Welsh outlaw."

"I think not of the One-eyed robber," said Wilkin; "although the increase and audacity of such robbers as Dawfyd is no good sign of a quiet country. But thou, who livest within yonder walls, hearest but little of what passes without, and your estate is less anxious;—you had known nothing of the news from me, unless in case I had found it necessary to remove to another country."

"To remove, my dearest father, from the land where your thrift and industry have gained you an honourable competency?"

"Ay, and where the hunger of wicked men, who envy me the produce of my thrift, may likely bring me to a dishonourable death. There have been tumults among the English rabble in more than one county, and their wrath is directed against those of our nation, as if we were Jews or heathens, and not better Christians and better men than themselves. They have, at York, Bristol, and elsewhere, sacked the houses of the Flemings, spoiled their goods, misused their families, and murdered themselves.—And why?—except that we have brought among them the skill and industry which they possessed not; and because wealth, which they would never else have seen in Britain, was the reward of our art and our toil. Roschen, this evil spirit is spreading wider daily. Here we are more safe than elsewhere, because we form a colony of some numbers and strength. But I confide not in our neighbours; and hadst not thou, Rose, been in security, I would long ere this have given up all, and left Britain."

"Given up all, and left Britain!"—The words sounded prodigious in the ears of his daughter, who knew better than any one how successful her father had been in his industry, and how unlikely one of his firm and sedate temper was to abandon known and present advantages for the dread of distant or contingent peril. At length she replied, "If such be your peril, my father, methinks your house and goods cannot have a better protection than the presence of this noble knight. Where lives the man who dare aught of violence against the house which harbours Damian de Lacy?"

"I know not that," said the Fleming, in the same composed and steady, but ominous tone—"May Heaven forgive it me, if it be sin! but I see little save folly in these Crusades, which the priesthood have preached up so successfully. Here has the Constable been absent for nearly three years, and no certain tidings of his life or death, victory or defeat. He marched from hence, as if he meant not to draw bridle or sheathe sword until the Holy Sepulchre was won from the Saracens, yet we can hear with no certainty whether even a hamlet has been taken from the Saracens. In the meanwhile, the people that are at home grow discontented; their lords, with the better part of their followers, are in Palestine—dead or alive we scarcely know; the people themselves are oppressed and flayed by stewards and deputies, whose yoke is neither so light nor so lightly endured as that o. the actual lord. The commons, who naturally hate the knights and gentry, think it no bad time to make some head against them — ay, and there be some of noble blood who would not care to be their leaders, that they may have their share in the spoil; for foreign expeditions and profligate habits have made many poor; and he that is poor will murder his father for money. I hate poor people; and I would the devil had every man who cannot keep himself by the work of his own hand!"

The Fleming concluded, with this characteristic imprecation, a speech which gave Rose a more frightful view of the state of England, than, shut up as she was within the Garde Doloureuse, she had before had an opportunity of learning. "Surely," she said — "surely these violences of which you speak are not to be dreaded by those who live under the banner of De Lacy and of Berenger?"

"Berenger subsists but in name," answered Wilkin Flammock, "and Damian, though a brave youth, hath not his uncle's ascendency of character, and authority. His men also complain that they are harassed with the duty of watching for protection of a castle, in itself impregnable, and sufficiently garrisoned, and that they lose all opportunity of honourable enterprise, as they call it — that is, of fight and spoil — in this inactive and inglorious manner of life. They say that Damian the beardless was a man, but that Damian with the mustache is no better than a woman; and that age, which has darkened his upper lip, hath at the same time blenched his courage. — And they say more, which were but wearisome to tell."

"Nay, but, let me know what they say; let me know it, for Heaven's sake!" answered Rose, "if it concern, as it must concern, my dear lady."

"Even so, Roschen," answered Wilkin. "There are many among the Norman men-at-arms who talk, over their wine-cups, how that Damian de Lacy is in love with his uncle's betrothed bride; ay, and that they correspond together by art magic."

"By art magic, indeed, it must be," said Rose, smiling scornfully, "for by no earthly means do they correspond, as I, for one, can bear witness."

"To art magic, accordingly, they impute it," quoth Wilkin Flammock, "that so soon as ever my lady stirs beyond the portal of her castle, De Lacy is in the saddle with a party of his cavalry, though they are positively certain that he has received no messenger, letter, or other ordinary notice of her purpose; nor have they ever, on such occasions, scoured the passes long, ere they have seen or heard of my Lady Eveline's being abroad."

"This has not escaped me," said Rose; "and my lady has expressed herself even displeased at the accuracy which Damian displayed in procuring a knowledge of her motions, as well as at the officious punctuality with which he has attended and guarded them. To-day has, however, shown," she continued, "that his vigilance may serve a good purpose; and as they never met upon these occasions, but continued at such distance as excluded even the possibility of intercourse, methinks they might have escaped the censure of the most suspicious."

"Ay, my daughter Roschen," replied Wilkin; "but it is possible to drive caution so far as to excite suspicion. Why, say the men-at-arms, should these two observe such constant, yet such guarded intelligence with one another? Why should their approach be so near, and why, yet, should they never meet? If they had been merely the nephew, and the uncle's bride, they must have had interviews avowedly and frankly; and, on the other hand, if they be two secret lovers, there is reason to believe that they do find their own private places of meeting, though they have art sufficient to conceal them."

"Every word that you speak, my father," replied the generous Rose, "increases the absolute necessity that you receive this wounded youth into your house. Be the evils you dread ever so great, yet, may you rely upon it, that they cannot be augmented by admitting him, with a few of his faithful followers."

"Not one follower," said the Fleming, hastily, "not one beef-fed knave of them, save the page that is to tend him, and the doctor that is to attempt his cure."

"But I may offer the shelter of your roof to these three, at least?" answered Rose.

"Do as thou wilt, do as thou wilt," said the doating father. "By my faith, Roschen, it is well for thee thou hast sense and moderation in asking, since I am so foolishly prompt in granting. This is one of your freaks, now, of honour or generosity—but commend me to prudence and honesty.— Ah! Rose, Rose, those who would do what is better than good, sometimes bring about what is worse than bad!—But I think I shall be quit of the trouble for the fear; and that thy mistress, who is, with reverence, something of a damsel errant, will stand stoutly for the chivalrous privilege of lodging her knight in her own bower, and tending him in person."

The Fleming prophesied true. Rose had no sooner made the proposal to Eveline, that the wounded Damian should be left at her father's house for his recovery, than her mistress briefly and positively rejected the proposal. "He has been my preserver," she said, "and if there be one being left for whom the gates of the Garde Doloureuse should of themselves fly open, it is to Damian de Lacy. Nay, damsel, look not upon me with that suspicious and yet sorrowful countenance—they that are beyond disguise, my girl, contemn suspicion—It is to God and Our Lady that I must answer, and to them my bosom lies open!"

They proceeded in silence to the castle gate, when the Lady Eveline issued her orders that her Guardian, as she emphatically termed Damian, should be lodged in her father's apartment; and, with the prudence of more advanced age, she gave the necessary direction for the reception and accommodation of his followers, and the arrangements which such an accession of guests required in the fortress. All this she did with the utmost composure and presence of mind, even before she altered or arranged her own disordered dress.

Another step still remained to be taken. She hastened to the Chapel of the Virgin, and prostrating herself before her divine protectress, returned thanks for her second deliverance, and implored her guidance and direction, and, through her intercession, that of Almighty God, for the disposal and regulation of her conduct. "Thou knowest," she said, "that from no confidence in my own strength, have I thrust myself into danger. Oh, make me strong where I am most weak—Let not my gratitude and my compassion be a snare to me; and while I strive to discharge the duties which thankfulness imposes on me, save me from the evil tongues of men—and save—oh, save me from the insidious devices of my own heart!"

She then told her rosary with devout fervour, and retiring from the chapel to her own apartment, summoned her women to adjust her dress, and remove the external appearance of the violence to which she had been so lately subjected.

Chapter the Twenty-Seventh.

Julia. ————— Gentle sir,
You are our captive — but we'll use you so,
That you shall think your prison joys may match
Whate'er your liberty hath known of pleasure.
Roderick. No, fairest, we have trifled here too long ;
And, lingering to see your roses blossom,
I've let my laurels wither.

OLD PLAY.

ARRAYED in garments of a mourning colour, and of a fashion more matronly than perhaps altogether befitted her youth — plain to an extremity, and devoid of all ornament, save her rosary — Eveline now performed the duty of waiting upon her wounded deliverer; a duty which the etiquette of the time not only permitted, but peremptorily enjoined. She was attended by Rose and Dame Gillian. Margery, whose element was a sick-chamber, had been already despatched to that of the young knight, to attend to whatever his condition might require.

Eveline entered the room with a light step, as if unwilling to disturb the patient. She paused at the door, and cast her eyes around her. It had been her father's chamber; nor had she entered it since his violent death. Around the walls hung a part of his armour and weapons, with hawking-gloves, hunting-poles, and other instruments of silvan sport. These relics brought as it were in living form before her the stately presence of old Sir Raymond. ."Frown not, my father," — her lips formed the words, though her voice did not utter them—"Frown not—Eveline will never be unworthy of thee."

Father Aldrovand, and Amelot, the page of Damian, were seated by the bedside. They rose as Lady Eveline entered; and the first, who meddled a little with the healing art, said to Eveline "that the knight had slumbered for some time, and was now about to awake."

Amelot at the same time came forward, and in a hasty and low voice, begged that the chamber might be kept quiet, and the spectators requested to retire. "My lord," he said, "ever since his illness at Gloucester, is apt to speak something wildly as he awakes from sleep, and will be displeased with me should I permit any one to be near him."

Eveline accordingly caused her women and the monk to retire into the anteroom, while she herself remained standing by the door-communication which connected the apartments, and heard Damian mention her name as he turned himself painfully on his couch. "Is she safe and unharmed?" was his first question, and it was asked with an eagerness which intimated how far it preceded all other considerations. When Amelot replied in the affirmative, he sighed, as one whose bosom is relieved from some weighty load, and in a less animated voice, asked of the page where they were. "This apartment," he said, "with its furniture, are all strange to me."

"My dear master," said Amelot, "you are at present too weak to ask questions and receive explanations."

"Be I where I will," said Damian, as if recovering his recollection, "I am not in the place where my duty calls me. Tell my trumpets to sound to horse — to horse, and let Ralph Genvil carry my banner. To horse — to horse! we have not a moment to lose!"

The wounded knight made some effort to rise, which, in his state of weakness, Amelot was easily able to frustrate. "Thou art right," he said, as he sunk back into his reclining posture —"thou art right — I am weak —·but why should strength remain when honour is lost?"

The unhappy young man covered his face with his hands, and groaned in agony, which seemed more that of the mind than of the body. Lady Eveline approached his bedside with unassured steps, fearing she knew not what, yet earnest to testify the interest she felt in the distresses of the sufferer. Damian looked up and beheld her, and again hid his face with his hands.

"What means this strange passion, Sir Knight?" said Eveline, with a voice which, at first weak and trembling, gradually obtained steadiness and composure. "Ought it to grieve you so much, sworn as you are to the duties of chivalry, that Heaven hath twice made you its instrument to save the unfortunate Eveline Berenger?"

"Oh no, no!" he exclaimed with rapidity; "since you are saved, all is well — but time presses — it is necessary I should presently depart — nowhere ought I now to tarry — least of all, within this castle — Once more, Amelot, let them get to horse!"

"Nay, my good lord," said the damsel, "this must not be. As your ward, I cannot let my guardian part thus suddenly—as a physician, I cannot allow my patient to destroy himself—It is impossible that you can brook the saddle."

"A litter — a bier — a cart, to drag forth the dishonoured knight and traitor — all were too good for me — a coffin were best of all!—But see, Amelot, that it be framed like that of the meanest churl — no spurs displayed on the pall — no shield with the ancient coat of the De Lacys — no helmet with their knightly crest must deck the hearse of him whose name is dishonoured!"

"Is his brain unsettled?" said Eveline, looking with terror from the wounded man to his attendant; "or is there some dreadful mystery in these broken words?—If so, speak it forth; and if it may be amended by life or goods, my deliverer will sustain no wrong."

Amelot regarded her with a dejected and melancholy air, shook his head, and looked down on his master with a countenance which seemed to express, that the questions which she asked could not be prudently answered in Sir Damian's presence. The Lady Eveline, observing this gesture, stepped back into the outer apartment, and made Amelot a sign to follow her. He obeyed, after a glance at his master, who remained in the same disconsolate posture as formerly, with his hands crossed over his eyes, like one who wished to exclude the light, and all which the light made visible.

When Amelot was in the wardrobe, Eveline, making signs to her attendants to keep at such distance as the room permitted, questioned him closely on the cause of his master's desperate expression of terror and remorse. "Thou knowest," she said, "that I am bound to succour thy lord, if I may, both from gratitude, as one whom he hath served to the peril of his life — and also from kinsmanship. Tell me, therefore, in what case he stands, that I may help him if I can — that is," she added, her pale cheeks deeply colouring, "if the cause of the distress be fitting for me to hear."

The page bowed low, yet showed such embarrassment when he began to speak, as produced a corresponding degree of confusion in the Lady Eveline, who, nevertheless, urged him as before "to speak without scruple or delay — so that the tenor of his discourse was fitting for her ears."

"Believe me, noble lady," said Amelot, "your commands had been instantly obeyed, but that I fear my master's displeasure if I talk of his affairs without his warrant; nevertheless, on your command, whom I know he honours above all earthly beings, I will speak thus far, that if his life be safe from the wounds he has received, his honour and worship may be in great danger, if it please not Heaven to send a remedy."

"Speak on," said Eveline; "and be assured you will do Sir Damian de Lacy no prejudice by the confidence you may rest in me."

"I well believe it, lady," said the page. "Know, then, if it be not already known to you, that the clowns and rabble, who have taken arms against the nobles in the west, pretend to be favoured in their insurrection, not only by Randal Lacy, but by my master, Sir Damian."

"They lie that dare charge him with such foul treason to his own blood, as well as to his sovereign!" replied Eveline.

"Well do I believe they lie," said Amelot; "but this hinders not their falsehoods from being believed by those who know him less inwardly. More than one runaway from our troop have joined this rabblement, and that gives some credit to the scandal. And then they say—they say—that—in short, that my master longs to possess the lands in his proper right which he occupies as his uncle's administrator; and that if the old Constable—I crave your pardon, madam—should return from Palestine, he should find it difficult to obtain possession of his own again."

"The sordid wretches judge of others by their own base minds, and conceive those temptations too powerful for men of worth, which they are themselves conscious they would be unable to resist. But are the insurgents then so insolent and so powerful? We have heard of their violences, but only as if it had been some popular tumult."

"We had notice last night that they have drawn together in great force, and besieged or blockaded Wild Wenlock, with his men-at-arms, in a village about ten miles hence. He hath sent to my master, as his kinsman and companion-at-arms, to come to his assistance. We were on horseback this morning to march to the rescue—when ——"

He paused, and seemed unwilling to proceed. Eveline caught at the word. "When you heard of my danger?" she said. "I would ye had rather heard of my death!"

"Surely, noble lady," said the page, with his eyes fixed on the ground, "nothing but so strong a cause could have made my master halt his troop, and carry the better part of them to the Welsh mountains, when his countryman's distress, and the commands of the King's Lieutenant, so peremptorily demanded his presence elsewhere."

"I knew it," she said—"I knew I was born to be his destruction! yet methinks this is worse than I dreamed of, when the worst was in my thoughts. I feared to occasion his death, not his loss of fame. For God's sake, young Amelot, do what thou canst, and that without loss of time! Get thee straightway to horse, and join to thy own men as many as thou canst gather of mine—Go—ride, my brave youth—show thy master's banner, and let them see that his forces and his heart are with them, though his person be absent. Haste, haste, for the time is precious."

"But the safety of this castle—But your own safety?" said the page. "God knows how willingly I would do aught to save his fame! But I know my master's mood; and were you to suffer by my leaving the Garde Doloureuse, even although I were to save him lands, life, and honour, by my doing so, I should be more like to taste of his dagger, than of his thanks or bounty."

"Go, nevertheless, dear Amelot," said she; "gather what force thou canst make, and begone."

"You spur a willing horse, madam," said the page, springing to his feet; "and in the condition of my master, I see nothing better than that his banner should be displayed against these churls."

"To arms, then," said Eveline, hastily; "to arms, and win thy spurs. Bring me assurance that thy master's honour is safe, and will myself buckle them on thy heels. Here—take this blessed osary—bind it on thy crest, and be the thought of the Virgin of the Garde Doloureuse, that never failed a votary, strong with thee in the hour of conflict."

She had scarcely ended, ere Amelot flew from her presence, and summoning together such horse as he could assemble, both of his master's, and of those belonging to the castle, there were soon forty cavaliers mounted in the court-yard.

But although the page was thus far readily obeyed, yet when the soldiers heard they were to go forth on a dangerous expedition, with no more experienced general than a youth of fifteen, they showed a decided reluctance to move from the castle. The old soldiers of De Lacy said, Damian himself was almost too youthful to command them, and had no right to delegate his authority to a mere boy; while the followers of Berenger said, their mistress might be satisfied with her deliverance of the morning, without trying farther dangerous conclusions by diminishing the garrison of her castle — "The times," they said, "were stormy, and it was wisest to keep a stone roof over their heads."

The more the soldiers communicated their ideas and apprehensions to each other, the stronger their disinclination to the undertaking became; and when Amelot, who, page-like, had gone to see that his own horse was accoutred and brought forth, returned to the castle-yard, he found them standing confusedly together, some mounted, some on foot, all men speaking loud, and all in a state of disorder. Ralph Genvil, a veteran whose face had been seamed with many a scar, and who had long followed the trade of a soldier of fortune, stood apart from the rest, holding his horse's bridle in one hand, and in the other the banner-spear, around which the banner of De Lacy was still folded.

"What means this, Genvil?" said the page, angrily. "Why do you not mount your horse and display the banner? and what occasions all this confusion?"

"Truly, Sir Page," said Genvil, composedly, "I am not in my saddle, because I have some regard for this old silken rag, which I have borne to honour in my time, and I will not willingly carry it where men are unwilling to follow and defend it."

"No march—no sally—no lifting of banner to-day!" cried the soldiers, by way of burden to the banner-man's discourse.

"How now, cowards! do you mutiny?" said Amelot, laying his hand upon his sword.

"Menace not me, Sir Boy," said Genvil; "nor shake your sword my way. I tell thee, Amelot, were my weapon to cross with yours, never flail sent abroad more chaff than I would make splinters of your hatched and gilded toasting-iron. Look you, there are gray-bearded men here that care not to be led about on any boy's humour. For me, I stand little upon that; and I care not whether one boy or another commands me. But I am the Lacy's man for the time; and I am not sure that, in marching to the aid of this Wild Wenlock, we shall do an errand the Lacy will thank us for. Why led he us not thither in the morning when we were commanded off into the mountains?"

"You well know the cause," said the page.

"Yes, we do know the cause; or, if we do not, we can guess it," answered the banner-man, with a horse laugh, which was echoed by several of his companions.

"I will cram the calumny down thy false throat, Genvil!" said the page; and, drawing his sword, threw himself headlong on the banner-man, without considering their great difference of strength.

Genvil was contented to foil his attack by one, and, as it seemed, a slight movement of his gigantic arm, with which he forced the page aside, parrying, at the same time, his blow with the standard-spear.

There was another loud laugh, and Amelot, feeling all his efforts baffled, threw his sword from him, and weeping in pride and indignation, hastened back to tell the Lady Eveline of his bad success. "All," he said, "is lost — the cowardly villains have mutinied, and will not move; and the blame of their sloth and faintheartedness will be laid on my dear master."

"That shall never be," said Eveline, "should I die to prevent it.—Follow me, Amelot."

She hastily threw a scarlet scarf over her dark garments, and hastened down to the court-yard, followed by Gillian, assuming, as she went, various attitudes and actions expressing astonishment and pity, and by Rose, carefully suppressing all appearance of the feelings which she really entertained.

Eveline entered the castle-court, with the kindling eye and glowing brow which her ancestors were wont to bear in danger and extremity, when their soul was arming to meet the storm, and displayed in their mien and looks high command and contempt of danger. She seemed at the moment taller than her usual size; and it was with a voice distinct and clearly heard, though not exceeding the delicacy of feminine tone, that the mutineers heard her address them. "How is this, my masters?" she said; and as she spoke, the bulky forms of the armed soldiers seemed to draw closer together, as if to escape her individual censure. It was like a group of heavy water-fowl, when they close to avoid the stoop of the slight and beautiful merlin, dreading the superiority of its nature and breeding over their own inert physical strength.—"How now?" again she demanded of them; "is it a time, think ye, to mutiny, when your lord is absent, and his nephew and lieutenant lies stretched on a bed of sickness?—Is it thus you keep your oaths?—Thus ye merit your leader's bounty?—Shame on ye, craven hounds, that quail and give back the instant you lose sight of the huntsman!"

There was a pause—the soldiers looked on each other, and then again on Eveline, as if ashamed alike to hold out in their mutiny, or to return to their usual discipline.

"I see how it is, my brave friends—ye lack a leader here; but stay not for that—I will guide you myself, and, woman as I am, there need not a man of you fear disgrace where a Berenger commands.—Trap my palfrey with a steel saddle," she said, "and that instantly." She snatched from the ground the page's light head-piece, and threw it over her hair, caught up his drawn sword, and went on. "Here I promise you my countenance and guidance — this gentleman," she pointed to Genvil, "shall supply my lack of military skill. He looks like a man that hath seen many a day of battle, and can well teach a young leader her devoir."

"Certes," said the old soldier, smiling in spite of himself, and shaking his head at the same time, "many a battle have I seen, but never under such a commander."

"Nevertheless," said Eveline, seeing how the eyes of the rest turned on Genvil, "you do not—cannot—will not—refuse to follow me? You do not as a soldier, for my weak voice supplies your captain's orders—you cannot as a gentleman, for a lady, a forlorn and distressed female, asks you a boon — you will not as an Englishman, for your country requires your sword, and your comrades are in danger. Unfurl your banner, then, and march."

"I would do so, upon my soul, fair lady," answered Genvil, as if preparing to unfold the banner — "And Amelot might lead us well enough, with advantage of some lessons from me. But I wot not whether you are sending us on the right road."

"Surely, surely," said Eveline, earnestly, "it must be the right road which conducts you to the relief of Wenlock and his followers, besieged by the insurgent boors."

"I know not," said Genvil, still hesitating. "Our leader here, Sir Damian de Lacy, protects the commons — men say he befriends them — and I know he quarrelled with Wild Wenlock once for some petty wrong he did to the miller's wife at Twyford. We should be finely off, when our fiery young leader is on foot again, if he should find we had been fighting against the side he favoured."

"Assure yourself," said the maiden, anxiously, "the more he would protect the commons against oppression, the more he would put them down when oppressing others. Mount and ride — save Wenlock and his men — there is life and death in every moment. I will warrant, with my life and lands, that whatsoever you do will be held good service to De Lacy. Come, then, follow me."

"None surely can know Sir Damian's purpose better than you, fair damsel," answered Genvil; "nay, for that matter, you can make him change as ye list. — And so I will march with the men, and we will aid Wenlock, if it is yet time, as I trust it may; for he is a rugged wolf, and when he turns to bay, will cost the boors blood enough ere they sound a mort. But do you remain within the castle, fair lady, and trust to Amelot and me. — Come, Sir Page, assume the command, since so it must be; though, by my faith, it is pity to take the head-piece from that pretty head, and the sword from that pretty hand — By Saint George! to see them there is a credit to the soldier's profession."

The Lady accordingly surrendered the weapons to Amelot, exhorting him in few words to forget the offence he had received, and do his devoir manfully. Meanwhile Genvil slowly unrolled the pennon—then shook it abroad, and without putting his foot in the stirrup, aided himself a little with resting on the spear, and threw himself into the saddle, heavily armed as he was. "We are ready now, an it like your juvenility," said he to Amelot; and then, while the page was putting the band into order, he whispered to his nearest comrade, "Methinks, instead of this old swallow's tail,* we should muster rarely under a broidered petticoat — a furbelowed petticoat has no fellow in my mind. — Look you, Stephen Pontoys — I can forgive Damian now for forgetting his uncle and his own credit, about this wench; for, by my faith, she is one I could have doated to death upon *par amours.* Ah! evil luck be the women's portion! — they govern us at every turn, Stephen, and at every age. When they are young, they bribe us with fair looks, and sugared words, sweet kisses and love tokens; and when they are of middle age, they work us to their will by presents and courtesies, red wine and red gold; and when they are old, we are fain to run their errands to get out of sight of their old leathern visages. Well, old De Lacy should have staid at home and watched his falcon. But it is all one to us, Stephen, and we may make some vantage to-day, for these boors have plundered more than one castle."

"Ay, ay," answered Pontoys, "the boor to the booty, and the banner-man to the boor, a right pithy proverb. But, prithee, canst thou say why his pageship leads us not forward yet?"

"Pshaw!" answered Genvil, "the shake I gave him has addled his brains — or perchance he has not swallowed all his tears yet; sloth it is not, for 'tis a forward cockeril for his years, wherever honour is to be won. — See, they now begin to move. — Well, it is a singular thing this gentle blood, Stephen; for here is a child whom I but now baffled like a schoolboy, must lead us graybeards where we may get our heads broken, and that at the command of a light lady."

"I warrant Sir Damian is secretary to my pretty lady," answered Stephen Pontoys, "as this springald Amelot is to Sir Damian; and so we poor men must obey and keep our mouths shut."

"But our eyes open, Stephen Pontoys—forget not that."

They were by this time out of the gates of the castle, and upon the road leading to the village, in which, as they understood by the intelligence of the morning, Wenlock was besieged or blockaded by a greatly superior number of the insurgent commons. Amelot rode at the head of the troop, still embarrassed at the affront which he had received in presence of the

---

* The pennon of a Knight was, in shape, a long streamer, and forked like a swallow's tail: the banner of a Banneret was square, and was formed into the other by cutting the ends from the pennon. It was 'hee the ceremony was performed on the pennon of John Chandos, by the Black Prince, before the battle of Najara.

soldiers, and lost in meditating how he was to eke out that deficiency of experience, which on former occasions had been supplied by the counsels of the banner-man, with whom he was ashamed to seek a reconciliation. But Genvil was not of a nature absolutely sullen, though a habitual grumbler. He rode up to the page, and having made his obeisance, respectfully asked him whether it were not well that some one or two of their number pricked forward upon good horses to learn how it stood with Wenlock, and whether they should be able to come up in time to his assistance.

"Methinks, banner-man," answered Amelot, "you should take the ruling of the troop, since you know so fittingly what should be done. You may be the fitter to command, because—But I will not upbraid you."

"Because I know so ill how to obey," replied Genvil; "that is what you would say; and, by my faith, I cannot deny but there may be some truth in it. But is it not peevish in thee to let a fair expedition be unwisely conducted, because of a foolish word or a sudden action?—Come, let it be peace with us."

"With all my heart," answered Amelot; "and I will send out an advanced party upon the adventure, as thou hast advised me."

"Let it be old Stephen Pontoys and two of the Chester spears—he is as wily as an old fox, and neither hope nor fear will draw him a hairbreadth farther than judgment warrants."

Amelot eagerly embraced the hint, and, at his command, Pontoys and two lances started forward to reconnoitre the road before them, and inquire into the condition of those whom they were advancing to succour. "And now that we are on the old terms, Sir Page," said the banner-man, "tell me, if thou canst, doth not yonder fair lady love our handsome knight *par amours?*"

"It is a false calumny," said Amelot, indignantly; "betrothed as she is to his uncle, I am convinced she would rather die than have such a thought, and so would our master. I have noted this heretical belief in thee before now, Genvil, and I have prayed thee to check it. You know the thing cannot be, for you know they have scarce ever met."

"How should I know that," said Genvil, "or thou either? Watch them ever so close—much water slides past the mill that Hob Miller never wots of. They do correspond; that, at least, thou canst not deny?"

"I do deny it," said Amelot, "as I deny all that can touch their honour."

"Then how, in Heaven's name, comes he by such perfect knowledge of her motions, as he has displayed no longer since than the morning?"

"How should I tell?" answered the page; "there be such things. surely, as saints and good angels, and if there be one on earth deserves their protection, it is Dame Eveline Berenger."

"Well said, Master Counsel-keeper," replied Genvil, laughing; "but that will hardly pass on an old trooper.—Saint and angels, quotha? most saint-like doings, I warrant you."

The page was about to continue his angry vindication, when Stephen Pontoys and his followers returned upon the spur. "Wenlock holds out bravely," he exclaimed, "though he is felly girded in with these boors. The large crossbows are doing good service; and I little doubt his making his place good till we come up, if it please you to ride something sharply. They have assailed the barriers, and were close up to them even now, but were driven back with small success."

The party were now put in as rapid motion as might consist with order, and soon reached the top of a small eminence, beneath which lay the village where Wenlock was making his defence. The air rung with the cries and shouts of the insurgents, who, numerous as bees, and possessed of that dogged spirit of courage so peculiar to the English, thronged like ants to the barriers, and endeavoured to break down the palisades, or to climb over them, in despite of the showers of stones and arrows from within, by which they suffered great loss, as well as by the swords and battle-axes of the men-at-arms, whenever they came to hand-blows.

"We are in time, we are in time," said Amelot, dropping the reins of his bridle, and joyfully clapping his hands; "shake thy banner abroad, Genvil —give Wenlock and his fellows a fair view of it.—Comrades, halt—breathe your horses for a moment.—Hark hither, Genvil—If we descend by yonder broad pathway into the meadow where the cattle are———"

"Bravo, my young falcon!" replied Genvil, whose love of battle, like that of the war-horse of Job, kindled at the sight of the spears, and at the sound of the trumpet; "we shall have then an easy field for a charge on yonder knaves."

"What a thick black cloud the villains make!" said Amelot; "but we will let daylight through it with our lances—See, Genvil, the defenders hoist a signal to show they have seen us."

"A signal to us?" exclaimed Genvil. "By Heaven, it is a white flag—a signal of surrender!"

"Surrender! they cannot dream of it, when we are advancing to their succour," replied Amelot; when two or three melancholy notes from the trumpets of the besieged, with a thundering and tumultuous acclamation from the besiegers, rendered the fact indisputable.

"Down goes Wenlock's pennon," said Genvil, "and the churls enter the barricades on all points.—Here has been cowardice or treachery—What is to be done?"

"Advance on them," said Amelot, "retake the place, and deliver the prisoners."

"Advance, indeed!" answered the banner-man—"Not a horse's length by my counsel—we should have every nail in our corslets counted with arrow-shot, before we got down the hill in the face of such a multitude; and the place to storm afterwards—it were mere insanity."

"Yet come a little forward along with me," said the page; "perhaps we may find some path by which we could descend unperceived."

Accordingly they rode forward a little way to reconnoitre the face of the hill, the page still urging the possibility of descending it unperceived amid the confusion, when Genvil answered impatiently, "Unperceived!—you are already perceived—here comes a fellow, pricking towards us as fast as his beast may trot."

As he spoke, the rider came up to them. He was a short, thick-set peasant, in an ordinary frieze jacket and hose, with a blue cap on his head, which he had been scarcely able to pull over a shock head of red hair, that seemed in arms to repel the covering. The man's hands were bloody, and he carried at his saddlebow a linen bag, which was also stained with blood. "Ye be of Damian de Lacy's company, be ye not?" said this rude messenger; and, when they answered in the affirmative, he proceeded with the same blunt courtesy, "Hob Miller of Twyford commends him to Damian de Lacy, and knowing his purpose to amend disorders in the commonwealth, Hob Miller sends him toll of the grist which he has grinded;" and with that he took from the bag a human head, and tendered it to Amelot.

"It is Wenlock's head," said Genvil—"how his eyes stare!"

"They will stare after no more wenches now," said the boor—"I have cured him of caterwauling."

"Thou!" said Amelot, stepping back in disgust and indignation.

"Yes, I myself," replied the peasant; "I am Grand Justiciar of the Commons, for lack of a better."

"Grand hangman, thou wouldst say," replied Genvil.

"Call it what thou list," replied the peasant. "Truly, it behoves men in state to give good example. I'll bid no man do that I am not ready to do myself. It is as easy to hang a man, as to say hang him; we will have no splitting of offices in this new world, which is happily set up in old England."

"Wretch!" said Amelot, "take back thy bloody token to them that sent thee! Hadst thou not come upon assurance, I had pinned thee to the earth with my lance—But, be assured, your cruelty shall be fearfully avenged.—Come, Genvil, let us to our men; there is no farther use in abiding here."

The fellow, who had expected a very different reception, stood staring after them for a few moments, then replaced his bloody trophy in the wallet, and rode back to those who sent him.

"This comes of meddling with men's *amourettes*," said Genvil; "Sir Damian would needs brawl with Wenlock about his dealings with this miller's daughter, and you see they account him a favourer of their enterprise; it will be well if others do not take up the same opinion.—I wish we were rid of the trouble which such suspicions may bring upon us—ay, were it at the price of my best horse—I am like to lose him at any rate with the day's hard service, and I would it were the worst it is to cost us."

The party returned, wearied and discomforted, to the castle of the Garde Doloureuse, and not without losing several of their number by the way, some straggling owing to the weariness of their horses, and others taking the opportunity of desertion, in order to join the bands of insurgents and plunderers, who had now gathered together in different quarters, and were augmented by recruits from the dissolute soldiery.

Amelot, on his return to the castle, found that the state of his master was still very precarious, and that the Lady Eveline, though much exhausted, had not yet retired to rest, but was awaiting his return with impatience. He was introduced to her accordingly, and, with a heavy heart, mentioned the ineffectual event of his expedition.

"Now the saints have pity upon us!" said the Lady Eveline; "for it seems as if a plague or pest attached to me, and extended itself to all who interest themselves in my welfare. From the moment they do so, their very virtues become snares to them; and what would, in every other case, recommend them to honour, is turned to destruction to the friends of Eveline Berenger."

"Fear not, fair lady," said Amelot; "there are still men enough in my master's camp to put down these disturbers of the public peace. I will but abide to receive his instructions, and will hence to-morrow, and draw out a force to restore quiet in this part of the country."

"Alas! you know not yet the worst of it," replied Eveline. "Since you went hence, we have received certain notice, that when the soldiers at Sir Damian's camp heard of the accident which he this morning met with, already discontented with the inactive life which they had of late led, and dispirited by the hurts and reported death of their leader, they have altogether broken up and dispersed their forces. Yet be of good courage, Amelot," she said; "this house is strong enough to bear out a worse tempest than any that is likely to be poured on it; and if all men desert your master in wounds and affliction, it becomes yet more the part of Eveline Berenger to shelter and protect her deliverer."

Chapter the Twenty-Eighth.

Let our proud trumpet shake their castle wall,
Menacing death and ruin.
                                        OTWAY.

THE evil news with which the last chapter concluded were necessarily told to Damian de Lacy, as the person whom they chiefly concerned; and Lady Eveline herself undertook the task of communicating them, mingling what she said with tears, and again interrupting those tears to suggest topics of hope and comfort, which carried no consolation to her own bosom.

The wounded knight continued with his face turned towards her, listening to the disastrous tidings, as one who was not otherwise affected by them, than as they regarded her who told the story. When she had done speaking, he continued as in a reverie, with his eyes so intently fixed upon her, that she rose up, with the purpose of withdrawing from looks by which she felt herself embarrassed. He hastened to speak, that he might prevent her departure. "All that you have said, fair lady," he replied, "had been enough, if told by another, to have broken my heart; for it tells me that the power and honour of my house, so solemnly committed to my charge, have been blasted in my misfortunes. But when I look upon you, and hear your voice, I forget every thing, saving that you have been rescued, and are here in honour and safety. Let me therefore pray of your goodness that I may be removed from the castle which holds you, and sent elsewhere. I am in no shape worthy of your farther care, since I have no longer the swords of others at my disposal, and am totally unable for the present to draw my own."

"And if you are generous enough to think of me in your own misfortunes, noble knight," answered Eveline, "can you suppose that I forget wherefore, and in whose rescue, these wounds were incurred? No, Damian, speak not of removal—while there is a turret of the Garde Douloureuse standing, within that turret shall you find shelter and protection. Such, I am well assured, would be the pleasure of your uncle, were he here in person."

It seemed as if a sudden pang of his wound had seized upon Damian; for, repeating the words "My uncle!" he writhed himself round, and averted his face from Eveline; then again composing himself, replied, "Alas! knew my uncle how ill I have obeyed his precepts, instead of sheltering me within this house, he would command me to be flung from the battlements!"

"Fear not his displeasure," said Eveline, again preparing to withdraw; "but endeavour, by the composure of your spirit, to aid the healing of your wounds; when, I doubt not, you will be able again to establish good order in the Constable's jurisdiction, long before his return."

She coloured as she pronounced the last words, and hastily left the apartment. When she was in her own chamber, she dismissed her other attendants and retained Rose. "What dost thou think of these things, my wise maiden and monitress?" said she.

"I would," replied Rose, "either that this young knight had never entered this castle — or that, being here, he could presently leave it — or, that he could honourably remain here for ever."

"What dost thou mean by remaining here for ever?" said Eveline sharply and hastily.

"Let me answer that question with another — How long has the Constable of Chester been absent from England?"

"Three years come Saint Clement's day," said Eveline; "and what of that?"

"Nay, nothing; but ——"

"But what? — I command you to speak out."

"A few weeks will place your hand at your own disposal."

"And think you, Rose," said Eveline, rising with dignity, "that there are no bonds save those which are drawn by the scribe's pen?—We know little of the Constable's adventures; but we know enough to show that his towering hopes have fallen, and his sword and courage proved too weak to change the fortunes of the Sultan Saladin. Suppose him returning some brief time hence, as we have seen so many crusaders regain their homes, poor and broken in health — suppose that he finds his lands laid waste, and his followers dispersed, by the consequence of their late misfortunes, how would it sound should he also find that his betrothed bride had wedded and endowed with her substance the nephew whom he most trusted? — Dost thou think such an engagement is like a Lombard's mortgage, which must be redeemed on the very day, else forfeiture is sure to be awarded?"

"I cannot tell, madam," replied Rose; "but they that keep their covenant to the letter, are, in my country, held bound to no more."

"That is a Flemish fashion, Rose," said her mistress; "but the honour of a Norman is not satisfied with an observance so limited. What! wouldst thou have my honour, my affections, my duty, all that is most valuable to a woman, depend on the same progress of the kalendar which an usurer watches for the purpose of seizing on a forfeited pledge? — Am I such a mere commodity, that I must belong to one man if he claims me before Michaelmas, to another if he comes afterwards? —No, Rose; I did not thus interpret my engagement, sanctioned as it was by the special providence of Our Lady of the Garde Doloureuse."

"It is a feeling worthy of you, my dearest lady," answered the attendant; "yet you are so young—so beset with perils—so much exposed to calumny — that I, at least, looking forward to the time when you may have a legal companion and protector, see it as an extrication from much doubt and danger."

"Do not think of it, Rose," answered Eveline; "do not liken your mistress to those provident dames, who, while one husband yet lives, though in old age or weak health, are prudently engaged in plotting for another."

"Enough, my dearest lady," said Rose; — "yet not so. Permit me one word more. Since you are determined not to avail yourself of your freedom, even when the fatal period of your engagement is expired, why suffer this young man to share our solitude?—He is surely well enough to be removed to some other place of security. Let us resume our former sequestered mode of life, until Providence send us some better or more certain prospects."

Eveline sighed — looked down — then looking upwards, once more had opened her lips to express her willingness to enforce so reasonable an arrangement, but for Damian's recent wounds, and the distracted state of the country, when she was interrupted by the shrill sound of trumpets, blown before the gate of the castle; and Raoul, with anxiety on his brow, came limping to inform his lady, that a knight, attended by a pursuivant-at-arms, in the royal livery, with a strong guard, was in front of the castle, and demanded admittance in the name of the King.

Eveline paused a moment ere she replied, "Not even to the King's order shall the castle of my ancestors be opened, until we are well assured of the person by whom, and the purpose for which, it is demanded. We will ourself to the gate, and learn the meaning of this summons — My veil, Rose; and call my women. — Again that trumpet sounds! Alas! it rings like a signal to death and ruin."

The prophetic apprehensions of Eveline were not false; for scarce had she reached the door of the apartment, when she was met by the page

Amelot, in a state of such disordered apprehension as an elève of chivalry was scarce on any occasion permitted to display. "Lady, noble lady," he said, hastily bending his knee to Eveline, "save my dearest master!—You, and you alone, can save him at this extremity."

"I!" said Eveline, in astonishment—"I save him?—And from what danger?—God knows how willingly!"

There she stopped short, as if afraid to trust herself with expressing what rose to her lips.

"Guy Monthermer, lady, is at the gate, with a pursuivant and the royal banner. The hereditary enemy of the House of Lacy, thus accompanied, comes hither for no good—the extent of the evil I know not, but for evil he comes. My master slew his nephew at the field of Malpas, and therefore "—— He was here interrupted by another flourish of trumpets, which rung, as if in shrill impatience, through the vaults of the ancient fortress.

The Lady Eveline hasted to the gate, and found that the wardens, and others who attended there, were looking on each other with doubtful and alarmed countenances, which they turned upon her at her arrival, as if to seek from their mistress the comfort and the courage which they could not communicate to each other. Without the gate, mounted, and in complete armour, was an elderly and stately knight, whose raised visor and beaver depressed, showed a beard already grizzled. Beside him appeared the pursuivant on horseback, the royal arms embroidered on his heraldic dress of office, and all the importance of offended consequence on his countenance, which was shaded by his barret-cap and triple plume. They were attended by a body of about fifty soldiers, arranged under the guidon of England.

When the Lady Eveline appeared at the barrier, the knight, after a slight reverence, which seemed more in formal courtesy than in kindness, demanded if he saw the daughter of Raymond Berenger. "And is it," he continued, when he had received an answer in the affirmative, "before the castle of that approved and favoured servant of the House of Anjou, that King Henry's trumpets have thrice sounded, without obtaining an entrance for those who are honoured with their Sovereign's command?"

"My condition," answered Eveline, "must excuse my caution. I am a lone maiden, residing in a frontier fortress. I may admit no one without inquiring his purpose, and being assured that his entrance consists with the safety of the place, and mine own honour."

"Since you are so punctilious, lady," replied Monthermer, "know, that in the present distracted state of the country, it is his Grace the King's pleasure to place within your walls a body of men-at-arms, sufficient to guard this important castle, both from the insurgent peasants, who burn and slay, and from the Welsh, who, it must be expected, will, according to their wont in time of disturbance, make incursions on the frontiers. Undo your gates, then, Lady of Berenger, and suffer his Grace's forces to enter the castle."

"Sir Knight," answered the lady, "this castle, like every other fortress in England, is the King's by law; but by law also I am the keeper and defender of it; and it is the tenure by which my ancestors held these lands. I have men enough to maintain the Garde Doloureuse in my time, as my father, and my grandfather before him, defended it in theirs. The King is gracious to send me succours, but I need not the aid of hirelings; neither do I think it safe to admit such into my castle, who may, in this lawless time, make themselves master of it for other than its lawful mistress."

"Lady," replied the old warrior, "his Grace is not ignorant of the motives which produce a contumacy like this. It is not any apprehension for the royal forces which influences you, a royal vassal, in this refractory conduct. I might proceed upon your refusal to proclaim you a traitor to the Crown, but the King remembers the services of your father. Know, then, we are not ignorant that Damian de Lacy, accused of instigating and heading this insurrection, and of deserting his duty in the field, and abandoning a noble comrade to the swords of the brutal peasants, has found shelter under this roof, with little credit to your loyalty as a vassal, or your conduct as a high-born maiden. Deliver him up to us, and I will draw off these men-at-arms, and dispense, though I may scarce answer doing so, with the occupation of the castle."

"Guy de Monthermer," answered Eveline, "he that throws a stain on my name, speaks falsely and unworthily; as for Damian de Lacy, he knows how to defend his own fame. This only let me say, that, while he takes his abode in the castle of the betrothed of his kinsman, she delivers him to no one, least of all to his well-known feudal enemy — Drop the portcullis, wardens, and let it not be raised without my special order."

The portcullis, as she spoke, fell rattling and clanging to the ground, and Monthermer, in baffled spite, remained excluded from the castle. "Unworthy lady"—he began in passion, then, checking himself, said calmly to the pursuivant, "Ye are witness that she hath admitted that the traitor is within that castle, — ye are witness that, lawfully summoned, this Eveline Berenger refuses to deliver him up. Do your duty, Sir Pursuivant, as is usual in such cases."

The pursuivant then advanced and proclaimed, in the formal and fatal phrase befitting the occasion, that Eveline Berenger, lawfully summoned, refusing to admit the King's forces into her castle, and to deliver up the body of a false traitor, called Damian de Lacy, had herself incurred the penalty of high treason, and had involved within the same doom all who aided, abetted, or maintained her in holding out the said castle against their allegiance to Henry of Anjou. The trumpets, so soon as the voice of the herald had ceased, confirmed the doom he had pronounced, by a long and ominous peal, startling from their nests the owl and the raven, who replied to it by their ill-boding screams.

The defenders of the castle looked on each other with blank and dejected countenances, while Monthermer, raising aloft his lance, exclaimed, as he turned his horse from the castle gate, "When I next approach the Garde Doloureuse, it will be not merely to intimate, but to execute, the mandate of my Sovereign."

As Eveline stood pensively to behold the retreat of Monthermer and his associates, and to consider what was to be done in this emergency, she heard one of the Flemings, in a low tone, ask an Englishman, who stood beside him, what was the meaning of a traitor.

"One who betrayeth a trust reposed — a betrayer," said the interpreter.

The phrase which he used recalled to Eveline's memory her boding vision or dream. "Alas!" she said, "the vengeance of the fiend is about to be accomplished. Widow'd wife and wedded maid — these epithets have long been mine. Betrothed! — wo's me! it is the key-stone of my destiny. Betrayer I am now denounced, though, thank God, I am clear from the guilt! It only follows that I should be betrayed, and the evil prophecy will be fulfilled to the very letter."

Chapter the Twenty-Ninth.

Out on ye, owls; Nothing but songs of death!
RICHARD III.

MORE than three months had elapsed since the event narrated in the last chapter, and it had been the precursor of others of still greater importance, which will evolve themselves in the course of our narrative. But, as we profess to present to the reader not a precise detail of circumstances, according to their order and date, but a series of pictures, endeavouring to exhibit the most striking incidents before the eye or imagination of those whom it may concern, we therefore open a new scene, and bring other actors upon the stage.

Along a wasted tract of country, more than twelve miles distant from the Garde Doloureuse, in the heat of a summer noon, which shed a burning lustre on the silent valley, and the blackened ruins of the cottages with which it had been once graced, two travellers walked slowly, whose palmer cloaks, pilgrims' staves, large slouched hats, with a scallop shell bound on the front of each, above all, the cross, cut in red cloth upon their shoulders, marked them as pilgrims who had accomplished their vow, and had returned from that fatal bourne, from which, in those days, returned so few of the thousands who visited it, whether in the love of enterprise, or in the ardour of devotion.

The pilgrims had passed, that morning, through a scene of devastation similar to, and scarce surpassed in misery by, those which they had often trod during the wars of the Cross. They had seen hamlets which appeared to have suffered all the fury of military execution, the houses being burned to the ground; and in many cases the carcasses of the miserable inhabitants, or rather relics of such objects, were suspended on temporary gibbets, or on the trees, which had been allowed to remain standing, only, it would seem, to serve the convenience of the executioners. Living creatures they saw none, excepting those wild denizens of nature who seemed silently resuming the now wasted district, from which they might have been formerly expelled by the course of civilization. Their ears were no less disagreeably occupied than their eyes. The pensive travellers might indeed hear the screams of the raven, as if lamenting the decay of the carnage on which he had been gorged; and now and then the plaintive howl of some dog, deprived of his home and master; but no sounds which argued either labour or domestication of any kind.

The sable figures, who, with wearied steps, as it appeared, travelled through these scenes of desolation and ravage, seemed assimilated to them in appearance. They spoke not with each other — they looked not to each other — but one, the shorter of the pair, keeping about half a pace in front of his companion, they moved slowly, as priests returning from a sinner's death-bed, or rather as spectres flitting along the precincts of a churchyard.

At length they reached a grassy mound, on the top of which was placed one of those receptacles for the dead of the ancient British chiefs of distinction, called Kist-ven, which are composed of upright fragments of granite, so placed as to form a stone coffin, or something bearing that resemblance. The sepulchre had been long violated by the victorious Saxons, either in scorn or in idle curiosity, or because treasures were supposed to be sometimes concealed in such spots. The huge flat stone which had once been the cover of the coffin, if so it might be termed, lay broken in two pieces at some distance from the sepulchre; and, overgrown as the fragments were with grass and lichens, showed plainly that the lid had been removed to its present situation many years before. A stunted and doddered oak still spread its branches over the open and rude mausoleum, as if the Druid's badge and emblem, shattered and storm-broken, was still bending to offer its protection to the last remnants of their worship.

"This, then, is the _Kist-vaen_," said the shorter pilgrim; "and here we must abide tidings of our scout. But what, Philip Guarine, have we to expect as an explanation of the devastation which we have traversed?"

"Some incursion of the Welsh wolves, my lord," replied Guarine; "and, by Our Lady, here lies a poor Saxon sheep whom they have snapped up."

The Constable (for he was the pilgrim who had walked foremost) turned as he heard his squire speak, and saw the corpse of a man amongst the long grass; by which, indeed, it was so hidden, that he himself had passed without notice, what the esquire, in less abstracted mood, had not failed to observe. The leathern doublet of the slain bespoke him an English peasant — the body lay on its face, and the arrow which had caused his death still stuck in his back.

Philip Guarine, with the cool indifference of one accustomed to such scenes, drew the shaft from the man's back, as composedly as he would have removed it from the body of a deer. With similar indifference the Constable signed to his esquire to give him the arrow — looked at it with indolent curiosity, and then said, "Thou hast forgotten thy old craft, Guarine, when thou callest that a Welsh shaft. Trust me, it flew from a Norman bow; but why it should be found in the body of that English churl, I can ill guess."

"Some runaway serf, I would warrant — some mongrel cur, who had joined the Welsh pack of hounds," answered the esquire.

"It may be so," said the Constable; "but I rather augur some civil war among the Lords Marchers themselves. The Welsh, indeed, sweep the villages, and leave nothing behind them but blood and ashes, but here even castles seem to have been stormed and taken. May God send us good news of the Garde Doloureuse!"

"Amen!" replied his squire; "but if Renault Vidal brings it, 'twill be the first time he has proved a bird of good omen."

"Philip," said the Constable, "I have already told thee thou art a jealous-pated fool. How many times has Vidal shown his faith in doubt — his address in difficulty — his courage in battle — his patience under suffering?"

"It may be all very true, my lord," replied Guarine; "yet — but what avails to speak? — I own he has done you sometimes good service; but loath were I that your life or honour were at the mercy of Renault Vidal."

"In the name of all the saints, thou peevish and suspicious fool, what is it thou canst found upon to his prejudice?"

"Nothing, my lord," replied Guarine, "but instinctive suspicion and aversion. The child that, for the first time, sees a snake, knows nothing of its evil properties, yet he will not chase it and take it up as he would a butterfly. Such is my dislike of Vidal — I cannot help it. I could pardon the man his malicious and gloomy sidelong looks, when he thinks no one observes him; but his sneering laugh I cannot forgive — it is like the beast we heard of in Judea, who laughs, they say, before he tears and destroys."

"Philip," said De Lacy, "I am sorry for thee — sorry, from my soul, to see such a predominating and causeless jealousy occupy the brain of a gallant old soldier. Here, in this last misfortune, to recall no more ancient proofs of his fidelity, could he mean otherwise than well with us, when, thrown by shipwreck upon the coast of Wales, we would have been doomed to instant death, had the Cymri recognized in me the Constable of Chester, and in thee his trusty esquire, the executioner of his commands against the Welsh in so many instances?"

"I acknowledge," said Philip Guarine, "death had surely been our fortune, had not that man's ingenuity represented us as pilgrims, and, under that character, acted as our interpreter — and in that character he entirely precluded us from getting information from any one respecting the state of things here, which it behoved your lordship much to know, and which I must needs say looks gloomy and suspicious enough."

"Still art thou a fool, Guarine," said the Constable; "for, look you, had Vidal meant ill by us, why should he not have betrayed us to the Welsh, or suffered us, by showing such knowledge as thou and I may have of their gibberish, to betray ourselves?"

"Well, my lord," said Guarine, "I may be silenced, but not satisfied. All the fair words he can speak — all the fine tunes he can play — Renault

Vidal will be to my eyes ever a dark and suspicious man, with features always ready to mould themselves into the fittest form to attract confidence; with a tongue framed to utter the most flattering and agreeable words at one time, and at another to play shrewd plainness or blunt honesty; and an eye which, when he thinks himself unobserved, contradicts every assumed expression of features, every protestation of honesty, and every word of courtesy or cordiality to which his tongue has given utterance. But I speak not more on the subject; only I am an old mastiff, of the true breed — I love my master, but cannot endure some of those whom he favours; and yonder, as I judge, comes Vidal, to give us such an account of our situation as it shall please him."

A horseman was indeed seen advancing in the path towards the Kist-vaen, with a hasty pace; and his dress, in which something of the Eastern fashion was manifest, with the fantastic attire usually worn by men of his profession, made the Constable aware that the minstrel, of whom they were speaking, was rapidly approaching them.

Although Hugo de Lacy rendered this attendant no more than what in justice he supposed his services demanded, when he vindicated him from the suspicions thrown out by Guarine, yet at the bottom of his heart he had sometimes shared those suspicions, and was often angry at himself, as a just and honest man, for censuring, on the slight testimony of looks, and sometimes casual expressions, a fidelity which seemed to be proved by many acts of zeal and integrity.

When Vidal approached and dismounted to make his obeisance, his master hasted to speak to him in words of favour, as if conscious he had been partly sharing Guarine's unjust judgment upon him, by even listening to it. "Welcome, my trusty Vidal," he said; "thou hast been the raven that fed us on the mountains of Wales, be now the dove that brings us good tidings from the Marches.—Thou art silent. What mean these downcast looks — that embarrassed carriage — that cap plucked down o'er thine eyes? — In God's name, man, speak!—Fear not for me — I can bear worse than tongue of man may tell. Thou hast seen me in the wars of Palestine, when my brave followers fell, man by man, around me, and when I was left well-nigh alone — and did I blench then? — Thou hast seen me when the ship's keel lay grating on the rock, and the billows flew in foam over her deck — did I blench then? — No — nor will I now."

"Boast not," said the minstrel, looking fixedly upon the Constable, as the former assumed the port and countenance of one who sets Fortune and her utmost malice at defiance—"boast not, lest thy bands be made strong."

There was a pause of a minute, during which the group formed at this instant a singular picture.

Afraid to ask, yet ashamed to *seem* to fear the ill tidings which impended, the Constable confronted his messenger with person erect, arms folded, and brow expanded with resolution; while the minstrel, carried beyond his usual and guarded apathy by the interest of the moment, bent on his master a keen fixed glance, as if to observe whether his courage was real or assumed.

Philip Guarine, on the other hand, to whom Heaven, in assigning him a rough exterior, had denied neither sense nor observation, kept his eye in turn firmly fixed on Vidal, as if endeavouring to determine what was the character of that deep interest which gleamed in the minstrel's looks apparently, and was unable to ascertain whether it was that of a faithful domestic sympathetically agitated by the bad news with which he was about to afflict his master, or that of an executioner standing with his knife suspended over his victim, deferring his blow until he should discover where it would be most sensibly felt. In Guarine's mind, prejudiced, perhaps, by the previous opinion he had entertained, the latter sentiment so decidedly predominated, that he longed to raise his staff, and strike down to the earth the servant, who seemed thus to enjoy the protracted sufferings of their common master.

At length a convulsive movement crossed the brow of the Constable, and Guarine, when he beheld a sardonic smile begin to curl Vidal's lip, could keep silence no longer. "Vidal," he said, "thou art a——"

"A bearer of bad tidings," said Vidal, interrupting him, "therefore subject to the misconstruction of every fool who cannot distinguish between the author of harm, and him who unwillingly reports it."

"To what purpose this delay?" said the Constable. "Come, Sir Minstrel, I will spare you a pang — Eveline has forsaken and forgotten me?"

The minstrel assented by a low inclination.

Hugo de Lacy paced a short turn before the stone monument, endeavouring to conquer the deep emotion which he felt. "I forgive her," he said. "Forgive, did I say — Alas! I have nothing to forgive. She used but the right I left in her hand — yes — our date of engagement was out — she had heard of my losses — my defeats — the destruction of my hopes — the expenditure of my wealth; and has taken the first opportunity which strict law afforded to break off her engagement with one bankrupt in fortune and fame. Many a maiden would have done — perhaps in prudence should have done — this; — but that woman's name should not have been Eveline Berenger."

He leaned on his esquire's arm, and for an instant laid his head on his shoulder with a depth of emotion which Guarine had never before seen him betray, and which, in awkward kindness, he could only attempt to console, by bidding his master "be of good courage — he had lost but a woman."

"This is no selfish emotion, Philip," said the Constable, resuming self-command. "I grieve less that she has left me, than that she has misjudged me — that she has treated me as the pawnbroker does his wretched creditor, who arrests the pledge as the very moment elapses within which it might have been relieved. Did she then think that I in my turn would have been a creditor so rigid? — that I, who, since I knew her, scarce deemed myself worthy of her when I had wealth and fame, should insist on her sharing my diminished and degraded fortunes? How little she ever knew me, or how selfish must she have supposed my misfortunes to have made me! But be it so — she is gone, and may she be happy. The thought that she disturbed me shall pass from my mind; and I will think she has done that which I myself, as her best friend, must in honour have advised."

So saying, his countenance, to the surprise of his attendants, resumed its usual firm composure.

"I give you joy," said the esquire, in a whisper to the minstrel; "your evil news have wounded less deeply than, doubtless, you believed was possible."

"Alas!" replied the minstrel, "I have others and worse behind."

This answer was made in an equivocal tone of voice, corresponding to the peculiarity of his manner, and like that seeming emotion of a deep but very doubtful character.

"Eveline Berenger is then married," said the Constable; "and, let me make a wild guess,—she has not abandoned the family, though she has forsaken the individual—she is still a Lacy? ha?—Dolt that thou art, wilt thou not understand me? She is married to Damian de Lacy—to my nephew?"

The effort with which the Constable gave breath to this supposition formed a strange contrast to the constrained smile to which he compelled his features while he uttered it. With such a smile a man about to drink poison might name a health, as he put the fatal beverage to his lips.

"No, my lord—not *married*," answered the minstrel, with an emphasis on the word, which the Constable knew how to interpret.

"No, no," he replied quickly, "not married, perhaps, but engaged—

troth-plighted. Wherefore not? The date of her old affiance was out, why not enter into a new engagement?"

"The Lady Eveline and Sir Damian de Lacy are not affianced that I know of," answered his attendant.

This reply drove De Lacy's patience to extremity.

"Dog! dost thou trifle with me?" he exclaimed: "Vile wire-pincher, thou torturest me! Speak the worst at once, or I will presently make thee minstrel to the household of Satan."

Calm and collected did the minstrel reply,—"The Lady Eveline and Sir Damian are neither married nor affianced, my lord. They have loved and lived together—*par amours*."

"Dog, and son of a dog," said De Lacy, "thou liest!" And, seizing the minstrel by the breast, the exasperated baron shook him with his whole strength. But great as that strength was, it was unable to stagger Vidal, a practised wrestler, in the firm posture which he had assumed, any more than his master's wrath could disturb the composure of the minstrel's bearing.

"Confess thou hast lied," said the Constable, releasing him, after having effected by his violence no greater degree of agitation than the exertion of human force produces upon the Rocking Stones of the Druids, which may be shaken, indeed, but not displaced.

"Were a lie to buy my own life, yea, the lives of all my tribe," said the minstrel, "I would not tell one. But truth itself is ever termed falsehood when it counteracts the train of our passions."

"Hear him, Philip Guarine, hear him!" exclaimed the Constable, turning hastily to his squire: "He tells me of my disgrace—of the dishonour of my house—of the depravity of those whom I have loved the best in the world—he tells me of it with a calm look, an eye composed, an unfaltering tongue.—Is this—can it be natural? Is De Lacy sunk so low, that his dishonour shall be told by a common strolling minstrel, as calmly as if it were a theme for a vain ballad? Perhaps thou wilt make it one, ha!" as he concluded, darting a furious glance at the minstrel.

"Perhaps I might, my lord," replied the minstrel, "were it not that I must record therein the disgrace of Renault Vidal, who served a lord without either patience to bear insults and wrongs, or spirit to revenge them on the authors of his shame."

"Thou art right, thou art right, good fellow," said the Constable, hastily; "it is vengeance now alone which is left us—And yet upon whom?"

As he spoke he walked shortly and hastily to and fro; and, becoming suddenly silent, stood still and wrung his hands with deep emotion.

"I told thee," said the minstrel to Guarine, "that my muse would find a tender part at last. Dost thou remember the bull-fight we saw in Spain? A thousand little darts perplexed and annoyed the noble animal, ere he received the last deadly thrust from the lance of the Moorish Cavalier."

"Man, or fiend, be which thou wilt," replied Guarine, "that can thus drink in with pleasure, and contemplate at your ease, the misery of another, I bid thee beware of me! Utter thy cold-blooded taunts in some other ear; for if my tongue be blunt, I wear a sword that is sharp enough."

"Thou hast seen me amongst swords," answered the minstrel, "and knowest how little terror they have for such as I am." Yet as he spoke he drew off from the esquire. He had, in fact, only addressed him in that sort of fulness of heart, which would have vented itself in soliloquy if alone, and now poured itself out on the nearest auditor, without the speaker being entirely conscious of the sentiments which his speech excited.

Few minutes had elapsed before the Constable of Chester had regained the calm external semblance with which, until this last dreadful wound, he had borne all the inflictions of fortune. He turned towards his followers, and addressed the minstrel with his usual calmness, "Thou art right, good

2 o

fellow," he said, "in what thou saidst to me but now, and I forgive thee the taunt which accompanied thy good counsel. Speak out, in God's name! and speak to one prepared to endure the evil which God hath sent him. Certes, a good knight is best known in battle, and a Christian in the time of trouble and adversity."

The tone in which the Constable spoke, seemed to produce a corresponding effect upon the deportment of his followers. The minstrel dropped at once the cynical and audacious tone in which he had hitherto seemed to tamper with the passions of his master; and in language simple and respectful, and which even approached to sympathy, informed him of the evil news which he had collected during his absence. It was indeed disastrous.

The refusal of the Lady Eveline Berenger to admit Monthermer and his forces into her castle, had of course given circulation and credence to all the calumnies which had been circulated to her prejudice, and that of Damian de Lacy; and there were many who, for various causes, were interested in spreading and supporting these slanders. A large force had been sent into the country to subdue the insurgent peasants; and the knights and nobles despatched for that purpose, failed not to avenge to the uttermost, upon the wretched plebeians, the noble blood which they had spilled during their temporary triumph.

The followers of the unfortunate Wenlock were infected with the same persuasion. Blamed by many for a hasty and cowardly surrender of a post which might have been defended, they endeavoured to vindicate themselves by alleging the hostile demonstrations of De Lacy's cavalry as the sole cause of their premature submission.

These rumours, supported by such interested testimony, spread wide and far through the land; and, joined to the undeniable fact that Damian had sought refuge in the strong castle of Garde Doloureuse, which was now defending itself against the royal arms, animated the numerous enemies of the house of De Lacy, and drove its vassals and friends almost to despair, as men reduced either to disown their feudal allegiance, or renounce that still more sacred fealty which they owed to their sovereign.

At this crisis they received intelligence that the wise and active monarch by whom the sceptre of England was then swayed, was moving towards that part of England, at the head of a large body of soldiers, for the purpose at once of pressing the siege of the Garde Doloureuse, and completing the suppression of the insurrection of the peasantry, which Guy Monthermer had nearly accomplished.

In this emergency, and when the friends and dependents of the House of Lacy scarcely knew which hand to turn to, Randal, the Constable's kinsman, and, after Damian, his heir, suddenly appeared amongst them, with a royal commission to raise and command such followers of the family as might not desire to be involved in the supposed treason of the Constable's delegate. In troublesome times, men's vices are forgotten, provided they display activity, courage, and prudence, the virtues then most required; and the appearance of Randal, who was by no means deficient in any of these attributes, was received as a good omen by the followers of his cousin. They quickly gathered around him, surrendered to the royal mandate such strongholds as they possessed, and, to vindicate themselves from any participation in the alleged crimes of Damian, they distinguished themselves, under Randal's command, against such scattered bodies of peasantry as still kept the field, or lurked in the mountains and passes; and conducted themselves with such severity after success, as made the troops even of Monthermer appear gentle and clement in comparison with those of De Lacy. Finally, with the banner of his ancient house displayed, and five hundred good men assembled under it, Randal appeared before the Garde Doloureuse, and joined Henry's camp there.

The castle was already hardly pressed, and the few defenders, disabled by wounds, watching, and privation, had now the additional discouragement to see displayed against their walls the only banner in England under which they had hoped forces might be mustered for their aid.

The high-spirited entreaties of Eveline, unbent by adversity and want, gradually lost effect on the defenders of the castle; and proposals for surrender were urged and discussed by a tumultuary council, into which not only the inferior officers, but many of the common men, had thrust themselves, as in a period of such general distress as unlooses all the bonds of discipline, and leaves each man at liberty to speak and act for himself. To their surprise, in the midst of their discussions, Damian de Lacy, arisen from the sick-bed to which he had been so long confined, appeared among them, pale and feeble, his cheek tinged with the ghastly look which is left by long illness — he leaned on his page Amelot. "Gentlemen," he said, "and soldiers — yet why should I call you either? — Gentlemen are ever ready to die in behalf of a lady — soldiers hold life in scorn compared to their honour."

"Out upon him! out upon him!" exclaimed some of the soldiers, interrupting him; "he would have us, who are innocent, die the death of traitors, and be hanged in our armour over the walls, rather than part with his leman."

"Peace, irreverent slave!" said Damian, in a voice like thunder, "or my last blow shall be a mean one, aimed against such a caitiff as thou art. — And you," he continued, addressing the rest, — "you, who are shrinking from the toils of your profession, because if you persist in a course of honour, death may close them a few years sooner than it needs must—you, who are scared like children at the sight of a death's-head, do not suppose that Damian de Lacy would desire to shelter himself at the expense of those lives which you hold so dear. Make your bargain with King Henry. Deliver me up to his justice, or his severity; or, if you like it better, strike my head from my body, and hurl it, as a peace-offering, from the walls of the castle. To God, in his good time, will I trust for the clearance of mine honour. In a word, surrender me, dead or alive, or open the gates and permit me to surrender myself. Only, as ye are men, since I may not say better of ye, care at least for the safety of your mistress, and make such terms as may secure HER safety, and save yourselves from the dishonour of being held cowardly and perjured caitiffs in your graves."

"Methinks the youth speaks well and reasonably," said William Flammock. "Let us e'en make a grace of surrendering his body up to the King, and assure thereby such terms as we can for ourselves and the lady, ere the last morsel of our provision is consumed."

"I would hardly have proposed this measure," said, or rather mumbled, Father Aldrovand, who had recently lost four of his front teeth by a stone from a sling, — "yet, being so generously offered by the party principally concerned, I hold with the learned scholiast, *Volenti non fit injuria.*"

"Priest and Fleming," said the old banner-man, Ralph Genvil, "I see how the wind stirreth you; but you deceive yourselves if you think to make our young master, Sir Damian, a scape-goat for your light lady. — Nay, never frown nor fume, Sir Damian; if you know not your safest course, we know it for you. — Followers of De Lacy, throw yourselves on your horses, and two men on one, if it be necessary—we will take this stubborn boy in the midst of us, and the dainty squire Amelot shall be prisoner too, if he trouble us with his peevish opposition. Then let us make a fair sally upon the siegers. Those who can cut their way through will shift well enough; those who fall, will be provided for."

A shout from the troopers of Lacy's band approved this proposal. Whilst the followers of Berenger expostulated in loud and angry tone, Eveline, summoned by the tumult, in vain endeavoured to appease it; and the anger and entreaties of Damian were equally lost on his followers. To each and either the answer was the same.

"Have you no care of it—Because you love *par amours*, is it reasonable you should throw away your life and ours?" So exclaimed Genvil to De Lacy; and in softer language, but with equal obstinacy, the followers of Raymond Berenger refused on the present occasion to listen to the commands or prayers of his daughter.

Wilkin Flammock had retreated from the tumult, when he saw the turn which matters had taken. He left the castle by a sally-port, of which he had been intrusted with the key, and proceeded without observation or opposition to the royal camp, where he requested access to the Sovereign. This was easily obtained, and Wilkin speedily found himself in the presence of King Henry. The monarch was in his royal pavilion, attended by two of his sons, Richard and John, who afterwards swayed the sceptre of England with very different auspices.

"How now?—What art thou?" was the royal question.

"An honest man, from the castle of the Garde Doloureuse."

"Thou may'st be honest," replied the Sovereign, "but thou comest from a nest of traitors."

"Such as they are, my lord, it is my purpose to put them at your royal disposal; for they have no longer the wisdom to guide themselves, and lack alike prudence to hold out, and grace to submit. But I would first know of your grace to what terms you will admit the defenders of yonder garrison?"

"To such as kings give to traitors," said Henry, sternly—"sharp knives and tough cords."

"Nay, my gracious lord, you must be kinder than that amounts to, if the castle is to be rendered by my means; else will your cords and knives have only my poor body to work upon, and you will be as far as ever from the inside of the Garde Doloureuse."

The King looked at him fixedly. "Thou knowest," he said, "the law of arms. Here, provost-marshal, stands a traitor, and yonder stands a tree."

"And here is a throat," said the stout-hearted Fleming, unbuttoning the collar of his doublet.

"By mine honour," said Prince Richard, "a sturdy and faithful yeoman! It were better send such fellows their dinners, and then buffet it out with them for the castle, than to starve them as the beggarly Frenchmen famish their hounds."

"Peace, Richard," said his father; "thy wit is over green, and thy blood over hot, to make thee my counsellor here. — And you, knave, speak you some reasonable terms, and we will not be over strict with thee."

"First, then," said the Fleming, "I stipulate full and free pardon for life, limb, body, and goods, to me, Wilkin Flammock, and my daughter Rose."

"A true Fleming," said Prince John; "he takes care of himself in the first instance."

"His request," said the King, "is reasonable. What next?"

"Safety in life, honour, and land, for the demoiselle Eveline Berenger."

"How, sir knave!" said the King, angrily, "is it for such as thou to dictate to our judgment or clemency in the case of a noble Norman Lady? Confine thy mediation to such as thyself; or rather render us this castle without farther delay; and be assured thy doing so will be of more service to the traitors within, than weeks more of resistance, which must and shall be bootless."

The Fleming stood silent, unwilling to surrender without some specific terms, yet half convinced, from the situation in which he had left the garrison of the Garde Doloureuse, that his admitting the King's forces would be, perhaps, the best he could do for Lady Eveline.

"I like thy fidelity, fellow," said the King, whose acute eye perceived the struggle in the Fleming's bosom; "but carry not thy stubbornness too far. Have we not said we will be gracious to yonder offenders, as far as our royal duty will permit?"

"And, royal father," said Prince John, interposing, "I pray you let me have the grace to take first possession of the Garde Doloureuse, and the wardship or forfeiture of the offending lady."

"*I* pray you also, my royal father, to grant John's boon," said his brother Richard, in a tone of mockery. "Consider, royal father, it is the first desire he hath shown to approach the barriers of the castle, though we have attacked them forty times at least. Marry, crossbow and mangonel were busy on the former occasions, and it is like they will be silent now."

"Peace, Richard," said the King; "your words, aimed at thy brother's honour, pierce my heart.—John, thou hast thy boon as concerns the castle; for the unhappy young lady, we will take her in our own charge.—Fleming, how many men wilt thou undertake to admit?"

Ere Flammock could answer, a squire approached Prince Richard, and whispered in his ear, yet so as to be heard by all present, "We have discovered that some internal disturbance, or other cause unknown, has withdrawn many of the warders from the castle walls, and that a sudden attack might——"

"Dost thou hear that, John?" exclaimed Richard. "Ladders, man—get ladders, and to the wall. How I should delight to see thee on the highest round—thy knees shaking—thy hands grasping convulsively, like those of one in an ague fit—all air around thee, save a baton or two of wood—the moat below—half-a-dozen pikes at thy throat——"

"Peace, Richard, for shame, if not for charity!" said his father, in a tone of anger, mingled with grief. "And thou, John, get ready for the assault."

"As soon as I have put on my armour, father," answered the Prince; and withdrew slowly, with a visage so blank as to promise no speed in his preparations.

His brother laughed as he retired, and said to his squire, "It were no bad jest, Alberick, to carry the place ere John can change his silk doublet for a steel one."

So saying, he hastily withdrew, and his father exclaimed in paternal distress, "Out, alas! as much too hot as his brother is too cold; but it is the manlier fault.—Gloucester," said he to that celebrated earl, "take sufficient strength, and follow Prince Richard to guard and sustain him. If any one can rule him, it must be a knight of thy established fame. Alas, alas! for what sin have I deserved the affliction of these cruel family feuds!"

"Be comforted, my lord," said the chancellor, who was also in attendance. "Speak not of comfort to a father, whose sons are at discord with each other, and agree only in their disobedience to him!"

Thus spoke Henry the Second, than whom no wiser, or, generally speaking, more fortunate monarch ever sat upon the throne of England; yet whose life is a striking illustration, how family dissensions can tarnish the most brilliant lot to which Heaven permits humanity to aspire; and how little gratified ambition, extended power, and the highest reputation in war and in peace, can do towards curing the wounds of domestic affliction.

The sudden and fiery attack of Richard, who hastened to the escalade at the head of a score of followers, collected at random, had the complete effect of surprise; and having surmounted the walls with their ladders, before the contending parties within were almost aware of the assault, the assailants burst open the gates, and admitted Gloucester, who had hastily followed with a strong body of men-at-arms. The garrison, in their state of surprise, confusion, and disunion, offered but little resistance, and would have been put to the sword, and the place plundered, had not Henry himself entered it, and by his personal exertions and authority, restrained the excesses of the dissolute soldiery.

The King conducted himself, considering the times and the provocation, with laudable moderation. He contented himself with disarming and dismissing the common soldiers, giving them some trifle to carry them out of the country, lest want should lead them to form themselves into bands of robbers. The officers were more severely treated, being for the greater part thrown into dungeons, to abide the course of the law. In particular, imprisonment was the lot of Damian de Lacy, against whom, believing the various charges with which he was loaded, Henry was so highly incensed, that he purposed to make him an example to all false knights and disloyal subjects. To the Lady Eveline Berenger he assigned her own apartment as a prison, in which she was honourably attended by Rose and Alice, but guarded with the utmost strictness. It was generally reported that her demesnes would be declared a forfeiture to the crown, and bestowed, at least in part, upon Randal de Lacy, who had done good service during the siege. Her person, it was thought, was destined to the seclusion of some distant French nunnery, where she might at leisure repent her of her follies and her rashness.

Father Aldrovand was delivered up to the discipline of the convent, long experience having very effectually taught Henry the imprudence of infringing on the privileges of the church; although, when the King first beheld him with a rusty corslet clasped over his frock, he with difficulty repressed the desire to cause him be hanged over the battlements, to preach to the ravens.

With Wilkin Flammock, Henry held much conference, particularly on his subject of manufactures and commerce; on which the sound-headed, though blunt-spoken Fleming, was well qualified to instruct an intelligent monarch. "Thy intentions," he said, "shall not be forgotten, good fellow, though they have been anticipated by the headlong valour of my son Richard, which has cost some poor caitiffs their lives—Richard loves not to sheathe a bloodless weapon. But thou and thy countrymen shall return to thy mills yonder, with a full pardon for past offences, so that you meddle no more with such treasonable matters."

"And our privileges and duties, my liege?" said Flammock. "Your Majesty knows well we are vassals to the lord of this castle, and must follow him in battle."

"It shall no longer be so," said Henry; "I will form a community of Flemings here, and thou, Flammock, shalt be Mayor, that thou may'st not plead feudal obedience for a relapse into treason."

"Treason, my liege!" said Flammock, longing, yet scarce venturing, to interpose a word in behalf of Lady Eveline, for whom, despite the constitutional coolness of his temperament, he really felt much interest—"I would that your Grace but justly knew how many threads went to that woof."

"Peace, sirrah!—meddle with your loom," said Henry; "and if we deign to speak to thee concerning the mechanical arts which thou dost profess, take it for no warrant to intrude farther on our privacy."

The Fleming retired, rebuked, and in silence; and the fate of the unhappy prisoners remained in the King's bosom. He himself took up his lodging in the castle of the Garde Doloureuse, as a convenient station for sending abroad parties to suppress and extinguish all the embers of rebellion; and so active was Randal de Lacy on these occasions, that he appeared daily to rise in the King's grace, and was gratified with considerable grants out of the domains of Berenger and Lacy, which the King seemed already to treat as forfeited property. Most men considered this growing favour of Randal as a perilous omen, both for the life of young De Lacy, and for the fate of the unfortunate Eveline.

Chapter the Thirtieth.

A vow, a vow—I have a vow in Heaven.
Shall I bring perjury upon my soul?
No, not for Venice.

MERCHANT OF VENICE.

THE conclusion of the last chapter contains the tidings with which the minstrel greeted his unhappy master, Hugo de Lacy; not indeed with the same detail of circumstances with which we have been able to invest the narrative, but so as to infer the general and appalling facts, that his betrothed bride, and beloved and trusted kinsman, had leagued together for his dishonour—had raised the banner of rebellion against their lawful sovereign, and, failing in their audacious attempt, had brought the life of one of them, at least, into the most imminent danger, and the fortunes of the House of Lacy, unless some instant remedy could be found, to the very verge of ruin.

Vidal marked the countenance of his master as he spoke, with the same keen observation which the chirurgeon gives to the progress of his dissecting-knife. There was grief on the Constable's features — deep grief— but without the expression of abasement or prostration which usually accompanies it; anger and shame were there—but they were both of a noble character, seemingly excited by his bride and nephew's transgressing the laws of allegiance, honour, and virtue, rather than by the disgrace and damage which he himself sustained through their crime.

The minstrel was so much astonished at this change of deportment, from the sensitive acuteness of agony which attended the beginning of his narrative, that he stepped back two paces, and gazing on the Constable with wonder, mixed with admiration, exclaimed, "We have heard of martyrs in Palestine, but this exceeds them!"

"Wonder not so much, good friend," said the Constable, patiently; "it is the first blow of the lance or mace which pierces or stuns — those which follow are little felt." *

"Think, my lord," said Vidal, "all is lost — love, dominion, high office, and bright fame—so late a chief among nobles, now a poor palmer!"

"Wouldst thou make sport with my misery?" said Hugo, sternly; "but even that comes of course behind my back, and why should it not be endured when said to my face?—Know, then, minstrel, and put it in song if you list, that Hugo de Lacy, having lost all he carried to Palestine, and all which he left at home, is still lord of his own mind; and adversity can no more shake him, than the breeze which strips the oak of its leaves can tear up the trunk by the roots."

"Now, by the tomb of my father," said the minstrel, rapturously, "this man's nobleness is too much for my resolve!" and stepping hastily to the Constable, he kneeled on one knee, and caught his hand more freely than the state maintained by men of De Lacy's rank usually permitted.

"Here," said Vidal, "on this hand—this noble hand—I renounce——"

But ere he could utter another word, Hugo de Lacy, who, perhaps, felt the freedom of the action as an intrusion on his fallen condition, pulled

---

* Such an expression is said to have been used by Mandrin, the celebrated smuggler, while in the act of being broken upon the wheel. This dreadful punishment consists in the executioner, with a bar of iron, breaking the shoulder-bones, arms, thigh-bones, and legs of the criminal, taking his alternate sides. The punishment is concluded by a blow across the breast, called the coup de grace, because it removes the sufferer from his agony. When Mandrin received the second blow over the left shoulder-bone, he laughed. His confessor inquired the reason of demeanour so unbecoming his situation. "I only laugh at my own folly, my father," answered Mandrin, "who could suppose that sensibility of pain should continue after the nervous system had been completely deranged by the first blow."

back his hand, and bid the minstrel, with a stern frown, arise, and remember that misfortune made not De Lacy a fit personage for a mummery.

Renault Vidal rose rebuked. "I had forgot," he said, "the distance between an Armorican violer and a high Norman baron. I thought that the same depth of sorrow, the same burst of joy, levelled, for a moment at least, those artificial barriers by which men are divided. But it is well as it is. Live within the limits of your rank, as heretofore within your donjon tower and your fosses, my lord, undisturbed by the sympathy of any mean man like me. I, too, have my duties to discharge."

"And now to the Garde Douloureuse," said the baron, turning to Philip Guarine—"God knoweth how well it deserveth the name!—there to learn, with our own eyes and ears, the truth of these woful tidings. Dismount, minstrel, and give me thy palfrey — I would, Guarine, that I had one for thee—as for Vidal, his attendance is less necessary. I will face my foes, or my misfortunes, like a man — that be assured of, violer; and look not so sullen, knave—I will not forget old adherents."

"One of them, at least, will not forget you, my lord," replied the minstrel, with his usual dubious tone of look and emphasis.

But just as the Constable was about to prick forwards, two persons appeared on the path, mounted on one horse, who, hidden by some dwarf-wood, had come very near them without being perceived. They were male and female; and the man, who rode foremost, was such a picture of famine, as the eyes of the pilgrims had scarce witnessed in all the wasted land through which they had travelled. His features, naturally sharp and thin, had disappeared almost entirely among the uncombed gray beard and hairs with which they were overshadowed; and it was but the glimpse of a long nose, that seemed as sharp as the edge of a knife, and the twinkling glimpse of his gray eyes, which gave any intimation of his lineaments. His leg, in the wide old boot which enclosed it, looked like the handle of a mop left by chance in a pail — his arms were about the thickness of riding-rods — and such parts of his person as were not concealed by the tatters of a huntsman's cassock, seemed rather the appendages of a mummy than a live man.

The female who sat behind this spectre exhibited also some symptoms of extenuation; but being a brave jolly dame naturally, famine had not been able to render her a spectacle so rueful as the anatomy behind which she rode. Dame Gillian's cheek (for it was the reader's old acquaintance) had indeed lost the rosy hue of good cheer, and the smoothness of complexion which art and easy living had formerly substituted for the more delicate bloom of youth; her eyes were sunken, and had lost much of their bold and roguish lustre; but she was still in some measure herself, and the remnants of former finery, together with the tight-drawn scarlet hose, though sorely faded, showed still a remnant of coquettish pretension.

So soon as she came within sight of the pilgrims, she began to punch Raoul with the end of her riding-rod. "Try thy new trade, man, since thou art unfit for any other — to the good man — to them — crave their charity."

"Beg from beggars?" muttered Raoul; "that were hawking at sparrows, dame."

"It will bring our hand in use though," said Gillian; and commenced, in a whining tone, "God love you, holy men, who have had the grace to go to the Holy Land, and, what is more, have had the grace to come back again; I pray, bestow some of your alms upon my poor old husband, who is a miserable object, as you see, and upon one who has the bad luck to be his wife—Heaven help me!"

"Peace, woman, and hear what I have to say," said the Constable, laying his hand upon the bridle of the horse — "I have present occasion for that horse, and——"

"By the hunting-horn of St. Hubert, but thou gettest him not without blows!" answered the old huntsman ~ "A fine world it is, when palmers turn horse-stealers."

"Peace, fellow!" said the Constable, sternly, — "I say I have occasion presently for the service of thy horse. Here be two gold bezants for a day's use of the brute; it is well worth the fee-simple of him, were he never returned."

"But the palfrey is an old acquaintance, master," said Raoul; "and if perchance——"

"Out upon *if* and *perchance* both," said the dame, giving her husband so determined a thrust as well-nigh pushed him out of the saddle. "Off the horse! and thank God and this worthy man for the help he hath sent us in this extremity. What signifies the palfrey, when we have not enough to get food either for the brute or ourselves? not though we would eat grass and corn with him, like King Somebody, whom the good father used to read us to sleep about."

"A truce with your prating, dame," said Raoul, offering his assistance to help her from the croupe; but she preferred that of Guarine, who, though advanced in years, retained the advantage of his stout soldierly figure.

"I humbly thank your goodness," said she, as, (having first kissed her,) the squire set her on the ground. "And, pray, sir, are ye come from the Holy Land? — Heard ye any tidings there of him that was Constable of Chester?"

De Lacy, who was engaged in removing the pillion from behind the saddle, stopped short in his task, and said, "Ha, dame! what would you with him?"

"A great deal, good palmer, an I could light on him; for his lands and offices are all to be given, it's like, to that false thief, his kinsman."

"What!—to Damian, his nephew?" exclaimed the Constable, in a harsh and hasty tone.

"Lord, how you startle me, sir!" said Gillian; then continued, turning to Philip Guarine, "Your friend is a hasty man, belike."

"It is the fault of the sun he has lived under so long," said the squire; "but look you answer his questions truly, and he will make it the better for you."

Gillian instantly took the hint. "Was it Damian de Lacy you asked after? — Alas! poor young gentleman! no offices or lands for him — more likely to have a gallows-cast, poor lad — and all for nought, as I am a true dame. Damian!—no, no, it is not Damian, or damson neither—but Randal Lacy, that must rule the roast, and have all the old man's lands, and livings, and lordships."

"What?" said the Constable — "before they know whether the old man is dead or no?—Methinks that were against law and reason both."

"Ay, but Randal Lacy has brought about less likely matters. Look you, he hath sworn to the King that they have true tidings of the Constable's death — ay, and let him alone to make them soothfast enough, if the Constable were once within his danger."

"Indeed!" said the Constable. "But you are forging tales on a noble gentleman. Come, come, dame, you say this because you like not Randal Lacy."

"Like him not!—And what reason have I to like him, I trow?" answered Gillian. "Is it because he seduced my simplicity to let him into the castle of the Garde Douloureuse—ay, oftener than once or twice either,—when he was disguised as a pedlar, and told him all the secrets of the family, and how the boy Damian, and the girl Eveline, were dying of love with each other, but had not courage to say a word of it, for fear of the Constable, though he were a thousand miles off? — You seem concerned, worthy sir — may I offer your reverend worship a trifling sup from my bottle, which is sovereign for *tremor cordis*, and fits of the spleen?"

"No, no," ejaculated De Lacy—"I was but grieved with the shooting of an old wound. But, dame, I warrant me this Damian and Eveline, as you call them, became better, closer friends, in time?"

"They?—not they indeed, poor simpletons!" answered the dame; "they wanted some wise counsellor to go between and advise them. For, look you, sir, if old Hugo be dead, as is most like, it were more natural that his bride and his nephew should inherit his lands, than this same Randal who is but a distant kinsman, and a foresworn caitiff to boot.—Would you think it, reverend pilgrim, after the mountains of gold he promised me?—when the castle was taken, and he saw I could serve him no more, he called me old beldame, and spoke of the beadle and the cucking-stool.—Yes, reverend sir, old beldame and cucking-stool were his best words, when he knew I had no one to take my part, save old Raoul, who cannot take his own. But if grim old Hugh bring back his weatherbeaten carcass from Palestine, and have but half the devil in him which he had when he was fool enough to go away, Saint Mary, but I will do his kinsman's office to him!"

There was a pause when she had done speaking.

"Thou say'st," at length exclaimed the Constable, "that Damian de Lacy and Eveline love each other, yet are unconscious of guilt or falsehood, or ingratitude to me—I would say, to their relative in Palestine?"

"Love, sir!—in troth and so it is—they do love each other," said Gillian; "but it is like angels—or like lambs—or like fools, if you will; for they would never so much as have spoken together, but for a prank of that same Randal Lacy's."

"How!" demanded the Constable—"a prank of Randal's?—What motive had he that these two should meet?"

"Nay, their meeting was none of his seeking; but he had formed a plan to carry off the Lady Eveline himself, for he was a wild rover, this same Randal; and so he came disguised as a merchant of falcons, and trained out my old stupid Raoul, and the Lady Eveline, and all of us, as if to have an hour's mirth in hawking at the heron. But he had a band of Welsh kites in readiness to pounce upon us; and but for the sudden making in of Damian to our rescue, it is undescribable to think what might have come of us; and Damian being hurt in the onslaught, was carried to the Garde Douloureuse in mere necessity; and but to save his life, it is my belief my lady would never have asked him to cross the drawbridge, even if he had offered."

"Woman," said the Constable, "think what thou say'st! If thou hast done evil in these matters heretofore, as I suspect from thine own story, think not to put it right by a train of new falsehoods, merely from spite at missing thy reward."

"Palmer," said old Raoul, with his broken-toned voice, cracked by many a hollo, "I am wont to leave the business of tale-bearing to my wife Gillian, who will tongue-pad it with any shrew in Christendom. But thou speak'st like one having some interest in these matters, and therefore I will tell thee plainly, that although this woman has published her own shame in avowing her correspondence with that same Randal Lacy, yet what she has said is true as the gospel; and, were it my last word, I would say that Damian and the Lady Eveline are innocent of all treason and all dishonesty, as is the babe unborn.—But what avails what the like of us say, who are even driven to the very begging for mere support, after having lived at a good house, and in a good lord's service—blessing be with him!"

"But hark you," continued the Constable, "are there left no ancient servants of the house, that could speak out as well as you?"

"Humph!" answered the huntsman—"men are not willing to babble when Randal Lacy is cracking his thong above their heads. Many are slain, or starved to death—some disposed of—some spirited away. But there are the weaver Flammock and his daughter Rose, who know as much of the matter as we do."

"What!—Wilkin Flammock the stout Netherlander?" said the Constable; "he and his blunt but true daughter Rose?—I will venture my life on their faith. Where dwell they?—What has been their lot amidst these changes?"

"And in God's name who are *you* that ask these questions?" said Dame Gillian. "Husband, husband—we have been too free; there is something in that look and that tone which I should remember."

"Yes, look at me more fixedly," said the Constable, throwing back the hood which had hitherto in some degree obscured his features.

"On your knees—on your knees, Raoul!" exclaimed Gillian, dropping on her own at the same time; "it is the Constable himself, and he has heard me call him old Hugh!"

"It is all that is left of him who was the Constable, at least," replied De Lacy; "and old Hugh willingly forgives your freedom, in consideration of your good news. Where are Flammock and his daughter?"

"Rose is with the Lady Eveline," said Dame Gillian; "her ladyship, belike, chose her for bower-woman in place of me, although Rose was never fit to attire so much as a Dutch doll."

"The faithful girl!" said the Constable. "And where is Flammock?"

"Oh, for him, he has pardon and favour from the King," said Raoul; "and is at his own house, with his rabble of weavers, close beside the Battle-bridge, as they now call the place where your lordship quelled the Welsh."

"Thither will I then," said the Constable; "and will then see what welcome King Henry of Anjou has for an old servant. You two must accompany me."

"My lord," said Gillian, with hesitation, "you know poor folk are little thanked for interference with great men's affairs. I trust your lordship will be able to protect us if we speak the truth; and that you will not look back with displeasure on what I did, acting for the best."

"Peace, dame, with a wanion to ye!" said Raoul. "Will you think of your own old sinful carcass, when you should be saving your sweet young mistress from shame and oppression?—And for thy ill tongue, and worse practices, his lordship knows they are bred in the bone of thee."

"Peace, good fellow!" said the Constable; "we will not look back on thy wife's errors, and your fidelity shall be rewarded.—For you, my faithful followers," he said, turning towards Guarine and Vidal, "when De Lacy shall receive his rights, of which he doubts nothing, his first wish shall be to reward your fidelity."

"Mine, such as it is, has been and shall be its own reward," said Vidal. "I will not accept favours from him in prosperity, who, in adversity, refused me his hand—our account stands yet open."

"Go to, thou art a fool; but thy profession hath a privilege to be humorous," said the Constable, whose weatherbeaten and homely features looked even handsome, when animated by gratitude to Heaven and benevolence towards mankind. "We will meet," he said, "at Battle-bridge, an hour before vespers—I shall have much achieved before that time."

"The space is short," said his esquire.

"I have won a battle in yet shorter," replied the Constable.

"In which," said the minstrel, "many a man has died that thought himself well assured of life and victory."

"Even so shall my dangerous cousin Randal find his schemes of ambition blighted," answered the Constable; and rode forwards, accompanied by Raoul and his wife, who had remounted their palfrey, while the minstrel and squire followed a-foot, and, of course, much more slowly.

Chapter the Thirty-First.

"Oh, fear not, fear not, good Lord John,
That I would you betray,
Or sue requital for a debt,
Which nature cannot pay.

"Bear witness, all ye sacred powers—
Ye lights that 'gin to shine—
This night shall prove the sacred tie
That binds your faith and mine."

ANCIENT SCOTTISH BALLAD.

LEFT behind by their master, the two dependants of Hugh de Lacy marched on in sullen silence, like men who dislike and distrust each other, though bound to one common service, and partners, therefore, in the same hopes and fears. The dislike, indeed, was chiefly upon Guarine's side; for nothing could be more indifferent to Renault Vidal than was his companion, farther than as he was conscious that Philip loved him not, and was not unlikely, so far as lay in his power, to thwart some plans which he had nearly at heart. He took little notice of his companion, but hummed over to himself, as for the exercise of his memory, romances and songs, many of which were composed in languages which Guarine, who had only an ear for his native Norman, did not understand.

They had proceeded together in this sullen manner for nearly two hours, when they were met by a groom on horseback, leading a saddled palfrey. "Pilgrims," said the man, after looking at them with some attention, "which of you is called Philip Guarine?"

"I, for fault of a better," said the esquire, "reply to that name."

"Thy lord, in that case, commends him to you," said the groom; "and sends you this token, by which you shall know that I am his true messenger."

He showed the esquire a rosary, which Philip instantly recognized as that used by the Constable.

"I acknowledge the token," he said; "speak my master's pleasure."

"He bids me say," replied the rider, "that his visit thrives as well as is possible, and that this very evening, by time that the sun sets, he will be possessed of his own. He desires, therefore, you will mount this palfrey, and come with me to the Garde Doloureuse, as your presence would be wanted there."

"It is well, and I obey him," said the esquire, much pleased with the import of the message, and not dissatisfied at being separated from his travelling companion.

"And what charge for me?" said the minstrel, addressing the messenger.

"If you, as I guess, are the minstrel, Renault Vidal, you are to abide your master at the Battle-bridge, according to the charge formerly given."

"I will meet him, as in duty bound," was Vidal's answer; and scarce was it uttered, ere the two horsemen, turning their backs on him, rode briskly forward, and were speedily out of sight.

It was now four hours past noon, and the sun was declining, yet there was more than three hours' space to the time of rendezvous, and the distance from the place did not now exceed four miles. . Vidal, therefore, either for the sake of rest or reflection, withdrew from the path into a thicket on the left hand, from which gushed the waters of a streamlet, fed by a small fountain that bubbled up amongst the trees. Here the traveller sat himself down, and with an air which seemed unconscious of what he was doing, bent his eye on the little sparkling font for more than half an hour, without change of posture; so that he might, in Pagan times, have represented the statue of a water-god bending over his urn, and attentive only to the supplies which it was pouring forth. At length, however, he seemed to recall himself from this state of deep abstraction, drew himself up, and took some coarse food from his pilgrim's scrip, as if suddenly reminded that life is not supported without means. But he had probably something at his heart which affected his throat or appetite. After a vain attempt to swallow a morsel, he threw it from him in disgust, and applied him to a small flask, in which he had some wine or other liquor. But seemingly this also turned distasteful, for he threw from him both scrip and bottle, and, bending down to the spring, drank deeply of the pure element, bathed in it his hands and face, and arising from the fountain apparently refreshed, moved slowly on his way, singing as he went, but in a low and saddened tone, wild fragments of ancient poetry, in a tongue equally ancient.

Journeying on in this melancholy manner, he at length came in sight of the Battle-bridge; near to which arose, in proud and gloomy strength, the celebrated castle of the Garde Doloureuse. "Here, then," he said—"here, then, I am to await the proud De Lacy. Be it so, in God's name!—he shall know me better ere we part."

So saying, he strode, with long and resolved steps, across the bridge, and ascending a mound which arose on the opposite side at some distance, he gazed for a time upon the scene beneath—the beautiful river, rich with the reflected tints of the western sky—the trees, which were already brightened to the eye, and saddened to the fancy, with the hue of autumn — and the darksome walls and towers of the feudal castle, from which, at times, flashed a glimpse of splendour, as some sentinel's arms caught and gave back a transient ray of the setting sun.

The countenance of the minstrel, which had hitherto been dark and troubled, seemed softened by the quiet of the scene. He threw loose his pilgrim's dress, yet suffering part of its dark folds to hang around him mantle-wise; under which appeared his minstrel's tabard. He took from his side a *rote*, and striking, from time to time, a Welsh descant, sung at others a lay, of which we can offer only a few fragments, literally translated from the ancient language in which they were chanted, premising that they are in that excursive symbolical style of poetry, which Taliessin, Llewarch Hen, and other bards, had derived perhaps from the time of the Druids.

> "I asked of my harp, 'Who hath injured thy chords?'
> And she replied, 'The crooked finger, which I mocked in my tune.'
> A blade of silver may be bended—a blade of steel abideth—
> Kindness fadeth away, but vengeance endureth.
>
> "The sweet taste of mead passeth from the lips,
> But they are long corroded by the juice of wormwood;
> The lamb is brought to the shambles, but the wolf rangeth the mountain;
> Kindness fadeth away, but vengeance endureth.
>
> "I asked the red-hot iron, when it glimmered on the anvil,
> 'Wherefore glowest thou longer than the firebrand?'—
> 'I was born in the dark mine, and the brand in the pleasant greenwood.'
> Kindness fadeth away, but vengeance endureth.
>
> "I asked the green oak of the assembly, wherefore its boughs were dry and seared
>   like the horns of the stag?
> And it showed me that a small worm had gnawed its roots.
> The boy who remembered the scourge, undid the wicket of the castle at midnight.
> Kindness fadeth away, but vengeance endureth.
>
> "Lightning destroyeth temples, though their spires pierce the clouds;
> Storms destroy armadas, though their sails intercept the gale.
> He that is in his glory falleth, and that by a contemptible enemy.
> Kindness fadeth away, but vengeance endureth."

More of the same wild images were thrown out, each bearing some analogy, however fanciful and remote, to the theme, which occurred like a chorus at the close of each stanza; so that the poetry resembled a piece of music, which, after repeated excursions through fanciful variations, returns ever and anon to the simple melody which is the subject of ornament.

As the minstrel sung, his eyes were fixed on the bridge and its vicinity; but when, near the close of his chant, he raised up his eyes towards the distant towers of the Garde Doloureuse, he saw that the gates were opened, and that there was a mustering of guards and attendants without the barriers, as if some expedition were about to set forth, or some person of importance to appear on the scene. At the same time, glancing his eyes around, he discovered that the landscape, so solitary when he first took his seat on the gray stone from which he overlooked it, was now becoming filled with figures.

During his reverie, several persons, solitary and in groups, men, women, and children, had begun to assemble themselves on both sides of the river, and were loitering there, as if expecting some spectacle. There was also much bustling at the Fleming's mills, which, though at some distance, were also completely under his eye. A procession seemed to be arranging itself there, which soon began to move forward, with pipe and tabor, and various other instruments of music, and soon approached, in regular order, the place where Vidal was seated.

It appeared the business in hand was of a pacific character; for the gray-bearded old men of the little settlement, in their decent russet gowns, came first after the rustic band of music, walking in ranks of three and three, supported by their staves, and regulating the motion of the whole procession by their sober and staid pace. After these fathers of the settlement came Wilkin Flammock, mounted on his mighty war-horse, and in complete armor, save his head, like a vassal prepared to do military service for his lord. After him followed, and in battle rank, the flower of the little colony, consisting of thirty men, well armed and appointed, whose steady march, as well as their clean and glittering armour, showed steadiness and discipline, although they lacked alike the fiery glance of the French soldiery, or the look of dogged defiance which characterized the English, or the wild ecstatic impetuosity of eye which then distinguished the Welsh. The mothers and the maidens of the colony came next; then followed the children, with faces as chubby, and features as serious, and steps as grave as their parents; and last, as a rear-guard, came the youths from fourteen to twenty, armed with light lances, bows, and similar weapons becoming their age.

This procession wheeled around the base of the mound or embankment on which the minstrel was seated; crossed the bridge with the same slow and regular pace, and formed themselves into a double line, facing inwards, as if to receive some person of consequence, or witness some ceremonial. Flammock remained at the extremity of the avenue thus formed by his countrymen, and quietly, yet earnestly, engaged in making arrangements and preparations.

In the meanwhile, stragglers of different countries began to draw together, apparently brought there by mere curiosity, and formed a motley assemblage at the farther end of the bridge, which was that nearest to the castle. Two English peasants passed very near the stone on which Vidal sat—"Wilt thou sing us a song, minstrel," said one of them, "and here is a tester for thee?" throwing into his hat a small silver coin.

"I am under a vow," answered the minstrel, "and may not practise the gay science at present."

"Or you are too proud to play to English churls," said the elder peasant, "for thy tongue smacks of the Norman."

"Keep the coin, nevertheless," said the younger man. "Let the palmer have what the minstrel refuses to earn."

"I pray you reserve your bounty, kind friend," said Vidal, "I need it not;—and tell me of your kindness, instead, what matters are going forward here."

"Why, know you not that we have got our Constable de Lacy again, and that he is to grant solemn investiture to the Flemish weavers of all these fine things Harry of Anjou has given?—Had Edward the Confessor been alive, to give the Netherland knaves their guerdon, it would have been a cast of the gallows-tree. But come, neighbour, we shall lose the show."

So saying, they pressed down the hill.

Vidal fixed his eyes on the gates of the distant castle; and the distant waving of banners, and mustering of men on horseback, though imperfectly seen at such a distance, apprized him that one of note was about to set forth at the head of a considerable train of military attendants. Distant flourishes of trumpets, which came faintly yet distinctly on his ear, seemed to attest the same. Presently he perceived, by the dust which began to arise in columns betwixt the castle and the bridge, as well as by the nearer sound of the clarions, that the troop was advancing towards him in procession.

Vidal, on his own part, seemed as if irresolute whether to retain his present position, where he commanded a full but remote view of the whole scene, or to obtain a nearer but more partial one, by involving himself in the crowd which now closed around on either hand of the bridge, unless where the avenue was kept open by the armed and arrayed Flemings.

A monk next hurried past Vidal, and on his enquiring as formerly the cause of the assembly, answered, in a muttering tone, from beneath his hood, that it was the Constable de Lacy, who, as the first act of his authority, was then and there to deliver to the Flemings a royal charter of their immunities.

"He is in haste to exercise his authority, methinks," said the minstrel.

"He that has just gotten a sword is impatient to draw it," replied the monk, who added more which the minstrel understood imperfectly; for Father Aldrovand had not recovered the injury which he had received during the siege.

Vidal, however, understood him to say, that he was to meet the Constable there, to beg his favourable intercession.

"I also will meet him," said Renault Vidal, rising suddenly from the stone which he occupied.

"Follow me, then," mumbled the priest; "the Flemings know me, and will let me forward."

But Father Aldrovand being in disgrace, his influence was not so potent as he had flattered himself; and both he and the minstrel were jostled to and fro in the crowd, and separated from each other.

Vidal, however, was recognized by the English peasants who had before spoke to him. "Canst thou do any jugglers' feats, minstrel?" said one. "Thou may'st earn a fair largess, for our Norman masters love *jonglerie.*"

"I know but one," said Vidal, "and I will show it, if you will yield me some room."

They crowded a little off from him, and gave him time to throw aside his bonnet, bare his legs and knees, by stripping off the leathern buskins which swathed them, and retaining only his sandals. He then tied a parti-coloured handkerchief around his swarthy and sunburnt hair, and casting off his upper doublet, showed his brawny and nervous arms naked to the shoulder.

But while he amused those immediately about him with these preparations, a commotion and rush among the crowd, together with the close sound of trumpets, answered by all the Flemish instruments of music, as well as the shouts in Norman and English, of "Long live the gallant Constable!— Our Lady for the bold De Lacy!" announced that the Constable was close at hand.

Vidal made incredible exertions to approach the leader of the procession, whose morion, distinguished by its lofty plumes, and right hand holding his truncheon, or leading-staff, was all he could see, on account of the crowd of officers and armed men around him. At length his exertions prevailed, and he came within three yards of the Constable, who was then in a small circle which had been with difficulty kept clear for the purpose of the ceremonial of the day. His back was towards the minstrel, and he was in the act of bending from his horse to deliver the royal charter to Wilkin Flammock, who had knelt on one knee to receive it the more reverentially. His discharge of this duty occasioned the Constable to stoop so low that his plume seemed in the act of mixing with the flowing mane of his noble charger.

At this moment, Vidal threw himself, with singular agility, over the heads of the Flemings who guarded the circle; and, ere an eye could twinkle, his right knee was on the croupe of the Constable's horse — the grasp of his left hand on the collar of De Lacy's buff-coat; then, clinging to its prey like a tiger after its leap, he drew, in the same instant of time, a short, sharp dagger — and buried it in the back of the neck, just where the spine, which was severed by the stroke, serves to convey to the trunk of the human body the mysterious influences of the brain. The blow was struck with the utmost accuracy of aim and strength of arm. The unhappy horseman dropped from his saddle, without groan or struggle, like a bull in the amphitheatre, under the steel of the tauridor; and in the same saddle sat his murderer, brandishing the bloody poniard, and urging the horse to speed.

There was indeed a possibility of his having achieved his escape, so much were those around paralyzed for the moment by the suddenness and audacity of the enterprise; but Flammock's presence of mind did not forsake him — he seized the horse by the bridle, and, aided by those who wanted but an example, made the rider prisoner, bound his arms, and called aloud that he must be carried before King Henry. This proposal, uttered in Flammock's strong and decided tone of voice, silenced a thousand wild cries of murder and treason, which had arisen while the different and hostile natives, of which the crowd was composed, threw upon each other reciprocally the charge of treachery.

All the streams, however, now assembled in one channel, and poured with unanimous assent towards the Garde Douloureuse, excepting a few of the murdered nobleman's train, who remained to transport their master's body, in decent solemnity of mourning, from the spot which he had sought with so much pomp and triumph.

When Flammock reached the Garde Douloureuse, he was readily admitted with his prisoner, and with such witnesses as he had selected to prove the execution of the crime. To his request of an audience, he was answered, that the King had commanded that none should be admitted to him for some time; yet so singular were the tidings of the Constable's slaughter, that the captain of the guard ventured to interrupt Henry's privacy, in order to communicate that event; and returned with orders that Flammock and his prisoner should be instantly admitted to the royal apartment. Here they found Henry, attended by several persons, who stood respectfully behind the royal seat, in a darkened part of the room.

When Flammock entered, his large bulk and massive limbs were strangely contrasted with cheeks pale with horror at what he had just witnessed, and with awe at finding himself in the royal presence-chamber. Beside him stood his prisoner, undaunted by the situation in which he was placed. The blood of his victim, which had spirted from the wound, was visible on his bare limbs and his scanty garments; but particularly upon his brow and the handkerchief with which it was bound.

Henry gazed on him with a stern look, which the other not only endured without dismay, but seemed to return with a frown of defiance.

"Does no one know this caitiff?" said Henry, looking around him.

There was no immediate answer, until Philip Guarine, stepping from the group which stood behind the royal chair, said, though with hesitation, "So please you, my liege, but for the strange guise in which he is now arrayed, I should say there was a household minstrel of my master, by name Renault Vidal."

"Thou art deceived, Norman," replied the minstrel; "my menial place and base lineage were but assumed,—I am Cadwallon the Briton—Cadwallon of the Nine Lays — Cadwallon, the chief bard of Gwenwyn of Powys-land — and his avenger!"

As he uttered the last word, his looks encountered those of a palmer, who had gradually advanced from the recess in which the attendants were stationed, and now confronted him.

The Welshman's eyes looked eagerly ghastly, as if flying from their sockets, while he exclaimed, in a tone of surprise, mingled with horror, "Do the dead come before monarchs? — Or, if thou art alive, *whom* have I slain? — I dreamed not, surely, of that bound, and of that home-blow? — yet my victim stands before me! Have I not slain the Constable of Chester?"

"Thou hast indeed slain the Constable," answered the King; "but know, Welshman, it was Randal de Lacy, on whom that charge was this morning conferred, by our belief of our loyal and faithful Hugh de Lacy's having been lost upon his return from the Holy Land, as the vessel in which he had taken passage was reported to have suffered shipwreck. Thou hast cut short, Randal's brief elevation but by a few hours; for to-morrow's sun would have again seen him without land or lordship."

The prisoner dropped his head on his bosom in evident despair. "I thought," he murmured, "that he had changed his slough, and come forth so glorious, all too soon. May the eyes drop out that were cheated with those baubles, a plumed cap and a lacquered baton!"

"I will take care, Welshman, thine eyes cheat thee not again," said the King, sternly; "before the night is an hour older, they shall be closed on all that is earthly."

"May I request of your nobleness," said the Constable, "that you will permit me to ask the unhappy man a few questions?"

"When I have demanded of him myself," said the King, "why he has dipt his hands in the blood of a noble Norman."

"Because he at whom I aimed my blow," said the Briton, his eye glancing fiercely from the King to De Lacy, and back, "had spilled the blood of the descendant of a thousand kings; to which his own gore, or thine, proud Count of Anjou, is but as the puddle of the highway to the silver fountain."

Henry's eye menaced the audacious speaker; but the King reined in his wrath when he beheld the imploring look of his servant. — "What wouldst thou ask of him?" he said; "be brief, for his time is short."

"So please you, my liege, I would but demand wherefore he has for years forborne to take the life he aimed at, when it was in his power—nay, when it must have been lost but for his seemingly faithful service?"

"Norman," said Cadwallon, "I will answer thee. When I first took upon me thy service, it was well my purpose to have slain thee that night. There stands the man," pointing to Philip Guarine, "to whose vigilance thou owedst thy safety."

"Indeed," said De Lacy, "I do remember some indications of such a purpose; but why didst thou forego it, when following opportunities put it in thy power?"

"When the slayer of my sovereign became God's soldier," answered Cadwallon, "and served his cause in Palestine, he was safe from my earthly vengeance."

"A wonderful forbearance on the part of a Welsh assassin!" said the King, scornfully.

"Ay," answered Cadwallon; "and which certain Christian princes have scarce attained to, who have never neglected the chance of pillage or conquest afforded by the absence of a rival in the Holy Crusade."

"Now, by the Holy Rood" — said Henry, on the point of bursting out, for the insult affected him peculiarly; but, suddenly stopping, he said, with an air of contempt, "To the gallows with the knave!"

"But one other question," said De Lacy, "Renault, or by whatever name thou art called. Ever since my return thou hast rendered me service inconsistent with thy stern resolution upon my life — thou didst aid me in my shipwreck — and didst guide me safely through Wales, where my name would have ensured my death; and all this after the crusade was accomplished?"

"I could explain thy doubt," said the bard, "but that it might be thought I was pleading for my life."

"Hesitate not for that," said the King; "for were our Holy Father to intercede for thee, his prayer were in vain."

"Well then," said the bard, "know the truth — I was too proud to permit either wave or Welshman to share in my revenge. Know also, what is perhaps Cadwallon's weakness — use and habit had divided my feelings towards De Lacy, between aversion and admiration. I still contemplated my revenge, but as something which I might never complete, and which seemed rather an image in the clouds, than an object to which I must one day draw near. And when I beheld thee," he said, turning to De Lacy, "this very day so determined, so sternly resolved, to bear thy impending fate like a man — that you seemed to me to resemble the last tower of a ruined palace, still holding its head to heaven, when its walls of splendour, and its bowers of delight, lay in desolation around — may I perish, I said to myself in secret, ere I perfect its ruin! Yes, De Lacy, then, even then — but some hours since—hadst thou accepted my proffered hand, I had served thee as never follower served master. You rejected it with scorn—and yet notwithstanding that insult, it required that I should have seen you, as I thought, trampling over the field in which you slew my master, in the full pride of Norman insolence, to animate my resolution to strike the blow, which, meant for you, has slain at least one of your usurping race.—I will answer no more questions — lead on to axe or gallows — it is indifferent to Cadwallon—my soul will soon be with my free and noble ancestry, and with my beloved and royal patron."

"My liege and prince," said De Lacy, bending his knee to Henry, "can you hear this, and refuse your ancient servant one request? — Spare this man! — Extinguish not such a light, because it is devious and wild."

"Rise, rise, De Lacy; and shame thee of thy petition," said the King "Thy kinsman's blood—the blood of a noble Norman, is on the Welshman's hands and brow. As I am crowned King, he shall die ere it is wiped off.— Here I have him to present execution!"

Cadwallon was instantly withdrawn under a guard. The Constable seemed, by action rather than words, to continue his intercession.

"Thou art mad, De Lacy — thou art mad, mine old and true friend, to urge me thus," said the King, compelling De Lacy to rise. "See'st thou not that my care in this matter is for thee?—This Randal, by largesses and promises, hath made many friends, who will not, perhaps, easily again be brought to your allegiance, returning as thou dost, diminished in power and wealth. Had he lived, we might have had hard work to deprive him entirely of the power which he had acquired. We thank the Welsh assassin who hath rid us of him; but his adherents would cry foul play were the murderer spared. When blood is paid for blood, all will be forgotten, and their loyalty will once more flow in its proper channel to thee, their lawful lord."

Hugo de Lacy arose from his knees, and endeavoured respectfully to combat the politic reasons of his wily sovereign, which he plainly saw were resorted to less for his sake than with the prudent purpose of effecting the change of feudal authority, with the least possible trouble to the country or Sovereign.

Henry listened to De Lacy's arguments patiently, and combated them with temper, until the death-drum began to beat, and the castle bell to toll.

He then led De Lacy to the window: on which, for it was now dark, a strong ruddy light began to gleam from without. A body of men-at-arms, each holding in his hand a blazing torch, were returning along the terrace from the execution of the wild but high-soul'd Briton, with cries of "Long live King Henry! and so perish all enemies of the gentle Norman men!"

Conclusion.

A sun hath set—a star hath risen,
O, Geraldine! since arms of thine
Have been the lovely lady's prison.
                    COLERIDGE.

POPULAR fame had erred in assigning to Eveline Berenger, after the capture of her castle, any confinement more severe than that of her aunt the Lady Abbess of the Cistertians' convent afforded. Yet that was severe enough; for maiden aunts, whether abbesses or no, are not tolerant of the species of errors of which Eveline was accused; and the innocent damosel was brought in many ways to eat her bread in shame of countenance and bitterness of heart. Every day of her confinement was rendered less and less endurable by taunts, in the various forms of sympathy, consolation, and exhortation; but which, stript of their assumed forms, were undisguised anger and insult. The company of Rose was all which Eveline had to sustain her under these inflictions, and that was at length withdrawn on the very morning when so many important events took place at the Garde Douloureuse.

The unfortunate young lady inquired in vain of a grim-faced nun, who appeared in Rose's place to assist her to dress, why her companion and friend was debarred attendance. The nun observed on that score an obstinate silence, but threw out many hints on the importance attached to the vain ornaments of a frail child of clay, and on the hardship that even a spouse of Heaven was compelled to divert her thoughts from her higher duties, and condescend to fasten clasps and adjust veils.

The Lady Abbess, however, told her niece after matins, that her attendant had not been withdrawn from her for a space only, but was likely to be shut up in a house of the severest profession, for having afforded her mistress assistance in receiving Damian de Lacy into her sleeping apartment at the castle of Baldringham.

A soldier of De Lacy's band, who had hitherto kept what he had observed a secret, being off his post that night, had now in Damian's disgrace found he might benefit himself by telling the story. This new blow, so unexpected, so afflictive — this new charge, which it was so difficult to explain, and so impossible utterly to deny, seemed to Eveline to seal Damian's fate and her own; while the thought that she had involved in ruin her single-hearted and high-soul'd attendant, was all that had been wanting to produce a state which approached to the apathy of despair. "Think of me what you will," she said to her aunt, "I will no longer defend myself—say what you will, I will no longer reply — carry me where you will, I will no longer resist — God will, in his good time, clear my fame — may he forgive my persecutors!"

After this, and during several hours of that unhappy day, the Lady Eveline, pale, cold, silent, glided from chapel to refectory, from refectory to chapel again, at the slightest beck of the Abbess or her official sisters, and seemed to regard the various privations, penances, admonitions, and reproaches, of which she, in the course of that day, was subjected to an extraordinary share, no more than a marble statue minds the inclemency of the external air, or the rain-drops which fall upon it, though they must in time waste and consume it.

The Abbess, who loved her niece, although her affection showed itself often in a vexatious manner, became at length alarmed — countermanded her orders for removing Eveline to an inferior cell—attended herself to see her laid in bed, (in which, as in every thing else, the young lady seemed entirely passive,) and, with something like reviving tenderness, kissed and blessed her on leaving the apartment. Slight as the mark of kindness was, it was unexpected; and, like the rod of Moses, opened the hidden fountains of waters. Eveline wept, a resource which had been that day denied to her —she prayed—and, finally, sobbed herself to sleep, like an infant, with a mind somewhat tranquillized by having given way to this tide of natural emotion.

She awoke more than once in the night to recall mingled and gloomy dreams of cells and of castles, of funerals and of bridals, of coronets and of racks and gibbets; but towards morning she fell into sleep more sound than she had hitherto enjoyed, and her visions partook of its soothing character. The Lady of the Garde Doloureuse seemed to smile on her amid her dreams, and to promise her votaress protection. The shade of her father was there also; and with the boldness of a dreamer, she saw the paternal resemblance with awe, but without fear; his lips moved, and she heard words—their import she did not fully comprehend, save that they spoke of hope, consolation, and approaching happiness. There also glided in, with bright blue eyes fixed upon hers, dressed in a tunic of saffron-coloured silk, with a mantle of cerulean blue of antique fashion, the form of a female, resplendent in that delicate species of beauty which attends the fairest complexion. It was, she thought, the Britoness Vanda; but her countenance was no longer resentful — her long yellow hair flew not loose on her shoulders, but was mysteriously braided with oak and mistletoe; above all, her right hand was gracefully disposed of under her mantle; and it was an unmutilated, unspotted, and beautifully formed hand which crossed the brow of Eveline. Yet, under these assurances of favour, a thrill of fear passed over her as the vision seemed to repeat, or chant,

> "Widow'd wife and wedded maid,
> Betrothed, betrayer, and betray'd,
> All is done that has been said;
> Vanda's wrong has been y-wroken—
> Take her pardon by this token."

She bent down, as if to kiss Eveline, who started at that instant, and then awoke. Her hand was indeed gently pressed, by one as pure and white as her own. The blue eyes and fair hair of a lovely female face, with halfveiled bosom and dishevelled locks, flitted through her vision, and indeed its lips approached to those of the lovely sleeper at the moment of her awakening; but it was Rose in whose arms her mistress found herself pressed, and who moistened her face with tears, as in a passion of affection she covered it with kisses.

"What means this, Rose?" said Eveline; "thank God, you are restored to me!—But what mean these bursts of weeping?"

"Let me weep — let me weep," said Rose; "it is long since I have wept for joy, and long, I trust, it will be ere I again weep for sorrow. News are come on the spur from the Garde Doloureuse—Amelot has brought them — he is at liberty — so is his master, and in high favour with Henry. Hear yet more, but let me not tell it too hastily — You grow pale."

"No, no," said Eveline; "go on—go on—I think I understand you—I think I do."

"The villain Randal de Lacy, the master-mover of all our sorrows, will plague you no more; he was slain by an honest Welshman, and grieved am

I that they have hanged the poor man for his good service. Above all, the stout old Constable is himself returned from Palestine, as worthy, and somewhat wiser, than he was; for it is thought he will renounce his contract with your ladyship."

"Silly girl," said Eveline, crimsoning as high as she had been before pale, "jest not amidst such a tale. — But can this be reality? — Is Randal indeed slain? — and the Constable returned?"

These were hasty and hurried questions, answered as hastily and confusedly, and broken with ejaculations of surprise and thanks to Heaven, and to Our Lady, until the ecstasy of delight sobered down into a sort of tranquil wonder.

Meanwhile Damian Lacy also had his explanations to receive, and the mode in which they were conveyed had something remarkable. Damian had for some time been the inhabitant of what our age would have termed a dungeon, but which, in the ancient days, they called a prison. We are perhaps censurable in making the dwelling and the food of acknowledged and convicted guilt more comfortable and palatable than what the parties could have gained by any exertions when at large, and supporting themselves by honest labour; but this is a venial error compared to that of our ancestors, who, considering a charge and a conviction as synonymous, treated the accused before sentence in a manner which would have been of itself a severe punishment after he was found guilty. Damian, therefore, notwithstanding his high birth and distinguished rank, was confined after the manner of the most atrocious criminal, was heavily fettered, fed on the coarsest food, and experienced only this alleviation, that he was permitted to indulge his misery in a solitary and separate cell, the wretched furniture of which was a mean bedstead, and a broken table and chair. A coffin — and his own arms and initials were painted upon it — stood in one corner, to remind him of his approaching fate; and a crucifix was placed in another, to intimate to him that there was a world beyond that which must soon close upon him. No noise could penetrate into the iron silence of his prison — no rumour, either touching his own fate or that of his friends. Charged with being taken in open arms against the King, he was subject to military law, and to be put to death even without the formality of a hearing; and he foresaw no milder conclusion to his imprisonment.

This melancholy dwelling had been the abode of Damian for nearly a month, when, strange as it may seem, his health, which had suffered much from his wounds, began gradually to improve, either benefited by the abstemious diet to which he was reduced, or that certainty, however melancholy, is an evil better endured by many constitutions than the feverish contrast betwixt passion and duty. But the term of his imprisonment seemed drawing speedily to a close; his jailer, a sullen Saxon of the lowest order, in more words than he had yet used to him, warned him to look to a speedy change of dwelling; and the tone in which he spoke convinced the prisoner there was no time to be lost. He demanded a confessor, and the jailer, though he withdrew without reply, seemed to intimate by his manner that the boon would be granted.

Next morning, at an unusually early hour, the chains and bolts of the cell were heard to clash and groan, and Damian was startled from a broken sleep, which he had not enjoyed for above two hours. His eyes were bent on the slowly opening door, as if he had expected the headsman and his assistants; but the jailer ushered in a stout man in a pilgrim's habit. "Is it a priest whom you bring me, warden?" said the unhappy prisoner. "He can best answer the question himself," said the surly official, and presently withdrew.

The pilgrim remained standing on the floor, with his back to the small window, or rather loophole, by which the cell was imperfectly lighted, and gazed intently upon Damian, who was seated on the side of his bed; his pale cheek and dishevelled hair bearing a melancholy correspondence to his heavy irons. He returned the pilgrim's gaze, but the imperfect light only showed him that his visiter was a stout old man, who wore the scallop-shell on his bonnet, as a token that he had passed the sea, and carried a palm branch in his hand, to show he had visited the Holy Land.

"Benedictine, reverend father," said the unhappy young man; "are you a priest come to unburden my conscience?"

"I am not a priest," replied the Palmer, "but one who brings you news of discomfort."

"You bring them to one to whom comfort has been long a stranger, and to a place which perchance never knew it," replied Damian.

"I may be the bolder in my communication," said the Palmer; "those in sorrow will better hear ill news than those whom they surprise in the possession of content and happiness."

"Yet even the situation of the wretched," said Damian, "can be rendered more wretched by suspense. I pray you, reverend sir, to speak the worst at once—if you come to announce the doom of this poor frame, may God be gracious to the spirit which must be violently dismissed from it!"

"I have no such charge," said the Palmer. "I come from the Holy Land, and have the more grief in finding you thus, because my message to you was one addressed to a free man, and a wealthy one."

"For my freedom," said Damian, "let these fetters speak, and this apartment for my wealth.—But speak out thy news—should my uncle—for I fear thy tale regards him—want either my arm or my fortune, this dungeon and my degradation have farther pangs than I had yet supposed, as they render me unable to aid him."

"Your uncle, young man," said the Palmer, "is prisoner, I should rather say slave, to the great Soldan, taken in a battle in which he did his duty, though unable to avert the defeat of the Christians, with which it was concluded. He was made prisoner while covering the retreat, but not until he had slain with his own hand, for his misfortune as it has proved, Hassan Ali, a favourite of the Soldan. The cruel pagan has caused the worthy knight to be loaded with irons heavier than those you wear, and the dungeon to which he is confined would make this seem a palace. The infidel's first resolution was to put the valiant Constable to the most dreadful death which his tormentors could devise. But fame told him that Hugo de Lacy was a man of great power and wealth; and he has demanded a ransom of ten thousand bezants of gold. Your uncle replied that the payment would totally impoverish him, and oblige him to dispose of his whole estates; even then he pleaded, time must be allowed him to convert them into money. The Soldan replied, that it imported little to him whether a hound like the Constable were fat or lean, and that he therefore insisted upon the full amount of the ransom. But he so far relaxed as to make it payable in three portions, on condition that, along with the first portion of the price, the nearest of kin and heir of De Lacy must be placed in his hands as a hostage for what remained due. On these conditions he consented your uncle should be put at liberty so soon as you arrive in Palestine with the gold."

"Now may I indeed call myself unhappy," said Damian, "that I cannot show my love and duty to my noble uncle, who hath ever been a father to me in my orphan state."

"It will be a heavy disappointment, doubtless, to the Constable," said the Palmer, "because he was eager to return to this happy country, to fulfil a contract of marriage which he had formed with a lady of great beauty and fortune."

Damian shrunk together in such sort that his fetters clashed, but he made no answer.

"Were he not your uncle," continued the Pilgrim, "and well known as a wise man, I should think he is not quite prudent in this matter. Whatever be was before he left England, two summers spent in the wars of Palestine, and another amid the tortures and restraints of a heathen prison, have made him a sorry bridegroom."

"Peace, pilgrim," said De Lacy, with a commanding tone. "It is not thy part to censure such a noble knight as my uncle, nor is it meet that I should listen to your strictures."

"I crave your pardon, young man," said the Palmer. "I spoke not without some view to your interest, which, methinks, does not so well consort with thine uncle having an heir of his body."

"Peace, base man!" said Damian. "By Heaven, I think worse of my cell than I did before, since its doors opened to such a counsellor, and of my chains, since they restrain me from chastising him. — Depart, I pray thee."

"Not till I have your answer for your uncle," answered the Palmer. "My age scorns the anger of thy youth, as the rock despises the foam of the rivulet dashed against it."

"Then, say to my uncle," answered Damian, "I am a prisoner, or I would have come to him — I am a confiscated beggar, or I would have sent him my all."

"Such virtuous purposes are easily and boldly announced," said the Palmer, "when he who speaks them knows that he cannot be called upon to make good the boast of his tongue. But could I tell thee of thy restoration to freedom and wealth, I trow thou wouldst consider twice ere thy act confirmed the sacrifice thou hast in thy present state promised so glibly."

"Leave me, I prithee, old man," said Damian; "thy thought cannot comprehend the tenor of mine—go, and add not to my distress insults which I have not the means to avenge."

"But what if I had it in my power to place thee in the situation of a free and wealthy man, would it please thee *then* to be reminded of thy present boast? for if not, thou may'st rely on my discretion never to mention the difference of sentiment between Damian bound and Damian at liberty."

"How meanest thou?—or hast thou any meaning, save to torment me?" said the youth.

"Not so," replied the old Palmer, plucking from his bosom a parchment scroll to which a heavy seal was attached.—"Know that thy cousin Randal hath been strangely slain, and his treacheries towards the Constable and thee as strangely discovered. The King, in requital of thy sufferings, hath sent thee this full pardon, and endowed thee with a third part of those ample estates, which, by his death, revert to the crown."

"And hath the King also restored my freedom and my right of blood?" exclaimed Damian.

"From this moment, forthwith," said the Palmer—"look upon the parchment—behold the royal hand and seal."

"I must have better proof.—Here," he exclaimed, loudly clashing his irons at the same time, "Here, thou Dogget—warder, son of a Saxon wolfhound!"

The Palmer, striking on the door, seconded the previous exertions for summoning the jailer, who entered accordingly.

"Warder," said Damian de Lacy, in a stern tone, "am I yet thy prisoner, or no?"

The sullen jailer consulted the Palmer by a look, and then answered to Damian that he was a free man.

"Then, death of thy heart, slave," said Damian, impatiently, "why hang these fetters on the free limbs of a Norman noble? each moment they confine him are worth a lifetime of bondage to such a serf as thou!"

"They are soon rid of, Sir Damian," said the man; "and I pray you to take some patience, when you remember that ten minutes since you had little right to think these bracelets would have been removed for any other purpose than your progress to the scaffold."

"Peace, ban-dog," said Damian, "and be speedy;—And thou, who hast brought me these good tidings, I forgive thy former bearing—thou thoughtest, doubtless, that it was prudent to extort from me professions during my bondage which might in honour decide my conduct when at large. The suspicion inferred in it was somewhat offensive, but thy motive was to ensure my uncle's liberty."

"And it is really your purpose," said the Palmer, "to employ your newly-gained freedom in a voyage to Syria, and to exchange your English prison for the dungeon of the Soldan?"

"If thou thyself wilt act as my guide," answered the undaunted youth, "you shall not say I dally by the way."

"And the ransom," said the Palmer, "how is that to be provided?"

"How, but from the estates, which, nominally restored to me, remain in truth and justice my uncle's, and must be applied to his use in the first instance? If I mistake not greatly, there is not a Jew or Lombard who would not advance the necessary sums on such security.—Therefore, dog," he continued, addressing the jailer, "hasten thy unclenching and undoing of rivets, and be not dainty of giving me a little pain, so thou break no limb, for I cannot afford to be stayed on my journey."

The Palmer looked on a little while, as if surprised at Damian's determination, then exclaimed, "I can keep the old man's secret no longer—such high-souled generosity must not be sacrificed.—Hark thee, brave Sir Damian, I have a mighty secret still to impart, and as this Saxon churl understands no French, this is no unfit opportunity to communicate it. Know that thine uncle is a changed man in mind, as he is debilitated and broken down in body. Peevishness and jealousy have possessed themselves of a heart which was once strong and generous; his life is now on the dregs, and I grieve to speak it, these dregs are foul and bitter."

"Is this thy mighty secret?" said Damian. "That men grow old, I know; and if with infirmity of body comes infirmity of temper and mind, their case the more strongly claims the dutiful observance of those who are bound to them in blood or affection."

"Ay," replied the Pilgrim, "but the Constable's mind has been poisoned against thee by rumours which have reached his ear from England, that there have been thoughts of affection betwixt thee and his betrothed bride, Eveline Berenger.—Ha! have I touched you now?"

"Not a whit," said Damian, putting on the strongest resolution with which his virtue could supply him—"it was but this fellow who struck my shin-bone somewhat sharply with his hammer. Proceed. My uncle heard such a report, and believed it?"

"He did," said the Palmer—"I can well aver it, since he concealed no thought from me. But he prayed me carefully to hide his suspicions from you, 'otherwise,' said he, 'the young wolf-cub will never thrust himself into the trap for the deliverance of the old he-wolf. Were he once in my prison-house,' your uncle continued to speak of you, 'he should rot and die ere I sent one penny of ransom to set at liberty the lover of my betrothed bride.'"

"Could this be my uncle's sincere purpose?" said Damian, all aghast. "Could he plan so much treachery towards me as to leave me in the captivity into which I threw myself for his redemption?—Tush! it cannot be."

"Flatter not yourself with such a vain opinion," said the Palmer—"if you go to Syria, you go to eternal captivity, while your uncle returns to possession of wealth little diminished—and of Eveline Berenger."

"Ha!" ejaculated Damian; and looking down for an instant, demanded of the Palmer, in a subdued voice, what he would have him do in such an extremity.

"The case is plain, according to my poor judgment," replied the Palmer. "No one is bound to faith with those who mean to observe none with him. Anticipate this treachery of your uncle, and let his now short and infirm existence moulder out in the pestiferous cell to which he would condemn your youthful strength. The royal grant has assigned you lands enough for your honourable support; and wherefore not unite with them those of the Garde Doloureuse?—Eveline Berenger, if I do not greatly mistake, will scarcely say nay. Ay, more—I vouch it on my soul that she will say yes, for I have sure information of her mind; and for her precontract, a word from Henry to his Holiness, now that they are in the heyday of their reconciliation, will obliterate the name Hugh from the parchment, and insert Damian in its stead."

"Now, by my faith," said Damian, arising and placing his foot upon the stool, that the warder might more easily strike off the last ring by which he was encumbered,—"I have heard of such things as this—I have heard of beings who, with seeming gravity of word and aspect--with subtle counsels, artfully applied to the frailties of human nature—have haunted the cells of despairing men, and made them many a fair promise, if they would but exchange for their by-ways the paths of salvation. Such are the fiend's dearest agents, and in such a guise hath the fiend himself been known to appear. In the name of God, old man, if human thou art, begone!—I like not thy words or thy presence—I spit at thy counsels. And mark me," he added, with a menacing gesture, "Look to thine own safety—I shall presently be at liberty!"

"Boy," replied the Palmer, folding his arms contemptuously in his cloak, "I scorn thy menaces—I leave thee not till we know each other better!"

"I too," said Damian, "would fain know whether thou be'st man or fiend; and now for the trial!" As he spoke, the last shackle fell from his leg, and clashed on the pavement, and at the same moment he sprung on the Palmer, caught him by the waist, and exclaimed, as he made three distinct and separate attempts to lift him up, and dash him headlong to the earth, "This for maligning a nobleman—this for doubting the honour of a knight—and this (with a yet more violent exertion) for belying a lady!"

Each effort of Damian seemed equal to have rooted up a tree; yet though they staggered the old man, they overthrew him not; and while Damian panted with his last exertion, he replied, "And take this, for so roughly entreating thy father's brother."

As he spoke, Damian de Lacy, the best youthful wrestler in Cheshire, received no soft fall on the floor of the dungeon. He arose slowly and astounded; but the Palmer had now thrown back both hood and dalmatique, and the features, though bearing marks of age and climate, were those of his uncle the Constable, who calmly observed, "I think, Damian, thou art become stronger, or I weaker, since my breast was last pressed against yours in our country's celebrated sport. Thou hadst nigh had me down in that last turn, but that I knew the old De Lacy's back-trip as well as thou.—But wherefore kneel, man?" He raised him with much kindness, kissed his cheek, and proceeded; "Think not, my dearest nephew, that I meant in my late disguise to try your faith, which I myself never doubted. But evil tongues had been busy, and it was this which made me resolve on an experiment, the result of which has been, as I expected, most honourable for you. And know, (for these walls have sometimes ears, even according to the letter,) there are ears and eyes not far distant which have heard and seen the whole. Marry, I wish though, thy last hug had not been so severe a one. My ribs still feel the impression of thy knuckles."

"Dearest and honoured uncle," said Damian—"excuse——"

"There is nothing to excuse," replied his uncle, interrupting him. "**Have** we not wrestled a turn before now?—But there remains yet one trial for thee to go through—Get thee out of this hole speedily—don thy best array to accompany me to the Church at noon ; for, Damian, thou must be present at the marriage of the Lady Eveline Berenger."

This proposal at once struck to the earth the unhappy young man. "For mercy's sake," he exclaimed, "hold me excused in this, my gracious uncle ! —I have been of late severely wounded, and am very weak."

"As my bones can testify," said his uncle. "Why, man, thou hast the strength of a Norway bear."

"Passion," answered Damian, "might give me strength for a moment ; but, dearest uncle, ask any thing of me rather than this. Methinks, if I have been faulty, some other punishment might suffice."

"I tell thee," said the Constable, "thy presence is necessary — indispensably necessary. Strange reports have been abroad, which thy absence on this occasion would go far to confirm. Eveline's character and mine own are concerned in this."

"If so," said Damian, "if it be indeed so, no task will be too hard for me. But I trust, when the ceremony is over, you will not refuse me your consent to take the cross, unless you should prefer my joining the troops destined, as I heard, for the conquest of Ireland."

"Ay, ay," said the Constable ; "if Eveline grant you permission, I will not withhold mine."

"Uncle," said Damian, somewhat sternly, "you do not know the feelings which you jest with."

"Nay," said the Constable, "I compel nothing ; for if thou goest to the church, and likest not the match, thou may'st put a stop to it if thou wilt— the sacrament cannot proceed without the bridegroom's consent."

"I understand you not, uncle," said Damian ; "you have already consented."

"Yes, Damian," he said, "I have — to withdraw my claim, and to relinquish it in thy favour ; for if Eveline Berenger is wedded to-day, thou art her bridegroom ! The Church has given her sanction—the King his approbation—the lady says not nay—and the question only now remains, whether the bridegroom will say yes."

The nature of the answer may be easily conceived ; nor is it necessary to dwell upon the splendour of the ceremonial, which, to atone for his late unmerited severity, Henry honoured with his own presence. Amelot and Rose were shortly afterwards united, old Flammock having been previously created a gentleman of coat armour, that the gentle Norman blood might without utter derogation, mingle with the meaner stream that coloured the cheek with crimson, and meandered in azure over the lovely neck and bosom of the fair Fleming. There was nothing in the manner of the Constable towards his nephew and his bride, which could infer a regret of the generous self-denial which he had exercised in favour of their youthful passion. But he soon after accepted a high command in the troops destined to invade Ireland ; and his name is found amongst the highest in the roll of the chivalrous Normans who first united that fair island to the English crown.

Eveline, restored to her own fair castle and domains, failed not to provide for her Confessor, as well as for her old soldiers, servants, and retainers, forgetting their errors, and remembering their fidelity. The Confessor was restored to the flesh-pots of Egypt, more congenial to his habits than the meagre fare of his convent. Even Gillian had the means of subsistence, since to punish her would have been to distress the faithful Raoul. They quarrelled for the future part of their lives in plenty, just as they had formerly quarrelled in poverty ; for wrangling curs will fight over a banquet as fiercely as over a bare bone. Raoul died first, and Gillian having lost her whetstone, found that as her youthful looks decayed her wit turned somewhat blunt. She therefore prudently commenced devotee, and spent hours in long panegyrics on her departed husband.

The only serious cause of vexation which I can trace the Lady Eveline having been tried with, arose from a visit of her Saxon relative, made with much form, but, unfortunately, at the very time which the Lady Abbess had selected for that same purpose. The discord which arose between these honoured personages was of a double character, for they were Norman and Saxon, and, moreover, differed in opinion concerning the time of holding Easter. This, however, was but a slight gale to disturb the general serenity of Eveline; for with her unhoped-for union with Damian, ended the trials and sorrows of THE BETROTHED.

END OF THE BETROTHED.

Tales of the Crusaders.

~~~~~~~~~~~~~~~~~~

THE TALISMAN.

THE TALISMAN.

INTRODUCTION — (1832.)

The "Betrothed" did not greatly please one or two friends, who thought that it did not well correspond to the general title of "The Crusaders." They urged, therefore, that, without direct allusion to the manners of the Eastern tribes, and to the romantic conflicts of the period, the title of a "Tale of the Crusaders" would resemble the play-bill, which is said to have announced the tragedy of Hamlet, the character of the Prince of Denmark being left out. On the other hand, I felt the difficulty of giving a vivid picture of a part of the world with which I was almost totally unacquainted, unless by early recollections of the Arabian Nights' Entertainments; and not only did I labour under the incapacity of ignorance, in which, as far as regards Eastern manners, I was as thickly wrapped as an Egyptian in his fog; but my contemporaries were, many of them, as much enlightened upon the subject, as if they had been inhabitants of the favoured land of Goshen. The love of travelling had pervaded all ranks, and carried the subjects of Britain into all quarters of the world. Greece, so attractive by its remains of art, by its struggles for freedom against a Mahomedan-tyrant, by its very name, where every fountain had its classical legend;—Palestine, endeared to the imagination by yet more sacred remembrances, had been of late surveyed by British eyes, and described by recent travellers. Had I, therefore, attempted the difficult task of substituting manners of my own invention, instead of the genuine costume of the East, almost every traveller I met, who had extended his route beyond what was anciently called "The Grand Tour," had acquired a right, by ocular inspection, to chastise me for my presumption. Every member of the Travellers' Club, who could pretend to have thrown his shoe over Edom, was, by having done so, constituted my lawful critic and corrector. It occurred, therefore, that where the author of Anastasius, as well as he of Hadji Baba, had described the manners and vices of the Eastern nations, not only with fidelity, but with the humour of Le Sage and the ludicrous power of Fielding himself, one who was a perfect stranger to the subject must necessarily produce an unfavourable contrast. The Poet Laureate also, in the charming tale of "Thalaba," had shown how extensive might be the researches of a person of acquirements and talent, by dint of investigation alone, into the ancient doctrines, history, and manners of the Eastern countries, in which we are probably to look for the cradle of mankind; Moore, in his "Lallah Rookh," had successfully trod the same path; in which, too, Byron, joining ocular experience to extensive reading, had written some of his most attractive poems. In a word, the Eastern themes had been already so successfully handled by those who were acknowledged to be masters of their craft, that I was diffident of making the attempt.

These were powerful objections, nor did they lose force when they became the subject of anxious reflection, although they did not finally prevail. The arguments on the other side were, that though I had no hope of rivalling the contemporaries whom I have mentioned, yet it occurred to me as possible to acquit myself of the task I was engaged in, without entering into competition with them.

The period relating more immediately to the Crusades which I at last fixed upon, was that at which the warlike character of Richard I., wild and generous, a pattern of chivalry, with all its extravagant virtues, and its no less absurd errors, was opposed to that of Saladin, in which the Christian and English monarch showed all the cruelty and violence of an Eastern sultan; and Saladin, on the other hand, displayed the deep policy and prudence of a European sovereign, whilst each contended which should excel the other in the knightly qualities of bravery and generosity. This singular contrast afforded, as the author conceived, materials for a work of fiction, possessing peculiar interest. One of the inferior characters introduced, was a supposed relation of Richard Cœur de Lion; a violation of the truth of history, which gave offence to Mr. Mills, the Author of the History of Chivalry and the Crusades, who was not, it may be presumed, aware that romantic fiction naturally includes the power of such invention, which is indeed one of the requisites of the art.

Prince David of Scotland, who was actually in the host, and was the hero of some very romantic adventures on his way home, was also pressed into my service, and constitutes one of my *dramatis personæ*.

It is true I had already brought upon the field Him of the Lion Heart. But it was in a more private capacity than he was here to be exhibited in the Talisman; then as a disguised knight, now in the avowed character of a conquering monarch; so that I doubted not a name so dear to Englishmen as that of King Richard I. might contribute to their amusement for more than once.

I had access to all which antiquity believed, whether of reality or fable, on the subject of that magnificent warrior, who was the proudest boast of Europe and their chivalry, and with whose dreadful name the Saracens, according to a historian of their own country, were wont to rebuke their startled horses. "Do you think," said they, "that King Richard is on the track, that you stray so wildly from it?" The most curious register of the history of King Richard, is an ancient romance, translated originally from the Norman; and at first certainly having a pretence to be termed a work of chivalry, but latterly becoming stuffed with the most astonishing and monstrous fables. There is perhaps no metrical romance upon record, where, along with curious and genuine history, are mingled more absurd and exaggerated incidents. We have placed in the Appendix to this Introduction (p. 491), the passage of the romance in which Richard figures as an Ogre, or literal cannibal.

A principal incident in the story, is that from which the title is derived. Of all people who ever lived, the Persians were perhaps most remarkable for their unshaken credulity in amulets, spells, periapts, and similar charms, framed, it was said, under the influence of particular planets, and bestowing high medical powers, as well as the means of advancing men's fortunes in various manners. A story of this kind, relating to a Crusader of eminence, is often told in the west of Scotland, and the relic alluded to is still in existence, and even yet held in veneration.

Sir Simon Lockhart of Lee and Cartland made a considerable figure in the reigns of Robert the Bruce and of his son David. He was one of the chief of that band of Scottish chivalry, who accompanied James, the Good Lord Douglas, on his expedition to the Holy Land, with the heart of King Robert Bruce. Douglas, impatient to get at the Saracens, entered into war with those of Spain, and was killed there. Lockhart proceeded to the Holy Land with such Scottish knights as had escaped the fate of their leader, and assisted for some time in the wars against the Saracens.

The following adventure is said by tradition to have befallen him :—

He made prisoner in battle an Emir of considerable wealth and consequence. The aged mother of the captive came to the Christian camp, to redeem her son from his state of captivity. Lockhart is said to have fixed the price at which his prisoner should ransom himself; and the lady, pulling out a large embroidered purse, proceeded to tell down the ransom, like a mother who pays little respect to gold in comparison of her son's liberty. In this operation, a pebble inserted in a coin, some say of the Lower Empire, fell out of the purse, and the Saracen matron testified so much haste to recover it, as gave the Scottish knight a high idea of its value, when compared with gold or silver. " I will not consent," he said, " to grant your son's liberty, unless that amulet be added to his ransom." The lady not only consented to this, but explained to Sir Simon Lockhart the mode in which the Talisman was to be used, and the uses to which it might be put. The water in which it was dipt, operated as a styptic, as a febrifuge, and possessed several other properties as a medical talisman.

Sir Simon Lockhart, after much experience of the wonders which it wrought, brought it to his own country, and left it to his heirs, by whom, and by Clydesdale in general, it was, and is still, distinguished by the name of the Lee-penny, from the name of his native seat of Lee.

The most remarkable part of its history, perhaps, was, that it so especially escaped condemnation when the Church of Scotland chose to impeach many other cures which savoured of the miraculous, as occasioned by sorcery, and censured the appeal to them, " excepting only that to the amulet, called the Lee-penny, to which it had pleased God to annex certain healing virtues which the Church did not presume to condemn." It still, as has been said, exists, and its powers are sometimes resorted to. Of late, they have been chiefly restricted to the cure of persons bitten by mad dogs ; and as the illness in such cases frequently arises from imagination, there can be no reason for doubting that water which has been poured on the Lee-penny furnishes a congenial cure.*

---

* [THE Publisher has to acknowledge the politeness of the owner of the LEE PENNY, Sir Norman Macdonald Lockhart, Bart., of Lee and Carnwath, who kindly transmitted it to Edinburgh, to be drawn for the engraver ; and to Hector Maclean, Esq. he is also indebted for the following additional particulars regarding this singularly curious relic of antiquity.]

* Although the age of miracles has departed, and the belief in supernatural appearances been almost entirely eradicated, in these days of the *march of intellect*, still there are who place a kind of faith in nostrums and such like things : and, amongst others, the *Lee Penny* has had, and still has, its votaries, who firmly believe in its efficacy to cure all diseases to which man and beast are subject, particularly in cases of hydrophobia. Far be it from us to disturb the faith of these. Even the immortal Author of the following pages thought it not beneath the dignity of his mighty genius to take as his groundwork this very Talisman. It is a stone of a dark red colour and triangular shape, and its size about half an inch each side. It is set in a piece of silver coin, now almost entirely defaced, but, from some letters still remaining, is supposed to be a shilling of Edward I., the cross a few years ago, having been very plain, as on that shilling. It is used by dipping the stone in water, which is given to the diseased cattle to drink, or the person who has been bit ; and the wound or part infected is washed with the water, then held to have a certain healing property communicated, and from drinking which the patient is restored to health. There are no words used in the dipping of the stone. Many and wonderful are the cures said to have been wrought by this singular relic. People came from all parts of Scotland, and even from England, to procure the water in which it was dipped, to give to their cattle when ill with the murrain and the black-leg. During the time that Scotland was convulsed with religious zeal, the Talisman did not escape the attention of the Church, a complaint having been made to the Ecclesiastical Courts against the Laird of Lee, then Sir James Lockhart, for using witchcraft. The Act of the Synod and Assembly, held at Glasgow, gave deliverance in the matter, as pretty illustrative of the extent to which Church *discipline* was carried in those days ; and to what a degree of faith the people held the Talisman.* The inhabitants of Newcastle, when infected with the plague, sent for the Lee Penny, and granted a bond

---

* " *Copy of an Act of the Synod and Assemblie. Apud Glasgow, 25th October.*

" Quhilk dye, amongest the referries of the brethern of the ministrie of Lanark, it was propondit to the Synode, that Gawen Hammiltonne of Raplocke had preferit ane complaint before them against Sir James Lockhart of Lee, anent the superstitious using of ane stone set in silver, for the curing of diseased cattell, qlk the said Gawen affirmet could not be lawfully used, and that they had defferit to give ony decisionne therein till the advice of the Assemblie might he had concerning the same. The Assemblie having inquirit of the manner of using thereof, and particularlie understoode, by examinationne of the said Laird of Lee, and otherwise, that the custome is onlie to casts the stane in sume water, and give the diseasit cattill thereof to drink ; and qt the sam is done wtout using onie words such as charmers and sorcerers use in their unlawful practisese ; and considering that in nature they are mony things seen to work straunge effects, qr. of no human witt can give a reason, it haying pleasit God to give unto stones and herbes special virtues for the healing of mony infirmities in man and beast, advises the brethern to surrease thir process, as qr. in they perceive no grond of offence : And admonishes the said Laird of Lee, in the useing of the said stone to tak heed that it be used hereafter wt the least scandal that possible may be.

" Extract out of the books of the Assemblie holden at Glasgow, and subscribed be their Clark, at their command.

"Mr. ROBERT YOUNG, Clark."

Such is the tradition concerning the Talisman, which the author has taken the liberty to vary in applying it to his own purposes.

"Considerable liberties have also been taken with the truth of history, both with respect to Conrade of Montserrat's life, as well as his death. That Conrade, however, was reckoned the enemy of Richard, is agreed both in history and romance. The general opinion of the terms upon which they stood, may be guessed from the proposal of the Saracens, that the Marquis of Montserrat should be invested with certain parts of Syria, which they were to yield to the Christians. Richard, according to the romance which bears his name, "could no longer repress his fury. The Marquis, he said, was a traitor, who had robbed the Knights Hospitallers of sixty thousand pounds, the present of his father Henry; that he was a renegade, whose treachery had occasioned the loss of Acre; and he concluded by a solemn oath, that he would cause him to be drawn to pieces by wild horses, if he should ever venture to pollute the Christian camp by his presence. Philip attempted to intercede in favour of the Marquis, and throwing down his glove, offered to become a pledge for his fidelity to the Christians; but his offer was rejected, and he was obliged to give way to Richard's impetuosity." — *History of Chivalry.*

Conrade of Montserrat makes a considerable figure in those wars, and was at length put to death by one of the followers of the Scheik, or Old Man of the Mountain; nor did Richard remain free of the suspicion of having instigated his death.

It may be said, in general, that most of the incidents introduced in the following tale are fictitious; and that reality, where it exists, is only retained in the characters of the piece.

ABBOTSFORD, 1st *July*, 1832.

—————

APPENDIX TO INTRODUCTION.

WHILE warring in the Holy Land, Richard was seized with an ague. The best leeches of the camp were unable to effect the cure of the King's disease; but the prayers of the army were more successful. He became

for a large sum for its safe return; and such was their belief in its virtues, and the good which it did, that they offered to pay the money, and keep the Penny. A copy of this bond is well known to have been among the family papers. It would be endless to recount the many cures said to have been performed by it. We may, however, adduce one, and which is recorded in the papers of the family. About a century and a-half ago, Lady Baird, of Sauchtonhall, near Edinburgh, having been bitten by a mad dog, and symptoms of hydrophobia appearing, great anxiety and alarm was excited in the minds of the family. They sent immediately to beg the loan of the Lee Penny; on procuring which, she used it for some weeks, both drinking and bathing in the water in which it had been dipped. When she quite recovered her wonted health, the Laird of Lee and his lady were entertained at Sauchtonhall by Lady Baird and her husband for many days, in the most sumptuous manner, on account of her recovery, and in gratitude for the loan of the Penny. It will, doubtless, be thought by some that now it can only be looked upon as a mere subject of curiosity; such, however, is not the case. The water is still frequently applied for, and we can vouch for the fact, by the inhabitants of the different villages at a considerable distance from Lee. But the most recent case of which we have heard, happened a few months ago, and fully exemplified the great faith placed in it even by our southern neighbours, and their recollection of its talismanic influence upon the sick and afflicted. The neighbourhood of Kirkwhelpington and Birtley, Northumberland, had been subject to much alarm by the visits of dogs in a rabid state: no fewer than seven of these animals were killed. The dread of the inhabitants was naturally great, and the injury done excessive, principally among the farm stock: the number of sheep and cattle bitten, and which died of hydrophobia, is almost incredible. A horse having bitten a man's hand severely at Guunerton, the dreadful nature of the complaint, and the hitherto impossibility of its cure, excited great alarm in the minds of the people, and a desire to resort to any means whereby to avert its fatal effects. In this state of doubt and anxiety, they bethought themselves of the Lee Penny, in which they still had a belief; and hoped that its waters would effect what no mortal means could do. They accordingly sent express to Lee for a large quantity of the water. The person sent, having arrived on Sunday morning, procured a barrel full, and started back immediately, with that which was looked upon as the only hope for the man labouring under the complaint: and, strange as it may seem, no bad effects resulted from the wound. The sceptic may doubt, but we merely state a fact, and for the accuracy of which we can vouch. One of the English newspapers, at the time, taking notice of the circumstance, adds, 'The "spirit of the age" has not yet banished the popular belief in the *Lockerie water,* a large supply having been procured by voluntary subscription,' &c."

convalescent, and the first symptom of his recovery was a violent longing for pork. But pork was not likely to be plentiful in a country whose inhabitants had an abhorrence for swine's flesh; and

―――――"though his men should be hanged
They ne might, in that countrey,
For gold, ne silver, ne no money,
No pork find, take, ne get,
That King Richard might aught of eat.
An old knight with Richard biding,
When he heard of that tiding,
That the kinges wants were swyche,
To the steward he spake privyliche—
'Our lord the king sore is sick, I wiss,
After porck he alonged is;
Ye may none find to selle;
No man he hardy him so to telle!
If he did he might die.
Now behoves to done as I shall say,
Tho' he wets nought of that.
Take a Saracen, young and fat;
In haste let the thief be slain,
Opened, and his skin off flayn;
And sudden full hastily,
With powder and with spicery,
And with saffrun of good colour.
When the king thereof feels savour,
Out of agne if he be went,
He shall have thereto good talent.

When he has a good taste,
And eaten well a good repast,
And supped of the brewis a sup,
Slept after and swet a drop,
Through Goddis help and my counsail.
Soon he shall be fresh and hail.'
The sooth to say, at wordes few,
Slain and sodden was the heathen shrew.
Before the king it was forth brought;
Quod his men, 'Lord, we have pork sought,
Eates and soups of the brewis soote.†
Thorough grace of God it shall be your boot.
Before King Richard carff a knight,
He ate faster than he carve might.
The king ate the flesh and gnaw‡ the bones,
And drank well after for the nonce.
And when he had eaten enough,
His folk hem turned away, and lough.§
He lay still and drew in his arm;
His chamberlain him wrapped warm,
He lay and slept, and swet a stound,
And became whole and sound.
King Richard clad him and arose,
And walked abouten in the close."

An attack of the Saracens was repelled by Richard in person, the consequence of which is told in the following lines:

"When King Richard had rested a whyle,
A knight his arms 'gan unlace,
Him to comfort and solace.
Him was brought a sop in wine.
'The head of that ilke swine,
That I of ate!' (the cook be bade.)
'For feeble I am, and faint and mad.
Of mine evil now I am fear;
Serve me therewith at my soupere!'

Quod the cook, 'That head I ne have.'
Then said the king. 'So God me save,
But I see the head of that swine
For sooth, thou shalt lesen thine!'
The cook saw none other might be;
He fet the head and let him see.
He fell on knees, and made a cry—
'Lo, here the head! my Lord, mercy!'"

The cook had certainly some reason to fear that his master would be struck with horror at the recollection of the dreadful banquet to which he owed his recovery, but his fears were soon dissipated.

"The swarte visg when the king seeth,
His black beard and white teeth,
How his lippes grinned wide.
'What devil is this?' the king cried,
And 'gan to laugh as he were wode.
'What! is Saracen's flesh thus good?
That, never erst I nought wist!
By God's death and his uprist,

Shall we never die for default,
While we may in any assault,
Slee Saracens, the flesh may take,
And seethen and roasten and do hem bake,
[And] Gnawen her flesh to the bones!
Now I have it proved ones,
For hunger ere I be wo,
I and my folk shall eat mo!'"

The besieged now offered to surrender, upon conditions of safety to the inhabitants; while all the public treasury, military machines, and arms, were delivered to the victors, together with the further ransom of one hundred thousand bezants. After this capitulation, the following extraordinary scene took place. We shall give it in the words of the humorous and amiable George Ellis, the collector and the editor of these Romances.

"Though the garrison had faithfully performed the other articles of their contract, they were unable to restore the cross, which was not in their possession, and were therefore treated by the Christians with great cruelty. Daily reports of their sufferings were carried to Saladin; and as many of them were persons of the highest distinction, that monarch, at the solicitation of their friends, despatched an embassy to King Richard with magnificent presents, which he offered for the ransom of the captives. The ambassadors were persons the most respectable from their age, their rank, and their eloquence. They delivered their message in terms of the utmost humility, and without arraigning the justice of the conqueror in his severe treatment of their countrymen, only solicited a period to that severity, laying at his feet the treasures with which they were entrusted, and pledging themselves and their master for the payment of any farther sums which he might demand as the price of mercy.

---

* Bruth.   † Sweet.   ‡ Gnawed.   § Laughed.   ‖ Black face.

> " King Richard spake with wordes mild,
> ' The gold to take, God me shield !
> Among you partina' every charge.
> I brought in shippes and in barge,
> More gold and silver with me,
> Than has your lord, and swilke three.
>
> To his treasure have I no need !
> But for my love I you bid,
> To ment with me that ye dwell ;
> And afterward I shall you tell.
> Thorough counsel I shall you answer,
> What budet ye shall to your lord bear.'

" The invitation was gratefully accepted. Richard, in the meantime, gave secret orders to his marshal that he should repair to the prison, select a certain number of the most distinguished captives, and, after carefully noting their names on a roll of parchment, cause their heads to be instantly struck off ; that these heads should be delivered to the cook with instructions to clear away the hair, and after boiling them in a caldron, to distribute them on several platters, one to each guest, observing to fasten on the forehead of each the piece of parchment expressing the name and family of the victim.

> " ' An hot head bring me beforn,
> As I were well spayed withal,
> Eat thereof fast I shall :
> As it were a tender chick,
> To see how the others will like.'

" This horrible order was punctually executed. At noon the guests were summoned to wash by the music of the waits ; the king took his seat, attended by the principal officers of his court, at the high table, and the rest of the company were marshalled at a long table below him. On the cloth were placed portions of salt at the usual distances, but neither bread, wine, nor water. The ambassadors, rather surprised at this omission, but still free from apprehension, awaited in silence the arrival of the dinner, which was announced by the sounds of pipes, trumpets, and tabours ; and beheld, with horror and dismay, the unnatural banquet introduced by the steward and his officers. Yet their sentiments of disgust and abhorrence, and even their fears, were for a time suspended by their curiosity. Their eyes were fixed on the king, who, without the slightest change of countenance, swallowed the morsels as fast as they could be supplied by the knight who carved them.

> " Every man then poked other :
> They said, ' This is the devil's brother,
> That slays oer men, and thus hem eats !"

" Their attention was then involuntarily fixed on the smoking heads' before them ; they traced in the swollen and distorted features the resemblance of a friend or near relation, and received from the fatal scroll which accompanied each dish the sad assurance that this resemblance was not imaginary. They sat in torpid silence, anticipating their own fate in that of their countrymen, while their ferocious entertainer, with fury in his eyes, but with courtesy on his lips, insulted them by frequent invitations to merriment. At length this first course was removed, and its place supplied by venison, cranes, and other dainties, accompanied by the richest wines. The king then apologized to them for what had passed, which he attributed to his ignorance of their taste ; and assured them of his religious respect for their character as ambassadors, and of his readiness to grant them a safe-conduct for their return. This boon was all that they now wished to claim ; and

> " King Richard spake to an old man,
> ' Wendes home to your Soudan !
> His melancholy that ye abate ;
> And sayes that ye came too late.
> Too slowly was your time y-guessed ;
> Ere he came, the flesh was dressed,
> That men shoulden serve with me,
> Thus at noon, and my meynie.
> Say him, it shall him nought avail,
> Though he forbar us our vitail,
> Bread, wine, fish, flesh, salmon, and conger
> Of us none shall die with hunger,
> While we may wenden to fight,
> And slay the Saracens downright.
>
> Wash the flesh, and roast the head.
> With no ‡ Saracen I may well feed
> Well a nine or a ten
> Of my good Christian men.
> King Richard shall warrant,
> There is no flesh so nourissant
> Unto an English man.
> Partridge, plover, heron, ne swan,
> Cow ne ox, sheep ne swine,
> As the head of a Saracyn.
> There he is fat, and therein tender,
> And my men be lean and slender,
> While any Saracen quick be,
> Livand now in this Syrie.

Divide.   † Message.   ‡ One.

For meat will we nothing care,
Abouten fast we shall fare.
And every day we shall eat
All so many as we may get.

To England will be nought gon,
Till they be eaten every one.'"
*Ellis's Specimens of Early English Metrical
Romances,* vol. ii. p. 236.

The reader may be curious to know owing to what circumstances so extraordinary an invention as that which imputed cannibalism to the King of England, should have found its way into his history. Mr. James, to whom we owe so much that is curious, seems to have traced the origin of this extraordinary rumour.

"With the army of the cross also was a multitude of men," the same author declares, "who made it a profession to be without money; they walked barefoot, carried no arms, and even preceded the beasts of burden in their march, living upon roots and herbs, and presenting a spectacle both disgusting and pitiable.

"A Norman, who, according to all accounts, was of noble birth, but who, having lost his horse, continued to follow as a foot soldier, took the strange resolution of putting himself at the head of this race of vagabonds, who willingly received him as their king. Amongst the Saracens these men became well-known under the name of *Thafurs*, (which Guibert translates *Trudentes*,) and were beheld with great horror, from the general persuasion that they fed on the dead bodies of their enemies; a report which was occasionally justified, and which the king of the Thafurs took care to encourage. This respectable monarch was frequently in the habit of stopping his followers, one by one, in a narrow defile, and of causing them to be searched carefully, lest the possession of the least sum of money should render them unworthy of the name of his subjects. If even two sous were found upon any one, he was instantly expelled the society of his tribe, the king bidding him contemptuously buy arms and fight.

"This troop, so far from being cumbersome to the army, was infinitely serviceable, carrying burdens, bringing in forage, provisions, and tribute; working the machines in the sieges, and, above all, spreading consternation among the Turks, who feared death from the lances of the knights less than that farther consummation they heard of under the teeth of the Thafurs." *

It is easy to conceive, that an ignorant minstrel, finding the taste and ferocity of the Thafurs commemorated in the historical accounts of the Holy Wars, has ascribed their practices and propensities to the Monarch of England, whose ferocity was considered as an object of exaggeration as legitimate as his valour.

ABBOTSFORD, 1st *July*, 1832.

---

* James's History of Chivalry, p. 173.

THE TALISMAN.

Chapter the First.

—— They, too, retired
To the wilderness, but 'twas with arms.
PARADISE REGAINED.

THE burning sun of Syria had not yet attained its highest point in the horizon, when a knight of the Red-cross, who had left his distant northern home, and joined the host of the Crusaders in Palestine, was pacing slowly along the sandy deserts which lie in the vicinity of the Dead Sea, or, as it is called, the Lake Asphaltites, where the waves of the Jordan pour themselves into an inland sea, from which there is no discharge of waters.

The warlike pilgrim had toiled among cliffs and precipices during the earlier part of the morning; more lately, issuing from those rocky and dangerous defiles, he had entered upon that great plain, where the accursed cities provoked, in ancient days, the direct and dreadful vengeance of the Omnipotent.

The toil, the thirst, the dangers of the way, were forgotten, as the traveller recalled the fearful catastrophe, which had converted into an arid and dismal wilderness the fair and fertile valley of Siddim, once well watered, even as the Garden of the Lord, now a parched and blighted waste, condemned to eternal sterility.

Crossing himself, as he viewed the dark mass of rolling waters, in colour as in quality unlike those of every other lake, the traveller shuddered as he remembered, that beneath these sluggish waves lay the once proud cities of the plain, whose grave was dug by the thunder of the heavens, or the eruption of subterraneous fire, and whose remains were hid, even by that sea which holds no living fish in its bosom, bears no skiff on its surface, and, as if its own dreadful bed were the only fit receptacle for its sullen waters, sends not, like other lakes, a tribute to the ocean. The whole land around, as in the days of Moses, was "brimstone and salt; it is not sown, nor beareth, nor any grass groweth thereon;" the land as well as the lake might be termed dead, as producing nothing having resemblance to vegetation, and even the very air was entirely devoid of its ordinary winged inhabitants, deterred probably by the odour of bitumen and sulphur, which the burning sun exhaled from the waters of the lake, in steaming clouds, frequently assuming the appearance of waterspouts. Masses of the slimy and sulphurous substance called naphtha, which floated idly on the sluggish and sullen waves, supplied those rolling clouds with new vapours, and afforded awful testimony to the truth of the Mosaic history.

Upon this scene of desolation the sun shone with almost intolerable splendour, and all living nature seemed to have hidden itself from the rays, excepting the solitary figure which moved through the flitting sand at a foot's pace, and appeared the sole breathing thing on the wide surface of the plain. The dress of the rider and the accoutrements of his horse, were peculiarly unfit for the traveller in such a country. A coat of linked mail, with long sleeves, plated gauntlets, and a steel breastplate, had not been esteemed a sufficient weight of armour; there was also his triangular shield suspended round his neck, and his barred helmet of steel, over which he had a hood and collar of mail, which was drawn around the warrior's shoulders and throat, and filled up the vacancy between the hauberk and the head-piece. His lower limbs were sheathed, like his body, in flexible mail, securing the legs and thighs, while the feet rested in plated shoes, which corresponded with the gauntlets. A long, broad, straight-shaped, double-edged falchion, with a handle formed like a cross, corresponded with a stout poniard, on the other side. The Knight also bore, secured to his saddle, with one end resting on his stirrup, the long steel-headed lance, his own proper weapon, which, as he rode, projected backwards, and displayed its little pennoncelle, to dally with the faint breeze, or drop in the dead calm. To this cumbrous equipment must be added a surcoat of embroidered cloth, much frayed and worn, which was thus far useful, that it excluded the burning rays of the sun from the armour, which they would otherwise have rendered intolerable to the wearer. The surcoat bore, in several places, the arms of the owner, although much defaced. These seemed to be a couchant leopard, with the motto, "I sleep—wake me not." An outline of the same device might be traced on his shield, though many a blow had almost effaced the painting. The flat top of his cumbrous cylindrical helmet was unadorned with any crest. In retaining their own unwieldy defensive armour, the northern Crusaders seemed to set at defiance the nature of the climate and country to which they had come to war.

The accoutrements of the horse were scarcely less massive and unwieldy than those of the rider. The animal had a heavy saddle plated with steel, uniting in front with a species of breast-plate, and behind with defensive armour made to cover the loins. Then there was a steel axe, or hammer, called a mace-of-arms, and which hung to the saddle-bow; the reins were secured by chain-work, and the front-stall of the bridle was a steel plate, with apertures for the eyes and nostrils, having in the midst a short sharp pike, projecting from the forehead of the horse like the horn of the fabulous unicorn.

But habit had made the endurance of this load of panoply a second nature, both to the knight and his gallant charger. Numbers, indeed, of the western warriors who hurried to Palestine, died ere they became inured to the burning climate; but there were others to whom that climate became innocent and even friendly, and among this fortunate number was the solitary horseman who now traversed the border of the Dead Sea.

Nature, which cast his limbs in a mould of uncommon strength, fitted to wear his linked hauberk with as much ease as if the meshes had been formed of cobwebs, had endowed him with a constitution as strong as his limbs, and which bade defiance to almost all changes of climate, as well as to fatigue and privations of every kind. His disposition seemed, in some degree, to partake of the qualities of his bodily frame; and as the one possessed great strength and endurance, united with the power of violent exertion, the other, under a calm and undisturbed semblance, had much of the fiery and enthusiastic love of glory which constituted the principal attribute of the renowned Norman line, and had rendered them sovereigns in every corner of Europe, where they had drawn their adventurous swords.

It was not, however, to all the race that fortune proposed such tempting rewards; and those obtained by the solitary knight during two years' campaign in Palestine, had been only temporal fame, and, as he was taught to believe, spiritual privileges. Meantime, his slender stock of money had melted away, the rather that he did not pursue any of the ordinary modes by which the followers of the Crusade condescended to recruit their diminished resources, at the expense of the people of Palestine · he exacted no gifts from the wretched natives for sparing their possessions when engaged in warfare with the Saracens, and he had not availed himself of any opportunity of enriching himself by the ransom of prisoners of consequence. The small train which had followed him from his native country, had been gradually diminished, as the means of maintaining them disappeared, and his only remaining squire was at present on a sick-bed, and unable to attend his master, who travelled, as we have seen, singly and alone. This was of little consequence to the Crusader, who was accustomed to consider his good sword as his safest escort, and devout thoughts as his best companion.

Nature had, however, her demands for refreshment and repose, even on the iron frame and patient disposition of the Knight of the Sleeping Leopard; and at noon, when the Dead Sea lay at some distance on his right, he joyfully hailed the sight of two or three palm-trees, which arose beside the well which was assigned for his mid-day station. His good horse, too, which had plodded forward with the steady endurance of his master, now lifted his head, expanded his nostrils, and quickened his pace, as if he snuffed afar off the living waters, which marked the place of repose and refreshment. But labour and danger were doomed to intervene ere the horse or horseman reached the desired spot.

As the Knight of the Couchant Leopard continued to fix his eyes attentively on the yet distant cluster of palm-trees, it seemed to him as if some object was moving among them. The distant form separated itself from the trees, which partly hid its motions, and advanced towards the knight with a speed which soon showed a mounted horseman, whom his turban, long spear, and green caftan floating in the wind, on his nearer approach, showed to be a Saracen cavalier. "In the desert," saith an Eastern proverb, "no man meets a friend." The Crusader was totally indifferent whether the infidel, who now approached on his gallant barb, as if borne on the wings of an eagle, came as friend or foe — perhaps, as a vowed champion of the Cross, he might rather have preferred the latter. He disengaged his lance from his saddle, seized it with the right hand, placed it in rest with its point half elevated, gathered up the reins in the left, waked his horse's mettle with the spur, and prepared to encounter the stranger with the calm self-confidence, belonging to the victor in many contests.

The Saracen came on at the speedy gallop of an Arab horseman, managing his steed more by his limbs, and the inflection of his body, than by any use of the reins, which hung loose in his left hand; so that he was enabled to wield the light round buckler of the skin of the rhinoceros, ornamented with silver loops, which he wore on his arm, swinging it as if he meant to oppose its slender circle to the formidable thrust of the western lance. His own long spear was not couched or levelled like that of his antagonist, but grasped by the middle with his right hand, and brandished at arm's length above his head. As the cavalier approached his enemy at full career, he seemed to expect that the Knight of the Leopard should put his horse to the gallop to encounter him. But the Christian knight, well acquainted with the customs of Eastern warriors, did not mean to exhaust his good horse by any unnecessary exertion; and, on the contrary, made a dead halt, confident that if the enemy advanced to the actual shock, his own weight, and that of his powerful charger, would give him sufficient advantage, without the additional momentum of rapid motion. Equally sensible and apprehensive of such a probable result, the Saracen cavalier, when he had approached towards the Christian within twice the length of his lance, wheeled his steed to the left with inimitable dexterity, and rode twice round his antagonist, who, turning without quitting his ground, and presenting his front constantly to his enemy, frustrated his attempts to attack him on an unguarded point; so that the Saracen, wheeling his horse, was fain to retreat to the distance of an hundred yards. A second time, like a hawk attacking a heron, the Heathen renewed the charge, and a second time was fain to retreat without coming to a close struggle. A third time he approached in the same manner, when the Christian knight, desirous to terminate this elusory warfare, in which he might at length have been worn out by the activity of his foeman, suddenly seized the mace which hung at his saddle-bow, and, with a strong hand and unerring aim, hurled it against the head of the Emir, for such and not less his enemy appeared. The Saracen was just aware of the formidable missile in time to interpose his light buckler betwixt the mace and his head; but the violence of the blow forced the buckler down on his turban, and though that defence also contributed to deaden its violence, the Saracen was beaten from his horse. Ere the Christian could avail himself of this mishap, his nimble foeman sprung from the ground, and calling on his horse, which instantly returned to his side, he leaped into his seat without touching the stirrup, and regained all the advantage of which the Knight of the Leopard hoped to deprive him. But the latter had in the meanwhile recovered his mace, and the Eastern cavalier, who remembered the strength and dexterity with which his antagonist had aimed it, seemed to keep cautiously out of reach of that weapon, of which he had so lately felt the force, while he showed his purpose of waging a distant warfare with missile weapons of his own. Planting his long spear in the sand at a distance from the scene of combat, he strung, with great address, a short bow, which he carried at his back, and putting his horse to the gallop, once more described two or three circles of a wider extent than formerly, in the course of which he discharged six arrows at the Christian with such unerring skill, that the goodness of his harness alone saved him from being wounded in as many places. The seventh shaft apparently found a less perfect part of the armour, and the Christian dropped heavily from his horse. But what was the surprise of the Saracen, when, dismounting to examine the condition of his prostrate enemy, he found himself suddenly within the grasp of the European, who had had recourse to this artifice to bring his enemy within his reach! Even in this deadly grapple, the Saracen was saved by his agility and presence of mind. He unloosed the sword-belt, in which the Knight of the Leopard had fixed his hold, and, thus eluding his fatal grasp, mounted his horse, which seemed to watch his motions with the intelligence of a human being, and again rode off. But in the last encounter the Saracen had lost his sword and his quiver of arrows, both of which were attached to the girdle, which he was obliged to abandon. He had also lost his turban in the struggle. These disadvantages seemed to incline the Moslem to a truce: He approached the Christian with his right hand extended, but no longer in a menacing attitude.

"There is truce betwixt our nations," he said, in the lingua franca commonly used for the purpose of communication with the Crusaders; "wherefore should there be war betwixt thee and me? — Let there be peace betwixt us."

"I am well contented," answered he of the Couchant Leopard; "but what security dost thou offer that thou wilt observe the truce?"

"The word of a follower of the Prophet was never broken," answered the Emir. "It is thou, brave Nazarene, from whom I should demand security, did I not know that treason seldom dwells with courage."

The Crusader felt that the confidence of the Moslem made him ashamed of his own doubts.

"By the cross of my sword," he said, laying his hand on the weapon as he spoke, "I will be true companion to thee, Saracen, while our fortune wills that we remain in company together."

"By Mahommed, Prophet of God, and by Allah, God of the Prophet," replied his late foeman, "there is not treachery in my heart towards thee.

And now wend we to yonder fountain, for the hour of rest is at hand, and the stream had hardly touched my lip when I was called to battle by thy approach."

The Knight of the Couchant Leopard yielded a ready and courteous assent; and the late foes, without an angry look, or gesture of doubt, rode side by side to the little cluster of palm-trees.

Chapter the Second.

TIMES of danger have always, and in a peculiar degree, their seasons of good-will and of security; and this was particularly so in the ancient feudal ages, in which, as the manners of the period had assigned war to be the chief and most worthy occupation of mankind, the intervals of peace, or rather of truce, were highly relished by those warriors to whom they were seldom granted, and endeared by the very circumstances which rendered them transitory. It is not worth while preserving any permanent enmity against a foe, whom a champion has fought with to-day, and may again stand in bloody opposition to on the next morning. The time and situation afforded so much room for the ebullition of violent passions, that men, unless when peculiarly opposed to each other, or provoked by the recollection of private and individual wrongs, cheerfully enjoyed in each other's society the brief intervals of pacific intercourse, which a warlike life admitted.

The distinctions of religion, nay, the fanatical zeal which animated the followers of the Cross and of the Crescent against each other, was much softened by a feeling so natural to generous combatants, and especially cherished by the spirit of chivalry. This last strong impulse had extended itself gradually from the Christians to their mortal enemies, the Saracens, both of Spain and of Palestine. The latter were indeed no longer the fanatical savages, who had burst from the centre of Arabian deserts, with the sabre in one hand, and the Koran in the other, to inflict death or the faith of Mahommed, or at the best, slavery and tribute, upon all who dared to oppose the belief of the prophet of Mecca. These alternatives indeed had been offered to the unwarlike Greeks and Syrians; but in contending with the western Christians, animated by a zeal as fiery as their own, and possessed of as unconquerable courage, address, and success in arms, the Saracens gradually caught a part of their manners, and especially of those chivalrous observances, which were so well calculated to charm the minds of a proud and conquering people. They had their tournaments and games of chivalry; they had even their knights, or some rank analogous; and above all, the Saracens observed their plighted faith with an accuracy which might sometimes put to shame those who owned a better religion. Their truces, whether national or betwixt individuals, were faithfully observed; and thus it was, that war, in itself perhaps the greatest of evils, yet gave occasion for display of good faith, generosity, clemency, and even kindly affections, which less frequently occur in more tranquil periods, where the passions of men, experiencing wrongs or entertaining quarrels which cannot be brought to instant decision, are apt to smoulder for a length of time in the bosoms of those who are so unhappy as to be their prey.

It was under the influence of these milder feelings, which soften the horrors of warfare, that the Christian and Saracen, who had so lately done their best for each other's mutual destruction, rode at a slow pace towards the fountain of palm-trees, to which the Knight of the Couchant Leopard had been tending, when interrupted in mid-passage by his fleet and dangerous adversary. Each was wrapt for some time in his own reflections, and took breath after an encounter which had threatened to be fatal to one or both; and their good horses seemed no less to enjoy the interval of repose. That of the Saracen, however, though he had been forced into much the more violent and extended sphere of motion, appeared to have suffered less from fatigue than the charger of the European knight. The sweat hung still clammy on the limbs of the last, when those of the noble Arab were completely dried by the interval of tranquil exercise, all saving the foam-flakes which were still visible on his bridle and housings. The loose soil on which he trod so much augmented the distress of the Christian's horse, heavily loaded by his own armour and the weight of his rider, that the latter jumped from his saddle, and led his charger along the deep dust of the loamy soil, which was burnt in the sun into a substance more impalpable than the finest sand, and thus gave the faithful horse refreshment at the expense of his own additional toil; for, iron-sheathed as he was, he sunk over the mailed shoes at every step, which he placed on a surface so light and unresisting.

"You are right," said the Saracen; and it was the first word that either had spoken since their truce was concluded, — "your strong horse deserves your care; but what do you in the desert with an animal, which sinks over the fetlock at every step, as if he would plant each foot deep as the root of a date-tree?"

"Thou speakest rightly, Saracen," said the Christian knight, not delighted at the tone with which the infidel criticised his favourite horse, — "rightly, according to thy knowledge and observation. But my good horse hath ere now borne me, in mine own land, over as wide a lake as thou seest yonder spread out behind us, yet not wet one hair above his hoof."

The Saracen looked at him with as much surprise as his manners permitted him to testify, which was only expressed by a slight approach to a disdainful smile, that hardly curled perceptibly the broad thick mustache which enveloped his upper lip.

"It is justly spoken," he said, instantly composing himself to his usual serene gravity, — "list to a Frank, and hear a fable."

"Thou are not courteous, misbeliever," replied the Crusader, "to doubt the word of a dubbed knight; and were it not that thou speakest in ignorance, and not in malice, our truce had its ending ere it is well begun. Thinkest thou I tell thee an untruth when I say, that I, one of five hundred horsemen, armed in complete mail, have ridden — ay, and ridden for miles, upon water as solid as the crystal, and ten times less brittle!"

"What wouldst thou tell me?" answered the Moslem; "yonder inland sea thou dost point at is peculiar in this, that, by the special curse of God, it suffereth nothing to sink in its waves, but wafts them away, and casts them on its margin; but neither the Dead Sea, nor any of the seven oceans which environ the earth, will endure on their surface the pressure of a horse's foot, more than the Red Sea endured to sustain the advance of Pharaoh and his host."

"You speak truth after your knowledge, Saracen," said the Christian knight; "and yet, trust me, I fable not, according to mine. Heat, in this climate, converts the soil into something almost as unstable as water; and in my land cold often converts the water itself into a substance as hard as rock. Let us speak of this no longer; for the thoughts of the calm, clear, blue refulgence of a winter's lake, glimmering to stars and moonbeams, aggravate the horrors of this fiery desert, where, methinks, the very air which we breathe is like the vapour of a fiery furnace seven times heated."

The Saracen looked on him with some attention, as if to discover in what sense he was to understand words, which, to him, must have appeared either to contain something of mystery, or of imposition. At length he seemed determined in what manner to receive the language of his new companion.

"You are," he said, "of a nation that loves to laugh, and you make sport with yourselves, and with others, by telling what is impossible, and reporting what never chanced. Thou art one of the knights of France, who hold it for glee and pastime to *gab*,* as they term it, of exploits that are beyond human power. I were wrong to challenge, for the time, the privilege of thy speech, since boasting is more natural to thee than truth."

"I am not of their land, neither of their fashion," said the Knight, "which is, as thou well sayest, to *gab* of that which they dare not undertake, or undertaking cannot perfect. But in this I have imitated their folly, brave Saracen, that in talking to thee of what thou canst not comprehend, I have, even in speaking most simple truth, fully incurred the character of a braggart in thine eyes ; so, I pray you, let my words pass."

They had now arrived at the knot of palm-trees, and the fountain which welled out from beneath their shade in sparkling profusion.

We have spoken of a moment of truce in the midst of war ; and this, a spot of beauty in the midst of a steril desert, was scarce less dear to the imagination. It was a scene which, perhaps, would elsewhere have deserved little notice ; but as the single speck, in a boundless horizon, which promised the refreshment of shade and living water, these blessings, held cheap where they are common, rendered the fountain and its neighbourhood a little paradise. Some generous or charitable hand, ere yet the evil days of Palestine began, had walled in and arched over the fountain, to preserve it from being absorbed in the earth, or choked by the flitting clouds of dust with which the least breath of wind covered the desert. The arch was now broken, and partly ruinous : but it still so far projected over, and covered in the fountain, that it excluded the sun in a great measure from its waters, which, hardly touched by a straggling beam, while all around was blazing, lay in a steady repose, alike delightful to the eye and the imagination. Stealing from under the arch, they were first received in a marble basin, much defaced indeed, but still cheering the eye, by showing that the place was anciently considered as a station, that the hand of man had been there, and that man's accommodation had been in some measure attended to. The thirsty and weary traveller was reminded by these signs, that others had suffered similar difficulties, reposed in the same spot, and, doubtless, found their way in safety to a more fertile country. Again, the scarce visible current which escaped from the basin, served to nourish the few trees which surrounded the fountain, and where it sunk into the ground and disappeared, its refreshing presence was acknowledged by a carpet of velvet verdure.

In this delightful spot the two warriors halted, and each, after his own fashion, proceeded to relieve his horse from saddle, bit, and rein, and permitted the animals to drink at the basin ere they refreshed themselves from the fountain head, which arose under the vault. They then suffered the steeds to go loose, confident that their interest, as well as their domesticated habits, would prevent their straying from the pure water and fresh grass.

Christian and Saracen next sat down together on the turf, and produced each the small allowance of store which they carried for their own refreshment. Yet, ere they severally proceeded to their scanty meal, they eyed each other with that curiosity which the close and doubtful conflict in which they had been so lately engaged was calculated to inspire. Each was desirous to measure the strength, and form some estimate of the character, of an adversary so formidable ; and each was compelled to acknowledge, that had he fallen in the conflict, it had been by a noble hand.

* *Gabr.* This French word signified a sort of sport much used among the French chivalry, which consisted in vying with each other in making the most romantic gasconades. The verb and the meaning are retained in Scottish.

The champions formed a striking contrast to each other in person and features, and might have formed no inaccurate representatives of their different nations. The Frank seemed a powerful man, built after the ancient Gothic cast of form, with light brown hair, which, on the removal of his helmet, was seen to curl thick and profusely over his head. His features had acquired, from the hot climate, a hue much darker than those parts of his neck which were less frequently exposed to view, or than was warranted by his full and well-opened blue eye, the colour of his hair, and of the mustaches which thickly shaded his upper lip, while his chin was carefully divested of beard, after the Norman fashion. His nose was Grecian and well formed; his mouth a little large in proportion, but filled with well-set, strong, and beautifully white teeth; his head small, and set upon the neck with much grace. His age could not exceed thirty, but if the effects of toil and climate were allowed for, might be three or four years under that period. His form was tall, powerful, and athletic, like that of a man whose strength might, in later life, become unwieldy, but which was hitherto united with lightness and activity. His hands, when he withdrew the mailed gloves, were long, fair, and well-proportioned; the wrist-bones peculiarly large and strong; and the arms themselves remarkably well-shaped and brawny. A military hardihood, and careless frankness of expression, characterized his language and his motions; and his voice had the tone of one more accustomed to command than to obey, and who was in the habit of expressing his sentiments aloud and boldly, whenever he was called upon to announce them.

The Saracen Emir formed a marked and striking contrast with the western Crusader. His stature was indeed above the middle size, but he was at least three inches shorter than the European, whose size approached the gigantic. His slender limbs, and long spare hands and arms, though well proportioned to his person, and suited to the style of his countenance, did not at first aspect promise the display of vigour and elasticity which the Emir had lately exhibited. But on looking more closely, his limbs, where exposed to view, seemed divested of all that was fleshy or cumbersome; so that nothing being left but bone, brawn, and sinew, it was a frame fitted for exertion and fatigue, far beyond that of a bulky champion, whose strength and size are counterbalanced by weight, and who is exhausted by his own exertions. The countenance of the Saracen naturally bore a general national resemblance to the Eastern tribe from whom he descended, and was as unlike as possible to the exaggerated terms in which the minstrels of the day were wont to represent the infidel champions, and the fabulous description which a sister art still presents as the Saracen's head upon signposts. His features were small, well-formed, and delicate, though deeply embrowned by the Eastern sun, and terminated by a flowing and curled black beard, which seemed trimmed with peculiar care. The nose was straight and regular, the eyes keen, deep-set, black, and glowing, and his teeth equalled in beauty the ivory of his deserts. The person and proportions of the Saracen, in short, stretched on the turf near to his powerful antagonist, might have been compared to his sheeny and crescent-formed sabre, with its narrow and light, but bright and keen Damascus blade, contrasted with the long and ponderous Gothic war-sword which was flung unbuckled on the same sod. The Emir was in the very flower of his age, and might perhaps have been termed eminently beautiful, but for the narrowness of his forehead, and something of too much thinness and sharpness of feature, or at least what might have seemed such in a European estimate of beauty.

The manners of the Eastern warrior were grave, graceful, and decorous; indicating, however, in some particulars, the habitual restraint which men of warm and choleric tempers often set as a guard upon their native impetuosity of disposition, and at the same time a sense of his own dignity, which seemed to impose a certain formality of behaviour in him who entertained it.

This haughty feeling of superiority was perhaps equally entertained by his new European acquaintance, but the effect was different; and the same feeling, which dictated to the Christian knight a bold, blunt, and somewhat careless bearing, as one too conscious of his own importance to be anxious about the opinions of others, appeared to prescribe to the Saracen a style of courtesy more studiously and formally observant of ceremony. Both were courteous; but the courtesy of the Christian seemed to flow rather from a good-humoured sense of what was due to others; that of the Moslem, from a high feeling of what was to be expected from himself.

The provision which each had made for his refreshment was simple, but the meal of the Saracen was abstemious. A handful of dates, and a morsel of coarse barley-bread, sufficed to relieve the hunger of the latter, whose education had habituated him to the fare of the desert, although, since their Syrian conquests, the Arabian simplicity of life frequently gave place to the most unbounded profusion of luxury. A few draughts from the lovely fountain by which they reposed completed his meal. That of the Christian, though coarse, was more genial. Dried hog's-flesh, the abomination of the Moslemah, was the chief part of his repast; and his drink, derived from a leathern bottle, contained something better than pure element. He fed with more display of appetite, and drank with more appearance of satisfaction, than the Saracen judged it becoming to show in the performance of a mere bodily function; and, doubtless, the secret contempt which each entertained for the other, as the follower of a false religion, was considerably increased by the marked difference of their diet and manners. But each had found the weight of his opponent's arm, and the mutual respect which the bold struggle had created, was sufficient to subdue other and inferior considerations. Yet the Saracen could not help remarking the circumstances which displeased him in the Christian's conduct and manners; and, after he had witnessed for some time in silence the keen appetite which protracted the knight's banquet long after his own was concluded, he thus addressed him:—

"Valiant Nazarene, is it fitting that one who can fight like a man should feed like a dog or a wolf? Even a misbelieving Jew would shudder at the food which you seem to eat with as much relish as if it were fruit from the trees of Paradise."

"Valiant Saracen," answered the Christian, looking up with some surprise at the accusation thus unexpectedly brought, "know thou that I exercise my Christian freedom, in using that which is forbidden to the Jews, being, as they esteem themselves, under the bondage of the old law of Moses. We, Saracen, be it known to thee, have a better warrant for what we do—Ave Maria!—be we thankful." And, as if in defiance of his companion's scruples, he concluded a short Latin grace with a long draught from the leathern bottle.

"That, too, you call a part of your liberty," said the Saracen; "and as you feed like the brutes, so you degrade yourself to the bestial condition, by drinking a poisonous liquor which even they refuse!"

"Know, foolish Saracen," replied the Christian, without hesitation, "that thou blasphemest the gifts of God, even with the blasphemy of thy father Ishmael. The juice of the grape is given to him that will use it wisely, as that which cheers the heart of man after toil, refreshes him in sickness, and comforts him in sorrow. He who so enjoyeth it may thank God for his wine-cup as for his daily bread; and he who abuseth the gift of Heaven, is not a greater fool in his intoxication than thou in thine abstinence."

The keen eye of the Saracen kindled at this sarcasm, and his hand sought the hilt of his poniard. It was but a momentary thought, however, and died away in the recollection of the powerful champion with whom he had to deal, and the desperate grapple, the impression ot which still throbbed in bis limbs and veins; and he contented himself with pursuing the contest in colloquy, as more convenient for the time.

"Thy words," he said, "O Nazarene, might create anger, did not thy ignorance raise compassion. See'st thou not, O thou more blind than any who ask alms at the door of the Mosque, that the liberty thou dost boast of is restrained even in that which is dearest to man's happiness, and to his household; and that thy law, if thou dost practise it, binds thee in marriage to one single mate, be she sick or healthy, be she fruitful or barren, bring she comfort and joy, or clamour and strife, to thy table and to thy bed? This, Nazarene, I do indeed call slavery; whereas, to the faithful, hath the Prophet assigned upon earth the patriarchal privileges of Abraham our father, and of Solomon, the wisest of mankind, having given us here a succession of beauty at our pleasure, and beyond the grave the black-eyed houris of Paradise."

"Now, by His name that I most reverence in Heaven," said the Christian, "and by hers whom I most worship on earth, thou art but a blinded and a bewildered infidel!—That diamond signet, which thou wearest on thy finger, thou holdest it, doubtless, as of inestimable value?"

"Balsora and Bagdad cannot show the like," replied the Saracen; "but what avails it to our purpose?"

"Much," replied the Frank, "as thou shalt thyself confess. Take my war-axe, and dash the stone into twenty shivers;—would each fragment be as valuable as the original gem, or would they, all collected, bear the tenth part of its estimation?"

"That is a child's question," answered the Saracen; "the fragments of such a stone would not equal the entire jewel in the degree of hundreds to one."

"Saracen," replied the Christian warrior, "the love which a true knight binds on one only, fair and faithful, is the gem entire; the affection thou flingest among thy enslaved wives, and half-wedded slaves, is worthless, comparatively, as the sparkling shivers of the broken diamond."

"Now, by the Holy Caaba," said the Emir, "thou art a madman, who hugs his chain of iron as if it were of gold! — Look more closely. This ring of mine would lose half its beauty were not the signet encircled and enchased with these lesser brilliants, which grace it and set it off. The central diamond is man, firm and entire, his value depending on himself alone; and this circle of lesser jewels are women, borrowing his lustre, which he deals out to them as best suits his pleasure or his convenience. Take the central stone from the signet, and the diamond itself remains as valuable as ever, while the lesser gems are comparatively of little value. And this is the true reading of thy parable; for, what sayeth the poet Mansour; "It is the favour of man which giveth beauty and comeliness to woman, as the stream glitters no longer when the sun ceases to shine."

"Saracen," replied the Crusader, "thou speakest like one who never saw a woman worthy the affection of a soldier. Believe me, couldst thou look upon those of Europe, to whom, after Heaven, we of the order of knighthood vow fealty and devotion, thou wouldst loathe for ever the poor sensual slaves who form thy haram. The beauty of our fair ones gives point to our spears, and edge to our swords; their words are our law; and as soon will a lamp shed lustre when unkindled, as a knight distinguish himself by feat of arms, having no mistress of his affection."

"I have heard of this frenzy among the warriors of the west," said the Emir, "and have ever accounted it one of the accompanying symptoms of that insanity which brings you hither to obtain possession of an empty sepulchre. But yet, methinks, so highly have the Franks whom I have met with extolled the beauty of their women, I could be well contented to behold with mine own eyes those charms, which can transform such brave warriors into the tools of their pleasure."

"Brave Saracen," said the Knight, "if I were not on a pilgrimage to the Holy Sepulchre, it should be my pride to conduct you, on assurance of safety, to the camp of Richard of England, than whom none knows better how to do honour to a noble foe; and though I be poor and unattended, yet have I interest to secure for thee, or any such as thou seemest, not safety only, but respect and esteem. There shouldst thou see several of the fairest beauties of France and Britain form a small circle, the brilliancy of which exceeds ten-thousand-fold the lustre of mines of diamonds such as thine."

"Now, by the corner-stone of the Caaba," said the Saracen, "I will accept thy invitation as freely as it is given, if thou wilt postpone thy present intent; and, credit me, brave Nazarene, it were better for thyself to turn back thy horse's head towards the camp of thy people, for, to travel towards Jerusalem without a passport, is but a wilful casting away of thy life."

"I have a pass," answered the Knight, producing a parchment, "under Saladin's hand and signet."

The Saracen bent his head to the dust as he recognized the seal and handwriting of the renowned Soldan of Egypt and Syria; and having kissed the paper with profound respect, he pressed it to his forehead, then returned it to the Christian, saying, "Rash Frank, thou hast sinned against thine own blood and mine, for not showing this to me when we met."

"You came with levelled spear," said the Knight; "had a troop of Saracens so assailed me, it might have stood with my honour to have shown the Soldan's pass, but never to one man."

"And yet one man," said the Saracen, haughtily, "was enough to interrupt your journey."

"True, brave Moslem," replied the Christian; "but there are few such as thou art. Such falcons fly not in flocks, or if they do, they pounce not in numbers upon one."

"Thou dost us but justice," said the Saracen, evidently gratified by the compliment, as he had been touched by the implied scorn of the European's previous boast; "from us thou shouldst have had no wrong; but well was it for me that I failed to slay thee, with the safeguard of the king of kings upon thy person. Certain it were, that the cord or the sabre had justly avenged such guilt."

"I am glad to hear that its influence shall be availing to me," said the Knight; "for I have heard that the road is infested with robber-tribes, who regard nothing in comparison of an opportunity of plunder."

"The truth has been told to thee, brave Christian," said the Saracen; "but I swear to thee, by the turban of the Prophet, that shouldst thou miscarry in any haunt of such villains, I will myself undertake thy revenge with five thousand horse; I will slay every male of them, and send their women into such distant captivity, that the name of their tribe shall never again be heard within five hundred miles of Damascus. I will sow with salt the foundations of their village, and there shall never live thing dwell there, even from that time forward."

"I had rather the trouble which you design for yourself, were in revenge of some other more important person than of me, noble Emir," replied the Knight; "but my vow is recorded in Heaven, for good or for evil, and I must be indebted to you for pointing me out the way to my resting-place for this evening."

"That," said the Saracen, "must be under the black covering of my father's tent."

"This night," answered the Christian, "I must pass in prayer and penitence with a holy man, Theodorick of Engaddi, who dwells amongst these wilds, and spends his life in the service of God."

"I will at least see you safe thither," said the Saracen.

"That would be pleasant convoy for me," said the Christian, "yet might endanger the future security of the good father; for the cruel hand of your people has been red with the blood of the servants of the Lord, and therefore do we come hither in plate and mail, with sword and lance, to open the road to the Holy Sepulchre, and protect the chosen saints and anchorites who yet dwell in this land of promise and of miracle."

"Nazarene," said the Moslem, "in this the Greeks and Syrians have much belied us, seeing we do but after the word of Abubeker Alwakel, the successor of the Prophet, and, after him, the first commander of true believers. 'Go forth,' he said, 'Yezed Ben Sophian,' when he sent that renowned general to take Syria from the infidels, 'quit yourselves like men in battle, but slay neither the aged, the infirm, the women, nor the children. Waste not the land, neither destroy corn and fruit-trees, they are the gifts of Allah. Keep faith when you have made any covenant, even if it be to your own harm. If ye find holy men labouring with their hands, and serving God in the desert, hurt them not, neither destroy their dwellings. But when you find them with shaven crowns, they are of the synagogue of Satan! smite with the sabre, slay, cease not till they become believers or tributaries.' As the Caliph, companion of the Prophet, hath told us, so have we done, and those whom our justice has smitten are but the priests of Satan. But unto the good men who, without stirring up nation against nation, worship sincerely in the faith of Issa Ben Marian, we are a shadow and a shield; and such being he whom you seek, even though the light of the Prophet hath not reached him, from me he will only have love, favour, and regard."

"The anchorite, whom I would now visit," said the warlike pilgrim, "is, I have heard, no priest; but were he of that anointed and sacred order, I would prove with my good lance, against paynim and infidel——"

"Let us not defy each other, brother," interrupted the Saracen; "we shall find, either of us, enough of Franks or of Moslemah on whom to exercise both sword and lance. This Theodorick is protected both by Turk and Arab; and, though one of strange conditions at intervals, yet, on the whole, he bears himself so well as the follower of his own prophet, that he merits the protection of him who was sent——"

"Now, by Our Lady, Saracen," exclaimed the Christian, "if thou darest name in the same breath, the camel-driver of Mecca with——"

An electrical shock of passion thrilled through the form of the Emir; but it was only momentary, and the calmness of his reply had both dignity and reason in it, when he said, "Slander not him whom thou knowest not; the rather that we venerate the founder of thy religion, while we condemn the doctrine which priests have spun from it. I will myself guide thee to the cavern of the hermit, which, methinks, without my help, thou wouldst find it a hard matter to reach. And, on the way, let us leave to mollahs and to monks, to dispute about the divinity of our faith, and speak on themes which belong to youthful warriors,—upon battles, upon beautiful women, upon sharp swords, and upon bright armour."

Chapter the Third.

THE warriors arose from their place of brief rest and simple refreshment, and courteously aided each other while they carefully replaced and adjusted the harness, from which they had relieved for the time their trusty steeds. Each seemed familiar with an employment, which, at that time, was a part of necessary, and, indeed, of indispensable duty. Each also seemed to possess, as far as the difference betwixt the animal and rational species admitted, the confidence and affection of the horse, which was the constant companion of his travels and his warfare. With the Saracen, this familiar intimacy was a part of his early habits; for, in the tents of the Eastern military tribes, the horse of the soldier ranks next to, and almost equal in importance with, his wife and his family; and, with the European warrior, circumstances, and indeed necessity, rendered his war-horse scarcely less than his brother-in-arms. The steeds, therefore, suffered themselves quietly to be taken from their food and liberty, and neighed and snuffled fondly around their masters, while they were adjusting their accoutrements for farther travel and additional toil. And each warrior, as he prosecuted his own task, or assisted with courtesy his companion, looked with observant curiosity at the equipments of his fellow-traveller, and noted particularly what struck him as peculiar in the fashion in which he arranged his riding accoutrements.

Ere they remounted to resume their journey, the Christian knight again moistened his lips, and dipt his hands in the living fountain, and said to his Pagan associate of the journey—"I would I knew the name of this delicious fountain, that I might hold it in my grateful remembrance; for never did water make more deliciously a more oppressive thirst than I have this day experienced."

"It is called in the Arabic language," answered the Saracen, "by a name which signifies the Diamond of the Desert."

"And well is it so named," replied the Christian. "My native valley hath a thousand springs, but not to one of them shall I attach hereafter such precious recollection as to this solitary fount, which bestows its liquid treasures where they are not only delightful, but nearly indispensable."

"You say truth," said the Saracen; "for the curse is still on yonder sea of death, and neither man nor beast drink of its waves, nor of the river which feeds without filling it, until this inhospitable desert be passed."

They mounted, and pursued their journey across the sandy waste. The ardour of noon was now past, and a light breeze somewhat alleviated the terrors of the desert, though not without bearing on its wings an impalpable dust, which the Saracen little heeded, though his heavily-armed companion felt it as such an annoyance, that he hung his iron casque at his saddlebow, and substituted the light riding-cap, termed in the language of the time a *mortier*, from its resemblance in shape to an ordinary mortar. They rode together for some time in silence, the Saracen performing the part of director and guide of the journey, which he did by observing minute marks and bearings of the distant rocks, to a ridge of which they were gradually approaching. For a little time he seemed absorbed in the task, as a pilot when navigating a vessel through a difficult channel; but they had not proceeded half a league when he seemed secure of his route, and disposed, with more frankness than was usual to his nation, to enter into conversation.

"You have asked the name," he said, "of a mute fountain, which hath the semblance, but not the reality, of a living thing. Let me be pardoned to ask the name of the companion with whom I have this day encountered, both in danger and in repose, and which I cannot fancy unknown, even here among the deserts of Palestine?"

"It is not yet worth publishing," said the Christian. "Know, however, that among the soldiers of the Cross I am called Kenneth — Kenneth of the Couching Leopard; at home I have other titles, but they would sound harsh in an Eastern ear. Brave Saracen, let me ask which of the tribes of Arabia claims your descent, and by what name you are known?"

"Sir Kenneth," said the Moslem, "I joy that your name is such as my lips can easily utter. For me, I am no Arab, yet derive my descent from a line neither less wild nor less warlike. Know, Sir Knight of the Leopard, that I am Sheerkohf, the Lion of the Mountain, and that Kurdistan, from which I derive my descent, holds no family more noble than that of Seljook."

"I have heard," answered the Christian, "that your great Soldan claims his blood from the same source?"

"Thanks to the Prophet, that hath so far honoured our mountains, as to send from their bosom him whose word is victory," answered the Paynim. "I am but as a worm before the King of Egypt and Syria, and yet in my own land something my name may avail. — Stranger, with how many men didst thou come on this warfare?"

"By my faith," said Sir Kenneth, "with aid of friends and kinsmen, I was hardly pinched to furnish forth ten well-appointed lances, with maybe some fifty more men, archers, and varlets included. Some have deserted my unlucky pennon — some have fallen in battle — several have died of disease — and one trusty armour-bearer, for whose life I am now doing my pilgrimage, lies on the bed of sickness."

"Christian," said Sheerkohf, "here I have five arrows in my quiver, each feathered from the wing of an eagle. When I send one of them to my tents, a thousand warriors mount on horseback — when I send another, an equal force will arise — for the five I can command five thousand men; and if I send my bow, ten thousand mounted riders will shake the desert. And with thy fifty followers thou hast come to invade a land in which I am one of the meanest!"

"Now, by the rood, Saracen," retorted the western warrior, "thou shouldst know ere thou vauntest thyself, that one steel glove can crush a whole handful of hornets."

"Ay, but it must first enclose them within its grasp," said the Saracen, with a smile which might have endangered their new alliance, had he not changed the subject by adding, "And is bravery so much esteemed amongst the Christian princes, that thou, thus void of means, and of men, canst offer, as thou didst of late, to be my protector and security in the camp of thy brethren?"

"Know, Saracen," said the Christian, "since such is thy style, that the name of a knight, and the blood of a gentleman, entitle him to place himself on the same rank with sovereigns even of the first degree, in so far as regards all but regal authority and dominion. Were Richard of England himself to wound the honour of a knight as poor as I am, he could not, by the law of chivalry, deny him the combat."

"Methinks I should like to look upon so strange a scene," said the Emir, "in which a leathern belt and a pair of spurs put the poorest on a level with the most powerful."

"You must add free blood and a fearless heart," said the Christian; "then, perhaps you will not have spoken untruly of the dignity of knighthood."

"And mix you as boldly amongst the females of your chiefs and leaders?" asked the Saracen.

"God forbid," said the Knight of the Leopard, "that the poorest Knight in Christendom should not be free, in all honourable service, to devote his hand and sword, the fame of his actions, and the fixed devotion of his heart, to the fairest princess who ever wore coronet on her brow!"

"But a little while since," said the Saracen, "and you described love as the highest treasure of the heart — thine hath undoubtedly been high and nobly bestowed?"

"Stranger," answered the Christian, blushing deeply as he spoke, "we tell not rashly where it is we have bestowed our choicest treasures — it is enough for thee to know, that, as thou sayest, my love is highly and nobly bestowed—most highly—most nobly; but if thou wouldst hear of love and broken lances, venture thyself, as thou sayest, to the Camp of the Crusaders, and thou wilt find exercise for thine ears, and, if thou wilt, for thy hands too."

The Eastern warrior, raising himself in his stirrups, and shaking aloft his lance, replied, "Hardly, I fear, shall I find one with a crossed shoulder, who will exchange with me the cast of the jerrid."

"I will not promise for that," replied the knight, "though there be in the camp certain Spaniards, who have right good skill in your Eastern game of hurling the javelin."

"Dogs, and sons of dogs!" ejaculated the Saracen; "what have these Spaniards to do to come hither to combat the true believers, who, in their own land, are their lords and taskmasters? with them I would mix in no warlike pastime."

"Let not the knights of Leon or Asturias hear you speak thus of them," said the Knight of the Leopard; "but," added he, smiling at the recollection of the morning's combat, "if, instead of a reed, you were inclined to stand the cast of a battle-axe, there are enough of western warriors who would gratify your longing."

"By the beard of my father, sir," said the Saracen, with an approach to laughter, "the game is too rough for mere sport — I will never shun them in battle, but my head" (pressing his hand to his brow) "will not, for a while, permit me to seek them in sport."

"I would you saw the axe of King Richard," answered the western warrior, "to which that which hangs at my saddlebow weighs but as a feather."

"We hear much of that island sovereign," said the Saracen; "art thou one of his subjects?"

"One of his followers I am, for this expedition," answered the Knight, "and honoured in the service; but not born his subject, although a native of the island in which he reigns."

"How mean you?" said the Eastern soldier; "have you then two kings in one poor island?"

"As thou sayest," said the Scot, for such was Sir Kenneth by birth,— "It is even so; and yet, although the inhabitants of the two extremities of that island are engaged in frequent war, the country can, as thou seest, furnish forth such a body of men-at-arms, as may go far to shake the unholy hold which your master hath laid on the cities of Zion."

"By the beard of Saladin, Nazarene, but that it is a thoughtless and boyish folly, I could laugh at the simplicity of your great Sultan, who comes hither to make conquests of deserts and rocks, and dispute the possession of them with those who have tenfold numbers at command, while he leaves a part of his narrow islet, in which he was born a sovereign, to the dominion of another sceptre than his. Surely, Sir Kenneth, you and the other good men of your country should have submitted yourself to the dominion of this King Richard, ere you left your native land, divided against itself, to set forth on this expedition?"

Hasty and fierce was Kenneth's answer. "No, by the bright light of Heaven! if the King of England had not set forth to the Crusade till he was sovereign of Scotland, the crescent might, for me, and all true-hearted Scots, glimmer for ever on the walls of Zion."

Thus far he had proceeded, when, suddenly recollecting himself, he muttered, "*Mea culpa! mea culpa!* what have I, a soldier of the Cross, to do with recollection of war betwixt Christian nations?"

The rapid expression of feeling corrected by the dictates of duty, did not escape the Moslem, who, if he did not entirely understand all which it conveyed, saw enough to convince him with the assurance, that Christians, as well as Moslemah, had private feelings of personal pique, and national quarrels, which were not entirely reconcilable. But the Saracens were a race, polished, perhaps, to the utmost extent which their religion permitted, and particularly capable of entertaining high ideas of courtesy and politeness; and such sentiments prevented his taking any notice of the inconsistency of Sir Kenneth's feelings, in the opposite characters of a Scot and a Crusader.

Meanwhile, as they advanced, the scene began to change around them. They were now turning to the eastward, and had reached the range of steep and barren hills, which binds in that quarter the naked plain, and varies the surface of the country, without changing its steril character. Sharp rocky eminences began to arise around them, and, in a short time, deep declivities, and ascents, both formidable in height, and difficult from the narrowness of the path, offered to the travellers obstacles of a different kind from those with which they had recently contended. Dark caverns and chasms amongst the rocks, those grottoes so often alluded to in Scripture, yawned fearfully on either side as they proceeded, and the Scottish knight was informed by the Emir, that these were often the refuge of beasts of prey, or of men still more ferocious, who, driven to desperation by the constant war, and the oppression exercised by the soldiery, as well of the Cross as of the Crescent, had become robbers, and spared neither rank nor religion, neither sex nor age, in their depredations.

The Scottish knight listened with indifference to the accounts of ravages committed by wild beasts or wicked men, secure as he felt himself in his own valour and personal strength; but he was struck with mysterious dread, when he recollected that he was now in the awful wilderness of the forty days' fast, and the scene of the actual personal temptation, wherewith the Evil Principle was permitted to assail the Son of Man. He withdrew his attention gradually from the light and worldly conversation of the infidel warrior beside him, and, however acceptable his gay and gallant bravery would have rendered him as a companion elsewhere, Sir Kenneth felt as if, in those wildernesses — the waste and dry places, in which the foul spirits were wont to wander when expelled the mortals whose forms they possessed — a bare-footed friar would have been a better associate than the gay but unbelieving Paynim.

These feelings embarrassed him; the rather that the Saracen's spirits appeared to rise with the journey, and because the farther he penetrated into the gloomy recesses of the mountains, the lighter became his conversation, and when he found that unanswered, the louder grew his song. Sir Kenneth knew enough of the Eastern languages, to be assured that he chanted sonnets of love, containing all the glowing praises of beauty, in which the Oriental poets are so fond of luxuriating, and which, therefore, were peculiarly unfitted for a serious or devotional train of thought, the feeling best becoming the Wilderness of the Temptation. With inconsistency enough, the Saracen also sung lays in praise of wine, the liquid ruby of the Persian poets, and his gaiety at length became so unsuitable to the Christian knight's contrary train of sentiments, as, but for the promise of amity which they had exchanged, would most likely have made Sir Kenneth take measures to change his note. As it was, the Crusader felt as if he had by his side some gay licentious fiend, who endeavoured to ensnare his soul, and endanger his immortal salvation, by inspiring loose thoughts of earthly pleasure, and thus polluting his devotion, at a time when his faith as a

Christian, and his vow as a pilgrim, called on him for a serious and penitential state of mind. He was thus greatly perplexed, and undecided how to act; and it was in a tone of hasty displeasure, that, at length breaking silence, he interrupted the lay of the celebrated Rudpiki, in which he prefers the mole on his mistress's bosom to all the wealth of Bokhara and Samarcand.

"Saracen," said the Crusader, sternly, "blinded as thou art, and plunged amidst the errors of a false law, thou shouldst yet comprehend that there are some places more holy than others, and that there are some scenes also, in which the Evil One hath more than ordinary power over sinful mortals. I will not tell thee for what awful reason this place — these rocks — these caverns with their gloomy arches, leading as it were to the central abyss — are held an especial haunt of Satan and his angels. It is enough, that I have been long warned to beware of this place by wise and holy men, to whom the qualities of the unholy region are well known. Wherefore, Saracen, forbear thy foolish and ill-timed levity, and turn thy thoughts to things more suited to the spot; although, alas, for thee! thy best prayers are but as blasphemy and sin."

The Saracen listened with some surprise, and then replied, with good-humour and gaiety, only so far repressed as courtesy required, "Good Sir Kenneth, methinks you deal unequally by your companion, or else ceremony is but indifferently taught amongst your western tribes. I took no offence when I saw you gorge hog's flesh and drink wine, and permitted you to enjoy a treat which you called your Christian liberty, only pitying in my heart your foul pastimes — Wherefore, then, shouldst thou take scandal, because I cheer, to the best of my power, a gloomy road with a cheerful verse? — What saith the poet, — 'Song is like the dews of Heaven on the bosom of the desert; it cools the path of the traveller.'"

"Friend Saracen," said the Christian, "I blame not the love of minstrelsy and of the *gai science;* albeit, we yield unto it even too much room in our thoughts when they should be bent on better things. But prayers and holy psalms are better fitting than lais of love or of wine-cups, when men walk in this Valley of the Shadow of Death, full of fiends and demons, whom the prayers of holy men have driven forth from the haunts of humanity to wander amidst scenes as accursed as themselves."

"Speak not thus of the Genii, Christian," answered the Saracen, "for know, thou speakest to one whose line and nation drew their origin from the immortal race, which your sect fear and blaspheme."

"I well thought," answered the Crusader, "that your blinded race had their descent from the foul fiend, without whose aid you would never have been able to maintain this blessed land of Palestine against so many valiant soldiers of God. I speak not thus of thee in particular, Saracen, but generally of thy people and religion. Strange is it to me, however, not that you should have the descent from the Evil One, but that you should boast of it."

"From whom should the bravest boast of descending, saving from him that is bravest?" said the Saracen; "from whom should the proudest trace their line so well as from the Dark Spirit, which would rather fall headlong by force, than bend the knee by His will? Eblis may be hated, stranger, but he must be feared; and such as Eblis are his descendants of Kurdistan."

Tales of magic and of necromancy were the learning of the period, and Sir Kenneth heard his companion's confession of diabolical descent without any disbelief, and without much wonder; yet not without a secret shudder at finding himself in this fearful place, in the company of one who avouched himself to belong to such a lineage. Naturally unsusceptible, however, of fear, he crossed himself, and stoutly demanded of the Saracen an account of the pedigree which he had boasted. The latter readily complied.

"Know, brave stranger," he said, "that when the cruel Zohauk, one of the descendants of Giamschid, held the throne of Persia, he formed a league with the Powers of Darkness, amidst the secret vaults of Istakhar, vaults which the hands of the elementary spirits had hewn out of the living rock long before Adam himself had an existence. Here he fed, with daily oblations of human blood, two devouring serpents, which had become, according to the poets, a part of himself, and to sustain whom he levied a tax of daily human sacrifices, till the exhausted patience of his subjects caused some to raise up the scimitar of resistance, like the valiant Blacksmith, and the victorious Feridoun, by whom the tyrant was at length dethroned, and imprisoned for ever in the dismal caverns of the mountain Damavend. But ere that deliverance had taken place, and whilst the power of the bloodthirsty tyrant was at its height, the band of ravening slaves, whom he had sent forth to purvey victims for his daily sacrifice, brought to the vaults of the palace of Istakhar seven sisters so beautiful, that they seemed seven houris. These seven maidens were the daughters of a sage, who had no treasures save those beauties and his own wisdom. The last was not sufficient to foresee this misfortune, the former seemed ineffectual to prevent it. The eldest exceeded not her twentieth year, the youngest had scarce attained her thirteenth; and so like were they to each other, that they could not have been distinguished but for the difference of height, in which they gradually rose in easy gradation above each other, like the ascent which leads to the gates of Paradise. So lovely were these seven sisters when they stood in the darksome vault, disrobed of all clothing saving a cymar of white silk, that their charms moved the hearts of those who were not mortal. Thunder muttered, the earth shook, the wall of the vault was rent, and at the chasm entered one dressed like a hunter, with bow and shafts, and followed by six others, his brethren. They were tall men, and, though dark, yet comely to behold, but their eyes had more the glare of those of the dead, than the light which lives under the eyelids of the living. 'Zeneib,' said the leader of the band—and as he spoke he took the eldest sister by the hand, and his voice was soft, low, and melancholy,—'I am Cothrob, king of the subterranean world, and supreme chief of Ginnistan. I and my brethren are of those, who, created out of the pure elementary fire, disdained, even at the command of Omnipotence, to do homage to a clod of earth, because it was called Man. Thou may'st have heard of us as cruel, unrelenting, and persecuting. It is false. We are by nature kind and generous; only vengeful when insulted, only cruel when affronted. We are true to those who trust us; and we have heard the invocations of thy father, the sage Mithrasp, who wisely worships not alone the Origin of Good, but that which is called the Source of Evil. You and your sisters are on the eve of death; but let each give to us one hair from your fair tresses, in token of fealty, and we will carry you many miles from hence to a place of safety, where you may bid defiance to Zohauk and his ministers.' The fear of instant death, saith the poet, is like the rod of the prophet Haroun, which devoured all other rods when transformed into snakes before the King of Pharaoh; and the daughters of the Persian sage were less apt than others to be afraid of the addresses of a spirit. They gave the tribute which Cothrob demanded, and in an instant the sisters were transported to an enchanted castle on the mountains of Tugrut, in Kurdistan, and were never again seen by mortal eye. But in process of time seven youths, distinguished in the war and in the chase, appeared in the environs of the castle of the demons. They were darker, taller, fiercer, and more resolute, than any of the scattered inhabitants of the valleys of Kurdistan; and they took to themselves wives, and became fathers of the seven tribes of the Kurdmans, whose valour is known throughout the universe."

The Christian knight heard with wonder the wild tale, of which Kurdistan still possesses the traces, and, after a moment's thought, replied,—

"Verily, Sir Knight, you have spoken well—your genealogy may be dreaded and hated, but it cannot be contemned. Neither do I any longer wonder at your obstinacy in a false faith; since, doubtless, it is part of the fiendish disposition which hath descended from your ancestors, those infernal huntsmen, as you have described them, to love falsehood rather than truth; and I no longer marvel that your spirits become high and exalted, and vent themselves in verse and in tunes, when you approach to the places encumbered by the haunting of evil spirits, which must excite in you that joyous feeling which others experience when approaching the land of their human ancestry."

"By my father's beard, I think thou hast the right," said the Saracen, rather amused than offended by the freedom with which the Christian had uttered his reflections; "for, though the Prophet (blessed be his name!) hath sown amongst us the seed of a better faith than our ancestors learned in the ghostly halls of Tugrut, yet we are not willing, like other Moslemah, to pass hasty doom on the lofty and powerful elementary spirits from whom we claim our origin. These Genii, according to our belief and hope, are not altogether reprobate, but are still in the way of probation, and may hereafter be punished or rewarded. Leave we this to the mollahs and the imaums. Enough that with us the reverence of these spirits is not altogether effaced by what we have learned from the Koran, and that many of us still sing, in memorial of our fathers' more ancient faith, such verses as these."

So saying, he proceeded to chant verses, very ancient in the language and structure, which some have thought derive their source from the worshippers of Aimanes, the Evil Principle.

AHRIMAN.

Dark Ahriman, whom Irak still
Holds origin of woe and ill!
  When bending at thy shrine,
We view the world with troubled eye,
Where see we 'neath the extended sky,
  An empire matching thine?

If the Benigner Power can yield
A fountain in the desert field,
  Where weary pilgrims drink;
Thine are the waves that lash the rock,
Thine the tornado's deadly shock,
  Where countless navies sink!

Or if He bid the soil dispense
Balsams to cheer the sinking sense,
  How few can they deliver
From lingering pains, or pang intense,
Red Fever, spotted Pestilence,
  The arrows of thy quiver!

Chief in Man's bosom sits thy sway,
And frequent, while in words we pray
  Before another throne,
Whate'er of specious form be there,
The secret meaning of the prayer
  Is, Ahriman, thine own.

Say, hast thou feeling, sense, and form,
Thunder thy voice, thy garments storm,
  As Eastern Magi say;
With sentient soul of hate and wrath,
And wings to sweep thy deadly path,
  And fangs to tear thy prey?

Or art thou mix'd in Nature's source,
An ever-operating force,
  Converting good to ill;
An evil principle innate,
Contending with our better fate,
  And oh! victorious still?

Howe'er it be, dispute is vain,
On all without thou hold'st thy reign,
  Nor less on all within;
Each mortal passion's fierce career,
Love, hate, ambition, joy, and fear,
  Thou goadest into sin.

Whene'er a sunny gleam appears,
To brighten up our vale of tears,
  Thou art not distant far;
'Mid such brief solace of our lives,
Thou whett'st our very banquet-knives
  To tools of death and war.

Thus from the moment of our birth,
Long as we linger on the earth,
  Thou rul'st the fate of men;
Thine are the pangs of life's last hour,
And—who dare answer?—is thy power,
  Dark Spirit! ended THEN?*

These verses may perhaps have been the not unnatural effusion of some half-enlightened philosopher, who, in the fabled deity, Arimanes, saw but the prevalence of moral and physical evil; but in the ears of Sir Kenneth of the Leopard, they had a different effect, and, sung as they were by one who had just boasted himself a descendant of demons, sounded very like an

---

* The worthy and learned clergyman, by whom this species of hymn has been translated, desires, that, for fear of misconception, we should warn the reader to recollect, that it is composed by a heathen, to whom the real causes of moral and physical evil are unknown, and who views their predominance in the system of the universe, as all must view that appalling fact, who have not the benefit of the Christian Revelation. On our own part, we beg to add, that we understand the style of the translator is more paraphrastic than can be approved by those who are acquainted with the singularly curious original. The translator seems to have despaired of rendering into English verse the flights of Oriental poetry; and, possibly, like many learned and ingenious men, finding it impossible to discover the sense of the original, he may have tacitly substituted his own.

address of worship to the Arch-fiend himself. He weighed within himself, whether, on hearing such blasphemy in the very desert where Satan had stood rebuked for demanding homage, taking an abrupt leave of the Saracen was sufficient to testify his abhorrence; or whether he was not rather constrained by his vow as a Crusader, to defy the infidel to combat on the spot, and leave him food for the beasts of the wilderness, when his attention was suddenly caught by an unexpected apparition.

The light was now verging low, yet served the knight still to discern that they two were no longer alone in the forest, but were closely watched by a figure of great height and very thin, which skipped over rocks and bushes with so much agility, as, added to the wild and hirsute appearance of the individual, reminded him of the fauns and silvans, whose images he had seen in the ancient temples of Rome. As the single-hearted Scotsman had never for a moment doubted these gods of the ancient Gentiles to be actually devils, so he now hesitated not to believe that the blasphemous hymn of the Saracen had raised up an infernal spirit.

"But what recks it!" said stout Sir Kenneth to himself; "down with the fiend and his worshippers!"

He did not, however, think it necessary to give the same warning of defiance to two enemies, as he would unquestionably have afforded to one. His hand was upon his mace, and perhaps the unwary Saracen would have been paid for his Persian poetry, by having his brains dashed out on the spot, without any reason assigned for it; but the Scottish knight was spared from committing what would have been a sore blot in his shield of arms. The apparition, on which his eyes had been fixed for some time, had at first appeared to dog their path by concealing itself behind rocks and shrubs, using those advantages of the ground with great address, and surmounting its irregularities with surprising agility. At length, just as the Saracen paused in his song, the figure, which was that of a tall man clothed in goat-skins, sprung into the midst of the path, and seized a rein of the Saracen's bridle in either hand, confronting thus and bearing back the noble horse, which, unable to endure the manner in which this sudden assailant pressed the long-armed bit, and the severe curb, which, according to the Eastern fashion, was a solid ring of iron, reared upright, and finally fell backwards on his master, who, however, avoided the peril of the fall, by lightly throwing himself to one side.

The assailant then shifted his grasp from the bridle of the horse to the throat of the rider, flung himself above the struggling Saracen, and, despite of his youth and activity, kept him undermost, wreathing his long arms above those of his prisoner, who called out angrily, and yet, half-laughing at the same time—"Hamako—fool—unloose me—this passes thy privilege—unloose me, or I will use my dagger."

"Thy dagger!—infidel dog!" said the figure in the goat-skins, "hold it in thy gripe if thou canst!" and in an instant he wrenched the Saracen's weapon out of its owner's hand, and brandished it over his head.

"Help, Nazarene!" cried Sheerkohf, now seriously alarmed; "help, or the Hamako will slay me."

"Slay thee!" replied the dweller of the desert; "and well hast thou merited death, for singing thy blasphemous hymns, not only to the praise of thy false prophet, who is the foul fiend's harbinger, but to the Author of Evil himself."

The Christian Knight had hitherto looked on as one stupified, so strangely had this rencontre contradicted, in its progress and event, all that he had previously conjectured. He felt, however, at length, that it touched his honour to interfere in behalf of his discomfited companion; and therefore addressed himself to the victorious figure in the goat-skins.

"Whosoe'er thou art," he said, "and whether of good or of evil, know that I am sworn for the time to be true companion to the Saracen whom thou holdest under thee ;—therefore, I pray thee to let him arise, else I will do battle with thee in his behalf."

"And a proper quarrel it were," answered the Hamako, "for a Crusader to do battle in—for the sake of an unbaptized dog to combat one of his own holy faith! Art thou come forth to the wilderness to fight for the Crescent against the Cross? A goodly soldier of God art thou to listen to those who sing the praises of Satan!"

Yet, while he spoke thus, he arose himself, and, suffering the Saracen to arise also, returned him his cangiar, or poniard.

"Thou seest to what a point of peril thy presumption has brought thee," continued he of the goat-skins, now addressing Sheerkohf, "and by what weak means thy practised skill and boasted agility can be foiled, when such is Heaven's pleasure. Wherefore, beware, O Ilderim! for know that, were there not a twinkle in the star of thy nativity, which promises for thee something that is good and gracious in Heaven's good time, we two had not parted till I had torn asunder the throat which so lately thrilled forth blasphemies."

"Hamako," said the Saracen, without any appearance of resenting the violent language, and yet more violent assault, to which he had been subjected, "I pray thee, good Hamako, to beware how thou dost again urge thy privilege over far; for though, as a good Moslem, I respect those whom Heaven hath deprived of ordinary reason, in order to endow them with the spirit of prophecy, yet I like not other men's hands on the bridle of my horse, neither upon my own person. Speak, therefore, what thou wilt, secure of any resentment from me; but gather so much sense as to apprehend, that if thou shalt again proffer me any violence, I will strike thy shagged head from thy meagre shoulders.—And to thee, friend Kenneth," he added, as he remounted his steed, "I must needs say, that, in a companion through the desert, I love friendly deeds better than fair words. Of the last thou hast given me enough; but it had been better to have aided me more speedily in my struggle with this Hamako, who had wellnigh taken my life in his frenzy."

"By my faith," said the Knight, "I did somewhat fail—was somewhat tardy in rendering thee instant help; but the strangeness of the assailant, the suddenness of the scene—it was as if thy wild and wicked lay had raised the devil among us—and such was my confusion, that two or three minutes elapsed ere I could take to my weapon."

"Thou art but a cold and considerate friend," said the Saracen; "and, had the Hamako been one grain more frantic, thy companion had been slain by thy side, to thy eternal dishonour, without thy stirring a finger in his aid, although thou satest by, mounted and in arms."

"By my word, Saracen," said the Christian, "if thou wilt have it in plain terms, I thought that strange figure was the devil; and being of thy lineage, I knew not what family secret you might be communicating to each other, as you lay lovingly rolling together on the sand."

"Thy gibe is no answer, brother Kenneth," said the Saracen; "for know, that had my assailant been in very deed the Prince of Darkness, thou wert bound not the less to enter into combat with him in thy comrade's behalf. Know, also, that whatever there may be of foul or of fiendish about the Hamako, belongs more to your lineage than to mine; this Hamako being, in truth, the anchorite whom thou art come hither to visit."

"This!" said Sir Kenneth, looking at the athletic yet wasted figure before him—"this!—thou mockest, Saracen—this cannot be the venerable Theodorick!"

"Ask himself, if thou wilt not believe me," answered Sheerkohf; and ere the words had left his mouth, the hermit gave evidence in his own behalf.

"I am Theodorick of Engaddi," he said—"I am the walker of the desert

— I am friend of the cross, and flail of all infidels, heretics, and devil-worshippers. Avoid ye, avoid ye!—Down with Mahound, Termagaunt, and all their adherents!"—So saying, he pulled from under his shaggy garment a sort of flail, or jointed club, bound with iron, which he brandished round his head with singular dexterity.

"Thou see'st thy saint," said the Saracen, laughing, for the first time, at the unmitigated astonishment with which Sir Kenneth looked on the wild gestures, and heard the wayward muttering of Theodorick, who, after swinging his flail in every direction, apparently quite reckless whether it encountered the head of either of his companions, finally showed his own strength, and the soundness of the weapon, by striking into fragments a large stone which lay near him.

"This is a madman," said Sir Kenneth.

"Not the worse saint," returned the Moslem, speaking according to the well-known Eastern belief, that madmen are under the influence of immediate inspiration. "Know, Christian, that when one eye is extinguished, the other becomes more keen—when one hand is cut off, the other becomes more powerful; so, when our reason in human things is disturbed or destroyed, our view heavenward becomes more acute and perfect."

Here the voice of the Saracen was drowned in that of the hermit, who began to hollo aloud in a wild chanting tone,—"I am Theodorick of Engaddi—I am the torch-brand of the desert—I am the flail of the infidels! The lion and the leopard shall be my comrades, and draw nigh to my cell for shelter; neither shall the goat be afraid of their fangs—I am the torch and the lantern—Kyrie Eleison!"

He closed his song by a short race, and ended that again by three forward bounds, which would have done him great credit in a gymnastic academy, but became his character of hermit so indifferently, that the Scottish knight was altogether confounded and bewildered.

The Saracen seemed to understand him better. "You see," he said, "that he expects us to follow him to his cell, which, indeed, is our only place of refuge for the night. You are the leopard, from the portrait on your shield—I am the lion, as my name imports—and, by the goat, alluding to his garb of goat-skins, he means himself. We must keep him in sight, however, for he is as fleet as a dromedary."

In fact, the task was a difficult one, for though the reverend guide stopped from time to time, and waved his hand, as if to encourage them to come on, yet, well acquainted with all the winding dells and passes of the desert, and gifted with uncommon activity, which, perhaps, an unsettled state of mind kept in constant exercise, he led the knights through chasms, and along footpaths, where even the light-armed Saracen, with his well-trained barb, was in considerable risk, and where the iron-sheathed European, and his over-burdened horse, found themselves in such imminent peril, as the rider would gladly have exchanged for the dangers of a general action. Glad he was when, at length, after this wild race, he beheld the holy man who had led it standing in front of a cavern, with a large torch in his hand, composed of a piece of wood dipped in bitumen, which cast a broad and flickering light, and emitted a strong sulphurous smell.

Undeterred by the stifling vapour, the knight threw himself from his horse and entered the cavern, which afforded small appearance of accommodation. The cell was divided into two parts, in the outward of which were an altar of stone, and a crucifix made of reeds: This served the anchorite for his chapel. On one side of this outward cave the Christian knight, though not without scruple, arising from religious reverence to the objects around, fastened up his horse, and arranged him for the night, in imitation of the Saracen, who gave him to understand that such was the custom of the place. The hermit, meanwhile, was busied putting his inner apartment in order to receive his guests, and there they soon joined him.

At the bottom of the outer cave, a small aperture, closed with a door of rough plank, led into the sleeping apartment of the hermit, which was more commodious. The floor had been brought to a rough level by the labour of the inhabitant, and then strewed with white sand, which he daily sprinkled with water from a small fountain which bubbled out of the rock in one corner, affording, in that stifling climate, refreshment alike to the ear and the taste. Mattrasses, wrought of twisted flags, lay by the side of the cell; the sides, like the floor, had been roughly brought to shape, and several herbs and flowers were hung around them. Two waxen torches, which the hermit lighted, gave a cheerful air to the place, which was rendered agreeable by its fragrance and coolness.

There were implements of labour in one corner of the apartment, in another was a niche for a rude statue of the Virgin. A table and two chairs showed that they must be the handywork of the anchorite, being different in their form from Oriental accommodations. The former was covered, not only with reeds and pulse, but also with dried flesh, which Theodorick assiduously placed in such arrangement as should invite the appetite of his guests. This appearance of courtesy, though mute and expressed by gesture only, seemed to Sir Kenneth something entirely irreconcilable with his former wild and violent demeanour. The movements of the hermit were now become composed, and apparently it was only a sense of religious humiliation which prevented his features, emaciated as they were by his austere mode of life, from being majestic and noble. He trode his cell as one who seemed born to rule over men, but who had abdicated his empire to become the servant of Heaven. Still it must be allowed that his gigantic size, the length of his unshaven locks and beard, and the fire of a deep-set and wild eye, were rather attributes of a soldier than of a recluse.

Even the Saracen seemed to regard the anchorite with some veneration, while he was thus employed, and he whispered in a low tone to Sir Kenneth, "The Hamako is now in his better mind, but he will not speak until we have eaten — such is his vow."

It was in silence, accordingly, that Theodorick motioned to the Scot to take his place on one of the low chairs, while Sheerkohf placed himself, after the custom of his nation, upon a cushion of mats. The hermit then held up both hands, as if blessing the refreshment which he had placed before his guests, and they proceeded to eat in silence as profound as his own. To the Saracen this gravity was natural, and the Christian imitated his taciturnity, while he employed his thoughts on the singularity of his own situation, and the contrast betwixt the wild, furious gesticulations, loud cries, and fierce actions of Theodorick, when they first met him, and the demure, solemn, decorous assiduity with which he now performed the duties of hospitality.

When their meal was ended, the hermit, who had not himself eaten a morsel, removed the fragments from the table, and placing before the Saracen a pitcher of sherbet, assigned to the Scot a flask of wine.

"Drink," he said, "my children," — they were the first words he had spoken, — "the gifts of God are to be enjoyed, when the Giver is remembered."

Having said this, he retired to the outward cell, probably for performance of his devotions, and left his guests together in the inner apartment; when Sir Kenneth endeavoured, by various questions, to draw from Sheerkohf what that Emir knew concerning his host. He was interested by more than mere curiosity in these inquiries. Difficult as it was to reconcile the outrageous demeanour of the recluse at his first appearance, to his present humble and placid behaviour, it seemed yet more impossible to think it consistent with the high consideration in which, according to what Sir Kenneth had learned, this Hermit was held by the most enlightened divines of the Christian world. Theodorick, the Hermit of Engaddi, had, in that character, been the correspondent of popes and councils; to whom his letters, full of eloquent fervour, had described the miseries imposed by the unbelievers upon the Latin Christians in the Holy Land, in colours scarce inferior to those employed at the Council of Clermont by the Hermit Peter, when he preached the first Crusade. To find, in a person so reverend, and so much revered, the frantic gestures of a mad fakir, induced the Christian knight to pause ere he could resolve to communicate to him certain important matters, which he had in charge from some of the leaders of the Crusade.

It had been a main object of Sir Kenneth's pilgrimage, attempted by a route so unusual, to make such communications; but what he had that night seen, induced him to pause and reflect ere he proceeded to the execution of his commission. From the Emir he could not extract much information, but the general tenor was as follows: — That, as he had heard, the hermit had been once a brave and valiant soldier, wise in council, and fortunate in battle, which last he could easily believe from the great strength and agility which he had often seen him display;—that he had appeared at Jerusalem in the character not of a pilgrim, but in that of one who had devoted himself to dwell for the remainder of his life in the Holy Land. Shortly afterwards he fixed his residence amid the scenes of desolation where they now found him, respected by the Latins for his austere devotion, and by the Turks and Arabs on account of the symptoms of insanity which he displayed, and which they ascribed to inspiration. It was from them he had the name of Hamako, which expresses such a character in the Turkish language. Sheerkohf himself seemed at a loss how to rank their host. He had been, he said, a wise man, and could often for many hours together speak lessons of virtue or wisdom, without the slightest appearance of inaccuracy. At other times he was wild and violent, but never before had he seen him so mischievously disposed as he had that day appeared to be. His rage was chiefly provoked by any affront to his religion; and there was a story of some wandering Arabs, who had insulted his worship and defaced his altar, and whom he had on that account attacked and slain with the short flail, which he carried with him in lieu of all other weapons. This incident had made a great noise, and it was as much the fear of the hermit's iron flail, as regard for his character as a Hamako, which caused the roving tribes to respect his dwelling and his chapel. His fame had spread so far, that Saladin had issued particular orders that he should be spared and protected. He himself, and other Moslem lords of rank, had visited the cell more than once, partly from curiosity, partly that they expected from a man so learned as the Christian Hamako, some insight into the secrets of futurity. "He had," continued the Saracen, "a rashid, or observatory, of great height, contrived to view the heavenly bodies, and particularly the planetary system; by whose movements and influences, as both Christian and Moslem believed, the course of human events was regulated, and might be predicted.

This was the substance of the Emir Sheerkohf's information, and it left Sir Kenneth in doubt whether the character of insanity arose from the occasional excessive fervour of the hermit's zeal, or whether it was not altogether fictitious, and assumed for the sake of the immunities which it afforded. Yet it seemed that the infidels had carried their complaisance towards him to an uncommon length, considering the fanaticism of the followers of Mohammed, in the midst of whom he was living, though the professed enemy of their faith. He thought also there was more intimacy of acquaintance betwixt the hermit and the Saracen, than the words of the latter had induced him to anticipate; and it had not escaped him, that the former had called the latter by a name different from that which he himself had assumed. All these considerations authorized caution, if not suspicion. He determined to observe his host closely, and not to be over hasty in communicating with him on the important charge intrusted to him.

2 T

"Beware, Saracen," he said; "methinks our host's imagination wanders as well on the subject of names as upon other matters. Thy name is Sheerkohf, and he called thee but now by another."

"My name, when in the tent of my father," replied the Kurdman, "was Ilderim, and by this I am still distinguished by many. In the field, and to soldiers, I am known as the Lion of the Mountain, being the name my good sword hath won for me. — But hush, the Hamako comes — it is to warn us to rest—I know his custom—none must watch him at his vigils."

The anchorite accordingly entered, and folding his arms on his bosom as he stood before them, said with a solemn voice,—"Blessed be His name, who hath appointed the quiet night to follow the busy day, and the calm sleep to refresh the wearied limbs, and to compose the troubled spirit!"

Both warriors replied "Amen!" and, arising from the table, prepared to betake themselves to the couches, which their host indicated by waving his hand, as, making a reference to each, he again withdrew from the apartment.

The Knight of the Leopard then disarmed himself of his heavy panoply, his Saracen companion kindly assisting him to undo his buckler and clasps, until he remained in the close dress of chamois leather, which knights and men-at-arms used to wear under their harness. The Saracen, if he had admired the strength of his adversary when sheathed in steel, was now no less struck with the accuracy of proportion displayed in his nervous and well-compacted figure. The knight, on the other hand, as, in exchange of courtesy, he assisted the Saracen to disrobe himself of his upper garments, that he might sleep with more convenience, was, on his side, at a loss to conceive how such slender proportions and slimness of figure could be reconciled with the vigour he had displayed in personal contest.

Each warrior prayed, ere he addressed himself to his place of rest. The Moslem turned towards his *kebla*, the point to which the prayer of each follower of the Prophet was to be addressed, and murmured his heathen orisons, while the Christian, withdrawing from the contamination of the infidel's neighbourhood, placed his huge cross-handled sword upright, and kneeling before it as the sign of salvation, told his rosary with a devotion, which was enhanced by the recollection of the scenes through which he had passed, and the dangers from which he had been rescued in the course of the day. Both warriors, worn by toil and travel, were soon fast asleep, each on his separate pallet.

Chapter the Fourth.

KENNETH the Scot was uncertain how long his senses had been lost in profound repose, when he was roused to recollection by a sense of oppression on his chest, which at first suggested a flitting dream of struggling with a powerful opponent, and at length recalled him fully to his senses. He was about to demand who was there, when, opening his eyes, he beheld the figure of the anchorite, wild and savage-looking as we have described him, standing by his bedside, and pressing his right hand upon his breast, while he held a small silver lamp in the other.

"Be silent," said the hermit, as the prostrate knight looked up in surprise; "I have that to say to you which yonder infidel must not hear."

These words he spoke in the French language, and not in the Lingua Franca, or compound of Eastern and European dialects, which had hitherto been used amongst them.

Arise," he continued, "put on thy mantle—speak not, but tread lightly, and follow me."

Sir Kenneth arose, and took his sword.

"It needs not," answered the anchorite, in a whisper; "we are going where spiritual arms avail much, and fleshly weapons are but as the reed and the decayed gourd."

The knight deposited his sword by the bedside as before, and, armed only with his dagger, from which in this perilous country he never parted, prepared to attend his mysterious host.

The hermit then moved slowly forwards, and was followed by the knight, still under some uncertainty whether the dark form which glided on before to show him the path, was not, in fact, the creation of a disturbed dream. They passed, like shadows, into the outer apartment, without disturbing the paynim Emir, who lay still buried in repose. Before the cross and altar, in the outward room, a lamp was still burning, a missal was displayed, and on the floor lay a discipline, or penitential scourge of small cord and wire, the lashes of which were stained with recent blood, a token, no doubt, of the severe penance of the recluse. Here Theodorick kneeled down, and pointed to the knight to take his place beside him upon the sharp flints, which seemed placed for the purpose of rendering the posture of reverential devotion as uneasy as possible; he read many prayers of the Catholic Church, and chanted, in a low but earnest voice, three of the penitential psalms. These last he intermixed with sighs and tears, and convulsive throbs, which bore witness how deeply he felt the divine poetry which he recited. The Scottish knight assisted with profound sincerity at these acts of devotion, his opinions of his host beginning, in the meantime, to be so much changed, that he doubted whether, from the severity of his penance, and the ardour of his prayers, he ought not to regard him as a saint; and when they arose from the ground, he stood with reverence before him, as a pupil before an honoured master. The hermit was on his side silent and abstracted, for the space of a few minutes.

"Look into yonder recess, my son," he said, pointing to the farther corner of the cell; "there thou wilt find a veil — bring it hither."

The knight obeyed; and, in a small aperture cut out of the wall, and secured with a door of wicker, he found the veil inquired for. When he brought it to the light, he discovered that it was torn, and soiled in some places with some dark substance. The anchorite looked at it with a deep but smothered emotion, and ere he could speak to the Scottish knight, was compelled to vent his feelings in a convulsive groan.

"Thou art now about to look upon the richest treasure that the earth possesses," he at length said; "woe is me, that my eyes are unworthy to be lifted towards it! Alas! I am but the vile and despised sign, which points out to the wearied traveller a harbour of rest and security, but must itself remain for ever without doors. In vain have I fled to the very depths of the rocks, and the very bosom of the thirsty desert. Mine enemy hath found me — even he whom I have denied has pursued me to my fortresses."

He paused again for a moment, and turning to the Scottish knight, said, in a firmer tone of voice, "You bring me a greeting from Richard of England?"

"I come from the Council of Christian Princes," said the knight; "but the King of England being indisposed, I am not honoured with his Majesty's commands."

"Your token?" demanded the recluse.

Sir Kenneth hesitated — former suspicions, and the marks of insanity which the hermit had formerly exhibited, rushed suddenly on his thoughts; but how suspect a man whose manners were so saintly?—"My pass-word," he said at length, "is this — Kings begged of a beggar."

"It is right," said the hermit, while he paused; "I know you well; but the sentinel upon his post—and mine is an important one—challenges friend as well as foe."

He then moved forward with the lamp, leading the way into the room which they had left. The Saracen lay on his couch, still fast asleep. The hermit paused by his side, and looked down on him."

"He sleeps," he said, "in darkness, and must not be awakened.

The attitude of the Emir did indeed convey the idea of profound repose. One arm, flung across his body, as he lay with his face half turned to the wall, concealed, with its loose and long sleeve, the greater part of his face; but the high forehead was yet visible. Its nerves, which during his waking hours were so uncommonly active, were now motionless, as if the face had been composed of dark marble, and his long silken eyelashes closed over his piercing and hawk-like eyes. The open and relaxed hand, and the deep, regular, and soft breathing, gave all tokens of the most profound repose. The slumberer formed a singular group along with the tall forms of the hermit in his shaggy dress of goat-skins, bearing the lamp, and the knight in his close leathern coat; the former with an austere expression of ascetic gloom, the latter with anxious curiosity deeply impressed on his manly features.

"He sleeps soundly," said the hermit, in the same low tone as before, and repeating the words, though he had changed the meaning from that which is literal to a metaphorical sense, — "He sleep in darkness, but there shall be for him a day-spring. — O, Ilderim, thy waking thoughts are yet as vain and wild as those which are wheeling their giddy dance through thy sleeping brain; but the trumpet shall be heard, and the dream shall be dissolved."

So saying, and making the knight a sign to follow him, the hermit went towards the altar, and passing behind it, pressed a spring, which, opening without noise, showed a small iron door wrought on the side of the cavern, so as to be almost imperceptible, unless upon the most severe scrutiny. The hermit, ere he ventured fully to open the door, dropt some oil on the hinges, which the lamp supplied. A small staircase, hewn in the rock, was discovered, when the iron door was at length completely opened.

"Take the veil which I hold," said the hermit, in a melancholy tone, "and blind mine eyes; for I may not look on the treasure which thou art presently to behold, without sin and presumption."

Without reply, the knight hastily muffled the recluse's head in the veil, and the latter began to ascend the staircase as one too much accustomed to the way to require the use of light, while at the same time he held the lamp to the Scot, who followed him for many steps up the narrow ascent. At length they rested in a small vault of irregular form, in one nook of which the staircase terminated, while in another corner a corresponding stair was seen to continue the ascent. In a third angle was a Gothic door, very rudely ornamented with the usual attributes of clustered columns and carving, and defended by a wicket, strongly guarded with iron, and studded with large nails. To this last point the hermit directed his steps, which seemed to falter as he approached it.

"Put off thy shoes," he said to his attendant; "the ground on which thou standest is holy. Banish from thy innermost heart each profane and carnal thought, for to harbour such while in this place, were a deadly impiety."

The knight laid aside his shoes as he was commanded, and the hermit stood in the meanwhile as if communing with his soul in secret prayer, and when he again moved, commanded the knight to knock at the wicket three times. He did so. The door opened spontaneously, at least Sir Kenneth beheld no one, and his senses were at once assailed by a stream of the purest light, and by a strong and almost oppressive sense of the richest perfumes. He stepped two or three paces back, and it was the space of a minute ere he recovered the dazzling and overpowering effects of the sudden change from darkness to light.

When he entered the apartment in which this brilliant lustre was displayed, he perceived that the light proceeded from a combination of silver lamps, fed with purest oil, and sending forth the richest odours, hanging by silver chains from the roof of a small Gothic chapel, hewn, like most part of the hermit's singular mansion, out of the sound and solid rock. But, whereas, in every other place which Sir Kenneth had seen, the labour employed upon the rock had been of the simplest and coarsest description, it had in this chapel employed the invention and the chisels of the most able architects. The groined roof rose from six columns on each side, carved with the rarest skill; and the manner in which the crossings of the concave arches were bound together, as it were, with appropriate ornaments, were all in the finest tone of the architecture, and of the age. Corresponding to the line of pillars, there were on each side six richly wrought niches, each of which contained the image of one of the twelve apostles.

At the upper and eastern end of the chapel stood the altar, behind which a very rich curtain of Persian silk, embroidered deeply with gold, covered a recess, containing, unquestionably, some image or relic of no ordinary sanctity, in honour of whom this singular place of worship had been erected. Under the persuasion that this must be the case, the knight advanced to the shrine, and kneeling down before it, repeated his devotions with fervency, during which his attention was disturbed by the curtain being suddenly raised, or rather pulled aside, how or by whom he saw not; but in the niche which was thus disclosed, he beheld a cabinet of silver and ebony, with a double folding door, the whole formed into the miniature resemblance of a Gothic church.

As he gazed with anxious curiosity on the shrine, the two folding doors also flew open, discovering a large piece of wood, on which were blazoned the words, VERA CRUX, at the same time a choir of female voices sung GLORIA PATRI. The instant the strain had ceased, the shrine was closed, and the curtain again drawn, and the knight who knelt at the altar might now continue his devotions undisturbed, in honour of the holy relic which had been just disclosed to his view. He did this under the profound impression of one who had witnessed, with his own eyes, an awful evidence of the truth of his religion, and it was some time ere, concluding his orisons, he arose, and ventured to look around him for the hermit, who had guided him to this sacred and mysterious spot. He beheld him, his head still muffled in the veil, which he had himself wrapped around it, couching, like a rated hound, upon the threshold of the chapel; but apparently, without venturing to cross it; the holiest reverence, the most penitential remorse, was expressed by his posture, which seemed that of a man borne down and crushed to the earth by the burden of his inward feelings. It seemed to the Scot, that only the sense of the deepest penitence, remorse, and humiliation, could have thus prostrated a frame so strong, and a spirit so fiery.

He approached him as if to speak, but the recluse anticipated his purpose, murmuring in stifled tones, from beneath the fold in which his head was muffled, and which sounded like a voice proceeding from the cerements of a corpse,—" Abide, abide—happy thou that may'st—the vision is not yet ended." — So saying, he reared himself from the ground, drew back from the threshold on which he had hitherto lain prostrate, and closed the door of the chapel, which, secured by a spring bolt within, the snap of which resounded through the place, appeared so much like a part of the living rock from which the cavern was hewn, that Kenneth could hardly discern where the aperture had been. He was now alone in the lighted chapel, which contained the relic to which he had lately rendered his homage, without other arms than his dagger, or other companion than his pious thoughts and dauntless courage.

2 T 2

Uncertain what was next to happen, but resolved to abide the course of events, Sir Kenneth paced the solitary chapel till about the time of the earliest cock crowing. At this dead season, when night and morning met together, he heard, but from what quarter he could not discover, the sound of such a small silver bell as is rung at the elevation of the host, in the ceremony, or sacrifice, as it has been called, of the mass. The hour and the place rendered the sound fearfully solemn, and, bold as he was, the knight withdrew himself into the farther nook of the chapel, at the end opposite to the altar, in order to observe, without interruption, the consequences of this unexpected signal.

He did not wait long ere the silken curtain was again withdrawn, and the relic again presented to his view. As he sunk reverentially on his knee, he heard the sound of the lauds, or earliest office of the Catholic church, sung by female voices, which united together in the performance as they had done in the former service. The knight was soon aware that the voices were no longer stationary in the distance, but approached the chapel and became louder, when a door, imperceptible when closed, like that by which he had himself entered, opened on the other side of the vault, and gave the tones of the choir more room to swell along the ribbed arches of the roof.

The knight fixed his eyes on the opening with breathless anxiety, and, continuing to kneel in the attitude of devotion which the place and scene required, expected the consequence of these preparations. A procession appeared about to issue from the door. First, four beautiful boys, whose arms, neck, and legs were bare, showing the bronze complexion of the East, and contrasting with the snow-white tunics which they wore, entered the chapel by two and two. The first pair bore censers, which they swung from side to side, adding double fragrance to the odours with which the chapel already was impregnated. The second pair scattered flowers.

After these followed, in due and majestic order, the females who composed the choir; six, who, from their black scapularies, and black veils over their white garments, appeared to be professed nuns of the order of Mount Carmel; and as many whose veils, being white, argued them to be novices, or occasional inhabitants in the cloister, who were not as yet bound to it by vows. The former held in their hands large rosaries, while the young and lighter figures who followed, carried each a chaplet of red and white roses. They moved in procession around the chapel, without appearing to take the slightest notice of Kenneth, although passing so near him that their robes almost touched him; while they continued to sing, the knight doubted not that he was in one of those cloisters where the noble Christian maidens had formerly openly devoted themselves to the services of the church. Most of them had been suppressed since the Mahometans had reconquered Palestine, but many, purchasing connivance by presents, or receiving it from the clemency or contempt of the victors, still continued to observe in private the ritual to which their vows had consecrated them. Yet, though Kenneth knew this to be the case, the solemnity of the place and hour, the surprise at the sudden appearance of these votaresses, and the visionary manner in which they moved past him, had such influence on his imagination, that he could scarce conceive that the fair procession which he beheld was formed of creatures of this world, so much did they resemble a choir of supernatural beings, rendering homage to the universal object of adoration.

Such was the knight's first idea, as the procession passed him, scarce moving, save just sufficiently to continue their progress; so that, seen by the shadowy and religious light, which the lamps shed through the clouds of incense which darkened the apartment, they appeared rather to glide than to walk.

But as a second time, in surrounding the chapel, they passed the spot on which he kneeled, one of the white-stoled maidens, as she glided by him, detached from the chaplet which she carried a rose bud, which dropped from her fingers, perhaps unconsciously, on the foot of Sir Kenneth. The knight started as if a dart had suddenly struck his person; for, when the mind is wound up to a high pitch of feeling and expectation, the slightest incident, if unexpected, gives fire to the train which imagination has already laid. But he suppressed his emotion, recollecting how easily an incident so indifferent might have happened, and that it was only the uniform monotony of the movement of the choristers, which made the incident in the slightest degree remarkable.

Still, while the procession, for the third time, surrounded the chapel, the thoughts and the eyes of Kenneth followed exclusively the one among the novices who had dropped the rose-bud. Her step, her face, her form, were so completely assimilated to the rest of the choristers, that it was impossible to perceive the least marks of individuality, and yet Kenneth's heart throbbed like a bird that would burst from its cage, as if to assure him, by its sympathetic suggestions, that the female who held the right file on the second rank of the novices, was dearer to him, not only than all the rest that were present, but than the whole sex besides. The romantic passion of love, as it was cherished, and indeed enjoined, by the rules of chivalry, associated well with the no less romantic feelings of devotion; and they might be said much more to enhance than to counteract each other. It was, therefore, with a glow of expectation, that had something even of a religious character, that Sir Kenneth, his sensations thrilling from his heart to the ends of his fingers, expected some second sign of the presence of one, who he strongly fancied, had already bestowed on him the first. Short as the space was during which the procession again completed a third perambulation of the chapel, it seemed an eternity to Kenneth. At length the form, which he had watched with such devoted attention, drew nigh—there was no difference betwixt that shrouded figure and the others, with whom it moved in concert and in unison, until, just as she passed for the third time the kneeling Crusader, a part of a little and well-proportioned hand, so beautifully formed as to give the highest idea of the perfect proportions of the form to which it belonged, stole through the folds of the gauze, like a moonbeam through the fleecy cloud of a summer night, and again a rosebud lay at the feet of the Knight of the Leopard.

This second intimation could not be accidental—it could not be fortuitous the resemblance of that half-seen, but beautiful female hand, with one which his lips had once touched, and, while they touched it, had internally sworn allegiance to the lovely owner. Had farther proof been wanting, there was the glimmer of that matchless ruby ring on that snow-white finger, whose invaluable worth Kenneth would yet have prized less than the slightest sign which that finger could have made — and, veiled too, as she was, he might see, by chance, or by favour, a stray curl of the dark tresses, each hair of which was dearer to him a hundred times than a chain of massive gold. It was the lady of his love! But that she should be here — in the savage and sequestered desert — among vestals, who rendered themselves habitants of wilds and of caverns, that they might perform in secret those Christian rites which they dared not assist in openly — that this should be so—in truth and in reality—seemed too incredible—it must be a dream—a delusive trance of the imagination. While these thoughts passed through the mind of Kenneth, the same passage, by which the procession had entered the chapel, received them on their return. The young sacristans, the sable nuns, vanished successively through the open door—at length she from whom he had received this double intimation, passed also — yet, in passing, turned her head, slightly indeed, but perceptibly, towards the place where he remained fixed as an image. He marked the last wave of her veil—it was gone—and a darkness sunk upon his soul, scarce less palpable, than that which almost immediately enveloped the external sense; for the last chorister had no sooner crossed the threshold of the door, than it shut with a loud sound, and at the same instant the voices of the choir were silent, the lights of the chapel were at once extinguished, and Sir Kenneth remained solitary, and in total darkness. But to Kenneth, solitude, and darkness, and the uncertainty of his mysterious situation, were as nothing—he thought not of them—cared not for them—cared for nought in the world save the flitting vision which had just glided past him, and the tokens of her favour which she had bestowed. To grope on the floor for the buds which she had dropped—to press them to his lips—to his bosom—now alternately, now together — to rivet his lips to the cold stones on which, as near as he could judge, she had so lately stept — to play all the extravagances which strong affection suggests and vindicates to those who yield themselves up to it, were but the tokens of passionate love, proper to all ages. But it was peculiar to the times of chivalry, that in his wildest rapture the knight imagined of no attempt to follow or to trace the object of such romantic attachment; that he thought of her as of a deity, who, having deigned to show herself for an instant to her devoted worshipper, had again returned to the darkness of her sanctuary — or as an influential planet, which, having darted in some auspicious minute one favourable ray, wrapped itself again in its veil of mist. The motions of the lady of his love were to him those of a superior being, who was to move without watch or control, rejoice him by her appearance, or depress him by her absence, animate him by her kindness, or drive him to despair by her cruelty—all at her own free will, and without other importunity or remonstrance than that expressed by the most devoted services of the heart and sword of the champion, whose sole object in life was to fulfil her commands, and, by the splendour of his own achievements, to exalt her fame.

Such were the rules of chivalry, and of the love which was its ruling principle. But Sir Kenneth's attachment was rendered romantic by other and still more peculiar circumstances. He had never even heard the sound of his lady's voice, though he had often beheld her beauty with rapture. She moved in a circle, which his rank of knighthood permitted him indeed to approach, but not to mingle with; and highly as he stood distinguished for warlike skill and enterprise, still the poor Scottish soldier was compelled to worship his divinity at a distance, almost as great as divides the Persian from the sun which he adores. But when was the pride of woman too lofty to overlook the passionate devotion of a lover, however inferior in degree? Her eye had been on him in the tournament, her ear had heard his praises in the report of the battles which were daily fought: and while count, duke, and lord, contended for her grace, it flowed, unwillingly perhaps at first, or even unconsciously, towards the poor Knight of the Leopard, who, to support his rank, had little besides his sword. When she looked, and when she listened, the lady saw and heard enough to encourage her in her partiality, which had at first crept on her unawares. If a knight's personal beauty was praised, even the most prudish dames of the military court of England would make an exception in favour of the Scottish Kenneth; and it oftentimes happened, that notwithstanding the very considerable largesses which princes and peers bestowed on the minstrels, an impartial spirit of independence would seize the poet, and the harp was swept to the heroism of one, who had neither-palfreys nor garments to bestow in guerdon of his applause.

The moments when she listened to the praises of her lover became gradually more and more dear to the high-born Edith, relieving the flattery with which her ear was weary, and presenting to her a subject of secret contemplation, more worthy, as she seemed by general report, than those who surpassed him in rank and in the gifts of fortune. As her attention became constantly, though cautiously, fixed on Sir Kenneth, she grew more and more convinced of his personal devotion to herself, and more and more certain in her mind, that in Kenneth of Scotland she beheld the fated knight doomed to share with her through weal and woe — and the prospect looked gloomy and dangerous — the passionate attachment to which the poets of the age ascribed such universal dominion, and which its manners and morals placed nearly on the same rank with devotion itself.

Let us not disguise the truth from our readers. When Edith became aware of the state of her own sentiments, chivalrous as were her sentiments, becoming a maiden not distant from the throne of England — gratified as her pride must have been with the mute though unceasing homage rendered to her by the knight whom she had distinguished, there were moments when the feelings of the woman, loving and beloved, murmured against the restraints of state and form by which she was surrounded, and when she almost blamed the timidity of her lover, who seemed resolved not to infringe them. The etiquette, to use a modern phrase, of birth and rank, had drawn around her a magical circle, beyond which Sir Kenneth might indeed bow and gaze, but within which he could no more pass, than an evoked spirit can transgress the boundaries prescribed by the rod of a powerful enchanter. The thought involuntarily pressed on her that she herself must venture, were it but the point of her fairy foot, beyond the prescribed boundary, if she ever hoped to give a lover, so reserved and bashful, an opportunity of so slight a favour, as but to salute her shoe-tie. There was an example, the noted precedent of the "King's daughter of Hungary," who thus generously encouraged the "Squire of low degree;" and Edith, though of kingly blood, was no King's daughter, any more than her lover was of low degree — fortune had put no such extreme barrier in obstacle to their affections. Something, however, within the maiden's bosom—that modest pride, which throws fetters even on love itself—forbade her, notwithstanding the superiority of her condition, to make those advances, which, in every case, delicacy assigns to the other sex; above all, Sir Kenneth was a knight so gentle and honourable, so highly accomplished, as her imagination at least suggested, together with the strictest feelings of what was due to himself and to her, that however constrained her attitude might be while receiving his adorations, like the image of some deity, who is neither supposed to feel nor to reply to the homage of its votaries, still the idol feared that to step prematurely from her pedestal, would be to degrade herself in the eyes of her devoted worshipper.

Yet the devout adorer of an actual idol can even discover signs of approbation in the rigid and immovable features of a marble image, and it is no wonder that something, which could be as favourably interpreted, glanced from the bright eye of the lovely Edith, whose beauty, indeed, consisted rather more in that very power of expression, than on absolute regularity of contour, or brilliancy of complexion. Some light marks of distinction had escaped from her, notwithstanding her own jealous vigilance, else how could Sir Kenneth have so readily, and so undoubtingly, recognized the lovely hand, of which scarce two fingers were visible from under the veil, or how could he have rested so thoroughly assured that two flowers, successively dropt on the spot, were intended as a recognition on the part of his lady-love? By what train of observation — by what secret signs, looks, or gestures—by what instinctive free-masonry of love, this degree of intelligence came to subsist between Edith and her lover, we cannot attempt to trace; for we are old, and such slight vestiges of affection, quickly discovered by younger eyes, defy the power of ours. Enough, that such affection did subsist between parties who had never even spoken to one another, though, on the side of Edith, it was checked by a deep sense of the difficulties and dangers which must necessarily attend the farther progress of their attachment, and upon that of the knight by a thousand doubts and fears, lest he had over-estimated the slight tokens of the lady's notice, varied, as they necessarily were, by long intervals of apparent coldness, during which, either the fear of exciting the observation of others, and thus drawing danger upon her lover, or that of sinking in his esteem by seeming too willing to be won, made her behave with indifference, as if unobservant of his presence.

This narrative, tedious perhaps, but which the story renders necessary, may serve to explain the state of intelligence, if it deserves so strong a name, betwixt the lovers, when Edith's unexpected appearance in the chapel produced so powerful an effect on the feelings of her knight.

Chapter the Fifth.

Their necromantic forms in vain
Haunt us on the tented plain;
We bid those spectre shapes avaunt,
Ashtaroth and Termagaunt.
WARTON.

THE most profound silence, the deepest darkness, continued to brood for more than an hour over the chapel in which we left the Knight of the Leopard still kneeling, alternately expressing thanks to Heaven, and gratitude to his lady, for the boon which had been vouchsafed to him. His own safety, his own destiny, for which he was at all times little anxious, had not now the weight of a grain of dust in his reflections. He was in the neighbourhood of Lady Edith, he had received tokens of her grace, he was in a place hallowed by relics of the most awful sanctity. A Christian soldier, a devoted lover, could fear nothing, think of nothing, but his duty to Heaven, and his devoir to his lady.

At the lapse of the space of time which we have noticed, a shrill whistle, like that with which a falconer calls his hawk, was heard to ring sharply through the vaulted chapel. It was a sound ill suited to the place, and reminded Sir Kenneth how necessary it was he should be upon his guard. He started from his knee, and laid his hand upon his poniard. A creaking sound, as of a screw or pulleys, succeeded, and a light streaming upwards, as from an opening in the floor, showed that a trap-door had been raised or depressed. In less than a minute, a long skinny arm, partly naked, partly clothed in a sleeve of red samite, arose out of the aperture, holding a lamp as high as it could stretch upwards, and the figure to which the arm belonged ascended step by step to the level of the chapel floor. The form and face of the being who thus presented himself, were those of a frightful dwarf, with a large head, a cap fantastically adorned with three peacock-feathers, a dress of red samite, the richness of which rendered his ugliness more conspicuous, distinguished by gold bracelets and armlets, and a white silk sash, in which he wore a gold-hilted dagger. This singular figure had in his left hand a kind of broom. So soon as he had stepped from the aperture through which he arose, he stood still, and, as if to show himself more distinctly, moved the lamp which he held slowly over his face and person, successively illuminating his wild and fantastic features, and his misshapen, but nervous limbs. Though disproportioned in person, the dwarf was not so distorted as to argue any want of strength or activity. While Sir Kenneth gazed on this disagreeable object, the popular creed occurred to his remembrance, concerning gnomes, or earthly spirits, which make their abode in the caverns of the earth; and so much did this figure correspond with ideas he had formed of their appearance, that he looked on it with disgust, mingled not indeed with fear, but that sort of awe which the presence of a supernatural creature may infuse into the most steady bosom.

The dwarf again whistled, and summoned from beneath a companion. This second figure ascended in the same manner as the first; but it was a female arm, in this second instance, which upheld the lamp from the subterranean vault out of which these presentments arose, and it was a female form, much resembling the first in shape and proportions, which slowly emerged from the floor. Her dress was also of red samite, fantastically cut and flounced, as if she had been dressed for some exhibition of mimes or jugglers; and with the same minuteness which her predecessor had exhibited, she passed the lamp over her face and person, which seemed to rival the male in ugliness. But, with all this most unfavourable exterior, there was one trait in the features of both which argued alertness and intelligence in the most uncommon degree. This arose from the brilliancy of their eyes, which, deep set beneath black and shaggy brows, gleamed with a lustre which, like that in the eye of the toad, seemed to make some amends for the extreme ugliness of countenance and person.

Sir Kenneth remained as if spell-bound, while this unlovely pair, moving round the chapel close to each other, appeared to perform the duty of sweeping it, like menials; but, as they used only one hand, the floor was not much benefited by the exercise, which they plied with such oddity of gestures and manner, as befitted their bizarre and fantastic appearance. When they approached near to the knight, in the course of their occupation, they ceased to use their brooms, and placing themselves side by side, directly opposite to Sir Kenneth, they again slowly shifted the lights which they held, so as to allow him distinctly to survey features which were not rendered more agreeable by being brought nearer, and to observe the extreme quickness and keenness with which their black and glittering eyes flashed back the light of the lamps. They then turned the gleam of both lights upon the knight, and having accurately surveyed him, turned their faces to each other, and set up a loud yelling laugh, which resounded in his ears. The sound was so ghastly, that Sir Kenneth started at hearing it, and hastily demanded, in the name of God, who they were who profaned that holy place with such antic gestures and elritch exclamations.

"I am the dwarf Nectabanus," said the abortion-seeming male, in a voice corresponding to his figure, and resembling that of the night-crow more than any sound which is heard by daylight.

"And I am Guenevra, his lady and his love," replied the female, in tones which, being shriller, were yet wilder than those of her companion.

"Wherefore are you here?" again demanded the knight, scarcely yet assured that it was human beings which he saw before him.

"I am," replied the male dwarf, with much assumed gravity and dignity, "the twelfth Imaum—I am Mahommed Mohadi, the guide and the conductor of the faithful. An hundred horses stand ready saddled for me and my train at the Holy City, and as many at the City of Refuge. I am he who shall bear witness, and this is one of my houris."

"Thou liest!" answered the female, interrupting her companion, in tones yet shriller than his own; "I am none of thy houris, and thou art no such infidel trash as the Mahommed of whom thou speakest. May my curse rest upon his coffin!—I tell thee, thou ass of Issachar, thou art King Arthur of Britain, whom the fairies stole away from the field of Avalon; and I am Dame Guenevra, famed for her beauty."

"But in truth, noble sir," said the male, "we are distressed princes, dwelling under the wing of King Guy of Jerusalem, until he was driven out from his own nest by the foul infidels—Heaven's bolts consume them!"

"Hush," said a voice from the side upon which the knight had entered—"Hush, fools, and begone; your ministry is ended."

The dwarfs had no sooner heard the command, than gibbering in discord-ant whispers to each other, they blew out their lights at once, and left the knight in utter darkness, which, when the pattering of their retiring feet had died away, was soon accompanied by its fittest companion, total silence.

The knight felt the departure of these unfortunate creatures a relief. He could not, from their language, manners, and appearance, doubt that they belonged to the degraded class of beings, whom deformity of person, and weakness of intellect, recommended to the painful situation of appendages to great families, where their personal appearance and imbecility were food for merriment to the household. Superior in no respect to the ideas and manners of his time, the Scottish knight might, at another period, have been much amused by the mummery of these poor effigies of humanity; but now, their appearance, gesticulations, and language, broke the train of deep and solemn feeling with which he was impressed, and he rejoiced in the disappearance of the unhappy objects.

A few minutes after they had retired, the door at which he had entered opened slowly, and, remaining ajar, discovered a faint light arising from a lantern placed upon the threshold. Its doubtful and wavering gleam showed a dark form reclined beside the entrance, but without its precincts, which, on approaching it more nearly, he recognized to be the hermit, couching in the same humble posture in which he had at first laid himself down, and which doubtless he had retained during the whole time of his guest's continuing in the chapel.

"All is over," said the hermit, as he heard the knight approaching — "and the most wretched of earthly sinners, with him, who should think himself most honoured and most happy among the race of humanity, must retire from this place. Take the light, and guide me down the descent, for I may not uncover my eyes until I am far from this hallowed spot."

The Scottish knight obeyed in silence, for a solemn and yet ecstatic sense of what he had seen had silenced even the eager workings of curiosity. He led the way, with considerable accuracy, through the various secret passages and stairs by which they had ascended, until at length they found themselves in the outward cell of the hermit's cavern.

"The condemned criminal is restored to his dungeon, reprieved from one miserable day to another, until his awful judge shall at length appoint the well-deserved sentence to be carried into execution."

As the hermit spoke these words, he laid aside the veil with which his eyes had been bound, and looked at it with a suppressed and hollow sigh. No sooner had he restored it to the crypt from which he had caused the Scot to bring it, than he said hastily and sternly to his companion — "Begone, begone — to rest, to rest. You may sleep — you can sleep — I neither can nor may."

Respecting the profound agitation with which this was spoken, the knight retired into the inner cell; but, casting back his eye as he left the exterior grotto, he beheld the anchorite stripping his shoulders with frantic haste, of their shaggy mantle, and ere he could shut the frail door which separated the two compartments of the cavern, he heard the clang of the scourge, and the groans of the penitent under his self-inflicted penance. A cold shudder came over the knight as he reflected what could be the foulness of the sin, what the depth of the remorse, which, apparently, such severe penance could neither cleanse or assuage. He told his beads devoutly, and flung himself on his rude couch, after a glance at the still sleeping Moslem, and, wearied by the various scenes of the day and the night, soon slept as sound as infancy. Upon his awaking in the morning, he held certain conferences with the hermit upon matters of importance, and the result of their intercourse induced him to remain for two days longer in the grotto. He was regular, as became a pilgrim, in his devotional exercises, but was not again admitted to the chapel in which he had seen such wonders.

Chapter the Sixth.

Now change the scene — and let the trumpets sound,
For we must rouse the lion from his lair.

OLD PLAY.

THE scene must change, as our program has announced, from the mountain wilderness of Jordan to the camp of King Richard of England, then stationed betwixt Jean d'Acre and Ascalon; and containing that army with which he of the Lion Heart had promised himself a triumphant march to Jerusalem, and in which he would probably have succeeded, if not hindered by the jealousies of the Christian princes engaged in the same enterprise, and the offence taken by them at the uncurbed haughtiness of the English monarch, and Richard's unveiled contempt for his brother sovereigns, who, his equals in rank, were yet far his inferiors in courage, hardihood, and military talents. Such discords, and particularly those betwixt Richard and Philip of France, created disputes and obstacles which impeded every active measure proposed by the heroic though impetuous Richard, while the ranks of the Crusaders were daily thinned, not only by the desertion of individuals, but of entire bands, headed by their respective feudal leaders, who withdrew from a contest in which they had ceased to hope for success.

The effects of the climate became, as usual, fatal to soldiers from the north, and the more so that the dissolute license of the Crusaders, forming a singular contrast to the principles and purpose of their taking up arms, rendered them more easy victims to the insalubrious influence of burning heat and chilling dews. To these discouraging causes of loss was to be added the sword of the enemy. Saladin, than whom no greater name is recorded in Eastern history, had learnt, to his fatal experience, that his light-armed followers were little able to meet in close encounter with the iron-clad Franks, and had been taught, at the same time, to apprehend and dread the adventurous character of his antagonist Richard. But if his armies were more than once routed with great slaughter, his numbers gave the Saracen the advantage in those lighter skirmishes, of which many were inevitable.

As the army of his assailants decreased, the enterprises of the Sultan became more numerous and more bold in this species of petty warfare. The camp of the Crusaders was surrounded, and almost besieged, by clouds of light cavalry, resembling swarms of wasps, easily crushed when they are once grasped, but furnished with wings to elude superior strength, and stings to inflict harm and mischief. There was perpetual warfare of posts and foragers, in which many valuable lives were lost, without any corresponding object being gained; convoys were intercepted, and communications were cut off. The Crusaders had to purchase the means of sustaining life, by life itself; and water, like that of the well of Bethlehem, longed for by King David, one of its ancient monarchs, was then, as before, only obtained by the expenditure of blood.

These evils were, in a great measure, counterbalanced by the stern resolution and reckless activity of King Richard, who, with some of his best knights, was ever on horseback, ready to repair to any point where danger occurred, and often, not only bringing unexpected succour to the Christians, but discomfiting the infidels when they seemed most secure of victory. But even the iron frame of Cœur de Lion could not support, without injury, the alternations of the unwholesome climate, joined to ceaseless exertions of body and mind. He became afflicted with one of those slow and wasting fevers peculiar to Asia, and, in despite of his great strength, and still greater courage, grew first unfit to mount on horseback, and then unable to attend

the councils of war, which were, from time to time, held by the Crusaders.
It was difficult to say whether this state of personal inactivity was rendered
more galling or more endurable to the English monarch, by the resolution
of the council to engage in a truce of thirty days with the Sultan Saladin;
for, on the one hand, if he was incensed at the delay which this interposed
to the progress of the great enterprise, he was, on the other, somewhat consoled by knowing that others were not acquiring laurels, while he remained
inactive upon a sick-bed.

That, however, which Cœur de Lion could least excuse, was the general
inactivity which prevailed in the camp of the Crusaders, so soon as his illness assumed a serious aspect; and the reports which he extracted from his
unwilling attendants gave him to understand, that the hopes of the host had
abated in proportion to his illness, and that the interval of truce was employed, not in recruiting their numbers, reanimating their courage, fostering
their spirit of conquest, and preparing for a speedy and determined advance
upon the Holy City, which was the object of their expedition, but in securing the camp occupied by their diminished followers, with trenches, palisades, and other fortifications, as if preparing rather to repel an attack from
a powerful enemy so soon as hostilities should recommence, than to assume
the proud character of conquerors and assailants.

The English king chafed under these reports, like the imprisoned lion
viewing his prey from the iron barriers of his cage. Naturally rash and
impetuous, the irritability of his temper preyed on itself. He was dreaded
by his attendants, and even the medical assistants feared to assume the necessary authority, which a physician, to do justice to his patient, must needs
exercise over him. One faithful baron, who, perhaps, from the congenial
nature of his disposition, was devoutly attached to the King's person, dared
alone to come between the dragon and his wrath, and quietly, but firmly,
maintained a control which no other dared assume over the dangerous in
valid, and which Thomas de Multon only exercised, because he esteemed his
sovereign's life and honour more than he did the degree of favour which he
might lose, or even the risk which he might incur, in nursing a patient so
intractable, and whose displeasure was so perilous.

Sir Thomas was the Lord of Gilsland, in Cumberland, and, in an age
when surnames and titles were not distinctly attached, as now, to the individuals who bore them, he was called by the Normans the Lord de Vaux,
and in English, by the Saxons, who clung to their native language, and were
proud of the share of Saxon blood in this renowned warrior's veins, he was
termed Thomas, or more familiarly, Thom of the Gills, or Narrow Valleys,
from which his extensive domains derived their well-known appellation.

This chief had been exercised in almost all the wars, whether waged
betwixt England and Scotland, or amongst the various domestic factions
which then tore the former country asunder, and in all had been distinguished, as well from his military conduct as his personal prowess. He
was, in other respects, a rude soldier, blunt and careless in his bearing, and
taciturn, nay, almost sullen in his habits of society, and seeming, at least,
to disclaim all knowledge of policy and of courtly art. There were men,
however, who pretended to look deeply into character, who asserted that the
Lord de Vaux was not less shrewd and aspiring, though he was blunt and
bold, and who thought that, while he assimilated himself to the king's own
character of blunt hardihood, it was, in some degree at least, with an eye
to establish his favour, and to gratify his own hopes of deep-laid ambition.
But no one cared to thwart his schemes, if such he had, by rivalling him in
the dangerous occupation of daily attendance on the sick-bed of a patient,
whose disease was pronounced infectious, and more especially when it was
remembered that the patient was Cœur de Lion, suffering under all the
furious impatience of a soldier withheld from battle, and a sovereign sequestered from authority; and the common soldiers, at least in the English

army, were generally of opinion that De Vaux attended on the King like comrade upon comrade, in the honest and disinterested frankness of military friendship, contracted between the partakers of daily dangers.

It was on the decline of a Syrian day that Richard lay on his couch of sickness, loathing it as much in his mind as his illness made it irksome to his body. His bright blue eye, which at all times shone with uncommon keenness and splendour, had its vivacity augmented by fever and mental impatience, and glanced from among his curled and unshorn locks of yellow hair, as fitfully and as vividly, as the last gleams of the sun shoot through the clouds of an approaching thunder-storm, which still, however, are gilded by its beams. His manly features showed the progress of wasting illness, and his beard, neglected and untrimmed, had overgrown both lips and chin. Casting himself from side to side, now clutching towards him the coverings, which at the next moment he flung as impatiently from him, his tossed couch and impatient gestures showed at once the energy and the reckless impatience of a disposition, whose natural sphere was that of the most active exertion.

Beside his couch stood Thomas de Vaux, in face, attitude, and manner, the strongest possible contrast to the suffering monarch. His stature approached the gigantic, and his hair in thickness might have resembled that of Samson, though only after the Israelitish champion's locks had passed under the shears of the Philistines, for those of De Vaux were cut short, that they might be enclosed under his helmet. The light of his broad, large hazel eye, resembled that of the autumn morn, and it was only perturbed for a moment, when from time to time it was attracted by Richard's vehement marks of agitation and restlessness. His features, though massive like his person, might have been handsome before they were defaced with scars; his upper lip, after the fashion of the Normans, was covered with thick mustaches, which grew so long and luxuriantly as to mingle with his hair, and, like his hair, were dark brown, slightly brindled with gray. His frame seemed of that kind which most readily defies both toil and climate, for he was thin flanked, broad chested, long armed, deep breathed, and strong limbed. He had not laid aside his buff-coat, which displayed the cross-cut on the shoulder, for more than three nights, enjoying but such momentary repose as the warder of a sick monarch's couch might by snatches indulge. This Baron rarely changed his posture, except to administer to Richard the medicine or refreshments, which none of his less favoured attendants could persuade the impatient monarch to take; and there was something affecting in the kindly, yet awkward manner in which he discharged offices so strangely contrasted with his blunt and soldierly habits and manners.

The pavilion in which these personages were, had, as became the time, as well as the personal character of Richard, more of a warlike than a sumptuous or royal character. Weapons offensive and defensive, several of them of strange and newly-invented construction, were scattered about the tented apartment, or disposed upon the pillars which supported it. Skins of animals slain in the chase were stretched on the ground, or extended along the sides of the pavilion, and, upon a heap of these sylvan spoils, lay three *alans*, as they were then called, (wolf-gray-hounds, that is,) of the largest size, and as white as snow. Their faces, marked with many a scar from clutch and fang, showed their share in collecting the trophies upon which they reposed, and their eyes, fixed from time to time with an expressive stretch and yawn upon the bed of Richard, evinced how much they marvelled at and regretted the unwonted inactivity which they were compelled to share. These were but the accompaniments of the soldier and huntsman; but, on a small table close by the bed, was placed a shield of wrought steel, of triangular form, bearing the three lions passant, first assumed by the chivalrous monarch, and before it the golden circlet, revembling much a ducal coronet, only that it was higher in front than behind, which, with the purple velvet and embroidered tiara that lined it, formed then the emblem of England's sovereignty. Beside it, as if prempt for defending the regal symbol, lay a mighty curtal axe, which would have wearied the arm of any other than Cœur de Lion.

In an outer partition of the pavilion waited two or three officers of the royal household, depressed, anxious for their master's health, and not less so for their own safety, in case of his decease. Their gloomy apprehensions spread themselves to the warders without, who paced about in downcast and silent contemplation, or, resting on their halberds, stood motionless on their post, rather like armed trophies than living warriors.

"So thou hast no better news to bring me from without, Sir Thomas?" said the King, after a long and perturbed silence, spent in the feverish agitation which we have endeavoured to describe. "All our knights turned women, and our ladies become devotees, and neither a spark of valour nor of gallantry to enlighten a camp which contains the choicest of Europe's chivalry — Ha!"

"The truce, my lord," said De Vaux, with the same patience with which he had twenty times repeated the explanation—"the truce prevents us bearing ourselves as men of action; and, for the ladies, I am no great reveller, as is well known to your Majesty, and seldom exchange steel and buff for velvet and gold—but thus far I know, that our choicest beauties are waiting upon the Queen's Majesty and the Princess, to a pilgrimage to the convent of Engaddi, to accomplish their vows for your Highness's deliverance from this trouble."

"And is it thus," said Richard, with the impatience of indisposition, "that royal matrons and maidens should risk themselves, where the dogs who defile the land have as little truth to man, as they have faith towards God?"

"Nay, my lord," said De Vaux, "they have Saladin's word for their safety."

"True, true!" replied Richard, "and I did the heathen Soldan injustice — I owe him reparation for it. — Would God I were but fit to offer it him upon my body between the two hosts—Christendom and Heathenesse both looking on!"

As Richard spoke, he thrust his right arm out of bed, naked to the shoulder, and, painfully raising himself in his couch, shook his clenched hand, as if it grasped sword or battle-axe, and was then brandished over the jewelled turban of the Soldan. It was not without a gentle degree of violence, which the King would scarce have endured from another, that De Vaux, in his character of sick-nurse, compelled his royal master to replace himself in the couch, and covered his sinewy arm, neck, and shoulders, with the care which a mother bestows upon an impatient child.

"Thou art a rough nurse, though a willing one, De Vaux," said the King, laughing with a bitter expression, while he submitted to the strength which he was unable to resist; "methinks a coif would become thy lowering features as well as a child's biggin would beseem mine. We should be a babe and nurse to frighten girls with."

"We have frightened men in our time, my liege," said De Vaux; "and, I trust, may live to frighten them again. What is a fever-fit, that we should not endure it patiently, in order to get rid of it easily?"

"Fever-fit!" exclaimed Richard impetuously; "thou mayest think, and justly, that it is a fever-fit with me; but what is it with all the other Christian princes — with Philip of France — with that dull Austrian — with him of Montserrat—with the Hospitallers—with the Templars—what is it with all them? — I will tell thee — it is a cold palsy — a dead lethargy — a disease that deprives them of speech and action — a canker that has eaten into the heart of all that is noble, and chivalrous, and virtuous among them

—that has made them false to the noblest vow ever knights were sworn to—has made them indifferent to their fame, and forgetful of their God!"

"For the love of Heaven, my liege," said De Vaux, "take it less violently—you will be heard without doors, where such speeches are but too current already among the common soldiery, and engender discord and contention in the Christian host. Bethink you that your illness mars the mainspring of their enterprise: a mangonel will work without screw and lever better than the Christian host without King Richard."

"Thou flatterest me, De Vaux," said Richard; and, not insensible to the power of praise, he reclined his head on the pillow, with a more deliberate attempt to repose than he had yet exhibited. But Thomas de Vaux was no courtier; the phrase which had offered had risen spontaneously to his lips; and he knew not how to pursue the pleasing theme, so as to soothe and prolong the vein which he had excited. He was silent, therefore, until, relapsing into his moody contemplations, the King demanded of him sharply, "Despardieux! This is smoothly said to soothe a sick man; but does a league of monarchs, an assemblage of nobles, a convocation of all the chivalry of Europe, droop with the sickness of one man, though he chances to be King of England? Why should Richard's illness, or Richard's death, check the march of thirty thousand men, as brave as himself? When the master-stag is struck down, the herd do not disperse upon his fall—when the falcon strikes the leading crane, another takes the guidance of the phalanx.—Why do not the powers assemble and choose some one, to whom they may intrust the guidance of the host?"

"Forsooth, and if it please your Majesty," said De Vaux, "I hear consultations have been held among the royal leaders for some such purpose."

"Ha!" exclaimed Richard, his jealousy awakened, giving his mental irritation another direction—"Am I forgot by my allies ere I have taken the last sacrament?—do they hold me dead already?—But no, no—they are right—And whom do they select as leader of the Christian host?"

"Rank and dignity," said De Vaux, "point to the King of France."

"Oh, ay," answered the English monarch, "Philip of France and Navarre—Dennis Mountjoie—his Most Christian Majesty! mouth-filling words these! There is but one risk—that he might mistake the words *En arrière* for *En avant*, and lead us back to Paris, instead of marching to Jerusalem. His politic head has learned by this time, that there is more to be gotten by oppressing his feudatories, and pillaging his allies, than fighting with the Turks for the Holy Sepulchre."

"They might choose the Archduke of Austria," said De Vaux.

"What! because he is big and burly like thyself, Thomas—nearly as thick-headed, but without thy indifference to danger, and carelessness of offence? I tell thee that Austria has in all that mass of flesh no bolder animation, than is afforded by the peevishness of a wasp, and the courage of a wren. Out upon him!—*he* a leader of chivalry to deeds of glory!—Give him a flagon of Rhenish to drink with his besmirched baaren-hauters and lancknechts."

"There is the Grand Master of the Templars," continued the baron, not sorry to keep his master's attention engaged on other topics than his own illness, though at the expense of the characters of prince and potentate—"There is the Grand Master of the Templars," he continued, "undaunted, skilful, brave in battle, and sage in council, having no separate kingdoms of his own to divert his exertions from the recovery of the Holy Land—what thinks your Majesty of the Master as a general leader of the Christian host?"

"Ha, Beau-Seant!" answered the King. "Oh, no exception can be taken to Brother Giles Amaury—he understands the ordering of a battle, and the fighting in front when it begins. But, Sir Thomas, were it fair to take the Holy Land from the heathen Saladin, so full of all the virtues which may distinguish unchristened man, and give it to Giles Amaury, a worse Pagan than himself — an idolator — a devil-worshipper — a necromancer — who practises crimes the most dark and unnatural, in the vaults and secret places of abomination and darkness ?''

"The Grand Master of the Hospitallers of St. John of Jerusalem is not tainted by fame, either with heresy or magic," said Thomas de Vaux.

"But is he not a sordid miser?" said Richard, hastily; "has he not been suspected — ay, more than suspected — of selling to the infidels those advantages which they would never have won by fair force? Tush, man, better give the army to be made merchandise of by Venetian skippers and Lombardy pedlars, than trust it to the Grand Master of St. John."

"Well, then, I will venture but another guess," said the Baron de Vaux —"What say you to the gallant Marquis of Montserrat, so wise, so elegant, such a good man-at-arms?''

"Wise? cunning, you would say," replied Richard; "elegant in a lady's chamber, if you will. Oh, ay, Conrade of Montserrat,—who knows not the popinjay? Politic and versatile, he will change you his purposes as often as the trimmings of his doublet, and you shall never be able to guess the hue of his inmost vestments from their outward colours. A man-at-arms? ay, a fine figure on horseback, and can bear him well in the tilt-yard, and at the barriers, when swords are blunted at point and edge, and spears are tipped with trenchers of wood, instead of steel pikes. Wert thou not with me, when I said to that same gay Marquis, 'Here be three good Christians, and on yonder plain there pricks a band of some threescore Saracens, what say you to charge them briskly? There are but twenty unbelieving miscreants to each true knight.'''

"I recollect the Marquis replied," said De Vaux, "that his limbs were of flesh, not of iron, and that he would rather bear the heart of a man than of a beast, though that beast were the lion. But I see how it is — we shall end where we began, without hope of praying at the Sepulchre, until Heaven shall restore King Richard to health.''

At this grave remark, Richard burst out into a hearty fit of laughter, the first which he had for some time indulged in. "Why, what a thing is conscience," he said, "that through its means even such a thick-witted northern lord as thou canst bring thy sovereign to confess his folly! It is true, that, did they not propose themselves as fit to hold my leading-staff, little should I care for plucking the silken trappings off the puppets thou hast shown me in succession— What concerns it me what fine tinsel robes they swagger in, unless when they are named as rivals in the glorious enterprise to which I have vowed myself? Yes, De Vaux, I confess my weakness, and the wilfulness of my ambition. The Christian camp contains, doubtless, many a better knight than Richard of England, and it would be wise and worthy to assign to the best of them the leading of the host — but," continued the warlike monarch, raising himself in his bed, and shaking the cover from his head, while his eyes sparkled as they were wont to do on the eve of battle, "were such a knight to plant the banner of the Cross on the Temple of Jerusalem, while I was unable to bear my share in the noble task, he should, so soon as I was fit to lay lance in rest, undergo my challenge to mortal combat, for having diminished my fame, and pressed in before to the object of my enterprise. — But hark, what trumpets are those at a distance ?''

"Those of King Philip, as I guess, my liege," said the stout Englishman.

"Thou art dull of ear, Thomas," said the King, endeavouring to start up —"hearest thou not that clash and clang? By Heaven, the Turks are in the camp — I hear their lelies.''*

He again endeavoured to get out of bed, and De Vaux was obliged to

---

* The war-cries of the Moslemah.

exercise his own great strength, and also to summon the assistance of the chamberlains from the inner tent, to restrain him.

" Thou art a false traitor, De Vaux," said the incensed monarch, when, breathless and exhausted with struggling, he was compelled to submit to superior strength, and to repose in quiet on his couch. " I would I were— I would I were but strong enough to dash thy brains out with my battle-axe !"

" I would you had the strength, my liege," said De Vaux, " and would even take the risk of its being so employed. The odds would be great in favour of Christendom, were Thomas Multon dead, and Cœur de Lion himself again."

" Mine honest faithful servant," said Richard, extending his hand, which the baron reverentially saluted, " forgive thy master's impatience of mood. It is this burning fever which chides thee, and not thy kind master, Richard of England. But go, I prithee, and bring me word what strangers are in the camp, for these sounds are not of Christendom."

De Vaux left the pavilion on the errand assigned, and, in his absence, which he had resolved should be brief, he charged the chamberlains, pages, and attendants to redouble their attention on their sovereign, with threats of holding them to responsibility, which rather added to than diminished their timid anxiety in the discharge of their duty ; for next perhaps to the ire of the monarch himself, they dreaded that of the stern and inexorable Lord of Gilsland.*

Chapter the Seventh.

There never was a time on the March parts yet,
When Scottish with English met,
But it was marvel if the red blood ran not
As the rain does in the street.
                    BATTLE OF OTTERBOURN.

A CONSIDERABLE band of Scottish warriors had joined the Crusaders, and had naturally placed themselves under the command of the English monarch, being, like his native troops, most of them of Saxon and Norman descent, speaking the same languages, possessed, some of them, of English as well as Scottish demesnes, and allied, in some cases, by blood and intermarriage. The period also preceded that when the grasping ambition of Edward I. gave a deadly and envenomed character to the wars betwixt the two nations ; the English fighting for the subjugation of Scotland, and the Scottish, with all the stern determination and obstinacy which has ever characterized their nation, for the defence of their independence, by the most violent means, under the most disadvantageous circumstances, and at the most ex-

* He was a historical hero, faithfully attached, as is here expressed, to King Richard, and is noticed with distinction in the romance mentioned in the Introduction. At the beginning of the romance, mention is made of a tournament, in which the king returns three times with a fresh suit of armour, which acted as a disguise ; and at each appearance, some knight of great prowess had a sharp encounter with him. When Richard returned the second time, the following is Mr. Ellis's account of his proceedings : —" He now mounted a bay horse, assumed a suit of armour painted red, and a helmet, the crest of which was a red hound, with a long tail which reached to the earth : an emblem intended to convey his indignation against the heathen hounds who defiled the Holy Land, and his determination to attempt their destruction. Having sufficiently signalized himself in his new disguise, he rode into the ranks for the purpose of selecting a more formidable adversary ; and, delivering his spear to his squire, took his mace, and assaulted Sir Thomas de Multon, a knight whose prowess was deservedly held in the highest estimation. Sir Thomas, apparently not at all disordered by a blow which would have felled a common adversary, calmly advised him to go and amuse himself elsewhere ; but Richard, having aimed at him a second and more violent stroke, by which his helmet was nearly crushed, he returned it with such vigour that the king lost his stirrups, and recovering himself with some difficulty rode off with all speed into the forest."—Ellis's Specimens, pp. 193, 194.

treme hazard. As yet, wars betwixt the two nations, though fierce and frequent, had been conducted on principles of fair hostility, and admitted of those softening shades by which courtesy, and the respect for open and generous foemen, qualify and mitigate the horrors of war. In time of peace, therefore, and especially when both, as at present, were engaged in war, waged in behalf of a common cause, and rendered dear to them by their ideas of religion, the adventurers of both countries frequently fought side by side, their national emulation serving only to stimulate them to excel each other in their efforts against the common enemy.

The frank and martial character of Richard, who made no distinction betwixt his own subjects and those of William of Scotland, excepting as they bore themselves in the field of battle, tended much to conciliate the troops of both nations. But upon his illness, and the disadvantageous circumstances in which the Crusaders were placed, the national disunion between the various bands united in the Crusade, began to display itself, just as old wounds break out afresh in the human body, when under the influence of disease or debility.

The Scottish and English, equally jealous and high-spirited, and apt to take offence, — the former the more so, because the poorer and the weaker nation, — began to fill up, by internal dissension, the period when the truce forbade them to wreak their united vengeance on the Saracens. Like the contending Roman chiefs of old, the Scottish would admit no superiority, and their southern neighbours would brook no equality. There were charges and recriminations, and both the common soldiery, and their leaders and commanders, who had been good comrades in time of victory, lowered on each other in the period of adversity, as if their union had not been then more essential than ever, not only to the success of their common cause, but to their joint safety. The same disunion had begun to show itself betwixt the French and English, the Italians and the Germans, and even between the Danes and Swedes; but it is only that which divided the two nations whom one island bred, and who seemed more animated against each other for the very reason, that our narrative is principally concerned with.

Of all the English nobles who had followed their King to Palestine, De Vaux was most prejudiced against the Scottish; they were his near neighbours, with whom he had been engaged during his whole life in private or public warfare, and on whom he had inflicted many calamities, while he had sustained at their hands not a few. His love and devotion to the King was like the vivid affection of the old English mastiff to his master, leaving him churlish and inaccessible to all others, even towards those to whom he was indifferent, and rough and dangerous to any against whom he entertained a prejudice. De Vaux had never observed, without jealousy and displeasure, his King exhibit any mark of courtesy or favour to the wicked, deceitful, and ferocious race, born on the other side of a river, or an imaginary line drawn through waste and wilderness, and he even doubted the success of a Crusade in which they were suffered to bear arms, holding them in his secret soul little better than the Saracens whom he came to combat. It may be added, that, as being himself a blunt and downright Englishman, unaccustomed to conceal the slightest movement either of love or of dislike, he accounted the fair-spoken courtesy, which the Scots had learned, either from imitation of their frequent allies, the French, or which might have arisen from their own proud and reserved character, as a false and astucious mark of the most dangerous designs against their neighbours, over whom he believed, with genuine English confidence, they could, by fair manhood, never obtain any advantage.

Yet, though De Vaux entertained these sentiments concerning his northern neighbours, and extended them, with little mitigation, even to such as had assumed the Cross, his respect for the King, and a sense of the duty imposed by his vow as a Crusader, prevented him from displaying them otherwise than by regularly shunning all intercourse with his Scottish brethren-at-arms, as far as possible,—by observing a sullen taciturnity, when compelled to meet them occasionally,—and by looking scornfully upon them when they encountered on the march and in camp. The Scottish barons and knights were not men to bear his scorn unobserved or unreplied to; and it came to that pass, that he was regarded as the determined and active enemy of a nation, whom, after all, he only disliked, and in some sort despised. Nay, it was remarked by close observers, that, if he had not towards them the charity of Scripture, which suffereth long, and judges kindly, he was by no means deficient in the subordinate and limited virtue, which alleviates and relieves the wants of others. The wealth of Thomas of Gilsland procured supplies of provisions and medicines, and some of these usually flowed by secret channels into the quarters of the Scottish; his surly benevolence proceeding on the principle, that, next to a man's friend, his foe was of most importance to him, passing over all the intermediate relations, as too indifferent to merit even a thought. This explanation is necessary, in order that the reader may fully understand what we are now to detail.

Thomas de Vaux had not made many steps beyond the entrance of the royal pavilion, when he was aware of what the far more acute ear of the English monarch, no mean proficient in the art of minstrelsy, had instantly discovered, that the musical strains, namely, which had reached their ears, were produced by the pipes, shalms, and kettle-drums of the Saracens; and, at the bottom of an avenue of tents, which formed a broad access to the pavilion of Richard, he could see a crowd of idle soldiers assembled around the spot from which the music was heard, almost in the centre of the camp; and he saw, with great surprise, mingled amid the helmets of various forms worn by the Crusaders of different nations, white turbans and long pikes, announcing the presence of armed Saracens, and the huge deformed heads of several camels or dromedaries, overlooking the multitude by aid of their long disproportioned necks.

Wondering and displeased at a sight so unexpected and singular,—for it was customary to leave all flags of truce and other communications from the enemy in an appointed place without the barriers,—the baron looked eagerly round for some one of whom he might inquire the cause of this alarming novelty.

The first person whom he met advancing to him, he set down at once, by his grave and haughty step, as a Spaniard or a Scot; and presently after muttered to himself—"And a Scot it is—he of the Leopard.—I have seen him fight indifferently well, for one of his country."

Loath to ask even a passing question, he was about to pass Sir Kenneth, with that sullen and lowering port which seems to say, "I know thee, but I will hold no communication with thee; but his purpose was defeated by the Northern Knight, who moved forward directly to him, and accosting him with formal courtesy, said, "My Lord de Vaux of Gilsland, I have in charge to speak with you."

"Ha!" returned the English baron, "with me? But, say your pleasure, so it be shortly spoken—I am on the King's errand."

"Mine touches King Richard yet more nearly," answered Sir Kenneth; "I bring him, I trust, health."

The Lord of Gilsland measured the Scot with incredulous eyes, and replied, "Thou art no leech, I think, Sir Scot—I had as soon thought of your bringing the King of England wealth."

Sir Kenneth, though displeased with the manner of the baron's reply, answered calmly; "Health to Richard is glory and wealth to Christendom.—But my time presses; I pray you may I see the King?"

"Surely not, fair sir," said the baron, "until your errand be told more distinctly. The sick chambers of princes open not to all who inquire, like a northern hostelry."

"My lord," said Kenneth, "the cross which I wear in common with yourself, and the importance of what I have to tell, must, for the present, cause me to pass over a bearing, which else I were unapt to endure. In plain language, then, I bring with me a Moorish physician, who undertakes to work a cure on King Richard."

"A Moorish physician!" said De Vaux; "and who will warrant that he brings not poisons instead of remedies?"

"His own life, my lord — his head, which he offers as a guarantee."

"I have known many a resolute ruffian," said De Vaux, "who valued his own life as little as it deserved, and would troop to the gallows as merrily as if the hangman were his partner in a dance."

"But thus it is, my lord," replied the Scot; "Saladin, to whom none will deny the credit of a generous and valiant enemy, hath sent this leech hither with an honourable retinue and guard, befitting the high estimation in which El Hakim * is held by the Soldan, and with fruits and refreshments for the King's private chamber, and such message as may pass betwixt honourable enemies, praying him to be recovered of his fever, that he may be the fitter to receive a visit from the Soldan, with his naked scimitar in his hand, and an hundred thousand cavaliers at his back. Will it please you, who are of the King's secret council, to cause these camels to be discharged of their burdens, and some order taken as to the reception of the learned physician?"

"Wonderful!" said De Vaux, as speaking to himself. — "And who will vouch for the honour of Saladin, in a case when bad faith would rid him at once of his most powerful adversary?"

"I myself," replied Sir Kenneth, "will be his guarantee, with honour, life, and fortune."

"Strange!" again ejaculated De Vaux; "the North vouches for the South — the Scot for the Turk! — May I crave of you, Sir Knight, how you became concerned in this affair?"

"I have been absent on a pilgrimage, in the course of which," replied Sir Kenneth, "I had a message to discharge towards the holy hermit of Engaddi."

"May I not be intrusted with it, Sir Kenneth, and with the answer of the holy man?"

"It may not be, my lord," answered the Scot.

"I am of the secret council of England," said the Englishman, haughtily.

"To which land I know no allegiance," said Kenneth. "Though I have voluntarily followed in this war the personal fortunes of England's sovereign, I was despatched by the General Council of the kings, princes, and supreme leaders of the army of the Blessed Cross, and to them only I render my errand."

"Ha! say'st thou?" said the proud Baron de Vaux. "But know, messenger of the kings and princes as thou may'st be, no leech shall approach the sick-bed of Richard of England, without the consent of him of Gilsland; and they will come on evil errand who dare to intrude themselves against it."

He was turning loftily away, when the Scot, placing himself closer, and more opposite to him, asked, in a calm voice, yet not without expressing his share of pride, whether the Lord of Gilsland esteemed him a gentleman and a good knight.

"All Scots are ennobled by their birthright," answered Thomas de Vaux, something ironically; but, sensible of his own injustice, and perceiving that Kenneth's colour rose, he added, "For a good knight it were sin to

* The Physician.

doubt you, in one at least who has seen you well and bravely discharge your devoir."

"Well, then," said the Scottish knight, satisfied with the frankness of the last admission, "and let me swear to you, Thomas of Gilsland, that as I am true Scottish man, which I hold a privilege equal to my ancient gentry, and as sure as I am a belted knight, and come hither to acquire *los** and fame in this mortal life, and forgiveness of my sins in that which is to come — so truly, and by the blessed Cross which I wear, do I protest unto you, that I desire but the safety of Richard Cœur de Lion, in recommending the ministry of this Moslem physician."

The Englishman was struck with the solemnity of the obtestation, and answered with more cordiality than he had yet exhibited, "Tell me, Sir Knight of the Leopard, granting (which I do not doubt) that thou art thyself satisfied in this matter, shall I do well, in a land where the art of poisoning is as general as that of cooking, to bring this unknown physician to practise with his drugs on a health so valuable to Christendom?"

"My lord," replied the Scot, "thus only can I reply; that my squire, the only one of my retinue whom war and disease had left in attendance on me, has been of late suffering dangerously under this same fever, which, in valiant King Richard, has disabled the principal limb of our holy enterprise. This leech, this El Hakim, hath ministered remedies to him not two hours since, and already he hath fallen into a refreshing sleep. That he *can* cure the disorder, which has proved so fatal, I nothing doubt; that he hath the purpose to do it, is, I think, warranted by his mission from the royal Soldan, who is true-hearted and loyal, so far as a blinded infidel may be called so; and, for his eventual success, the certainty of reward in case of succeeding, and punishment in case of voluntary failure, may be a sufficient guarantee."

The Englishman listened with downcast looks, as one who doubted, yet was not unwilling to receive conviction. At length he looked up and said, "May I see your sick squire, fair sir?"

The Scottish knight hesitated and coloured, yet answered at last, "Willingly, my Lord of Gilsland; but you must remember, when you see my poor quarter, that the nobles and knights of Scotland feed not so high, sleep not so soft, and care not for the magnificence of lodgment, which is proper to their southern neighbours. I am poorly lodged, my Lord of Gilsland," he added with a haughty emphasis on the word, while, with some unwillingness, he led the way to his temporary place of abode.

Whatever were the prejudices of De Vaux against the nation of his new acquaintance, and though we undertake not to deny that some of these were excited by its proverbial poverty, he had too much nobleness of disposition to enjoy the mortification of a brave individual, thus compelled to make known wants which his pride would gladly have concealed.

"Shame to the soldier of the Cross," he said, "who thinks of worldly splendour, or of luxurious accommodation, when pressing forward to the conquest of the Holy City. Fare as hard as we may, we shall yet be better than the host of martyrs and of saints, who, having trod these scenes before us, now hold golden lamps, and evergreen palms."

This was the most metaphorical speech which Thomas of Gilsland was ever known to utter, the rather, perhaps, (as will sometimes happen,) that it did not entirely express his own sentiments, being somewhat a lover of good cheer and splendid accommodation. By this time they reached the place of the camp, where the Knight of the Leopard had assumed his abode.

Appearances here did indeed promise no breach of the laws of mortification, to which the Crusaders, according to the opinion expressed by him of Gilsland, ought to subject themselves. A space of ground, large enough

---

* *Los* — laus, praise, or renown.

to accommodate perhaps thirty tents, according to the Crusader's rules of castrametation, was partly vacant—because, in ostentation, the knight had demanded ground to the extent of his original retinue—partly occupied by a few miserable huts, hastily constructed of boughs, and covered with palm-leaves. These habitations seemed entirely deserted, and several of them were ruinous. The central hut, which represented the pavilion of the leader, was distinguished by the swallow-tailed pennon, placed on the point of a spear; from which its long folds dropt motionless to the ground, as if sickening under the scorching rays of the Asiatic sun. But no pages or squires, not even a solitary warder, was placed by the emblem of feudal power and knightly degrees. If its reputation defended it not from insult, it had no other guard.

Sir Kenneth cast a melancholy look around him, but, suppressing his feelings, entered the hut, making a sign to the Baron of Gilsland to follow. He also cast around a glance of examination, which implied pity not altogether unmingled with contempt, to which, perhaps, it is as nearly akin as it is said to be to love. He then stooped his lofty crest, and entered a lowly hut, which his bulky form seemed almost entirely to fill.

The interior of the hut was chiefly occupied by two beds. One was empty, but composed of collected leaves, and spread with an antelope's hide. It seemed, from the articles of armour laid beside it, and from a crucifix of silver, carefully and reverentially disposed at the head, to be the couch of the knight himself. The other contained the invalid, of whom Sir Kenneth had spoken, a strong-built and harsh-featured man, past, as his looks betokened, the middle-age of life. His couch was trimmed more softly than his master's, and it was plain, that the more courtly garments of the latter, the loose robe, in which the knights showed themselves on pacific occasions, and the other little spare articles of dress and adornment, had been applied by Sir Kenneth to the accommodation of his sick domestic. In an outward part of the hut, which yet was within the range of the English Baron's eye, a boy, rudely attired with buskins of deer's hide, a blue cap or bonnet, and a doublet, whose original finery was much tarnished, sat on his knees by a chafing-dish filled with charcoal, cooking upon a plate of iron the cakes of barley-bread, which were then, and still are, a favourite food with the Scottish people. Part of an antelope was suspended against one of the main props of the hut, nor was it difficult to know how it had been procured; for a large stag greyhound, nobler in size and appearance than those even which guarded King Richard's sick-bed, lay eyeing the process of baking the cake. The sagacious animal, on their first entrance, uttered a stifled growl, which sounded from his deep chest like distant thunder. But he saw his master, and acknowledged his presence by wagging his tail and couching his head, abstaining from more tumultuous or noisy greeting, as if his noble instinct had taught him the propriety of silence in a sick man's chamber.

Beside the couch, sat on a cushion, also composed of skins, the Moorish physician of whom Sir Kenneth had spoken, cross-legged, after the Eastern fashion. The imperfect light showed little of him, save that the lower part of his face was covered with a long black beard, which descended over his breast—that he wore a high *tolpach*, a Tartar cap of the lamb's wool manufactured at Astracan, bearing the same dusky colour, and that his ample caftan, or Turkish robe, was also of a dark hue. Two piercing eyes, which gleamed with unusual lustre, were the only lineaments of his visage that could be discerned amid the darkness in which he was enveloped. The English lord stood silent with a sort of reverential awe; for, notwithstanding the roughness of his general bearing, a scene of distress and poverty, firmly endured without complaint or murmur, would at any time have claimed more reverence from Thomas de Vaux, than would all the splendid formalities of a royal presence-chamber, unless that presence-chamber were

King Richard's own. Nothing was, for a time, heard, but the heavy and regular breathings of the invalid, who seemed in profound repose.

"He hath not slept for six nights before," said Sir Kenneth, "as I am assured by the youth, his attendant."

"Noble Scot," said Thomas de Vaux, grasping the Scottish knight's hand, with a pressure which had more of cordiality than he permitted his words to utter, "this gear must be mended — Your esquire is but too evil fed and looked to."

In the latter part of this speech, he naturally raised his voice to its usual decided tone. The sick man was disturbed in his slumbers.

"My master," he said, murmuring as in a dream, "noble Sir Kenneth— taste not, to you as to me, the waters of the Clyde cold and refreshing, after the brackish springs of Palestine?"

"He dreams of his native land, and is happy in his slumbers," whispered Sir Kenneth to De Vaux; but had scarce uttered the words, when the physician, arising from the place which he had taken near the couch of the sick, and laying the hand of the patient, whose pulse he had been carefully watching, quietly upon the couch, came to the two knights, and taking them each by the arm, while he intimated to them to remain silent, led them to the front of the hut.

"In the name of Issa Bon Mariam," he said, "whom we honour as you, though not with the same blinded superstition, disturb not the effect of the blessed medicine of which he hath partaken. To awaken him now, is death or deprivation of reason ; but return at the hour when the Muezzin calls from the minaret to evening prayer in the mosque, and, if left undisturbed until then, I promise you, this same Frankish soldier shall be able, without prejudice to his health, to hold some brief converse with you, on any matters on which either, and especially his master, may have to question him."

The knights retreated before the authoritative commands of the leech, who seemed fully to comprehend the importance of the Eastern proverb, that the sick chamber of the patient is the kingdom of the physician.

They paused, and remained standing together at the door of the hut, Sir Kenneth, with the air of one who expected his visiter to say farewell—and De Vaux, as if he had something on his mind which prevented him from doing so. The hound, however, had pressed out of the tent after them, and now thrust his long rough countenance into the hand of his master as if modestly soliciting some mark of his kindness. He had no sooner received the notice which he desired, in the shape of a kind word and slight caress, than eager to acknowledge his gratitude, and joy for his master's return, he flew off at full speed, galloping in full career, and with outstretched tail, here and there, about and around, crossways and endlong, through the decayed huts, and the esplanade we have described, but never transgressing those precincts which his sagacity knew were protected by his master's pennon. After a few gambols of this kind, the dog, coming close up to his master, laid at once aside his frolicsome mood, relapsed into his usual gravity and slowness of gesture and deportment, and looked as if he were ashamed that any thing should have moved him to depart so far out of his sober self-control.

Both knights looked on with pleasure; for Sir Kenneth was justly proud of his noble hound, and the northern English baron was of course an admirer of the chase, and a judge of the animal's merits.

"A right able dog," he said ; "I think, fair sir, King Richard hath not an *alan* which may match him, if he be as staunch as he is swift. But let me pray you, speaking in all honour and kindness—have you not heard the proclamation, that no one, under the rank of earl, shall keep hunting dogs within King Richard's camp, without the royal license, which, I think, Sir Kenneth, hath not been issued to you? — I speak as Master of the Horse."

2 v

"And I answer as a free Scottish knight," said Kenneth sternly. "For the present I follow the banner of England, but I cannot remember that I have ever subjected myself to the forest-laws of that kingdom, nor have I such respect for them as would incline me to do so. When the trumpet sounds to arms, my foot is in the stirrup as soon as any — when it clangs for the charge, my lance has not yet been the last laid in the rest. But for my hours of liberty or of idleness, King Richard has no title to bar my recreation."

"Nevertheless," said De Vaux, "it is a folly to disobey the King's ordinance—so, with your good leave, I, as having authority in that matter, will send you a protection for my friend here."

"I thank you," said the Scot coldly; "but he knows my allotted quarters, and within these I can protect him myself.—And yet," he said, suddenly changing his manner, "this is but a cold return for a well-meant kindness. I thank you, my lord, most heartily. The King's equerries, or prickers, might find Roswal at disadvantage, and do him some injury, which I should not, perhaps, be slow in returning, and so ill might come of it. You have seen so much of my housekeeping, my lord," he added with a smile, "that I need not shame to say that Roswal is our principal purveyor; and well I hope our Lion Richard will not be like the lion in the minstrel fable, that went a-hunting and kept the whole booty to himself. I cannot think he would grudge a poor gentleman, who follows him faithfully, his hour of sport, and his morsel of game, more especially when other food is hard enough to come by."

"By my faith, you do the King no more than justice—and yet," said the baron, "there is something in these words, vert and venison, that turns the very brains of our Norman princes."

"We have heard of late," said the Scot, "by minstrels and pilgrims, that your outlawed yeomen have formed great bands in the shires of York and Nottingham, having at their head a most stout archer, called Robin Hood, with his lieutenant, Little John. Methinks it were better that Richard relaxed his forest-code in England, than endeavoured to enforce it in the Holy Land."

"Wild work, Sir Kenneth," replied De Vaux, shrugging his shoulders, as one who would avoid a perilous or unpleasing topic —"a mad world, sir.— I must now bid you adieu, having presently to return to the King's pavilion. At vespers, I will again, with your leave, visit your quarters, and speak with this same infidel physician. I would, in the mean time, were it no offence, willingly send you what would somewhat mend your cheer."

"I thank you, sir," said Sir Kenneth, "but it needs not; Roswal hath already stocked my larder for two weeks, since the sun of Palestine, if it brings diseases, serves also to dry venison."

The two warriors parted much better friends than they had met; but ere they separated, Thomas de Vaux informed himself at more length of the circumstances attending the mission of the Eastern physician, and received from the Scottish knight the credentials which he had brought to King Richard on the part of Saladin.

Chapter the Eighth.

A wise physician, skill'd our wounds to heal,
Is more than armies to the common weal.

POPE'S ILIAD.

"THIS is a strange tale, Sir Thomas," said the sick monarch, when he had heard the report of the trusty Baron of Gilsland; "art thou sure this Scottish man is a tall man and true?"

"I cannot say, my lord," replied the jealous Borderer; "I live a little too near the Scots to gather much truth among them, having found them ever fair and false. But this man's bearing is that of a true man, were he a devil as well as a Scot — that I must needs say for him in conscience."

"And for his carriage as a knight, how say'st thou, De Vaux?" demanded the King.

"It is your Majesty's business more than mine to note men's bearings; and I warrant you have noted the manner in which this man of the Leopard hath borne himself. He hath been well spoken of."

"And justly, Thomas," said the King. "We have ourselves witnessed him. It is indeed our purpose, in placing ourselves ever in the front of battle, to see how our liegemen and followers acquit themselves, and not from a vain desire to accumulate vainglory to ourselves, as some have supposed. We know the vanity of the praise of man, which is but a vapour, and buckle on our armour for other purposes than to win it."

De Vaux was alarmed when he heard the King make a declaration so inconsistent with his nature, and believed at first that nothing short of the approach of death could have brought him to speak in depreciating terms of military renown, which was the very breath of his nostrils. But recollecting he had met the royal confessor in the outer pavilion, he was shrewd enough to place this temporary self-abasement to the effect of the reverend man's lesson, and suffered the King to proceed without reply.

"Yes," continued Richard, "I have indeed marked the manner in which this knight does his devoir. My leading-staff were not worth a fool's bauble, had he escaped my notice — and he had ere now tasted of our bounty, but that I have also marked his overweening and audacious presumption."

"My liege," said the Baron of Gilsland, observing the King's countenance change, "I fear I have transgressed your pleasure in lending some countenance to his transgression."

"How, De Multon, thou?" said the King, contracting his brows, and speaking in a tone of angry surprise, — "Thou countenance his insolence? —It cannot be."

"Nay, your Majesty will pardon me to remind you, that I have by mine office right to grant liberty to men of gentle blood, to keep them a hound or two within the camp, just to cherish the noble art of venerie; and besides, it were a sin to have maimed or harmed a thing so noble as this gentleman's dog."

"Has he then a dog so handsome?" said the King.

"A most perfect creature of Heaven," said the baron, who was an enthusiast in field-sports — "of the noblest Northern breed — deep in the chest, strong in the stern, black colour, and brindled on the breast and legs, not spotted with white, but just shaded into gray—strength to pull down a bull —swiftness to cote an antelope."

The King laughed at his enthusiasm. "Well, thou hast given him leave to keep the hound, so there is an end of it. Be not, however, liberal of your licenses among those knights adventurers, who have no prince or leader to depend upon — they are ungovernable, and leave no game in

Palestine.—But to this piece of learned heathenesse — say'st thou the Scot met him in the desert?"

"No, my liege, the Scot's tale runs thus:—He was despatched to the old hermit of Engaddi, of whom men talk so much——"

"'Sdeath and hell!' said Richard, starting up, "By whom despatched, and for what? Who dared send any one thither, when our Queen was in the Convent of Engaddi, upon her pilgrimage for our recovery?"

"The Council of the Crusade sent him, my lord," answered the Baron de Vaux; "for what purpose he declined to account to me. I think it is scarce known in the camp that your royal consort is on a pilgrimage — and even the princes may not have been aware, as the Queen has been sequestered from company since your love prohibited her attendance in case of infection."

"Well, it shall be looked into," said Richard. — "So this Scottish man, this envoy, met with a wandering physician at the grotto of Engaddi — ha?"

"Not so, my liege," replied De Vaux; "but he met, I think, near that place, with a Saracen Emir, with whom he had some mêlée in the way of proof of valour, and finding him worthy to bear brave men company, they went together, as errant knights are wont, to the grotto of Engaddi."

Here De Vaux stopped, for he was not one of those who can tell a long story in a sentence.

"And did they there meet the physician?" demanded the King, impatiently.

"No, my liege," replied De Vaux; "but the Saracen, learning your Majesty's grievous illness, undertook that Saladin should send his own physician to you, and with many assurances of his eminent skill; and he came to the grotto accordingly, after the Scottish Knight had tarried a day for him and more. He is attended as if he were a prince, with drums and atabals, and servants on horse and foot, and brings with him letters of credence from Saladin."

"Have they been examined by Giacomo Loredani?"

"I showed them to the interpreter ere bringing them hither, and behold their contents in English."

Richard took a scroll, in which were inscribed these words:—"The blessing of Allah and his Prophet Mahommed, ['Out upon the hound!' said Richard, spitting in contempt, by way of interjection;] Saladin, king of kings, Soldan of Egypt and of Syria, the light and refuge of the earth, to the great Melech Ric, Richard of England, greeting. Whereas, we have been informed that the hand of sickness hath been heavy upon thee, our royal brother, and that thou hast with thee only such Nazarene and Jewish mediciners, as work without the blessing of Allah and our holy Prophet, ['Confusion on his head!' again muttered the English monarch,] we have therefore sent to tend and wait upon thee at this time, the physician to our own person, Adonbec el Hakim, before whose face the angel Azrael* spreads his wings and departs from the sick chamber; who knows the virtues of herbs and stones, the path of the sun, moon, and stars, and can save man from all that is not written on his forehead. And this we do, praying you heartily to honour and make use of his skill; not only that we may do service to thy worth and valour, which is the glory of all the nations of Frangistan, but that we may bring the controversy which is at present between us to an end, either by honourable agreement, or by open trial thereof with our weapons, in a fair field; seeing that it neither becomes thy place and courage, to die the death of a slave who hath been overwrought by his taskmaster, nor befits it our fame that a brave adversary be snatched from our weapon by such a disease. And, therefore, may the holy——"

---

* The Angel of Death.

"Hold, hold," said Richard, "I will have no more of his dog of a Prophet! It makes me sick to think the valiant and worthy Soldan should believe in a dead dog. — Yes, I will see his physician. I will put myself into the charge of this Hakim—I will repay the noble Soldan his generosity —I will meet Saladin in the field, as he so worthily proposes, and he shall have no cause to term Richard of England ungrateful. I will strike him to the earth with my battle-axe — I will convert him to Holy Church with such blows as he has rarely endured—He shall recant his errors before my good cross-handled sword, and I will have him baptized in the battle-field, from my own helmet, though the cleansing waters were mixed with the blood of us both. — Haste, De Vaux, why dost thou delay a conclusion so pleasing? Fetch the Hakim hither."

"My lord," said the baron, who perhaps saw some accession of fever in this overflow of confidence,—"bethink you, the Soldan is a pagan, and that you are his most formidable enemy——"

"For which reason he is the more bound to do me service in this matter, lest a paltry fever end the quarrel betwixt two such kings. I tell thee, he loves me as I love him — as noble adversaries ever love each other — by my honour, it were sin to doubt his good faith!"

"Nevertheless, my lord, it were well to wait the issue of those medicines upon the Scottish squire," said the Lord of Gilsland; "my own life depends upon it, for worthy were I to die like a dog, did I proceed rashly in this matter, and make shipwreck of the weal of Christendom."

"I never knew thee before hesitate for fear of life," said Richard, upbraidingly.

"Nor would I now, my liege," replied the stout-hearted baron, "save that yours lies at pledge as well as my own."

"Well, thou suspicious mortal," answered Richard, "begone then, and watch the progress of this remedy. I could almost wish it might either cure or kill me, for I am weary of lying here like an ox dying of the murrain, when tambours are beating, horses stamping, and trumpets sounding without."

The Baron hastily departed, resolved, however, to communicate his errand to some churchman, as he felt something burdened in conscience at the idea of his master being attended by an unbeliever.

The Archbishop of Tyre was the first to whom he confided his doubts, knowing his interest with his master, Richard, who both loved and honoured that sagacious prelate. The bishop heard the doubts which De Vaux stated, with that acuteness of intelligence which distinguishes the Roman Catholic clergy. The religious scruples of De Vaux he treated with as much lightness as propriety permitted him to exhibit on such a subject to a layman.

"Mediciners," he said, "like the medicines which they employed, were often useful, though the one were by birth or manners, the vilest of humanity, as the others are, in many cases, extracted from the basest materials. Men may use the assistance of pagans and infidels," he continued, "in their need, and there is reason to think, that one cause of their being permitted to remain on earth, is that they might minister to the convenience of true Christians — Thus, we lawfully make slaves of heathen captives. — Again," proceeded the prelate, "there is no doubt that the primitive Christians used the services of the unconverted heathen — thus, in the ship of Alexandria, in which the blessed Apostle Paul sailed to Italy, the sailors were doubtless pagans; yet what said the holy saint when their ministry was needful — '*Nisi hi in navi manserint, vos salvi fieri non potestis* — Unless these men abide in the ship, ye cannot be saved.' Again, Jews are infidels to Christianity, as well as Mahommedans. But there are few physicians in the camp excepting Jews, and such are employed without scandal or scruple Therefore, Mahommedans may be used for their service in that capacity — *quod erat demonstrandum.*"

This reasoning entirely removed the scruples of Thomas de Vaux, who was particularly moved by the Latin quotation, as he did not understand a word of it.

But the bishop proceeded with far less fluency, when he considered the possibility of the Saracen's acting with bad faith; and here he came not to a speedy decision. The baron showed him the letters of credence. He read and re-read them, and compared the original with the translation. "It is a dish choicely cooked," he said, "to the palate of King Richard, and I cannot but have my suspicions of the wily Saracen. They are curious in the art of poisons, and can so temper them that they shall be weeks in acting upon the party, during which time, the perpetrator has leisure to escape. They can impregnate cloth and leather, nay, even paper and parchment, with the most subtle venom—Our Lady forgive me!—And wherefore, knowing this, hold I these letters of credence so close to my face? — Take them, Sir Thomas, take them speedily."

Here he gave them at arm's-length, and with some appearance of haste, to the baron. "But come, my Lord De Vaux," he continued, "wend we to the tent of this sick squire, where we shall learn whether this Hakim hath really the art of curing which he professeth, ere we consider whether there be safety in permitting him to exercise his art upon King Richard. — Yet hold! let me first take my pouncet-box, for these fevers spread like an infection. I would advise you to use dried rosemary steeped in vinegar, my lord. I, too, know something of the healing art."

"I thank your reverend lordship," replied Thomas of Gilsland; "but had I been accessible to the fever, I had caught it long since by the bed of my master."

The Bishop of Tyre blushed, for he had rather avoided the presence of the sick monarch; and he bid the baron lead on.

As they paused before the wretched hut in which Kenneth of the Leopard and his follower abode, the bishop said to De Vaux, "Now, of a surety, my lord, these Scottish knights have worse care of their followers than we of our dogs. Here is a knight, valiant they say in battle, and thought fitting to be graced with charges of weight in time of truce, whose esquire of the body is lodged worse than in the worst dog-kennel in England. What say you of your neighbours?"

"That a master doth well enough for his servant, when he lodgeth him in no worse dwelling than his own," said De Vaux, and entered the hut.

The bishop followed, not without evident reluctance; for though he lacked not courage in some respects, yet it was tempered with a strong and lively regard for his own safety. He recollected, however, the necessity there was for judging personally of the skill of the Arabian physician, and entered the hut with a stateliness of manner, calculated, as he thought, to impose respect on the stranger.

The prelate was, indeed, a striking and commanding figure. In his youth he had been eminently handsome, and, even in age, was unwilling to appear less so. His episcopal dress was of the richest fashion, trimmed with costly fur, and surrounded by a cope of curious needle-work. The rings on his fingers were worth a goodly barony, and the hood which he wore, though now unclasped and thrown back for heat, had studs of pure gold to fasten it around his throat and under his chin when he so inclined. His long beard, now silvered with age, descended over his breast. One of two youthful acolytes who attended him, created an artificial shade, peculiar then to the East, by bearing over his head an umbrella of palmetto leaves, while the other refreshed his reverend master by agitating a fan of peacock feathers.

When the Bishop of Tyre entered the hut of the Scottish knight, the master was absent; and the Moorish physician, whom he had come to see, sat in the very posture in which De Vaux had left him several hours before, cross-legged upon a mat made of twisted leaves, by the side of the patient, who appeared in deep slumber, and whose pulse he felt from time to time. The bishop remained standing before him in silence for two or three minutes, as if expecting some honourable salutation, or at least that the Saracen would seem struck with the dignity of his appearance. But Adonbec el Hakim took no notice of him beyond a passing glance, and when the prelate at length saluted him in the lingua franca current in the country, he only replied by the ordinary Oriental greeting, "*Salam alicum* — peace be with you."

"Art thou a physician, infidel?" said the bishop, somewhat mortified at this cold reception. "I would speak with thee on that art."

' If thou knowest aught of medicine," answered El Hakim, "thou wouldst be aware, that physicians hold no counsel or debate in the sick chamber of their patient. Hear," he added, as the low growling of the stag-hound was heard from the inner hut, "even the dog might teach thee reason, Ulemat. His instinct teaches him to suppress his barking in the sick man's hearing. — Come without the tent," said he, rising and leading the way, "if thou hast aught to say with me."

Notwithstanding the plainness of the Saracen leech's dress, and his inferiority of size, when contrasted with the tall prelate and gigantic English baron, there was something striking in his manner and countenance, which prevented the Bishop of Tyre from expressing strongly the displeasure he felt at this unceremonious rebuke. When without the hut, he gazed upon Adonbec in silence, for several minutes, before he could fix on the best manner to renew the conversation. No locks were seen under the high bonnet of the Arabian, which hid also part of a brow that seemed lofty and expanded, smooth, and free from wrinkles, as were his cheeks, where they were seen under the shade of his long beard. We have elsewhere noticed the piercing quality of his dark eyes.

The prelate, struck with his apparent youth, at length broke a pause, which the other seemed in no haste to interrupt, by demanding of the Arabian how old he was?

"The years of ordinary men," said the Saracen, "are counted by their wrinkles; those of sages by their studies. I dare not call myself older than an hundred revolutions of the Hegira." *

The Baron of Gilsland, who took this for a literal assertion, that he was a century old, looked doubtfully upon the prelate, who, though he better understood the meaning of El Hakim, answered his glance by mysteriously shaking his head. He resumed an air of importance, when he again authoritatively demanded, what evidence Adonbec could produce of his medical proficiency.

"Ye have the word of the mighty Saladin," said the sage, touching his cap in sign of reverence; "a word which was never broken towards friend or foe—what, Nazarene, wouldst thou demand more?"

"I would have ocular proof of thy skill," said the baron, "and without it thou approachest not to the couch of King Richard."

"The praise of the physician," said the Arabian, "is in the recovery of his patient. Behold this sergeant, whose blood has been dried up by the fever which has whitened your camp with skeletons, and against which the art of your Nazarene leeches hath been like a silken doublet against a lance of steel. Look at his fingers and arms, wasted like the claws and shanks of the crane. Death had this morning his clutch on him; but had Azrael been on one side of the couch, I being on the other, his soul should not have been reft from his body. Disturb me not with farther questions, but await the critical minute, and behold in silent wonder the marvellous event."

---

* Meaning, that his attainments were those which might have been made in a hundred years.

The physician had then recourse to his astrolabe, the oracle of Eastern science, and, watching with grave precision until the precise time of the evening prayer had arrived, he sunk on his knees, with his face turned to Mecca, and recited the petitions which close the Moslemah's day of toil. The bishop and the English baron looked on each other, meanwhile, with symptoms of contempt and indignation, but neither judged it fit to interrupt El Hakim in his devotions, unholy as they considered them to be.

The Arab arose from the earth, on which he had prostrated himself, and, walking into the hut where the patient lay extended, he drew a sponge from a small silver box, dipt perhaps in some aromatic distillation; for when he put it to the sleeper's nose, he sneezed, awoke, and looked wildly around. He was a ghastly spectacle, as he sat up almost naked on his couch, the bones and cartilages as visible through the surface of his skin, as if they had never been clothed with flesh; his face was long, and furrowed with wrinkles, but his eye, though it wandered at first, became gradually more settled. He seemed to be aware of the presence of his dignified visiters, for he attempted feebly to pull the covering from his head, in token of reverence, as he inquired, in a subdued and submissive voice, for his master.

"Do you know us, vassal?" said the Lord of Gilsland.

"Not perfectly, my lord," replied the Squire, faintly. "My sleep has been long and full of dreams. Yet I know that you are a great English lord, as seemeth by the red cross, and this a holy prelate, whose blessing I crave on me a poor sinner."

"Thou hast it—*Benedictio Domini sit vobiscum*," said the prelate, making the sign of the cross, but without approaching nearer to the patient's bed.

"Your eyes witness," said the Arabian, "the fever hath been subdued— he speaks with calmness and recollection—his pulse beats composedly as yours—try its pulsations yourself."

The prelate declined the experiment; but Thomas of Gilsland, more determined on making the trial, did so, and satisfied himself that the fever was indeed gone.

"This is most wonderful," said the knight, looking to the bishop; "the man is assuredly cured. I must conduct this mediciner presently to King Richard's tent—What thinks your reverence?"

"Stay, let me finish one cure ere I commence another," said the Arab; "I will pass with you when I have given my patient the second cup of this most holy elixir."

So saying, he pulled out a silver cup, and filling it with water from a gourd which stood by the bedside, he next drew forth a small silken bag made of network, twisted with silver, the contents of which the bystanders could not discover, and immersing it in the cup, continued to watch it in silence during the space of five minutes. It seemed to the spectators as if some effervescence took place during the operation, but if so, it instantly subsided.

"Drink," said the physician to the sick man — "sleep, and awaken free from malady."

"And with this simple-seeming draught, thou wilt undertake to cure a monarch?" said the Bishop of Tyre.

"I have cured a beggar, as you may behold," replied the sage. "Are the Kings of Frangistan made of other clay than the meanest of their subjects?"

"Let us have him presently to the King," said the Baron of Gilsland. "He hath shown that he possesses the secret which may restore his health. If he fails to exercise it, I will put himself past the power of medicine."

As they were about to leave the hut, the sick man, raising his voice as much as his weakness permitted, exclaimed, "Reverend father, noble knight, and you, kind leech, if you would have me sleep and recover, tell me in charity what is become of my dear master?"

"He is upon a distant expedition, friend," replied the Prelate; "on an honourable embassy, which may detain him for some days."

"Nay," said the Baron of Gilsland, "why deceive the poor fellow?— Friend, thy master has returned to the camp, and you will presently see him."

The invalid held up, as if in thankfulness, his wasted hands to Heaven, and resisting no longer the soporiferous operation of the elixir, sunk down in a gentle sleep.

"You are a better physician than I, Sir Thomas," said the prelate; "a soothing falsehood is fitter for a sick room than an unpleasing truth."

"How mean you, my reverend lord?" said De Vaux, hastily. "Think you I would tell a falsehood to save the lives of a dozen such as he?"

"You said," replied the bishop, with manifest symptoms of alarm — "you said, the esquire's master was returned—he, I mean, of the Couchant Leopard."

"And he *is* returned," said De Vaux. "I spoke with him but a few hours since. This learned leech came in his company."

"Holy Virgin! why told you not of his return to me?" said the bishop, in evident perturbation.

"Did I not say that this same Knight of the Leopard had returned in company with the physician?— I thought I had," replied De Vaux, carelessly; "but what signified his return, to the skill of the physician, or the cure of his Majesty?"

"Much, Sir Thomas — it signified much," said the bishop, clenching his hands, pressing his foot against the earth, and giving signs of impatience, as if in an involuntary manner. "But, where can he be gone now, this same knight?—God be with us—here may be some fatal errors!"

"Yonder serf in the outer space," said De Vaux, not without wonder at the bishop's emotion, "can probably tell us whither his master has gone."

The lad was summoned, and, in a language nearly incomprehensible to them, gave them at length to understand, that an officer had summoned his master to the royal tent, some time before their arrival at that of his master. The anxiety of the bishop appeared to rise to the highest, and became evident to De Vaux, though neither an acute observer, nor of a suspicious temper. But with his anxiety seemed to increase his wish to keep it subdued and unobserved. He took a hasty leave of De Vaux, who looked after him with astonishment; and, after shrugging up his shoulders in silent wonder, proceeded to conduct the Arabian physician to the tent of King Richard.

Chapter the Ninth.

This is the prince of leeches; fever, plague,
Cold rheum, and hot podagra, do but look on him,
And quit their grasp upon the tortured sinews.
ANONYMOUS.

THE Baron of Gilsland walked with slow step and an anxious countenance towards the royal pavilion. He had much diffidence of his own capacity, except in a field of battle, and conscious of no very acute intellect, was usually contented to wonder at circumstances, which a man of livelier imagination would have endeavoured to investigate and understand, or at least would have made the subject of speculation. But it seemed very extraordinary, even to him, that the attention of the bishop should have been at once abstracted from all reflection on the marvellous cure which they had witnessed, and upon the probability it afforded of Richard being restored to health, by what seemed a very trivial piece of information, announcing the motions of a beggarly Scottish knight, than whom Thomas of Gilsland knew nothing within the circle of gentle blood more unimportant or contemptible; and, despite his usual habit of passively beholding passing events, the baron's spirit toiled with unwonted attempts to form conjectures on the cause.

At length the idea occurred at once to him, that the whole might be a conspiracy against King Richard, formed within the camp of the allies, and to which the bishop, who was by some represented as a politic and unscrupulous person, was not unlikely to have been accessary. It was true, that, in his own opinion, there existed no character so perfect as that of his master; for Richard being the flower of chivalry, and the chief of Christian leaders, and obeying in all points the commands of Holy Church, De Vaux's ideas of perfection went no farther. Still he knew that, however unworthily, it had been always his master's fate to draw as much reproach and dislike, as honour and attachment, from the display of his great qualities; and that in the very camp, and amongst those princes bound by oath to the Crusade, were many who would have sacrificed all hope of victory over the Saracens, to the pleasure of ruining, or at least of humbling, Richard of England.

"Wherefore," said the baron to himself, "it is in no sense impossible that this El Hakim, with this his cure, or seeming cure, wrought on the body of the Scottish squire, may mean nothing but a trick, to which he of the Leopard may be accessary, and wherein the Bishop of Tyre, prelate as he is, may have some share."

This hypothesis, indeed, could not be so easily reconciled with the alarm manifested by the bishop, on learning that, contrary to his expectation, the Scottish knight had suddenly returned to the Crusaders' camp. But De Vaux was influenced only by his general prejudices, which dictated to him the assured belief, that a wily Italian priest, a false-hearted Scot, and an infidel physician, formed a set of ingredients from which all evil, and no good, was likely to be extracted. He resolved, however, to lay his scruples bluntly before the King, of whose judgment he had nearly as high an opinion as of his valour.

Meantime, events had taken place very contrary to the suppositions which Thomas De Vaux had entertained. Scarce had he left the royal pavilion, when, betwixt the impatience of the fever, and that which was natural to his disposition, Richard began to murmur at his delay, and express an earnest desire for his return. He had seen enough to try to reason himself out of this irritation, which greatly increased his bodily malady. He wearied his attendants by demanding from them amusements, and the breviary of the priest, the romance of the clerk, even the harp of his favourite minstrel, were had recourse to in vain. At length, some two hours before sundown, and long, therefore, ere he could expect a satisfactory account of the process of the cure which the Moor or Arabian had undertaken, he sent, as we have already heard, a messenger, commanding the attendance of the Knight of the Leopard, determined to soothe his impatience by obtaining from Sir Kenneth a more particular account of the cause of his absence from the camp, and the circumstances of his meeting with this celebrated physician.

The Scottish knight, thus summoned, entered the royal presence, as one who was no stranger to such scenes. He was scarcely known to the King of England,—even by sight, although, tenacious of his rank, as devout in the adoration of the lady of his secret heart, he had never been absent on those occasions when the munificence and hospitality of England opened the Court of its monarch to all who held a certain rank in chivalry. The King gazed fixedly on Sir Kenneth approaching his bedside, while the knight bent his knee for a moment, then arose, and stood before him in a posture of deference, but not of subservience or humility, as became an officer in the presence of his sovereign.

"Thy name," said the King, "is Kenneth of the Leopard—From whom hadst thou degree of knighthood?"

"I took it from the sword of William the Lion, King of Scotland," replied the Scot.

"A weapon," said the King, "well worthy to confer honour, nor has it been laid on an undeserving shoulder. We have seen thee bear thyself knightly and valiantly in press of battle, when most need there was; and thou hadst not been yet to learn that thy deserts were known to us, but that thy presumption in other points has been such, that thy services can challenge no better reward than that of pardon for thy transgression. What sayest thou — ha?"

Kenneth attempted to speak, but was unable to express himself distinctly; the consciousness of his too ambitious love, and the keen falcon glance with which Cœur de Lion seemed to penetrate his inmost soul, combining to disconcert him.

"And yet," said the King, "although soldiers should obey command, and vassals be respectful towards their superiors, we might forgive a brave knight greater offence than the keeping a simple hound, though it were contrary to our express public ordinance."

Richard kept his eye fixed on the Scot's face, beheld, and beholding, smiled inwardly at the relief produced by the turn he had given to his general accusation.

"So please you, my lord," said the Scot, "your Majesty must be good to us poor gentlemen of Scotland in this matter. We are far from home, scant of revenues, and cannot support ourselves as your wealthy nobles, who have credit of the Lombards. The Saracens shall feel our blows the harder that we eat a piece of dried venison from time to time, with our herbs and barley-cakes."

"It skills not asking my leave," said Richard, "since Thomas de Vaux, who doth, like all around me, that which is fittest in his own eyes, hath already given thee permission for hunting and hawking."

"For hunting only, and please you," said the Scot; "but if it please your Majesty to indulge me with the privilege of hawking also, and you list to trust me with a falcon on fist, I trust I could supply your royal mess with some choice waterfowl."

"I dread me, if thou hadst but the falcon," said the King, "thou wouldst scarce wait for the permission. I wot well it is said abroad that we of the line of Anjou resent offence against our forest-laws, as highly as we would do treason against our crown. To brave and worthy men, however, we could pardon either misdemeanour.—But enough of this—I desire to know of you, Sir Knight, wherefore, and by whose authority, you took this recent journey to the wilderness of the Dead Sea, and Engaddi?"

"By order," replied the knight, "of the Council of Princes of the Holy Crusade."

"And how dared any one to give such an order, when I — not the least, surely, in the league — was unacquainted with it?"

"It was not my part, please your highness," said the Scot, "to inquire into such particulars. I am a soldier of the Cross—serving, doubtless, for the present, under your highness's banner, and proud of the permission to do so—but still, one who hath taken on him the holy symbol for the rights of Christianity, and the recovery of the Holy Sepulchre, and bound, therefore, to obey, without question, the orders of the princes and chiefs by whom the blessed enterprise is directed. That indisposition should seclude, I trust for but a short time, your highness from their councils, in which you hold so potential a voice, I must lament with all Christendom; but, as a soldier, I must obey those on whom the lawful right of command devolves, or set but an evil example in the Christian camp."

"Thou say'st well," said King Richard; "and the blame rests not with thee, but with those with whom, when it shall please Heaven to raise me from this accursed bed of pain and inactivity, I hope to reckon roundly. What was the purport of thy message?"

"Methinks, and please your highness," replied Sir Kenneth, "that were best asked of those who sent me, and who can render the reasons of mine errand: whereas I can only tell its outward form and purport."

"Palter not with me, Sir Scot — it were ill for thy safety," said the irritated monarch.

"My safety, my lord," replied the knight firmly, "I cast behind me as a regardless thing when I vowed myself to this enterprise, looking rather to my immortal welfare, than to that which concerns my earthly body."

"By the mass," said King Richard, "thou art a brave fellow! Hark thee, Sir Knight, I love the Scottish people: they are hardy, though dogged and stubborn, and, I think, true men in the main, though the necessity of state has sometimes constrained them to be dissemblers. I deserve some love at their hand, for I have voluntarily done what they could not by arms have extorted from me, any more than from my predecessors — I have re-established the fortresses of Roxburgh and Berwick, which lay in pledge to England — I have restored your ancient boundaries — and, finally, I have renounced a claim to homage upon the crown of England, which I thought unjustly forced on you. I have endeavoured to make honourable and independent friends where former kings of England attempted only to compel unwilling and rebellious vassals."

"All this you have done, my Lord King," said Sir Kenneth, bowing — "All this you have done, by your royal treaty with our sovereign at Canterbury. Therefore have you me, and many better Scottish men, making war against the infidels, under your banners, who would else have been ravaging your frontiers in England. If their numbers are now few, it is because their lives have been freely waged and wasted."

"I grant it true," said the King; "and for the good offices I have done your land, I require you to remember, that, as a principal member of the Christian league, I have a right to know the negotiations of my confederates. Do me, therefore, the justice to tell me what I have a title to be acquainted with, and which I am certain to know more truly from you than from others."

"My lord," said the Scot, "thus conjured, I will speak the truth; for I well believe that your purposes towards the principal object of our expedition are single-hearted and honest; and it is more than I dare warrant for others of the Holy League. Be pleased, therefore, to know, that my charge was to propose, through the medium of the hermit of Engaddi—a holy man, respected and protected by Saladin himself——"

"A continuation of the truce, I doubt not," said Richard, hastily interrupting him.

"No, by Saint Andrew, my liege," said the Scottish knight, "but the establishment of a lasting peace, and the withdrawing our armies from Palestine."

"Saint George!" said Richard, in astonishment — "Ill as I have justly thought of them, I could not have dreamed they would have humbled themselves to such dishonour. Speak, Sir Kenneth, with what will did you carry such a message?"

"With right good will, my lord," said Kenneth; "because, when we had lost our noble leader, under whose guidance alone I hoped for victory, I saw none who could succeed him likely to lead us to conquest, and I accounted it well in such circumstances to avoid defeat."

"And on what conditions was this hopeful peace to be contracted?" said King Richard, painfully suppressing the passion with which his heart was almost bursting.

"These were not intrusted to me, my lord," answered the Knight of the Couchant Leopard. "I delivered them sealed to the hermit."

"And for what hold you this reverend hermit?—for fool, madman, traitor, cr saint?" said Richard.

"His folly, sire," replied the shrewd Scottishman, "I hold to be assumed to win favour and reverence from the Paynimrie, who regard madmen as the inspired of Heaven; at least it seemed to me as exhibited only occasionally, and not as mixing, like naturaly folly, with the general tenor of his mind."

"Shrewdly replied," said the monarch, throwing himself back on his couch, from which he had half-raised himself. — "Now of his penitence?"

"His penitence," continued Kenneth, "appears to me sincere, and the fruits of remorse for some dreadful crime, for which he seems, in his own opinion, condemned to reprobation."

"And for his policy?" said King Richard.

"Methinks, my lord," said the Scottish knight, " he despairs of the security of Palestine, as of his own salvation, by any means short of a miracle —at least since the arm of Richard of England hath ceased to strike for it."

"And, therefore, the coward policy of this hermit is like that of these miserable princes, who, forgetful of their knighthood and their faith, are only resolved and determined when the question is retreat, and, rather than go forward against an armed Saracen, would trample in their flight over a dying ally!"

"Might I so far presume, my Lord King," said the Scottish knight," this discourse but heats your disease, the enemy from which Christendom dreads more evil, than from armed hosts of infidels."

The countenance of King Richard was, indeed, more flushed, and his action became more feverishly vehement, as, with clenched hand, expanded arm, and flashing eyes, he seemed at once to suffer under bodily pain, and at the same time under vexation of mind, while his high spirit led him to speak on, as if in contempt of both.

"You can flatter, Sir Knight," he said, "but you escape me not. I must know more from you than you have yet told me. Saw you my royal consort when at Engaddi?"

"To my knowledge — no, my lord," replied Sir Kenneth, with considerable perturbation; for he remembered the midnight procession in the chapel of the rocks.

"I ask you," said the King, in a sterner voice, "whether you were not in the chapel of the Carmelite nuns at Engaddi, and there saw Berengaria, Queen of England, and the ladies of her Court, who went thither on pilgrimage?"

"My lord," said Sir Kenneth, "I will speak the truth as in the confessional. In a subterranean chapel, to which the anchorite conducted me, I beheld a choir of ladies do homage to a relic of the highest sanctity; but as I saw not their faces, nor heard their voices, unless in the hymns which they chanted, I cannot tell whether the Queen of England was of the bevy."

"And was there no one of these ladies known to you?"

Sir Kenneth stood silent.

"I ask you," said Richard, raising himself on his elbow, "as a knight and a gentleman, and I shall know by your answer how you value either character — did you, or did you not, know any lady amongst that band of worshippers?"

"My lord," said Kenneth, not without much hesitation, "I might guess."

"And I also may guess," said the King, frowning sternly; "but it is enough. Leopard as you are, Sir Knight, beware tempting the lion's paw. Hark ye — to become enamoured of the moon would be but an act of folly; but to leap from the battlements of a lofty tower, in the wild hope of coming within her sphere, were self-destructive madness."

At this moment some bustling was heard in the outer apartment, and the King, hastily changing to his more natural manner, said, "Enough — begone —speed to De Vaux, and send him hither with the Arabian physician. My life for the faith of the Soldan! Would he but abjure his false law, I would aid him with my sword to drive this scum of French and Austrians from his dominions, and think Palestine as well ruled by him as when her kings were anointed by the decree of Heaven itself."

The Knight of the Leopard retired, and presently afterwards the chamberlain announced a deputation from the Council, who had come to wait on the Majesty of England.

"It is well they allow that I am living yet," was his reply. "Who are the reverend ambassadors?"

"The Grand Master of the Templars, and the Marquis of Montserrat."

"Our brother of France loves not sick-beds," said Richard; "yet, had Philip been ill, I had stood by his couch long since. —Jocelyn, lay me the couch more fairly, it is tumbled like a stormy sea — reach me yonder steel mirror — pass a comb through my hair and beard. They look, indeed, liker a lion's mane than a Christian man's locks — bring water."

"My lord," said the trembling chamberlain, "the leeches say that cold water may be fatal."

"To the foul fiend with the leeches!" replied the monarch; "if they cannot cure me, think you I will allow them to torment me? — There, then"— he said, after having made his ablutions, "admit the worshipful envoys; they will now, I think, scarcely see that disease has made Richard negligent of his person."

The celebrated Master of the Templars was a tall, thin, war-worn man, with a slow yet penetrating eye, and a brow on which a thousand dark intrigues had stamped a portion of their obscurity. At the head of that singular body, to whom their order was every thing, and their individuality nothing — seeking the advancement of its power, even at the hazard of that very religion which the fraternity were originally associated to protect— accused of heresy and witchcraft, although by their character Christian priests—suspected of secret league with the Soldan, though by oath devoted to the protection of the Holy Temple, or its recovery—the whole order, and the whole personal character of its commander, or Grand Master, was a riddle, at the exposition of which most men shuddered. The Grand Master was dressed in his white robes of solemnity, and he bore the *abacus*, a mystic staff of office, the peculiar form of which has given rise to such singular conjectures and commentaries, leading to suspicions that this celebrated fraternity of Christian knights were embodied under the foulest symbols of Paganism.

Conrade of Montserrat had a much more pleasing exterior than the dark and mysterious priest-soldier by whom he was accompanied. He was a handsome man, of middle age, or something past that term, bold in the field, sagacious in council, gay and gallant in times of festivity; but, on the other hand, he was generally accused of versatility, of a narrow and selfish ambition, of a desire to extend his own principality, without regard to the weal of the Latin Kingdom of Palestine, and of seeking his own interest, by private negotiations with Saladin, to the prejudice of the Christian leaguers.

When the usual salutations had been made by these dignitaries, and courteously returned by King Richard, the Marquis of Montserrat commenced an explanation of the motives of their visit, sent, as he said they were, by the anxious Kings and Princes who composed the Council of the Crusaders, to "inquire into the health of their magnanimous ally, the valiant King of England."

"We know the importance in which the Princes of the Council hold our health," replied the English King; "and are well aware how much they must have suffered by suppressing all curiosity concerning it for fourteen days, for fear doubtless, of aggravating our disorder, by showing their anxiety regarding the event."

The flow of the Marquis's eloquence being checked, and he himself thrown into some confusion by this reply, his more austere companion took up the thread of the conversation, and, with as much dry and brief gravity as was consistent with the presence which he addressed, informed the King that they came from the Council, to pray, in the name of Christendom, "that he would not suffer his health to be tampered with by an infidel physician, said to be dispatched by Saladin, until the Council had taken measures to remove or confirm the suspicion, which they at present conceived did attach itself to the mission of such a person."

"Grand Master of the Holy and Valiant Order of Knights Templars, and you, Most Noble Marquis of Montserrat," replied Richard, "if it please you to retire into the adjoining pavilion, you shall presently see what account we make of the tender remonstrances of our royal and princely colleagues in this most religious warfare."

The Marquis and Grand Master retired accordingly; nor had they been many minutes in the outward pavilion when the Eastern physician arrived, accompanied by the Baron of Gilsland and Kenneth of Scotland. The baron, however, was a little later of entering the tent than the other two, stopping, perchance, to issue some orders to the warders without.

As the Arabian physician entered, he made his obeisance, after the Oriental fashion, to the Marquis and Grand Master, whose dignity was apparent, both from their appearance and their bearing. The Grand Master returned the salutation with an expression of disdainful coldness, the Marquis, with the popular courtesy which he habitually practised to men of every rank and nation. There was a pause; for the Scottish knight, waiting for the arrival of De Vaux, presumed not, of his own authority, to enter the tent of the King of England, and, during this interval, the Grand Master sternly demanded of the Moslem,—"Infidel, hast thou the courage to practise thine art upon the person of an anointed sovereign of the Christian host?"

"The sun of Allah," answered the sage, "shines on the Nazarene as well as on the true believer, and his servant dare make no distinction betwixt them, when called on to exercise his art of healing."

"Misbelieving Hakim," said the Grand Master, "or whatsoever they call thee for an unbaptized slave of darkness, dost thou well know, that thou shalt be torn asunder by wild horses should King Richard die under thy charge?"

"That were hard justice," answered the physician: "seeing that I can but use human means, and that the issue is written in the book of light."

"Nay, reverend and valiant Grand Master," said the Marquis of Montserrat, "consider that this learned man is not acquainted with our Christian order, adopted in the fear of God, and for the safety of his anointed. — Be it known unto thee, grave physician, whose skill we doubt not, that your wisest course is to repair to the presence of the illustrious Council of our Holy League, and there to give account and reckoning to such wise and learned leeches as they shall nominate, concerning your means of process and cure of this illustrious patient; so shall you escape all the danger, which, rashly taking such a high matter upon your sole answer, you may else most likely incur."

"My lords," said El Hakim, "I understand you well. But knowledge hath its champions as well as your military art, nay, hath sometimes had its martyrs as well as religion. I have the command of my sovereign, the Soldan Saladin, to heal this Nazarene King, and, with the blessing of the Prophet, I will obey his commands. If I fail, ye wear swords thirsting for the blood of the faithful, and I proffer my body to your weapons. But I will not reason with one uncircumcised upon the virtue of the medicines of which I have obtained knowledge, through the grace of the Prophet, and I pray you interpose no delay between me and my office."

"Who talks of delay?" said the Baron De Vaux, hastily entering the tent; "we have had but too much already.—I salute you, my Lord of Mont-serrat, and you, valiant Grand Master. But I must presently pass with this learned physician to the bedside of my master."

"My lord," said the Marquis, in Norman French, or the language of Ouie, as it was then called, "are you well advised that we came to expostu-late on the part of the Council of the Monarchs and Princes of the Crusade, against the risk of permitting an infidel and Eastern physician to tamper with a health so valuable as that of your master King Richard?"

"Noble Lord Marquis," replied the Englishman, bluntly, "I can neither use many words, nor do I delight in listening to them — moreover, I am much more ready to believe what my eyes have seen, than what my ears have heard. I am satisfied that this heathen can cure the sickness of King Richard, and I believe and trust he will labour to do so. Time is precious. If Mahommed—may God's curse be on him!—stood at the door of the tent, with such fair purpose as this Adonbec el Hakim entertains, I would hold it sin to delay him for a minute.—So, give ye God'en, my lords."

"Nay, but," said Conrade of Montserrat, "the King himself said we should be present when this same physician dealt upon him."

The baron whispered the chamberlain, probably to know whether the Marquis spoke truly, and then replied, "My lords, if you will hold your patience, you are welcome to enter with us; but if you interrupt, by action or threat, this accomplished physician in his duty, be it known, that, with-out respect to your high quality, I will enforce your absence from Richard's tent; for know, I am so well satisfied with the virtue of this man's medi-cines, that were Richard himself to refuse them, by our Lady of Lanercost, I think I could find in my heart to force him to take the means of his cure whether he would or no.—Move onward, El Hakim."

The last word was spoken in the lingua franca, and instantly obeyed by the physician. The Grand Master looked grimly on the unceremonious old soldier, but, on exchanging a glance with the Marquis, smoothed his frown-ing brow as well as he could, and both followed De Vaux and the Arabian into the inner tent, where Richard lay expecting them, with that impatience with which the sick patient watches the step of his physician. Sir Kenneth, whose attendance seemed neither asked nor prohibited, felt himself, by the circumstances in which he stood, entitled to follow these high dignitaries, but, conscious of his inferior power and rank, remained aloof during the scene which took place.

Richard, when they entered his apartment, immediately exclaimed, "So ho! a goodly fellowship come to see Richard take his leap in the dark. — My noble allies, I greet you as the representatives of our assembled league; Richard will again be amongst you in his former fashion, or ye shall bear to the grave what is left of him. — De Vaux, lives he or dies he, thou hast the thanks of thy prince.—There is yet another—but this fever hath wasted my eyesight — what, the bold Scot, who would climb Heaven without a ladder?—he is welcome too.—Come, Sir Hakim, to the work, to the work."

The physician, who had already informed himself of the various symp-toms of the King's illness, now felt his pulse for a long time, and with deep attention, while all around stood silent, and in breathless expectation. The sage next filled a cup with spring water, and dipt into it the small red purse which, as formerly, he took from his bosom. When he seemed to think it sufficiently medicated, he was about to offer it to the sovereign, who prevented him, by saying, "Hold an instant.— Thou hast felt my pulse — let me lay my finger on thine. — I too, as becomes a good knight, know something of thine art."

The Arabian yielded his hand without hesitation, and his long slender dark fingers were, for an instant, enclosed, and almost buried, in the large enfoldment of King Richard's hand.

"His blood beats calm as an infant's"— said the King; "so throb not theirs who poison princes. De Vaux, whether we live or die, dismiss this Hakim with honour and safety—Commend us, friend, to the noble Saladin. Should I die, it is without doubt of his faith — should I live, it will be to thank him as a warrior would desire to be thanked."

He then raised himself in bed, took the cup in his hand, and, turning to the Marquis and the Grand Master, — "Mark what I say, and let my royal brethren pledge me in Cyprus wine — 'To the immortal honour of the first Crusader, who shall strike lance or sword on the gate of Jerusalem; and to the shame and eternal infamy of whomsoever shall turn back from the plough on which he hath laid his hand!'"

He drained the cup to the bottom, resigned it to the Arabian, and sunk back, as if exhausted, upon the cushions which were arranged to receive him. The physician, then, with silent but expressive signs, directed that all should leave the tent excepting himself and De Vaux, whom no remonstrance could induce to withdraw. The apartment was cleared accordingly.

Chapter the Tenth.

And now I will unclasp a secret book.
And, to your quick-conceiving discontent,
I'll read you matter deep and dangerous.
                                    HENRY IV. PART I.

THE Marquis of Montserrat, and the Grand Master of the Knights Templars, stood together in the front of the royal pavilion, within which this singular scene had passed, and beheld a strong guard of bills and bows drawn out to form a circle around it and keep at distance all which might disturb the sleeping monarch. The soldiers wore the downcast, silent, and sullen looks, with which they trail their arms at a funeral, and stepped with such caution that you could not hear a buckler ring, or a sword clatter, though so many men in armour were moving around the tent. They lowered their weapons in deep reverence, as the dignitaries passed through their files, but with the same profound silence.

"There is a change of cheer among these island dogs," said the Grand Master to Conrade, when they had passed Richard's guards. "What hoarse tumult and revel used to be before this pavilion! nought but pitching the bar, hurling the ball, wrestling, roaring of songs, clattering of wine-pots, and quaffing of flagons, among these burly yeomen, as if they were holding some country wake, with a Maypole in the midst of them, instead of a royal standard."

"Mastiffs are a faithful race," said Conrade; "and the King their master has won their love by being ready to wrestle, brawl, or revel amongst the foremost of them whenever the humour seized him."

"He is totally compounded of humours," said the Grand Master.

2 W 2

"Marked you the pledge he gave us, instead of a prayer, over his grace-cup yonder?"

"He would have felt it a grace-cup, and a well spiced one too," said the Marquis, "were Saladin like any other Turk that ever wore turban, or turned him to Mecca at call of the Muezzin. But he affects faith, and honour, and generosity, — as if it were for an unbaptized dog like him to practise the virtuous bearing of a Christian knight! It is said he hath applied to Richard to be admitted within the pale of chivalry."

"By Saint Bernard!" exclaimed the Grand Master, "it were time then to throw off our belts and spurs, Sir Conrade, deface our armorial bearings, and renounce our burgonets, if the highest honour of Christianity were conferred on an unchristened Turk of tenpence."

"You rate the Soldan cheap," replied the Marquis; "yet though he be a likely man, I have seen a better heathen sold for forty pence at the bagnio."

They were now near their horses, which stood at some distance from the royal tent, prancing among the gallant train of esquires and pages by whom they were attended, when Conrade, after a moment's pause, proposed that they should enjoy the coolness of the evening breeze which had arisen, and, dismissing their steeds and attendants, walk homewards to their own quarters, through the lines of the extended Christian camp. The Grand Master assented, and they proceeded to walk together accordingly, avoiding, as if by mutual consent, the more inhabited parts of the canvass city, and tracing the broad esplanade which lay between the tents and the external defences, where they could converse in private, and unmarked, save by the sentinels as they passed them.

They spoke for a time upon the military points and preparations for defence; but this sort of discourse, in which neither seemed to take interest, at length died away, and there was a long pause, which terminated by the Marquis of Montserrat stopping short, like a man who has formed a sudden resolution, and, gazing for some moments on the dark inflexible countenance of the Grand Master, he at length addressed him thus:—"Might it consist with your valour and sanctity, reverend Sir Giles Amaury, I would pray you for once to lay aside the dark vizor which you wear, and to converse with a friend barefaced."

The Templar half smiled.

"There are light-coloured masks," he said, "as well as dark vizors, and the one conceals the natural features as completely as the other."

"Be it so," said the Marquis, putting his hand to his chin, and withdrawing it with the action of one who unmasks himself; "there lies my disguise. And now, what think you, as touching the interests of your own order, of the prospects of this Crusade?"

"This is tearing the veil from *my* thoughts rather than exposing your own," said the Grand Master; "yet I will reply with a parable told to me by a santon of the desert. — 'A certain farmer prayed to Heaven for rain, and murmured when it fell not at his need. To punish his impatience, Allah,' said the santon, 'sent the Euphrates upon his farm, and he was destroyed with all his possessions, even by the granting of his own wishes.'"

"Most truly spoken," said the Marquis Conrade; "would that the ocean had swallowed up nineteen parts of the armaments of these western princes! what remained would better have served the purpose of the Christian nobles of Palestine, the wretched remnant of the Latin Kingdom of Jerusalem. Left to ourselves, we might have bent to the storm, or, moderately supported with money and troops, we might have compelled Saladin to respect our valour, and grant us peace and protection on easy terms. But from the extremity of danger with which this powerful Crusade threatens the Soldan, we cannot suppose, should it pass over, that the Saracen will suffer any one of us to hold possessions or principalities in Syria, far less permit the existence of the Christian military fraternities, from whom they have experienced so much mischief."

"Ay, but," said the Templar, "these adventurous Crusaders may succeed, and again plant the Cross on the bulwarks of Zion."

"And what will that advantage either the Order of the Templars, or Conrade of Montserrat?" said the Marquis.

"You it may advantage," replied the Grand Master. "Conrade of Montserrat might become Conrade King of Jerusalem."

"That sounds like something," said the Marquis, "and yet it rings but hollow.—Godfrey of Bouillon might well choose the crown of thorns for his emblem. Grand Master, I will confess to you I have caught some attachment to the Eastern form of government: A pure and simple monarchy should consist but of king and subjects. Such is the simple and primitive structure — a shepherd and his flock. All this internal chain of feudal dependence is artificial and sophisticated, and I would rather hold the baton of my poor marquisate with a firm gripe, and wield it after my pleasure, than the sceptre of a monarch, to be in effect restrained and curbed by the will of as many proud feudal barons as hold land under the Assize of Jerusalem.* A King should tread freely, Grand Master, and should not be controlled by here a ditch, and there a fence—here a feudal privilege, and there a mail-clad baron, with his sword in his hand to maintain it. To sum the whole, I am aware that Guy de Lusignan's claims to the throne would be preferred to mine, if Richard recovers, and has aught to say in the choice."

"Enough," said the Grand Master; "thou hast indeed convinced me of thy sincerity. Others may hold the same opinions, but few, save Conrade of Montserrat, dared frankly avow that he desires not the restitution of the kingdom of Jerusalem, but rather prefers being master of a portion of its fragments; like the barbarous islanders who labour not for the deliverance of a goodly vessel from the billows, expecting rather to enrich themselves at the expense of the wreck."

"Thou wilt not betray my counsel?" said Conrade, looking sharply and suspiciously. "Know, for certain, that my tongue shall never wrong my head, nor my hand forsake the defence of either. Impeach me if thou wilt —I am prepared to defend myself in the lists against the best Templar who ever laid lance in rest."

"Yet thou start'st somewhat suddenly for so bold a steed," said the Grand Master. "However, I swear to thee by the Holy Temple, which our Order is sworn to defend, that I will keep counsel with thee as a true comrade."

"By which Temple?" said the Marquis of Montserrat, whose love of sarcasm often outran his policy and discretion; "swearest thou by that on the hill of Zion, which was built by King Solomon, or by that symbolical, emblematical edifice, which is said to be spoken of in the councils held in the vaults of your Preceptories, as something which infers the aggrandisement of thy valiant and venerable Order?"

The Templar scowled upon him with an eye of death, but answered calmly, "By whatever Temple I swear, be assured, Lord Marquis, my oath is sacred. —I would I knew how to bind *thee* by one of equal obligation."

"I will swear truth to thee," said the Marquis, laughing, "by the Earl's coronet, which I hope to convert, ere these wars are over, into something better. It feels cold on my brow, that same slight coronal; a duke's cap of maintenance were a better protection against such a night-breeze as now blows, and a king's crown more preferable still, being lined with comfortable ermine and velvet. In a word, our interests bind us together; for think not, Lord Grand Master, that, were these allied Princes to regain Jeru-

---

* The Assizes de Jerusalem were the direst of feudal law, composed by Godfrey of Boulogne, for the government of the Latin kingdom of Palestine, when reconquered from the Saracens. "It was composed with advice of the patriarch and barons, the clergy and laity, and is," says the historian Gibbon, "a precious monument of feudatory jurisprudence, founded upon those principles of freedom which were essential to the system."

salem, and place a king of their own choosing there, they would suffer your Order, any more than my poor marquisate, to retain the independence which we now hold. No, by Our Lady! In such case, the proud Knights of Saint John must again spread plasters, and dress plague-sores, in the hospitals; and you, most puissant and venerable Knights of the Temple, must return to your condition of simple men-at-arms, sleep three on a pallet, and mount two upon one horse, as your present seal still expresses to have been your ancient most simple custom."

"The rank, privileges, and opulence of our Order prevent so much degradation as you threaten," said the Templar, haughtily.

"These are your bane," said Conrade of Montserrat; "and you, as well as I, reverend Grand Master, know, that, were the allied Princes to be successful in Palestine, it would be their first point of policy to abate the independence of your Order, which, but for the protection of our holy father the Pope, and the necessity of employing your valour in the conquest of Palestine, you would long since have experienced. Give them complete success, and you will be flung aside, as the splinters of a broken lance are tossed out of the tilt-yard."

"There may be truth in what you say," said the Templar, darkly smiling; "but what were our hopes should the allies withdraw their forces, and leave Palestine in the grasp of Saladin?"

"Great and assured," replied Conrade; "the Soldan would give large provinces to maintain at his behest a body of well-appointed Frankish lances. In Egypt, in Persia, an hundred such auxiliaries, joined to his own light cavalry, would turn the battle against the most fearful odds. This dependence would be but for a time—perhaps during the life of this enterprising Soldan — but, in the East, empires arise like mushrooms. Suppose him dead, and us strengthened with a constant succession of fiery and adventurous spirits from Europe, what might we not hope to achieve, uncontrolled by these monarchs, whose dignity throws us at present into the shade —and, were they to remain here, and succeed in this expedition, would willingly consign us for ever to degradation and dependence?"

"You say well, my Lord Marquis," said the Grand Master; "and your words find an echo in my bosom. Yet must we be cautious; Philip of France is wise as well as valiant."

"True, and will be therefore the more easily diverted from an expedition, to which, in a moment of enthusiasm, or urged by his nobles, he rashly bound himself. He is jealous of King Richard, his natural enemy, and longs to return to prosecute plans of ambition nearer to Paris than Palestine. Any fair pretence will serve him for withdrawing from a scene, in which he is aware he is wasting the force of his kingdom."

"And the Duke of Austria?" said the Templar.

"Oh, touching the Duke," returned Conrade, "his self-conceit and folly lead him to the same conclusions as do Philip's policy and wisdom. He conceives himself, God help the while, ungratefully treated, because men's mouths—even those of his own *minne-singers*,*—are filled with the praises of King Richard, whom he fears and hates, and in whose harm he would rejoice, like those unbred dastardly curs, who, if the foremost of the pack is hurt by the gripe of the wolf, are much more likely to assail the sufferer from behind, than to come to his assistance. — But wherefore tell I this to thee, save to show that I am in sincerity in desiring that this league be broken up, and the country freed of these great monarchs with their hosts? and thou well knowest, and hast thyself seen, how all the princes of influence and power, one alone excepted, are eager to enter into treaty with the Soldan."

"I acknowledge it," said the Templar; "he were blind that had not seen

---

* The German minstrels were so termed.

this in their last deliberations. But lift yet thy mask an inch higher, and tell me thy real reason for pressing upon the Council that Northern Englishman, or Scot, or whatever you call yonder Knight of the Leopard, to carry their proposals for a treaty?"

"There was a policy in it," replied the Italian; "his character of native of Britain was sufficient to meet what Saladin required, who knew him to belong to the band of Richard, while his character of Scot, and certain other personal grudges which I wot of, rendered it most unlikely that our envoy should, on his return, hold any communication with the sick-bed of Richard, to whom his presence was ever unacceptable."

"Oh, too fine-spun policy," said the Grand Master; "trust me, that Italian spiders' webs will never bind this unshorn Samson of the Isle—well if you can do it with new cords, and those of the toughest. See you not that the envoy whom you have selected so carefully, hath brought us in this physician, the means of restoring the lion-hearted, bull-necked Englishman, to prosecute his Crusading enterprise; and, so soon as he is able once more to rush on, which of the princes dare hold back?—They must follow him for very shame, although they would march under the banner of Satan as soon."

"Be content," said Conrade of Montserrat; "ere this physician, if he work by any thing short of miraculous agency, can accomplish Richard's cure, it may be possible to put some open rupture betwixt the Frenchman, at least the Austrian, and his allies of England, so that the breach shall be irreconcilable; and Richard may arise from his bed, perhaps to command his own native troops, but never again, by his sole energy, to wield the force of the whole Crusade."

"Thou art a willing archer," said the Templar; "but, Conrade of Montserrat, thy bow is over slack to carry an arrow to the mark."

He then stopt short, cast a suspicious glance to see that no one overheard him, and taking Conrade by the hand, pressed it eagerly as he looked the Italian in the face, and repeated slowly,—"Richard arise from his bed, say'st thou?—Conrade, he must never arise!"

The Marquis of Montserrat started—"What!—spoke you of Richard of England—of Cœur de Lion—the champion of Christendom?"

His cheek turned pale, and his knees trembled as he spoke. The Templar looked at him, with his iron visage contorted into a smile of contempt.

"Know'st thou what thou look'st like, Sir Conrade, at this moment? Not like the politic and valiant Marquis of Montserrat—not like him who would direct the Council of Princes, and determine the fate of empires—but like a novice, who, stumbling upon a conjuration in his master's book of gramarye, has raised the devil when he least thought of it, and now stands terrified at the spirit which appears before him."

"I grant you," said Conrade, recovering himself, "that—unless some other sure road could be discovered—thou hast hinted at that which leads most direct to our purpose. But, blessed Mary! we shall become the curse of all Europe, the malediction of every one, from the Pope on his throne to the very beggar at the church-gate, who, ragged and leprous, in the last extremity of human wretchedness, shall bless himself that he is neither Giles Amaury, nor Conrade of Montserrat."

"If thou takest it thus," said the Grand Master, with the same composure which characterized him all through this remarkable dialogue, "let us hold there has nothing passed between us—that we have spoken in our sleep—have awakened, and the vision is gone."

"It never can depart," answered Conrade.

"Visions of ducal crowns and kingly diadems are, indeed, somewhat tenacious of their place in the imagination," replied the Grand Master.

"Well," answered Conrade, "let me, but first try to break peace between Austria and England."

They parted.—Conrade remained standing still upon the spot, and watching the flowing white cloak of the Templar, as he stalked slowly away, and gradually disappeared amid the fast-sinking darkness of the Oriental night. Proud, ambitious, unscrupulous, and politic, the Marquis of Montserrat was yet not cruel by nature. He was a voluptuary and an epicurean, and, like many who profess this character, was averse, even upon selfish motives, from inflicting pain, or witnessing acts of cruelty; and he retained also a general sense of respect for his own reputation, which sometimes supplies the want of the better principles by which reputation is to be maintained.

" I have," he said, as his eyes still watched the point at which he had seen the last slight wave of the Templar's mantle,—" I have, in truth, raised the devil with a vengeance ! Who would have thought this stern ascetic Grand Master, whose whole fortune and misfortune is merged in that of his order, would be willing to do more for its advancement, than I who labour for my own interest ? To check this wild Crusade was my motive, indeed, but I durst not think on the ready mode which this determined priest has dared to suggest—yet it is the surest—perhaps even the safest."

Such were the Marquis's meditations, when his muttered soliloquy was broken by a voice at a little distance, which proclaimed with the emphatic tone of a herald,—" Remember the Holy Sepulchre !"

The exhortation was echoed from post to post, for it was the duty of the sentinels to raise this cry from time to time upon their periodical watch, that the host of the Crusaders might always have in their remembrance the purpose of their being in arms. But though Conrade was familiar with the custom, and had heard the warning voice on all former occasions as a matter of habit; yet it came at the present moment so strongly in contact with his own train of thought, that it seemed a voice from Heaven warning him against the iniquity which his heart meditated. He looked around anxiously, as if, like the patriarch of old, though from very different circumstances, he was expecting some ram caught in a thicket — some substitution for the sacrifice, which his comrade proposed to offer, not to the Supreme Being, but to the Moloch of their own ambition. As he looked, the broad folds of the ensign of England, heavily distending itself to the failing night-breeze, caught his eye. It was displayed upon an artificial mound, nearly in the midst of the camp, which perhaps of old some Hebrew chief or champion had chosen as a memorial of his place of rest. If so, the name was now forgotten, and the Crusaders had christened it Saint George's Mount, because from that commanding height the banner of England was supereminently displayed, as if an emblem of sovereignty over the many distinguished, noble, and even royal ensigns, which floated in lower situations.

A quick intellect like that of Conrade catches ideas from the glance of a moment. A single look on the standard seemed to dispel the uncertainty of mind which had affected him. He walked to his pavilion with the hasty and determined step of one who has adopted a plan which he is resolved to achieve, dismissed the almost princely train who waited to attend him, and, as he committed himself to his couch, muttered his amended resolution, that the milder means are to be tried before the more desperate are resorted to.

" To-morrow," he said, " I sit at the board of the Archduke of Austria —we will see what can be done to advance our purpose, before prosecuting the dark suggestions of this Templar."

Chapter the Eleventh.

One thing is certain in our Northern land.
Allow that birth, or valour, wealth, or wit,
Give each precedence to their possessor,
Envy, that follows on such eminence,
As comes the lyme-hound on the roebuck's trace,
Shall pull them down each one.
SIR DAVID LINDSAY.

LEOPOLD, Grand Duke of Austria, was the first possessor of that noble country to whom the princely rank belonged. He had been raised to the ducal sway in the German empire, on account of his near relationship to the Emperor, Henry the Stern, and held under his government the finest provinces which are watered by the Danube. His character has been stained in history, on account of one action of violence and perfidy, which arose out of these very transactions in the Holy Land; and yet the shame of having made Richard a prisoner, when he returned through his dominions, unattended, and in disguise, was not one which flowed from Leopold's natural disposition. He was rather a weak and a vain, than an ambitious or tyrannical prince. His mental powers resembled the qualities of his person. He was tall, strong, and handsome, with a complexion in which red and white was strongly contrasted, and had long flowing locks of fair hair. But there was an awkwardness in his gait, which seemed as if his size was not animated by energy sufficient to put in motion such a mass; and in the same manner, wearing the richest dresses, it always seemed as if they became him not. As a prince, he appeared too little familiar with his own dignity, and being often at a loss how to assert his authority when the occasion demanded it, he frequently thought himself obliged to recover, by acts and expressions of ill-timed violence, the ground which might have been easily and gracefully maintained by a little more presence of mind in the beginning of the controversy.

Not only were these deficiencies visible to others, but the Archduke himself could not but sometimes entertain a painful consciousness that he was not altogether fit to maintain and assert the high rank which he had acquired; and to this was joined the strong, and sometimes the just suspicion, that others esteemed him lightly accordingly.

When he first joined the Crusade, with a most princely attendance, Leopold had desired much to enjoy the friendship and intimacy of Richard, and had made such advances towards cultivating his regard, as the King of England ought, in policy, to have received and answered. But the Archduke, though not deficient in bravery, was so infinitely inferior to Cœur de Lion in that ardour of mind which wooed danger as a bride, that the King very soon held him in a certain degree of contempt. Richard, also, as a Norman Prince, a people with whom temperance was habitual, despised the inclination of the German for the pleasures of the table, and particularly his liberal indulgence in the use of wine. For these and other personal reasons, the King of England very soon looked upon the Austrian Prince with feelings of contempt, which he was at no pains to conceal or modify, and which, therefore, were speedily remarked, and returned with deep hatred, by the suspicious Leopold. The discord between them was fanned by the secret and politic arts of Philip of France, one of the most sagacious monarchs of his time, who, dreading the fiery and overbearing character of Richard, considering him as his natural rival, and feeling offended, moreover, at the dictatorial manner in which he, a vassal of France for his continental domains, conducted himself towards his liege lord, endeavoured to strengthen his own party, and weaken that of Richard, by uniting the Crusading princes of inferior degree, in resistance to what he termed the usurping authority of the King of England. Such was the state of politics and opinions entertained by the Archduke of Austria, when Conrade of Montserrat resolved upon employing his jealousy of England as the means of dissolving, or loosening at least, the league of the Crusaders.

The time which he chose for his visit was noon, and the pretence, to present the Archduke with some choice Cyprus wine which had lately fallen into his hands, and discuss its comparative merits with those of Hungary and of the Rhine. An intimation of his purpose was of course answered by a courteous invitation to partake of the Archducal meal, and every effort was used to render it fitting the splendour of a sovereign prince. Yet, the refined taste of the Italian saw more cumbrous profusion, than elegance or splendour, in the display of provisions under which the board groaned.

The Germans, though still possessing the martial and frank character of their ancestors, who subdued the Roman empire, had retained withal no slight tinge of their barbarism. The practices and principles of chivalry were not carried to such a nice pitch amongst them, as amongst the French and English knights, nor were they strict observers of the prescribed rules of society, which among those nations were supposed to express the height of civilization. Sitting at the table of the Archduke, Conrade was at once stunned and amused, with the clang of Teutonic sounds assaulting his ears on all sides, notwithstanding the solemnity of a princely banquet. Their dress seemed equally fantastic to him, many of the Austrian nobles retaining their long beards, and almost all of them wearing short jerkins of various colours, cut, and flourished, and fringed, in a manner not common in Western Europe.

Numbers of dependents, old and young, attended in the pavilion, mingled at times in the conversation, received from their masters the relics of the entertainment, and devoured them as they stood behind the backs of the company. Jesters, dwarfs, and minstrels, were there in unusual numbers, and more noisy and intrusive than they were permitted to be in better regulated society. As they were allowed to share freely in the wine, which flowed round in large quantities, their licensed tumult was the more excessive.

All this while, and in the midst of a clamour and confusion, which would better have become a German tavern during a fair, than the tent of a sovereign prince, the Archduke was waited upon with a minuteness of form and observance, which showed how anxious he was to maintain rigidly the state and character to which his elevation had entitled him. He was served on the knee, and only by pages of noble blood, fed upon plate of silver, and drank his Tokay and Rhenish wines from a cup of gold. His ducal mantle was splendidly adorned with ermine, his coronet might have equalled in value a royal crown, and his feet, cased in velvet shoes (the length of which, peaks included, might be two feet), rested upon a footstool of solid silver. But it served partly to intimate the character of the man, that, although desirous to show attention to the Marquis of Montserrat, whom he had courteously placed at his right hand, he gave much more of his attention to his *spruch-sprecher*, that is, his man of conversation, or *sayer of sayings*, who stood behind the Duke's right shoulder.

This personage was well attired, in a coat and doublet of black velvet, the last of which was decorated with various silver and gold coins, stitched upon it, in memory of the munificent princes who had conferred them, and bearing a short staff, to which also bunches of silver coins were attached by rings, which he jingled by way of attracting attention, when he was about to say any thing which he judged worthy of it. This person's capacity in the household of the Archduke, was somewhat betwixt that of a minstrel and a counsellor; he was by turns a flatterer, a poet, and an orator; and those who desired to be well with the Duke, generally studied to gain the good-will of the *spruch-sprecher*.

Lest too much of this officer's wisdom should become tiresome, the Duke's other shoulder was occupied by his *hoff-narr*, or court jester, called Jonas Schwanker, who made almost as much noise with his fool's-cap, bells, and bauble, as did the orator, or man of talk, with his jingling baton.

These two persons threw out grave and comic nonsense alternately, while their master, laughing or applauding them himself, yet carefully watched the countenance of his noble guest, to discern what impressions so accomplished a cavalier received from this display of Austrian eloquence and wit. It is hard to say whether the man of wisdom or the man of folly contributed most to the amusement of the party, or stood highest in the estimation of their princely master; but the sallies of both seemed excellently well received. Sometimes they became rivals for the conversation, and clanged their flappers in emulation of each other, with a most alarming contention; but, in general, they seemed on such good terms, and so accustomed to support each other's play, that the *spruch-sprecher* often condescended to follow up the jester's witticisms with an explanation, to render them more obvious to the capacity of the audience; so that his wisdom became a sort of commentary on the buffoon's folly. And sometimes, in requital, the *hoff-narr*, with a pithy jest, wound up the conclusion of the orator's tedious harangue.

Whatever his real sentiments might be, Conrade took especial care that his countenance should express nothing but satisfaction with what he heard, and smiled or applauded, as zealously, to all appearance, as the Archduke himself, at the solemn folly of the *spruch-sprecher*, and the gibbering wit of the fool. In fact, he watched carefully until the one or other should introduce some topic, favourable to the purpose which was uppermost in his mind.

It was not long ere the King of England was brought on the carpet by the jester, who had been accustomed to consider Dickon of the Broom (which irreverent epithet he substituted for Richard Plantagenet) as a subject of mirth, acceptable and inexhaustible. The orator, indeed, was silent, and it was only when applied to by Conrade, that he observed, "The *genista*, or broom-plant was an emblem of humility; and it would be well, when those who wore it would remember the warning."

The allusion to the illustrious badge of Plantagenet was thus rendered sufficiently manifest, and Jonas Schwanker observed, that they who humbled themselves had been exalted with a vengeance.

"Honour unto whom honour is due," answered the Marquis of Montserrat; "we have all had some part in these marches and battles, and methinks other princes might share a little in the renown which Richard of England engrosses amongst minstrels and *minne-singers*. Has no one of the Joyeuse science here present a song in praise of the royal Archduke of Austria, our princely entertainer?"

Three minstrels emulously stepped forward with voice and harp. Two were silenced with difficulty by the *spruch-sprecher*, who seemed to act as master of the revels, and a hearing was at length procured for the poet preferred, who sung, in high German, stanzas which may be thus translated:—

> What brave chief shall head the forces,
>   Where the red-cross legions gather?
> Best of horsemen, best of horses,
>   Highest head and fairest feather.

Here the orator, jingling his staff, interrupted the bard to intimate to the party, what they might not have inferred from the description, that their royal host was the party indicated, and a full-crowned goblet went round to the acclamation — *Hoch lebe der Herzog Leopold!* Another stanza followed.

> Ask not Austria why, midst princes,
>   Still her banner rises highest;
> Ask as well the strong-wing'd eagle,
>   Why to Heaven he soars the nighest.

2 x

"The eagle," said the expounder of dark sayings, "is the cognizance of our noble lord the Archduke — of his royal Grace, I would say — and the eagle flies the highest and nearest to the sun of all the feathered creation."

"The lion hath taken a spring above the eagle," said Conrade, carelessly.

The Archduke reddened, and fixed his eyes on the speaker, while the *spruch-sprecher* answered, after a minute's consideration, "The Lord Marquis will pardon me—a lion cannot fly above an eagle, because no lion hath got wings."

"Except the Lion of Saint Mark," responded the jester.

"That is the Venetian banner," said the Duke; "but assuredly, that amphibious race, half nobles, half merchants, will not dare to place their rank in comparison with ours?"

"Nay, it was not of the Venetian lion that I spoke," said the Marquis of Montserrat; "but of the three lions passant of England—formerly, it is said, they were leopards, but now they are become lions at all points, and must take precedence of beast, fish, or fowl, or wo worth the gainstander."

"Mean you seriously, my lord?" said the Austrian, now considerably flushed with wine; "think you that Richard of England asserts any pre-eminence over the free sovereigns who have been his voluntary allies in this Crusade?"

"I know not but from circumstances," answered Conrade; "yonder hangs his banner alone in the midst of our camp, as if he were king and generalissimo of our whole Christian army."

"And do you endure this so patiently, and speak of it so coldly?" said the Archduke.

"Nay, my lord," answered Conrade, "it cannot concern the poor Marquis of Montserrat to contend against an injury, patiently submitted to by such potent princes as Philip of France and Leopold of Austria. What dishonour you are pleased to submit to, cannot be a disgrace to me."

Leopold closed his fist, and struck on the table with violence.

"I have told Philip of this," he said; "I have often told him that it was our duty to protect the inferior princes against the usurpation of this islander — but he answers me ever with cold respects of their relations together as suzerain and vassal, and that it were impolitic in him to make an open breach at this time and period."

"The world knows that Philip is wise," said Conrade, "and will judge his submission to be policy. — Yours, my lord, you can yourself alone account for; but I doubt not you have deep reasons for submitting to English domination."

"*I* submit!" said Leopold, indignantly — "*I*, the Archduke of Austria, so important and vital a limb of the Holy Roman empire—*I* submit myself to this King of half an island—this grandson of a Norman bastard! — No, by Heaven! The camp, and all Christendom, shall see that I know how to right myself, and whether I yield ground one inch to the English bandog. — Up, my lieges and merry-men, up and follow me! We will — and that without losing one instant—place the eagle of Austria, where she shall float as high as ever floated the cognizance of king or kaisar."

With that he started from his seat, and, amidst the tumultuous cheering of his guests and followers, made for the door of the pavilion, and seized his own banner, which stood pitched before it.

"Nay, my lord," said Conrade, affecting to interfere, "it will blemish your wisdom to make an affray in the camp at this hour, and perhaps it is better to submit to the usurpation of England a little longer than to ——"

"Not an hour — not a moment longer," vociferated the Duke; and, with the banner in his hand, and followed by his shouting guests and attendants, marched hastily to the central mount, from which the banner of England floated, and laid his hand on the standard-spear, as if to pluck it from the ground.

"My master, my dear master!" said Jonas Schwanker, throwing his arms about the Duke — "take heed — lions have teeth ——"

"And eagles have claws," said the Duke, not relinquishing his hold on the banner-staff, yet hesitating to pull it from the ground.

The speaker of sentences, notwithstanding such was his occupation, had nevertheless some intervals of sound sense. He clashed his staff loudly, and Leopold, as if by habit, turned his head towards his man of counsel.

"The eagle is king among the fowls of the air," said the *spruch-sprecher*, "as is the lion among the beasts of the field — each has his dominion, separated as wide as England and Germany — do thou, noble eagle, no dishonour to the princely lion, but let your banners remain floating in peace side by side."

Leopold withdrew his hand from the banner-spear, and looked round for Conrade of Montserrat, but he saw him not; for the Marquis, so soon as he saw the mischief afoot, had withdrawn himself from the crowd, taking care, in the first place, to express before several neutral persons his regret, that the Archduke should have chosen the hours after dinner to avenge any wrong of which he might think he had a right to complain. Not seeing his guest, to whom he wished more particularly to have addressed himself, the Archduke said aloud, that, having no wish to breed dissension in the army of the Cross, he did but vindicate his own privileges and right to stand upon an equality with the King of England, without desiring, as he might have done, to advance his banner, which he derived from Emperors, his progenitors, above that of a mere descendant of the Counts of Anjou; and, in the meantime, he commanded a cask of wine to be brought hither and pierced, for regaling the bystanders, who, with tap of drum and sound of music, quaffed many a carouse round the Austrian standard.

This disorderly scene was not acted without a degree of noise, which alarmed the whole camp.

The critical hour had arrived, at which the physician, according to the rules of his art, had predicted that his royal patient might be awakened with safety, and the spunge had been applied for that purpose; and the leech had not made many observations ere he assured the Baron of Gilsland that the fever had entirely left his sovereign, and that such was the happy strength of his constitution, it would not be even necessary, as in most cases, to give a second dose of the powerful medicine. Richard himself seemed to be of the same opinion, for, sitting up and rubbing his eyes, he demanded of De Vaux what present sum of money was in the royal coffers.

The baron could not exactly inform him of the amount.

"It matters not," said Richard; "be it greater or smaller, bestow it all on this learned leech, who hath, I trust, given me back again to the service of the Crusade. If it be less than a thousand bezants, let him have jewels to make it up."

"I sell not the wisdom with which Allah has endowed me," answered the Arabian physician; "and be it known to you, great Prince, that the divine medicine, of which you have partaken, would lose its effects in my unworthy hands, did I exchange its virtues either for gold or diamonds."

"The physician refuseth a gratuity!" said De Vaux to himself. "This is more extraordinary than his being an hundred years old."

"Thomas de Vaux," said Richard, "thou knowest no courage but what belongs to the sword, no bounty and virtue but what are used in chivalry — I tell thee that this Moor, in his independence, might set an example to them who account themselves the flower of knighthood."

"It is reward enough for me," said the Moor, folding his arms on his bosom, and maintaining an attitude at once respectful and dignified, "that so great a King as the Melech Ric* should thus speak of his servant.—But

---

* Richard was thus called by the Eastern nations.

now, let me pray you again to compose yourself on your couch; for though I think there needs no farther repetition of the divine draught, yet injury might ensue from any too early exertion, ere your strength be entirely restored."

"I must obey thee, Hakim," said the King; "yet believe me, my bosom feels so free from the wasting fire, which for so many days hath scorched it, that I care not how soon I expose it to a brave man's lance.—But hark! what mean these shouts, and that distant music, in the camp? Go, Thomas de Vaux, and make inquiry."

"It is the Archduke Leopold," said De Vaux, returning after a minute's absence, "who makes with his pot-companions some procession through the camp."

"The drunken fool!" exclaimed King Richard, "can he not keep his brutal inebriety within the veil of his pavilion, that he must needs show his shame to all Christendom?—What say you, Sir Marquis?" he added, addressing himself to Conrade of Montserrat, who at that moment entered the tent.

"Thus much, honoured Prince," answered the Marquis, "that I delight to see your Majesty so well, and so far recovered; and that is a long speech for any one to make who has partaken of the Duke of Austria's hospitality."

"What! you have been dining with the Teutonic wine-skin," said the monarch; "and what frolic has he found out to cause all this disturbance? Truly, Sir Conrade, I have still held you so good a reveller, that I wonder at your quitting the game."

De Vaux, who had got a little behind the King, now exerted himself, by look and sign, to make the Marquis understand that he should say nothing to Richard of what was passing without. But Conrade understood not, or heeded not, the prohibition.

"What the Archduke does," he said, "is of little consequence to any one, least of all to himself, since he probably knows not what he is acting—yet, to say truth, it is a gambol I should not like to share in, since he is pulling down the banner of England from Saint George's Mount in the centre of the camp yonder, and displaying his own in its stead."

"WHAT say'st thou?" said the King, in a tone which might have waked the dead.

"Nay," said the Marquis, "let it not chafe your Highness, that a fool should act according to his folly——"

"Speak not to me," said Richard, springing from his couch, and casting on his clothes with a despatch which seemed marvellous—"speak not to me, Lord Marquis!—De Multon, I command thee speak not a word to me—he that breathes but a syllable, is no friend to Richard Plantagenet.—Hakim, be silent, I charge thee!"

All this while the King was hastily clothing himself, and, with the last word, snatched his sword from the pillar of the tent, and without any other weapon, or calling any attendance, he rushed out of the tent. Conrade, holding up his hands, as if in astonishment, seemed willing to enter into conversation with De Vaux, but Sir Thomas pushed rudely past him, and calling to one of the royal equerries, said hastily,—"Fly to Lord Salisbury's quarters, and let him get his men together, and follow me instantly to Saint George's Mount. Tell him the King's fever has left his blood, and settled in his brain."

Imperfectly heard, and still more imperfectly comprehended, by the startled attendant whom De Vaux addressed thus hastily, the equerry and his fellow-servants of the royal chamber rushed hastily into the tents of the neighbouring nobility, and quickly spread an alarm, as general as the cause seemed vague, through the whole British forces. The English soldiers, waked in alarm from that noon-day rest which the heat of the climate had taught them to enjoy as a luxury, hastily asked each other the cause of the tumult, and, without waiting an answer, supplied, by the force of their own fancy, the want of information. Some said the Saracens were in the camp, some that the King's life was attempted, some that he had died of the fever the preceding night, many that he was assassinated by the Duke of Austria. The nobles and officers, at an equal loss with the common men to ascertain the real cause of the disorder, laboured only to get their followers under arms and under authority, lest their rashness should occasion some great misfortune to the Crusading army. The English trumpets sounded loud, shrill, and continuously. The alarm-cry of "Bows and bills — bows and bills!" was heard from quarter to quarter, again and again shouted, and again and again answered by the presence of the ready warriors, and their national invocation, "Saint George for Merry England!"

The alarm went through the nearest quarter of the camp, and men of all the various nations assembled, where, perhaps, every people in Christendom had their representatives, flew to arms, and drew together under circumstances of general confusion, of which they knew neither the cause nor the object. It was, however, lucky, amid a scene so threatening, that the Earl of Salisbury, while he hurried after De Vaux's summons, with a few only of the readiest English men-at-arms, directed the rest of the English host to be drawn up and kept under arms, to advance to Richard's succour if necessity should require, but in fit array, and under due command, and not with the tumultuary haste which their own alarm, and zeal for the King's safety, might have dictated.

In the meanwhile, without regarding for one instant the shouts, the cries, the tumult, which began to thicken around him, Richard, with his dress in the last disorder, and his sheathed blade under his arm, pursued his way with the utmost speed, followed only by De Vaux, and one or two household servants, to Saint George's Mount.

He outsped even the alarm which his impetuosity only had excited, and passed the quarter of his own gallant troops of Normandy, Poitou, Gascony, and Anjou, before the disturbance had reached them, although the noise accompanying the German revel had induced many of the soldiery to get on foot to listen. The handful of Scots were also quartered in the vicinity, nor had they been disturbed by the uproar. But the King's person, and his haste, were both remarked by the Knight of the Leopard, who, aware that danger must be afoot, and hastening to share in it, snatched his shield and sword, and united himself to De Vaux, who with some difficulty kept with his impatient and fiery master. De Vaux answered a look of curiosity, which the Scottish knight directed towards him, with a shrug of his broad shoulders, and they continued, side by side, to pursue Richard's steps.

The King was soon at the foot of Saint George's Mount, the sides as well as platform of which were now surrounded and crowded, partly by those belonging to the Duke of Austria's retinue, who were celebrating, with shouts of jubilee, the act which they considered as an assertion of national honour; partly by bystanders of different nations, whom dislike to the English, or mere curiosity, had assembled together, to witness the end of these extraordinary proceedings. Through this disorderly troop Richard burst his way, like a goodly ship under full sail, which cleaves her forcible passage through the rolling billows, and heeds not that they unite after her passage, and roar upon her stern.

The summit of the eminence was a small level space, on which were pitched the rival banners, surrounded still by the Archduke's friends and retinue. In the midst of the circle was Leopold himself, still contemplating with self-satisfaction the deed he had done, and still listening to the shouts of applause which his partisans bestowed with no sparing breath. While he was in this state of self-gratulation, Richard burst into the circle, at tended, indeed, only by two men, but in his own headlong energies an irresistible host.

"Who has dared," he said, laying his hands upon the Austrian standard, and speaking in a voice like the sound which precedes an earthquake : "who has dared to place this paltry rag beside the banner of England ?"

The Archduke wanted not personal courage, and it was impossible he could hear this question without reply. Yet, so much was he troubled and surprised by the unexpected arrival of Richard, and affected by the general awe inspired by his ardent and unyielding character, that the demand was twice repeated, in a tone which seemed to challenge heaven and earth, ere the Archduke replied with such firmness as he could command, "It was I, Leopold of Austria."

"Then shall Leopold of Austria," replied Richard, "presently see the rate at which his banner and his pretensions are held by Richard of England."

So saying, he pulled up the standard-spear, splintered it to pieces, threw the banner itself on the ground, and placed his foot upon it.

"Thus," said he, "I trample on the banner of Austria—Is there a knight among your Teutonic chivalry, dare impeach my deed ?"

There was a momentary silence; but there are no braver men than the Germans.

"I," and "I," and "I," was heard from several knights of the Duke's followers : and he himself added his voice to those which accepted the King of England's defiance.

"Why do we dally thus ?" said the Earl Wallenrode, a gigantic warrior from the frontiers of Hungary: "Brethren, and noble gentlemen, this man's foot is on the honour of your country — Let us rescue it from violation, and down with the pride of England !"

So saying, he drew his sword, and struck at the King a blow which might have proved fatal, had not the Scot intercepted and caught it upon his shield.

"I have sworn," said King Richard — and his voice was heard above all the tumult, which now waxed wild and loud — "never to strike one whose shoulder bears the cross ; therefore live, Wallenrode—but live to remember Richard of England."

As he spoke, he grasped the tall Hungarian round the waist, and, unmatched in wrestling, as in other military exercises, hurled him backwards with such violence that the mass flew as if discharged from a military engine, not only through the ring of spectators who witnessed the extraordinary scene, but over the edge of the mount itself, down the steep side of which Wallenrode rolled headlong, until, pitching at length upon his shoulder, he dislocated the bone, and lay like one dead. This almost supernatural display of strength did not encourage either the Duke or any of his followers, to renew a personal contest so inauspiciously commenced. Those who stood farthest back did, indeed, clash their swords, and cry out, "Cut the island mastiff to pieces !" but those who were nearer, veiled, perhaps, their personal fears under an affected regard for order, and cried, for the most part, "Peace ! peace ! the peace of the Cross—the peace of Holy Church, and our Father the Pope !"

These various cries of the assailants, contradicting each other, showed their irresolution ; while Richard, his foot still on the archducal banner, glared around him, with an eye that seemed to seek an enemy, and from which the angry nobles shrunk appalled, as from the threatened grasp of a lion. De Vaux and the Knight of the Leopard kept their places beside him ; and though the swords which they held were still sheathed, it was plain that they were prompt to protect Richard's person to the very last, and their size and remarkable strength plainly showed the defence would be a desperate one.

Salisbury and his attendants were also now drawing near, with bills and partisans brandished, and bows already bended.

At this moment, King Philip of France, attended by one or two of his nobles, came on the platform to inquire the cause of the disturbance, and made gestures of surprise at finding the King of England raised from his sick-bed, and confronting their common ally the Duke of Austria, in such a menacing and insulting posture. Richard himself blushed at being discovered by Philip, whose sagacity he respected as much as he disliked his person, in an attitude neither becoming his character as a monarch, nor as a Crusader; and it was observed that he withdrew his foot, as if accidentally, from the dishonoured banner, and exchanged his look of violent emotion for one of affected composure and indifference. Leopold also struggled to attain some degree of calmness, mortified as he was by having been seen by Philip in the act of passively submitting to the insults of the fiery King of England.

Possessed of many of those royal qualities for which he was termed by his subjects the August, Philip might be termed the Ulysses, as Richard was indisputably the Achilles, of the Crusade. The King of France was sagacious, wise, deliberate in council, steady and calm in action, seeing clearly, and steadily pursuing, the measures most for the interest of his kingdom — dignified and royal in his deportment, brave in person, but a politician rather than a warrior. The Crusade would have been no choice of his own, but the spirit was contagious, and the expedition was enforced upon him by the church, and by the unanimous wish of his nobility. In any other situation, or in a milder age, his character might have stood higher than that of the adventurous Cœur de Lion. But in the Crusade, itself an undertaking wholly irrational, sound reason was the quality, of all others, least estimated, and the chivalric valour which both the age and the enterprise demanded, was considered as debased, if mingled with the least touch of discretion. So that the merit of Philip, compared with that of his haughty rival, showed like the clear but minute flame of a lamp, placed near the glare of a huge blazing torch, which, not possessing half the utility, makes ten times more impression on the eye. Philip felt his inferiority in public opinion, with the pain natural to a high-spirited prince; and it cannot be wondered at if he took such opportunities as offered, for placing his own character in more advantageous contrast with that of his rival. The present seemed one of those occasions, in which prudence and calmness might reasonably expect to triumph over obstinacy and impetuous violence.

"What means this unseemly broil betwixt the sworn brethren of the Cross—the royal Majesty of England and the princely Duke Leopold? How is it possible that those who are the chiefs and pillars of this holy expedition ——"

"A truce with thy remonstrance, France," said Richard, enraged inwardly at finding himself placed on a sort of equality with Leopold, yet not knowing how to resent it,—"this duke, or prince, or pillar, if you will, hath been insolent, and I have chastised him — that is all. Here is a coil, forsooth, because of spurning a hound!"

"Majesty of France," said the Duke, "I appeal to you and every sovereign prince against the foul indignity which I have sustained. This King of England hath pulled down my banner — torn and trampled on it."

"Because he had the audacity to plant it beside mine," said Richard.

"My rank as thine equal entitled me," replied the Duke, imboldened by the presence of Philip.

"Assert such equality for thy person," said King Richard, "and, by Saint George, I will treat thy person as I did thy broidered kerchief there, fit but for the meanest use to which kerchief may be put."

"Nay, but patience, brother of England," said Philip, "and I will presently show Austria that he is wrong in this matter. — Do not think, noble duke," he continued, "that, in permitting the standard of England to occupy the highest point in our camp, we, the independent sovereigns of the Crusade, acknowledge any inferiority to the royal Richard. It were inconsistent to think so; since even the oriflamme itself—the great banner of France, to which the royal Richard himself, in respect of his French possessions, is but a vassal—holds for the present an inferior place to the Lions of England. But as sworn brethren of the Cross, military pilgrims, who, laying aside the pomp and pride of this world, are hewing with our swords the way to the Holy Sepulchre, I myself, and the other princes, have renounced to King Richard, from respect to his high renown and great feats of arms, that precedence, which elsewhere, and upon other motives, would not have been yielded. I am satisfied, that when your royal grace of Austria shall have considered this, you will express sorrow for having placed your banner on this spot, and that the royal Majesty of England will then give satisfaction for the insult he has offered."

The *spruch-sprecher* and the jester had both retired to a safe distance when matters seemed coming to blows, but returned when words, their own commodity, seemed again about to become the order of the day.

The man of proverbs was so delighted with Philip's politic speech, that he clashed his baton at the conclusion, by way of emphasis, and forgot the presence in which he was, so far as to say aloud, that he himself had never said a wiser thing in his life.

"It may be so," whispered Jonas Schwanker, "but we shall be whipt if you speak so loud."

The Duke answered sullenly, that he would refer his quarrel to the General Council of the Crusade—a motion which Philip highly applauded, as qualified to take away a scandal most harmful to Christendom.

Richard, retaining the same careless attitude, listened to Philip, until his oratory seemed exhausted, and then said aloud, "I am drowsy—this fever hangs about me still. Brother of France, thou art acquainted with my humour, and that I have at all times but few words to spare—know, therefore, at once, I will submit a matter touching the honour of England neither to Prince, Pope, nor Council. Here stands my banner—whatsoever pennon shall be reared within three butts' length of it—ay, were it the oriflamme, of which you were, I think, but now speaking, shall be treated as that dishonoured rag; nor will I yield other satisfaction than that which these poor limbs can render in the lists to any bold challenge—ay, were it against five champions instead or one."

"Now," said the jester, whispering his companion, "that is as complete a piece of folly, as if I myself had said it—but yet, I think, there may be in this matter a greater fool than Richard yet."

"And who may that be?" asked the man of wisdom.

"Philip," said the jester; "or our own Royal Duke, should either accept the challenge—But oh, most sage *spruch-sprecher*, what excellent kings would thou and I have made, since those on whose heads these crowns have fallen, can play the proverb-monger and the fool as completely as ourselves!"

While these worthies plied their offices apart, Philip answered calmly to the almost injurious defiance of Richard,—"I came not hither to awaken fresh quarrels, contrary to the oath we have sworn, and the holy cause in which we have engaged. I part from my brother of England as brothers should part, and the holy strife between the Lions of England and the Lilies of France shall be, which shall be carried deepest into the ranks of the infidels."

"It is a bargain, my royal brother," said Richard, stretching out his hand with all the frankness which belonged to his rash but generous disposition; "and soon may we have the opportunity to try this gallant and fraternal wager!"

. "Let this noble Duke also partake in the friendship of this happy moment," said Philip; and the Duke approached half-sullenly, half-willing to enter into some accommodation.

"I think not of fools, nor of their folly," said Richard, carelessly; and the Archduke, turning his back on him, withdrew from the ground.

Richard looked after him as he retired.

"There is a sort of glow-worm courage," he said, "that shows only by night. I must not leave this banner unguarded in darkness — by daylight the look of the Lions will alone defend it. Here, Thomas of Gilsland, I give thee the charge of the standard—watch over the honour of England."

"Her safety is yet more dear to me," said De Vaux, "and the life of Richard is the safety of England—I must have your Highness back to your tent, and that without farther tarriance."

"Thou art a rough and peremptory nurse, De Vaux," said the King, smiling; and then added, addressing Sir Kenneth, "Valiant Scot, I owe thee a boon, and I will pay it richly. There stands the banner of England! Watch it as a novice does his armour on the night before he is dubbed — Stir not from it three spears' length, and defend it with thy body against injury or insult—Sound thy bugle, if thou art assailed by more than three at once. Dost thou undertake the charge?"

"Willingly," said Kenneth; "and will discharge it upon penalty of my head. I will but arm me, and return hither instantly."

The Kings of France and England then took formal leave of each other, hiding, under an appearance of courtesy, the grounds of complaint which either had against the other,—Richard against Philip, for what he deemed an officious interference betwixt him and Austria, and Philip against Cœur de Lion, for the disrespectful manner in which his mediation had been received. Those whom this disturbance had assembled, now drew off in different directions, leaving the contested mount in the same solitude which had subsisted till interrupted by the Austrian bravado. Men judged of the events of the day according to their partialities; and while the English charged the Austrian with having afforded the first ground of quarrel, those of other nations concurred in casting the greater blame upon the insular haughtiness and assuming character of Richard.

"Thou seest," said the Marquis of Montserrat to the Grand Master of the Templars, "that subtle courses are more effective than violence. I have unloosed the bonds which held together this bunch of sceptres and lances— thou wilt see them shortly fall asunder."

"I would have called thy plan a good one," said the Templar, "had there been but one man of courage among yonder cold-blooded Austrians, to sever the bonds of which you speak, with his sword. A knot that is unloosed may again be fastened, but not so the cord which has been cut to pieces."

Chapter the Twelfth.

'Tis woman that seduces all mankind.

GAY.

In the days of chivalry, a dangerous post, or a perilous adventure, was a reward frequently assigned to military bravery as a compensation for its former trials — just as, in ascending a precipice, the surmounting one crag only lifts the climber to points yet more dangerous.

It was midnight, and the moon rode clear and high in heaven, when Kenneth of Scotland stood upon his watch on Saint George's Mount, beside the banner of England, a solitary sentinel, to protect the emblem of that nation against the insults which might be meditated among the thousands whom Richard's pride had made his enemies. High thoughts rolled, one after another, upon the mind of the warrior. It seemed to him as if he had gained some favour in the eyes of the chivalrous monarch, who till now had not seemed to distinguish him among the crowds of brave men whom his renown had assembled under his banner, and Sir Kenneth little recked that the display of royal regard consisted in placing him upon a post so perilous. The devotion of his ambitious and high-placed affection, inflamed his military enthusiasm.

Hopeless as that attachment was, in almost any conceivable circumstances, those which had lately occurred had, in some degree, diminished the distance between Edith and himself. He upon whom Richard had conferred the distinction of guarding his banner, was no longer an adventurer of slight note, but placed within the regard of a princess, although he was as far as ever from her level. An unknown and obscure fate could not now be his. If he was surprised and slain on the post which had been assigned him, his death — and he resolved it should be glorious — must deserve the praises, as well as call down the vengeance, of Cœur de Lion, and be followed by the regrets, and even the tears, of the high-born beauties of the English Court. He had now no longer reason to fear that he should die as a fool dieth.

Sir Kenneth had full leisure to enjoy these and similar high-souled thoughts, fostered by that wild spirit of chivalry, which, amid its most extravagant and fantastic flights, was still pure from all selfish alloy — generous, devoted, and perhaps only thus far censurable, that it proposed objects and courses of action inconsistent with the frailties and imperfections of man. All nature around him slept in calm moonshine, or in deep shadow. The long rows of tents and pavilions, glimmering or darkening as they lay in the moonlight or in the shade, were still and silent as the streets of a deserted city. Beside the banner-staff lay the large stag-hound already mentioned, the sole companion of Kenneth's watch, on whose vigilance he trusted for early warning of the approach of any hostile footstep. The noble animal seemed to understand the purpose of their watch, for he looked from time to time at the rich folds of the heavy pennon, and, when the cry of the sentinels came from the distant lines and defences of the camp, he answered them with one deep and reiterated bark, as if to affirm that he too was vigilant in his duty. From time to time, also, he lowered his lofty head, and wagged his tail, as his master passed and repassed him in the short turns which he took upon his post; or, when the knight stood silent and abstracted leaning on his lance, and looking up towards heaven, his faithful attendant ventured sometimes, in the phrase of romance, "to disturb his thoughts," and awaken him from his reverie, by thrusting his large rough snout into the knight's gauntleted hand, to solicit a transitory caress.

Thus passed two hours of the knight's watch without any thing remarkable occurring. At length, and upon a sudden, the gallant stag-hound bayed furiously, and seemed about to dash forward where the shadow lay the darkest, yet waited, as if in the slips, till he should know the pleasure of his master.

"Who goes there?" said Sir Kenneth, aware that there was something creeping forward on the shadowy side of the mount.

"In the name of Merlin and Maugis," answered a hoarse disagreeable voice, "tie up your four-footed demon there, or I come not at you."

"And who art thou, that would approach my post?" said Sir Kenneth, bending his eyes as keenly as he could on some object which he could just observe at the bottom of the ascent, without being able to distinguish its form. "Beware—I am here for death and life."

"Take up thy long-fanged Sathanas," said the voice, "or I will conjure him with a bolt from my arblast."

At the same time was heard the sound of a spring or check, as when a crossbow is bent.

"Unbend thy arblast, and come into the moonlight," said the Scot, "or, by Saint Andrew, I will pin thee to the earth, be what or whom thou wilt!"

As he spoke, he poised his long lance by the middle, and, fixing his eye upon the object which seemed to move, he brandished the weapon, as if meditating to cast it from his hand—a use of the weapon sometimes, though rarely, resorted to, when a missile was necessary. But Sir Kenneth was ashamed of his purpose, and grounded his weapon, when there stepped from the shadow into the moonlight, like an actor entering upon the stage, a stunted decrepit creature, whom, by his fantastic dress and deformity, he recognized, even at some distance, for the male of the two dwarfs whom he had seen at the chapel of Engaddi. Recollecting, at the same moment, the other, and far different, visions of that extraordinary night, he gave his dog a signal, which he instantly understood, and, returning to the standard, laid himself down beside it with a stifled growl.

The little distorted miniature of humanity, assured of his safety from an enemy so formidable, came panting up the ascent, which the shortness of his legs rendered laborious, and, when he arrived on the platform on the top, shifted to his left hand the little crossbow, which was just such a toy as children at that period were permitted to shoot small birds with, and, assuming an attitude of great dignity, gracefully extended his right hand to Sir Kenneth, in an attitude as if he expected he would salute it. But such a result not following, he demanded in a sharp and angry tone of voice, "Soldier, wherefore renderest thou not to Nectabanus the homage due to his dignity?—Or, is it possible that thou canst have forgotten him?"

"Great Nectabanus," answered the knight, willing to soothe the creature's humour, "that were difficult for any one who has ever looked upon thee. Pardon me, however, that, being a soldier upon my post, with my lance in my hand, I may not give to one of thy puissance the advantage of coming within my guard, or of mastering my weapon. Suffice it, that I reverence thy dignity, and submit myself to thee as humbly as a man-at-arms in my place may."

"It shall suffice," said Nectabanus, "so that you presently attend me to the presence of those who have sent me hither to summon you."

"Great sir," replied the knight, "neither in this can I gratify thee, for my orders are to abide by this banner till daybreak—so I pray you to hold me excused in that matter also."

So saying, he resumed his walk upon the platform; but the dwarf did not suffer him so easily to escape from his importunity.

"Look you," he said, placing himself before Sir Kenneth, so as to interrupt his way, "either obey me, Sir Knight, as in duty bound, or I will lay the command upon thee, in the name of one whose beauty could call down the genii from their sphere, and whose grandeur could command the immortal race when they had descended."

A wild and improbable conjecture arose in the knight's mind, but he repelled it. It was impossible, he thought, that the lady of his love should have sent him such a message by such a messenger—yet his voice trembled as he said, "Go to, Nectabanus. Tell me at once, and as a true man, whether this sublime lady, of whom thou speakest, be other than the houri, with whose assistance I beheld thee sweeping the chapel at Engaddi?"

"How! presumptuous knight," replied the dwarf, "think'st thou the mistress of our own royal affections, the sharer of our greatness, and the partner of our comeliness, would demean herself by laying charge on such a vassal as thou?   No, highly as thou art honoured, thou hast not yet deserved the notice of Queen Guenevra, the lovely bride of Arthur, from whose high seat even princes seem but pigmies.   But look thou here, and as thou knowest or disownest this token, so obey or refuse her commands, who hath deigned to impose them on thee."

So saying, he placed in the knight's hands a ruby ring, which, even in the moonlight, he had no difficulty to recognize as that which usually graced the finger of the high-born lady to whose service he had devoted himself. Could he have doubted the truth of the token, he would have been convinced by the small knot of carnation-coloured ribbon, which was fastened to the ring.   This was his lady's favourite colour, and more than once had he himself, assuming it for that of his own liveries, caused the carnation to triumph over all other hues in the lists and in the battle.

Sir Kenneth was struck nearly mute, by seeing such a token in such hands.

"In the name of all that is sacred, from whom didst thou receive this witness?" said the knight; "bring, if thou canst, thy wavering understanding to a right settlement for a minute or two, and tell me the person by whom thou art sent, and the real purpose of thy message—and take heed what thou say'st, for this is no subject for buffoonery."

"Fond and foolish knight," said the dwarf, "wouldst thou know more of this matter, than that thou art honoured with commands from a princess, delivered to thee by a king?—We list not to parley with thee farther than to command thee, in the name, and by the power of that ring, to follow us to her who is the owner of the ring.   Every minute that thou tarriest is a crime against thy allegiance."

"Good Nectabanus—bethink thyself," said the knight,—"Can my lady know where and upon what duty I am this night engaged?—Is she aware that my life—Pshaw, why should I speak of life—but that my honour depends on my guarding this banner till daybreak—and can it be her wish that I should leave it even to pay homage to her?—It is impossible—the princess is pleased to be merry with her servant, in sending him such a message: and I must think so the rather that she hath chosen such a messenger."

"Oh, keep your belief," said Nectabanus, turning round as if to leave the platform; "it is little to me whether you be traitor or true man to this royal lady—so fare thee well."

"Stay, stay—I entreat you stay," said Sir Kenneth; "answer me but one question—Is the lady who sent thee near to this place?"

"What signifies it?" said the dwarf; "ought fidelity to reckon furlongs, or miles, or leagues—like the poor courier, who is paid for his labour by the distance which he traverses?   Nevertheless, thou soul of suspicion, I tell thee, the fair owner of the ring, now sent to so unworthy a vassal, in whom there is neither truth nor courage, is not more distant from this place, than this arblast can send a bolt."

The knight gazed again on the ring, as if to ascertain that there was no possible falsehood in the token.—"Tell me," he said to the dwarf, "is my presence required for any length of time?"

"Time!" answered Nectabanus, in his flighty manner; "what call you time?   I see it not—I feel it not—it is but a shadowy name—a succession of breathings measured forth by night by the clank of a bell, by day by a shadow crossing along a dial-stone.   Know'st thou not a true knight's time should only be reckoned by the deeds that he performs in behalf of God and his lady?"

"The words of truth, though in the mouth of folly," said the knight. "And doth my lady really summon me to some deed of action, in her name and for her sake?—and may it not be postponed for even the few hours till daybreak?"

"She requires thy presence instantly," said the dwarf, "and without the loss of so much time as would be told by ten grains of the sand-glass — Hearken, thou cold-blooded and suspicious knight, these are her very words —'Tell him, that the hand which dropped roses can bestow laurels.'"

This allusion to their meeting in the chapel of Engaddi, sent a thousand recollections through Sir Kenneth's brain, and convinced him that the message delivered by the dwarf was genuine. The rose-buds, withered as they were, were still treasured under his cuirass, and nearest to his heart. He paused, and could not resolve to forego an opportunity—the only one which might ever offer, to gain grace in her eyes, whom he had installed as sovereign of his affections. The dwarf, in the meantime, augmented his confusion by insisting either that he must return the ring, or instantly attend him.

"Hold, hold, yet a moment hold," said the knight, and proceeded to mutter to himself—"Am I either the subject or slave of King Richard, more than as a free knight sworn to the service of the Crusade? And whom have I come hither to honour with lance and sword? Our holy cause and my transcendent lady!"

"The ring, the ring!" exclaimed the dwarf impatiently; "false and slothful knight, return the ring, which thou art unworthy to touch or to look upon."

"A moment, a moment, good Nectabanus," said Sir Kenneth; "disturb not my thoughts.—What if the Saracens were just now to attack our lines? Should I stay here like a sworn vassal of England, watching that her king's pride suffered no humiliation; or should I speed to the breach, and fight for the Cross? — To the breach, assuredly; and, next to the cause of God, come the commands of my liege lady.—And, yet, Cœur de Lion's behest—my own promise!—Nectabanus, I conjure thee once more to say, are you to conduct me far from hence?"

"But to yonder pavilion; and since you must needs know," replied Nectabanus, "the moon is glimmering on the gilded ball which crowns its roof, and which is worth a king's ransom."

"I can return in an instant," said the knight, shutting his eyes desperately to all farther consequences. "I can hear from thence the bay of my dog, if any one approaches the standard—I will throw myself at my lady's feet, and pray her leave to return to conclude my watch. — Here, Roswal," (calling his hound, and throwing down his mantle by the side of the standard-spear,) "watch thou here, and let no one approach."

The majestic dog looked in his master's face, as if to be sure that he understood his charge, then sat down beside the mantle, with ears erect and head raised, like a sentinel, understanding perfectly the purpose for which he was stationed there.

"Come now, good Nectabanus," said the knight, "let us hasten to obey the commands thou hast brought."

"Haste he that will," said the dwarf, sullenly; "thou hast not been in haste to obey my summons, nor can I walk fast enough to follow your long strides — you do not walk like a man, but bound like an ostrich in the desert."

There were but two ways of conquering the obstinacy of Nectabanus, who, as he spoke, diminished his walk into a snail-pace. For bribes Sir Kenneth had no means — for soothing no time, so in his impatience he snatched the dwarf up from the ground, and bearing him along, notwithstanding his entreaties and his fear, reached nearly to the pavilion pointed out as that of the Queen. In approaching it, however, the Scot observed there was a small guard of soldiers sitting on the ground, who had been concealed from him by the intervening tents. Wondering that the clash of his own armour had not yet attracted their attention, and supposing that his motions might, on the present occasion, require to be conducted with secrecy, he placed the little panting guide upon the ground to recover his breath, and point out what was next to be done. Nectabanus was both frightened and angry; but he had felt himself as completely in the power of the robust knight, as an owl in the claws of an eagle, and therefore cared not to provoke him to any farther display of his strength.

He made no complaints, therefore, of the usage he had received, but, turning amongst the labyrinth of tents, he led the knight in silence to the opposite side of the pavilion, which thus screened them from the observation of the warders, who seemed either too negligent or too sleepy to discharge their duty with much accuracy. Arrived there the dwarf raised the under part of the canvass from the ground, and made signs to Sir Kenneth that he should introduce himself to the inside of the tent, by creeping under it. The knight hesitated — there seemed an indecorum in thus privately introducing himself into a pavilion, pitched, doubtless, for the accommodation of noble ladies, but he recalled to remembrance the assured tokens which the dwarf had exhibited, and concluded that it was not for him to dispute his lady's pleasure.

He stoopt accordingly, crept beneath the canvass enclosure of the tent, and heard the dwarf whisper from without, — "Remain there until I call thee."

Chapter the Thirteenth.

You talk of Gaiety and Innocence!
The moment when the fatal fruit was eaten,
They parted ne'er to meet again; and Malice
Has ever since been playmate to light Gaiety.
From the first moment when the smiling infant
Destroys the flower or butterfly he toys with,
To the last chuckle of the dying miser,
Who on his deathbed laughs his last to hear
His wealthy neighbour has become a bankrupt.
                                        OLD PLAY.

SIR KENNETH was left for some minutes alone, and in darkness. Here was another interruption, which must prolong his absence from his post, and he began almost to repent the facility with which he had been induced to quit it. But to return without seeing the Lady Edith, was now not to be thought of. He had committed a breach of military discipline, and was determined at least to prove the reality of the seductive expectations which had tempted him to do so. Meanwhile, his situation was unpleasant. There was no light to show him into what sort of an apartment he had been led — the Lady Edith was in immediate attendance on the Queen of England — and the discovery of his having introduced himself thus furtively into the royal pavilion, might, were it discovered, lead to much and dangerous suspicion. While he gave way to these unpleasant reflections, and began almost to wish that he could achieve his retreat unobserved, he heard a noise of female voices, laughing, whispering, and speaking, in an adjoining apartment, from which, as the sounds gave him reason to judge, he could only be separated by a canvass partition. Lamps were burning, as he might perceive by the shadowy light which extended itself even to his side of the veil which divided the tent, and he could see shades of several figures sitting and moving in the adjoining apartment. It cannot be termed discourtesy in Sir Kenneth, that, situated as he was, he overheard a conversation, in which he found himself deeply interested.

"Call her — call her, for Our Lady's sake," said the voice of one of these laughing invisibles. "Nectabanus, thou shalt be made ambassador to Prester John's court, to show them how wisely thou canst discharge thee of a mission.

The shrill tone of the dwarf was heard, yet so much subdued, that Sir Kenneth could not understand what he said, except that he spoke something of the means of merriment given to the guard.

"But how shall we rid us of the spirit which Nectabanus hath raised, my maidens?"

"Hear me, royal madam," said another voice; "if the sage and princely Nectabanus be not over jealous of his most transcendent bride and empress, let us send her to get us rid of this insolent knight-errant, who can be so easily persuaded that high-born dames may need the use of his insolent and overweening valour."

"It were but justice, methinks," replied another, "that the Princess Guenevra should dismiss, by her courtesy, him, whom her husband's wisdom has been able to entice hither."

Struck to the heart with shame and resentment at what he had heard, Sir Kenneth was about to attempt his escape from the tent at all hazards, when what followed arrested his purpose.

"Nay, truly," said the first speaker, "our cousin Edith must first learn how this vaunted wight hath conducted himself, and we must reserve the power of giving her ocular proof that he hath failed in his duty. It may be a lesson will do good upon her; for, credit me, Calista, I have sometimes thought she has let this northern adventurer sit nearer her heart than prudence would sanction."

One of the other voices was then heard to mutter something of the Lady Edith's prudence and wisdom.

"Prudence, wench!" was the reply—"It is mere pride, and the desire to be thought more rigid than any of us. Nay, I will not quit my advantage. You know well, that when she has us at fault, no one can, in a civil way, lay your error before you more precisely than can my Lady Edith — But here she comes."

A figure, as if entering the apartment, cast upon the partition a shade, which glided along slowly until it mixed with those which already clouded it. Despite of the bitter disappointment which he had experienced — despite the insult and injury with which it seemed he had been visited by the malice, or, at best, by the idle humour of Queen Berengaria, (for he already concluded that she who spoke loudest, and in a commanding tone, was the wife of Richard,) the knight felt something so soothing to his feelings in learning that Edith had been no partner to the fraud practised on him, and so interesting to his curiosity in the scene which was about to take place, that, instead of prosecuting his more prudent purpose of an instant retreat, he looked anxiously, on the contrary, for some rent or crevice by means of which he might be made eye as well as ear-witness to what was to go forward.

"Surely," said he to himself, "the Queen, who hath been pleased for an idle frolic to endanger my reputation, and perhaps my life, cannot complain if I avail myself of the chance which fortune seems willing to afford me, to obtain knowledge of her farther intentions."

It seemed, in the meanwhile, as if Edith were waiting for the commands of the Queen, and as if the other were reluctant to speak, for fear of being unable to command her laughter, and that of her companions; for Sir Kenneth could only distinguish a sound as of suppressed tittering and merriment.

"Your Majesty," said Edith, at last, "seems in a merry mood, though, methinks, the hour of night prompts a sleepy one. I was well disposed bedward, when I had your Majesty's commands to attend you."

"I will not long delay you, cousin, from your repose," said the Queen;

"though I fear you will sleep less soundly when I tell you your wager is lost."

"Nay, royal madam," said Edith, "this, surely, is dwelling on a jest which has rather been worn out. I laid no wager, however it was your Majesty's pleasure to suppose, or to insist, that I did so."

"Nay, now, despite our pilgrimage, Satan is strong with you, my gentle cousin, and prompts thee to leasing. Can you deny that you gaged your ruby ring against my golden bracelet, that yonder Knight of the Libbard, or how call you him, could not be seduced from his post?"

"Your Majesty is too great for me to gainsay you," replied Edith; "but these ladies can, if they will, bear me witness, that it was your highness who proposed such a wager, and took the ring from my finger, even while I was declaring that I did not think it maidenly to gage any thing on such a subject."

"Nay, but, my Lady Edith," said another voice, "you must needs grant, under your favour, that you expressed yourself very confident of the valour of that same Knight of the Leopard."

"And if I did, minion," said Edith, angrily, "is that a good reason why thou shouldst put in thy word to flatter her Majesty's humour? I spoke of that knight but as all men speak who have seen him in the field, and had no more interest in defending than thou in detracting from him. In a camp, what can women speak of save soldiers and deeds of arms?"

"The noble Lady Edith," said a third voice, "hath never forgiven Calista and me, since we told your Majesty that she dropped two rose-buds in the chapel."

"If your Majesty," said Edith, in a tone which Sir Kenneth could judge to be that of respectful remonstrance, "have no other commands for me than to hear the gibes of your waiting-women, I must crave your permission to withdraw."

"Silence, Florise," said the Queen, "and let not our indulgence lead you to forget the difference betwixt yourself and the kinswoman of England. — But you, my dear cousin," she continued, resuming her tone of raillery, "how can you, who are so good-natured, begrudge us poor wretches a few minutes' laughing when we have had so many days devoted to weeping and gnashing of teeth?"

"Great be your mirth, royal lady," said Edith; "yet would I be content not to smile for the rest of my life, rather than ——"

She stopped, apparently out of respect; but Sir Kenneth could hear that she was in much agitation.

"Forgive me," said Berengaria, a thoughtless but good-humoured princess of the House of Navarre, — "but what is the great offence after all? A young knight has been wiled hither—has stolen — or has *been* stolen — from his post, which no none will disturb in his absence, for the sake of a fair lady; for, to do your champion justice, sweet one, the wisdom of Nectabanus could conjure him hither in no name but yours."

"Gracious Heaven! your Majesty does not say so?" said Edith, in a voice of alarm quite different from the agitation she had previously evinced, — "you cannot say so, consistently with respect for your own honour and for mine, your husband's kinswoman! — Say you were jesting with me, my royal mistress, and forgive me that I could, even for a moment, think it possible you could be in earnest!"

"The Lady Edith," said the Queen, in a displeased tone of voice, "regrets the ring we have won of her. — We will restore the pledge to you, gentle cousin, only you must not grudge us in turn a little triumph over the wisdom which has been so often spread over us as a banner over a host."

"A triumph!" exclaimed Edith, indignantly; "a triumph!—the triumph will be with the infidel, when he hears that the Queen of England can make the reputation of her husband's kinswoman the subject of a light frolic."

"You are angry, fair cousin, at losing your favourite ring," said the Queen ——"Come, since you grudge to pay your wager, we will renounce our right; it was your name and that pledge brought him hither, and we care not for the bait after the fish is caught."

"Madam," replied Edith, impatiently, "you know well that your Grace could not wish for any thing of mine but it becomes instantly yours. But I would give a bushel of rubies ere ring or name of mine had been used to bring a brave man into a fault, and perhaps to disgrace and punishment."

"Oh, it is for the safety of our true knight that we fear!" said the Queen. "You rate our power too low, fair cousin, when you speak of a life being lost for a frolic of ours. Oh, Lady Edith, others have influence on the iron breasts of warriors as well as you—the heart even of a lion is made of flesh, not of stone; and, believe me, I have interest enough with Richard to save this knight, in whose faith Lady Edith is so deeply concerned, from the penalty of disobeying his royal commands."

"For the love of the blessed Cross, most royal lady," said Edith — and Sir Kenneth, with feelings which it were hard to unravel, heard her prostrate herself at the Queen's feet, — "for the love of our blessed Lady, and of every holy saint in the calendar, beware what you do! You know not King Richard — you have been but shortly wedded to him — your breath might as well combat the west wind when it is wildest, as your words persuade my royal kinsman to pardon a military offence. Oh! for God's sake, dismiss this gentleman, if indeed you have lured him hither! I could almost be content to rest with the shame of having invited him, did I know that he was returned again where his duty calls him!"

"Arise, cousin, arise," said Queen Berengaria, "and be assured all will be better than you think. Rise, dear Edith; I am sorry I have played my foolery with a knight in whom you take such deep interest — Nay, wring not thy hands — I will believe thou carest not for him — believe any thing rather than see thee look so wretchedly miserable — I tell thee I will take the blame on myself with King Richard in behalf of thy fair northern friend — thine acquaintance, I would say, since thou own'st him not as a friend. — Nay, look not so reproachfully — We will send Nectabanus to dismiss this Knight of the Standard to his post; and we ourselves will grace him on some future day, to make amends for his wild-goose chase. He is, I warrant, but lying perdue in some neighbouring tent."

"By my crown of lilies, and my sceptre of a specially good water-reed," said Nectabanus, "your Majesty is mistaken — he is nearer at hand than you wot — he lieth esconced there behind that canvass partition."

"And within hearing of each word we have said!" exclaimed the Queen, in her turn violently surprised and agitated — "Out, monster of folly and malignity!"

As she uttered these words, Nectabanus fled from the pavilion with a yell of such a nature, as leaves it still doubtful whether Berengaria had confined her rebuke to words, or added some more emphatic expression of her displeasure.

"What can now be done?" said the Queen to Edith, in a whisper of undisguised uneasiness.

"That which must," said Edith, firmly. "We must see this gentleman, and place ourselves in his mercy."

So saying, she began hastily to undo a curtain, which at one place covered an entrance or communication.

"For Heaven's sake, forbear—consider," said the Queen, "my apartment — our dress — the hour — my honour!"

But ere she could detail her remonstrances, the curtain fell, and there was no division any longer betwixt the armed knight and the party of ladies. The warmth of an Eastern night occasioned the undress of Queen Berengaria and her household to be rather more simple and unstudied than their station, and the presence of a male spectator of rank, required. This the Queen remembered, and with a loud shriek fled from the apartment where Sir Kenneth was disclosed to view in a copartment of the ample pavilion, now no longer separated from that in which they stood. The grief and agitation of the Lady Edith, as well as the deep interest she felt in a hasty explanation with the Scottish knight, perhaps occasioned her forgetting that her locks were more dishevelled, and her person less heedfully covered, than was the wont of high-born damsels, in an age which was not, after all, the most prudish or scrupulous period of the ancient time. A thin loose garment of pink-coloured silk made the principal part of her vestments, with Oriental slippers, into which she had hastily thrust her bare feet, and a scarf hurriedly and loosely thrown about her shoulders. Her head had no other covering than the veil of rich and dishevelled locks falling round it on every side, that half hid a countenance, which a mingled sense of modesty, and of resentment, and other deep and agitating feelings, had covered with crimson.

But although Edith felt her situation with all that delicacy which is her sex's greatest charm, it did not seem that for a moment she placed her own bashfulness in comparison with the duty, which, as she thought, she owed to him, who had been led into error and danger on her account. She drew, indeed, her scarf more closely over her neck and bosom, and she hastily laid from her hand a lamp, which shed too much lustre over her figure; but, while Sir Kenneth stood motionless on the same spot in which he was first discovered, she rather stepped towards than retired from him, as she exclaimed, "Hasten to your post, valiant knight!—you are deceived in being trained hither—ask no questions."

"I need ask none," said the knight, sinking upon one knee, with the reverential devotion of a saint at the altar, and bending his eyes on the ground, lest his looks should increase the lady's embarrassment.

"Have you heard all?" said Edith, impatiently—"Gracious saints! then wherefore wait you here, when each minute that passes is loaded with dishonour!"

"I have heard that I am dishonoured, lady, and I have heard it from you," answered Kenneth. "What reck I how soon punishment follows? I have but one petition to you, and then I seek, among the sabres of the infidels, whether dishonour may not be washed out with blood."

"Do not so, neither," said the lady. "Be wise—dally not here—all may yet be well, if you will but use despatch."

"I wait but for your forgiveness," said the knight, still kneeling, "for my presumption in believing my poor services could have been required or valued by you."

"I do forgive you — Oh, I have nothing to forgive!—I have been the means of injuring you—But oh, begone!—I will forgive—I will value you —that is, as I value every brave Crusader—if you will but begone!"

"Receive, first, this precious yet fatal pledge," said the knight, tendering the ring to Edith, who now showed gestures of impatience.

"Oh, no, no," she said, declining to receive it. "Keep it—keep it as a mark of my regard — my regret, I would say. Oh, begone, if not for your own sake, for mine!"

Almost recompensed for the loss even of honour, which her voice had denounced to him, by the interest which she seemed to testify in his safety, Sir Kenneth rose from his knee, and, casting a momentary glance on Edith, bowed low and seemed about to withdraw. At the same instant, that maidenly bashfulness, which the energy of Edith's feelings had till then triumphed over, became conqueror in its turn, and she hastened from the apartment, extinguishing her lamp as she went, and leaving, in Sir Kenneth's thoughts, both mental and natural gloom behind her.

She must be obeyed, was the first distinct idea which waked him from his reverie, and he hastened to the place by which he had entered the pavilion. To pass under the canvass in the manner he had entered, required time and attention, and he made a readier aperture by slitting the canvass wall with his poniard. When in the free air, he felt rather stupified and overpowered by a conflict of sensations, than able to ascertain what was the real import of the whole. He was obliged to spur himself to action, by recollecting that the commands of the Lady Edith had required haste. Even then, engaged as he was amongst tent ropes and tents, he was compelled to move with caution until he should regain the path or avenue, aside from which the dwarf had led him, in order to escape the observation of the guards before the Queen's pavilion ; and he was obliged also to move slowly, and with precaution, to avoid giving an alarm, either by falling or by the clashing of his armour. A thin cloud had obscured the moon, too, at the very instant of his leaving the tent, and Sir Kenneth had to struggle with this inconvenience at a moment when the dizziness of his head, and the fulness of his heart, scarce left him powers of intelligence sufficient to direct his motions.

But at once sounds came upon his ear, which instantly recalled him to the full energy of his faculties. These proceeded from the Mount of Saint George. He heard first a single fierce, angry, and savage bark, which was immediately followed by a yell of agony. No deer ever bounded with a wilder start at the voice of Roswal, than did Sir Kenneth at what he feared was the death-cry of that noble hound, from whom no ordinary injury could have extracted even the slightest acknowledgment of pain. He surmounted the space which divided him from the avenue, and, having attained it, began to run towards the mount, although loaded with his mail, faster than most men could have accompanied him even if unarmed, relaxed not his pace for the steep sides of the artificial mound, and in a few minutes stood on the platform upon its summit.

The moon broke through the cloud at this moment, and showed him that the standard of England was vanished, that the spear on which it floated lay broken on the ground, and beside it was his faithful hound, apparently in the agonies of death.

Chapter the Fourteenth.

———— All my long arrear of honour lost,
Heap'd up in youth, and hoarded up for age.
Hath Honour's fountain then suck'd up the stream?
He hath — and hooting boys may barefoot pass,
And gather pebbles from the naked ford!

　　　　　　　　　　DON SEBASTIAN.

AFTER a torrent of afflicting sensations, by which he was at first almost stunned and confounded, Sir Kenneth's first thought was to look for the authors of this violation of the English banner ; but in no direction could he see traces of them. His next, which to some persons, but scarce to any who have made intimate acquaintances among the canine race, may appear strange, was to examine the condition of his faithful Roswal, mortally wounded, as it seemed, in discharging the duty which his master had been seduced to abandon. He caressed the dying animal, who, faithful to the last, seemed to forget his own pain in the satisfaction he received from his master's presence, and continued wagging his tail and licking his hand, even while by low moanings he expressed that his agony was increased by the attempts which Sir Kenneth made to withdraw from the wound the fragment of the lance or javelin, with which it had been inflicted; then redoubled his feeble endearments, as if fearing he had offended his master by showing a sense of the pain to which his interference had subjected him. There was something in the display of the dying creature's attachment, which mixed as a bitter ingredient with the sense of disgrace and desolation by which Sir Kenneth was oppressed. His only friend seemed removed from him, just when he had incurred the contempt and hatred of all besides. The knight's strength of mind gave way to a burst of agonized distress, and he groaned and wept aloud.

While he thus indulged his grief, a clear and solemn voice, close beside him, pronounced these words in the sonorous tones of the readers of the mosque, and in the lingua Franca, mutually understood by Christians and Saracens: —

"Adversity is like the period of the former and of the latter rain — cold, comfortless, unfriendly to man and to animal; yet from that season have their birth the flower and the fruit, the date, the rose, and the pomegranate."

Sir Kenneth of the Leopard turned towards the speaker, and beheld the Arabian physician, who, approaching unheard, had seated himself a little behind him cross-legged, and uttered with gravity, yet not without a tone of sympathy, the moral sentences of consolation with which the Koran and its commentators supplied him; for, in the East, wisdom is held to consist, less in a display of the sage's own inventive talents, than in his ready memory, and happy application of, and reference to, "that which is written."

Ashamed at being surprised in a woman-like expression of sorrow, Sir Kenneth dashed his tears indignantly aside, and again busied himself with his dying favourite.

"The poet hath said," continued the Arab, without noticing the knight's averted looks and sullen deportment—"'the ox for the field, and the camel for the desert.' Were not the hand of the leech fitter than that of the soldier to cure wounds, though less able to inflict them?"

"This patient, Hakim, is beyond thy help," said Sir Kenneth; "and, besides, he is, by thy law, an unclean animal."

"Where Allah hath deigned to bestow life, and a sense of pain and pleasure," said the physician, "it were sinful pride should the sage, whom he has enlightened, refuse to prolong existence, or assuage agony. To the sage, the cure of a miserable groom, of a poor dog, and of a conquering monarch, are events of little distinction. Let me examine this wounded animal."

Sir Kenneth acceded in silence, and the physician inspected and handled Roswal's wound with as much care and attention as if he had been a human being. He then took forth a case of instruments, and by the judicious and skilful application of pincers, withdrew from the wounded shoulder the fragment of the weapon, and stopped with styptics and bandages the effusion of blood which followed; the creature all the while suffering him patiently to perform these kind offices, as if he had been aware of his kind intentions.

"The animal may be cured," said El Hakim, addressing himself to Sir Kenneth, "if you will permit me to carry him to my tent, and treat him with the care which the nobleness of his nature deserves. For know, that thy servant Adonbec is no less skilful in the race and pedigree, and distinctions of good dogs and of noble steeds, than in the diseases which affect the human race."

"Take him with you," said the knight. "I bestow him on you freely if he recovers. I owe thee a reward for attendance on my squire, and have nothing else to pay it with. For myself,—I will never again wind bugle, or halloo to hound!"

The Arabian made no reply, but gave a signal with a clapping of his hands, which was instantly answered by the appearance of two black slaves. He gave them his orders in Arabic, received the answer, that "to hear was to obey," when, taking the animal in their arms, they removed him, without much resistance on his part; for though his eyes turned to his master, he was too weak to struggle.

"Fare thee well, Roswal, then," said Sir Kenneth,—"fare thee well, my last and only friend — thou art too noble a possession to be retained by one such as I must in future call myself. — I would," he said, as the slaves retired, "that, dying as he is, I could exchange conditions with that noble animal."

"It is written," answered the Arabian, although the exclamation had not been addressed to him, "that all creatures are fashioned for the service of man ; and the master of the earth speaketh folly when he would exchange, in his impatience, his hopes here and to come, for the servile condition of an inferior being."

"A dog who dies in discharging his duty," said the knight, sternly, "is better than a man who survives the desertion of it. Leave me, Hakim ; thou hast, on this side of miracle, the most wonderful science which man ever possessed, but the wounds of the spirit are beyond thy power."

"Not if the patient will explain his calamity, and be guided by the physician," said Adonbec El Hakim.

"Know, then," said Sir Kenneth, "since thou art so importunate, that last night the Banner of England was displayed from this mound — I was its appointed guardian — morning is now breaking — there lies the broken banner-spear — the standard itself is lost — and here sit I a living man !"

"How !" said El Hakim, examining him ; "thy armour is whole — there is no blood on thy weapons, and report speaks thee one unlikely to return thus from fight.—Thou hast been trained from thy post—ay, trained by the rosy cheek and black eye of one of those houris, to whom you Nazarenes vow rather such service as is due to Allah, than such love as may lawfully be rendered to forms of clay like our own. It has been thus assuredly ; for so hath man ever fallen, even since the days of Sultan Adam."

"And if it were so, physician," said Sir Kenneth, sullenly, "what remedy ?"

"Knowledge is the parent of power," said El Hakim, "as valour supplies strength.—Listen to me. Man is not as a tree, bound to one spot of earth —nor is he framed to cling to one bare rock, like the scarce animated shellfish. Thine own Christian writings command thee, when persecuted in one city to flee to another; and we Moslem also know that Mohammed, the Prophet of Allah, driven forth from the holy city of Mecca, found his refuge and his helpmates at Medina."

"And what does this concern me ?" said the Scot.

"Much," answered the physician. "Even the sage flies the tempest which he cannot control. Use thy speed, therefore, and fly from the vengeance of Richard to the shadow of Saladin's victorious banner."

"I might indeed hide my dishonour," said Sir Kenneth, ironically, "in a camp of infidel heathens, where the very phrase is unknown. But had I not better partake more fully in their reproach ? Does not thy advice stretch so far as to recommend me to take the turban ?—Methinks I want but apostasy to consumate my infamy."

"Blaspheme not, Nazarene," said the physician, sternly; "Saladin makes no converts to the law of the Prophet, save those on whom its precepts shall work conviction. Open thine eyes to the light, and the great Soldan, whose liberality is as boundless as his power, may bestow on thee a kingdom ; remain blinded if thou wilt, and, being one whose second life is doomed to misery, Saladin will yet, for this span of present time, make thee rich and happy. But fear not that thy brows shall be bound with a turban, save at thine own free choice."

"My choice were rather," said the knight, "that my writhen features should blacken, as they are like to do, in this evening's setting sun."

"Yet thou art not wise, Nazarene," said El Hakim, "to reject this fair offer ; for I have power with Saladin, and can raise thee high in his grace. Look you, my son—this Crusade, as you call your wild enterprise, is like a large dromond* parting asunder in the waves. Thou thyself hast borne terms of truce from the Kings and Princes, whose force is here assembled, to the mighty Soldan, and know'st not, perchance, the full tenor of thine own errand."

"I know not, and I care not," said the knight, impatiently ; "what avails it to me that I have been of late the envy of princes, when, ere night, I shall be a gibbeted and dishonoured corse !"

"Nay, I speak that it may not be so with thee," said the physician. "Saladin is courted on all sides ; the combined Princes of this league formed against him, have made such proposals of composition and peace, as, in other circumstances, it might have become his honour to have granted to them. Others have made private offers, on their own separate account, to disjoin their forces from the camp of the Kings of Frangistan, and even to lend their arms to the defence of the standard of the Prophet. But Saladin will not be served by such treacherous and interested defection. The King of kings will treat only with the Lion King. Saladin will hold treaty with none but the Melech Ric, and with him he will treat like a prince, or fight like a champion. To Richard he will yield such conditions of his free liberality, as the swords of all Europe could never compel from him by force or terror. He will permit a free pilgrimage to Jerusalem, and all the places where the Nazarenes list to worship ; nay, he will so far share even his empire with his brother Richard, that he will allow Christian garrisons in the six strongest cities of Palestine, and one in Jerusalem itself, and suffer them to be under the immediate command of the officers of Richard, who, he consents, shall bear the name of King Guardian of Jerusalem. Yet farther, strange and incredible as you may think it, know, Sir Knight—for to your honour I can commit even that almost incredible secret—know that Saladin will put a sacred seal on this happy union betwixt the bravest and noblest of Frangistan and Asia, by raising to the rank of his royal spouse a Christian damsel, allied in blood to King Richard, and known by the name of the Lady Edith of Plantagenet."[†]

"Ha !—say'st thou !" exclaimed Sir Kenneth, who, listening with indifference and apathy to the preceding part of El Hakim's speech, was touched by this last communication, as the thrill of a nerve, unexpectedly jarred, will awaken the sensation of agony, even in the torpor of palsy. Then, moderating his tone, by dint of much effort, he restrained his indignation, and, veiling it under the appearance of contemptuous doubt, he prosecuted the conversation in order to get as much knowledge as possible of the plot, as he deemed it, against the honour and happiness of her, whom he loved not the less that his passion had ruined, apparently, his fortunes, at once, and his honour.—"And what Christian," he said, with tolerable calmness, "would sanction a union so unnatural, as that of a Christian maiden with an unbelieving Saracen ?"

"Thou art but an ignorant, bigoted Nazarene," said the Hakim. "See'st thou not how the Mohammedan princes daily intermarry with the noble Nazarene maidens in Spain, without scandal either to Moor or Christian ? And the noble Soldan will, in his full confidence in the blood of Richard, permit the English maid the freedom which your Frankish manners have assigned to women. He will allow her the free exercise of her religion,—

* The largest sort of vessels then known were termed *dromonds*, or dromedaries.
† This may appear so extraordinary and improbable a proposition, that it is necessary to say such a one was actually made   The historians, however, substitute the widowed Queen of Naples, sister of Richard, for the bride, and Saladin's brother for the bridegroom.   They appear to have been ignorant of the existence of Edith of Plantagenet.—*See Mill's History of the Crusades*, vol. ii. p. 61

seeing that, in very truth, it signifies but little to which faith females are addicted,—and he will assign her such place and rank over all the women of his zenana, that she shall be in every respect his sole and absolute Queen."

"What!" said Sir Kenneth, "darest thou think, Moslem, that Richard would give his kinswoman—a high-born and virtuous princess, to be, at best, the foremost concubine in the haram of a misbeliever? Know, Hakim, the meanest free Christian noble would scorn, on his child's behalf, such splendid ignominy."

"Thou errest," said the Hakim; "Philip of France, and Henry of Champagne, and others of Richard's principal allies, have heard the proposal without starting, and have promised, as far as they may, to forward an alliance that may end these wasteful wars; and the wise arch-priest of Tyre hath undertaken to break the proposal to Richard, not doubting that he shall be able to bring the plan to good issue. The Soldan's wisdom hath as yet kept his proposition secret from others, such as he of Montserrat, and the Master of the Templars, because he knows they seek to thrive by Richard's death or disgrace, not by his life or honour. — Up, therefore, Sir Knight, and to horse. I will give thee a scroll which shall advance thee highly with the Soldan; and deem not that you are leaving your country, or her cause, or her religion, since the interest of the two monarchs will speedily be the same. To Saladin thy counsel will be most acceptable, since thou canst make him aware of much concerning the marriages of the Christians, the treatment of their wives, and other points of their laws and usages, which, in the course of such treaty, it much concerns him that he should know. The right hand of the Soldan grasps the treasures of the East, and is the fountain of generosity. Or, if thou desirest it, Saladin, when allied with England, can have but little difficulty to obtain from Richard not only thy pardon and restoration to favour, but an honourable command in the troops which may be left of the King of England's host, to maintain their joint government in Palestine. Up, then, and mount, there lies a plain path before thee."

"Hakim," said the Scottish knight, "thou art a man of peace — also, thou hast saved the life of Richard of England—and, moreover, of my own poor esquire, Strauchan. I have, therefore, heard to an end a matter, which, being propounded by another Moslem than thyself, I would have cut short with a blow of my dagger! Hakim, in return for thy kindness, I advise thee to see that the Saracen, who shall propose to Richard a union betwixt the blood of Plantagenet and that of his accursed race, do put on a helmet, which is capable to endure such a blow of a battle-axe as that which struck down the gate of Acre. Certes, he will be otherwise placed beyond the reach even of thy skill."

"Thou art, then, wilfully determined not to fly to the Saracen host?" said the physician — "Yet, remember, thou stayest to certain destruction; and the writings of thy law, as well as ours, prohibit man from breaking into the tabernacle of his own life."

"God forbid!" replied the Scot, crossing himself; "but we are also forbidden to avoid the punishment which our crimes have deserved. And, since so poor are thy thoughts of fidelity, Hakim, it grudges me that I have bestowed my good hound on thee, for, should he live, he will have a master ignorant of his value."

"A gift that is begrudged, is already recalled," said El Hakim, "only we physicians are sworn not to send away a patient uncured. If the dog recover, he is once more yours."

"Go to, Hakim," answered Sir Kenneth; "men speak not of hawk and hound when there is but an hour of day-breaking betwixt them and death. Leave me to recollect my sins, and reconcile myself to Heaven."

"I leave thee in thine obstinacy," said the physician; "the mist hides the precipice from those who are doomed to fall over it."

He withdrew slowly, turning from time to time his head, as if to observe whether the devoted knight might not recall him either by word or signal. At last his turbaned figure was lost among the labyrinth of tents which lay extended beneath, whitening in the pale light of the dawning, before which the moonbeam had now faded away.

But although the physician Adonbec's words had not made that impression upon Kenneth which the sage desired, they had inspired the Scot with a motive for desiring life, which, dishonoured as he conceived himself to be, he was before willing to part from as from a sullied vestment no longer becoming his wear. Much that had passed betwixt himself and the hermit, besides what he had observed between the anchorite and Sheerkohf, (or Ilderim,) he now recalled to recollection, and tended to confirm what the Hakim had told him of the secret article of the treaty.

"The reverend impostor!" he exclaimed to himself; "the hoary hypocrite! He spoke of the unbelieving husband converted by the believing wife — and what do I know but that the traitor exhibited to the Saracen, accursed of God, the beauties of Edith Plantagenet, that the hound might judge if the princely Christian lady were fit to be admitted into the haram of a misbeliever? If I had yonder infidel Ilderim, or whatsoever he is called, again in the gripe with which I once held him fast as ever hound held hare, never again should he at least come on errand disgraceful to the honour of Christian king, or noble and virtuous maiden. But I—my hours are fast dwindling into minutes — yet, while I have life and breath, something must be done, and speedily."

He paused for a few minutes, threw from him his helmet, then strode down the hill, and took the road to King Richard's pavilion.

Chapter the Fifteenth.

> The feather'd songster, chanticleer
>   Had wound his bugle-horn,
> And told the early villager
>   The coming of the morn.
> King Edward saw the ruddy streaks
>   Of light eclipse the gray,
> And heard the raven's croaking throat
>   Proclaim the fated day.
> "Thou'rt right," he said, "for, by the God
>   That sits enthroned on high,
> Charles Bawdwin, and his fellows twain,
>   This day shall surely die."
>   CHATTERTON.

ON the evening on which Sir Kenneth assumed his post, Richard, after the stormy event which disturbed its tranquillity, had retired to rest in the plenitude of confidence inspired by his unbounded courage, and the superiority which he had displayed in carrying the point he aimed at in presence of the whole Christian host, and its leaders, many of whom, he was aware, regarded in their secret souls the disgrace of the Austrian Duke as a triumph over themselves; so that his pride felt gratified, that in prostrating one enemy he had mortified a hundred.

Another monarch would have doubled his guards on the evening after such a scene, and kept at least a part of his troops under arms. But Cœur de Lion dismissed, upon the occasion, even his ordinary watch, and assigned to his soldiers a donative of wine to celebrate his recovery, and to drink to the Banner of Saint George; and his quarter of the camp would have assumed a character totally devoid of vigilance and military preparation, but that Sir Thomas de Vaux, the Earl of Salisbury, and other nobles, took precautions to preserve order and discipline among the revellers.

The physician attended the King from his retiring to bed till midnight was past, and twice administered medicine to him during that period, always previously observing the quarter of heaven occupied by the full moon, whose influences he declared to be most sovereign, or most baleful, to the effect of his drugs. It was three hours after midnight ere El Hakim withdrew from the royal tent, to one which had been pitched for himself and his retinue. In his way thither he visited the tent of Sir Kenneth of the Leopard, in order to see the condition of his first patient in the Christian camp, old Strauchan, as the knight's esquire was named. Inquiring there for Sir Kenneth himself, El Hakim learned on what duty he was employed, and probably this information led him to Saint George's Mount, where he found him whom he sought in the disastrous circumstances alluded to in the last chapter.

It was about the hour of sunrise, when a slow, armed tread was heard approaching the King's pavilion; and ere De Vaux, who slumbered beside his master's bed as lightly as ever sleep sat upon the eyes of a watch-dog, had time to do more than arise and say, "Who comes?" the Knight of the Leopard entered the tent, with a deep and devoted gloom seated upon his manly features.

"Whence this bold intrusion, Sir Knight?" said De Vaux, sternly, yet in a tone which respected his master's slumbers.

"Hold! De Vaux," said Richard, awakening on the instant; "Sir Kenneth cometh like a good soldier to render an account of his guard—to such the General's tent is ever accessible."—Then rising from his slumbering posture, and leaning on his elbow, he fixed his large bright eye upon the warrior—"Speak, Sir Scot; thou comest to tell me of a valiant, safe, and honourable watch, dost thou not? The rustling of the folds of the Banner of England were enough to guard it, even without the body of such a knight as men hold thee."

"As men will hold me no more," said Sir Kenneth—"my watch hath neither been vigilant, safe, nor honourable. The Banner of England has been carried off."

"And thou alive to tell it?" said Richard, in a tone of derisive incredulity.—"Away, it cannot be. There is not even a scratch on thy face.—Why dost thou stand thus mute? Speak the truth—it is ill jesting with a king—yet I will forgive thee if thou hast lied."

"Lied! Sir King!" returned the unfortunate knight, with fierce emphasis, and one glance of fire from his eye, bright and transient as the flash from the cold and stony flint. "But this also must be endured—I have spoken the truth."

"By God, and by Saint George!" said the King, bursting into fury, which, however, he instantly checked—"De Vaux, go view the spot—This fever has disturbed my brain—This cannot be—The man's courage is proof —It *cannot* be! Go speedily—or send, if thou wilt not go."

The King was interrupted by Sir Henry Neville, who came, breathless, to say that the banner was gone, and the knight who guarded it overpowered, and most probably murdered, as there was a pool of blood where the banner-spear lay shivered.

"But whom do I see here?" said Neville, his eyes suddenly resting upon Sir Kenneth.

"A traitor," said the King, starting to his feet, and seizing the curtalaxe, which was ever near his bed — "a traitor! whom thou shalt see die a traitor's death."—And he drew back the weapon as in act to strike.

Colourless, but firm as a marble statue, the Scot stood before him, with his bare head uncovered by any protection, his eyes cast down to the earth, his lips scarcely moving, yet muttering probably in prayer. Opposite to him, and within the due reach for a blow, stood King Richard, his large person wrapt in the folds of his camiscia, or ample gown of linen, except where the violence of his action had flung the covering from his right arm, shoulder, and a part of his breast, leaving to view a specimen of a frame which might have merited his Saxon predecessor's epithet of Ironside. He stood for an instant, prompt to strike—then sinking the head of the weapon towards the ground, he exclaimed, " But there was blood, Neville — there was blood upon the place. Hark thee, Sir Scot—brave thou wert once, for I have seen thee fight—Say thou hast slain two of the thieves in defence of the Standard — say but one — say thou hast struck but a good blow in our behalf, and get thee out of the camp with thy life and thy infamy!"

" You have called me liar, my Lord King," replied Kenneth, firmly ; " and therein, at least, you have done me wrong—Know, that there was no blood shed in defence of the Standard save that of a poor hound, which, more faithful than his master, defended the charge which he deserted."

" Now, by Saint George!" said Richard, again heaving up his arm—But De Vaux threw himself between the King and the object of his vengeance, and spoke with the blunt truth of his character, " My liege, this must not be — here, not by your own hand. It is enough of folly for one night and day, to have intrusted your banner to a Scot—said I not they were ever fair and false ?"*

" Thou didst, De Vaux ; thou wast right, and I confess it," said Richard. " I should have known him better—I should have remembered how the fox William deceived me touching this Crusade."

" My Lord," said Sir Kenneth, " William of Scotland never deceived ; but circumstances prevented his bringing his forces."

" Peace, shameless!" said the King ; " thou sulliest the name of a prince, even by speaking it.—And yet, De Vaux, it is strange," he added, " to see the bearing of the man. Coward or traitor he must be, yet he abode the blow of Richard Plantagenet, as our arm had been raised to lay knighthood on his shoulder. Had he shown the slightest sign of fear — had but a joint trembled, or an eyelid quivered, I had shattered his head like a crystal goblet. But I cannot strike where there is neither fear nor resistance."

There was a pause.

" My lord," said Kenneth ——

" Ha!" replied Richard, interrupting him, " hast thou found thy speech? Ask grace from Heaven, but none from me, for England is dishonoured through thy fault ; and wert thou mine own and only brother, there is no pardon for thy fault."

" I speak not to demand grace of mortal man," said the Scot ; " it is in your Grace's pleasure to give or refuse me time for Christian shrift—if man denies it, may God grant me the absolution which I would otherwise ask of his Church! But whether I die on the instant, or half an hour hence, I equally beseech your Grace for one moment's opportunity to speak that to your royal person, which highly concerns your fame as a Christian King."

" Say on," said the King, making no doubt that he was about to hear some confession concerning the loss of the Banner.

" What I have to speak," said Sir Kenneth, " touches the royalty of England, and must be said to none ears but thine own."

" Begone with yourselves, sirs," said the King to Neville and De Vaux.

---

* Such were the terms in which the English used to speak of their poor northern neighbours, forgetting that their own encroachments upon the independence of Scotland obliged the weaker nation to defend themselves by policy as well as force. The disgrace must be divided between Edward I. and III., who enforced their domination over a free country, and the Scots who were compelled to take compulsory oaths, without any purpose of keeping them.

The first obeyed, but the latter would not stir from the King's presence.

"If you said I was in the right," replied De Vaux to his sovereign, "I will be treated as one should be who hath been found to be right — that is, I will have my own will. I leave you not with this false Scot."

"How! De Vaux," said Richard, angrily, and stamping slightly, "darest thou not venture our person with one traitor?"

"It is in vain you frown and stamp, my lord," said De Vaux; "I venture not a sick man with a sound one, a naked man with one armed in proof."

"It matters not," said the Scottish knight, "I seek no excuse to put off time — I will speak in presence of the Lord of Gilsland. He is good lord and true."

"But half an hour since," said De Vaux, with a groan, implying a mixture of sorrow and vexation, "and I had said as much for thee!"

"There is treason around you, King of England," continued Sir Kenneth.

"It may well be as thou say'st," replied Richard, "I have a pregnant example."

"Treason that will injure thee more deeply than the loss of an hundred banners in a pitched field. The — the" — Sir Kenneth hesitated, and at length continued, in a lower tone, "The Lady Edith ——"

"Ha!" said the King, drawing himself suddenly into a state of haughty attention, and fixing his eye firmly on the supposed criminal; "What of her? — what of her? — what has she to do with this matter?"

"My lord," said the Scot, "there is a scheme on foot to disgrace your royal lineage by bestowing the hand of the Lady Edith on the Saracen Soldan, and thereby to purchase a peace most dishonourable to Christendom, by an alliance most shameful to England."

This communication had precisely the contrary effect from that which Sir Kenneth expected. Richard Plantagenet was one of those, who, in Iago's words, would not serve God because it was the devil who bade him; advice or information often affected him less according to its real import, than through the tinge which it took from the supposed character and views of those by whom it was communicated. Unfortunately, the mention of his relative's name renewed his recollection of what he considered as extreme presumption in the Knight of the Leopard, even when he stood high in the rolls of chivalry, but which, in his present condition, appeared an insult sufficient to drive the fiery monarch into a frenzy of passion.

"Silence," he said, "infamous and audacious! By Heaven, I will have thy tongue torn out with hot pincers, for mentioning the very name of a noble Christian damsel! Know, degenerate traitor, that I was already aware to what height thou hadst dared to raise thine eyes, and endured it, though it were insolence, even when thou hadst cheated us — for thou art all a deceit — into holding thee as of some name and fame. But now, with lips blistered with the confession of thine own dishonour — that thou shouldst now dare to name our noble kinswoman as one in whose fate thou hast part or interest! What is it to thee if she marry Saracen or Christian? — what is it to thee, if in a camp where princes turn cowards by day, and robbers by night — where brave knights turn to paltry deserters and traitors — what is it, I say, to thee, or any one, if I should please to ally myself to truth, and to valour, in the person of Saladin?"

"Little to me, indeed, to whom all the world will soon be as nothing," answered Sir Kenneth, boldly; "but were I now stretched on the rack, I would tell thee, that what I have said is much to thine own conscience and thine own fame. I tell thee, Sir King, that if thou dost but in thought entertain the purpose of wedding thy kinswoman, the Lady Edith ——"

"Name her not — and for an instant think not of her," said the King, again straining the curtal-axe in his gripe, until the muscles started above his brawny arm, ██████rdage formed by the ivy around the limb of an oak.

"Not name — not think of her!" answered Sir Kenneth, his spirits, stunned as they were by self-depression, beginning to recover their elasticity from this species of controversy, — "Now, by the Cross, on which I place my hope, her name shall be the last word in my mouth, her image the last thought in my mind. Try thy boasted strength on this bare brow, and see if thou canst prevent my purpose."

"He will drive me mad!" said Richard, who, in his despite, was once more staggered in his purpose by the dauntless determination of the criminal.

Ere Thomas of Gilsland could reply, some bustle was heard without, and the arrival of the Queen was announced from the outer part of the pavilion.

"Detain her — detain her, Neville," said the King; "this is no sight for women — Fie, that I have suffered such a paltry traitor to chafe me thus! — Away with him, De Vaux," he whispered, "through the back-entrance of our tent — coop him up close, and answer for his safe custody with your life. — And hark ye — he is presently to die — let him have a ghostly father — we would not kill soul and body. — And stay — hark thee — we will not have him dishonoured — he shall die knight-like, in his belt and spurs; for if his treachery be as black as hell, his boldness may match that of the devil himself."

De Vaux, right glad, if the truth may be guessed, that the scene ended without Richard's descending to the unkingly act of himself slaying an un-resisting prisoner, made haste to remove Sir Kenneth by a private issue to a separate tent, where he was disarmed and put in fetters for security. De Vaux looked on with a steady and melancholy attention, while the provost's officers, to whom Sir Kenneth was now committed, took these severe precautions.

When they were ended, he said solemnly to the unhappy criminal — "It is King Richard's pleasure that you die undegraded — without mutilation of your body, or shame to your arms — and that your head be severed from the trunk by the sword of the executioner."

"It is kind," said the knight, in a low and rather submissive tone of voice, as one who received an unexpected favour; "my family will not then hear the worst of the tale — Oh, my father — my father!"

This muttered invocation did not escape the blunt but kindly-natured Englishman, and he brushed the back of his large hand over his rough features, ere he could proceed.

"It is Richard of England's farther pleasure," he said at length, "that you have speech with a holy man, and I have met on the passage hither with a Carmelite friar, who may fit you for your passage. He waits without, until you are in a habit of mind to receive him."

"Let it be instantly," said the knight. "In this also Richard is kind. I cannot be more fit to see the good father at any time than now; for life and I have taken farewell, as two travellers who have arrived at the cross-way, where their roads separate."

"It is well," said De Vaux, slowly and solemnly; "for it irks me some-what to say that which sums my message. It is King Richard's pleasure that you prepare for instant death."

"God's pleasure and the King's be done," replied the knight, patiently "I neither contest the justice of the sentence, nor desire delay of the execu-tion."

De Vaux began to leave the tent, but very slowly — paused at the door, and looked back at the Scot, from whose aspect thoughts of the world seemed banished, as if he was composing himself into deep devotion. The feelings of the stout English Baron were in general none of the most acute, and yet, on the present occasion, his sympathy overpowered him in an unusual manner. He came hastily back to the bundle of reeds on which the captive lay, took one of his fettered hands, and said, with as much softness as his rough voice was capable of expressing, "Sir Kenn▓▓▓▓▓u art young—yet thou hast a father. My Ralph, whom I left training his little galloway nag on the banks of the Irthing, may one day attain thy years — and, but for last night, I would to God I saw his youth bear such promise as thine—Can nothing be said or done in thy behalf?"

"Nothing," was the melancholy answer. "I have deserted my charge—the banner intrusted to me is lost — when the headsman and block are prepared, the head and trunk are ready to part company."

"Nay, then, God have mercy!" said De Vaux; "yet would I rather than my best horse I had taken that watch myself. There is mystery in it, young man, as a plain man may descry, though he cannot see through it. — Cowardice? pshaw! No coward ever fought as I have seen thee do.—Treachery? I cannot think traitors die in their treason so calmly. Thou hast been trained from thy post by some deep guile — some well-devised stratagem — the cry of some distressed maiden has caught thine ear, or the laughful look of some merry one has taken thine eye. Never blush for it, we have all been led aside by such gear. Come, I pray thee, make a clean conscience of it to me, instead of the priest. Richard is merciful when his mood is abated. Hast thou nothing to intrust to me?"

The unfortunate knight turned his face from the kind warrior, and answered — "NOTHING."

And De Vaux, who had exhausted his topics of persuasion, arose and left the tent, with folded arms, and in melancholy deeper than he thought the occasion merited—even angry with himself, to find that so simple a matter as the death of a Scottish man could affect him so nearly.

"Yet," as he said to himself, "though the rough-footed knaves be our enemies in Cumberland, in Palestine one almost considers them as brethren."

Chapter the Sixteenth.

'Tis not her sense — for sure, in that
There's nothing more than common;
And all her wit is only that,
Like any other woman.

SONG.

THE high-born Berengaria, daughter of Sanchez, King of Navarre, and the Queen-Consort of the heroic Richard, was accounted one of the most beautiful women of the period. Her form was slight, though exquisitely moulded. She was graced with a complexion not common in her country, a profusion of fair hair, and features so extremely juvenile, as to make her look several years younger than she really was, though in reality she was not above one-and-twenty. Perhaps it was under the consciousness of this extremely juvenile appearance, that she affected, or at least practised, a little childish petulance, and wilfulness of manner, not unbefitting, she might suppose, a youthful bride, whose rank and age gave her a right to have her fantasies indulged and attended to. She was by nature perfectly good-humoured, and if her due share of admiration and homage (in her opinion a very large one) was duly resigned to her, no one could possess better temper, or a more friendly disposition; but then, like all despots, the more power that was voluntarily yielded to her, the more she desired to extend her sway. Sometimes, even when all her ambition was gratified, she chose to be a little out of health, and a little out of spirits; and physicians had to toil to invent names for imaginary maladies, while her ladies racked their imagination for new games, new headgear and new court-scandal, to pass away those unpleasant hours, during which their own situation was scarce to be greatly envied. Their most frequent resource for diverting this malady was some trick, or piece of mischief, practised upon each other; and the good Queen, in the buoyancy of her reviving spirits, was, to speak truth, rather too indifferent whether the frolics thus practised were entirely befitting her own dignity, or whether the pain which those suffered upon whom they were inflicted, was not beyond the proportion of pleasure which she herself derived from them. She was confident in her husband's favour, in her high rank, and in her supposed power to make good whatever such pranks might cost others. In a word, she gamboled with the freedom of a young lioness, who is unconscious of the weight of her own paws when laid on those whom she sports with.

The Queen Berengaria loved her husband passionately, but she feared the loftiness and roughness of his character, and as she felt herself not to be his match in intellect, was not much pleased to see that he would often talk with Edith Plantagenet in preference to herself, simply because he found more amusement in her conversation, a more comprehensive understanding, and a more noble cast of thoughts and sentiments, than his beautiful consort exhibited. Berengaria did not hate Edith on this account, far less meditate her any harm: for, allowing for some selfishness, her character was, on the whole, innocent and generous. But the ladies of her train, sharp-sighted in such matters, had for some time discovered, that a poignant jest at the expense of the Lady Edith was a specific for relieving her Grace of England's low spirits, and the discovery saved their imagination much toil.

There was something ungenerous in this, because the Lady Edith was understood to be an orphan; and though she was called Plantagenet, and the Fair Maid of Anjou, and admitted by Richard to certain privileges only granted to the royal family, and held her place in the circle accordingly, yet few knew, and none acquainted with the Court of England ventured to ask, in what exact degree of relationship she stood to Cœur de Lion. She had come with Eleanor, the celebrated Queen Mother of England, and joined Richard at Messina, as one of the ladies destined to attend on Berengaria, whose nuptials then approached. Richard treated his kinswoman with much respectful observance, and the Queen made her her most constant attendant, and, even in despite of the petty jealousy which we have observed, treated her, generally, with suitable respect.

The ladies of the household had, for a long time, no farther advantage over Edith, than might be afforded by an opportunity of censuring a less artfully disposed head attire, or an unbecoming robe; for the lady was judged to be inferior in these mysteries. The silent devotion of the Scottish Knight did not, indeed, pass unnoticed; his liveries, his cognizance, his feats of arms, his mottoes and devices, were nearly watched, and occasionally made the subject of a passing jest. But then came the pilgrimage of the Queen and her ladies to Engaddi, a journey which the Queen had undertaken under a vow for the recovery of her husband's health, and which she had been encouraged to carry into effect by the Archbishop of Tyre for a political purpose. It was then, and in the chapel at that holy place, connected from above with a Carmelite nunnery, from beneath with the cell of the anchorite, that one of the Queen's attendants remarked that secret sign of intelligence which Edith had made to her lover, and failed not instantly to communicate it to her Majesty. The Queen returned from her pilgrimage enriched with this admirable recipe against dulness or ennui, and her train was at the same time augmented by a present of two wretched dwarfs from the dethroned Queen of Jerusalem, as deformed and as crazy (the excellence of that unhappy species) as any Queen could have desired. One of Berengaria's idle amusements had been to t████████ct of the sudden appearance of such ghastly and fantastic forms on the nerves of the Knight when left alone in the chapel; but the jest had been lost by the composure of the Scot, and the interference of the anchorite. She had now tried another, of which the consequences promised to be more serious.

The ladies again met after Sir Kenneth had retired from the tent; and the Queen, at first little moved by Edith's angry expostulations, only replied to her by upbraiding her prudery, and by indulging her wit at the expense of the garb, nation, and, above all, the poverty of the Knight of the Leopard, in which she displayed a good deal of playful malice, mingled with some humour, until Edith was compelled to carry her anxiety to her separate apartment. But when, in the morning, a female, whom Edith had intrusted to make inquiry, brought word that the Standard was missing, and its champion vanished, she burst into the Queen's apartment, and implored her to rise and proceed to the King's tent without delay, and use her powerful mediation to prevent the evil consequences of her jest.

The Queen, frightened in her turn, cast, as is usual, the blame of her own folly on those around her, and endeavoured to comfort Edith's grief, and appease her displeasure, by a thousand inconsistent arguments. She was sure no harm had chanced — the knight was sleeping, she fancied, after his night-watch. What though, for fear of the King's displeasure, he had deserted with the standard — it was but a piece of silk, and he but a needy adventurer — or if he was put under warding for a time, she would soon get the King to pardon him — it was but waiting to let Richard's mood pass away.

Thus she continued talking thick and fast, and heaping together all sorts of inconsistencies, with the vain expectation of persuading both Edith and herself that no harm could come of a frolic, which in her heart she now bitterly repented. But while Edith in vain strove to intercept this torrent of idle talk, she caught the eye of one of the ladies who entered the Queen's apartment. There was death in her look of affright and horror, and Edith, at the first glance of her countenance, had sunk at once on the earth had not strong necessity, and her own elevation of character, enabled her to maintain at least external composure.

"Madam," she said to the Queen, "lose not another word in speaking, but save life—if, indeed," she added, her voice choking as she said it, "life may yet be saved."

"It may — it may," answered the lady Calista. "I have just heard that he has been brought before the King—it is not yet over—but," she added, bursting into a vehement flood of weeping, in which personal apprehensions had some share — "it will soon — unless some course be taken."

"I will vow a golden candlestick to the Holy Sepulchre — a shrine of silver to our Lady of Engaddi—a pall, worth one hundred bezants, to Saint Thomas of Orthez," said the Queen in extremity.

"Up, up, madam!" said Edith; "call on the saints if you list, but be your own best saint."

"Indeed, madam," said the terrified attendant, "the Lady Edith speaks truth. Up, madam, and let us to King Richard's tent, and beg the poor gentleman's life."

"I will go — I will go instantly," said the Queen, rising and trembling excessively; while her women, in as great confusion as herself, were unable to render her those duties which were indispensable to her levee. Calm, composed, only pale as death, Edith ministered to the Queen with her own hand, and alone supplied the deficiencies of her numerous attendants.

"How you wait, wenches!" said the Queen, not able even then to forget frivolous distinctions. "Suffer ye the Lady Edith to do the duties of your attendance? — See'st thou, Edith, they can do nothing — I shall never be attired in time. We will send for the Archbishop of Tyre, and employ him as a mediator."

"Oh, no, no!" exclaimed Edith—"Go yourself, ma▮▮n—you have done ▮▮il, do you confer the remedy."

"▮▮▮ go—I will go," said the Queen; "but if Richard be in his mood, I dare not speak to him—he will kill me!"

"Yet go, gracious madam," said the Lady Calista, who best knew her mistress's temper; "not a lion, in his fury, could look upon such a face and form, and retain so much as an angry thought—far less a love-true knight like the royal Richard, to whom your slightest word would be a command."

"Dost thou think so, Calista?" said the Queen. "Ah, thou little knowest—yet I will go—But see you here—what means this? You have bedizened me in green, a colour he detests. Lo you! let me have a blue robe, and—search for the ruby carcanet, which was part of the King of Cyprus's ransom—it is either in the steel-casket, or somewhere else."

"This, and a man's life at stake!" said Edith, indignantly: "it passes human patience. Remain at your ease, madam—I will go to King Richard—I am a party interested—I will know if the honour of a poor maiden of his blood is to be so far tampered with, that her name shall be abused to train a brave gentleman from his duty, bring him within the compass of death and infamy, and make, at the same time, the glory of England a laughing-stock to the whole Christian army."

At this unexpected burst of passion, B▮▮▮garia listened with an almost stupified look of fear and wonder. But as Edith was about to leave the tent, she exclaimed, though faintly, "Stop her—stop her."

"You must, indeed, stop, noble Lady Edith," said Calista, taking her arm gently; "and you, royal madam, I am sure, will go, and without farther dallying. If the Lady Edith goes alone to the King, he will be dreadfully incensed, nor will it be one life that will stay his fury."

"I will go—I will go," said the Queen, yielding to necessity; and Edith reluctantly halted to wait her movements.

They were now as speedy as she could have desired. The Queen hastily wrapped herself in a large loose mantle, which covered all inaccuracies of the toilet. In this guise, attended by Edith and her women, and preceded and followed by a few officers and men-at-arms, she hastened to the tent of her lion-like husband.

Chapter the Seventeenth.

Were every hair upon his head a life,
And every life were to be supplicated
By numbers equal to those hairs quadrupled,
Life after life should out like waning stars
Before the daybreak—or as festive lamps,
Which have lent lustre to the midnight revel,
Each after each are quench'd when guests depart!

OLD PLAY.

THE entrance of Queen Berengaria into the interior of Richard's pavilion was withstood—in the most respectful and reverential manner indeed—but still withstood, by the chamberlains who watched in the outer tent. She could hear the stern command of the King from within, prohibiting their entrance.

"You see," said the Queen, appealing to Edith, as if she had exhausted all means of intercession in her power—"I knew it—the King will not receive us."

At the same time, they heard Richard speak to ▮▮▮ within—"Go, speed thine office quickly, sirrah — for in that consists thy mercy — ten bezants if thou deal'st on him at one blow. — And, hark thee, villain, observe if his cheek loses colour, or his eye falters — mark me the smallest twitch of the features, or wink of the eyelid—I love to know how brave souls meet death."

"If he sees my blade waved aloft without shrinking, he is the first ever did so," answered a harsh deep voice, which a sense of unusual awe had softened into a sound much lower than its usual coarse tones.

Edith could remain silent no longer. "If your Grace," she said to the Queen, "make not your own way, I make it for you; or if not for your Majesty, for myself, at least. — Chamberlains, the Queen demands to see King Richard—the wife to speak with her husband."

"Noble lady," said the officer, lowering his wand of office, "it grieves me to gainsay you; but his Majesty is busied on matters of life and death."

"And we seek also to speak with him on matters of life and death," said Edith. — "I will make entrance for your Grace." — And putting aside the chamberlain with one hand, she laid hold on the curtain with the other.

"I dare not gainsay her Majesty's pleasure," said the chamberlain, yielding to the vehemence of the fair petitioner; and as he gave way, the Queen found herself obliged to enter the apartment of Richard.

The Monarch was lying on his couch, and at some distance, as awaiting his farther commands, stood a man whose profession it was not difficult to conjecture. He was clothed in a jerkin of red cloth, which reached scantly below the shoulders, leaving the arms bare from about halfway above the elbow, and, as an upper garment, he wore, when about as at present to betake himself to this dreadful office, a coat or tabard without sleeves, something like that of a herald, made of dressed bull's hide, and stained in the front with many a broad spot and speckle of dull crimson. The jerkin, and the tabard over it, reached the knee, and the nether stocks, or covering of the legs, were of the same leather which composed the tabard. A cap of rough shag served to hide the upper part of a visage, which, like that of a screech-owl, seemed desirous to conceal itself from light — the lower part of the face being obscured by a huge red beard, mingling with shaggy locks of the same colour. What features were seen were stern and misanthropical. The man's figure was short, strongly made, with a neck like a bull, very broad shoulders, arms of great and disproportioned length, a huge square trunk, and thick bandy legs. This truculent official leant on a sword, the blade of which was nearly four feet and a half in length, while the handle of twenty inches, surrounded by a ring of lead plummets to counterpoise the weight of such a blade, rose considerably above the man's head, as he rested his arm upon its hilt, waiting for King Richard's farther directions.

On the sudden entrance of the ladies, Richard, who was then lying on his couch, with his face towards the entrance, and resting on his elbow as he spoke to his grisly attendant, flung himself hastily, as if displeased and surprised, to the other side, turning his back to the Queen and the females of her train, and drawing around him the covering of his couch, which, by his own choice, or more probably the flattering selection of his chamberlains, consisted of two large lions' skins, dressed in Venice with such admirable skill that they seemed softer than the hide of the deer.

Berengaria, such as we have described her, knew well — what woman knows not? — her own road to victory. After a hurried glance of undisguised and unaffected terror at the ghastly companion of her husband's secret counsels, she rushed at once to the side of Richard's couch, dropped on her knees, flung her mantle from her shoulders, showing, as they hung down at their full length, her beautiful golden tresses, and while her countenance seemed like a sun bursting through a cloud, yet bearing on its pallid front traces that its splendours have been obscured, she seized upon the right hand of the King, which, as he assumed his wonted posture, had been employed in dragging the covering of his couch, and gradually pulling it to her with a force which was resisted, though but faintly, she possessed herself of that arm, the prop of Christendom, and the dread of Heathenesse, and imprisoning its strength in both her little fairy hands, she bent upon it her brow, and united it to her lips.

"What needs this, Berengaria?" said Richard, his head still averted, but his hand remaining under her control.

"Send away that man—his look kills me!" muttered Berengaria.

"Begone, sirrah," said Richard, still without looking round. "What wait'st thou for? art thou fit to look on these ladies?"

"Your Highness's pleasure touching the head," said the man.

"Out with thee, dog!" answered Richard—"a Christian burial!"

The man disappeared, after casting a look upon the beautiful Queen, in her deranged dress and natural loveliness, with a smile of admiration more hideous in its expression than even his usual scowl of cynical hatred against humanity.

"And now, foolish wench, what wishest thou?" said Richard, turning slowly and half reluctantly round to his royal suppliant.

But it was not in nature for any one, far less an admirer of beauty like Richard, to whom it stood only in the second rank to glory, to look without emotion on the countenance and the tremor of a creature so beautiful as Berengaria, or to feel, without sympathy, that her lips, her brow, were on his hand, and that it was wetted by her tears. By degrees he turned on her his manly countenance, with the softest expression of which his large blue eye, which so often gleamed with insufferable light, was capable. Caressing her fair head, and mingling his large fingers in her beautiful and dishevelled locks, he raised and tenderly kissed the cherub countenance which seemed desirous to hide itself in his hand. The robust form, the broad, noble brow, and majestic looks, the naked arm and shoulder, the lions' skins among which he lay, and the fair fragile feminine creature that kneeled by his side, might have served for a model of Hercules reconciling himself, after a quarrel, to his wife Dejanira.

"And, once more, what seeks the lady of my heart in her knight's pavilion, at this early and unwonted hour?"

"Pardon, my most gracious liege, pardon," said the Queen, whose fears began again to unfit her for the duty of intercessor.

"Pardon! for what?" said the King.

"First, for entering your royal presence too boldly and unadvisedly——" She stopped.

"Thou too boldly!—the sun might as well ask pardon, because his rays entered the windows of some wretch's dungeon. But I was busied with work unfit for thee to witness, my gentle one, and I was unwilling besides, that thou shouldst risk thy precious health where sickness has been so lately rife."

"But thou art now well?" said the Queen, still delaying the communication which she feared to make.

"Well enough to break a lance on the bold crest of that champion who shall refuse to acknowledge thee the fairest dame in Christendom."

"Thou wilt not then refuse me one boon—only one—only a poor life?"

"Ha!—proceed," said King Richard, bending his brows.

"This unhappy Scottish knight"—said the Queen.

"Speak not of him, madam," said Richard, sternly; "he dies—his doom is fixed."

"Nay, my royal liege and love, 'tis but a silken banner neglected—Berengaria will give thee another broidered with her own hand, and rich as ever dallied with the wind. Every pearl I have shall go to bedeck it, and with every pearl I will drop a tear of thankfulness to my generous knight."

"Thou know'st not what thou say'st," said the King, interrupting her in anger. — "Pearls! can all the pearls of the East atone for a speck upon England's honour — all the tears that ever woman's eye wept wash away a stain on Richard's fame?—Go to, madam, know your place, and your time, and your sphere. At present we have duties, in which you cannot be our partner."

"Thou hear'st, Edith," whispered the Queen, "we shall but incense him."

"Be it so," said Edith, stepping forward.—"My lord—I, your poor kinswoman, crave you for justice rather than mercy; and, to the cry of justice, the ears of a monarch should be open at every time, place, and circumstance."

"Ha! our cousin Edith?" said Richard, rising and sitting upright on the side of his couch, covered with his long camiscia — "She speaks ever kinglike, and king-like will I answer her, so she bring no request unworthy of herself or me."

The beauty of Edith was of a more intellectual and less voluptuous cast than that of the Queen; but impatience and anxiety had given her countenance a glow, which it sometimes wanted, and her mien had a character of energetic dignity that imposed silence for a moment even on Richard himself, who, to judge by his looks, would willingly have interrupted her.

"My lord," she said, "this good knight, whose blood you are about to spill, hath done, in his time, service to Christendom. He hath fallen from his duty, through a snare set for him in mere folly and idleness of spirit. A message sent to him in the name of one who—why should I not speak it? — it was in my own — induced him for an instant to leave his post—And what knight in the Christian camp might not have thus far transgressed at the command of a maiden, who, poor howsoever in other qualities, hath yet the blood of Plantagenet in her veins."

"And you saw him, then, cousin?" replied the King, biting his lips, to keep down his passion.

"I did, my liege," said Edith. "It is no time to explain wherefore — I am here neither to exculpate myself nor to blame others."

"And where did you do him such a grace?"

"In the tent of her Majesty the Queen."

"Of our royal consort!" said Richard. "Now by Heaven, by Saint George of England, and every other saint that treads its crystal floor, this is too audacious! I have noticed and overlooked this warrior's insolent admiration of one so far above him, and I grudged him not that one of my blood should shed from her high-born sphere such influence as the sun bestows on the world beneath—But, heaven and earth! that you should have admitted him to an audience by night, in the very tent of our royal consort! — and dare to offer this as an excuse for his disobedience and desertion! By my father's soul, Edith, thou shalt rue this thy life-long in a monastery!"

"My liege," said Edith, "your greatness licenses tyranny. My honour, Lord King, is as little touched as yours, and my Lady the Queen can prove it if she think fit.—But I have already said, I am not here to excuse myself or inculpate others — I ask you but to extend to one, whose fault was committed under strong temptation, that mercy which even you yourself, Lord King, must one day supplicate at a higher tribunal, and for faults, perhaps, less venial."

"Can this be Edith Plantagenet?" said the King bitterly.—"Edith Plantagenet, the wise and the noble?—Or is it some love-sick woman, who cares not for her own fame in comparison of the life of her paramour? Now, by King Henry's soul! little hinders but I order thy minion's skull to be brought from the gibbet, and fixed as a perpetual ornament by the crucifix in thy cell!"

"And if thou dost send it from the gibbet to be placed for ever in my sight," said Edith, "I will say it is a relic of a good knight, cruelly and unworthily done to death by"—(she checked herself)—"by one of whom I shall only say, he should have known better how to reward chivalry. —— Minion call'st thou him!" she continued with increasing vehemence,—"He was indeed my lover, and a most true one—but never sought he grace from me by look or word—contented with such humble observance as men pay to the saints—And the good—the valiant—the faithful—must die for this!"

"Oh, peace, peace, for pity's sake," whispered the Queen; "you do but offend him more!"

"I care not," said Edith; "the spotless virgin fears not the raging lion. Let him work his will on this worthy knight. Edith, for whom he dies, will know how to weep his memory—to me no one shall speak more of politic alliances, to be sanctioned with this poor hand. I could not—I would not—have been his bride living—our degrees were too distant. But death unites the high and the low—I am henceforward the spouse of the grave."

The King was about to answer with much anger, when a Carmelite monk entered the apartment hastily, his head and person muffled in the long mantle and hood of striped cloth of the coarsest texture, which distinguished his order, and, flinging himself on his knees before the King, conjured him, by every holy word and sign, to stop the execution.

"Now, by both sword and sceptre!" said Richard, "the world are leagued to drive me mad!—fools, women, and monks, cross me at every step. How comes he to live still?"

"My gracious liege," said the monk, "I entreated of the Lord of Gilsland to stay the execution until I had thrown myself at your royal——"

"And he was wilful enough to grant thy request," said the King; "but it is of a piece with his wonted obstinacy—And what is it thou hast to say? Speak in the fiend's name!"

"My lord, there is a weighty secret—but it rests under the seal of confession—I dare not tell or even whisper it—but I swear to thee by my holy order—by the habit which I wear—by the blessed Elias, our founder, even him who was translated without suffering the ordinary pangs of mortality—that this youth hath divulged to me a secret, which, if I might confide it to thee, would utterly turn thee from thy bloody purpose in regard to him."

"Good father," said Richard, "that I reverence the church, let the arms which I now wear for her sake bear witness. Give me to know this secret, and I will do what shall seem fitting in the matter. But I am no blind Bayard, to take a leap in the dark under the stroke of a pair of priestly spurs."

"My lord," said the holy man, throwing back his cowl and upper vesture, and discovering under the latter a garment of goatskin, and from beneath the former a visage so wildly wasted by climate, fast, and penance, as to resemble rather the apparition of an animated skeleton than a human face, "for twenty years have I macerated this miserable body in the caverns of Engaddi, doing penance for a great crime. Think you I, who am dead to the world, would contrive a falsehood to endanger my own soul, or that one, bound by the most sacred oaths to the contrary—one such as I, who have but one longing wish connected with earth, to wit, the rebuilding of our Christian Zion,—would betray the secrets of the confessional? Both are alike abhorrent to my very soul."

"So," answered the King, "thou art that hermit of whom men speak so much? Thou art, I confess, like enough to those spirits which walk in dry places, but Richard fears no hobgoblins—and thou art he, too, as I bethink me, to whom the Christian princes sent this very criminal to open a communication with the Soldan, even while I, who ought to have been first consulted, lay on my sick-bed? Thou and they may content themselves—I will not put my neck into the loop of a Carmelite's girdle—And, for your envoy, he shall die, the rather and the sooner that thou dost entreat for him."

"Now God be gracious to thee, Lord King!" said the hermit, with much emotion; "thou art setting that mischief on foot which thou wilt hereafter wish thou hadst stopt though it had cost thee a limb. Rash, blinded man, yet forbear!"

"Away, away," said the King, stamping; "the sun has risen on the dishonour of England, and it is not yet avenged.—Ladies and priest, withdraw, if ye would not hear orders which would displease you; for, by St. George, I swear ——"

"Swear NOT!" said the voice of one who had just then entered the pavilion.

"Ha! my learned Hakim," said the King; "come, I hope, to tax our generosity."

"I come to request instant speech with you—instant—and touching matters of deep interest."

"First look on my wife, Hakim, and let her know in you the preserver of her husband."

"It is not for me," said the physician, folding his arms with an air of Oriental modesty and reverence, and bending his eyes on the ground,—"It is not for me to look upon beauty unveiled, and armed in its splendours."

"Retire, then, Berengaria," said the Monarch; "and, Edith, do you retire also;— nay, renew not your importunities! This I give to them, that the execution shall not be till high noon.— Go, and be pacified — dearest Berengaria, begone.— Edith," he added, with a glance which struck terror even into the courageous soul of his kinswoman, "go, if you are wise."

The females withdrew, or rather hurried from the tent, rank and ceremony forgotten, much like a flock of wild-fowl huddled together, against whom the falcon has made a recent stoop.

They returned from thence to the Queen's pavilion, to indulge in regrets and recriminations, equally unavailing. Edith was the only one who seemed to disdain these ordinary channels of sorrow. Without a sigh, without a tear, without a word of upbraiding, she attended upon the Queen, whose weak temperament showed her sorrow in violent hysterical ecstasies, and passionate hypochondriacal effusions, in the course of which Edith sedulously, and even affectionately, attended her.

"It is impossible she can have loved this knight," said Florise to Calista, her senior in attendance upon the Queen's person. "We have been mistaken; she is but sorry for his fate, as for a stranger who has come to trouble on her account."

"Hush, hush," answered her more experienced and more observant comrade, she is of that proud house of Plantagenet, who never own that a hurt grieves them. While they have themselves been bleeding to death, under a mortal wound, they have been known to bind up the scratches sustained by their more faint-hearted comrades.—Floriso, we have done frightfully wrong; and, for my own part, I would buy with every jewel I have, that our fatal jest had remained unacted."

Chapter the Eighteenth.

This work desires a planetary intelligence
Of Jupiter and Sol; and those great spirits
Are proud, fantastical. It asks great charges
To entice them from the guiding of their spheres
To wait on mortals.
                                    ALBUMAZAR.

THE hermit followed the ladies from the pavilion of Richard, as shadow follows a beam of sunshine when the clouds are driving over the face of the sun. But he turned on the threshold, and held up his hand towards the King in a warning, or almost a menacing posture, as he said—"Wo to him who rejects the counsel of the Church, and betaketh himself to the foul divan of the infidel! King Richard, I do not yet shake the dust from my feet and depart from thy encampment — the sword falls not — but it hangs but by a hair.—Haughty monarch, we shall meet again."

"Be it so, haughty priest," returned Richard, "prouder in thy goatskins than princes in purple and fine linen."

The hermit vanished from the tent, and the King continued, addressing the Arabian, — "Do the dervises of the East, wise Hakim, use such familiarity with their princes?"

"The dervise," replied Adonbec, "should be either a sage or a madman; there is no middle course for him who wears the khirkhah,* who watches by night, and fasts by day. Hence, hath he either wisdom enough to bear himself discreetly in the presence of princes, or else, having no reason bestowed on him, he is not responsible for his own actions."

"Methinks our monks have adopted chiefly the latter character," said Richard — "But to the matter. — In what can I pleasure you, my learned physician?"

"Great King," said El Hakim, making his profound Oriental obeisance, "let thy servant speak one word, and yet live. I would remind thee that thou owest—not to me, their humble instrument—but to the Intelligences, whose benefits I dispense to mortals, a life——"

"And I warrant me thou wouldst have another in requital, ha?" interrupted the King.

"Such is my humble prayer," said the Hakim, "to the great Melech Ric —even the life of this good knight, who is doomed to die, and but for such fault as was committed by the Sultan Adam, surnamed Aboulbeschar, or the father of all men."

"And thy wisdom might remind thee, Hakim, that Adam died for it," said the King, somewhat sternly, and then began to pace the narrow space of his tent with some emotion, and to talk to himself. "Why, God-a-mercy —I knew what he desired as soon as ever he entered the pavilion!—Here is one poor life justly condemned to extinction, and I, a king and a soldier, who have slain thousands by my command, and-scores with my own hand, am to have no power over it, although the honour of my arms, of my house, of my very Queen, hath been attainted by the culprit—By Saint George, it makes me laugh! — By Saint Louis, it reminds me of Blondel's tale of an enchanted castle, where the destined knight was withstood successively in his purpose of entrance by forms and figures the most dissimilar, but all hostile to his undertaking! No sooner one sunk than another appeared!— Wife—Kinswoman—Hermit—Hakim—each appears in the lists as soon as the other is defeated!—Why, this is a single knight fighting against the whole mêlée of the tournament—ha! ha! ha!"—And Richard laughed

---

* Literally, the torn robe. The habit of the dervises is so called.

aloud; for he had, in fact, begun to change his mood, his resentment being usually too violent to be of long endurance.

The physician meanwhile looked on him with a countenance of surprise, not unmingled with contempt; for the Eastern people make no allowance for those mercurial changes in the temper, and consider open laughter, upon almost any account, as derogatory to the dignity of man, and becoming only to women and children. At length, the sage addressed the King, when he saw him more composed.

"A doom of death should not issue from laughing lips.—Let thy servant hope that thou hast granted him this man's life."

"Take the freedom of a thousand captives instead," said Richard; "restore so many of thy countrymen to their tents and families, and I will give the warrant instantly. This man's life can avail thee nothing, and it is forfeited."

"All our lives are forfeited," said the Hakim, putting his hand to his cap. "But the great Creditor is merciful, and exacts not the pledge rigorously nor untimely."

"Thou canst show me," said Richard, "no special interest thou hast to become intercessor betwixt me and the execution of justice, to which I am sworn as a crowned king."

"Thou art sworn to the dealing forth mercy as well as justice," said El Hakim; "but what thou seekest, great King, is the execution of thine own will. And, for the concern I have in this request, know that many a man's life depends upon thy granting this boon."

"Explain thy words," said Richard; "but think not to impose upon me by false pretexts."

"Be it far from thy servant!" said Adonbec. "Know, then, that the medicine to which thou, Sir King, and many one beside, owe their recovery, is a talisman, composed under certain aspects of the heavens, when the Divine Intelligences are most propitious. I am but the poor administrator of its virtues. I dip it in a cup of water, observe the fitting hour to administer it to the patient, and the potency of the draught works the cure."

"A most rare medicine," said the King, "and a commodious! and, as it may be carried in the leech's purse, would save the whole caravan of camels which they require to convey drugs and physic-stuff—I marvel there is any other in use."

"It is written," answered the Hakim, with imperturbable gravity, "'abuse not the steed which hath borne thee from the battle.' Know, that such talismans might indeed be framed, but rare has been the number of adepts who have dared to undertake the application of their virtue. Severe restrictions, painful observances, fasts, and penance, are necessary on the part of the sage who uses this mode of cure; and if, through neglect of these preparations, by his love of ease, or his indulgence of sensual appetite, he omits to cure at least twelve persons within the course of each moon, the virtue of the divine gift departs from the amulet, and both the last patient and the physician will be exposed to speedy misfortune, neither will they survive the year. I require yet one life to make up the appointed number."

"Go out into the camp, good Hakim, where thou wilt find a-many," said the King, "and do not seek to rob my headsman of his patients; it is unbecoming a mediciner of thine eminence to interfere with the practice of another. — Besides, I cannot see how delivering a criminal from the death he deserves, should go to make up thy tale of miraculous cures."

"When thou canst show why a draught of cold water should have cured thee, when the most precious drugs failed," said the Hakim, "thou mayst reason on the other mysteries attendant on this matter. For myself, I am inefficient to the great work, having this morning touched an unclean animal. Ask, therefore, no farther questions; it is enough that, by sparing this man's life at my request, you will deliver yourself, great King, and thy servant, from a great danger."

"Hark thee, Adonbec," replied the King, "I have no objection that leeches should wrap their words in mist, and pretend to derive knowledge from the stars; but when you bid Richard Plantagenet fear that a danger will fall upon *him* from some idle omen, or omitted ceremonial, you speak to no ignorant Saxon, or doting old woman, who foregoes her purpose because a hare crosses the path, a raven croaks, or a cat sneezes."

"I cannot hinder your doubt of my words," said Adonbec; "but yet, let my Lord the King grant that truth is on the tongue of his servant,—will he think it just to deprive the world, and every wretch who may suffer by the pains which so lately reduced him to that couch, of the benefit of this most virtuous talisman, rather than extend his forgiveness to one poor criminal? Bethink you, Lord King, that though thou canst slay thousands, thou canst not restore one man to health. Kings have the power of Satan to torment, sages that of Allah to heal—beware how thou hinderest the good to humanity, which thou canst not thyself render. Thou canst cut off the head, but not cure the aching tooth."

"This is over insolent," said the King, hardening himself, as the Hakim assumed a more lofty, and almost a commanding tone. "We took thee for our leech, not for our counsellor, or conscience-keeper."

"And is it thus the most renowned Prince of Frangistan repays benefit done to his royal person?" said El Hakim, exchanging the humble and stooping posture, in which he had hitherto solicited the King, for an attitude lofty and commanding. "Know, then," he said, "that through every court of Europe and Asia—to Moslem and Nazarene—to knight and lady—wherever harp is heard and sword worn—wherever honour is loved and infamy detested—to every quarter of the world will I denounce thee, Melech Ric, as thankless and ungenerous; and even the lands—if there be any such—that never heard of thy renown, shall yet be acquainted with thy shame!"

"Are these terms to me, vile infidel!" said Richard, striding up to him in fury.—"Art weary of thy life?"

"Strike!" said El Hakim; "thine own deed shall then paint thee more worthless than could my words, though each had an hornet's sting."

Richard turned fiercely from him, folded his arms, traversed the tent as before, and then exclaimed, "Thankless and ungenerous!—as well be termed coward and infidel!—Hakim, thou hast chosen thy boon; and though I had rather thou hadst asked my crown-jewels, yet I may not, king-like, refuse thee. Take this Scot, therefore, to thy keeping—the provost will deliver him to thee on this warrant."

He hastily traced one or two lines, and gave them to the physician. "Use him as thy bond-slave, to be disposed of as thou wilt—only, let him beware how he comes before the eyes of Richard. Hark thee—thou art wise—he hath been over bold among those in whose fair looks and weak judgments we trust our honour, as you of the East lodge your treasures in caskets of silver wire, as fine and as frail as the web of a gossamer."

"Thy servant understands the word of the King," said the sage, at once resuming the reverent style of address in which he had commenced. "When the rich carpet is soiled, the fool pointeth to the stain—the wise man covers it with his mantle. I have heard my lord's pleasure, and to hear is to obey."

"It is well," said the King; "let him consult his own safety, and never appear in my presence more.—Is there aught else in which I may do thee pleasure?"

"The bounty of the King hath filled my cup to the brim," said the sage; "yea, it hath been abundant as the fountain which sprung up amid the camp of the descendants of Israel, when the rock was stricken by the rod of Moussa Ben Amran."

"Ay, but," said the King, smiling, "it required, as in the desert, a hard blow on the rock ere it yielded its treasures. I would that I knew something to pleasure thee, which I might yield as freely as the natural fountain sends forth its waters."

"Let me touch that victorious hand," said the sage, "in token, that if Adonbec el Hakim should hereafter demand a boon of Richard of England, he may do so, yet plead his command."

"Thou hast hand and glove upon it, man," replied Richard; "only, if thou couldst consistently make up thy tale of patients without craving me to deliver from punishment those who have deserved it, I would more willingly discharge my debt in some other form."

"May thy days be multiplied!"—answered the Hakim, and withdrew from the apartment after the usual deep obeisance.

King Richard gazed after him as he departed, like one but half-satisfied with what had passed.

"Strange pertinacity," he said, "in this Hakim, and a wonderful chance to interfere between that audacious Scot and the chastisement he has merited so richly. Yet, let him live! there is one brave man the more in the world.—And now for the Austrian.—Ho, is the Baron of Gilsland there without?"

Sir Thomas de Vaux thus summoned, his bulky form speedily darkened the opening of the pavilion, while behind him glided as a spectre, unannounced, yet unopposed, the savage form of the hermit of Engaddi, wrapped in his goatskin mantle.

Richard, without noticing his presence, called in a loud tone to the Baron, "Sir Thomas de Vaux, of Lanercost and Gilsland, take trumpet and herald, and go instantly to the tent of him whom they call Archduke of Austria, and see that it be when the press of his knights and vassals is greatest around him,—as is likely at this hour, for the German boar breakfasts ere he hears mass—enter his presence with as little reverence as thou may'st, and impeach him, on the part of Richard of England, that he hath this night, by his own hand, or that of others, stolen from its staff the Banner of England. Wherefore, say to him our pleasure, that, within an hour from the time of my speaking, he restore the said banner with all reverence — he himself and his principal barons waiting the whilst with heads uncovered, and without their robes of honour.—And that, moreover, he pitch beside it, on the one hand, his own Banner of Austria reversed, as that which hath been dishonoured by theft and felony—and on the other, a lance, bearing the bloody head of him who was his nearest counsellor, or assistant, in this base injury—And say, that such our behests being punctually discharged, we will, for the sake of our vow, and the weal of the Holy Land, forgive his other forfeits."

"And how if the Duke of Austria deny all accession to this act of wrong and of felony?" said Thomas de Vaux.

"Tell him," replied the King, "we will prove it upon his body—ay, were he backed with his two bravest champions. Knight-like will we prove it, on foot or on horse, in the desert or in the field, time, place, and arms, all at his own choice."

"Bethink you of the peace of God and the Church, my liege lord," said the Baron of Gilsland, "among those princes engaged in this holy Crusade."

"Bethink you how to execute my commands, my liege vassal," answered Richard, impatiently. "Methinks men expect to turn our purpose by their breath, as boys blow feathers to and fro — Peace of the Church!—who, I prithee, minds it? The peace of the Church, among Crusaders, implies war with the Saracens, with whom the princes have made truce, and the one ends with the other. And, besides, see you not how every prince of them is seeking his own several ends?—I will seek mine also—and that is honour. For honour I came hither, and if I may not win it upon the Saracens, at least I will not lose a jot from any respect to this paltry Duke, though he were bulwarked and buttressed by every prince in the Crusade."

De Vaux turned to obey the King's mandate, shrugging his shoulders at the same time, the bluntness of his nature being unable to conceal that its tenor went against his judgment. But the hermit of Engaddi stepped forward, and assumed the air of one charged with higher commands than those of a mere earthly potentate. Indeed, his dress of shaggy skins, his uncombed and untrimmed hair and beard, his lean, wild, and contorted features, and the almost insane fire which gleamed from under his bushy eyebrows, made him approach nearly to our idea of some seer of Scripture, who, charged with high mission to the sinful Kings of Judah or Israel, descended from the rocks and caverns in which he dwelt in abstracted solitude, to abash earthly tyrants in the midst of their pride, by discharging on them the blighting denunciations of Divine Majesty, even as the cloud discharges the lightning with which it is fraught, on the pinnacles and towers of castles and palaces. In the midst of his most wayward mood, Richard respected the Church and its ministers, and though offended at the intrusion of the hermit into his tent, he greeted him with respect; at the same time, however, making a sign to Sir Thomas de Vaux to hasten on his message.

But the hermit prohibited the baron, by gesture, look, and word, to stir a yard on such an errand; and, holding up his bare arm, from which the goatskin mantle fell back in the violence of his action, he waved it aloft, meagre with famine, and wealed with the blows of the discipline.

"In the name of God, and of the most holy Father, the vicegerent of the Christian Church upon earth, I prohibit this most profane and blood-thirsty, and brutal defiance, betwixt two Christian princes, whose shoulders are signed with the blessed mark under which they swore brotherhood. Wo to him by whom it is broken!—Richard of England, recall the most unhallowed message thou hast given to that baron — Danger and death are nigh thee! —the dagger is glancing at thy very throat!——"

"Danger and Death are playmates to Richard," answered the monarch proudly; "and he hath braved too many swords to fear a dagger."

"Danger and Death are near," replied the seer; and, sinking his voice to a hollow, unearthly tone, he added, "And after death the judgment!"

"Good and holy father," said Richard, "I reverence thy person and thy sanctity——"

"Reverence not me!" interrupted the hermit; "reverence sooner the vilest insect that crawls by the shores of the Dead Sea, and feeds upon its accursed slime. But reverence Him whose commands I speak — Reverence Him whose sepulchre you have vowed to rescue—Revere the oath of concord which you have sworn, and break not the silver cord of union and fidelity with which you have bound yourself to your princely confederates."

"Good father," said the King, "you of the church seem to me to presume somewhat, if a layman may say so much, upon the dignity of your holy character. Without challenging your right to take charge of our consciences, methinks you might leave us the charge of our own honour."

"Presume!" repeated the hermit—"is it for me to presume, royal Richard, who am but the bell obeying the hand of the sexton—but the senseless and worthless trumpet, carrying the command of him who sounds it? — See, on my knees I throw myself before thee, imploring thee to have mercy on Christendom, on England, and on thyself!"

"Rise, rise," said Richard, compelling him to stand up; "it beseems not that knees, which are so frequently bended to the Deity, should press the ground in honour of man. What danger awaits us, reverend father? and when stood the power of England so low, that the noisy bluster of this new-made Duke's displeasure should alarm her, or her monarch?"

"I have looked forth from my mountain turret upon the starry host of heaven, as each in his midnight circuit uttered wisdom to another, and knowledge to the few who can understand their voice. There sits an enemy in thy House of Life, Lord King, malign at once to thy fame, and thy prosperity—an emanation of Saturn, menacing thee with instant and bloody peril, and which, but thou yield thy proud will to the rule of thy duty, will presently crush thee, even in thy pride."

"Away, away—this is heathen science," said the King. "Christians practise it not — wise men believe it not. — Old man, thou dotest."

"I dote not, Richard," answered the hermit — "I am not so happy. I know my condition, and that some portion of reason is yet permitted me, not for my own use, but that of the Church, and the advancement of the Cross. I am the blind man who holds a torch to others, though it yields no light to himself. Ask me touching what concerns the weal of Christendom, and of this Crusade, and I will speak with thee as the wisest counsellor on whose tongue persuasion ever sat. Speak to me of my own wretched being, and my words shall be those of the maniac outcast which I am."

"I would not break the bands of unity asunder among the Princes of the Crusade," said Richard, with a mitigated tone and manner; "but what atonement can they render me for the injustice and insult which I have sustained?"

"Even of that I am prepared and commissioned to speak by the Council, which, meeting hastily at the summons of Philip of France, have taken measures for that effect."

"Strange," replied Richard, "that others should treat of what is due to the wounded Majesty of England!"

"They are willing to anticipate your demands, if it be possible," answered the hermit. "In a body, they consent that the Banner of England be replaced on Saint George's Mount, and they lay under ban and condemnation the audacious criminal, or criminals, by whom it was outraged, and will announce a princely reward to any who shall denounce the delinquent's guilt, and give his flesh to the wolves and ravens."

"And Austria," said Richard—"upon whom rest such strong presumptions that he was the author of the deed?"

"To prevent discord in the host," replied the hermit, "Austria will clear himself of the suspicion, by submitting to whatsoever ordeal the Patriarch of Jerusalem shall impose."

"Will he clear himself by the trial by combat?" said King Richard.

"His oath prohibits it," said the hermit; "and, moreover, the Council of the Princes ——"

"Will neither authorize battle against the Saracens," interrupted Richard, "nor against any one else. But it is enough, father—thou hast shown me the folly of proceeding as I designed in this matter. You shall sooner light your torch in a puddle of rain, than bring a spark out of a cold-blooded coward. There is no honour to be gained on Austria, and so let him pass. — I will have him perjure himself, however; I will insist on the ordeal. — How I shall laugh to hear his clumsy fingers hiss, as he grasps the red-hot globe of iron!—Ay, or his huge mouth riven, and his gullet swelling to suffocation, as he endeavours to swallow the consecrated bread!"

"Peace, Richard," said the hermit — "Oh, peace, for shame if not for charity! Who shall praise or honour princes, who insult and calumniate each other?—Alas! that a creature so noble as thou art—so accomplished in princely thoughts and princely daring — so fitted to honour Christendom by thy actions, and, in thy calmer mood, to rule her by thy wisdom, should yet have the brute and wild fury of the lion, mingled with the dignity and courage of that king of the forest!"

He remained an instant musing with his eyes fixed on the ground, and then proceeded — " But Heaven, that knows our imperfect nature, accepts of our imperfect obedience, and hath delayed, though not averted, the bloody end of thy daring life. The destroying angel hath stood still, as of old by the threshing-floor of Araunah the Jebusite, and the blade is drawn in his hand, by which, at no distant date, Richard, the lion-hearted, shall be as low as the meanest peasant."

" Must it then be so soon ?"— said Richard. " Yet, even so be it. May my course be bright, if it be but brief !"

" Alas! noble King," said the solitary, and it seemed as if a tear (unwonted guest) were gathering in his dry and glazened eye—"short and melancholy, marked with mortification, and calamity, and captivity, is the span that divides thee from the grave which yawns for thee — a grave in which thou shalt be laid without lineage to succeed thee—without the tears of a people, exhausted by thy ceaseless wars, to lament thee —without having extended the knowledge of thy subjects — without having done aught to enlarge their happiness."

" But not without renown, monk — not without the tears of the lady of my love! These consolations, which thou canst neither know nor estimate, await upon Richard to his grave."

" Do I not know — can I not estimate, the value of minstrel's praise, and of lady's love !" retorted the hermit, in a tone, which for a moment seemed to emulate the enthusiasm of Richard himself. " King of England," he continued, extending his emaciated arm, "the blood which boils in thy blue veins is not more noble than that which stagnates in mine. Few and cold as the drops are, they still are of the blood of the royal Lusignan — of the heroic and sainted Godfrey. I am—that is, I was when in the world—Alberick Mortemar ——"

" Whose deeds," said Richard, "have so often filled Fame's trumpet ! Is it so — can it be so ? — Could such a light as thine fall from the horizon of chivalry, and yet men be uncertain where its embers had alighted ?"

" Seek a fallen star," said the hermit, " and thou shalt only light on some foul jelly, which, in shooting through the horizon, has assumed for a moment an appearance of splendour. Richard, if I thought that rending the bloody veil from my horrible fate could make thy proud heart stoop to the discipline of the church, I could find in my heart to tell thee a tale, which I have hitherto kept gnawing at my vitals in concealment, like the self-devoted youth of Heathenesse. — Listen, then, Richard, and may the grief and despair, which cannot avail this wretched remnant of what was once a man, be powerful as an example to so noble, yet so wild a being as thou art ! Yes — I will — I *will* tear open the long-hidden wounds, although in thy very presence they should bleed to death !"

King Richard, upon whom the history of Alberick of Mortemar had made a deep impression in his early years, when minstrels were regaling his father's halls with legends of the Holy Land, listened with respect to the outlines of a tale, which, darkly and imperfectly sketched, indicated sufficiently the cause of the partial insanity of this singular and most unhappy being.

" I need not," he said, "tell thee that I was noble in birth, high in fortune, strong in arms, wise in council. All these I was; but while the noblest ladies in Palestine strove which should wind garlands for my helmet, my love was fixed—unalterably and devotedly fixed—on a maiden of low degree. Her father, an ancient soldier of the Cross, saw our passion, and knowing the difference betwixt us, saw no other refuge for his daughter's honour than to place her within the shadow of the cloister. I returned from a distant expedition, loaded with spoils and honour, to find my happiness was destroyed for ever ! I, too, sought the cloister, and Satan, who had marked me for his own, breathed into my heart a vapour of spiritual pride, which could only have had its source in his own infernal regions. I had risen as high in the church as before in the state—I was, forsooth, the wise, the self-sufficient, the impeccable!—I was the counsellor of councils—I was the director of prelates—how should I stumble?—wherefore should I fear temptation?—Alas! I became confessor to a sisterhood, and amongst that sisterhood I found the long loved—the long lost. Spare me farther confession!—A fallen nun, whose guilt was avenged by self-murder, sleeps soundly in the vaults of Engaddi, while, above her very grave, gibbers, moans, and roars a creature, to whom but so much reason is left as may suffice to render him completely sensible to his fate!"

"Unhappy man!" said Richard, "I wonder no longer at thy misery. How didst thou escape the doom, which the canons denounce against thy offence?"

"Ask one who is yet in the gall of worldly bitterness," said the hermit, "and he will speak of a life spared for personal respects, and from consideration to high birth. But, Richard, I tell thee, that Providence hath preserved me, to lift me on high as a light and beacon, whose ashes, when this earthly fuel is burnt out, must yet be flung into Tophet. Withered and shrunk as this poor form is, it is yet animated with two spirits—one active, shrewd, and piercing, to advocate the cause of the Church of Jerusalem—one mean, abject, and despairing, fluctuating between madness and misery, to mourn over my own wretchedness, and to guard holy relics, on which it would be most sinful for me even to cast my eye. Pity me not!—it is but sin to pity the loss of such an abject—pity me not, but profit by my example. Thou standest on the highest, and, therefore, on the most dangerous pinnacle, occupied by any Christian prince. Thou art proud of heart, loose of life, bloody of hand. Put from thee the sins which are to thee as daughters—though they be dear to the sinful Adam, expel these adopted furies from thy breast—thy pride, thy luxury, thy blood-thirstiness."

"He raves," said Richard, turning from the solitary to De Vaux, as one who felt some pain from a sarcasm which yet he could not resent—then turned him calmly, and somewhat scornfully to the anchoret, as he replied—"Thou hast found a fair bevy of daughters, reverend father, to one who hath been but few months married; but since I must put them from my roof, it were but like a father to provide them with suitable matches. Wherefore, I will part with my pride to the noble Canons of the Church—my luxury, as thou call'st it, to the Monks of the rule—and my blood-thirstiness to the Knights of the Temple."

"Oh, heart of steel, and hand of iron," said the anchoret, "upon whom example, as well as advice, is alike thrown away!—Yet shalt thou be spared for a season, in case it so be thou shouldst turn and do that which is acceptable in the sight of Heaven.—For me, I must return to my place.—Kyrie Eleison!—I am he through whom the rays of heavenly grace dart like those of the sun through a burning glass, concentrating them on other objects, until they kindle and blaze, while the glass itself remains cold and uninfluenced. — Kyrie Eleison!—the poor must be called, for the rich have refused the banquet—Kyrie Eleison!"

So saying, he burst from the tent, uttering loud cries.

"A mad priest!"—said Richard, from whose mind the frantic exclamations of the hermit had partly obliterated the impression produced by the detail of his personal history and misfortunes. "After him, De Vaux, and see he comes to no harm; for, Crusaders as we are, a juggler hath more reverence amongst our varlets than a priest or a saint, and they may, perchance, put some scorn upon him."

The knight obeyed, and Richard presently gave way to the thoughts which the wild prophecy of the monk had inspired.—"To die early—without lineage—without lamentation?—a heavy sentence, and well that it is not passed by a more competent judge. Yet the Saracens, who are accomplished in mystical knowledge, will often maintain, that He, in whose eyes the wisdom of the sage is but as folly, inspires wisdom and prophecy into the seeming folly of the madman. Yonder hermit is said to read the stars too, an art generally practised in these lands, where the heavenly host was of yore the object of idolatry. I would I had asked him touching the loss of my banner; for not the blessed Tishbite, the founder of his order, could seem more wildly rapt out of himself, or speak with a tongue more resembling that of a prophet. — How now, De Vaux, what news of the mad priest?"

"Mad priest, call you him, my lord?" answered De Vaux. "Methinks he resembles more the blessed Baptist himself, just issued from the wilderness. He has placed himself on one of the military engines, and from thence he preaches to the soldiers, as never man preached since the time of Peter the Hermit. The camp, alarmed by his cries, crowd around him in thousands; and breaking off every now and then from the main thread of his discourse, he addresses the several nations, each in their own language, and presses upon each the arguments best qualified to urge them to perseverance in the delivery of Palestine."

"By this light, a noble hermit!" said King Richard. "But what else could come from the blood of Godfrey? *He* despair of safety, because he hath in former days lived *par amours?* I will have the Pope send him an ample remission, and I would not less willingly be intercessor had his *belle amie* been an abbess."

As he spoke, the Archbishop of Tyre craved audience, for the purpose of requesting Richard's attendance, should his health permit, on a secret conclave of the chiefs of the Crusade, and to explain to him the military and political incidents which had occurred during his illness.

Chapter the Nineteenth.

Must we then sheathe our still victorious sword;
Turn back our forward step, which ever trode
O'er foemen's necks the onward path of glory;
Unclasp the mail, which with a solemn vow,
In God's own house, we hung upon our shoulders,
That vow, as unaccomplish'd as the promise
Which village nurses make to still their children,
And after think no more of?——
            THE CRUSADE, A *Tragedy.*

THE Archbishop of Tyre was an emissary well chosen to communicate to Richard tidings, which from another voice the lion-hearted King would not have brooked to hear, without the most unbounded explosions of resentment. Even this sagacious and reverend prelate found difficulty in inducing him to listen to news, which destroyed all his hopes of gaining back the Holy Sepulchre by force of arms, and acquiring the renown, which the universal all-hail of Christendom was ready to confer upon him, as the Champion of the Cross.

But, by the Archbishop's report, it appeared that Saladin was assembling all the force of his hundred tribes, and that the monarchs of Europe, already disgusted from various motives with the expedition, which had proved so hazardous, and was daily growing more so, had resolved to abandon their purpose. In this they were countenanced by the example of Philip of France, who, with many protestations of regard, and assurances that he would first see his brother of England in safety, declared his intention to return to Europe. His great vassal, the Earl of Champagne, had adopted the same resolution; and it could not excite surprise, that Leopold of Austria, affronted as he had been by Richard, was glad to embrace an opportunity of deserting a cause, in which his haughty opponent was to be considered as chief. Others announced the same purpose; so that it was plain that the King of England was to be left, if he chose to remain, supported only by such volunteers as might, under such depressing circumstances, join themselves to the English army; and by the doubtful aid of Conrade of Montserrat, and the military orders of the Temple, and of Saint John, who, though they were sworn to wage battle against the Saracens, were at least equally jealous of any European monarch achieving the conquest of Palestine, where, with shortsighted and selfish policy, they proposed to establish independent dominions of their own.

It needed not many arguments to show Richard the truth of his situation; and, indeed, after his first burst of passion, he sat him calmly down, and with gloomy looks, head depressed, and arms folded on his bosom, listened to the Archbishop's reasoning on the impossibility of his carrying on the Crusade when deserted by his companions. Nay, he forbore interruption, even when the prelate ventured, in measured terms, to hint that Richard's own impetuosity had been one main cause of disgusting the princes with the expedition.

"*Confiteor*," answered Richard, with a dejected look, and something of a melancholy smile; "I confess, reverend father, that I ought on some accounts to sing *culpa mea*. But is it not hard that my frailties of temper should be visited with such a penance, that, for a burst or two of natural passion, I should be doomed to see fade before me ungathered such a rich harvest of glory to God and honour to chivalry?—But it shall *not* fade.—By the soul of the Conqueror, I will plant the Cross on the towers of Jerusalem, or it shall be planted over Richard's grave!"

"Thou mayst do it," said the prelate, "yet not another drop of Christian blood be shed in the quarrel."

"Ah, you speak of compromise, Lord Prelate—but the blood of the infidel hounds must also cease to flow," said Richard.

"There will be glory enough," replied the Archbishop, "in having extorted from Saladin, by force of arms, and by the respect inspired by your fame, such conditions, as at once restore the Holy Sepulchre, open the Holy Land to pilgrims, secure their safety by strong fortresses, and, stronger than all, assure the safety of the Holy City, by conferring on Richard the title of King Guardian of Jerusalem."

"How!" said Richard, his eyes sparkling with unusual light—"I—I—I the King Guardian of the Holy City! Victory itself, but that it *is* victory, could not gain more — scarce so much, when won with unwilling and disunited forces. — But Saladin still proposes to retain his interest in the Holy Land?"

"As a joint sovereign, the sworn ally," replied the Prelate, "of the mighty Richard — his relative — if it may be permitted by marriage."

"By marriage!" said Richard, surprised, yet less so than the Prelate had expected. "Ha! — Ay — Edith Plantagenet. Did I dream this? — or did some one tell me? My head is still weak from this fever, and has been agitated.—Was it the Scot, or the Hakim, or yonder holy hermit, that hinted such a wild bargain?"

"The hermit of Engaddi, most likely," said the Archbishop; "for he hath toiled much in this matter; and since the discontent of the princes has become apparent, and a separation of their forces unavoidable, he hath had many consultations, both with Christian and Pagan, for arranging such a pacification, as may give to Christendom, at least in part, the objects of this holy warfare."

"My kinswoman to an infidel — Ha!" exclaimed Richard, as his eyes began to sparkle.

The Prelate hastened to avert his wrath.

"The Pope's consent must doubtless be first attained, and the holy hermit, who is well known at Rome, will treat with the Holy Father."

"How? — without our consent first given?" said the King.

"Surely no," said the Bishop, in a quiet and insinuating tone of voice; "only with and under your special sanction."

"My sanction to marry my kinswoman to an infidel?" said Richard; yet he spoke rather in a tone of doubt than as distinctly reprobating the measure proposed. "Could I have dreamed of such a composition when I leaped upon the Syrian shore from the prow of my galley, even as a lion springs on his prey!— And now — But proceed — I will hear with patience."

Equally delighted and surprised to find his task so much easier than he had apprehended, the Archbishop hastened to pour forth before Richard the instances of such alliances in Spain — not without countenance from the Holy See—the incalculable advantages which all Christendom would derive from the union of Richard and Saladin, by a bond so sacred; and, above all, he spoke with great vehemence and unction on the probability that Saladin would, in case of the proposed alliance, exchange his false faith for the true one.

"Hath the Soldan shown any disposition to become Christian?" said Richard; "if so, the king lives not on earth to whom I would grant the hand of a kinswoman, ay, or sister, sooner than to my noble Saladin — ay, though the one came to lay crown and sceptre at her feet, and the other had nothing to offer but his good sword and better heart!"

"Saladin hath heard our Christian teachers," said the Bishop, somewhat evasively,—"my unworthy self—and others—and as he listens with patience, and replies with calmness, it can hardly be but that he be snatched as a brand from the burning. *Magna est veritas, et prevalebit!* Moreover, the hermit of Engaddi, few of whose words have fallen fruitless to the ground, is possessed fully with the belief that there is a calling of the Saracens and the other heathen approaching, to which this marriage shall be matter of induction. He readeth the course of the stars; and dwelling, with maceration of the flesh, in those divine places which the saints have trodden of old, the spirit of Elijah the Tishbite, the founder of his blessed order, hath been with him as it was with the prophet Elisha, the son of Shaphat, when he spread his mantle over him."

King Richard listened to the Prelate's reasoning, with a downcast brow and a troubled look.

"I cannot tell," he said, "how it is with me; but methinks these cold counsels of the Princes of Christendom have infected me too with a lethargy of spirit. The time hath been, that, had a layman proposed such alliance to me, I had struck him to the earth—if a churchman, I had spit at him as a renegade and priest of Baal — yet now this counsel sounds not so strange in mine ear; for why should I not seek for brotherhood and alliance with a Saracen, brave, just, generous, — who loves and honours a worthy foe, as if he were a friend, — whilst the Princes of Christendom shrink from the side of their allies, and forsake the cause of Heaven and good knighthood? — But I will possess my patience, and will not think of them. Only one attempt will I make to keep this gallant brotherhood together, if it be possible; and if I fail, Lord Archbishop, we will speak together of thy counsel, which, as now, I neither accept nor altogether reject. Wend we to the Council, my lord — the hour calls us. Thou say'st Richard is hasty and proud—thou shalt see him humble himself like the lowly broom-plant, from which he derives his surname."

With the assistance of those of his privy chamber, the King then hastily robed himself in a doublet and mantle of a dark and uniform colour; and without any mark of regal dignity, excepting a ring of gold upon his head, he hastened with the Archbishop of Tyre to attend the Council, which waited but his presence to commence its sitting.

The pavilion of the Council was an ample tent, having before it the large Banner of the Cross displayed, and another, on which was portrayed a female kneeling, with dishevelled hair and disordered dress, meant to represent the desolate and distressed Church of Jerusalem, and bearing the motto, *Afflictæ sponsæ ne obliviscaris.* Warders, carefully selected, kept every one at a distance from the neighbourhood of this tent, lest the debates, which were sometimes of a loud and stormy character, should reach other ears than those they were designed for.

Here, therefore, the Princes of the Crusade were assembled, awaiting Richard's arrival: and even the brief delay which was thus interposed, was turned to his disadvantage by his enemies; various instances being circulated of his pride, and undue assumption of superiority, of which even the necessity of the present short pause was quoted as an instance. Men strove to fortify each other in their evil opinion of the King of England, and vindicated the offence which each had taken, by putting the most severe construction upon circumstances the most trifling; and all this, perhaps, because they were conscious of an instinctive reverence for the heroic monarch, which it would require more than ordinary efforts to overcome.

They had settled, accordingly, that they should receive him on his entrance with slight notice, and no more respect than was exactly necessary to keep within the bounds of cold ceremonial. But when they beheld that noble form, that princely countenance, somewhat pale from his late illness — the eye which had been called by minstrels the bright star of battle and victory —when his feats, almost surpassing human strength and valour, rushed on their recollection, the Council of Princes simultaneously arose — even the jealous King of France, and the sullen and offended Duke of Austria, arose with one consent, and the assembled princes burst forth with one voice in the acclamation, "God save King Richard of England!—Long life to the valiant Lion's heart!"

With a countenance frank and open as the summer sun when it rises, Richard distributed his thanks around, and congratulated himself on being once more among his royal brethren of the Crusades.

"Some brief words he desired to say," such was his address to the assembly, "though on a subject so unworthy as himself, even at the risk of delaying for a few minutes their consultations for the weal of Christendom, and the advancement of their holy enterprise."

The assembled princes resumed their seats, and there was a profound silence.

"This day," continued the King of England, "is a high festival of the Church; and well becomes it Christian men, at such a tide, to reconcile themselves with their brethren, and confess their faults to each other. Noble princes, and fathers of this holy expedition, Richard is a soldier — his hand is ever readier than his tongue—and his tongue is but too much used to the rough language of his trade. But do not, for Plantagenet's hasty speeches and ill-considered actions, forsake the noble cause of the redemption of Palestine—do not throw away earthly renown and eternal salvation, to be won here if ever they can be won by man, because the act of a soldier may have been hasty, and his speech as hard as the iron which he has worn from childhood. Is Richard in default to any of you, Richard will make compensation both by word and action.—Noble brother of France, have I been so unlucky as to offend you?"

"The Majesty of France has no atonement to seek from that of England," answered Philip with knightly dignity, accepting, at the same time, the offered hand of Richard; "and whatever opinion I may adopt concerning the prosecution of this enterprise, will depend on reasons arising out of the state of my own kingdom, certainly on no jealousy or disgust at my royal and valorous brother."

"Austria," said Richard, walking up to the Archduke, with a mixture of frankness and dignity, while Leopold arose from his seat, as if involuntarily, and with the action of an automaton, whose motions depended upon some external impulse,—"Austria thinks he hath reason to be offended with England; England, that he hath cause to complain of Austria. Let them exchange forgiveness, that the peace of Europe, and the concord of this host, may remain unbroken. We are now joint supporters of a more glorious banner than ever blazed before an earthly prince,—even the Banner of Salvation: let not, therefore, strife be betwixt us, for the symbol of our more worldly dignities; but let Leopold restore the pennon of England, if he has it in his power, and Richard will say, though from no motive save his love for Holy Church, that he repents him of the hasty mood in which he did insult the standard of Austria."

The Archduke stood still, sullen, and discontented, with his eyes fixed on the floor, and his countenance lowering with smothered displeasure, awe, mingled with awkwardness, prevented his giving vent to in w

The Patriarch of Jerusalem hastened to break the embarrassing and to bear witness for the Archduke of Austria, that he had ex himself, by a solemn oath, from all knowledge, direct, or indirect, aggression done to the Banner of England.

"Then we have done the noble Archduke the gre r," said Richard; "and craving his pardon for imputing to h rage so cowardly, we extend our hand to him in token of renewed d amity.—But how is this? Austria refuses our uncovered hand, he formerly refused our mailed glove? What! are we neither to be his mate in peace, nor his antagonist in war? Well, let it be so. We will take the slight esteem in which he holds us, as a penance for aught which we may have done against him in heat of blood, and therefore hold the account between us cleared."

So saying, he turned from the Archduke with an air rather of dignity than scorn, leaving the Austrian apparently as much relieved by the removal of his eye, as is a sullen and truant schoolboy when the glance of his severe pedagogue is withdrawn.

"Noble Earl of Champagne—Princely Marquis of Montserrat—Valiant Grand Master of the Templars—I am here a penitent in the confessional—Do any of you bring a charge, or claim amends from me?"

"I know not on what we could ground any," said the smooth-tongued Conrade, "unless it were that the King of England carries off from the poor brothers of the war all the fame which they might have hoped to gain in the expedition."

"My charge, if I am called to make one," said the Master of the Templars, "is graver and deeper than that of the Marquis of Montserrat. It may be thought ill to beseem a military monk such as I to raise his voice where so many noble princes remain silent; but it concerns our whole host, and not least this noble King of England, that he should hear from some one to his face those charges, which there are enow to bring against him in his absence. We laud and honour the courage and high achievements of the King of England, but we feel aggrieved that he should, on all occasions, seize and maintain a precedence and superiority over us, which it becomes not independent princes to submit to. Much we might yield of our free will to his bravery, his zeal, his wealth, and his power; but he who snatches all, as matter of right, and leaves nothing to grant out of courtesy and favour, degrades us from allies into retainers and vassals, and sullies, in the eyes of our soldiers and subjects, the lustre of our authority, which is no longer independently exercised. Since the royal Richard has asked the truth from us, he must neither be surprised nor angry when he hears one, to whom worldly pomp is prohibited, and secular authority is nothing, saving so far as it advances the prosperity of God's Temple, and the prostration of the lion which goeth about seeking whom he may devour—when he hears, I say, such a one as I tell him the truth in reply to his question ; which truth, even while I speak it, is, I know, confirmed by the heart of every one who hears me, however respect may stifle their voices."

Richard coloured very highly while the Grand Master was making this direct and unvarnished attack upon his conduct, and the murmur of assent which followed it showed plainly, that almost all who were present acquiesced in the justice of the accusation. Incensed, and at the same time mortified, he yet foresaw that to give way to his headlong resentment, would be to give the cold and wary accuser the advantage over him which it was the Templar's principal object to obtain. He, therefore, with a strong effort, remained silent till he had repeated a pater noster, being the course which his confessor had enjoined him to pursue, when anger was likely to obtain dominion over him. The King then spoke with composure, though not without an imbittered tone, especially at the outset.

"And is it even so? And are our brethren at such pains to note the infirmities of our natural temper, and the rough precipitance of our zeal, which may sometimes have urged us to issue commands when there was little time to hold council? I could not have thought that offences, casual and unpremeditated like mine, could find such deep root in the hearts of my allies in this most holy cause ; that for my sake they should withdraw their hand from the plough when the furrow was near the end ; for my sake turn aside from the direct path to Jerusalem, which their swords have opened. I vainly thought that my small services might have outweighed my rash errors—that if it were remembered that I pressed to the van in an assault, it would not be forgotten that I was ever the last in the retreat — that, if I elevated my banner upon conquered fields of battle, it was all the advantage that I sought, while others were dividing the spoil. I may have called the conquered city by my name, but it was to others that I yielded the dominion. If I have been headstrong in urging bold counsels, I have not, methinks, spared my own blood or my people's in carrying them into as bold execution — or if I have, in the hurry of march or battle, assumed a command over the soldiers of others, such have been ever treated as my own, when my wealth purchased the provisions and medicines which their own sovereigns could not procure.—But it shames me to remind you of what all but myself seem to have forgotten. — Let us rather look forward to our future measures ; and believe me, brethren," he continued, his face kindling with eagerness, "you shall not find the pride, or the wrath, or the ambition of Richard, a stumbling-block of offence in the path to which religion and glory summon you, as with the trumpet of an archangel. Oh, no, no! never would I survive the thought, that my frailties and infirmities had been the means to sever this goodly fellowship of assembled princes. I would cut off my left hand with my right, could my doing so attest my sincerity. I will yield up voluntarily, all right to command in the host, even mine own liege subjects. They shall be led by such sovereigns as you may nominate, and their King, ever but too apt to exchange the leader's baton for the adventurer's lance, will serve under the banner of Beau-Seant among the Templars —ay, or under that of Austria, if Austria will name a brave man to lead his forces. Or, if ye are yourselves a-weary of war, and feel your armour chafe your tender bodies, leave but with Richard some ten or fifteen thousand of your soldiers to work out the accomplishment of your vow ; and when Zion is won," he exclaimed, waving his hand aloft, as if displaying the standard of the Cross over Jerusalem — "when Zion is won, we will write upon her gates, NOT the name of Richard Plantagenet, but of those generous Princes who intrusted him with the means of conquest!"

The rough eloquence and determined expression of the military monarch, at once roused the drooping spirits of the Crusaders, reanimated their devotion, and, fixing their attention on the principal object of the expedition, made most of them who were present blush for having been moved by such petty subjects of complaint as had before engrossed them. Eye caught fire from eye, voice lent courage to voice. They resumed, as with one accord, the war-cry with which the sermon of Peter the Hermit was echoed back, and shouted aloud, "Lead us on, gallant Lion's heart—none so worthy to lead where brave men follow. Lead us on—to Jerusalem—to Jerusalem! It is the will of God—it is the will of God! Blessed is he who shall lend an arm to its fulfilment!"

The shout, so suddenly and generally raised, was heard beyond the ring of sentinels who guarded the pavilion of Council, and spread among the soldiers of the host, who, inactive and dispirited by disease and climate, had begun, like their leaders, to droop in resolution; but the reappearance of Richard in renewed vigour, and the well-known shout which echoed from the assembly of the princes, at once rekindled their enthusiasm, and thousands and tens of thousands answered with the same shout of "Zion, Zion!—War, war!—instant battle with the infidels! It is the will of God—it is the will of God!"

The acclamations from without increased in their turn the enthusiasm which prevailed within the pavilion. Those who did not actually catch the flame, were afraid, at least for the time, to seem colder than others. There was no more speech except of a proud advance towards Jerusalem upon the expiry of the truce, and the measures to be taken in the meantime for supplying and recruiting the army. The council broke up, all apparently filled with the same enthusiastic purpose,—which, however, soon faded in the bosom of most, and never had an existence in that of others.

Of the latter class were the Marquis Conrade and the Grand Master of the Templars, who retired together to their quarters ill at ease, and malcontent with the events of the day.

"I ever told it to thee," said the latter, with the cold sardonic expression peculiar to him, "that Richard would burst through the flimsy wiles you spread for him, as would a lion through a spider's web. Thou seest he has but to speak, and his breath agitates these fickle fools as easily as the whirlwind catcheth scattered straws, and sweeps them together, or disperses them at its pleasure."

"When the blast has passed away," said Conrade, "the straws, which it made dance to its pipe, will settle to earth again."

"But know'st thou not besides," said the Templar, "that it seems, if this new purpose of conquest shall be abandoned and pass away, and each mighty prince shall again be left to such guidance as his own scanty brain can supply, Richard may yet probably become King of Jerusalem by compact, and establish those terms of treaty with the Soldan, which thou thyself thought'st him so likely to spurn at?"

"Now, by Mahound and Termagaunt, for Christian oaths are out of fashion," said Conrade, "say'st thou the proud King of England would unite his blood with a heathen Soldan?—My policy threw in that ingredient to make the whole treaty an abomination to him.—As bad for us that he become our master by an agreement, as by victory."

"Thy policy hath ill calculated Richard's digestion," answered the Templar; "I know his mind by a whisper from the Archbishop.—And then thy master-stroke respecting yonder banner, it has passed off with no more respect than two cubits of embroidered silk merited. Marquis Conrade, thy wit begins to halt—I will trust thy fine-spun measures no longer, but will try my own. Know'st thou not the people whom the Saracens call Charegites?"

"Surely," answered the Marquis; "they are desperate and besotted enthusiasts, who devote their lives to the advancement of religion—somewhat like Templars — only they are never known to pause in the race of their calling."

"Jest not," answered the scowling monk; "know, that one of these men has set down, in his bloody vow, the name of the Island Emperor yonder, to be hewn down as the chief enemy of the Moslem faith."

"A most judicious paynim," said Conrade. "May Mahomet send him his paradise for a reward!"

"He was taken in the camp by one of our squires, and, in private examination, frankly avowed his fixed and determined purpose to me," said the Grand Master.

"Now the Heavens pardon them who prevented the purpose of this most judicious Charegite!" answered Conrade.

"He is my prisoner," added the Templar, "and secluded from speech with others, as thou may'st suppose — but prisons have been broken——"

"Chains left unlocked, and captives have escaped," answered the Marquis. "It is an ancient saying,—no sure dungeon but the grave."

"When loose he resumes his quest," continued the military priest; "for it is the nature of this sort of bloodhound never to quit the slot of the prey he has once scented."

"Say no more of it," said the Marquis; "I see thy policy—it is dreadful, but the emergency is imminent."

"I only told thee of it," said the Templar, "that thou mayst keep thyself on thy guard, for the uproar will be dreadful, and there is no knowing on whom the English may vent their rage—Ay, and there is another risk—my page knows the counsels of this Charegite," he continued; "and, moreover, he is a peevish, self-willed fool, whom I would I were rid of, as he thwarts me by presuming to see with his own eyes, not mine. But our holy Order gives me power to put a remedy to such inconvenience. Or stay — the Saracen may find a good dagger in his cell, and I warrant you he uses it as he breaks forth, which will be of a surety so soon as the page enters with his food."

"It will give the affair a colour," said Conrade; "and yet——"

"Yet and but," said the Templar, "are words for fools—wise men neither hesitate nor retract — they resolve and they execute."

Chapter the Twentieth.

When beauty leads the lion in her toils,
Such are her charms, he dare not raise his mane,
Far less expand the terror of his fangs.
So great Alcides made his club a distaff,
And spun to please fair Omphale.
ANONYMOUS.

RICHARD, the unsuspicious object of the dark treachery detailed in the closing part of the last chapter, having effected, for the present at least, the triumphant union of the Crusading princes, in a resolution to prosecute the war with vigour, had it next at heart to establish tranquillity in his own family; and, now that he could judge more temperately, to inquire distinctly into the circumstances leading to the loss of his banner, and the nature and the extent of the connection betwixt his kinswoman Edith, and the banished adventurer from Scotland.

Accordingly, the Queen and her household were startled with a visit from

Sir Thomas De Vaux, requesting the present attendance of the Lady Calista, of Montfaucon, the Queen's principal bower-woman, upon King Richard.

"What am I to say, madam?" said the trembling attendant to the Queen. "He will slay us all."

"Nay, fear not, madam," said De Vaux. "His Majesty hath spared the life of the Scottish knight, who was the chief offender, and bestowed him upon the Moorish physician — he will not be severe upon a lady, though faulty."

"Devise some cunning tale, wench," said Berengaria. "My husband hath too little time to make inquiry into the truth."

"Tell the tale as it really happened," said Edith, "lest I tell it for thee."

"With humble permission of her Majesty," said De Vaux, "I would say Lady Edith adviseth well; for although King Richard is pleased to believe what it pleases your Grace to tell him, yet I doubt his having the same deference for the Lady Calista, and in this especial matter."

"The Lord of Gilsland is right," said the Lady Calista, much agitated at the thoughts of the investigation which was to take place: "and, besides, if I had presence of mind enough to forge a plausible story, beshrew me if I think I should have the courage to tell it."

In this candid humour, the Lady Calista was conducted by De Vaux to the King, and made, as she had proposed, a full confession of the decoy by which the unfortunate Knight of the Leopard had been induced to desert his post; exculpating the Lady Edith, who, she was aware, would not fail to exculpate herself, and laying the full burden on the Queen, her mistress, whose share of the frolic, she well knew, would appear the most venial in the eyes of Cœur de Lion. In truth, Richard was a fond — almost an uxorious husband. The first burst of his wrath had long since passed away, and he was not disposed severely to censure what could not now be amended. The wily Lady Calista, accustomed from her earliest childhood to fathom the intrigues of a court, and watch the indications of a sovereign's will, hastened back to the Queen with the speed of a lapwing charged with the King's commands that she should expect a speedy visit from him; to which the bower-lady added a commentary founded on her own observation, tending to show that Richard meant just to preserve so much severity as might bring his royal consort to repent of her frolic, and then to extend to her and all concerned, his gracious pardon.

"Sits the wind in that corner, wench?" said the Queen, much relieved by this intelligence; "believe me, that, great commander as he is, Richard will find it hard to circumvent us in this matter; and that, as the Pyrenean shepherds are wont to say in my native Navarre, many a one comes for wool and goes back shorn."

Having possessed herself of all the information which Calista could communicate, the royal Berengaria arrayed herself in her most becoming dress, and awaited with confidence the arrival of the heroic Richard.

He arrived, and found himself in the situation of a prince entering an offending province, in the confidence that his business will only be to inflict rebuke, and receive submission, when he unexpectedly finds it in a state of complete defiance and insurrection. Berengaria well knew the power of her charms, and the extent of Richard's affection, and felt assured that she could make her own terms good, now that the first tremendous explosion of his anger had expended itself without mischief. Far from listening to the King's intended rebuke, as what the levity of her conduct had justly deserved, she extenuated, nay, defended as a harmless frolic, that which she was accused of. She denied, indeed, with many a pretty form of negation, that she had directed Nectabanus absolutely to entice the knight farther than the brink of the Mount on which he kept watch—and indeed this was so far true, that she had not designed Sir Kenneth to be introduced into her tent, — and then, eloquent in urging her own defence, the Queen was far more so in pressing upon Richard the charge of unkindness, in refusing her so poor a boon as the life of an unfortunate knight, who, by her thoughtless prank, had been brought within the danger of martial law. She wept and sobbed while she enlarged on her husband's obduracy on this score, as a rigour which had threatened to make her unhappy for life, whenever she should reflect that she had given, unthinkingly, the remote cause for such a tragedy. The vision of the slaughtered victim would have haunted her dreams — nay, for aught she knew, since such things often happened, his actual spectre might have stood by her waking couch. To all this misery of the mind, was she exposed by the severity of one, who, while he pretended to dote upon her slightest glance, would not forego one act of poor revenge, though the issue was to render her miserable.

All this flow of female eloquence was accompanied with the usual arguments of tears and sighs, and uttered with such tone and action, as seemed to show that the Queen's resentment arose neither from pride nor sullenness, but from feelings hurt at finding her consequence with her husband less than she had expected to possess.

The good King Richard was considerably embarrassed. He tried in vain to reason with one, whose very jealousy of his affection rendered her incapable of listening to argument, nor could he bring himself to use the restraint of lawful authority to a creature so beautiful in the midst of her unreasonable displeasure. He was, therefore, reduced to the defensive, endeavoured gently to chide her suspicions, and soothe her displeasure, and recalled to her mind that she need not look back upon the past with recollections either of remorse or supernatural fear, since Sir Kenneth was alive and well, and had been bestowed by him upon the great Arabian physician, who, doubtless, of all men, knew best how to keep him living. But this seemed the unkindest cut of all, and the Queen's sorrow was renewed at the idea of a Saracen — a mediciner — obtaining a boon, for which, with bare head, and on bended knee, she had petitioned her husband in vain. At this new charge, Richard's patience began rather to give way, and he said, in a serious tone of voice, " Berengaria, the physician saved my life. If it is of value in your eyes, you will not grudge him a higher recompense than the only one I could prevail on him to accept."

The Queen was satisfied she had urged her coquettish displeasure to the verge of safety.

" My Richard," she said, " why brought you not that sage to me, that England's Queen might show how she esteemed him, who could save from extinction the lamp of chivalry, the glory of England, and the light of poor Berengaria's life and hope ?"

In a word, the matrimonial dispute was ended ; but, that some penalty might be paid to justice, both King and Queen accorded in laying the whole blame on the agent Nectabanus, who (the Queen being by this time well weary of the poor dwarf's humour) was, with his royal consort Guenevra, sentenced to be banished from the court ; and the unlucky dwarf only escaped a supplementary whipping, from the Queen's assurances that he had already sustained personal chastisement. It was decreed farther, that as an envoy was shortly to be despatched to Saladin, acquainting him with the resolution of the Council to resume hostilities so soon as the truce was ended, and as Richard proposed to send a valuable present to the Soldan, in acknowledgment of the high benefit he had derived from the services of El Hakim, the two unhappy creatures should be added to it as curiosities, which, from their extremely grotesque appearance, and the shattered state of their intellect, were gifts that might well pass between sovereign and sovereign.

Richard had that day yet another female encounter to sustain ; but he advanced to it with comparative indifference, for Edith, though beautiful, and highly esteemed by her royal relative—nay, although she had from his unjust suspicions actually sustained the injury of which Berengaria only affected to complain, still was neither Richard's wife nor mistress, and he feared her reproaches less, although founded in reason, than those of the Queen, though unjust and fantastical. Having requested to speak with her apart, he was ushered into her apartment, adjoining that of the Queen, whose two female Coptish slaves remained on their knees in the most remote corner during the interview. A thin black veil extended its ample folds over the tall and graceful form of the high-born maiden, and she wore not upon her person any female ornament of what kind soever. She arose and made a low reverence when Richard entered, resumed her seat at his command, and, when he sat down beside her, waited, without uttering a syllable, until he should communicate his pleasure.

Richard, whose custom it was to be familiar with Edith, as their relationship authorized, felt this reception chilling, and opened the conversation with some embarrassment.

"Our fair cousin," he at length said, "is angry with us; and we own that strong circumstances have induced us, without cause, to suspect her of conduct alien to what we have ever known in her course of life. But while we walk in this misty valley of humanity, men will mistake shadows for substances. Can my fair cousin not forgive her somewhat vehement kinsman, Richard?"

"Who can refuse forgiveness to *Richard*," answered Edith, "provided Richard can obtain pardon of the *King?*"

"Come, my kinswoman," replied Cœur de Lion, "this is all too solemn. By Our Lady, such a melancholy countenance, and this ample sable veil, might make men think thou wert a new-made widow, or had lost a betrothed lover, at least. Cheer up — thou hast heard doubtless that there is no real cause for wo—why then keep up the form of mourning?"

"For the departed honour of Plantagenet—for the glory which hath left my father's house."

Richard frowned. "Departed honour! glory which hath left our house!" —he repeated, angrily; "but my cousin Edith is privileged. I have judged her too hastily, she has therefore a right to deem of me too harshly. But tell me at least in what I have faulted."

"Plantagenet," said Edith, "should have either pardoned an offence, or punished it. It mis-becomes him to assign free men, Christians, and brave knights, to the fetters of the infidels. It becomes him not to compromise and barter, or to grant life under the forfeiture of liberty. To have doomed the unfortunate to death might have been severity, but had a show of justice; to condemn him to slavery and exile, was barefaced tyranny."

"I see, my fair cousin," said Richard, "you are of those pretty ones who think an absent lover as bad as none, or as a dead one. Be patient; half a score of light horsemen may yet follow and redeem the error, if thy gallant have in keeping any secret which might render his death more convenient than his banishment."

"Peace with thy scurril jests!" answered Edith, colouring deeply — "Think rather, that for the indulgence of thy mood thou hast lopped from is great enterprise one goodly limb, deprived the Cross of one of its most ... supporters, and placed a servant of the true God in the hands of the ... given, too, to minds as suspicious as thou hast shown thine ow... ...ter, some right to say that Richard Cœur de Lion banished the brav... ...ldier in his camp, lest his name in battle might match his own."

"I — I !" exclaimed Richard, now indeed greatly moved — "am I one to be jealous of renown? — I would he were here to profess such equality! I would waive my rank and my crown, and meet him, man-like, in the lists, that it might appear whether Richard Plantagenet had room to fear or to envy the prowess of mortal man. Come, Edith, thou think'st not as thou say'st. Let not anger or grief for the absence of thy lover, make thee unjust to thy kinsman, who, notwithstanding all thy tetchiness, values thy good report as high as that of any one living."

"The absence of my lover?" said the lady Edith. "But yes—he may be well termed my lover, who hath paid so dear for the title. Unworthy as I might be of such homage, I was to him like a light, leading him forward in the noble path of chivalry; but that I forgot my rank, or that he presumed beyond his, is false, were a king to speak it."

"My fair cousin," said Richard, "do not put words in my mouth which I have not spoken. I said not you had graced this man beyond the favour which a good knight may earn, even from a princess, whatever be his native condition. But, by Our Lady, I know something of this love-gear—it begins with mute respect and distant reverence: but, when opportunities occur, familiarity increases, and so—But it skills not talking with one who thinks herself wiser than all the world."

"My kinsman's counsels I willingly listen to, when they are such," said Edith, "as convey no insult to my rank and character."

"Kings, my fair cousin, do not counsel, but rather command," said Richard.

"Soldans do indeed command," said Edith, "but it is because they have slaves to govern."

"Come, you might learn to lay aside this scorn of Soldanrie, when you hold so high of a Scot," said the King. "I hold Saladin to be truer to his word than this William of Scotland, who must needs be called a Lion, forsooth — he hath foully faulted towards me, in failing to send the auxiliary aid he promised. Let me tell thee, Edith, thou may'st live to prefer a true Turk to a false Scot."

"No—never!" answered Edith — "not should Richard himself embrace the false religion, which he crossed the seas to expel from Palestine."

"Thou wilt have the last word," said Richard, "and thou shalt have it. Even think of me what thou wilt, pretty Edith. I shall not forget that we are near and dear cousins."

So saying, he took his leave in fair fashion, but very little satisfied with the result of his visit.

It was the fourth day after Sir Kenneth had been dismissed from the camp; and King Richard sat in his pavilion, enjoying an evening breeze from the west, which, with unusual coolness on her wings, seemed breathed from merry England for the refreshment of her adventurous monarch, as he was gradually recovering the full strength which was necessary to carry on his gigantic projects. There was no one with him, De Vaux having been sent to Ascalon to bring up reinforcements and supplies of military munition, and most of his other attendants being occupied in different departments, all preparing for the re-opening of hostilities, and for a grand preparatory review of the army of the Crusaders, which was to take place the next day. The King sat, listening to the busy hum among the soldiery, the clatter from the forges, where horse-shoes were preparing, and from the tents of the armourers, who were repairing harness — the voice of the soldiers too, as they passed and repassed, was loud and cheerful, carrying with its very tone an assurance of high and excited courage, and an omen of approaching victory. While Richard's ear drank in these sounds with delight, and while he yielded himself to the visions of conquest and of glory which they suggested, an equerry told him that a messenger from Saladin waited without.

"Admit him instantly," said the King, "and with due honour, Josceline."

The English knight accordingly introduced a person, apparently of no higher rank than a Nubian slave, whose appearance was nevertheless highly interesting. He was of superb stature and nobly formed, and his commanding features, although almost jet-black, showed nothing of negro descent. He wore over his coal-black locks a milk-white turban, and over his shoulders, a short mantle of the same colour, open in front and at the sleeves, under which appeared a doublet of dressed leopard's skin reaching within a handbreadth of the knee. The rest of his muscular limbs, both legs and arms, were bare, excepting that he had sandals on his feet, and wore a collar and bracelets of silver. A straight broadsword, with a handle of boxwood, and a sheath covered with snake-skin, was suspended from his waist. In his right hand he held a short javelin, with a broad, bright, steel head, of a span in length, and in his left he led, by a leash of twisted silk and gold, a large and noble stag-hound.

The messenger prostrated himself, at the same time partially uncovering his shoulders, in sign of humiliation, and having touched the earth with his forehead, arose so far as to rest on one knee, while he delivered to the King a silken napkin, enclosing another of cloth of gold, within which was a letter from Saladin in the original Arabic, with a translation into Norman-English, which may be modernized thus:—

"Saladin, King of kings, to Melech Ric, the Lion of England. Whereas, we are informed by thy last message, that thou hast chosen war rather than peace, and our enmity rather than our friendship, we account thee as one blinded in this matter, and trust shortly to convince thee of thine error, by the help of our invincible forces of the thousand tribes, when Mohammed, the Prophet of God, and Allah, the God of the Prophet, shall judge the controversy betwixt us. In what remains, we make noble account of thee, and of the gifts which thou hast sent us, and of the two dwarfs, singular in their deformity as Ysop, and mirthful as the lute of Isaack. And in requital of these tokens from the treasure-house of thy bounty, behold we have sent thee a Nubian slave, named Zohauk, of whom judge not by his complexion, according to the foolish ones of the earth, in respect the dark-rinded fruit hath the most exquisite flavour. Know that he is strong to execute the will of his master, as Rustan of Zablestan; also he is wise to give counsel when thou shalt learn to hold communication with him, for the Lord of Speech hath been stricken with silence betwixt the ivory walls of his palace. We commend him to thy care, hoping the hour may not be distant when he may render thee good service. And herewith we bid thee farewell; trusting that our most holy Prophet may yet call thee to a sight of the truth, failing which illumination, our desire is, for the speedy restoration of thy royal health, that Allah may judge between thee and us in a plain field of battle."

And the missive was sanctioned by the signature and seal of the Soldan.

Richard surveyed the Nubian in silence as he stood before him, his looks bent upon the ground, his arms folded on his bosom, with the appearance of a black marble statue of the most exquisite workmanship, waiting life from the touch of a Prometheus. The king of England, who, as it was emphatically said of his successor Henry the Eighth, loved to look upon A MAN, was well pleased with the thewes, sinews, and symmetry of him whom he now surveyed, and questioned him in the lingua Franca, "Art thou a pagan?"

The slave shook his head, and raising his finger to his brow, crossed himself in token of his Christianity, then resumed his posture of motionless humility.

"A Nubian Christian, doubtless," said Richard, "and mutilated of the organ of speech by these heathen dogs?"

The mute again slowly shook his head in token of negative, pointed with his forefinger to Heaven, and then laid it upon his own lips.

"I understand thee," said Richard; "thou dost suffer under the infliction of God, not by the cruelty of man. Canst thou clean an armour and belt, and buckle it in time of need?"

Jeoffrey died 1186 - 3 years before the death of
his father I was not alive at the point of this
place

THE TALISMAN.   627

The mute nodded, and stepping towards the coat of mail, which hung with the shield and helmet of the chivalrous monarch, upon the pillar of the tent, he handled it with such nicety of address, as sufficiently to show that he ful'y understood the business of the armour-bearer.

"Thou art an apt, and wilt doubtless be a useful knave—thou shalt wait in my chamber, and on my person," said the King, "to show how much I value the gift of the royal Soldan. If thou hast no tongue, it follows thou canst carry no tales, neither provoke me to be sudden by any unfit reply."

The Nubian again prostrated himself till his brow touched the earth, then stood erect, at some paces distant, as waiting for his new master's commands.

"Nay, thou shalt commence thy office presently," said Richard, "for I see a speck of rust darkening on that shield; and when I shake it in the face of Saladin, it should be bright and unsullied as the Soldan's honour and mine own."

A horn was winded without, and presently Sir Henry Neville entered with a packet of despatches. — "From England, my lord," he said, as he delivered it.

"From England — our own England!" repeated Richard, in a tone of melancholy enthusiasm—"Alas! they little think how hard their Sovereign has been beset by sickness and sorrow — faint friends and forward enemies." Then opening the despatches, he said, hastily, "Ha! this comes from no peaceful land — they too have their feuds. — Neville, begone — I must peruse these tidings alone, and at leisure."

Neville withdrew accordingly, and Richard was soon absorbed in the melancholy details which had been conveyed to him from England, concerning the factions that were tearing to pieces his native dominions — the disunion of his brothers, John and Geoffrey, and the quarrels of both with the High Justiciary Longchamp, Bishop of Ely, — the oppressions practised by the nobles upon the peasantry, and rebellion of the latter against their masters, which had produced every where scenes of discord, and in some instances the effusion of blood. Details of incidents mortifying to his pride, and derogatory from his authority, were intermingled with the earnest advice of his wisest and most attached counsellors, that he should presently return to England, as his presence offered the only hope of saving the kingdom from all the horrors of civil discord, of which France and Scotland were likely to avail themselves. Filled with the most painful anxiety, Richard read, and again read, the ill-omened letters, compared the intelligence which some of them contained with the same facts as differently stated in others, and soon became totally insensible to whatever was passing around him, although seated, for the sake of coolness, close to the entrance of his tent, and having the curtains withdrawn, so that he could see and be seen by the guards and others who were stationed without.

Deeper in the shadow of the pavilion, and busied with the task his new master had imposed, sat the Nubian slave, with his back rather turned towards the King. He had finished adjusting and cleaning the hauberk and brigandine, and was now busily employed on a broad pavesse, or buckler, of unusual size, and covered with steel-plating, which Richard often used in reconnoitring, or actually storming fortified places, as a more effectual protection against missile weapons, than the narrow triangular shield used on horseback. This pavesse bore neither the royal lions of England, nor any other device, to attract the observation of the defenders of the walls against which it was advanced; the care, therefore, of the armour was addressed to causing its surface to shine as bright as crystal, in which he seemed to be peculiarly successful. Beyond the Nubian, and scarce visible from without, lay the large dog, which might be termed his brother slave, and which, as if he felt awed by being transferred to a royal owner, was couched close to the side of the mute, with head and ears on the ground, and his limbs and tail drawn close around and under him.

While the Monarch and his new attendant were thus occupied, another actor crept upon the scene, and mingled among the group of English yeomen, about a score of whom, respecting the unusually pensive posture and close occupation of their sovereign, were, contrary to their wont, keeping a silent guard in front of his tent. It was not, however, more vigilant than usual. Some were playing at games of hazard with small pebbles, others spoke together in whispers of the approaching day of battle, and several lay asleep, their bulky limbs folded in their green mantles.

Amid these careless warders glided the puny form of a little old Turk, poorly dressed like a marabout or santon of the desert, a sort of enthusiasts, who sometimes ventured into the camp of the Crusaders, though treated always with contumely, and often with violence. Indeed, the luxury and profligate indulgence of the Christian leaders had occasioned a motley concourse in their tents, of musicians, courtezans, Jewish merchants, Copts, Turks, and all the varied refuse of the Eastern nations; so that the caftan and turban, though to drive both from the Holy Land was the professed object of the expedition, were nevertheless neither an uncommon or an alarming sight in the camp of the Crusaders. When, however, the little insignificant figure we have described approached so nigh as to receive some interruption from the warders, he dashed his dusky green turban from his head, showed that his beard and eye-brows were shaved like those of a professed buffoon, and that the expression of his fantastic and writhen features, as well as of his little black eyes, which glittered like jet, was that of a crazed imagination.

"Dance, marabout," cried the soldiers, acquainted with the manners of these wandering enthusiasts — "dance, or we will scourge thee with our bowstrings, till thou spin as never top did under school-boy's lash."—Thus shouted the wreckless warders, as much delighted at having a subject to teaze, as a child when he catches a butterfly, or a school-boy upon discovering a bird's nest.

The marabout, as if happy to do their behests, bounded from the earth, and spun his giddy round before them with singular agility, which, when contrasted with his slight and wasted figure, and diminutive appearance, made him resemble a withered leaf twirled round and around at the pleasure of the winter's breeze. His single lock of hair streamed upwards from his bald and shaven head, as if some genie upheld him by it; and indeed it seemed as if supernatural art were necessary to the execution of the wild whirling dance, in which scarce the tiptoe of the performer was seen to touch the ground. Amid the vagaries of his performance, he flew here and there, from one spot to another, still approaching, however, though almost imperceptibly, to the entrance of the royal tent; so that, when at length he sunk exhausted on the earth, after two or three bounds still higher than those which he had yet executed, he was not above thirty yards from the King's person.

"Give him water," said one yeoman; "they always crave a drink after their merry-go-round."

"Aha, water, say'st thou, Long Allen?"—exclaimed another archer, with a most scornful emphasis on the despised element; "how wouldst like such beverage thyself, after such a morrice dancing?"

"The devil a water-drop he gets here," said a third. "We will teach the light-footed old infidel to be a good Christian, and drink wine of Cyprus."

"Ay, ay," said a fourth; "and in case he be restive, fetch thou Dick Hunter's horn, that he drenches his mare withal."

A circle was instantly formed around the prostrate and exhausted dervise, and while one tall yeoman raised his feeble form from the ground, another presented to him a huge flagon of wine. Incapable of speech, the old man shook his head, and waved away from him with his hand the liquor forbidden by the Prophet; but his tormentors were not thus to be appeased.

"The horn, the horn!" exclaimed one. "Little difference between a Turk and a Turkish horse, and we will use him conforming."

"By Saint George, you will choke him!" said Long Allen; "and, besides, it is a sin to throw away upon a heathen dog as much wine as would serve a good Christian for a treble night-cap."

"Thou know'st not the nature of these Turks and pagans, Long Allen," replied Henry Woodstall; "I tell thee, man, that this flagon of Cyprus will set his brains a-spinning, just in the opposite direction that they went whirling in the dancing, and so bring him, as it were, to himself again.— Choke? he will no more choke on it than Ben's black bitch on the pound of butter."

"And for grudging it," said Tomalin Blacklees, "why shouldst thou grudge the poor paynim devil a drop of drink on earth, since thou know'st he is not to have a drop to cool the tip of his tongue through a long eternity?"

"That were hard laws, look ye," said Long Allen, "only for being a Turk, as his father was before him. Had he been Christian turned heathen, I grant you the hottest corner had been good winter quarters for him."

"Hold thy peace, Long Allen," said Henry Woodstall; "I tell thee that tongue of thine is not the shortest limb about thee, and I prophesy that it will bring thee into disgrace with Father Francis, as once about the black-eyed Syrian wench.—But here comes the horn.—Be active a bit, man, wilt thou, and just force open his teeth with the haft of thy dudgeon-dagger."

"Hold, hold — he is comfortable," said Tomalin; "see, see, he signs for the goblet—give him room, boys. *Oop sey es*, quoth the Dutchman—down it goes like lamb's-wool! Nay, they are true topers when once they begin —your Turk never coughs in his cup, or stints in his liquoring."

In fact, the dervise, or whatever he was, drank, or at least seemed to drink, the large flagon to the very bottom at a single pull; and when he took it from his lips, after the whole contents were exhausted, only uttered, with a deep sigh, the words Allah kerim, or God is merciful. There was a laugh among the yeomen who witnessed this pottle-deep potation, so obstreperous, as to rouse and disturb the King, who, raising his finger, said, angrily, "How, knaves, no respect, no observance?"

All were at once hushed into silence, well acquainted with the temper of Richard, which at some times admitted of much military familiarity, and at others exacted the most precise respect, although the latter humour was of much more rare occurrence. Hastening to a more reverent distance from the royal person, they attempted to drag along with them the marabout, who, exhausted apparently by previous fatigue, or overpowered by the potent draught he had just swallowed, resisted being moved from the spot, both with struggles and groans.

"Leave him still, ye fools," whispered Long Allen to his mates; "by Saint Christopher, you will make our Dickon go beside himself, and we shall have his dagger presently fly at our costards. Leave him alone, in less than a minute he will sleep like a dormouse."

At the same moment, the Monarch darted another impatient glance to the spot, and all retreated in haste, leaving the dervise on the ground, unable, as it seemed, to stir a single limb or joint of his body. In a moment afterward, and all was as still and quiet as it had been before the intrusion.

Chapter the Twenty-First.

—— and wither'd Murder,
Alarum'd by his sentinel, the wolf,
Whose howl's his watch, thus with his stealthy pace,
With Tarquin's ravishing strides, towards his design
Moves like a ghost.

               MACBETH.

FOR the space of a quarter of an hour, or longer, after the incident related, all remained perfectly quiet in the front of the royal habitation. The King read, and mused in the entrance of his pavilion—behind, and with his back turned to the same entrance, the Nubian slave still burnished the ample pavesse—in front of all, at an hundred paces distant, the yeomen of the guard stood, sat, or lay extended on the grass, attentive to their own sports, but pursuing them in silence, while, on the esplanade betwixt them and the front of the tent, lay, scarcely to be distinguished from a bundle of rags, the senseless form of the marabout.

But the Nubian had the advantage of a mirror, from the brilliant reflection which the surface of the highly polished shield now afforded, by means of which he beheld, to his alarm and surprise, that the marabout raised his head gently from the ground, so as to survey all around him, moving with a well-adjusted precaution, which seemed entirely inconsistent with a state of ebriety. He couched his head instantly, as if satisfied he was unobserved, and began, with the slightest possible appearance of voluntary effort, to drag himself, as if by chance, ever nearer and nearer to the King, but stopping, and remaining fixed at intervals, like the spider, which, moving towards her object, collapses into apparent lifelessness, when she thinks she is the subject of observation. This species of movement appeared suspicious to the Ethiopian, who, on his part, prepared himself, as quietly as possible, to interfere, the instant that interference should seem to be necessary.

The marabout meanwhile glided on gradually and imperceptibly, serpent-like, or rather snail-like, till he was about ten yard's distance from Richard's person, when, starting on his feet, he sprung forward with the bound of a tiger, stood at the King's back in less than an instant, and brandished aloft the cangiar, or poniard, which he had hidden in his sleeve. Not the presence of his whole army could have saved their heroic Monarch — but the motions of the Nubian had been as well calculated as those of the enthusiast, and ere the latter could strike, the former caught his uplifted arm. Turning his fanatical wrath upon what thus unexpectedly interposed betwixt him and his object, the Charegite, for such was the seeming marabout, dealt the Nubian a blow with the dagger, which, however, only grazed his arm, while the far superior strength of the Ethiopian easily dashed him to the ground. Aware of what had passed, Richard had now arisen, and with little more of surprise, anger, or interest of any kind in his countenance, than an ordinary man would show in brushing off and crushing an intrusive wasp, caught up the stool on which he had been sitting, and exclaiming only, " Ha, dog!" dashed almost to pieces the skull of the assassin, who uttered twice, once in a loud, and once in a broken tone, the words, " Allah ackbar!" —— God is victorious — and expired at the King's feet.

" Ye are careful warders," said Richard to his archers, in a tone of scornful reproach, as, aroused by the bustle of what had passed, in terror and tumult they now rushed into his tent ;—" watchful sentinels ye are, to leave me to do such hangman's work with my own hand. — Be silent all of you, and cease your senseless clamour! saw ye never a dead Turk before?—

Here — cast that carrion out of the camp, strike the head from the trunk, and stick it on a lance, taking care to turn the face to Mecca, that he may the easier tell the foul impostor, on whose inspiration he came hither, how he has sped on his errand.—For thee, my swart and silent friend," he added, turning to the Ethiopian—" But how's this ?—thou art wounded—and with a poisoned weapon, I warrant me, for by force of stab so weak an animal as that could scarce hope to do more than raze the lion's hide. — Suck the poison from his wound, one of you — the venom is harmless on the lips, though fatal when it mingles with the blood."

The yeomen looked on each other confusedly and with hesitation, the apprehension of so strange a danger prevailing with those who feared no other.

" How now, sirrahs," continued the King, " are you dainty-lipped, or do you fear death that you dally thus ?"

" Not the death of a man," said Long Allen, to whom the King looked as he spoke, " but methinks I would not die like a poisoned rat for the sake of a black chattel there, that is bought and sold in a market like a Martlemas ox."

" His Grace speaks to men of sucking poison," muttered another yeoman, " as if he said, Go to, swallow a gooseberry !"

" Nay," said Richard, " I never bade man do that which I would not do myself."

And, without farther ceremony, and in spite of the general expostulations of those around, and the respectful opposition of the Nubian himself, the King of England applied his lips to the wound of the black slave, treating with ridicule all remonstrances, and overpowering all resistance. He had no sooner intermitted his singular occupation, than the Nubian started from him, and, casting a scarf over his arm, intimated by gestures, as firm in purpose as they were respectful in manner, his determination not to permit the Monarch to renew so degrading an employment. Long Allen also interposed, saying that if it were necessary to prevent the King engaging again in a treatment of this kind, his own lips, tongue, and teeth, were at the service of the negro, (as he called the Ethiopian,) and that he would eat him up bodily, rather than King Richard's mouth should again approach him.

Neville, who entered with other officers, added his remonstrances.

" Nay, nay, make not a needless halloo about a hart that the hounds have lost, or a danger when it is over," said the King — " the wound will be a trifle, for the blood is scarce drawn — an angry cat had dealt a deeper scratch — and for me, I have but to take a drachm of orvietan by way of precaution, though it is needless."

Thus spoke Richard, a little ashamed, perhaps, of his own condescension, though sanctioned both by humanity and gratitude. But when Neville continued to make remonstrances on the peril to his royal person, the King imposed silence on him.

" Peace, I prithee — make no more of it — I did it but to show these ignorant prejudiced knaves how they might help each other when these cowardly caitiffs come against us with sarbacanes and poisoned shafts.— But," he added, " take thee this Nubian to thy quarters, Neville — I have changed my mind touching him — let him be well cared for — But, hark in thine ear — see that he escapes thee not — there is more in him than seems. Let him have all liberty, so that he leave not the camp.—And you, ye beef-devouring, wine-swilling English mastiffs, get ye to your guard again, and be sure you keep it more warily. Think not you are now in your own land of fair play, where men speak before they strike, and shake hands ere they cut throats. Danger in our land walks openly, and with his blade drawn, and defies the foe whom he means to assault ; but here, he challenges you with a silk glove instead of a steel-gauntlet, cuts your throat with the feather of a turtle-dove, stabs you with the tongue of a priest's brooch, or throttles you with the lace of my lady's boddice. Go to — keep your eyes open as I your mouths shut — drink less and look sharper about you; or I will place your huge stomachs on such short allowance, as would pinch that of a patient Scotchman."

The yoemen, abashed and mortified, withdrew to their post, and Neville was beginning to remonstrate with his master upon the risk of passing over thus slightly their negligence upon their duty, and the propriety of an example in a case so peculiarly aggravated as the permitting one so suspicious as the marabout to approach within dagger's length of his person, when Richard interrupted him with "Speak not of it, Neville—wouldst thou have me avenge a petty risk to myself more severely than the loss of England's banner? It has been stolen—stolen by a thief, or delivered up by a traitor, and nô blood has been shed for it.—My sable friend, thou art an expounder of mysteries, saith the illustrious Soldan — now would I give thee thine own weight in gold, if, by raising one still blacker than thyself, or by what other means thou wilt, thou couldst show me the thief who did mine honour that wrong. What say'st thou? ha!"

The youth seemed desirous to speak, but uttered only that imperfect sound proper to his melancholy condition, then folded his arms, looked on the King with an eye of intelligence, and nodded in answer to his question.

"How!" said Richard, with joyful impatience. "Wilt thou undertake to make discovery in this matter?"

The Nubian slave repeated the same motion.

"But how shall we understand each other?" said the King. — "Canst thou write, good fellow?"

The slave again nodded in assent.

"Give him writing-tools," said the King. "They were readier in my father's tent than mine — but they be somewhere about, if this scorching climate hath not dried up the ink. — Why, this fellow is a jewel — a black diamond, Neville."

"So please you, my liege," said Neville, "if I might speak my poor mind, it were ill dealing in this ware. This man must be a wizard, and wizards deal with the Enemy, who hath most interest to sow tares among the wheat, and bring dissension into our councils, and ——"

"Peace, Neville," said Richard. "Hollo to your northern hound when he is close on the haunch of the deer, and hope to recall him, but seek not to stop Plantagenet when he hath hope to retrieve his honour."

The slave, who during this discussion had been writing, in which art he seemed skilful, now arose, and pressing what he had written to his brow, prostrated himself as usual, ere he delivered it into the King's hands. The scroll was in French, although their intercourse had hitherto been conducted by Richard in the lingua Franca.

"To Richard, the conquering and invincible King of England, this from the humblest of his slaves. Mysteries are the sealed caskets of Heaven, but wisdom may devise means to open the lock. Were your slave stationed where the leaders of the Christian host were made to pass before him in order, doubt nothing, that if he who did the injury whereof my King complains shall be among the number, he may be made manifest in his iniquity, though it be hidden under seven veils."

"Now, by Saint George!" said King Richard, "thou hast spoken most opportunely. — Neville, thou know'st, that when we muster our troops to-morrow, the princes have agreed, that to expiate the affront offered to England in the theft of her Banner, the leaders should pass our new standard as it floats on Saint George's Mount, and salute it with formal regard. Believe me, the secret traitor will not dare to absent himself from an expurgation so solemn, lest his very absence should be matter of suspicion. There will we place our sable man of counsel, and, if his art can detect the villain, leave me to deal with him."

"My liege," said Neville, with the frankness of an English baron, "beware what work you begin. Here is the concord of our holy league unexpectedly renewed — will you, upon such suspicions as a negro slave can instil, tear open wounds so lately closed — or will you use the solemn procession, adopted for the reparation of your honour, and the establishment of unanimity amongst the discording princes, as the means of again finding out new cause of offence, or reviving ancient quarrels? It were scarce too strong to say, this were a breach of the declaration your Grace made to the assembled Council of the Crusade."

"Neville," said the King, sternly interrupting him, "thy zeal makes thee presumptuous and unmannerly. Never did I promise to abstain from taking whatever means were most promising, to discover the infamous author of the attack on my honour. Ere I had done so, I would have renounced my kingdom — my life. All my declarations were under this necessary and absolute qualification; — only, if Austria had stepped forth and owned the injury like a man, I proffered, for the sake of Christendom, to have forgiven him."

"But," continued the baron, anxiously, "what hope that this juggling slave of Saladin will not palter with your Grace?"

"Peace, Neville," said the King; "thou think'st thyself mighty wise, and art but a fool. Mind thou my charge touching this fellow — there is more in him than thy Westmoreland wit can fathom. — And thou, swart and silent, prepare to perform the feat thou hast promised, and, by the word of a King, thou shalt choose thine own recompense. — Lo, he writes again."

The mute accordingly wrote and delivered to the King, with the same form as before, another slip of paper, containing these words. — "The will of the King is the law to his slave — nor doth it become him to ask guerdon for discharge of his devoir."

"*Guerdon* and *devoir*!" said the King, interrupting himself as he read, and speaking to Neville in the English tongue with some emphasis on the words, — "These Eastern people will profit by the Crusaders — they are acquiring the language of chivalry! — And see, Neville, how discomposed that fellow looks — were it not for his colour, he would blush. I should not think it strange if he understood what I say — they are perilous linguists."

"The poor slave cannot endure your Grace's eye," said Neville; "it is nothing more."

"Well, but," continued the King, striking the paper with his finger, as he proceeded, "this bold scroll proceeds to say, that our trusty mute is charged with a message from Saladin to the Lady Edith Plantagenet, and craves means and opportunity to deliver it. What think'st thou of a request so modest — ha! Neville?"

"I cannot say," said Neville, "how such freedom may relish with your Grace; but the lease of the messenger's neck would be a short one, who should carry such a request to the Soldan on the part of your Majesty."

"Nay, I thank Heaven that I covet none of his sunburnt beauties," said Richard; "and for punishing this fellow for discharging his master's errand, and that when he has just saved my life — methinks it were something too summary. I'll tell thee, Neville, a secret — for, although our sable and mute minister be present, he cannot, thou know'st, tell it over again, even if he should chance to understand us — I tell thee, that for this fortnight past, I have been under a strange spell, and I would I were disenchanted. There has no sooner any one done me good service, but lo you, he cancels his interest in me by some deep injury; and, on the other hand, he who hath deserved death at my hands for some treachery or some insult, is sure to be the very person, of all others, who confers upon me some obligation that overbalances his demerits, and renders respite of his sentence a debt due from my honour. Thus, thou see'st, I am deprived of the best

3 c 2

part of my royal function, since I can neither punish men nor reward them. Until the influence of this disqualifying planet be passed away, I will say nothing concerning the request of this our sable attendant, save that it is an unusually bold one, and that his best chance of finding grace in our eyes will be, to endeavour to make the discovery which he proposes to achieve in our behalf. Meanwhile, Neville, do thou look well to him, and let him be honourably cared for.—And hark thee once more," he said, in a low whisper, "seek out yonder hermit of Engaddi, and bring him to me forthwith, be he saint or savage, madman or sane. Let me see him privately."

Neville retired from the tent, signing to the Nubian to follow him, and much surprised at what he had seen and heard, and especially at the unusual demeanour of the King. In general, no task was so easy as to discover Richard's immediate course of sentiment and feeling, though it might, in some cases, be difficult to calculate its duration : for no weather-cock obeyed the changing wind more readily, than the King his gusts of passion. But, on the present occasion, his manner seemed unusually constrained and mysterious, nor was it easy to guess whether displeasure or kindness predominated in his conduct towards his new dependant, or in the looks with which, from time to time, he regarded him. The ready service which the King had rendered to counteract the bad effects of the Nubian's wound, might seem to balance the obligation conferred on him by the slave, when he intercepted the blow of the assassin ; but it seemed, as a much longer account remained to be arranged between them, that the Monarch was doubtful whether the settlement might leave him, upon the whole, debtor or creditor, and that, therefore, he assumed, in the meantime, a neutral demeanour, which might suit with either character. As for the Nubian, by whatever means he had acquired the art of writing the European languages, the King remained convinced that the English tongue at least was unknown to him, since having watched him closely during the last part of the interview, he conceived it impossible for any one understanding a conversation, of which he was himself the subject, to have so completely avoided the apppearance of taking an interest in it.

Chapter the Twenty-Second.

Who's there ? — Approach — 'tis kindly done —
My learn'd physician and a friend.
　　　　　　　Sir Eustace Grey.

Our narrative retrogrades to a period shortly previous to the incidents last mentioned, when, as the reader must remember, the unfortunate Knight of the Leopard, bestowed upon the Arabian physician by King Richard, rather as a slave than in any other capacity, was exiled from the camp of the Crusaders, in whose ranks he had so often and so brilliantly distinguished himself. He followed his new master, for so he must now term the Hakim, to the Moorish tents which contained his retinue and his property, with the stupid feelings of one who, fallen from the summit of a precipice, and escaping unexpectedly with life, is just able to drag him from the fatal spot, but without the power of estimating the extent of the damage which he has sustained. Arrived at the tent, he threw himself, without speech of any kind, upon a couch of dressed buffalo's hide, which was pointed out to him by his conductor, and, hiding his face betwixt his hands, groaned heavily, as if his heart was on the point of bursting. The physician heard him, as he was giving orders to his numerous domestics to prepare for their departure the next morning before daybreak, and, moved with compassion, interrupted his occupation, to sit down cross-legged, by the side of his couch, and administer comfort according to the Oriental manner.

"My friend," he said, "be of good comfort—for what sayeth the poet—'It is better that a man should be the servant of a kind master, than be the slave of his own wild passions.' Again, be of good courage; because, whereas Ysouf Ben Yagoube was sold to a King by his brethren, even to Pharaoh King of Egypt, thy king hath, on the other hand, bestowed thee on one who will be to thee as a brother."

Sir Kenneth made an effort to thank the Hakim, but his heart was too full, and the indistinct sounds which accompanied his abortive attempts to reply, induced the kind physician to desist from his premature endeavours at consolation. He left his new domestic, or guest, in quiet, to indulge his sorrows, and having commanded all the necessary preparations for their departure on the morning, sat down upon the carpet of the tent, and indulged himself in a moderate repast. After he had thus refreshed himself, similar viands were offered to the Scottish Knight; but though the slaves let him understand that the next day would be far advanced ere they would halt for the purpose of refreshment, Sir Kenneth could not overcome the disgust which he felt against swallowing any nourishment, and could be prevailed upon to taste nothing, saving a draught of cold water.

He was awake, long after his Arab host had performed his usual devotions, and betaken himself to his repose, nor had sleep visited him at the hour of midnight, when a movement took place among the domestics, which, though attended with no speech, and very little noise, made him aware they were loading the camels and preparing for departure. In the course of these preparations, the last person who was disturbed, excepting the physician himself, was the Knight of Scotland, whom, about three in the morning, a sort of major-domo, or master of the household, acquainted that he must arise. He did so, without farther answer, and followed him into the moonlight, where stood the camels, most of which were already loaded, and one only remained kneeling until its burden should be completed.

A little apart from the camels stood a number of horses ready bridled and saddled, and the Hakim himself, coming forth, mounted on one of them with as much agility as the grave decorum of his character permitted, and directed another, which he pointed out, to be led towards Sir Kenneth. An English officer was in attendance, to escort them through the camp of the Crusaders, and to ensure their leaving it in safety, and all was ready for their departure. The pavilion which they had left, was, in the meanwhile, struck with singular despatch, and the tent-poles and coverings composed the burden of the last camel—when the physician, pronouncing solemnly the verse of the Koran, "God be our guide, and Mohammed our protector in the desert as in the watered field," the whole cavalcade was instantly in motion.

In traversing the camp, they were challenged by the various sentinels who maintained guard there, and suffered to proceed in silence, or with a muttered curse upon their prophet, as they passed the post of some more zealous Crusader. At length, the last barriers were left behind them, and the party formed themselves for the march with military precaution. Two or three horsemen advanced in front as a vanguard; one or two remained a bowshot in the rear; and, wherever the ground admitted, others were detached to keep an outlook on the flanks. In this manner they proceeded onward, while Sir Kenneth, looking back on the moonlight camp, might now indeed seem banished, deprived at once of honour and liberty, from the glimmering banners under which he had hoped to gain additional renown, and the tented dwellings of chivalry, of Christianity, and—of Edith Plantagenet.

The Hakim, who rode by his side, observed, in his usual tone of sententious consolation — "It is unwise to look back when-the journey lieth forward;" and as he spoke, the horse of the knight made such a perilous stumble, as threatened to add a practical moral to the tale.

The knight was compelled by this hint to give more attention to the management of his steed, which more than once required the assistance and support of the check-bridle, although, in other respects, nothing could be more easy at once, and active, than the ambling pace at which the animal (which was a mare) proceeded.

"The conditions of that horse," observed the sententious physician, "are like those of human fortune: seeing that amidst his most swift and easy pace, the rider must guard himself against a fall, and that it is when prosperity is at the highest, that our prudence should be awake and vigilant to prevent misfortune."

The overloaded appetite loathes even the honeycomb, and it is scarce a wonder that the knight, mortified and harassed with misfortunes and abasement, became something impatient of hearing his misery made, at every turn, the ground of proverbs and apothegms, however just and apposite.

"Methinks," he said, rather peevishly, "I wanted no additional illustration of the instability of fortune — though I would thank thee, Sir Hakim, for thy choice of a steed for me, would the jade but stumble so effectually as at once to break my neck and her own."

"My brother," answered the Arab sage, with imperturbable gravity, "thou speakest as one of the foolish. Thou say'st in thy heart, that the sage should have given you, as his guest, the younger and better horse, and reserved the old one for himself; but know, that the defects of the older steed may be compensated by the energies of the young rider, whereas the violence of the young horse requires to be moderated by the cold temper of the older."

So spoke the sage; but neither to this observation did Sir Kenneth return any answer which could lead to a continuance of their conversation, and the physician, wearied, perhaps, of administering comfort to one who would not be comforted, signed to one of his retinue.

"Hassan," he said, "hast thou nothing wherewith to beguile the way?"

Hassan, story-teller and poet by profession, spurred up, upon this summons, to exercise his calling. — "Lord of the palace of life," he said, addressing the physician, "thou, before whom the angel Azrael spreadeth his wings for flight—thou, wiser than Solimaun Ben Daoud, upon whose signet was inscribed the REAL NAME which controls the spirits of the elements—forbid it, Heaven, that while thou travellest upon the track of benevolence, bearing healing and hope wherever thou comest, thine own course should be saddened for lack of the tale and of the song. Behold, while thy servant is at thy side, he will pour forth the treasures of his memory, as the fountain sendeth her stream beside the pathway, for the refreshment of him that walketh thereon."

After this exordium, Hassan uplifted his voice, and began a tale of love and magic, intermixed with feats of warlike achievement, and ornamented with abundant quotations from the Persian poets, with whose compositions the orator seemed familiar. The retinue of the physician, such excepted as were necessarily detained in attendance on the camels, thronged up to the narrator, and pressed as close as deference for their master permitted, to enjoy the delight which the inhabitants of the East have ever derived from this species of exhibition.

At another time, notwithstanding his imperfect knowledge of the language, Sir Kenneth might have been interested in the recitation, which, though dictated by a more extravagant imagination, and expressed in more inflated and metaphorical language, bore yet a strong resemblance to the romances of chivalry, then so fashionable in Europe. But as matters stood with him, he was scarcely even sensible that a man in the centre of the cavalcade recited and sung, in a low tone, for nearly two hours, modulating his voice to the various moods of passion introduced into the tale, and receiving, in return, now low murmurs of applause, now muttered expressions of wonder, now sighs and tears, and sometimes, what it was far more difficult to extract from such an audience, a tribute of smiles, and even laughter.

During the recitation, the attention of the exile, however abstracted by his own deep sorrow, was occasionally awakened by the low wail of a dog, secured in a wicker enclosure suspended on one of the camels, which, as an experienced woodsman, he had no hesitation in recognizing to be that of his own faithful hound; and from the plaintive tone of the animal, he had no doubt that he was sensible of his master's vicinity, and, in his way, invoking his assistance for liberty and rescue.

"Alas! poor Roswal," he said, "thou callest for aid and sympathy upon one in stricter bondage than thou thyself art. I will not seem to heed thee, or return thy affection, since it would serve but to load our parting with yet more bitterness."

Thus passed the hours of night, and the space of dim hazy dawn, which forms the twilight of a Syrian morning. But when the very first line of the sun's disk began to rise above the level horizon, and when the very first level ray shot glimmering in dew along the surface of the desert, which the travellers had now attained, the sonorous voice of El Hakim himself overpowered and cut short the narrative of the tale-teller, which he caused to resound along the sands the solemn summons, which the muezzins thunder at morning from the minaret of every mosque.

"To prayer!—to prayer! God is the one God.—To prayer!—to prayer! Mohammed is the prophet of God.—To prayer—to prayer! Time is flying from you.— To prayer—to prayer! Judgment is drawing nigh to you."

In an instant each Moslem cast himself from his horse, turned his face towards Mecca, and performed with sand an imitation of those ablutions, which were elsewhere required to be made with water, while each individual, in brief but fervent ejaculations, recommended himself to the care, and his sins to the forgiveness, of God and the Prophet. Even Sir Kenneth, whose reason at once and prejudices were offended by seeing his companions engaged in that which he considered as an act of idolatry, could not help respecting the sincerity of their misguided zeal, and being stimulated by their fervour to apply supplications to Heaven in a purer form, wondering, meanwhile, what new-born feelings could teach him to accompany in prayer, though with varied invocation, those very Saracens, whose heathenish worship he had conceived a crime dishonourable to the land in which high miracles had been wrought, and where the day-star of redemption had arisen.

The act of devotion, however, though rendered in such strange society, burst purely from his natural feelings of religious duty, and had its usual effect in composing the spirits, which had been long harassed by so rapid a succession of calamities. The sincere and earnest approach of the Christian to the throne of the Almighty teaches the best lesson of patience under affliction; since wherefore should we mock the Deity with supplications, when we insult him by murmuring under his decrees? or how, while our prayers have in every word admitted the vanity and nothingness of the things of time in comparison to those of eternity, should we hope to deceive the Searcher of Hearts, by permitting the world and worldly passions to reassume the reins even immediately after a solemn address to Heaven? But Sir Kenneth was not of these. He felt himself comforted and strengthened, and better prepared to execute or submit to whatever his destiny might call upon him to do or to suffer.

Meanwhile, the party of Saracens regained their saddles, and continued their route, and the tale-teller, Hassan, resumed the thread of his narrative; but it was no longer to the same attentive audience. A horseman, who had ascended some high ground on the right hand of the little column, had returned on a speedy gallop to El Hakim, and communicated with him. Four or five more cavaliers had then been despatched, and the little band, which might consist of about twenty or thirty persons, began to follow them with their eyes, as men from whose gestures, and advance or retreat, they were to augur good or evil. Hassan, finding his audience inattentive, or being himself attracted by the dubious appearances on the flank, stinted in his song; and the march became silent, save when a camel-driver called out to his patient charge, or some anxious follower of the Hakim communicated with his next neighbour, in a hurried and low whisper.

This suspense continued until they had rounded a ridge, composed of hillocks of sand, which concealed from their main body the object that had created this alarm among their scouts. Sir Kenneth could now see, at the distance of a mile or more, a dark object moving rapidly on the bosom of the desert, which his experienced eye recognized for a party of cavalry, much superior to their own in numbers, and, from the thick and frequent flashes which flung back the level beams of the rising sun, it was plain that these were Europeans in their complete panoply.

The anxious looks which the horsemen of El Hakim now cast upon their leader, seemed to indicate deep apprehension; while he, with gravity as undisturbed as when he called his followers to prayer, detached two of his best-mounted cavaliers, with instructions to approach as closely as prudence permitted to these travellers of the desert, and observe more minutely their numbers, their character, and, if possible, their purpose. The approach of danger, or what was feared as such, was like a stimulating draught to one in apathy, and recalled Sir Kenneth to himself and his situation.

"What fear you from these Christian horsemen, for such they seem?" he said to the Hakim.

"Fear!" said El Hakim, repeating the word disdainfully — "The sage fears nothing but Heaven — but ever expects from wicked men the worst which they can do."

"They are Christians," said Sir Kenneth, "and it is the time of truce — why should you fear a breach of faith?"

"They are the priestly soldiers of the Temple," answered El Hakim, "whose vow limits them to know neither truce nor faith with the worshippers of Islam. May the prophet blight them, both root, branch, and twig! —Their peace is war, and their faith is falsehood. Other invaders of Palestine have their times and moods of courtesy. The Lion Richard will spare when he has conquered — the eagle Philip will close his wing when he has stricken a prey—even the Austrian bear will sleep when he is gorged; but this horde of ever-hungry wolves know neither pause nor satiety in their rapine. See'st thou not that they are detaching a party from their main body, and that they take an eastern direction? Yon are their pages and squires, whom they train up in their accursed mysteries, and whom, as lighter mounted, they send to cut us off from our watering-place. But they will be disappointed; I know the war of the desert yet better than they."

He spoke a few words to his principal officer, and his whole demeanour and countenance was at once changed from the solemn repose of an eastern sage, accustomed more to contemplation than to action, into the prompt and proud expression of a gallant soldier, whose energies are roused by the near approach of a danger, which he at once foresees and despises.

To Sir Kenneth's eyes the approaching crisis had a different aspect, and when Adonbec said to him, "Thou must tarry close by my side," he answered solemnly in the negative.

"Yonder," he said, "are my comrades in arms—the men in whose society

I have vowed to fight or fall — on their banner gleams the sign of our most blessed redemption — I cannot fly from the Cross in company with the Crescent."

"Fool!" said the Hakim; "their first action would be to do thee to death, were it only to conceal their breach of the truce."

"Of that I must take my chance," replied Sir Kenneth; "but I wear not the bonds of the infidels an instant longer than I can cast them from me."

"Then will I compel thee to follow me," said El Hakim.

"Compel!" answered Sir Kenneth, angrily. "Wert thou not my benefactor, or one who has showed will to be such, and were it not that it is to thy confidence I owe the freedom of these hands, which thou mightest have loaded with fetters, I would show thee that, unarmed as I am, compulsion would be no easy task."

"Enough, enough," replied the Arabian physician, "we lose time even when it is becoming precious."

So saying, he threw his arm aloft, and uttered a loud and shrill cry, as a signal to those of his retinue, who instantly dispersed themselves on the face of the desert, in as many different directions as a chaplet of beads when the string is broken. Sir Kenneth had no time to note what ensued; for, at the same instant, the Hakim seized the rein of his steed, and putting his own to its mettle, both sprung forth at once with the suddenness of light, and at a pitch of velocity which almost deprived the Scottish knight of the power of respiration, and left him absolutely incapable, had he been desirous, to have checked the career of his guide. Practised as Sir Kenneth was in horsemanship from his earliest youth, the speediest horse he had ever mounted was a tortoise in comparison to those of the Arabian sage. They spurned the sand from behind them — they seemed to devour the desert before them — miles flew away with minutes, and yet their strength seemed unabated, and their respiration as free as when they first started upon the wonderful race. The motion, too, as easy as it was swift, seemed more like flying through the air than riding on the earth, and was attended with no unpleasant sensation, save the awe naturally felt by one who is moving at such astonishing speed, and the difficulty of breathing occasioned by their passing through the air so rapidly.

It was not until after an hour of this portentous motion, and when all human pursuit was far, far behind, that the Hakim at length relaxed his speed, and slackening the pace of the horses into a hand gallop, began, in a voice as composed and even as if he had been walking for the last hour, a descant upon the excellence of his coursers to the Scot, who, breathless, half blind, half deaf, and altogether giddy, from the rapidity of this singular ride, hardly comprehended the words which flowed so freely from his companion.

"These horses," he said, "are of the breed called the Winged, equal in speed to aught excepting the Borak of the prophet. They are fed on the golden barley of Yemen, mixed with spices, and with a small portion of dried sheep's flesh. Kings have given provinces to possess them, and their age is active as their youth. Thou, Nazarene, art the first, save a true believer, that ever had beneath his loins one of this noble race, a gift of the prophet himself to the blessed Ali, his kinsman and lieutenant, well called the Lion of God. Time lays his touch so lightly on these generous steeds, that the mare on which thou sittest has seen five times five years pass over her, yet retains her pristine speed and vigour, only that in the career the support of a bridle, managed by a hand more experienced than thine, hath now become necessary. May the prophet be blessed, who hath bestowed on the true believers the means of advance and retreat, which causeth their iron-clothed enemies to be worn out with their own ponderous weight! How the horses of yonder dog Templars must have snorted and blown, when they had toiled fetlock-deep in the desert for one-twentieth part of the space which these brave steeds have left behind them, without one thick pant, or a drop of moisture upon their sleek and velvet coats !"

The Scottish knight, who had now begun to recover his breath and powers of attention, could not help acknowledging in his heart the advantage possessed by these Eastern warriors in a race of animals, alike proper for advance or retreat, and so admirably adapted to the level and sandy deserts of Arabia and Syria. But he did not choose to augment the pride of the Moslem by acquiescing in his proud claim of superiority, and therefore suffered the conversation to drop, and looking around him, could now, at the more moderate pace at which they moved, distinguish that he was in a country not unknown to him.

The blighted borders, and sullen waters of the Dead Sea, the ragged and precipitous chain of mountains arising on the left, the two or three palms clustered together, forming the single green speck on the bosom of the waste wilderness,—objects which once seen, were scarcely to be forgotten, —showed to Sir Kenneth that they were approaching the fountain called the Diamond of the Desert, which had been the scene of his interview, on a former occasion, with the Saracen Emir Sheerkohf, or Ilderim. In a few minutes they checked their horses beside the spring, and the Hakim invited Sir Kenneth to descend from horseback, and repose himself as in a place of safety. They unbridled their steeds, El Hakim observing that farther care of them was unnecessary, since they would be speedily joined by some of the best mounted among his slaves, who would do what farther was needful.

"Meantime," he said, spreading some food on the grass, "eat and drink, and be not discouraged. Fortune may raise up or abase the ordinary mortal, but the sage and the soldier should have minds beyond her control."

The Scottish knight endeavoured to testify his thanks by showing himself docile ; but though he strove to eat out of complaisance, the singular contrast between his present situation, and that which he had occupied on the same spot, when the envoy of princes, and the victor in combat, came like a cloud over his mind, and fasting, lassitude, and fatigue, oppressed his bodily powers. El Hakim examined his hurried pulse, his red and inflamed eye, his heated hand, and his shortened respiration.

"The mind," he said, "grows wise by watching, but her sister the body, of coarser materials, needs the support of repose. Thou must sleep ; and that thou mayest do so to refreshment, thou must take a draught mingled with this elixir."

He drew from his bosom a small crystal vial, cased in silver filigree-work, and dropped into a little golden drinking-cup a small portion of a dark-coloured fluid.

"This," he said, "is one of those productions which Allah hath sent on earth for a blessing, though man's weakness and wickedness have sometimes converted it into a curse. It is powerful as the wine-cup of the Nazarene to drop the curtain on the sleepless eye, and to relieve the burden of the over-loaded bosom ; but when applied to the purposes of indulgence and debauchery, it rends the nerves, destroys the strength, weakens the intellect, and undermines life. But fear not thou to use its virtues in the time of need, for the wise man warms him by the same firebrand with which the madman burneth the tent."*

"I have seen too much of thy skill, sage Hakim," said Sir Kenneth, "to debate thine hest ;" and swallowed the narcotic, mingled as it was with some water from the spring, then wrapped him in the haik, or Arab cloak, which had been fastened to his saddle-pommel, and, according to the directions of the physician, stretched himself at ease in the shade to await the

---

* Some preparation of opium seems to be intimated.

promised repose.   Sleep came not at first, but in her stead a train of pleasing yet not rousing or awakening sensations.   A state ensued, in which, still conscious of his own identity and his own condition, the knight felt enabled to consider them not only without alarm and sorrow, but as composedly as he might have viewed the story of his misfortunes acted upon a stage, or rather as a disembodied spirit might regard the transactions of its past existence.   From this state of repose, amounting almost to apathy respecting the past, his thoughts were carried forward to the future, which, in spite of all that existed to overcloud the prospect, glittered with such hues, as under much happier auspices his unstimulated imagination had not been able to produce, even in its most exalted state.   Liberty, fame, successful love, appeared to be the certain, and not very distant prospect, of the enslaved exile, the dishonoured knight, even of the despairing lover, who had placed his hopes of happiness so far beyond the prospect of chance, in her wildest possibilities, serving to countenance his wishes.   Gradually as the intellectual sight became overclouded, these gay visions became obscure, like the dying hues of sunset, until they were at last lost in total oblivion ; and Sir Kenneth lay extended at the feet of El Hakim, to all appearance, but for his deep respiration, as inanimate a corpse, as if life had actually departed.

Chapter the Twenty-Third.

Mid these wild scenes Enchantment waves her hand,
To change the face of the mysterious land :
Till the bewildering scenes around us seem
The vain productions of a feverish dream.
                                        ASTOLPHO, *a Romance.*

WHEN the Knight of the Leopard awoke from his long and profound repose, he found himself in circumstances so different from those in which he had lain down to sleep, that he doubted whether he was not still dreaming, or whether the scene had not been changed by magic.   Instead of the damp grass, he lay on a couch of more than Oriental luxury, and some kind hands had, during his repose, stripped him of the cassock of chamois which he wore under his armour, and substituted a night dress of the finest linen, and a loose gown of silk.   He had been canopied only by the palm trees of the desert, but now he lay beneath a silken pavilion, which blazed with the richest colours of the Chinese loom, while a slight curtain of gauze, displayed around his couch, was calculated to protect his repose from the insects, to which he had, ever since his arrival in these climates, been a constant and passive prey.   He looked around, as if to convince himself that he was actually awake, and all that fell beneath his eye partook of the splendour of his dormitory.   A portable bath of cedar, lined with silver, was ready for use, and steamed with the odours which had been used in preparing it.   On a small stand of ebony beside the couch, stood a silver vase, containing sherbet of the most exquisite quality, cold as snow, and which the thirst that followed the use of the strong narcotic rendered peculiarly delicious.   Still farther to dispel the dregs of intoxication which it had left behind, the knight resolved to use the bath, and experienced in doing so a delightful refreshment.   Having dried himself with napkins of the Indian wool, he would willingly have resumed his own coarse garments, that he might go forth to see whether the world was as

3 D

much changed without as within the place of his repose. These, however, were nowhere to be seen, but in their place he found a Saracen dress of rich materials, with sabre and poniard, and all befitting an emir of distinction. He was able to suggest no motive to himself for this exuberance of care, excepting a suspicion that these attentions were intended to shake him in his religious profession; as indeed it was well known that the high esteem of the European knowledge and courage, made the Soldan unbounded in his gifts to those who, having become his prisoners, had been induced to take the turban. Sir Kenneth, therefore, crossing himself devoutly, resolved to set all such snares at defiance; and that he might do so the more firmly, conscientiously determined to avail himself as moderately as possible of the attentions and luxuries thus liberally heaped upon him. Still, however, he felt his head oppressed and sleepy, and aware, too, that his undress was not fit for appearing abroad, he reclined upon the couch, and was again locked in the arms of slumber.

But this time his rest was not unbroken; for he was awakened by the voice of the physician at the door of the tent, inquiring after his health, and whether he had rested sufficiently.—" May I enter your tent;" he concluded, " for the curtain is drawn before the entrance."

" The master," replied Sir Kenneth, determined to show that he was not surprised into forgetfulness of his own condition, " need demand no permission to enter the tent of the slave."

" But if I come not as a master?" said El Hakim, still without entering.

" The physician," answered the knight, " hath free access to the bedside of his patient."

" Neither come I now as a physician," replied El Hakim; " and therefore I still request permission, ere I come under the covering of thy tent."

" Whoever comes as a friend," said Sir Kenneth, " and such thou hast hitherto shown thyself to me, the habitation of the friend is ever open to him."

" Yet once again," said the Eastern sage, after the periphrastical manner of his countrymen, " supposing that I come not as a friend?"

" Come as thou wilt," said the Scottish knight, somewhat impatient of this circumlocution,—" be what thou wilt—thou knowest well it is neither in my power nor my inclination to refuse thee entrance."

" I come, then," said El Hakim, " as your ancient foe; but a fair and a generous one."

He entered as he spoke; and when he stood before the bedside of Sir Kenneth, the voice continued to be that of Adonbec the Arabian physician, but the form, dress, and features, were those of Ilderim of Kurdistan, called Sheerkohf. Sir Kenneth gazed upon him, as if he expected the vision to depart, like something created by his imagination.

" Doth it so surprise thee," said Ilderim, " and thou an approved warrior, to see that a soldier knows somewhat of the art of healing?—I say to thee, Nazarene, that an accomplished cavalier should know how to dress his steed as well as how to ride him; how to forge his sword upon the stithy, as well as how to use it in battle; how to burnish his arms, as well as how to wear them; and above all, how to cure wounds as well as how to inflict them."

As he spoke, the Christian knight repeatedly shut his eyes, and while they remained closed, the idea of the Hakim, with his long flowing dark robes, high Tartar cap, and grave gestures, was present to his imagination; but so soon as he opened them, the graceful and richly-gemmed turban, the light hauberk of steel rings entwisted with silver, which glanced brilliantly as it obeyed every inflection of the body, the features freed from their formal expression, less swarthy, and no longer shadowed by the mass of hair, (now limited to a well-trimmed beard,) announced the soldier and not the sage.

"Art thou still so much surprised," said the Emir, "and hast thou walked in the world with such little observance, as to wonder that men are not always what they seem? — Thou thyself — art thou what thou seemest?"

"No, by St. Andrew!" exclaimed the knight; "for to the whole Christian camp I seem a traitor, and I know myself to be a true though an erring man."

"Even so I judged thee," said Ilderim, "and as we had eaten salt together, I deemed myself bound to rescue thee from death and contumely.— But wherefore lie you still on your couch, since the sun is high in the heavens? or are the vestments which my sumpter-camels have afforded unworthy of your wearing?"

"Not unworthy, surely, but unfitting for it," replied the Scot; "give me the dress of a slave, noble Ilderim, and I will don it with pleasure; but I cannot brook to wear the habit of the free Eastern warrior, with the turban of the Moslem."

"Nazarene," answered the Emir, "thy nation so easily entertain suspicion, that it may well render themselves suspected. Have I not told thee that Saladin desires no converts saving those whom the holy prophet shall dispose to submit themselves to his law? violence and bribery are alike alien to his plan for extending the true faith. Hearken to me, my brother. When the blind man was miraculously restored to sight, the scales dropped from his eyes at the Divine pleasure — think'st thou that any earthly leech could have removed them? No. Such mediciner might have tormented the patient with his instruments, or perhaps soothed him with his balsams and cordials, but dark as he was must the darkened man have remained; and it is even so with the blindness of the understanding. If there be those among the Franks, who, for the sake of worldly lucre, have assumed the turban of the Prophet, and followed the laws of Islam, with their own consciences be the blame. Themselves sought out the bait — It was not flung to them by the Soldan. And when they shall hereafter be sentenced, as hypocrites, to the lowest gulf of hell, below Christian and Jew, magician and idolater, and condemned to eat the fruit of the tree Yacoun, which is the heads of demons — to themselves, not to the Soldan, shall their guilt and their punishment be attributed. Wherefore wear, without doubt or scruple, the vesture prepared for you, since if you proceed to the camp of Saladin, your own native dress will expose you to troublesome observation, and perhaps to insult."

"If I go to the camp of Saladin?" said Sir Kenneth, repeating the words of the Emir; "Alas! am I a free agent, and rather must I not go wherever your pleasure carries me?"

"Thine own will may guide thine own motions," said the Emir, "as freely as the wind which moveth the dust of the desert in what direction it chooseth. The noble enemy who met, and well-nigh mastered my sword, cannot become my slave like him who has crouched beneath it. If wealth and power would tempt thee to join our people, I could ensure thy possessing them; but the man who refused the favours of the Soldan when the axe was at his head, will not, I fear, now accept them, when I tell him he has his free choice."

"Complete your generosity, noble Emir," said Sir Kenneth, "by forbearing to show me a mode of requital, which conscience forbids me to comply with. Permit me rather to express, as bound in courtesy, my gratitude for this most chivalrous bounty, this undeserved generosity."

"Say not undeserved," replied the Emir Ilderim; "was it not through thy conversation, and thy account of the beauties which grace the court of the Melech Ric, that I ventured me thither in disguise, and thereby procured a sight the most blessed that I have ever enjoyed — that I ever shall enjoy, until the glories of Paradise beam on my eyes?"

"I understand you not," said Sir Kenneth, colouring alternately, and turning pale, as one who felt that the conversation was taking a tone of the most painful delicacy.

"Not understand me!" exclaimed the Emir. "If the sight I saw in the tent of King Richard escaped thine observation, I will account it duller than the edge of a buffoon's wooden falchion. True, thou wert under sentence of death at the time; but, in my case, had my head been dropping from the trunk, the last strained glances of my eyeballs had distinguished with delight such a vision of loveliness, and the head would have rolled itself towards the incomparable houris, to kiss with its quivering lips the hem of their vestments.—Yonder royalty of England, who for her superior loveliness deserves to be Queen of the universe — what tenderness in her blue eye!—what lustre in her tresses of dishevelled gold!—By the tomb of the prophet, I scarce think that the houri who shall present to me the diamond cup of immortality, will deserve so warm a caress!"

"Saracen," said Sir Kenneth, sternly, "thou speakest of the wife of Richard of England, of whom men think not and speak not as a woman to be won, but as a Queen to be revered."

"I cry you mercy," said the Saracen. "I had forgotten your superstitious veneration for the sex, which you consider rather fit to be wondered at and worshipped, than wooed and possessed. I warrant, since thou exactest such profound respect to yonder tender piece of frailty, whose every motion, step, and look, bespeaks her very woman, less than absolute adoration must not be yielded to her of the dark tresses, and nobly speaking eye. She, indeed, I will allow, hath in her noble port and majestic mien something at once pure and firm — yet even she, when pressed by opportunity and a forward lover, would, I warrant thee, thank him in her heart, rather for treating her as a mortal than as a goddess."

"Respect the kinswoman of Cœur de Lion!" said Sir Kenneth, in a tone of unrepressed anger.

"Respect her!" answered the Emir, in scorn—"by the Caaba, and if I do, it shall be rather as the bride of Saladin."

"The Infidel Soldan is unworthy to salute even a spot that has been pressed by the foot of Edith Plantagenet!" exclaimed the Christian, springing from his couch.

"Ha! what said the Giaour?" exclaimed the Emir, laying his hand on his poniard hilt, while his forehead glowed like glancing copper, and the muscles of his lips and cheeks wrought till each curl of his beard seemed to twist and screw itself, as if alive with instinctive wrath. But the Scottish knight, who had stood the lion anger of Richard, was unappalled at the tiger-like mood of the chafed Saracen.

"What I have said," continued Sir Kenneth, with folded arms and dauntless look. "I would, were my hands loose, maintain on foot or horseback against all mortals: and would hold it not the most memorable deed of my life to support it with my good broadsword against a score of these sickles and bodkins," pointing at the curved sabre and small poniard of the Emir.

The Saracen recovered his composure as the Christian spoke, so far as to withdraw his hand from his weapon, as if the motion had been without meaning; but still continued in deep ire.

"By the sword of the prophet," he said, "which is the key both of Heaven and Hell, he little values his own life, brother, who uses the language thou dost! Believe me, that were thine hands loose, as thou term'st it, one single true believer would find them so much to do, that thou wouldst soon wish them fettered again in manacles of iron."

"Sooner would I wish them hewn off by the shoulder-blades!" replied Sir Kenneth.

"Well. Thy hands are bound at present," said the Saracen, in a more amicable tone, "bound by thine own gentle sense of courtesy, nor have I any present purpose of setting them at liberty. We have proved each other's strength and courage ere now, and we may again meet in a fair field ;—and shame befall him who shall be the first to part from his foeman! But now we are friends, and I look for aid from thee, rather than hard terms or defiances."

"We *are* friends," repeated the knight; and there was a pause, during which the fiery Saracen paced the tent, like the lion, who, after violent irritation, is said to take that method of cooling the distemperature of his blood, ere he stretches himself to repose in his den. The colder European remained unaltered in posture and aspect; yet he, doubtless, was also engaged in subduing the angry feelings which had been so unexpectedly awakened.

"Let us reason of this calmly," said the Saracen; "I am a physician, as thou know'st, and it is written, that he who would have his wound cured, must not shrink when the leech probes and tents it. Seest thou, I am about to lay my finger on the sore. Thou lovest this kinswoman of the Melech Ric — Unfold the veil that shrouds thy thoughts — or unfold it not if thou wilt, for mine eyes see through its coverings."

"I *loved* her," answered Sir Kenneth, after a pause, "as a man loves Heaven's grace, and sued for her favour like a sinner for Heaven's pardon."

"And you love her no longer?" said the Saracen.

"Alas!" answered Sir Kenneth, "I am no longer worthy to love her.—I prithee cease this discourse — thy words are poniards to me."

"Pardon me but a moment," continued Ilderim. "When thou, a poor and obscure soldier, didst so boldly and so highly fix thine affection, tell me, hadst thou good hope of its issue?"

"Love exists not without hope," replied the knight; "but mine was as nearly allied to despair, as that of the sailor swimming for his life, who, as he surmounts billow after billow, catches by intervals some gleam of the distant beacon, which shows him there is land in sight, though his sinking heart and wearied limbs assure him that he shall never reach it."

"And now," said Ilderim, "those hopes are sunk — that solitary light is quenched for ever?"

"For ever," answered Sir Kenneth, in the tone of an echo from the bosom of a ruined sepulchre.

"Methinks," said the Saracen, "if all thou lackest were some such distant meteoric glimpse of happiness as thou hadst formerly, thy beacon-light might be rekindled, thy hope fished up from the ocean in which it has sunk, and thou thyself, good knight, restored to the exercise and amusement of nourishing thy fantastic fashion upon a diet as unsubstantial as moonlight; for, if thou stoodst to-morrow fair in reputation as ever thou wert, she whom thou lovest will not be less the daughter of princes, and the elected bride of Saladin."

"I would it so stood," said the Scot, "and if I did not——"

He stopt short, like a man who is afraid of boasting, under circumstances which did not permit his being put to the test. The Saracen smiled as he concluded the sentence.

"Thou wouldst challenge the Soldan to single combat?" said he.

"And if I did," said Sir Kenneth, haughtily, "Saladin's would neither be the first nor the best turban that I have couched lance at."

"Ay, but methinks the Soldan might regard it as too unequal a mode of periling the chance of a royal bride, and the event of a great war," said the Emir.

"He may be met with in the front of battle," said the knight, his eyes gleaming with the ideas which such a thought inspired.

"He has been ever found there," said Ilderim: "nor is it his wont to turn his horse's head from any brave encounter.—But it was not of the Soldan that I meant to speak. In a word, if it will content thee to be placed in such reputation as may be attained by detection of the thief who stole the Banner of England, I can put thee in a fair way of achieving this task — that is, if thou wilt be governed; for what says Lokman, 'If the child would walk, the nurse must lead him — if the ignorant would understand, the wise must instruct.'"

"And thou art wise, Ilderim," said the Scot, "wise though a Saracen, and generous though an infidel. I have witnessed that thou art both. Take, then, the guidance of this matter; and so thou ask nothing of me contrary to my loyalty and my Christian faith, I will obey thee punctually. Do what thou hast said, and take my life when it is accomplished."

"Listen thou to me, then," said the Saracen. "Thy noble hound is now recovered, by the blessing of that divine medicine which healeth man and beast, and by his sagacity shall those who assailed him be discovered."

"Ha!" said the knight, — "methinks I comprehend thee — I was dull not to think of this!"

"But tell me," added the Emir, "hast thou any followers or retainers in the camp, by whom the animal may be known?"

"I dismissed," said Sir Kenneth, "my old attendant, thy patient, with a varlet that waited on him, at the time when I expected to suffer death, giving him letters for my friends in Scotland — there are none other to whom the dog is familiar. But then my own person is well known — my very speech will betray me, in a camp where I have played no mean part for many months."

"Both he and thou shall be disguised, so as to escape even close examination — I tell thee," said the Saracen, "that not thy brother in arms — not thy brother in blood—shall discover thee, if thou be guided by my counsels. Thou hast seen me do matters more difficult—he that can call the dying from the darkness of the shadow of death, can easily cast a mist before the eyes of the living. But mark me—there is still the condition annexed to this service, that thou deliver a letter of Saladin to the niece of the Melech Ric, whose name is difficult to our Eastern tongue and lips, as her beauty is delightful to our eyes."

Sir Kenneth paused before he answered, and the Saracen observing his hesitation, demanded of him, "if he feared to undertake this message?"

"Not if there were death in the execution," said Sir Kenneth; "I do but pause to consider whether it consists with my honour to bear the letter of the Soldan, or with that of the Lady Edith to receive it from a heathen prince."

"By the head of Mohammed, and by the honour of a Soldier—by the tomb of Mecca, and by the soul of my father," said the Emir, "I swear to thee that the letter is written in all honour and respect. The song of the nightingale will sooner blight the rose-bower she loves, than will the words of the Soldan offend the ears of the lovely kinswoman of England."

"Then," said the knight, "I will bear the Soldan's letter faithfully, as if I were his born vassal, — understanding, that beyond this simple act of service, which I will render with fidelity, from me of all men he can least expect mediation or advice in this his strange love-suit."

"Saladin is noble," answered the Emir, "and will not spur a generous horse to a leap which he cannot achieve.—Come with me to my tent," he added, "and thou shalt be presently equipped with a disguise as unsearchable as midnight; so thou mayst walk the camp of the Nazarenes as if thou hadst on thy finger the signet of the Giaougi."*

---

* Perhaps the same with Gyges.

Chapter the Twenty-Fourth.

——A grain of dust
Soiling our cup, will make our sense reject
Fastidiously the draught which we did thirst for;
A rusted nail, placed near the faithful compass,
Will sway it from the truth, and wreck the argosy
Even this small cause of anger and disgust
Will break the bonds of amity 'mongst princes,
And wreck their noblest purposes.
THE CRUSADE.

THE reader can now have little doubt who the Ethiopian slave really was, with what purpose he had sought Richard's camp, and wherefore and with what hope he now stood close to the person of that monarch, as, surrounded by his valiant peers of England and Normandy, Cœur de Lion stood on the summit of Saint George's Mount, with the Banner of England by his side, borne by the most goodly person in the army, being his own natural brother, William with the Long Sword, Earl of Salisbury, the offspring of Henry the Second's amour with the celebrated Rosamond of Woodstock.

From several expressions in the King's conversation with Neville on the preceding day, the Nubian was left in anxious doubt whether his disguise had not been penetrated, especially as that the King seemed to be aware in what manner the agency of the dog was expected to discover the thief who stole the banner, although the circumstance of such an animal's having been wounded on the occasion, had been scarce mentioned in Richard's presence. Nevertheless, as the King continued to treat him in no other manner than his exterior required, the Nubian remained uncertain whether he was or was not discovered, and determined not to throw his disguise aside voluntarily.

Meanwhile, the powers of the various Crusading princes, arrayed under their royal and princely leaders, swept in long order around the base of the little mound; and as those of each different country passed by, their commanders advanced a step or two up the hill, and made a signal of courtesy to Richard and to the Standard of England, "in sign of regard and amity," as the protocol of the ceremony heedfully expressed it, "not of subjection or vassalage." The spiritual dignitaries, who in those days veiled not their bonnets to created being, bestowed on the King and his symbol of command their blessing instead of rendering obeisance.

Thus the long files marched on, and, diminished as they were by so many causes, appeared still an iron host, to whom the conquest of Palestine might seem an easy task. The soldiers, inspired by the consciousness of united strength, sat erect in their steel saddles, while it seemed that the trumpets sounded more cheerfully shrill, and the steeds, refreshed by rest and provender, chafed on the bit, and trode the ground more proudly. On they passed, troop after troop, banners waving, spears glancing, plumes dancing, in long perspective——a host composed of different nations, complexions, languages, arms, and appearances, but all fired, for the time, with the holy yet romantic purpose of rescuing the distressed daughter of Zion from her thraldom, and redeeming the sacred earth, which more than mortal had trodden, from the yoke of the unbelieving Pagan. And it must be owned, that if, in other circumstances, the species of courtesy rendered to the King of England by so many warriors, from whom he claimed no natural allegiance, had in it something that might have been thought humiliating, yet the nature and cause of the war was so fitted to his pre-eminently chivalrous character, and renowned feats in arms, that claims, which might elsewhere have been urged, were there forgotten; and the brave did willing homage to the bravest, in an expedition where the most undaunted and energetic courage was necessary to success.

The good King was seated on horseback about half way up the Mount, a morion on his head, surmounted by a crown, which left his manly features exposed to public view, as, with cool and considerate eye, he perused each rank as it passed him, and returned the salutation of the leaders. His tunic was of sky-coloured velvet, covered with plates of silver, and his hose of crimson silk, slashed with cloth of gold. By his side stood the seeming Ethiopian slave, holding the noble dog in a leash, such as was used in woodcraft. It was a circumstance which attracted no notice, for many of the princes of the Crusade had introduced black slaves into their household, in imitation of the barbarous splendour of the Saracens. Over the King's head streamed the large folds of the banner, and, as he looked to it from time to time, he seemed to regard a ceremony, indifferent to himself personally, as important, when considered as atoning an indignity offered to the kingdom which he ruled. In the background, and on the very summit of the Mount, a wooden turret, erected for the occasion, held the Queen Berengaria and the principal ladies of the court. To this the King looked from time to time, and then ever and anon his eyes were turned on the Nubian and the dog, but only when such leaders approached, as, from circumstances of previous ill-will, he suspected of being accessary to the theft of the standard, or whom he judged capable of a crime so mean.

Thus, he did not look in that direction when Philip Augustus of France approached at the head of his splendid troops of Gallic chivalry — nay, he anticipated the motions of the French King, by descending the Mount as the latter came up the ascent, so that they met in the middle space, and blended their greetings so gracefully, that it appeared they met in fraternal equality. The sight of the two greatest princes in Europe, in rank at once and power, thus publicly avowing their concord, called forth bursts of thundering acclaim from the Crusading host at many miles' distance, and made the roving Arab scouts of the desert alarm the camp of Saladin with intelligence, that the army of the Christians was in motion. Yet who but the King of kings can read the hearts of monarchs? Under this smooth show of courtesy, Richard nourished displeasure and suspicion against Philip, and Philip meditated withdrawing himself and his host from the army of the Cross, and leaving Richard to accomplish or fail in the enterprise with his own unassisted forces.

Richard's demeanour was different when the dark-armed knights and squires of the Temple chivalry approached—men with countenances bronzed to Asiatic blackness by the suns of Palestine, and the admirable state of whose horses and appointments far surpassed even that of the choicest troops of France and England. The King cast a hasty glance aside, but the Nubian stood quiet, and his trusty dog sat at his feet, watching, with a sagacious yet pleased look, the ranks which now passed before them. The King's look turned again on the chivalrous Templars, as the Grand Master, availing himself of his mingled character, bestowed his benediction on Richard as a priest, instead of doing him reverence as a military leader.

"The misproud and amphibious caitiff puts the monk upon me," said Richard to the Earl of Salisbury. "But, Long-Sword, we will let it pass. A punctilio must not lose Christendom the services of these experienced lances, because their victories have rendered them overweening. — Lo you, here comes our valiant adversary, the Duke of Austria — mark his manner and bearing, Long-Sword — and thou, Nubian, let the hound have full view of him. By Heaven, he brings his buffoons along with him."

In fact, whether from habit, or, which is more likely, to intimate contempt of the ceremonial he was about to comply with, Leopold was attended by his *spruch-sprecher* and his jester, and as he advanced towards Richard, he whistled in what he wished to be considered as an indifferent manner, though his heavy features evinced the sullenness, mixed with the fear, with which a truant schoolboy may be seen to approach his master.

As the reluctant dignitary made, with discomposed and sulky look, the obeisance required, the *spruch-sprecher* shook his baton, and proclaimed, like a herald, that, in what he was now doing, the Archduke of Austria was not to be held derogating from the rank and privileges of a sovereign prince; to which the jester answered with a sonorous *amen*, which provoked much laughter among the bystanders.

King Richard looked more than once at the Nubian and his dog; but the former moved not, nor did the latter strain at the leash, so that Richard said to the slave with some scorn, "Thy success in this enterprise, my sable friend, even though thou hast brought thy hound's sagacity to back thine own, will not, I fear, place thee high in the rank of wizards, or much augment thy merits towards our person."

The Nubian answered, as usual, only by a low obeisance.

Meantime the troops of the Marquis of Montserrat next passed in order before the King of England. That powerful and wily baron, to make the greater display of his forces, had divided them into two bodies. At the head of the first, consisting of his vassals and followers, and levied from his Syrian possessions, came his brother Enguerrand, and he himself followed, leading on a gallant band of twelve hundred Stradiots, a kind of light cavalry raised by the Venetians in their Dalmatian possessions, and of which they had entrusted the command to the Marquis, with whom the republic had many bonds of connexion. These Stradiots were clothed in a fashion partly European, but partaking chiefly of the Eastern fashion. They wore, indeed, short hauberks, but had over them parti-coloured tunics of rich stuffs, with large wide pantaloons and half-boots. On their heads were straight upright caps, similar to those of the Greeks, and they carried small round targets, bows, and arrows, scimitars, and poniards. They were mounted on horses, carefully selected, and well maintained at the expense of the State of Venice; their saddles and appointments resembled those of the Turks, and they rode in the same manner, with short stirrups and upon a high seat. These troops were of great use in skirmishing with the Arabs, though unable to engage in close combat, like the iron-sheathed men-at-arms of Western and Northern Europe.

Before this goodly band came Conrade, in the same garb with the Stradiots, but of such rich stuff that he seemed to blaze with gold and silver, and the milk-white plume fastened in his cap by a clasp of diamonds, seemed tall enough to sweep the clouds. The noble steed which he reined bounded and caracoled, and displayed his spirit and agility in a manner which might have troubled a less admirable horseman than the Marquis, who gracefully ruled him with the one hand, while the other displayed the baton, whose predominancy over the ranks which he led seemed equally absolute. Yet his authority over the Stradiots was more in show than in substance; for there paced beside him, on an ambling palfrey of soberest mood, a little old man, dressed entirely in black, without beard or mustaches, and having an appearance altogether mean and insignificant, when compared with the blaze of splendour around him. But this mean-looking old man was one of those deputies whom the Venetian government sent into camps to overlook the conduct of the generals to whom the leading was consigned, and to maintain that jealous system of espial and control which had long distinguished the policy of the republic.

Conrade, who, by cultivating Richard's humour, had attained a certain degree of favour with him, no sooner was come within his ken than the King of England descended a step or two to meet him, exclaiming, at the same time, "Ha, Lord Marquis, thou at the head of the fleet Stradiots, and thy black shadow attending thee as usual, whether the sun shines or not!—

May not one ask thee whether the rule of the troops remains with the sha
dow or the substance?"

Conrade was commencing his reply with a smile, when Roswal, the noble
hound, uttering a furious and savage yell, sprung forward. The Nubian,
at the same time, slipped the leash, and the hound, rushing on, leaped upon
Conrade's noble charger, and seizing the Marquis by the throat, pulled him
down from the saddle. The plumed rider lay rolling on the sand, and the
frightened horse fled in wild career through the camp.

"Thy hound hath pulled down the right quarry, I warrant him," said
the King to the Nubian, "and I vow to Saint George he is a stag of ten
tynes!—Pluck the dog off, lest he throttle him."

The Ethiopian, accordingly, though not without difficulty, disengaged the
dog from Conrade, and fastened him up, still highly excited, and struggling
in the leash. Meanwhile many crowded to the spot, especially followers of
Conrade and officers of the Stradiots, who, as they saw their leader lie
gazing wildly on the sky, raised him up amid a tumultuary cry of — "Cut
the slave and his hound to pieces!"

But the voice of Richard, loud and sonorous, was heard clear above all
other exclamations—"He dies the death who injures the hound! He hath
but done his duty, after the sagacity with which God and nature have endowed the brave animal. — Stand forward for a false traitor, thou Conrade,
Marquis of Montserrat! I impeach thee of treason."

Several of the Syrian leaders had now come up, and Conrade, vexation,
and shame, and confusion struggling with passion in his manner and voice,
exclaimed, "What means this?—With what am I charged?—Why this base
usage, and these reproachful terms? — Is this the league of concord which
England renewed but so lately?"

"Are the Princes of the Crusade turned hares or deers in the eyes of
King Richard, that he should slip hounds on them?" said the sepulchral
voice of the Grand Master of the Templars.

"It must be some singular accident—some fatal mistake," said Philip of
France, who rode up at the same moment.

"Some deceit of the Enemy," said the Archbishop of Tyre.

"A stratagem of the Saracens," cried Henry of Champagne — "It were
well to hang up the dog, and put the slave to the torture."

"Let no man lay hand upon them," said Richard, "as he loves his own
life! — Conrade, stand forth, if thou darest, and deny the accusation which
this mute animal hath in his noble instinct brought against thee, of injury
done to him, and foul scorn to England!"

"I never touched the banner," said Conrade, hastily.

"Thy words betray thee, Conrade!" said Richard; "for how didst thou
know, save from conscious guilt, that the question is concerning the banner?"

"Hast thou then not kept the camp in turmoil on that and no other
score?" answered Conrade; "and dost thou impute to a prince and an ally
a crime, which, after all, was probably committed by some paltry felon for
the sake of the gold thread? Or wouldst thou now impeach a confederate
on the credit of a dog?"

By this time the alarm was becoming general, so that Philip of France
interposed.

"Princes and nobles," he said, "you speak in presence of those whose
swords will soon be at the throats of each other, if they hear their leaders
at such terms together. In the name of Heaven, let us draw off, each his
own troops, into their separate quarters, and ourselves meet an hour hence
in the Pavilion of Council, to take some order in this new state of confusion."

"Content," said King Richard, "though I should have liked to have in-

terrogated that caitiff while his gay doublet was yet besmirched with sand—
But the pleasure of France shall be ours in this matter."

The leaders separated as was proposed, each prince placing himself at
the head of his own forces; and then was heard on all sides the crying of
war-cries, and the sounding of gathering-notes upon bugles and trumpets,
by which the different stragglers were summoned to their prince's banner;
and the troops were shortly seen in motion, each taking different routes
through the camp to their own quarters. But although any immediate act
of violence was thus prevented, yet the accident which had taken place
dwelt on every mind; and those foreigners, who had that morning hailed
Richard as the worthiest to lead their army, now resumed their prejudices
against his pride and intolerance, while the English, conceiving the honour
of their country connected with the quarrel, of which various reports had
gone about, considered the natives of other countries jealous of the fame
of England and her King, and disposed to undermine it by the meanest arts
of intrigue. Many and various were the rumours spread upon the occasion,
and there was one which averred that the Queen and her ladies had been
much alarmed by the tumult, and that one of them had swooned.

The Council assembled at the appointed hour. Conrade had in the
meanwhile laid aside his dishonoured dress, and with it the shame and confusion which, in spite of his talents and promptitude, had at first overwhelmed him, owing to the strangeness of the accident, and suddenness of
the accusation. He was now robed like a prince, and entered the council-
chamber attended by the Archduke of Austria, the Grand Masters both of
the Temple and of the order of St. John, and several other potentates, who
made a show of supporting him and defending his cause, chiefly perhaps
from political motives, or because they themselves nourished a personal
enmity against Richard.

This appearance of union in favour of Conrade was far from influencing
the King of England. He entered the Council with his usual indifference
of manner, and in the same dress in which he had just alighted from horseback. He cast a careless and somewhat scornful glance on the leaders, who
had with studied affectation arranged themselves around Conrade, as if
owning his cause, and in the most direct terms charged Conrade of Montserrat with having stolen the Banner of England, and wounded the faithful
animal who stood in its defence.

Conrade arose boldly to answer, and in despite, as he expressed himself,
of man and brute, king or dog, avouched his innocence of the crime charged.

"Brother of England," said Philip, who willingly assumed the character
of moderator of the assembly, "this is an unusual impeachment. We do
not hear you avouch your own knowledge of this matter, farther than your
belief, resting upon the demeanour of this hound towards the Marquis of
Montserrat. Surely the word of a knight and a prince should bear him out
against the barking of a cur?"

"Royal brother," returned Richard, "recollect that the Almighty, who
gave the dog to be companion of our pleasures and our toils, hath invested
him with a nature noble and incapable of deceit. He forgets neither friend
nor foe—remembers, and with accuracy, both benefit and injury. He hath
a share of man's intelligence, but no share of man's falsehood. You may
bribe a soldier to slay a man with his sword, or a witness to take life by
false accusation; but you cannot make a hound tear his benefactor — he is
the friend of man, save when man justly incurs his enmity. Dress yonder
Marquis in what peacock-robes you will—disguise his appearance—alter his
complexion with drugs and washes — hide him amidst an hundred men — I
will yet pawn my sceptre that the hound detects him, and expresses his resentment, as you have this day beheld. This is no new incident, although
a strange one. Murderers and robbers have been, ere now, convicted, and
suffered death under such evidence, and men have said that the finger of

God was in it. In thine own land, royal brother, and upon such an occasion, the matter was tried by a solemn duel betwixt the man and the dog, as appellant and defendant in a challenge of murder. The dog was victorious, the man was punished, and the crime was confessed. Credit me, royal brother, that hidden crimes have often been brought to light by the testimony even of inanimate substances, not to mention animals far inferior in instinctive sagacity to the dog, who is the friend and companion of our race."

"Such a duel there hath indeed been, royal brother," answered Philip, "and that in the reign of one of our predecessors, to whom God be gracious. But it was in the olden time, nor can we hold it a precedent fitting for this occasion. The defendant in that case was a private gentleman, of small rank or respect; his offensive weapons were only a club, his defensive a leathern jerkin. But we cannot degrade a prince to the disgrace of using such rude arms, or to the ignominy of such a combat."

"I never meant that you should," said King Richard; "it were foul play to hazard the good hound's life against that of such a double-faced traitor as this Conrade hath proved himself. But there lies our own glove — we appeal him to the combat in respect of the evidence we brought forth against him — a king, at least, is more than the mate of a marquis."

Conrade made no hasty effort to seize on the pledge which Richard cast into the middle of the assembly, and King Philip had time to reply, ere the Marquis made a motion to lift the glove.

"A king," said he of France, "is as much more than a match for the Marquis Conrade as a dog would be less. Royal Richard, this cannot be permitted. You are the leader of our expedition — the sword and buckler of Christendom."

"I protest against such a combat," said the Venetian proveditore, "until the King of England shall have repaid the fifty thousand bezants which he is indebted to the republic. It is enough to be threatened with the loss of our debt, should our debtor fall by the hands of the pagans, without the additional risk of his being slain in brawls amongst Christians, concerning dogs and banners."

"And I," said William with the Long Sword, Earl of Salisbury, "protest in my turn against my royal brother periling his life, which is the property of the people of England, in such a cause. — Here, noble brother, receive back your glove, and think only as if the wind had blown it from your hand. Mine shall lie in its stead. A king's son, though with the bar sinister on his shield, is at least a match for this marmozet of a Marquis."

"Princes and nobles," said Conrade, "I will not accept of King Richard's defiance. He hath been chosen our leader against the Saracens, and if *his* conscience can answer the accusation of provoking an ally to the field on a quarrel so frivolous, *mine*, at least, cannot endure the reproach of accepting it. But touching his bastard brother, William of Woodstock, or against any other who shall adopt or shall dare to stand godfather to this most false charge, I will defend my honour in the lists, and prove whosoever impeaches it a false liar."

"The Marquis of Montserrat," said the Archbishop of Tyre, "hath spoken like a wise and moderate gentleman; and methinks this controversy might, without dishonour to any party, end at this point."

"Methinks it might so terminate," said the King of France, "provided King Richard will recall his accusation, as made upon over-slight grounds."

"Philip of France," answered Cœur de Lion, "my words shall never do my thoughts so much injury. I have charged yonder Conrade as a thief, who, under cloud of night, stole from its place the emblem of England's dignity. I still believe and charge him to be such; and when a day is appointed for the combat, doubt not that, since Conrade declines to meet us in person, I will find a champion to appear in support of my challenge; for thou, William, must not thrust thy long sword into this quarrel without our special licence."

" Since my rank makes me arbiter in this most unhappy matter," said Philip of France, " I appoint the fifth day from hence for the decision thereof, by way of combat, according to knightly usage—Richard, King of England, to appear by his champion as appellant, and Conrade, Marquis of Montserrat, in his own person as defendant. Yet I own, I know not where to find neutral ground where such a quarrel may be fought out; for it must not be in the neighbourhood of this camp, where the soldiers would make faction on the different sides."

" It were well," said Richard, " to apply to the generosity of the royal Saladin, since, heathen as he is, I have never known knight more fulfilled of nobleness, or to whose good faith we may so peremptorily intrust ourselves. I speak thus for those who may be doubtful of mishap—for myself, wherever I see my foe I make that spot my battle-ground."

" Be it so," said Philip; " we will make this matter known to Saladin, although it be showing to an enemy the unhappy spirit of discord which we would willingly hide from ourselves, were it possible. Meanwhile, I dismiss this assembly, and charge you all, as Christian men and noble knights, that ye let this unhappy feud breed no farther brawling in the camp, but regard it as a thing solemnly referred to the judgment of God, to whom each of you should pray that he will dispose of victory in the combat according to the truth of the quarrel; and therewith may His will be done!"

" Amen, Amen!" was answered on all sides; while the Templar whispered the Marquis, " Conrade, wilt thou not add a petition to be delivered from the power of the dog, as the Psalmist hath it?"

" Peace, thou ——!" replied the Marquis; " there is a revealing demon abroad, which may report, amongst other tidings, how far thou dost carry the motto of the order — *Feriatur Leo*."

" Thou wilt stand the brunt of challenge?" said the Templar.

" Doubt me not," said Conrade. " I would not, indeed, have willingly met the iron arm of Richard himself, and I shame not to confess that I rejoice to be free of his encounter. But, from his bastard brother downward, the man breathes not in his ranks whom I fear to meet."

" It is well you are so confident," continued the Templar; " and in that case, the fangs of yonder hound have done more to dissolve this league of princes, than either thy devices, or the dagger of the Charegite. Seest thou how, under a brow studiously overclouded, Philip cannot conceal the satisfaction which he feels at the prospect of release from the alliance which sat so heavy on him? Mark how Henry of Champagne smiles to himself, like a sparkling goblet of his own wine — and see the chuckling delight of Austria, who thinks his quarrel is about to be avenged, without risk or trouble of his own. Hush, he approaches — A most grievous chance, most royal Austria, that these breaches in the walls of our Zion ——"

" If thou meanest this Crusade," replied the Duke, " I would it were crumbled to pieces, and each were safe at home!—I speak this in confidence."

" But," said the Marquis of Montserrat, " to think this disunion should be made by the hands of King Richard, for whose pleasure we have been contented to endure so much, and to whom we have been as submissive as slaves to a master, in hopes that he would use his valour against our enemies, instead of exercising it upon our friends!"

" I see not that he is so much more valorous than others," said the Archduke. " I believe, had the noble Marquis met him in the lists, he would have had the better; for, though the islander deals heavy blows with the pole-axe, he is not so very dexterous with the lance. I should have cared little to have met him myself on our old quarrel, had the weal of Christen-

dom permitted to sovereign princes to breathe themselves in the lists——
And if thou desirest it, noble Marquis, I will myself be your godfather in
this combat."

"And I also," said the Grand Master.

"Come, then, and take your nooning in our tent, noble sirs," said the
Duke, "and we'll speak of this business, over some right *nierenstein*."

They entered together accordingly.

"What said our patron and these great folks together?" said Jonas
Schwanker to his companion, the *spruch-sprecher*, who had used the freedom
to press nigh to his master when the council was dismissed, while the jester
waited at a more respectful distance.

"Servant of Folly," said the *spruch-sprecher*, "moderate thy curiosity—
it beseems not that I should tell to thee the counsels of our master."

"Man of wisdom, you mistake," answered Jonas; "we are both the constant attendants on our patron, and it concerns us alike to know whether
thou or I—Wisdom or Folly, have the deeper interest in him."

"He told to the Marquis," answered the *spruch-sprecher*, "and to the
Grand Master, that he was aweary of these wars, and would be glad he was
safe at home."

"That is a drawn cast, and counts for nothing in the game," said the
jester; "it was most wise to think thus, but great folly to tell it to others
—proceed."

"Ha, hem!" said the *spruch-sprecher*; "he next said to them, that Richard was not more valorous than others, or over dexterous in the tilt-yard."

"Woodcock of my side," said Schwanker; "this was egregious folly.
What next?"

"Nay, I am something oblivious," replied the man of wisdom, "he invited
them to a goblet of *nierenstein*."

"That hath a show of wisdom in it," said Jonas, "thou may'st mark it
to thy credit in the meantime; but an he drink too much, as is most likely,
I will have it pass to mine. Any thing more?"

"Nothing worth memory," answered the orator, "only he wished he had
taken the occasion to meet Richard in the lists."

"Out upon it—out upon it!" said Jonas—"this is such dotage of folly,
that I am well-nigh ashamed of winning the game by it—Ne'ertheless, fool
as he is, we will follow him, most sage *spruch-sprecher*, and have our share
of the wine of *nierenstein*."

Chapter the Twenty-Fifth.

Yet this inconsistency is such,
As thou too shalt adore;
I could not love thee, love, so much,
Loved I not honour more.

MONTROSE'S LINES.

WHEN King Richard returned to his tent, he commanded the Nubian to
be brought before him. He entered with his usual ceremonial reverence,
and having prostrated himself, remained standing before the King, in the
attitude of a slave awaiting the orders of his master. It was perhaps well
for him, that the preservation of his character required his eyes to be fixed
on the ground, since the keen glance with which Richard for some time surveyed him in silence, would, if fully encountered, have been difficult to
sustain.

"Thou canst well of woodcraft," said the King, after a pause, "and hast started thy game and brought him to bay, as ably as if Tristrem himself had taught thee.* But this is not all — he must be brought down at force, I myself would have liked to have levelled my hunting-spear at him. There are, it seems, respects which prevent this. Thou art about to return to the camp of the Soldan, bearing a letter, requiring of his courtesy to appoint neutral ground for the deed of chivalry, and, should it consist with his pleasure, to concur with us in witnessing it. Now, speaking conjecturally, we think thou might'st find in that camp some cavalier, who, for the love of truth, and his own augmentation of honour, will do battle with this same traitor of Montserrat."

The Nubian raised his eyes and fixed them on the King with a look of eager ardour; then raised them to Heaven with such solemn gratitude, that the water soon glistened in them — then bent his head, as affirming what Richard desired, and resumed his usual posture of submissive attention.

"It is well," said the King; "and I see thy desire to oblige me in this matter. And herein, I must needs say, lies the excellence of such a servant as thou, who hast not speech either to debate our purpose, or to require explanation of what we have determined. An English serving-man, in thy place, had given me his dogged advice to trust the combat with some good lance of my household, who, from my brother Long-Sword downwards, are all on fire to do battle in my cause; and a chattering Frenchman had made a thousand attempts to discover wherefore I look for a champion from the camp of the infidels. But thou, my silent agent, canst do mine errand without questioning or comprehending it; with thee, to hear is to obey."

A bend of the body, and a genuflection, were the appropriate answer of the Ethiopian to these observations.

"And now to another point," said the King, and speaking suddenly and rapidly. — "Have you yet seen Edith Plantagenet?"

The mute looked up as in the act of being about to speak, — nay, his lips had begun to utter a distinct negative, — when the abortive attempt died away in the imperfect murmurs of the dumb.

"Why, lo you there!" said the King. "The very sound of the name of a royal maiden, of beauty so surpassing as that of our lovely cousin, seems to have power enough wellnigh to make the dumb speak. What miracles then might her eye work upon such a subject! I will make the experiment, friend slave. Thou shalt see this choice beauty of our court, and do the errand of the princely Soldan."

Again a joyful glance — again a genuflection — but, as he arose, the King laid his hand heavily on his shoulder, and proceeded with stern gravity thus. — "Let me in one thing warn you, my sable envoy. Even if thou shouldst feel that the kindly influence of her, whom thou art soon to behold, should loosen the bonds of thy tongue, presently imprisoned, as the good Soldan expresses it, within the ivory walls of its castle, beware how thou changest thy taciturn character, or speakest a word in her presence, even if thy powers of utterance were to be miraculously restored. Believe me, that I should have thy tongue extracted by the roots, and its ivory palace, that is, I presume, its range of teeth, drawn out one by one. Wherefore, be wise and silent still."

The Nubian, so soon as the King had removed his heavy grasp from his shoulder, bent his head, and laid his hand on his lips, in token of silent obedience.

But Richard again laid his hand on him more gently, and added, "This behest we lay on thee as on a slave. Wert thou knight and gentleman, we

would require thine honour in pledge of thy silence, which is one especial
condition of our present trust."

The Ethiopian raised his body proudly, looked full at the King, and laid
his right hand on his heart.

Richard then summoned his chamberlain.

"Go, Neville," he said, "with this slave, to the tent of our royal consort,
and say it is our pleasure that he have an audience—a private audience—
of our cousin Edith. He is charged with a commission to her. Thou canst
show him the way also, in case he requires thy guidance, though thou
may'st have observed it is wonderful how familiar he already seems to be
with the purlieus of our camp. — And thou, too, friend Ethiop," the King
continued, "what thou dost, do quickly, and return hither within the half
hour."

"I stand discovered," thought the seeming Nubian, as, with downcast
looks and folded arms, he followed the hasty stride of Neville towards the
tent of Queen Berengaria.—"I stand undoubtedly discovered and unfolded
to King Richard, yet I cannot perceive that his resentment is hot against
me. If I understood his words, and surely it is impossible to misinterpret
them, he gives me a noble chance of redeeming my honour upon the crest
of this false Marquis, whose guilt I read in his craven eye and quivering
lip, when the charge was made against him. — Roswal, faithfully hast thou
served thy master, and most dearly shall thy wrong be avenged!—But what
is the meaning of my present permission to look upon her, whom I had
despaired ever to see again?—And why, or how, can the royal Plantagenet
consent that I should see his divine kinswoman, either as the messenger of
the heathen Saladin, or as the guilty exile whom he so lately expelled from
his camp — his audacious avowal of the affection which is his pride, being
the greatest enhancement of his guilt? That Richard should consent to
her receiving a letter from an infidel lover, by the hands of one of such disproportioned rank, are either of them circumstances equally incredible,
and, at the same time, inconsistent with each other. But Richard, when
unmoved by his heady passions, is liberal, generous, and truly noble, and
as such I will deal with him, and act according to his instructions, direct
or implied, seeking to know no more than may gradually unfold itself without my officious inquiry. To him who has given me so brave an opportunity to vindicate my tarnished honour, I owe acquiescence and obedience,
and, painful as it may be, the debt shall be paid. And yet," — thus the
proud swelling of his heart farther suggested, — "Cœur de Lion, as he is
called, might have measured the feelings of others by his own. I urge an
address to his kinswoman! I, who never spoke word to her when I took a
royal prize from her hand — when I was accounted not the lowest in feats
of chivalry among the defenders of the Cross! I approach her when in a
base disguise, and in a servile habit—and, alas! when my actual condition
is that of a slave, with a spot of dishonour on that which was once my
shield! I do this! He little knows me. Yet I thank him for the opportunity which may make us all better acquainted with each other."

As he arrived at this conclusion, they paused before the entrance of the
Queen's pavilion.

They were of course admitted by the guards, and Neville, leaving the
Nubian in a small apartment, or antechamber, which was but too well
remembered by him, passed into that which was used as the Queen's
presence-chamber. He communicated his royal master's pleasure in a low
and respectful tone of voice, very different from the bluntness of Thomas
de Vaux, to whom Richard was every thing, and the rest of the court, in-
cluding Berengaria herself, was nothing. A burst of laughter followed the
communication of his errand.

"And what like is the Nubian slave, who comes ambassador on such an
errand from the Soldan? - Negro, De Neville, is he not?" said a female

voice easily recognized for that of Berengaria. "A Negro, is he not, De Neville, with black skin, a head curled like a ram's, a flat nose, and blubber lips—ha, worthy Sir Henry?"

"Let not your Grace forget the shin-bones," said another voice, "bent outwards like the edge of a Saracen scimitar."

"Rather like the bow of a Cupid, since he comes upon a lover's errand," said the Queen. "Gentle Neville, thou art ever prompt to pleasure us poor women, who have so little to pass away our idle moments. We must see this messenger of love. Turks and Moors have I seen many, but Negro never."

"I am created to obey your Grace's commands, so you will bear me out with my sovereign for doing so," answered the debonair knight. "Yet, let me assure your Grace, you will see somewhat different from what you expect."

"So much the better — uglier yet than our imaginations can fancy, yet the chosen love-messenger of this gallant Soldan!"

"Gracious madam," said the Lady Calista, "may I implore you would permit the good knight to carry this messenger straight to the Lady Edith, to whom his credentials are addressed? We have already escaped hardly for such a frolic."

"Escaped?"—repeated the Queen, scornfully. "Yet thou mayst be right, Calista, in thy caution — let this Nubian, as thou callest him, first do his errand to our cousin — Besides, he is mute too — is he not?"

"He is, gracious madam," answered the knight.

"Royal sport have these Eastern ladies," said Berengaria, "attended by those before whom they may say any thing, yet who can report nothing. Whereas, in our camp, as the Prelate of St. Jude's is wont to say, a bird of the air will carry the matter."

"Because," said De Neville, "your Grace forgets that you speak within canvass walls."

The voices sunk on this observation, and after a little whispering, the English knight again returned to the Ethiopian, and made him a sign to follow. He did so, and Neville conducted him to a pavilion, pitched somewhat apart from that of the Queen, for the accommodation, it seemed, of the Lady Edith and her attendants. One of her Coptic maidens received the message communicated by Sir Henry Neville, and, in the space of a very few minutes, the Nubian was ushered into Edith's presence, while Neville was left on the outside of the tent. The slave who introduced him withdrew on a signal from her mistress, and it was with humiliation, not of the posture only, but of the very inmost soul, that the unfortunate knight, thus strangely disguised, threw himself on one knee, with looks bent on the ground, and arms folded on his bosom, like a criminal who expects his doom. Edith was clad in the same manner as when she received King Richard, her long transparent dark veil hanging around her like the shade of a summer night on a beautiful landscape, disguising and rendering obscure the beauties which it could not hide. She held in her hand a silver lamp, fed with some aromatic spirit, which burned with unusual brightness.

When Edith came within a step of the kneeling and motionless slave, she held the light towards his face, as if to peruse his features more attentively, then turned from him, and placed her lamp so as to throw the shadow of his face in profile upon the curtain which hung beside. She at length spoke in a voice composed, yet deeply sorrowful.

"Is it you?—is it indeed you, brave Knight of the Leopard—gallant Sir Kenneth of Scotland — is it indeed you? — thus servilely disguised — thus surrounded by an hundred dangers?"

At hearing the tones of his lady's voice thus unexpectedly addressed to him, and in a tone of compassion approaching to tenderness, a corresponding reply rushed to the knight's lips, and scarce could Richard's commands, and his own promised silence, prevent his answering, that the sight he saw, the sounds he just heard, were sufficient to recompense the slavery of a life, and dangers which threatened that life every hour. He *did* recollect himself, however, and a deep and impassioned sigh was his only reply to the high-born Edith's question.

"I see—I know I have guessed right"—continued Edith. "I marked you from your first appearance near the platform on which I stood with the Queen. I knew, too, your valiant hound. She is no true lady, and is unworthy of the service of such a knight as thou art, from whom disguises of dress or hue could conceal a faithful servant. Speak, then, without fear, to Edith Plantagenet. She knows how to grace in adversity the good knight who served, honoured, and did deeds of arms in her name, when fortune befriended him.—Still silent! Is it fear or shame that keeps thee so? Fear should be unknown to thee; and for shame, let it remain with those who have wronged thee."

The knight, in despair at being obliged to play the mute in an interview so interesting, could only express his mortification by sighing deeply, and laying his finger upon his lips. Edith stepped back, as if somewhat displeased.

"What!" she said, "the Asiatic mute in very deed, as well as in attire? This I looked not for — Or thou mayst scorn me, perhaps, for thus boldly acknowledging that I have heedfully observed the homage thou hast paid me? Hold no unworthy thoughts of Edith on that account. She knows well the bounds which reserve and modesty prescribe to high-born maidens, and she knows when and how far they should give place to gratitude—to a sincere desire that it were in her power to repay services and repair injuries, arising from the devotion which a good knight bore towards her. — Why fold thy hands together, and wring them with so much passion? — Can it be," she added, shrinking back at the idea—"that their cruelty has actually deprived thee of speech? Thou shakest thy head. Be it a spell — be it obstinacy, I question thee no farther, but leave thee to do thine errand after thine own fashion. I also can be mute."

The disguised knight made an action as if at once lamenting his own condition, and deprecating her displeasure, while at the same time he presented to her, wrapped, as usual, in fine silk and cloth of gold, the letter of the Soldan. She took it, surveyed it carelessly, then laid it aside, and bending her eyes once more on the knight, she said in a low tone—"Not even a word to do thine errand to me?"

He pressed both his hands to his brow, as if to intimate the pain which he felt at being unable to obey her; but she turned from him in anger.

"Begone!" she said. "I have spoken enough — too much — to one who will not waste on me a word in reply. Begone!—and say if I have wronged thee, I have done penance; for if I have been the unhappy means of dragging thee down from a station of honour, I have, in this interview, forgotten my own worth, and lowered myself in thy eyes and in my own."

She covered her eyes with her hand, and seemed deeply agitated. Sir Kenneth would have approached, but she waved him back.

"Stand off! thou whose soul Heaven hath suited to its new station! Aught less dull and fearful than a slavish mute had spoken a word of gratitude, were it but to reconcile me to my own degradation. Why pause you? — begone!"

The disguised knight almost involuntarily looked towards the letter as an apology for protracting his stay. She snatched it up, saying in a tone of irony and contempt, "I had forgotten — the dutiful slave waits an answer to his message. — How's this — from the Soldan!"

She hastily ran over the contents, which were expressed both in Arabic and French, and when she had done, she laughed in bitter anger.

"Now this passes imagination!" she said; "no jongleur can show so deft a transmutation! His legerdemain can transform zechins and bezants into doits and maravedies; but can his art convert a Christian knight, ever esteemed among the bravest of the Holy Crusade, into the dust-kissing slave of a heathen Soldan — the bearer of a Paynim's insolent proposals to a Christian maiden — nay, forgetting the laws of honourable chivalry, as well as of religion? But it avails not talking to the willing slave of a heathen hound. Tell your master, when his scourge shall have found thee a tongue, that which thou hast seen me do. — So saying, she threw the Soldan's letter on the ground, and placed her foot upon it — "And say to him, Edith Plantagenet scorns the homage of an unchristened Pagan."

With these words she was about to shoot from the knight, when, kneeling at her feet in bitter agony, he ventured to lay his hand upon her robe and oppose her departure.

"Heardst thou not what I said, dull slave?" she said, turning short round on him, and speaking with emphasis; "tell the heathen Soldan, thy master, that I scorn his suit as much as I despise the prostration of a worthless renegade to religion and chivalry — to God and to his lady!"

So saying, she burst from him, tore her garment from his grasp, and left the tent.

The voice of Neville, at the same time, summoned him from without. Exhausted and stupified by the distress he had undergone during this interview, from which he could only have extricated himself by breach of the engagement which he had formed with King Richard, the unfortunate knight staggered rather than walked after the English baron, till they reached the royal pavilion, before which a party of horsemen had just dismounted. There was light and motion within the tent, and when Neville entered with his disguised attendant, they found the king, with several of his nobility, engaged in welcoming those who were newly arrived.

Chapter the Twenty-Sixth.

"The tears I shed must ever fall!
I weep not for an absent swain,
For time may happier hours recall,
And parted lovers meet again.

"I weep not for the silent dead,
Their pains are passed, their sorrows o'er,
And those that loved their steps must tread,
When death shall join to part no more."

But worse than absence, worse than death,
She wept her lover's sullied fame,
And, fired with all the pride of birth,
She wept a soldier's injured name.
BALLAD.

THE frank and bold voice of Richard was heard in joyous gratulation.

"Thomas de Vaux! stout Tom of the Gills! by the head of King Henry, thou art welcome to me as ever was flask of wine to a jolly toper! I should scarce have known how to order my battle array, unless I had thy bulky form in my eye as a landmark to form my ranks upon. We shall have blows anon, Thomas, if the saints be gracious to us; and had we fought in thine absence, I would have looked to hear of thy being found hanging upon an elder tree."

"I should have borne my disappointment with more Christian patience, I trust," said Thomas de Vaux, "than to have died the death of an apostate. But I thank your Grace for my welcome, which is the more generous, as it respects a banquet of blows, of which, saving your pleasure, you are ever too apt to engross the larger share; but here have I brought one, to whom your Grace will, I know, give a yet warmer welcome."

The person who now stepped forward to make obeisance to Richard, was a young man of low stature and slight form. His dress was as modest as his figure was unimpressive, but he bore on his bonnet a gold buckle, with a gem, the lustre of which could only be rivalled by the brilliancy of the eye which the bonnet shaded. It was the only striking feature in his countenance; but when once noticed, it uniformly made a strong impression on the spectator. About his neck there hung in a scarf of sky-blue silk a _wrest_, as it was called, — that is, the key with which a harp is tuned, and which was of solid gold.

This personage would have kneeled reverently to Richard, but the monarch raised him in joyful haste, pressed him to his bosom warmly, and kissed him on either side of the face.

"Blondel de Nesle!" he exclaimed joyfully—"welcome from Cyprus, my king of minstrels!—welcome to the King of England, who rates not his own dignity more highly than he does thine. I have been sick, man, and, by my soul, I believe it was for lack of thee; for, were I half way to the gate of Heaven, methinks thy strains could call me back.—And what news, my gentle master, from the land of the lyre? Any thing fresh from the _trouveurs_ of Provence?—any thing from the minstrels of merry Normandy? above all, hast thou thyself been busy?—But I need not ask thee—thou canst not be idle, if thou wouldst—thy noble qualities are like a fire burning within, and compel thee to pour thyself out in music and song."

"Something I have learned, and something I have done, noble King," answered the celebrated Blondel, with a retiring modesty, which all Richard's enthusiastic admiration of his skill had been unable to banish.

"We will hear thee, man — we will hear thee instantly," said the King; — then touching Blondel's shoulder kindly, he added, "that is, if thou art not fatigued with thy journey; for I would sooner ride my best horse to death, than injure a note of thy voice."

"My voice is, as ever, at the service of my royal patron," said Blondel; "but your Majesty," he added, looking at some papers on the table, "seems more importantly engaged, and the hour waxes late."

"Not a whit, man, not a whit, my dearest Blondel. I did but sketch an array of battle against the Saracens, a thing of a moment—almost as soon done as the routing of them."

"Methinks, however," said Thomas de Vaux, "it were not unfit to inquire what soldiers your Grace hath to array. I bring reports on that subject from Ascalon."

"Thou art a mule, Thomas," said the King — "a very mule for dulness and obstinacy!—Come, nobles—a hall—a hall!—range ye around him— Give Blondel the tabouret—Where is his harp-bearer?—or, soft—lend him my harp, his own may be damaged by the journey."

"I would your Grace would take my report," said Thomas de Vaux. "I have ridden far, and have more list to my bed than to have my ears tickled."

"_Thy_ ears tickled!" said the King; "that must be with a woodcock's feather, and not with sweet sounds. Hark thee, Thomas, do thine ears know the singing of Blondel from the braying of an ass?"

"In faith, my liege," replied Thomas, "I cannot well say; but setting Blondel out of the question, who is a born gentleman, and doubtless of high acquirements, I shall never, for the sake of your Grace's question, look on a minstrel, but I shall think upon an ass."

"And might not your manners," said Richard, "have excepted me, who am a gentleman born as well as Blondel, and, like him, a guild-brother of the Joyeuse science?"

"Your Grace should remember," said De Vaux, smiling, "that 'tis useless asking for manners from a mule."

"Most truly spoken," said the King; "and an ill-conditioned animal thou art—But come hither, master mule, and be unloaded, that thou may'st get thee to thy litter, without any music being wasted on thee.—Meantime, do thou, good brother of Salisbury, go to our consort's tent, and tell her that Blondel has arrived, with his budget fraught with the newest minstrelsy — Bid her come hither instantly, and do thou escort her, and see that our cousin, Edith Plantagenet, remain not behind."

His eye then rested for a moment on the Nubian, with that expression of doubtful meaning, which his countenance usually displayed when he looked at him.

"Ha, our silent and secret messenger returned?—Stand up, slave, behind the back of De Neville, and thou shalt hear presently sounds which will make thee bless God that he afflicted thee rather with dumbness than deafness."

So saying, he turned from the rest of the company towards De Vaux, and plunged immediately into the military details which that baron laid before him.

About the time that the Lord of Gilsland had finished his audience, a messenger announced that the Queen and her attendants were approaching the royal tent. — "A flask of wine, ho!" said the King; "of old King Isaac's long-saved Cyprus, which we won when we stormed Famagosta—fill to the stout Lord of Gilsland, gentles — a more careful and faithful servant never had any prince."

"I am glad," said Thomas de Vaux, "that your Grace finds the mule a useful slave, though his voice be less musical than horse-hair or wire."

"What, thou canst not yet digest that quip of the mule?" said Richard. "Wash it down with a brimming flagon, man, or thou wilt choke upon it. — Why, so — well pulled!—and now I will tell thee, thou art a soldier as well as I, and we must brook each other's jests in the hall, as each other's blows in the tourney, and love each other the harder we hit. By my faith, if thou didst not hit me as hard as I did thee in our late encounter, thou gavest all thy wit to the thrust. But here lies the difference betwixt thee and Blondel. Thou art but my comrade—I might say my pupil—in the art of war; Blondel is my master in the science of minstrelsy and music. To thee I permit the freedom of intimacy — to him I must do reverence, as to my superior in his art. Come, man, be not peevish, but remain and hear our glee."

"To see your Majesty in such cheerful mood," said the Lord of Gilsland, "by my faith, I could remain till Blondel had achieved the great Romance of King Arthur, which lasts for three days."

"We will not tax your patience so deeply," said the King. "But see yonder glare of torches without shows that our consort approaches—Away to receive her, man, and win thyself grace in the brightest eyes of Christendom.—Nay, never stop to adjust thy cloak. See, thou hast let Neville come between the wind and the sails of thy galley."

"He was never before me in the field of battle," said De Vaux, not greatly pleased to see himself anticipated by the more active service of the chamberlain.

"No, neither he nor any one went before thee there, my good Tom of the Gills," said the King, "unless it was ourself now and then."

"Ay, my liege," said De Vaux, "and let us do justice to the unfortunate; —the unhappy Knight of the Leopard hath been before me too, at a season; for, look you, he weighs less on horseback, and so ——"

"Hush!" said the King, interrupting him in a peremptory tone—"not a word of him"—and instantly stepped forward to greet his royal consort; and when he had done so, he presented to her Blondel, as king of minstrelsy, and his master in the gay science. Berengaria, who well knew that her royal husband's passion for poetry and music almost equalled his appetite for warlike fame, and that Blondel was his special favourite, took anxious care to receive him with all the flattering distinctions due to one whom the King delighted to honour. Yet it was evident that, though Blondel made suitable returns to the compliments showered on him something too abundantly by the royal beauty, he owned with deeper reverence and more humble gratitude the simple and graceful welcome of Edith, whose kindly greeting appeared to him, perhaps, sincere in proportion to its brevity and simplicity.

Both the Queen and her royal husband were aware of this distinction, and Richard, seeing his consort somewhat piqued at the preference assigned to his cousin, by which perhaps he himself did not feel much gratified, said in the hearing of both,—"We minstrels, Berengaria, as thou may'st see by the bearing of our master Blondel, pay more reverence to a severe judge, like our kinswoman, than to a kindly partial friend, like thyself, who is willing to take our worth upon trust."

Edith was moved by this sarcasm of her royal kinsman, and hesitated not to reply, that, "To be a harsh and severe judge, was not an attribute proper to her alone of all the Plantagenets."

She had perhaps said more, having some touch of the temper of that house, which, deriving their name and cognizance from the lowly broom, (*Planta Genista*) assumed as an emblem of humility, were perhaps one of the proudest families that ever ruled in England; but her eye, when kindling in her reply, suddenly caught those of the Nubian, although he endeavoured to conceal himself behind the nobles who were present, and she sunk upon a seat, turning so pale, that the Queen Berengaria deemed herself obliged to call for water and essences, and to go through the other ceremonies appropriate to a lady's swoon. Richard, who better estimated Edith's strength of mind, called to Blondel to assume his seat and commence his lay, declaring that minstrelsy was worth every other recipe to recall a Plantagenet to life.—"Sing us," he said, "that song of the Bloody Vest, of which thou didst formerly give me the argument, ere I left Cyprus; thou must be perfect in it by this time, or, as our yeomen say, thy bow is broken."

The anxious eye of the minstrel, however, dwelt on Edith, and it was not till he observed her returning colour that he obeyed the repeated commands of the King. Then, accompanying his voice with the harp, so as to grace, but yet not drown, the sense of what he sung, he chanted in a sort of recitative, one of those ancient adventures of love and knighthood, which were wont of yore to win the public attention. So soon as he began to prelude, the insignificance of his personal appearance seemed to disappear, and his countenance glowed with energy and inspiration. His full, manly, mellow voice, so absolutely under command of the purest taste, thrilled on every ear, and to every heart. Richard, rejoiced as after victory, called out the appropriate summons for silence,

> "Listen, lords, in bower and hall;"

while with the zeal of a patron at once and a pupil, he arranged the circle around, and hushed them into silence; and he himself sat down with an air of expectation and interest, not altogether unmixed with the gravity of the professed critic. The courtiers turned their eyes on the King, that they might be ready to trace and imitate the emotions his features should express, and Thomas De Vaux yawned tremendously, as one who submitted unwillingly to a wearisome penance. The song of Blondel was of course in the Norman language; but the verses which follow, express its meaning and its manner.

The Bloody Vest.

'Twas near the fair city of Benevent,
When the sun was setting on bough and bent,
And knights were preparing in bower and tent,
On the eve of the Baptist's tournament;
When in Lincoln green a stripling gent,
Well seeming a page by a princess sent,
Wander'd the camp, and, still as he went,
Enquired for the Englishman, Thomas a Kent.

Far hath he fared, and farther must fare,
Till he finds his pavilion nor stately nor rare,—
Little save iron and steel was there;
And, as lacking the coin to pay armourer's care,
With his sinewy arms to the shoulders bare,
The good knight with hammer and file did repair
The mail that to-morrow must see him wear,
For the honour of Saint John and his lady fair.

"Thus speaks my lady," the page said he,
And the knight bent lowly both head and knee,
"She is Benevent's Princess so high in degree,
And thou art as lowly as knight may well be—
He that would climb so lofty a tree,
Or spring such a gulf as divides her from thee,
Must dare some high deed, by which all men may see
His ambition is back'd by his his chivalrie."

"Therefore thus speaks my lady," the fair page he said,
And the knight lowly louted with hand and with head,
"Fling aside thy good armour in which thou art clad,
And don thou this weed of her night-gear instead,
For a hauberk of steel, a kirtle of thread:
And charge thus attired, in the tournament dread,
And fight as thy wont is where most blood is shed,
And bring honour away, or remain with the dead."

Untroubled in his look, and untroubled in his breast,
The knight the weed hath taken, and reverently hath kiss'd: —
" Now blessed be the moment, the messenger be blest !
Much honour'd do I hold me in my lady's high behest ;
And say unto my lady, in this dear night-weed dress'd,
To the best armed champion I will not vail my crest :
But if I live and bear me well 'tis her turn to take the test."
Here, gentles, ends the foremost fytte of the Lay of the Bloody Vest.

"Thou hast changed the measure upon us unawares in that last couplet, my Blondel?" said the King.

"Most true, my lord," said Blondel. "I rendered the verses from the Italian of an old harper, whom I met in Cyprus, and not having had time either to translate it accurately, or commit it to memory, I am fain to supply gaps in the music and the verse as I can upon the spur of the moment, as you see boors mend a quickset fence with a faggot."

"Nay, on my faith," said the King, "I like these rattling rolling Alexandrines — methinks they come more twangingly off to the music than that briefer measure."

"Both are licensed, as is well known to your Grace," answered Blondel.

"They are so, Blondel," said Richard ; "yet methinks the scene, where there is like to be fighting, will go best on in these same thundering Alexandrines, which sound like the charge of cavalry ; while the other measure is but like the sidelong amble of a lady's palfrey."

"It shall be as your Grace pleases," replied Blondel, and began again to prelude.

"Nay, first cherish thy fancy with a cup of fiery Chios wine," said the King; "and hark thee, I would have thee fling away that new-fangled restriction of thine, of terminating in accurate and similar rhymes — They are a constraint on thy flow of fancy, and make thee resemble a man dancing in fetters."

"The fetters are easily flung off, at least," said Blondel, again sweeping his fingers over the strings, as one who would rather have played than listened to criticism.

"But why put them on, man?" continued the King— "Wherefore thrust thy genius into iron bracelets? I marvel how you got forward at all — I am sure I should not have been able to compose a stanza in yonder hampered measure."

Blondel looked down and busied himself with the strings of his harp, to hide an involuntary smile which crept over his features ; but it escaped not Richard's observation.

"By my faith, thou laugh'st at me, Blondel," he said; "and, in good truth, every man deserves it, who presumes to play the master when he should be the pupil ; but we kings get bad habits of self-opinion.—Come, on with thy lay, dearest Blondel — on after thine own fashion, better than aught that we can suggest, though we must needs be talking."

Blondel resumed the lay ; but, as extemporaneous composition was familiar to him, he failed not to comply with the King's hints, and was perhaps not displeased to show with how much ease he could new-model a poem, even while in the act of recitation.

The Bloody Vest.

FYTTE SECOND.

The Baptist's fair morrow beheld gallant feats—
There was winning of honour, and losing of seats—
There was hewing with falchions, and splintering of staves.
The victors won glory, the vanquish'd won graves.

Oh, many a knight there fought bravely and well,
Yet one was accounted his peers to excel,
And 'twas he whose sole armour on body and breast
Seem'd the weed of a damsel when bound for her rest.

There were some dealt him wounds, that were bloody
    and sore,
But others respected his plight, and forbore.
"It is some oath of honour." they said, "and I trow,
'Twere unknightly to slay him achieving his vow."
Then the Prince, for his sake, bade the tournament
    cease,
He flung down his warder, the trumpets sung peace;
And the judges declare, and competitors yield,
That the Knight of the Night-gear was first in the field.

The feast it was nigh, and the mass it was nigher,
When before the fair Princess low louted a squire,
And deliver'd a garment unseemly to view,   [through;
With sword-cut and spear-thrust all hack'd and pierced
All rent and all tatter'd, all clotted with blood,
With foam of the horses, with dust, and with mud,
Not the point of that lady's small finger, I ween,
Could have rested on spot was unsullied and clean.

"This token my master, Sir Thomas a Kent,
Restores to the Princess of fair Benevent;
He that climbs the tall tree has won right to the fruit,
He that leaps the wide gulf should prevail in his
    suit;
Through life's utmost peril the prize I have won,
And now must the faith of my mistress be shown;
For she who prompts knights on such danger to run,
Must avouch his true service in front of the sun.

"I restore," says my master, "the garment I've wore,
And I claim of the Princess to don it in turn;
For its stains and its rents she should prize it the more,
Since by shame 'tis unsullied, though crimson'd with
    gore."
Then deep blush'd the Princess—yet kiss'd she and
    press'd
The blood-spotted robes to her lips and her breast.
"Go tell my true knight, church and chamber shall
    show,
If I value the blood on this garment or no."   [show,

And when it was time for the nobles to pass
In solemn procession to minster and mass,
The first walk'd the Princess in purple and pall,
But the blood-besmear'd night-robe she wore over all;
And eke, in the hall, where they all sat at dine,
When she knelt to her father and proffer'd the wine,
Over all her rich robes and state jewels she wore
That wimple unseemly bedabbled with gore.

Then lords whisper'd ladies, as well you may think,
And ladies replied, with nod, titter and wink;
And the Prince, who in anger and shame had look'd
    down,   [frown.
Turn'd at length to his daughter, and spoke with a
"Now since thou hast publish'd thy folly and guilt,
E'en atone with thy hand for the blood thou hast spilt;
Yet sore for your boldness you both will repent,
When you wander as exiles from fair Benevent."

Then out spoke stout Thomas, in hall where he stood,
Exhausted and feeble, but dauntless of mood,
"The blood that I lost for this daughter of thine,
I pour'd forth as freely as flask gives its wine,
And if for my sake she brooks penance and blame,
Do not doubt I will save her from suffering and shame,
And light will she reck of thy princedom and rent,
When I hail her, in England, the Countess of Kent."

A murmur of applause ran through the assembly, following the example
of Richard himself, who loaded with praises his favourite minstrel, and
ended by presenting him with a ring of considerable value. The Queen
hastened to distinguish the favourite by a rich bracelet, and many of the
nobles who were present followed the royal example.

"Is our cousin Edith," said the King, "become insensible to the sound
of the harp she once loved?"

"She thanks Blondel for his lay," replied Edith, "but doubly the kindness of the kinsman who suggested it."

"Thou art angry, cousin," said the King; "angry because thou hast
heard of a woman more wayward than thyself. But you escape me not—
I will walk a space homeward with you towards the Queen's pavilion—we
must have conference together ere the night has waned into morning."

The Queen and her attendants were now on foot, and the other guests
withdrew from the royal tent. A train with blazing torches, and an escort
of archers, awaited Berengaria without the pavilion, and she was soon on
her way homeward. Richard, as he had proposed, walked beside his kinswoman, and compelled her to accept of his arm as her support, so that they
could speak to each other without being overheard.

"What answer, then, am I to return to the noble Soldan?" said Richard.
"The Kings and Princes are falling from me, Edith—this new quarrel hath
alienated them once more. I would do something for the Holy Sepulchre
by composition, if not by victory; and the chance of my doing this depends, alas! on the caprice of a woman. I would lay my single spear in
the rest against ten of the best lances in Christendom, rather than argue
with a wilful wench, who knows not what is for her own good.—What answer, coz, am I to return to the Soldan? It must be decisive."

"Tell him," said Edith, "that the poorest of the Plantagenets will rather
wed with misery than with misbelief."

"Shall I say with slavery, Edith?" said the King—"Methinks that is
nearer thy thoughts."

"There is no room," said Edith, "for the suspicion you so grossly insinuate. Slavery of the body might have been pitied, but that of the soul
is only to be despised. Shame to thee, King of merry England. Thou

hast enthralled both the limbs and the spirit of a knight, one scarce less famed than thyself."

"Should I not prevent my kinswoman from drinking poison, by sullying the vessel which contained it, if I saw no other means of disgusting her with the fatal liquor?" replied the King.

"It is thyself," answered Edith, "that would press me to drink poison, because it is proffered in a golden chalice."

"Edith," said Richard, "I cannot force thy resolution; but beware you shut not the door which heaven opens. The hermit of Engaddi, he whom Popes and Councils have regarded as a prophet, hath read in the stars that thy marriage shall reconcile me with a powerful enemy, and that thy husband shall be Christian, leaving thus the fairest ground to hope, that the conversion of the Soldan, and the bringing in of the sons of Ishmael to the pale of the church, will be the consequence of thy wedding with Saladin. Come, thou must make some sacrifice rather than mar such happy prospects."

"Men may sacrifice rams and goats," said Edith, "but not honour and conscience. I have heard that it was the dishonour of a Christian maiden which brought the Saracens into Spain — the shame of another is no likely mode of expelling them from Palestine."

"Dost thou call it shame to become an Empress?" said the King.

"I call it shame and dishonour to profane a Christian sacrament, by entering into it with an infidel whom it cannot bind; and I call it foul dishonour, that I, the descendant of a Christian princess, should become of free will the head of a haram of heathen concubines."

"Well, kinswoman," said the King, after a pause, "I must not quarrel with thee, though I think thy dependent condition might have dictated more compliance."

"My liege," replied Edith, "your Grace hath worthily succeeded to all the wealth, dignity, and dominion of the House of Plantagenet, — do not, therefore, begrudge your poor kinswoman some small share of their pride."

"By my faith, wench," said the King, "thou hast unhorsed me with that very word; so we will kiss and be friends. I will presently despatch thy answer to Saladin. But after all, coz, were it not better to suspend your answer till you have seen him? Men say he is pre-eminently handsome."

"There is no chance of our meeting, my lord," said Edith.

"By Saint George, but there is next to a certainty of it," said the King; "for Saladin will doubtless afford us a free field for the doing of this new battle of the Standard, and will witness it himself. Berengaria is wild to behold it also, and I dare be sworn not a feather of you, her companions and attendants, will remain behind—least of all thou thyself, fair coz. But come, we have reached the pavilion, and must part — not in unkindness though—nay, thou must seal it with thy lip as well as thy hand, sweet Edith —it is my right as a sovereign to kiss my pretty vassals."

He embraced her respectfully and affectionately, and returned through the moonlight camp, humming to himself such snatches of Blondel's lay as he could recollect.

On his arrival, he lost no time in making up his despatches for Saladin, and delivered them to the Nubian, with a charge to set out by peep of day on his return to the Soldan.

3 r

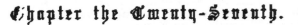

Chapter the Twenty-Seventh.

We heard the Tecbir,—so these Arabs call
Their shout of onset, when, with loud acclaim,
They challenge heaven to give them victory.
SIEGE OF DAMASCUS.

ON the subsequent morning, Richard was invited to a conference by Philip of France, in which the latter, with many expressions of his high esteem for his brother of England, communicated to him, in terms extremely courteous, but too explicit to be misunderstood, his positive intention to return to Europe, and to the cares of his kingdom, as entirely despairing of future success in their undertaking, with their diminished forces and civil discords. Richard remonstrated, but in vain; and when the conference ended, he received without surprise a manifesto from the Duke of Austria, and several other princes, announcing a resolution similar to that of Philip, and in no modified terms, assigning, for their defection from the cause of the Cross, the inordinate ambition and arbitrary domination of Richard of England. All hopes of continuing the war with any prospect of ultimate success, were now abandoned, and Richard, while he shed bitter tears over his disappointed hopes of glory, was little consoled by the recollection, that the failure was in some degree to be imputed to the advantages which he had given his enemies by his own hasty and imprudent temper.

"They had not dared to have deserted my father thus," he said to De Vaux, in the bitterness of his resentment.—"No slanders they could have uttered against so wise a king would have been believed in Christendom; whereas,—fool that I am!—I have not only afforded them a pretext for deserting me, but even a colour for casting all the blame of the rupture upon my unhappy foibles."

These thoughts were so deeply galling to the King, that De Vaux was rejoiced when the arrival of an ambassador from Saladin turned his reflections into a different channel.

This new envoy was an Emir much respected by the Soldan, whose name was Abdallah el Hadgi. He derived his descent from the family of the Prophet, and the race or tribe of Hashem, in witness of which genealogy he wore a green turban of large dimensions. He had also three times performed the journey to Mecca, from which he derived his epithet of El Hadji, or the Pilgrim. Notwithstanding these various pretensions to sanctity, Abdallah was (for an Arab) a boon companion, who enjoyed a merry tale, and laid aside his gravity so far as to quaff a blithe flagon, when secrecy ensured him against scandal. He was likewise a statesman, whose abilities had been used by Saladin in various negotiations with the Christian Princes, and particularly with Richard, to whom El Hadgi was personally known and acceptable. Animated by the cheerful acquiescence with which the envoy of Saladin afforded a fair field for the combat, a safe conduct for all who might choose to witness it, and offered his own person as a guarantee of his fidelity, Richard soon forgot his disappointed hopes, and the approaching dissolution of the Christian league, in the interesting discussions preceding a combat in the lists.

The station, called the Diamond of the Desert, was assigned for the place of conflict, as being nearly at an equal distance betwixt the Christian and Saracen camps. It was agreed that Conrade of Montserrat, the defendant, with his godfathers, the Archduke of Austria and the Grand Master of the Templars, should appear there on the day fixed for the combat, with an hundred armed followers, and no more; that Richard of England, and his brother Salisbury, who supported the accusation, should attend with the same number, to protect his champion; and that the Soldan should bring with him a guard of five hundred chosen followers, a band considered as not more than equal to the two hundred Christian lances. Such persons of consideration as either party chose to invite to witness the contest, were to wear no other weapons than their swords, and to come without defensive armour. The Soldan undertook the preparations of the lists, and to provide accommodations and refreshments of every kind for all who were to assist at the solemnity; and his letters expressed, with much courtesy, the pleasure which he anticipated in the prospect of a personal and peaceful meeting with the Melech Ric, and his anxious desire to render his reception as agreeable as possible.

All preliminaries being arranged, and communicated to the defendant and his godfathers, Abdallah the Hadgi was admitted to a more private interview, where he heard with delight the strains of Blondel. Having first carefully put his green turban out of sight, and assumed a Greek cap in its stead, he requited the Norman minstrel's music with a drinking song from the Persian, and quaffed a hearty flagon of Cyprus wine, to show that his practice matched his principles. On the next day, grave and sober as the water-drinker Mirglip, he bent his brow to the ground before Saladin's footstool, and rendered to the Soldan an account of his embassy.

On the day before that appointed for the combat, Conrade and his friends set off by daybreak to repair to the place assigned, and Richard left the camp at the same hour, and for the same purpose; but, as had been agreed upon, he took his journey by a different route, a precaution which had been judged necessary, to prevent the possibility of a quarrel betwixt their armed attendants.

The good King himself was in no humour for quarrelling with any one. Nothing could have added to his pleasurable anticipations of a desperate and bloody combat in the lists, except his being in his own royal person one of the combatants; and he was half in charity again even with Conrade of Montserrat. Lightly armed, richly dressed, and gay as a bridegroom on the eve of his nuptials, Richard caracoled along by the side of Queen Berengaria's litter, pointing out to her the various scenes through which they passed, and cheering with tale and song the bosom of the inhospitable wilderness. The former route of the Queen's pilgrimage to Engaddi had been on the other side of the chain of mountains, so that the ladies were strangers to the scenery of the desert; and though Berengaria knew her husband's disposition too well not to endeavour to seem interested in what he was pleased either to say or to sing, she could not help indulging some female fears when she found herself in the howling wilderness with so small an escort, which seemed almost like a moving speck on the bosom of the plain, and knew, at the same time, they were not so distant from the camp of Saladin but what they might be in a moment surprised and swept off by an overpowering host of his fiery-footed cavalry, should the Pagan be faithless enough to embrace an opportunity thus tempting. But when she hinted these suspicions to Richard, he repelled them with displeasure and disdain. "It were worse than ingratitude," he said, "to doubt the good faith of the generous Soldan."

Yet the same doubts and fears recurred more than once, not to the timid mind of the Queen alone, but to the firmer and more candid soul of Edith Plantagenet, who had no such confidence in the faith of the Moslem as to render her perfectly at ease when so much in their power; and her surprise had been far less than her terror, if the desert around had suddenly resounded with the shout of Alla hu! and a band of Arab cavalry had pounced on them like vultures on their prey. Nor were these suspicions lessened, when, as evening approached, they were aware of a single Arab horseman, distinguished by his turban and long lance, hovering on the edge of a small eminence like a hawk poised in the air, and who instantly, on the appearance of the royal retinue, darted off with the speed of the same bird, when it shoots down the wind and disappears from the horizon.

"We must be near the station," said King Richard; "and yonder cavalier is one of Saladin's outposts—methinks I hear the noise of the Moorish horns and cymbals. Get you into order, my hearts, and form yourselves around the ladies soldier-like and firmly."

As he spoke, each knight, squire, and archer, hastily closed in upon his appointed ground, and they proceeded in the most compact order, which made their numbers appear still smaller; and to say the truth, though there might be no fear, there was anxiety as well as curiosity in the attention with which they listened to the wild bursts of Moorish music, which came ever and anon more distinctly from the quarter in which the Arab horseman had been seen to disappear.

De Vaux spoke in a whisper to the King — "Were it not well, my liege, to send a page to the top of that sand-bank? Or would it stand with your pleasure that I prick forward? Methinks, by all yonder clash and clang, if there be no more than five hundred men beyond the sand-hills, half of the Soldan's retinue must be drummers and cymbal tossers.— Shall I spur on?"

The Baron had checked his horse with the bit, and was just about to strike him with the spurs, when the King exclaimed—"Not for the world. Such a caution would express suspicion, and could do little to prevent surprise, which, however, I apprehend not."

They advanced accordingly in close and firm order till they surmounted the line of low sand-hills, and came in sight of the appointed station, when a splendid, but at the same time a startling spectacle, awaited them.

The Diamond of the Desert, so lately a solitary fountain, distinguished only amid the waste by solitary groups of palm-trees, was now the centre of an encampment, the embroidered flags and gilded ornaments of which glittered far and wide, and reflected a thousand rich tints against the setting sun. The coverings of the large pavilions were of the gayest colours, scarlet, bright yellow, pale blue, and other gaudy and gleaming hues, and the tops of their pillars, or tent-poles, were decorated with golden pomegranates, and small silken flags. But, besides these distinguished pavilions, there were, what Thomas de Vaux considered as a portentous number of the ordinary black tents of the Arabs, being sufficient, as he conceived, to accommodate, according to the Eastern fashion, a host of five thousand men. A number of Arabs and Curds, fully corresponding to the extent of the encampment, were hastily assembling, each leading his horse in his hand, and their muster was accompanied by an astonishing clamour of their noisy instruments of martial music, by which, in all ages, the warfare of the Arabs has been animated.

They soon formed a deep and confused mass of dismounted cavalry in front of their encampment, when, at the signal of a shrill cry, which arose high over the clangour of the music, each cavalier sprung to his saddle. A cloud of dust arising at the moment of this manoeuvre, hid from Richard and his attendants the camp, the palm-trees, and the distant ridge of mountains, as well as the troops whose sudden movement had raised the cloud, and ascending high over their heads, formed itself into the fantastic forms of writhed pillars, domes, and minarets. Another shrill yell was heard from the bosom of this cloudy tabernacle. It was the signal for the cavalry to advance, which they did at full gallop, disposing themselves as they came forward, so as to come in at once on the front, flanks and rear, of Richard's little body-guard, who were thus surrounded and almost choked by the dense clouds of dust enveloping them on each side, through which were seen alternately, and lost, the grim forms and wild faces of the Saracens, brandishing and tossing their lances in every possible direction, with the wildest cries and halloos, and frequently only reining up their horses when within a spear's length of the Christians, while those in the rear discharged over the heads of both parties thick volleys of arrows. One of these struck the litter in which the Queen was seated, who loudly screamed, and the red spot was on Richard's brow in an instant.

"Ha! Saint George," he exclaimed, "we must take some order with this infidel scum!"

But Edith, whose litter was near, thrust her head out, and with her hand holding one of the shafts, exclaimed, "Royal Richard, beware what you do! see, these arrows are headless!"

"Noble, sensible wench!" exclaimed Richard; "by Heaven, thou shamest us all by thy readiness of thought and eye. — Be not moved, my English hearts," he exclaimed to his followers—"their arrows have no heads—and their spears, too, lack the steel points. It is but a wild welcome, after their savage fashion, though doubtless they would rejoice to see us daunted or disturbed. Move onward, slow and steady."

The little phalanx moved forward accordingly, accompanied on all sides by the Arabs, with the shrillest and most piercing cries, the bowmen, meanwhile, displaying their agility by shooting as near the crests of the Christians as possible, without actually hitting them, while the lancers charged each other with such rude blows of their blunt weapons, that more than one of them lost his saddle, and well-nigh his life, in this rough sport. All this, though designed to express welcome, had rather a doubtful appearance in the eyes of the Europeans.

As they had advanced nearly halfway towards the camp, King Richard and his suite forming, as it were, the nucleus round which this tumultuary body of horsemen howled, whooped, skirmished, and galloped, creating a scene of indescribable confusion, another shrill cry was heard, on which all these irregulars, who were on the front and upon the flanks of the little body of Europeans, wheeled off, and forming themselves into a long and deep column, followed with comparative order and silence in the rear of Richard's troop. The dust began now to dissipate in their front, when there advanced to meet them, through that cloudy veil, a body of cavalry of a different and more regular description, completely armed with offensive and defensive weapons, and who might well have served as a body-guard to the proudest of Eastern monarchs. This splendid troop consisted of five hundred men, and each horse which it contained was worth an earl's ransom. The riders were Georgian and Circassian slaves in the very prime of life; their helmets and hauberks were formed of steel rings, so bright that they shone like silver; their vestures were of the gayest colours, and some of cloth of gold or silver; the sashes were twisted with silk and gold, their rich turbans were plumed and jewelled, and their sabres and poniards, of Damascene steel, were adorned with gold and gems on hilt and scabbard.

This splendid array advanced to the sound of military music, and when they met the Christian body, they opened their files to the right and left, and let them enter between their ranks. Richard now assumed the foremost place in his troop, aware that Saladin himself was approaching. Nor was it long when, in the centre of his body-guard, surrounded by his domestic officers, and those hideous negroes who guard the Eastern haram, and whose misshapen forms were rendered yet more frightful by the richness of their attire, came the Soldan, with the look and manners of one on whose brow Nature had written, This is a King! In his snow-white turban, vest, and wide Eastern trowsers, wearing a sash of scarlet silk, without any other ornament, Saladin might have seemed the plainest dressed man in his own guard. But closer inspection discerned in his turban that inestimable gem, which was called by the poets, the Sea of Light; the diamond on which his signet was engraved, and which he wore in a ring, was pro-

3 r 2

bably worth all the jewels of the English crown, and a sapphire, which terminated the hilt of his canjiar, was of not much inferior value. It should be added, that to protect him from the dust, which, in the vicinity of the Dead Sea, resembles the finest ashes, or, perhaps, out of Oriental pride, the Soldan wore a sort of veil attached to his turban, which partly obscured the view of his noble features. He rode a milk-white Arabian, which bore him as if conscious and proud of his noble burden.

There was no need of farther introduction. The two heroic monarchs, for such they both were, threw themselves at once from horseback, and the troops halting and the music suddenly ceasing, they advanced to meet each other in profound silence, and, after a courteous inclination on either side, they embraced as brethren and equals. The pomp and display upon both sides attracted no farther notice—no one saw aught save Richard and Saladin, and they too beheld nothing but each other. The looks with which Richard surveyed Saladin, were, however, more intently curious than those which the Soldan fixed upon him; and the Soldan also was the first to break silence.

"The Melech Ric is welcome to Saladin as water to this desert. I trust he hath no distrust of this numerous array. Excepting the armed slaves of my household, those who surround you with eyes of wonder and of welcome, are, even the humblest of them, the privileged nobles of my thousand tribes; for who that could claim a title to be present, would remain at home when such a Prince was to be seen as Richard, with the terrors of whose name, even on the sands of Yemen, the nurse stills her child, and the free Arab subdues his restive steed!"

"And these are all nobles of Araby?" said Richard, looking around on wild forms with their persons covered with haicks, their countenances swart with the sunbeams, their teeth as white as ivory, their black eyes glancing with fierce and preternatural lustre from under the shade of their turbans, and their dress being in general simple, even to meanness.

"They claim such rank," said Saladin; "but though numerous, they are within the conditions of the treaty, and bear no arms but the sabre—even the iron of their lances is left behind."

"I fear," muttered De Vaux in English, "they have left them where they can be soon found.—A most flourishing House of Peers, I confess, and would find Westminster-Hall something too narrow for them."

"Hush, De Vaux," said Richard, "I command thee.—Noble Saladin," he said, "suspicion and thou cannot exist on the same ground—See'st thou," pointing to the litters—"I too have brought some champions with me, though armed, perhaps, in breach of agreement, for bright eyes and fair features are weapons which cannot be left behind."

The Soldan, turning to the litters, made an obeisance as lowly as if looking towards Mecca, and kissed the sand in token of respect.

"Nay," said Richard,—"they will not fear a closer encounter, brother; wilt thou not ride towards their litters, and the curtains will be presently withdrawn?"

"That may Allah prohibit!" said Saladin, "since not an Arab looks on who would not think it shame to the noble ladies to be seen with their faces uncovered."

"Thou shalt see them, then, in private, brother," answered Richard.

"To what purpose?" answered Saladin, mournfully. "Thy last letter was, to the hopes which I had entertained, like water to fire; and wherefore should I again light a flame, which may indeed consume, but cannot cheer me?—But will not my brother pass to the tent which his servant hath prepared for him? My principal black slave hath taken order for the reception of the Princesses—the officers of my household will attend your followers, and ourself will be the chamberlain of the royal Richard."

He led the way accordingly to a splendid pavilion, where was every thing that royal luxury could devise. De Vaux, who was in attendance, then removed the chappe, (*capa*,) or long riding-cloak which Richard wore, and he stood before Saladin in the close dress which showed to advantage the strength and symmetry of his person, while it bore a strong contrast to the flowing robes which disguised the thin frame of the Eastern monarch. It was Richard's two-handed sword that chiefly attracted the attention of the Saracen, a broad straight blade, the seemingly unwieldy length of which extended well-nigh from the shoulder to the heel of the wearer.

"Had I not," said Saladin, "seen this brand flaming in the front of battle, like that of Azrael, I had scarce believed that human arm could wield it. Might I request to see the Melech Ric strike one blow with it in peace, and in pure trial of strength?"

"Willingly, noble Saladin," answered Richard; and looking around for something whereon to exercise his strength, he saw a steel mace, held by one of the attendants, the handle being of the same metal, and about an inch and a half in diameter—this he placed on a block of wood.

The anxiety of De Vaux for his master's honour led him to whisper in English—"For the blessed Virgin's sake, beware what you attempt, my liege! Your full strength is not as yet returned—give no triumph to the infidel."

"Peace, fool!" said Richard, standing firm on his ground, and casting a fierce glance around—"thinkest thou that I can fail in *his* presence?"

The glittering broadsword, wielded by both his hands, rose aloft to the King's left shoulder, circled round his head, descended with the sway of some terrific engine, and the bar of iron rolled on the ground in two pieces, as a woodman would sever a sapling with a hedging-bill.

"By the head of the Prophet, a most wonderful blow!" said the Soldan, critically and accurately examining the iron bar which had been cut asunder; and the blade of the sword was so well tempered as to exhibit not the least token of having suffered by the feat it had performed. He then took the King's hand, and looking on the size and muscular strength which it exhibited, laughed as he placed it beside his own, so lank and thin, so inferior in brawn and sinew.

"Ay, look well," said De Vaux, in English, "it will be long ere your long jackanape's fingers do such a feat with your fine gilded reaping-hook there."

"Silence, De Vaux," said Richard; "by Our Lady, he understands or guesses thy meaning—be not so broad, I pray thee."

The Soldan, indeed, presently said—"Something I would fain attempt—though, wherefore should the weak show their inferiority in presence of the strong? Yet, each land hath its own exercises, and this may be new to the Melech Ric."—So saying, he took from the floor a cushion of silk and down, and placed it upright on one end.—"Can thy weapon, my brother, sever that cushion?" he said to King Richard.

"No surely," replied the King; "no sword on earth, were it the Excalibar of King Arthur, can cut that which opposes no steady resistance to the blow."

"Mark, then," said Saladin; and tucking up the sleeve of his gown, showed his arm, thin indeed and spare, but which constant exercise had hardened into a mass consisting of nought but bone, brawn, and sinew. He unsheathed his scimitar, a curved and narrow blade, which glittered not like the swords of the Franks, but was, on the contrary, of a dull blue colour, marked with ten millions of meandering lines, which showed how anxiously the metal had been welded by the armourer. Wielding this weapon, apparently so inefficient when compared to that of Richard, the Soldan stood resting his weight upon his left foot, which was slightly advanced; he balanced himself a little as if to steady his aim, then stepping at once forward, drew the scimitar across the cushion, applying the edge so dexterously, and with so little apparent effort, that the cushion seemed rather to fall asunder than to be divided by violence.

"It is a juggler's trick," said De Vaux, darting forward and snatching up the portion of the cushion which had been cut off, as if to assure himself of the reality of the feat, — "there is gramarye in this."

The Soldan seemed to comprehend him, for he undid the sort of veil which he had hitherto worn, laid it double along the edge of his sabre, extended the weapon edgeways in the air, and drawing it suddenly through the veil, although it hung on the blade entirely loose, severed that also into two parts, which floated to different sides of the tent, equally displaying the extreme temper and sharpness of the weapon, and the exquisite dexterity of him who used it.

"Now, in good faith, my brother," said Richard, "thou art even matchless at the trick of the sword, and right perilous were it to meet thee! Still, however, I put some faith in a downright English blow, and what we cannot do by sleight, we eke out by strength. Nevertheless, in truth thou art as expert in inflicting wounds, as my sage Hakim in curing them. I trust I shall see the learned leech—I have much to thank him for, and had brought some small present."

As he spoke, Saladin exchanged his turban for a Tartar cap. He had no sooner done so, than De Vaux opened at once his extended mouth and his large round eyes, and Richard gazed with scarce less astonishment, while the Soldan spoke in a grave and altered voice: "The sick man, saith the poet, while he is yet infirm, knoweth the physician by his step; but when he is recovered, he knoweth not even his face when he looks upon him."

"A miracle! — a miracle!" exclaimed Richard.

"Of Mahound's working, doubtless," said Thomas de Vaux.

"That I should lose my learned Hakim," said Richard, "merely by absence of his cap and robe, and that I should find him again in my royal brother Saladin!"

"Such is oft the fashion of the world," answered the Soldan; "the tattered robe makes not always the dervisch."

"And it was through thy intercession," said Richard, "that yonder Knight of the Leopard was saved from death — and by thy artifice that he revisited my camp in disguise?"

"Even so," replied Saladin; "I was physician enough to know, that unless the wounds of his bleeding honour were stanched, the days of his life must be few. His disguise was more easily penetrated than I had expected from the success of my own."

"An accident," said King Richard, (probably alluding to the circumstance of his applying his lips to the wound of the supposed Nubian,) "let me first know that his skin was artificially discoloured; and that hint once taken, detection became easy, for his form and person are not to be forgotten. I confidently expect that he will do battle on the morrow."

"He is full in preparation, and high in hope," said the Soldan. "I have furnished him with weapons and horse, thinking nobly of him from what I have seen under various disguises."

"Knows he now," said Richard, "to whom he lies under obligation?"

"He doth," replied the Saracen — "I was obliged to confess my person when I unfolded my purpose."

"And confessed he aught to you?" said the King of England.

"Nothing explicit," replied the Soldan; "but from much that passed between us, I conceive his love is too highly placed to be happy in its issue."

"And thou knowest, that his daring and insolent passion crossed thine own wishes?" said Richard.

"I might guess so much," said Saladin; "but his passion had existed ere my wishes had been formed — and, I must now add, is likely to survive them. I cannot, in honour, revenge me for my disappointment on him who had no hand in it Or, if this high-born dame loved him better than myself, who can say that she did not justice to a knight of her own religion, who is full of nobleness?"

"Yet of too mean lineage to mix with the blood of Plantagenet," said Richard, haughtily.

"Such may be your maxims in Frangistan," replied the Soldan. "Our poets of the Eastern countries say, that a valiant camel-driver is worthy to kiss the lip of a fair Queen, when a cowardly prince is not worthy to salute the hem of her garment.—But with your permission, noble brother, I must take leave of thee for the present, to receive the Duke of Austria and yonder Nazarene knight, much less worthy of hospitality, but who must yet be suitably entreated, not for their sakes, but for mine own honour—for what saith the sage Lokman? 'Say not that the food is lost unto thee which is given to the stranger—for if his body be strengthened and fattened therewithal, not less is thine own worship and good name cherished and augmented.'"

The Saracen monarch departed from King Richard's tent, and having indicated to him, rather with signs than with speech, where the pavilion of the Queen and her attendants was pitched, he went to receive the Marquis of Montserrat and his attendants, for whom, with less good-will, but with equal splendour, the magnificent Soldan had provided accommodations. The most ample refreshments, both in the Oriental, and after the European fashion, were spread before the royal and princely guests of Saladin, each in their own separate pavilion; and so attentive was the Soldan to the habits and taste of his visiters, that Grecian slaves were stationed to present them with the goblet, which is the abomination of the sect of Mahommed. Ere Richard had finished his meal, the ancient Omrah, who had brought the Soldan's letter to the Christian's camp, entered with a plan of the ceremonial to be observed on the succeeding day of combat. Richard, who knew the taste of his old acquaintance, invited him to pledge him in a flagon of wine of Schiraz; but Abdallah gave him to understand, with a rueful aspect, that self-denial, in the present circumstances, was a matter in which his life was concerned; for that Saladin, tolerant in many respects, both observed, and enforced by high penalties, the laws of the Prophet.

"Nay, then," said Richard, "if he loves not wine, that lightener of the human heart, his conversion is not to be hoped for, and the prediction of the mad priest of Engaddi goes like chaff down the wind."

The King then addressed himself to settle the articles of combat, which cost a considerable time, as it was necessary on some points to consult with the opposite parties, as well as with the Soldan.

They were at length finally agreed upon, and adjusted by a protocol in French and in Arabian, which was subscribed by Saladin, as umpire of the field, and by Richard and Leopold as guarantees for the two combatants. As the Omrah took his final leave of King Richard for the evening, De Vaux entered.

"The good knight," he said, "who is to do battle to-morrow, requests to know, whether he may not to-night pay duty to his royal godfather?"

"Hast thou seen him, De Vaux?" said the King, smiling; "and didst thou know an ancient acquaintance?"

"By our Lady of Lanercost," answered De Vaux, "there are so many surprises and changes in this land, that my poor brain turns. I scarce knew Sir Kenneth of Scotland, till his good hound, that had been for a short while under my care, came and fawned on me; and even then I only knew the tyke by the depth of his chest, the roundness of his foot, and his manner of baying; for the poor gaze-hound was painted like any Venetian courtezan."

"Thou art better skilled in brutes than men, De Vaux," said the King.

"I will not deny," said De Vaux, "I have fo u d them ofttimes the honester animals. Also, your Grace is pleased to term me sometimes a brute myself; besides that I serve the Lion, whom all men acknowledge the king of brutes."

"By Saint George, there thou brokest thy lance fairly on my brow," said the King. "I have ever said thou hast a sort of wit, De Vaux—marry, one must strike thee with a sledge-hammer ere it can be made to sparkle. But to the present gear—is the good knight well armed and equipped?"

"Fully, my liege, and nobly," answered De Vaux; "I know the armour well—it is that which the Venetian commissary offered your highness, just ere you became ill, for five hundred bezants."

"And he hath sold it to the infidel Soldan, I warrant me, for a few ducats more, and present payment. These Venetians would sell the sepulchre itself!"

"The armour will never be borne in a nobler cause," said De Vaux.

"Thanks to the nobleness of the Saracen," said the King, "not to the avarice of the Venetians."

"I would to God your Grace would be more cautious," said the anxious De Vaux. — "Here are we deserted by all our allies, for points of offence given to one or another; we cannot hope to prosper upon the land, and we have only to quarrel with the amphibious republic, to lose the means of retreat by sea!"

"I will take care," said Richard, impatiently, "but school me no more. Tell me rather, for it is of interest, hath the knight a confessor?"

"He hath," answered De Vaux; "the hermit of Engaddi, who erst did him that office when preparing for death, attends him on the present occasion; the fame of the duel having brought him hither."

"'Tis well," said Richard; "and now for the knight's request. Say to him, Richard will receive him when the discharge of his devoir beside the Diamond of the Desert shall have atoned for his fault beside the Mount of Saint George; and as thou passest through the camp, let the Queen know I will visit her pavilion — and tell Blondel to meet me there."

De Vaux departed, and in about an hour afterwards, Richard, wrapping his mantle around him, and taking his ghittern in his hand, walked in the direction of the Queen's pavilion. Several Arabs passed him, but always with averted heads, and looks fixed upon the earth, though he could observe that all gazed earnestly after him when he was past. This led him justly to conjecture that his person was known to them; but that either the Soldan's commands, or their own Oriental politeness, forbade them to seem to notice a sovereign who desired to remain incognito.

When the King reached the pavilion of his Queen, he found it guarded by those unhappy officials whom Eastern jealousy places around the zenana. Blondel was walking before the door, and touched his rote from time to time, in a manner which made the Africans show their ivory teeth, and bear burden with their strange gestures and shrill unnatural voices.

"What art thou after with this herd of black cattle, Blondel?" said the King; "wherefore goest thou not into the tent?"

"Because my trade can neither spare the head nor the fingers," said Blondel; "and these honest blackamoors threatened to cut me joint from joint if I pressed forward."

"Well, enter with me," said the King, "and I will be thy safeguard."

The blacks accordingly lowered pikes and swords to King Richard, and bent their eyes on the ground, as if unworthy to look upon him. In the interior of the pavilion, they found Thomas de Vaux in attendance on the Queen. While Berengaria welcomed Blondel, King Richard spoke for some time secretly and apart with his fair kinswoman.

At length, "Are we still foes, my fair Edith?" he said, in a whisper.

"No, my liege," said Edith, in a voice just so low, as not to interrupt the music — "none can bear enmity against King Richard, when he deigns to show himself, as he really is, generous and noble, as well as valiant and honourable."

So saying, she extended her hand to him. The King kissed it in token of reconciliation, and then proceeded.

"You think, my sweet cousin, that my anger in this matter was feigned; but you are deceived. The punishment I inflicted upon this knight was just; for he had betrayed—no matter for how tempting a bribe, fair cousin—the trust committed to him. But I rejoice, perchance as much as you, that to-morrow gives him a chance to win the field, and throw back the stain which for a time clung to him, upon the actual thief and traitor. No!—future times may blame Richard for impetuous folly; but they shall say, that in rendering judgment, he was just when he should, and merciful when he could."

"Laud not thyself, cousin King," said Edith. "They may call thy justice cruelty—thy mercy caprice."

"And do not thou pride thyself," said the King, "as if thy knight, who hath not yet buckled on his armour, were unbelting it in triumph—Conrade of Montserrat is held a good lance. What if the Scot should lose the day?"

"It is impossible!" said Edith, firmly—"My own eyes saw yonder Conrade tremble and change colour, like a base thief. He is guilty—and the trial by combat is an appeal to the justice of God—I myself, in such a cause, would encounter him without fear."

"By the mass, I think thou wouldst, wench," said the King, "and beat him to boot; for there never breathed a truer Plantagenet than thou."

He paused, and added in a very serious tone,—"See that thou continue to remember what is due to thy birth."

"What means that advice, so seriously given at this moment?" said Edith. "Am I of such light nature as to forget my name—my condition?"

"I will speak plainly, Edith," answered the King, "and as to a friend,—What will this knight be to you, should he come off victor from yonder lists?"

"To me?" said Edith, blushing deep with shame and displeasure,—"What *can* he be to me more than an honoured knight, worthy of such grace as Queen Berengaria might confer on him, had he selected her for his lady, instead of a more unworthy choice? The meanest knight may devote himself to the service of an empress, but the glory of his choice," she said proudly, "must be his reward."

"Yet he hath served and suffered much for you," said the King.

"I have paid his services with honour and applause, and his sufferings with tears," answered Edith. "Had he desired other reward, he would have done wisely to have bestowed his affections within his own degree."

"You would not then wear the bloody night-gear for his sake?" said King Richard.

"No more," answered Edith, "than I would have required him to expose his life by an action, in which there was more madness than honour."

"Maidens talk ever thus," said the King; "but when the favoured lover presses his suit, she says, with a sigh, her stars had decreed otherwise."

"Your Grace has now, for the second time, threatened me with the influence of my horoscope," Edith replied, with dignity. "Trust me, my liege, whatever be the power of the stars, your poor kinswoman will never wed either infidel, or obscure adventurer.—Permit me, that I listen to the music of Blondel, for the tone of your royal admonitions is scarce so grateful to the ear."

The conclusion of the evening offered nothing worthy of notice.

Chapter the Twenty-Eighth.

Heard ye the din of battle bray,
Lance to lance and horse to horse!
         GRAY.

It had been agreed, on account of the heat of the climate, that the judicial combat, which was the cause of the present assemblage of various nations at the Diamond of the Desert, should take place at one hour after sunrise. The wide lists, which had been constructed under the inspection of the Knight of the Leopard, enclosed a space of hard sand, which was one hundred and twenty yards long by forty in width. They extended in length from north to south, so as to give both parties the equal advantage of the rising sun. Saladin's royal seat was erected on the western side of the enclosure, just in the centre, where the combatants were expected to meet in mid encounter. Opposed to this was a gallery with closed casements, so contrived that the ladies, for whose accommodation it was erected, might see the fight without being themselves exposed to view. At either extremity of the lists was a barrier, which could be opened or shut at pleasure. Thrones had been also erected, but the Archduke, perceiving that his was lower than King Richard's, refused to occupy it; and Cœur de Lion, who would have submitted to much ere any formality should have interfered with the combat, readily agreed that the sponsors, as they were called, should remain on horseback during the fight. At one extremity of the lists were placed the followers of Richard, and opposed to them were those who accompanied the defender, Conrade. Around the throne destined for the Soldan, were ranged his splendid Georgian Guards, and the rest of the enclosure was occupied by Christian and Mahomedan spectators.

Long before daybreak, the lists were surrounded by even a larger number of Saracens than Richard had seen on the preceding evening. When the first ray of the sun's glorious orb arose above the desert, the sonorous call, "To prayer, to prayer!" was poured forth by the Soldan himself, and answered by others, whose rank and zeal entitled them to act as muezzins. It was a striking spectacle to see them all sink to earth, for the purpose of repeating their devotions, with their faces turned to Mecca. But when they arose from the ground, the sun's rays, now strengthening fast, seemed to confirm the Lord of Gilsland's conjecture of the night before. They were flashed back from many a spear-head, for the pointless lances of the preceding day were certainly no longer such. De Vaux pointed it out to his master, who answered with impatience, that he had perfect confidence in the good faith of the Soldan; but if De Vaux was afraid of his bulky body, he might retire.

Soon after this the noise of timbrels was heard, at the sound of which the whole Saracen cavaliers threw themselves from their horses, and prostrated themselves, as if for a second morning prayer. This was to give an opportunity to the Queen, with Edith and her attendants, to pass from the pavilion to the gallery intended for them. Fifty guards of Saladin's seraglio escorted them, with naked sabres, whose orders were, to cut to pieces whomsoever, were he prince or peasant, should venture to gaze on the ladies as they passed, or even presume to raise his head until the cessation of the music should make all men aware that they were lodged in their gallery, not to be gazed on by the curious eye.

This superstitious observance of Oriental reverence to the fair sex, called forth from Queen Berengaria some criticisms very unfavourable to Saladin and his country. But their den, as the royal fair called it, being securely closed and guarded by their sable attendants, she was under the necessity of contenting herself with seeing, and laying aside for the present the still more exquisite pleasure of being seen.

Meantime the sponsors of both champions went, as was their duty, to see that they were duly armed, and prepared for combat. The Archduke of Austria was in no hurry to perform this part of the ceremony, having had rather an unusually severe debauch upon wine of Schiraz the preceding evening. But the Grand Master of the Temple, more deeply concerned in the event of the combat, was early before the tent of Conrade of Montserrat. To his great surprise, the attendants refused him admittance.

"Do you not know me, ye knaves?" said the Grand Master in great anger.

"We do, most valiant and reverend," answered Conrade's squire; "but even *you* may not at present enter—the Marquis is about to confess himself."

"Confess himself!" exclaimed the Templar, in a tone where alarm mingled with surprise and scorn — "and to whom, I pray thee?"

"My master bid me be secret," said the squire; on which the Grand Master pushed past him, and entered the tent almost by force.

The Marquis of Montserrat was kneeling at the feet of the Hermit of Engaddi, and in the act of beginning his confession.

"What means this, Marquis?" said the Grand Master, "up, for shame—or, if you must needs confess, am not I here?"

"I have confessed to you too often already," replied Conrade, with a pale cheek and a faltering voice. "For God's sake, Grand Master, begone, and let me unfold my conscience to this holy man."

"In what is he holier than I am?" said the Grand Master. — "Hermit, prophet, madman — say, if thou darest, in what thou excellest me?"

"Bold and bad man," replied the Hermit, "know that I am like the latticed window, and the divine light passes through to avail others, though, alas! it helpeth not me. Thou art like the iron stanchions, which neither receive light themselves, nor communicate it to any one."

"Prate not to me, but depart from this tent," said the Grand Master; "the Marquis shall not confess this morning, unless it be to me, for I part not from his side."

"Is this *your* pleasure?" said the Hermit to Conrade; "for think not I will obey that proud man, if you continue to desire my assistance."

"Alas! said Conrade, irresolutely, "what would you have me say? — Farewell for a while — we will speak anon."

"Oh, procrastination!" exclaimed the Hermit, "thou art a soul-murderer! — Unhappy man, farewell — not for a while, but until we both shall meet — no matter where. — And for thee," he added, turning to the Grand Master, "TREMBLE!"

"Tremble!" replied the Templar, contemptuously, "I cannot if I would." The Hermit heard not his answer, having left the tent.

"Come! to this gear hastily," said the Grand Master, "since thou wilt needs go through the foolery. — Hark thee — I think I know most of thy frailties by heart, so we may omit the detail, which may be somewhat a long one, and begin with the absolution. What signifies counting the spots of dirt that we are about to wash from our hands?"

"Knowing what thou art thyself," said Conrade, "it is blasphemous to speak of pardoning another."

"That is not according to the canon, Lord Marquis," said the Templar,— "thou art more scrupulous than orthodox. The absolution of the wicked priest is as effectual as if he were himself a saint,— otherwise God help the poor penitent! What wounded man inquires whether the surgeon that tents his gashes have clean hands or no! — Come, shall we to this toy?"

"No," said Conrade, "I will rather die unconfessed than mock the sacrament."

"Come, noble Marquis," said the Templar, "rouse up your courage, and speak not thus. In an hour's time thou shalt stand victorious in the lists, or confess thee in thy helmet, like a valiant knight."

"Alas, Grand Master!" answered Conrade, "all augurs ill for this affair. The strange discovery by the instinct of a dog — the revival of this Scottish knight, who comes into the lists like a spectre — all betokens evil."

"Pshaw!" said the Templar, "I have seen thee bend thy lance boldly against him in sport, and with equal chance of success—think thou art but in a tournament, and who bears him better in the tilt-yard than thou ? — Come, squires and armourers, your master must be accoutred for the field."

The attendants entered accordingly, and began to arm the Marquis.

"What morning is without ?" said Conrade.

"The sun rises dimly." answered a squire.

"Thou seest, Grand Master," said Conrade, "nought smiles on us."

"Thou wilt fight the more coolly," answered the Templar; "thank Heaven, that bath tempered the sun of Palestine to suit thy occasion."

Thus jested the Grand Master; but his jests had lost their influence on the harassed mind of the Marquis, and, notwithstanding his attempts to seem gay, his gloom communicated itself to the Templar.

"This craven," he thought, "will lose the day in pure faintness and cowardice of heart, which he calls tender conscience. I, whom visions and auguries shake not — who am firm in my purpose as the living rock — I should have fought the combat myself.—Would to God the Scot may strike him dead on the spot — it were next best to his winning the victory. But come what will, he must have no other confessor than myself—our sins are too much in common, and he might confess my share with his own."

While these thoughts passed through his mind, he continued to assist the Marquis in arming, but it was in silence.

The hour at length arrived, the trumpets sounded, the knights rode into the lists armed at all points, and mounted like men who were to do battle for a kingdom's honour. They wore their vizors up, and riding around the lists three times, showed themselves to the spectators. Both were goodly persons, and both had noble countenances. But there was an air of manly confidence on the brow of the Scot — a radiancy of hope, which amounted even to cheerfulness, while, although pride and effort had recalled much of Conrade's natural courage, there lowered still on his brow a cloud of ominous despondence. Even his steed seemed to tread less lightly and blithely to the trumpet-sound than the noble Arab which was bestrode by Sir Kenneth ; and the *spruch-sprecher* shook his head while he observed, that while the challenger rode about the lists in the course of the sun, that is, from right to left, the defender made the same circuit *widdersins*, that is, from left to right, which is in most countries held ominous.

A temporary altar was erected just beneath the gallery occupied by the Queen, and beside it stood the Hermit in the dress of his order, as a Carmelite friar. Other churchmen were also present. To this altar the challenger and defender were successively brought forward, conducted by their respective sponsors. Dismounting before it, each knight avouched the justice of his cause by a solemn oath on the Evangelists, and prayed that his success might be according to the truth or falsehood of what he then swore. They also made oath, that they came to do battle in knightly guise, and with the usual weapons, disclaiming the use of spells, charms, or magical devices, to incline victory to their side. The challenger pronounced his vow with a firm and manly voice, and a bold and cheerful countenance. When the ceremony was finished, the Scottish Knight looked at the gallery, and bent his head to the earth, as if in honour of those invisible beauties which were enclosed within ; then, loaded with armour as he was, sprung to the saddle without the use of the stirrup, and made his courser carry him in a succession of caracoles to his station at the eastern extremity of the lists. Conrade also presented himself before the altar with boldness enough ; but his voice, as he took the oath, sounded hollow, as if drowned in his helmet. The lips with which he appealed to heaven to adjudge victory to the just quarrel, grew white as they uttered the impious mockery. As he turned to remount his horse, the Grand Master approached him closer, as if to rectify something about the sitting of his gorget, and whispered,—"Coward and fool! — recall thy senses, and do me this battle bravely, else, by Heaven, shouldst thou escape him, thou escapest not *me!*"

The savage tone in which this was whispered, perhaps completed the confusion of the Marquis's nerves, for he stumbled as he made to horse; and though he recovered his feet, sprung to the saddle with his usual agility, and displayed his address in horsemanship as he assumed his position opposite to the challenger's, yet the accident did not escape those who were on the watch for omens, which might predict the fate of the day.

The priests, after a solemn prayer, that God would show the rightful quarrel, departed from the lists. The trumpets of the challenger then rung a flourish, and a herald-at-arms proclaimed at the eastern end of the lists.— "Here stands a good knight, Sir Kenneth of Scotland, champion for the royal King Richard of England, who accuseth Conrade, Marquis of Montserrat, of foul treason and dishonour done to the said King."

When the words Kenneth of Scotland announced the name and character of the champion, hitherto scarce generally known, a loud and cheerful acclaim burst from the followers of King Richard, and hardly, notwithstanding repeated commands of silence, suffered the reply of the defendant to be heard. He, of course, avouched his innocence, and offered his body for battle. The esquires of the combatants now approached, and delivered to each his shield and lance, assisting to hang the former around his neck, that his two hands might remain free, one for the management of the bridle, the other to direct the lance.

The shield of the Scot displayed his old bearing, the leopard, but with the addition of a collar and broken chain, in allusion to his late captivity. The shield of the Marquis bore, in reference to his title, a serrated and rocky mountain. Each shook his lance aloft, as if to ascertain the weight and toughness of the unwieldy weapon, and then laid it in the rest. The sponsors, heralds, and squires, now retired to the barriers, and the combatants sat opposite to each other, face to face, with couched lance and closed vizor, the human form so completely enclosed, that they looked more like statues of molten iron, than beings of flesh and blood. The silence of suspense was now general — men breathed thicker, and their very souls seemed seated in their eyes, while not a sound was to be heard save the snorting and pawing of the good steeds, who, sensible of what was about to happen, were impatient to dash into career. They stood thus for perhaps three minutes, when, at a signal given by the Soldan, an hundred instruments rent the air with their brazen clamours, and each champion striking his horse with the spurs, and slacking the rein, the horses started into full gallop, and the knights met in mid space with a shock like a thunderbolt. The victory was not in doubt — no, not one moment. Conrade, indeed, showed himself a practised warrior; for he struck his antagonist knightly in the midst of his shield, bearing his lance so straight and true, that it shivered into splinters from the steel spear-head up to the very gauntlet. The horse of Sir Kenneth recoiled two or three yards and fell on his haunches, but the rider easily raised him with hand and rein. But for Conrade, there was no recovery. Sir Kenneth's lance had pierced through the shield, through a plated corslet of Milan steel, through a *secret*, or coat of linked mail, worn beneath the corslet, had wounded him deep in the bosom, and borne him from his saddle, leaving the truncheon of the lance fixed in his wound. The sponsors, heralds, and Saladin himself, descending from his throne, crowded around the wounded man; while Sir Kenneth, who had drawn his sword ere yet he discovered his antagonist was totally helpless, now commanded him to avow his guilt. The belmet was hastily unclosed, and the wounded man, gazing wildly on the skies, replied,—"What would you more?—God hath decided justly—I am guilty—but there are worse traitors in the camp than I.—In pity to my soul, let me have a confessor!"

He revived as he uttered these words.

"The talisman—the powerful remedy, royal brother," said King Richard to Saladin.

"The traitor," answered the Soldan, "is more fit to be dragged from the lists to the gallows by the heels, than to profit by its virtues:—and some such fate is in his look," he added, after gazing fixedly upon the wounded man; "for though his wound may be cured, yet Azrael's seal is on the wretch's brow."

"Nevertheless," said Richard, "I pray you do for him what you may, that he may at least have time for confession—Slay not soul and body! .m one half hour of time may be worth more, by ten thousand fold, ..an the life of the oldest patriarch."

"My royal brother's wish shall be obeyed," said Saladin.—"Slaves, bear this wounded man to our tent."

"Do not so," said the Templar, who had hitherto stood gloomily looking on in silence.—"The royal Duke of Austria and myself will not permit this unhappy Christian Prince to be delivered over to the Saracens, that they may try their spells upon him. We are his sponsors, and demand that he be assigned to our care."

"That is, you refuse the certain means offered to recover him?" said Richard.

"Not so," said the Grand Master, recollecting himself. — "If the Soldan useth lawful medicines, he may attend the patient in my tent."

"Do so, I pray thee, good brother," said Richard to Saladin, "though the permission be ungraciously yielded.—But now to a more glorious work.— Sound, trumpets — shout England — in honour of England's champion!"

Drum, clarion, trumpet, and cymbal, rung forth at once, and the deep and regular shout, which for ages has been the English acclamation, sounded amidst the shrill and irregular yells of the Arabs, like the diapason of the organ amid the howling of a storm. There was silence at length.

"Brave Knight of the Leopard," resumed Cœur de Lion, "thou hast shown that the Ethiopian *may* change his skin and the Leopard his spots, though clerks quote Scripture for the impossibility. Yet I have more to say to you when I have conducted you to the presence of the ladies, the best judges, and best rewarders, of deeds of chivalry."

The Knight of the Leopard bowed assent.

"And thou, princely Saladin, wilt also attend them. I promise thee our Queen will not think herself welcome, if she lacks the opportunity to thank her royal host for her most princely reception."

Saladin bent his head gracefully, but declined the invitation.

"I must attend the wounded man," he said. "The leech leaves not his patient more than the champion the lists, even if he be summoned to a bower like those of Paradise. And farther, royal Richard, know that the blood of the East flows not so temperately in the presence of beauty, as that of your land. What saith the Book itself? — Her eye is as the edge of the sword of the Prophet, who shall look upon it? He that would not be burnt avoideth to tread on hot embers — wise men spread not the flax before a bickering torch — He, saith the sage, who hath forfeited a treasure, doth not wisely to turn back his head to gaze at it."

Richard, it may be believed, respected the motives of delicacy which flowed from manners so different from his own, and urged his request no farther.

"At noon," said the Soldan, as he departed, "I trust ye will all accept a collation under the black camel-skin tent of a chief of Curdistan."

The same invitation was circulated among the Christians, comprehending all those of sufficient importance to be admitted to sit at a feast made for princes.

"Hark!" said Richard, the timbrels announce that our Queen and her attendants are leaving their gallery—and see, the turbans sink on the ground, as if struck down by a destroying angel. All lie prostrate, as if the glance of an Arab's eye could sully the lustre of a lady's cheek! Come, we will to the pavilion, and lead our conqueror thither in triumph.—How I pity that noble Soldan, who knows but of love as it is known to those of inferior nature!"

Blondel tuned his harp to its boldest measure, to welcome the introduction of the victor into the pavilion of Queen Berengaria. He entered, supported on either side by his sponsors, Richard and Thomas Longsword, and knelt gracefully down before the Queen, though more than half the homage was silently rendered to Edith, who sat on her right hand.

"Unarm him, my mistresses," said the King, whose delight was in the execution of such chivalrous usages—"Let Beauty honour Chivalry! Undo his spurs, Berengaria; Queen though thou be, thou owest him what marks of favour thou canst give.—Unlace his helmet, Edith—by this hand thou shalt, wert thou the proudest Plantagenet of the line, and he the poorest knight on earth!"

Both ladies obeyed the royal commands.—Berengaria with bustling assiduity, as anxious to gratify her husband's humour, and Edith blushing and growing pale alternately, as slowly and awkwardly she undid, with Longsword's assistance, the fastenings, which secured the helmet to the gorget.

"And what expect you from beneath this iron shell?" said Richard, as the removal of the casque gave to view the noble countenance of Sir Kenneth, his face glowing with recent exertion, and not less so with present emotion. "What think ye of him, gallants and beauties?" said Richard. "Doth he resemble an Ethiopian slave, or doth he present the face of an obscure and nameless adventurer? No, by my good sword!—Here terminate his various disguises. He hath knelt down before you, unknown save by his worth—he arises, equally distinguished by birth and fortune. The adventurous knight, Kenneth, arises David, Earl of Huntingdon, Prince Royal of Scotland!"

There was a general exclamation of surprise, and Edith dropped from her hand the helmet, which she had just received.

"Yes, my masters," said the King, "it is even so. Ye know how Scotland deceived us when she proposed to send this valiant Earl, with a bold company of her best and noblest, to aid our arms in this conquest of Palestine, but failed to comply with her engagements. This noble youth, under whom the Scottish Crusaders were to have been arrayed, thought foul scorn that his arm should be withheld from the holy warfare, and joined us at Sicily with a small train of devoted and faithful attendants, which was augmented by many of his countrymen to whom the rank of their leader was unknown. The confidants of the Royal Prince had all, saving one old follower, fallen by death, when his secret, but too well kept, had nearly occasioned my cutting off, in a Scottish adventurer, one of the noblest hopes of Europe.—Why did you not mention your rank, noble Huntingdon, when endangered by my hasty and passionate sentence?—Was it that you thought Richard capable of abusing the advantage I possessed over the heir of a King whom I have so often found hostile?"

"I did you not that injustice, royal Richard," answered the Earl of Huntingdon; "but my pride brooked not that I should avow myself Prince of Scotland in order to save my life, endangered for default of loyalty. And, moreover, I had made my vow to preserve my rank unknown till the

Crusade should be accomplished; nor did I mention it save *in articulo mortis*, and under the seal of confession, to yonder reverend hermit."

"It was the knowledge of that secret, then, which made the good man so urgent with me to recall my severe sentence?" said Richard. "Well did he say, that, had this good knight fallen by my mandate, I should have wished the deed undone though it had cost me a limb—A limb!—I should have wished it undone had it cost me my life — since the world would have said that Richard had abused the condition in which the heir of Scotland had placed himself, by his confidence in his generosity."

"Yet, may we know of your Grace by what strange and happy chance this riddle was at length read?" said the Queen Berengaria.

"Letters were brought to us from England," said the King, "in which we learnt, among other unpleasant news, that the King of Scotland had seized upon three of our nobles, when on a pilgrimage to Saint Ninian, and alleged as a cause, that his heir, being supposed to be fighting in the ranks of the Teutonic Knights, against the heathen of Borussia, was, in fact, in our camp and in our power; and, therefore, William proposed to hold these nobles as hostages for his safety. This gave me the first light on the real rank of the Knight of the Leopard, and my suspicions were confirmed by De Vaux, who, on his return from Askalon, brought back with him the Earl of Huntingdon's sole attendant, a thick-skulled slave, who had gone thirty miles to unfold to De Vaux a secret he should have told to me."

"Old Strauchan must be excused," said the Lord of Gilsland. "He knew from experience that my heart is somewhat softer than if I wrote myself Plantagenet."

"Thy heart soft? thou commodity of old iron — and Cumberland flint, that thou art!" exclaimed the King. — "It is we Plantagenets who boast soft and feeling hearts, Edith," turning to his cousin, with an expression which called the blood into her cheek—"Give me thy hand, my fair cousin, and, Prince of Scotland, thine."

"Forbear, my lord," said Edith, hanging back, and endeavouring to hide her confusion, under an attempt to rally her royal kinsman's credulity. "Remember you not that my hand was to be the signal of converting to the Christian faith the Saracen and Arab, Saladin and all his turbaned host?"

"Ay, but the wind of prophecy hath chopped about, and sits now in another corner," replied Richard.

"Mock not, lest your bonds be made strong," said the Hermit, stepping forward. "The heavenly host write nothing but truth in their brilliant records — it is man's eyes which are too weak to read their characters aright. Know, that when Saladin and Kenneth of Scotland slept in my grotto, I read in the stars, that there rested under my roof a prince, the natural foe of Richard, with whom the fate of Edith Plantagenet was to be united. Could I doubt that this must be the Soldan, whose rank was well known to me, as he often visited my cell to converse on the revolutions of the heavenly bodies? — Again, the lights of the firmament proclaimed that this Prince, the husband of Edith Plantagenet, should be a Christian; and I—weak and wild interpreter!—argued thence the conversion of the noble Saladin, whose good qualities seemed often to incline him towards the better faith. The sense of my weakness hath humbled me to the dust, but in the dust I have found comfort! I have not read aright the fate of others — who can assure me but that I may have miscalculated mine own? God will not have us break into his council-house or spy out his hidden mysteries. We must wait his time with watching and prayer—with fear and with hope. I came hither the stern seer—the proud prophet—skilled, as I thought, to instruct princes, and gifted even with supernatural powers, but burdened with a weight which I deemed no shoulders but mine could have borne. But my bands have been broken! I go hence humble in mine ignorance, penitent —and not hopeless."

With these words he withdrew from the assembly; and it is recorded, that, from that period, his frenzy fits seldom occurred, and his penances were of a milder character, and accompanied with better hopes of the future. So much is there of self-opinion, even in insanity, that the conviction of his having entertained and expressed an unfounded prediction with so much vehemence, seemed to operate like loss of blood on the human frame, to modify and lower the fever of the brain.

It is needless to follow into farther particulars the conferences at the royal tent, or to inquire whether David, Earl of Huntingdon, was as mute in the presence of Edith Plantagenet, as when he was bound to act under the character of an obscure and nameless adventurer. It may be well believed that he there expressed, with suitable earnestness, the passion to which he had so often before found it difficult to give words.

The hour of noon now approached, and Saladin waited to receive the Princes of Christendom in a tent, which, but for its large size, differed little from that of the ordinary shelter of the common Curdman, or Arab; yet, beneath its ample and sable covering, was prepared a banquet after the most gorgeous fashion of the East, extended upon carpets of the richest stuffs, with cushions laid for the guests. But we cannot stop to describe the cloth of gold and silver — the superb embroidery in Arabesque — the shawls of Caschmere—and the muslins of India, which were here unfolded in all their splendour; far less to tell the different sweetmeats, ragouts edged with rice coloured in various manners, with all the other niceties of Eastern cookery. Lambs roasted whole, and game and poultry dressed in pilaus, were piled in vessels of gold, and silver, and porcelain, and intermixed with large mazers of sherbet, cooled in snow and ice from the caverns of Mount Lebanon. A magnificent pile of cushions at the head of the banquet, seemed prepared for the master of the feast, and such dignitaries as he might call to share that place of distinction, while from the roof of the tent in all quarters, but over this seat of eminence in particular, waved many a banner and pennon, the trophies of battles won, and kingdoms overthrown. But amongst and above them all, a long lance displayed a shroud, the banner of Death, with this impressive inscription—" SALADIN, KING OF KINGS—SALADIN, VICTOR OF VICTORS—SALADIN MUST DIE." Amid these preparations, the slaves who had arranged the refreshments stood with drooped heads and folded arms, mute and motionless as monumental statuary, or as automata, which waited the touch of the artist to put them in motion.

Expecting the approach of his princely guests, the Soldan, imbued, as most were, with the superstitions of his time, paused over a horoscope and corresponding scroll, which had been sent to him by the Hermit of Engaddi when he departed from the camp.

"Strange and mysterious science," he muttered to himself, "which, pretending to draw the curtain of futurity, misleads those whom it seems to guide, and darkens the scene which it pretends to illuminate! Who would not have said that I was that enemy most dangerous to Richard, whose enmity was to be ended by marriage with his kinswoman? Yet it now appears that a union betwixt this gallant Earl and the lady will bring about friendship betwixt Richard and Scotland, an enemy more dangerous than I, as a wild-cat in a chamber is more to be dreaded than a lion in a distant desert, — But then," he continued to mutter to himself, "the combination intimates, that this husband was to be Christian.—Christian?" he repeated, after a pause,—"That gave the insane fanatic star-gazer hopes that I might renounce my faith! but me, the faithful follower of our Prophet — me it should have undeceived. Lie there, mysterious scroll," he added, thrusting it under the pile of cushions; "strange are thy bodements and fatal, since, even when true in themselves, they work upon those who attempt to decipher their meaning, all the effects of falsehood. — How now, what means this intrusion?"

He spoke to the dwarf Nectabanus, who rushed into the tent fearfully agitated, with each strange and disproportioned feature wrenched by horror into still more extravagant ugliness,—his mouth open, his eyes staring, his hands, with their shrivelled and deformed fingers, widely expanded.

"What now?" said the Soldan, sternly.

"*Accipe hoc!*" groaned out the dwarf.

"Ha! say'st thou?" answered Saladin.

"*Accipe hoc!*" replied the panic-struck creature, unconscious, perhaps, that he repeated the same words as before.

"Hence! I am in no vein for foolery," said the Emperor.

"Nor am I farther fool," said the dwarf, "than to make my folly help out my wits to earn my bread, poor helpless wretch!—Hear, hear me, great Soldan!"

"Nay, if thou hast actual wrong to complain of," said Saladin, "fool or wise, thou art entitled to the ear of a King. — Retire hither with me;" and he led him into the inner tent.

Whatever their conference related to, it was soon broken off by the fanfare of the trumpets, announcing the arrival of the various Christian princes, whom Saladin welcomed to his tent with a royal courtesy well becoming their rank and his own; but chiefly he saluted the young Earl of Huntingdon, and generously congratulated him upon prospects, which seemed to have interfered with and overclouded those which he had himself entertained.

"But think not," said the Soldan, "thou noble youth, that the Prince of Scotland is more welcome to Saladin, than was Kenneth to the solitary Ilderim when they met in the desert, or the distressed Ethiop to the Hakim Adonbec. A brave and generous disposition like thine hath a value independent of condition and birth, as the cool draught which I here proffer thee, is as delicious from an earthen vessel as from a goblet of gold."

The Earl of Huntingdon made a suitable reply, gratefully acknowledging the various important services he had received from the generous Soldan; but when he had pledged Saladin in the bowl of sherbet, which the Soldan had proffered to him, he could not help remarking with a smile, "The brave cavalier, Ilderim, knew not of the formation of ice, but the munificent Soldan cools his sherbet with snow."

"Wouldst thou have an Arab or a Curdman as wise as a Hakim?" said the Soldan. "He who dons a disguise must make the sentiments of his heart and the learning of his head accord with the dress which he assumes. I desired to see how a brave and single-hearted cavalier of Frangistan would conduct himself in debate with such a chief as I then seemed; and I questioned the truth of a well-known fact, to know by what arguments thou wouldst support thy assertion."

While they were speaking, the Archduke of Austria, who stood a little apart, was struck with the mention of iced sherbet, and took with pleasure and some bluntness the deep goblet, as the Earl of Huntingdon was about to replace it.

"Most delicious!" he exclaimed, after a deep draught, which the heat of the weather, and the feverishness following the debauch of the preceding day, had rendered doubly acceptable. He sighed as he handed the cup to the Grand Master of the Templars. Saladin made a sign to the dwarf, who advanced and pronounced, with a harsh voice, the words, *Accipe hoc!* The Templar started, like a steed who sees a lion under a bush, beside the pathway; yet instantly recovered, and to hide, perhaps, his confusion, raised the goblet to his lips—but those lips never touched that goblet's rim. The sabre of Saladin left its sheath as lightning leaves the cloud. It was waved in the air, — and the head of the Grand Master rolled to the extremity of the tent, while the trunk remained for a second standing, with the goblet still clenched in its grasp, then fell, the liquor mingling with the blood that spurted from the veins.*

There was a general exclamation of treason, and Austria, nearest to whom Saladin stood with the bloody sabre in his hand, started back as if apprehensive that his turn was to come next. Richard and others laid hand on their swords.

"Fear nothing, noble Austria," said Saladin, as composedly as if nothing had happéned, "nor you, royal England, be wroth at what you have seen. Not for his manifold treason;—not for the attempt which, as may be vouched by his own squire, he instigated against King Richard's life;—not that he pursued the Prince of Scotland and myself in the desert, reducing us to save our lives by the speed of our horses;—not that he had stirred up the Maronites to attack us upon this very occasion, had I not brought up unexpectedly so many Arabs as rendered the scheme abortive;—not for any or all of these crimes does he now lie there, although each were deserving such a doom;—but because, scarce half an hour ere he polluted our presence, as the simoom empoisons the atmosphere, he poniarded his comrade and accomplice, Conrade of Montserrat, lest he should confess the infamous plots in which they had both been engaged."

"How! Conrade murdered?—And by the Grand Master, his sponsor and most intimate friend!" exclaimed Richard. "Noble Soldan, I would not doubt thee—yet this must be proved—otherwise——"

"There stands the evidence," said Saladin, pointing to the terrified dwarf. "Allah, who sends the fire-fly to illuminate the night-season, can discover secret crimes by the most contemptible means."

The Soldan proceeded to tell the dwarf's story, which amounted to this.—In his foolish curiosity, or, as he partly confessed, with some thoughts of pilfering, Nectabanus had strayed into the tent of Conrade, which had been deserted by his attendants, some of whom had left the encampment to carry the news of his defeat to his brother, and others were availing themselves of the means which Saladin had supplied for revelling. The wounded man slept under the influence of Saladin's wonderful talisman, so that the dwarf had opportunity to pry about at pleasure, until he was frightened into concealment by the sound of a heavy step. He skulked behind a curtain, yet could see the motions, and hear the words of the Grand Master, who entered, and carefully secured the covering of the pavilion behind him. His victim started from sleep, and it would appear that he instantly suspected the purpose of his old associate, for it was in a tone of alarm that he demanded wherefore he disturbed him?

"I come to confess and absolve thee," answered the Grand Master.

Of their farther speech the terrified dwarf remembered little, save that Conrade implored the Grand Master not to break a wounded reed, and that the Templar struck him to the heart with a Turkish dagger, with the words *Accipe hoc*—words which long afterwards haunted the terrified imagination of the concealed witness.

"I verified the tale," said Saladin, "by causing the body to be examined; and I made this unhappy being, whom Allah hath made the discoverer of the crime, repeat in your own presence words which the murderer spoke; and you yourselves saw the effect which they produced upon his conscience!"

---

* The manner of the death of the supposed Grand Master of the Templars, was taken from the real tragedy enacted by Saladin, upon the person of Arnold or Reginald de Chatillon. This person, a soldier of fortune, had seized a castle on the verge of the desert, from whence he made plundering excursions, and insulted and abused the pilgrims who were on their journey to Mecca. It was chiefly on his account that Saladin declared war against Guy de Lusignan, the last Latin King of the Holy Land. The Christian monarch was defeated by Saladin with the loss of thirty thousand men, and having been made prisoner, with Chatillon and others, was conducted before the Soldan. The victor presented to his exhausted captive a cup of sherbet, cooled in snow. Lusignan having drank, was about to hand the cup to Chatillon when the Sultan interfered. "Your person," he said, "my royal prisoner, is sacred, but the cup of Saladin must not be profaned by a blasphemous robber and ruffian." So saying, he slew the captive knight by a blow of his scimitar.—See *Gibbon's History*.

The Soldan paused, and the King of England broke silence:—

"If this be true, as I doubt not, we have witnessed a great act of justice, though it bore a different aspect. But wherefore in this presence? wherefore with thine own hand?"

"I had designed otherwise," said Saladin; "but had I not hastened his doom, it had been altogether averted, since, if I had permitted him to taste of my cup, as he was about to do, how could I, without incurring the brand of inhospitality, have done him to death as he deserved? Had he murdered my father, and afterwards partaken of my food and my bowl, not a hair of his head could have been injured by me. But enough of him—let his carcass and his memory be removed from amongst us."

The body was carried away, and the marks of the slaughter obliterated or concealed with such ready dexterity, as showed that the case was not altogether so uncommon as to paralyse the assistants and officers of Saladin's household.

But the Christian princes felt that the scene which they had beheld weighed heavily on their spirits, and although, at the courteous invitation of the Soldan, they assumed their seats at the banquet, yet it was with the silence of doubt and amazement. The spirits of Richard alone surmounted all cause for suspicion or embarrassment. Yet he, too, seemed to ruminate on some proposition, as if he were desirous of making it in the most insinuating and acceptable manner which was possible. At length he drank off a large bowl of wine, and, addressing the Soldan, desired to know whether it was not true that he had honoured the Earl of Huntingdon with a personal encounter.

Saladin answered with a smile, that he had proved his horse and his weapons with the heir of Scotland, as cavaliers are wont to do with each other when they meet in the desert—and modestly added, that though the combat was not entirely decisive, he had not, on his part, much reason to pride himself on the event. The Scot, on the other hand, disclaimed the attributed superiority, and wished to assign it to the Soldan.

"Enough of honour thou hast had in the encounter," said Richard, "and I envy thee more for that, than for the smiles of Edith Plantagenet, though one of them might reward a bloody day's work.—But what say you, noble princes; is it fitting that such a royal ring of chivalry should break up without something being done for future times to speak of? What is the overthrow and death of a traitor, to such a fair garland of honour as is here assembled, and which ought not to part without witnessing something more worthy of their regard? How say you, princely Soldan—What if we two should now, and before this fair company, decide the long-contended question for this land of Palestine, and end at once these tedious wars? Yonder are the lists ready, nor can Paynimrie ever hope a better champion than thou. I, unless worthier offers, will lay down my gauntlet in behalf of Christendom, and, in all love and honour, we will do mortal battle for the possession of Jerusalem."

There was a deep pause for the Soldan's answer. His cheek and brow coloured highly, and it was the opinion of many present, that he hesitated whether he should accept the challenge. At length he said, "Fighting for the Holy City against those whom we regard as idolaters, and worshippers of stocks and stones, and graven images, I might confide that Allah would strengthen my arm; or if I fell beneath the sword of the Melech Ric, I could not pass to Paradise by a more glorious death. But Allah has already given Jerusalem to the true believers, and it were a tempting the God of the Prophet to peril, upon my own personal strength and skill, that which I hold securely by the superiority of my forces."

"If not for Jerusalem, then," said Richard, in the tone of one who would entreat a favour of an intimate friend, "yet, for the love of honour, let us run at least three courses with grinded lances?"

Check Out More Titles From HardPress Classics Series In this collection we are offering thousands of classic and hard to find books. This series spans a vast array of subjects — so you are bound to find something of interest to enjoy reading and learning about.

Subjects:
Architecture
Art
Biography & Autobiography
Body, Mind &Spirit
Children & Young Adult
Dramas
Education
Fiction
History
Language Arts & Disciplines
Law
Literary Collections
Music
Poetry
Psychology
Science
…and many more.

Visit us at www.hardpress.net